OXFORD
HAMMOND

Concise Atlas of the World

OXFORD
HAMMOND

Concise

Atlas
of the World

OXFORD UNIVERSITY PRESS

OXFORD • MELBOURNE • TORONTO

Contents

INDEX

68/B3 **Flixecourt** A 60,000-entry Master Index
69/D4 **Flize, Fran** lists places and features appear-
69/D4 **Floing, Fra** ing in this atlas, complete with
69/H4 **Flonheim,**
69/F5 **Florange, I** page numbers and easy-to-use
69/D3 **Floreffe, B**
69/D2 **Florennes** alpha-numeric references.

Oxford University Press, Walton Street, Oxford OX2 6DP
Oxford New York
Athens Auckland Bangkok Bombay
Calcutta Cape Town Dar es Salaam Delhi
Florence Hong Kong Istanbul Karachi
Kuala Lumpur Madras Madrid Melbourne
Mexico City Nairobi Paris Singapore
Taipei Tokyo Toronto

and associated companies in
Berlin Ibadan

Oxford is a trade mark of Oxford University Press

This edition is not available in the USA

Hardback first published 1994
Reprinted 1995
Paperback first published 1995

ENTIRE CONTENTS © COPYRIGHT MCMXCIV BY HAMMOND INCORPORATED

British Library Cataloguing in Publication Data
Data available

Library of Congress Cataloging in Publication Data
Data available

Hardback ISBN 0–19–869253–6
Paperback ISBN 0–19–869286–2
T.S.P. Paperback ISBN 0–19–869254–4

Printed in Hong Kong

Evolution of Cartography

Early cartographers used optical instruments and mathematical analysis to survey and measure distances on the ground. Map-making was slow and time consuming, though accuracy was impressive.

Hot air balloons were occasionally used by military observers to map battle areas not accessible by land. More importantly, the application of photography by cartographers ushered in a new age of map-making.

Airplanes permitted aerial reconnaissance at higher altitudes, greatly reducing surveying time. Meanwhile, advances in photography allowed sharp images of increasingly larger areas.

Satellites gave cartographers a global vantage point beyond the earth's atmosphere. Technological advances, many derived from military and aerospace research, permitted images to be systematically sent from space to sophisticated computers, where they were organized and enhanced.

Digital geographic databases are revolutionizing map-making. As this brief history of cartography reveals, maps can now be created and updated with greater accuracy and speed than ever before.

The foundation of modern-day cartography was laid by the ancient Greeks, who recognized the spherical shape of the earth, developed our system of longitude and latitude, designed the first map projections and calculated the size of the earth — with surprising accuracy. Claudius Ptolemy's Geographia, produced in the 2nd century A.D., was the first bound collection of maps designed to serve both scholarship and administration.

During the Middle Ages, mapmakers made little attempt to show the world as it was. The typical medieval map represented a Christian ideal, usually placing Jerusalem in the center of the world. At the same time, however, Arab scholars were improving on Ptolemy's work, making significant advances in map presentation and accuracy.

At the end of the 13th century, the compass came into general use, and with it came a new kind of map, called a portolan chart, created by the Genovese fleet for navigational purposes. Based on compass surveys, these outline maps depicted the Mediterranean and Black seas with great accuracy. An elaborate system of lines indicating compass directions crisscrossed the maps' surfaces. In 1375, the Catalan Atlas used portolans to depict most of the world, following the text of Marco Polo.

Three key events contributed to the renaissance of cartography. First was the rediscovery of Ptolemy's Geographia in the West. Carefully preserved by devotees, the text eventually reached the Moorish rulers in Spain.

An eminent cartographer of the Age of Exploration, Gerardus Mercator, produced his first world map in 1538. As an aid to seamen, Mercator's map was unsurpassed, because all compass directions appeared as straight lines.

Second was the invention of printing, which greatly increased the number of available maps, and brought them within reach of the average person. In 1478, Ptolemy's Geographia became the first of the classical Greek works to be printed.

Third, and perhaps most important, was the age of the great discoveries, which was itself made possible by the development of new three-masted sailing vessels.

THE AGE OF EXPLORATION

European mariners set sail across the Atlantic beginning in the late 15th century. The great sea-going explorers of this era — Columbus, Cabot, Amerigo Vespucci, Magellan and Sir Francis Drake — all owed much to Ptolemy's ancient text, and to the refinements made at the navigational school founded by Prince Henry the Navigator. Ptolemy and others, however, considerably exaggerated the Eurasian landmass, showing it to occupy nearly half the globe. This error led Columbus to underestimate the distance to Asia; thus he failed to realize that he had reached the new world.

In 1572 a volume of maps published in Rome added the figure of Atlas holding up the world—hence the name "Atlas".

This map of Holland was reproduced from an original version of Theatrum Orbis Terrarum. (Courtesy of Federico Canobbio-Codelli)

Gerardus Mercator, an important cartographer of his age, was the first to produce a true world navigational chart on a flat surface. It became the favored depiction among map publishers.

Many new maps followed as great explorers, and later traders, returned to correct and fill in the blank spaces of the expanding world. The first modern atlas, Theatrum Orbis Terrarum, was published in 1570.

The first successful marine chronometer, in use by 1761, offered a reliable means of measuring longitude. By the late 18th century, mapmakers were already producing a reasonable picture of the world as we know it today.

With the invention of photography in the 19th century, cartographers could at last record the landscape with photo-realistic precision and detail. Then, in the early 1900's, airplanes dramatically extended the scope of our view. Advances in photography kept pace, permitting crisp images of ever expanding areas. Aerial reconnaissance became the standard method for gathering cartographic data. Infrared and ultra-violet photography extended the range of

satellite view of the area
hown on the map at left.
ote the addition of Dutch
olders" or land reclaimed
om the sea.

enetrated visual obstacles such as
clouds and fog.

IMAGES FROM SPACE

But a quantum leap forward occurred
in the 1970's, when remote sensing
satellites launched a new age of cartography, giving us a vantage point beyond
the earth's atmosphere. Satellites
provided the first exact measurements
of the earth's diameter and the distances between continents, and showed
the earth to be flattened at the poles by
precisely 26.6 miles (42.8 km.).

Today, satellites are mapping the
globe. Landsat digital images of the
earth are systematically broadcast from
space to sophisticated computers,
where the images are assembled and
enhanced. This marriage of computers
and satellites has given birth to radically new geographic information systems.

COMPUTER-ASSISTED MAPS

Computers were quickly employed in
the everyday production of maps. In
computer-assisted map-making systems, computers function as electronic
versions of traditional drafting tools.
Hand-drawn maps are scanned into a

perception
beyond the
visible spectrum,
while radar

computer, where revisions such as
name and color changes can be made
quickly and easily. However, because
these systems must use existing maps
as their source material, their ability to
output maps at various scales,
projections or with different levels of
detail is seriously limited.

CREATING A DIGITAL DATABASE

The Oxford Hammond Atlas of
the World is the first world
atlas created directly from
a digital database, and its
computer-generated
maps represent a new
phase in map-making
technology.

To build the database capable of generating this world
atlas, the latitude and
longitude of every
significant town, river,
coastline, natural and
political border, transportation network and
peak elevation was
researched and
digitized.

Engineering the complex data structure was critical to the success of the
system, which relies on powerful
computers and enormous data storage

**Traditional craftsmanship
still plays a vital role. To
vividly represent a region's
topography, hand-sculpted
TerraScape™ relief models
created by master cartographer Ernst Hofmann are
married to the computer-
generated world maps.**

capacity. Hundreds of millions of data
points describing nearly every important geographic feature on earth are
organized into over 1,000 different map
feature codes.

HOW COMPUTER-GENERATED MAPS ARE MADE

There are no maps in this unique
system. Rather, it consists entirely of
coded points, lines and polygons. To
create a map, cartographers determine
what city, region or continent they want
to show and select specific information
to include, based on editorial considerations such as scale, town size, population density, and the relative importance of different features. How does a
computer plot irregular rivers and
mountains — at many different scales?
Using fractal geometry to describe natural forms such as coastlines, mathematical physicist Mitchell Feigenbaum
developed software capable of reconfiguring coastlines, borders and
mountain ranges to fit a multitude of
map scales and projections.

Even map labeling has finally given
way to new technology. Dr. Feigenbaum
also created a new computerized type
placement program which places thousands of map labels in minutes, a
task which previously
required days of tedious
labor. The program
insures that the type
carefully follows the
curve of the graticule,
or map grid, for maximum legibility and aesthetic appeal. After these
steps have been completed, the computer then draws the final map. The benefits of such a system go far beyond
producing more timely and accurate
maps. For the first time, geographers
possess a uniquely creative mapmaking tool. Map projections can be
changed at whim. Revisions that once
took months can be completed in
hours. Because the maps are digitally
created, they can be utilized in a wide
variety of electronic media.

A traditionally-produced
map may require ten to forty
film overlays, each containing a portion of the final
map. Updating city names
and political boundaries in
the conventional manner is
a tedious manual effort
requiring light tables, ink
pens and opaquing brushes.

The computer-generated
maps in this atlas represent
a new phase in cartography.
They are derived from a
digital world database that
contains the precise latitude
and longitude coordinates
for every significant point
on the globe. A single
change with a computer
control can alter the entire
look of a map.

Once the map design is
approved, a sophisticated
laser plotter prints the final
artwork onto film, producing
a complete set of film
positives for the standard
four-color printing process
in close to an hour — a
savings of many days over
conventional methods. Or,
the image can be electronically transmitted anywhere
in the world.

Map Projections

S imply stated, the mapmaker's challenge is to project the earth's curved surface onto a flat plane. To achieve this elusive goal, cartographers have developed map projections — equations which govern this conversion of geographic data.

This section explores some of the most widely used projections. It also introduces a new projection, Hammond's Optimal Conformal.

GENERAL PRINCIPLES AND TERMS

The earth rotates around its axis once a day. Its end points are the North and South poles; the line circling the earth midway between the poles is the equator. The arc from the equator to either pole is divided into 90 degrees of latitude. The equator represents 0° latitude. Circles of equal latitude, called parallels, are traditionally shown at every fifth or tenth degree.

The equator is divided into 360 degrees. Lines circling the globe from pole to pole through the degree points on the equator are called meridians, or great circles. All meridians are equal in length, but by international agreement the meridian passing through the Greenwich Observatory near London has been chosen as the prime meridian or 0° longitude. The distance in degrees from the prime meridian to any point east or west is its longitude.

While meridians are all equal in length, parallels become shorter as they approach the poles. Whereas one degree of latitude represents approximately 69 miles (112 km.) anywhere on the globe, a degree of longitude varies from 69 miles (112 km.) at the equator to zero at the poles. Each degree of latitude and longitude is divided into 60 minutes. One minute of latitude equals one nautical mile (1.15 land miles or 1.85 km.).

HOW TO FLATTEN A SPHERE: THE ART OF CONTROLLING DISTORTION

There is only one way to represent a sphere with absolute precision: on a globe. All attempts to project our planet's surface onto a plane unevenly stretch or tear the sphere as it flattens, inevitably distorting shapes, distances, area (sizes appear larger or smaller than actual size), angles or direction.

Since representing a sphere on a flat plane always creates distortion, only the parallels or the meridians (or some other set of lines) can maintain the same length as on a globe of corresponding scale. All other lines must be either too long or too short. Accordingly, the scale on a flat map cannot be true everywhere; there will always be different scales in different parts of a map. On world maps or very large areas, variations in scale may be extreme. Most maps seek to preserve either true area relationships (equal area projections) or true angles and shapes (conformal projections); some attempt to achieve overall balance.

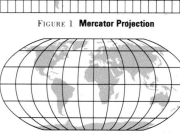

FIGURE 1 **Mercator Projection**

FIGURE 2 **Robinson Projection**

PROJECTIONS: SELECTED EXAMPLES

Mercator (Fig. 1): This projection is especially useful because all compass directions appear as straight lines, making it a valuable navigational tool. Moreover, every small region conforms to its shape on a globe — hence the name conformal. But because its meridians are evenly-spaced vertical lines which never converge (unlike the globe), the horizontal parallels must be drawn farther and farther apart at higher latitudes to maintain a correct relationship. Only the equator is true to scale, and the size of areas in the higher latitudes is dramatically distorted.

Robinson (Fig. 2): To create the thematic maps in Global Relationships and the two-page world map in the Maps of the World section, the Robinson projection was used. It combines elements of both conformal and equal area projections to show the whole earth with relatively true shapes and reasonably equal areas.

Conic (Fig. 3): This projection has been used frequently for air navigation charts and to create most of the national and regional maps in this atlas. (See text in margin at left).

HAMMOND'S OPTIMAL CONFORMAL

As its name implies, this new conformal projection presents the optimal view of an area by reducing shifts in scale over an entire region to the minimum degree possible. While conformal maps generally preserve all small shapes, large shapes can become very distorted because of varying scales, causing considerable inaccuracy in distance measurements. The concept underlying the Optimal Conformal is that for any region on the globe, there is an ideal projection for which scale variation can be made as small as possible. Consequently, unlike other projections, the Optimal Conformal does not use one standard formula to construct a map. Each map is a unique projection — the optimal projection for that particular area.

In practice, the cartographer first defines the map subject, then, working on a computer, draws a band around the region to be mapped. Next, a sophisticated software program evaluates the size and shape of the region to determine the most accurate way to project it. The result is the most distortion-free

Optimal Conformal
Projection

ACCURACY COMPARED

CITIES	SPHERICAL (TRUE) DISTANCE	OPTIMAL CONFORMAL DISTANCE	LAMBERT AZIMUTHAL DISTANCE
CARACAS TO RIO GRANDE	4,443 MI. (7,149 KM.)	4,429 MI. (7,126 KM.)	4,316 MI. (6,944 KM.)
MARACAIBO TO RECIFE	2,834 MI. (4,560 KM.)	2,845 MI. (4,578 KM.)	2,817 MI. (4,533 KM.)
FORTALEZA TO PUNTA ARENAS	3,882 MI. (6,246 KM.)	3,907 MI. (6,266 KM.)	3,843 MI. (6,163 KM.)

Continent maps drawn using the Lambert Azimuthal Equal Area projection (Fig. 4) contain distortions ranging from 2.3 percent for Europe up to 15 percent for Asia. The Optimal Conformal cuts that distortion in half, improving distance measurements on these continent maps. Less distortion means greater visual fidelity, so the shape of a continent on an Optimal projection more closely represents its True shape. The table above compares measurements on the Optimal projection to those of the Lambert Azimuthal Equal Area projection for selected cities.

conformal map possible, and the most accurate projections that have ever been made. All of the continents maps in this atlas (with the exception of Antarctica) have been drawn using this projection.

PROJECTIONS COMPARED

Because the true shapes of earth's landforms are unfamiliar to most people, distinguishing between various projections can be difficult. The following diagrams reveal the distortions introduced by several commonly used projections. By using a simple face with familiar shapes as the starting point (The Plan), it is easy to see the benefits — and drawbacks — of each. Think of the facial features as continents. Note that distortion appears not only in the features themselves, but in the changing shapes, angles and areas of the background grid, or graticule.

Figure 5: The Plan
The Plan indicates that the continents are either perfect concentric circles or are true straight lines *on the earth*. They should appear that way on a "perfect" map.

Figure 6: Orthographic Projection
This view shows the continents on the earth as seen from space. The facial features occupy half of the earth, which is all that you can see from this perspective. As you move outward towards the edge, note how the eyes become elliptical, the nose appears larger and less straight, and the mouth is curved into a smile.

Figure 7: Mercator
This cylindrical projection preserves angles exactly, but the mouth is now smiling broadly, and shows extreme distortion at the map's outer edge. This rapid expansion as you move away from the map's center is typified by the extreme enlargement of Greenland found on Mercator world maps (also see Fig. 1).

Figure 8: Peters
The Peters projection is a square equal area projection elongated, or stretched vertically, by a factor of two. While representing areas in their correct proportions, it does not closely resemble the Plan, and angles, local shapes and global relations are significantly distorted.

Figure 9: Hammond's Optimal Conformal
As you can see, this projection minimizes inaccuracies between the angles and shapes of the Plan, yielding a near-perfect map of the given area, up to a complete hemisphere. Like all conformal maps, the Optimal projection preserves every angle exactly, but it is more successful than previous projections at spreading the inevitable curvature across the entire map. Note that the sides of the triangle appear almost straight while correctly containing more than 180°. And though the eyes are slightly too large, it is the only map with eyes which appear concentric. Both mathematically and visually, it offers the best conformal map that can be made of the ideal Plan.

FIGURE 5
The Plan

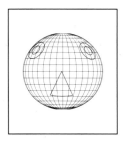

FIGURE 6
Orthographic Projection

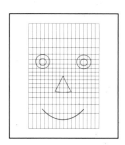

FIGURE 7
Mercator Projection

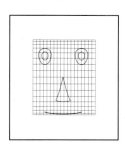

FIGURE 8
Peters Projection

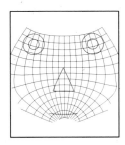

FIGURE 9
Optimal Conformal Projection

Using This Atlas

**How to Locate
Information Quickly**

For familiar locations such as continents, countries and major political divisions, the Quick Reference Guide helps you quickly pinpoint the map you need. For less familiar places, begin with the Master Index.

> Albania
> Alberta, Canada
> Algeria
> American Samoa
> Andorra
> Angola
> Anguilla

Quick Reference Guide

This concise guide lists continents, countries, states, provinces and territories in alphabetical order, complete with the size, population and capital of each. Red page numbers and alpha-numeric reference keys are visible at a glance.

Merlimont, Fran.
.9/F4 **Mersch**, Luxembou
68/A3 **Mers-les-Bains**, France
69/F4 **Mertert**, Luxembourg
69/F4 **Mertesdorf**, Germany
69/G6 **Mertzwiller**, France
68/B5 **Méru**, France
68/B2 **Merville**, France
69/F2 **Merzenich**, Germany
69/F5 **Merzig**, Germany
F4 **Messancy**, Belgi
attet Relr

Master Index of the World

When you're looking for an unfamiliar place or physical feature, your quickest route is the Master Index. This 60,000-entry alphabetical index lists both the page number and alpha-numeric reference key for places and features in Maps of the World.

T*he Oxford Hammond Concise Atlas of the World* has been thought-fully designed to be easy and enjoyable to use, both as a general reference, and for armchair exploration of the globe. A short time spent familiarizing yourself with its organization will help you to benefit fully from its use.

GLOBAL RELATIONSHIPS

This section highlights key social, cultural, economic and geographic factors. Together, these seven succinct chapters — from Population to Standards of Living— provide a fresh perspective on the world today. In the case of complex and rapidly evolving topics such as Environment, data analysis is in a relatively early stage, and projected outcomes are sometimes controversial.

THE PHYSICAL WORLD

These relief maps of the continents and major regions of the world depict the topography of the earth's surface, and represent our most current knowledge of the ocean floor. Because the maps are actual photographs of three-dimensional TerraScape™ models, they present the relationships of land and sea forms and the rugged contours of the terrain with startling realism.

GEOGRAPHIC COMPARISONS

World Statistics lists the dimensions of the earth's principal mountains, islands, rivers and lakes, along with other useful geographic information. The Time Zones map shows all standard time zones as well as those areas using half hour deviations. All countries plus selected major cities are included. Population of Major Cities contains the latest population figures for the world's largest cities, organized by country in alphabetical order. You'll find the size, population and location of major geographical areas, from countries, states and territories to continents, in the Quick Reference Guide.

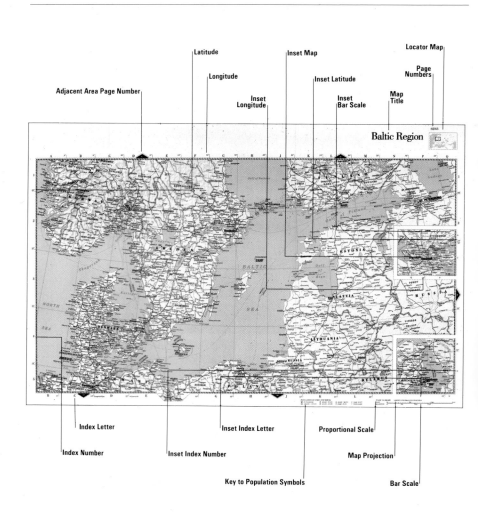

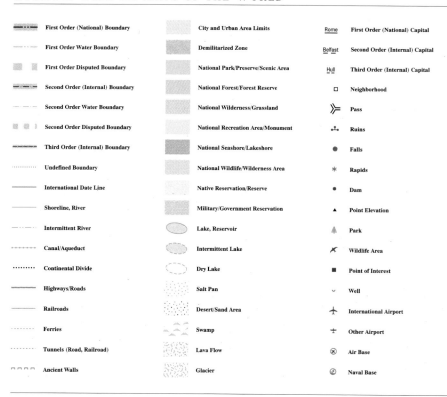

SYMBOLS USED ON MAPS OF THE WORLD

First Order (National) Boundary	City and Urban Area Limits	Rome First Order (National) Capital
First Order Water Boundary	Demilitarized Zone	Belfast Second Order (Internal) Capital
First Order Disputed Boundary	National Park/Preserve/Scenic Area	Hull Third Order (Internal) Capital
Second Order (Internal) Boundary	National Forest/Forest Reserve	Neighborhood
Second Order Water Boundary	National Wilderness/Grassland	Pass
Second Order Disputed Boundary	National Recreation Area/Monument	Ruins
Third Order (Internal) Boundary	National Seashore/Lakeshore	Falls
Undefined Boundary	National Wildlife/Wilderness Area	Rapids
International Date Line	Native Reservation/Reserve	Dam
Shoreline, River	Military/Government Reservation	Point Elevation
Intermittent River	Lake, Reservoir	Park
Canal/Aqueduct	Intermittent Lake	Wildlife Area
Continental Divide	Dry Lake	Point of Interest
Highways/Roads	Salt Pan	Well
Railroads	Desert/Sand Area	International Airport
Ferries	Swamp	Other Airport
Tunnels (Road, Railroad)	Lava Flow	Air Base
Ancient Walls	Glacier	Naval Base

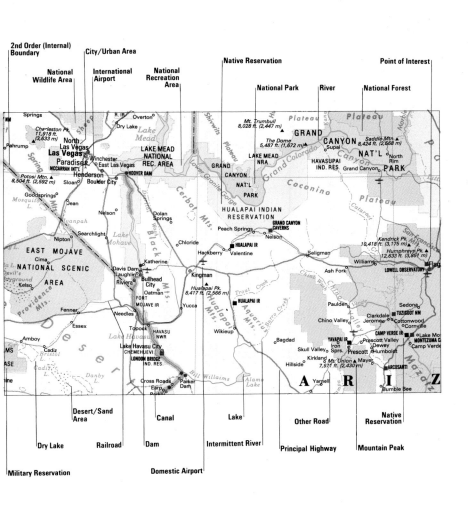

2nd Order (Internal) Boundary
National Wildlife Area
City/Urban Area
International Airport
National Recreation Area
Native Reservation
National Park
River
Point of Interest
National Forest

Desert/Sand Area
Canal
Lake
Other Road
Native Reservation

Dry Lake
Railroad
Dam
Intermittent River
Principal Highway
Mountain Peak

Military Reservation
Domestic Airport

PRINCIPAL MAP ABBREVIATIONS

ABOR. RSV.	ABORIGINAL RESERVE	IND. RES.	INDIAN RESERVATION	NWR	NATIONAL WILDLIFE RESERVE
ADMIN.	ADMINISTRATION	INT'L	INTERNATIONAL		
AFB	AIR FORCE BASE	IR	INDIAN RESERVATION	OBL.	OBLAST
AMM. DEP.	AMMUNITION DEPOT	ISTH.	ISTHMUS	OCC.	OCCUPIED
ARCH.	ARCHIPELAGO	JCT.	JUNCTION	OKR.	OKRUG
ARPT.	AIRPORT	L.	LAKE	PAR.	PARISH
AUT.	AUTONOMOUS	LAG.	LAGOON	PASSG.	PASSAGE
B.	BAY	LAKESH.	LAKESHORE	PEN.	PENINSULA
BFLD.	BATTLEFIELD	MEM.	MEMORIAL	PK.	PEAK
BK.	BROOK	MIL.	MILITARY	PLAT.	PLATEAU
BOR.	BOROUGH	MISS.	MISSILE	PN	PARK NATIONAL
BR.	BRANCH	MON.	MONUMENT	PREF.	PREFECTURE
C.	CAPE	MT.	MOUNT	PROM.	PROMONTORY
CAN.	CANAL	MTN.	MOUNTAIN	PROV.	PROVINCE
CAP.	CAPITAL	MTS.	MOUNTAINS	PRSV.	PRESERVE
C.G.	COAST GUARD	NAT.	NATURAL	PT.	POINT
CHAN.	CHANNEL	NAT'L	NATIONAL	R.	RIVER
CO.	COUNTY	NAV.	NAVAL	RA	RECREATION AREA
CR.	CREEK	NB	NATIONAL	RA.	RANGE
CTR.	CENTER		BATTLEFIELD	REC.	RECREATION(AL)
DEP.	DEPOT	NBP	NATIONAL	REF.	REFUGE
DEPR.	DEPRESSION		BATTLEFIELD PARK	REG.	REGION
DEPT.	DEPARTMENT	NBS	NATIONAL	REP.	REPUBLIC
DES.	DESERT		BATTLEFIELD SITE	RES.	RESERVOIR, RESERVATION
DIST.	DISTRICT	NHP	NATIONAL HISTORICAL		
DMZ	DEMILITARIZED ZONE		PARK	RVWY.	RIVERWAY
DPCY.	DEPENDENCY	NHPP	NATIONAL HISTORICAL	SA.	SIERRA
ENG.	ENGINEERING		PARK AND PRESERVE	SD.	SOUND
EST.	ESTUARY	NHS	NATIONAL HISTORIC	SEASH.	SEASHORE
FD.	FIORD, FJORD		SITE	SO.	SOUTHERN
FED.	FEDERAL	NL	NATIONAL LAKESHORE	SP	STATE PARK
FK.	FORK	NM	NATIONAL MONUMENT	SPR., SPRS.	SPRING, SPRINGS
FLD.	FIELD	NMEMP	NATIONAL MEMORIAL	ST.	STATE
FOR.	FOREST		PARK	STA.	STATION
FT.	FORT	NMILP	NATIONAL MILITARY	STM.	STREAM
G.	GULF		PARK	STR.	STRAIT
GOV.	GOVERNOR	NO.	NORTHERN	TERR.	TERRITORY
GOVT.	GOVERNMENT	NP	NATIONAL PARK	TUN.	TUNNEL
GD.	GRAND	NPP	NATIONAL PARK AND	TWP.	TOWNSHIP
GT.	GREAT		PRESERVE	VAL.	VALLEY
HAR.	HARBOR	NPRSV	NATIONAL PRESERVE	VILL.	VILLAGE
HD.	HEAD	NRA	NATIONAL	VOL.	VOLCANO
HIST.	HISTORIC(AL)		RECREATION AREA	WILD.	WILDLIFE, WILDERNESS
HTS.	HEIGHTS	NRSV	NATIONAL RESERVE		
I., IS.	ISLAND(S)	NS	NATIONAL SEASHORE	WTR.	WATER

MAPS OF THE WORLD

These detailed regional maps are arranged by continent, and introduced by a political map of that continent. The continent maps, which utilize Hammond's new Optimal Conformal projection, are distinguished by individual colors for each country to highlight political divisions.

On the regional maps, different colors and textures highlight distinctive features such as parks, forests, deserts and urban areas. These maps also provide considerable information concerning geographic features and political divisions. The realistic topography is achieved by combining the computer-generated political maps with the hand-sculpted TerraScape™ relief maps.

MASTER INDEX

This is an A-Z listing of names found on the political maps. It also has its own abbreviation list which, along with other Index keys, appears on page 170.

MAP SCALES

A map's scale is the relationship of any length on the map to an identical length on the earth's surface. A scale of 1:3,000,000 means that one inch on the map represents 3,000,000 inches (47 miles, 76 km.) on the earth's surface. Thus, a 1:1,000,000 scale is larger than 1:3,000,000, just as 1/1 is larger than 1/3.

The most densely populated areas are shown at a scale of 1:1,170,000, while selected metropolitan areas are covered at either 1:587,000 or 1:1,170,000. Other populous areas are presented at 1:3,500,000 and 1:7,000,000, allowing you to accurately compare areas and distances of similar regions. Remaining regions are scaled at 1:10,500,000. The continent maps, as well as the United States, Canada, Russia, Pacific and World have smaller scales.

Boundary Policies

This atlas observes the boundary policies of the U.S. Department of State. Boundary disputes are customarily handled with a special symbol treatment, but de facto boundaries are favored if they seem to have any degree of permanence, in the belief that boundaries should reflect current geographic and political realities. The portrayal of independent nations in the atlas follows their recognition by the United Nations and/or the United States government.

The atlas also uses accepted conventional names for certain major foreign places. Usually, space permits the inclusion of the local form in parentheses. To make the maps more readily understandable to English-speaking readers, many foreign physical features are translated into more recognizable English forms.

A Word About Names

Our source for all foreign names and physical names in the United States is the decision lists of the U.S. Board of Geographic Names, which contain hundreds of thousands of place names. If a place is not listed, the Atlas follows the name form appearing on official foreign maps or in official gazetteers of the country concerned. For rendering domestic city, town and village names, this atlas follows the forms and spelling of the U.S. Postal Service.

Quick Reference Guide

This concise alphabetical reference lists continents, countries, states, territories, possessions and other major geographical areas, complete with the size, population and capital or chief town of each. Blue page numbers and alpha-numeric reference keys (which refer to the grid squares of latitude and longitude on each map) are visible at a glance. The population figures are the latest and most reliable figures obtainable.

	Place	Square Miles	Square Kilometers	Population	Capital or Chief Town	Page/ Index Ref.
A	Afghanistan	250,775	649,507	16,450,000	Kabul	95/H 2
	Africa	11,707,000	30,321,130	648,000,000	....	122
	Alabama, U.S.	51,705	133,916	4,040,587	Montgomery	163/G 3
	Alaska, U.S.	591,004	1,530,700	550,043	Juneau	151
	Albania	11,100	28,749	3,335,000	Tiranë	81/F 2
	Alberta, Canada	255,285	661,185	2,545,553	Edmonton	152/E 3
	Algeria	919,591	2,381,740	26,022,000	Algiers	124/F 2
	American Samoa	77	199	46,773	Pago Pago	121/J 6
	Andorra	188	487	53,000	Andorra la Vella	75/F 1
	Angola	481,351	1,246,700	8,668,000	Luanda	126/C 3
	Anguilla, U.K.	35	91	7,000	The Valley	150/F 3
	Antarctica	5,500,000	14,245,000	....	....	113
	Antigua and Barbuda	171	443	64,000	St. John's	150/F 3
	Argentina	1,072,070	2,776,661	32,664,000	Buenos Aires	135/C 4
	Arizona, U.S.	114,000	295,260	3,665,228	Phoenix	158/D 4
	Arkansas, U.S.	53,187	137,754	2,350,725	Little Rock	162/E 3
	Armenia	11,506	29,800	3,283,000	Yerevan	87/H 4
	Aruba, Netherlands	75	193	64,000	Oranjestad	150/D 4
	Ascension Island, St. Helena	34	88	719	Georgetown	52/J 6
	Ashmore & Cartier Islands, Australia	61	159	....	(Canberra, Austr.)	114/C 2
	Asia	17,128,500	44,362,815	3,176,000,000	....	90
	Australia	2,966,136	7,682,300	16,850,540	Canberra	114
	Australian Capital Territory	927	2,400	280,132	Canberra	119/D 2
	Austria	32,375	83,851	7,666,000	Vienna	73/L 3
	Azerbaijan	33,436	86,600	7,029,000	Baku	87/H 4
	Azores, Portugal	902	2,335	275,900	Ponta Delgada	75/R12
B	Bahamas	5,382	13,939	252,000	Nassau	150/B 2
	Bahrain	240	622	537,000	Manama	94/F 3
	Baker Island, U.S.	1	2.6	....	....	121/H 4
	Balearic Islands, Spain	1,936	5,014	655,909	Palma	75/F 3
	Bangladesh	55,126	142,776	116,601,000	Dhaka	106/E 3
	Barbados	166	430	255,000	Bridgetown	150/G 4
	Belarus	80,154	207,600	10,200,000	Minsk	52/G 3
	Belgium	11,781	30,513	9,922,000	Brussels	64/C 3
	Belize	8,867	22,966	228,000	Belmopan	148/D 2
	Benin	43,483	112,620	4,832,000	Porto-Novo	129/F 4
	Bermuda, U.K.	21	54	58,000	Hamilton	145/L 6
	Bhutan	18,147	47,000	1,598,000	Thimphu	106/E 2
	Bolivia	424,163	1,098,582	7,157,000	La Paz; Sucre	136/F 7
	Bonaire, Neth. Antilles	112	291	8,087	Kralendijk	150/D 4
	Bosnia & Hercegovina	19,940	51,129	4,124,256	Sarajevo	82/C 3
	Botswana	224,764	582,139	1,258,000	Gaborone	126/D 5
	Bouvet Island, Norway	22	57	....	....	51/K 8
	Brazil	3,284,426	8,506,663	155,356,000	Brasília	134/D 3
	British Columbia, Canada	366,253	948,596	3,282,061	Victoria	152/D 3
	British Indian Ocean Terr., U.K.	29	75	2,000	(London, U.K.)	90/G10
	British Virgin Islands	59	153	12,000	Road Town	150/E 3
	Brunei	2,226	5,765	398,000	Bandar Seri Begawan	112/A 4
	Bulgaria	42,823	110,912	8,911,000	Sofia	83/G 4
	Burkina Faso	105,869	274,200	9,360,000	Ouagadougou	129/E 3
	Burma (Myanmar)	261,789	678,034	42,112,000	Rangoon	107/G 2
	Burundi	10,747	27,835	5,831,000	Bujumbura	130/A 3
C	California, U.S.	158,706	411,049	29,760,021	Sacramento	158/B 3
	Cambodia (Kampuchea)	69,898	181,036	7,146,000	Phnom Penh	109/D 3
	Cameroon	183,568	475,441	11,390,000	Yaoundé	124/H 7
	Canada	3,851,787	9,976,139	27,296,859	Ottawa	152
	Canary Islands, Spain	2,808	7,273	1,367,646	Las Palmas; Santa Cruz	75/X16
	Cape Province, South Africa	261,705	677,816	5,543,506	Cape Town	132/C 3
	Cape Verde	1,557	4,033	387,000	Praia	122/J 9
	Cayman Islands, U.K.	100	259	27,000	Georgetown	149/F 2

	Place	Square Miles	Square Kilometers	Population	Capital or Chief Town	Page/ Index R
	Celebes, Indonesia	72,986	189,034	7,732,383	Ujung Pandang	111/E 4
	Central African Republic	242,000	626,780	2,952,000	Bangui	125/J 6
	Chad	495,752	1,283,998	5,122,000	N'Djamena	125/J 4
	Channel Islands, U.K.	75	194	133,000	St. Helier; St. Peter Port	72/B 2
	Chile	292,257	756,946	13,287,000	Santiago	135/B 3
	China, People's Rep. of	3,691,000	9,559,690	1,151,487,000	Beijing	90/J 6
	China, Republic of (Taiwan)	13,971	36,185	20,659,000	Taipei	105/J 3
	Christmas Island, Australia	52	135	1,275	Flying Fish Cove	90/K1
	Clipperton Island, France	2	5.2	....	....	50/D 9
	Cocos (Keeling) Islands, Australia	5.4	14	647	West Island	90/J1
	Colombia	439,513	1,138,339	33,778,000	Bogotá	138/C 4
	Colorado, U.S.	104,091	269,596	3,294,394	Denver	158/F 3
	Comoros	719	1,862	477,000	Moroni	133/G 5
	Congo	132,046	342,000	2,309,000	Brazzaville	122/D 5
	Connecticut, U.S.	5,018	12,997	3,287,116	Hartford	161/F 3
	Cook Islands, New Zealand	91	236	18,000	Avarua	121/J 6
	Coral Sea Islands, Australia	8.5	22	....	....	115/J 2
	Corsica, France	3,352	8,682	289,842	Ajaccio; Bastia	80/A 1
	Costa Rica	19,575	50,700	3,111,000	San José	149/F 4
	Côte d'Ivoire, see Ivory Coast					
	Croatia	22,050	56,538	4,601,469	Zagreb	82/B 3
	Cuba	44,206	114,494	10,732,000	Havana	149/F 1
	Curaçao, Neth. Antilles	178	462	145,430	Willemstad	150/D 4
	Cyprus	3,473	8,995	709,000	Nicosia	91/C 2
	Czech Republic	30,449	78,863	10,291,927	Prague	65/H 4
D	Delaware, U.S.	2,044	5,294	666,168	Dover	160/F 4
	Denmark	16,629	43,069	5,133,000	Copenhagen	62/C 4
	District of Columbia, U.S.	69	179	606,900	Washington	166/B 6
	Djibouti	8,880	23,000	346,000	Djibouti	125/P 5
	Dominica	290	751	86,000	Roseau	150/F 4
	Dominican Republic	18,704	48,443	7,385,000	Santo Domingo	150/D 3
E	Ecuador	109,483	283,561	10,752,000	Quito	136/C 4
	Egypt	386,659	1,001,447	54,452,000	Cairo	127/B 3
	El Salvador	8,260	21,393	5,419,000	San Salvador	148/D 3
	England, U.K.	50,516	130,836	46,220,955	London	55/K1
	Equatorial Guinea	10,831	28,052	379,000	Malabo	124/G 7
	Eritrea	36,170	93,679	3,500,000	Āsmera	125/N 4
	Estonia	17,413	45,100	1,573,000	Tallinn	63/L 2
	Ethiopia	435,606	1,128,220	51,617,000	Addis Ababa	125/N 5
	Europe	4,057,000	10,507,630	689,000,000	....	52
F	Falkland Is. & Depdcs., U.K.	6,198	16,053	1,813	Stanley	143/M 8
	Faroe Islands, Denmark	540	1,399	48,000	Tórshavn	52/D 2
	Fiji	7,055	18,272	744,000	Suva	120/G 6
	Finland	130,128	337,032	4,991,000	Helsinki	61/H 2
	Florida, U.S.	58,664	151,940	12,937,926	Tallahassee	163/H 4
	France	210,038	543,998	56,596,000	Paris	72/D 3
	French Guiana	35,135	91,000	102,000	Cayenne	137/H 3
	French Polynesia	1,544	4,000	195,000	Papeete	121/M 6
G	Gabon	103,346	267,666	1,080,000	Libreville	124/H 7
	Gambia	4,127	10,689	875,000	Banjul	128/B 1
	Gaza Strip	139	360	642,000	Gaza	91/C 4
	Georgia	26,911	69,700	5,449,000	Tbilisi	87/G 4
	Georgia, U.S.	58,910	152,577	6,478,216	Atlanta	163/G 3
	Germany	137,753	356,780	79,548,000	Berlin	64/E 3
	Ghana	92,099	238,536	15,617,000	Accra	129/E 4
	Gibraltar, U.K.	2.28	5.91	30,000	Gibraltar	74/C 4
	Great Britain & Northern Ireland (United Kingdom)	94,399	244,493	57,236,000	London	55
	Greece	50,944	131,945	10,043,000	Athens	81/G 3
	Greenland, Denmark	840,000	2,175,600	57,000	Nuuk (Godthåb)	145/N 2
	Grenada	133	344	84,000	St. George's	150/F 5

Place	Square Miles	Square Kilometers	Population	Capital or Chief Town	Page/ Index Ref.
Guadeloupe & Dependencies, France	687	1,779	345,400	Basse-Terre	150/F 3
Guam, U.S.	209	541	133,152	Agaña	120/D 3
Guatemala	42,042	108,889	9,266,000	Guatemala	148/D 3
Guinea	94,925	245,856	7,456,000	Conakry	128/C 4
Guinea-Bissau	13,948	36,125	1,024,000	Bissau	128/B 3
Guyana	83,000	214,970	750,000	Georgetown	139/G 3
Haiti	10,694	27,697	6,287,000	Port-au-Prince	149/H 2
Hawaii, U.S.	6,471	16,760	1,108,229	Honolulu	154/S10
Heard & McDonald Islands, Australia	113	293	....	....	51/P 8
Holland, see Netherlands					
Honduras	43,277	112,087	4,949,000	Tegucigalpa	148/E 3
Hong Kong, U.K.	403	1,044	5,856,000	Victoria	105/G 4
Howland Island, U.S.	1	2.6	....	....	121/H 4
Hungary	35,919	93,030	10,558,000	Budapest	82/D 2
Iceland	39,768	103,000	260,000	Reykjavík	61/N 7
Idaho, U.S.	83,564	216,431	1,006,749	Boise	156/E 5
Illinois, U.S.	56,345	145,934	11,430,602	Springfield	160/B 4
India	1,269,339	3,287,588	869,515,000	New Delhi	106/C 3
Indiana, U.S.	36,185	93,719	5,544,159	Indianapolis	160/C 3
Indonesia	788,430	2,042,034	193,560,000	Jakarta	111/E 4
Iowa, U.S.	56,275	145,752	2,776,755	Des Moines	157/K 5
Iran	636,293	1,648,000	59,051,000	Tehran	90/E 6
Iraq	172,476	446,713	19,525,000	Baghdad	92/E 3
Ireland	27,136	70,282	3,489,000	Dublin	55/G10
Ireland, Northern, U.K.	5,452	14,121	1,543,000	Belfast	55/H 9
Isle of Man, U.K.	227	588	64,000	Douglas	56/D 3
Israel	7,847	20,324	4,558,000	Jerusalem	91/D 3
Italy	116,303	301,225	57,772,000	Rome	52/E 4
Ivory Coast (Côte d'Ivoire)	124,504	322,465	12,978,000	Yamoussoukro	128/D 5
Jamaica	4,411	11,424	2,489,000	Kingston	149/G 2
Jan Mayen, Norway	144	373	....	....	52/D 1
Japan	145,730	377,441	124,017,000	Tokyo	97/M 4
Jarvis Island, U.S.	1	2.6	....	....	121/J 5
Java, Indonesia	48,842	126,500	73,712,411	Jakarta	110/C 5
Johnston Atoll, U.S.	.91	2.4	327	....	121/J 3
Jordan	35,000	90,650	3,413,000	Amman	92/D 4
Kampuchea (Cambodia)	69,898	181,036	5,200,000	Phnom Penh	109/D 3
Kansas, U.S.	82,277	213,097	2,477,574	Topeka	159/H 3
Kazakhstan	1,048,300	2,715,100	16,538,000	Alma-Ata	88/G 5
Kentucky, U.S.	40,409	104,659	3,685,296	Frankfort	160/C 4
Kenya	224,960	582,646	25,242,000	Nairobi	130/C 2
Kermadec Islands, New Zealand	13	33	5	....	120/G 7
Kingman Reef, U.S.	0.1	0.26	....	....	121/J 4
Kiribati	291	754	71,000	Bairiki	120/H 5
Korea, North	46,540	120,539	21,815,000	P'yŏngyang	101/D 2
Korea, South	38,175	98,873	43,134,000	Seoul	101/D 4
Kuwait	6,532	16,918	2,204,000	Al Kuwait	93/F 4
Kyrgyzstan	76,641	198,500	4,291,000	Bishkek	102/B 3
Laos	91,428	236,800	4,113,000	Vientiane	109/C 2
Latvia	24,595	63,700	2,681,000	Riga	63/L 3
Lebanon	4,015	10,399	3,385,000	Beirut	91/D 3
Lesotho	11,720	30,355	1,801,000	Maseru	132/D 3
Liberia	43,000	111,370	2,730,000	Monrovia	128/C 5
Libya	679,358	1,759,537	4,353,000	Tripoli	125/J 2
Liechtenstein	61	158	28,000	Vaduz	77/F 3
Lithuania	25,174	65,200	3,690,000	Vilnius	63/K 4
Louisiana, U.S.	47,752	123,678	4,219,973	Baton Rouge	162/E 4
Luxembourg	999	2,587	388,000	Luxembourg	69/E 4
Macau, Portugal	6	16	446,000	Macau	105/G 4
Macedonia	9,889	25,713	1,909,136	Skopje	81/G 2
Madagascar	226,657	587,041	12,185,000	Antananarivo	133/H 8
Madeira Islands, Portugal	307	796	262,800	Funchal	75/V15
Maine, U.S.	33,265	86,156	1,227,928	Augusta	161/G 2
Malawi	45,747	118,485	9,438,000	Lilongwe	131/D 2
Malaya, Malaysia	50,806	131,588	11,138,227	Kuala Lumpur	110/B 3

Place	Square Miles	Square Kilometers	Population	Capital or Chief Town	Page/ Index Ref.
Malaysia	128,308	332,318	17,982,000	Kuala Lumpur	110/C 2
Maldives	115	298	226,000	Male	90/G 9
Mali	464,873	1,204,021	8,339,000	Bamako	124/E 4
Malta	122	316	356,000	Valletta	80/D 5
Manitoba, Canada	250,999	650,087	1,091,942	Winnipeg	152/F 3
Marquesas Islands, French Polynesia	492	1,274	5,419	Atuona	121/M 5
Marshall Islands	70	181	48,000	Majuro	120/G 3
Martinique, France	425	1,101	345,000	Fort-de-France	150/F 4
Maryland, U.S.	10,460	27,091	4,781,468	Annapolis	160/E 4
Massachusetts, U.S.	8,284	21,456	6,016,425	Boston	161/F 3
Mauritania	419,229	1,085,803	1,996,000	Nouakchott	124/C 4
Mauritius	790	2,046	1,081,000	Port Louis	133/S15
Mayotte, France	144	373	75,000	Dzaoudzi	133/H 6
Mexico	761,601	1,972,546	90,007,000	Mexico City	145/G 7
Michigan, U.S.	58,527	151,585	9,295,297	Lansing	160/C 2
Micronesia, Federated States of	....	....	108,000	Kolonia	120/D 4
Midway Islands, U.S.	1.9	4.9	453	....	120/H 2
Minnesota, U.S.	84,402	218,601	4,375,099	St. Paul	157/K 4
Mississippi, U.S.	47,689	123,515	2,573,216	Jackson	163/F 3
Missouri, U.S.	69,697	180,515	5.117.073	Jefferson City	159/J 3
Moldova	13,012	33,700	4,341,000	Kishinev	83/J 2
Monaco	368 acres	149 hectares	30,000	....	78/A 5
Mongolia	606,163	1,569,962	2,247,000	Ulaanbaatar	96/D 2
Montana, U.S.	147,046	380,849	799,065	Helena	156/F 4
Montserrat, U.K.	40	104	13,000	Plymouth	150/F 3
Morocco	172,414	446,550	26,182,000	Rabat	124/C 1
Mozambique	303,769	786,762	15,113,000	Maputo	126/G 4
Myanmar, see Burma					
Namibia	317,827	823,172	1,521,000	Windhoek	126/C 5
Natal, South Africa	33,578	86,967	5,722,215	Pietermaritzburg	133/E 3
Nauru	7.7	20	9,000	Yaren (district)	120/F 5
Navassa Island, U.S.	2	5	....	....	149/H 2
Nebraska, U.S.	77,355	200,349	1,578,385	Lincoln	159/G 2
Nepal	54,663	141,577	19,612,000	Kathmandu	106/D 2
Netherlands	15,892	41,160	15,022,000	The Hague; Amsterdam	64/C 3
Netherlands Antilles	320	817	184,000	Willemstad	150/D 5
Nevada, U.S.	110,561	286,353	1,201,833	Carson City	158/C 3
New Brunswick, Canada	28,354	73,437	723,900	Fredericton	161/H 2
New Caledonia & Dependencies, France	7,335	18,998	172,000	Nouméa	120/F 6
Newfoundland, Canada	156,184	404,517	568,474	St. John's	153/K 3
New Hampshire, U.S.	9,279	24,033	1,109,252	Concord	161/G 3
New Jersey, U.S.	7,787	20,168	7,730,188	Trenton	166/D 3
New Mexico, U.S.	121,593	314,926	1,515,069	Santa Fe	158/F 4
New South Wales, Australia	309,498	801,600	5,731,906	Sydney	119/C 1
New York, U.S.	49,108	127,190	17,990,455	Albany	160/F 3
New Zealand	103,736	268,676	3,309,000	Wellington	115/Q10
Nicaragua	45,698	118,358	3,752,000	Managua	149/E 3
Niger	489,189	1,267,000	8,154,000	Niamey	124/G 4
Nigeria	357,000	924,630	122,471,000	Abuja	124/G 6
Niue, New Zealand	100	259	3,578	Alofi	121/J 7
Norfolk Island, Australia	13.4	34.6	1,478	Kingston	115/M 5
North America	9,363,000	24,250,170	427,000,000	....	145
North Carolina, U.S.	52,669	136,413	6,628,637	Raleigh	163/H 3
North Dakota, U.S.	70,702	183,118	638,800	Bismarck	157/H 4
Northern Ireland, U.K.	5,452	14,121	1,543,000	Belfast	55/H 9
Northern Marianas, U.S.	184	477	43,345	Capitol Hill	120/D 3
Northern Territory, Australia	519,768	1,346,200	175,876	Darwin	114/E 3
North Korea	46,540	120,539	21,815,000	P'yŏngyang	101/D 2
Northwest Territories, Canada	1,304,896	3,379,683	57,649	Yellowknife	152/E 2
Norway	125,053	323,887	4,273,000	Oslo	61/C 3
Nova Scotia, Canada	21,425	55,491	899,942	Halifax	161/J 2
Oceania (Pacific Ocean)	3,292,000	8,526,280	23,000,000	....	120
Ohio, U.S.	41,330	107,045	10,847,115	Columbus	160/D 3
Oklahoma, U.S.	69,956	181,186	3,145,585	Oklahoma City	159/H 4
Oman	120,000	310,800	1,534,000	Muscat	95/G 4

Place	Square Miles	Square Kilometers	Population	Capital or Chief Town	Page/Index Ref.
Ontario, Canada	412,580	1,068,582	10,084,885	Toronto	152/H 3
Orange Free State, South Africa	49,866	129,153	1,833,216	Bloemfontein	132/D 3
Oregon, U.S.	97,073	251,419	2,842,321	Salem	156/C 4
Orkney Islands, Scotland	376	974	17,675	Kirkwall	55/N13
P Pakistan	310,403	803,944	117,490,000	Islamabad	95/H 3
Palau	188	487	14,000	Koror	120/C 4
Palmyra Atoll, U.S.	3.85	1	....	....	121/J 4
Panama	29,761	77,082	2,476,000	Panamá	149/F 4
Papua New Guinea	183,540	475,369	3,913,000	Port Moresby	120/D 5
Paracel Islands	....	....	....	....	105/F 5
Paraguay	157,047	406,752	4,799,000	Asunción	134/C 5
Pennsylvania, U.S.	45,308	117,348	11,881,643	Harrisburg	160/E 3
Peru	496,222	1,285,215	22,362,000	Lima	144/C 3
Philippines	115,707	299,681	65,759,000	Manila	112
Pitcairn Islands, U.K.	18	47	54	Adamstown	121/N 7
Poland	120,725	312,678	37,800,000	Warsaw	65/K 2
Portugal	35,549	92,072	10,388,000	Lisbon	74/A 3
Prince Edward Island, Canada	2,184	5,657	129,765	Charlottetown	161/J 2
Puerto Rico, U.S.	3,515	9,104	3,522,037	San Juan	150/E 3
Q Qatar	4,247	11,000	518,000	Doha	94/F 3
Québec, Canada	594,857	1,540,680	6,895,963	Québec	153/J 3
Queensland, Australia	666,872	1,727,200	2,977,813	Brisbane	118/B 3
R Réunion, France	969	2,510	607,000	St-Denis	133/R15
Rhode Island, U.S.	1,212	3,139	1,003,464	Providence	161/F 3
Romania	91,699	237,500	23,397,000	Bucharest	83/F 3
Russia	6,592,812	17,075,400	147,386,000	Moscow	88/H 3
Rwanda	10,169	26,337	7,903,000	Kigali	130/A 3
S Sabah, Malaysia	29,300	75,887	1,002,608	Kota Kinabalu	111/E 2
Saint Helena & Dependencies, U.K.	162	420	7,000	Jamestown	122/B 6
Saint Kitts and Nevis	104	269	40,000	Basseterre	150/F 3
Saint Lucia	238	616	153,000	Castries	150/F 4
Saint Pierre & Miquelon, France	93.5	242	6,000	Saint-Pierre	161/K 2
Saint Vincent & the Grenadines	150	388	114,000	Kingstown	150/F 4
Sakhalin, Russia	29,500	76,405	655,000	Yuzhno-Sakhalinsk	89/Q 4
San Marino	23.4	60.6	23,000	San Marino	79/F 5
São Tomé and Príncipe	372	963	128,000	São Tomé	124/G 7
Sarawak, Malaysia	48,202	124,843	1,294,753	Kuching	110/D 3
Sardinia, Italy	9,301	24,090	1,450,483	Cagliari	80/A 2
Saskatchewan, Canada	251,699	651,900	988,928	Regina	152/F 3
Saudi Arabia	829,995	2,149,687	17,870,000	Riyadh	94/D 4
Scotland, U.K.	30,414	78,772	5,117,146	Edinburgh	55/J 8
Senegal	75,954	196,720	7,953,000	Dakar	128/B 3
Seychelles	145	375	.69,000	Victoria	123/H 5
Shetland Islands, Scotland	552	1,430	18,494	Lerwick	55/N 2
Siam, see Thailand					
Sicily, Italy	9,926	25,708	4,628,918	Palermo	80/C 3
Sierra Leone	27,925	72,325	4,275,000	Freetown	128/B 4
Singapore	226	585	2,756,000	Singapore	110/B 3
Slovakia	18,924	49,014	4,991,168	Bratislava	65/K 4
Slovenia	7,898	20,251	1,891,864	Ljubljana	82/B 3
Society Islands, French Polynesia	677	1,753	117,703	Papeete	121/K 6
Solomon Islands	11,500	29,785	347,000	Honiara	120/E 6
Somalia	246,200	637,658	6,709,000	Mogadishu	125/Q 6
South Africa	455,318	1,179,274	40,601,000	Cape Town; Pretoria	126/D 6
South America	6,875,000	17,806,250	297,000,000	....	134
South Australia, Australia	379,922	984,000	1,400,630	Adelaide	114/E 5
South Carolina, U.S.	31,113	80,583	3,486,703	Columbia	163/H 3
South Dakota, U.S.	77,116	199,730	696,004	Pierre	157/H 4
South Korea	38,175	98,873	43,134,000	Seoul	101/D 4
Spain	194,881	504,742	39,385,000	Madrid	74/C 2
Spratly Islands	....	....	....	....	110/D 2
Sri Lanka	25,332	65,610	17,424,000	Colombo	106/D 6
Sudan	967,494	2,505,809	27,220,000	Khartoum	125/L 5
Sumatra, Indonesia	164,000	424,760	19,360,400	Medan	110/B 4
Suriname	55,144	142,823	402,000	Paramaribo	139/G 3
Svalbard, Norway	23,957	62,049	3,431	Longyearbyen	88/C 2
Swaziland	6,705	17,366	859,000	Mbabane	133/E 2
Sweden	173,665	449,792	8,564,000	Stockholm	61/E 3
Switzerland	15,943	41,292	6,784,000	Bern	76/D 4
Syria	71,498	185,180	12,966,000	Damascus	92/D 3
T Tahiti, French Polynesia	402	1,041	95,604	Papeete	121/X13
Taiwan	13,971	36,185	16,609,961	Taipei	105/J 3
Tajikistan	55,251	143,100	5,112,000	Dushanbe	88/H 6
Tanzania	363,708	942,003	26,869,000	Dar es Salaam	130/B 4
Tasmania, Australia	26,178	67,800	452,851	Hobart	119/C 4
Tennessee, U.S.	42,144	109,153	4,877,185	Nashville	163/G 3
Texas, U.S.	266,807	691,030	16,986,510	Austin	162/C 4
Thailand	198,455	513,998	56,814,000	Bangkok	109/C 3
Tibet, China	463,320	1,200,000	1,790,000	Lhasa	102/D 5
Togo	21,622	56,000	3,811,000	Lomé	129/F 4
Tokelau, New Zealand	3.9	10	1,575	Fakaofo	121/H 5
Tonga	270	699	102,000	Nuku'alofa	121/H 7
Transvaal, South Africa	109,621	283,918	10,673,033	Pretoria	132/E 2
Trinidad and Tobago	1,980	5,128	1,285,000	Port-of-Spain	150/F 5
Tristan da Cunha, St. Helena	38	98	251	Edinburgh	50/J 7
Tuamotu Archipelago, French Polynesia	341	883	9,052	Apataki	121/L 6
Tunisia	63,378	164,149	8,276,000	Tunis	124/G 1
Turkey	300,946	779,450	58,581,000	Ankara	92/C 2
Turkmenistan	188,455	488,100	3,534,000	Ashkhabad	88/F 6
Turks and Caicos Islands, U.K.	166	430	10,000	Cockburn Town, Grand Turk	150/D 2
Tuvalu	9.78	25.33	9,000	Fongafale, Funafuti	120/G 5
U Uganda	91,076	235,887	18,690,000	Kampala	130/B 3
Ukraine	233,089	603,700	51,704,000	Kiev	86/D 2
United Arab Emirates	32,278	83,600	2,390,000	Abu Dhabi	94/F 4
United Kingdom	94,399	244,493	57,515,000	London	55
United States	3,623,420	9,384,658	252,502,000	Washington	154
Uruguay	72,172	186,925	3,121,000	Montevideo	135/E 3
Utah, U.S.	84,899	219,888	1,722,850	Salt Lake City	158/E 3
Uzbekistan	173,591	449,600	19,906,000	Tashkent	88/G 5
V Vanuatu	5,700	14,763	170,000	Vila	120/F 6
Vatican City	108.7 acres	44 hectares	1,000	....	80/C 2
Venezuela	352,143	912,050	20,189,000	Caracas	139/E 3
Vermont, U.S.	9,614	24,900	562,758	Montpelier	161/F 2
Victoria, Australia	87,876	227,600	4,244,282	Melbourne	119/C 3
Vietnam	128,405	332,569	67,568,000	Hanoi	109/D 2
Virginia, U.S.	40,767	105,587	6,187,358	Richmond	160/E 5
Virgin Islands, British	59	153	12,000	Road Town	150/E 3
Virgin Islands, U.S.	132	342	101,809	Charlotte Amalie	150/E 3
W Wake Island, U.S.	2.5	6.5	302	Wake Islet	120/F 3
Wales, U.K.	8,017	20,764	2,790,462	Cardiff	55/J10
Wallis and Futuna, France	106	275	17,000	Mata Utu	120/G 6
Washington, U.S.	68,139	176,480	4,866,692	Olympia	156/C 4
West Bank	2,100	5,439	1,105,000	....	91/D 3
Western Australia, Australia	975,096	2,525,500	1,587,050	Perth	114/B 4
Western Sahara	102,703	266,000	197,000	....	124/B 3
Western Samoa	1,133	2,934	190,000	Apia	121/R 9
West Virginia, U.S.	24,231	62,758	1,793,477	Charleston	160/D 4
Wisconsin, U.S.	56,153	145,436	4,891,769	Madison	160/B 2
World	(land) 57,970,000	150,142,300	5,292,000,000		50
Wyoming, U.S.	97,809	253,325	453,588	Cheyenne	156/F 5
Y Yemen	188,321	487,752	10,063,000	Sanaa	94/E 5
Yugoslavia	38,989	100,982	11,371,275	Belgrade	82/D 3
Yukon Territory, Canada	207,075	536,324	27,797	Whitehorse	152/C 2
Z Zaire (Congo)	905,063	2,344,113	37,832,000	Kinshasa	122/E 5
Zambia	290,586	752,618	8,446,000	Lusaka	126/E 3
Zimbabwe	150,803	390,580	10,720,000	Harare	131/C 3

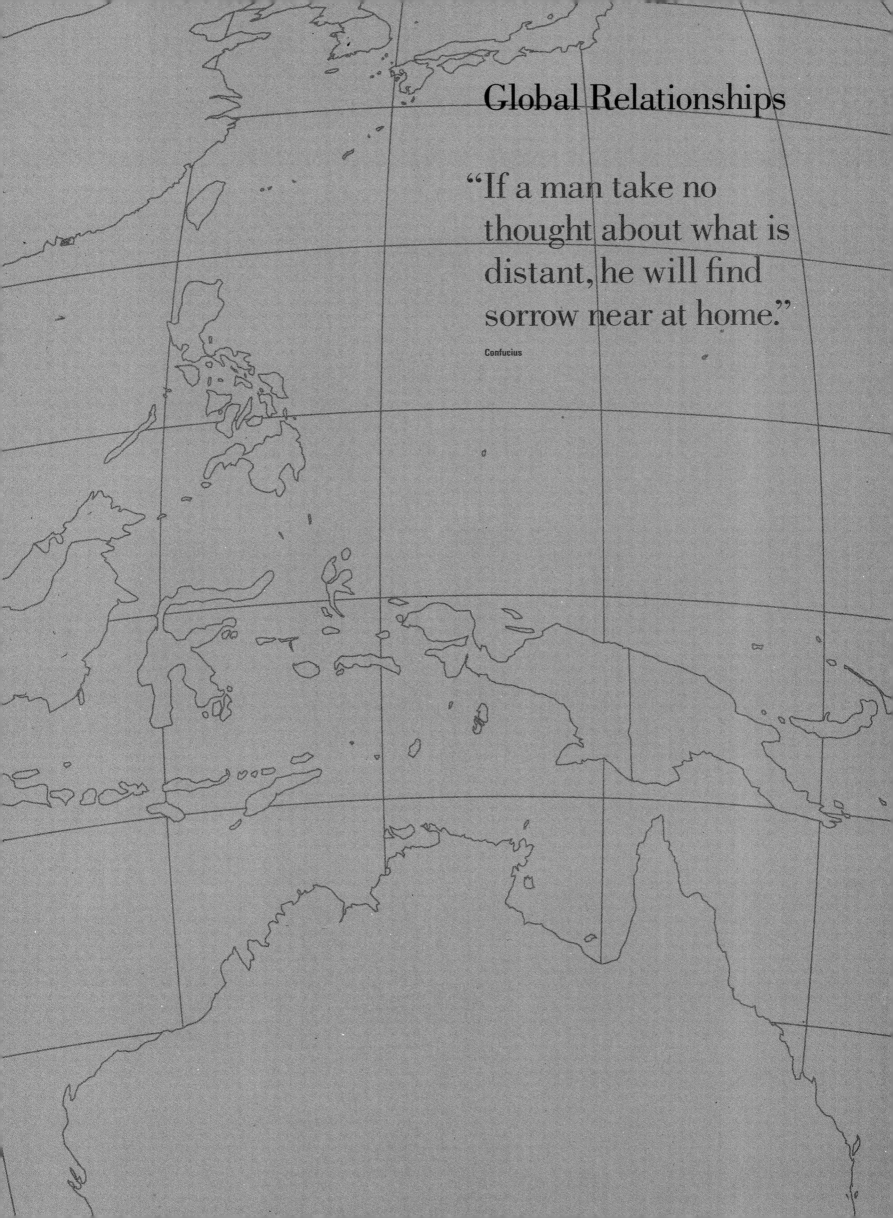

Global Relationships

"If a man take no thought about what is distant, he will find sorrow near at home."

Confucius

Environmental Concerns

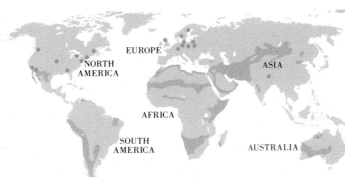

DESERTIFICATION AND ACID RAIN DAMAGE

AREAS OF PRODUCTIVE DRYLANDS
DESERTIFIED BY EARLY 1980's

AREAS OF DAMAGE FROM ACID RAIN
AND OTHER AIRBORNE POLLUTANTS

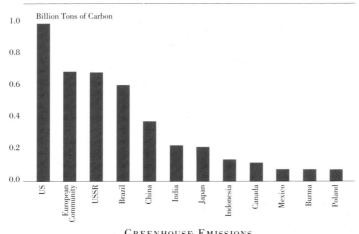

Billion Tons of Carbon

1.0
0.8
0.6
0.4
0.2
0.0

US | European Community | USSR | Brazil | China | India | Japan | Indonesia | Canada | Mexico | Burma | Poland

GREENHOUSE EMISSIONS

CARBON DIOXIDE EQUIVALENTS, 1987 NET EMISSIONS

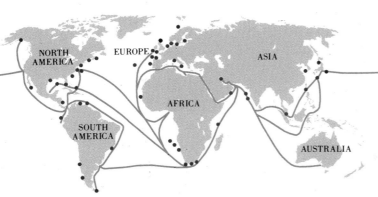

MAIN TANKER ROUTES AND MAJOR OIL SPILLS

ROUTES OF VERY LARGE CRUDE OIL CARRIERS   ● MAJOR OIL SPILLS

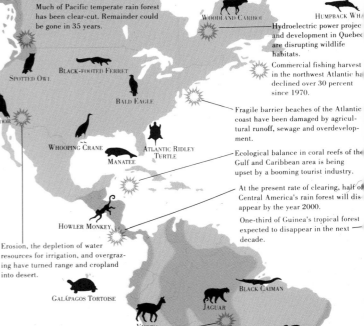

GRIZZLY BEAR
Much of Pacific temperate rain forest has been clear-cut. Remainder could be gone in 35 years.

WOODLAND CARIBOU

HUMPBACK WHA
Hydroelectric power projec and development in Quebec are disrupting wildlife habitats.

Commercial fishing harvest in the northwest Atlantic ha declined over 30 percent since 1970.

SPOTTED OWL

BLACK-FOOTED FERRET

BALD EAGLE

Fragile barrier beaches of the Atlantic coast have been damaged by agricultural runoff, sewage and overdevelopment.

CONDOR

WHOOPING CRANE

ATLANTIC RIDLEY TURTLE

MANATEE

Ecological balance in coral reefs of the Gulf and Caribbean area is being upset by a booming tourist industry.

At the present rate of clearing, half of Central America's rain forest will dis appear by the year 2000.

One-third of Guinea's tropical forest expected to disappear in the next decade.

HOWLER MONKEY

Erosion, the depletion of water resources for irrigation, and overgrazing have turned range and cropland into desert.

GALÁPAGOS TORTOISE

VICUNA

JAGUAR

BLACK CAIMAN

Every year over 5000 square miles (13,000 sq km) of rain forest is destroyed in Brazil's Amazon Basin.

CHINCHILLA

GOLDEN LION TAMARIN

GIANT ARMADILLO

The Atlantic waters off Patagonia have suffered fro over-fishing and oil spills.

Southern Chile's rain forest is threatened by development.

BLUE WHALE

Acid Rain

Acid rain of nitric and sulfuric acids has killed all life in thousands of lakes, and over 15 million acres (6 million hectares) of virgin forest in Europe and North America are dead or dying.

Deforestation

Each year, 50 million acres (20 million hectares) of tropical rainforests are being felled by loggers. Trees remove carbon-dioxide from the atmosphere and are vital to the prevention of soil erosion.

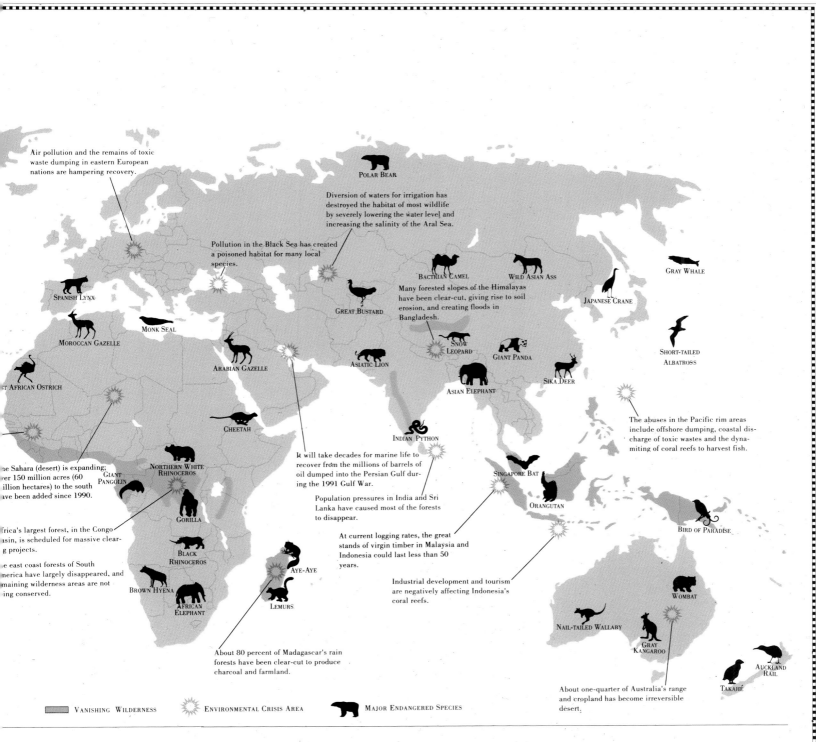

Air pollution and the remains of toxic waste dumping in eastern European nations are hampering recovery.

POLAR BEAR

Diversion of waters for irrigation has destroyed the habitat of most wildlife by severely lowering the water level and increasing the salinity of the Aral Sea.

Pollution in the Black Sea has created a poisoned habitat for many local species.

BACTRIAN CAMEL   WILD ASIAN ASS

GRAY WHALE

SPANISH LYNX

GREAT BUSTARD

Many forested slopes of the Himalayas have been clear-cut, giving rise to soil erosion, and creating floods in Bangladesh.

JAPANESE CRANE

MONK SEAL

MOROCCAN GAZELLE

ARABIAN GAZELLE

ASIATIC LION

SNOW LEOPARD

GIANT PANDA

SHORT-TAILED ALBATROSS

...T AFRICAN OSTRICH

ASIAN ELEPHANT

SIKA DEER

CHEETAH

INDIAN PYTHON

The abuses in the Pacific rim areas include offshore dumping, coastal discharge of toxic wastes and the dynamiting of coral reefs to harvest fish.

It will take decades for marine life to recover from the millions of barrels of oil dumped into the Persian Gulf during the 1991 Gulf War.

...he Sahara (desert) is expanding; ...er 150 million acres (60 ...illion hectares) to the south ...ave been added since 1990.

GIANT PANGOLIN

NORTHERN WHITE RHINOCEROS

Population pressures in India and Sri Lanka have caused most of the forests to disappear.

SINGAPORE BAT

ORANGUTAN

...rica's largest forest, in the Congo ...asin, is scheduled for massive clear...g projects.

GORILLA

At current logging rates, the great stands of virgin timber in Malaysia and Indonesia could last less than 50 years.

BIRD OF PARADISE

...e east coast forests of South ...merica have largely disappeared, and ...maining wilderness areas are not ...ing conserved.

BLACK RHINOCEROS

AYE-AYE

Industrial development and tourism are negatively affecting Indonesia's coral reefs.

WOMBAT

BROWN HYENA

AFRICAN ELEPHANT

LEMURS

NAIL-TAILED WALLABY

GRAY KANGAROO

AUCKLAND RAIL

About 80 percent of Madagascar's rain forests have been clear-cut to produce charcoal and farmland.

TAKAHĒ

About one-quarter of Australia's range and cropland has become irreversible desert.

▬ VANISHING WILDERNESS   ✦ ENVIRONMENTAL CRISIS AREA   🐻 MAJOR ENDANGERED SPECIES

Extinction

Biologists estimate that over 50,000 plant and animal species inhabiting the world's rain forests are disappearing each year due to pollution, unchecked hunting and the destruction of natural habitats.

Air Pollution

Billions of tons of industrial emissions and toxic pollutants are released into the air each year, depleting our ozone layer, killing our forests and lakes with acid rain and threatening our health.

Water Pollution

Only 3 percent of the earth's water is fresh. Pollution from cities, farms and factories has made much of it unfit to drink. In the developing world, most sewage flows untreated into lakes and rivers.

Ozone Depletion

The layer of ozone in the stratosphere shields earth from harmful ultraviolet radiation. But man-made gases are destroying this vital barrier, increasing the risk of skin cancer and eye disease.

Population

CURRENT POPULATION COMPARISONS

EACH AREA'S SIZE IS PROPORTIONATE TO ITS POPULATION

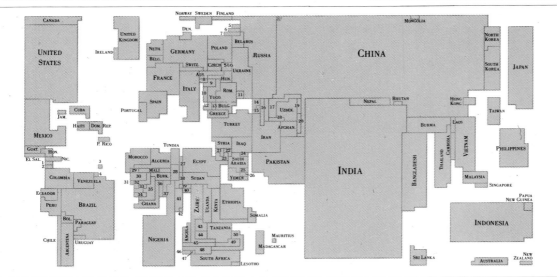

COUNTRIES INDICATED BY NUMBER

1 COSTA RICA	10 BOSNIA AND	20 TAJIKISTAN	30 SENEGAL	40 CONGO	51 CYPRUS
2 PANAMA	HERCEGOVINA	21 LEBANON	31 GUINEA-BISSAU	41 CAMEROON	52 CAPE VERDE
3 TRINIDAD AND	11 MOLDOVA	22 JORDAN	32 GUINEA	42 GABON	53 GAMBIA
TOBAGO	12 ALBANIA	23 ISRAEL	33 SIERRA LEONE	43 RWANDA	54 EQUATORIAL GUINEA
4 GUYANA	13 MACEDONIA	24 KUWAIT	34 LIBERIA	44 BURUNDI	55 BAHRAIN
5 ESTONIA	14 GEORGIA	25 UNITED ARAB	35 IVORY COAST	45 ZAMBIA	56 QATAR
6 LATVIA	15 ARMENIA	EMIRATES	36 TOGO	46 NAMIBIA	57 BRUNEI
7 LITHUANIA	16 AZERBAIJAN	26 OMAN	37 BENIN	47 ZIMBABWE	58 SOLOMON ISLANDS
8 SLOVENIA	17 KAZAKHSTAN	27 LIBYA	38 CHAD	48 ZIMBABWE	
9 CROATIA	18 TURKMENISTAN	28 NIGER	39 CENTRAL AFRICAN	49 MOZAMBIQUE	
	19 KYRGYZSTAN	29 MAURITANIA	REPUBLIC	50 MALAWI	

PROJECTED POPULATION COMPARISONS - 2020

EACH AREA'S SIZE IS PROPORTIONATE TO ITS POPULATION

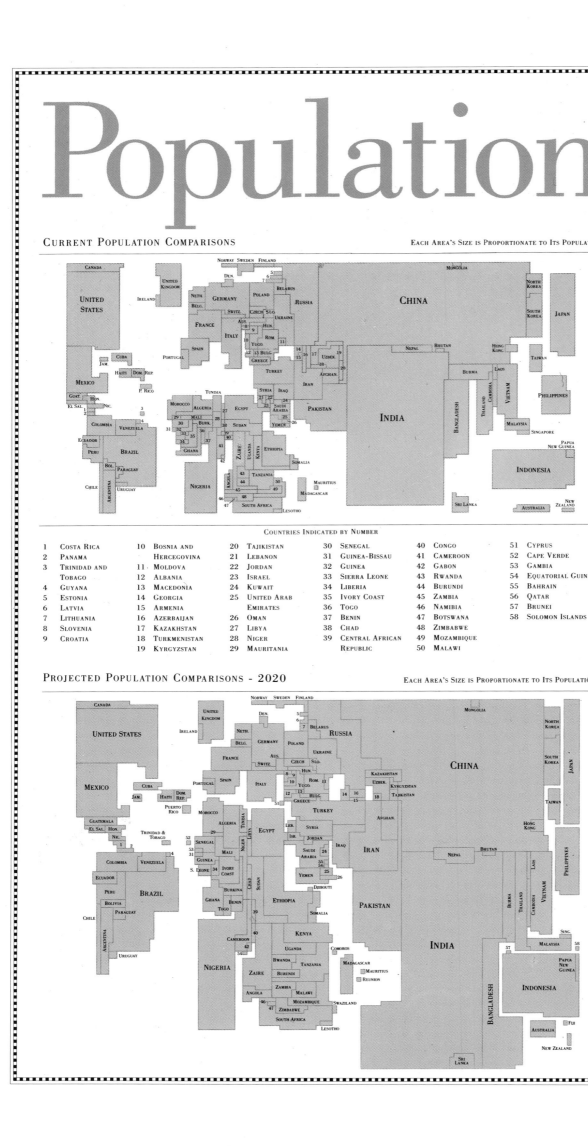

3.5 PERCENT OR M

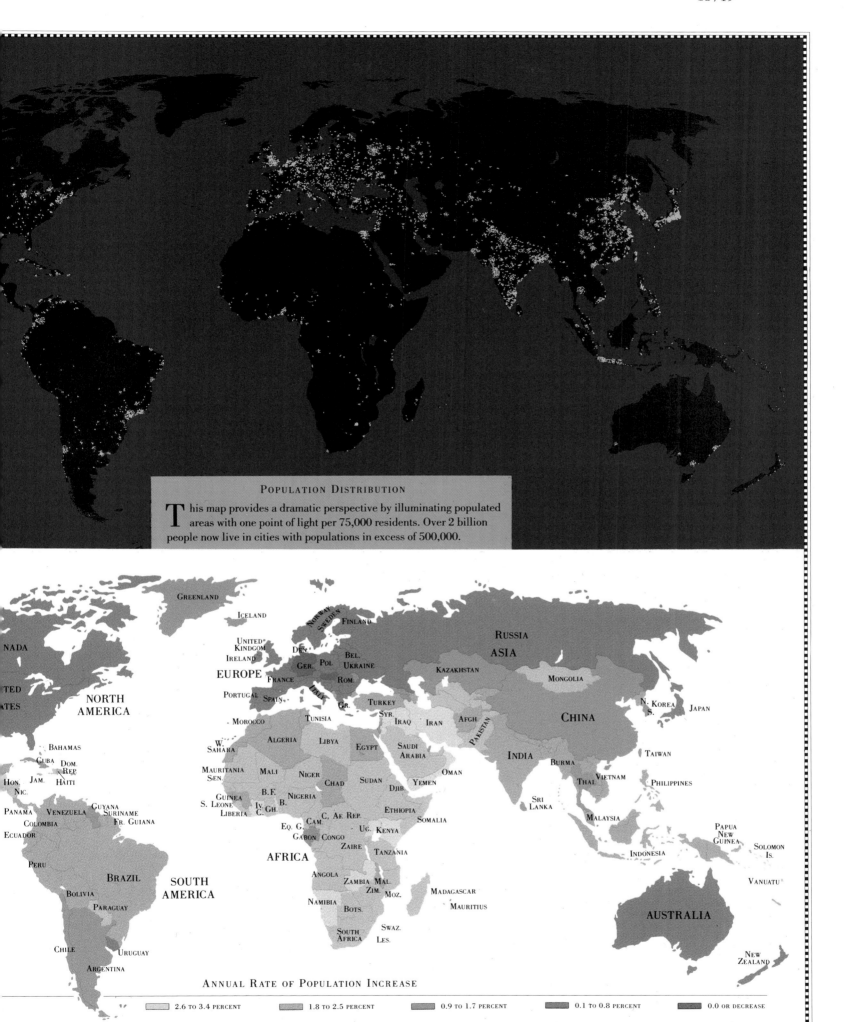

POPULATION DISTRIBUTION

This map provides a dramatic perspective by illuminating populated areas with one point of light per 75,000 residents. Over 2 billion people now live in cities with populations in excess of 500,000.

ANNUAL RATE OF POPULATION INCREASE

| | 2.6 TO 3.4 PERCENT | 1.8 TO 2.5 PERCENT | 0.9 TO 1.7 PERCENT | 0.1 TO 0.8 PERCENT | 0.0 OR DECREASE |

Standards of Living

LITERATE PERCENT OF POPULATION

80 AND ABOVE	40-59	0-19
60-79	20-39	

YEARS OF LIFE EXPECTANCY (MEN AND WOMEN)

70 AND ABOVE	50-59	0-39
60-69	40-49	

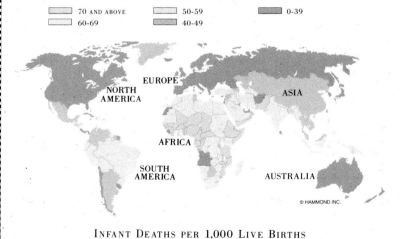

© HAMMOND INC.

INFANT DEATHS PER 1,000 LIVE BIRTHS

150 AND MORE	50-99	0-24
100-149	25-49	

ALASKA

CANADA

UNITED STATES

UNITED STATES
The economic and political influence of women has risen substantially. In a number of fields, women's salaries are now nearly equal to men's.

MEXICO

BAHAMAS

CUBA

JAM. DOM. REP.
HAITI

BEL.
HON.
GUAT.
EL. SAL. NIC.

C.R.

PANAMA VENEZUELA GUYANA
COLOMBIA SURINAME
FR. GUIANA

LATIN AMERICA
The gulf between rich and poor continues to widen, despite efforts to reform oppressive governments, increase literacy and relieve overburdened cities.

ECUADOR

SOUTH AMERICA
Political unrest, rising inflation and slow economic growth continue to thwart efforts to bring unity and prosperity to the nations of South America

PERU BRAZIL

BOLIVIA

PARAGUAY

CHILE

URUGUAY

ARGENTINA

GREE

COMPARISON OF EUROPEAN, U.S. AND JAPANESE WORKERS

COUNTRY	SCHEDULED WEEKLY HOURS	ANNUAL LEAVE DAYS/HOLIDAYS	ANNUAL HOURS WORKED
GERMANY	39	42	1708
NETHERLANDS	40	43.5	1740
BELGIUM	38	31	1748
AUSTRIA	39.3	38	1751
FRANCE	39	34	1771
ITALY	40	39	1776
UNITED KINGDOM	39	33	1778
LUXEMBOURG	40	37	1792
FINLAND	40	37	1792
SWEDEN	40	37	1792
SPAIN	40	36	1800
DENMARK	40	34	1816
NORWAY	40	30	1848
GREECE	40	28	1864
IRELAND	40	28	1864
UNITED STATES	40	22	1912
SWITZERLAND	41.5	30.5	1913
PORTUGAL	45	36	2025
JAPAN	44	23.5	2116

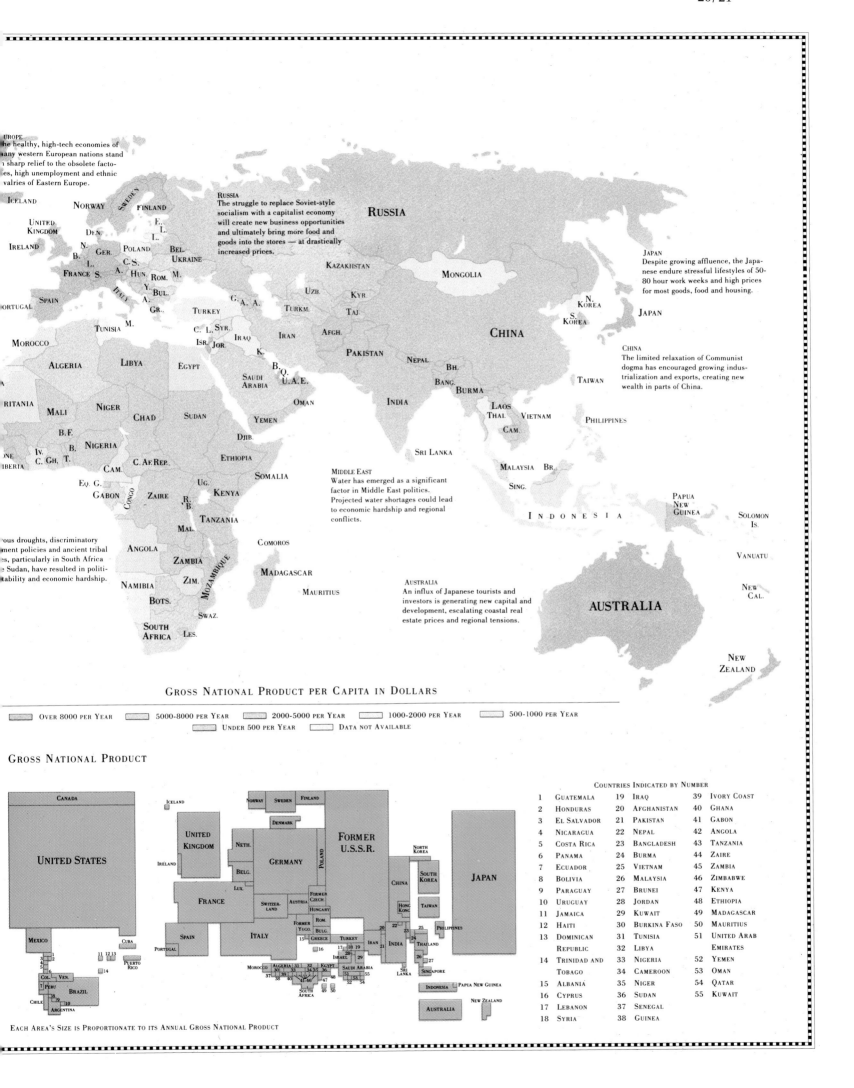

EUROPE
The healthy, high-tech economies of many western European nations stand in sharp relief to the obsolete factories, high unemployment and ethnic valries of Eastern Europe.

RUSSIA
The struggle to replace Soviet-style socialism with a capitalist economy will create new business opportunities and ultimately bring more food and goods into the stores — at drastically increased prices.

JAPAN
Despite growing affluence, the Japanese endure stressful lifestyles of 50-80 hour work weeks and high prices for most goods, food and housing.

CHINA
The limited relaxation of Communist dogma has encouraged growing industrialization and exports, creating new wealth in parts of China.

MIDDLE EAST
Water has emerged as a significant factor in Middle East politics. Projected water shortages could lead to economic hardship and regional conflicts.

AUSTRALIA
An influx of Japanese tourists and investors is generating new capital and development, escalating coastal real estate prices and regional tensions.

...rous droughts, discriminatory ...ment policies and ancient tribal ...es, particularly in South Africa ... Sudan, have resulted in politi-...ability and economic hardship.

GROSS NATIONAL PRODUCT PER CAPITA IN DOLLARS

OVER 8000 PER YEAR   5000-8000 PER YEAR   2000-5000 PER YEAR   1000-2000 PER YEAR   500-1000 PER YEAR

UNDER 500 PER YEAR   DATA NOT AVAILABLE

GROSS NATIONAL PRODUCT

EACH AREA'S SIZE IS PROPORTIONATE TO ITS ANNUAL GROSS NATIONAL PRODUCT

COUNTRIES INDICATED BY NUMBER

1	GUATEMALA	19	IRAQ	39	IVORY COAST
2	HONDURAS	20	AFGHANISTAN	40	GHANA
3	EL SALVADOR	21	PAKISTAN	41	GABON
4	NICARAGUA	22	NEPAL	42	ANGOLA
5	COSTA RICA	23	BANGLADESH	43	TANZANIA
6	PANAMA	24	BURMA	44	ZAIRE
7	ECUADOR	25	VIETNAM	45	ZAMBIA
8	BOLIVIA	26	MALAYSIA	46	ZIMBABWE
9	PARAGUAY	27	BRUNEI	47	KENYA
10	URUGUAY	28	JORDAN	48	ETHIOPIA
11	JAMAICA	29	KUWAIT	49	MADAGASCAR
12	HAITI	30	BURKINA FASO	50	MAURITIUS
13	DOMINICAN REPUBLIC	31	TUNISIA	51	UNITED ARAB EMIRATES
14	TRINIDAD AND TOBAGO	32	LIBYA	52	YEMEN
		33	NIGERIA	53	OMAN
15	ALBANIA	34	CAMEROON	54	QATAR
16	CYPRUS	35	NIGER	55	KUWAIT
17	LEBANON	36	SUDAN		
18	SYRIA	37	SENEGAL		
		38	GUINEA		

Energy & Resources

TOP FIVE WORLD PRODUCERS OF SELECTED MINERAL COMMODITIES

MINERAL FUELS	1	2	3	4	5
CRUDE OIL	RUSSIA	UNITED STATES	SAUDI ARABIA	CHINA	IRAQ
REFINED OIL	UNITED STATES	RUSSIA	JAPAN	CHINA	UNITED KINGDOM
NATURAL GAS	RUSSIA	UNITED STATES	CANADA	NETHERLANDS	UNITED KINGDOM
COAL (ALL GRADES)	CHINA	UNITED STATES	GERMANY	RUSSIA	POLAND
MINE URANIUM	CANADA	SOUTH AFRICA	UNITED STATES	AUSTRALIA	NAMIBIA

METALS					
CHROMITE	SOUTH AFRICA	KAZAKHSTAN	ALBANIA	FINLAND	INDIA
IRON ORE	BRAZIL	UKRAINE	RUSSIA	CHINA	AUSTRALIA
MANGANESE ORE	FORMER USSR	SOUTH AFRICA	CHINA	GABON	AUSTRALIA
MINE NICKEL	CANADA	RUSSIA	NEW CALEDONIA	AUSTRALIA	INDONESIA
MINE SILVER	MEXICO	UNITED STATES	PERU	FORMER USSR	CANADA
BAUXITE	AUSTRALIA	GUINEA	BRAZIL	JAMAICA	FORMER USSR
ALUMINIUM	UNITED STATES	FORMER USSR	CANADA	AUSTRALIA	BRAZIL
GOLD	SOUTH AFRICA	FORMER USSR	UNITED STATES	AUSTRALIA	CANADA
MINE COPPER	CHILE	UNITED STATES	CANADA	FORMER USSR	ZAIRE
MINE LEAD	AUSTRALIA	FORMER USSR	UNITED STATES	CANADA	CHINA
MINE TIN	BRAZIL	INDONESIA	MALAYSIA	CHINA	FORMER USSR
MINE ZINC	CANADA	FORMER USSR	AUSTRALIA	CHINA	PERU

NONMETALS					
NATURAL DIAMOND	AUSTRALIA	ZAIRE	BOTSWANA	FORMER USSR	SOUTH AFRICA
POTASH	FORMER USSR	CANADA	GERMANY	UNITED STATES	FRANCE
PHOSPHATE ROCK	UNITED STATES	FORMER USSR	MOROCCO	CHINA	TUNISIA
ELEMENTAL SULFUR	UNITED STATES	FORMER USSR	CANADA	POLAND	CHINA

Names in Black Indicate More Than 10% of Total World Production

NUCLEAR POWER PRODUCTION

PERCENTAGE OF WORLD TOTAL

United States 27.4

France 15.1

Japan 11.4

Germany 8.6

Canada 4.6

Sweden 4.1

United Kingdom 3.3

Belgium 2.5

Spain 2.5

South Korea 2.4

Czechoslovakia 1.3

Switzerland 1.3

Finland 1.2

COMMERCIAL ENERGY CONSUMPTION/PRODUCTION

PERCENTAGE OF WORLD TOTAL

0.0 PRODUCTION   ■ 0.0 CONSUMPTION

Former USSR 23.2 / 19.3

United States 19.8 / 24.1

China 8.8 / 8.3

Canada 3.3 / 2.7

United Kingdom 3.3 / 3.0

Saudi Arabia 3.3 / 0.8

Mexico 2.5 / 1.5

Germany 2.5 / 4.9

India 2.1 / 2.3

Australia 1.9 / 1.1

Iran 1.9 / 0.7

Poland 1.8 / 1.9

Venezuela 1.7 / 0.6

ALASKA

UNIT

ME

- ▨ OIL FIELDS
- ■ NATURAL GAS FIELDS
- ● MAJOR COAL DEPOSITS
- ▲ OIL SANDS
- ◆ OIL SHALE
- ✳ MAJOR URANIUM DEPOSITS
- ■ IMPORTANT PEAT DEPOSITS

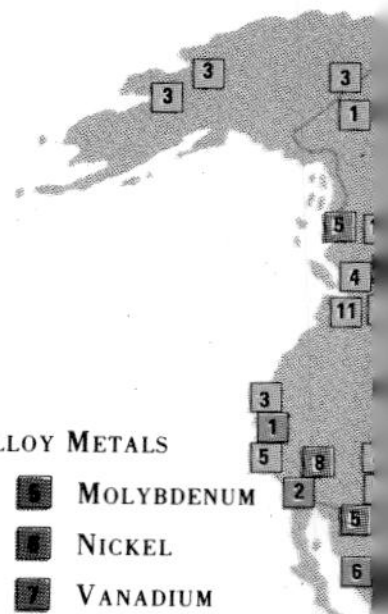

IRON AND FERROALLOY METALS

1	COBALT	5	MOLYBDENUM
2	CHROMIUM	6	NICKEL
3	IRON ORE	7	VANADIUM
4	MANGANESE	8	TUNGSTEN

OTHER METALS

1	SILVER	7	PLATINUM
2	BAUXITE	8	ANTIMONY
3	GOLD	9	TIN
4	COPPER	10	TITANIUM
5	MERCURY	11	ZINC
6	LEAD		

NONMETALS

1	ASBESTOS	10	MICA
2	BORAX	11	NITRATES
3	DIAMONDS	12	OPALS
4	EMERALDS	13	PHOSPHATES
5	FLUORSPAR	14	PEARLS
6	GRAPHITE	15	RUBIES
7	IODINE	16	SULFUR
8	JADE	17	SAPPHIRES
9	POTASH		

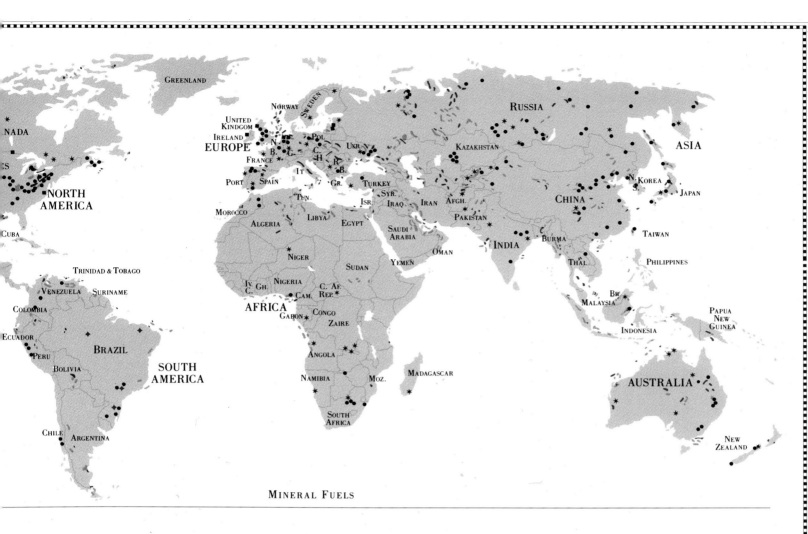

MINERAL FUELS

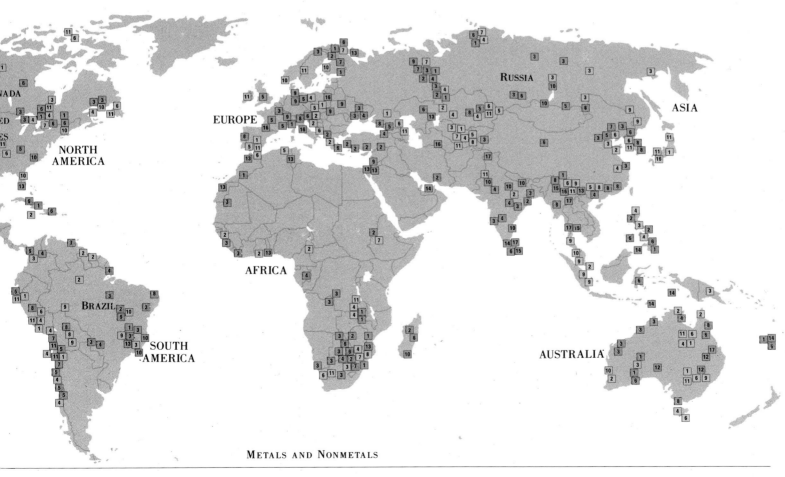

METALS AND NONMETALS

Agriculture & Manufacturing

Top Five World Producers of Selected Agricultural Commodities

	1	2	3	4	5
WHEAT	CHINA	FORMER USSR	UNITED STATES	INDIA	FRANCE
RICE	CHINA	INDIA	INDONESIA	BANGLADESH	THAILAND
OATS	FORMER USSR	UNITED STATES	CANADA	GERMANY	POLAND
CORN (MAIZE)	UNITED STATES	CHINA	BRAZIL	ROMANIA	FORMER USSR
SOYBEANS	UNITED STATES	BRAZIL	CHINA	ARGENTINA	CANADA
POTATOES	RUSSIA	POLAND	CHINA	GERMANY	UKRAINE
COFFEE	BRAZIL	COLOMBIA	INDONESIA	MEXICO	IVORY COAST
TEA	INDIA	CHINA	SRI LANKA	KENYA	FORMER USSR
TOBACCO	CHINA	UNITED STATES	INDIA	BRAZIL	FORMER USSR
COTTON	CHINA	UNITED STATES	FORMER USSR	PAKISTAN	INDIA
CATTLE	AUSTRALIA	BRAZIL	UNITED STATES	CHINA	RUSSIA
SHEEP	AUSTRALIA	CHINA	NEW ZEALAND	RUSSIA	INDIA
HOGS	CHINA	UNITED STATES	RUSSIA	GERMANY	BRAZIL
COW'S MILK	UNITED STATES	GERMANY	RUSSIA	FRANCE	POLAND
HEN'S EGGS	CHINA	UNITED STATES	RUSSIA	JAPAN	BRAZIL
WOOL	AUSTRALIA	FORMER USSR	NEW ZEALAND	CHINA	ARGENTINA
ROUNDWOOD	UNITED STATES	RUSSIA	CHINA	INDIA	BRAZIL
NATURAL RUBBER	MALAYSIA	INDONESIA	THAILAND	CHINA	INDIA
FISH CATCHES	JAPAN	FORMER USSR	CHINA	UNITED STATES	CHILE

Names in Black Indicate More Than 10% of Total World Production

Percent of Total Employment in Agriculture, Manufacturing and Other Industries

Legend:
- AGRICULTURE (INCLUDES FORESTRY AND FISHING)
- MANUFACTURING
- CONSTRUCTION
- TRADE AND COMMERCE
- FINANCE, INSURANCE, REAL ESTATE
- SERVICES
- OTHER (INCLUDES MINING, UTILITIES, TRANSPORTATION)

Scale: 0 — 20 — 40 — 60 — 80 — 100

India
China
Indonesia
Pakistan
Mexico
Brazil
Spain
Argentina
Italy
Japan
France
Canada
Australia
Germany
United States
United Kingdom

Finance, Insurance, Real Estate Data Included With "Other" for India, China, Indonesia and Pakistan

CEREALS, LIVESTOCK

LIVESTOCK RANCHING AND HE...

SEATTLE - TACOMA
SAN FRANCISCO - SAN JOSE
SOUTHERN CALIFORNIA
CHICAGO - G...
ST. LOU...
DET...
HOU...
MEXICO CITY - PUEBLA
SANTIAGO - VALPARA...

▲ AIRCRAFT
△ MOTOR VEHICLES
▽ SHIPBUILDING

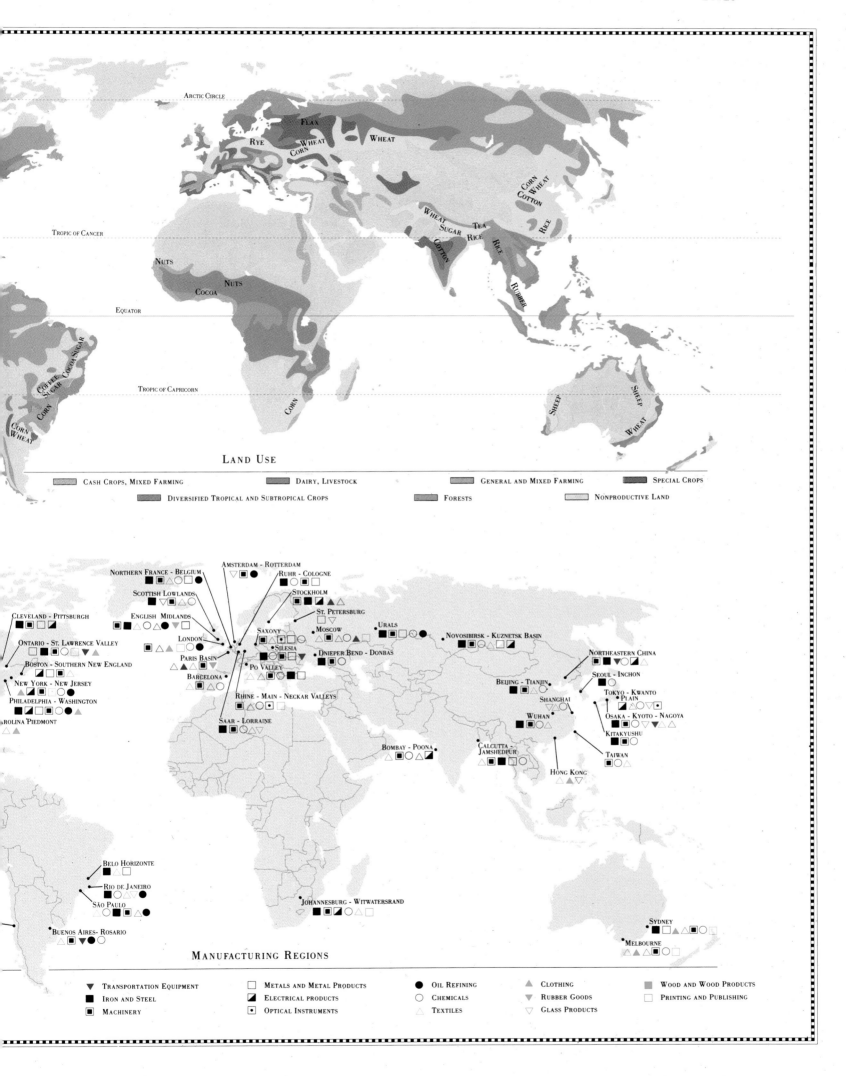

ARCTIC CIRCLE

FLAX

RYE
CORN
WHEAT
WHEAT
WHEAT
CORN
WHEAT
COTTON

TROPIC OF CANCER

WHEAT
SUGAR
TEA
RICE
COTTON
RICE
RICE

NUTS

NUTS
COCOA

RUBBER

EQUATOR

COFFEE COCOA SUGAR
SUGAR COCOA SUGAR

CORN
CORN

TROPIC OF CAPRICORN

CORN

SHEEP
SHEEP
WHEAT

CORN
WHEAT

LAND USE

CASH CROPS, MIXED FARMING	DAIRY, LIVESTOCK	GENERAL AND MIXED FARMING	SPECIAL CROPS
DIVERSIFIED TROPICAL AND SUBTROPICAL CROPS	FORESTS	NONPRODUCTIVE LAND

AMSTERDAM - ROTTERDAM
NORTHERN FRANCE - BELGIUM
RUHR - COLOGNE
SCOTTISH LOWLANDS
STOCKHOLM
CLEVELAND - PITTSBURGH
ENGLISH MIDLANDS
ST. PETERSBURG
SAXONY
MOSCOW
URALS
NOVOSIBIRSK - KUZNETSK BASIN
ONTARIO - ST. LAWRENCE VALLEY
LONDON
SILESIA
BOSTON - SOUTHERN NEW ENGLAND
PARIS BASIN
DNIEPER BEND - DONBAS
NEW YORK - NEW JERSEY
PO VALLEY
BEIJING - TIANJIN
NORTHEASTERN CHINA
PHILADELPHIA - WASHINGTON
BARCELONA
SEOUL - INCHON
ROLINA PIEDMONT
SHANGHAI
TOKYO - KWANTO PLAIN
RHINE - MAIN - NECKAR VALLEYS
WUHAN
OSAKA - KYOTO - NAGOYA
SAAR - LORRAINE
KITAKYUSHU
BOMBAY - POONA
CALCUTTA - JAMSHEDPUR
TAIWAN
HONG KONG

BELO HORIZONTE
RIO DE JANEIRO
SÃO PAULO
JOHANNESBURG - WITWATERSRAND
SYDNEY
BUENOS AIRES - ROSARIO
MELBOURNE

MANUFACTURING REGIONS

▼ TRANSPORTATION EQUIPMENT	☐ METALS AND METAL PRODUCTS	● OIL REFINING	▲ CLOTHING	■ WOOD AND WOOD PRODUCTS
■ IRON AND STEEL	◪ ELECTRICAL PRODUCTS	○ CHEMICALS	▼ RUBBER GOODS	☐ PRINTING AND PUBLISHING
▣ MACHINERY	⊡ OPTICAL INSTRUMENTS	△ TEXTILES	▽ GLASS PRODUCTS	

Climate

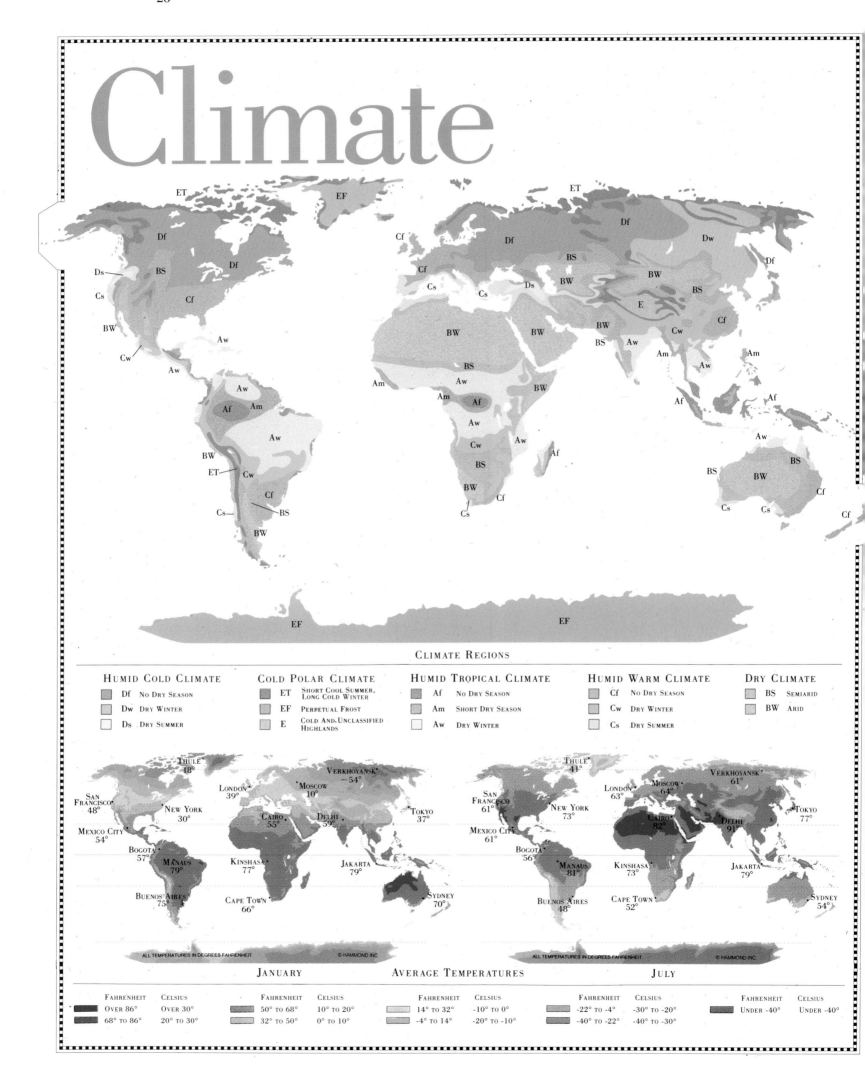

CLIMATE REGIONS

HUMID COLD CLIMATE
- Df NO DRY SEASON
- Dw DRY WINTER
- Ds DRY SUMMER

COLD POLAR CLIMATE
- ET SHORT COOL SUMMER, LONG COLD WINTER
- EF PERPETUAL FROST
- E COLD AND UNCLASSIFIED HIGHLANDS

HUMID TROPICAL CLIMATE
- Af NO DRY SEASON
- Am SHORT DRY SEASON
- Aw DRY WINTER

HUMID WARM CLIMATE
- Cf NO DRY SEASON
- Cw DRY WINTER
- Cs DRY SUMMER

DRY CLIMATE
- BS SEMIARID
- BW ARID

JANUARY   AVERAGE TEMPERATURES   JULY

ALL TEMPERATURES IN DEGREES FAHRENHEIT   © HAMMOND INC.

FAHRENHEIT	CELSIUS	FAHRENHEIT	CELSIUS	FAHRENHEIT	CELSIUS	FAHRENHEIT	CELSIUS	FAHRENHEIT	CELSIUS
OVER 86°	OVER 30°	50° TO 68°	10° TO 20°	14° TO 32°	-10° TO 0°	-22° TO -4°	-30° TO -20°	UNDER -40°	UNDER -40°
68° TO 86°	20° TO 30°	32° TO 50°	0° TO 10°	-4° TO 14°	-20° TO -10°	-40° TO -22°	-40° TO -30°		

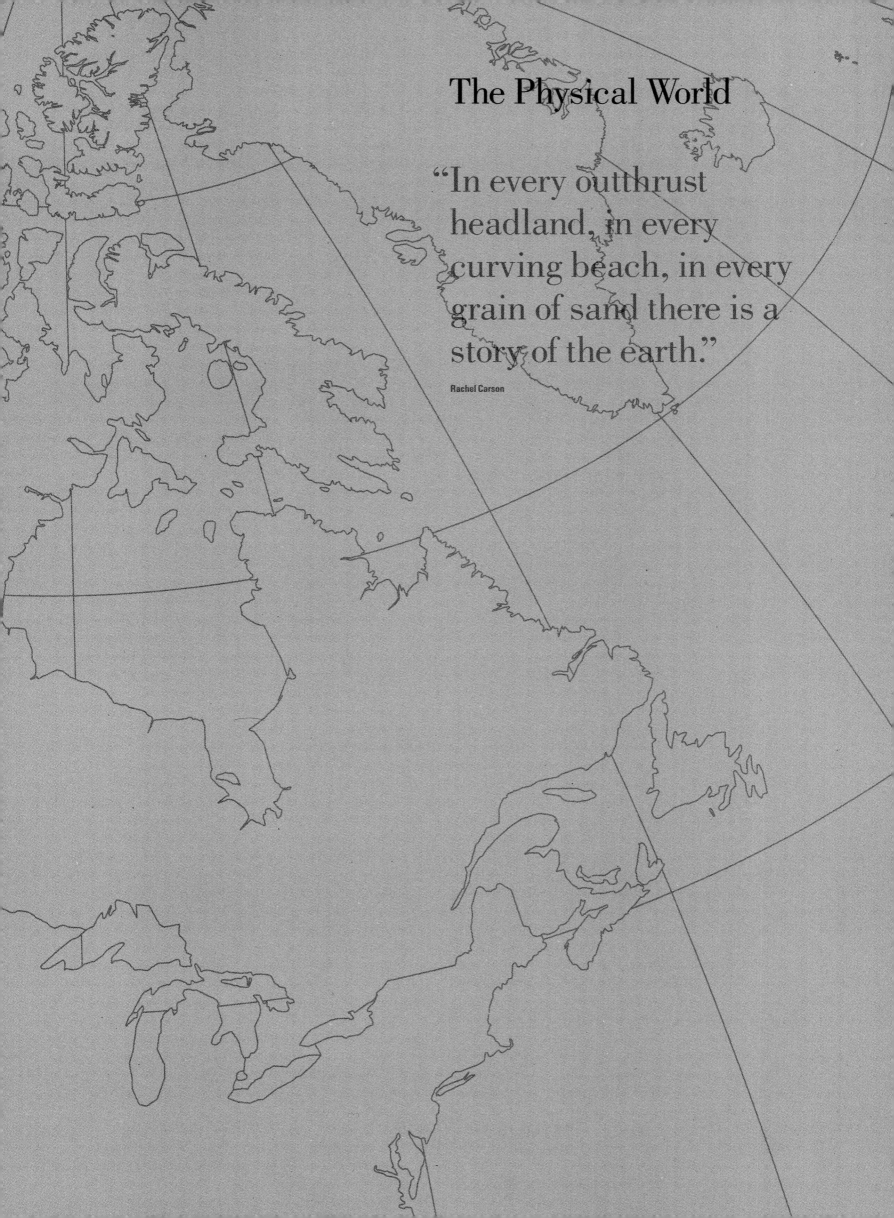

The Physical World

"In every outthrust headland, in every curving beach, in every grain of sand there is a story of the earth."

Rachel Carson

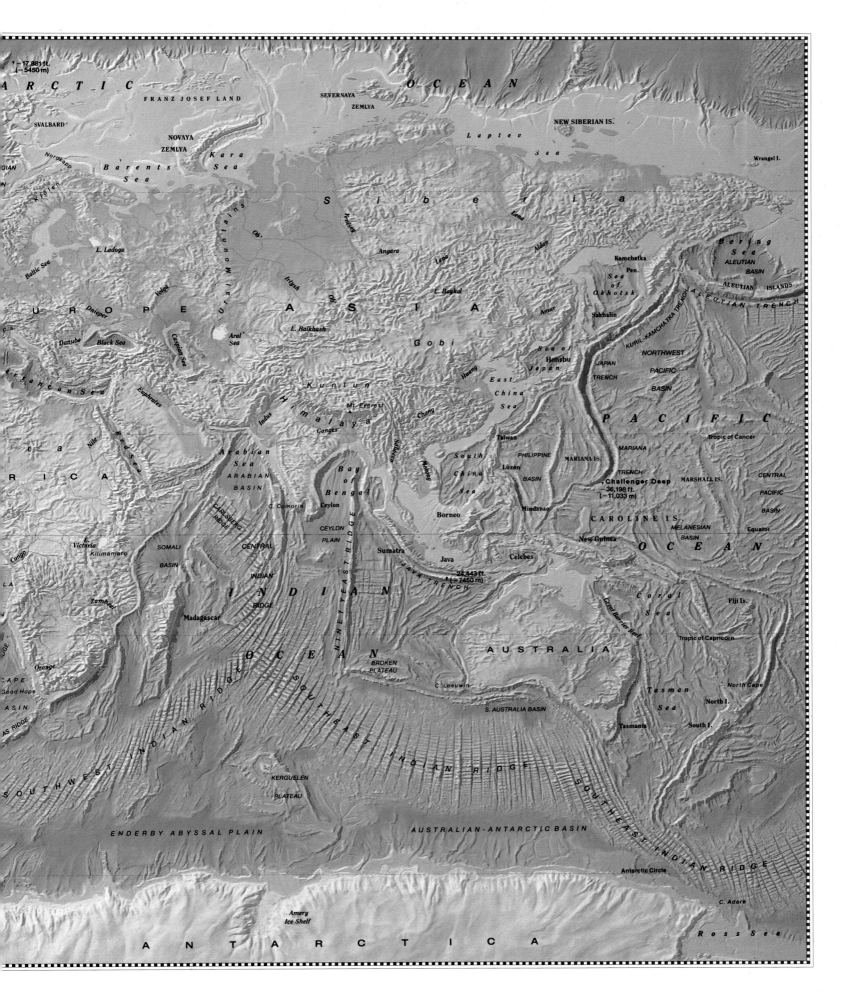

▼ −17,881 ft.
(−5450 m)

ARCTIC — OCEAN

FRANZ JOSEF LAND

SEVERNAYA
ZEMLYA

NEW SIBERIAN IS.

SVALBARD

NOVAYA
ZEMLYA

Kara
Sea

Laptev
Sea

Wrangel I.

Nordkapp

Barents
Sea

GIAN

Kjölen

Baltic Sea

L. Ladoga

S i b e r i a

Yenisey

Lena

Aldan

Bering
Sea

Kamchatka
Pen.

ALEUTIAN
BASIN

EUROPE

Ural Mountains

Ob'

Irtysh

Angara

Lena

L. Baykal

Amur

Sea
of
Okhotsk

Sakhalin

ALEUTIAN ISLANDS

ALEUTIAN TRENCH

Volga

Caspian Sea

ASIA

KURIL-KAMCHATKA TRENCH

Dnieper

Aral'
Sea

L. Balkhash

Gobi

NORTHWEST

Danube

Black Sea

Honshu
Japan

JAPAN
TRENCH

PACIFIC

BASIN

Euphrates

Kunlun

Huang

Sea of
Japan

ranean Sea

Nile

Red Sea

Indus

Himalaya

Mt. Everest

Ganges

Chang

East
China
Sea

RICA

Arabian
Sea

ARABIAN
BASIN

Salween

Mekong

South
China
Sea

Taiwan

PHILIPPINE

Luzon
BASIN

MARIANA IS.

MARIANA

TRENCH

▼Challenger Deep
−36,198 ft.
(−11,033 m)

Tropic of Cancer

MARSHALL IS.

CENTRAL

PACIFIC

BASIN

PACIFIC

C. Comorin

Ceylon

Bay
of
Bengal

CEYLON
PLAIN

CARLSBERG
RIDGE

L.
Victoria
Kilimanjaro

Congo

SOMALI
BASIN

CENTRAL

INDIAN

RIDGE

Sumatra

Java

Borneo

Celebes

Mindanao

CAROLINE IS.

MELANESIAN
BASIN

New Guinea

Equator

OCEAN

Zambezi

Madagascar

INDIAN

NINETYEAST RIDGE

▼−24,343 ft.
(−7450 m)
JAVA TRENCH

AUSTRALIA

Coral
Sea

Fiji Is.

Tropic of Capricorn

Great Barrier Reef

Orange

C. Good Hope

ASIN

AS RIDGE

OCEAN

BROKEN
PLATEAU

C. Leeuwin

S. AUSTRALIA BASIN

Tasman
Sea

North Cape

North I.

SOUTHWEST INDIAN RIDGE

SOUTHEAST INDIAN RIDGE

KERGUELEN

PLATEAU

Tasmania

South I.

SOUTHEAST INDIAN RIDGE

ENDERBY ABYSSAL PLAIN

AUSTRALIAN-ANTARCTIC BASIN

Antarctic Circle

C. Adare

Amery
Ice Shelf

Ross Sea

A N T A R C T I C A

Europe

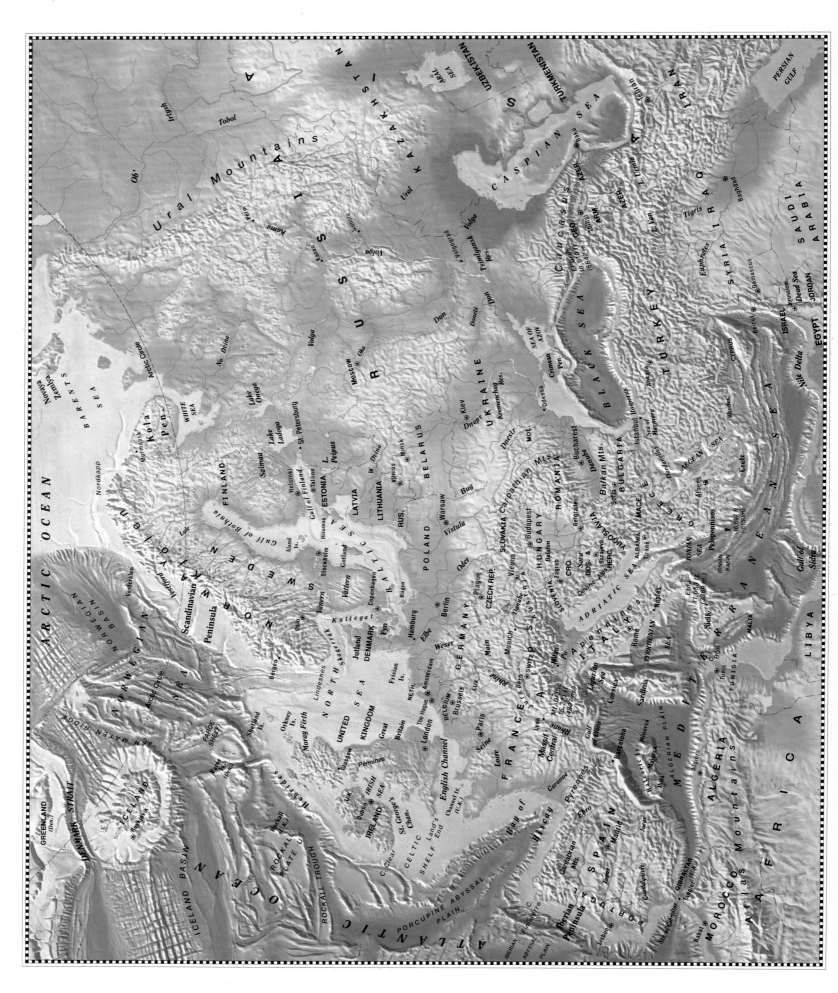

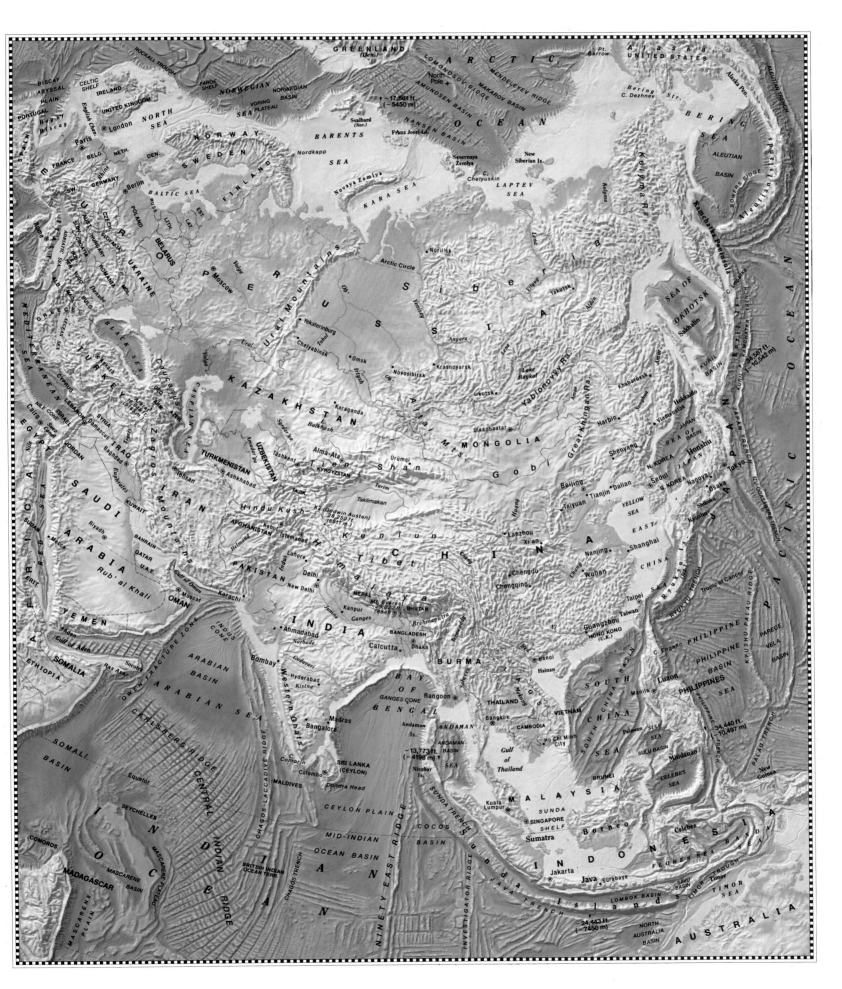

Near and Middle East

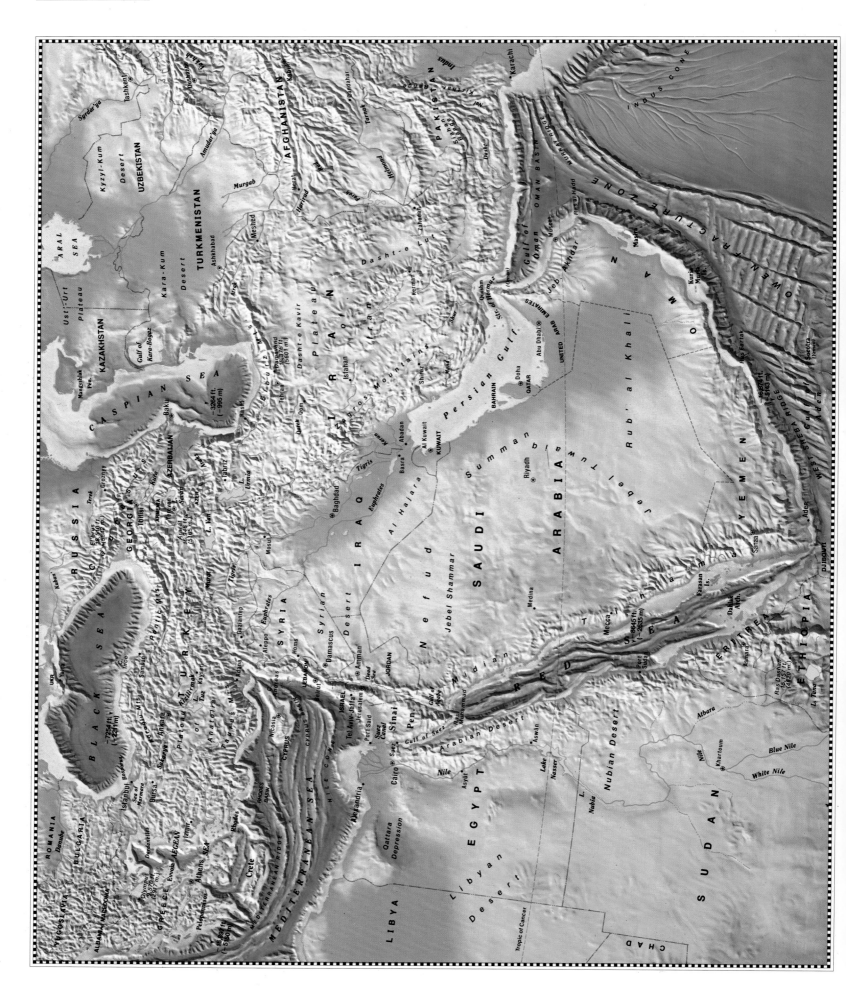

Southern Asia

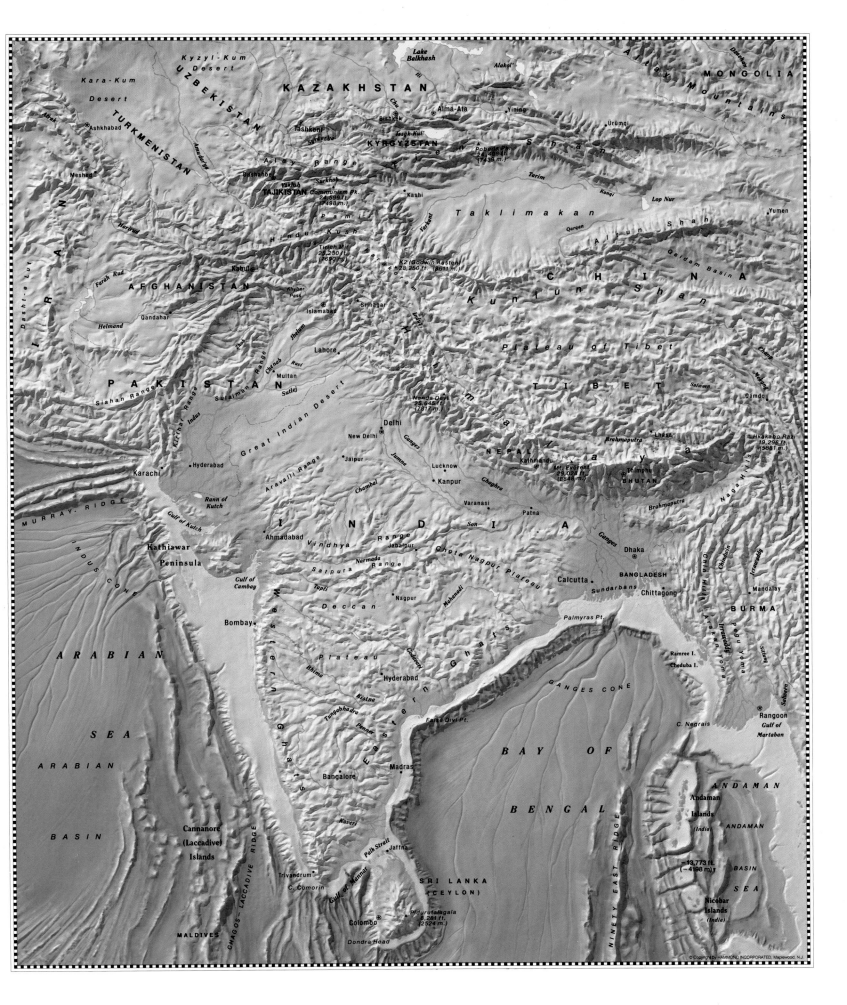

MONGOLIA

Lake
Balkhash

Kyzyl-Kum
Desert

Kara-Kum
Desert

UZBEKISTAN

KAZAKHSTAN

Alakol'

Altai Mountains

Aral

Ashkhabad

TURKMENISTAN

Tashkent

Bishkek

Alma-Ata

Yining

Ürümqi

Issyk-Kul'

Meshed

Aley Range

KYRGYZSTAN

Pobeda Pk.
24,406 ft.
(7439 m.)

Tien Shan

Tarim

Konqi

Lop Nur

Yumen

Bashahbeg

Kashi

Yarkant

Yakhsh
Surkhob
TAJIKISTAN Communism Pk.
24,590 ft.
(7498 m.)

Pamir

Taklimakan

Qarqan

Amu

Hindu Kush

K2 (Godwin Austen)
28,250 ft. (8611 m.)

Altun Shan

Qaidam Basin

Harirud

Tirich Mir
25,280 ft.
(7690 m.)

Kabul

C H I N A

Kunlun Shan

Farah Rud

AFGHANISTAN

Khyber
Pass

Islamabad

Srinagar

Plateau of Tibet

Qandahar

Indus

T I B E T

Salween

Helmand

Zhob

Jhelum

Lahore

Chenab

Ravi

Qamdo

Nanda Devi
25,645 ft.
(7817 m.)

Brahmaputra

Lhasa

Hkakabo Razi
19,296 ft.
(5881 m.)

Kirthar Range

Sulaimana Range

Multan

Sutlej

H i m a l a y a

PAKISTAN

Siahan Range

Great Indian Desert

Delhi

New Delhi

Ganges

NEPAL

Kathmandu

Mt. Everest
29,028 ft.
(8848 m.)

Thimphu

BHUTAN

Naga Hills

Karachi

Hyderabad

Jaipur

Jumna

Lucknow

Kanpur

Ghaghra

Brahmaputra

Murghab

Rann of
Kutch

Aravalli Range

Chambal

Varanasi

Son

Patna

Ganges

Dhaka

Mandalay

MURRAY RIDGE

Gulf of Kutch

I N D I A

Chindwin

INDUS CONE

Ahmadabad

Vindhya Range

Jabalpur

Chota Nagpur Plateau

BANGLADESH

Calcutta

Chittagong

BURMA

Kathiawar
Peninsula

Narmada

Range

Sundarbans

Irrawaddy

Satpura Range

Deccan

Tapti

Nagpur

Mahanadi

Palmyras Pt.

Pegu Yoma

Gulf of
Cambay

Bombay

Plateau

Bhima

Hyderabad

Godavari

Ramree I.

Cheduba I.

Arakan Yoma

A R A B I A N

Western Ghats

Kistna

Eastern Ghats

GANGES CONE

Sittang

Salween

S E A

Tungabhadra

Penner

False Divi Pt.

C. Negrais

Rangoon
Gulf of
Martaban

ARABIAN

BASIN

Madras

Bangalore

B A Y   O F

Kaveri

A N D A M A N

Cannanore
(Laccadive)
Islands

CHAGOS–LACCADIVE RIDGE

Polk Strait

Jaffna

B E N G A L

Andaman
Islands
(India)

ANDAMAN

Trivandrum

C. Comorin

SRI LANKA
(CEYLON)

NINETY EAST RIDGE

–13,773 ft.
(–4198 m.)

BASIN

S E A

MALDIVES

Gulf of Mannar

Pidurutalagala
8,281 ft.
(2524 m.)

Colombo

Nicobar
Islands
(India)

Dondra Head

I
R
A
N

Dasht-e Lut

Abraq

© Copyright by HAMMOND INCORPORATED, Maplewood, N.J.

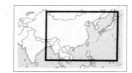

East Asia

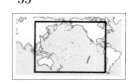

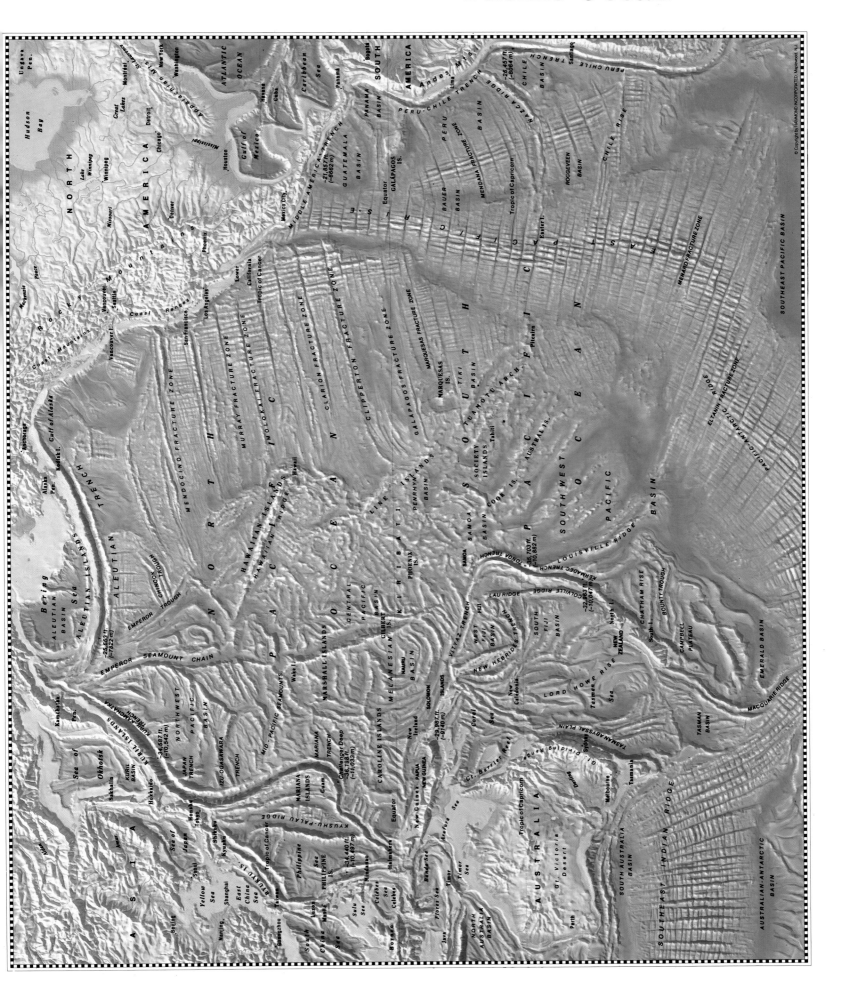

Africa

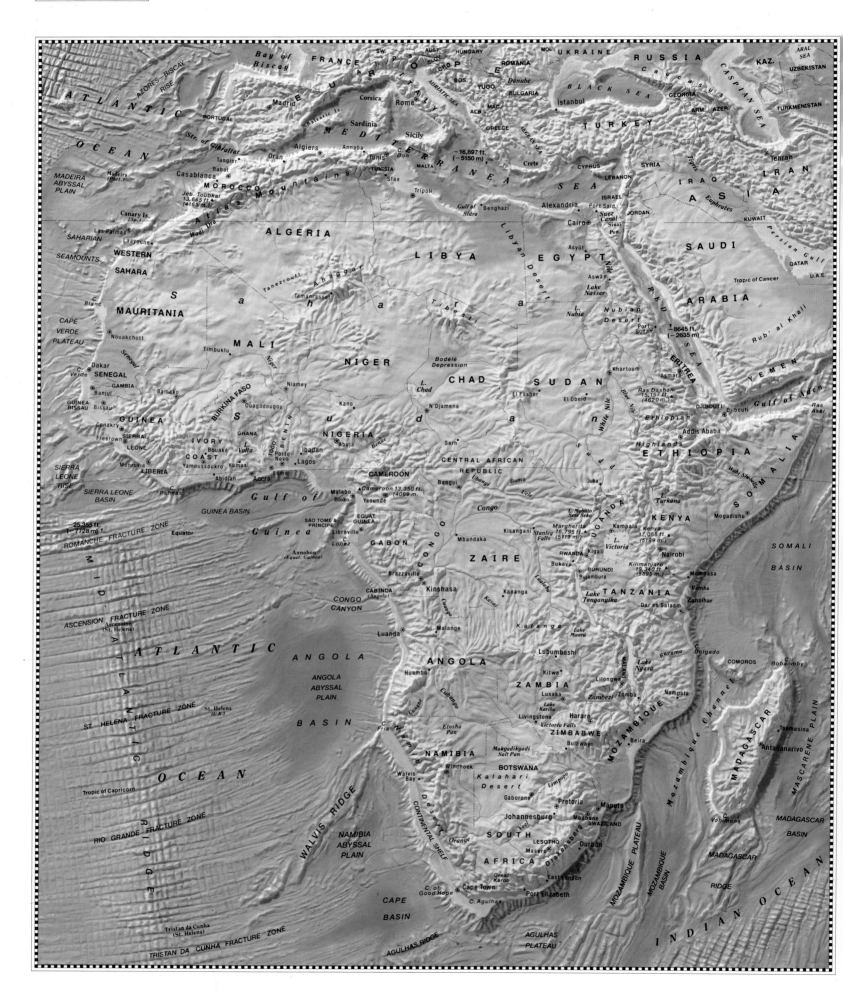

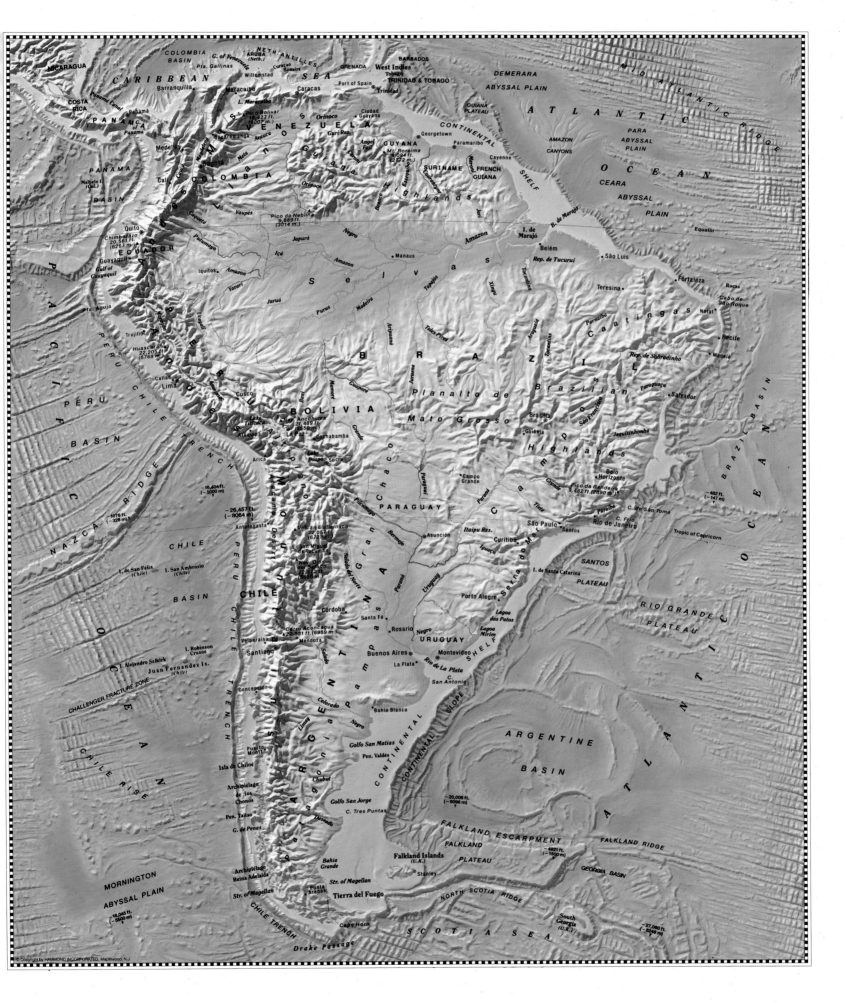

North America

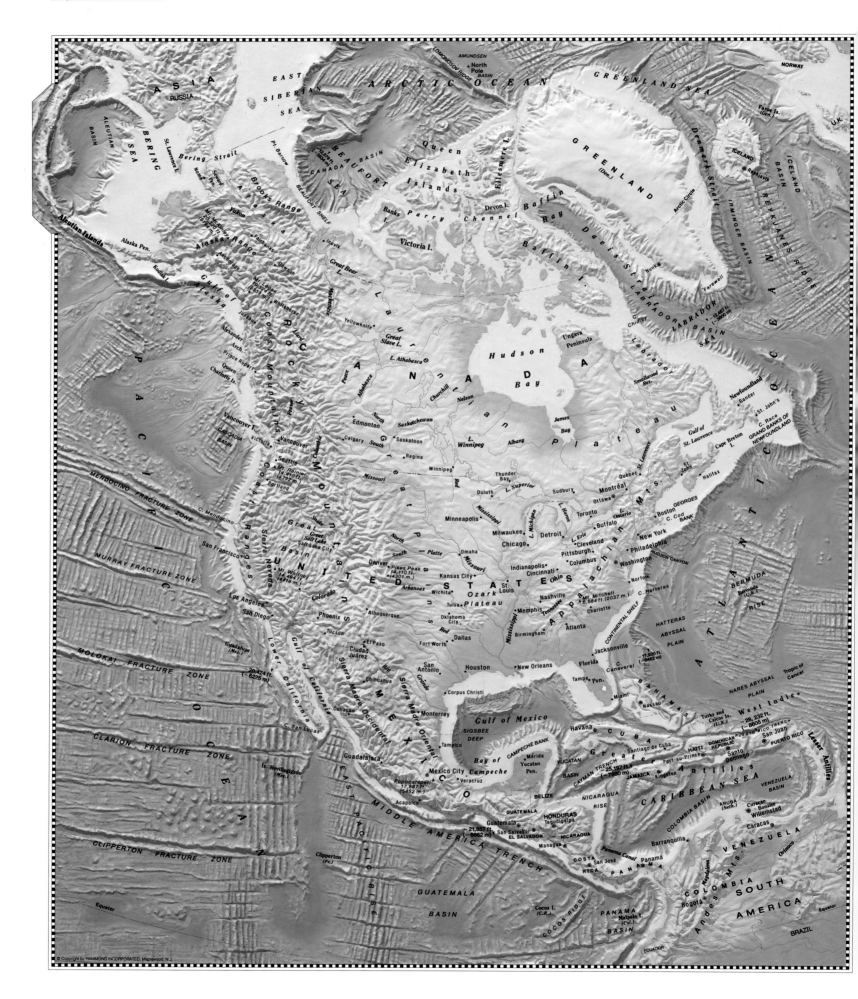

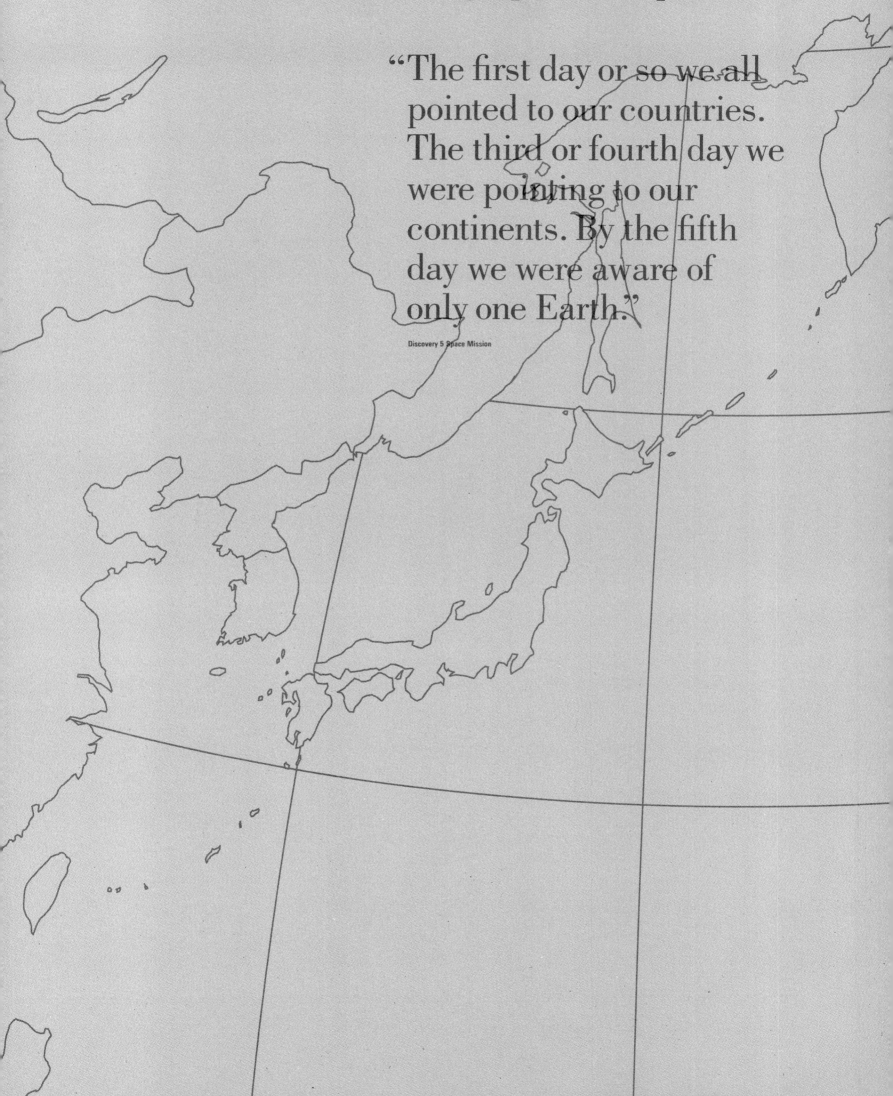

Geographic Comparisons

"The first day or so we all
pointed to our countries.
The third or fourth day we
were pointing to our
continents. By the fifth
day we were aware of
only one Earth."

Discovery 5 Space Mission

World Statistics

ELEMENTS OF THE SOLAR SYSTEM

	Mean Distance from Sun: in Miles	in Kilometers	Period of Revolution around Sun	Period of Rotation on Axis	Equatorial Diameter in Miles	in Kilometers	Surface Gravity (Earth = 1)	Mass (Earth = 1)	Mean Density (Water = 1)	Number of Satellites
Mercury	35,990,000	57,900,000	87.97 days	59 days	3,032	4,880	0.38	0.055	5.5	0
Venus	67,240,000	108,200,000	224.70 days	243 days†	7,523	12,106	0.90	0.815	5.25	0
Earth	93,000,000	149,700,000	365.26 days	23h 56m	7,926	12,755	1.00	1.00	5.5	1
Mars	141,730,000	228,100,000	687.00 days	24h 37m	4,220	6,790	0.38	0.107	4.0	2
Jupiter	483,880,000	778,700,000	11.86 years	9h 50m	88,750	142,800	2.87	317.9	1.3	16
Saturn	887,130,000	1,427,700,000	29.46 years	10h 39m	74,580	120,020	1.32	95.2	0.7	23
Uranus	1,783,700,000	2,870,500,000	84.01 years	17h 24m†	31,600	50,900	0.93	14.6	1.3	15
Neptune	2,795,500,000	4,498,800,000	164.79 years	17h 50m	30,200	48,600	1.23	17.2	1.8	8
Pluto	3,667,900,000	5,902,800,000	247.70 years	6.39 days(?)	1,500	2,400	0.03(?)	0.01(?)	0.7(?)	1

† Retrograde motion

DIMENSIONS OF THE EARTH

	Area in: Sq. Miles	Sq. Kilometers
Superficial area	196,939,000	510,073,000
Land surface	57,506,000	148,941,000
Water surface	139,433,000	361,132,000

	Distance in: Miles	Kilometers
Equatorial circumference	24,902	40,075
Polar circumference	24,860	40,007
Equatorial diameter	7,926.4	12,756.4
Polar diameter	7,899.8	12,713.6
Equatorial radius	3,963.2	6,378.2
Polar radius	3,949.9	6,356.8

Volume of the Earth	2.6×10^{11} cubic miles	10.84×10^{11} cubic kilometers
Mass or weight	6.6×10^{21} short tons	6.0×10^{21} metric tons
Maximum distance from Sun	94,600,000 miles	152,000,000 kilometers
Minimum distance from Sun	91,300,000 miles	147,000,000 kilometers

OCEANS AND MAJOR SEAS

	Area in: Sq. Miles	Sq. Kms.	Greatest Depth in: Feet	Meters
Pacific Ocean	64,186,000	166,241,700	36,198	11,033
Atlantic Ocean	31,862,000	82,522,600	28,374	8,648
Indian Ocean	28,350,000	73,426,500	25,344	7,725
Arctic Ocean	5,427,000	14,056,000	17,880	5,450
Caribbean Sea	970,000	2,512,300	24,720	7,535
Mediterranean Sea	969,000	2,509,700	16,896	5,150
South China Sea	895,000	2,318,000	15,000	4,600
Bering Sea	875,000	2,266,250	15,800	4,800
Gulf of Mexico	600,000	1,554,000	12,300	3,750
Sea of Okhotsk	590,000	1,528,100	11,070	3,370
East China Sea	482,000	1,248,400	9,500	2,900
Yellow Sea	480,000	1,243,200	350	107
Sea of Japan	389,000	1,007,500	12,280	3,740
Hudson Bay	317,500	822,300	846	258
North Sea	222,000	575,000	2,200	670
Black Sea	185,000	479,150	7,365	2,245
Red Sea	169,000	437,700	7,200	2,195
Baltic Sea	163,000	422,170	1,506	459

THE CONTINENTS

	Area in: Sq. Miles	Sq. Kms.	Percent of World's Land
Asia	17,128,500	44,362,815	29.5
Africa	11,707,000	30,321,130	20.2
North America	9,363,000	24,250,170	16.2
South America	6,875,000	17,806,250	11.8
Antarctica	5,500,000	14,245,000	9.5
Europe	4,057,000	10,507,630	7.0
Australia	2,966,136	7,682,300	5.1

MAJOR SHIP CANALS

	Length in: Miles	Kms.	Minimum Depth in: Feet	Meters
Volga-Baltic, Russia	225	362	–	–
Baltic-White Sea, Russia	140	225	16	5
Suez, Egypt	100.76	162	42	13
Albert, Belgium	80	129	16.5	5
Moscow-Volga, Russia	80	129	18	6
Volga-Don, Russia	62	100	–	–
Göta, Sweden	54	87	10	3
Kiel (Nord-Ostsee), Germany	53.2	86	38	12
Panama Canal, Panama	50.72	82	41.6	13
Houston Ship, U.S.A.	50	81	36	11

LARGEST ISLANDS

	Area in: Sq. Miles	Sq. Kms.
Greenland	840,000	2,175,600
New Guinea	305,000	789,950
Borneo	290,000	751,100
Madagascar	226,400	586,376
Baffin, Canada	195,928	507,454
Sumatra, Indonesia	164,000	424,760
Honshu, Japan	88,000	227,920
Great Britain	84,400	218,896
Victoria, Canada	83,896	217,290
Ellesmere, Canada	75,767	196,236
Celebes, Indonesia	72,986	189,034
South I., New Zealand	58,393	151,238
Java, Indonesia	48,842	126,501
North I., New Zealand	44,187	114,444
Newfoundland, Canada	42,031	108,860
Cuba	40,533	104,981
Luzon, Philippines	40,420	104,688
Iceland	39,768	103,000
Mindanao, Philippines	36,537	94,631
Ireland	31,743	82,214
Sakhalin, Russia	29,500	76,405
Hispaniola, Haiti & Dom. Rep.	29,399	76,143

	Area in: Sq. Miles	Sq. Kms.
Hokkaido, Japan	28,983	75,066
Banks, Canada	27,038	70,028
Ceylon,Sri Lanka	25,332	65,610
Tasmania, Australia	24,600	63,710
Svalbard, Norway	23,957	62,049
Devon, Canada	21,331	55,247
Novaya Zemlya (north isl.), Russia	18,600	48,200
Marajó, Brazil	17,991	46,597
Tierra del Fuego, Chile & Argentina	17,900	46,360
Alexander, Antarctica	16,700	43,250
Axel Heiberg, Canada	16,671	43,178
Melville, Canada	16,274	42,150
Southhampton, Canada	15,913	41,215
New Britain, Papua New Guinea	14,100	36,519
Taiwan, China	13,836	35,835
Kyushu, Japan	13,770	35,664
Hainan, China	13,127	33,999
Prince of Wales, Canada	12,872	33,338
Spitsbergen, Norway	12,355	31,999
Vancouver, Canada	12,079	31,285
Timor, Indonesia	11,527	29,855
Sicily, Italy	9,926	25,708

	Area in: Sq. Miles	Sq. Kms.
Somerset, Canada	9,570	24,786
Sardinia, Italy	9,301	24,090
Shikoku, Japan	6,860	17,767
New Caledonia, France	6,530	16,913
Nordaustlandet, Norway	6,409	16,599
Samar, Philippines	5,050	13,080
Negros, Philippines	4,906	12,707
Palawan, Philippines	4,550	11,785
Panay, Philippines	4,446	11,515
Jamaica	4,232	10,961
Hawaii, United States	4,038	10,458
Viti Levu, Fiji	4,010	10,386
Cape Breton, Canada	3,981	10,311
Mindoro, Philippines	3,759	9,736
Kodiak, Alaska, U.S.A.	3,670	9,505
Cyprus	3,572	9,251
Puerto Rico, U.S.A.	3,435	8,897
Corsica, France	3,352	8,682
New Ireland, Papua New Guinea	3,340	8,651
Crete, Greece	3,218	8,335
Anticosti, Canada	3,066	7,941
Wrangel, Russia	2,819	7,301

PRINCIPAL MOUNTAINS

	Height in: Feet	Meters		Height in: Feet	Meters		Height in: Feet	Meters
verest, Nepal-China	29,028	8,848	Llullaillaco, Chile-Argentina	22,057	6,723	Blanc, France	15,771	4,807
2 (Godwin Austen), Pakistan-China	28,250	8,611	Nevada Ancohuma, Bolivia	21,489	6,550	Klyuchevskaya Sopka, Russia	15,584	4,750
Makalu, Nepal-China	27,789	8,470	Chimborazo, Ecuador	20,561	6,267	Fairweather, Br. Col., Canada	15,300	4,663
haulagiri, Nepal	26,810	8,172	McKinley, Alaska	20,320	6,194	Dufourspitze (Mte. Rosa), Italy-Switzerland	15,203	4,634
langa Parbat, Pakistan	26,660	8,126	Logan, Yukon, Canada	19,524	5,951	Ras Dashen, Ethiopia	15,157	4620
nnapurna, Nepal	26,504	8,078	Cotopaxi, Ecuador	19,347	5,897	Matterhorn, Switzerland	14,691	4,478
akaposhi, Pakistan	25,550	7,788	Kilimanjaro, Tanzania	19,340	5,895	Whitney, California, U.S.A.	14,494	4,418
ongur Shan, China	25,325	7,719	El Misti, Peru	19,101	5,822	Elbert, Colorado, U.S.A.	14,433	4,399
irich Mir, Pakistan	25,230	7,690	Pico Cristóbal Colón, Colombia	18,947	5,775	Rainier, Washington, U.S.A.	14,410	4,392
ongga Shan, China	24,790	7,556	Huila, Colombia	18,865	5,750	Shasta, California, U.S.A.	14,162	4,317
ommunism Peak, Tajikistan	24,590	7,495	Citlaltépetl (Orizaba), Mexico	18,701	5,700	Pikes Peak, Colorado, U.S.A.	14,110	4,301
obedy Peak, Kyrgyzstan	24,406	7,439	Damavand, Iran	18,606	5,671	Finsteraarhorn, Switzerland	14,022	4, 274
homo Lhari, Bhutan-China	23,997	7,314	El'brus, Russia	18,510	5,642	Mauna Kea, Hawaii, U.S.A.	13,796	4,205
Muztag, China	23,891	7,282	St. Elias, Alaska, U.S.A.-Yukon, Canada	18,008	5,489	Mauna Loa, Hawaii, U.S.A.	13,677	4,169
erro Aconcagua, Argentina	22,831	6,959	Dykh-tau, Russia	17,070	5,203	Jungfrau, Switzerland	13,642	4,158
jos del Salado, Chile-Argentina	22,572	6,880	Batian (Kenya), Kenya	17,058	5,199	Grossglockner, Austria	12,457	3,797
onete, Chile-Argentina	22,546	6,872	Ararat, Turkey	16,946	5,165	Fujiyama, Japan	12,389	3,776
upungato, Chile-Argentina	22,310	6,800	Vinson Massif, Antarctica	16,864	5,140	Cook, New Zealand	12,349	3,764
issis, Argentina	22,241	6,779	Margherita (Ruwenzori), Africa	16,795	5,119	Etna, Italy	10,902	3,323
Mercedario, Argentina	22,211	6,770	Kazbek, Georgia-Russia	16,558	5,047	Kosciusko, Australia	7,310	2,228
uascarán, Peru	22,205	6,768	Puncak Jaya, Indonesia	16,503	5,030	Mitchell, North Carolina, U.S.A.	6,684	2,037

LONGEST RIVERS

	Length in: Miles	Kms.		Length in: Miles	Kms.		Length in: Miles	Kms.
ile, Africa	4,145	6,671	Indus, Asia	1,800	2,897	Don, Russia	1,222	1,967
mazon, S. America	3,915	6,300	Danube, Europe	1,775	2,857	Red, U.S.A.	1,222	1,966
hang Jiang (Yangtze), China	3,900	6,276	Salween, Asia	1,770	2,849	Columbia, U.S.A.-Canada	1,214	1,953
Mississippi-Missouri-Red Rock, U.S.A.	3,741	6,019	Brahmaputra, Asia	1,700	2,736	Saskatchewan, Canada	1,205	1,939
b'-Irtysh-Black Irtysh, Russia-Kazakhstan	3,362	5,411	Euphrates, Asia	1,700	2,736	Peace-Finlay, Canada	1,195	1,923
enisey-Angara, Russia	3,100	4,989	Tocantins, Brazil	1,677	2,699	Tigris, Asia	1,181	1,901
uang He (Yellow), China	2,877	4,630	Xi (Si), China	1,650	2,601	Darling, Australia	1,160	1,867
mur-Shilka-Onon, Asia	2,744	4,416	Amudar'ya, Asia	1,616	2,601	Angara, Russia	1,135	1,827
ena, Russia	2,734	4,400	Nelson-Saskatchewan, Canada	1,600	2,575	Sungari, Asia	1,130	1,819
ongo (Zaire), Africa	2,718	4,374	Orinoco, S. America	1,600	2,575	Pechora, Russia	1,124	1,809
Mackenzie-Peace-Finlay,Canada	2,635	4,241	Zambezi, Africa	1,600	2,575	Snake, U.S.A.	1,038	1,670
Mekong, Asia	2,610	4,200	Paraguay, S. America	1,584	2,549	Churchill, Canada	1,000	1,609
Missouri-Red Rock, U.S.A.	2,564	4,125	Kolyma, Russia	1,562	2,514	Pilcomayo, S. America	1,000	1,609
iger, Africa	2,548	4,101	Ganges, Asia	1,550	2,494	Uruguay, S. America	994	1.600
araná-La Plata, S. America	2,450	3,943	Ural, Russia-Kazakhstan	1,509	2,428	Platte-N. Platte, U.S.A.	990	1,593
Mississippi, U.S.A.	2,348	3,778	Japurá, S. America	1,500	2,414	Ohio, U.S.A.	981	1,578
Murray-Darling, Australia	2,310	3,718	Arkansas, U.S.A.	1,450	2,334	Magdalena, Colombia	956	1,538
olga, Russia	2,194	3,531	Colorado, U.S.A.-Mexico	1,450	2,334	Pecos, U.S.A.	926	1,490
Madeira, S. America	2,013	3,240	Negro, S. America	1,400	2,253	Oka, Russia	918	1,477
urus, S. America	1,995	3,211	Dnieper, Russia-Belarus-Ukraine	1,368	2,202	Canadian, U.S.A.	906	1,458
ukon, Alaska-Canada	1,979	3,185	Orange, Africa	1,350	2,173	Colorado, Texas, U.S.A.	894	1,439
t. Lawrence, Canada-U.S.A.	1,900	3,058	Irrawaddy, Burma	1,325	2,132	Dniester, Ukraine-Moldova	876	1,410
io Grande, Mexico-U.S.A.	1,885	3,034	Brazos, U.S.A.	1,309	2,107	Fraser, Canada	850	1,369
yrdar'ya-Naryn, Asia	1,859	2,992	Ohio-Allegheny, U.S.A.	1,306	2,102	Rhine, Europe	820	1,319
ão Francisco, Brazil	1,811	2,914	Kama, Russia	1,252	2,031	Northern Dvina, Russia	809	1,302

PRINCIPAL NATURAL LAKES

	Area in: Sq. Miles	Sq. Kms.	Max. Depth in: Feet	Meters		Area in: Sq. Miles	Sq. Kms.	Max. Depth in: Feet	Meters
aspian Sea, Asia	143,243	370,999	3,264	995	Lake Eyre, Australia	3,500-0	9,000-0	–	–
ake Superior, U.S.A.-Canada	31,820	82,414	1,329	405	Lake Titicaca, Peru-Bolivia	3,200	8,288	1, 000	305
ake Victoria, Africa	26,724	69,215	270	82	Lake Nicaragua, Nicaragua	3,100	8,029	230	70
ake Huron, U.S.A.-Canada	23,010	59,596	748	228	Lake Athabasca, Canada	3,064	7,936	400	122
ake Michigan, U.S.A.	22,400	58,016	923	281	Reindeer Lake, Canada	2,568	6,651	–	–
Aral Sea, Kazakhstan-Uzbekistan	15,830	41,000	213	65	Lake Turkana (Rudolf), Africa	2,463	6,379	240	73
Lake Tanganyika, Africa	12,650	32,764	4,700	1,433	Issyk-Kul', Kyrgyzstan	2,425	6,281	2,303	702
ake Baykal, Russia	12,162	31,500	5,316	1,620	Lake Torrens, Australia	2,230	5,776	–	–
reat Bear Lake, Canada	12,096	31,328	1,356	413	Vänern, Sweden	2,156	5,584	328	100
ake Nyasa (Malawi), Africa	11,555	29,928	2,320	707	Nettilling Lake, Canada	2,140	5,543	–	–
reat Slave Lake, Canada	11,031	28,570	2,015	614	Lake Winnipegosis, Canada	2,075	5,374	38	12
ake Erie, U.S.A.-Canada	9,940	25,745	210	64	Lake Mobutu Sese Seko (Albert), Africa	2,075	5,374	160	49
ake Winnipeg, Canada	9,417	24,390	60	18	Kariba Lake, Zambia-Zimbabwe	2,050	5,310	295	90
ake Ontario, U.S.A.-Canada	7,540	19,529	775	244	Lake Nipigon, Canada	1,872	4,848	540	165
ake Ladoga, Russia	7,104	18,399	738	225	Lake Mweru, Zaire-Zambia	1,800	4,662	60	18
ake Balkhash, Kazakhstan	7,027	18,200	87	27	Lake Manitoba, Canada	1,799	4,659	12	4
ake Maracaibo, Venezuela	5,120	13,261	100	31	Lake Taymyr, Russia	1,737	4,499	85	26
ake Chad, Africa	4,000 –	10,360 –			Lake Khanka, China-Russia	1,700	4,403	33	10
	10,000	25,900	25	8	Lake Kioga, Uganda	1,700	4,403	25	8
ake Onega, Russia	3,710	9,609	377	115	Lake of the Woods, U.S.A.-Canada	1,679	4,349	70	21

Time Zones of the World

ARCTIC OCEAN

SVALBARD

FRANZ JOSEF LAND

WRANGEL I.

RUSSIA

Anadyr'

2 P.M.
FINLAND
Helsinki
St. Petersburg
EST.
LAT.
RUS. LITH.
Moscow
Yekaterinburg
Novosibirsk
Irkutsk
Chita
Magadan

ALASKA
2 A.M.

POLAND
BELARUS
n
SLVK. UKRAINE Kiev
HUN. MOL.
BOSN. ROMANIA
YUGO. BULGARIA
ALB. MAC.
GREECE Istanbul
Athens TURKEY
LTA CYPRUS LEB.
ISRAEL
oli JOR.
Cairo
LIBYA EGYPT
4 P.M.
Volgograd
KAZAKHSTAN
6 P.M.
UZBEKISTAN
Baku Tashkent
AZER. KYRGYZSTAN
TURKMENISTAN TAJIKISTAN
Tehran AFGHANISTAN
IRAN 4:30 P.M.
3:30 P.M. 5 P.M.
PAKISTAN
BAHRAIN
QATAR
U.A.E. Karachi
OMAN
MONGOLIA

8 P.M.
Beijing
CHINA

Vladivostok

N. KOREA
Seoul
S. KOREA
JAPAN
Tokyo

PACIFIC

MONDAY
SUNDAY

HAWAII

Riyadh
SAUDI
ARABIA
YEMEN
Delhi
NEPAL
INDIA
5:30 P.M.
Bombay
5:40 P.M.
Bh.
Calcutta
BANG.
BURMA
6:30
P.M.
LAOS
THAI-
LAND
TAIWAN
HONG KONG

9 P.M.
NORTHERN
MARIANAS

OCEAN

MARSHALL
ISLANDS

CHAD
Khartoum
SUDAN
ERIT.
DJIBOUTI
SRI
LANKA
5:30
P.M.
Bangkok
CAMB.
VIETNAM
Manila
PHILIPPINES

mena
. AFR. REP.
ETHIOPIA
SOMALIA
MALDIVES
BRUNEI
MALAYSIA
SING.

FED. STATES OF
MICRONESIA

NAURU

ZAIRE
(CONGO)
RWANDA
BURUNDI
UGA.
KENYA
TANZANIA Dar es
Salaam
SEYCHELLES
BRITISH INDIAN
OCEAN TERR.
INDIAN
Jakarta
INDONESIA
PAPUA
NEW GUINEA

SOLOMON
ISLANDS

KIRIBATI

2 A.M.

NGOLA
ZAMBIA MALAWI
Comoros
ZIMB.
MOZAMBIQUE
MADAGASCAR
MAURITIUS
OCEAN
6:30 P.M.
Cocos
Is.
Darwin
TUVALU
TOKELAU
W. SAMOA
AMER.
SAMOA

VANUATU
FIJI
TONGA

BIA
BOTSWANA
Johannesburg
SWAZILAND
SOUTH
AFRICA LESOTHO
Cape Town
AUSTRALIA
9:30
P.M.
Perth
Adelaide
Sydney

1 A.M.

11:30 P.M.
NORFOLK I.
LORD HOWE I.
10:30
P.M.

NEW
ZEALAND
Wellington
12:45 A.M.
CHATHAM
IS.

PRINCE
EDWARD IS.
CROZET IS.

Population of Major Cities

The following pages include population figures for all cities with more than 100,000 inhabitants, and for all national capitals, regardless of size. Cities are listed alphabetically, and grouped alphabetically by country.

Three dependencies, Hong Kong, Puerto Rico and Macau, follow the country listing. Capitals are indicated with an asterisk (*). The population figures, given in thousands, represent the most current information available.

Country / City	Population in thousands
A **Afghanistan**	
Herát	177
Kábul*	1,424
Mazār-e Sharīf	131
Qandahar	226
Albania	
Tiranë*	171
Algeria	
Algiers*	1,688
Annaba	228
Batna	185
Bechar	107
Bejaïa	118
Biskra	130
Blida	132
Chelif	130
Constantine	450
Mostaganem	115
Oran	599
Sétif	186
Sidi Bel-Abbes	155
Skikda	129
Tébessa	108
Tiaret	106
Tlemcen	108
Andorra	
Andorra la Vella*	12
Angola	
Luanda*	475
Antigua and Barbuda	
Saint John's*	22
Argentina	
Avellaneda	331
Bahía Blanca	233
Buenos Aires*	2,908
Concordia	122
Córdoba	990
Corrientes	186
Formosa	102
General Roca	210
General San Martin	384
Godoy Cruz	142
Lanús	466
La Plata	473
Lomas de Zamora	509
Mar del Plata	302
Mendoza	118
Merlo	293
Morón	597
Paraná	224
Posadas	148
Resistencia	143
Río Cuarto	191
Rosario	935
Salta	266
San Fernando	129
San Juan	118
San Miguel de Tucumán	393
San Nicolás de los Arroyes	114
San Rafael	144
San Salvador de Jujuy	167
Santa Fé	375
Santiago del Estero	163
Tigre	199
Vicente López	290
Armenia	
Kirovakan	146
Kumayri	120
Yerevan*	1,199
Australia	
Adelaide	978
Brisbane	1,149
Canberra*	247
Geelong	140
Gold Coast	135
Hobart	175
Melbourne	2,833
Newcastle	256
Perth	994
Sydney	3,365
Wollongong	207
Austria	
Graz	243
Innsbruck	116
Linz	198

Country / City	Population in thousands
Salzburg	138
Vienna*	1,516
Azerbaijan	
Baku*	1,150
Gyandzhe	278
Sumgait	231
B **Bahamas**	
Nassau*	135
Bahrain	
Manama*	109
Bangladesh	
Barisāl	159
Chittagong	1,388
Comilla	126
Dhākā*	3,459
Jessore	149
Khulna	623
Nārāyanganj	496
Pābna	101
Rājshāhi	172
Barbados	
Bridgetown*	7
Belarus	
Baranovichi	159
Bobruysk	223
Borisov	144
Brest	258
Gomel'	500
Grodno	270
Minsk*	1,589
Mogilëv	356
Mozyr'	101
Orsha	123
Pinsk	119
Vitebsk	350
Belgium	
Antwerp	186
Brugge	118
Brussels*	997
Charleroi	222
Ghent	239
Liège	214
Namur	102
Schaerbeek	107
Belize	
Belmopan*	3
Benin	
Cotonou	383
Porto-Novo*	144
Bhutan	
Thimphu*	12
Bolivia	
Cochabamba	205
La Paz*	635
Oruro	124
Santa Cruz	255
Sucre*	64
Bosnia & Hercegovina	
Banja Luka	184
Mostar	110
Prijedor	109
Sarajevo*	449
Tuzla	122
Zenica	133
Botswana	
Gaborone*	120
Brazil	
Americana	122
Anápolis	161
Aracaju	293
Araçatuba	113
Barra Mansa	123
Baurú	179
Belém	934
Belo Horizonte	1,775
Blumenau	145
Brasília*	411
Campina Grande	222
Campinas	567
Campo Grande	291
Campos	174
Canoas	214
Carapicuíba	186
Caruaru	138
Caxias do Sul	199

Country / City	Population in thousands
Contegem	112
Cuiabá	213
Curitiba	1,026
Diadema	229
Divinópolis	108
Duque du Caxias	306
Feira de Santana	225
Florianópolis	188
Fortaleza	1,309
Franca	144
Goiânia	718
Governador Valadares	174
Guarulhos	395
Imperatriz	112
Ipatinga	105
Itabuna	130
Jacareí	104
João Pessoa	330
Joinvile	217
Juazeiro do Norte	125
Juiz de Fora	300
Jundiaí	210
Lages	109
Limeira	138
Londrina	258
Macapá	138
Maceió	400
Manaus	635
Marília	104
Maringá	158
Mauá	206
Mogi das Cruzes	122
Montes Claros	152
Mossoró	118
Natal	420
Nilópolis	103
Niterói	386
Nova Iguaçu	492
Novo Hamburgo	132
Olinda	266
Osasco	474
Passo Fundo	103
Pelotas	197
Petrópolis	149
Piracicaba	179
Ponta Grossa	171
Porto Alegre	1,126
Porto Velho	135
Presidente Prudente	128
Recife	1,205
Ribeirão Preto	301
Rio Branco	117
Rio Claro	103
Rio de Janeiro	5,093
Rio Grande	125
Salvador	1,501
Santa Maria	151
Santarém	102
Santo André	549
Santos	411
São Bernardo do Campo	381
São Caetano do Sul	163
São Carlos	109
São Gonçalo	221
São João de Meriti	211
São José do Rio Preto	172
São José dos Campos	268
São Luís	450
São Paulo	8,491
São Vicente	193
Sorocaba	255
Taguatinga	480
Taubaté	155
Teresina	378
Uberaba	180
Uberlândia	230
Vitória	208
Vitória da Conquista	126
Volta Redonda	178
Brunei	
Bandar Seri Begawan*	64
Bulgaria	
Burgas	183
Pleven	130
Plovdiv	343
Shumen	100
Sofia*	1,122
Stara Zagora	151

Country / City	Population in thousands
Tolbukhin	109
Varna	303
Burkina	
Bobo Dioulasso	231
Ouagadougou*	308
Burma	
Akyab	108
Bassein	144
Insein	144
Mandalay	533
Monywa	107
Moulmein	220
Pegu	151
Rangoon*	2,513
Taunggyi	108
Burundi	
Bujumbura*	141
C **Cambodia**	
Phnom Penh*	300
Cameroon	
Douala	784
N'Kongsamba	102
Yaoundé*	552
Canada	
Brampton	188
Burlington	117
Burnaby	145
Calgary	671
Edmonton	785
Halifax	114
Hamilton	307
Kitchener	151
Laval	284
London	269
Longueuil	125
Markham	115
Mississauga	374
Montréal	1,015
Oshawa	124
Ottawa*	301
Québec	165
Regina	175
Richmond	108
Saint Catharines	123
Saskatoon	201
Surrey	181
Thunder Bay	112
Toronto	2,193
Vancouver	431
Windsor	193
Winnipeg	625
Cape Verde	
Praia*	57
Central African Republic	
Bangui*	474
Chad	
N'Djamena*	179
Chile	
Antofagasta	203
Arica	158
Barrancas	184
Chillán	127
Concepción	281
Iquique	127
Maipú	118
Osorno	102
Puente Alto	126
Puerto Montt	119
Punta Arenas	107
Rancagua	157
San Bernardo	136
Santiago*	4,100
Talca	138
Talcahuano	218
Temuco	168
Valdivia	105
Valparaiso	273
Viña del Mar	261
China	
Anda	423
Anqing	449
Anshan	1,196
Anshun	201
Anyang	501
Baicheng	276
Baiyin	325

Country / City	Population in thousands
Baoding	495
Baoji	341
Baotou	1,076
Beihai	174
Beijing*	5,531
Beipiao	605
Bengbu	550
Benxi	774
Binzhou	186
Botou	1,076
Cangzhou	280
Changchun	1,747
Changde	214
Changsha	1,066
Changshu	100
Changshun	1,747
Changzhi	450
Changzhou	534
Chaoyang	207
Chaozhou	162
Chengde	327
Chengdu	2,499
Chenzhou	166
Chifeng	293
Chongqing	2,673
Conghua	280
Da Xian	193
Dafang	962
Dalian	1,480
Dandong	545
Daqing	758
Datong	962
Da Xian	193
Dezhou	259
Ding Xian	938
Dongguan	1,230
Dongying	540
Duyun	102
Echeng	119
Fengcheng	996
Foshan	274
Fushun	1,185
Fuxin	647
Fuyang	178
Fuzhou	1,112
Ganzhou	363
Gejiu	353
Guangzhou	3,182
Guilin	432
Guiyang	1,350
Haicheng	992
Haikou	263
Hailar	157
Haining	600
Handan	930
Hangzhou	1,171
Hanzhong	374
Harbin	2,519
Hebi	336
Hefei	795
Hegang	592
Hengshui	101
Hengyang	532
Heshan	112
Hohhot	754
Houma	144
Huaibei	445
Huaihua	436
Huainan	1,029
Huangshi	376
Huaying	321
Huizhou	158
Hunjiang	694
Huzhou	953
Jiamusi	540
Ji'an	168
Jiangmen	212
Jiaojiang	391
Jiaozuo	484
Jiaxing	655
Jilin	1,888
Jinan	1,359
Jingdezhen	611
Jingmen	957
Jinhua	869
Jining (Nei Mong.)	159
Jining (Shandong)	190
Jinzhou	599

Country / City	Population in thousands
Jiujiang	351
Jixi	782
Kaifeng	602
Kaiyuan	223
Karamay	152
Kashi	252
Korla	118
Kunming	1,419
Kuytun	240
Langfang	533
Lanxi	612
Lanzhou	1,364
Laohekou	102
Lengshuijiang	255
Lengshuitan	371
Leshan	958
Lhasa	343
Lianyungang	397
Liaocheng	737
Liaoyang	589
Liaoyuan	772
Lichuan	718
Linchuan	619
Linfen	208
Liuzhou	582
Longyan	347
Loudi	268
Lu'an	146
Luohe	158
Luoyang	952
Luzhou	305
Ma'anshan	352
Manzhouli	104
Maoming	413
Meizhou	111
Mianyang	769
Mudanjiang	581
Nanchang	1,076
Nanchong	228
Nanjing	2,091
Nanning	890
Nanping	408
Nantong	403
Nanyang	288
Neijiang	271
Ningbo	479
Pingdingshan	470
Pingxiang	1,189
Pingyang	510
Qingdao	1,172
Qingjiang	235
Qinhuangdao	394
Qiqihar	1,209
Qitaihe	283
Quanzhou	403
Qufu	545
Quzhou	981
Renqiu	591
Rizhao	988
Sanmenxia	147
Sanming	199
Shanghai	6,293
Shangqiu	187
Shangrao	665
Shantou	718
Shaoguan	371
Shaoxing	1,091
Shaoyang	397
Shashi	239
Shenyang	3,944
Shihezi	564
Shijiazhuang	1,069
Shishou	558
Shiyan	307
Shizuishan	298
Shuangyashan	400
Siping	334
Suizhou	143
Suzhou	192
Tai'an	1,275
Taiyuan	1,746
Taizhou	161
Tangshan	1,408
Tianjin	5,152
Tianshui	185
Tieling	221
Tongchuan	354
Tonghua	360

Country City	Population in thousands
Tongliao	213
Tongling	184
Ulanhot	174
Ürümqi	961
Wanxian	267
Weifang	393
Weihai	205
Wenzhou	516
Wuhan	3,288
Wuhu	449
Wuxi	798
Wuzhou	245
Xiaguan	117
Xiamen	507
Xi'an	2,185
Xiangfan	323
Xiangtan	492
Xianning	406
Xianyang	502
Xichang	146
Xifeng	237
Xingtai	334
Xining Shi	567
Xinji	532
Xinxiang	525
Xinyang	240
Xinyu	622
Xuchang	219
Xuzhou	777
Ya'an	254
Yangquan	478
Yangzhou	302
Yanji	176
Yantai	385
Yibin	245
Yichang	365
Yichun	756
Yinchuan	354
Yingcheng	546
Yingkou	423
Yingtan	120
Yining	257
Yiyang	165
Yong'an	272
Yuci	271
Yueyang	972
Yumen	195
Yushu	150
Yuyao	778
Zaozhuang	1,244
Zhangjiakou	617
Zhangzhou	283
Zhanjiang	854
Zhaoqing	172
Zhaotong	133
Zhengzhou	1,404
Zhenjiang	346
Zhongshan	135
Zhoukou	214
Zhuhai	132
Zhumadian	150
Zhuo Xian	478
Zhuzhou	383
Zibo	2,198
Zigong	866
Zixing	340
Zunyi	351
Colombia	
Armenia	180
Barrancabermeja	137
Barranquilla	897
Bello	206
Bogotá*	3,975
Bucaramanga	342
Buenaventura	160
Cali	1,324
Cartagena	491
Cúcuta	357
Floridablanca	138
Ibagué	269
Itagüí	136
Manizales	275
Medellín	1,419
Montería	157
Neiva	178
Palmira	175
Pasto	197
Pereira	233
Popayán	142
Santa Marta	178
Sincelejo	121
Soledad	164
Valledupar	143
Villavicencio	161
Comoros	
Moroni*	20

Country City	Population in thousands
Congo	
Brazzaville*	299
Pointe-Noire	142
Costa Rica	
San José*	241
Croatia	
Osijek	159
Rijeka	193
Slavonski Brod	106
Split	236
Zadar	116
Zagreb*	681
Cuba	
Bayamo,	122
Camagüey	279
Cienfuegos	119
Guantánamo	198
Havana*	2,078
Holguín	223
Marianao	128
Matanzas	112
Pinar del Río	117
Santa Clara	191
Santiago de Cuba	397
Victoria de las Tunas	115
Cyprus	
Limassol	120
Nicosia*	167
Czech Republic	
Brno	371
Olomouc	102
Ostrava	322
Pilsen	171
Prague*	1,182
Denmark	
Ålborg	155
Århus	182
Copenhagen*	494
Odense	137
Djibouti	
Djibouti*	96
Dominica	
Roseau*	8
Dominican Republic	
Santiago de los Caballeros	279
Santo Domingo*	1,313
Ecuador	
Ambato	113
Cuenca	157
Guayaquil	1,205
Machala	108
Manta	104
Portoviejo	123
Quito*	890
Santo Domingo de los Colorados	128
Egypt	
Alexandria	2,319
Al Fayyum	167
Al Jīzah	1,247
Al Maḩallah al Kubrá	293
Al Mansūra	258
Al Minyā	146
Aswān	144
Asyūt	214
Az Zaqāzīq	203
Banī Suwayf	118
Cairo*	5,084
Damanhūr	189
Ismailia	146
Kafr ad Dawwār	161
Port Said	263
Shibīn al Kaum	103
Shubrā al Khaymah	394
Suez	194
Tantā	285
El Salvador	
San Miguel	179
San Salvador*	471
Santa Ana	228
Equatorial Guinea	
Malabo*	37
Eritrea	
Āsmera*	275
Estonia	
Tallinn*	482
Tartu	114
Ethiopia	
Addis Ababa*	1,413
Dirē Dawa	105
Gonder	108

Country City	Population in thousands
Fiji	
Suva*	70
Finland	
Esbo (Espoo)	157
Helsinki*	486
Tampere	169
Turku	161
Vantaa	144
France	
Aix-en-Provence	100
Amiens	130
Angers	135
Besançon	112
Bordeaux	202
Boulogne-Billancourt	103
Brest	154
Caen	112
Clermont-Ferrand	146
Dijon	139
Grenoble	156
Le Havre	199
Le Mans	146
Lille	168
Limoges	138
Lyon	410
Marseille	868
Metz	113
Montpellier	190
Mulhouse	112
Nantes	238
Nice	331
Nîmes	121
Paris*	2,166
Perpignan	108
Reims	176
Rennes	191
Roubaix	101
Rouen	101
Saint-Étienne	194
Strasbourg	247
Toulon	177
Toulouse	345
Tours	131
Gabon	
Libreville*	105
Gambia	
Banjul*	49
Georgia	
Batumi	136
Kutaisi	235
Rustavi	159
Sukhumi	121
Tbilisi*	1,260
Germany	
Aachen	233
Augsburg	248
Bergisch Gladbach	102
Berlin*	3,305
Bielefeld	312
Bochum	389
Bonn	282
Bottrop	116
Braunschweig	254
Bremen	535
Bremerhaven	127
Chemnitz	314
Cologne	937
Cottbus	127
Darmstadt	136
Dessau	104
Dortmund	587
Dresden	520
Duisburg	527
Düsseldorf	570
Erfurt	217
Erlangen	101
Essen	621
Frankfurt am Main	625
Freiburg	184
Gelsenkirchen	287
Gera	113
Göttingen	118
Hagen	211
Halle	236
Hamburg	1,603
Hamm	174
Hannover	498
Heidelberg	131
Heilbronn	112
Herne	175
Hildesheim	104
Jena	108
Karlsruhe	265
Kassel	189

Country City	Population in thousands
Kiel	241
Koblenz	107
Köpenick	118
Krefeld	235
Leipzig	551
Leverkusen	157
Lübeck	211
Ludwigshafen	158
Magdeburg	289
Mainz	175
Mannheim	300
Moers	102
Mönchengladbach	253
Mülheim an der Ruhr	175
Munich	1,212
Münster	249
Neuss	144
Nürnberg	249
Oberhausen	221
Offenbach	112
Oldenburg	141
Osnabrück	155
Paderborn	114
Pforzheim	109
Potsdam	141
Recklinghausen	122
Regensburg	119
Remscheid	121
Reutlingen	100
Rostock	249
Saarbrücken	188
Salzgitter	112
Schwerin	128
Siegen	106
Solingen	161
Stuttgart	563
Ulm	197
Wiesbaden	254
Witten	104
Wolfsburg	126
Wuppertal	371
Würzburg	126
Zwickau	121
Ghana	
Accra*	860
Kumasi	349
Tamale	137
Greece	
Athens*	886
Iráklion	102
Kallithéa	117
Lárisa	102
Pátrai	142
Peristérion	141
Piraiévs	196
Thessaloníki	406
Grenada	
Saint George's*	6
Guatemala	
Guatemala*	750
Guinea	
Conakry*	526
Guinea-Bissau	
Bissau*	109
Guyana	
Georgetown*	63
Haiti	
Port-au-Prince*	461
Honduras	
La Ceiba	104
San Pedro Sula	397
Tegucigalpa*	598
Hungary	
Budapest*	2,104
Debrecen	217
Győr	131
Kecskemét	105
Miskolc	210
Nyíregyháza	119
Pécs	182
Szeged	188
Székesfehérvár	113
Iceland	
Reykjavík*	96
India	
Ādoni	109
Āgra	747
Agartala	132
Ahmadābād	2,548
Ahmadnagar	181
Ajmer	376
Akola	225

Country City	Population in thousands
Alīgarh	321
Allahābād	650
Alleppey	170
Alwar	146
Ambāla	121
Amravati	261
Amritsar	595
Amroha	113
Anantapur	120
Arrah	125
Asansol	366
Aurangābād	316
Bīkaner	288
Bally	148
Bālurghāt	113
Bangalore	2,922
Baranagar	170
Bareilly	449
Baroda	745
Barrackpur	116
Batāla	102
Belgaum	300
Bellary	202
Berhampore	102
Berhampur	163
Bhadrāvati	131
Bhāgalpur	225
Bhārātpur	105
Bharuch	121
Bhatinda	127
Bhātpāra	265
Bhavnagar	309
Bhilai	376
Bhīlwāra	123
Bhīmavaram	102
Bhiwandi	115
Bhiwāni	101
Bhopāl	671
Bhubaneswar	219
Bhusawal	132
Bīhar	151
Bijāpur	147
Bilāspur	187
Bokaro Steel City	264
Bombay	8,243
Bulandshahr	103
Burdwān	167
Burhānpur	141
Calcutta	9,194
Cannanore	158
Chandannagar	102
Chandigarh	423
Chandrapur	116
Chāpra	112
Cochin	686
Coimbatore	920
Cuddalore	128
Cuddapah	103
Cuttack	327
Darbhanga	176
Dāvangere	197
Dehra Dūn	293
Delhi	4,884
Dhānbād	621
Dhārwār	379
Dhūlia	211
Dindigul	164
Dombivli	103
Durg	115
Durgāpur	312
Elūru	168
Erode	276
Etāwah	112
Faizābād	143
Farīdābād	331
Farrukhābād	161
Firozābād	202
Firozpur	106
Gadag-Betigeri	117
Garden Reach	191
Gauhāti	152
Gayā	247
Ghaziābād	287
Gondia	100
Gorakhpur	308
Gulbarga	221
Guntūr	368
Gurgaon	101
Gwalior	556
Hābra	130
Hāpur	103
Hardwār	146
Hisār	137
Hooghly-Chinsura	125
Hospet	115
Howrah	744
Hubli-Dhārwār	527

Country City	Population in thousands
Hyderābād	2,546
Ichalkaranji	134
Imphāl	157
Indore	829
Jabalpur	757
Jaipur	1,015
Jālgaon	145
Jālna	122
Jammu	223
Jāmnagar	317
Jamshedpur	670
Jaridih	102
Jaunpur	105
Jhānsi	284
Jodhpur	506
Jullundur	442
Junāgadh	120
Kākināda	226
Kalyān	136
Kāmārhāti	235
Kānchīpuram	145
Kānpur	1,639
Kāraikkudi	100
Karnāl	132
Katihār	122
Khandwa	115
Kharagpur	233
Kolār Gold Fields	144
Kolhāpur	351
Kota	358
Kozhikode	546
Kumbakonam	142
Kurnool	206
Lātūr	112
Lucknow	1,008
Ludhiāna	607
Machilipatnam	139
Madras	4,289
Madurai	908
Mālegaon	246
Mandya	100
Mangalore	306
Mathurā	159
Meerut	537
Miraj	105
Mirzāpur	128
Monghyr	129
Morādābād	345
Murwāra	123
Muzaffarnagar	172
Muzaffarpur	190
Mysore	479
Nabadwīp	130
Nadiād	143
Nāgercoil	172
Nāgpur	1,302
Naihāti	115
Nānded	191
Nāsik	429
Navsāri	129
Nellore	237
New Delhi*	273
Nizāmābād	183
Pālghāt	118
Pānīpat	138
Pānihāti	206
Parbhani	109
Pātan	105
Pathānkot	110
Patiāla	206
Patna	919
Pimpri-Chinchwad	221
Pollāchi	115
Pondicherry	251
Poona	1,686
Porbandar	133
Proddatūr	107
Purī	101
Purnia	110
Quilon	168
Raichūr	125
Raipur	338
Rājahmundry	268
Rājapālaiyam	102
Rājkot	445
Rāmpur	205
Rānchī	503
Rānīganj	119
Ratlām	156
Raurkela	321
Rewa	101
Rohtak	167
Sāgar	207
Sahāranpur	295
Salem	498
Sambalpur	162
Sambhal	108

Country / City	Population in thousands
Sāngli	269
Secunderābād	136
Serampore	127
Shāhjahānpur	205
Shillong	175
Shimoga	152
Sholāpur	515
Sīkar	103
Sīliguri	154
Sītāpur	101
Sonepat	109
South Dum Dum	230
South Suburban	395
Sri Gangānagar	124
Srīnagar	606
Surat	914
Tenāli	119
Thāna	390
Thanjavur	184
Tiruchchirāppalli	545
Tirunelveli	178
Tirupati	115
Tiruppūr	203
Tītāgarh	105
Trichūr	170
Trivandrum	520
Tumkūr	109
Tuticorin	251
Udaipur	233
Ujjain	282
Ulhāsnagar	315
Vālpārai	115
Vāranāsi	797
Vellore	247
Verāval	105
Vijayawada	543
Visākhapatnam	604
Vizianagaram	115
Warangal	335
Yamunānagar	160
Indonesia	
Ambon	209
Balikpapan	281
Bandung	1,463
Banjarmasin	381
Bekasi	123
Bogor	247
Ciamis	105
Cianjur	132
Cilacap	119
Cimahi	157
Cirebon	224
Jakarta*	6,503
Jambi	230
Jember	115
Kediri	222
Kuningan	105
Madiun	151
Magelang	123
Malang	512
Manado	217
Medan	1,379
Padang	481
Padangsidempuan	135
Pakanbaru	186
Palembang	787
Pare	108
Pekalongan	133
Pemalang	110
Pematangsiantar	150
Pontianak	305
Probolinggo	100
Purwokerto	125
Samarinda	265
Semarang	1,027
Sukabumi	110
Surabaya	2,028
Surakarta	470
Tanjungkarang	284
Tanjungpriok	148
Tasikmalaya	136
Tegal	132
Ujung Pandang	709
Yogyakarta	399
Iran	
Abādān	296
Amol	118
Ahvāz	580
Arāk	265
Ardabīl	147
Bābol	115
Bākhtarān	561
Bandar-e 'Abbās	202
Borūjerd	184
Būshehr	121
Dezfūl	151
Eşfahān	987
Gorgān	139
Hamadān	272
Karaj	275
Kāshān	139
Kermān	257
Khomeynīshahr	105
Khorramābād	209
Khorramshahr	147
Khvoy	115
Malāyer	104
Marāgheh	101
Mashhad	1,464
Masjed-e Soleymān	105
Najafābād	129
Neyshābūr	109
Orūmīyeh	301
Qā'emshahr	109
Qazvīn	249
Qom	543
Rasht	291
Sabzevār	129
Sanandaj	205
Sārī	141
Shīrāz	848
Tabrīz	971
Tajrīsh	157
Tehrān*	6,043
Yazd	230
Zāhedān	282
Zanjān	215
Iraq	
Al Başrah	313
An Najaf	128
Baghdad*	1,900
Kirkūk	167
Mosul	315
Ireland	
Cork	133
Dublin*	503
Israel	
Bat Yam	129
Beersheba	111
Hefa	226
Holon	133
Jerusalem*	429
Netanya	102
Petah Tiqwa	124
Ramat Gan	117
Rishon LeZiyyon	102
Tel Aviv-Yafo	327
Italy	
Bari	369
Bergamo	121
Bologna	455
Bolzano	103
Brescia	203
Cagliari	219
Catania	380
Cosenza	101
Ferrara	118
Florence	443
Foggia	150
Genoa	755
La Spezia	111
Livorno	172
Messina	240
Mestre	198
Milan	1,602
Modena	165
Monza	123
Naples	1,210
Padua	228
Palermo	698
Parma	160
Perugia	104
Pescara	131
Piacenza	104
Prato	157
Reggio di Calabria	159
Reggio nell'Emilia	107
Rimini	112
Rome*	2,605
Salerno	150
Sassari	104
Siracusa	109
Taranto	231
Trieste	237
Turin	1,115
Udine	102
Venice	317
Verona	239
Vicenza	111
Ivory Coast	
Abidjan	686
Bouaké	173
Yamoussoukro*	36
J Jamaica	
Kingston*	494
Japan	
Abiko	101
Ageo	166
Aizu-Wakamatsu	115
Akashi	255
Akita	285
Amagasaki	524
Anjō	124
Aomori	288
Asahikawa	353
Ashikaga	166
Atsugi	145
Beppu	136
Chiba	793
Chigasaki	171
Chofu	181
Daitō	117
Fuchū	192
Fuji	206
Fujieda	103
Fujinomiya	108
Fujisawa	300
Fukui	241
Fukuoka	1,089
Fukushima	263
Fukuyama	346
Funabashi	479
Gifu	410
Habikino	103
Hachiōji	387
Hachinohe	238
Hadano	123
Hakodate	320
Hamamatsu	491
Higashikurume	107
Higashimurayama	119
Higashi-Ōsaka	522
Himeji	446
Hino	145
Hirakata	353
Hiratsuka	214
Hirosaki	175
Hiroshima	899
Hitachi	205
Hōfu	111
Ibaraki	234
Ichihara	216
Ichikawa	364
Ichinomiya	253
Ikeda	101
Imabari	123
Iruma	104
Ise	106
Isesaki	106
Ishinomaki	121
Itami	178
Iwaki	342
Iwakuni	113
Izumi	124
Jōetsu	128
Kadoma	139
Kagoshima	505
Kakamigahara	115
Kakogawa	212
Kamakura	173
Kanazawa	418
Kariya	106
Kashihara	107
Kashiwa	239
Kasugai	244
Kasukabe	156
Kawagoe	259
Kawaguchi	379
Kawanishi	130
Kawasaki	1,041
Kiryū	133
Kisarazu	111
Kishiwada	180
Kitakyūshū	1,065
Kitami	103
Kōbe	1,367
Kōchi	301
Kōfu	199
Kōriyama	286
Kodaira	155
Koganei	102
Komaki	103
Komatsu	104
Koshigaya	223
Kumagaya	137
Kumamoto	526
Kurashiki	404
Kure	235
Kurume	217
Kushiro	215
Kyōto	1,473
Machida	295
Maebashi	265
Matsubara	136
Matsudo	401
Matsue	136
Matsumoto	192
Matsusaka	113
Matsuyama	402
Mino'o	104
Mitaka	165
Mito	216
Miyakonojō	129
Miyazaki	265
Moriguchi	166
Morioka	229
Muroran	150
Musashino	137
Nagano	324
Nagaoka	180
Nagareyama	107
Nagasaki	447
Nagoya	2,088
Naha	296
Nara	298
Narashino	125
Neyagawa	256
Niigata	458
Niihama	132
Niiza	119
Nishinomiya	410
Nobeoka	137
Numazu	204
Obihiro	154
Odawara	177
Ogaki	143
Oita	360
Okayama	546
Okazaki	262
Omiya	354
Omuta	163
Onomichi	102
Osaka	2,648
Ota	123
Otaru	181
Otsu	215
Oyama	127
Saga	164
Sagamihara	439
Sakai	810
Sakata	103
Sakura	101
Sapporo	1,402
Sasebo	251
Sayama	124
Sendai	665
Seto	121
Shimizu	242
Shimonoseki	269
Shizuoka	458
Sōka	187
Suita	332
Suzuka	156
Tachikawa	143
Takamatsu	317
Takaoka	175
Takarazuka	184
Takasaki	221
Takatsuki	341
Tokorozawa	236
Tokushima	249
Tokuyama	111
Tōkyō*	8,352
Tomakomai	152
Tottori	131
Toyama	305
Toyohashi	304
Toyokawa	103
Toyonaka	403
Toyota	282
Tsu	145
Tsuchiura	113
Ube	169
Ueda	112
Uji	153
Urawa	358
Utsunomiya	378
Wakayama	401
Yachiyo	134
Yaizu	104
Yamagata	237
Yamaguchi	115
Yamato	168
Yao	273
Yatsushiro	108
Yokkaichi	255
Yokohama	2,774
Yokosuka	421
Yonago	127
Jordan	
'Ammān*	624
Az Zarqā'	216
Irbid	113
K Kazakhstan	
Aktyubinsk	253
Alma-Ata*	1,128
Chimkent	393
Dzhambul	307
Dzhezkazgan	109
Ekibastuz	135
Gur'yev	149
Karaganda	614
Kokchetav	137
Kustanay	224
Kzyl-Orda	153
Pavlodar	331
Petropavlovsk	241
Rudnyy	110
Semipalatinsk	334
Shevchenko	159
Taldy-Kurgan	119
Temirtau	212
Tselinograd	277
Ural'sk	200
Ust'-Kamenogorsk	324
Kenya	
Mombasa	247
Nairobi*	509
Kiribati	
Bairiki*	2
Korea, North	
Ch'ŏngjin	306
Haeju	140
Hamhŭng	484
Kaesŏng	175
Kimch'aek	100
Nampb	140
P'yŏngyang*	1,250
Sinŭiju	300
Wŏnsan	275
Korea, South	
Andong	102
Anyang	254
Cheju	168
Chinhae	112
Chinju	203
Ch'ŏnan	121
Ch'ŏngju	253
Chŏnju	367
Ch'unch'ŏn	155
Ch'ungju	113
Inch'ŏn	1,085
Iri	145
Kangnŭng	117
Kimhae	203
Kimje	221
Kohŭng	217
Kunsan	165
Kwangju	728
Kyŏngju	122
Masan	387
Mokp'o	222
Nonsan	226
P'ohang	201
Puch'on	221
Pusan	3,160
Seoul*	8,367
Sunch'ŏn	114
Suwŏn	311
Taegu	1,607
Taejŏn	652
Ulsan	418
Wŏnju	137
Yanggu	278
Yŏsu	161
Kuwait	
Al Kuwait*	182
As Sālimīyah	153
Hawallī	145
Jalīb ash Shuyūkh	115
Kyrgyzstan	
Bishkek*	616
Osh	213
L Laos	
Vientiane*	377
Latvia	
Daugavpils	127
Liepāja	114
Riga*	916
Lebanon	
Beirut*	475
Tripoli	128
Lesotho	
Maseru*	13
Liberia	
Monrovia*	167
Libya	
Benghāzī	284
Mişrātah	102
Tripoli*	55
Liechtenstein	
Vaduz*	
Lithuania	
Kaunas	42
Klaipėda	20
Panevėžys	12
Šiauliai	14
Vilnius*	58
Luxembourg	
Luxembourg*	7
M Macedonia	
Bitola	13
Gostivar	10
Kumanovo	12
Skopje*	50
Tetovo	16
Madagascar	
Antananarivo*	45
Fandriana	10
Malawi	
Blantyre	33
Lilongwe*	23
Malaysia	
Georgetown	24
Ipoh	29
Johor Baharu	24
Kelang	19
Kota Baharu	16
Kuala Lumpur*	92
Kuala Terengganu	18
Kuantan	13
Seremban	13
Taiping	14
Maldives	
Male*	4
Mali	
Bamako*	40
Malta	
Valletta*	1
Marshall Islands	
Majuro*	
Mauritania	
Nouakchott*	13
Mauritius	
Port Louis*	13
Mexico	
Acapulco de Juárez	301
Aguascalientes	29
Campeche	128
Celaya	14
Chihuahua	38
Ciudad Juárez	54
Ciudad Madero	13
Ciudad Obregón	16
Ciudad Victoria	14
Coatzacoalcos	12
Cuernavaca	19
Culiacán	30
Durango de Victoria	25
Ecatepec de Morelos	742
Ensenada	12
Gómez Palacio	11
Guadalajara	1,62
Guadalupe	37
Hermosillo	29
Irapuato	17
Jalapa Enríquez	20
León	59
Los Mochis	12
Matamoros	18
Mazatlán	20
Mérida	40
Mexicali	34
Mexico City*	8,83
Minatitlán	10
Monclova	11
Monterrey	1,08

Country / City	Population in thousands
Morelia	298
Naucalpan de Juárez	724
Netzahualcóyotl	1,341
Nuevo Laredo	202
Oaxaca de Juárez	154
Orizaba	115
Pachuca de Soto	110
Poza Rica	167
Puebla de Zaragoza	773
Querétaro	216
Reynosa	195
Saltillo	285
San Luis Potosí	362
San Nicolás de los Garzas	281
Tampico	268
Tepic	146
Tijuana	430
Tlalnepantla de Galeana	778
Tlaquepaque	134
Toluca de Lerdo	200
Torreón	328
Tuxtla Gutiérrez	131
Uruapan del Progreso	123
Veracruz Llave	285
Villahermosa	158
Zapopan	345
Micronesia, Federated States of	
Kolonia*	6
Moldova	
Bel'tsy	159
Bendery	130
Kishinëv*	665
Tiraspol'	182
Monaco	
Monaco*	30
Mongolia	
Ulaanbaatar*	515
Morocco	
Casablanca	1,506
Fès	325
Kenitra	139
Marrakech	333
Meknès	248
Oujda	176
Rabat*	368
Safi	129
Salé	156
Tangier	188
Tétouan	139
Mozambique	
Maputo*	883
Nampula	183
Namibia	
Windhoek*	96
Nepal	
Käthmändu*	423
Netherlands	
Amsterdam*	695
Apeldoorn	147
Arnhem	129
Breda	121
Dordrecht	109
Eindhoven	191
Enschede	145
Groningen	168
Haarlem	149
Leiden	109
Maastricht	116
Nijmegen	145
Rotterdam	576
The Hague*	444
Tilburg	155
Utrecht	240
Zaandam	130
New Zealand	
Auckland	149
Christchurch	168
Manukau	177
Wellington*	137
Nicaragua	
Managua*	608
Niger	
Niamey*	225
Nigeria	
Aba	177
Abeokuta	253
Abuja*	1
Ado	213
Benin City	136
Calabar	103
Ede	182
Enugu	187
Ibadan	847
Ife	176
Ilesha	224
Ilorin	282
Iseyin	115
Iwo	214
Kaduna	202
Kano	399
Katsina	109
Lagos	1,061
Maiduguri	189
Ogbomosho	432
Onitsha	220
Oshogbo	282
Oyo	152
Port Harcourt	242
Zaria	224
Norway	
Bergen	207
Oslo*	447
Trondheim	134
Oman	
Muscat*	8
Pakistan	
Bahäwalpur	180
Chiniot	106
Dera Ghäzi Khän	102
Faisalabad	1,104
Gujränwäla	659
Gujrät	155
Hyderäbäd	752
Islämäbäd*	204
Jhang Sadar	196
Jhelum	106
Karächi	5,076
Kasür	156
Lahore	2,953
Lärkäna	124
Mardän	148
Mirpur Khäs	124
Multän	732
Nawäbshäh	102
Okära	127
Peshäwar	566
Quetta	286
Rahïmyär Khän	119
Räwalpindi	795
Sähiwäl	151
Sargodha	291
Shekhüpura	141
Siälkot	302
Sukkur	191
Wäh	127
Panama	
Panamá*	432
Papua New Guinea	
Port Moresby*	124
Paraguay	
Asunción*	388
Peru	
Arequipa	108
Callao	261
Chiclayo	280
Chimbote	216
Comas	287
Huancayo	165
Ica	111
Iquitos	174
Lima*	376
Piura	186
Trujillo	355
Philippines	
Angeles	189
Bacolod City	262
Baguio	119
Batangas	144
Butuan	173
Butuan City	172
Cabanatuan City	138
Cadiz	130
Cagayan de Oro City	227
Calamba	121
Calbayog City	107
Caloocan City	468
Cebu City	490
Davao City	610
General Santos	149
Iligan	167
Iligan City	167
Iloilo	245
Lipa City	121
Lucena	108
Makati	373
Malabon	191
Mandaue	111
Manila City*	1,630
Marikina	212
Olongapo	156
Ormoc City	105
Paranaque	209
Pasay City	288
Pasig	269
Quezon City	1,166
San Carlos	101
San Fernando	111
San Pablo City	132
Silay	111
Tacloban	103
Tarlac	176
Valenzuela	212
Zamboanga City	344
Poland	
Białystok	268
Bielsko-Biała	181
Bydgoszcz	380
Bytom	230
Chorzów	132
Częstochowa	257
Dąbrowa Górnicza	135
Elbląg	126
Gdańsk	462
Gdynia	251
Gliwice	212
Gorzów Wielkopolski	123
Grudziądz	102
Jastrzębie Zdroj	102
Kalisz	106
Katowice	366
Kielce	213
Koszalin	108
Kraków	746
Legnica	104
Łódź	849
Lublin	349
Olsztyn	161
Opole	127
Płock	121
Poznań	587
Radom	226
Ruda Śląska	169
Rybnik	142
Rzeszów	151
Słupsk	100
Sosnowiec	259
Szczecin	411
Tarnów	121
Toruń	201
Tychy	190
Wałbrzych	142
Warsaw*	1,651
Włocławek	121
Wodzisław Śląski	111
Wrocław	641
Zabrze	203
Zielona Góra	113
Portugal	
Lisbon*	818
Porto	330
Qatar	
Doha*	217
Romania	
Arad	188
Bacău	180
Baia Mare	140
Botoşani	109
Brăila	236
Braşov	351
Bucharest*	1,990
Buzău	136
Cluj-Napoca	310
Constanţa	328
Craiova	281
Galaţi	295
Iaşi	313
Oradea	214
Piatra Neamţ	109
Piteşti	157
Ploieşti	235
Reşiţa	106
Satu Mare	130
Sibiu	178
Timisoara	325
Tirgu Mures	159
Russia	
Abakan	154
Achinsk	122
Al'met'yevsk	129
Angarsk	266
Anzhero-Sudzhensk	108
Archangel	416
Armavir	161
Arzamas	109
Astrakhan'	509
Balakovo	198
Balashikha	136
Barnaul	602
Belgorod	300
Belovo	112
Berezniki	201
Biysk	233
Blagoveshchensk	206
Bratsk	255
Bryansk	452
Cheboksary	420
Chelyabinsk	1,143
Cherepovets	310
Cherkessk	113
Chita	366
Dimitrovgrad	124
Dzerzhinsk	285
Elektrostal'	153
Engel's	182
Glazov	104
Groznyy	401
Irkutsk	626
Ivanovo	481
Izhevsk	635
Kaliningrad (Kalin.)	401
Kaliningrad (Moscow)	160
Kaluga	312
Kamensk-Ural'skiy	209
Kamyshin	122
Kansk	110
Kazan'	1,094
Kemerovo	520
Khabarovsk	601
Khimki	133
Kineshma	105
Kiselevsk	128
Kislovodsk	114
Kolomna	162
Kolpino	142
Komsomol'sk-na-Amure	315
Kopeysk	146
Kostroma	278
Kovrov	160
Krasnodar	620
Krasnoyarsk	912
Kurgan	356
Kursk	424
Leninsk-Kuznetskiy	165
Lipetsk	450
Lyubertsy	165
Magadan	152
Magnitogorsk	440
Makhachkala	315
Maykop	149
Mezhdurechensk	107
Miass	168
Michurinsk	109
Moscow*	8,769
Murmansk	468
Murom	124
Mytishchi	154
Naberezhnye Chelny	501
Nakhodka	165
Nal'chik	235
Neftekamsk	107
Nevinnomyssk	121
Nizhnekamsk	191
Nizhnevartovsk	242
Nizhniy Novgorod	1,438
Nizhniy Tagil	440
Noginsk	123
Noril'sk	174
Novgorod	229
Novocheboksarsk	115
Novocherkassk	187
Novokuybyshevsk	113
Novokuznetsk	600
Novomoskovsk	146
Novorossiysk	186
Novoshakhtinsk	106
Novosibirsk	1,436
Novotroitsk	106
Obninsk	100
Odintsovo	125
Oktyabr'skiy	105
Omsk	1,148
Orekhovo-Zuyevo	137
Orël	337
Orenburg	547
Orsk	271
Penza	483
Perm'	1,091
Pervoural'sk	142
Petropavlovsk-Kamchatskiy	269
Petrozavodsk	270
Podol'sk	210
Prokop'yevsk	274
Pskov	204
Pyatigorsk	129
Rostov	1,020
Rubtsovsk	172
Ryazan'	515
Rybinsk	252
Saint Petersburg	4,456
Salavat	150
Samara	1,257
Saransk	312
Sarapul	111
Saratov	905
Sergiyev Posad	115
Serov	104
Serpukhov	144
Severodvinsk	249
Shakhty	224
Shchelkovo	109
Simbirsk	625
Smolensk	341
Sochi	337
Solikamsk	110
Staryy Oskol'	174
Stavropol'	318
Sterlitamak	248
Surgut	248
Syktyvkar	233
Syzran'	174
Taganrog	291
Tambov	305
Tol'yatti	630
Tomsk	502
Tula	540
T'ver	451
Tyumen'	477
Ufa	1,083
Ukhta	111
Ulan-Ude	353
Usol'ye-Sibirskoye	107
Ussuriysk	162
Ust'-Ilimsk	109
Velikiye Luki	114
Vladikavkaz	300
Vladimir	350
Vladivostok	648
Volgograd	999
Vologda	283
Volzhskiy	269
Vorkuta	116
Voronezh	887
Votkinsk	103
Vyatka	441
Yakutsk	187
Yaroslavl'	633
Yekaterinburg	1,367
Yelets	120
Yoshkar-Ola	242
Yuzhno-Sakhalinsk	157
Zelenograd	158
Zhukovskiy	101
Zlatoust	208
Rwanda	
Kigali*	118
Saint Kitts and Nevis	
Basseterre*	15
Saint Lucia	
Castries*	56
Saint Vincent and the Grenadines	
Kingstown*	17
San Marino	
San Marino*	4
Sao Tome and Principe	
São Tomé*	8
Saudi Arabia	
Ad Dammäm	128
Al Hufüf	101
Aţ Ţä'if	205
Jiddah	561
Mecca	367
Medina	198
Riyadh*	667
Senegal	
Dakar*	799
Kaolack	107
Thiès	117
Seychelles	
Victoria*	16
Sierra Leone	
Freetown*	274
Singapore	
Singapore*	2,756
Slovak Republic	
Bratislava*	380
Košice	202
Slovenia	
Ljubljana*	305
Maribor	186
Solomon Islands	
Honiara*	30
Somalia	
Mogadishu*	371
South Africa	
Bloemfontein	104
Boksburg	111
Cape Town*	777
Durban	634
East London	120
Germiston	117
Johannesburg	632
Kimberley	105
Pietermaritzburg	115
Port Elizabeth	273
Pretoria*	443
Roodepoort-Maraisburg	142
Soweto	522
Springs	143
Tembisa	149
Wes-Rand	647
Spain	
Albacete	116
Alcalá de Henares	137
Alcorcón	141
Alicante	246
Almería	141
Badajoz	111
Badalona	230
Baracaldo	119
Barcelona	1,753
Bilbao	433
Burgos	153
Cádiz	157
Cartagena	168
Castellón de la Plana	124
Córdoba	279
Elche	165
Getafe	127
Gijón	256
Granada	247
Huelva	128
Jerez de la Frontera	176
La Coruña	232
La Laguna	106
Las Palmas de Gran Canaria	360
Leganés	164
León	127
L'Hospitalet de Llobregat	295
Lleida	107
Logroño	110
Madrid*	3,159
Málaga	502
Móstoles	150
Murcia	285
Oviedo	184
Palma	290
Pamplona	178
Sabadell	186
Salamanca	154
San Sebastián	172
Santa Cruz de Tenerife	186
Santander	180
Saragossa	572
Seville	646
Tarragona	109
Terrassa	156
Valencia	745
Valladolid	320
Vigo	261
Vitoria	190
Sri Lanka	
Colombo*	609
Dehiwala-Mount Lavinia	190
Galle	109
Jaffna	127
Kandy	102
Kotte	107
Moratuwa	165
Sudan	
Khartoum*	334
Khartoum North	151

Country / City	Population in thousands
Omdurman	299
Port Sudan	133
Wad Medani	107
Suriname	
Paramaribo*	68
Swaziland	
Mbabane*	38
Sweden	
Borås	101
Göteborg	431
Hälsingborg	107
Jönköping	110
Linköping	119
Malmö	232
Norrköping	119
Örebro	120
Stockholm*	669
Uppsala	162
Västerås	118
Switzerland	
Basel	182
Bern*	145
Geneva	157
Lausanne	127
Zürich	370
Syria	
Aleppo	977
Damascus*	1,251
Ḥamāh	177
Ḥimṣ	355
Latakia	197
T Taiwan	
Changhua	186
Chiayi	252
Kaohsiung	1,227
Keelung	348
Pingtung	189
Taichung	565
Tainan	541
Taipei*	2,108
Taoyuan	106
Tajikistan	
Dushanbe*	595
Khudzhand	160
Tanzania	
Dar es Salaam*	757
Mwanza	111
Tanga	103
Zanzibar	111
Thailand	
Bangkok*	4,697
Chiang Mai	102
Chon Buri	116
Nakhon Si Thammarat	102
Songkhla	173
Thon Buri	628
Togo	
Lomé*	370
Tonga	
Nuku'alofa*	18
Trinidad and Tobago	
Port-of-Spain*	60
Tunisia	
Safāqis	232
Tūnis*	597
Turkey	
Adana	778
Adapazarı	152
Ankara*	2,235
Antalya	261
Antioch	108
Balıkesir	150
Batman	110
Bursa	613
Denizli	169
Diyarbakır	306
Elazığ	182
Erzurum	246
Eskişehir	367
Gaziantep	479
İskenderun	152
İsparta	101
İstanbul	5,476
İzmir	1,490
İzmit	233
Kağıthane	164
Kahramanmaraş	210
Kayseri	374
Kırıkkale	208
Konya	439
Kütahya	119
Malatya	243
Manisa	127

Country / City	Population in thousands
Mersin	314
Osmaniye	104
Samsun	241
Sivas	199
Tarsus	147
Trabzon	142
Urfa	195
Van	111
Zonguldak	118
Turkmenistan	
Ashkhabad*	398
Chardzhou	161
Tashauz	112
Tuvalu	
Fongafale*	1,500
U Uganda	
Kampala*	479
Ukraine	
Aleksandriya	103
Belaya Tserkov'	197
Berdyansk	132
Cherkassy	290
Chernigov	296
Chernovtsy	257
Dneprodzerzhinsk	282
Dnepropetrovsk	1,179
Donetsk	1,110
Gorlovka	337
Ivano-Frankovsk	214
Kamenets-Podol'skiy	102
Kerch'	174
Khar'kov	1,611
Kherson	355
Khmel'nitskiy	237
Kirovograd	269
Kiev*	2,587
Kommunarsk	126
Konstantinovka	108
Kramatorsk	198
Krasnyy Luch	113
Kremenchug	236
Krivoy Rog	713
Lisichansk	127
Lugansk	497
Lutsk	198
L'viv	790
Makeyevka	430
Mariupol'	517
Melitopol'	174
Nikolayev	503
Nikopol'	158
Odessa	1,115
Pavlograd	131
Poltava	315
Rovno	228
Sevastopol'	356
Severodonetsk	131
Simferopol'	344
Slavyansk	135
Stakhanov	112
Sumy	291
Ternopol'	205
Uzhgorod	117
Vinnitsa	374
Yenakiyevo	121
Yevpatoriya	108
Zaporozh'ye	884
Zhitomir	292
United Arab Emirates	
Abu Dhabi*	243
Ash Shāriqah	125
Dubayy	266
United Kingdom	
Aberdeen	190
Belfast	295
Birkenhead	156
Birmingham	1,014
Blackburn	110
Blackpool	146
Bolton	144
Bournemouth	143
Bradford	293
Brighton	135
Bristol	414
Cardiff	262
Coventry	319
Derby	218
Dudley	187
Dundee	174
Edinburgh	420
Glasgow	765
Gloucester	107
Hillingdon	227
Huddersfield	148

Country / City	Population in thousands
Hull	322
Ipswich	130
Kingston upon Thames	131
Leeds	452
Leicester	324
Liverpool	539
London*	7,567
Luton	163
Manchester	449
Middlesbrough	159
Newcastle upon Tyne	199
Newport	116
Northampton	154
Norwich	170
Nottingham	273
Oldham	107
Oxford	114
Peterborough	113
Plymouth	239
Poole	123
Portsmouth	174
Preston	167
Reading	195
Rotherham	122
Saint Helens	114
Sheffield	471
Slough	106
Southampton	211
Southend-on-Sea	156
Stockport	135
Stoke-on-Trent	272
Sunderland	195
Sutton Coldfield	103
Swansea	172
Swindon	127
Walsall	178
Warley	152
Warrington	129
Watford	110
West Bromwich	154
Wolverhampton	264
York	123
United States	
Abilene	107
Akron	223
Albany	101
Albuquerque	385
Alexandria	111
Allentown	105
Amarillo	158
Amherst	112
Anaheim	266
Anchorage	226
Ann Arbor	110
Arlington (Tex.)	262
Arlington (Va.)	171
Atlanta	394
Aurora	222
Austin	466
Bakersfield	175
Baltimore	736
Baton Rouge	220
Beaumont	114
Berkeley	103
Birmingham	266
Boise	126
Boston	574
Bridgeport	142
Buffalo	328
Cedar Rapids	109
Charlotte	396
Chattanooga	152
Chesapeake	152
Chicago	2,784
Chula Vista	135
Cincinnati	364
Citrus Heights	107
Cleveland	506
Colorado Springs	281
Columbus (Ga.)	179
Columbus (Ohio)	633
Concord	111
Corpus Christi	257
Dallas	1,007
Dayton	182
Denver	468
Des Moines	193
Detroit	1,028
Durham	137
East Los Angeles	126
Elizabeth	110
El Monte	106
El Paso	515
Erie	109
Escondido	109
Eugene	113

Country / City	Population in thousands
Evansville	126
Flint	141
Fort Lauderdale	149
Fort Wayne	173
Fort Worth	448
Fremont	173
Fresno	354
Fullerton	114
Garden Grove	143
Garland	181
Gary	117
Glendale (Ariz.)	148
Glendale (Calif.)	180
Grand Rapids	189
Greensboro	184
Hampton	134
Hartford	140
Hayward	111
Hialeah	188
Hollywood	122
Honolulu	365
Houston	1,631
Huntington Beach	182
Huntsville	160
Independence	112
Indianapolis	742
Inglewood	110
Irvine	110
Irving	155
Jackson	197
Jacksonville	635
Jersey City	229
Kansas City (Kans.)	150
Kansas City (Mo.)	435
Knoxville	165
Lakewood	126
Lansing	127
Laredo	123
Las Vegas	258
Lexington	225
Lincoln	192
Little Rock	176
Livonia	101
Long Beach	429
Los Angeles	3,485
Louisville	269
Lowell	103
Lubbock	186
Macon	107
Madison	191
Memphis	610
Mesa	288
Mesquite	101
Metairie	149
Miami	359
Milwaukee	628
Minneapolis	368
Mobile	196
Modesto	165
Montgomery	187
Moreno Valley	119
Nashville	488
Newark	275
New Haven	130
New Orleans	497
Newport News	170
New York	7,323
Norfolk	261
Oakland	372
Oceanside	128
Oklahoma City	445
Omaha	336
Ontario	133
Orange	111
Orlando	165
Overland Park	112
Oxnard	142
Paradise	125
Pasadena (Calif.)	132
Pasadena (Tex.)	119
Paterson	141
Peoria	114
Philadelphia	1,586
Phoenix	983
Pittsburgh	370
Plano	129
Pomona	132
Portland	437
Portsmouth	104
Providence	161
Raleigh	208
Rancho Cucamonga	101
Reno	134
Richmond	203
Riverside	227
Rochester	232

Country / City	Population in thousands
Rockford	139
Sacramento	369
Saint Louis	397
Saint Paul	272
Saint Petersburg	239
Salem	108
Salinas	109
Salt Lake City	160
San Antonio	936
San Bernardino	164
San Diego	1,111
San Francisco	724
San Jose	782
Santa Ana	294
Santa Clarita	111
Santa Rosa	113
Savannah	138
Scottsdale	130
Seattle	516
Shreveport	199
Simi Valley	100
Sioux Falls	101
South Bend	106
Spokane	177
Springfield (Ill.)	105
Springfield (Mo.)	140
Springfield (Mass.)	157
Stamford	108
Sterling Heights	118
Stockton	211
Sunnyvale	117
Syracuse	164
Tacoma	177
Tallahassee	125
Tampa	280
Tempe	142
Thousand Oaks	104
Toledo	333
Topeka	120
Torrance	133
Tucson	405
Tulsa	367
Vallejo	109
Virginia Beach	393
Waco	104
Warren	145
Washington*	607
Waterbury	109
Wichita	304
Winston-Salem	143
Worcester	170
Yonkers	188
Uruguay	
Montevideo*	1,173
Uzbekistan	
Almalyk	114
Andizhan	293
Angren	131
Bukhara	224
Chirchik	156
Dzhizak	102
Fergana	200
Karshi	156
Kokand	182
Margilan	125
Namangan	308
Navoi	107
Nukus	169
Samarkand	366
Tashkent*	2,073
Urgench	128
V Vanuatu	
Vila*	5
Vatican City	
Vatican City*	1
Venezuela	
Barinas	158
Barquisimeto	661
Cabimas	162
Caracas*	1,247
Ciudad Bolivar	241
Ciudad Guayana	459
Cumaná	218
Guarenas	104
Los Teques	149
Maracaibo	1,124
Maracay	497
Maturín	205
Mérida	188
Petare	396
San Cristóbal	235
San Francisco	198
Valencia	856
Valera	132

Country / City	Population in thousands
Vietnam	
Biên Hòa	187
Cam Ranh	118
Can Tho	183
Đà Lat	105
Đà Nang	319
Haiphong	1,279
Hanoi*	2,571
Ho Chi Minh City	3,420
Hong Gai	115
Hue	168
Long Xuyên	112
My Tho	101
Nam Dinh	160
Nha Trang	173
Qui Nhon	127
Thái Nguyên	110
Vinh	160
Vũng Tàu	108
W Western Samoa	
Apia*	32
Y Yemen	
Aden	240
Sanaa*	135
Yugoslavia	
Belgrade*	1,470
Čačak	111
Kragujevac	165
Kraljevo	122
Kruševac	133
Leskovac	159
Niš	231
Novi Sad	258
PanČevo	124
Peć	111
Priština	210
Prizren	135
Šabac	120
Smederevo	107
Subotica	155
Titograd	132
Uroševac	114
Zrenjanin	139
Z Zaire	
Bukavu	135
Kananga	429
Kikwit	112
Kinshasa*	1,323
Kisangani	230
Lubumbashi	318
Matadi	110
Mbandaka	108
Mbuji-Mayi	256
Zambia	
Chingola	146
Kabwe	144
Kitwe	315
Luanshya	132
Lusaka*	538
Mufulira	150
Ndola	282
Zimbabwe	
Bulawayo	414
Harare*	656
Dependency	
Hong Kong (U.K.)	
Kowloon	2,450
Victoria*	1,183
Puerto Rico (U.S.)	
Bayamón	202
Carolina	162
Ponce	159
San Juan*	426
Macau (Port.)	
Macau*	238

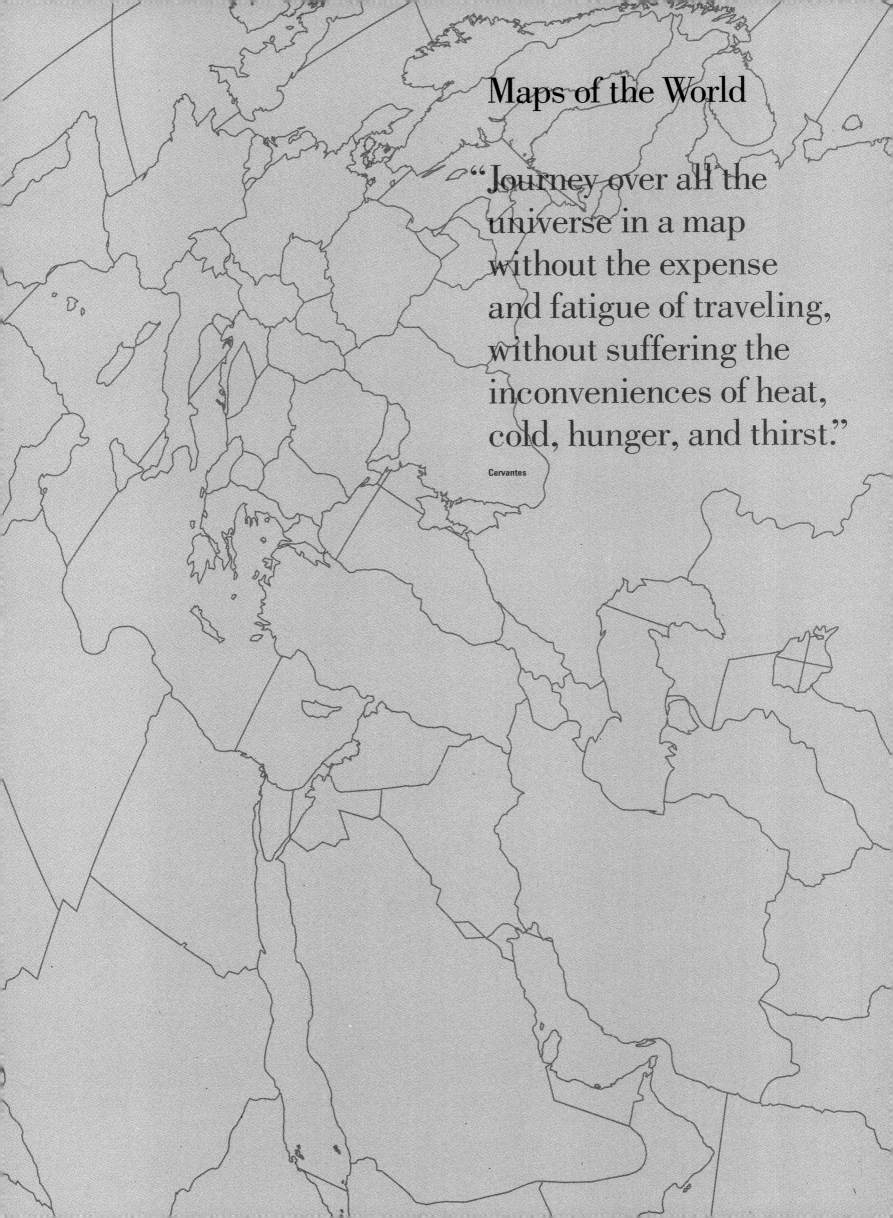

Maps of the World

"Journey over all the universe in a map without the expense and fatigue of traveling, without suffering the inconveniences of heat, cold, hunger, and thirst."

Cervantes

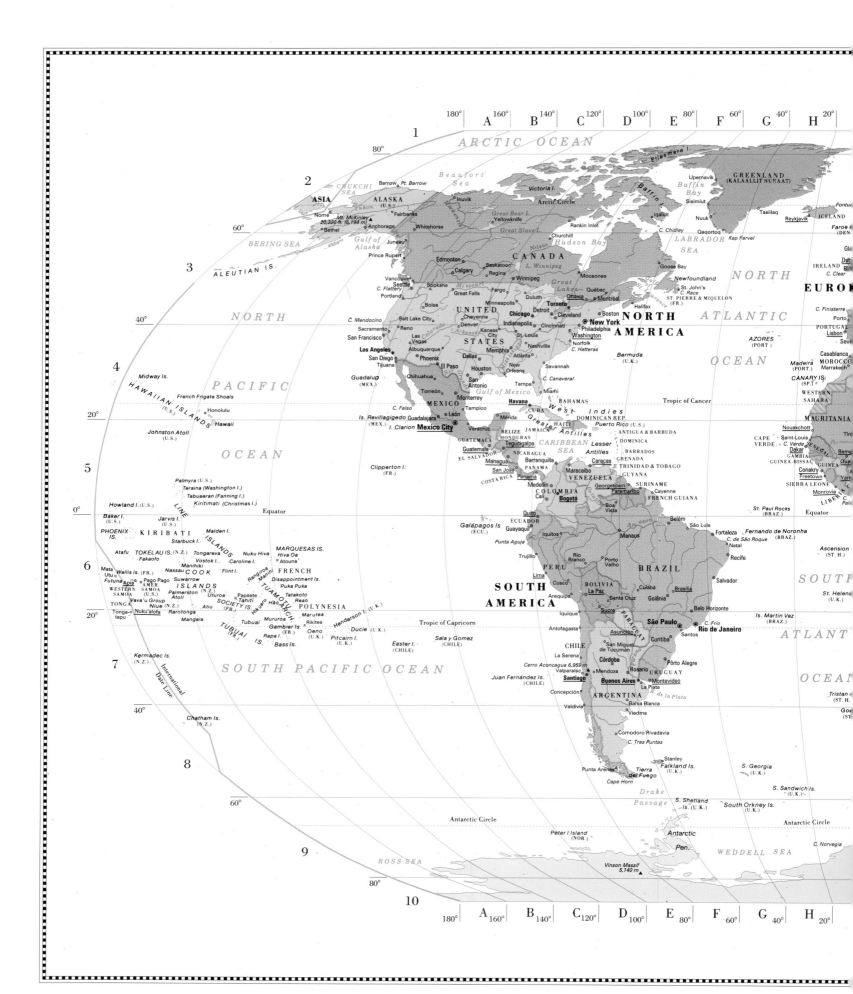

World

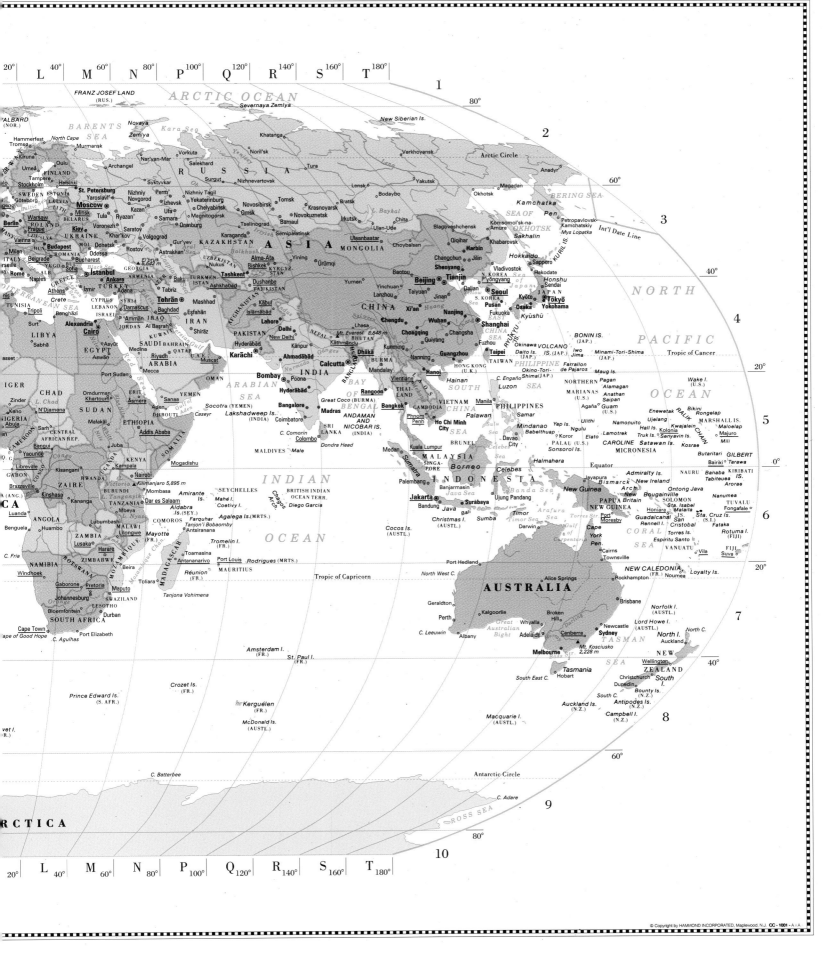

POPULATION OF CITIES AND TOWNS

◉ OVER 5,000,000   ● 500,000 - 1,999,999
● 2,000,000 - 4,999,999   ○ UNDER 500,000

SCALE 1:81,700,000   ROBINSON PROJECTION   STANDARD PARALLELS 38°N AND 38°S

MILES   0 ———————— 1000 ———— 2000 ———— 3000 ———— 4000
KILOMETERS   0 ———————— 1000 ———— 2000 ———— 3000 ———— 4000

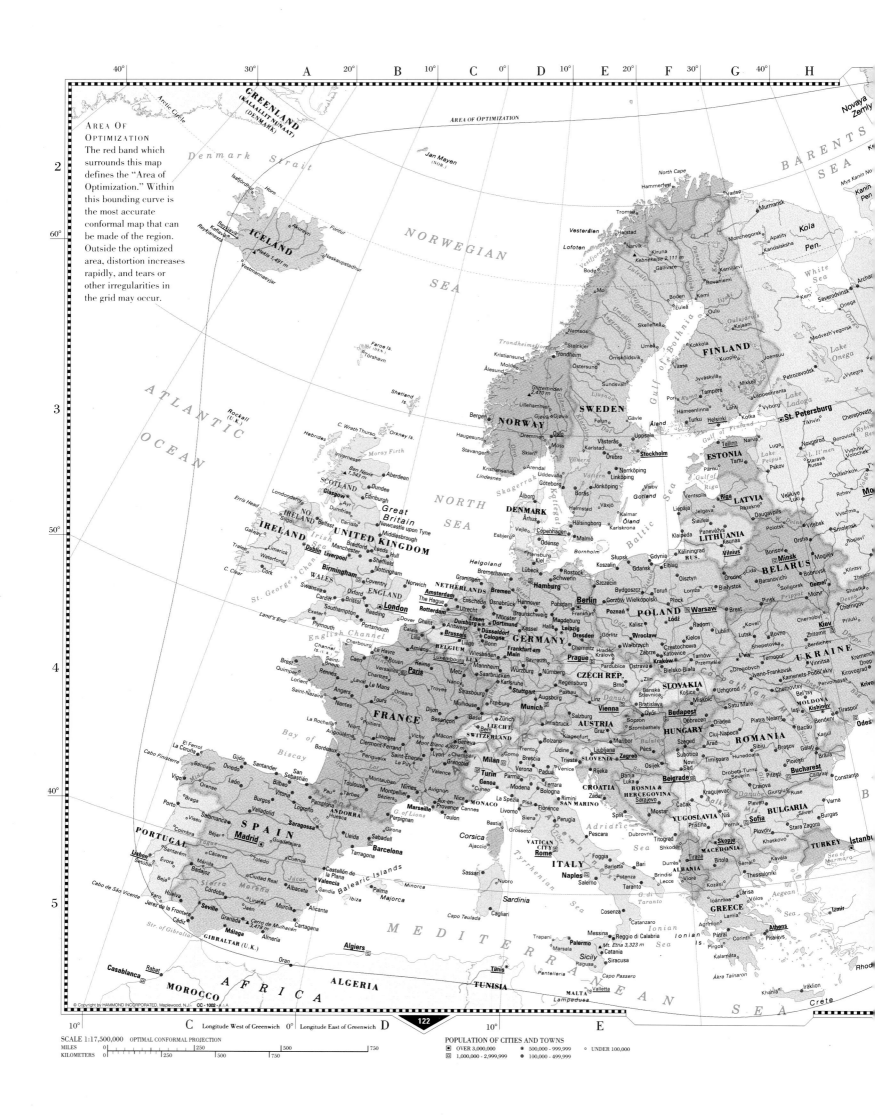

AREA OF OPTIMIZATION

The red band which surrounds this map defines the "Area of Optimization." Within this bounding curve is the most accurate conformal map that can be made of the region. Outside the optimized area, distortion increases rapidly, and tears or other irregularities in the grid may occur.

SCALE 1:17,500,000 OPTIMAL CONFORMAL PROJECTION

MILES
KILOMETERS

POPULATION OF CITIES AND TOWNS

| ⊡ OVER 3,000,000 | ✴ 500,000 - 999,999 | ○ UNDER 100,000 |
| ⊡ 1,000,000 - 2,999,999 | ● 100,000 - 499,999 | |

Europe

Central Scotland

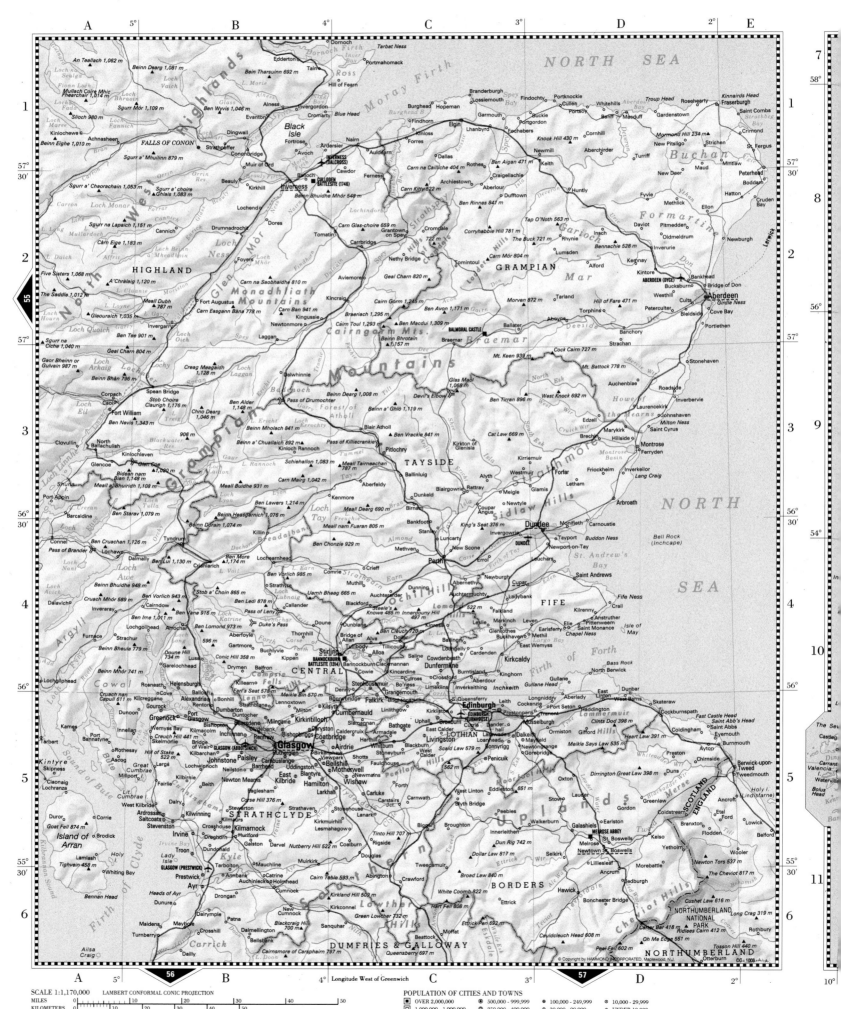

SCALE 1:1,170,000   LAMBERT CONFORMAL CONIC PROJECTION

MILES
KILOMETERS

POPULATION OF CITIES AND TOWNS

◻ OVER 2,000,000	● 500,000 - 999,999	● 100,000 - 249,999	● 10,000 - 29,999
◻ 1,000,000 - 1,999,999	● 250,000 - 499,999	● 30,000 - 99,999	○ UNDER 10,000

Longitude West of Greenwich

United Kingdom, Ireland

SCALE 1:3,500,000   LAMBERT CONFORMAL CONIC PROJECTION

Longitude West of Greenwich 0°   Longitude East of Greenwich

MILES 0   50   100   150
KILOMETERS 0   50   100   150

Northeastern Ireland, Northern England and Wales

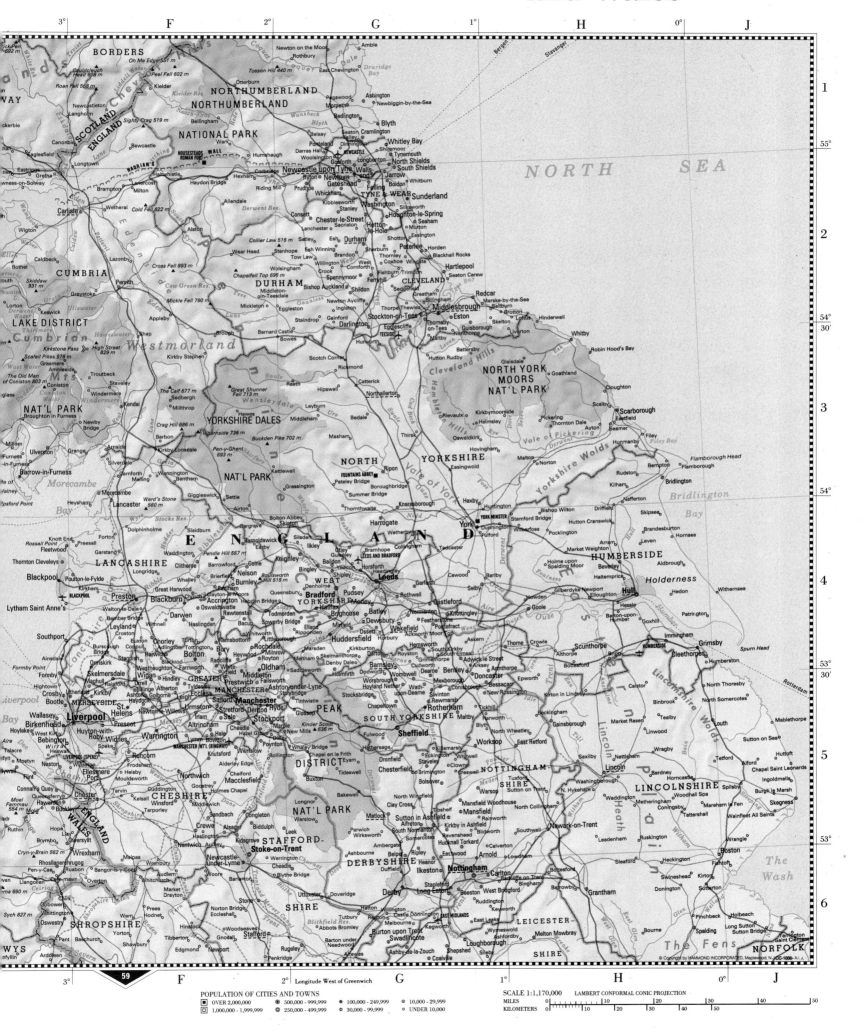

POPULATION OF CITIES AND TOWNS

- ■ OVER 2,000,000
- □ 1,000,000 - 1,999,999
- ● 500,000 - 999,999
- ● 250,000 - 499,999
- ● 100,000 - 249,999
- ● 30,000 - 99,999
- ⊙ 10,000 - 29,999
- ○ UNDER 10,000

SCALE 1:1,170,000   LAMBERT CONFORMAL CONIC PROJECTION

MILES 0 ... 10 ... 20 ... 30 ... 40 ... 50
KILOMETERS 0 ... 10 ... 20 ... 30 ... 40 ... 50

Longitude West of Greenwich

© Copyright by HAMMOND INCORPORATED, Maplewood, N.J.

Southern England and Wales

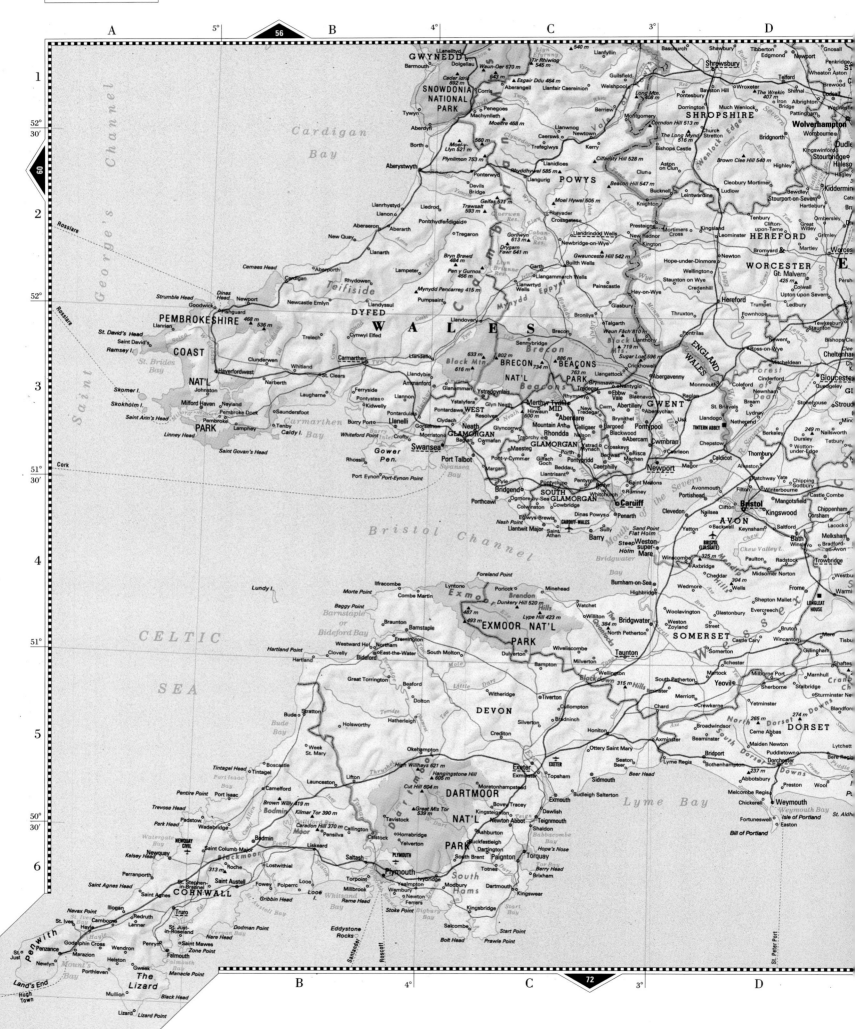

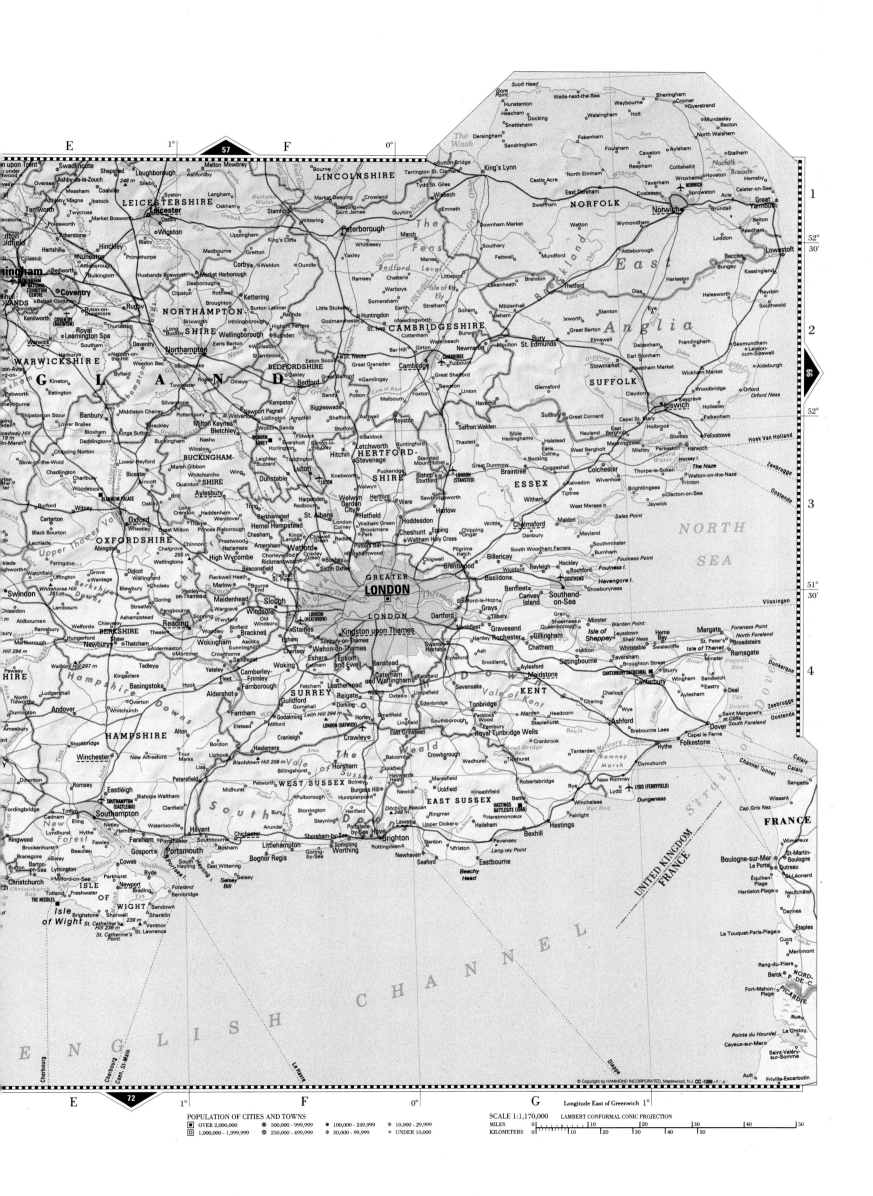

1

52°
30'

2

59

52°

3

51°
30'

4

POPULATION OF CITIES AND TOWNS

■ OVER 2,000,000 ⊛ 500,000 - 999,999 ● 100,000 - 249,999 ⊙ 10,000 - 29,999
▣ 1,000,000 - 1,999,999 ⊛ 250,000 - 499,999 ● 30,000 - 99,999 ○ UNDER 10,000

SCALE 1:1,170,000   LAMBERT CONFORMAL CONIC PROJECTION
MILES 0   10   20   30   40   50
KILOMETERS 0   10   20   30   40   50

© Copyright by HAMMOND INCORPORATED, Maplewood, N.J.

Central and Southern Ireland

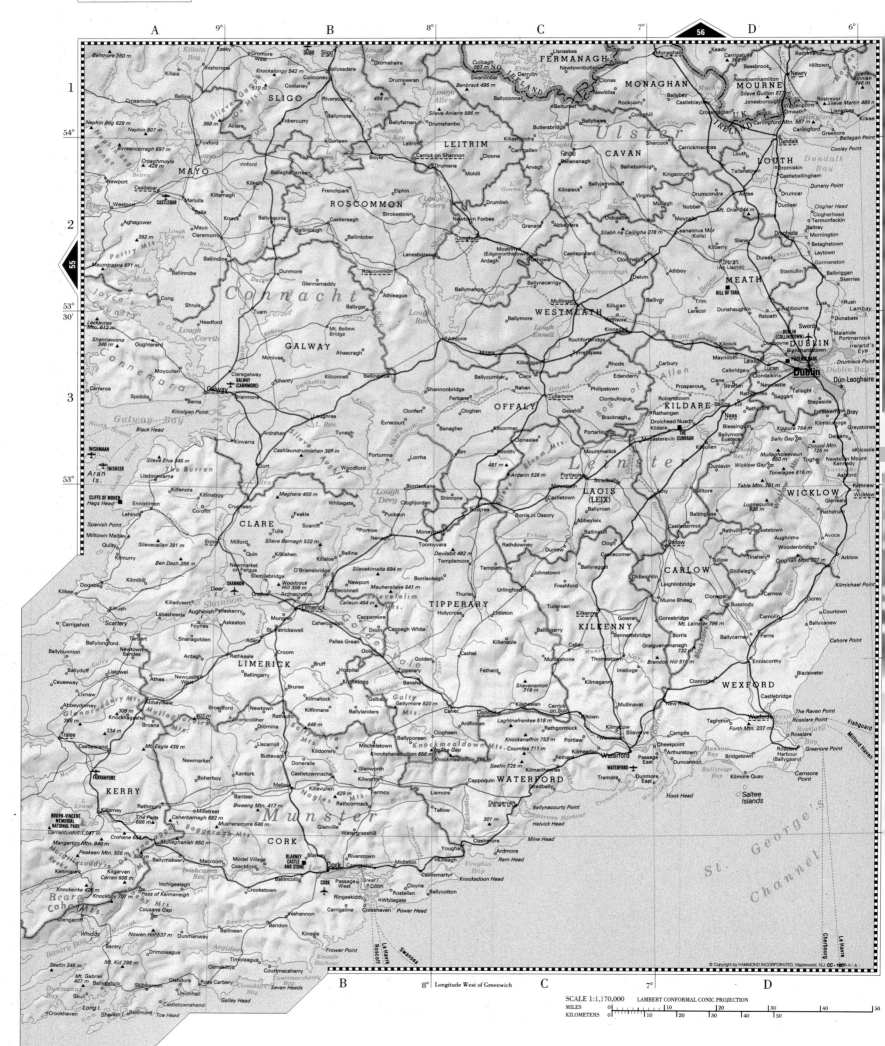

SCALE 1:1,170,000   LAMBERT CONFORMAL CONIC PROJECTION

MILES 0   10   20   30   40   50

KILOMETERS 0   10   20   30   40   50

Scandinavia and Finland, Iceland

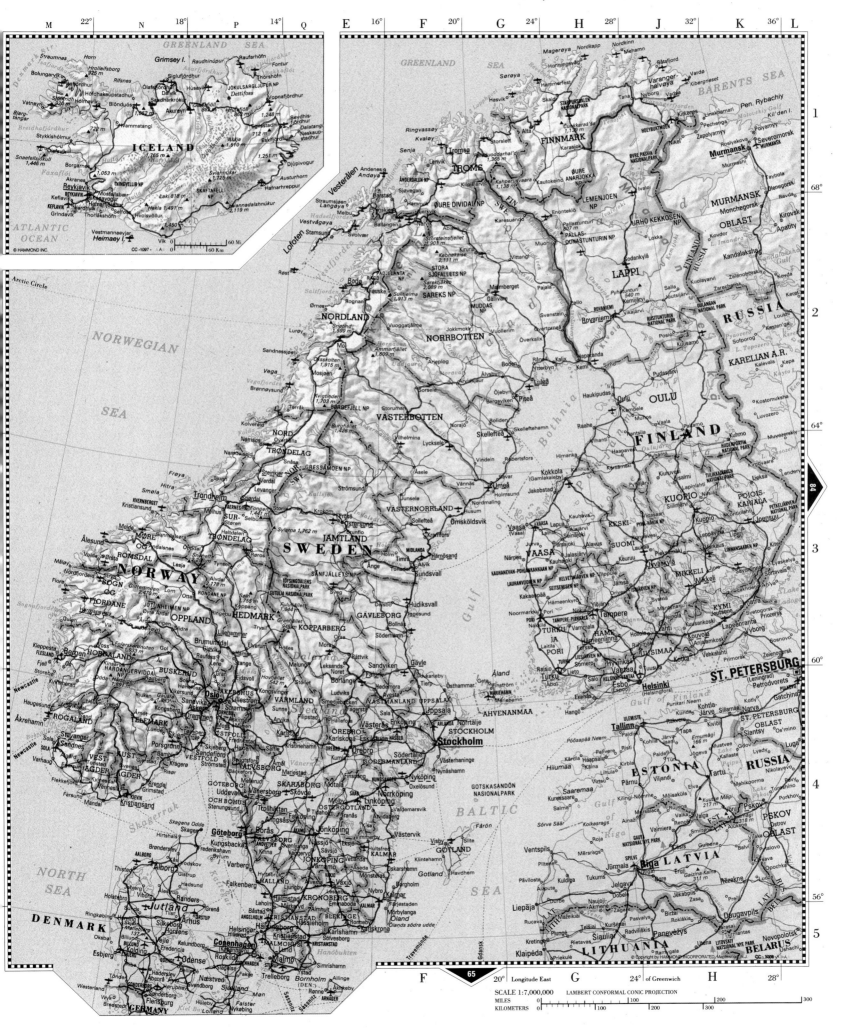

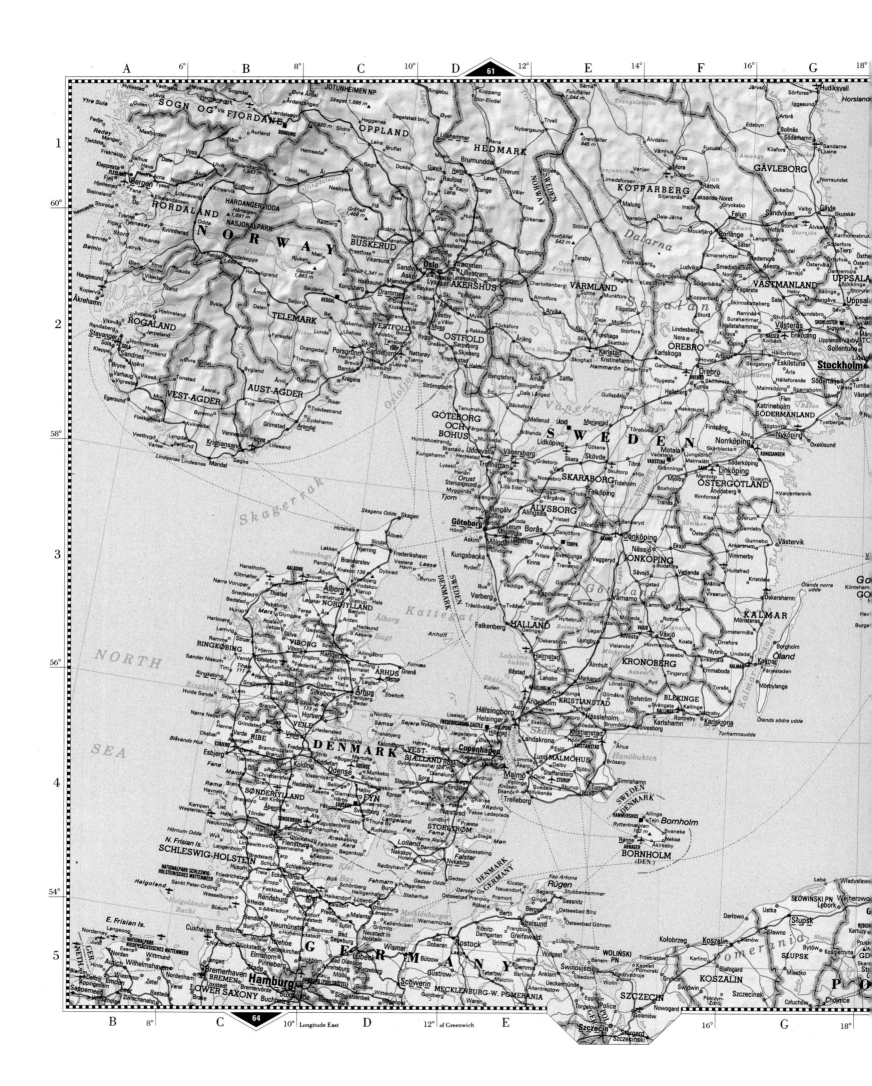

Baltic Region

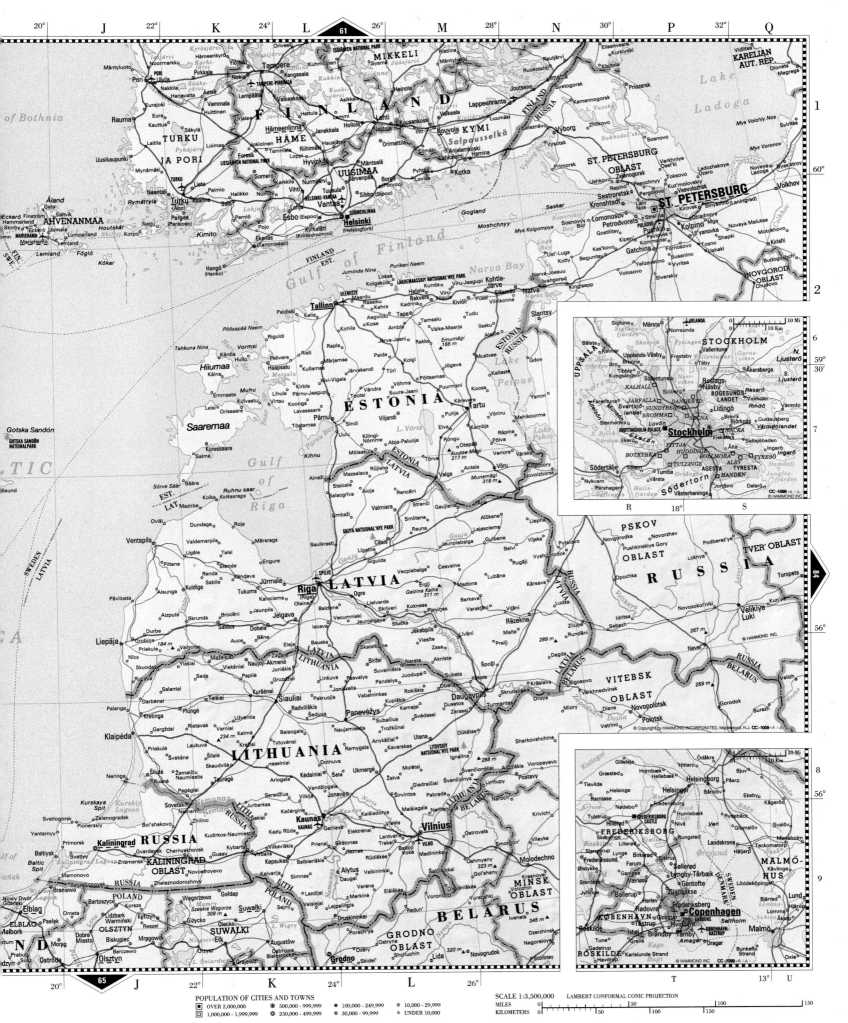

POPULATION OF CITIES AND TOWNS

■ OVER 2,000,000	● 500,000 - 999,999	● 100,000 - 249,999	● 10,000 - 29,999
□ 1,000,000 - 1,999,999	● 250,000 - 499,999	● 30,000 - 99,999	● UNDER 10,000

SCALE 1:3,500,000   LAMBERT CONFORMAL CONIC PROJECTION

MILES

KILOMETERS

North Central Europe

POPULATION OF CITIES AND TOWNS

■ OVER 2,000,000   ◉ 500,000 - 999,999   ● 100,000 - 249,999   ⊕ 10,000 - 29,999
▣ 1,000,000 - 1,999,999   ◎ 250,000 - 499,999   ● 30,000 - 99,999   ○ UNDER 10,000

SCALE 1:3,500,000   LAMBERT CONFORMAL CONIC PROJECTION

MILES 0   50   100   150

KILOMETERS 0   50   100   150

Netherlands, Northwestern Germany

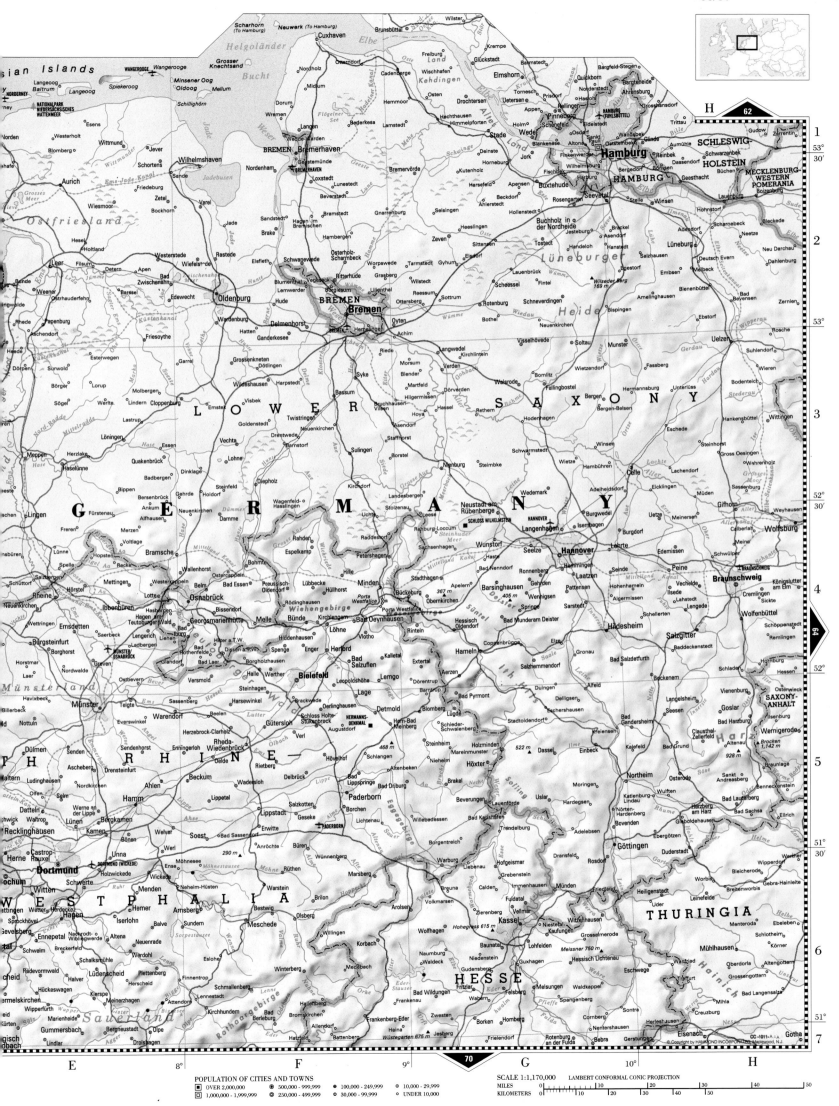

POPULATION OF CITIES AND TOWNS

■ OVER 2,000,000 ● 500,000 - 999,999 ● 100,000 - 249,999 ● 10,000 - 29,999
▣ 1,000,000 - 1,999,999 ● 250,000 - 499,999 ● 30,000 - 99,999 ○ UNDER 10,000

SCALE 1:1,170,000   LAMBERT CONFORMAL CONIC PROJECTION
MILES
KILOMETERS

Belgium, Northern France, Western Germany

POPULATION OF CITIES AND TOWNS

■ OVER 2,000,000   ◉ 500,000 - 999,999   ● 100,000 - 249,999   ⊙ 10,000 - 29,999
□ 1,000,000 - 1,999,999   ◎ 250,000 - 499,999   ⊚ 30,000 - 99,999   ○ UNDER 10,000

SCALE 1:1,170,000   LAMBERT CONFORMAL CONIC PROJECTION

MILES   0   10   20   30   40   50

KILOMETERS   0   10   20   30   40   50

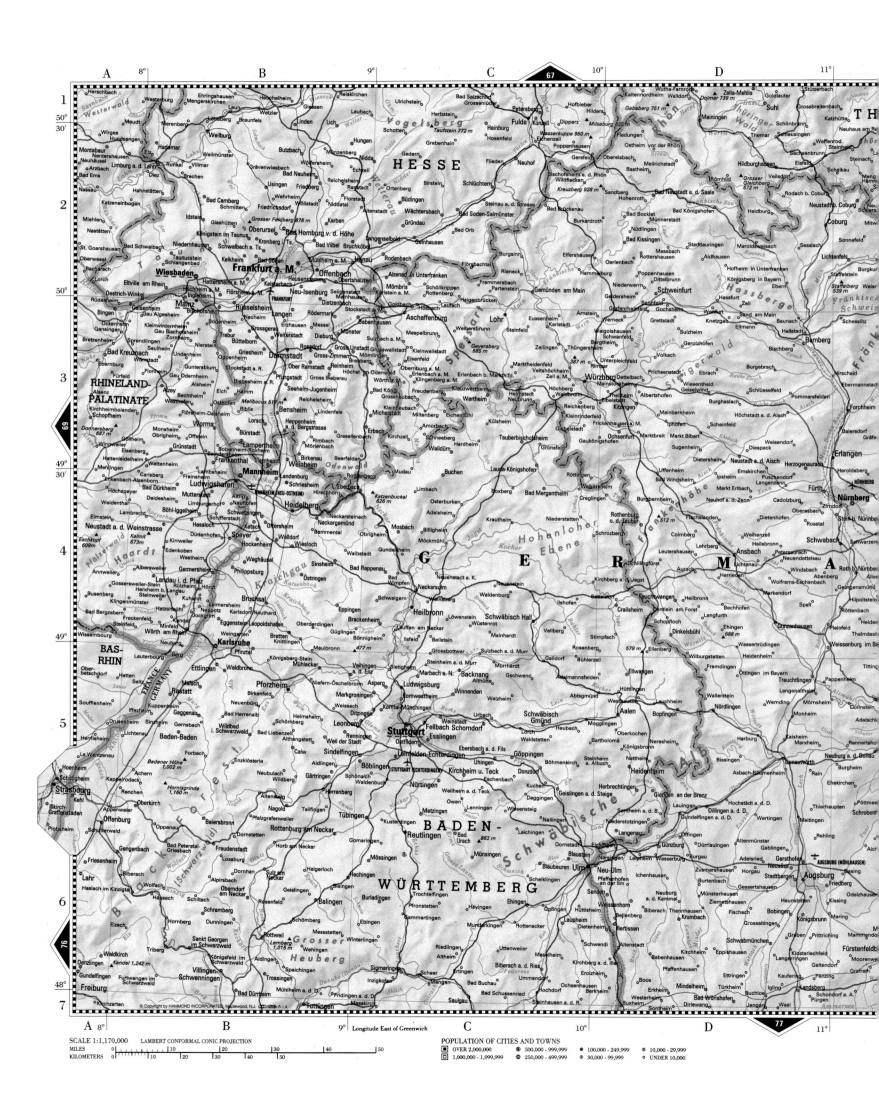

This is a map of central Germany, showing parts of Hesse, Rhineland-Palatinate, Baden-Württemberg, and neighboring regions.

A 8°   B   9°   C   10°   D 11°

50°
30'

Westerwald

Herschbach · Westerburg · Ehringshausen · Mengerskirchen · Leun · Reiskirchen · Ulrichstein · Bad Salzschlirf · Grossenlüder · Petersberg · Hofbieber · Hilders · Wutha-Farnrode · Kaltennordheim Walldorf · Dolmar 739 m · Zella-Mehlis · Goldlauter · Stützerbach

Meudt · Mengerskirchen · Wetzlar · Linden · Giessen · Laubach · Herbstein · Fulda · Künzell · Dipperz · Gebaberg 751 m · Meiningen · Schönbrunn · Grossbreitenbach

THÜRINGER WALD

Montabaur · Nentershausen · Weilburg · Braunfels · Lich · Hungen · Grebenhain · Hosenfeld · Neuhof · Wasserkuppe 950 m · Eichenzell · Poppenhausen · Gersfeld · Oberelsbach · Bastheim · Fladungen · Ostheim vor der Rhön · Römhild · Hildburghausen

HESSE

Limburg a. d. Lahn · Runkel · Villmar · Butzbach · Münzenberg · Nidda · Echzell · Ortenberg · Birstein · Schlüchtern · Bischofsheim a. d. Rhön · Kreuzberg 928 m · Sandberg · Bad Neustadt a. d. Saale · Rodach b. Coburg · Neustadt b. Coburg

Diez · Brechen · Gräven-wiesbach · Bad Nauheim · Reichelsheim · Ramstadt · Florstadt · Büdingen · Gründau · Bad Soden-Salmünster · Burkardroth · Hohenroth · Nüdlingen · Münnerstadt · Heldburg · Coburg

Nassau · Katzenelnbogen · Bad Camberg · Schmitten · Friedberg · Wöllstadt · Niddatal · Wächtersbach · Bad Orb · Burgsinn · Eltershausen · Massbach · Stadtlauringen · Maroldsweisach · Sesslach · Sonnefeld

Miehlen · Idstein · Glashütten · Grosser Feldberg 878 m · Oberursel · Karben · Langenselbold · Gelnhausen · Flörsbachtal · Rieneck · Gemünden am Main · Geldersheim · Oerlenbach · Poppenhausen · Dittelbrunn · Königsberg in Bayern · Staffelstein

SCALE 1:1,170,000   LAMBERT CONFORMAL CONIC PROJECTION

MILES 0   10   20   30   40   50
KILOMETERS 0   10   20   30   40   50

POPULATION OF CITIES AND TOWNS

- OVER 2,000,000
- 1,000,000 - 1,999,999
- 500,000 - 999,999
- 250,000 - 499,999
- 100,000 - 249,999
- 30,000 - 99,999
- 10,000 - 29,999
- UNDER 10,000

© Copyright by HAMMOND INCORPORATED, Maplewood, N.J. OD-1018-A-LA

A 8°   B   9° Longitude East of Greenwich   C   10°   D 11°

Southern Germany, Czech Republic, Upper Austria

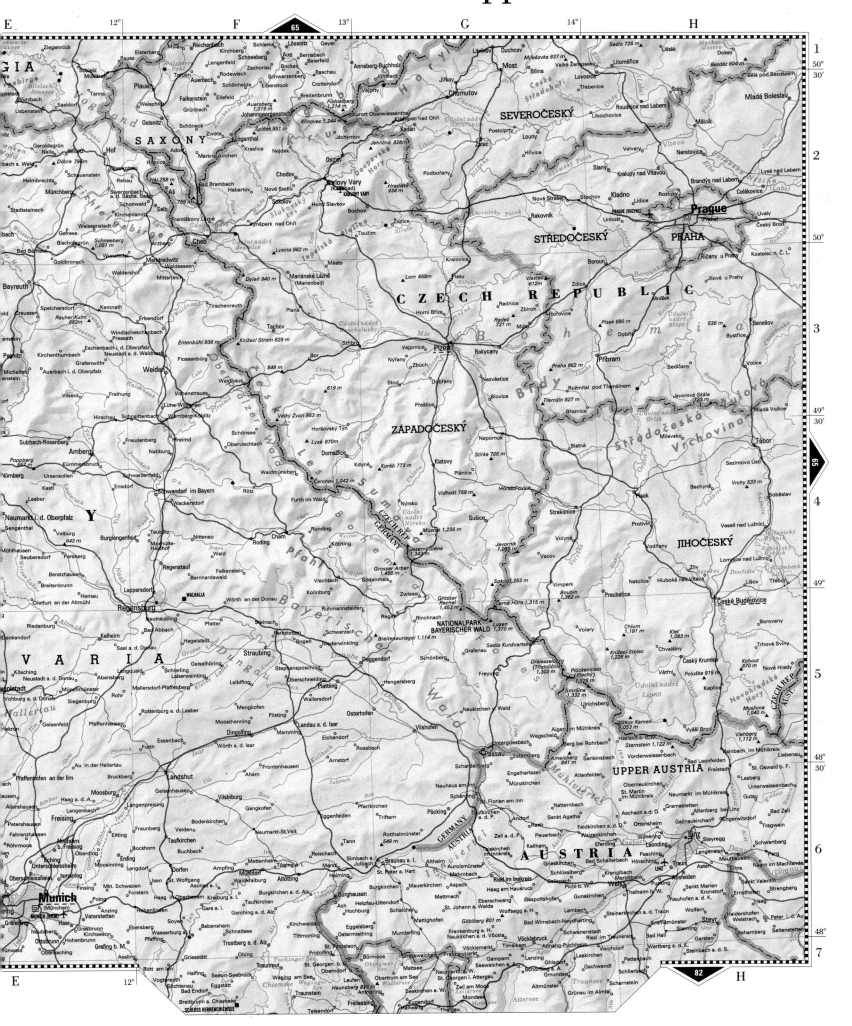

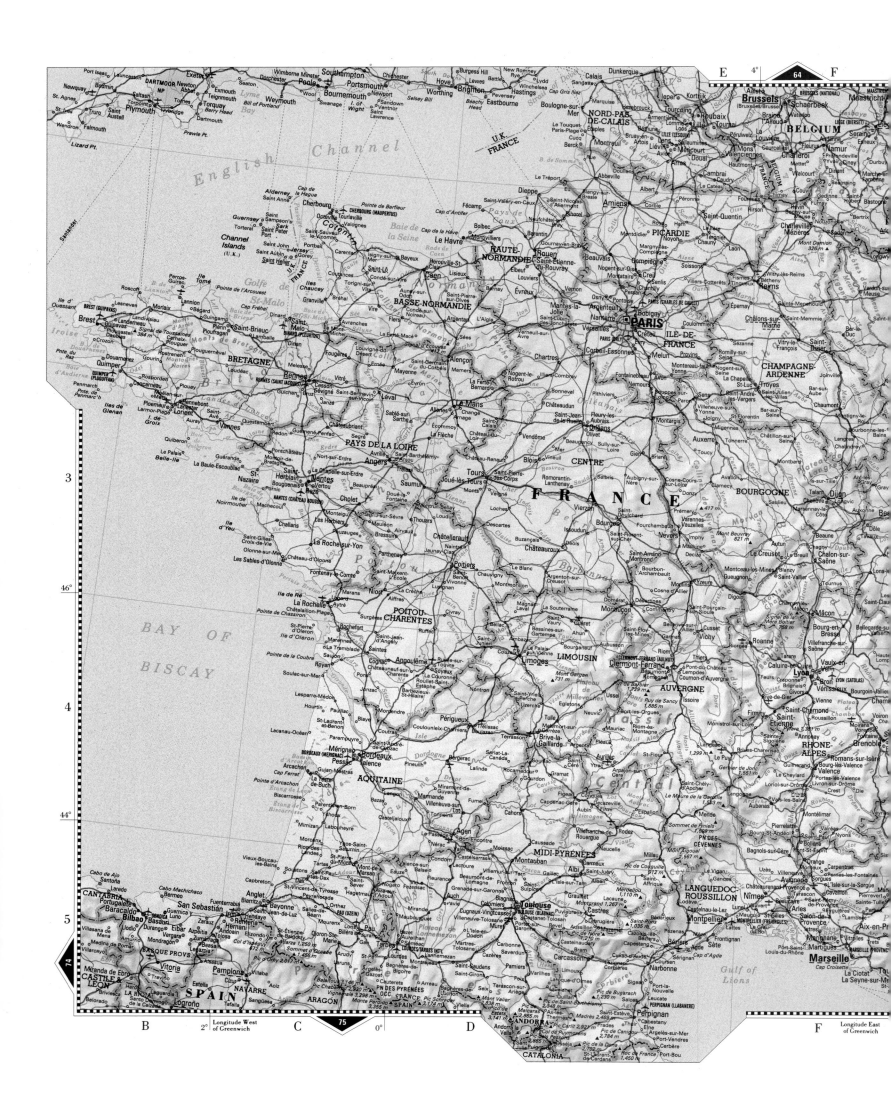

West Central Europe

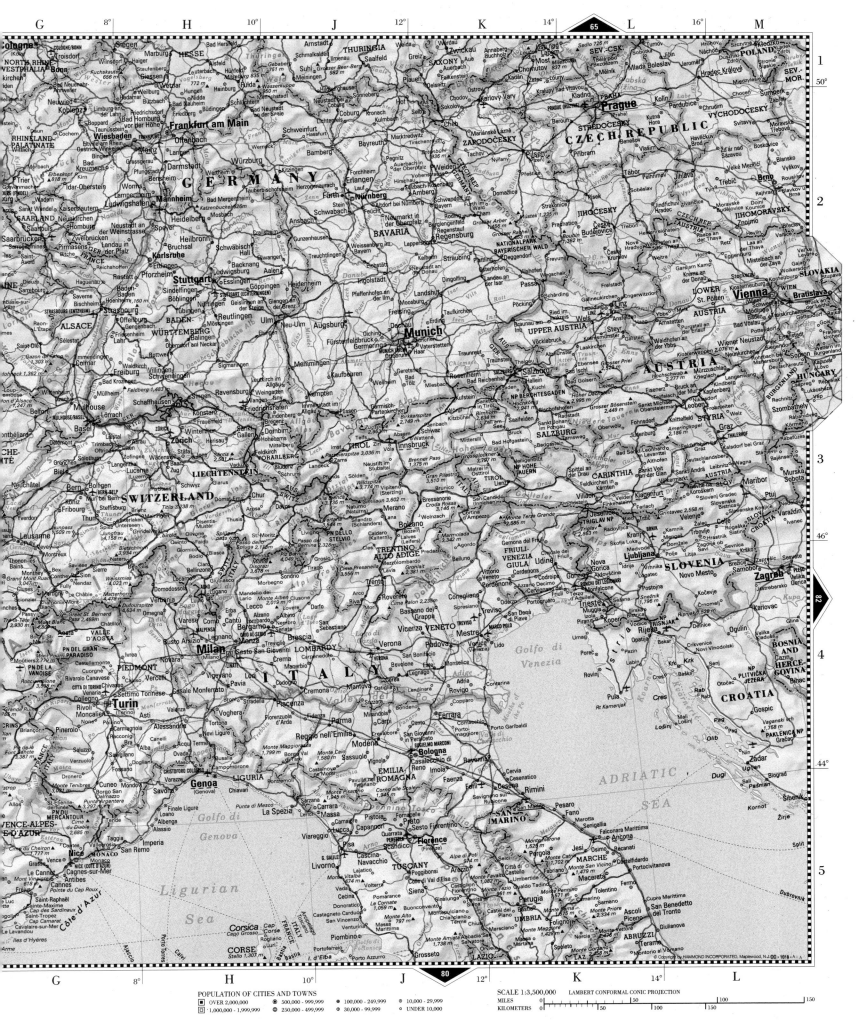

POPULATION OF CITIES AND TOWNS

☐ OVER 2,000,000	● 500,000 - 999,999	● 100,000 - 249,999	◦ 10,000 - 29,999
☐ 1,000,000 - 1,999,999	● 250,000 - 499,999	● 30,000 - 99,999	◦ UNDER 10,000

SCALE 1:3,500,000   LAMBERT CONFORMAL CONIC PROJECTION

MILES 0   50   100   150

KILOMETERS 0   50   100   150

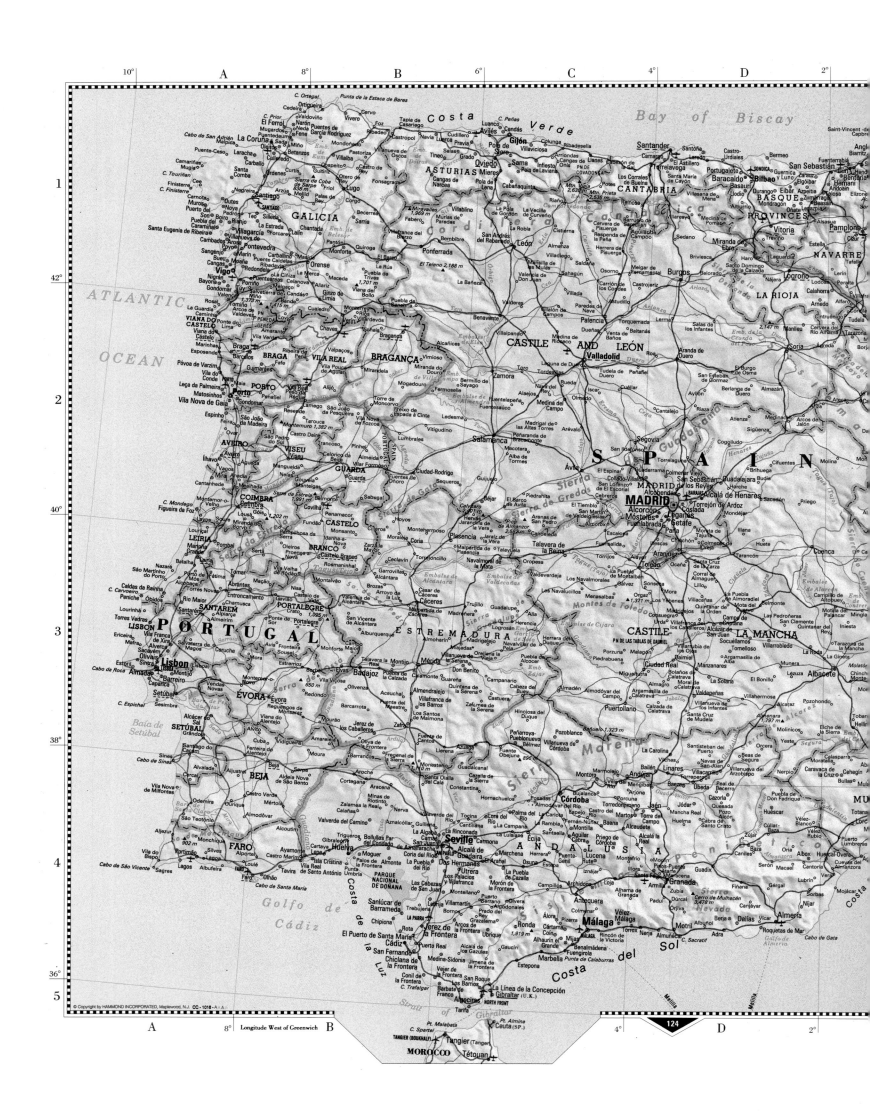

Spain, Portugal

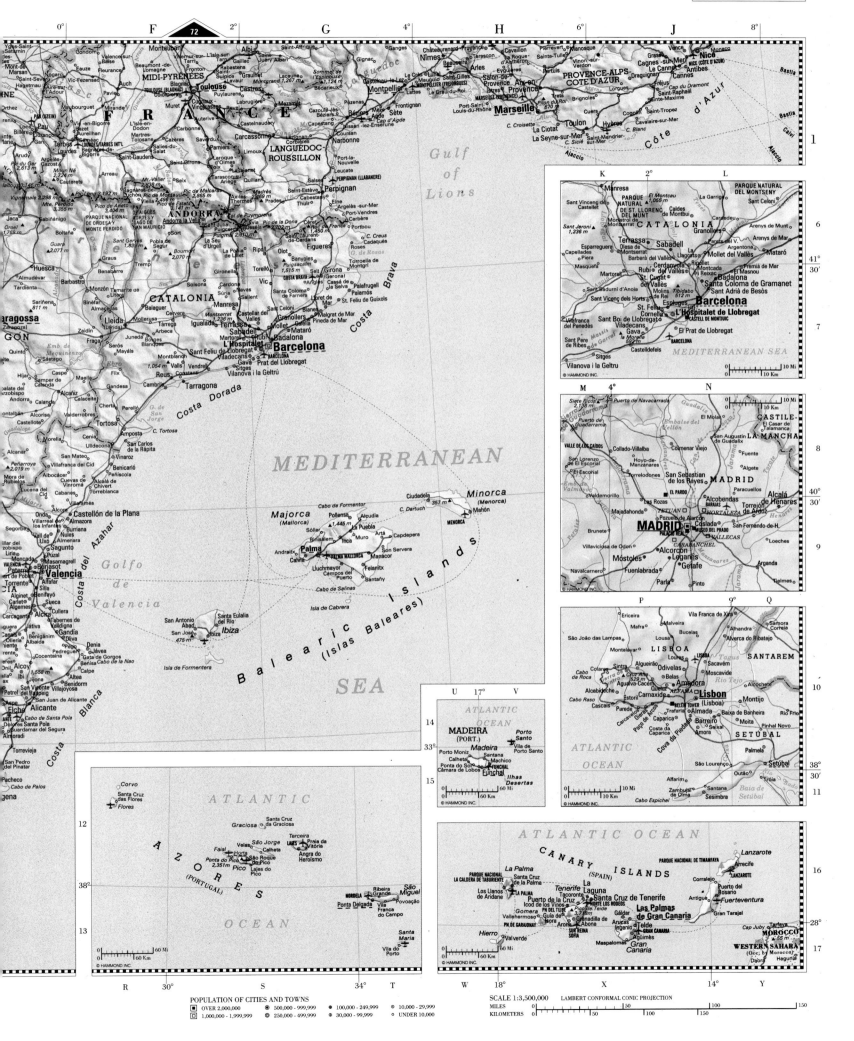

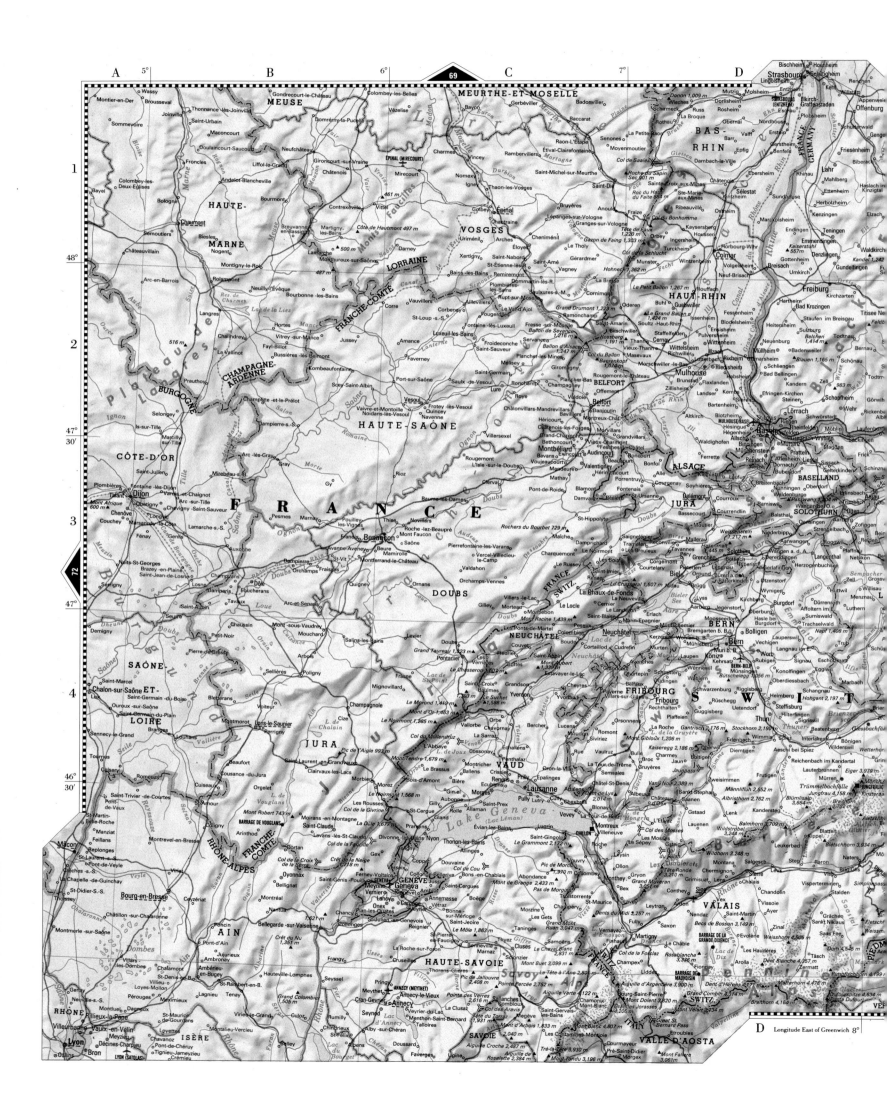

Central Alps Region

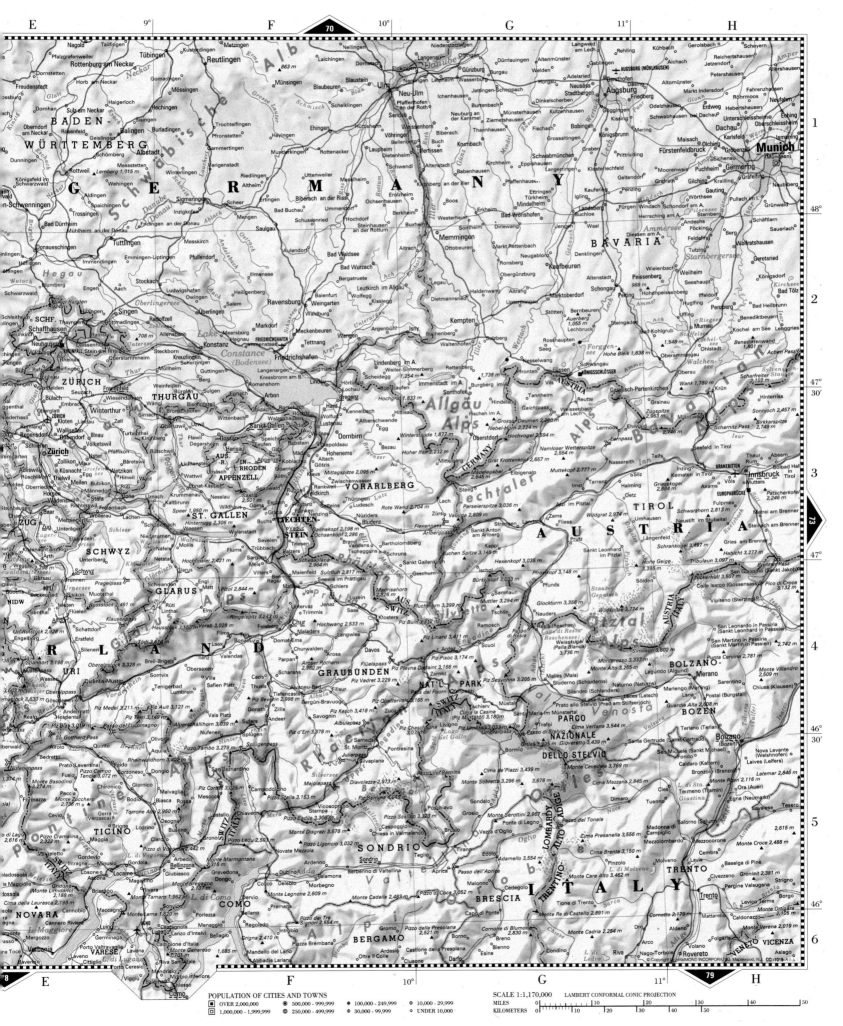

Northern Italy

Longitude East of Greenwich

POPULATION OF CITIES AND TOWNS

■ OVER 2,000,000   ● 500,000 - 999,999   ● 100,000 - 249,999   ○ 10,000 - 29,999
□ 1,000,000 - 1,999,999   ● 250,000 - 499,999   ● 30,000 - 99,999   ○ UNDER 10,000

SCALE 1:1,170,000   LAMBERT CONFORMAL CONIC PROJECTION

MILES   0   10   20   30   40   50
KILOMETERS   0   10   20   30   40   50

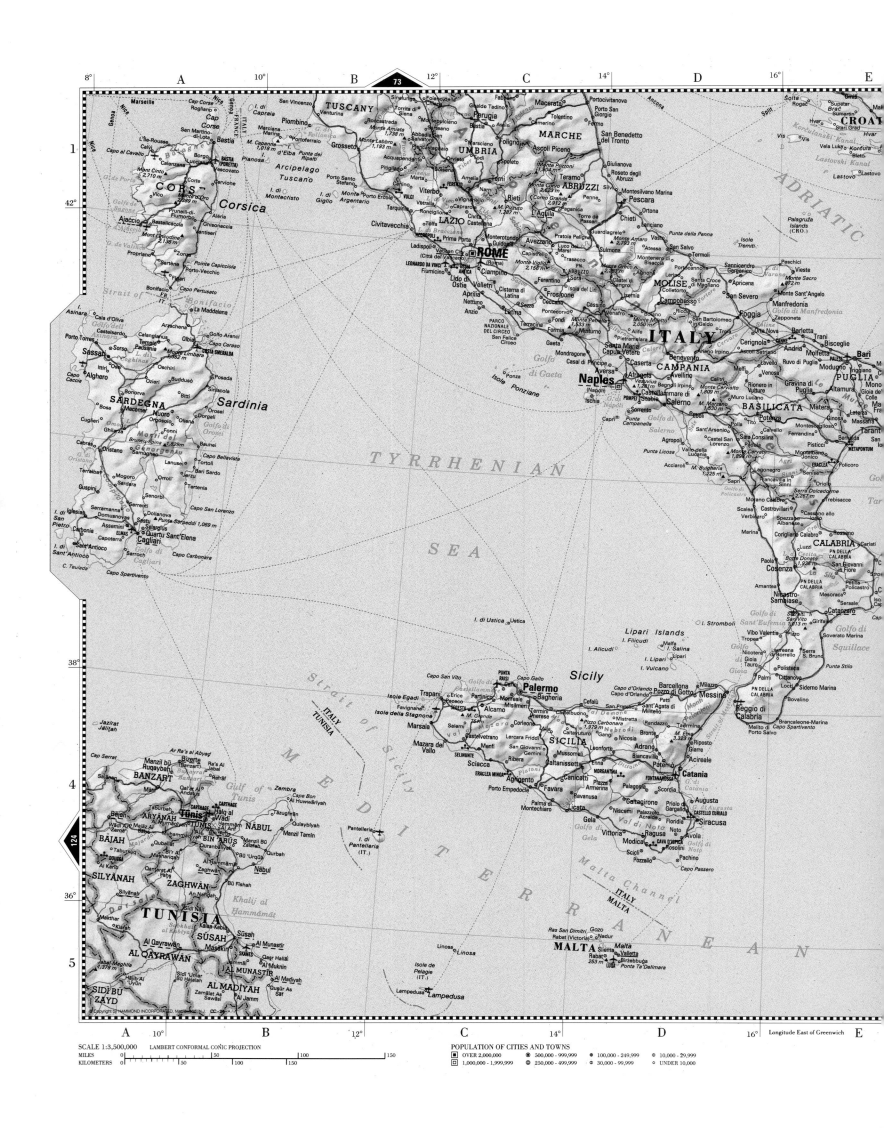

Map Labels

8° A 10° B 73 12° C 14° D 16° E

1
42°
38°
4
36°
5

A 10° B 12° C 14° D 16° E Longitude East of Greenwich

FRANCE

Marseille
Nice
Genoa
Cap Corse
Rogliano
I. di Capraia
San Vincenzo
TUSCANY
Sinalunga
Foiano della Chiana
Macerata
Portocivitanova
Ancona
Solta
Rogac
Supetar
Stari
Grad
Brač
Sumartin
CROA

L'Île-Rousse
Calvi
Cap Corse
Corse
San Martino-di-Lota
BASTIA (PORETTA)
Piombino
Venturina
Marciana Marina
Portoferraio
d'Elba
Grosseto
Monte Amiata 1,738 m
Torrita di Siena
Montepulciano
Castiglione
PERUGIA
Assisi
Gualdo Tadino
MARCHE
Camerino
Tolentino
Fermo
Porto San Giorgio
Vis
Vela Luka
Korčula
Lastovo

Capo al Cavallo
Capo al Cavallo
M. Capanne 1,018 m
Pianosa
I. di Pianosa
Abbadia San Salvatore
Acquapendente
Pitigliano
UMBRIA
Todi
Spoleto
Ascoli Piceno
San Benedetto del Tronto
Giulianova
Teramo
Corno Grande 2,912 m
ADRIATIC

Mont Cinto 2,710 m
Calenzana
Borgo
Lucciana
CORS-
Corte
Cervione
Arcipelago Tuscano
Porto Santo Stefano
Monte Argentario
I. di Giglio
Orvieto
Tiber
Marta
Narni
Terni
Rieti
Monte Pozzoni 2,104 m
ABRUZZI
Penne
Pescara
Montesilvano Marina
Ortona
Palagruža Islands (CRO.)
Isole Tremiti

42°
Monte d'Oro 2,389 m
Vescovato
Corsica
Ghisonaccia
I. di Montecristo
Civitavecchia
LAZIO
Viterbo
Tarquinia
Civita Castellana
Amelia
Monte Viglio 2,156 m
M. Pizuto 1,287 m
L'Aquila
Corno Grande
Chieti
Lanciano
Vasto
San Salvo
Peschici
Vieste
Isole Sacro
Gargano

Ajaccio
Bastelicaccia
Mont Incudine 2,136 m
Prunelli-di-Flumorbo
Aléria
Porto Ercole
Ladispoli
Vatican City (Città del Vaticano)
ROME (Roma)
Tivoli
Avezzano
Sulmona
Monte Amaro 2,793 m
Guardiagrele
Atessa
Punta della Penna
Termoli
Sannicandro Gargano

Sartène
Porto-Vecchio
Propriano
Zonza
Fiumicino
Ciampino
Velletri
Anzio
Nettuno
Latina
Frosinone
Cassino
Isernia
Campobasso
MOLISE
San Severo
Manfredonia
Golfo di Manfredonia

I. Asinara
Cala d'Oliva
Castelsardo
Santa Teresa
La Maddalena
Arzachena
Golfo Aranci
Olbia
Bonifacio
Capo Pertusato
Strait of Bonifacio
Ponza
Isole Ponziane
Gaeta
Formia
Mondragone
Casal di Principe
Aversa
Caserta
CAMPANIA
Benevento
Avellino
Foggia
Cerignola
Barletta
Trani
Bisceglie
Andria
Molfetta
BARI
PUGLIA

Porto Torres
Sorso
Sassari
Alghero
Capo Caccia
Bonorva
Ozieri
Buddusò
Posada
Nuoro
Siniscola
SARDEGNA
Macomer
Orgosolo
Oliena
Dorgali
Golfo di Orosei
Naples (Napoli)
Vesuvius 1,277 m
Castellammare di Stabia
Salerno
Muro Lucano
Potenza
BASILICATA
Matera
Altamura
Gravina di Puglia
Ruvo di Puglia
Gioia del Colle

Bosa
Cuglieri
Ghilarza
Samugheo
Fonni
Bruncu Spina 1,829 m
Monti del Gennargentu
Baunei
Capo Bellavista
Lanusei
Tortolì
Sardinia
Ischia
Capri
Punta Campanella
Golfo di Salerno
Agropoli
Acciaroli
Vallo della Lucania
Sapri
Sala Consilina
Polla
Monte Cervati 1,898 m
Serra Dolcedorme 2,267 m
Policoro
Trebisacce
TYRRHENIAN

Oristano
Terralba
Guspini
Mogoro
Sardara
Senorbì
Jerzu
Tertenia
Capo San Lorenzo
Punta Licosa
M. Bulgheria 1,225 m
Morano Calabro
Castrovillari
Cassano allo Ionio
Corigliano Calabro
Rossano
Cariati

San Pietro
I. di Iglesias
Carbonia
Assemini
ELMAS
Selargius
Quartu Sant'Elena
Dolianova
Serramanna
Samassi
Capoterra
Sarroch
Punta Serpeddi 1,069 m
SEA
Marina
Amantea
Paola
Monte Cocuzzo 1,541 m
Botte Donato 1,928 m
San Giovanni in Fiore
CALABRIA
Petilia Policastro
Capo Rizzuto

Sant'Antioco
I. di Sant'Antioco
Cagliari
Golfo di Cagliari
Capo Carbonara
Capo Spartivento
C. Teulada
Cosenza
Nicastro-Sambiase
Catanzaro
Golfo di Squillace
Soverato Marina

I. di Ustica
Ustica
Lipari Islands
I. Filicudi
I. Salina
I. Lipari
I. Vulcano
I. Stromboli
Vibo Valentia
Tropea
Nicotera
Gioia Tauro
Palmi
Golfo di Gioia
Sant'Eufemia
Serra S. Bruno
Punta Stilo

38°
Sicily
Capo San Vito
Golfo di Castellammare
Capo Gallo
Palermo
Bagheria
Cefalù
Capo d'Orlando
Barcellona
Milazzo
Pozzo di Gotto
Messina
PN DELLA CALABRIA
Bovalino
Locri
Siderno Marina

Trapani
Erice
Partinico
Monreale
Misilmeri
Termini Imerese
Caltavuturo
Mistretta
Sant'Agata di Militello
San Fratello
Randazzo
Taormina
Strait of Messina
Reggio di Calabria
Melito di Porto Salvo
Brancaleone-Marina
Capo Spartivento

Strait of Sicily
Isole Egadi
Favignana
Isole della Stagnone
SEGESTA
Alcamo
Salemi
M. Grande
Corleone
Lercara Friddi
Petralia
Nicosia
Bronte
Adrano
M. Etna 3,323 m
Riposto
Giarre
Acireale

ITALY / TUNISIA
Marsala
Mazara del Vallo
SELINUNTE
Castelvetrano
Menfi
Sciacca
ERACLEA MINOA
Ribera
Agrigento
Canicattì
Favara
Caltanissetta
SICILIA
Enna
Leonforte
Piazza Armerina
Caltagirone
Palagonia
FONTANAROSSA
Biancavilla
Paternò
Catania
G. di Catania

4
Ar Ra's al Abyad
Jazirat Jālītah
Cap Serrat
BANZART
Bizerte
Ra's al Jabal
Gulf of Tunis
Zembra
Cape Bon
Al Huwwārīyah
Pantelleria
I. di Pantelleria (IT.)
Porto Empedocle
Palma di Montechiaro
Licata
Gela
Ravanusa
Niscemi
Gela
Gela
Vittoria
Comiso
Priolo Gargallo
CASTELLO EURIALO
Augusta
Siracusa

124
TUNIS
Carthage
CARTHAGE
ARYĀNAH
Wad Milian
NĀBUL
Zaghwān
Nābul
Qurbah
Ragusa
Modica
CAVA D'ISPICA
Rosolini
Avola
Noto
Val di Noto

BĀJAH
Manzil Bū Ruqaybah
Muhammadiyah
Qal'at al Andalus
Tāzūghrān
Manzil Tamīm
Linosa
I. di Pantelleria
Scicli
Pozzallo
Capo Passero

36°
SILYĀNAH
ZAGHWĀN
An Nafidah
BQ Fishah
Khalīj al Hammāmāt
Ras San Dimitri
Rabat (Victoria)
Gozo
Nadur
Malta

TUNISIA
Mākthar
Sīdī Nāji
Kalaa-Kebira
Sūsah
SŪSAH
ITALY / MALTA
MALTA
Sliema
Valletta
Birżebbuġa
LUQA

5
Jebel Maghila 1,378 m
Al Qayrawān
AL QAYRAWĀN
Al Munastīr
AL MUNASTĪR
Al Madīyah
Isole di Pelagie (IT.)
Linosa
Linosa
Rabat
253 m
Ponte Ta' Delimara

SIDI BŪ ZAYD
AL MADĪYAH
Al Jamm
Lampedusa
Lampedusa

POPULATION OF CITIES AND TOWNS
■ OVER 2,000,000   ◉ 500,000 - 999,999   ● 100,000 - 249,999   ◦ 10,000 - 29,999
▣ 1,000,000 - 1,999,999   ◉ 250,000 - 499,999   ● 30,000 - 99,999   ○ UNDER 10,000

Southern Italy, Albania, Greece

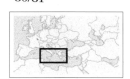

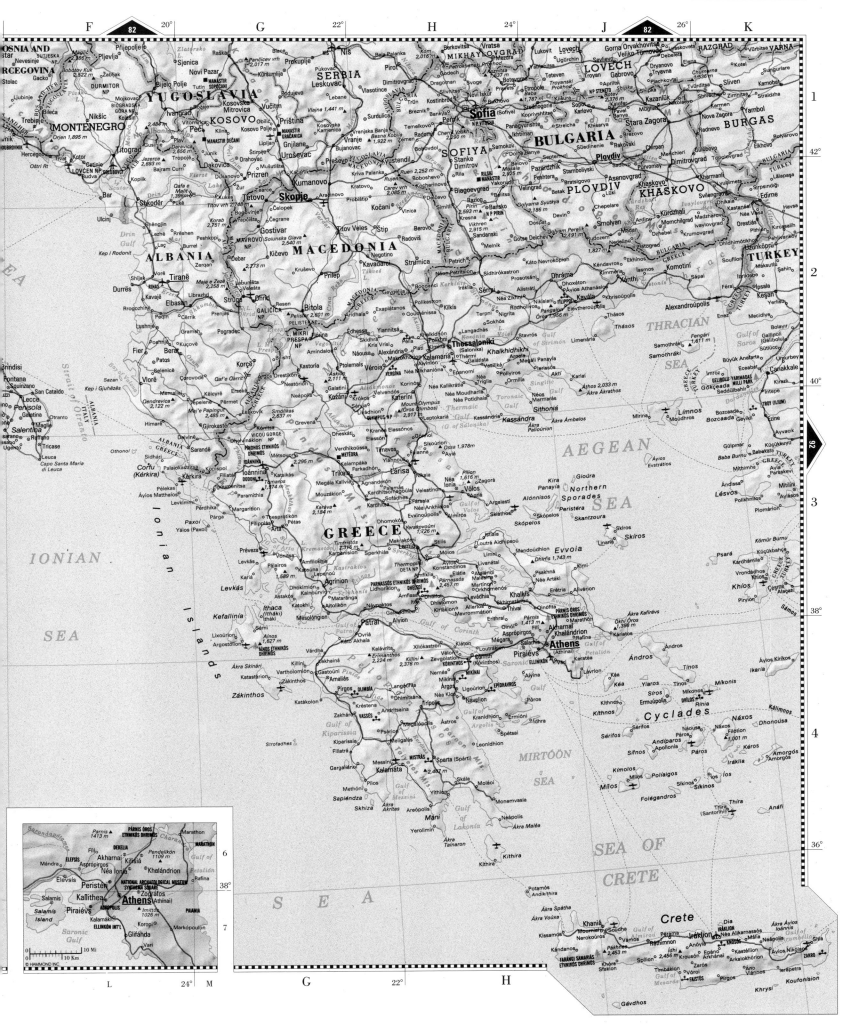

Hungary, Northern Balkan States

Northeastern Europe

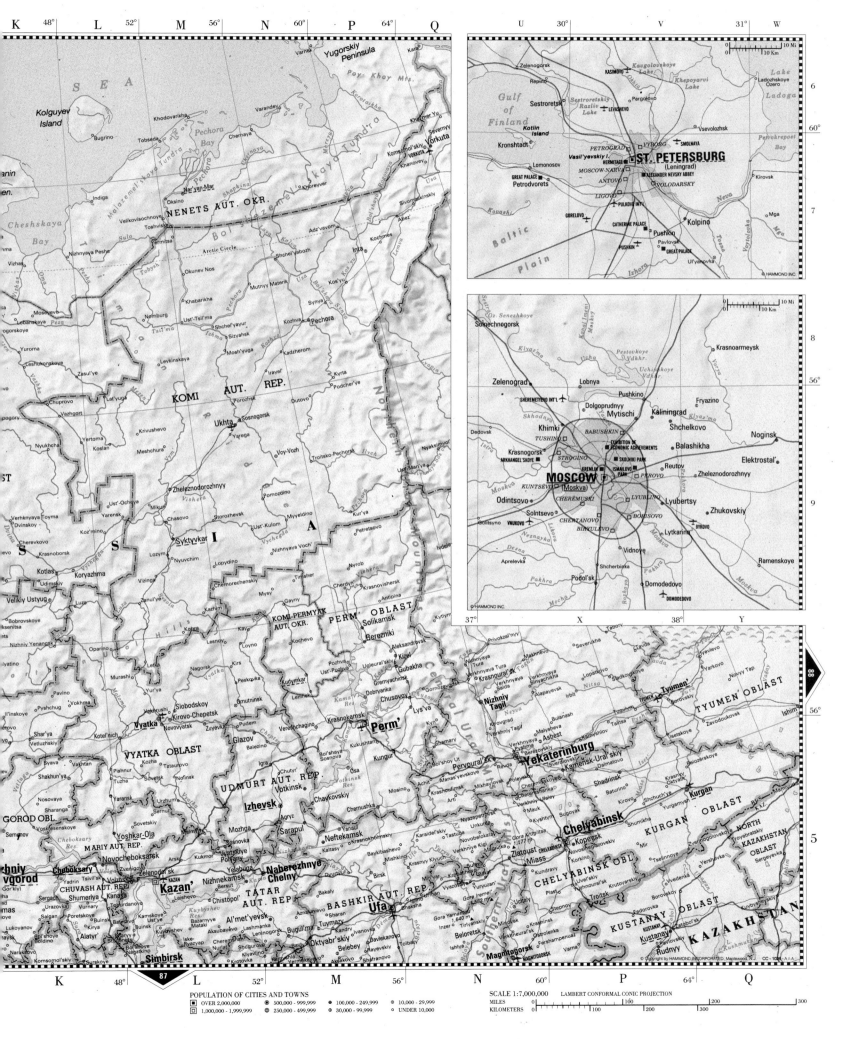

POPULATION OF CITIES AND TOWNS

■ OVER 2,000,000	● 500,000 - 999,999
▣ 1,000,000 - 1,999,999	● 250,000 - 499,999

● 100,000 - 249,999   ● 10,000 - 29,999
● 30,000 - 99,999   ○ UNDER 10,000

SCALE 1:7,000,000   LAMBERT CONFORMAL CONIC PROJECTION

MILES 0   100   200   300
KILOMETERS 0   100   200   300

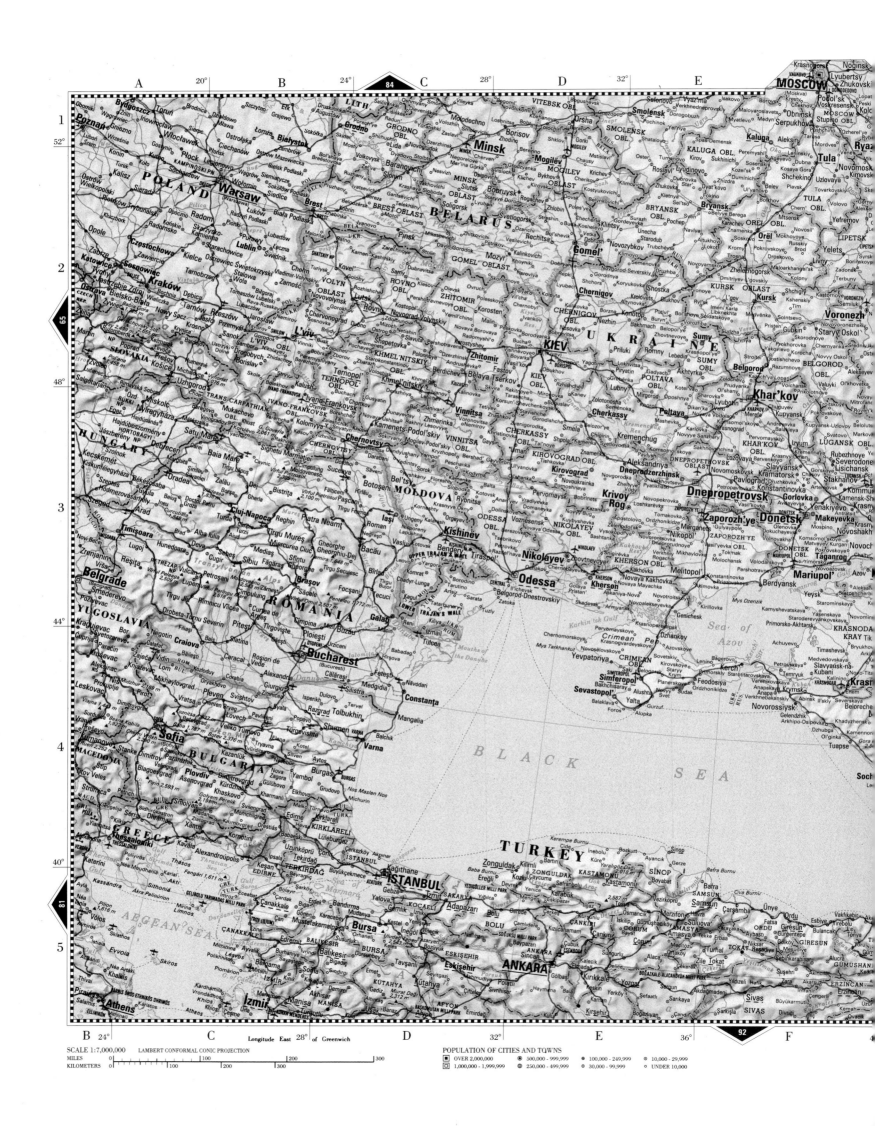

Southeastern Europe

Russia and Neighboring Countries

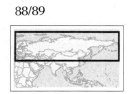

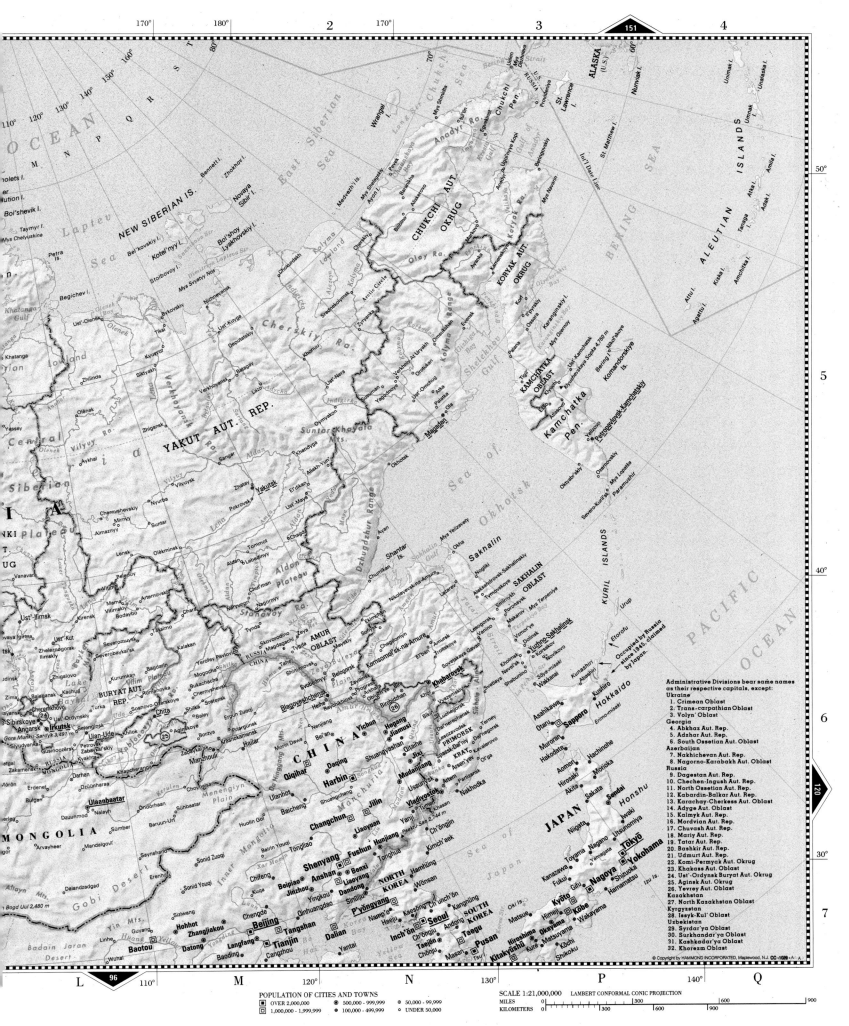

Asia

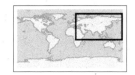

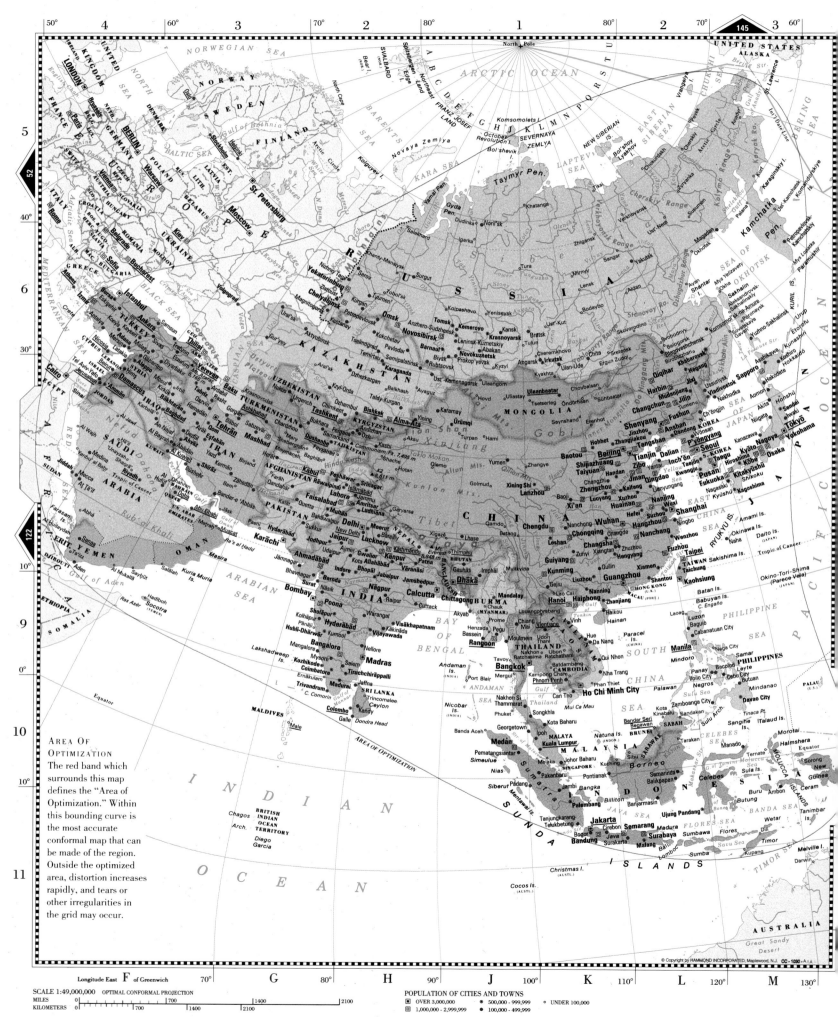

AREA OF
OPTIMIZATION
The red band which
surrounds this map
defines the "Area of
Optimization." Within
this bounding curve is
the most accurate
conformal map that can
be made of the region.
Outside the optimized
area, distortion increases
rapidly, and tears or
other irregularities in
the grid may occur.

SCALE 1:49,000,000   OPTIMAL CONFORMAL PROJECTION

Longitude East **F** of Greenwich

MILES

KILOMETERS

POPULATION OF CITIES AND TOWNS
- ▣ OVER 3,000,000
- ▣ 1,000,000 - 2,999,999
- ● 500,000 - 999,999
- ● 100,000 - 499,999
- ○ UNDER 100,000

© Copyright by HAMMOND INCORPORATED, Maplewood, N.J.

Eastern Mediterranean Region

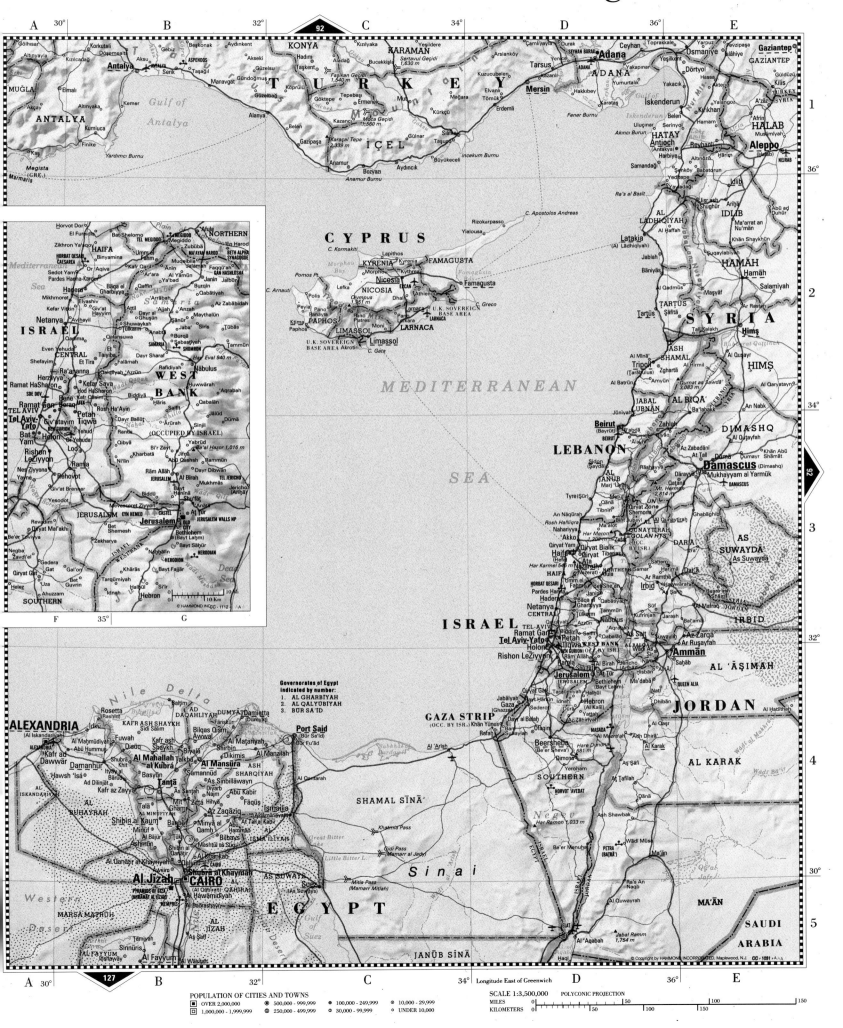

SCALE 1:7,000,000   LAMBERT CONFORMAL CONIC PROJECTION

MILES   0   100   200   300
KILOMETERS 0   100   200   300

Longitude East of Greenwich

POPULATION OF CITIES AND TOWNS

- ■ OVER 2,000,000
- □ 1,000,000 - 1,999,999
- ● 500,000 - 999,999
- ● 250,000 - 499,999
- ● 100,000 - 249,999
- ● 30,000 - 99,999
- ⊙ 10,000 - 29,999
- ○ UNDER 10,000

Governorates of Egypt
indicated by number:

1. AL ISKANDARIYAH
2. KAFR ASH SHAYKH
3. AL GHARBIYAH
4. AL MINÚFIYAH
5. AD DAQAHLIYAH
6. DUMYÁT
7. BUR SA'ID
8. ASH SHARQIYAH
9. AL ISMA'ILIYAH
10. AL QALYUBIYAH
11. AL QAHIRAH
12. AL FAYYÚM
13. BANI SUWAYF

© Copyright HAMMOND INCORPORATED, Maplewood, N.J. CC-1092-A-J-A

Northern Middle East

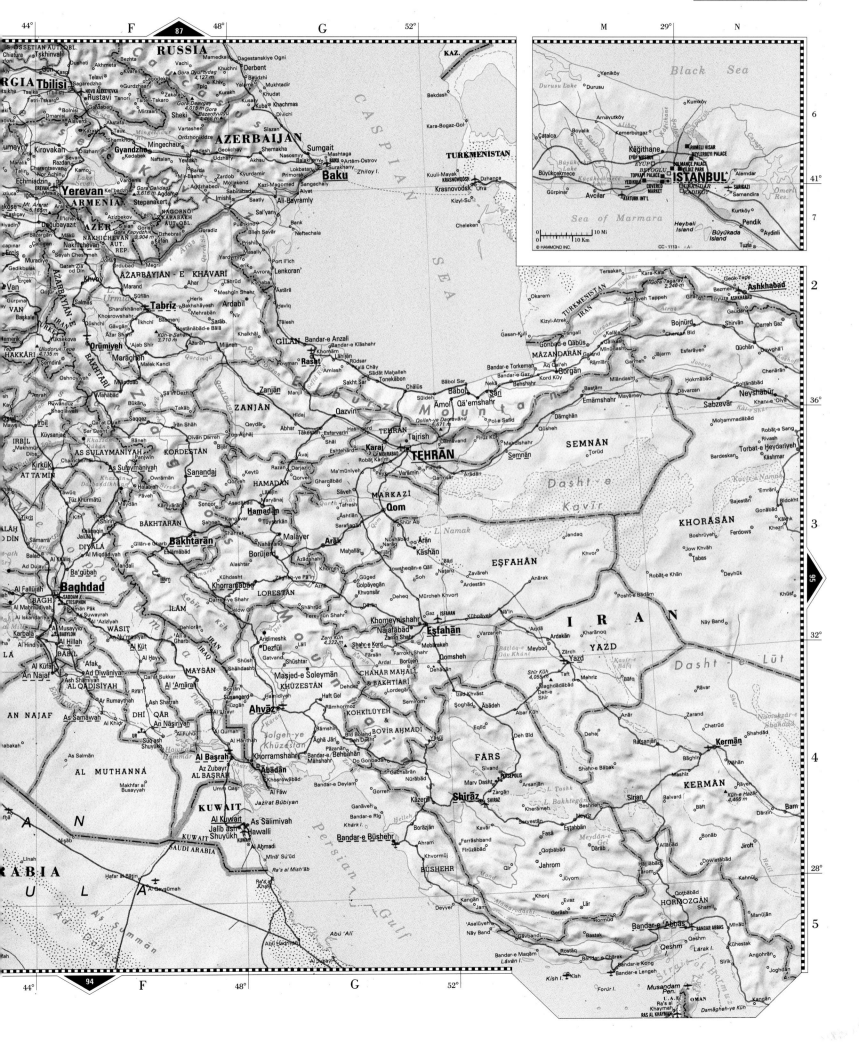

Southwestern Asia

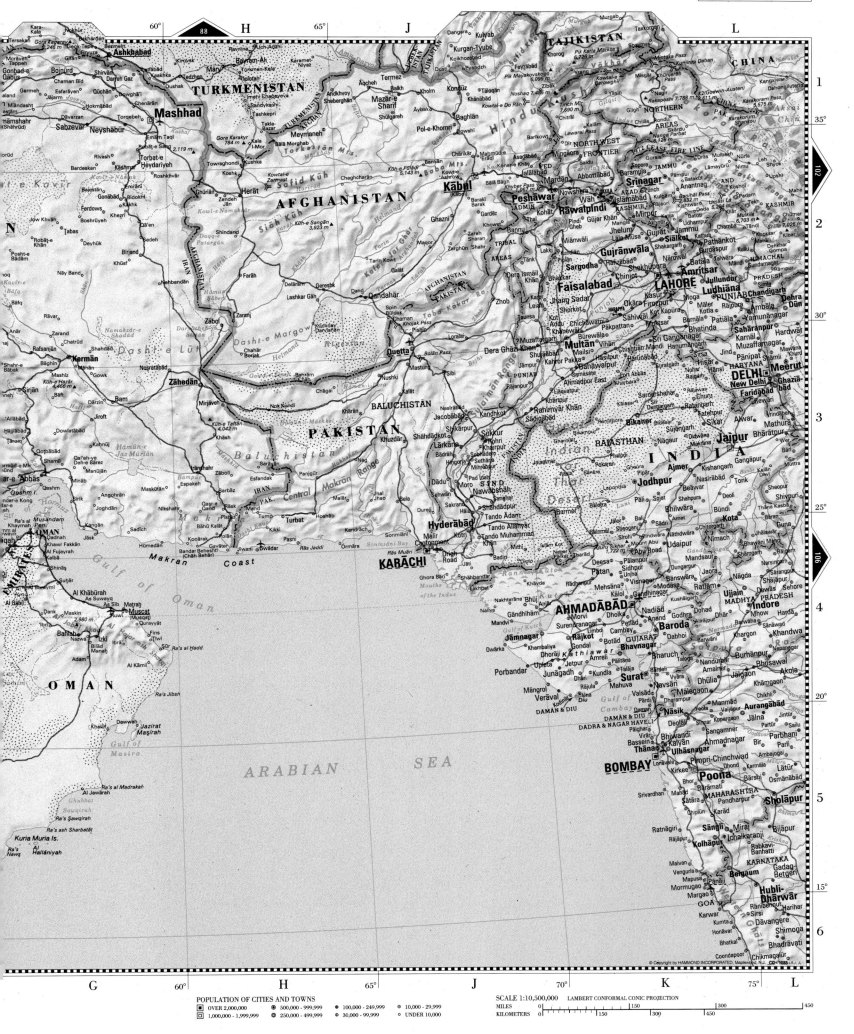

POPULATION OF CITIES AND TOWNS

| ■ OVER 2,000,000 | ● 500,000 - 999,999 | ● 100,000 - 249,999 | ○ 10,000 - 29,999 |
| ▣ 1,000,000 - 1,999,999 | ● 250,000 - 499,999 | ● 30,000 - 99,999 | ○ UNDER 10,000 |

SCALE 1:10,500,000   LAMBERT CONFORMAL CONIC PROJECTION

MILES   0   150   300   450
KILOMETERS   0   150   300   450

© Copyright by HAMMOND INCORPORATED, Maplewood, N.J.   CO-1033-A A A

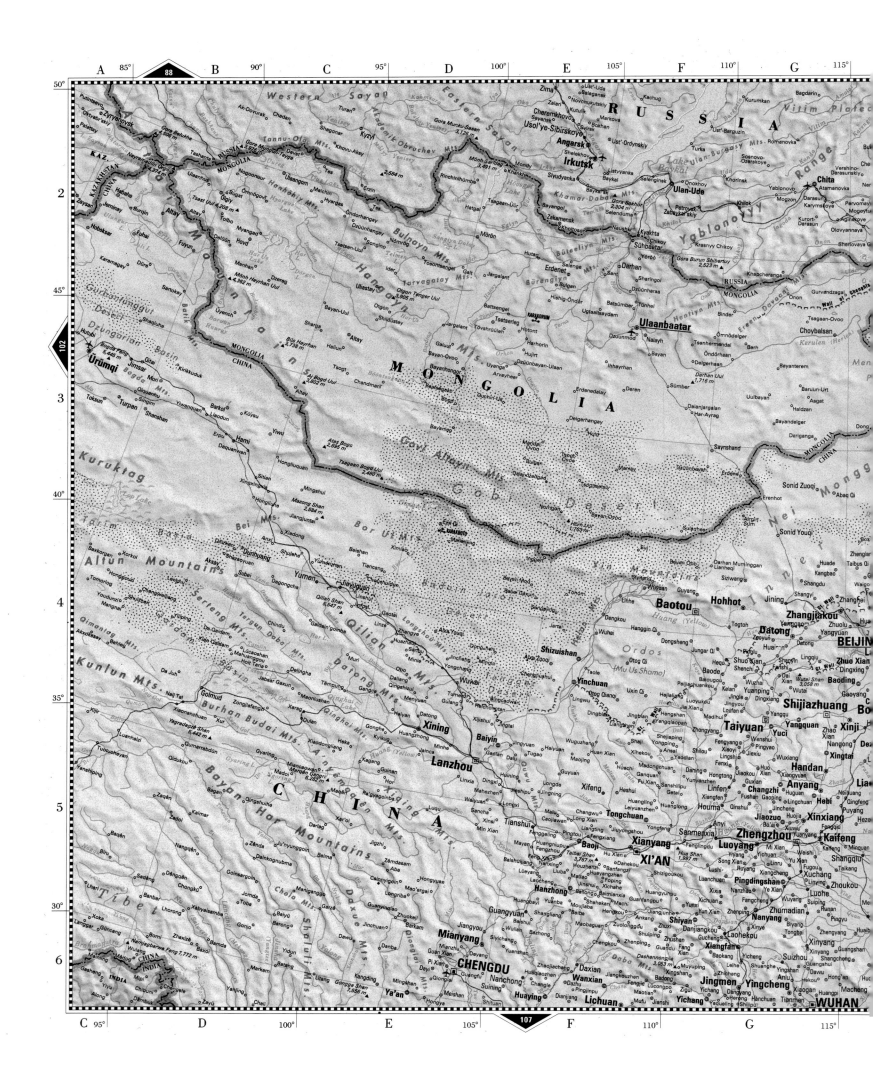

POPULATION OF CITIES AND TOWNS

■ OVER 2,000,000   ⊡ 500,000 - 999,999   ● 100,000 - 249,999   ⊙ 10,000 - 29,999
⊡ 1,000,000 - 1,999,999   ⊛ 250,000 - 499,999   ⊕ 30,000 - 99,999   ○ UNDER 10,000

SCALE 1:10,500,000   LAMBERT CONFORMAL CONIC PROJECTION

MILES   0   150   300   450
KILOMETERS   0   150   300   450

© Copyright by HAMMOND INCORPORATED, Maplewood, N.J.   CC - 1004 - A - A

Central and Southern Japan

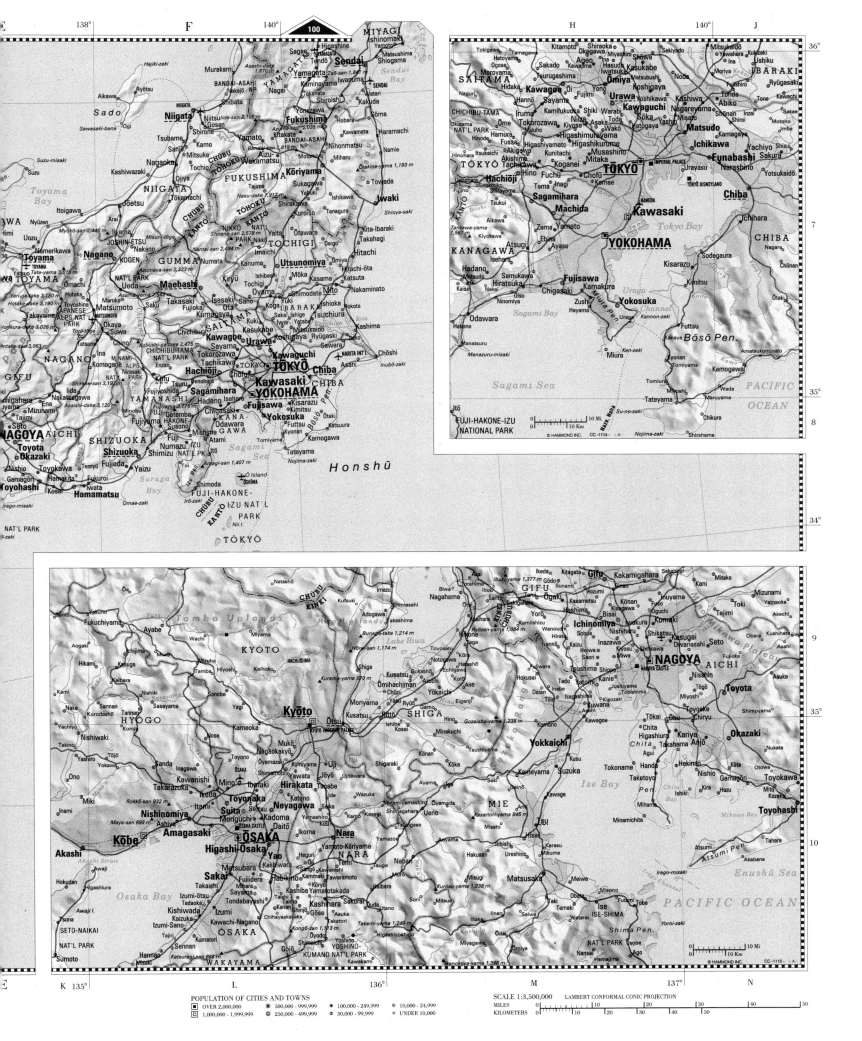

Northern Japan, Ryukyu Islands

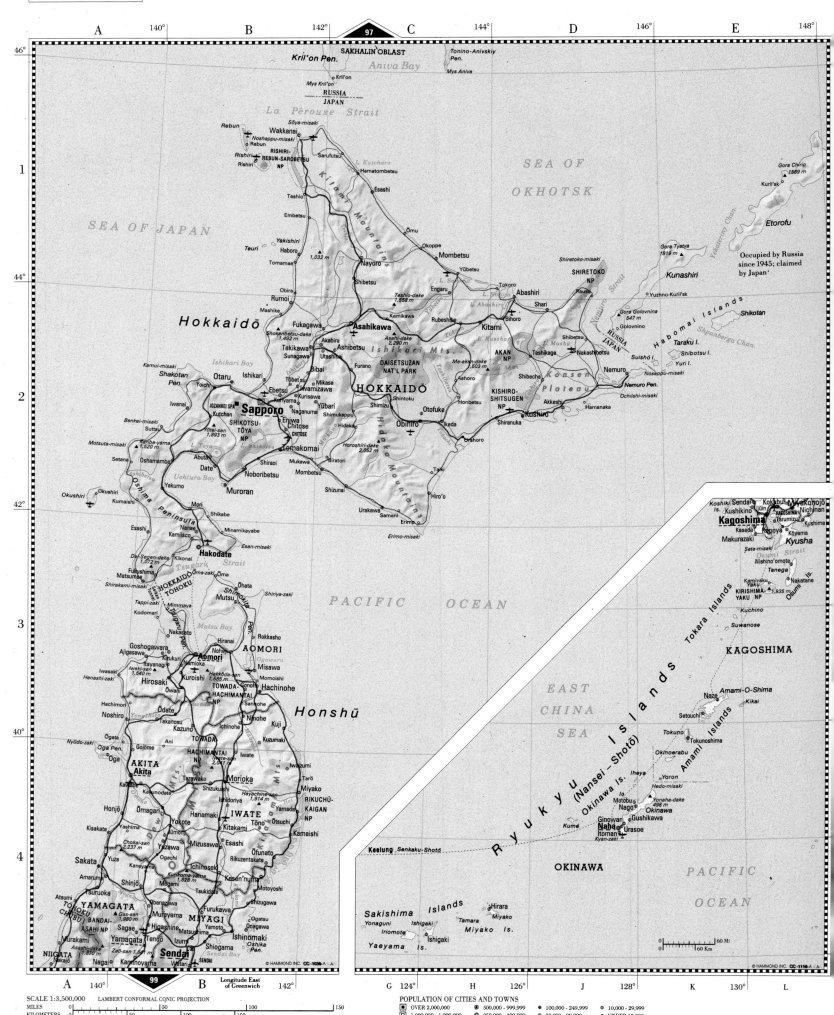

A 140° B 142° 97 C 144° D 146° E 148°

46°

SAKHALIN OBLAST

Kril'on Pen.
Tonino-Anivskiy Pen.
Aniva Bay
Mys Aniva

Mys Kril'on
RUSSIA
JAPAN
La Pérouse Strait

SEA OF
OKHOTSK

Gora Chirip
1589 m

Kuril'sk

Rebun
Wakkanai
Noshappu-misaki
Sōya-misaki
RISHIRI-
REBUN-SAROBETSU
NP
Rishiri
Rishiri

Sarufutsu
L. Kutcharo
Hamatombetsu

Etorofu

1

Teshio
Esashi
Ōmu
Okoppe

Mombetsu

SEA OF JAPAN

Embetsu
Yakishiri
Haboro
Teuri
Tomamae

Yūbetsu

Shiretoko-misaki

Gora Tyatya
1819 m

Kunashiri

Occupied by Russia
since 1945; claimed
by Japan

44°

1,032 m
Obira
Nayoro
Shibetsu

Engaru
Kamikawa

Tokoro
Abashiri
Shari

SHIRETOKO
NP

Rausu

Gora Golovnina
547 m
Golovnino

Rumoi
Mashike
Fukagawa

Asahikawa
Teshio-dake
1,558 m
Rubeshibe
Kitami

Yuzhno-Kuril'sk

RUSSIA
JAPAN

Shikotan

Habomai Islands

Shokanbetsu-dake
1,492 m
Takikawa
Akabira
Ashibetsu
Asahi-dake
2,290 m

Taraku I.
Shpanberga Chan.

Hokkaidō

Kamui-misaki
Shakotan
Pen.
Ishikari Bay
Otaru
Yoichi
Ishikari
Sunagawa
Utashinai
DAISETSUZAN
NAT'L PARK
Me-akan-dake
1,503 m
AKAN
NP
Teshikaga
Shibetsu
Nakashibetsu

Suishō I.

Yuri I.

2

Iwanai
Bibai
Mikasa
Iwamizawa
Furano
Ashoro
Shibecha
Konsen
Plateau

Nosappu-misaki

Nemuro

JŌZANKEI SPA
Kutchan
Sapporo
Kuriyama
Yūbari
Shimukappu
Hidaka
Shimizu
HOKKAIDŌ
Honbetsu
KUSHIRO-
SHITSUGEN
NP
Akkeshi
Hamanaka

Nemuro Pen.

Benkei-misaki
Suttsu
SHIKOTSU-
TŌYA
NP
Iōtei-san
1,893 m
Eniwa
Chitose
CHITOSE
Naganuma
Otofuke
Obihiro
Ikeda
Urahoro
Kushiro
Ochiishi-misaki

Motsuta-misaki
Kariba-yama
1,520 m
L. Tōya
L. Shikotsu
Tomakomai
Horoshiri-dake
2,052 m
Urahoro
Teiki

Setana
Oshamambe
Abuta
Date
Shiraoi
Mukawa
Biratori

42°

Okushiri
Okushiri
Kumaishi
Mori
Shikabe
Minamikayabe
Yakumo
Noboribetsu
Muroran
Mombetsu
Shizunai
Urakawa
Samani
Erimo
Hiro'o

Esashi
Nanae
Kamiiso
Esan-misaki
Erimo-misaki

PACIFIC   OCEAN

Kagashima inset:

Dai-Segen-dake
1,072 m
Hakodate
Kikonai
Ōma
Koshiki
Is.
Sendai
Kushikino
Kokubu
Miyekonojō
Nichinan

Fukushima
Matsumae
Kikonai
Ōma-zaki
Ōma
Ōhata
Kaseda
Kagoshima
Nagoya
Kōyama
Kushima

3

Shirakami-misaki
HOKKAIDŌ
TŌHOKU
Tsugaru Strait
Shimokita
Mutsu
Shiriya-zaki
Makurazaki
Sata-misaki
Ōsumi
Strait
Nishino'omote
Tanega

Kyusha

Tappi-zaki
Kodomari
Mimmaya
Ōhata

Kirishima-
Yaku
NP
1,935 m
Nakatane

Goshogawara
Ajigasawa
Kizukuri
Nohej
Hiranai
Rokkasho
Mutsu Bay

Kamiyaku
Yaku

40°

Iwaki-san
1,625 m
Namioka
Aomori
Misawa
EAST
CHINA
SEA
Kuchino
Suwanose
KAGOSHIMA

Iwasaki
Henashi-zaki
Hirosaki
Kuroishi
Hakköda-san
1,585 m
Momoishi
Hachinohe

Hachimori
Ōwani
Ōdate
TOWADA-
HACHIMANTAI
NP
Sannohe
Ninohe
Kuji
Naze
Amami-O-Shima
Kikai

Noshiro
Takanosu
Kazuno
Ichinohe
Kuzumaki
Setouchi

Tokara Islands

Ōga Pen.
Ōgata
TOWADA
Iwate
Iwaizumi
Tokuno

Nyūdo-zaki
Oga
Gojōme
HACHIMANTAI
NP
Iwate-san
2,041 m
Tarō
Tokunoshima
Amami Islands

AKITA
Akita
Tazawako
Morioka
Hayachine-san
1,914 m
Miyako
Okinoerabu

Honshū

Kakunodate
Shizukuishi
Ishidoriya
RIKUCHŪ-
KAIGAN
NP
Yoron
Hedo-misaki

Honjō
Ōmagari
Hanamaki
Yamada
Ōtsuchi
Iō
Motobu
Yonaha-dake
498 m

Kisakata
Yashima
IWATE
Kitakami
Tōno
Kamaishi
Nago
Okinawa

4

Sakata
Yuza
Ōfunato
Kumé
Ginowan
Gushikawa

Chokai-san
2,237 m
Mizusawa
Esashi
Rikuzentakata
Naha
Urasoe

Amarume
Ogachi
Ichinoseki
Kesen'numa
Itoman
Kyan-zaki

Kurikoma-yama
1,628 m
Tsukidate

Atsumi
Kaneyama
Mogami
Motoyoshi

Tsuruoka
Shinjō
Shizugawa

YAMAGATA
Obanazawa
Furukawa
Ogatsu
OKINAWA

TŌHOKU
CHIBU
BANDAI
ASAHI NP
Gas-san
1,980 m
Murayama
MIYAGI
Matsushima
Naruko
Ogatsu
Oshika
Pen.

NIIGATA
Asahi-dake
1,870 m
Tendō
Higashine
Yamato
Ishinomaki

Nagai
Kaminoyama
Yamagata
Sagae
Zaō-san
1,841 m
Sendai
Shiogama
Oshika
Pen.

Sakishima   Islands
Hirara
Miyako
Tamara
Ishigaki
Yonaguni
Iriomote
Ishigaki
Miyako Is.
Keelung
Senkaku-Shotō

Yaeyama   Is.

Sendai Bay

© HAMMOND INC. CC-1036-A A

A 140° 99 B Longitude East
of Greenwich 142°

G 124° H 126° J 128° K 130° L

SCALE 1:3,500,000   LAMBERT CONFORMAL CONIC PROJECTION
MILES 0   50   100   150
KILOMETERS 0   50   100   150

POPULATION OF CITIES AND TOWNS
■ OVER 2,000,000   ◉ 500,000 - 999,999   ● 100,000 - 249,999   ⊙ 10,000 - 29,999
□ 1,000,000 - 1,999,999   ◎ 250,000 - 499,999   • 30,000 - 99,999   ○ UNDER 10,000

0   60 Mi
0   60 Km

Korea

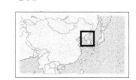

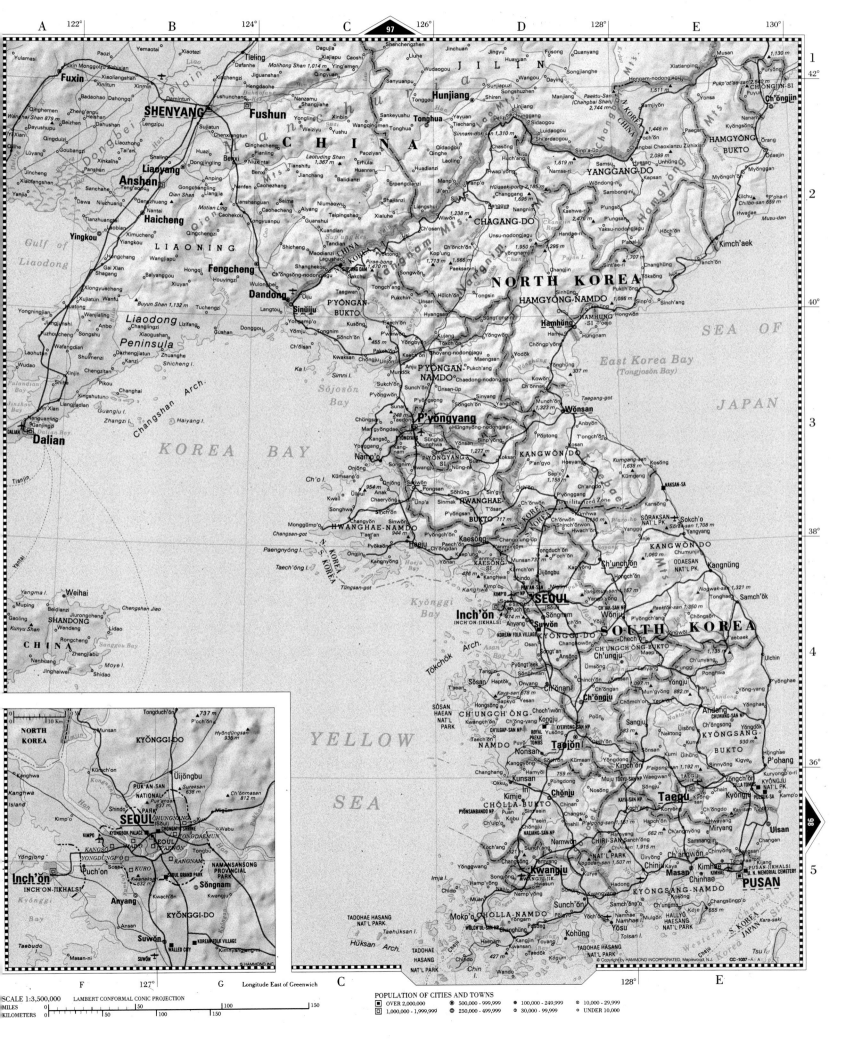

Central Asia

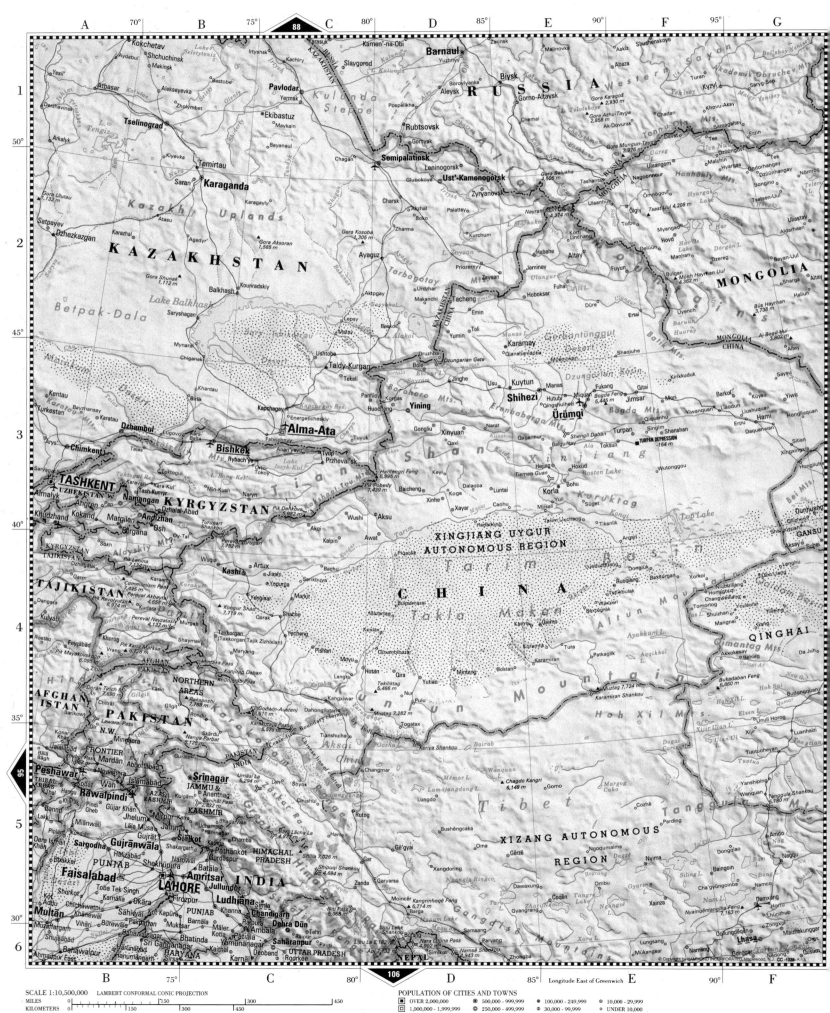

Northeastern China

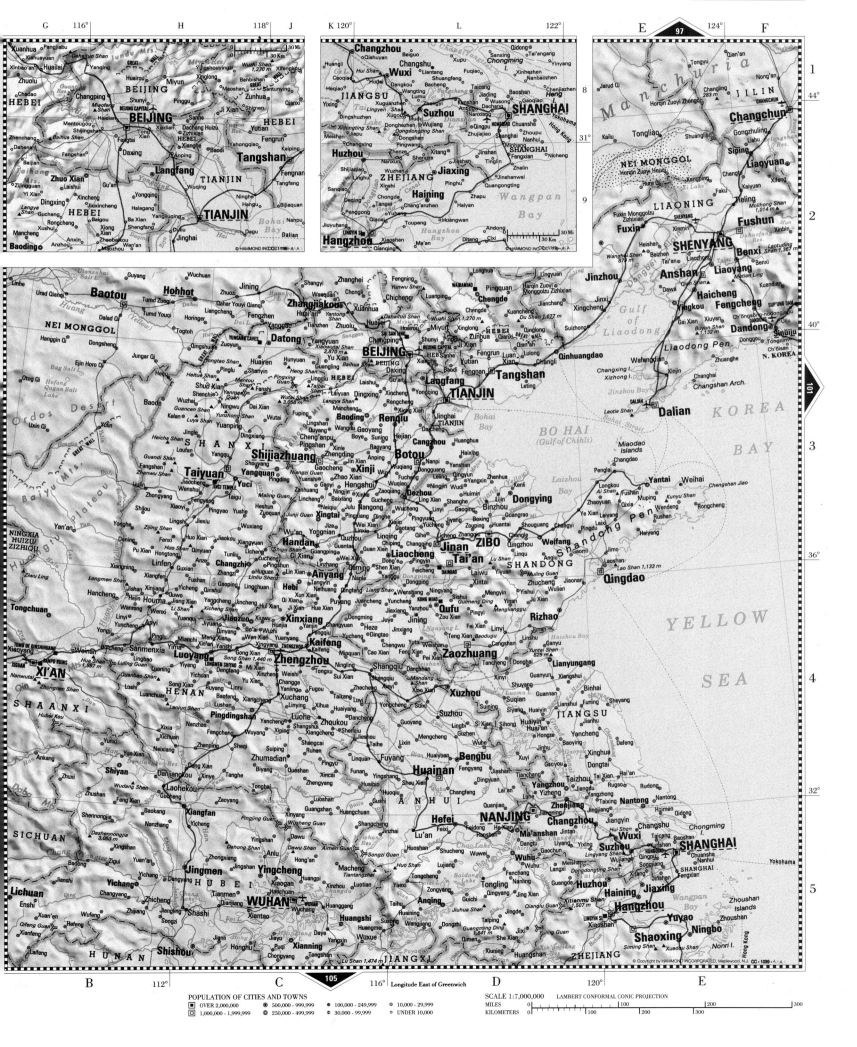

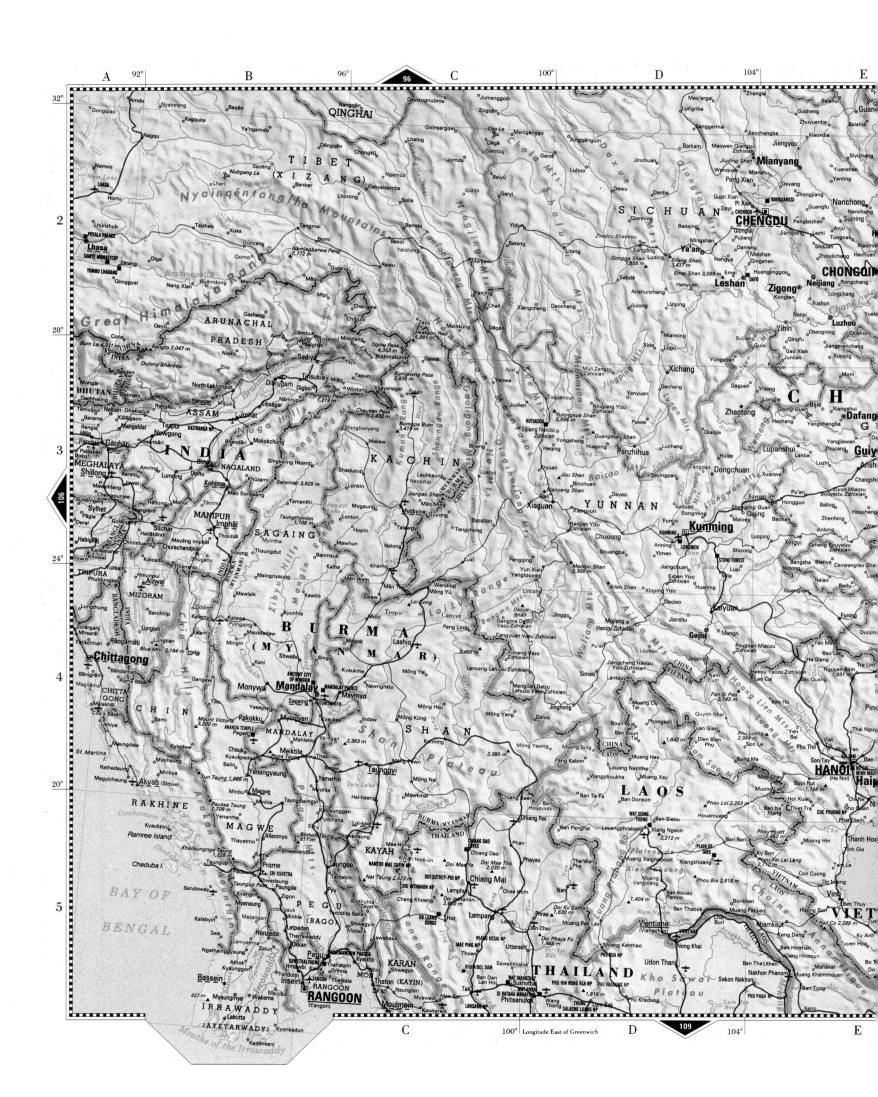

Southeastern China, Burma

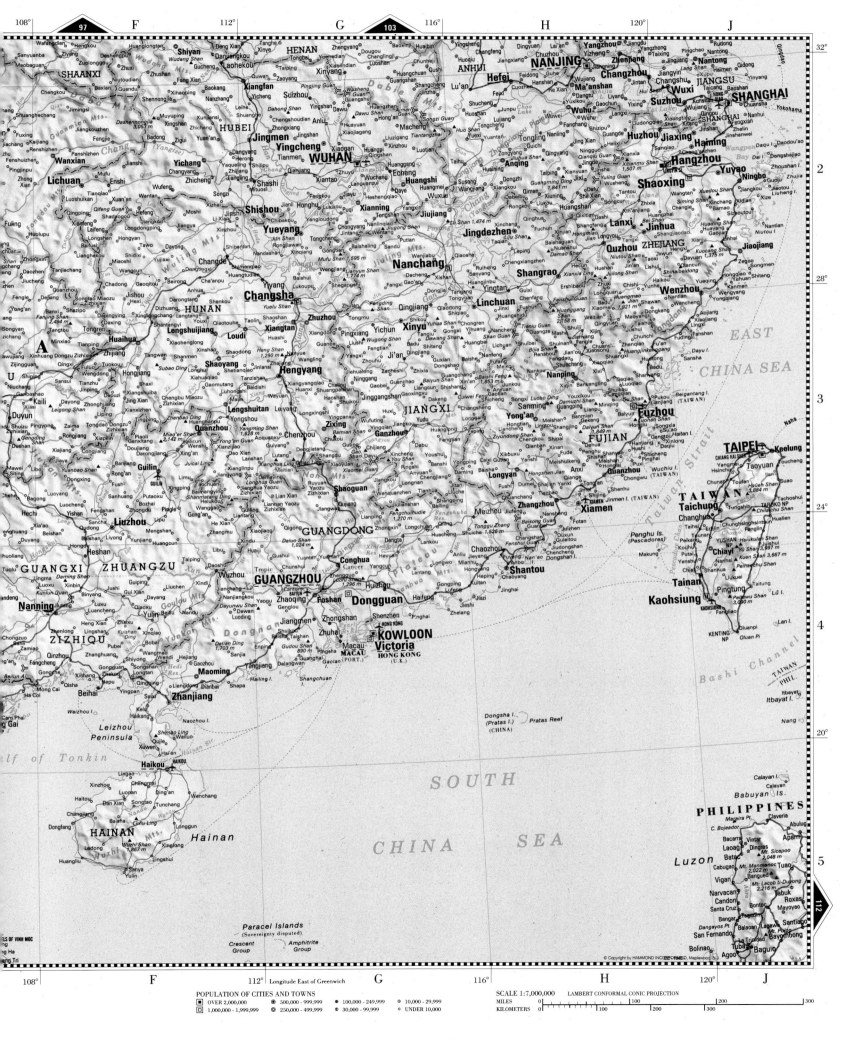

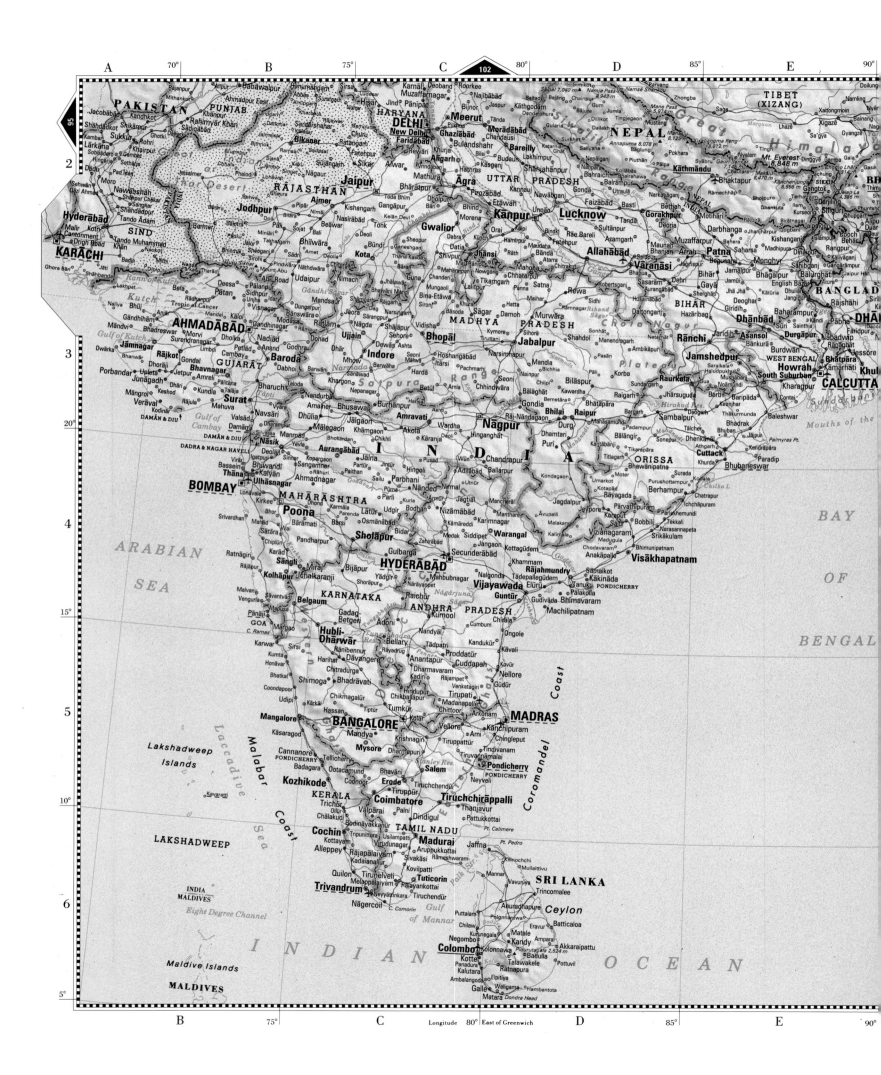

Southern Asia

POPULATION OF CITIES AND TOWNS

■ OVER 2,000,000	◉ 500,000 - 999,999	● 100,000 - 249,999	◎ 10,000 - 29,999
▣ 1,000,000 - 1,999,999	◉ 250,000 - 499,999	● 30,000 - 99,999	○ UNDER 10,000

SCALE 1:10,500,000   LAMBERT CONFORMAL CONIC PROJECTION

MILES 0   150   300   450

KILOMETERS 0   150   300   450

Longitude 100° East of Greenwich

© Copyright by HAMMOND INCORPORATED, Maplewood, N.J.   CC - 1041 -A-: A

Punjab Plain, Southern India

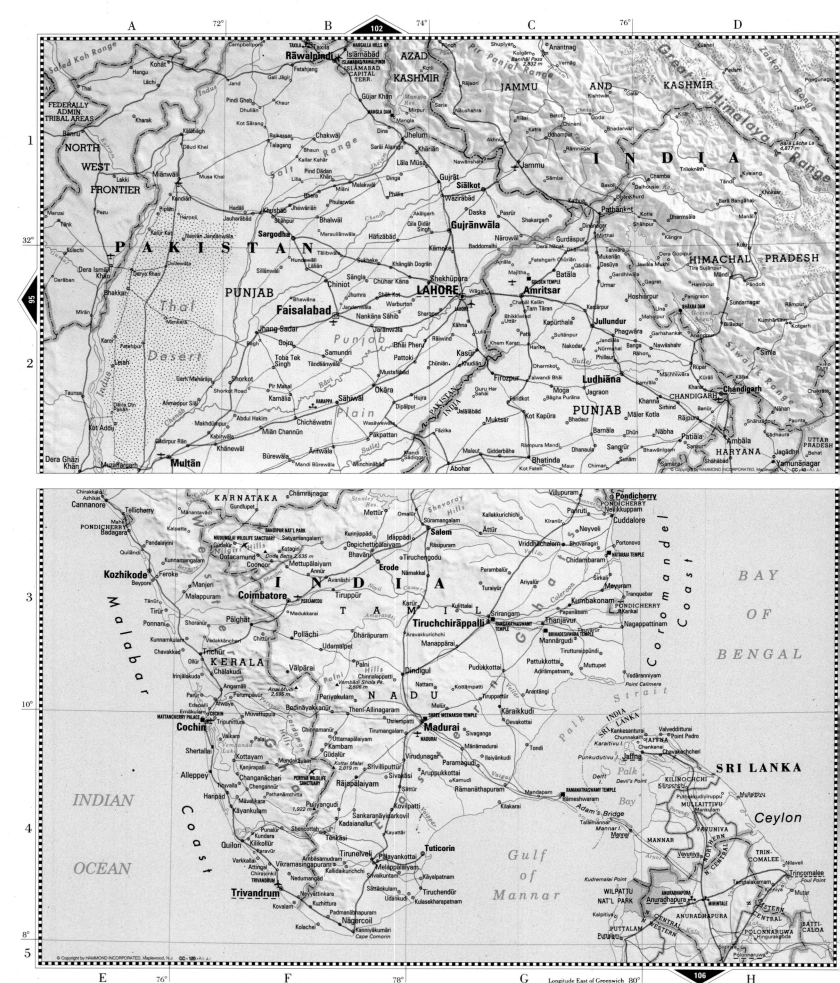

SCALE 1:3,500,000   LAMBERT CONFORMAL CONIC PROJECTION

MILES   0   50   100   150

KILOMETERS   0   50   100   150

POPULATION OF CITIES AND TOWNS

■ OVER 2,000,000	● 500,000 - 999,999	● 100,000 - 249,999	○ 10,000 - 29,999
▢ 1,000,000 - 1,999,999	● 250,000 - 499,999	● 30,000 - 99,999	○ UNDER 10,000

Longitude East of Greenwich 80°

Eastern Burma, Thailand, Indochina

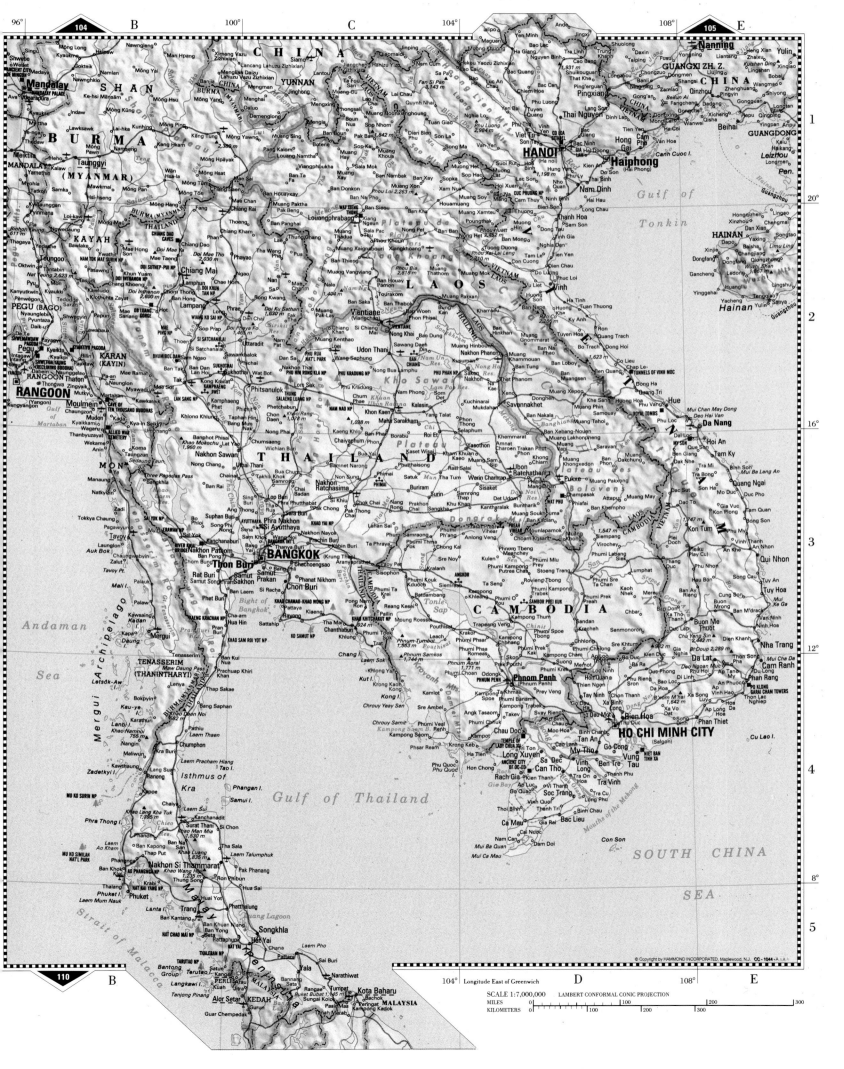

SCALE 1:7,000,000   LAMBERT CONFORMAL CONIC PROJECTION

MILES   0   100   200   300
KILOMETERS   0   100   200   300

Longitude East of Greenwich

© Copyright by HAMMOND INCORPORATED, Maplewood, N.J.   CC-1044

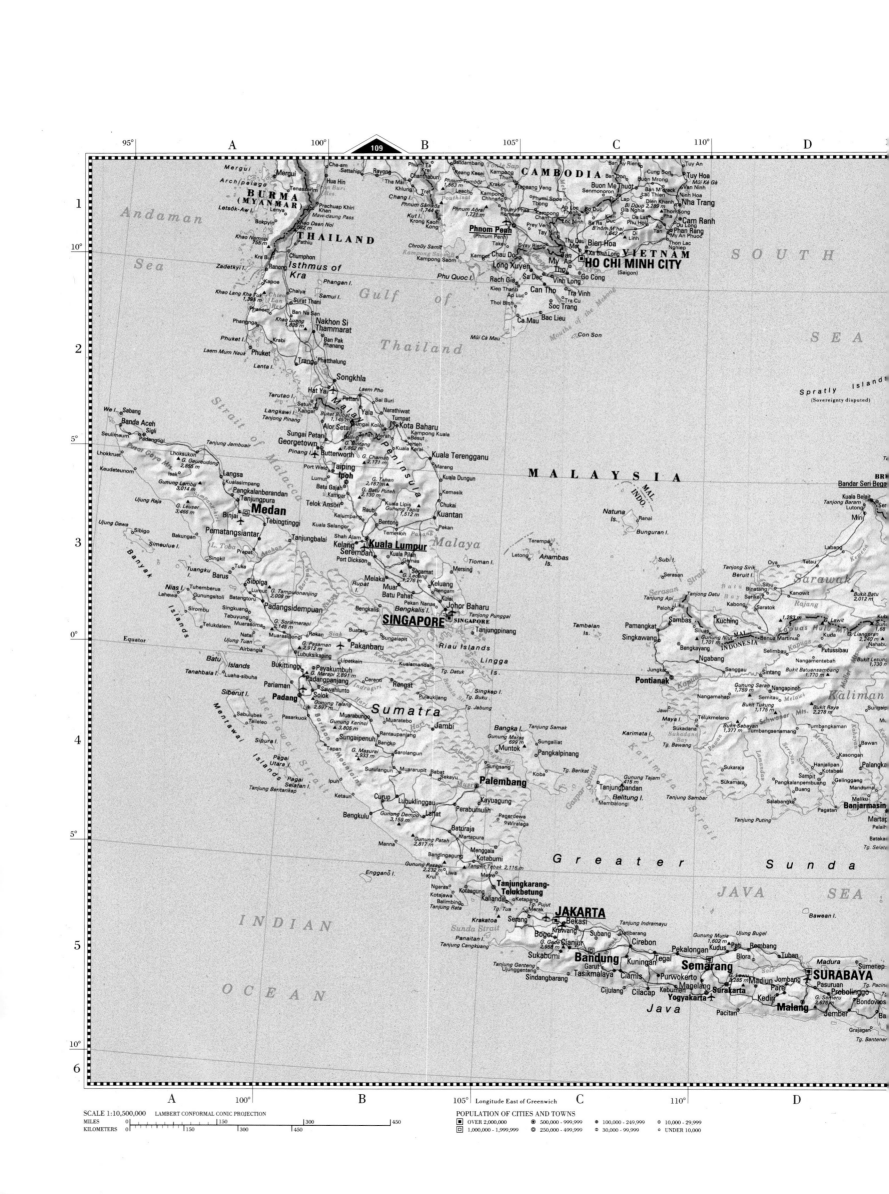

Southeastern Asia

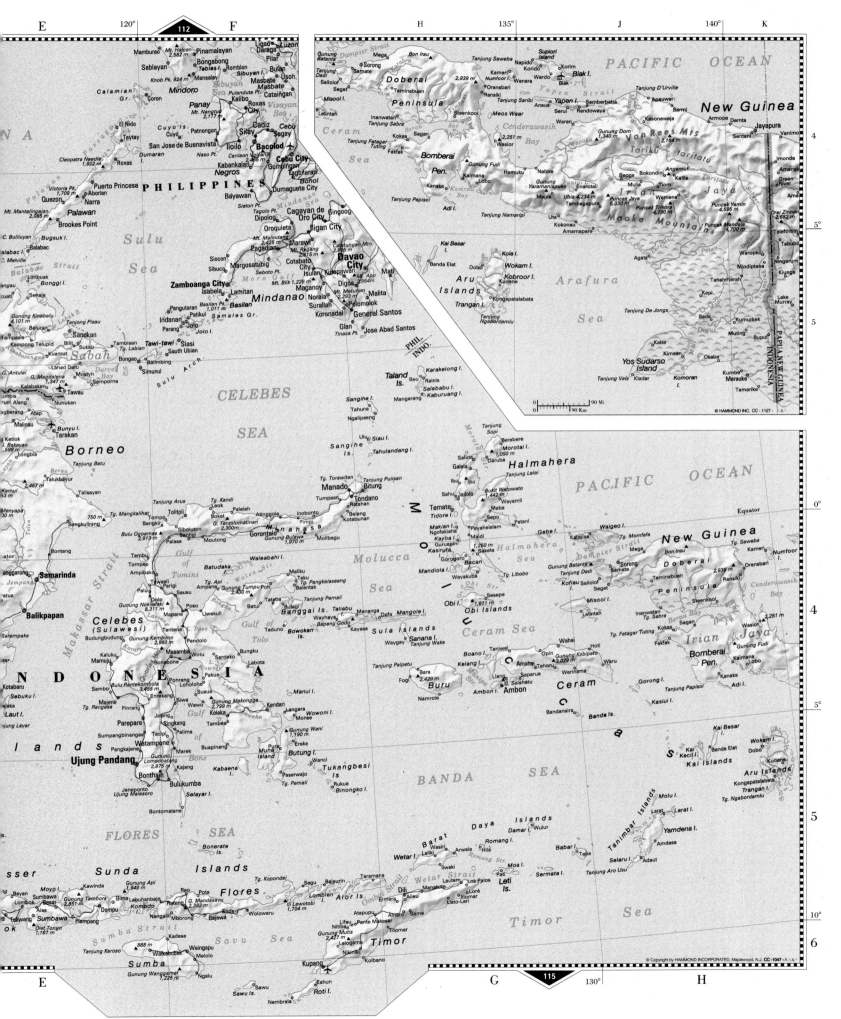

Philippines

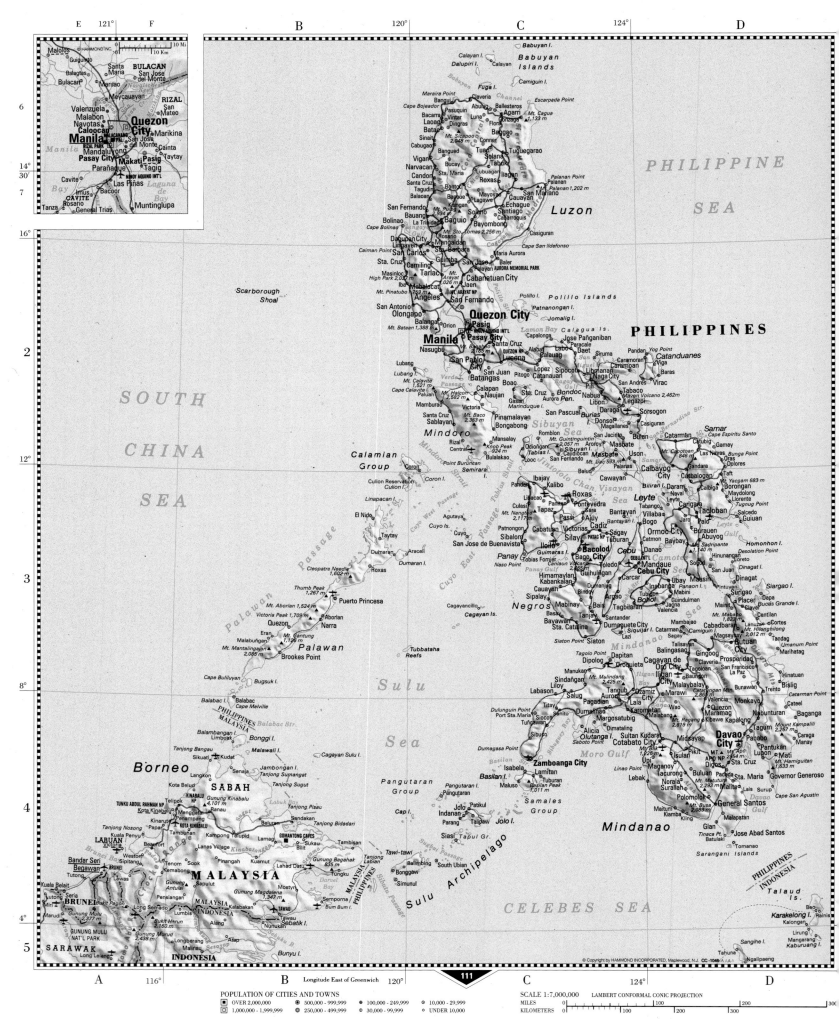

POPULATION OF CITIES AND TOWNS

- ■ OVER 2,000,000
- ◉ 500,000 - 999,999
- ● 100,000 - 249,999
- ⊙ 10,000 - 29,999
- ▣ 1,000,000 - 1,999,999
- ● 250,000 - 499,999
- ● 30,000 - 99,999
- ○ UNDER 10,000

Longitude East of Greenwich

SCALE 1:7,000,000   LAMBERT CONFORMAL CONIC PROJECTION

MILES 0 — 100 — 200 — 300

KILOMETERS 0 — 100 — 200 — 300

Antarctica

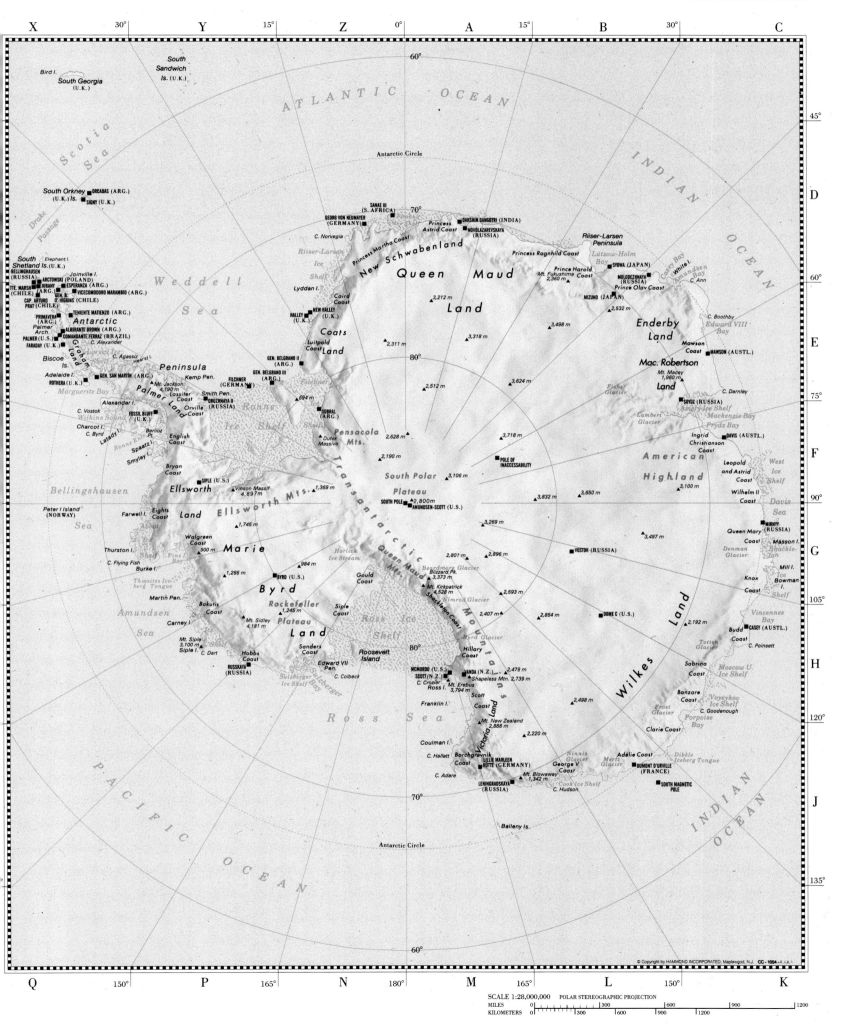

SCALE 1:28,000,000 POLAR STEREOGRAPHIC PROJECTION

MILES 0 300 600 900 1200
KILOMETERS 0 300 600 900 1200

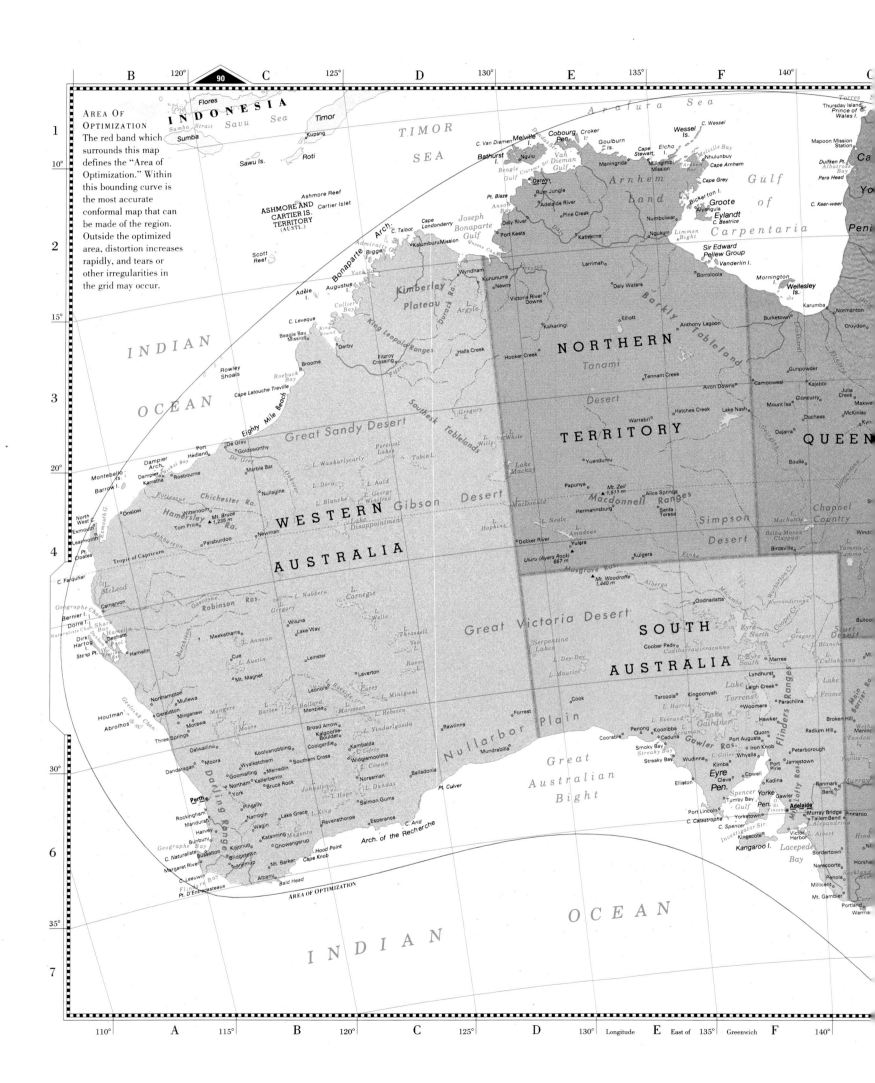

AREA OF OPTIMIZATION
The red band which surrounds this map defines the "Area of Optimization." Within this bounding curve is the most accurate conformal map that can be made of the region. Outside the optimized area, distortion increases rapidly, and tears or other irregularities in the grid may occur.

INDONESIA

Flores

Sumba Strait Savu Sea

Sumba Roti

Timor

Kupang

TIMOR SEA

Arafura Sea

Sawu Is.

Ashmore Reef Cartier Islet

ASHMORE AND CARTIER IS. TERRITORY (AUSTL.)

Scott Reef

C. Van Diemen Melville Cobourg Croker I.
Bathurst Pen. I.
I. Nguiu Goulburn Is.
Cape Stewart Elcho Is.

Wessel Is. C. Wessel

Melville Bay
Nhulunbuy Cape Arnhem

Mapoon Mission Station

Thursday Island Prince of Wales I.
Torres

Van Dieman Gulf Maningrida Milingimbi Mission
Cape Grey

Duifken Pt.
Albatross Bay
Pera Head

Ca

Darwin
Pt. Blaze Rum Jungle
Adelaide River
Pine Creek

Arnhem Land Numbulwar

Bickerton I.
Alyangula Groote Eylandt
C. Beatrice

C. Keer-weer

Yo

Ansoń Bay

Gulf of Carpentaria

Pen

Ashmore Reef

Bonaparte Arch.

York

C. Talbot

Cape Londonderry

Joseph Bonaparte Gulf

Daly River
Port Keats

Katherine

Queen

Ngukurr Limmen Bight

Sir Edward Pellew Group
Vanderlin I.

Bigge I.

Adèle I.

Augustus I.

KalumburuMission

Wyndham Kununurra Newry

Victoria River Downs

Larrimah

Borroloola

Mornington

Wellesley Is.

Collier Bay

Adele

Kimberley Plateau

L. Argyle

Daly Waters

Barkly Tableland

Karumba

Normanton

C. Leveque

King Leopold Ranges

Kalkaringi

Elliott

Anthony Lagoon

Burketown

Croydon

INDIAN

Beagle Bay
Missiòń

King Sound

Derby

Fitzroy Crossing

Halls Creek

Hooker Creek

NORTHERN

Tanami

Tennant Creek

Gunpowder

OCEAN

Rowley Shoals

Roebuck Bay

Broome

Furròs

Desert

Avon Downs

Camooweal

Kajabbi

Mount Isa

Cloncurry

Julia Creek

Maxwe

Cape Latouche Treville

Eighty Mile Beach

Great Sandy Desert

Southesk Tablelands

Gregory L.

Warrabri

Hatches Creek

Lake Nash

Duchess McKinlay

Dajarra

Kyn

Port De Grey
Goldsworthy

L. Waukarlycarly

Percival Lakes

Tobin L.

L. Will

TERRITORY

QUEEN

Dampier Arch.
Nickol Bay
Dampier Karratha Roebourne

Hedland
De Grey

Marble Bar

L. Dora

L. Auld

L. White

Lake Mackay

Yuendumu

Boulia

Montebello Is.
Barrow I.

Nullagine

L. Blanche

L. George
L. Winifred

WESTERN Gibson Desert

MacDonald

Papunya Mt. Zeil
1,511 m

Alice Springs
Macdonnell Ranges

Santa Teresa

Simpson

Chichester Ra.

Wittenoom Mt. Bruce
1,235 m

Hamersley

North West C.
Exmouth
Learmonth
Pt. Cloates

Fortescue

Onslow

Tom Price

Ra.

Paraburdoo

Newman

Ashburton

Lake Disappointment

L. Neale

D, Amadeus
Uluru (Ayers Rock)
867 m

Hermannsburg

Docker River
Yulara

Kulgera

MacArthur

Channel Country

Belba Morea
Claypan

Birdsville

Windor

Einas

Chapel

AUSTRALIA

Tropic of Capricorn

Mt. Woodroffe
1,440 m

Musgrave Ras.

Einte

Yamma Yamma

C. Farquhar

C. McLeod
Carnarvon

Gascoyne

Robinson Ras.

L. Nabberu

L. Carnegie

Alberga

Great Victoria Desert

SOUTH

Oodnadatta

Warrandirga

Bulloo

Bernier I.
Dorre I.

Geographe Chan.

Gregory

Wiluna

Wells

Serpentine Lakes

Eyre North

Cooper's Cr.

L. Gregory

Sturt

L. Blanche

Naturaliste Chan.

Shark Bay

Meekatharra

Lake Way

Coober Pedy

Cadibarrawirracanna

Marree

L. Callabonna

Dirk Hartog I.
Denham
Hamelin Pool

L. Annean

L. Austin

Throssell

Yeo L.

L. Dey-Dey

Lake Eyre South

AUSTRALIA

Lyndhurst

Steep Pt.

Hamelin

Cue

Mt. Magnet

Leinster

L. Maurice

L. Harris

Leigh Creek

Tarcoola

Kingoonyah

Lake Torrens

Hawker

Broken Hill

Frame

Laverton

Rason L.

Cook

Woomera
Parachilna

Menin

Leonora

Beadie

L. Minigwal

Forrest

Penong Koonibba
Coorabie

L. Everard
Ceduna

L. Harris

Port Augusta
Quorn

Radium Hill

Tandau

Northampton
Mullewa

Mingenew

Mongers

Ballard L.

Menzies

L. Rebecca

Rawlinna

Mundrabilla

Nullarbor Plain

Smoky Bay
Streaky Bay

Kimba
Wudinna

Iron Knob
Whyalla

Peterborough

Geraldton
Morawa

L. Moore

Broad Arrow

L. Yindarlgooda

Great

Streaky Bay

Cowell
L. Gilles

Jamestown

Houtman Abrolhos

Three Springs

Dalwallinu

Kalgoorlie
Boulder

Coolgardie

Australian

Port Augusta

Kadina
Snowtown

Renmark
Berri

Dandaragan

Goomalling
Moora

Merredin
Wyalkatchem

Southern Cross

Kambalda
L. Lefroy
Widgiemooltha

Balladonia

L. Cowan

Bight

Eyre Pen.

Cowell

Wallaroo
Moonta

Murray Bridge

Pinnaroo

Northam
Kellerberrin

Norseman

Port Lincoln

Tumby Bay
Port Pirie

Yorke

Gawler

Adelaide

Tailem Bend
Alexandrina

Perth

York

Bruce Rock

L. Dundas

Pt. Culver

C. Catastrophe
C. Spencer

Spencer
Gulf

Yorketown

Kingscote

Victor Harbor
L. Albert

Bordertown

Horsh

Rockingham
Mandurah

Pingelly

Narrogin

Lake Grace
L. King

Salmon Gums

Kangaroo I.

Lacepede
Bay

Naracoorte

Penola

Harvey

Wagin

Katanning Magenta

Ravensthorpe

C. Arid

Arch. of the Recherche

Millicent

Rocking

Geographe Bay

Bunbury

Busselton
Bridgetown

Kojonup
Gnowangerup

Hood Point

Mt. Gambier

Warrn

C. Naturaliste

Margaret River

Nannup
Mt. Barker

Cape Knob

Portland

Leeuwin

Flinders Bay

Albany

Bald Head

Pt. D'Entrecasteaux

AREA OF OPTIMIZATION

INDIAN

OCEAN

Australia; New Zealand

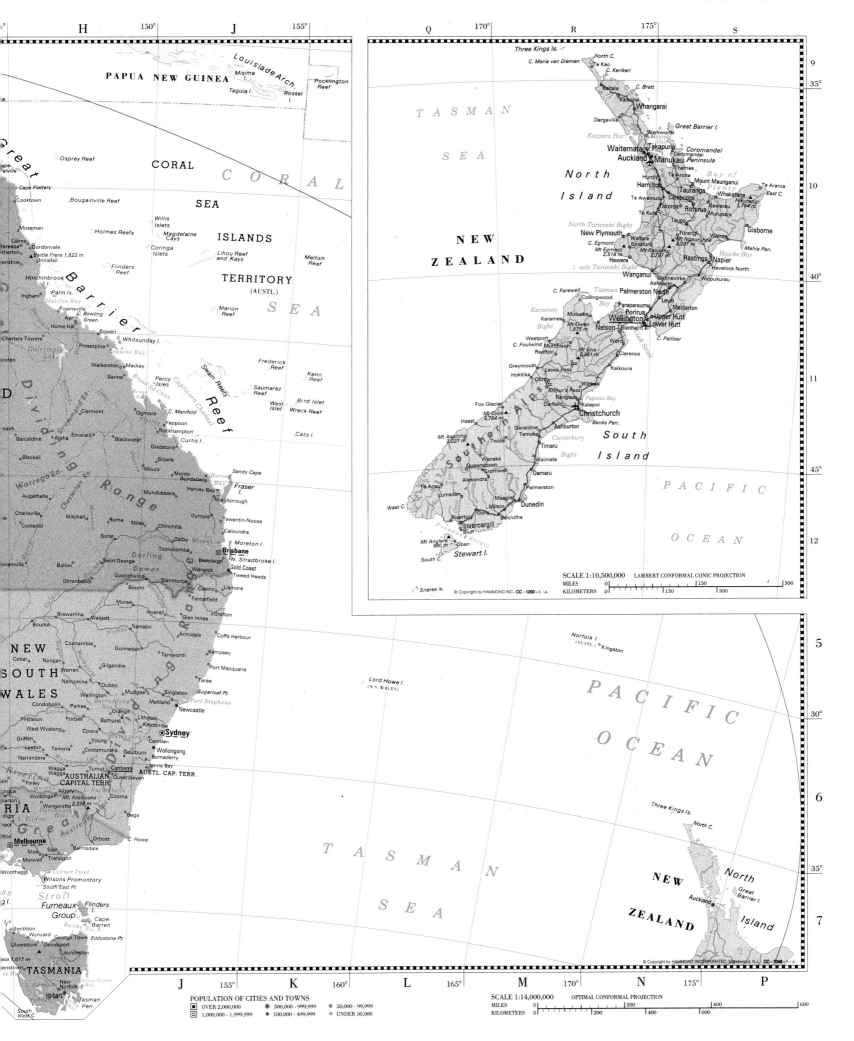

SCALE 1:10,500,000   LAMBERT CONFORMAL CONIC PROJECTION

MILES   0   150   300
KILOMETERS   0   150   300

© Copyright by HAMMOND INC. · CC - 1200 - A · A

POPULATION OF CITIES AND TOWNS
■ OVER 2,000,000   ● 500,000 - 999,999   ● 50,000 - 99,999
▣ 1,000,000 - 1,999,999   ● 100,000 - 499,999   ○ UNDER 50,000

SCALE 1:14,000,000   OPTIMAL CONFORMAL PROJECTION

MILES   0   200   400   600
KILOMETERS   0   200   400   600

© Copyright by HAMMOND INCORPORATED, Maplewood, N.J. · CC - 1048 - A · A

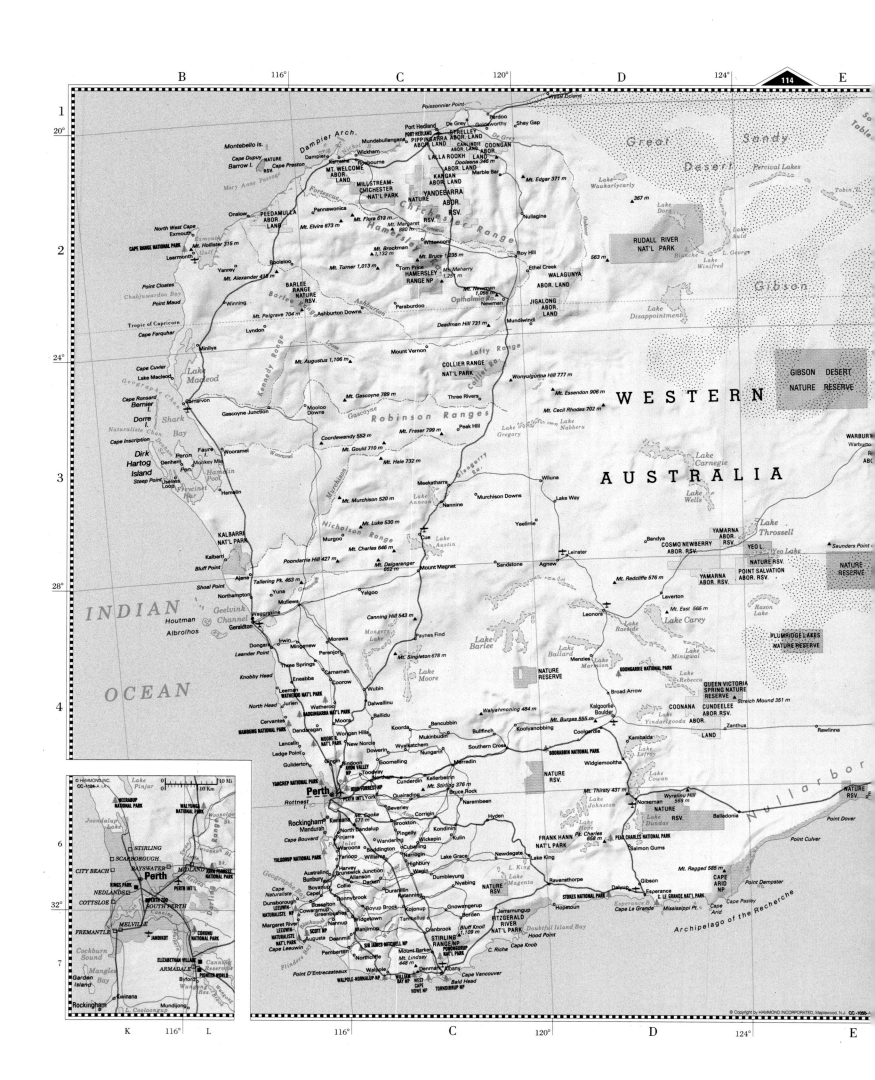

B • 116° • C • 120° • D • 124° • E

1

20°

Visual Downs

Poissonnier Point

Port Hedland • De Grey • Perdoo
Port Hedland • Goldsworthy • Shay Gap
STRELLEY • COONGAN
PIPPINGARRA ABOR. LAND • CARLINDIE • ABOR.
ABOR. LAND • ABOR. LAND
LALLA ROOKH • Doolena 346 m
LAND • Marble Bar
Montebello Is.
Mundabullangana • Wickham • KANGAN
Cape Dupuy • Dampier Arch. • ABOR.
Barrow I. • NATURE • Dampier • Roebourne • LAND • ▲ Mt. Edgar 371 m
Cape Preston • MT. WELCOME • YANDEEARRA
RSV. • ABOR. • ABOR.
LAND • ▲ 367 m
Mary Anne Passage • MILLSTREAM- • RSV.
CHICHESTER • Nullagine
NAT'L PARK • NATURE

Onslow • Pannawonica

Great Sandy Desert

Percival Lakes

Lake
Waukarlycarly

Lake
Dora

L. George

Tobin L.

PEEDAMULLA
ABOR.
North West Cape • LAND
Exmouth
Cape Range National Park • ▲ Mt. Hollister 315 m • Mt. Elvire 673 m • ▲ Mt. Flora 613 m • RSV. • Whitenoom
Learmonth • ▲ Mt. Margaret
Esmouth • 880 m
Gulf • ▲ Mt. Brockman • ▲ Roy Hill
Yanrey • 1,132 m • WALAGUNYA
Point Cloates • Boolaloo • ▲ Tom Price • ▲ Mt. Bruce 1,235 m • Ethel Creek • ABOR. LAND
▲ Mt. Alexander 418 m • ▲ Mt. Turner 1,013 m • HAMERSLEY • Mt. Meharry
2 • RANGE NP • 1,251 m • ▲ 563 m

RUDALL RIVER
NAT'L PARK

Lake
Auld

Lake
Winifred

Bianche

Gibson

Barlee • Mt. Newman
Point Maud • Winning • BARLEE • 1,056 m • JIGALONG
RANGE • ▲ Opthalmic Ra. • ABOR.
Tropic of Capricorn • NATURE • Newman • LAND
Cape Farquhar • RSV. • ▲ Mt. Palgrave 704 m • Ashburton Downs • Paraburdoo • Mundiwindi
Minilya • Lyndon • Deadman Hill 731 m ▲

Lake
Disappointment

24°

Cape Cuvier • Lake Macleod • ▲ Mt. Augustus 1,106 m • Mount Vernon • Lofty Range

COLLIER RANGE
NAT'L PARK • ▲ Wonyulgunna Hill 777 m

WESTERN

GIBSON DESERT
NATURE RESERVE

Cape Ronsard • Carnarvon • ▲ Mt. Gascoyne 789 m • Three Rivers • ▲ Mt. Essendon 906 m
Bernier I. • Mooloo
Dorre I. • Gascoyne Junction • Downs • Robinson Ranges • ▲ Mt. Cecil Rhodes 702 m
Cape Inscription • ▲ Coordewandy 552 m • ▲ Mt. Fraser 799 m • Peak Hill • Lake
Dirk • Faure I. • Wooramel • ▲ Mt. Gould 710 m • Gregory • Lake
Hartog • Peron • Denham • Nabberu • AUSTRALIA
Island • Monkey Mia • ▲ Mt. Hale 732 m
Steep Point • Useless • Hamelin • ▲ Mt. Murchison 520 m • Meekatharra • Wiluna • Lake
Loop • Pool • Nannine • Carnegie
3 • Hamelin • Murchison Downs • Lake Way • Lake
▲ Mt. Luke 530 m • Lake • Wells
Annean • Yeelirrie
Cue • Austin

Lake
Throssell

KALBARRI • Murgoo • ▲ Mt. Charles 646 m • YAMARNA
NAT'L PARK • Bandya • ABOR.
Kalbarri • ▲ Poondarrie Hill 427 m • COSMO NEWBERRY • RSV. • Yeo Lake
Bluff Point • ▲ Mt. Dalgaranger • ABOR. RSV. • YEO L.
Ajana • 652 m • Mount Magnet • Sandstone • Agnew • Leinster • NATURE RSV. • ▲ Saunders Point
Shoal Point • Tallering Pk. 453 m • POINT SALVATION
28° • Northampton • Yuna • ▲ Mt. Redcliffe 576 m • YAMARNA • ABOR. RSV. • NATURE
Houtman • Mullewa • Yalgoo • ABOR. RSV. • RESERVE
Abrolhos • Waggrakine • Laverton
Geelvink • Geraldton • Leonora • ▲ Mt. East 565 m • Rason
Channel • Canning Hill 543 m • Lake • Lake
Dongara • Irwin • Raeside • Carey • Lake
INDIAN • Mingenew • Morawa • Mongers • PLUMRIDGE LAKES
Leander Point • Perenjori • Lake • Paynes Find • Lake • NATURE RESERVE
Three Springs • ▲ Mt. Singleton 678 m • Barlee • Lake
Knobby Head • Carnamah • Ballard • Menzies • Minigwal
Eneabba • Lake
OCEAN • Coorow • Marmion • GOONGARRIE NATIONAL PARK
Wubin • Moore • NATURE • Lake
Leeman • WATHEROO NAT'L PARK • Dalwallinu • RESERVE • Rebecca
North Head • Jurien • Watheroo • Broad Arrow • QUEEN VICTORIA
4 • Cervantes • BADGINGARRA NAT'L PARK • Ballidu • SPRING NATURE
Moora • Kalgoorlie • RESERVE • Streich Mound 351 m
NAMBUNG NATIONAL PARK • Dandaragan • Wongan Hills • ▲ Walyahmoning 484 m • Boulder • COONANA • CUNDEELEE
Lancelin • New Norcia • Mukinbudin • ▲ Mt. Burges 555 m • ABOR. • ABOR. • Zanthus
Ledge Point • MOORE R. • Koorda • Bulfinch • Koolyanobbing • Lake • LAND • Rawlinna
NAT'L PARK • Dowerin • Coolgardie • Yindarlgooda
Guilderton • Bindoon • Goomalling • Nungarin • Southern Cross • Kambalda • Lake
AVON VALLEY • Toodyay • Merredin • Lefroy
YANCHEP NATIONAL PARK • NP • JOHN FORREST VP • Widgiemooltha • Lake
Perth • Northam • Cunderdin • Bencubbin • Cowan
Rottnest • PERTH INT'L • York • Wyalkatchem • BOORABBIN NATIONAL PARK
Kellerberrin
Quairading • ▲ Mt. Stirling 376 m • Lake
Beverley • ▲ Bruce Rock • Johnston
Rockingham • Kwinana • ▲ Mt. Cooke • Corrigin • Narembeen • Norseman • ▲ Wyralinu Hill
Mandurah • 571 m • Brookton • NATURE • 569 m • NATURE
Cape Bouvard • North Dandalup • Pingelly • Kondinin • Hyden • RSV. • RSV.
Pinjarra • Wandering • Wickepin • Kulin • Lake • Lake • Balladonia
Waroona • Baddington • Hope • Dundas
YALGORUP NATIONAL PARK • Yarloop • Williams • Narrogin • Lake Grace • FRANK HANN • ▲ Mt. Thirsty 431 m
Cape • Harvey • Cuballing • NAT'L PARK • ▲ Mt. Charles • PEAK CHARLES NATIONAL PARK
Naturaliste • Australind • Brunswick Junction • Wagin • Newdegate • Lake King • 658 m • Point Culver
Bunbury • Allanson • Highbury • Dumbleyung • Salmon Gums
6 • Capel • Collie • Darkan • Nyabing • NATURE • Mt. Ragged 585 m
Dunsborough • Boyanup • Duranillin • RSV. • ▲ • CAPE
Cape • Busselton • Donnybrook • Kojonup • Gnowangerup • Ravensthorpe • Gibson • ARID
Naturaliste • NATURALISTE • Capel • Boyup Brook • Kotanning • Borden • STOKES NATIONAL PARK • Dalyup • NP
LEEUWIN • Greenbushes • Cranbrook • JERRAMUNGUP • Esperance • Point Dempster
NAT'L PARK • Margaret River • Bridgetown • Tambellup • FITZGERALD • Hopetoun • C. LE GRANDE NAT'L PARK
Cape Leeuwin • Nannup • Manjimup • RIVER • Esperance B. • Cape Arid
LEEUWIN • Deanmill • STIRLING • NAT'L PARK • Cape Le Grande • Cape Pasley
NATURALISTE • SCOTT NP • ▲ Bluff Knoll • RANGE • Mississippi Pt.
NAT'L PARK • Augusta • Pemberton • 1,109 m • NP • Hood Point
Point D'Entrecasteaux • Northcliffe • ▲ Mt. Lindsay • PORONGURUP • Archipelago of the Recherche
7 • 448 m • NAT'L PARK • Doubtful Island Bay
Walpole • Denmark • Albany • C. Riche
WALPOLE-NORNALUP NP • MAY NP • WEST • TORNDIRRUP NP • Cape Knob
CAPE • Bald Head • Cape Vancouver
HOWE NP

© Copyright by HAMMOND INCORPORATED, Maplewood, N.J. • CC-1050-A

B • 116° • C • 120° • D • 124° • E

Inset map (lower left):

© HAMMOND INC. • Lake • 0 • 10 Mi
CC-1124-A • Pinjar • 0 • 10 Km

WEERABUP • WALYUNGA
NATIONAL PARK • NATIONAL PARK

Joondalup
Lake • Woongolgo
Bk.

6 • STIRLING
CITY BEACH • SCARBOROUGH • MIDLAND
BAYSWATER • JOHN FORREST
KINGS PARK • Perth • NATIONAL PARK
NEDLANDS • PERTH INT'L
32° • COTTESLOE • SOUTH PERTH
MELVILLE
FREMANTLE • JANDAKOT
COHUNU
NATIONAL PARK
Cockburn • ELIZABETHAN VILLAGE
Sound • ARMADALE • PIONEER WORLD
Garden • Byford
7 • Island • Canning
Reservoir
Mangles • Serpentine
Bay
Rockingham • Mundijong
L. Coolongup

K • 116° • L

Western and Central Australia

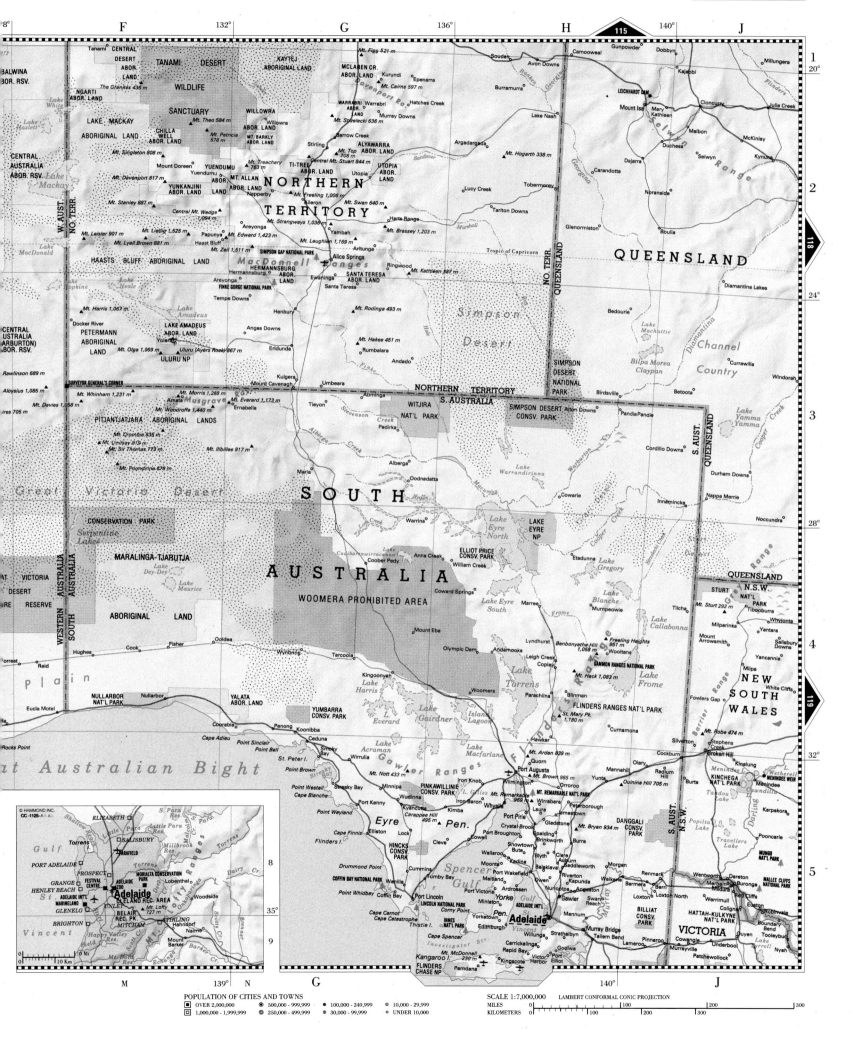

POPULATION OF CITIES AND TOWNS

■ OVER 2,000,000   ● 500,000 - 999,999   ● 100,000 - 249,999   ○ 10,000 - 29,999
□ 1,000,000 - 1,999,999   ● 250,000 - 499,999   ○ 30,000 - 99,999   ○ UNDER 10,000

SCALE 1:7,000,000   LAMBERT CONFORMAL CONIC PROJECTION

MILES   0   100   200   300
KILOMETERS   0   100   200   300

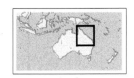

Northeastern Australia

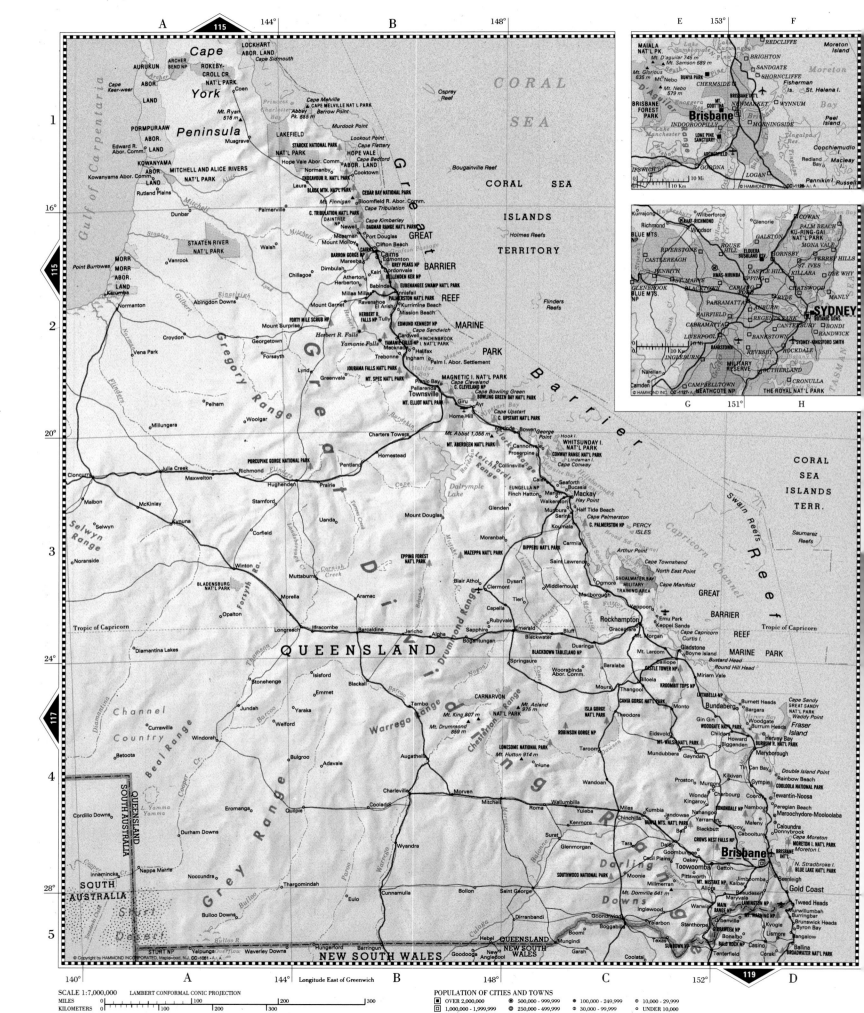

SCALE 1:7,000,000   LAMBERT CONFORMAL CONIC PROJECTION

MILES

KILOMETERS

POPULATION OF CITIES AND TOWNS

■ OVER 2,000,000   ● 500,000 - 999,999   ● 100,000 - 249,999   ○ 10,000 - 29,999

◻ 1,000,000 - 1,999,999   ● 250,000 - 499,999   ● 30,000 - 99,999   ○ UNDER 10,000

© Copyright by HAMMOND INCORPORATED, Maplewood, N.J. CC-1061 - A - A

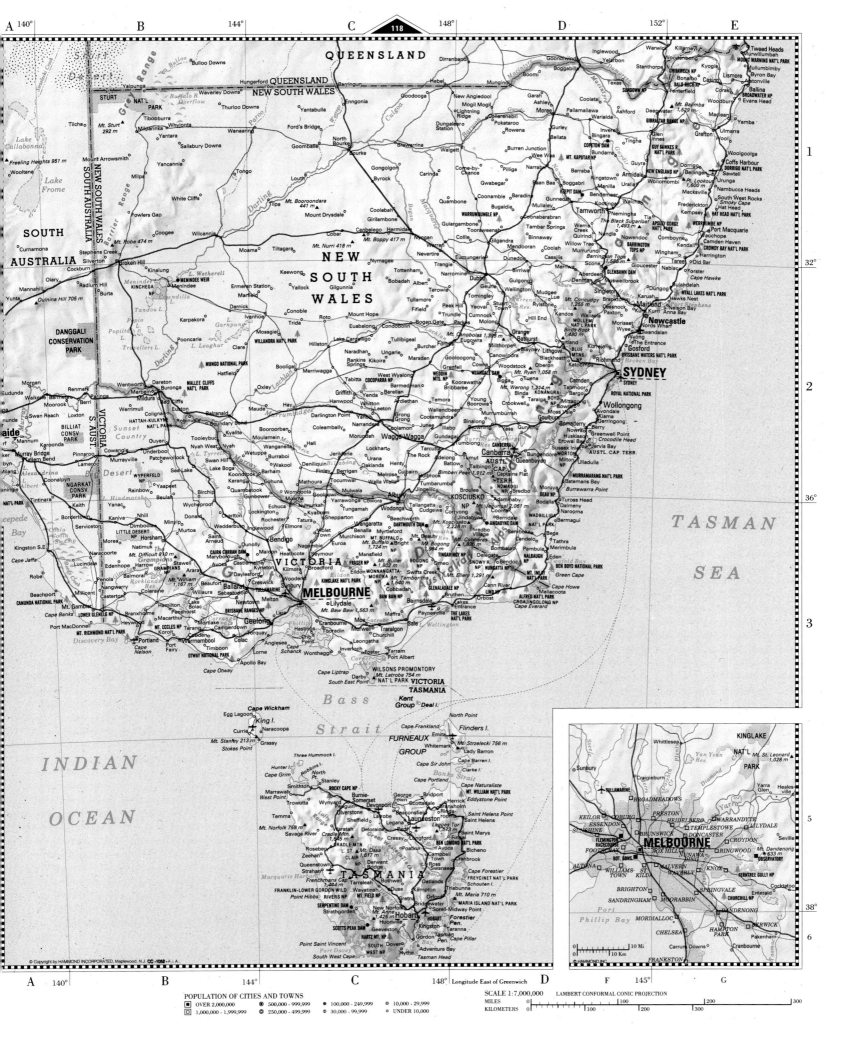

A   110°   120°   B   130°   C   140°   D   150°   E   160°   F   170°   G   180°

CHINA
Xiangtan Changsha Nanchang Jingdezhen Ningbo Tokara Is. Kyūshū
Hengyang Zhuzhou Ji'an Huangang Shan Wenzhou Naze Amami Is. Osumi Is.
Dayun Shan 2,150 m Tori-Shima
1,849 m Ganzhou Fuzhou RYUKYU JAPAN (JAPAN)
Guilin
Guangzhou Tonggu Zhang Xiamen Taipei Ogasawara Mukoshima Is.
1,526 m Zhaozhou BONIN IS. Chichishima Is.
MACAO Victoria Shantou Kaohsiung Taichung Ishigaki Sakishima Is. Daito Is. (JAPAN) Hahashima Is.
(PORT.) HONG KONG Tainan TAIWAN VOLCANO IS. Iwo Jima
(U.K.) Ritaið (JAPAN) Minamiið
Batan Is. Itbayat I. Tropic of Cancer
SOUTH Batan Is. Minami-Tori-Shima
CHINA Calayan I. Okino-Tori-Shima (JAPAN)
Vigan Laoag Babuyan Is. (JAPAN) Farallon de Pajaros
SEA Luzon PHILIPPINE Maug Is. NORTH
Dagupan City Baguio Asuncion
Mt. Pinatubo Cabanatuan City SEA Agrihan
1,759 m Quezon City Pagan NORTHERN Wake I.
Manila Quezon City Alamagan Guguan (U.S.)
Batangas Lucena Cataduanes Anathan Sarigan MARIANAS
Mindoro Legazpi Naga City Saipan Capitol Hill Farallon de Medinilla
PHILIPPINES Aguijan Tinian (U.S.)
Panay Masbate Samar Rota
Palawan Iloilo City Bacolod Leyte Tacloban Agaña Guam(U.S.)
Quezon Cebu City Micronesia
Negros Bohol Colonia Yap Is. Enewetak Bikini Rongerik Bikar
Cagayan de Ulithi Namonuito Utirik Ailuk MARSHALL
Kudat Zamboanga City Oro City Kavangel Babelthuap Faraulep West Hall Is. Ujelang Wotho RATAK ISLANDS
MALAYSIA Basilan Davao City Koror Ngulu Sorol Fayu Pikelot Oroluk Kwajalein Erikub Maloelap
SABAH General Santos Mindanao PALAU Woleai Olimarao Lamotrek Pulap Puluwat Moen Truk Is. Senyavin Is. Ujae Namu
Tawau Talaud Is. (U.S.) Eauripik Ifalik Elato Ant. Kolonia Mokil LAELAP Aur
Sulu Archipelago Sonsorol Is. Satawan CAROLINE ISLANDS Etal Lukunor Pohnpei Pingelap Lelu Namorik Majuro Arno
Tarakan Sangihe Is. Ngatik Kosrae Jaluit Mili
CELEBES Talaud Is. Nukuoro
Borneo SEA Morotai FEDERATED STATES OF MICRONESIA Makin
Kendari Abaiang Butaritari
Samarinda Manado Halmahera Kapingamarangi Tarawa
Palu Gorontalo Ternate Waigeo Tabiang Bairiki Birkenebeu
Celebes Equator Maiana Abemama
Gulf of Tomini Obi Sorong Schouten Is. NAURU Banaba GILBERT Nonouti Nikunau
Molucca Misool Manokwari Ninigo Admiralty St. Matthias Group Kuria Beru Onotoa
Ujung Sea Waigeo Is. Islands Lyra Reef ISLANDS Tabiteuea Tamana
Pandang Celebes Ceram Sea Yapen Is. Manus Lorengau Mussau Utiroa Arorae
Buru Ambon Fakfak Jayapura Vanimo Kavieng New Nuguria Is.
Buru Maoke Mts. Aitape Wewak Hanover Namatanai
INDONESIA Ceram Puncak Jaya New Guinea Karkar I. Madang New Rabaul Nissan I. Tauu Is. Lolua Nanumea
Sula Is. Aru Is. 5,030 m Sepik Mt. Wilhelm Ireland Kimbe Buka Nukumanu Atoll Nanumanga Niutao
Kai Is. Mt. Hagen 4,509 m Soroka Kundiawa Bougainville Ontong Java Nui Vaitupu
Salayar BANDA SEA Goroka New Kieta Nukufetau
Flores Sea Wetar Tanimbar Is. Bulolo Britain Arawa Choiseul Kia Santa Isabel TUVALU
Flores Alor Leti Babar Kolepom Wau PAPUA Trobriand Is. Shortland Is. Gizo Buala Funafuti
Sumbawa Dili Is. Is. Merauke NEW GUINEA D'Entrecasteaux Solomon New Aukia Malaita Niulakita
Sumba Kupang Timor Daru Gulf of Popondetta Is. Sea Georgia Honiara
SAVU SEA Papua Port Moresby Esa'ala Normanby Woodlark I. Kirakira San SANTA Ndende
ARAFURA SEA Alotau Samarai Pocklington Reef Guadalcanal Cristobal CRUZ Reef Is. WALLIS
Timor Torres Strait Louisiade Arch. Rossel Is. Tagula Rennell I. Utupua FUTUNA
Sea C. York SOLOMON Lata Vanikoro (FR.)
Melville I. Cape ISLANDS Torres Is. Rotuma I.
Darwin York Coen CORAL Banks Is. FIJI
Gulf of Peninsula CORAL SEA ISLANDS VANUATU Vanua Levu
Bonaparte Arch. Carpentaria Cooktown TERRITORY SEA Espiritu Santo Oba Maewo Lambasa
Pine Creek (AUSTL.) Tabwemasana Luganville Pentecost Yasawa
Katherine Cairns 1,879 m Norsup Ambrym Group Lautoka
Kimberley Wyndham Great Barrier Malekula Epi Shepherd Is. Nadi Viti Levu
Plateau Daly Waters Normanton NEW HEBRIDES Efate Suva
Broome Halls Creek Townsville Vila Erromango Kadavu
INDIAN Tennant Creek Bowen NEW Tanna Isangel
Port Hedland Camooweal Mackay CALEDONIA Aneityum
Roebourne Marble Bar Cloncurry Hughenden (FR.) Torres
OCEAN Onslow Clermont Rockhampton Chesterfield Koumac Hienghene We
Mt. Bruce Emerald Is. Mont Panié 1,628 m LOYALTY IS.
1,235 m Tropic of Capricorn Alice Springs Boulia Barcaldine Bundaberg Bellona New Koné Bourail Humboldt 1,618 m
Exmouth Longreach Reefs Caledonia Thio ile des Pins
Uluru (Ayers Rock) Gympie Nouméa
AUSTRALIA 867 m Birdsville Charleville Roma Toowoomba Brisbane
Carnarvon Musgrave Ras. Gold Coast
L. Carnegie Cunnamulla Saint Lismore Norfolk I.
Qdnadatta George Grafton Kingston (AUSTL.)
Meekatharra Wiluna Cooper Pedy Marree L. Eyre Moree Armidale Lord Howe I.
Leonora Bourke Tamworth (AUSTL.) Three
Northampton Geraldton Woomera Cobar Dubbo Port Macquarie Kings KERMADEC
Kalgoorlie Broken Hill Orange Is. (N.Z.)
Boulder Port Augusta Newcastle North Cape
Merredin Streaky Bay Whyalla Port Pirie Cootamundra Wollongong Whangarei NEW
Perth Northam Norseman Great Adelaide Wagga Wagga Sydney Auckland Manukau ZEALAND
Australian Port Lincoln Spencer Gulf Murray Bridge Canberra Hamilton Tauranga
Bight Mt. Kosciusko Albury TASMAN SEA Rotorua
2,228 m

INDONESIA   PAPUA NEW GUINEA   CORAL SEA   SOUTH   PACIFIC

Longitude East of Greenwich

A   110°   120°   B   130°   C   140°   D   150°   E   160°   F   170°   G   180°

Central Pacific Ocean

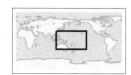

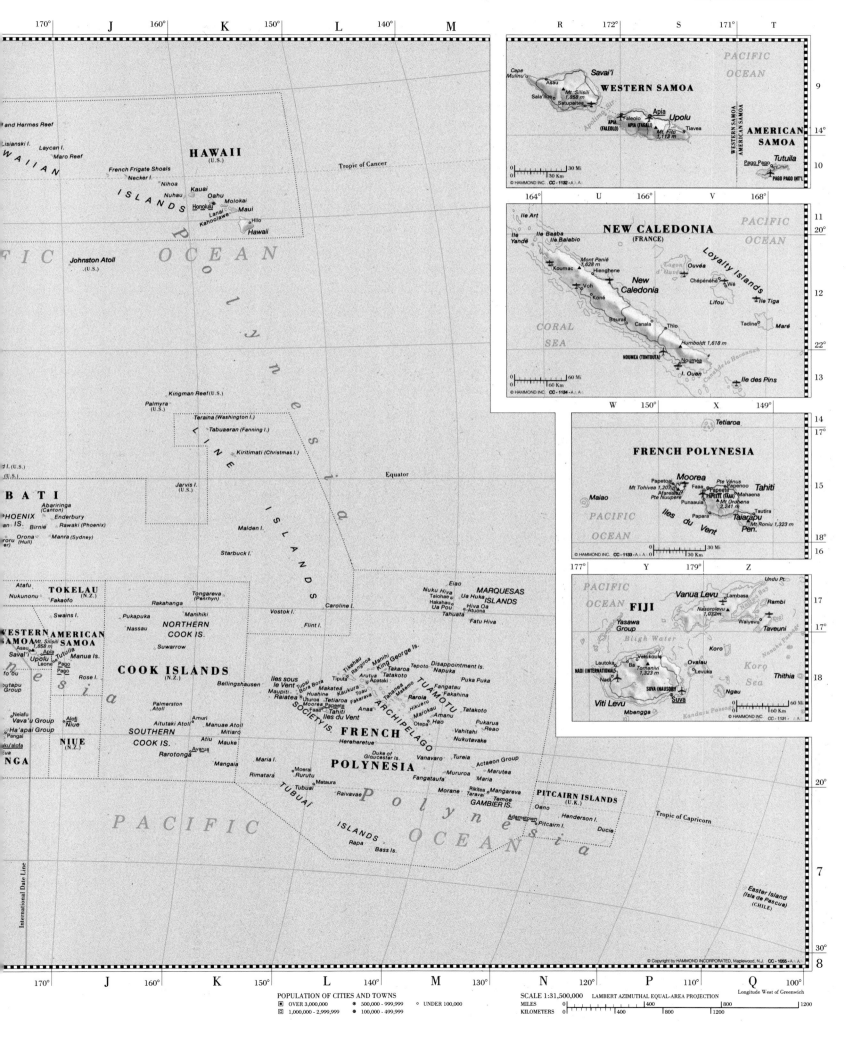

HAWAII (U.S.)

and Hermes Reef
Lisianski I.
Laycan I.
Maro Reef
French Frigate Shoals
Necker I.
Nihoa
Kauai
Nuhau
Oahu
Honolulu
Lanai Molokai
Kahoolawe Maui
Hilo
Hawaii

POLYNESIA

ISLANDS

PACIFIC OCEAN

Tropic of Cancer

Johnston Atoll (U.S.)

Kingman Reef (U.S.)
Palmyra (U.S.)
Teraina (Washington I.)
Tabuaeran (Fanning I.)
Kiritimati (Christmas I.)

LINE ISLANDS

Jarvis I. (U.S.)

Equator

WESTERN SAMOA

Cape Mulinu'u
Asau
Savai'i
Sala'ilua
Mt. Silisili 1,858 m
Setupaitea
Apolima Str.
faleolo
APIA (FALEOLO)
Apia
Upolu
APIA (FASGALI)
Mt. Fito 1,113 m
Tiavea

PACIFIC OCEAN

AMERICAN SAMOA

WESTERN SAMOA / AMERICAN SAMOA

Tutuila
Pago Pago
PAGO PAGO INT'L

© Hammond Inc. CC-1132-A-A-A

NEW CALEDONIA (FRANCE)

Ile Art
Ile
Yandé
Ile Baaba
Ile Balabio
Mont Panié 1,628 m
Koumac
Hienghene
Voh
Koné
New Caledonia
Bourail
Canala
Thio
Humboldt 1,618 m
NOUMEA (TONTOUTA)
Nouméa
I. Ouen
Ile des Pins

Lagon d'Ouvéa
Ouvéa
Chépénéhé
Wé
Lifou
Ile Tiga
Tadine
Maré
Loyalty Islands

CORAL SEA

PACIFIC OCEAN

Canal de la Havannah

© Hammond Inc. CC-1134-A-A-A

FRENCH POLYNESIA

Tetiaroa
Maiao
Papetoai
Moorea
Mt Tohivea 1,207 m
Afareaitu
Pte Nuupere
Papeete
PAPEETE (FAAA)
Faaa
Punaauia
Papara
Pte Vénus
Mahaena
Mt Orohena 2,241 m
Tautira
Tahiti
Taiarapu Pen.
Mt Roniu 1,323 m

Iles du Vent

PACIFIC OCEAN

© HAMMOND INC. CC-1133-A-A-A

FIJI

Undu Pt.
Vanua Levu
Lambasa
Nasorolevu 1,032m
Rambi
Yasawa Group
Walyevu
Taveuni
Bligh Water
Vetokoula
Koro
Lautoka
Ba
NADI (INTERNATIONAL)
Nadi
Ovalau
Levuka
Thithia
Viti Levu
Tomanivi 1,323 m
SUVA (NAUSORI)
Suva
Ngau
Koro Sea
Mbengga
Kandavu Passage

© HAMMOND INC. CC-1131-A-A-A

BATI
Abariringa (Canton)
PHOENIX IS.
Enderbury
Birnie
Rawaki (Phoenix)
Orona (Hull)
Manra (Sydney)

Malden I.

Starbuck I.

Atafu
Nukunonu
Fakaofo
TOKELAU (N.Z.)
Swains I.
Pukapuka
Nassau
Rakahanga
Manihiki
Tongareva (Penrhyn)
NORTHERN COOK IS.
Suwarrow

Vostok I.
Flint I.

Eiao
Nuku Hiva
Taiohae
Hakahau
Ua Pou
Ua Huka
Hiva Oa
Atuona
Tahuata
Fatu Hiva
MARQUESAS ISLANDS

Caroline I.

WESTERN SAMOA
Mt. Silisili 1,858 m
Saval'i
Asau
Apia
Upolu
Pago Pago
Leone
AMERICAN SAMOA
Tutuila
Manua Is.
Rose I.

COOK ISLANDS (N.Z.)
Palmerston Atoll
Amuri
Manuae Atoll
Bellingshausen
Iles sous le Vent
Tubai
Maupiti
Bora Bora
Huahine
Raiatea
Uturoa
Makatea
Tetiaroa
Moorea
Papeete
Tahiti
Faaa
Iles du Vent
SOCIETY IS.
Rangiroa
Tikehau
Manihi
Tiputa
King George Is.
Takaroa
Arutua
Tatakoto
Kaukura
Toau
Apataki
Anaa
Tahanea
Makemo
Raroia
Hikueru
Marokau
Amanu
Hao
Otepa
Nukutavake
Vahitahi

TUAMOTU ARCHIPELAGO

Disappointment Is.
Napuka
Tepoto
Puka Puka
Fangatau
Fakahina
Tatakoto
Pukarua
Reao

Neiafu
Vava'u Group
Alofi
Niue
NIUE (N.Z.)
Ha'apai Group
Pangai
Southern Cook Is.
Aitutaki Atoll
Mitiaro
Atiu
Mauke
Avarua
Rarotonga
Mangaia
Maria I.
Rimatara
Moerai
Rurutu
Mataura
Tubuai
Raivavae
Rapa
Bass Is.
FRENCH POLYNESIA
Hereheretue
Duke of Gloucester Is.
Vanavaro
Tureia
Actaeon Group
Mururoa
Marutea
Maria
Fangataufa
Morane
Rikitea
Mangareva
GAMBIER IS.
Temoe
PITCAIRN ISLANDS (U.K.)
Oeno
Adamstown
Pitcairn I.
Henderson I.
Ducie

Polynesia

TUBUAI ISLANDS

PACIFIC OCEAN

Tropic of Capricorn

Easter Island (Isla de Pascua) (CHILE)

International Date Line

TONGA

POPULATION OF CITIES AND TOWNS

▣ OVER 3,000,000	● 500,000 - 999,999	○ UNDER 100,000
▣ 1,000,000 - 2,999,999	● 100,000 - 499,999	

SCALE 1:31,500,000   LAMBERT AZIMUTHAL EQUAL-AREA PROJECTION

MILES 0 | 400 | 800 | 1200
KILOMETERS 0 | 400 | 800 | 1200

Longitude West of Greenwich

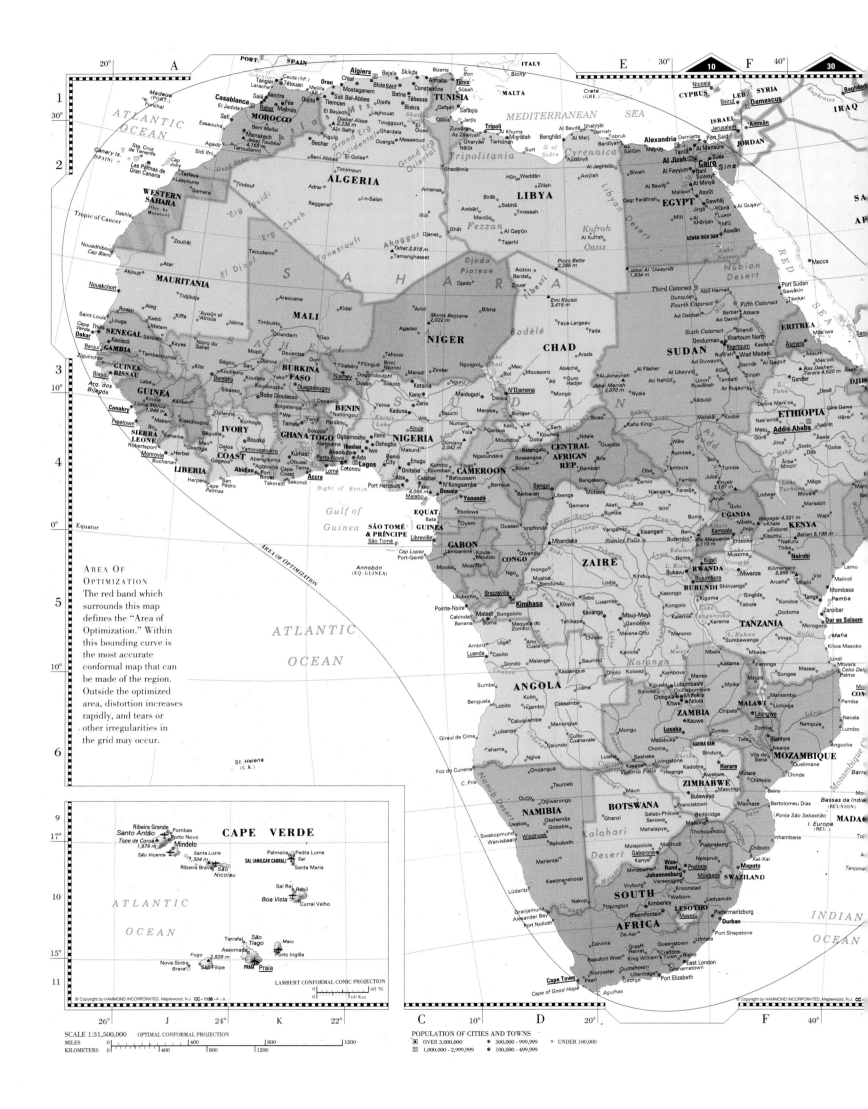

AREA OF
OPTIMIZATION
The red band which
surrounds this map
defines the "Area of
Optimization." Within
this bounding curve is
the most accurate
conformal map that can
be made of the region.
Outside the optimized
area, distortion increases
rapidly, and tears or
other irregularities in
the grid may occur.

CAPE VERDE

LAMBERT CONFORMAL CONIC PROJECTION

© Copyright by HAMMOND INCORPORATED, Maplewood, N.J. CC - 1136 - A - A

SCALE 1:31,500,000   OPTIMAL CONFORMAL PROJECTION

MILES
KILOMETERS

POPULATION OF CITIES AND TOWNS

■ OVER 3,000,000   ● 500,000 - 999,999   ○ UNDER 100,000
▣ 1,000,000 - 2,999,999   ● 100,000 - 499,999

Africa

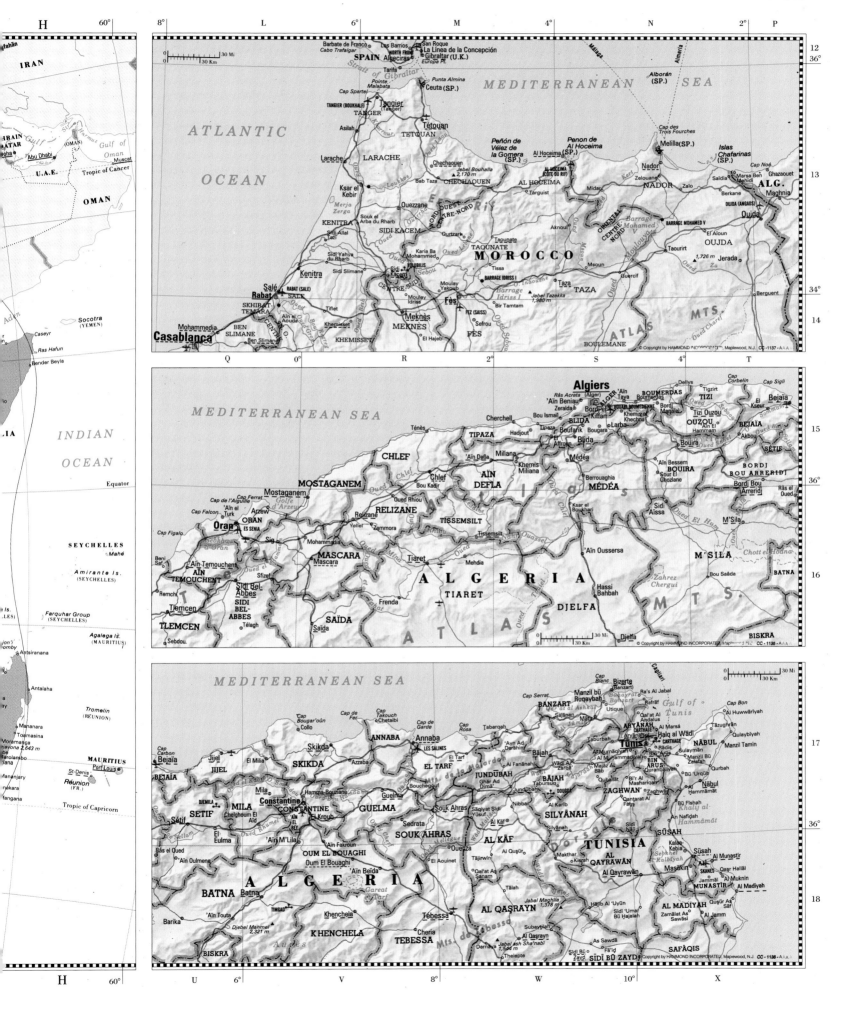

Northern Africa

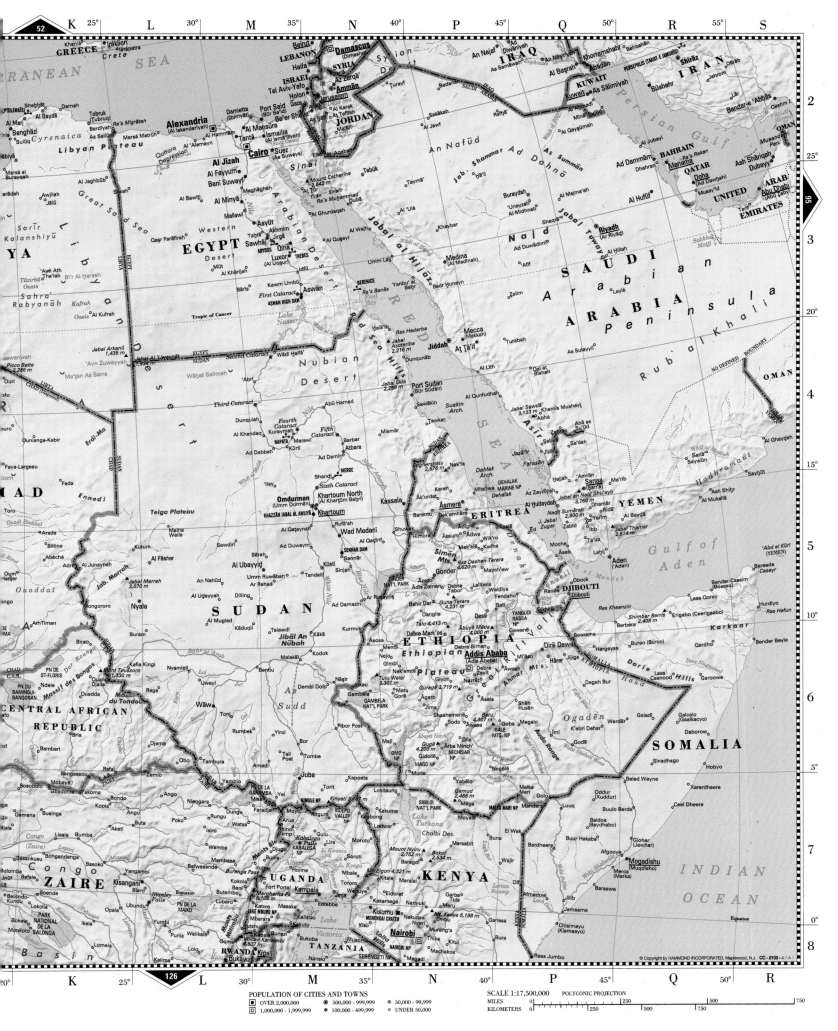

Southern Africa

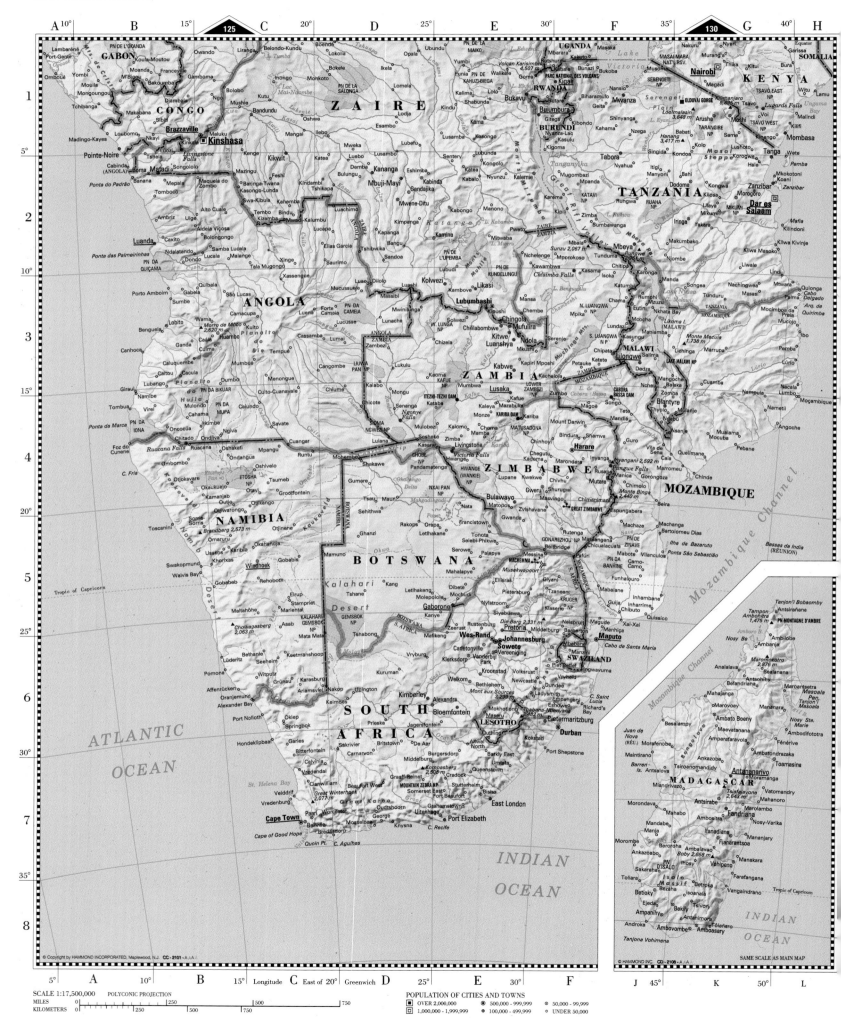

SCALE 1:17,500,000   POLYCONIC PROJECTION

MILES

KILOMETERS

POPULATION OF CITIES AND TOWNS

☐ OVER 2,000,000   ⊡ 500,000 - 999,999   ⊚ 50,000 - 99,999
☐ 1,000,000 - 1,999,999   ⊡ 100,000 - 499,999   ○ UNDER 50,000

Northeastern Africa

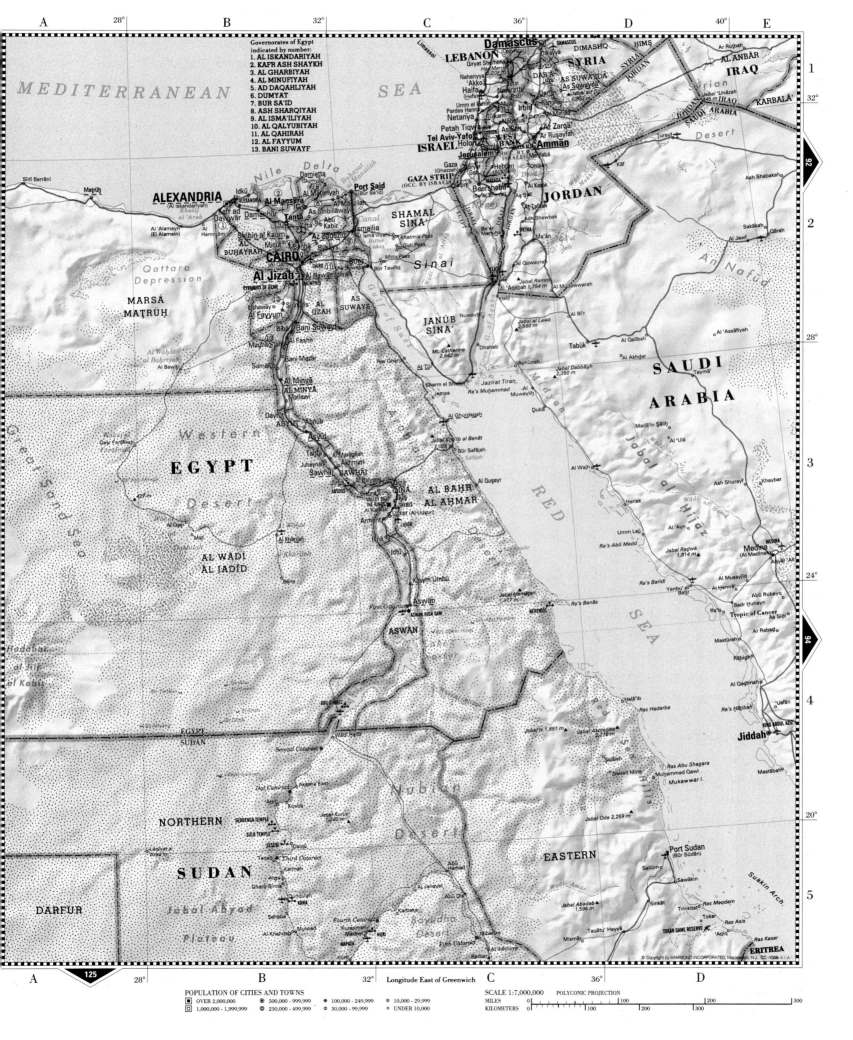

ATLANTIC

OCEAN

MAURITANIA

SENEGAL

GAMBIA

GUINEA-BISSAU

GUINEA

SIERRA LEONE

LIBERIA

IVORY COAST
(CÔTE D'IVOIRE)

SCALE 1:7,000,000   POLYCONIC PROJECTION

MILES   0   100   200   300

KILOMETERS 0   100   200   300

Longitude West of Greenwich

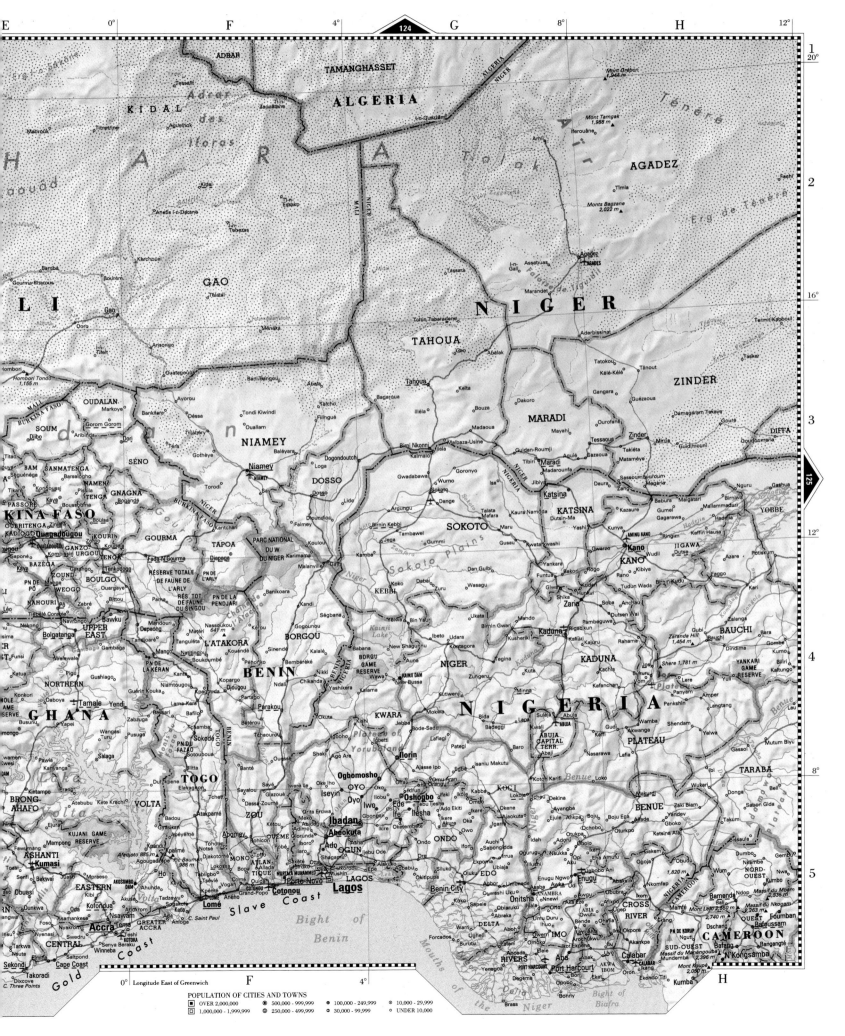

POPULATION OF CITIES AND TOWNS

| ■ OVER 2,000,000 | ⬤ 500,000 - 999,999 | ⬤ 100,000 - 249,999 | ⬤ 10,000 - 29,999 |
| ▣ 1,000,000 - 1,999,999 | ⬤ 250,000 - 499,999 | ⬤ 30,000 - 99,999 | ○ UNDER 10,000 |

Longitude East of Greenwich

East Africa

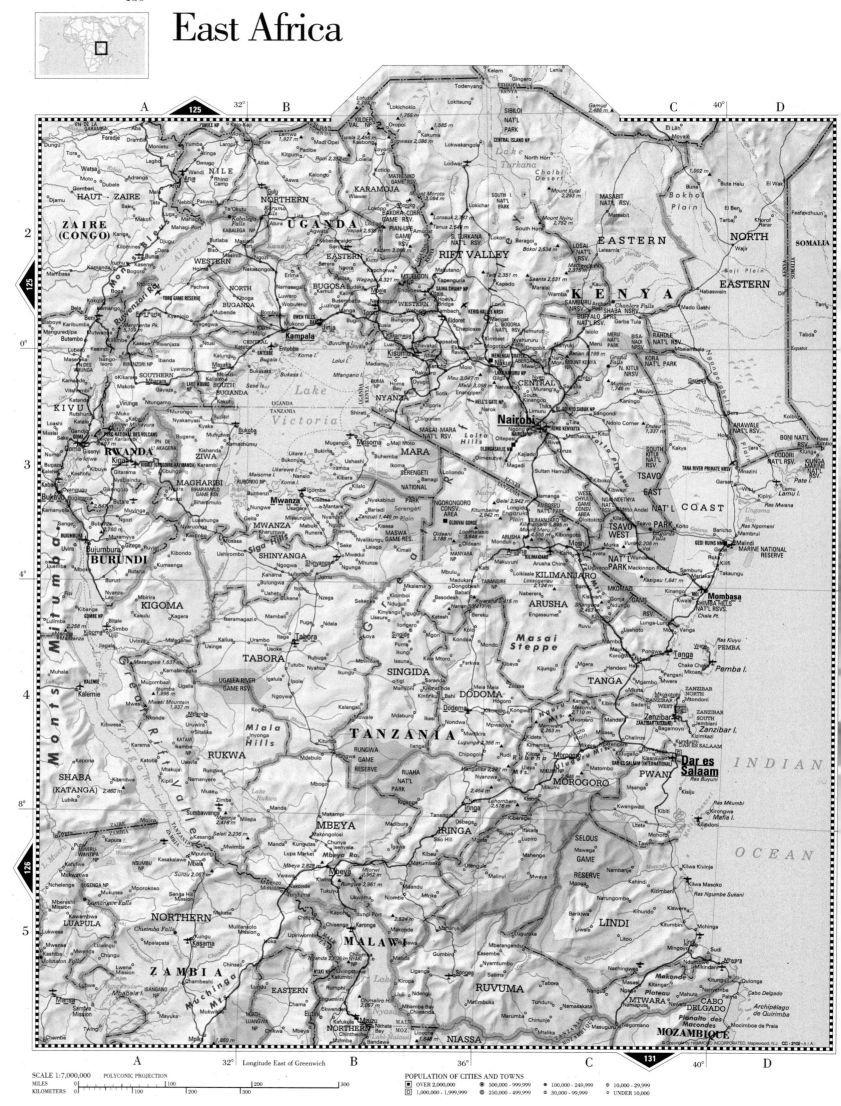

POPULATION OF CITIES AND TOWNS

▣ OVER 2,000,000	◉ 500,000 - 999,999
▢ 1,000,000 - 1,999,999	◉ 250,000 - 499,999

● 100,000 - 249,999	⊙ 10,000 - 29,999
● 30,000 - 99,999	○ UNDER 10,000

Longitude East of Greenwich

South Central Africa

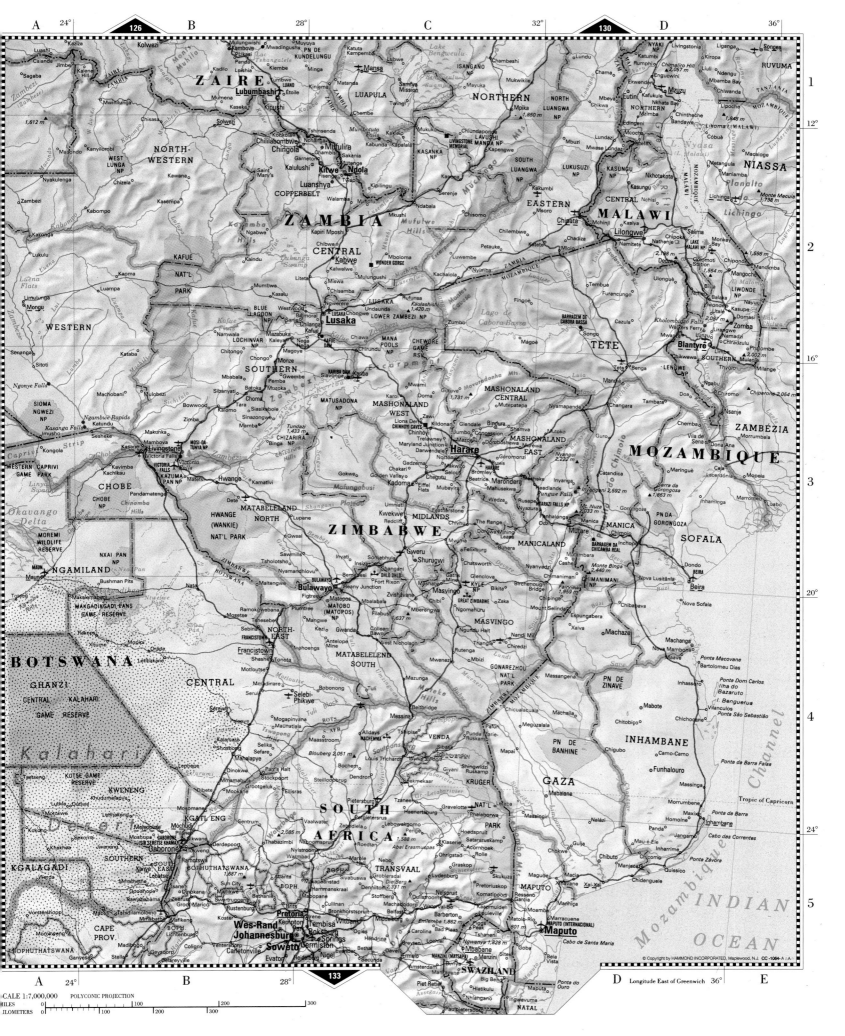

SCALE 1:7,000,000   POLYCONIC PROJECTION

Longitude East of Greenwich 36°

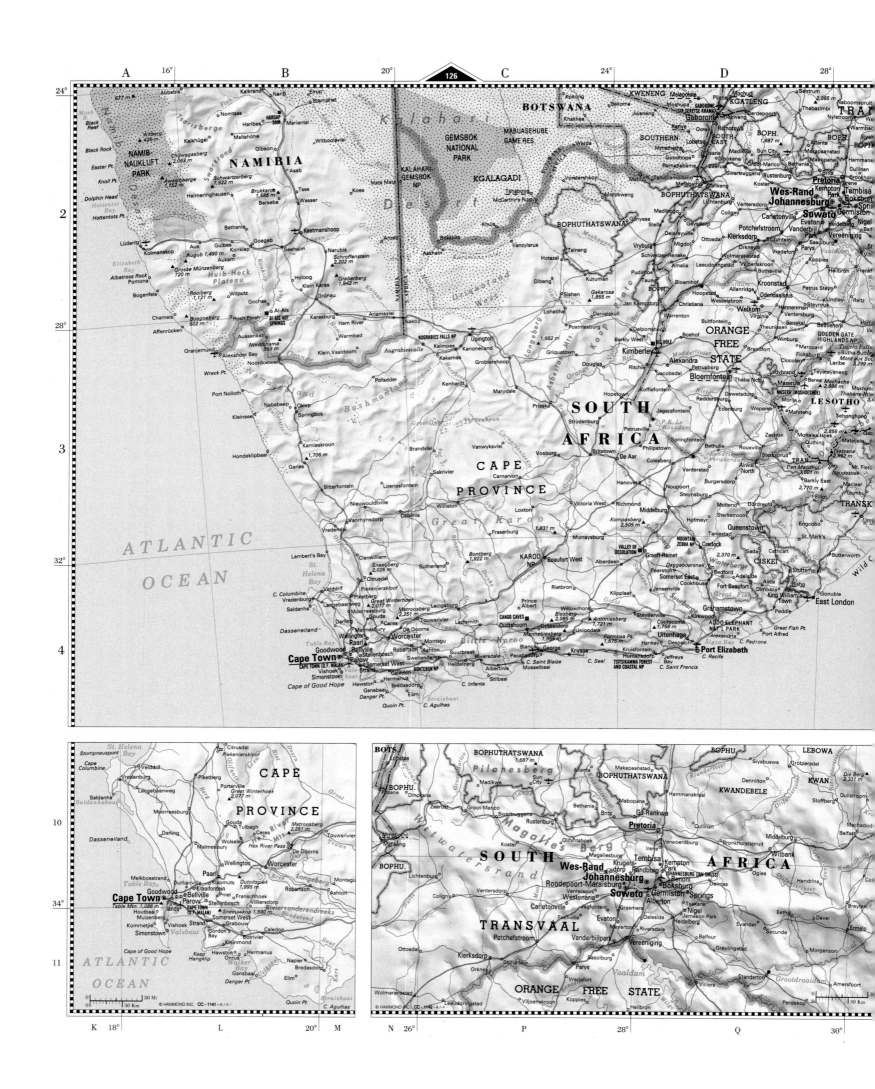

South Africa

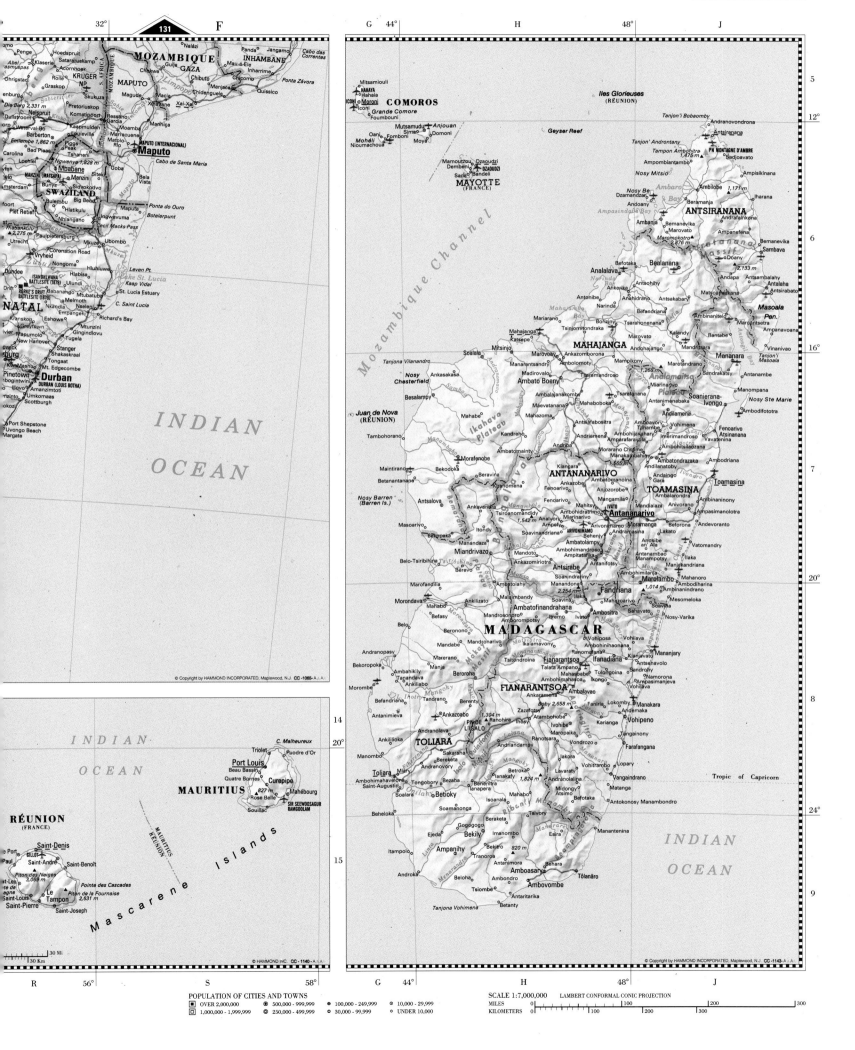

POPULATION OF CITIES AND TOWNS

| ■ OVER 2,000,000 | ● 500,000 - 999,999 | ● 100,000 - 249,999 | ○ 10,000 - 29,999 |
| □ 1,000,000 - 1,999,999 | ● 250,000 - 499,999 | ● 30,000 - 99,999 | ○ UNDER 10,000 |

SCALE 1:7,000,000   LAMBERT CONFORMAL CONIC PROJECTION

MILES 0 — 100 — 200 — 300
KILOMETERS 0 — 100 — 200 — 300

South America

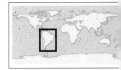

AREA OF OPTIMIZATION

The red band which surrounds this map defines the "Area of Optimization." Within this bounding curve is the most accurate conformal map that can be made of the region. Outside the optimized area, distortion increases rapidly, and tears or other irregularities in the grid may occur.

POPULATION OF CITIES AND TOWNS
- ■ OVER 3,000,000
- ◉ 500,000 - 999,999
- ○ UNDER 100,000
- ▣ 1,000,000 - 2,999,999
- ● 100,000 - 499,999

SCALE 1:28,000,000   OPTIMAL CONFORMAL PROJECTION

MILES   0   400   800   1200
KILOMETERS   0   400   800   1200

© Copyright by HAMMOND INCORPORATED, Maplewood, N.J. CC-1069 - A-A

Southern South America

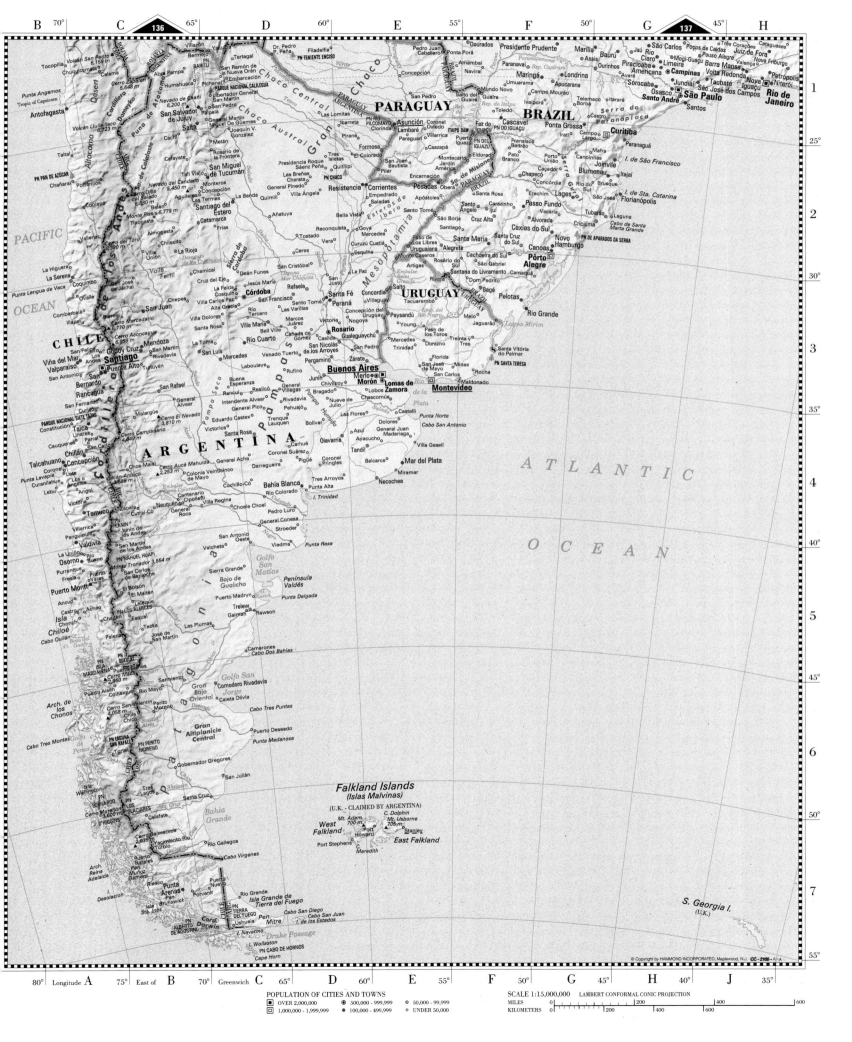

POPULATION OF CITIES AND TOWNS

- ■ OVER 2,000,000
- ◉ 500,000 - 999,999
- ○ 50,000 - 99,999
- ▣ 1,000,000 - 1,999,999
- ● 100,000 - 499,999
- ∘ UNDER 50,000

SCALE 1:15,000,000   LAMBERT CONFORMAL CONIC PROJECTION

MILES 0 — 200 — 400 — 600

KILOMETERS 0 — 200 — 400 — 600

Northern South America

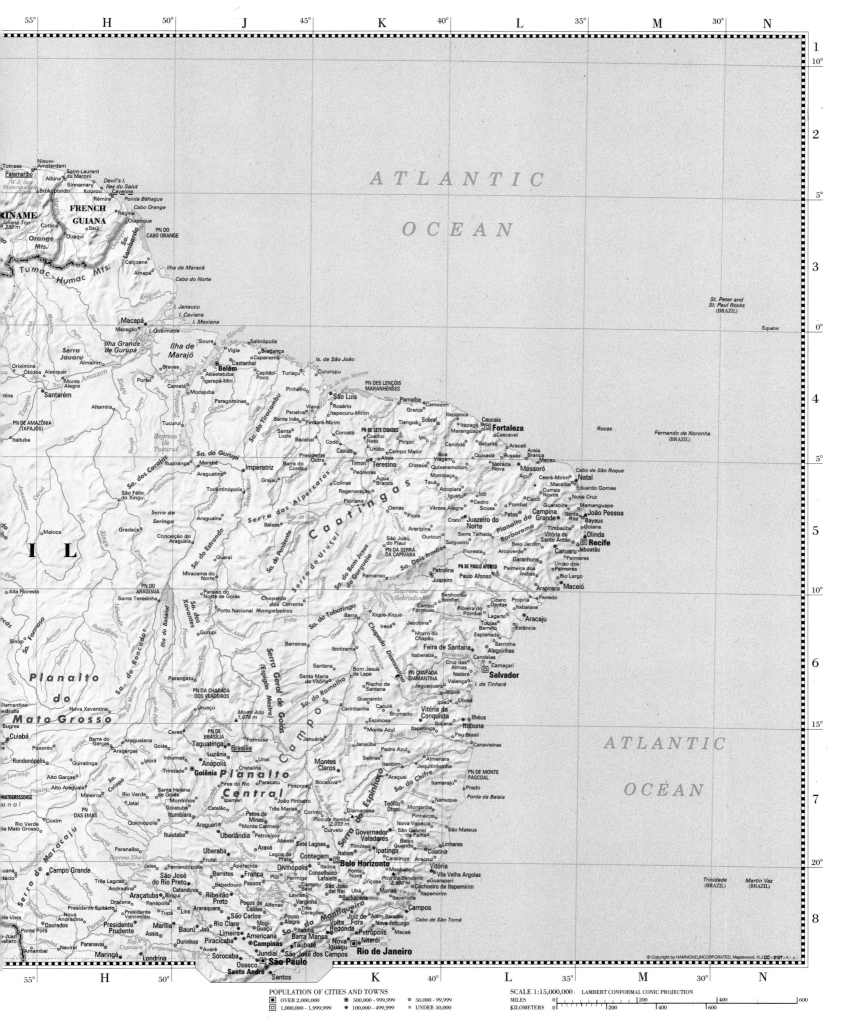

ATLANTIC

OCEAN

ATLANTIC

OCEAN

Equator

**FRENCH
GUIANA**

SURINAME

Orange
Mts.

Tumac-Humac Mts.

PN DO
CABO ORANGE

St. Peter and
St. Paul Rocks
(BRAZIL)

Rocas

Fernando de Noronha
(BRAZIL)

Serra
Javaru

Ilha Grande
de Gurupá

Ilha de
Marajó

Belém

Santarém

Amazon

PN DE AMAZÔNIA
(TAPAJÓS)

Serra dos Caraiós

Serra do Gurupi

Imperatriz

São Luís

Teresina

Fortaleza

Caatingas

Natal

Mossoró

João Pessoa

Recife

Maceió

Planalto
do
Mato Grosso

Campos

Planalto
Central

Brasília

Goiânia

Salvador

Feira de Santana

Vitória da
Conquista

Ilhéus

Montes
Claros

PN DE MONTE
PASCOAL

Trinidade
(BRAZIL)

Martin Vaz
(BRAZIL)

Belo Horizonte

Vitória

Campos

Campo Grande

Rio de Janeiro

Niterói

São Paulo

Santo André

Osasco

Santos

Londrina

I L

POPULATION OF CITIES AND TOWNS

■	OVER 2,000,000	◉	500,000 - 999,999	•	50,000 - 99,999
◻	1,000,000 - 1,999,999	●	100,000 - 499,999	○	UNDER 50,000

SCALE 1:15,000,000 · LAMBERT CONFORMAL CONIC PROJECTION

MILES   0   200   400   600
KILOMETERS   0   200   400   600

© Copyright by HAMMOND, INCORPORATED, Maplewood, N.J. CC-2107·A·A

Colombia, Venezuela, Ecuador

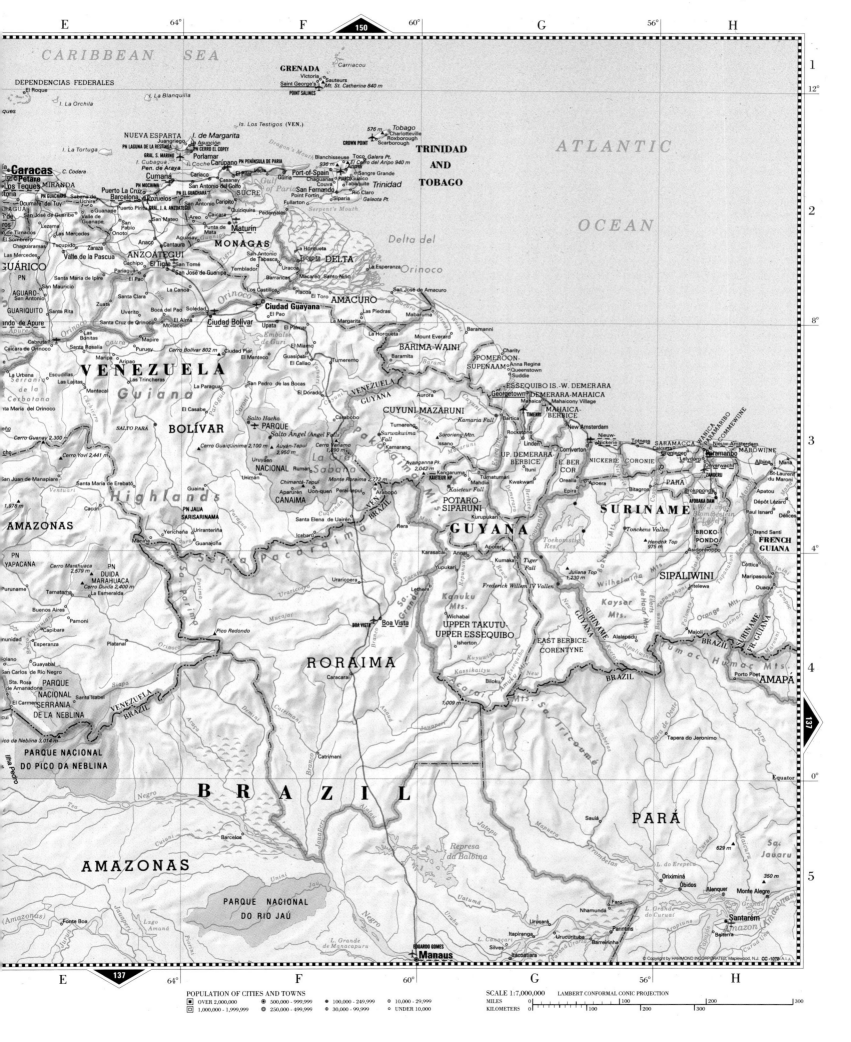

CARIBBEAN SEA

ATLANTIC

OCEAN

GRENADA
Victoria
Saint George's
POINT SALINES

NUEVA ESPARTA

Caracas

VENEZUELA

BOLÍVAR

AMAZONAS

Highlands

TRINIDAD AND TOBAGO

MONAGAS

ANZOÁTEGUI

GUÁRICO

DELTA

AMACURO

BARIMA-WAINI

POMEROON-SUPENAAM

ESSEQUIBO IS.-W. DEMERARA

DEMERARA-MAHAICA

MAHAICA-BERBICE

CUYUNI-MAZARUNI

GUYANA

POTARO-SIPARUNI

UP. DEMERARA-BERBICE

E. BER. COR.

SURINAME

FRENCH GUIANA

SIPALIWINI

RORAIMA

UPPER TAKUTU-UPPER ESSEQUIBO

EAST BERBICE-CORENTYNE

BRAZIL

AMAPÁ

PARÁ

AMAZONAS

PARQUE NACIONAL DO RIO JAÚ

PARQUE NACIONAL DO PICO DA NEBLINA

Manaus

Equator

© Copyright by HAMMOND INCORPORATED, Maplewood, N.J.

Northeastern Brazil

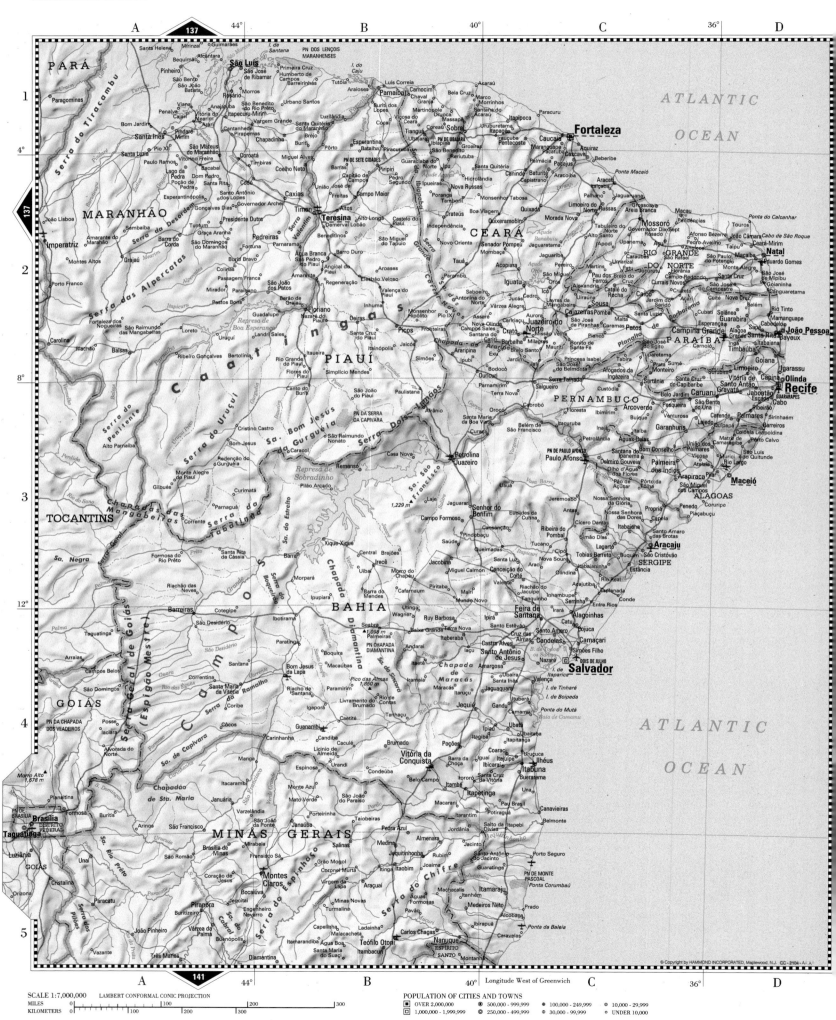

Longitude West of Greenwich

SCALE 1:7,000,000   LAMBERT CONFORMAL CONIC PROJECTION

MILES 0 ___ 100 ___ 200 ___ 300

KILOMETERS 0 ___ 100 ___ 200 ___ 300

POPULATION OF CITIES AND TOWNS
- ■ OVER 2,000,000
- ◉ 500,000 - 999,999
- ● 100,000 - 249,999
- ⊙ 10,000 - 29,999
- ▣ 1,000,000 - 1,999,999
- ◎ 250,000 - 499,999
- • 30,000 - 99,999
- ○ UNDER 10,000

Southeastern Brazil

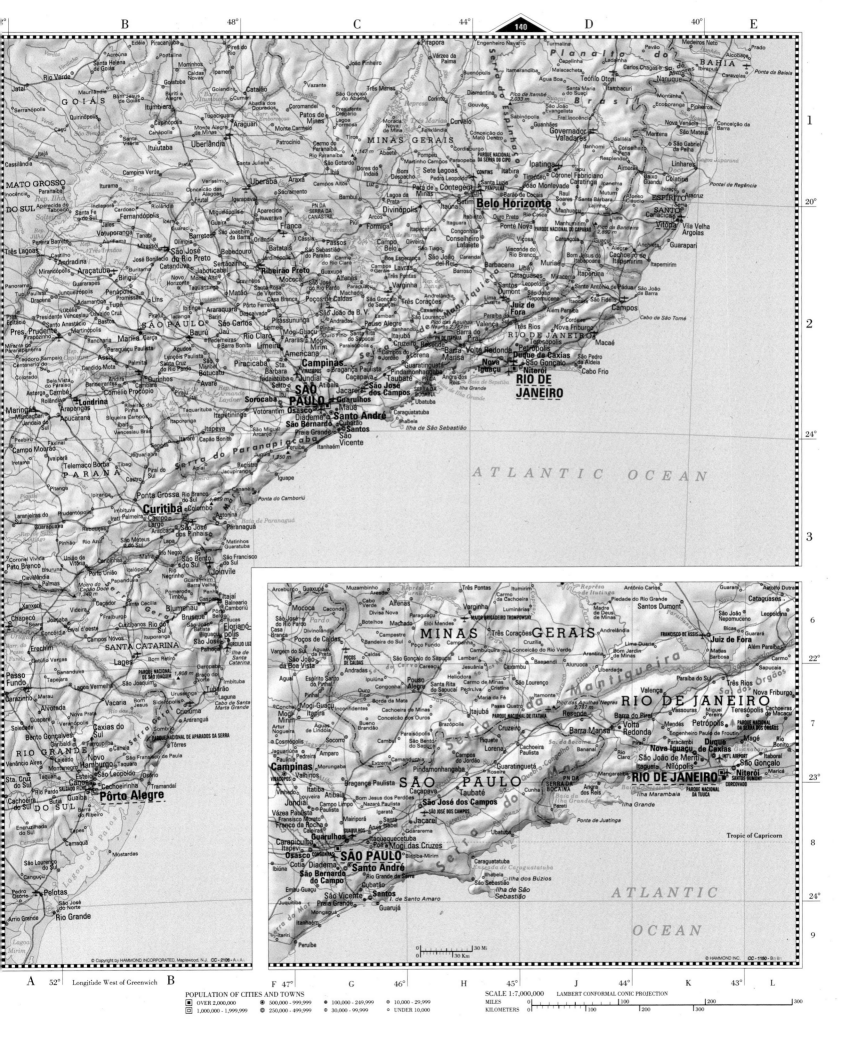

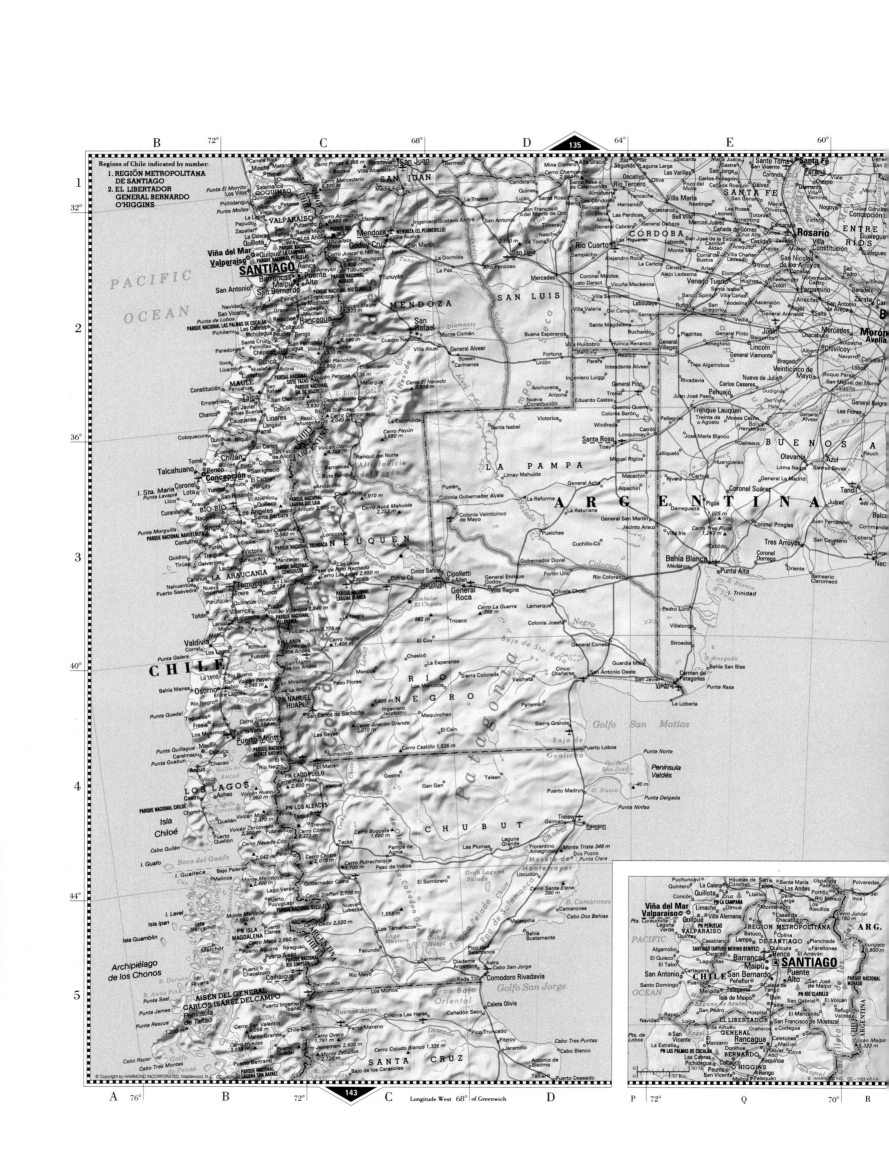

Southern Chile and Argentina

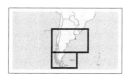

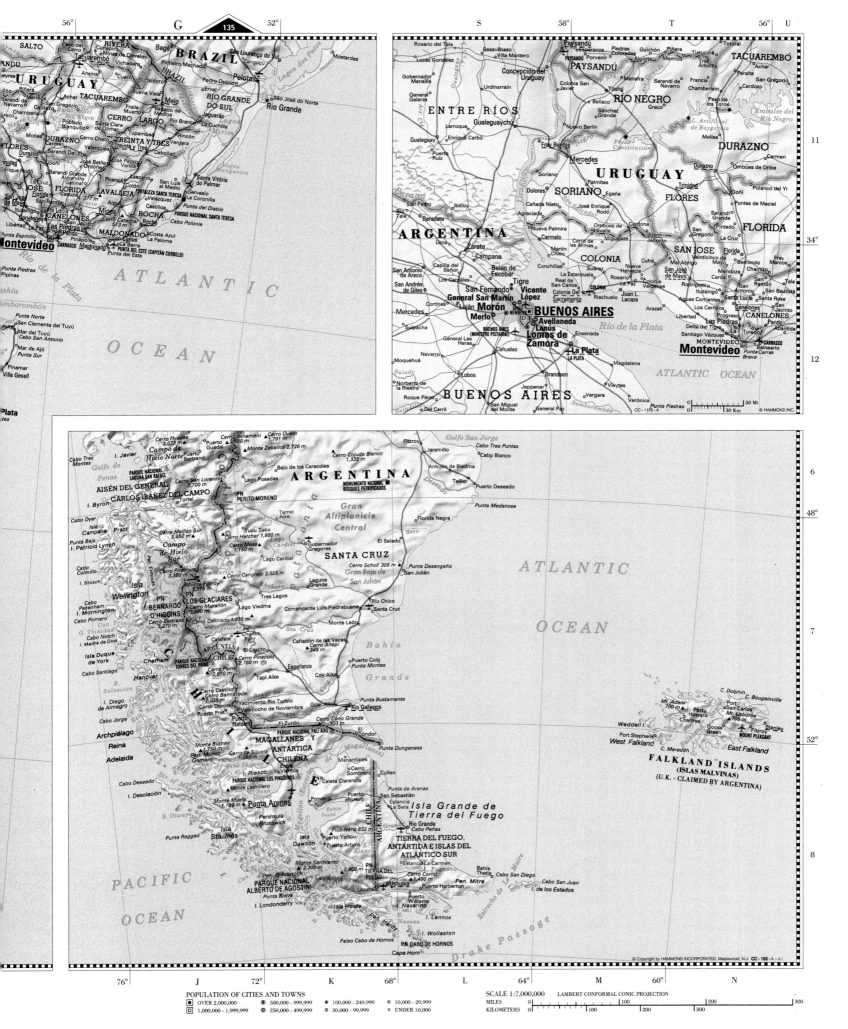

POPULATION OF CITIES AND TOWNS

- ■ OVER 2,000,000
- ◉ 500,000 - 999,999
- ⊕ 100,000 - 249,999
- ○ 10,000 - 29,999
- ▣ 1,000,000 - 1,999,999
- ◎ 250,000 - 499,999
- ⊙ 30,000 - 99,999
- ○ UNDER 10,000

SCALE 1:7,000,000   LAMBERT CONFORMAL CONIC PROJECTION

MILES   0   100   200   300

KILOMETERS   0   100   200   300

© Copyright by HAMMOND INCORPORATED, Maplewood, N.J.   CC-153

Peru

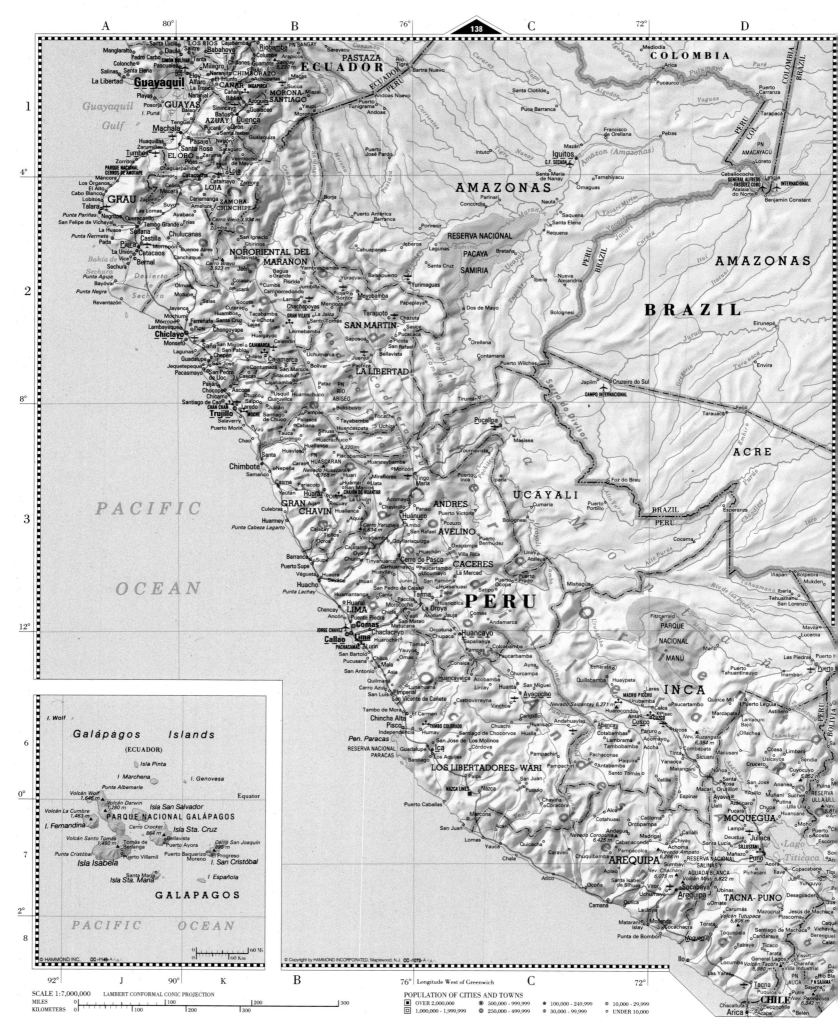

PACIFIC OCEAN

Galápagos Islands
(ECUADOR)

PARQUE NACIONAL GALÁPAGOS

GALAPAGOS

PACIFIC OCEAN

SCALE 1:7,000,000   LAMBERT CONFORMAL CONIC PROJECTION

MILES   0   100   200   300
KILOMETERS   0   100   200   300

Longitude West of Greenwich

POPULATION OF CITIES AND TOWNS

■ OVER 2,000,000	■ 500,000 - 999,999	● 100,000 - 249,999	● 10,000 - 29,999
◨ 1,000,000 - 1,999,999	◨ 250,000 - 499,999	● 30,000 - 99,999	○ UNDER 10,000

© Copyright by HAMMOND INCORPORATED, Maplewood, N.J.

North America

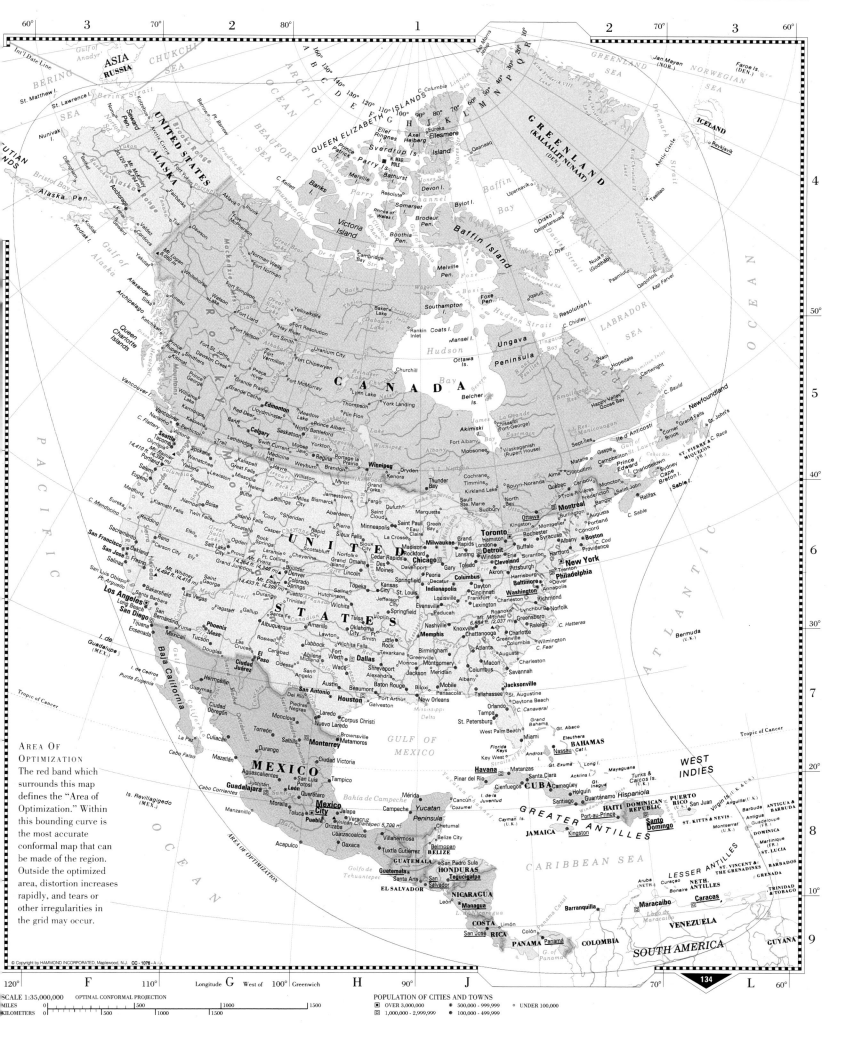

AREA OF OPTIMIZATION

The red band which surrounds this map defines the "Area of Optimization." Within this bounding curve is the most accurate conformal map that can be made of the region. Outside the optimized area, distortion increases rapidly, and tears or other irregularities in the grid may occur.

SCALE 1:35,000,000   OPTIMAL CONFORMAL PROJECTION

120°   F   110°   Longitude G West of 100° Greenwich   H   90°   J   70°   L   60°

MILES   0   500   1000   1500
KILOMETERS   0   500   1000   1500

POPULATION OF CITIES AND TOWNS

▣ OVER 3,000,000	● 500,000 - 999,999	○ UNDER 100,000
⊡ 1,000,000 - 2,999,999	● 100,000 - 499,999	

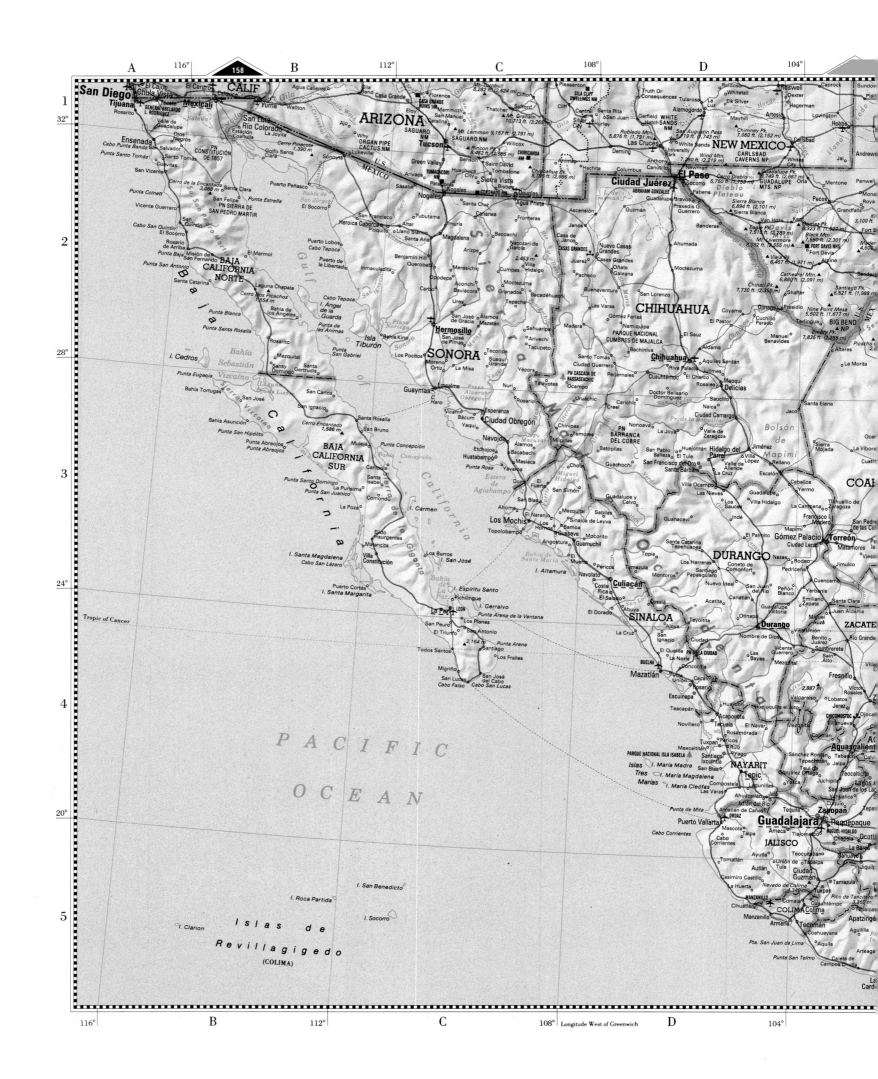

Northern and Central Mexico

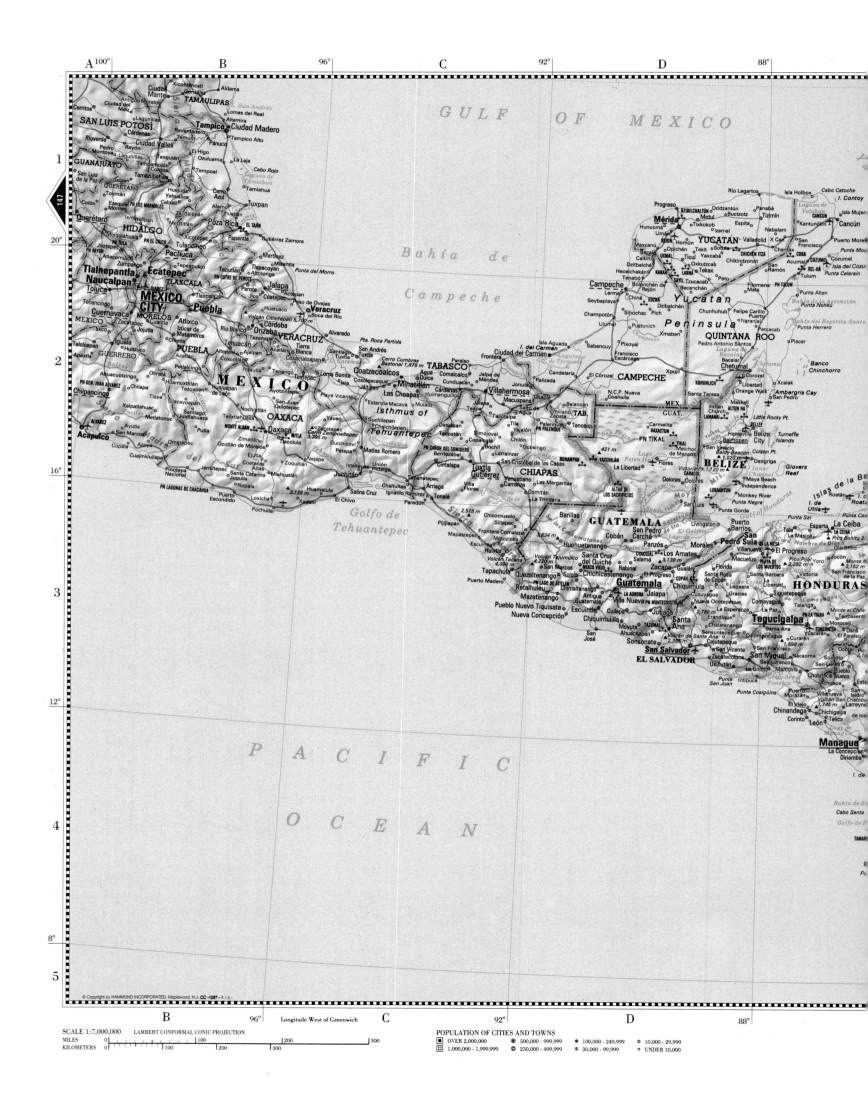

A 100°   B   96°   C   92°   D   88°

GULF OF MEXICO

Bahía de

Campeche

PACIFIC

OCEAN

Golfo de
Tehuantepec

MEXICO

GUATEMALA

HONDURAS

BELIZE

EL SALVADOR

Managua

SCALE 1:7,000,000   LAMBERT CONFORMAL CONIC PROJECTION

MILES 0   100   200   300
KILOMETERS 0   100   200   300

POPULATION OF CITIES AND TOWNS

■ OVER 2,000,000   ◉ 500,000 - 999,999   ● 100,000 - 249,999   ◦ 10,000 - 29,999
▫ 1,000,000 - 1,999,999   ◎ 250,000 - 499,999   • 30,000 - 99,999   ○ UNDER 10,000

Southern Mexico, Central America, Western Caribbean

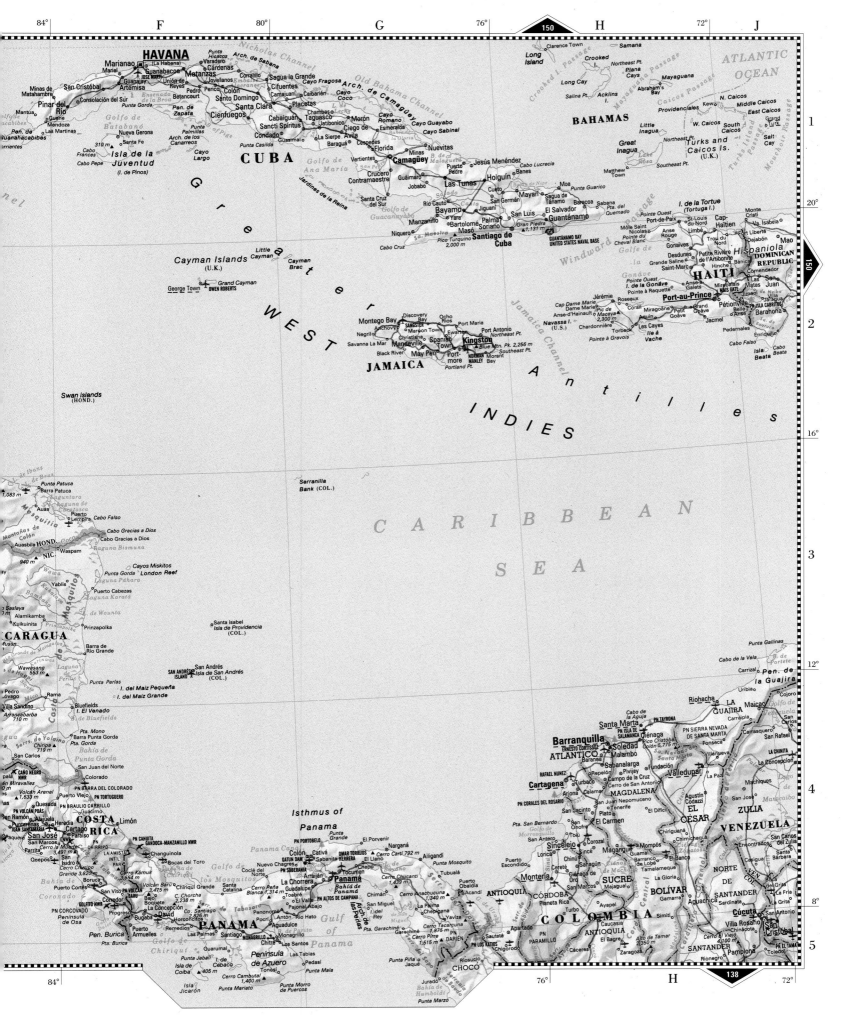

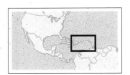

Eastern Caribbean, Bahamas

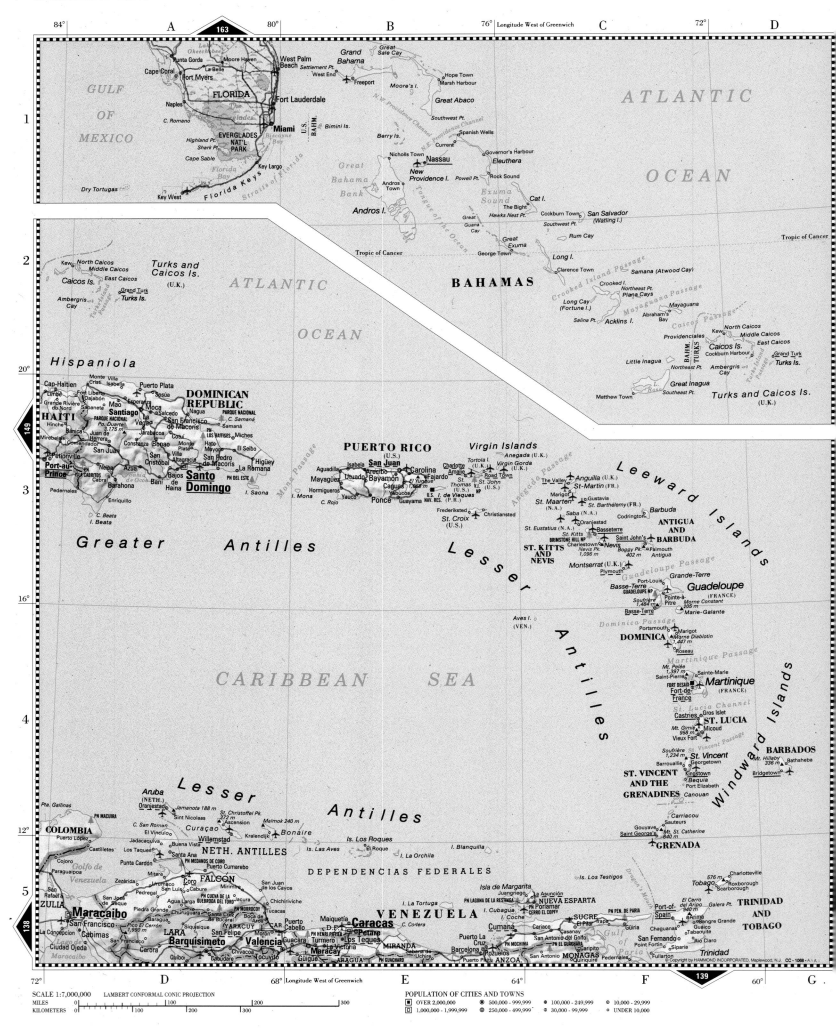

SCALE 1:7,000,000   LAMBERT CONFORMAL CONIC PROJECTION

MILES 0   100   200   300

KILOMETERS 0   100   200   300

POPULATION OF CITIES AND TOWNS

| ■ OVER 2,000,000 | ● 500,000 - 999,999 | • 100,000 - 249,999 | ◦ 10,000 - 29,999 |
| □ 1,000,000 - 1,999,999 | ◉ 250,000 - 499,999 | • 30,000 - 99,999 | ◦ UNDER 10,000 |

Alaska

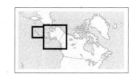

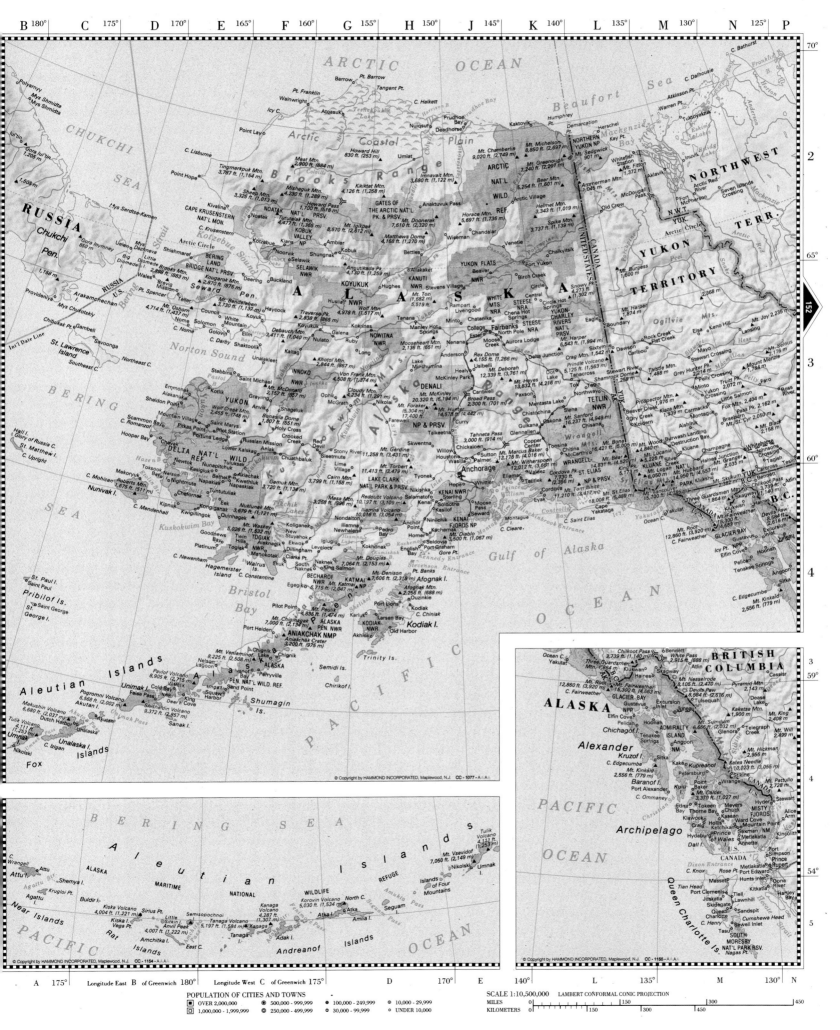

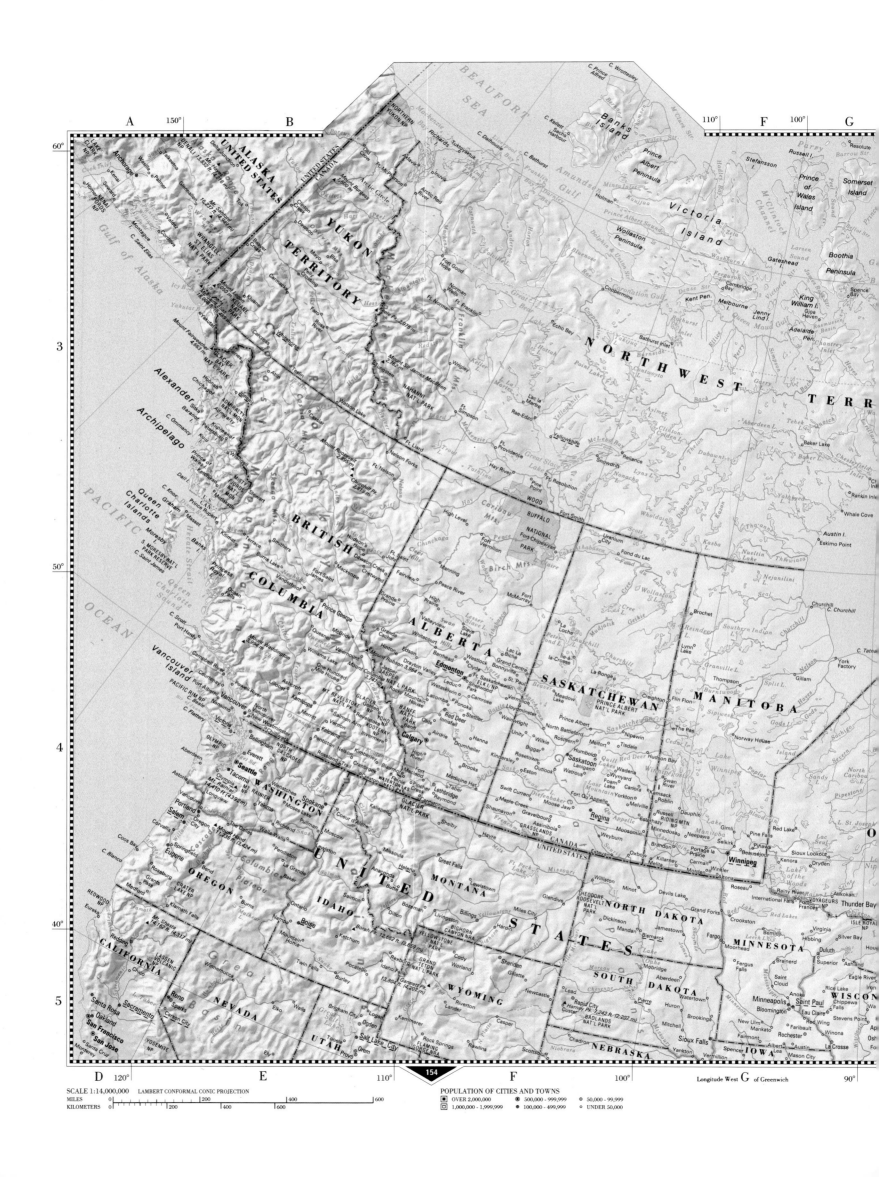

SCALE 1:14,000,000   LAMBERT CONFORMAL CONIC PROJECTION

MILES   0   200   400   600
KILOMETERS 0   200   400   600

POPULATION OF CITIES AND TOWNS

▪ OVER 2,000,000   ● 500,000 - 999,999   ∘ 50,000 - 99,999
□ 1,000,000 - 1,999,999   ⊙ 100,000 - 499,999   ∙ UNDER 50,000

Longitude West **G** of Greenwich

Canada

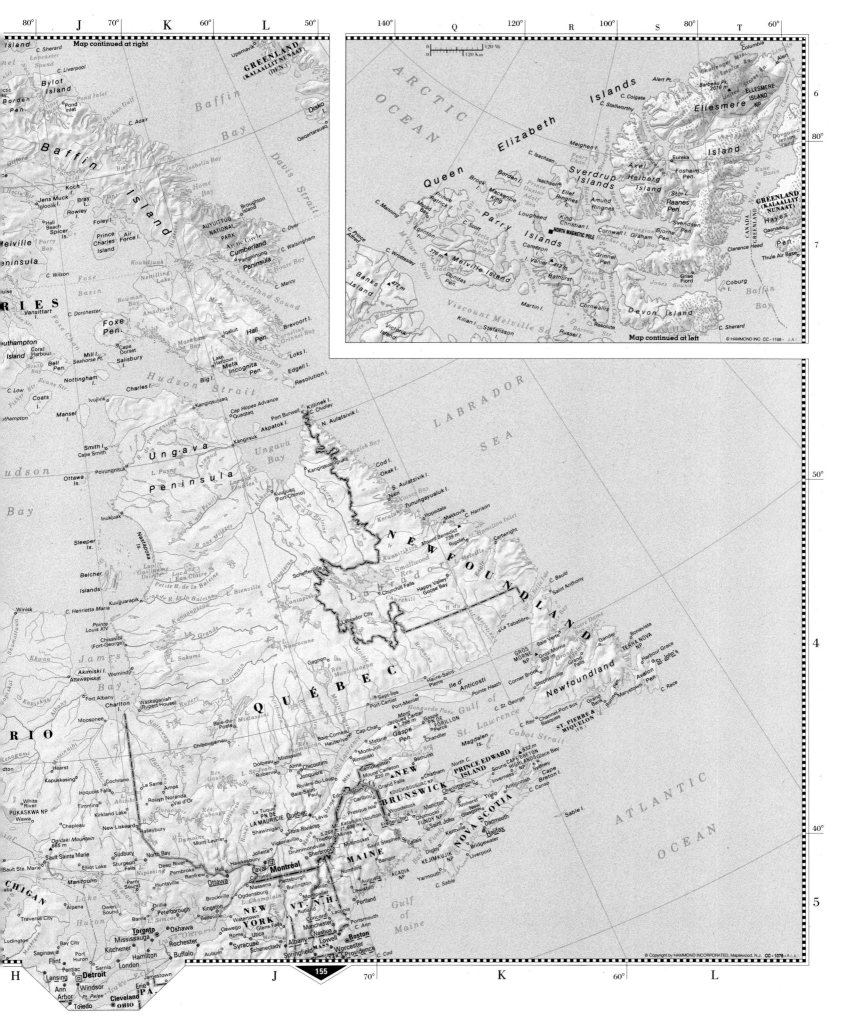

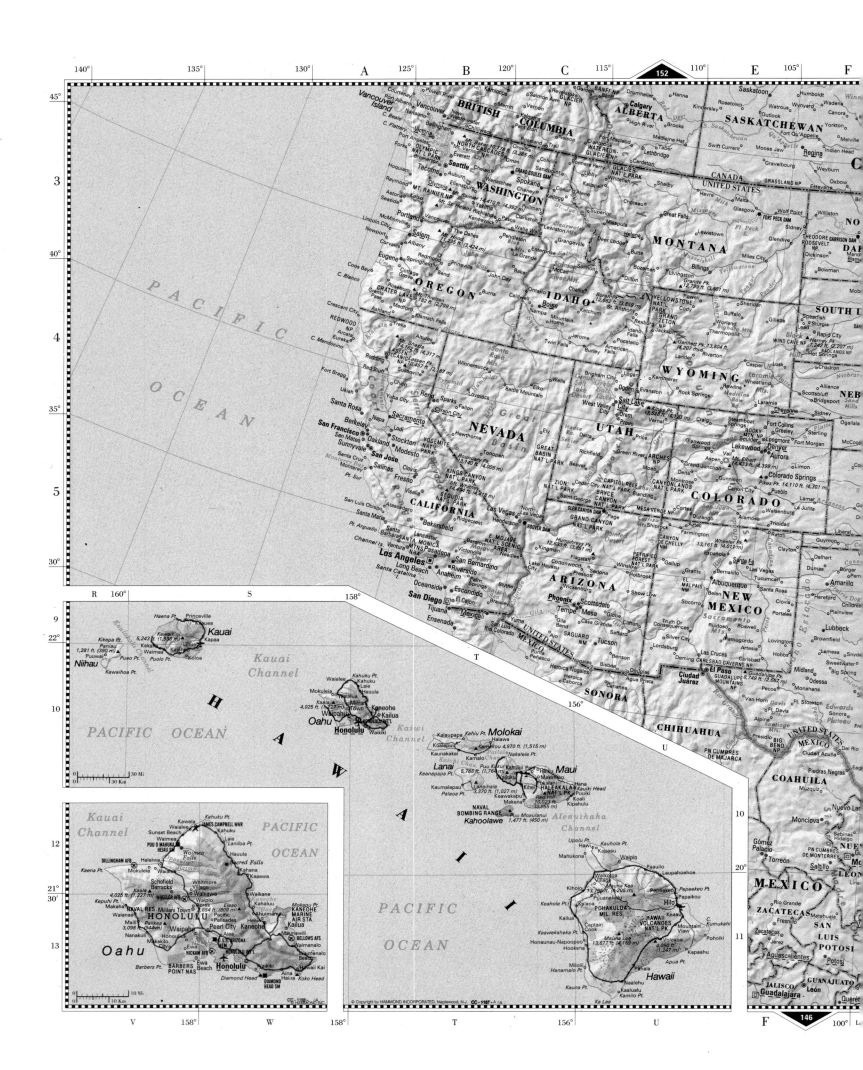

PACIFIC

OCEAN

BRITISH
COLUMBIA

ALBERTA

SASKATCHEWAN

CANADA
UNITED STATES

WASHINGTON

MONTANA

OREGON

IDAHO

WYOMING

NEVADA

UTAH

COLORADO

CALIFORNIA

Los Angeles

San Diego

ARIZONA

NEW
MEXICO

SONORA

CHIHUAHUA

COAHUILA

MEXICO

PACIFIC OCEAN

Kauai Channel

Kauai

Niihau

Oahu

Honolulu

HAWAII

Molokai

Lanai

Maui

Kahoolawe

Hawaii

Hilo

HAWAII VOLCANOES NAT'L PK

Kauai Channel

PACIFIC
OCEAN

HONOLULU

Oahu

Pearl City

Waipahu

Honolulu

Diamond Head

© Copyright by HAMMOND INCORPORATED, Maplewood, N.J. CC-1157-A

United States

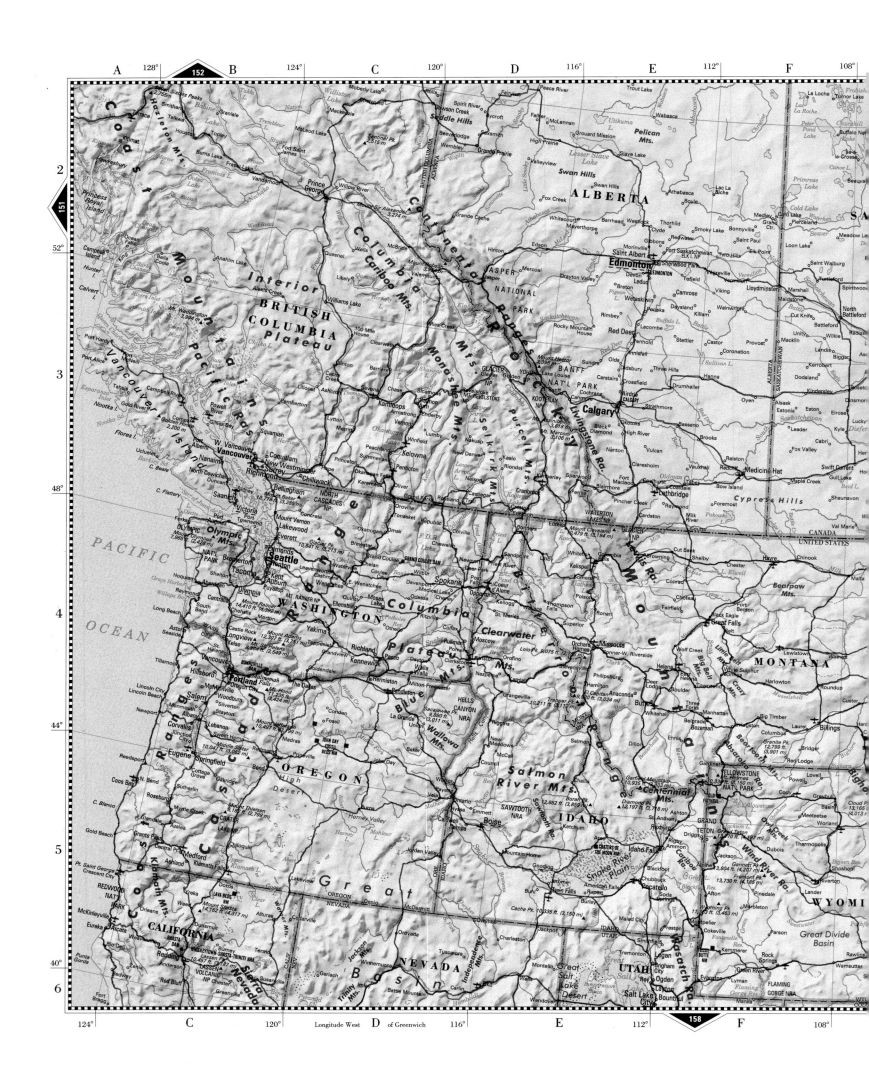

Southwestern Canada, Northwestern United States

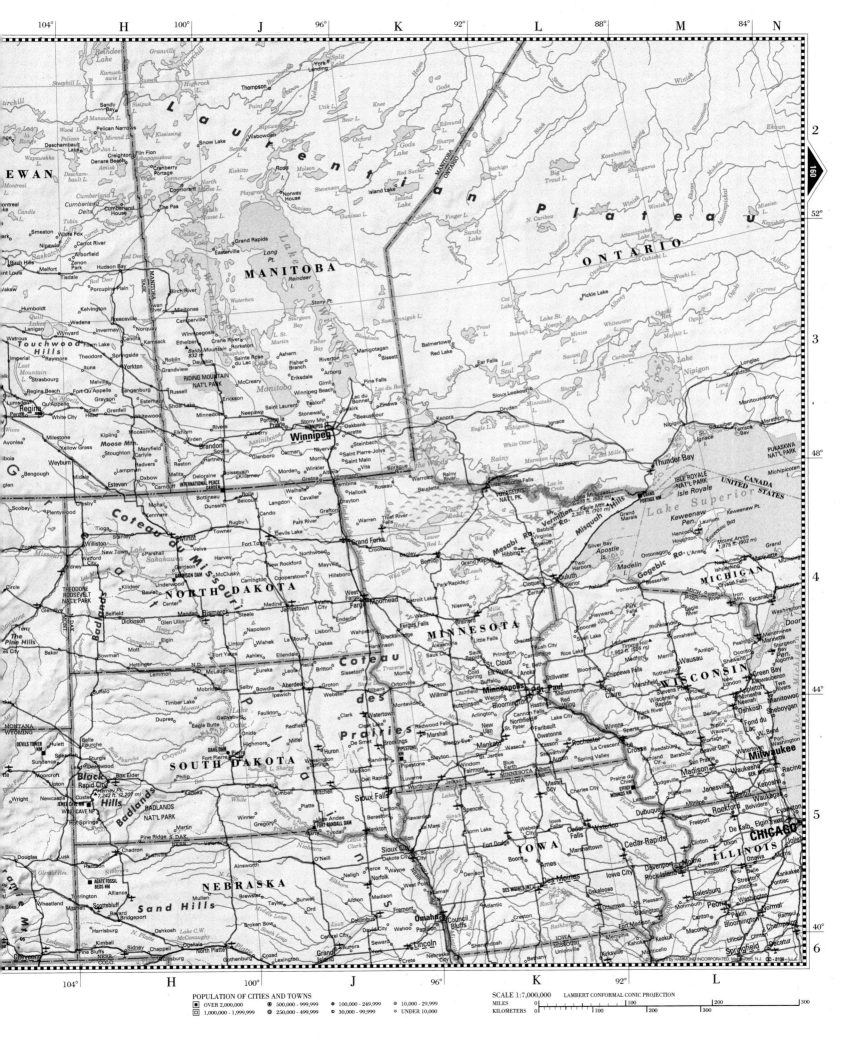

PACIFIC

OCEAN

Southwestern United States

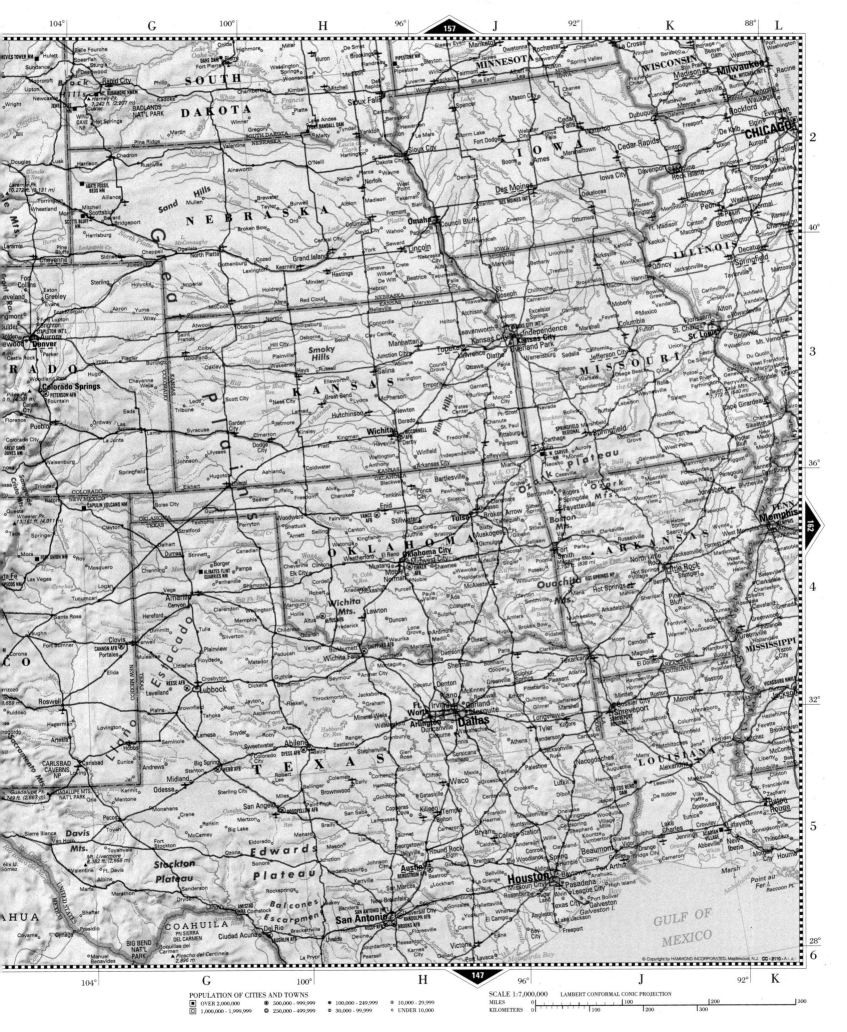

POPULATION OF CITIES AND TOWNS

■ OVER 2,000,000	◉ 500,000 - 999,999
▣ 1,000,000 - 1,999,999	◎ 250,000 - 499,999

● 100,000 - 249,999   ⊕ 10,000 - 29,999
● 30,000 - 99,999   ○ UNDER 10,000

SCALE 1:7,000,000   LAMBERT CONFORMAL CONIC PROJECTION

MILES   0   100   200   300

KILOMETERS   0   100   200   300

© Copyright by HAMMOND INCORPORATED, Maplewood, N.J.   CC - 2110 - A - A

Southeastern Canada, Northeastern United States

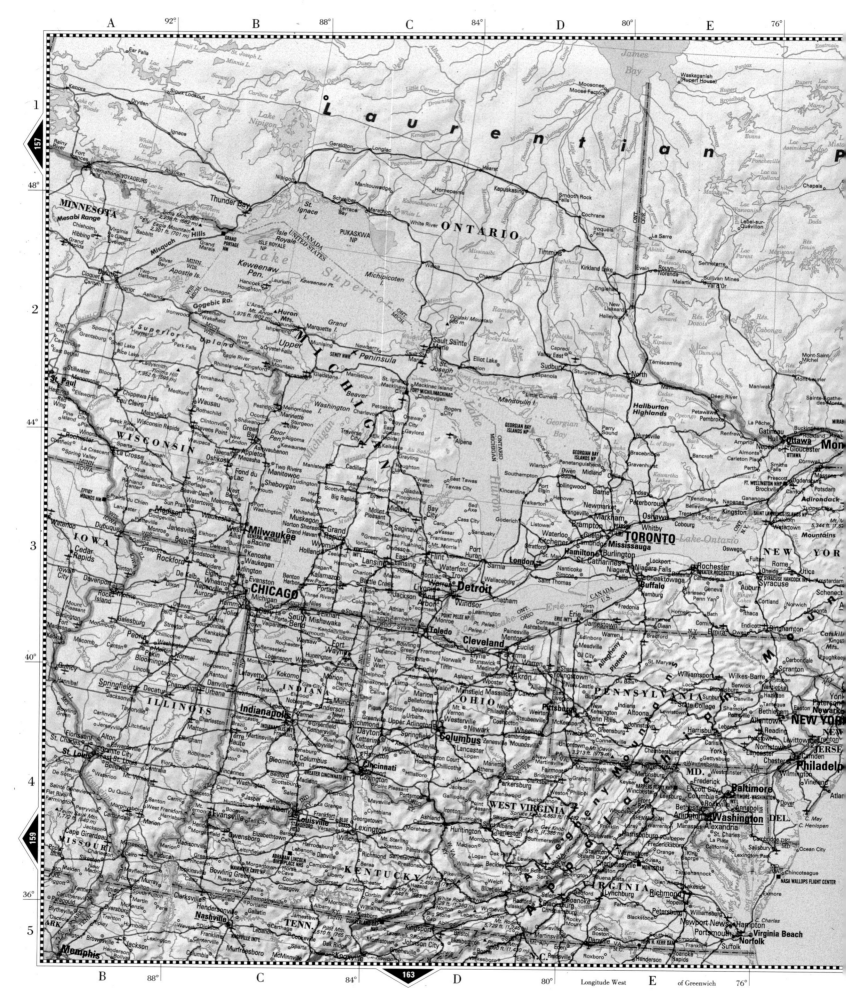

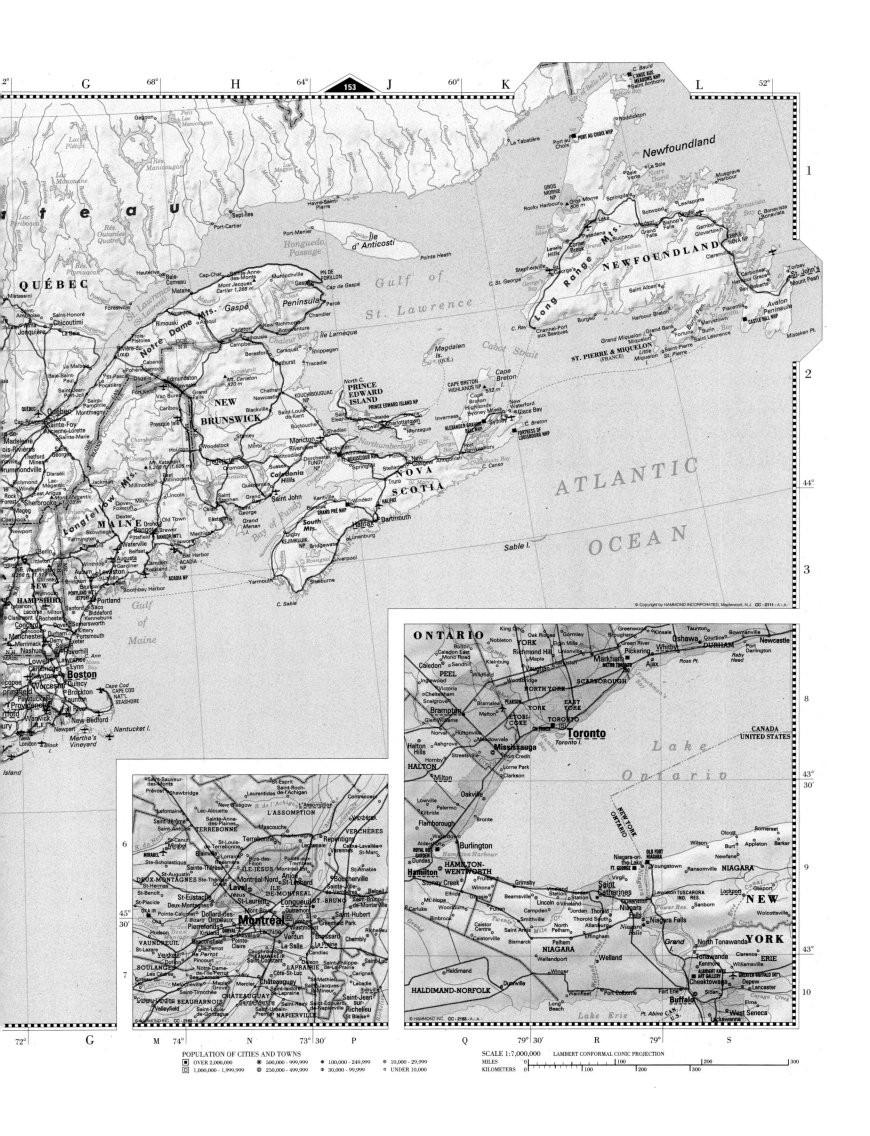

Southeastern United States

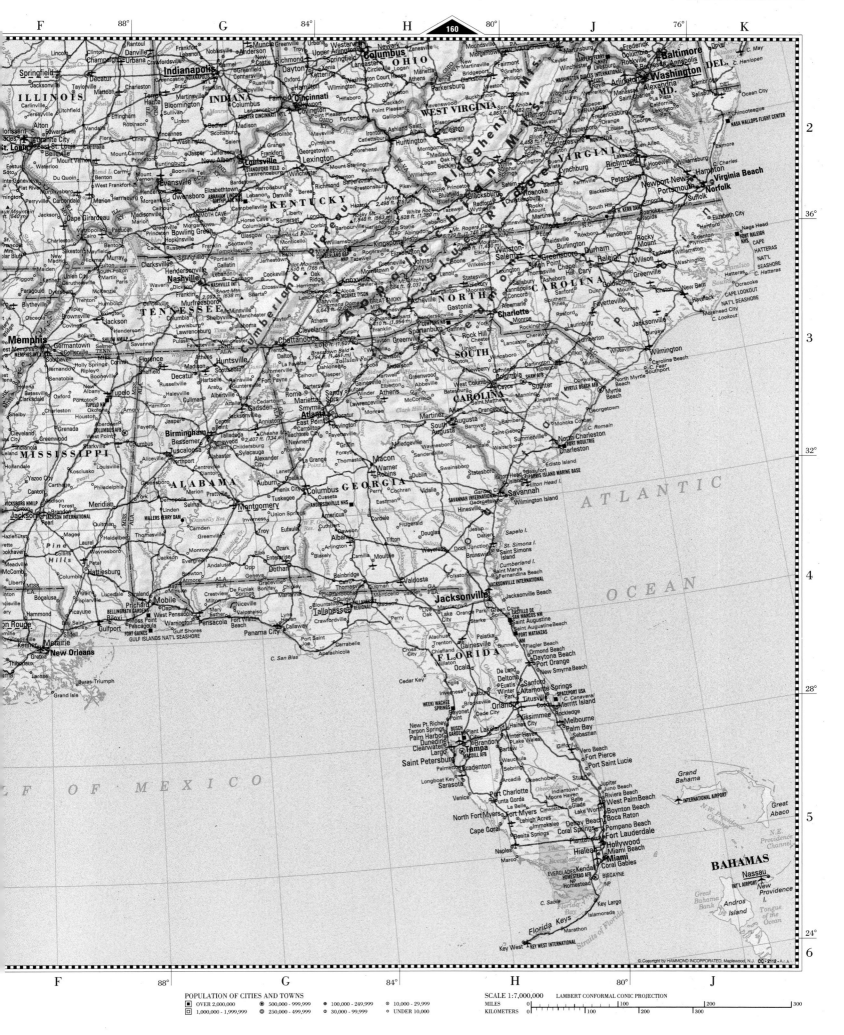

POPULATION OF CITIES AND TOWNS

■ OVER 2,000,000	● 500,000 - 999,999	● 100,000 - 249,999	○ 10,000 - 29,999
▣ 1,000,000 - 1,999,999	● 250,000 - 499,999	● 30,000 - 99,999	○ UNDER 10,000

SCALE 1:7,000,000   LAMBERT CONFORMAL CONIC PROJECTION

MILES   0   100   200   300
KILOMETERS   0   100   200   300

© Copyright by HAMMOND INCORPORATED, Maplewood, N.J.   CC-2112-A-A

Los Angeles-San Diego

Seattle, San Francisco, Detroit, Chicago

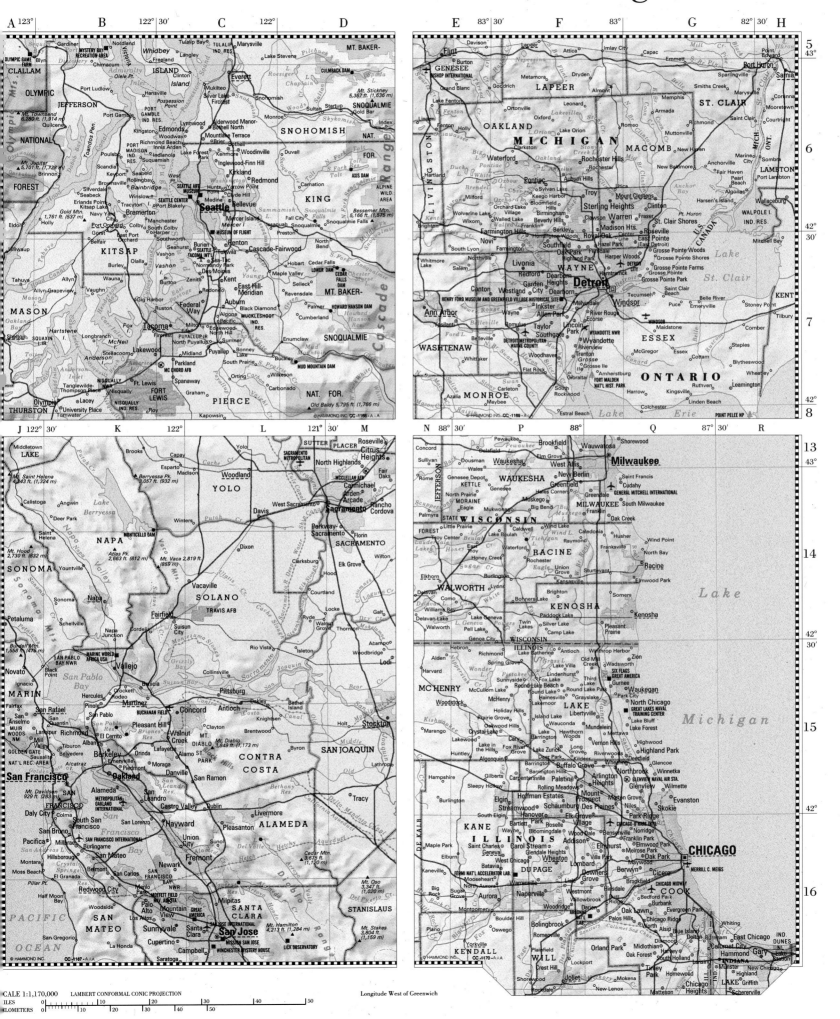

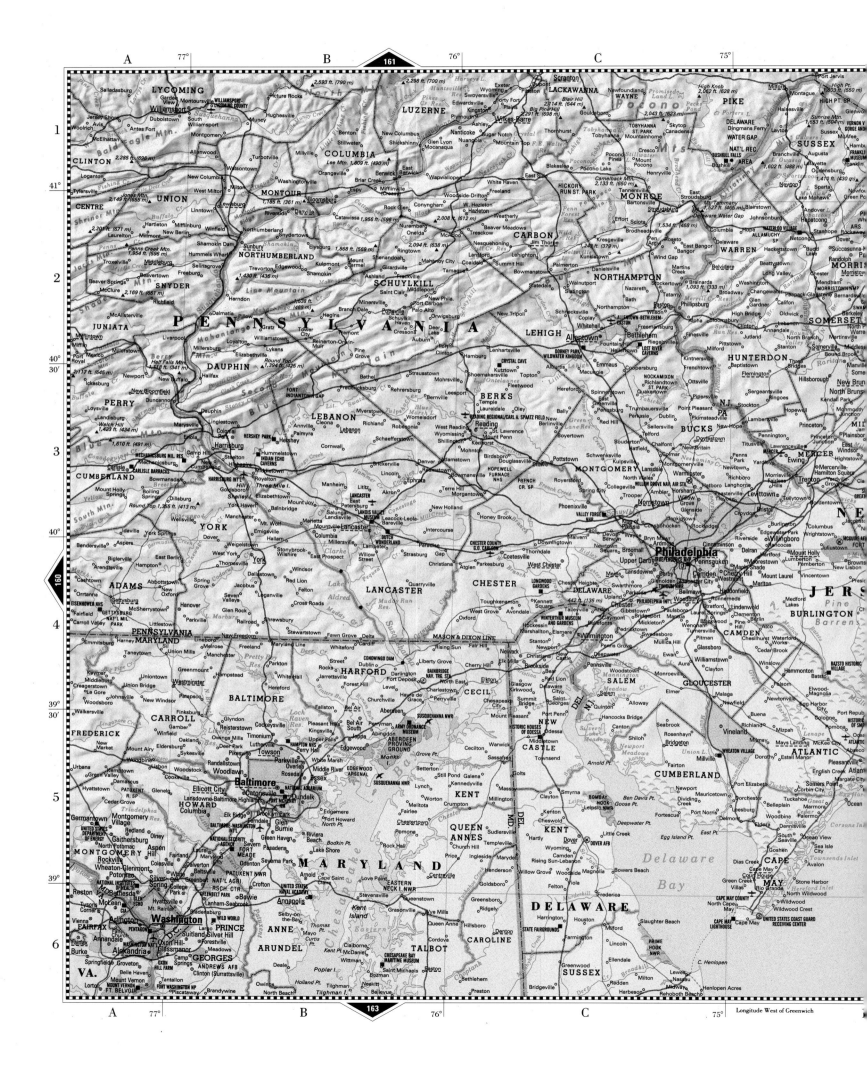

New York–Philadelphia–Washington

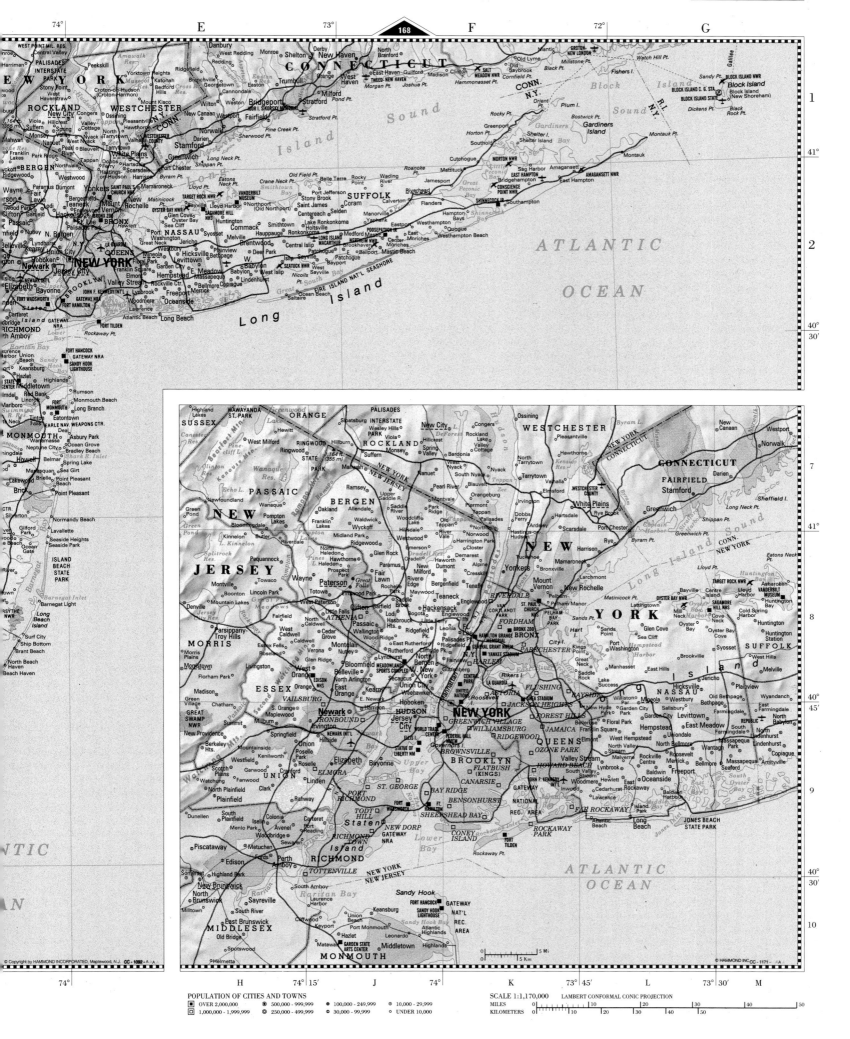

POPULATION OF CITIES AND TOWNS

- ■ OVER 2,000,000
- ◉ 500,000 - 999,999
- ● 100,000 - 249,999
- ◦ 10,000 - 29,999
- ▣ 1,000,000 - 1,999,999
- ◉ 250,000 - 499,999
- ◉ 30,000 - 99,999
- ○ UNDER 10,000

SCALE 1:1,170,000   LAMBERT CONFORMAL CONIC PROJECTION

MILES 0 10 20 30 40 50

KILOMETERS 0 10 20 30 40 50

Hartford-Boston, Cleveland-Pittsburgh

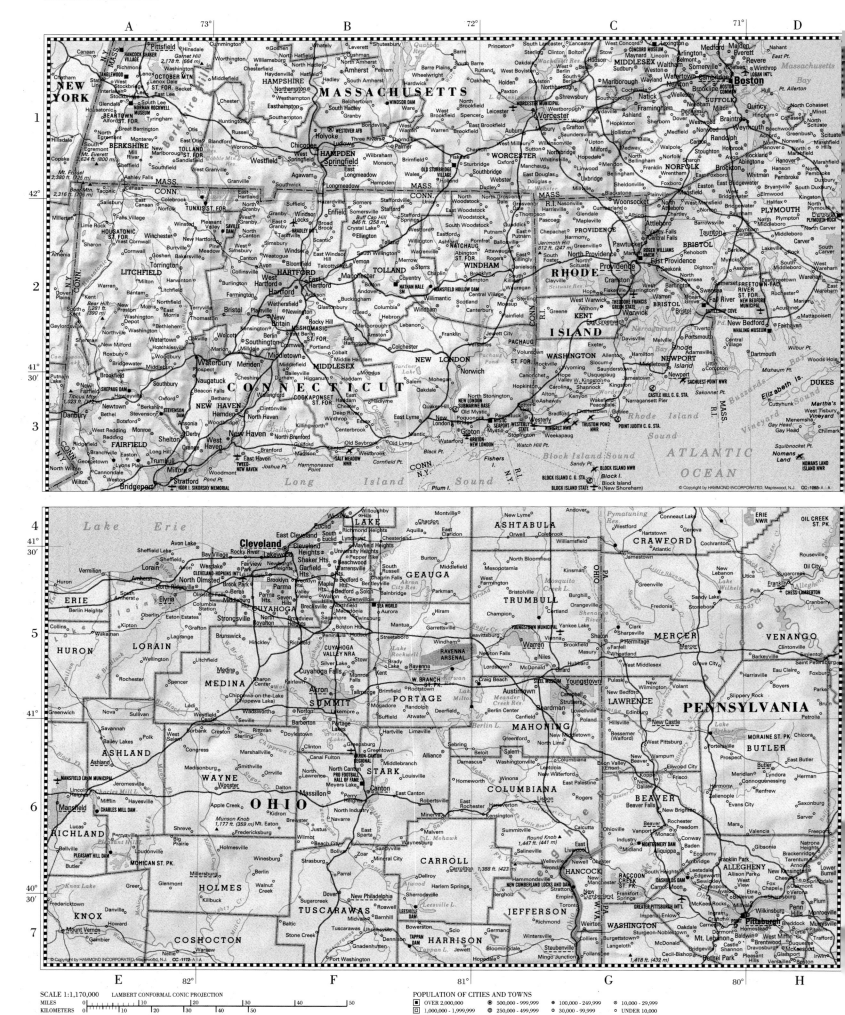

SCALE 1:1,170,000   LAMBERT CONFORMAL CONIC PROJECTION

POPULATION OF CITIES AND TOWNS

Index

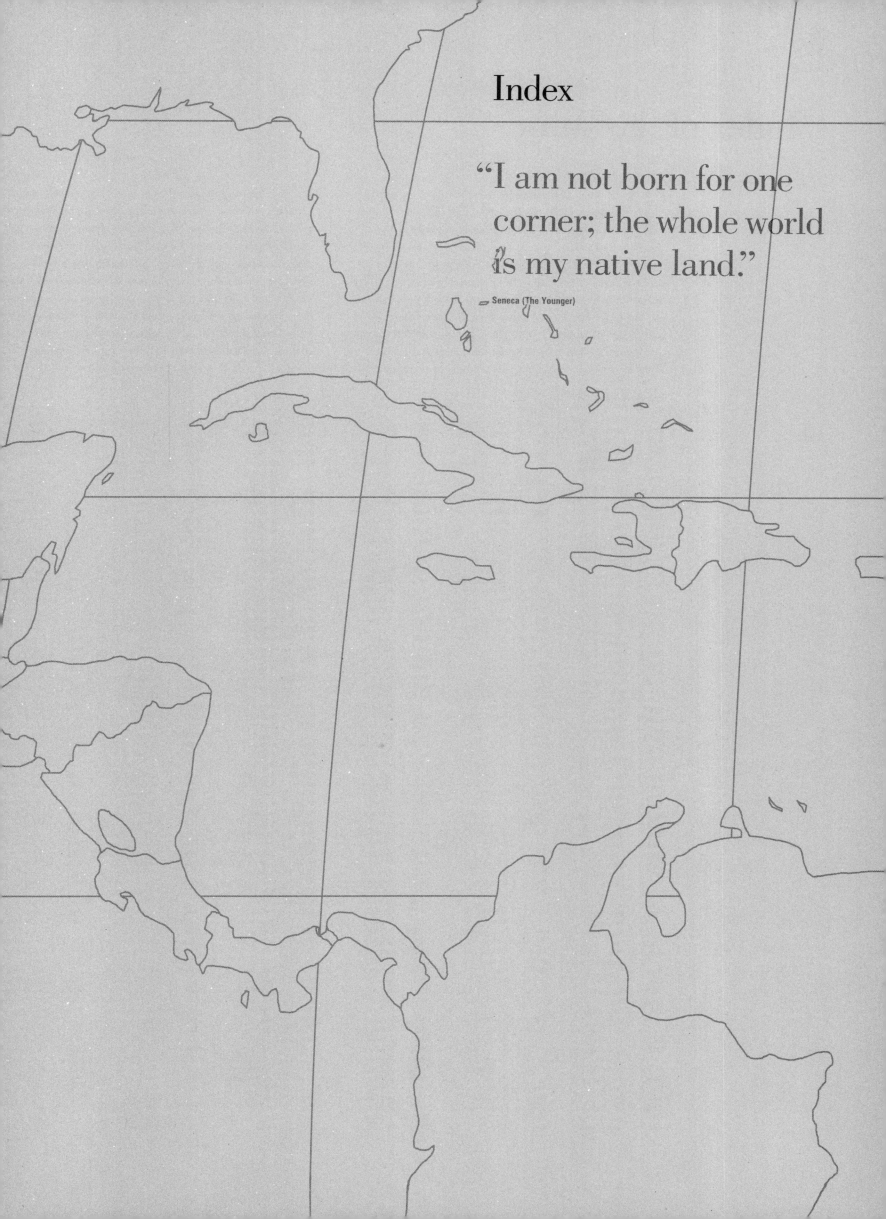

"I am not born for one corner; the whole world is my native land."

Seneca (The Younger)

Index of the World

This index is a comprehensive listing of the places and geographic features found in the atlas. Names are arranged in strict alphabetical order, without regard to hyphens or spaces. Every name is followed by the country or area to which it belongs. Except for cities, towns, countries and cultural areas, all entries include a reference to feature type, such as province, river, island, peak, and so on. The page number and alpha-numeric code appear in blue to the left of each listing. The page number directs you to the largest scale map on which the name can be found. The code refers to the grid squares formed by the horizontal

and vertical lines of latitude and longitude on each map. Following the letters from left to right and the numbers from top to bottom helps you to locate quickly the square containing the place or feature. Inset maps have their own alpha-numeric codes. Names that are accompanied by a point symbol are indexed to the symbol's location on the map. Other names are indexed to the initial letter of the name. When a map name contains a subordinate or alternate name, both names are listed in the index. To conserve space and provide room for more entries, many abbreviations are used in this index. The primary abbreviations are listed below.

Index Abbreviations

A Ab,Can	Alberta
Acad.	Academy
ACT	Australian Capital Territory
A.F.B.	Air Force Base
Afld.	Airfield
Afg.	Afghanistan
Afr.	Africa
Ak,US	Alaska
Al,US	Alabama
Alb.	Albania
Alg.	Algeria
Amm. Dep.	Ammunition Depot
And.	Andorra
Ang.	Angola
Angu.	Anguilla
Ant.	Antarctica
Anti.	Antigua and Barbuda
Ar,US	Arkansas
Arch.	Archipelago
Arg.	Argentina
Arm.	Armenia
Arpt.	Airport
Aru.	Aruba
ASam.	American Samoa
Ash.	Ashmore and Cartier Islands
Aus.	Austria
Austl.	Australia
Aut.	Autonomous
Az,US	Arizona
Azer.	Azerbaijan
Azor.	Azores
B Bahm.	Bahamas
Bahr.	Bahrain
Bang.	Bangladesh
Bar.	Barbados
BC,Can	British Columbia
Bela.	Belarus
Belg.	Belgium
Belz.	Belize
Ben.	Benin
Berm.	Bermuda
Bfld.	Battlefield
Bhu.	Bhutan
Bol.	Bolivia
Bor.	Borough
Bosn.	Bosnia and Hercegovina
Bots.	Botswana
Braz.	Brazil
BrIn.	British Indian Ocean Territory
Bru.	Brunei
Bul.	Bulgaria
Burk.	Burkina
Buru.	Burundi
BVI	British Virgin Islands
C Ca,US	California
CAfr.	Central African Republic
Camb.	Cambodia
Camr.	Cameroon
Can.	Canada
Can.	Canal
Canl.	Canary Islands
Cap.	Capital
Cap. Dist.	Capital District

Cap. Terr.	Capital Territory
Cay.	Cayman Islands
C.G.	Coast Guard
Chan.	Channel
Chl.	Channel Islands
Co.	County
Co,US	Colorado
Col.	Colombia
Com.	Comoros
Cont.	Continent
CpV.	Cape Verde Islands
CR	Costa Rica
Cr.	Creek
Cro.	Croatia
CSea.	Coral Sea Islands Territory
Ct,US	Connecticut
Ctr.	Center
Ctry.	Country
Cyp.	Cyprus
Czh.	Czech Republic
D DC,US	District of Columbia
De,US	Delaware
Den.	Denmark
Depr.	Depression
Dept.	Department
Des.	Desert
DF	Distrito Federal
Dist.	District
Djib.	Djibouti
Dom.	Dominica
Dpcy.	Dependency
DRep.	Dominican Republic
E Ecu.	Ecuador
Emb.	Embankment
Eng.	Engineering
Eng,UK	England
EqG.	Equatorial Guinea
Erit..	Eritrea
ESal.	El Salvador
Est.	Estonia
Eth.	Ethiopia
Eur.	Europe
F Falk.	Falkland Islands
Far.	Faroe Islands
Fed. Dist.	Federal District
Fin.	Finland
Fl,US	Florida
For.	Forest
Fr.	France
FrAnt.	French Southern and Antarctic Lands
FrG.	French Guiana
FrPol.	French Polynesia
G Ga,US	Georgia
Galp.	Galapagos Islands
Gam.	Gambia
Gaza	Gaza Strip
GBis.	Guinea-Bissau
Geo.	Georgia
Ger.	Germany

Gha.	Ghana
Gib.	Gibraltar
Glac.	Glacier
Gov.	Governorate
Govt.	Government
Gre.	Greece
Grld.	Greenland
Gren.	Grenada
Grsld.	Grassland
Guad.	Guadeloupe
Guat.	Guatemala
Gui.	Guinea
Guy.	Guyana
H Har.	Harbor
Hi,US	Hawaii
Hist.	Historic(al)
HK	Hong Kong
Hon.	Honduras
Hts.	Heights
Hun.	Hungary
I Ia,US	Iowa
Ice.	Iceland
Id,US	Idaho
Il,US	Illinois
IM	Isle of Man
In,US	Indiana
Ind. Res.	Indian Reservation
Indo.	Indonesia
Int'l	International
Ire.	Ireland
Isl., Isls.	Island, Islands
Isr.	Israel
Isth.	Isthmus
It.	Italy
IvC.	Ivory Coast
J Jam.	Jamaica
Jor.	Jordan
K Kaz.	Kazakhstan
Kiri.	Kiribati
Ks,US	Kansas
Kuw.	Kuwait
Ky,US	Kentucky
Kyr.	Kyrgyzstan
L La,US	Louisiana
Lab.	Laboratory
Lag.	Lagoon
Lakesh.	Lakeshore
Lat.	Latvia
Lcht.	Liechtenstein
Ldg.	Landing
Leb.	Lebanon
Les.	Lesotho
Libr.	Liberia
Lith.	Lithuania
Lux.	Luxembourg
M Ma,US	Massachusetts
Macd.	Macedonia
Madg.	Madagascar
Madr.	Madeira
Malay.	Malaysia
Mald.	Maldives
Malw.	Malawi
Mart.	Martinique
May.	Mayotte
Mb,Can	Manitoba
Md,US	Maryland

Me,US	Maine
Mem.	Memorial
Mex.	Mexico
Mi,US	Michigan
Micr.	Micronesia, Federated States of
Mil.	Military
Mn,US	Minnesota
Mo,US	Missouri
Mol.	Moldova
Mon.	Monument
Mona.	Monaco
Mong.	Mongolia
Monts.	Montserrat
Mor.	Morocco
Moz.	Mozambique
Mrsh.	Marshall Islands
Mrta.	Mauritania
Mrts.	Mauritius
Ms,US	Mississippi
Mt.	Mount
Mt,US	Montana
Mtn., Mts.	Mountain, Mountains
Mun. Arpt.	Municipal Airport
N NAm.	North America
Namb.	Namibia
NAnt.	Netherlands Antilles
Nat'l	National
Nav.	Naval
NB,Can	New Brunswick
Nbrhd.	Neighborhood
NC,US	North Carolina
NCal.	New Caledonia
ND,US	North Dakota
Ne,US	Nebraska
Neth.	Netherlands
Nf,Can	Newfoundland
Nga.	Nigeria
NH,US	New Hampshire
NI,UK	Northern Ireland
Nic.	Nicaragua
NJ,US	New Jersey
NKor.	North Korea
NM,US	New Mexico
NMar.	Northern Mariana Islands
Nor.	Norway
NS,Can	Nova Scotia
Nv,US	Nevada
NW,Can	Northwest Territories
NY,US	New York
NZ	New Zealand
O Obl.	Oblast
Oh,US	Ohio
Ok,US	Oklahoma
On,Can	Ontario
Or,US	Oregon
P Pa,US	Pennsylvania
PacUS	Pacific Islands, U.S.
Pak.	Pakistan
Pan.	Panama
Par.	Paraguay
Par.	Parish

PE,Can	Prince Edward Island
Pen.	Peninsula
Phil.	Philippines
Phys. Reg.	Physical Region
Pitc.	Pitcairn Islands
Plat.	Plateau
PNG	Papua New Guinea
Pol.	Poland
Port.	Portugal
Poss.	Possession
Pkwy.	Parkway
PR	Puerto Rico
Pref.	Prefecture
Prov.	Province
Prsv.	Preserve
Pt.	Point
Q Qu,Can	Quebec
R Rec.	Recreation(al)
Ref.	Refuge
Reg.	Region
Rep.	Republic
Res.	Reservoir, Reservation
Reun.	Réunion
RI,US	Rhode Island
Riv.	River
Rom.	Romania
Rsv.	Reserve
Rus.	Russia
Rvwy.	Riverway
Rwa.	Rwanda
S SAfr.	South Africa
SAm.	South America
SaoT.	São Tomé and Príncipe
SAr.	Saudi Arabia
Sc,UK	Scotland
SC,US	South Carolina
SD,US	South Dakota
Seash.	Seashore
Sen.	Senegal
Sey.	Seychelles
SGeo.	South Georgia and Sandwich Islands
Sing.	Singapore
Sk,Can	Saskatchewan
SKor.	South Korea
SLeo.	Sierra Leone
Slov.	Slovenia
Slvk.	Slovakia
SMar.	San Marino
Sol.	Solomon Islands
Som.	Somalia
Sp.	Spain
Spr., Sprs.	Spring, Springs
SrL.	Sri Lanka
Sta.	Station
StH.	Saint Helena
Str.	Strait
StK.	Saint Kitts and Nevis
StL.	Saint Lucia
StP.	Saint Pierre and Miquelon
StV.	Saint Vincent and the Grenadines
Sur.	Suriname

Sval.	Svalbard
Swaz.	Swaziland
Swe.	Sweden
Swi.	Switzerland
T Tah.	Tahiti
Tai.	Taiwan
Taj.	Tajikistan
Tanz.	Tanzania
Ter.	Terrace
Terr.	Territory
Thai.	Thailand
Tn,US	Tennessee
Tok.	Tokelau
Trg.	Training
Trin.	Trinidad and Tobago
Trkm.	Turkmenistan
Trks.	Turks and Caicos Islands
Tun.	Tunisia
Tun.	Tunnel
Turk.	Turkey
Tuv.	Tuvalu
Twp.	Township
Tx,US	Texas
U UAE	United Arab Emirates
Ugan.	Uganda
UK	United Kingdom
Ukr.	Ukraine
Uru.	Uruguay
US	United States
USVI	U.S. Virgin Islands
Ut,US	Utah
Uzb.	Uzbekistan
V Va,US	Virginia
Val.	Valley
Van.	Vanuatu
VatC.	Vatican City
Ven.	Venezuela
Viet.	Vietnam
Vill.	Village
Vol.	Volcano
Vt,US	Vermont
W Wa,US	Washington
Wal,UK	Wales
Wall.	Wallis and Futuna
WBnk.	West Bank
Wi,US	Wisconsin
Wild.	Wildlife, Wilderness
WSah.	Western Sahara
WSam.	Western Samoa
WV,US	West Virginia
Wy,US	Wyoming
Y Yem.	Yemen
Yk,Can	Yukon Territory
Yugo.	Yugoslavia
Z Zam.	Zambia
Zim.	Zimbabwe

A

68/B2 Aa (riv.), Fr.
66/D5 Aa (riv.), Ger.
67/G5 Aa (riv.), Ger.
77/E3 Aabach (riv.), Swi.
77/F2 Aach (riv.), Ger.
69/F2 Aachen, Ger.
70/C3 Aalbach (riv.), Ger.
66/C5 Aalburg, Neth.
70/D5 Aalen, Ger.
66/B4 Aalsmeer, Neth.
68/D2 Aalst, Belg.
66/D5 Aalten, Neth.
68/C1 Aalter, Belg.
70/B2 Aar (riv.), Ger.
76/E3 Aarau, Swi.
76/D3 Aare (riv.), Swi.
76/E3 Aargau (canton), Swi.
69/D2 Aarschot, Belg.
68/D1 Aartselaar, Belg.
96/E5 Aba, China
129/G5 Aba, Nga.
130/A2 Aba, Zaire
94/D5 Abā as Su'ūd, SAr.
136/G5 Abacaxis (riv.), Braz.
127/C5 Abadab, Jabal (peak), Sudan
93/G4 Ābādān, Iran
93/H4 Ābādeh, Iran
141/C1 Abadia dos Dourados, Braz.
82/E2 Abádszalók, Hun.
141/C1 Abaeté, Braz.
137/J4 Abaetetuba, Braz.
120/G4 Abaiang (atoll), Kiri.
154/D4 Abajo (mts.), Ut,US
88/K4 Abakan, Rus.
144/C4 Abancay, Peru
79/E2 Abano Terme, It.
96/G3 Abaq Qi, China
74/E3 Abarán, Sp.
121/H5 Abariringa (Canton) (atoll), Kiri.
93/H4 Abar Kūh, Iran
100/D1 Abashiri, Japan
100/C2 Abashiri (lake), Japan
147/E4 Abasolo, Mex.
88/H5 Abay, Kaz.
125/N6 Ābaya Hayk' (lake), Eth.
102/F1 Abaza, Rus.
80/B1 Abbadia San Salvatore, It.
60/B3 Abbert (riv.), Ire.
68/A3 Abbeville, Fr.
162/E4 Abbeville, La,US
163/H3 Abbeville, SC,US
56/E2 Abbey Head (pt.), Sc,UK
78/B2 Abbiategrasso, It.
113/T Abbot Ice Shelf, Ant.
57/G6 Abbots Bromley, Eng,UK
58/D5 Abbotsbury, Eng,UK
53/M6 Abbots Langley, Eng,UK
95/K2 Abbottābād, Pak.
66/B4 Abcoude, Neth.
92/D2 'Abd al 'Azīz, Jabal (mts.), Syria
108/B2 Abdul Hakīm, Pak.
87/K1 Abdulino, Rus.
125/K5 Abéché, Chad
133/E2 Abel Erasmuspas (pass), SAfr.
120/G4 Abemama (atoll), Kiri.
128/E5 Abengourou, IvC.
62/C4 Åbenrå, Den.
71/E5 Abens (riv.), Ger.
71/E5 Abensberg, Ger.
129/F5 Abeokuta, Nga.
56/D5 Aber, Wal,UK
58/B2 Aberaeron, Wal,UK
58/C1 Aberangell, Wal,UK
58/B2 Aberath, Wal,UK
58/C3 Abercarn, Wal,UK
54/D1 Aberchirder, Sc,UK
58/C3 Aberdare, Wal,UK
130/C3 Aberdare Nat'l Park, Kenya
56/D6 Aberdaron, Wal,UK
152/G2 Aberdeen (lake), NW,Can
54/D2 Aberdeen, Sc,UK
166/B4 Aberdeen, Md,US
163/F3 Aberdeen, Ms,US
157/J4 Aberdeen, SD,US
156/C4 Aberdeen, Wa,US
166/B5 Aberdeen Prov. Gnd. (mil. res.), Md,US
54/C4 Aberdour, Sc,UK
54/D1 Aberdour (bay), Sc,UK
58/B1 Aberdyfi, Wal,UK
54/C3 Aberfeldy, Sc,UK
54/B4 Aberfoyle, Sc,UK
58/C3 Abergavenny, Wal,UK
56/E5 Abergele, Wal,UK
54/D5 Aberlady, Sc,UK
54/C2 Aberlour, Sc,UK
54/C4 Abernethy, Sc,UK
58/B2 Aberporth, Wal,UK
56/D6 Abersoch, Wal,UK
58/C3 Abersychan, Wal,UK
158/B2 Abert (lake), Or,US
58/C3 Abertillery, Wal,UK
58/B2 Aberystwyth, Wal,UK
94/D5 Abhá, SAr.
93/G2 Abhar, Iran
125/P5 Abhe Bad (lake), Djib., Eth.
149/G4 Abide, Serraníade (range), Col.
128/D5 Abidjan, IvC.
99/J7 Abiko, Japan
159/H3 Abilene, Ks,US
162/D3 Abilene, Tx,US
59/E3 Abingdon, Eng,UK
160/D4 Abingdon, Va,US
54/C6 Abington, Sc,UK
168/D1 Abington, Ma,US
161/R10 Abino (pt.), On,Can
159/F3 Abiquiu, NM,US
160/E1 Abitibi (lake), On,Can
160/D1 Abitibi (riv.), On,Can
87/G4 Abkhaz Aut. Rep., Geo.
70/C6 Ablach (riv.), Ger.
127/B3 Abnūb, Egypt
108/C2 Abohar, India
128/E5 Aboisso, IvC.
129/F5 Abomey, Ben.
82/E2 Abony, Hun.
112/B3 Aborlan, Phil.
112/B3 Aborlan (mtn.), Phil.
63/K1 Åbo (Turku), Fin.
54/D2 Aboyne, Sc,UK
112/C1 Abra (riv.), Phil.
160/C4 Abraham Lincoln Birthplace Nat'l Hist. Site, Ky,US
150/C2 Abraham's Bay, Bahm.
74/A3 Abrantes, Port.
135/C1 Abra Pampa, Arg.
146/B3 Abreojos, Punta (pt.), Mex.
127/B4 'Abrī, Sudan
53/P7 Abridge, Eng,UK
82/F2 Abrud, Rom.
80/C1 Abruzzi (reg.), It.
80/C2 Abruzzo Nat'l Park, It.
156/F4 Absaroka (range), Mt, Wy,US
166/D5 Absecon, NJ,US
70/D5 Abtsgmünd, Ger.
94/F4 Abū al Abyaḑ (isl.), UAE
93/G5 Abū 'Alī (isl.), SAr.
95/F4 Abu Dhabi (Abū Ẓaby) (cap.), UAE
127/C5 Abū Dīs, Sudan
127/B4 Abu el-Husein, Bîr (well), Egypt
127/C5 Abū Ḩamad, Sudan
91/B4 Abū Ḩammād, Egypt
127/C4 Abu Hashim, Bi'r (well), Egypt
91/B4 Abū Ḩummuş, Egypt
129/G4 Abuja (cap.), Nga.
129/G4 Abuja Cap. Terr., Nga.
91/B4 Abū Kabīr, Egypt
92/E3 Abū Kamāl, Syria
99/G2 Abukuma (hills), Japan
99/G2 Abukuma (riv.), Japan
112/C1 Abulug, Phil.
127/A3 Abu Minqâr, Bîr (well), Egypt
136/E6 Abunā (riv.), Bol.
136/E5 Abunã (riv.), Braz.
106/B3 Abu Road, India
92/D3 Abu Rujmayn, Jabal (mts.), Syria
127/D4 Abu Shagara, Ras (cape), Sudan
127/B4 Abu Simbel (ruins), Egypt
100/B2 Abuta, Japan
125/N5 Ābuyē Mēda (peak), Eth.
112/D3 Abuyog, Phil.
95/F4 Abū Ẓaby (Abu Dhabi) (cap.), UAE
80/A4 Abyaḑ, Ar Ra's al (cape), Tun.
127/B3 Abydos (ruins), Egypt
138/C4 Acacías, Col.
161/G2 Acadia Nat'l Park, Me,US
162/E4 Acadian Village, La,US
140/C3 Acajutiba, Braz.
147/E4 Acámbaro, Mex.
146/D4 Acaponeta, Mex.
146/D4 Acaponeta (riv.), Mex.
147/E5 Acapulco, Mex.
139/G4 Acaraí (mts.), Braz., Guy.
140/B1 Acaraú, Braz.
140/B1 Acaraú (riv.), Braz.
140/C2 Acari, Braz.
136/G5 Acari (riv.), Braz.
138/D3 Acarigua, Ven.
147/F5 Acatlán, Mex.
147/M8 Acatzingo de Hidalgo, Mex.
129/E5 Accra (cap.), Gha.
57/F4 Accrington, Eng,UK
71/G6 Ach (riv.), Aus.
77/H2 Ach (riv.), Ger.
136/E7 Achacachi, Bol.
142/B4 Achao, Chile
129/H2 Achegour (well), Niger
77/H2 Achen (pass), Ger.
97/K2 Acheng, China
53/S10 Achères, Fr.
70/B5 Achern, Ger.
68/B3 Achicourt, Fr.
68/B3 Achiet-le-Grand, Fr.
161/N6 Achigan (riv.), Qu,Can
54/F10 Achill (isl.), Ire.
54/F10 Achill Head (pt.), Ire.
55/J7 Achiltibuie, Sc,UK
88/K4 Achinsk, Rus.
128/D2 Achmîm (well), Mrta.
54/A1 Achnasheen, Sc,UK
54/A2 A'Chràlaig (mtn.), Sc,UK
69/G3 Acht, Hohe (peak), Ger.
148/E3 Achuapa, Nic.
144/B1 Achupallas, Ecu.
92/B2 Acıpayam, Turk.
80/D4 Acireale, It.
150/C2 Acklins (isl.), Bahm.
57/G4 Ackworth Moor Top, Eng,UK
118/C4 Acland (peak), Austl.
59/H1 Acle, Eng,UK
142/C2 Aconcagua, Cerro (peak), Arg.
140/C2 Acopiara, Braz.
78/B3 Acqui Terme, It.
117/G5 Acraman (lake), Austl.
144/D3 Acre (state), Braz.
136/E6 Acre (riv.), Braz., Peru
141/B1 Acreúna, Braz.
81/L7 Acropolis, Gre.
121/M7 Actaeon Group (isls.), FrPol.
53/N7 Acton, Eng,UK
147/F5 Actopan, Mex.
140/C2 Açu, Braz.
147/P8 Acula, Mex.
142/Q9 Aculeo (lake), Chile
168/D2 Acushnet, Ma,US
160/D3 Ada, Oh,US
159/H4 Ada, Ok,US
82/E3 Ada, Yugo.
153/J1 Adair (cape), NW,Can
74/C2 Adaja (riv.), Sp.
151/C6 Adak (isl.), Ak,US
151/C6 Adak (str.), Ak,US
143/M7 Adam (peak), Falk.
141/B2 Adamantina, Braz.
129/H5 Adamawa (plat.), Camr., Nga.
77/G5 Adamello (peak), It.
156/D3 Adams (lake), BC,Can
166/A4 Adams (co.), Pa,US
156/C4 Adams (peak), Wa,US
108/G4 Adam's Bridge (shoals), SrL.
91/D1 Adana, Turk.
91/D1 Adana (prov.), Turk.
83/K5 Adapazarı, Turk.
113/M Adare (cape), Ant.
72/C5 Adarza (mtn.), Fr.
54/A4 Add (riv.), Sc,UK
78/C2 Adda (riv.), It.
125/M4 Ad Dabbah, Sudan
93/F5 Ad Dahnā' (des.), SAr.
125/M5 Ad Damazin, Sudan
125/M4 Ad Damīr, Sudan
94/F3 Ad Dammām, SAr.
91/B4 Ad Daqahlīyah (gov.), Egypt
94/F3 Ad Dawḩah (Doha) (cap.), Qatar
91/B4 Ad Dilinjāt, Egypt
125/N6 Addis Ababa (cap.), Eth.
165/Q16 Addison, Il,US
93/F4 Ad Dīwānīyah, Iraq
53/M7 Addlestone, Eng,UK
132/D4 Addo Elephant Nat'l Park, SAfr.
93/F3 Ad Dujayl, Iraq
125/M5 Ad Duwaym, Sudan
113/V Adelaide (isl.), Ant.
117/H5 Adelaide, Austl.
152/G2 Adelaide (pen.), NW,Can
132/D4 Adelaide, SAfr.
117/M8 Adelaide Zoo, Austl.
164/C1 Adelanto, Ca,US
114/C3 Adèle (isl.), Austl.
67/G5 Adelebsen, Ger.
113/K Adélie (coast), Ant.
63/R7 Adelsön (isl.), Swe.
125/Q5 Aden (gulf), Afr., Asia
94/D6 Aden, Yem.
67/H2 Adendorf, Ger.
111/H4 Adi (isl.), Indo.
130/A2 Adi, Zaire
117/G5 Adieu (cape), Austl.
73/J4 Adige (Etsch) (riv.), It.
125/N5 Ādīgrat, Eth.
106/C4 Adilābād, India
93/E2 Adilcevaz, Turk.
129/E2 Adiora (well), Mali
108/G3 Adirāmpatnam, India
160/F2 Adirondack (mts.), NY,US
125/N6 Ādīs Ābeba (Addis Ababa) (cap.), Eth.
125/N5 Ādīs Zemen, Eth.
92/D2 Adıyaman, Turk.
92/D2 Adıyaman (prov.), Turk.
83/H2 Adjud, Rom.
147/F4 Adjuntas (res.), Mex.
57/F4 Adlington, Eng,UK
77/E3 Adliswil, Swi.
114/D2 Admiralty (gulf), Austl.
153/H1 Admiralty (inlet), NW,Can
120/D5 Admiralty (isls.), PNG
165/B2 Admiralty (inlet), Wa,US
151/M4 Admiralty I. Nat'l Mon., Ak,US
99/L9 Ado (riv.), Japan
129/F5 Ado, Nga.
99/M9 Adogawa, Japan
106/C4 Ādoni, India
72/C5 Adour (riv.), Fr.
74/D4 Adra, Sp.
130/A2 Adranga, Zaire
80/D4 Adrano, It.
124/E2 Adrar, Alg.
129/F1 Adrar (wilaya), Alg.
128/B1 Adrar (reg.), Mrta.
124/E1 Adrar bou Nasser (peak), Mor.
129/F1 Adrar des Iforas (mts.), Mali
125/K5 Adré, Chad
79/F2 Adria, It.
160/C3 Adrian, Mi,US
52/E4 Adriatic, (sea)
59/F1 Adur (riv.), Eng,UK
125/N5 Ādwa, Eth.
57/G4 Adwick le Street, Eng,UK
89/P3 Adycha (riv.), Rus.
87/G4 Adzhar Aut. Rep., Geo.
85/N2 Adz'va (riv.), Rus.
81/J3 Aegean (sea), Gre., Turk.
62/D4 Aerø (isl.), Den.
58/B2 Aeron (riv.), Wal,UK
76/D3 Aesch, Swi.
56/E1 Ae, Water of (riv.), Sc,UK
129/F5 Afadjoto (peak), Gha.
93/F3 'Afak, Iraq
121/X15 Afareaitu, FrPol.
91/F7 Afek Nat'l Park, Isr.
72/B3 Aff (riv.), Fr.
54/A2 Affric, Loch (lake), Sc,UK
95/H2 Afghanistan
125/Q7 Afgooye, Som.
125/P7 Afmadow, Som.
139/H3 Afobaka (dam), Sur.
140/C2 Afogados da Ingàzeira, Braz.
151/H4 Afognak (isl.), Ak,US
151/H4 Afognak (mtn.), Ak,US
128/C2 Afollé (reg.), Mrta.
140/C2 Afonso Bezerra, Braz.
141/D2 Afonso Cláudio, Braz.
80/D2 Afragola, It.
140/B3 Afrânio, Braz.
122/* Africa
165/K10 Africa USA (Marine World), Ca,US
91/E1 'Afrīn, Syria
91/E1 'Afrīn (riv.), Syria
91/E1 Afrin (riv.), Turk.
76/A3 Afrique (mtn.), Fr.
92/D2 Afşin, Turk.
66/C2 Afsluitdijk (IJsselmeer) (dam), Neth.
67/E5 Afte (riv.), Ger.
156/F5 Afton, Wy,US
91/D3 'Afula, Isr.
92/B2 Afyon, Turk.
92/B2 Afyon (prov.), Turk.
124/H4 Agadem, Niger
129/G2 Agadez, Niger
129/H2 Agadez (dept.), Niger
124/D1 Agadir, Mor.
130/B2 Agago (riv.), Ugan.
123/H6 Agalega (isls.), Mrts.
129/F2 Agamor (well), Mali
120/D3 Agaña (cap.), Guam
99/F2 Agano (riv.), Japan
125/N6 Āgaro, Eth.
107/F3 Agartala, India
113/V Agassiz (cape), Ant.
153/T6 Agassiz (ice field), NW,Can
159/G2 Agate Fossil Beds Nat'l Mon., Ne,US
151/A5 Agattu (isl.), Ak,US
151/A5 Agattu (str.), Ak,US
168/B1 Agawam, Ma,US
129/G5 Agbor, Nga.
128/D5 Agboville, IvC.
87/H5 Ağdam, Azer.
72/E5 Agde, Fr.
72/E5 Agde, Cap d' (cape), Fr.
72/D4 Agen, Fr.
99/H7 Ageo, Japan
71/G7 Ager (riv.), Aus.
62/C4 Agerbæk, Den.
77/E3 Agerisee (lake), Swi.
63/S7 Agesta (reg. park), Swe.
67/E6 Agger (riv.), Ger.
82/E1 Aggteleki Nat'l Park, Hun.
56/B3 Aghagallon, NI,UK
93/G4 Aghā Jārī, Iran
146/C3 Agiabampo (lag.), Mex.
96/G1 Aginskoye, Rus.
56/B1 Agivey, NI,UK
79/E5 Agliana, It.
72/E5 Agly (riv.), Fr.
83/G3 Agnita, Rom.
79/E1 Agno (riv.), It.
77/E6 Agno, Swi.
99/M10 Ago, Japan
78/B2 Agogna (riv.), It.
105/J5 Agoo, Phil.
72/D5 Agout (riv.), Fr.
106/C2 Āgra, India
80/E2 Agri (riv.), It.
93/E2 Ağri (prov.), Turk.
87/H5 Ağri (Ararat) (peak), Turk.
80/C4 Agrigento, It.
120/D3 Agrihan (isl.), NMar.
81/G3 Agrínion, Gre.
142/C3 Agrio (riv.), Arg.
80/D2 Agropoli, It.
85/M4 Agryz, Rus.
147/L6 Agua Blanca Iturbide, Mex.
141/D1 Água Boa, Braz.
140/B2 Água Branca, Braz.
138/C2 Aguachica, Col.
138/C3 Aguadas, Col.
150/E3 Aguadilla, PR
148/C2 Agua Dulce, Mex.
149/F4 Aguadulce, Pan.
164/C4 Agua Hedionda (lag.), Ca,US
141/F7 Aguaí, Braz.
75/P10 Agualva-Cacém, Port.
148/E3 Aguan (riv.), Hon.
161/J1 Aguanus (riv.), Qu,Can
141/B2 Aguapeí (riv.), Braz.
138/C5 Aguarico (riv.), Ecu.
139/E2 Aguaro-Guariquito Nat'l Park, Ven.
141/H6 Águas (hills), Braz.
140/C3 Águas Belas, Braz.
146/E4 Aguascalientes, Mex.
146/E4 Aguascalientes (state), Mex.
141/G6 Águas da Prata, Braz.
141/G7 Águas de Lindóia, Braz.
140/B5 Águas Formosas, Braz.
141/B1 Aguavermelha (res.), Braz.
144/C3 Aguaytía (riv.), Peru
141/B2 Agudos, Braz.
74/A2 Águeda, Port.
74/B2 Águeda (riv.), Sp.
124/C3 Agüenit, WSah.
99/M10 Agui, Japan
120/D3 Aguijan (isl.), NMar.
74/C4 Aguilar, Sp.
74/C1 Aguilar de Campóo, Sp.
135/C2 Aguilares, Arg.
74/E4 Aguilas, Sp.
146/E5 Aguililla, Mex.
75/X17 Agüimes, Canl.,Sp.
144/A2 Aguja (pt.), Peru
132/M11 Agulhas (cape), SAfr.
141/C2 Agulhas Negras (peak), Braz.
111/E5 Agung (vol.), Indo.
112/D3 Agusan (riv.), Phil.
138/C2 Agustín Codazzi, Col.
130/B2 Agwata, Ugan.
124/G3 Ahaggar (plat.), Alg.
93/F2 Ahar, Iran
66/E4 Ahaus, Ger.
69/F3 Ahbach (riv.), Ger.
60/B5 Aherlow (riv.), Ire.
130/B3 Ahero, Kenya
92/E2 Ahlat, Turk.
67/E5 Ahlen, Ger.
106/B3 Ahmadābād, India
106/B4 Ahmadnagar, India
95/K3 Ahmadpur East, Pak.
108/A2 Ahmadpur Siāl, Pak.
125/P6 Ahmar (mts.), Eth.
56/B2 Ahoghill, NI,UK
69/F3 Ahr (riv.), Ger.
91/B5 Ahrāmāt al Jīzah (The Pyramids of Giza), Egypt
67/H1 Ahrensburg, Ger.
67/F5 Ahse (riv.), Ger.
147/K8 Ahuacatitlán, Mex.
148/D3 Ahuachapán, ESal.
154/W13 Ahuimanu, Hi,US
62/F4 Åhus, Swe.
93/G4 Ahvāz, Iran
63/H1 Ahvenanmaa (prov.), Fin.
101/C2 Ai (riv.), China
132/B2 Ai-Ais Hot Springs, Namb.
103/B2 Aibag Gol (riv.), China
70/E6 Aichach, Ger.
99/E3 Aichi (pref.), Japan
70/B5 Aidlingen, Ger.
154/W13 Aiea, Hi,US
76/C5 Aigle, Swi.
76/B4 Aigle, Pic de l' (peak), Fr.
72/E4 Aigoual (mtn.), Fr.
72/F4 Aigues (riv.), Fr.
75/F1 Aigues Tortes y Lago de San Mauricio Nat'l Park, Sp.
123/Q16 Aiguille, Cap de l' (cape), Alg.
99/F1 Aikawa, Japan
163/H3 Aiken, SC,US
104/D3 Ailao (mtn.), China
104/D4 Ailao (mts.), China
149/G4 Ailigandí, Pan.
120/F4 Ailinglapalap (atoll), Mrsh.
54/A6 Ailsa Craig (isl.), Sc,UK
120/G3 Ailuk (atoll), Mrsh.
105/G2 Aimen (pass), China
103/C5 Aimen Guan (pass), China
135/C2 Aimogasta, Arg.
141/D1 Aimorés, Braz.
72/F3 Ain (riv.), Fr.
123/V18 'Aïn Beïda, Alg.
123/S15 'Aïn Beniau, Alg.
124/D2 Aïn Ben Tili, Mrta.
123/S15 'Aïn Bessem, Alg.
123/R15 'Aïn Defla, Alg.
123/R15 'Aïn Defla (wilaya), Alg.
123/Q16 'Aïn el Turk, Alg.
123/V17 'Aïn Fakroun, Alg.
123/V17 'Aïn M'Lila, Alg.
81/G3 Aínos (peak), Gre.
81/G3 Ainos Nat'l Park, Gre.
123/U18 'Aïn Oulmene, Alg.
123/S16 'Aïn Oussersa, Alg.
57/E4 Ainsdale, Eng,UK
159/H2 Ainsworth, Ne,US
123/S15 'Aïn Taya, Alg.
123/Q16 'Aïn Temouchent, Alg.
123/Q16 'Aïn Temouchent (wilaya), Alg.
123/U18 'Aïn Touta, Alg.
129/G2 Aïr (plat.), Niger
156/E3 Airdrie, Ab,Can
54/C5 Airdrie, Sc,UK
68/D5 Aire (riv.), Fr.
57/G4 Aire (riv.), Eng,UK
68/B2 Aire, Canal de (can.), Fr.
57/E5 Aire, Point of (pt.), Wal,UK
68/B2 Aire-sur-la-Lys, Fr.
153/J2 Air Force (isl.), NW,Can
57/F3 Airton, Eng,UK
70/D3 Aisch (riv.), Ger.
68/D3 Aiseau-Presles, Belg.
142/B5 Aisén del General Carlos Ibáñez del Campo (reg.), Chile
103/E3 Ai Shan (mtn.), China
151/L3 Aishihik, Yk,Can
69/E3 Aisne (riv.), Belg.
68/C4 Aisne (dept.), Fr.
68/C5 Aisne (riv.), Fr.
124/E1 Aïssa (peak), Alg.
71/H6 Aist (riv.), Aus.
71/F5 Aiterach (riv.), Ger.
55/P12 Aith, Sc,UK
99/M9 Aitō, Japan
121/J6 Aitutaki (atoll), CookIs.
83/F2 Aiud, Rom.
141/J6 Aiuruoca, Braz.
141/J7 Aiuruoca (riv.), Braz.
72/F5 Aix-en-Provence, Fr.
72/F4 Aix-les-Bains, Fr.
81/H4 Aíyina, Gre.
81/H3 Aíyion, Gre.
99/F2 Aizu-Wakamatsu, Japan
104/B4 Āīzwal, India
80/A2 Ajaccio, Fr.
80/A2 Ajaccio (gulf), Fr.
147/F5 Ajalpan, Mex.
161/R8 Ajax, On,Can
96/D3 Aj Bogd (peak), Mong.
124/K1 Ajdābiyā, Libya
100/B3 Ajigasawa, Japan
127/C5 Aj Janayet, Sudan
82/C2 Ajka, Hun.
106/B2 Ajmer, India
158/D4 Ajo, Az,US
74/D1 Ajo, Cabo de (cape), Sp.
147/E5 Ajuchitlán, Mex.
147/Q10 Ajusco (mtn.), Mex.
112/C3 Ajuy, Phil.
99/F1 Aka (riv.), Japan
99/N10 Akabane, Japan
100/C2 Akabira, Japan
102/F1 Akademik Obruchev (mts.), Rus.
99/F3 Akaishi-dake (mtn.), Japan
100/D2 Akan (lake), Japan
100/D2 Akan Nat'l Park, Japan
127/B4 Akasha East, Sudan
98/D3 Akashi, Japan
99/K10 Akashi (str.), Japan
102/B4 Akbaytal (pass), Taj.
123/T15 Akbou, Alg.
92/D1 Akçaabat, Turk.
92/D2 Akçadağ, Turk.
92/D2 Akçakale, Turk.
83/K5 Akçakoca, Turk.
128/B2 Akchâr (reg.), Mrta.
92/C2 Akdağmadeni, Turk.
94/G4 Akdar, Al Jabal (mts.), Oman
99/N9 Akechi, Japan
62/H2 Åkersberga, Swe.
62/D2 Akershus (co.), Nor.
125/K7 Aketi, Zaire
87/G4 Akhaltsikhe, Geo.
81/H3 Akharnaí, Gre.
81/G3 Akhelóos (riv.), Gre.
92/A2 Akhisar, Turk.
127/B3 Akhmīm, Egypt
87/H3 Akhtuba (riv.), Rus.
87/H2 Akhtubinsk, Rus.
86/E2 Akhtyrka, Ukr.
98/C4 Aki, Japan
99/H7 Aki (riv.), Japan
99/H7 Akigawa, Japan
153/H3 Akimiski (isl.), NW,Can
91/D1 Akıncı (pt.), Turk.
99/H7 Akishima, Japan
100/B4 Akita, Japan
100/B4 Akita (pref.), Japan
128/B2 Akjoujt, Mrta.
106/D6 Akkaraipattu, SrL.
100/D2 Akkeshi, Japan
91/D3 'Akko, Isr.
128/D2 'Aklé 'Aouâna (dune), Mali, Mrta.
98/D3 Akō, Japan
124/H7 Akoga, Gabon
106/C3 Akola, India
125/N4 Ak'ordat, Erit.
92/C2 Akören, Turk.
129/F5 Akosombo (dam), Gha.
153/K2 Akpatok (isl.), NW,Can
102/C3 Akqi, China
81/J2 Akrathos, Ákra (cape), Gre.
62/A2 Åkrehamn, Nor.
81/G4 Akrítas, Ákra (cape), Gre.
159/G2 Akron, Co,US
168/F5 Akron, Oh,US
168/F5 Akron City (res.), Oh,US
102/C4 Aksai Chin (reg.), China, India
92/C2 Aksaray, Turk.
92/C2 Aksaray (prov.), Turk.
96/C4 Aksay, China
87/K2 Aksay, Kaz.
92/B2 Akşehir, Turk.
92/B2 Akşehir (lake), Turk.
91/B1 Akseki, Turk.
102/C2 Aksoran (peak), Kaz.
102/D3 Aksu, China
102/C3 Aksu (riv.), China
102/C2 Aksu (riv.), Kaz.
91/B1 Aksu (riv.), Turk.
125/N5 Āksum, Eth.
81/J2 Aktí (pen.), Gre.
87/L2 Aktyubinsk, Kaz.
87/L2 Aktyubinsk Obl., Kaz.
98/B4 Akune, Japan
61/N6 Akureyri, Ice.
151/E5 Akutan (isl.), Ak,US
151/E5 Akutan (passg.), Ak,US
129/G5 Akwa Ibom (state), Nga.
104/B4 Akyab (Sittwe), Burma
87/L2 Ak"yar, Rus.
83/K5 Akyazı, Turk.
96/B3 Ala (riv.), China
163/G3 Alabama (state), US
163/G4 Alabama (riv.), Al,US
163/G3 Alabama Space & Rocket Ctr., Al,US
163/G3 Alabaster, Al,US
112/C2 Alabat, Phil.
92/C1 Alaca, Turk.
92/C1 Alaçam, Turk.
163/H4 Alachua, Fl,US
149/F1 Alacranes, Embalse (res.), Cuba
87/H4 Alagir, Rus.
72/E4 Alagnon (riv.), Fr.
140/D2 Alagoa Grande, Braz.
140/C3 Alagoas (state), Braz.
140/C4 Alagoinhas, Braz.
74/B2 Alagón (riv.), Sp.
112/D4 Alah (riv.), Phil.
93/G4 Al Aḩmadi, Kuw.
61/G3 Alajärvi, Fin.
149/E4 Alajuela, CR
102/D2 Alakol' (lake), Kaz.
127/B2 Al 'Alamayn (El Alamein), Egypt
139/F5 Alalaú (riv.), Braz.
120/D3 Alamagan (isl.), NMar.
93/F4 Al 'Amārah, Iraq
93/H5 'Alāmarvdasht (riv.), Iran
165/K11 Alameda, Ca,US
165/L11 Alameda (co.), Ca,US
165/L11 Alameda (cr.), Ca,US
147/F4 Alamo, Mex.
158/D4 Alamo (lake), Az,US
165/K11 Alamo, Ca,US
158/D3 Alamo, Nv,US
159/F4 Alamogordo, NM,US
144/A2 Alamor, Ecu.
159/F3 Alamosa, Co,US
92/E3 Al Anbār (gov.), Iraq
63/H1 Åland (isls.), Fin.
64/F2 Aland (riv.), Ger.
91/C1 Alanya, Turk.
133/J7 Alaotra (lake), Madg.
163/H4 Alapaha (riv.), Ga,US
83/K5 Alaplı, Turk.
91/D5 Al 'Aqabah, Jor.
74/D3 Alarcón (res.), Sp.
92/B2 Alaşehir, Turk.
91/E4 Al 'Āsimah (gov.), Jor.
151/* Alaska (state), US
151/J4 Alaska (gulf), Ak,US
151/F4 Alaska (pen.), Ak,US
151/H3 Alaska (range), Ak,US
151/B5 Alaska Maritime Nat'l Wild. Ref., Ak,US
151/G4 Alaska Pen. Nat'l Wild. Ref., Ak,US
78/B5 Alassio, It.
85/K5 Alatyr', Rus.
87/H4 Alaverdi, Arm.
61/G3 Alavus, Fin.
56/D5 Alaw (riv.), Wal,UK
56/D5 Alaw, Llyn (lake), Wal,UK
102/B4 Alayskiy (mts.), Kyr.
89/R3 Alazeya (riv.), Rus.
93/F3 Al 'Azīzīyah, Iraq
124/H1 Al 'Azīzīyah, Libya
70/B5 Alb (riv.), Ger.
78/B3 Alba, It.
83/F2 Alba (co.), Rom.
92/D2 Al Bāb, Syria
74/E3 Albacete, Sp.
91/B5 Al Badrashayn, Egypt
127/C3 Al Baḩr al Aḩmar (gov.), Egypt
83/F2 Alba Iulia, Rom.
91/B4 Al Bājūr, Egypt
91/D3 Al Balqā' (gov.), Jor.
127/C3 Al Balyanā, Egypt
161/F1 Albanel (lake), Qu,Can
81/F2 Albania
116/C5 Albany, Austl.
153/H3 Albany (riv.), On,Can
165/K11 Albany, Ca,US
163/G4 Albany, Ga,US
160/C4 Albany, Ky,US
160/F3 Albany (cap.), NY,US
156/C4 Albany, Or,US
76/B6 Albarine (riv.), Fr.
93/F4 Al Başrah, Iraq
93/F4 Al Başrah (gov.), Iraq
114/G2 Albatross (bay), Austl.
132/A2 Albatross (pt.), Namb.
127/B2 Al Bawīţī, Egypt
125/K1 Al Bayḑā, Libya
76/E2 Albbruck, Ger.
144/J6 Albemarle (pt.), Ecu.
163/H3 Albemarle, NC,US
163/J2 Albemarle (sound), NC,US
78/B4 Albenga, It.
78/C1 Alben, Monte (peak), It.
76/B6 Albens, Fr.
74/C2 Alberche (riv.), Sp.
114/E5 Alberga (riv.), Austl.
119/A2 Albert (inlet), Austl.
114/F7 Albert (lake), Austl.
69/E2 Albert (canal), Belg.
68/B4 Albert, Fr.
130/A2 Albert (lake), Ugan., Zaire
152/E3 Alberta (prov.), Can.
142/E2 Alberti, Arg.
82/D2 Albertirsa, Hun.
157/K5 Albert Lea, Mn,US
130/A2 Albert Nile (riv.), Ugan.
143/J8 Alberto de Agostini Nat'l Park, Chile
132/Q13 Alberton, SAfr.
73/G4 Albertville, Fr.
163/G3 Albertville, Al,US
72/E5 Albi, Fr.
79/E2 Albignasego, It.
78/C1 Albino, It.
160/C3 Albion, Mi,US
159/H2 Albion, Ne,US
91/E2 Al Biqā' (gov.), Leb.
91/D3 Al Biqā' (Bekaa) (val.), Leb.
91/D4 Al Bīrah, WBnk.
78/B4 Albisola Superiore, It.
66/B5 Alblasserdam, Neth.
62/C3 Ålborg, Den.
62/D3 Ålborg (bay), Den.
74/D4 Albox, Sp.
161/S10 Albright Knox Art Gallery, NY,US
58/D1 Albrighton, Eng,UK
76/D5 Albristhorn (peak), Swi.
77/F1 Albstadt, Ger.
74/A4 Albufeira, Port.
91/B4 Al Buḩayrah (gov.), Egypt
77/F4 Albula (riv.), Swi.
77/F4 Albulapass (pass), Swi.
158/F4 Albuquerque, NM,US
74/B3 Alburquerque, Sp.
119/C3 Albury, Austl.
63/S7 Alby, Swe.
75/P10 Alcabideche, Port.
74/A3 Alcácer do Sal, Port.
74/C4 Alcalá de Guadaira, Sp.
74/D2 Alcalá de Henares, Sp.
74/D4 Alcalá la Real, Sp.
80/C4 Alcamo, It.
75/E2 Alcanadre (riv.), Sp.
75/E2 Alcanar, Sp.
75/E2 Alcañiz, Sp.
140/A1 Alcântara, Braz.
74/B3 Alcantara (res.), Sp.
74/E4 Alcantarilla, Sp.
74/D3 Alcarez (range), Sp.
165/K11 Alcatraz (isl.), Ca,US
74/C4 Alcaudete, Sp.
74/D3 Alcázar de San Juan, Sp.
59/E2 Alcester, Eng,UK
75/E3 Alcira, Sp.
163/H3 Alcoa, Tn,US
140/C5 Alcobaça, Braz.
74/D2 Alcobendas, Sp.
75/Q10 Alcochete, Port.
75/E2 Alcora, Sp.
74/D2 Alcorcón, Sp.
163/H3 Alcovy (riv.), Ga,US
75/E3 Alcoy, Sp.
123/G5 Aldabra (isls.), Sey.
162/B4 Aldama, Mex.
89/N4 Aldan, Rus.
89/N4 Aldan (plat.), Rus.
89/P3 Aldan (riv.), Rus.
102/G2 Aldarhaan, Mong.
59/E4 Aldbourne, Eng,UK
57/H4 Aldbrough, Eng,UK
59/H2 Alde (riv.), Eng,UK
59/H2 Aldeburgh, Eng,UK
126/B2 Aldeia Viçosa, Ang.
69/F2 Aldenhoven, Ger.
56/B2 Aldergrove, NI,UK
57/F5 Alderley Edge, Eng,UK
59/E4 Aldermaston, Eng,UK
72/B2 Alderney (isl.), Chl,UK
161/Q9 Aldershot, On,Can
59/F4 Aldershot, Eng,UK
165/C2 Alderwood Manor-Bothell North, Wa,US
162/E4 Aldine, Tx,US
70/B6 Aldingen, Ger.
166/B4 Aldred (lake), Pa,US
59/E1 Aldridge, Eng,UK
128/B2 Aleg, Mrta.
141/D2 Alegre, Braz.
135/E2 Alegrete, Braz.
134/A6 Alejandro Selkirk (isl.), Chile
86/E2 Aleksandriya, Ukr.
84/H4 Aleksandrov, Rus.
85/N4 Aleksandrovsk, Rus.
97/N1 Aleksandrovsk-Sakhalinskiy, Rus.
65/K2 Aleksandrów Kujawski, Pol.
65/K3 Aleksandrów Łódzki, Pol.
102/B1 Alekseyevka, Kaz.
86/F2 Alekseyevka, Rus.
84/H5 Aleksin, Rus.
82/E4 Aleksinac, Yugo.
93/N6 Alemdar, Turk.
141/L6 Além Paraíba, Braz.
72/D2 Alençon, Fr.
139/H5 Alenquer, Braz.
154/T10 Alenuihaha (chan.), Hi,US
91/E1 Aleppo (Ḩalab), Syria
142/B4 Alerce Andino Nat'l Park, Chile
153/S6 Alert (pt.), NW,Can
82/F2 Aleşd, Rom.
78/B3 Alessandria, It.
78/B3 Alessandria (prov.), It.
61/C3 Ålesund, Nor.
76/D5 Aletschhorn (peak), Swi.
151/E5 Aleutian (isls.), Ak,US
151/G4 Aleutian (range), Ak,US
54/D6 Ale Water (riv.), Sc,UK

172

Alexa – Annan

113/V **Alexander** (cape), Ant.
113/V **Alexander** (isl.), Ant.
116/B2 **Alexander** (peak), Austl.
151/L4 **Alexander** (arch.), Ak,US
163/G3 **Alexander City,** Al,US
161/J2 **Alexander Graham Bell Nat'l Hist. Park,** NS,Can
115/Q12 **Alexandra,** NZ
132/D3 **Alexandra,** SAfr.
140/C2 **Alexandria,** Braz.
81/H2 **Alexándria,** Gre.
83/G4 **Alexandria,** Rom.
54/B5 **Alexandria,** Sc,UK
162/E4 **Alexandria,** La,US
157/K4 **Alexandria,** Mn,US
166/A6 **Alexandria,** Va,US
127/B2 **Alexandria** (Al Iskandarīyah), Egypt
119/A2 **Alexandrina** (lake), Austl.
81/J2 **Alexandroúpolis,** Gre.
156/C2 **Alexis Creek,** BC,Can
102/D1 **Aley** (riv.), Rus.
102/D1 **Aleysk,** Rus.
75/E3 **Alfafar,** Sp.
93/E3 **Al Fallūjah,** Iraq
75/P10 **Alfama,** Port.
75/P11 **Alfarim,** Port.
74/E1 **Alfaro,** Sp.
125/L5 **Al Fāsher,** Sudan
127/B2 **Al Fashn,** Egypt
93/E3 **Al Fatḩah,** Iraq
93/G4 **Al Fāw,** Iraq
91/B5 **Al Fayyum,** Egypt
91/B5 **Al Fayyūm** (gov.), Egypt
69/F3 **Alfbach** (riv.), Ger.
67/G5 **Alfeld,** Ger.
141/H6 **Alfenas,** Braz.
81/G4 **Alfiós** (riv.), Gre.
79/F4 **Alfonsine,** It.
57/J5 **Alford,** Eng,UK
54/D2 **Alford,** Sc,UK
119/D3 **Alfred Nat'l Park,** Austl.
57/G5 **Alfreton,** Eng,UK
59/G5 **Alfriston,** Eng,UK
69/G2 **Alfter,** Ger.
87/L2 **Alga,** Kaz.
62/A2 **Ålgård,** Nor.
74/C4 **Algeciras,** Sp.
75/E3 **Algemesí,** Sp.
123/S15 **Alger** (wilaya), Alg.
123/S15 **Alger** (Algiers) (cap.), Alg.
124/F2 **Algeria**
67/G4 **Algermissen,** Ger.
75/N8 **Algete,** Sp.
93/F4 **Al Ghammās,** Iraq
127/B2 **Al Gharbīyah** (gov.), Egypt
80/A2 **Alghero,** It.
127/C3 **Al Ghurdaqah,** Egypt
123/S15 **Algiers** (Alger) (cap.), Alg.
75/E3 **Alginet,** Sp.
132/D4 **Algoa** (bay), SAfr.
144/C1 **Algodón** (riv.), Peru
165/P15 **Algonquin,** Il,US
75/P10 **Algueirão,** Port.
77/H4 **Algund** (Lagundo), It.
92/E3 **Al Ḩadīthah,** Iraq
95/G4 **Al Ḩajar ash Sharqī** (mts.), Oman
95/G5 **Al Ḩallānīyah** (isl.), Oman
74/D4 **Alhama de Granada,** Sp.
74/E4 **Alhama de Murcia,** Sp.
164/B2 **Alhambra,** Ca,US
127/B2 **Al Hammām,** Egypt
75/Q10 **Alhandra,** Port.
93/F4 **Al Hārithah,** Iraq
92/E2 **Al Ḩasakah,** Syria
92/E2 **Al Ḩasakah** (prov.), Syria
74/C4 **Alhaurín el Grande,** Sp.
91/B5 **Al Ḩawāmidīyah,** Egypt
93/F3 **Al Ḩayy,** Iraq
93/F3 **Al Ḩillah,** Iraq
93/F3 **Al Hindīyah,** Iraq
123/N13 **Al Hoceima,** Mor.
123/N13 **Al Hoceima** (isl.), Sp.
94/E3 **Al Hufūf,** SAr.
92/A2 **Aliağa,** Turk.
81/G2 **Aliákmon** (riv.), Gre.
81/G2 **Aliákmonos** (lake), Gre.
93/F3 **'Alī al Gharbī,** Iraq
93/F3 **'Alī ash Sharqī,** Iraq
162/C3 **Alibates Flint Quarries Nat'l Mon.,** Tx,US
87/J5 **Ali-Bayramly,** Azer.
127/C5 **Al Ibēdiyya,** Sudan
93/M6 **Alibey** (riv.), Turk.
83/J5 **Alibeyköy,** Turk.
75/E3 **Alicante,** Sp.
118/A1 **Alice** (riv.), Austl.
80/E3 **Alice** (pt.), It.
162/D5 **Alice,** Tx,US
117/G2 **Alice Springs,** Austl.
163/F3 **Aliceville,** Al,US
112/C4 **Alicia,** Phil.
80/D3 **Alicudi** (isl.), It.
106/C2 **Alīgarh,** India
94/E2 **Alīgudarz,** Iran
124/J8 **Alima** (riv.), Congo
62/E3 **Alingsås,** Swe.
106/B2 **Alīpur,** Pak.
106/E2 **Alīpur Duār,** India
168/G6 **Aliquippa,** Pa,US
91/A4 **Al Iskandarīyah** (gov.), Egypt
93/F3 **Al Iskandarīyah,** Iraq
91/A4 **Al Iskandarīyah** (Alexandria), Egypt
91/B4 **Al Ismā'īlīyah** (gov.), Egypt
91/C4 **Al Ismā'īlīyah** (Ismailia), Egypt
146/C2 **Alisos** (riv.), Mex.
132/D3 **Aliwal North,** SAfr.
125/K2 **Al Jaghbūb,** Libya
123/X18 **Al Jamm,** Tun.
91/D3 **Al Janūb** (gov.), Leb.
91/B4 **Al Jīzah,** Egypt
91/B5 **Al Jīzah** (gov.), Egypt
125/K5 **Al Junaynah,** Sudan
74/A4 **Aljustrel,** Port.
123/W17 **Al Kāf,** Tun.
123/W17 **Al Kāf** (gov.), Tun.
91/D4 **Al Karak,** Jor.
91/E4 **Al Karak** (gov.), Jor.
127/C3 **Al Karnak,** Egypt
69/E2 **Alken,** Belg.
95/G4 **Al Khābūrah,** Oman
91/D4 **Al Khalīl** (Hebron), WBnk.
93/F3 **Al Khāliş,** Iraq
127/B5 **Al Khandaq,** Sudan
91/B4 **Al Khānkah,** Egypt
127/B3 **Al Khārijah,** Egypt
125/M4 **Al Kharţūm Baḩrī** (Khartoum North), Sudan
94/F3 **Al Khobar,** SAr.
124/H1 **Al Khums,** Libya
66/B3 **Alkmaar,** Neth.
124/H3 **Alkoum** (well), Alg.
93/F3 **Al Kūfah,** Iraq
125/K3 **Al Kufrah,** Libya
93/F3 **Al Kūt,** Iraq
93/F4 **Al Kuwait** (Kuwait) (cap.), Kuw.
91/D2 **Al Lādhiqīyah** (prov.), Syria
91/D2 **Al Lādhiqīyah** (Latakia), Syria
106/D2 **Allahābād,** India
166/D2 **Allamuchy Saint Park,** NJ,US
157/G3 **Allan,** Sk,Can
157/G3 **Allan** (hills), Sk,Can
161/R9 **Allanburg,** On,Can
104/B5 **Allanmyo,** Burma
157/L3 **Allan Water** (riv.), On,Can
124/H1 **'Allāq** (well), Libya
127/C4 **'Allāqi, Wādī al** (dry riv.), Egypt
131/C4 **Alldays,** SAfr.
160/C3 **Allegan,** Mi,US
155/K4 **Allegheny** (mts.), US
168/G6 **Allegheny** (co.), Pa,US
160/E3 **Allegheny** (plat.), Pa,US
160/E3 **Allegheny** (riv.), Pa,US
142/D3 **Allen,** Arg.
58/B5 **Allen** (riv.), Eng,UK
60/C3 **Allen, Bog of** (swamp), Ire.
57/F2 **Allendale,** Eng,UK
163/H3 **Allendale,** SC,US
53/N7 **All England Lawn Tennis Club,** Eng,UK
60/B1 **Allen, Lough** (lake), Ire.
165/F7 **Allen Park,** Mi,US
77/F2 **Allensbach,** Ger.
166/C2 **Allentown,** Pa,US
108/F4 **Alleppey,** India
67/G3 **Aller** (riv.), Ger.
67/H4 **Allerkanal** (can.), Ger.
70/E4 **Allersberg,** Ger.
168/D1 **Allerton** (pt.), Ma,US
77/G3 **Allgäu** (mts.), Aus., Ger.
159/G2 **Alliance,** Ne,US
168/F6 **Alliance,** Oh,US
109/B2 **Allied War Cemetery,** Burma
72/E3 **Allier** (riv.), Fr.
54/C4 **Alloa,** Sc,UK
72/D3 **Allones,** Fr.
60/B5 **Allow** (riv.), Ire.
166/C4 **Alloway** (cr.), NJ,US
76/D2 **Allschwil,** Swi.
71/G7 **Alm** (riv.), Aus.
161/G1 **Alma,** Qu,Can
160/C3 **Alma,** Mi,US
159/H2 **Alma,** Ne,US
102/C3 **Alma-Ata** (cap.), Kaz.
74/A3 **Almada,** Port.
74/C3 **Almadén,** Sp.
92/B5 **Al Madīnah al Fikrīyah,** Egypt
80/B5 **Al Madīyah** (gov.), Tun.
91/E3 **Al Mafraq,** Jor.
142/D2 **Almafuerte,** Arg.
124/E1 **Al Maghrib** (reg.), Alg., Mor.
74/D3 **Almagro,** Sp.
91/B4 **Al Maḩallah al Kubrá,** Egypt
123/X18 **Al Mahdīyah,** Tun.
123/X18 **Al Mahdīyah** (gov.), Tun.
91/B4 **Al Maḩmūdīyah,** Egypt
93/F3 **Al Maḩmūdīyah,** Iraq
92/E2 **Al Mālikīyah,** Syria
102/A3 **Almalyk,** Uzb.
94/F3 **Al Manāmah** (Manama) (cap.), Bahr.
158/B2 **Almanor** (lake), Ca,US
75/E3 **Almansa,** Sp.
91/B4 **Al Mansūra,** Egypt
91/B4 **Al Manzilah,** Egypt
74/D4 **Almanzora** (riv.), Sp.
74/C2 **Almanzor, Pico de** (peak), Sp.
127/B3 **Al Marāghah,** Egypt
124/K1 **Al Marj,** Libya
140/B4 **Almas** (peak), Braz.
137/J6 **Almas** (riv.), Braz.
91/C4 **Al Maţarīyah,** Egypt
93/E2 **Al Mawşil** (Mosul), Iraq
92/E3 **Al Mayādin,** Syria
75/E3 **Almazora,** Sp.
67/F5 **Alme** (riv.), Ger.
137/H4 **Almeirim,** Braz.
74/A3 **Almeirim,** Port.
66/D4 **Almelo,** Neth.
140/B5 **Almenara,** Braz.
74/D3 **Almenara** (mtn.), Sp.
74/B2 **Almendra** (res.), Sp.
74/B3 **Almendralejo,** Sp.
66/C4 **Almere,** Neth.
74/D4 **Almería,** Sp.
75/D4 **Almeria** (gulf), Sp.
85/M5 **Al'met'yevsk,** Rus.
62/F3 **Älmhult,** Swe.
74/C5 **Almina** (pt.), Sp.
91/B4 **Al Minūfīyah** (gov.), Egypt
127/B2 **Al Minyā,** Egypt
127/B3 **Al Minyā** (gov.), Egypt
93/F3 **Al Miqdādiyah,** Iraq
143/J7 **Almirante Montt** (gulf), Chile
81/H3 **Almirós,** Gre.
81/J5 **Almiroú** (gulf), Gre.
74/C3 **Almodóvar del Campo,** Sp.
74/C4 **Almodóvar del Río,** Sp.
54/C4 **Almond** (riv.), Sc,UK
53/U11 **Almont** (riv.), Fr.
160/E2 **Almonte,** On,Can
74/B4 **Almonte,** Sp.
75/E3 **Almoradi,** Sp.
141/D1 **Almores** (range), Braz.
94/E3 **Al Mubarraz,** SAr.
125/L5 **Al Muglad,** Sudan
123/X18 **Al Muknīn,** Tun.
123/X18 **Al Munastīr,** Tun.
123/X18 **Al Munastīr** (gov.), Tun.
74/D4 **Almuñécar,** Sp.
93/F3 **Al Musayyib,** Iraq
93/F4 **Al Muthanná** (gov.), Iraq
54/B1 **Alness,** Sc,UK
54/B1 **Alness** (riv.), Sc,UK
55/L9 **Alnwick,** Eng,UK
121/J6 **Alofi** (cap.), Niue
120/H6 **Alofi** (isl.), Wall.
130/B2 **Aloi,** Ugan.
104/B2 **Along,** India
81/H3 **Alónnisos** (isl.), Gre.
111/F5 **Alor** (isls.), Indo.
74/C4 **Álora,** Sp.
110/B2 **Alor Setar,** Malay.
120/E6 **Alotau,** PNG
117/F3 **Aloysius** (peak), Austl.
79/E6 **Alpe di Poti** (peak), It.
78/D4 **Alpe di Succiso** (peak), It.
66/D5 **Alpen,** Ger.
160/D2 **Alpena,** Mi,US
140/A2 **Alpercatas** (mts.), Braz.
140/A2 **Alpercatas** (riv.), Braz.
77/F4 **Alperschällihorn** (peak), Swi.
66/B4 **Alphen aan de Rijn,** Neth.
74/A3 **Alpiarça,** Port.
78/A2 **Alpignano,** It.
162/C4 **Alpine,** Tx,US
156/F5 **Alpine,** Wy,US
165/D2 **Alpine Wild. Area,** Wa,US
70/B6 **Alpirsbach,** Ger.
74/B4 **Alportel,** Port.
73/G4 **Alps** (mts.), Eur.
99/F3 **Alps-Minami Nat'l Park,** Japan
95/G4 **Al Qābil,** Oman
125/N5 **Al Qaḑīrif,** Sudan
93/F4 **Al Qādisīyah** (gov.), Iraq
91/B4 **Al Qāhirah** (gov.), Egypt
91/B4 **Al Qāhirah** (Cairo) (cap.), Egypt
91/B4 **Al Qalyūbīyah** (gov.), Egypt
92/E2 **Al Qāmishlī,** Syria
91/B4 **Al Qanāţir al Khayrīyah,** Egypt
93/F3 **Al Qāsim,** Iraq
127/B3 **Al Qaşr,** Egypt
123/W18 **Al Qaşrayn,** Tun.
123/W18 **Al Qaşrayn** (gov.), Tun.
125/M5 **Al Qaţaynah,** Sudan
124/H3 **Al Qaţrūn,** Libya
123/X18 **Al Qayrawān,** Tun.
123/W18 **Al Qayrawān** (gov.), Tun.
91/D3 **Al Qunayţirah** (prov.), Syria
127/C3 **Al Quşayr,** Egypt
91/E2 **Al Quşayr,** Syria
91/E3 **Al Quţayfah,** Syria
59/E1 **Alrewas,** Eng,UK
62/C4 **Als** (isl.), Den.
76/D2 **Alsace** (hist. reg.), Fr.
73/G2 **Alsace** (reg.), Fr.
64/D5 **Alsace, Ballon d'** (mtn.), Fr.
57/F5 **Alsager,** Eng,UK
156/F3 **Alsask,** Sk,Can
74/D1 **Alsasua,** Sp.
69/F2 **Alsdorf,** Ger.
70/A3 **Alsenz** (riv.), Ger.
64/E3 **Alsfeld,** Ger.
165/Q16 **Alsip,** Il,US
67/H1 **Alster** (riv.), Ger.
57/F2 **Alston,** Eng,UK
57/F4 **Alt** (riv.), Eng,UK
61/G1 **Alta,** Nor.
63/S7 **Ålta,** Swe.
164/B2 **Altadena,** Ca,US
137/G6 **Alta Floresta,** Braz.
142/D1 **Alta Gracia,** Arg.
102/D1 **Altai** (mts.), Asia
163/H4 **Altamaha** (riv.), Ga,US
137/H4 **Altamira,** Braz.
147/F4 **Altamira,** Mex.
163/H4 **Altamonte Springs,** Fl,US
80/E2 **Altamura,** It.
146/C3 **Altamura** (isl.), Mex.
138/B5 **Altar** (vol.), Ecu.
148/D2 **Altar de los Sacrificios** (ruins), Guat.
96/B2 **Altay,** China
96/C3 **Altay,** Mong.
96/D2 **Altay,** Mong.
88/J4 **Altay Kray,** Rus.
77/E4 **Altdorf,** Swi.
71/E4 **Altdorf bei Nürnberg,** Ger.
75/E3 **Altea,** Sp.
67/E6 **Altena,** Ger.
67/F5 **Altenau** (riv.), Ger.
67/F5 **Altenbeken,** Ger.
64/G3 **Altenburg,** Ger.
70/B2 **Altenstadt,** Ger.
70/B5 **Altensteig,** Ger.
65/G2 **Altentreptow,** Ger.
147/F5 **Altepexi,** Mex.
66/D5 **Alter Rhein** (riv.), Ger.
67/G1 **Altes Land** (reg.), Ger.
70/B5 **Althengstett,** Ger.
57/H4 **Althorpe,** Eng,UK
92/D1 **Altındere Milli Park,** Turk.
91/E1 **Altınözü,** Turk.
136/E7 **Altiplano** (plat.), Bol., Peru
64/F2 **Altmark** (reg.), Ger.
71/E5 **Altmühl** (riv.), Ger.
71/G7 **Altmünster,** Aus.
140/A4 **Alto** (peak), Braz.
79/E2 **Alto** (riv.), It.
137/H7 **Alto Araguaia,** Braz.
126/C2 **Alto Cuale,** Ang.
149/H5 **Alto de Tamar** (peak), Col.
137/H7 **Alto Garças,** Braz.
140/B2 **Alto Longá,** Braz.
147/N7 **Alto Lucero,** Mex.
79/E2 **Alto, Monte** (peak), It.
59/F4 **Alton,** Eng,UK
160/B4 **Alton,** Il,US
119/F5 **Altona,** Austl.
157/J3 **Altona,** Mb,Can
160/E3 **Altoona,** Pa,US
140/A3 **Alto Parnaíba,** Braz.
144/C3 **Alto Purús** (riv.), Peru
140/B2 **Altos,** Braz.
140/C2 **Alto Santo,** Braz.
149/G4 **Altos de Campana Nat'l Park,** Pan.
147/F5 **Altotonga,** Mex.
71/F6 **Altötting,** Ger.
144/C3 **Alto Yuruá** (riv.), Peru
57/F5 **Altrincham,** Eng,UK
70/B4 **Altrip,** Ger.
96/C4 **Altun** (mts.), China
148/D2 **Altun Ha** (ruins), Belz.
158/B2 **Alturas,** Ca,US
159/H4 **Altus,** Ok,US
159/H4 **Altus** (res.), Ok,US
159/H4 **Altus A.F.B.,** Ok,US
125/M5 **Al Ubayyiḑ,** Sudan
92/D1 **Alucra,** Turk.
125/L5 **Al Uḑayyah,** Sudan
56/E5 **Alun** (riv.), Wal,UK
127/C3 **Al Uqşur** (Luxor), Egypt
86/E3 **Alushta,** Ukr.
125/L3 **Al 'Uwaynāt** (peak), Sudan
54/C4 **Alva,** Sc,UK
159/H3 **Alva,** Ok,US
147/G5 **Alvarado,** Mex.
146/C3 **Alvaro Obregón** (res.), Mex.
62/F1 **Älvdalen,** Swe.
59/E2 **Alvechurch,** Eng,UK
74/A3 **Alverca,** Port.
75/P10 **Alverca do Ribatejo,** Port.
62/F3 **Alvesta,** Swe.
58/D4 **Alveston,** Eng,UK
162/E4 **Alvin,** Tx,US
62/G1 **Älvkarleby,** Swe.
141/A4 **Alvorada,** Braz.
140/A4 **Alvorada do Norte,** Braz.
62/E3 **Älvsborg** (co.), Swe.
61/G2 **Älvsbyn,** Swe.
127/B3 **Al Wādī al Jadīd** (gov.), Egypt
92/B4 **Al Wāḩāt al Baḩrtyah** (oasis), Egypt
106/C2 **Alwar,** India
91/B5 **Al Wāsiţah,** Egypt
108/F3 **Alwaye,** India
96/E4 **Alxa Youqi,** China
96/F4 **Alxa Zuoqi,** China
117/G2 **Alyawarra Abor. Land,** Austl.
54/C3 **Alyth,** Sc,UK
63/L4 **Alytus,** Lith.
71/F7 **Alz** (riv.), Ger.
78/C1 **Alzano Lombardo,** It.
70/C2 **Alzenau in Unterfranken,** Ger.
69/F4 **Alzette** (riv.), Lux.
70/B3 **Alzey,** Ger.
71/F6 **Alzkanal** (can.), Ger.
144/D1 **Amacayacú Nat'l Park,** Col.
139/F2 **Amacuro** (riv.), Guy., Ven.
147/K8 **Amacuzac** (riv.), Mex.
94/B4 **Amada** (ruins), Egypt
117/F3 **Amadeus** (lake), Austl.
125/M6 **Amadi,** Sudan
153/J2 **Amadjuak** (lake), NW,Can
74/A3 **Amadora,** Port.
167/F2 **Amagansett Nat'l Wild. Ref.,** NY,US
99/L10 **Amagasaki,** Japan
63/T9 **Amager** (isl.), Den.
98/B4 **Amagi,** Japan
99/F3 **Amagi-san** (mtn.), Japan
138/B5 **Amaguaña,** Ecu.
111/G4 **Amahai,** Indo.
147/L6 **Amajac** (riv.), Mex.
98/A4 **Amakusa** (sea), Japan
62/E2 **Åmål,** Swe.
130/B3 **Amala** (riv.), Kenya
96/G1 **Amalat** (riv.), Rus.
138/C3 **Amalfi,** Col.
81/G4 **Amaliás,** Gre.
106/C3 **Amalner,** India
144/B2 **Amaluza,** Ecu.
135/E1 **Amambaí,** Braz.
137/H8 **Amambaí** (riv.), Braz.
100/K7 **Amami** (isls.), Japan
100/K6 **Amami-O-Shima** (isl.), Japan
139/E5 **Amaná** (lake), Braz.
80/E3 **Amantea,** It.
121/L6 **Amanu** (atoll), FrPol.
137/H3 **Amapá,** Braz.
139/H4 **Amapá** (state), Braz.
140/B2 **Amarante,** Braz.
74/A2 **Amarante,** Port.
140/A2 **Amarante do Marahão,** Braz.
104/C4 **Amarapura,** Burma
108/F3 **Amaravāti** (riv.), India
140/C4 **Amargosa,** Braz.
158/C3 **Amargosa** (dry riv.), Ca, Nv,US
162/C3 **Amarillo,** Tx,US
80/D1 **Amaro** (peak), It.
100/A4 **Amarume,** Japan
83/L5 **Amasra,** Turk.
92/C1 **Amasya,** Turk.
92/C1 **Amasya** (prov.), Turk.
99/J7 **Amatsukominato,** Japan
167/E1 **Amawalk** (res.), NY,US
69/E2 **Amay,** Belg.
147/L8 **Amayuca,** Mex.
137/H4 **Amazon** (riv.), SAm.
139/E5 **Amazonas** (state), Braz.
144/D2 **Amazonas** (state), Braz.
138/C5 **Amazonas** (comm.), Col.
144/C2 **Amazonas** (dept.), Peru
139/E3 **Amazonas** (terr.), Ven.
137/G4 **Amazônia** (Tapajós) Nat'l Park, Braz.
106/C4 **Ambajogai,** India
108/D2 **Ambāla,** India
106/D6 **Ambalangoda,** SrL.
133/H8 **Ambalavao,** Madg.
124/H7 **Ambam,** Camr.
133/J6 **Ambanja,** Madg.
133/H6 **Ambaro** (bay), Madg.
108/F4 **Ambāsamudram,** India
138/B5 **Ambato,** Ecu.
133/H7 **Ambato Boeny,** Madg.
133/H8 **Ambatofinandrahana,** Madg.
133/H7 **Ambatolampy,** Madg.
133/J7 **Ambatondrazaka,** Madg.
81/H4 **Ámbelos, Ákra** (cape), Gre.
71/E4 **Amberg,** Ger.
57/G5 **Ambergate,** Eng,UK
148/E2 **Ambergris** (cay), Belz.
150/C2 **Ambergris** (cay), Trks.
76/B6 **Ambérieu-en-Bugey,** Fr.
106/D3 **Ambikāpur,** India
133/J6 **Ambilobe,** Madg.
133/J7 **Ambinaninony,** Madg.
57/G1 **Amble,** Eng,UK
166/C3 **Ambler,** Pa,US
57/F3 **Ambleside,** Eng,UK
68/A2 **Ambleteuse,** Fr.
69/F3 **Amblève** (riv.), Belg.
133/H9 **Amboasary,** Madg.
133/J6 **Ambohitra, Tampon** (peak), Madg.
111/G4 **Ambon,** Indo.
111/G4 **Ambon** (isl.), Indo.
130/C2 **Amboseli Nat'l Park,** Kenya
133/H8 **Ambositra,** Madg.
133/H9 **Ambovombe,** Madg.
168/G6 **Ambridge,** Pa,US
126/B2 **Ambriz,** Ang.
76/B5 **Ambronay,** Fr.
120/F6 **Ambrym** (isl.), Van.
151/B6 **Amchitka** (isl.), Ak,US
151/B6 **Amchitka** (passg.), Ak,US
104/A1 **Amdo,** China
147/K6 **Amealco,** Mex.
146/D4 **Ameca,** Mex.
147/L7 **Amecameca de Juárez,** Mex.
71/G5 **Ameisberg** (peak), Aus.
69/F3 **Amel,** Belg.
66/C2 **Ameland** (isl.), Neth.
66/B5 **Amer** (chan.), Neth.
113/F **American** (highland), Ant.
165/M9 **American** (riv.), Ca,US
165/B3 **American** (lake), Wa,US
141/C2 **Americana,** Braz.
156/E5 **American Falls,** Id,US
158/D2 **American Falls** (res.), Id,US
158/E2 **American Fork,** Ut,US
158/B3 **American, North Fork** (riv.), Ca,US
121/J6 **American Samoa** (terr.), US
158/B3 **American, South Fork** (riv.), Ca,US
163/G3 **Americus,** Ga,US
73/L3 **Ameringkogel** (peak), Aus.
66/C4 **Amersfoort,** Neth.
59/F3 **Amersham,** Eng,UK
113/E **Amery Ice Shelf,** Ant.
157/K5 **Ames,** Ia,US
59/E4 **Amesbury,** Eng,UK
81/H3 **Ámfissa,** Gre.
89/N3 **Amga** (riv.), Rus.
89/T3 **Amguema** (riv.), Rus.
97/M1 **Amgun'** (riv.), Rus.
161/H2 **Amherst,** NS,Can
168/B1 **Amherst,** Ma,US
168/E5 **Amherst,** Oh,US
165/F7 **Amherstburg,** On,Can
80/B1 **Amiata** (peak), It.
68/B4 **Amiens,** Fr.
91/E1 **Amik** (lake), Turk.
89/U4 **Amila** (isl.), Ak,US
123/H5 **Amirante** (isls.), Sey.
157/H2 **Amisk** (lake), Sk,Can
162/C4 **Amistad** (res.), Mex., US
159/G5 **Amistad Nat'l Rec. Area,** Tx,US
159/K5 **Amite** (riv.), La,US
167/M9 **Amityville,** NY,US
106/C3 **Amla,** India
151/D6 **Amlia** (isl.), Ak,US
56/D5 **Amlwch,** Wal,UK
91/D4 **'Ammān** (cap.), Jor.
58/C3 **Amman** (riv.), Wal,UK
58/C3 **Ammanford,** Wal,UK
61/E2 **Ammarfjället** (peak), Swe.
70/B5 **Ammer** (riv.), Ger.
151/K2 **Ammerman** (mtn.), Yk,Can
70/E6 **Ammersee** (lake), Ger.
156/F5 **Ammon,** Id,US
109/D3 **Amnat Charoen,** Thai.
69/F5 **Amnéville,** Fr.
104/D4 **Amo** (riv.), China
93/H2 **Āmol,** Iran
75/P10 **Amora,** Port.
81/J4 **Amorgós** (isl.), Gre.
163/F3 **Amory,** Ms,US
160/E1 **Amos,** Qu,Can
133/J8 **Ampangalana** (can.), Madg.
133/H9 **Ampanihy,** Madg.
106/D6 **Amparai,** SrL.
141/G7 **Amparo,** Braz.
133/J6 **Ampasindava** (bay), Madg.
144/D4 **Ampato** (peak), Peru
71/E6 **Amper** (riv.), Ger.
105/G5 **Amphitrite Group** (isls.), China
75/F2 **Amposta,** Sp.
59/F2 **Ampthill,** Eng,UK
161/H1 **Amqui,** Qu,Can
106/C3 **Amravati,** India
106/B3 **Amreli,** India
92/C3 **'Amrīt** (ruins), Syria
108/C2 **Amritsar,** India
64/E1 **Amrun** (isl.), Ger.
66/B4 **Amstel** (riv.), Neth.
66/B4 **Amstelveen,** Neth.
51/N7 **Amsterdam** (isl.), FrAnt.
66/B4 **Amsterdam** (cap.), Neth.
160/F3 **Amsterdam,** NY,US
66/C5 **Amsterdam-Rijnkanaal** (can.), Neth.
73/L2 **Amstetten,** Aus.
125/K5 **Am Timan,** Chad
90/F5 **Amudar'ya** (riv.), Asia
130/B2 **Amudat,** Ugan.
151/D5 **Amukta** (passg.), Ak,US
139/G4 **Amuku** (mts.), Guy.
153/S7 **Amund Rignes** (isl.), NW,Can
113/D **Amundsen** (bay), Ant.
113/S **Amundsen** (sea), Ant.
152/D1 **Amundsen** (gulf), NW,Can
113/A **Amundsen-Scott,** Ant.
62/F1 **Amunge** (lake), Swe.
97/M1 **Amur** (riv.), China, Rus.
121/K6 **Amuri,** CookIs.
89/N4 **Amur Obl.,** Rus.
74/D1 **Amurrio,** Sp.
97/M1 **Amursk,** Rus.
127/C5 **'Amur, Wādī** (dry riv.), Sudan
91/D2 **Amyūn,** Leb.
121/L6 **Anaa** (atoll), FrPol.
89/L3 **Anabar** (riv.), Rus.
164/A2 **Anacapa** (isl.), Ca,US
149/G4 **Anachucuna** (mtn.), Pan.
139/E2 **Anaco,** Ven.
156/E4 **Anaconda,** Mt,US
159/H4 **Anadarko,** Ok,US
89/T3 **Anadyr',** Rus.
89/U3 **Anadyr'** (gulf), Rus.
89/T3 **Anadyr'** (range), Rus.
90/S3 **Anadyr'** (riv.), Rus.
81/J4 **Anáfi** (isl.), Gre.
92/E3 **'Ānah,** Iraq
164/C3 **Anaheim,** Ca,US
164/G8 **Anaheim Stadium,** Ca,US
156/B2 **Anahim Lake,** BC,Can
162/E4 **Anahuac,** Tx,US
108/F3 **Anai Mudi** (mtn.), India
140/A1 **Anajatuba,** Braz.
106/D4 **Anakāpalle,** India
133/H6 **Analalava,** Madg.
133/J7 **Analamaitso** (plat.), Madg.
149/G1 **Ana María** (gulf), Cuba
110/C3 **Anambas** (isls.), Indo.
129/G5 **Anambra** (state), Nga.
91/C1 **Anamur,** Turk.
91/C1 **Anamur** (pt.), Turk.
98/D4 **Anan,** Japan
106/B3 **Anand,** India
104/B4 **Ananda Temple,** Burma
106/C5 **Anantapur,** India
108/C1 **Anantnag,** India
102/C3 **Anan'yevo,** Kyr.
86/F3 **Anapa,** Rus.
143/K7 **Añapi** (peak), Arg.
137/J7 **Anápolis,** Braz.
137/H4 **Anapu** (riv.), Braz.
137/G8 **Anastácio,** Braz.
120/D3 **Anathan** (isl.), NMar.
92/B2 **Anatolia** (reg.), Turk.
135/D2 **Añatuya,** Arg.
139/F4 **Anauá** (riv.), Braz.
161/Q9 **Ancaster,** On,Can
141/D2 **Anchieta,** Braz.
165/G6 **Anchor** (bay), Mi,US
151/J3 **Anchorage,** Ak,US
161/G2 **Ancienne-Lorette,** Qu,Can
144/D4 **Ancohuma** (peak), Bol.
144/B3 **Ancón,** Peru
79/G5 **Ancona,** It.
79/G5 **Ancona** (prov.), It.
138/B4 **Ancón de Sardinas** (bay), Col., Ecu.
54/E5 **Ancroft,** Eng,UK
54/D6 **Ancrum,** Sc,UK
142/B4 **Ancud,** Chile
142/B4 **Ancud** (gulf), Chile
97/K2 **Anda,** China
144/C4 **Andahuaylas,** Peru
133/J7 **Andaingo Gara,** Madg.
61/C3 **Åndalsnes,** Nor.
74/C4 **Andalusia** (aut. comm.), Sp.
163/G4 **Andalusia,** Al,US
107/F5 **Andaman** (sea), Asia
107/F5 **Andaman** (isls.), India
107/F5 **Andaman & Nicobar Is.** (terr.), India
133/J6 **Andapa,** Madg.
140/B4 **Andaraí,** Braz.
68/A4 **Andelle** (riv.), Fr.
77/F2 **Andelsbach** (riv.), Ger.
61/F1 **Andenes,** Nor.
69/E3 **Andenne,** Belg.
61/F1 **Ånderdalen Nat'l Park,** Nor.
68/D3 **Anderlues,** Belg.
69/G3 **Andernach,** Ger.
151/N2 **Anderson** (riv.), NW,Can
158/B2 **Anderson,** Ca,US
160/C3 **Anderson,** In,US
163/H3 **Anderson,** SC,US
162/E4 **Anderson,** Tx,US
165/B3 **Anderson** (inlet), Wa,US
165/B3 **Anderson** (isl.), Wa,US
163/G3 **Andersonville Nat'l Hist. Site,** Ga,US
134/C4 **Andes** (mts.), SAm.
61/F1 **Andfjorden** (fjord), Nor.
106/C4 **Andhra Pradesh** (state), India
81/H5 **Andikíthira** (isl.), Gre.
133/J7 **Andilamena,** Madg.
93/G3 **Andīmeshk,** Iran
81/J4 **Andíparos** (isl.), Gre.
141/B2 **Andira,** Braz.
102/B3 **Andizhan,** Uzb.
74/D1 **Andoain,** Sp.
138/B5 **Andoas Nuevo,** Ecu.
101/E4 **Andong,** SKor.
101/E4 **Andong** (lake), SKor.
75/F1 **Andorra**
75/E2 **Andorra,** Sp.
75/F1 **Andorra la Vella** (cap.), And.
59/E4 **Andover,** Eng,UK
61/E1 **Andøya** (isl.), Nor.
141/G7 **Andradas,** Braz.
141/B2 **Andradina,** Braz.
75/G3 **Andraitx,** Sp.
133/H7 **Andranomavo** (riv.), Madg.
151/C6 **Andreanof** (isls.), Ak,US
141/J6 **Andrelândia,** Braz.
144/C3 **Andres Avelino Caceres** (dept.), Peru
53/S10 **Andrésy,** Fr.
162/C3 **Andrews,** Tx,US
166/B6 **Andrews A.F.B.,** Md,US
80/E2 **Andria,** It.
133/H8 **Andringitra** (mts.), Madg.
133/J6 **Androntany** (cape), Madg.
150/B1 **Andros** (isl.), Bahm.
81/J4 **Ándros** (isl.), Gre.
160/G2 **Androscoggin** (riv.), Me, NH,US
74/C3 **Andújar,** Sp.
142/C4 **Anecón Grande** (peak), Arg.
142/E4 **Anegada** (bay), Arg.
150/E3 **Anegada** (isl.), BVI
149/F5 **Anegada** (pt.), Pan.
150/E3 **Anegada** (passg.), West Indies
129/F5 **Aného,** Togo
120/G7 **Aneityum** (isl.), Van.
75/F1 **Aneto, Pico de** (peak), Sp.
107/K2 **Anfu,** China
108/F3 **Angamāli,** India
135/B1 **Angamos** (pt.), Chile
96/E1 **Angara** (riv.), Rus.
96/E1 **Angarsk,** Rus.
61/E3 **Ånge,** Swe.
67/E5 **Angel** (riv.), Ger.
139/F3 **Ángel** (falls), Ven.
146/B2 **Ángel de la Guarda** (isl.), Mex.
112/C2 **Angeles,** Phil.
164/B2 **Angeles Nat'l For.,** Ca,US
62/E3 **Ängelholm,** Swe.
162/E4 **Angelina** (riv.), Tx,US
64/E1 **Angeln** (reg.), Ger.
165/F6 **Angelus** (lake), Mi,US
164/D2 **Angelus Oaks,** Ca,US
111/J4 **Angemuk** (mtn.), Indo.
61/E2 **Ångermanälven** (riv.), Swe.
65/H2 **Angermünde,** Ger.
72/C3 **Angers,** Fr.
140/B2 **Angical do Piauí,** Braz.
140/C2 **Angicos,** Braz.
109/C3 **Angkor** (ruins), Camb.
109/D4 **Angk Tasaom,** Camb.
115/Q12 **Anglem** (peak), NZ
56/D5 **Anglesey** (isl.), Wal,UK
72/C5 **Anglet,** Fr.
162/E4 **Angleton,** Tx,US
72/D3 **Anglin** (riv.), Fr.
109/C2 **Ang Nam Ngum** (lake), Laos
125/L7 **Ango,** Zaire
126/G4 **Angoche,** Moz.
142/B3 **Angol,** Chile
126/C3 **Angola**
160/C3 **Angola,** In,US
148/C2 **Angostura** (res.), Mex.
72/D4 **Angoulême,** Fr.
75/S12 **Angra do Heroísmo,** Azor.,Port.
141/J8 **Angra dos Reis,** Braz.
102/B3 **Angren,** Uzb.
109/C3 **Ang Thong,** Thai.
125/K7 **Angu,** Zaire
150/F3 **Anguilla** (isl.), UK
151/G2 **Angutikada** (peak), Ak,US
131/C3 **Angwa** (riv.), Zim.
137/H8 **Anhanduí** (riv.), Braz.
69/D3 **Anhée,** Belg.
62/D3 **Anholt** (isl.), Den.
105/F2 **Anhua,** China
103/D4 **Anhui** (prov.), China
100/B3 **Ani,** Japan
151/G4 **Aniakchak** (crater), Ak,US
151/G4 **Aniakchak Nat'l Mon. & Prsv.,** Ak,US
68/C3 **Aniche,** Fr.
158/F3 **Animas** (riv.), Co, NM,US
146/B2 **Ánimas, Punta de las** (pt.), Mex.
82/E3 **Anina,** Rom.
97/N2 **Aniva** (bay), Rus.
100/C1 **Aniva, Mys** (cape), Rus.
63/M1 **Anjalamkoski,** Fin.
106/B3 **Anjār,** India
99/N10 **Anjō,** Japan
161/N6 **Anjou,** Qu,Can
72/C3 **Anjou** (hist. reg.), Fr.
133/H6 **Anjouan** (isl.), Com.
96/F5 **Ankang,** China
92/C2 **Ankara** (cap.), Turk.
92/C2 **Ankara** (prov.), Turk.
79/G1 **Ankaran,** Slov.
133/H7 **Ankaratra, Massif** (plat.), Madg.
162/C2 **Ankaree** (riv.), Co,US
133/H8 **Ankazoabo,** Madg.
109/E3 **An Khe,** Viet.
65/G2 **Anklam,** Ger.
104/E3 **Anlong,** China
109/D3 **Anlong Veng,** Camb.
66/D2 **Anloo,** Neth.
103/C5 **Anlu,** China
113/D **Ann** (cape), Ant.
161/G3 **Ann** (cape), Ma,US
160/E4 **Anna** (lake), Va,US
123/V17 **Annaba,** Alg.
123/V17 **Annaba** (wilaya), Alg.
71/G1 **Annaberg-Buchholz,** Ger.
91/E2 **An Nabk,** Syria
56/B3 **Annaclone,** NI,UK
92/D4 **An Nafūd** (des.), SAr.
125/L5 **An Nahūd,** Sudan
93/F4 **An Najaf,** Iraq
93/E4 **An Najaf** (gov.), Iraq
60/D1 **Annalee** (riv.), Ire.
56/C3 **Annalong,** NI,UK
109/D2 **Annamitique, Chaine** (mts.), Laos, Viet.
57/E2 **Annan,** Sc,UK

173
Annan – Athen

54/C6 Annan (riv.), Sc,UK
166/A6 Annandale, Va,US
66/B3 Anna Pavlowna, Neth.
142/B5 Anna Pink (bay), Chile
166/B6 Annapolis (cap.), Md,US
106/D2 Annapurna (mtn.), Nepal
94/C3 An Naqb, Ra's, Jor.
165/E7 Ann Arbor, Mi,US
93/F4 An Nāṣirīyah, Iraq
54/B6 Annbank Station, Sc,UK
119/C4 Anne (peak), Austl.
116/C3 Annean (lake), Austl.
166/B6 Anne Arundel (co.), Md,US
76/C6 Annecy, Fr.
76/C6 Annecy (lake), Fr.
76/C6 Annecy-le-Vieux, Fr.
76/C5 Annemasse, Fr.
53/U10 Annet-sur-Marne, Fr.
109/E3 An Nhon, Viet.
104/D3 Anning, China
104/D3 Anning (riv.), China
163/G3 Anniston, Al,US
124/F8 Annobón (isl.), EqG.
72/F4 Annonay, Fr.
93/F3 An Nu'manīyah, Iraq
108/F3 Annūr, India
70/A4 Annweiler, Ger.
99/M10 Anō, Japan
75/K7 Anoia (riv.), Sp.
157/K4 Anoka, Mn,US
133/J7 Anosibe an' Ala, Madg.
129/G2 Ânou-Zeggarene (wadi), Niger
109/E4 An Phuoc, Viet.
103/D5 Anqing, China
103/D3 Anqiu, China
107/K2 Anren, China
67/F5 Anröchte, Ger.
69/E2 Ans, Belg.
103/B3 Ansai, China
101/F7 Ansan, SKor.
70/D4 Ansbach, Ger.
138/C3 Anserma, Col.
71/H6 Ansfelden, Aus.
101/B2 Anshan, China
104/E3 Anshun, China
114/D2 Anson (bay), Austl.
162/D3 Anson, Tx,US
101/D4 Ansŏng, SKor.
168/A3 Ansonia, Ct,US
54/D4 Anstruther, Sc,UK
120/E4 Ant (atoll), Micr.
59/H1 Ant (riv.), Eng,UK
91/E1 Antakya (Antioch), Turk.
133/J6 Antalaha, Madg.
91/B1 Antalya, Turk.
91/B1 Antalya (gulf), Turk.
91/A1 Antalya (prov.), Turk.
133/H7 Antananarivo (cap.), Madg.
133/H7 Antananarivo (prov.), Madg.
113/W Antarctic (pen.), Ant.
113/* Antarctica
140/C3 Antas, Braz.
141/B4 Antas (riv.), Braz.
68/D5 Ante (riv.), Fr.
54/A1 An Teallach (mtn.), Sc,UK
131/C4 Antelope Mine, Zim.
74/C4 Antequera, Sp.
159/H3 Anthony, Ks,US
158/F4 Anthony, NM,US
124/D2 Anti-Atlas (mts.), Mor.
73/G5 Antibes, Fr.
161/J1 Anticosti (isl.), Qu,Can
71/G6 Antiesen (riv.), Aus.
72/D2 Antifer, Cap d' (cape), Fr.
160/B2 Antigo, Wi,US
161/J2 Antigonish, NS,Can
150/F3 Antigua (isl.), Anti.
150/F3 Antigua & Barbuda
148/D3 Antigua Guatemala, Guat.
91/D3 Anti-Lebanon (mts.), Leb.
165/L10 Antioch, Ca,US
165/P15 Antioch, Il,US
91/E1 Antioch (Antakya), Turk.
138/C3 Antioquia, Col.
138/C3 Antioquia (dept.), Col.
51/T8 Antipodes (isls.), NZ
138/B5 Antisana (vol.), Ecu.
159/J4 Antlers, Ok,US
135/B1 Antofagasta, Chile
68/C2 Antoing, Belg.
133/J6 Antongil (bay), Madg.
132/C4 Antoniesberg (peak), SAfr.
141/B3 Antonina, Braz.
140/C2 Antonina do Norte, Braz.
147/Q10 Antonio Alzate (lake), Mex.
141/K6 Antônio Carlos, Braz.
159/F3 Antonito, Co,US
147/P7 Antón Lizardo, Mex.
147/G5 Anton Lizardo, Punta (pt.), Mex.
53/S10 Antony, Fr.
56/B2 Antrim, NI,UK
56/B2 Antrim (dist.), NI,UK
56/B1 Antrim (mts.), NI,UK
133/H7 Antsalova, Madg.
133/H7 Antsirabe, Madg.
133/J6 Antsiranana, Madg.
133/J6 Antsiranana (prov.), Madg.
133/H6 Antsohihy, Madg.
142/C3 Antuco (vol.), Chile
112/B4 Antulai, Gunung (mtn.), Malay.
69/E1 Antwerp (prov.), Belg.
68/D1 Antwerp (Antwerpen), Belg.
68/D1 Antwerpen (Antwerp), Belg.
108/H4 Anuradhapura, SrL.
108/H4 Anuradhapura (dist.), SrL.
108/H4 Anuradhapura (ruins), SrL.
151/B6 Anvil (vol.), Ak,US
105/H3 Anxi, China
103/C3 Anyang, China
101/D4 Anyang, SKor.
101/F7 Anyang (riv.), SKor.
96/D4 A'nyêmaqên (mts.), China
103/B4 Anyi, China
105/G3 Anyuan, China
97/M2 Anyuy (riv.), Rus.
76/E6 Anza (riv.), It.
103/C3 Anze, China
68/C2 Anzegem, Belg.
88/J4 Anzhero-Sudzhensk, Rus.
68/C3 Anzin, Fr.
80/C2 Anzio, It.
139/E2 Anzoátegui (state), Ven.
99/L9 Aogaki, Japan
109/B4 Ao Kham (pt.), Thai.
100/B3 Aomori, Japan
100/B3 Aomori (dept.), Japan
81/G2 Aóos (riv.), Gre.
109/B4 Ao Phangnga Nat'l Park, Thai.
109/D3 Aoral (peak), Camb.
73/G4 Aosta, It.
78/A1 Aosta (prov.), It.
78/A1 Aosta, Valle d' (val.), It.
128/C2 Aoudaghost (ruins), Mrta.
125/K5 Aouk (riv.), CAfr., Chad
128/C2 Aoukar (reg.), Mrta.
124/F2 Aoulef, Alg.
99/M10 Aoyama, Japan
124/J3 Aozou, Chad
162/B4 Apache (mts.), Tx,US
163/G4 Apalachicola, Fl,US
147/L7 Apan, Mex.
138/D5 Apaporis (riv.), Braz., Col.
141/B4 Aparados da Serra Nat'l Park, Braz.
141/C2 Aparecida, Braz.
141/B2 Aparecida do Taboado, Braz.
112/C1 Aparri, Phil.
138/B3 Apartado, Col.
121/L6 Apataki, FrPol.
82/D3 Apatin, Yugo.
84/G2 Apatity, Rus.
146/E5 Apatzingán, Mex.
147/K7 Apaxco de Ocampo, Mex.
147/F5 Apaxtla, Mex.
109/D4 Ap Binh Chau, Viet.
66/C4 Apeldoorn, Neth.
66/D4 Apeldoornsch (can.), Neth.
67/E2 Apen, Ger.
52/E4 Apennines (mts.), It.
92/B2 Aphrodisias (ruins), Turk.
110/C3 Api (cape), Indo.
111/F4 Api (cape), Indo.
111/E5 Api (peak), Indo.
102/D5 Api (mtn.), Nepal
121/H6 Apia (cap.), WSam.
137/G6 Apiacás (mts.), Braz.
141/B3 Apiaí, Braz.
147/F5 Apizaco, Mex.
109/D4 Ap Loc Thanh, Viet.
109/E4 Ap Long Hoa, Viet.
109/D4 Ap Luc, Viet.
112/D4 Apo (mtn.), Phil.
147/E3 Apodaca, Mex.
140/C2 Apodi, Braz.
140/C2 Apodi (riv.), Braz.
139/G3 Apoera, Guy.
121/R9 Apolima (str.), WSam.
141/B1 Aporé (riv.), Braz.
148/E3 Aposentillo (pt.), Nic.
160/B2 Apostle (isls.), Wi,US
135/E2 Apóstoles, Arg.
91/D2 Apostolos Andreas (cape), Cyp.
155/K4 Appalachian (mts.), US
70/A5 Appenweier, Ger.
66/D2 Appingedam, Neth.
57/F2 Appleby, Eng,UK
59/E1 Appleby Magna, Eng,UK
161/S9 Appleton, NY,US
160/B2 Appleton, Wi,US
164/C1 Apple Valley, Ca,US
77/G5 Aprica, Passo dell' (pass), It.
80/D2 Apricena, It.
80/C2 Aprilia, It.
86/F3 Apsheronsk, Rus.
119/E1 Apsley Gorge Nat'l Park, Austl.
109/E4 Ap Tan My, Viet.
154/U11 Apua (pt.), Hi,US
78/D4 Apuane (mts.), It.
141/B2 Apucarana, Braz.
139/E3 Apure (riv.), Ven.
138/D3 Apure (state), Ven.
136/D6 Apurímac (riv.), Peru
109/E4 Ap Vinh Hao, Viet.
127/C2 Aqaba (gulf), Asia
92/C4 Aqaba (gulf), Egypt, SAr.
127/D5 'Aqīq, Sudan
102/E4 Aqqikkol (lake), China
93/E2 'Aqrah, Iraq
146/E3 Aquanaval (riv.), Mex.
137/G8 Aquidauana, Braz.
137/G8 Aquidauana (riv.), Braz.
140/C1 Aquiraz, Braz.
72/C4 Aquitaine (reg.), Fr.
96/D4 Ar (riv.), China
60/B5 Ara (riv.), Ire.
99/F2 Ara (riv.), Japan
125/L5 'Arab (riv.), Sudan
163/G3 Arab, Al,US
127/C2 'Arabah, Wādī (dry riv.), Egypt
92/D2 Araban, Turk.
94/D3 Arabian (pen.), Asia
95/H5 Arabian (sea), Asia
127/C3 Arabian (des.), Egypt
91/E3 'Arab, Jabal al (mts.), Syria
127/B2 'Arab, Kalīj al (gulf), Egypt
86/E4 Araç (riv.), Turk.
136/E7 Araca, Bol.
139/F4 Araça (riv.), Braz.
140/C3 Aracaju, Braz.
138/C2 Aracataca, Col.
140/C2 Aracati, Braz.
141/B2 Araçatuba, Braz.
112/B3 Araceli, Phil.
74/B4 Aracena, Sp.
140/C3 Araci, Braz.
140/C2 Aracoiba, Braz.
141/D1 Aracruz, Braz.
140/B5 Araçuaí, Braz.
140/B5 Araçuaí (riv.), Braz.
92/C4 'Arad, Isr.
82/E2 Arad, Rom.
82/E2 Arad (co.), Rom.
125/K4 Arada, Chad
93/H3 Ārādān, Iran
94/D4 'Arafāt, Jabal (mtn.), SAr.
114/E2 Arafura (sea), Austl.
137/H7 Aragarças, Braz.
87/H4 Aragats, Gora (peak), Arm.
60/B5 Araglin (riv.), Ire.
75/E2 Aragon (aut. comm.), Sp.
74/E1 Aragón (riv.), Sp.
139/E2 Aragua (state), Ven.
137/J5 Araguaia (riv.), Braz.
137/H7 Araguaiana, Braz.
137/H5 Araguaia Nat'l Park, Braz.
137/J5 Araguaína, Braz.
141/B1 Araguari, Braz.
137/H3 Araguari (riv.), Braz.
137/J7 Araguari (riv.), Braz.
141/C1 Araguari (Valhas) (riv.), Braz.
137/J5 Araguatins, Braz.
99/F2 Arai, Japan
140/B1 Araioses, Braz.
93/G3 Arāk, Iran
151/D3 Arakamchechan (isl.), Rus.
104/B4 Arakan (mts.), Burma
81/G3 Árakhthos (riv.), Gre.
92/E1 Araklı, Turk.
53/H5 Araks (riv.), Eur., Asia
88/G5 Aral (sea), Uzb., Kaz.
88/G5 Aral'sk, Kaz.
87/H2 Aralsor (lake), Kaz.
93/G3 Ārān, Iran
55/G9 Aran (isl.), Ire.
60/A3 Aran (isls.), Ire.
74/D2 Aranda de Duero, Sp.
146/E4 Arandas, Mex.
82/E3 Arandelovac, Yugo.
74/D2 Aranjuez, Sp.
56/E6 Aran Mawddwy (mtn.), Wal,UK
162/D5 Aransas Pass, Tx,US
108/G3 Arantāngi, India
141/J6 Arantina, Braz.
120/G4 Aranuka (atoll), Kiri.
140/C3 Arapiraca, Braz.
139/H5 Arapiuns (riv.), Braz.
92/D2 Arapkir, Turk.
141/B2 Arapongas, Braz.
141/B4 Araranguá, Braz.
141/B2 Araraquara, Braz.
141/C2 Araras, Braz.
119/B3 Ararat, Austl.
93/F2 Ararat (Ağri) (peak), Turk.
140/A1 Arari, Braz.
140/B2 Araripe (hills), Braz.
140/B2 Araripina, Braz.
92/F2 Aras (riv.), Asia
128/C2 Aratane (well), Mrta.
140/B2 Aratas (res.), Braz.
136/F4 Arauá (riv.), Braz.
138/D3 Arauca, Col.
138/D3 Arauca (inten.), Col.
139/E3 Arauca (riv.), Col., Ven.
141/B3 Araucária, Braz.
138/D2 Araure, Ven.
76/C6 Aravis, Col des (pass), Fr.
120/E5 Arawa, PNG
130/D3 Arawale Nat'l Rsv., Kenya
141/C1 Araxá, Braz.
139/E2 Araya (pen.), Ven.
112/C2 Arayat (mtn.), Phil.
125/N6 Ārba Minch', Eth.
62/F2 Arboga, Swe.
76/C6 Arbois, Mont d' (mtn.), Fr.
77/E5 Arbola, Punta d' (peak), It.
138/B2 Arboletes, Col.
77/F2 Arbon, Swi.
157/H2 Arborfield, Sk,Can
157/J3 Arborg, Mb,Can
54/D3 Arbroath, Sc,UK
72/F5 Arc (riv.), Fr.
73/G4 Arc (riv.), Fr.
72/C4 Arcachon, Fr.
72/C4 Arcachon (lag.), Fr.
72/C4 Arcachon, Pointe d' (pt.), Fr.
164/B2 Arcadia, Ca,US
163/H5 Arcadia, Fl,US
158/A2 Arcata, Ca,US
53/S10 Arc de Triomphe, Fr.
141/G6 Arceburgo, Braz.
84/J2 Archangel (Arkhangel'sk), Rus.
84/H3 Archangel Obl., Rus.
74/E3 Archena, Sp.
118/A1 Archer (riv.), Austl.
118/A1 Archer Bend Nat'l Park, Austl.
162/D3 Archer City, Tx,US
130/C2 Archers Post, Kenya
158/E3 Arches Nat'l Park, Ut,US
74/C4 Archidona, Sp.
54/C2 Archiestown, Sc,UK
78/B1 Arcisate, It.
142/C3 Arco (pass), Arg.
79/D1 Arco, It.
156/E5 Arco, Id,US
141/C2 Arcos, Braz.
74/C4 Arcos de la Frontera, Sp.
140/C3 Arcoverde, Braz.
50/A1 Arctic (ocean)
151/F2 Arctic (coast. pl.), Ak,US
151/J2 Arctic Nat'l Wild. Ref., Ak,US
151/M2 Arctic Red (riv.), NW,Can
83/G5 Arda (riv.), Bul.
78/C3 Arda (riv.), It.
93/G2 Ardabīl, Iran
93/E1 Ardahan, Turk.
93/H3 Ardakān, Iran
62/B1 Årdalstangen, Nor.
57/E6 Arddleen, Wal,UK
72/F4 Ardèche (riv.), Fr.
117/H5 Arden (peak), Austl.
165/M9 Arden-Arcade, Ca,US
69/E4 Ardennes (for.), Eur.
68/D4 Ardennes (dept.), Fr.
69/D4 Ardennes, Canal des (can.), Fr.
60/C3 Arderin (mtn.), Ire.
54/B1 Ardersier, Sc,UK
92/E1 Ardeşen, Turk.
56/C3 Ardglass, NI,UK
74/B3 Ardila (riv.), Sp.
55/H8 Ardivachar (pt.), Sc,UK
54/C3 Ardle (riv.), Sc,UK
159/H4 Ardmore, Ok,US
166/C3 Ardmore, Pa,US
55/H8 Ardnamurchan (pt.), Sc,UK
68/C2 Ardooie, Belg.
54/B5 Ardrossan, Sc,UK
56/C2 Ards (dist.), NI,UK
56/C3 Ards (pen.), NI,UK
61/E3 Åre, Swe.
141/G6 Areado, Braz.
150/E3 Arecibo, PR
140/C2 Areia Branca, Braz.
158/B3 Arena (pt.), Ca,US
146/C3 Arena de la Ventana, Punta (pt.), Mex.
149/E4 Arenal (vol.), CR
137/G6 Arenápolis, Braz.
146/C4 Arena, Punta (pt.), Mex.
74/C2 Arenas de San Pedro, Sp.
143/K8 Arenas, Punta de (pt.), Arg.
62/C2 Arendal, Nor.
66/C6 Arendonk, Belg.
56/E6 Arenig Fawr (mtn.), Wal,UK
75/L6 Arenys de Mar, Sp.
75/L6 Arenys de Munt, Sp.
78/B4 Arenzano, It.
144/D5 Arequipa, Peru
144/C4 Arequipa (dept.), Peru
74/C2 Arévalo, Sp.
79/E6 Arezzo, It.
79/E5 Arezzo (prov.), It.
72/C5 Arga (riv.), Sp.
74/D3 Argamasilla de Alba, Sp.
74/C3 Argamasilla de Calatrava, Sp.
75/N9 Arganda, Sp.
112/C3 Argao, Phil.
77/F2 Argen (riv.), Ger.
73/G5 Argens (riv.), Fr.
79/E3 Argenta, It.
72/C2 Argentan, Fr.
73/G4 Argentera (peak), It.
53/S10 Argenteuil, Fr.
76/D6 Argentière, Aiguille d' (peak), Swi.
135/C4 Argentina
78/A5 Argentina (riv.), It.
143/J7 Argentino (lake), Arg.
75/L6 Argentona, Sp.
83/G3 Argeş (co.), Rom.
83/G3 Argeş (riv.), Rom.
95/J2 Arghandab (riv.), Afg.
60/B6 Argideen (riv.), Ire.
127/B5 Argo, Sudan
81/H4 Argolis (gulf), Gre.
69/E5 Argonne (for.), Fr.
165/Q16 Argonne Nat'l Lab., Il,US
81/H4 Árgos, Gre.
81/G3 Argostólion, Gre.
68/A4 Argueil, Fr.
158/B4 Arguello (pt.), Ca,US
128/A1 Arguin (bay), Mrta.
97/H1 Argun (riv.), China, Rus.
102/E1 Argut (riv.), Rus.
114/D3 Argyle (lake), Austl.
54/A4 Argyll (dist.), Sc,UK
97/J3 Ar Horqin Qi, China
124/C3 Arhreijīt (well), Mrta.
62/D3 Århus, Den.
62/D3 Århus (co.), Den.
80/D2 Ariano Irpino, It.
74/C1 Arianza (riv.), Sp.
138/C4 Ariari (riv.), Col.
144/D5 Arica, Chile
116/D5 Arid (cape), Austl.
98/D3 Arida, Japan
164/A1 Arido (mtn.), Ca,US
72/D5 Ariège (riv.), Fr.
83/K5 Arifiye, Turk.
108/B2 Ārifwāla, Pak.
91/E2 Arīḥā, Syria
91/D4 Arīḥā (Jericho), WBnk.
159/G3 Arikaree (riv.), Co,US
150/F5 Arima, Trin.
130/A2 Aringa, Ugan.
140/A4 Arinos, Braz.
137/G6 Arinos (riv.), Braz.
136/F5 Aripuanã, Braz.
136/F5 Aripuanã (riv.), Braz.
136/F5 Ariquemes, Braz.
127/C2 'Arīsh, Wādī al (dry riv.), Egypt
133/H7 Arivonimamo, Madg.
108/G3 Ariyalūr, India
75/F1 Arize (riv.), Fr.
62/E2 Årjäng, Swe.
138/C2 Arjona, Col.
74/C4 Arjona, Sp.
162/E3 Arkadelphia, Ar,US
54/A3 Arkaig, Loch (lake), Sc,UK
102/A1 Arkalyk, Kaz.
155/H4 Arkansas (riv.), US
162/E3 Arkansas (state), US
163/F3 Arkansas City, Ar,US
159/H3 Arkansas City, Ks,US
159/H3 Arkansas, Salt Fork (riv.), Ks,US
125/K3 Arkanū (peak), Libya
84/J2 Arkhangel'sk (Archangel), Rus.
60/D4 Arklow, Ire.
65/G1 Arkona, Kap (cape), Ger.
106/C5 Arkonam, India
57/G4 Arksey, Eng,UK
88/H2 Arkticheskiy Institut (isls.), Rus.
74/C1 Arlanza (riv.), Sp.
74/C1 Arlazón (riv.), Sp.
77/G3 Arlbergpass (pass), Aus.
72/F5 Arles, Fr.
76/D3 Arlesheim, Swi.
68/C3 Arleux, Fr.
164/C3 Arlington, Ca,US
163/G4 Arlington, Ga,US
168/C1 Arlington, Ma,US
157/K4 Arlington, Mn,US
162/D3 Arlington, Tx,US
166/A6 Arlington, Va,US
165/Q15 Arlington Heights, Il,US
69/E4 Arlon, Belg.
78/B1 Arluno, It.
129/F4 Arly Nat'l Park, Burk.
129/F4 Arly Res., Ben.
165/G6 Armada, Mi,US
116/K7 Armadale, Austl.
54/C5 Armadale, Sc,UK
56/B3 Armagh, NI,UK
56/B3 Armagh (dist.), NI,UK
72/F3 Armançon (riv.), Fr.
141/B2 Armando Laydner (res.), Braz.
127/C3 Armant, Egypt
87/G3 Armavir, Rus.
73/G5 Arme, Cap d' (cape), Fr.
87/H4 Armenia
138/C3 Armenia, Col.
68/B2 Armentières, Fr.
146/E5 Armería, Mex.
138/C3 Armero, Col.
119/D1 Armidale, Austl.
74/D4 Armilla, Sp.
56/B1 Armoy, NI,UK
142/E2 Armstrong, Arg.
156/D3 Armstrong, BC,Can
57/G4 Armthorpe, Eng,UK
106/C4 Ārmūr, India
166/B5 Army Ordnance Museum, Md,US
153/J3 Arnaud (riv.), Qu,Can
91/C2 Arnauti (cape), Cyp.
93/M6 Arnavutköy, Turk.
59/E3 Arncott, Eng,UK
74/D1 Arnedo, Sp.
68/B2 Arnèke, Fr.
62/D1 Årnes, Nor.
159/H3 Arnett, Ok,US
114/F2 Arnhem (bay), Austl.
114/F2 Arnhem (cape), Austl.
66/C5 Arnhem, Neth.
114/E2 Arnhem Land (reg.), Austl.
106/C5 Arni, India
78/D5 Arno (riv.), It.
120/G4 Arno (atoll), Mrsh.
57/G5 Arnold, Eng,UK
166/B5 Arnold, Md,US
166/C5 Arnold (pt.), NJ,US
168/H6 Arnold, Pa,US
73/K3 Arnoldstein, Aus.
72/E3 Arnon (riv.), Fr.
53/T10 Arnouville-lès-Gonesse, Fr.
160/E2 Arnprior, On,Can
67/F6 Arnsberg, Ger.
57/F3 Arnside, Eng,UK
64/F3 Arnstadt, Ger.
70/C3 Arnstein, Ger.
140/B2 Aroases, Braz.
76/D6 Arolla, Swi.
67/G6 Arolsen, Ger.
72/E3 Aron (riv.), Fr.
75/X16 Arona, Canl.
78/B1 Arona, It.
68/B4 Aronde (riv.), Fr.
120/G5 Arorae (atoll), Kiri.
112/C2 Aroroy, Phil.
77/F4 Aroser Rothorn (peak), Swi.
111/H5 Aro Usu (cape), Indo.
53/S11 Arpajon, Fr.
68/B2 Arques, Fr.
106/D2 Arrah, India
125/M5 Ar Rahad, Sudan
140/A4 Arraias, Braz.
137/H6 Arraias (riv.), Braz.
149/G4 Arraiján, Pan.
57/H4 Arram, Eng,UK
93/E3 Ar Ramādī, Iraq
91/E3 Ar Ramthā, Jor.
54/A5 Arran (isl.), Sc,UK
149/E4 Arrancabarba (mtn.), Nic.
92/D3 Ar Raqqah, Syria
92/D2 Ar Raqqah (prov.), Syria
68/B3 Arras, Fr.
91/E2 Ar Rastan, Syria
75/F1 Arrats (riv.), Fr.
142/E2 Arrecifes, Arg.
72/B2 Arrée (mts.), Fr.
63/T9 Arresø (lake), Den.
148/C2 Arriaga, Mex.
93/F4 Ar Rifā'ī, Iraq
141/A5 Arrio Grande, Braz.
94/E4 Ar Riyāḍ (Riyadh) (cap.), SAr.
54/B4 Arrochar, Sc,UK
78/B4 Arroscia (riv.), It.
72/F3 Arroux (riv.), Fr.
60/B1 Arrow, Lough (lake), Ire.
74/B3 Arroyo de la Luz, Sp.
158/B4 Arroyo Grande, Ca,US
93/F4 Ar Rumaythah, Iraq
91/E3 Ar Ruṣayfah, Jor.
125/M5 Ar Ruṣayriṣ, Sudan
94/F4 Ar Ruways, SAr.
97/L3 Arsen'yev, Rus.
121/T11 Art (isl.), NCal.
81/G3 Árta, Gre.
81/G3 Arta (gulf), Gre.
147/E3 Arteaga, Mex.
74/A1 Arteijo, Sp.
97/L3 Artem, Rus.
149/F1 Artemisa, Cuba
164/B3 Artesia, Ca,US
159/F4 Artesia, NM,US
77/E3 Arth, Swi.
118/C3 Arthur (pt.), Austl.
116/C5 Arthur (riv.), Austl.
168/G6 Arthur (res.), Pa,US
167/J9 Arthur Kill (str.), NJ, NY,US
115/R11 Arthur's (pass), NZ
135/E3 Artigas, Uru.
68/A2 Artois (reg.), Fr.
68/B2 Artois, Collines de l' (hills), Fr.
141/F7 Artur Nogueira, Braz.
102/C4 Artux, China
92/E1 Artvin, Turk.
92/E1 Artvin (prov.), Turk.
111/H5 Aru (isls.), Indo.
130/A2 Aru, Zaire
130/A2 Arua, Ugan.
150/D4 Aruba (isl.), Neth.
141/G8 Arujá, Braz.
59/F5 Arun (riv.), Eng,UK
107/F2 Arunachal Pradesh (state), India
59/F5 Arundel, Eng,UK
108/G4 Aruppukkottai, India
111/F3 Arus (cape), Indo.
130/C3 Arusha, Tanz.
130/C4 Arusha (prov.), Tanz.
130/C3 Arusha Chini, Tanz.
130/C3 Arusha Nat'l Park, Tanz.
121/L6 Arutua (atoll), FrPol.
108/H4 Aruvi (riv.), SrL.
125/L7 Aruwimi (riv.), Zaire
96/E2 Arvayheer, Mong.
76/C6 Arve (riv.), Fr.
61/F2 Arvidsjaur, Swe.
62/E2 Arvika, Swe.
158/C4 Arvin, Ca,US
160/B2 Arvon (peak), Mi,US
123/X17 Aryānah (gov.), Tun.
102/A3 Arys', Kaz.
72/B3 Arz (riv.), Fr.
85/J5 Arzamas, Rus.
71/F2 Arzberg, Ger.
67/G4 Arzen, Ger.
123/Q16 Arzew, Alg.
69/F3 Arzfeld, Ger.
79/E1 Arzignano, It.
74/A1 Arzúa, Sp.
69/E1 As, Belg.
71/F2 Aš, Czh.
62/D2 Ås, Nor.
93/G3 Asadābād, Iran
128/D5 Asagny Nat'l Park, IvC.
110/A3 Asahan (riv.), Indo.
99/G3 Asahi, Japan
98/C3 Asahi (riv.), Japan
99/G2 Asahi-Bandai Nat'l Park, Japan
100/C2 Asahi-dake (mtn.), Japan
100/C2 Asahikawa, Japan
99/H7 Asaka, Japan
99/M9 Asake (riv.), Japan
125/P5 Āsalē, Eth.
99/F2 Asama-yama (mtn.), Japan
101/D4 Asan (bay), SKor.
106/E3 Asansol, India
124/J3 Asawanwah (well), Libya
85/P4 Asbest, Rus.
132/C3 Asbestos (mts.), SAfr.
167/D3 Asbury Park, NJ,US
136/F7 Ascención, Bol.
147/J5 Ascención (bay), Mex.
50/J6 Ascension (isl.), StH.
71/G6 Aschach (riv.), Aus.
70/C3 Aschaffenburg, Ger.
67/E5 Ascheberg, Ger.
64/F3 Aschersleben, Ger.
80/A1 Asco (riv.), Fr.
54/A5 Ascog, Sc,UK
80/C1 Ascoli Piceno, It.
80/D2 Ascoli Satriano, It.
144/B2 Ascope, Peru
59/F4 Ascot, Eng,UK
125/P5 Āseb, Erit.
125/N6 Āsela, Eth.
83/G4 Asenovgrad, Bul.
78/C3 Aserei, Monte (peak), It.
96/G2 Asgat, Mong.
59/G4 Ash, Eng,UK
59/E4 Ashampstead, Eng,UK
129/E5 Ashanti (reg.), Gha.
129/E5 Ashanti (uplands), Gha.
57/G5 Ashbourne, Eng,UK
116/C2 Ashburton (riv.), Austl.
115/R11 Ashburton, NZ
58/C5 Ashburton, Eng,UK
59/E1 Ashby (can.), Eng,UK
57/G6 Ashby-de-la-Zouch, Eng,UK
58/D3 Ashchurch, Eng,UK
156/C3 Ashcroft, BC,Can
163/J3 Asheboro, NC,US
157/J3 Ashern, Mb,Can
163/H3 Asheville, NC,US
157/M2 Asheweig (riv.), On,Can
53/M7 Ashford, Eng,UK
59/F1 Ashfordby, Eng,UK
161/Q8 Ashgrove, On,Can
115/S11 Ashhurst, NZ
100/C2 Ashibetsu, Japan
57/G1 Ashington, Eng,UK
99/L10 Ashiya, Japan
98/C4 Ashizuri-misaki (cape), Japan
123/W17 Ashkal (lake), Tun.
93/J2 Ashkhabad (cap.), Trkm.
159/H3 Ashland, Ks,US
160/D4 Ashland, Ky,US
168/C1 Ashland, Ma,US
168/E6 Ashland, Oh,US
168/E6 Ashland (co.), Oh,US
156/C5 Ashland, Or,US
160/B2 Ashland, Wi,US
157/J4 Ashley, ND,US
53/M6 Ashley Green, Eng,UK
114/C2 Ashmore (reef), Austl.
114/C2 Ashmore and Cartier Is. (terr.), Austl.
91/B4 Ashmūn, Egypt
100/C2 Ashoro, Japan
91/E2 Ash Shamāl (gov.), Leb.
93/F4 Ash Shāmīyah, Iraq
95/G3 Ash Shāriqah, UAE
91/B4 Ash Sharqīyah (gov.), Egypt
93/F4 Ash Shaṭrah, Iraq
106/C3 Ashta, India
160/D3 Ashtabula, Oh,US
168/G4 Ashtabula (co.), Oh,US
53/N8 Ashtead, Eng,UK
156/F4 Ashton, Id,US
57/F5 Ashton-in-Makerfield, Eng,UK
57/F5 Ashton-under-Lyne, Eng,UK
160/B2 Ashwaubenon, Wi,US
59/F2 Ashwell, Eng,UK
90/* Asia
63/L1 Asikkala, Fin.
123/L13 Asilah, Mor.
80/A2 Asinara (gulf), It.
80/A2 Asinara (isl.), It.
88/J4 Asino, Rus.
94/D5 'Asīr (mts.), SAr., Yemen
127/D5 Asis, Ras (cape), Sudan
92/E2 Aşkale, Turk.
57/E3 Askam in Furness, Eng,UK
62/D2 Asker, Nor.
57/G4 Askern, Eng,UK
62/D2 Askim, Nor.
62/D3 Askim, Swe.
81/G2 Áskion (peak), Gre.
61/P6 Askja (crater), Ice.
125/N4 Āsmera (cap.), Erit.
62/F3 Asnen (lake), Swe.
53/T9 Asnières-sur-Oise, Fr.
53/S10 Asnières-sur-Seine, Fr.
98/B4 Aso Nat'l Park, Japan
125/M5 Āsosa, Eth.
98/B4 Aso-san (mtn.), Japan
127/D4 Asoteriba, Jabal (peak), Sudan
57/E2 Aspatria, Eng,UK
75/E3 Aspe, Sp.
158/F3 Aspen, Co,US
91/B1 Aspendos (ruins), Turk.
166/A5 Aspen Hill, Md,US
70/C5 Asperg, Ger.
162/C3 Aspermont, Tx,US
167/E1 Aspetuck (riv.), Ct,US
75/F1 Aspin, Col d' (pass), Fr.
115/Q11 Aspiring (peak), NZ
81/H3 Asprópirgos, Gre.
156/G2 Asquith, Sk,Can
128/C2 'Assâba, Massif de l' (reg.), Mrta.
91/B5 Aş Şaff, Egypt
91/D4 Aş Şāfī, Jor.
93/G4 As Sālimīyah, Kuw.
94/E4 As Sālimīyah, SAr.
125/L1 As Sallūm, Egypt
91/D3 As Salṭ, Jor.
107/F2 Assam (state), India
93/F4 As Samāwah, Iraq
91/B4 As Sanṭah, Egypt
140/C2 Assaré, Braz.
91/D3 Aş Şarīḥ, Jor.
68/D2 Asse, Belg.
131/C5 Assegairivier (riv.), SAfr.
80/A3 Assemini, It.
66/D2 Assen, Neth.
68/C1 Assenede, Belg.
124/J1 As Sidr, Libya
91/B4 As Sinbillāwayn, Egypt
157/G3 Assiniboia, Sk,Can
156/E3 Assiniboine (peak), BC,Can
157/J3 Assiniboine (riv.), Mb,Can
160/F1 Assinika (lake), Qu,Can
141/B2 Assis, Braz.
75/G1 Assou (riv.), Fr.
125/M6 As Sudd (reg.), Sudan
93/F3 As Sulaymānīyah, Iraq
93/F3 As Sulaymānīyah (gov.), Iraq
93/F5 Aş Şummān (mts.), SAr.
91/E3 As Suwaydā', Syria
91/E3 As Suwaydā' (dist.), Syria
93/F3 Aş Şuwayrah, Iraq
91/C4 As Suways (gov.), Egypt
91/C5 As Suways (Suez), Egypt
66/C6 Asten, Neth.
78/B3 Asti, It.
78/B3 Asti (prov.), It.
79/E1 Astico (riv.), It.
141/L6 Astolfo Dutra, Braz.
59/E2 Aston, Eng,UK
58/D2 Aston on Clun, Eng,UK
141/B2 Astorga, Braz.
167/K8 Astoria, NY,US
156/C4 Astoria, Or,US
62/E3 Åstorp, Swe.
87/J3 Astrakhan', Rus.
87/H3 Astrakhan Obl., Rus.
74/B1 Asturias (aut. comm.), Sp.
59/E2 Astwood Bank, Eng,UK
99/L10 Asuka, Japan
99/N9 Asuke, Japan
120/D3 Asuncion (isl.), NMar.
135/E2 Asunción (cap.), Par.
147/F5 Asunción Nochixtlán, Mex.
62/F2 Asunden (lake), Swe.
130/B2 Aswa, Ugan.
130/B2 Aswa (riv.), Ugan.
127/C3 Aswān, Egypt
127/C4 Aswān (gov.), Egypt
127/C4 Aswan High (dam), Egypt
127/B3 Asyūṭ, Egypt
127/B3 Asyūṭ (gov.), Egypt
127/C2 Asyūṭī, Wādī al (dry riv.), Egypt
139/E4 Atabapo (riv.), Col., Ven.
135/C2 Atacama (des.), Chile
135/C1 Atacama, Puna de (plat.), Arg.
138/B4 Atacames, Ecu.
129/F4 Atacora (range), Ben.
121/H5 Atafu (atoll), Tok.
129/F5 Atakpamé, Togo
140/C3 Atalaia, Braz.
99/F3 Atami, Japan
128/B1 Atar, Mrta.
74/D4 Atarfe, Sp.
147/E4 Atarjea, Mex.
106/D2 Atarra, India
96/D3 Atas Bogd (peak), Mong.
158/B4 Atascadero, Ca,US
92/D2 Atatürk (dam), Turk.
92/D2 Atatürk (res.), Turk.
125/M4 Atbara, Sudan
125/M4 Atbara (Atbarah) (riv.), Eth., Sudan
102/A1 Atbasar, Kaz.
159/K5 Atchafalaya (bay), La,US
163/F4 Atchafalaya (riv.), La,US
159/J3 Atchison, Ks,US
129/E5 Atebubu, Gha.
61/G1 Ateelva (riv.), Nor.
146/D4 Atengo (riv.), Mex.
80/C1 Aterno (riv.), It.
68/C2 Ath, Belg.
156/E2 Athabasca, Ab,Can
152/E3 Athabasca (riv.), Ab,Can
152/F3 Athabasca (lake), Ab, Sk,Can
157/H2 Athapapuskow (lake), Mb,Can
124/K1 Āthār Ṭulmaythah (Ptolemaïs) (ruins), Libya
167/J8 Athenia, NJ,US
163/G3 Athens, Al,US
163/H3 Athens, Ga,US
160/D4 Athens, Oh,US
163/G3 Athens, Tn,US
162/E3 Athens, Tx,US

174

Athen – Bambe

81/H4 **Athens** (Athínai) (cap.), Gre.
81/L7 **Athens** (Athínai) (inset) (cap.), Gre.
59/E1 **Atherstone**, Eng,UK
57/F4 **Atherton**, Eng,UK
130/C3 **Athi** (riv.), Kenya
81/H4 **Athínai** (Athens) (cap.), Gre.
81/L7 **Athínai** (Athens) (inset) (cap.), Gre.
130/C3 **Athi River**, Kenya
53/T10 **Athis-Mons**, Fr.
60/C3 **Athlone**, Ire.
54/C3 **Atholl** (forest), Sc,UK
81/J2 **Athos** (peak), Gre.
124/J5 **Ati**, Chad
130/B2 **Atiak**, Ugan.
141/G8 **Atibaia**, Braz.
141/G7 **Atibaia** (riv.), Braz.
160/B1 **Atikokan**, On,Can
148/D3 **Atitlán** (lake), Guat.
121/K7 **Atiu** (isl.), Cookls.
151/C5 **Atka** (isl.), Ak,US
87/H2 **Atkarsk**, Rus.
151/M2 **Atkinson** (pt.), NW,Can
163/G3 **Atlanta** (cap.), Ga,US
162/E3 **Atlanta**, Tx,US
50/G3 **Atlantic** (ocean)
157/K5 **Atlantic**, Ia,US
166/D5 **Atlantic** (co.), NJ,US
166/D5 **Atlantic City**, NJ,US
138/C2 **Atlántico** (dept.), Col.
129/F5 **Atlantique** (prov.), Ben.
124/E2 **Atlas** (mts.), Afr.
165/K10 **Atlas** (peak), Ca,US
124/E1 **Atlas Saharien** (mts.), Alg., Mor.
147/M7 **Atlazayanca**, Mex.
151/M4 **Atlin** (lake), BC,Can
147/F5 **Atlixco**, Mex.
163/G4 **Atmore**, Al,US
136/E8 **Atocha**, Bol.
68/D2 **Atomium, The**, Belg.
147/L6 **Atotonilco el Grande**, Mex.
124/B3 **Atoui** (dry riv.), Mrta.
148/B2 **Atoyac** (riv.), Mex.
93/J2 **Atrak** (riv.), Iran
62/E3 **Ätran** (riv.), Swe.
138/B3 **Atrato** (riv.), Col.
99/H7 **Atsugi**, Japan
99/N10 **Atsumi**, Japan
99/N10 **Atsumi** (pen.), Japan
91/D4 **Aţ Ţafīlah**, Jor.
94/D4 **Aţ Ţā'if**, SAr.
91/E3 **At Tall**, Syria
163/G3 **Attalla**, Al,US
91/B4 **At Tall al Kabīr**, Egypt
93/E3 **At Ta'mīn** (gov.), Iraq
153/H3 **Attawapiskat** (riv.), On,Can
71/F6 **Attel** (riv.), Ger.
67/E6 **Attendorn**, Ger.
71/G7 **Attersee** (lake), Aus.
68/C5 **Attichy**, Fr.
108/F4 **Attingal**, India
168/C2 **Attleboro**, Ma,US
59/E2 **Attleborough**, Eng,UK
59/H2 **Attleborough**, Eng,UK
151/A5 **Attu** (isl.), Ak,US
127/C2 **Aţ Ţūr**, Egypt
108/G3 **Āttūr**, India
91/D4 **Aţ Ţūr**, WBnk.
94/D6 **At Turbah**, Yem.
142/D2 **Atuel** (riv.), Arg.
138/B4 **Atuntaqui**, Ecu.
130/B2 **Atura**, Ugan.
62/G2 **Åtvidaberg**, Swe.
158/B3 **Atwater**, Ca,US
159/G3 **Atwood**, Ks,US
168/F6 **Atwood** (lake), Oh,US
150/C2 **Atwood** (Samana) (cay), Bahm.
147/Q10 **Atzcapotzalco**, Mex.
139/E3 **Auari** (riv.), Braz.
69/E4 **Aubange**, Belg.
68/D6 **Aube** (dept.), Fr.
72/F2 **Aube** (riv.), Fr.
72/F4 **Aubenas**, Fr.
76/C4 **Aubert, Mont** (peak), Swi.
53/T10 **Aubervilliers**, Fr.
68/C6 **Aubetin** (riv.), Fr.
68/A5 **Aubette** (riv.), Fr.
72/E4 **Aubin**, Fr.
72/E4 **Aubrac** (mts.), Fr.
163/G3 **Auburn**, Al,US
158/B3 **Auburn**, Ca,US
160/C3 **Auburn**, In,US
168/C1 **Auburn**, Ma,US
161/G2 **Auburn**, Me,US
159/J2 **Auburn**, Ne,US
160/E3 **Auburn**, NY,US
165/C3 **Auburn**, Wa,US
165/F6 **Auburn Hills**, Mi,US
142/C3 **Aucá Mahuida** (peak), Arg.
72/D5 **Auch**, Fr.
68/B3 **Auchel**, Fr.
54/D3 **Auchenblae**, Sc,UK
56/E2 **Auchencairn**, Sc,UK
54/B6 **Auchinleck**, Sc,UK
54/C4 **Auchterarder**, Sc,UK
54/C4 **Auchtermuchty**, Sc,UK
115/R10 **Auckland**, NZ
51/S8 **Auckland** (isls.), NZ
72/E5 **Aude** (riv.), Fr.
68/D2 **Auderghem**, Belg.
76/C3 **Audeux** (riv.), Fr.
72/A3 **Audierne** (bay), Fr.
76/C3 **Audincourt**, Fr.
57/F6 **Audlem**, Eng,UK
57/F5 **Audley**, Eng,UK
125/P6 **Audo** (range), Eth.
69/E5 **Audun-le-Tiche**, Fr.
71/F1 **Aue**, Ger.
67/E2 **Aue** (riv.), Ger.
67/F3 **Aue** (riv.), Ger.
71/F1 **Auerbach**, Ger.
71/E3 **Auerbach in der Oberpfalz**, Ger.
77/G2 **Auerberg** (mtn.), Ger.
77/H5 **Auer** (Ora), It.
71/F2 **Auersberg** (peak), Ger.
70/E3 **Aufess** (riv.), Ger.
56/A3 **Augher**, NI,UK
60/A4 **Aughinish** (isl.), Ire.
56/B3 **Aughnacloy**, NI,UK
132/C3 **Augrabies Falls Nat'l Park**, SAfr.
132/C3 **Augrabiesvalle** (falls), SAfr.
70/D6 **Augsburg**, Ger.
132/A2 **Augub** (peak), Namb.
149/H4 **Augusta** (pt.), Col.
80/D4 **Augusta**, It.
80/D4 **Augusta** (gulf), It.
163/H3 **Augusta**, Ga,US
161/G2 **Augusta** (cap.), Me,US
67/F5 **Augustdorf**, Ger.
65/M2 **Augustów**, Pol.
114/C3 **Augustus** (isl.), Austl.
116/C3 **Augustus** (peak), Austl.
109/B3 **Auk Bok** (isl.), Burma
116/D2 **Auld** (lake), Austl.
54/C1 **Auldearn**, Sc,UK
75/M9 **Aulencia** (riv.), Sp.
77/F2 **Aulendorf**, Ger.
53/T10 **Aulnay-sous-Bois**, Fr.
72/B2 **Aulne** (riv.), Fr.
68/C3 **Aulnoye-Aymeries**, Fr.
77/F4 **Ault, Piz** (peak), Swi.
68/B5 **Aunette** (riv.), Fr.
132/B2 **Auob** (dry riv.), Namb.
132/C2 **Auobrivier** (dry riv.), SAfr.
120/G4 **Aur** (atoll), Mrsh.
70/D3 **Aurach** (riv.), Ger.
106/C4 **Aurangābād**, India
106/D3 **Aurangābād**, India
72/B3 **Auray**, Fr.
72/D5 **Aureilhan**, Fr.
67/E2 **Aurich**, Ger.
141/B2 **Auriflama**, Braz.
72/E4 **Aurillac**, Fr.
140/C2 **Aurora**, Braz.
112/C2 **Aurora**, Phil.
112/C4 **Aurora**, Phil.
159/F3 **Aurora**, Co,US
165/P16 **Aurora**, Il,US
159/J3 **Aurora**, Mo,US
159/H2 **Aurora**, Ne,US
168/F5 **Aurora**, Oh,US
112/C2 **Aurora Mem. Park**, Phil.
118/A1 **Aurukun Abor. Land**, Austl.
79/G1 **Ausa** (riv.), It.
160/C2 **Au Sable** (riv.), Mi,US
65/K3 **Auschwitz** (Oświęcim), Pol.
77/F3 **Ausserrhoden** (demi-canton), Swi.
72/E5 **Aussillon**, Fr.
62/B2 **Aust-Agder** (co.), Nor.
116/C3 **Austin** (lake), Austl.
152/G2 **Austin** (isl.), NW,Can
157/K5 **Austin**, Mn,US
158/C3 **Austin**, Nv,US
162/D4 **Austin** (cap.), Tx,US
168/G5 **Austintown**, Oh,US
114/* **Australia**
119/C3 **Australian Alps** (mts.), Austl.
119/D3 **Australian Cap. Terr.**, Austl.
73/L3 **Austria**
61/P7 **Austurhorn** (pt.), Ice.
68/B3 **Authie** (riv.), Fr.
146/D5 **Autlán**, Mex.
68/B5 **Automne** (riv.), Fr.
72/F3 **Autun**, Fr.
72/E4 **Auvergne** (reg.), Fr.
53/S9 **Auvers-sur-Oise**, Fr.
72/D4 **Auvézère** (riv.), Fr.
72/E3 **Auxerre**, Fr.
76/B3 **Auxonne**, Fr.
160/D2 **Aux Sables** (riv.), On,Can
139/F3 **Auyán-Tepuí** (peak), Ven.
153/K2 **Auyuittuq Nat'l Park**, NW,Can
144/D4 **Auzangate** (peak), Peru
72/E3 **Avallon**, Fr.
161/K2 **Avalon** (pen.), Nf,Can
108/F3 **Avanāshi**, India
141/B2 **Avaré**, Braz.
93/M7 **Avcılar**, Turk.
59/E4 **Avebury**, Eng,UK
59/E4 **Avebury Stone Circle** (ruins), Eng,UK
74/A2 **Aveiro**, Port.
74/A2 **Aveiro** (dist.), Port.
53/P7 **Aveley**, Eng,UK
68/C2 **Avelgem**, Belg.
142/F2 **Avellaneda**, Arg.
80/D2 **Avellino**, It.
68/A4 **Avelon** (riv.), Fr.
158/B3 **Avenal**, Ca,US
167/D2 **Avenel**, NJ,US
68/A6 **Aver** (riv.), Fr.
80/D2 **Aversa**, It.
150/E4 **Aves** (isl.), Ven.
62/G1 **Avesta**, Swe.
72/D4 **Aveyron** (riv.), Fr.
80/C1 **Avezzano**, It.
54/A4 **Avich, Loch** (lake), Sc,UK
54/C2 **Aviemore**, Sc,UK
72/F5 **Avignon**, Fr.
74/C2 **Ávila de los Caballeros**, Sp.
74/C1 **Avilés**, Sp.
68/B3 **Avion**, Fr.
74/B3 **Avis**, Port.
77/H5 **Avisio** (riv.), It.
56/B6 **Avoca**, Ire.
60/D4 **Avoca** (riv.), Ire.
54/B1 **Avoch**, Sc,UK
80/D4 **Avola**, It.
116/C5 **Avon** (riv.), Austl.
72/E2 **Avon**, Fr.
58/D4 **Avon** (co.), Eng,UK
58/C6 **Avon** (riv.), Eng,UK
58/D4 **Avon** (riv.), Eng,UK
59/E2 **Avon** (riv.), Eng,UK
59/E5 **Avon** (riv.), Eng,UK
54/C2 **Avon** (riv.), Sc,UK
54/C5 **Avon** (riv.), Sc,UK
168/B2 **Avon**, Ct,US
168/E5 **Avon**, Oh,US
60/D4 **Avonbeg** (riv.), Ire.
168/E4 **Avon Lake**, Oh,US
157/G3 **Avonlea**, Sk,Can
56/B6 **Avonmore** (riv.), Ire.
58/D4 **Avonmouth**, Eng,UK
116/C4 **Avon Valley Nat'l Park**, Austl.
54/B5 **Avon Water** (riv.), Sc,UK
72/C2 **Avranches**, Fr.
68/B4 **Avre** (riv.), Fr.
72/C3 **Avrillé**, Fr.
99/L10 **Awaji**, Japan
98/D3 **Awaji** (isl.), Japan
91/E3 **A'waj, Nahr al** (riv.), Syria
69/E2 **Awans**, Belg.
125/N6 **Āwasa**, Eth.
125/P6 **Āwash**, Eth.
125/P5 **Āwash Wenz** (riv.), Eth.
132/A2 **Awasibberge** (peak), Namb.
102/D3 **Awat**, China
124/H2 **Awbārī**, Libya
60/B5 **Awbeg** (riv.), Ire.
54/A4 **Awe, Loch** (lake), Sc,UK
125/K2 **Awjilah**, Libya
91/B4 **Awsīm**, Egypt
61/P6 **Axarfjördhur** (bay), Ice.
58/D4 **Axbridge**, Eng,UK
58/D4 **Axe** (riv.), Eng,UK
58/D5 **Axe** (riv.), Eng,UK
66/A6 **Axel**, Neth.
153/S7 **Axel Heiberg** (isl.), NW,Can
129/E5 **Axim**, Gha.
81/H2 **Axios** (riv.), Gre.
165/D2 **Axis** (dam), Wa,US
58/D5 **Axminster**, Eng,UK
147/L8 **Axochiapan**, Mex.
68/D5 **Ay**, Fr.
85/N5 **Ay** (riv.), Rus.
98/D3 **Ayabe**, Japan
142/F3 **Ayacucho**, Arg.
144/C4 **Ayacucho**, Peru
102/D2 **Ayaguz**, Kaz.
102/D2 **Ayaguz** (riv.), Kaz.
102/E4 **Ayakkum** (lake), China
99/M10 **Ayama**, Japan
128/E5 **Ayamé I, Barrage d'** (dam), IvC.
128/E5 **Ayamé II, Barrage d'** (dam), IvC.
74/B4 **Ayamonte**, Sp.
92/C1 **Ayancık**, Turk.
139/G3 **Ayanganna** (peak), Guy.
138/C2 **Ayapel**, Col.
149/H5 **Ayapel, Serranía** (range), Col.
92/C1 **Ayaş**, Turk.
99/H7 **Ayase**, Japan
144/D4 **Ayaviri**, Peru
95/J1 **Āybak**, Afg.
91/G7 **'Aybāl, Jabal** (Har Eval) (mtn.), WBnk.
92/D1 **Aybastı**, Turk.
92/A2 **Aydın**, Turk.
92/B2 **Aydın** (prov.), Turk.
93/N7 **Aydinli**, Turk.
117/F3 **Ayers Rock** (Uluru) (peak), Austl.
104/B5 **Ayeyarwady** (Irrawaddy) (div.), Burma
81/J3 **Ayios Evstrátios** (isl.), Gre.
81/J5 **Ayios Ioánnis, Ákra** (cape), Gre.
81/J5 **Ayios Nikólaos**, Gre.
59/F3 **Aylesbury**, Eng,UK
59/G4 **Aylesford**, Eng,UK
59/H4 **Aylesham**, Eng,UK
152/F2 **Aylmer** (lake), NW,Can
59/H1 **Aylsham**, Eng,UK
92/D2 **'Ayn al 'Arab**, Syria
125/K2 **'Ayn Ath Tha'lab**, Libya
94/D1 **'Ayn, Ra's al**, Syria
125/K3 **'Ayn Zuwayyah** (well), Libya
89/S3 **Ayon** (isl.), Rus.
75/E3 **Ayora**, Sp.
124/D3 **'Ayoûn 'Abd el Mâlek** (well), Mrta.
118/B2 **Ayr**, Austl.
54/B6 **Ayr**, Sc,UK
54/B6 **Ayr** (riv.), Sc,UK
56/D3 **Ayre, Point of** (pt.), Eng,UK
54/B6 **Ayr, Heads of** (pt.), Sc,UK
57/H3 **Ayton**, Eng,UK
54/D5 **Ayton**, Sc,UK
83/H4 **Aytos**, Bul.
72/C3 **Aytré**, Fr.
109/C3 **Ayutthaya** (ruins), Thai.
92/A2 **Ayvalık**, Turk.
69/E3 **Aywaille**, Belg.
108/B1 **Azad Kashmir** (terr.), Pak.
75/F3 **Azahar** (coast), Sp.
99/M9 **Azai**, Japan
156/C5 **Azalea**, Or,US
106/D2 **Azamgarh**, India
144/D4 **Azángaro**, Peru
144/D4 **Azángaro** (riv.), Peru
124/G2 **Azao** (peak), Alg.
129/E2 **Azaouād** (reg.), Mali
129/G2 **Azaouak, Vallée de l'** (wadi), Mali, Niger
93/F2 **Āzarbāyjān-e Bākhtarī** (gov.), Iran
93/F2 **Āzarbāyjān-e Khāvarī** (gov.), Iran
91/E1 **A'zāz**, Syria
87/H4 **Azerbaijan**
125/N5 **Āzezo**, Eth.
102/E1 **Azhu-Tayga, Gora** (peak), Rus.
92/D2 **'Azīz, Jabal 'Abd al** (mts.), Syria
138/B5 **Azogues**, Ecu.
75/R12 **Azores** (aut. reg.), Port.
75/R12 **Azores** (isls.), Port.
86/F3 **Azov**, Rus.
86/E3 **Azov** (sea), Rus., Ukr.
74/D1 **Azpeitia**, Sp.
158/F3 **Aztec**, NM,US
158/E3 **Aztec Ruins Nat'l Mon.**, NM,US
150/D3 **Azua**, DRep.
74/C3 **Azuaga**, Sp.
138/B5 **Azuay** (prov.), Ecu.
99/M9 **Azuchi**, Japan
149/F5 **Azuero** (pen.), Pan.
142/F3 **Azul**, Arg.
149/E4 **Azul** (mtn.), CR
147/H5 **Azul** (riv.), NAm.
144/B2 **Azul, Cordillera** (mts.), Peru
99/G2 **Azuma-san** (mtn.), Japan
99/F2 **Azumaya-san** (mtn.), Japan
73/G5 **Azur, Côte d'** (coast), Fr.
164/C2 **Azusa**, Ca,US
123/V17 **Azzaba**, Alg.
91/E3 **Az Zabadānī**, Syria
73/K4 **Azzano Decimo**, It.
91/B4 **Az Zaqāzīq**, Egypt
91/E3 **Az Zarqā'**, Jor.
124/H1 **Az Zāwiyah**, Libya
93/F4 **Az Zubayr**, Iraq

B

105/E2 **Ba** (riv.), China
121/Y18 **Ba**, Fiji
54/B3 **Ba** (riv.), Sc,UK
109/E3 **Ba** (riv.), Viet.
121/U11 **Baaba** (isl.), NCal.
91/G8 **Ba'al Ḩazor** (Tall 'Āşūr) (mtn.), WBnk.
77/E3 **Baar**, Swi.
122/G4 **Baarawe**, Som.
66/C4 **Baarn**, Neth.
96/D2 **Baatsagaan**, Mong.
95/J2 **Baba** (mts.), Afg.
83/F4 **Baba** (peak), Bul.
92/B1 **Baba** (pt.), Turk.
86/D4 **Baba Burnu** (pt.), Turk.
83/J3 **Babadag**, Rom.
83/H5 **Babaeski**, Turk.
138/B5 **Babahoyo**, Ecu.
111/G5 **Babar** (isl.), Indo.
130/B4 **Babati**, Tanz.
58/C5 **Babbacombe** (bay), Eng,UK
157/L4 **Babbitt**, Mn,US
158/C3 **Babbitt**, Nv,US
123/G3 **Bab el Mandeb** (str.), Afr., Asia
120/C4 **Babelthuap** (isl.), Palau
70/B3 **Babenhausen**, Ger.
86/A2 **Babia Gora** (peak), Pol.
104/D4 **Babian** (riv.), China
93/F3 **Bābil** (gov.), Iraq
156/B2 **Babine** (lake), BC,Can
152/D3 **Babine** (riv.), BC,Can
93/H2 **Bābol**, Iran
93/H2 **Bābol Sar**, Iran
112/C1 **Babuyan** (chan.), Phil.
112/C1 **Babuyan** (isl.), Phil.
112/C1 **Babuyan** (isls.), Phil.
93/F3 **Babylon** (ruins), Iraq
167/E2 **Babylon**, NY,US
140/A2 **Bacabal**, Braz.
137/H4 **Bacajá** (riv.), Braz.
148/D2 **Bacalar** (lag.), Mex.
111/G4 **Bacan** (isl.), Indo.
112/C1 **Bacarra**, Phil.
83/H2 **Bacău**, Rom.
83/H2 **Bacău** (co.), Rom.
109/D1 **Bac Can**, Viet.
79/F2 **Bacchiglione** (riv.), It.
109/D1 **Bac Giang**, Viet.
152/G2 **Back** (riv.), NW,Can
160/E2 **Back** (lake), On,Can
166/B5 **Back** (riv.), Md,US
82/D3 **Bačka** (reg.), Yugo.
82/D3 **Bačka Palanka**, Yugo.
82/D3 **Bačka Topola**, Yugo.
70/C5 **Backnang**, Ger.
58/D4 **Backwell**, Eng,UK
109/D4 **Bac Lieu**, Viet.
109/D1 **Bac Ninh**, Viet.
112/C2 **Baco** (mtn.), Phil.
112/C3 **Bacolod City**, Phil.
112/E7 **Bacoor**, Phil.
109/D1 **Bac Quang**, Viet.
82/D2 **Bácsalmás**, Hun.
82/D2 **Bács-Kiskun** (co.), Hun.
59/H1 **Bacton**, Eng,UK
57/F4 **Bacup**, Eng,UK
157/H4 **Bad** (riv.), SD,US
71/F5 **Bad Abbach**, Ger.
108/E3 **Badagara**, India
96/E3 **Badain Jaran** (des.), China
74/B3 **Badajoz**, Sp.
75/L7 **Badalona**, Sp.
160/D3 **Bad Axe**, Mi,US
70/B4 **Bad Bergzabern**, Ger.
67/F6 **Bad Berleberg**, Ger.
69/G2 **Bad Breisig**, Ger.
70/C2 **Bad Brückenau**, Ger.
70/B2 **Bad Camberg**, Ger.
64/F1 **Bad Doberan**, Ger.
108/C2 **Baddomalhi**, Pak.
67/G5 **Bad Driburg**, Ger.
70/B4 **Bad Dürkheim**, Ger.
70/B6 **Bad Dürrheim**, Ger.
70/A2 **Bad Ems**, Ger.
73/M2 **Baden**, Aus.
77/E3 **Baden**, Swi.
70/B5 **Baden-Baden**, Ger.
70/B5 **Badener** (peak), Ger.
54/B3 **Badenoch** (dist.), Sc,UK
70/C6 **Baden-Württemberg** (state), Ger.
79/G2 **Baderna**, Cro.
67/F4 **Bad Essen**, Ger.
65/H2 **Bad Freienwalde**, Ger.
67/H5 **Bad Gandersheim**, Ger.
116/B4 **Badgingarra Nat'l Park**, Austl.
73/K3 **Bad Goisern**, Aus.
67/H5 **Bad Harzburg**, Ger.
70/B5 **Bad Herrenalb**, Ger.
64/E3 **Bad Hersfeld**, Ger.
70/B2 **Bad Homburg vor der Höhe**, Ger.
69/G2 **Bad Honnef**, Ger.
77/F5 **Badile, Pizzo** (peak), It.
95/J4 **Badīn**, Pak.
73/K3 **Bad Ischl**, Aus.
70/D2 **Bad Kissingen**, Ger.
70/C3 **Bad König**, Ger.
70/D2 **Bad Königshofen**, Ger.
70/A3 **Bad Kreuznach**, Ger.
76/D2 **Bad Krozingen**, Ger.
157/H4 **Badlands** (uplands), ND,US
157/H5 **Badlands** (hills), SD,US
157/H5 **Badlands Nat'l Park**, SD,US
67/H6 **Bad Langensalza**, Ger.
67/H5 **Bad Lauterberg**, Ger.
70/B5 **Bad Liebenzell**, Ger.
67/F3 **Bad Lippspringe**, Ger.
70/C4 **Bad Mergentheim**, Ger.
67/G4 **Bad Munder am Deister**, Ger.
69/F2 **Bad Münstereifel**, Ger.
70/B2 **Bad Nauheim**, Ger.
67/G4 **Bad Nenndorf**, Ger.
69/G2 **Bad Neuenahr-Ahrweiler**, Ger.
70/D2 **Bad Neustadt an der Saale**, Ger.
67/F4 **Bad Oeynhausen**, Ger.
64/F2 **Bad Oldesloe**, Ger.
103/B5 **Badong**, China
70/C2 **Bad Orb**, Ger.
67/G5 **Bad Pyrmont**, Ger.
77/F3 **Bad Ragaz**, Swi.
95/J3 **Bādrāh**, Pak.
70/C4 **Bad Rappenau**, Ger.
64/G5 **Bad Reichenhall**, Ger.
67/H5 **Bad Sachsa**, Ger.
67/H4 **Bad Salzdetfurth**, Ger.
67/F4 **Bad Salzuflen**, Ger.
64/F3 **Bad Salzungen**, Ger.
67/F5 **Bad Sassendorf**, Ger.
70/C6 **Bad Schussenried**, Ger.
70/B2 **Bad Schwalbach**, Ger.
64/F2 **Bad Schwartau**, Ger.
64/F2 **Bad Segeberg**, Ger.
70/B2 **Bad Söden am Taunus**, Ger.
70/C2 **Bad Soden-Salmünster**, Ger.
67/G6 **Bad Sooden-Allendorf**, Ger.
77/H2 **Bad Tölz**, Ger.
106/D6 **Badulla**, SrL.
70/C6 **Bad Urach**, Ger.
70/B2 **Bad Vilbel**, Ger.
73/M3 **Bad Vöslau**, Aus.
77/F2 **Bad Waldsee**, Ger.
67/G6 **Bad Wildungen**, Ger.
70/C4 **Bad Wimpfen**, Ger.
70/D3 **Bad Windsheim**, Ger.
70/D6 **Bad Wörishofen**, Ger.
77/F2 **Bad Wurzach**, Ger.
67/E2 **Bad Zwischenahn**, Ger.
74/C4 **Baena**, Sp.
141/J6 **Baependi**, Braz.
76/C2 **Baerenkopf** (mtn.), Fr.
69/F2 **Baesweiler**, Ger.
74/D4 **Baeza**, Sp.
129/H5 **Bafang**, Camr.
153/H1 **Baffin** (isl.), NW,Can
153/K1 **Baffin** (bay), Can.,Grld.
162/D5 **Baffin** (bay), Tx,US
124/H7 **Bafia**, Camr.
128/D4 **Bafing** (riv.), Gui., IvC.
128/C3 **Bafing** (riv.), Gui., Mali
129/H5 **Bafoussam**, Camr.
92/C1 **Bafra**, Turk.
92/D1 **Bafra Burnu** (cape), Turk.
128/B2 **Bafrechié** (well), Mrta.
125/L7 **Bafwasende**, Zaire
103/B3 **Bag** (salt lake), China
124/H5 **Baga**, Nga.
112/B4 **Bagahak, Gunung** (peak), Malay.
130/C4 **Bagamoyo**, Tanz.
112/D4 **Baganga**, Phil.
129/G3 **Bagaroua**, Niger
112/E6 **Bagbag** (cr.), Phil.
102/E3 **Bagda** (mts.), China
143/G1 **Bagé**, Braz.
112/C1 **Baggao**, Phil.
58/B4 **Baggy** (pt.), Eng,UK
108/B2 **Bāgh**, Pak.
93/F3 **Baghdad** (gov.), Iraq
94/D2 **Baghdad** (Baghdād) (cap.), Iraq
80/C3 **Bagheria**, It.
95/J1 **Baghlān**, Afg.
92/E2 **Bağırpaşa** (peak), Turk.
58/C3 **Baglan**, Wal,UK
157/K4 **Bagley**, Mn,US
79/F4 **Bagnacavallo**, It.
72/D5 **Bagnères-de-Bigorre**, Fr.
53/S10 **Bagneux**, Fr.
79/E5 **Bagno di Romagna**, It.
53/T10 **Bagnolet**, Fr.
78/D2 **Bagnolo Mella**, It.
72/F4 **Bagnols-sur-Cèze**, Fr.
112/C3 **Bago**, Phil.
128/D3 **Bagoe** (riv.), IvC., Mali
104/B5 **Bago** (Pegu) (div.), Burma
144/B2 **Bagua Grande**, Peru
112/C1 **Baguio**, Phil.
124/J5 **Baguirmi** (reg.), Chad
129/H2 **Bagzane** (peak), Niger
150/B2 **Bahamas**
106/E3 **Baharampur**, India
102/B6 **Bahāwalnagar**, Pak.
95/K3 **Bahāwalpur**, Pak.
92/D2 **Bahçe**, Turk.
130/B4 **Bahi**, Tanz.
140/B4 **Bahia** (state), Braz.
142/E3 **Bahía Blanca**, Arg.
138/A5 **Bahía de Caráquez**, Ecu.
106/D3 **Bahía Honda**, Cuba
148/E2 **Bahía, Islas de la** (isls.), Hon.
125/N5 **Bahir Dar**, Eth.
95/G4 **Bahlah**, Oman
106/D2 **Bahraich**, India
94/F3 **Bahrain**
94/F3 **Bahrain** (gulf), Bahr., SAr.
122/E3 **Baḩr al Arab** (riv.), Sudan
93/E3 **Baḩr al Milḩ** (lake), Iraq
122/D4 **Bahr Aouk** (riv.), CAfr., Chad
127/B2 **Baḩrīyah, Al Wāḩāt al** (oasis), Egypt
103/C2 **Bai** (riv.), China
103/C4 **Bai** (riv.), China
83/F2 **Baia Mare**, Rom.
83/F2 **Baia Sprie**, Rom.
124/J6 **Baïbokoum**, Chad
104/D3 **Baicao** (mts.), China
102/D3 **Baicheng**, China
97/J2 **Baicheng**, China
83/G3 **Băicoi**, Rom.
125/P7 **Baidoa**, Som.
103/D5 **Baidong** (lake), China
161/G1 **Baie-Comeau**, Qu,Can
153/J3 **Baie-du-Poste**, Qu,Can
77/F2 **Baienfurt**, Ger.
70/B5 **Baiersbronn**, Ger.
70/E3 **Baiersdorf**, Ger.
161/G2 **Baie-Saint-Paul**, Qu,Can
161/K1 **Baie Verte**, Nf,Can
103/G7 **Baigou** (riv.), China
103/C3 **Baihua Shan** (mtn.), China
93/E3 **Ba'ījī**, Iraq
89/L4 **Baikal** (Baykal) (lake), Rus.
138/D2 **Bailadores**, Ven.
57/G4 **Baildon**, Eng,UK
74/D3 **Bailén**, Sp.
83/F3 **Băileşti**, Rom.
55/H8 **Bailivanish**, Sc,UK
68/B2 **Bailleul**, Fr.
96/E5 **Bailong** (riv.), China
103/C4 **Bailu** (riv.), China
96/E5 **Baima**, China
57/H5 **Bain** (riv.), Eng,UK
106/E2 **Bainang**, China
163/G4 **Bainbridge**, Ga,US
165/B2 **Bainbridge** (isl.), Wa,US
166/B4 **Bainbridge Nav. Trg. Sta.**, Md,US
102/E5 **Baingoin**, China
97/K2 **Baiquan**, China
102/D4 **Bairab** (lake), China
151/F3 **Baird** (inlet), Ak,US
162/D3 **Baird**, Tx,US
120/G4 **Bairiki** (cap.), Kiri.
97/H3 **Bairin Youqi**, China
119/C3 **Bairnsdale**, Austl.
91/E4 **Bā'ir, Wādī** (riv.), Jor.
112/C3 **Bais**, Phil.
72/D5 **Baïse** (riv.), Fr.
105/F5 **Baisha**, China
105/H3 **Baishi** (peak), China
105/H3 **Baisong** (pass), China
106/D2 **Baitadi**, Nepal
109/D2 **Bai Thuong**, Viet.
75/P10 **Baixa de Banheira**, Port.
140/B4 **Baixa Grande**, Braz.
103/C3 **Baixiang**, China
141/D1 **Baixo Guandu**, Braz.
96/E4 **Baiyin**, China
103/B3 **Baiyu** (mts.), China
105/G3 **Baiyun** (mtn.), China
143/J7 **Baja** (pt.), Chile
82/D2 **Baja**, Hun.
146/B2 **Baja California** (pen.), Mex.
146/B3 **Baja California Sur** (state), Mex.
123/W17 **Bājah**, Tun.
123/W17 **Bājah** (gov.), Tun.
146/B2 **Baja, Punta** (pt.), Mex.
111/F5 **Bajawa**, Indo.
82/D4 **Bajina Bašta**, Yugo.
119/E1 **Bajmba** (peak), Austl.
82/D3 **Bajmok**, Yugo.
150/D3 **Bajos de Haina**, DRep.
102/C2 **Bakanas** (riv.), Kaz.
111/E3 **Bakayan** (peak), Indo.
128/B3 **Bakel**, Sen.
152/G2 **Baker** (lake), NW,Can
143/J6 **Baker** (riv.), Chile
121/H4 **Baker** (isl.), PacUS
158/C4 **Baker**, Ca,US
157/G4 **Baker**, Mt,US
158/D3 **Baker**, Nv,US
156/D4 **Baker**, Or,US
156/C3 **Baker** (peak), Wa,US
158/C4 **Bakersfield**, Ca,US
57/G5 **Bakewell**, Eng,UK
86/E3 **Bakhchisaray**, Ukr.
86/E2 **Bakhmach**, Ukr.
93/F3 **Bākhtarān**, Iran
93/F3 **Bākhtarān** (gov.), Iran
93/H4 **Bakhtegān** (lake), Iran
93/G4 **Bakhtīārī & Chahār Maḩāll** (gov.), Iran
139/G4 **Bakhuis** (mts.), Sur.
61/P6 **Bakkaflói** (bay), Ice.
130/B2 **Bakora Corridor Game Rsv.**, Kenya
126/B1 **Bakoumba**, Gabon
71/G2 **Bakovský Potok** (riv.), Czh.
128/C4 **Bakoye** (riv.), Gui., Mali
87/J4 **Baku** (cap.), Azer.
130/A2 **Baku**, Zaire
113/S **Bakutis** (coast), Ant.
136/E6 **Bala** (mts.), Bol.
92/C2 **Balâ**, Turk.
56/E6 **Bala**, Wal,UK
111/E2 **Balabac** (str.), Malay., Phil.
112/B4 **Balabac**, Phil.
112/B4 **Balabac** (isl.), Phil.
91/E3 **Ba'labakk**, Leb.
121/U12 **Balabio** (isl.), NCal.
93/F3 **Balad**, Iraq
106/D3 **Bālāghāt**, India
80/A1 **Balagne** (range), Fr.
112/E6 **Balagtas**, Phil.
75/F2 **Balaguer**, Sp.
72/C5 **Balaïtous** (mtn.), Fr.
131/D2 **Balaka**, Malw.
85/J4 **Balakhna**, Rus.
87/H1 **Balakovo**, Rus.
112/B4 **Balambangan** (isl.), Malay.
95/H1 **Bālā Morghab**, Afg.
83/G2 **Bălan**, Rom.
147/H5 **Balancán**, Mex.
112/C2 **Balanga**, Phil.
109/E3 **Ba Lang An** (cape), Viet.
106/D3 **Bālāngir**, India
144/B1 **Balao**, Ecu.
112/C1 **Balaoan**, Phil.
85/X9 **Balashikha**, Rus.
87/G2 **Balashov**, Rus.
82/D1 **Balassagyarmat**, Hun.
82/C2 **Balaton** (lake), Hun.
82/C2 **Balatonfüred**, Hun.
139/G5 **Balbina** (res.), Braz.
164/G8 **Balboa**, Ca,US
142/F3 **Balcarce**, Arg.
56/E2 **Balcary** (pt.), Sc,UK
83/J4 **Balchik**, Bul.
115/Q12 **Balclutha**, NZ
59/F4 **Balcombe**, Eng,UK
162/D4 **Balcones Escarpment** (plat.), Tx,US
116/C5 **Bald** (pt.), Austl.
163/H2 **Bald** (peak), Va,US
166/A1 **Bald Eagle Mountain** (ridge), Pa,US
59/F3 **Baldock**, Eng,UK
119/E1 **Bald Rock Nat'l Park**, Austl.
167/L9 **Baldwin**, NY,US
168/H7 **Baldwin**, Pa,US
164/C2 **Baldwin Park**, Ca,US
157/H3 **Baldy** (peak), Mb,Can
148/D2 **Baldy Beacon** (mtn.), Belz.
79/G2 **Bale**, Cro.
75/F3 **Baleares** (Balearic) (isls.), Sp.
75/F3 **Balearic** (Baleares) (isls.), Sp.
141/E1 **Baleia, Ponta da** (pt.), Braz.
153/K3 **Baleine** (riv.), Qu,Can
153/J3 **Baleine, Grande Rivière de la** (riv.), Qu,Can
153/J3 **Baleine, Petite Rivière de la** (riv.), Qu,Can
125/N6 **Bale Mountains Nat'l Park**, Eth.
69/E1 **Balen**, Belg.
112/C2 **Baler**, Phil.
130/B2 **Balesa** (riv.), Kenya
106/E3 **Baleshwar**, India
96/H1 **Baley**, Rus.
54/B4 **Balfron**, Sc,UK
106/B2 **Bali**, India
110/D5 **Bali** (isl.), Indo.
110/D5 **Bali** (sea), Indo.
92/A2 **Balıkesir**, Turk.
92/A2 **Balıkesir** (prov.), Turk.
111/E4 **Balikpapan**, Indo.
112/D3 **Balingasag**, Phil.
70/B6 **Balingen**, Ger.
52/F4 **Balkan** (mts.), Eur.
87/K4 **Balkhan Obl.**, Trkm.
102/C2 **Balkhash**, Kaz.
102/B2 **Balkhash** (lake), Kaz.
60/D2 **Ballagan** (pt.), Ire.
56/C1 **Ballantrae**, Sc,UK
119/B3 **Ballarat**, Austl.
116/D4 **Ballard** (lake), Austl.
106/C4 **Ballarpur**, India
54/C2 **Ballater**, Sc,UK
56/D3 **Ballaugh**, IM,UK
113/L **Balleny** (isls.), Ant.
63/T9 **Ballerup**, Den.
112/C1 **Ballesteros**, Phil.
119/E1 **Ballina**, Austl.
60/A1 **Ballina**, Ire.
55/H9 **Ballinamallard**, NI,UK
60/B3 **Ballinasloe**, Ire.
56/B2 **Ballinderry** (riv.), NI,UK
162/D4 **Ballinger**, Tx,US
54/C4 **Ballingry**, Sc,UK
54/C3 **Ballinluig**, Sc,UK
56/B1 **Ballintoy**, NI,UK
54/B2 **Balloch**, Sc,UK
54/B5 **Balloch**, Sc,UK
76/C2 **Ballon, Col du** (pass), Fr.
76/C2 **Ballon d'Alsace** (mtn.), Fr.
76/C2 **Ballon de Sevance** (mtn.), Fr.
56/C2 **Ballycarry**, NI,UK
56/B1 **Ballycastle**, NI,UK
56/B2 **Ballyclare**, NI,UK
56/C2 **Ballyeaston**, NI,UK
56/A3 **Ballygawley**, NI,UK
56/C3 **Ballygowan**, NI,UK
56/C3 **Ballyhalbert**, NI,UK
60/B5 **Ballyhoura** (mts.), Ire.
56/A1 **Ballykelly**, NI,UK
56/B2 **Ballymena**, NI,UK
56/B2 **Ballymena** (dist.), NI,UK
56/B1 **Ballymoney**, NI,UK
56/B1 **Ballymoney** (dist.), NI,UK
60/C5 **Ballynacourty** (pt.), Ire.
56/C3 **Ballynahinch**, NI,UK
56/C2 **Ballynure**, NI,UK
56/C3 **Ballyquintin** (pt.), NI,UK
60/D5 **Ballyteige** (bay), Ire.
56/C2 **Ballywalter**, NI,UK
143/J7 **Balmaceda** (peak), Chile
82/E2 **Balmazújváros**, Hun.
157/K3 **Balmertown**, On,Can
76/D5 **Balmhorn** (peak), Swi.
131/C2 **Balmoral**, Zam.
54/C2 **Balmoral Castle**, Sc,UK
141/B3 **Balneario Camboriú**, Braz.
143/T12 **Balneario Carras**, Uru.
118/C4 **Balonne** (riv.), Austl.
106/B2 **Bālotra**, India
103/B3 **Balougou**, China
106/D2 **Balrāmpur**, India
83/G3 **Balş**, Rom.
59/E2 **Balsall Common**, Eng,UK
140/A2 **Balsas**, Braz.
140/A3 **Balsas** (riv.), Braz.
147/E5 **Balsas** (riv.), Mex.
147/M6 **Balsas de Agua**, Mex.
62/G1 **Bålsta**, Swe.
55/P12 **Baltasound**, Sc,UK
62/H2 **Baltic** (sea), Eur.
65/K1 **Baltic** (spit), Pol., Rus.
91/B4 **Balţīm**, Egypt
166/B5 **Baltimore**, Md,US
166/B4 **Baltimore** (co.), Md,US
166/B5 **Baltimore Highlands-Lansdown**, Md,US
63/H4 **Baltiysk**, Rus.
67/E1 **Baltrum** (isl.), Ger.
95/H3 **Baluchistan** (reg.), Iran, Pak.
112/C2 **Balud**, Phil.
106/E2 **Bālurghāt**, India
67/E6 **Balve**, Ger.
117/E2 **Balwina Abor. Rsv.**, Austl.
87/J3 **Balykshi**, Kaz.
138/B5 **Balzar**, Ecu.
129/E3 **Bam** (prov.), Burk.
102/F5 **Bam** (lake), China
93/J4 **Bam**, Iran
124/H5 **Bama**, Nga.
160/A1 **Bamaji** (lake), On,Can
128/D3 **Bamako** (cap.), Mali
128/D3 **Bamako** (reg.), Mali
105/E3 **Bama Yaozu Zizhixian**, China
136/C5 **Bambamarca**, Peru
149/E3 **Bambana** (riv.), Nic.
125/K6 **Bambari**, CAfr.
70/D3 **Bamberg**, Ger.

175
Bambe – Bejhi

163/H3 Bamberg, SC,US
57/F4 Bamber Ridge, Eng,UK
62/C2 Bamble, Nor.
141/C2 Bambuí, Braz.
129/H5 Bamenda, Camr.
95/J2 Bāmīān, Afg.
105/G3 Bamian (mtn.), China
125/K6 Bamingui-Bangoran Nat'l Park, CAfr.
70/B4 Bammental, Ger.
58/C5 Bampton, Eng,UK
95/H3 Bampūr (riv.), Iran
120/F5 Banaba (isl.), Kiri.
140/C2 Banabuiu (res.), Braz.
130/B3 Banagi, Tanz.
112/C2 Banahao (mtn.), Phil.
128/D3 Banamba, Mali
128/B4 Banana (isls.), SLeo.
126/B2 Banana, Zaire
141/J7 Bananal, Braz.
106/B2 Banās (riv.), India
127/C4 Banās, Ra's (pt.), Egypt
82/E3 Banatsko Novo Selo, Yugo.
112/C1 Banaue, Phil.
92/B2 Banaz, Turk.
104/B2 Banbar, China
56/B3 Banbridge, NI,UK
56/B3 Banbridge (dist.), NI,UK
59/E2 Banbury, Eng,UK
124/B3 Banc d'Arguin Nat'l Park, Mrta.
109/C2 Ban Chiang (ruins), Thai.
54/D2 Banchory, Sc,UK
149/F4 Banco (pt.), CR
160/E2 Bancroft, On,Can
111/H4 Banda (isls.), Indo.
111/G5 Banda (sea), Indo.
110/A2 Banda Aceh, Indo.
99/G2 Bandai-Asahi Nat'l Park, Japan
99/G2 Bandai-san (mtn.), Japan
128/D5 Bandama (riv.), IvC.
128/D4 Bandama Blanc (riv.), IvC.
128/D4 Bandama Rouge (riv.), IvC.
95/H3 Bandar Beheshtī (Chāh Behār), Iran
93/J5 Bandar-e 'Abbās, Iran
93/G2 Bandar-e Anzalī, Iran
93/G4 Bandar-e Būshehr, Iran
93/G4 Bandar-e Māhshahr, Iran
93/H2 Bandar-e Torkeman, Iran
112/A4 Bandar Seri Begawan (cap.), Bru.
131/D1 Bandawe, Malw.
141/D2 Bandeira (peak), Braz.
141/G6 Bandeira do Sul, Braz.
141/B2 Bandeirantes, Braz.
158/F4 Bandelier Nat'l Mon., NM,US
162/D4 Bandera, Tx,US
147/N7 Banderilla, Mex.
128/E3 Bandiagara, Mali
102/B5 Bandipura, India
108/F3 Bandipur Nat'l Park, India
83/H5 Bandırma, Turk.
83/J5 Bandirma (gulf), Turk.
60/B6 Bandon (riv.), Ire.
107/J5 Ban Don, Viet.
126/C1 Bandundu, Zaire
110/C5 Bandung, Indo.
75/E3 Bañeres, Sp.
149/H1 Banes, Cuba
54/D1 Banff, Sc,UK
156/E3 Banff Nat'l Park, Ab, BC,Can
128/D4 Banfora, Burk.
108/C2 Banga, India
106/C5 Bangalore, India
129/H5 Bangangté, Camr.
105/J5 Bangar, Phil.
125/K7 Bangassou, CAfr.
111/E2 Bangau, Tanjong (cape), Malay.
111/F4 Banggai (isls.), Indo.
102/C5 Banggong (lake), China
109/D2 Banghiang (riv.), Laos
110/C4 Bangka (isl.), Indo.
110/B4 Bangka (str.), Indo.
109/C3 Bangkok (bight), Thai.
109/C3 Bangkok (Krung Thep) (cap.), Thai.
106/E3 Bangladesh
109/C5 Bang Lang (res.), Thai.
104/C4 Bangma (mts.), China
56/C2 Bangor, NI,UK
56/D5 Bangor, Wal,UK
161/G2 Bangor, Me,US
57/F6 Bangor-is-y-Coed, Wal,UK
126/D2 Bangu, Zaire
112/C1 Bangued, Phil.
125/J7 Bangui (cap.), CAfr.
112/C1 Bangui, Phil.
91/B4 Banhā, Egypt
131/D4 Banhine Nat'l Park, Moz.
150/D3 Baní, DRep.
128/D3 Bani (riv.), Mali
128/D3 Banifing (riv.), Burk., Mali
95/L2 Banihāl (pass), India
127/B2 Banī Mazār, Egypt
163/J2 Banister (riv.), Va,US
91/D4 Banī Suhaylah, Gaza
127/B2 Banī Suwayf, Egypt
127/B2 Banī Suwayf (gov.), Egypt
91/D2 Bāniyās, Syria
82/C3 Banja Luka, Bosn.
110/D4 Banjarmasin, Indo.
128/A3 Banjul (cap.), Gam.
109/B5 Ban Kantang, Thai.
107/J4 Ban Kengkok, Laos
54/C4 Bankfoot, Sc,UK
109/D3 Ban Khampho, Laos
54/D2 Bankhead, Sc,UK
109/C5 Ban Khuan Niang, Thai.
119/B3 Banks (cape), Austl.
119/C4 Banks (str.), Austl.
152/C3 Banks (isl.), BC,Can
152/D1 Banks (isl.), NW,Can
115/R11 Banks (pen.), NZ
151/H4 Banks (pt.), Ak,US
156/D4 Banks (lake), Wa,US
120/F6 Banks (isls.), Van.
118/H8 Bankstown, Austl.
106/E3 Bānkurā, India
81/H1 Bankya, Bul.
109/D2 Ban Loboy, Laos
109/E3 Ban Mdrack, Viet.
109/D2 Ban Mong, Viet.
109/D2 Ban Muangsen, Laos
60/D4 Bann (riv.), Ire.
56/B2 Bann (riv.), NI,UK
78/A3 Banna (riv.), It.
109/D2 Ban Nape, Laos
54/C4 Bannockburn, Sc,UK
54/C4 Bannockburn Battlesite (1314), Sc,UK
60/D5 Bannow (bay), Ire.
108/A1 Bannu, Pak.
144/B1 Baños, Ecu.
82/D3 Banovići, Bosn.
109/C4 Ban Pak Phanang, Thai.
109/D3 Ban Phon, Laos
103/B4 Banpo (ruins), China
109/C2 Ban Sieou, Laos
65/K4 Banská Bystrica, Slvk.
83/F5 Bansko, Bul.
53/N8 Banstead, Eng,UK
106/B3 Bānswāra, India
112/C3 Bantayan, Phil.
112/C3 Bantayan (isl.), Phil.
110/D5 Bantenan (cape), Indo.
109/C2 Ban Thabok, Laos
109/B5 Bantong Group (isls.), Thai.
60/A6 Bantry (bay), Ire.
74/C3 Bañuelo (mtn.), Sp.
109/D3 Ban Xebang-Nouan, Laos
110/A3 Banyak (isls.), Indo.
75/G1 Banyoles, Sp.
110/D5 Banyuwangi, Indo.
113/J Banzare (coast), Ant.
123/W17 Banzart (gov.), Tun.
123/W17 Banzart (lake), Tun.
123/W17 Banzart (Bizerte), Tun.
103/B3 Baode, China
103/D3 Baodi, China
103/H7 Baodi, China
103/C3 Baoding, China
103/G7 Baoding, China
103/D4 Baodugu (mtn.), China
103/C4 Baofeng, China
104/E2 Baoguangsi, China
109/D1 Bao Ha, Viet.
96/F5 Baoji, China
107/J2 Baojing, China
103/B5 Baokang, China
109/D1 Bao Lac, Viet.
109/D4 Bao Loc, Viet.
149/J2 Baoruco, Sierra de (range), DRep.
103/E5 Baoshan, China
104/C3 Baoshan, China
105/J2 Baoshan, China
103/B2 Baotou, China
128/D4 Baoulé (riv.), IvC., Mali
128/C3 Baoulé (riv.), Mali
104/D2 Baoxing, China
103/D4 Baoying, China
106/D4 Bāpatla, India
91/D3 Bāqa el Gharbiyya, Isr.
104/B1 Baqên, China
109/D4 Ba Quan (cape), Viet.
93/F3 Ba'qūbah, Iraq
68/D5 Bar (riv.), Fr.
82/D4 Bar, Yugo.
109/D4 Ba Ra, Viet.
125/P7 Baraawe, Som.
110/E4 Barabai, Indo.
88/H4 Barabinsk, Rus.
160/B3 Baraboo, Wi,US
74/D1 Baracaldo, Sp.
149/H1 Baracoa, Cuba
91/E3 Baradá (riv.), Syria
142/F2 Baradero, Arg.
130/C2 Baragoi, Kenya
149/G1 Baraguá, Cuba
125/M5 Bārah, Sudan
150/D3 Barahona, DRep.
104/B3 Barāk (riv.), India
108/D1 Bāra Lācha La (pass), India
110/D3 Baram (cape), Malay.
112/A4 Baram (riv.), Malay.
139/G3 Barama (riv.), Guy.
106/B4 Bārāmati, India
95/K2 Baramula, India
106/C2 Bāran, India
138/C2 Baranoa, Col.
151/L4 Baranof (isl.), Ak,US
86/C1 Baranovichi, Bela.
82/C3 Baranya (co.), Hun.
141/D1 Barão de Cocais, Braz.
140/B2 Barão de Grajaú, Braz.
83/G2 Baraolt, Rom.
69/E3 Baraque de Fraiture (hill), Belg.
112/D2 Baras, Phil.
111/G5 Barat Daya (isls.), Indo.
141/D2 Barbacena, Braz.
150/G4 Barbados
140/C2 Barbalha, Braz.
127/C5 Barbar, Sudan
75/F1 Barbastro, Sp.
74/C4 Barbate de Franco, Sp.
153/T6 Barbeau (peak), NW,Can
75/L6 Barbera del Valles, Sp.
154/V13 Barbers (pt.), Hi,US
154/V13 Barbers Point Nav. Air Sta., Hi,US
133/E2 Barberton, SAfr.
168/F5 Barberton, Oh,US
72/C4 Barbezieux-Saint-Hilaire, Fr.
106/E3 Barbil, India
57/F3 Barbon, Eng,UK
78/D5 Barbona, Monte (peak), It.
138/C3 Barbosa, Col.
160/D4 Barbourville, Ky,US
150/F3 Barbuda (isl.), Anti.
54/A3 Barcaldine, Sc,UK
82/F2 Barcău (riv.), Rom.
80/D3 Barcellona Pozzo di Gotto, It.
75/G2 Barcelona, Sp.
139/E2 Barcelona, Ven.
75/L7 Barcelona (inset), Sp.
74/A2 Barcelos, Port.
65/J2 Barcin, Pol.
118/A4 Barcoo (riv.), Austl.
82/C3 Barcs, Hun.
65/L2 Barczewo, Pol.
124/J3 Bardaï, Chad
91/C4 Bardawīl, Sabkhat al (lag.), Egypt
65/L4 Bardejov, Slvk.
125/P7 Bardheere, Som.
125/L1 Bardīyah, Libya
57/H5 Bardney, Eng,UK
106/B3 Bārdoli, India
56/D6 Bardsey (isl.), Wal,UK
160/C4 Bardstown, Ky,US
125/R5 Bareeda, Som.
78/B2 Bareggio, It.
106/C2 Bareilly, India
66/B5 Barendrecht, Neth.
72/D2 Barentin, Fr.
51/L2 Barents (sea)
125/N4 Barentu, Erit.
166/B3 Bareville-Leacock-Leola, Pa,US
72/C2 Barfleur, Pointe de (pt.), Fr.
106/D3 Bargarh, India
58/C3 Bargoed, Wal,UK
67/H1 Bargteheide, Ger.
96/F1 Barguzin (riv.), Rus.
106/D2 Barhaj, India
161/G2 Bar Harbor, Me,US
59/G2 Bar Hill, Eng,UK
106/C2 Bāri, India
80/E2 Bari, It.
130/B3 Bariadi, Tanz.
130/C3 Baricho, Kenya
78/C3 Barigazzo, Monte (peak), It.
123/U18 Barika, Alg.
130/C5 Barikiwa, Tanz.
148/D3 Barillas, Guat.
139/G2 Barima (riv.), Guy., Ven.
139/F3 Barima-Waini (reg.), Guy.
138/D2 Barinas, Ven.
138/D2 Barinas (state), Ven.
126/C2 Baringa-Twana, Zaire
138/D2 Barinitas, Ven.
106/E3 Baripāda, India
141/B2 Bariri, Braz.
127/B3 Bārīs, Egypt
106/F3 Barisāl, Bang.
110/B4 Barisan (mts.), Indo.
110/D4 Barito (riv.), Indo.
135/C1 Baritu Nat'l Park, Arg.
165/N13 Bark (riv.), Wi,US
117/M9 Barker (cr.), Austl.
161/S9 Barker, NY,US
168/B1 Barkhamsted (res.), Ct,US
53/P7 Barking & Dagenham (bor.), Eng,UK
156/B3 Barkley (sound), BC,Can
160/C4 Barkley (lake), Ky,US
114/E3 Barkly (tablelands), Austl.
96/C3 Barkol (Barkol Kazak Zizhixian), China
57/F6 Barlaston, Eng,UK
57/G4 Barlby, Eng,UK
69/E6 Bar-le-Duc, Fr.
116/C4 Barlee (lake), Austl.
116/B2 Barlee (range), Austl.
116/B2 Barlee Range Nature Rsv., Austl.
80/E2 Barletta, It.
68/B3 Barlin, Fr.
65/H2 Barlinek, Pol.
135/E2 Barmejo (riv.), Arg.
106/B2 Barmer, India
58/B1 Barmouth, Wal,UK
67/G1 Barmstedt, Ger.
108/C2 Barnāla, India
57/G2 Barnard Castle, Eng,UK
102/D1 Barnaul, Rus.
167/D4 Barnegat (bay), NJ,US
167/D4 Barnegat (inlet), NJ,US
53/N7 Barnet, Eng,UK
53/N7 Barnet (bor.), Eng,UK
66/C4 Barneveld, Neth.
65/G2 Barnim (reg.), Ger.
57/F4 Barnoldswick, Eng,UK
57/G4 Barnsley, Eng,UK
58/B4 Barnstaple, Eng,UK
58/B4 Barnstaple (Bideford) (bay), Eng,UK
58/E2 Barnt Green, Eng,UK
67/G5 Barntrup, Ger.
163/H3 Barnwell, SC,US
106/B3 Baroda, India
78/B1 Barone, Monte (peak), It.
95/K1 Barowghīl (Khyber) (pass), Afg.
106/F2 Barpeta, India
138/D2 Barquisimeto, Ven.
56/D1 Barr, Sc,UK
140/B3 Barra, Braz.
55/H8 Barra (isl.), Sc,UK
141/B2 Barra Bonita, Braz.
141/B2 Barra Bonita (res.), Braz.
140/B4 Barra da Choça, Braz.
149/F4 Barra del Colorado Nat'l Park, CR
137/G7 Barra do Bugres, Braz.
140/A2 Barra do Corda, Braz.
137/H7 Barra do Garças, Braz.
140/B3 Barra do Mendes, Braz.
141/K7 Barra do Piraí, Braz.
141/B4 Barra do Ribeiro, Braz.
131/D4 Barra Falsa, Ponta da (pt.), Moz.
55/H8 Barra Head (pt.), Sc,UK
141/J7 Barra Mansa, Braz.
144/B3 Barranca, Peru
138/C3 Barrancabermeja, Col.
146/D3 Barranca del Cobre Nat'l Park, Mex.
142/C2 Barrancas, Chile
138/C2 Barranquilla, Col.
131/D4 Barra, Ponta da (pt.), Moz.
149/F4 Barra Punta Gorda, Nic.
140/B2 Barras, Braz.
141/B3 Barra Velha, Braz.
140/A4 Barreiras, Braz.
140/B1 Barreirinhas, Braz.
74/A3 Barreiro, Port.
140/D3 Barreiros, Braz.
133/G7 Barren, Nosy (isls.), Madg.
141/B2 Barretos, Braz.
156/E2 Barrhead, Ab,Can
54/B5 Barrhead, Sc,UK
56/D1 Barrhill, Sc,UK
160/E2 Barrie, On,Can
119/B1 Barrier (range), Austl.
156/C3 Barrière, BC,Can
165/P15 Barrington, Il,US
168/C2 Barrington, RI,US
165/P15 Barrington Hills, Il,US
119/D1 Barrington Tops (peak), Austl.
119/D1 Barrington Tops Nat'l Park, Austl.
140/B2 Barro Duro, Braz.
118/B2 Barron Gorge Nat'l Park, Austl.
141/D2 Barroso, Braz.
116/B2 Barrow (isl.), Austl.
118/B1 Barrow (pt.), Austl.
152/G1 Barrow (str.), NW,Can
60/D5 Barrow (riv.), Ire.
151/G1 Barrow (pt.), Ak,US
57/H6 Barrowby, Eng,UK
57/F4 Barrowford, Eng,UK
57/E3 Barrow-in-Furness, Eng,UK
58/C4 Barry, Wal,UK
87/L4 Barsakel'mes (salt pan), Uzb.
95/L5 Bārshi, India
67/G4 Barsinghausen, Ger.
63/T8 Bårslöv, Swe.
67/E2 Barssel, Ger.
158/C4 Barstow, Ca,US
146/E2 Barstow, Tx,US
72/F2 Bar-sur-Aube, Fr.
102/B4 Bartang (riv.), Taj.
64/G1 Barth, Ger.
83/L5 Bartın, Turk.
115/H3 Bartle Frere (peak), Austl.
159/J3 Bartlesville, Ok,US
165/P16 Bartlett, Il,US
149/G1 Bartolomé Masó, Cuba
131/D4 Bartolomeu Dias, Moz.
59/F3 Barton in the Clay, Eng,UK
59/E5 Barton on Sea, Eng,UK
59/E1 Barton under Needwood, Eng,UK
57/H4 Barton-upon-Humber, Eng,UK
65/L1 Bartoszyce, Pol.
163/H5 Bartow, Fl,US
149/F4 Barú (vol.), Pan.
110/B3 Barumun (riv.), Indo.
110/A3 Barus, Indo.
96/C2 Baruun Huuray (reg.), Mong.
96/G2 Baruun-Urt, Mong.
106/C3 Barwāha, India
106/B3 Barwāni, India
119/D1 Barwon (riv.), Austl.
65/J3 Barycz (riv.), Pol.
87/H1 Barysh, Rus.
125/J7 Basankusu, Zaire
74/D1 Basauri, Sp.
142/F2 Basavilbaso, Arg.
112/C3 Basay, Phil.
58/D1 Baschurch, Eng,UK
76/D2 Basel, Swi.
76/D3 Baselland (canton), Swi.
80/E2 Basento (riv.), It.
132/E3 Bashee (riv.), SAfr.
105/J4 Bashi (chan.), Phil., Tai.
102/E1 Bashkaus (riv.), Rus.
85/M5 Bashkir Aut. Rep., Rus.
112/C4 Basilan (isl.), Phil.
112/C4 Basilan (peak), Phil.
112/C4 Basilan (str.), Phil.
59/G3 Basildon, Eng,UK
78/C4 Basilica di Fieschi, It.
80/D2 Basilicata (reg.), It.
106/C3 Bāsim, India
156/F4 Basin, Wy,US
59/E4 Basingstoke, Eng,UK
53/M8 Basingstoke (can.), Eng,UK
91/D2 Basīt, Ra's al (pt.), Syria
93/F2 Başkale, Turk.
160/F2 Baskatong (res.), Qu,Can
92/B2 Başkomutan Nat'l Park, Turk.
92/B2 Başmakçı, Turk.
106/C3 Bāsoda, India
130/B4 Basodesh, Tanz.
77/E5 Basodino, Monte (peak), It.
125/K7 Basoko, Zaire
74/D1 Basque Provinces (aut. comm.), Sp.
76/D1 Bas-Rhin (dept.), Fr.
119/C3 Bass (str.), Austl.
121/L7 Bass (isls.), FrPol.
81/G4 Bassae (ruins), Gre.
156/E3 Bassano, Ab,Can
79/E1 Bassano del Grappa, It.
126/H5 Bassas da India (isl.), Reun.
104/B5 Bassein, Burma
104/B5 Bassein (riv.), Burma
106/B4 Bassein, India
69/E2 Bassenge, Belg.
72/C2 Basse-Normandie (reg.), Fr.
56/E2 Bassenthwaite (lake), Eng,UK
150/F3 Basse-Terre, Guad.
150/F3 Basse-Terre (isl.), Guad.
150/F3 Basseterre (cap.), StK.
54/D4 Bass Rock (isl.), Sc,UK
67/F3 Bassum, Ger.
160/B1 Basswood (lake), On,Can, Mn,US
62/E3 Båstad, Swe.
106/D2 Bastī, India
80/A1 Bastia, Fr.
80/C1 Bastia, It.
69/E3 Bastogne, Belg.
141/B2 Bastos, Braz.
162/F3 Bastrop, La,US
162/D4 Bastrop, Tx,US
91/B4 Basyūn, Egypt
124/G7 Bata, EqG.
112/C2 Bataan (mtn.), Phil.
149/F1 Batabanó (gulf), Cuba
112/C1 Batac, Phil.
89/P3 Batagay, Rus.
108/C2 Batāla, India
140/B2 Batalha, Braz.
74/A3 Batalha, Port.
120/B2 Batan (isls.), Phil.
104/C2 Batang, China
125/J6 Batangafo, CAfr.
112/C2 Batangas, Phil.
111/H4 Batanta (mtn.), Indo.
141/C2 Batatais, Braz.
165/P16 Batavia, Il,US
160/E3 Batavia, NY,US
86/F3 Bataysk, Rus.
107/H5 Batdambang, Camb.
118/H9 Bate (bay), Austl.
124/H8 Batéké (plat.), Congo
119/D2 Batemans Bay, Austl.
163/H3 Batesburg, SC,US
163/F3 Batesville, Ar,US
163/F3 Batesville, Ms,US
58/D4 Bath, Eng,UK
161/G3 Bath, Me,US
160/E3 Bath, NY,US
54/C5 Bathgate, Sc,UK
119/D2 Bathurst, Austl.
114/D2 Bathurst (isl.), Austl.
161/H2 Bathurst, NB,Can
151/N1 Bathurst (cape), NW,Can
152/F2 Bathurst (inlet), NW,Can
153/R7 Bathurst (isl.), NW,Can
125/P5 Batī, Eth.
130/C3 Batian (peak), Kenya
102/F2 Batik (mts.), China
94/E3 Bāţin, Wādī al (dry riv.), SAr.
164/C4 Batiquitos (lag.), Ca,US
93/H3 Bāţlāq-e Gāv Khūnī (marsh), Iran
57/G4 Batley, Eng,UK
92/E2 Batman, Turk.
123/V18 Batna, Alg.
123/T16 Batna (wilaya), Alg.
131/B3 Batoka, Zam.
163/F4 Baton Rouge (cap.), La,US
124/H7 Batouri, Camr.
91/D4 Baţrā' (Petra) (ruins), Jor.
161/F2 Batsican (riv.), Qu,Can
166/D4 Batsto (riv.), NJ,US
166/D4 Batsto Hist. Vill., NJ,US
96/F2 Batsümber, Mong.
51/M9 Batterbee (cape), Ant.
57/G3 Battersby, Eng,UK
53/N7 Battersea, Eng,UK
106/D6 Batticaloa, SrL.
108/H4 Batticaloa (dist.), SrL.
156/F2 Battle (riv.), Ab, Sk,Can
59/G5 Battle, Eng,UK
156/F3 Battle (cr.), Mt,US
160/C3 Battle Creek, Mi,US
156/F2 Battleford, Sk,Can
158/C2 Battle Mountain, Nv,US
168/C2 Battleship Cove, Ma,US
54/D3 Battock (mtn.), Sc,UK
82/E2 Battonya, Hun.
96/E2 Battsengel, Mong.
125/N6 Batu (peak), Eth.
111/E3 Batu (cape), Indo.
110/A4 Batu (isls.), Indo.
110/D3 Batu (bay), Malay.
110/D3 Batu (peak), Malay.
111/F4 Batudaka (isl.), Indo.
110/D3 Batuensambang (peak), Indo.
110/B3 Batu Gajah, Malay.
87/G4 Batumi, Geo.
110/B3 Batu Pahat, Malay.
110/B3 Batu Puteh (peak), Malay.
110/B4 Baturaja, Indo.
140/C2 Baturité, Braz.
91/F7 Bat Yam, Isr.
112/C1 Bauang, Phil.
129/H4 Bauchi (state), Nga.
157/K3 Baudette, Mn,US
138/B3 Baudó (mts.), Col.
138/B3 Baudó (riv.), Col.
149/G5 Baudo, Serranía de (range), Col.
153/L1 Bauld (cape), Nf,Can
129/F5 Bauman (peak), Togo
70/D2 Baunach (riv.), Ger.
67/G6 Baunatal, Ger.
112/D3 Bauñgon, Phil.
141/B2 Baurú, Braz.
65/H3 Bautzen, Ger.
71/E5 Bavaria (state), Ger.
77/H3 Bavarian Alps (mts.), Aus., Ger.
62/G2 Båven (lake), Swe.
146/C2 Bavispe (riv.), Mex.
110/C4 Bawang (cape), Indo.
119/C3 Baw Baw (peak), Austl.
119/C3 Baw Baw Nat'l Park, Austl.
110/D5 Bawean (isl.), Indo.
129/E4 Bawku, Gha.
104/C2 Baxoi, China
149/G1 Bayamo, Cuba
150/E3 Bayamón, PR
97/K2 Bayan, China
96/F2 Bayan, Mong.
96/G2 Bayandelger, Mong.
96/D5 Bayan Har (mts.), China
96/E2 Bayanhongor, Mong.
96/E3 Bayanleg, Mong.
96/F2 Bayannur, Mong.
149/G4 Bayano (res.), Pan.
96/E2 Bayan-Ovoo, Mong.
96/D2 Bayan-Uul, Mong.
159/G2 Bayard, Ne,US
112/C3 Bayawan, Phil.
69/G3 Baybach (riv.), Ger.
112/D3 Baybay, Phil.
92/E1 Bayburt, Turk.
92/E1 Bayburt (prov.), Turk.
160/D3 Bay City, Mi,US
162/E4 Bay City, Tx,US
88/G2 Baydaratskaya (bay), Rus.
125/P7 Baydhabo (Baidoa), Som.
96/D2 Baydrag (riv.), Mong.
71/F5 Bayerischer Wald (hills), Ger.
71/G5 Bayerischer Wald Nat'l Park, Ger.
140/D2 Bayeux, Braz.
72/C2 Bayeux, Fr.
143/T11 Baygorria, Artificial de (res.), Uru.
94/E6 Bayḩān al Qişāb, Yem.
92/A2 Bayındır, Turk.
96/F1 Baykal (lake), Rus.
89/L4 Baykal (mts.), Rus.
112/F7 Bay, Laguna de (lake), Phil.
163/G4 Bay Minette, Al,US
112/C1 Bayombong, Phil.
74/A1 Bayona, Sp.
163/H4 Bayonet Point, Fl,US
72/C5 Bayonne, Fr.
167/D2 Bayonne, NJ,US
167/E2 Bayport, NY,US
95/H1 Bayram-Ali, Trkm.
83/H5 Bayramiç, Turk.
71/E3 Bayreuth, Ger.
167/J9 Bay Ridge, NY,US
91/D3 Bayrūt (Beirut) (cap.), Leb.
160/E2 Bays (lake), On,Can
163/F4 Bay Saint Louis, Ms,US
75/E1 Bayse (riv.), Fr.
167/K8 Bayside, NY,US
58/D1 Bayston Hill, Eng,UK
116/K6 Bayswater, Austl.
91/D4 Bayt Laḩm (Bethlehem), WBnk.
162/E4 Baytown, Tx,US
127/C5 Bayudha (des.), Sudan
168/F5 Bay Village, Oh,US
167/E2 Bayville, NY,US
74/D4 Baza, Sp.
87/H4 Bazardyuzyu, Gora (peak), Rus.
131/D4 Bazaruto (isl.), Moz.
129/E4 Bazèga (prov.), Burk.
104/E2 Bazhong, China
160/F2 Bazin (riv.), Qu,Can
167/D4 Beachwood, NJ,US
168/F5 Beachwood, Oh,US
59/G5 Beachy Head (pt.), Eng,UK
58/C2 Beacon (hill), Wal,UK
161/N7 Beaconsfield, Qu,Can
59/F3 Beaconsfield, Eng,UK
58/B5 Beaford, Eng,UK
114/E2 Beagle (gulf), Austl.
118/A4 Beal (mts.), Austl.
133/J6 Bealanana, Madg.
156/B3 Beale (cape), BC,Can
159/G4 Beals (cr.), Tx,US
58/C3 Beaminster, Eng,UK
133/H9 Beampingaratra (ridge), Madg.
161/R9 Beamsville, On,Can
157/K2 Bear (lake), Mb,Can
88/C2 Bear (isl.), Nor.
151/K2 Bear (mtn.), Ak,US
151/K3 Bear (mtn.), Ak,US
165/M10 Bear (cr.), Ca,US
168/A2 Bear (hill), Ct,US
168/A1 Bear (mtn.), Ct,US
156/F5 Bear (lake), Id, Ut,US
156/F5 Bear (riv.), Id, Ut,US
60/A6 Beara (pen.), Ire.
113/M Beardmore (glac.), Ant.
167/H7 Bearfort (mtn.), NJ,US
156/F3 Bearpaw (mts.), Mt,US
54/B5 Bearsden, Sc,UK
156/F4 Beartooth (mts.), Mt, Wy,US
163/F4 Bear Town, Ms,US
168/A1 Beartown Saint For., Ma,US
108/D2 Beās (riv.), India
74/D1 Beasain, Sp.
74/D3 Beas de Segura, Sp.
150/D3 Beata (cape), DRep.
150/D3 Beata (isl.), DRep.
114/F2 Beatrice (cape), Austl.
159/H2 Beatrice, Ne,US
131/C3 Beatrice, Zim.
54/C6 Beattock, Sc,UK
158/C3 Beatty, Nv,US
72/F5 Beaucaire, Fr.
53/S9 Beauchamp, Fr.
145/C2 Beaufort (sea), Can., US
163/H3 Beaufort, SC,US
132/C4 Beaufort West, SAfr.
72/D3 Beaugency, Fr.
161/N7 Beauharnois, Qu,Can
161/N7 Beauharnois (co.), Qu,Can
72/F4 Beaujolais (mts.), Fr.
59/E5 Beaulieu, Eng,UK
54/B2 Beauly, Sc,UK
54/B2 Beauly (firth), Sc,UK
54/B2 Beauly (riv.), Sc,UK
56/D5 Beaumaris, Wal,UK
68/B3 Beaumetz-les-Loges, Fr.
72/E4 Beaumont, Fr.
164/D3 Beaumont, Ca,US
162/E4 Beaumont, Tx,US
53/S9 Beaumont-sur-Oise, Fr.
72/F3 Beaune, Fr.
72/C3 Beaupréau, Fr.
69/D3 Beauraing, Belg.
68/C3 Beaurevoir, Fr.
157/J3 Beauséjour, Mb,Can
68/B5 Beauvais, Fr.
156/G2 Beauval, Sk,Can
156/F2 Beaver (riv.), Ab, Sk,Can
152/D2 Beaver (riv.), Yk,Can
159/G3 Beaver (riv.), Co,US
159/G3 Beaver (riv.), Ks, Ne,US
160/C2 Beaver (isl.), Mi,US
159/G3 Beaver (riv.), NM, Ok,US
159/G3 Beaver, Ok,US
168/G6 Beaver (co.), Pa,US
168/G6 Beaver (riv.), Pa,US
158/D3 Beaver, Ut,US
151/K3 Beaver Creek, Yk,Can
160/B3 Beaver Dam, Wi,US
168/G6 Beaver Falls, Pa,US
156/E4 Beaverhead (riv.), Mt,US
156/D2 Beaverlodge, Ab,Can
157/L2 Beaver Stone (riv.), On,Can
106/B2 Beāwar, India
141/B2 Bebedouro, Braz.
140/C2 Beberibe, Braz.
57/E5 Bebington, Eng,UK
67/G7 Bebra, Ger.
59/H2 Beccles, Eng,UK
82/E3 Bečej, Yugo.
124/E1 Bechar, Alg.
151/G4 Becharof (lake), Ak,US
151/G4 Becharof Nat'l Wild. Ref., Ak,US
53/N7 Beckenham, Eng,UK
69/F5 Beckingen, Ger.
57/H5 Beckingham, Eng,UK
160/D4 Beckley, WV,US
67/F5 Beckum, Ger.
83/G2 Beclean, Rom.
76/D5 Becs de Bosson (peak), Swi.
57/G3 Bedale, Eng,UK
66/D7 Bedburg, Ger.
66/D5 Bedburg-Hau, Ger.
58/C3 Beddau, Wal,UK
56/D5 Beddgelert, Wal,UK
118/B1 Bedford (cape), Austl.
161/F2 Bedford, Qu,Can
59/F2 Bedford, Eng,UK
160/C4 Bedford, In,US
168/F5 Bedford, Oh,US
160/E4 Bedford, Va,US
168/F5 Bedford Heights, Oh,US
59/G2 Bedford Level (reg.), Eng,UK
59/F2 Bedfordshire (co.), Eng,UK
57/G1 Bedlington, Eng,UK
53/M6 Bedmond, Eng,UK
124/H4 Bedouaram (well), Niger
66/D2 Bedum, Neth.
58/C3 Bedwas, Wal,UK
59/E2 Bedworth, Eng,UK
118/D4 Beenleigh, Austl.
58/C5 Beer, Eng,UK
70/B3 Beerfelden, Ger.
58/C5 Beer Head (pt.), Eng,UK
68/C1 Beernem, Belg.
91/D4 Beersheba (Be'er Sheva'), Isr.
91/D4 Be'er Sheva' (Beersheba), Isr.
69/D1 Beerzel, Belg.
66/D6 Beesel, Neth.
57/G6 Beeston, Eng,UK
162/D4 Beeville, Tx,US
125/K7 Befale, Zaire
67/F5 Bega (riv.), Ger.
106/C3 Begamganj, India
87/K4 Begarslan (peak), Trkm.
82/E3 Bega Veche (riv.), Rom.
89/M2 Begichev (isl.), Rus.
56/B2 Beg, Lough (lake), NI,UK
62/C1 Begna (riv.), Nor.
106/E2 Begusarai, India
137/H3 Béhague (pt.), FrG.
110/B4 Behala (str.), Indo.
93/G4 Behbahān, Iran
69/F5 Behren-lès-Forbach, Fr.
93/H2 Behshahr, Iran
105/H2 Bei (mtn.), China
102/F3 Bei (mts.), China
105/F2 Bei (riv.), China
105/G3 Bei (riv.), China
97/K2 Bei'an, China
96/D4 Beida (riv.), China
105/J3 Beigantang (isl.), Tai.
78/B4 Beigua, Monte (peak), It.
105/F4 Beihai, China
103/D3 Beijing (cap.), China
103/H6 Beijing (prov.), China
103/H7 Beijing (inset) (cap.), China
66/D3 Beilen, Neth.
105/F4 Beiliu, China
71/E4 Beilngries, Ger.
96/C5 Beilu (riv.), China
105/E4 Beilun (pass), China
78/A2 Beinasco, It.
54/B3 Beinn a' Chuallaich (mtn.), Sc,UK
54/C3 Beinn a' Ghlò (mtn.), Sc,UK
54/B2 Beinn a' Mheadhoin, Loch (lake), Sc,UK
54/A3 Beinn Bhàn (mtn.), Sc,UK
54/B4 Beinn Bheula (mtn.), Sc,UK
54/C2 Beinn Bhrotain (mtn.), Sc,UK
54/B4 Beinn Bhuidhe (mtn.), Sc,UK
54/B2 Beinn Bhuidhe Mhór (mtn.), Sc,UK
54/B1 Beinn Dearg (mtn.), Sc,UK
54/C3 Beinn Dearg (mtn.), Sc,UK
54/B4 Beinn Dòrain (mtn.), Sc,UK
54/A1 Beinn Eighe (mtn.), Sc,UK
54/B3 Beinn Heasgarnich (mtn.), Sc,UK
54/B3 Beinn Mholach (mtn.), Sc,UK
54/A4 Beinn Mhór (mtn.), Sc,UK
54/B1 Bein Tharsuinn (mtn.), Sc,UK
103/E2 Beipiao, China
131/D3 Beira, Moz.
103/C4 Beiru (riv.), China
91/D3 Beirut (Bayrūt) (cap.), Leb.
131/C4 Beitbridge, Zim.
54/B5 Beith, Sc,UK
82/F2 Beiuş, Rom.
101/A2 Beizhen, China
74/B3 Beja, Port.
74/A4 Beja (dist.), Port.
123/T15 Bejaïa, Alg.
123/T15 Bejaïa (wilaya), Alg.
74/C2 Béjar, Sp.
95/J3 Bejhi (riv.), Pak.

176

Bekaa - Bismu

91/D3 Bekaa (Al Biqā') (val.), Leb.
110/C5 Bekasi, Indo.
82/E2 Békés, Hun.
82/E2 Békés (co.), Hun.
82/E2 Békéscsaba, Hun.
133/H8 Bekily, Madg.
129/E5 Bekwai, Gha.
106/B3 Bela, India
95/J3 Bela, Pak.
130/A2 Bela, Zaire
82/E3 Bela Crkva, Yugo.
140/B1 Bela Cruz, Braz.
166/B4 Bel Air, Md,US
117/M8 Belair Rec. Park, Austl.
166/B5 Bel Air South, Md,US
82/F4 Bela Palanka, Yugo.
86/C1 Belarus
75/P10 Belas, Port.
137/G8 Bela Vista, Braz.
131/D5 Bela Vista, Moz.
141/B2 Bela Vista do Paraiso, Braz.
85/M5 Belaya (riv.), Rus.
87/G2 Belaya Kalitva, Rus.
86/D2 Belaya Tserkov', Ukr.
78/B3 Belbo (riv.), It.
65/K3 Bełchatów, Pol.
76/D2 Belchen (peak), Ger.
153/S7 Belcher (chan.), NW,Can
153/H3 Belcher (isls.), NW,Can
157/J3 Belcourt, ND,US
85/M5 Belebey, Rus.
125/Q7 Beled Weyne, Som.
140/D2 Belém, Braz.
140/C3 Belém de São Francisco, Braz.
75/P10 Belem Tower, Port.
135/C2 Belén, Arg.
91/E1 Belen, Turk.
158/F4 Belen, NM,US
143/S12 Belén de Escobar, Arg.
83/G4 Belene, Bul.
74/B1 Belesar (res.), Sp.
125/N5 Beles Wenz (riv.), Eth.
86/F1 Belev, Rus.
56/C2 Belfast (cap.), NI,UK
56/C2 Belfast (dist.), NI,UK
161/G2 Belfast, Me,US
56/C2 Belfast Lough (inlet), NI,UK
157/H4 Belfield, ND,US
54/E5 Belford, Eng,UK
76/C2 Belfort, Fr.
76/C2 Belfort (dept.), Fr.
106/B4 Belgaum, India
64/C3 Belgium
86/F2 Belgorod, Rus.
86/D3 Belgorod-Dnestrovskiy, Ukr.
86/F2 Belgorod Obl., Rus.
156/F4 Belgrade, Mt,US
82/E3 Belgrade (Beograd) (cap.), Yugo.
60/B1 Belhavel (lake), Ire.
82/E4 Beli Drim (riv.), Yugo.
82/D3 Beli Manastir, Cro.
82/F4 Beli Timok (riv.), Yugo.
110/C4 Belitung (isl.), Indo.
148/D2 Belize
148/D2 Belize (riv.), Belz.
148/D2 Belize City, Belz.
82/E3 Beljanica (peak), Yugo.
89/P2 Bel'kovskiy (isl.), Rus.
117/G5 Bell (pt.), Austl.
153/H2 Bell (pen.), NW,Can
160/E1 Bell (riv.), Qu,Can
164/B3 Bell, Ca,US
156/B3 Bella Coola, BC,Can
56/B2 Bellaghy, NI,UK
106/C4 Bellary, India
135/E2 Bella Vista, Arg.
80/A3 Bellavista (cape), It.
165/G7 Belle (riv.), On,Can
165/G6 Belle (riv.), Mi,US
68/C5 Belleau, Fr.
56/B3 Belleek, NI,UK
160/D3 Bellefontaine, Oh,US
157/G4 Belle Fourche (riv.), SD, Wy,US
76/B5 Bellegarde-sur-Valserine, Fr.
163/H5 Belle Glade, Fl,US
166/A6 Belle Haven, Va,US
72/B3 Belle-Ile (isl.), Fr.
161/K1 Belle Isle (str.), Nf, Qu,Can
118/B2 Bellenden Ker Nat'l Park, Austl.
72/E3 Bellerive-sur-Allier, Fr.
160/E2 Belleville, On,Can
160/B4 Belleville, Il,US
159/H3 Belleville, Ks,US
165/E7 Belleville (lake), Mi,US
167/D2 Belleville, NJ,US
168/G7 Bellevue, Pa,US
165/C2 Bellevue, Wa,US
164/B3 Bellflower, Ca,US
164/F8 Bell Gardens, Ca,US
57/F1 Bellingham, Eng,UK
156/C3 Bellingham, Wa,US
163/F4 Bellingrath Gardens, Al,US
113/U Bellingshausen (sea), Ant.
121/K6 Bellingshausen (isl.), FrPol.
67/E2 Bellingwolde, Neth.
77/F5 Bellinzona, Swi.
166/C4 Bellmawr, NJ,US
167/E2 Bellmore, NY,US
138/C3 Bello, Col.
120/F7 Bellona (reefs), NCal.
152/G1 Bellot (str.), NW,Can
154/W13 Bellows A.F.B., Hi,US
54/D4 Bell Rock (Inchcape) (isl.), Sc,UK
54/B6 Bellsbank, Sc,UK
54/B5 Bellshill, Sc,UK
73/K3 Belluno, It.
79/E1 Belluno (prov.), It.
142/E2 Bell Ville, Arg.
132/B4 Bellville, SAfr.
162/D4 Bellville, Tx,US
67/F4 Belm, Ger.
165/K11 Belmont, Ca,US
168/C1 Belmont, Ma,US
140/C4 Belmonte, Braz.
148/D2 Belmopan (cap.), Belz.
140/B4 Belo Campo, Braz.
68/C2 Beloeil, Belg.
161/P6 Beloeil, Qu,Can
97/K1 Belogorsk, Rus.
82/F4 Belogradchik, Bul.
141/D1 Belo Horizonte, Braz.
159/H3 Beloit, Ks,US
160/B3 Beloit, Wi,US
140/C3 Belo Jardim, Braz.
84/G2 Belomorsk, Rus.
126/C1 Belondo-Kundu, Zaire
86/F3 Belorechensk, Rus.
85/N5 Beloretsk, Rus.
82/E4 Beloševac, Yugo.
83/H4 Beloslav, Bul.
88/J4 Belovo, Rus.
84/H3 Beloye (lake), Rus.
57/G5 Belper, Eng,UK
57/G1 Belsay, Eng,UK
156/F4 Belt, Mt,US
66/D3 Belterwijde (lake), Neth.
59/H1 Belton, Eng,UK
162/D4 Belton, Tx,US
60/A2 Beltra (lake), Ire.
166/B5 Beltsville, Md,US
83/H2 Bel'tsy, Mol.
166/C2 Beltzville (lake), Pa,US
102/E2 Belukha, Gora (peak), Rus.
160/B3 Belvidere, Il,US
118/B3 Belyando (riv.), Austl.
88/G2 Belyy (isl.), Rus.
64/G2 Belzig, Ger.
65/M3 Bełżyce, Pol.
133/H7 Bemaraha (plat.), Madg.
133/H7 Bemarivo (riv.), Madg.
131/C3 Bembezi (riv.), Zim.
74/B1 Bembibre, Sp.
59/E5 Bembridge, Eng,UK
131/C4 Bemebesi, Zim.
157/K4 Bemidji, Mn,US
66/C5 Bemmel, Neth.
57/H3 Bempton, Eng,UK
54/C1 Ben Aigan (hill), Sc,UK
54/B3 Ben Alder (mtn.), Sc,UK
117/C4 Benalla, Austl.
119/C4 Benalmádena, Sp.
74/C2 Benavente, Sp.
162/D5 Benavides, Tx,US
54/C2 Ben Avon (mtn.), Sc,UK
56/B1 Benbane Head (pt.), NI,UK
55/H8 Benbecula (isl.), Sc,UK
117/H4 Benbonyathe (peak), Austl.
119/D3 Ben Boyd Nat'l Park, Austl.
60/C1 Benbrack (mtn.), Ire.
56/B3 Benburb, NI,UK
54/C4 Ben Chonzie (mtn.), Sc,UK
54/C4 Ben Cleuch (mtn.), Sc,UK
54/A4 Ben Cruachan (mtn.), Sc,UK
156/C4 Bend, Or,US
60/A4 Ben Dash (mtn.), Ire.
166/C5 Ben Davis (pt.), NJ,US
129/G5 Bendel (state), Nga.
151/F2 Bendeleben (mtn.), Ak,US
83/J2 Bendery, Mol.
119/C3 Bendigo, Austl.
62/C4 Bendorf, Ger.
91/F7 Bene Beraq, Isr.
153/L3 Benedict (mtn.), Nf,Can
77/H2 Benediktenwand (peak), Ger.
140/B2 Beneditinos, Braz.
56/D1 Beneraid (hill), Sc,UK
71/H3 Benešov, Czh.
80/D2 Benevento, It.
59/G3 Benfleet, Eng,UK
131/D3 Benga, Moz.
106/E4 Bengal (bay), Asia
103/D4 Bengbu, China
125/K1 Benghāzī, Libya
109/D3 Ben Giang, Viet.
110/B3 Bengkalis, Indo.
110/B3 Bengkalis (isl.), Indo.
110/C3 Bengkayang, Indo.
110/B4 Bengkulu, Indo.
157/G3 Bengough, Sk,Can
62/E2 Bengtsfors, Swe.
126/B3 Benguela, Ang.
131/D4 Benguerua (isl.), Moz.
131/C1 Bengweulu (lake), Zam.
131/C1 Bengweulu (swamp), Zam.
55/J7 Ben Hope (mtn.), Sc,UK
136/E6 Beni (riv.), Bol.
130/A2 Beni, Zaire
124/E1 Beni Abbes, Alg.
75/F2 Benicarló, Sp.
165/K10 Benicia, Ca,US
75/E3 Benidorm, Sp.
75/E3 Benifayó, Sp.
54/B4 Ben Ime (mtn.), Sc,UK
124/D1 Beni Mellal, Mor.
129/F4 Benin
129/F5 Benin (bight), Ben., Nga.
129/G5 Benin City, Nga.
124/E1 Beni Ounif, Alg.
75/F3 Benisa, Sp.
142/B5 Benjamin (isl.), Chile
162/D3 Benjamin, Tx,US
144/D2 Benjamin Constant, Braz.
100/B2 Benkei-misaki (cape), Japan
159/G2 Benkelman, Ne,US
54/B3 Ben Lawers (mtn.), Sc,UK
54/B4 Ben Ledi (mtn.), Sc,UK
56/D5 Benllech, Wal,UK
54/B4 Ben Lomond (mtn.), Sc,UK
119/C4 Ben Lomond Nat'l Park, Austl.
54/B4 Ben Lui (mtn.), Sc,UK
54/C2 Ben Macdui (mtn.), Sc,UK
60/A1 Benmore (mtn.), Ire.
54/B4 Ben More (mtn.), Sc,UK
55/J7 Ben More Assynt (mtn.), Sc,UK
54/D2 Bennachie (hill), Sc,UK
56/C1 Bennane Head (pt.), Sc,UK
54/A6 Bennan Head (pt.), Sc,UK
89/R2 Bennett (isl.), Rus.
163/J3 Bennettsville, SC,US
54/B3 Ben Nevis (mtn.), Sc,UK
161/F3 Bennington, Vt,US
132/Q13 Benoni, SAfr.
133/J6 Be, Nosy (isl.), Madg.
124/H6 Bénoue Nat'l Park, Camr.
109/D2 Ben Quang, Viet.
54/C2 Ben Rinnes (mtn.), Sc,UK
165/Q16 Bensenville, Il,US
70/B3 Bensheim, Ger.
158/E5 Benson, Az,US
157/K4 Benson, Mn,US
167/K9 Bensonhurst, NY,US
54/A3 Ben Starav (mtn.), Sc,UK
54/B2 Ben Tee (mtn.), Sc,UK
57/F3 Bentham, Eng,UK
67/E4 Bentheim, Ger.
104/E5 Ben Thuy, Viet.
54/C3 Ben Tirran (mtn.), Sc,UK
125/L6 Bentiu, Sudan
57/G4 Bentley, Eng,UK
141/B4 Bento Gonçalves, Braz.
162/E3 Benton, Ar,US
160/B4 Benton, Il,US
160/B4 Benton, Ky,US
110/B3 Bentong, Malay.
160/C3 Benton Harbor, Mi,US
162/E2 Bentonville, Ar,US
109/D4 Ben Tre, Viet.
129/G4 Benue (riv.), Nga.
129/G5 Benue (state), Nga.
54/B4 Ben Vane (mtn.), Sc,UK
54/B4 Ben Vorlich (mtn.), Sc,UK
54/C3 Ben Vrackie (mtn.), Sc,UK
54/B1 Ben Wyvis (mtn.), Sc,UK
101/B2 Benxi, China
101/C2 Benxi, China
82/D3 Beočin, Yugo.
82/E3 Beograd (Belgrade) (cap.), Yugo.
98/B4 Beppu, Japan
98/B4 Beppu (bay), Japan
150/F4 Bequia (isl.), StV.
140/A1 Bequimão, Braz.
124/E1 Beraber (well), Alg.
56/A2 Beragh, NI,UK
81/F2 Berat, Alb.
111/E4 Beratus (peak), Indo.
111/H4 Berau (bay), Indo.
111/E3 Berau (riv.), Indo.
125/Q5 Berbera, Som.
124/J7 Berberati, CAfr.
139/G3 Berbice (riv.), Guy.
68/D1 Berchem, Belg.
71/E4 Berching, Ger.
73/K3 Berchtesgaden, Ger.
73/K3 Berchtesgaden Nat'l Park, Ger.
68/A3 Berck, Fr.
86/D2 Berdichev, Ukr.
88/J4 Berdsk, Rus.
86/F3 Berdyansk, Ukr.
160/C4 Berea, Ky,US
168/F5 Berea, Oh,US
86/B2 Beregovo, Ukr.
130/B4 Bereku, Tanz.
129/E5 Berekum, Gha.
127/C4 Berenice (ruins), Egypt
58/D5 Bere Regis, Eng,UK
161/H2 Beresford, NB,Can
157/J5 Beresford, SD,US
82/E2 Berettyo (riv.), Hun.
82/E2 Berettyóújfalu, Hun.
86/D1 Berezina (riv.), Bela.
85/N4 Berezniki, Rus.
132/B4 Berg (riv.), SAfr.
92/A2 Bergama, Turk.
77/F6 Bergamasque Alps (mts.), It.
78/C1 Bergamo, It.
78/C1 Bergamo (prov.), It.
67/G3 Bergen, Ger.
66/B3 Bergen, Neth.
62/A1 Bergen, Nor.
167/D1 Bergen (co.), NJ,US
67/G3 Bergen-Belsen, Ger.
167/E2 Bergenfield, NJ,US
66/B6 Bergen op Zoom, Neth.
72/D4 Bergerac, Fr.
66/C6 Bergeyk, Neth.
69/F2 Bergheim, Ger.
67/E6 Bergisch Gladbach, Ger.
67/E5 Bergkamen, Ger.
67/E6 Bergneustadt, Ger.
162/D4 Bergstrom A.F.B., Tx,US
66/C2 Bergum, Neth.
66/D2 Bergumermeer (lake), Neth.
62/G1 Bergviken (lake), Swe.
106/D4 Berhampur, India
110/C4 Berikat (cape), Indo.
89/S4 Bering (isl.), Rus.
50/A3 Bering (sea)
151/E3 Bering (str.), Rus., Ak,US
69/E1 Beringen, Belg.
151/E2 Bering Land Bridge Nat'l Prsv., Ak,US
110/B4 Beritarikap (cape), Indo.
74/D4 Berja, Sp.
66/D4 Berkel (riv.), Ger.
66/B5 Berkel, Neth.
58/D3 Berkeley, Eng,UK
165/K11 Berkeley, Ca,US
166/D2 Berkeley Heights, NJ,US
53/M6 Berkhamsted, Eng,UK
165/F6 Berkley, Mi,US
113/W Berkner (isl.), Ant.
83/F4 Berkovitsa, Bul.
166/C3 Berks (co.), Pa,US
59/E4 Berkshire (co.), Eng,UK
168/A1 Berkshire (co.), Ma,US
168/A1 Berkshire (hills), Ma,US
59/E4 Berkshire Downs (uplands), Eng,UK
68/C1 Berlare, Belg.
66/C5 Berlicum, Neth.
65/G2 Berlin (cap.), Ger.
168/B2 Berlin, Ct,US
161/G2 Berlin, NH,US
168/G6 Berlin (res.), Oh,US
113/V Berlioz (pt.), Ant.
134/C5 Bermejo (riv.), Arg.
135/D1 Bermejo, Bol.
74/D1 Bermeo, Sp.
145/L6 Bermuda (isl.), UK
166/A4 Bermudian (cr.), Pa,US
76/D3 Bern (canton), Swi.
76/D4 Bern (cap.), Swi.
144/A2 Bernal, Peru
80/E2 Bernalda, It.
158/F4 Bernalillo, NM,US
152/D1 Bernard (riv.), NW,Can
143/J7 Bernardo O'Higgins Nat'l Park, Chile
166/D2 Bernardsville, NJ,US
72/D2 Bernay, Fr.
64/F3 Bernburg, Ger.
67/F2 Berne (riv.), Ger.
76/D5 Bernese Alps (range), Swi.
53/S9 Bernes-sur-Oise, Fr.
116/B3 Bernier (isl.), Austl.
152/G1 Bernier (bay), NW,Can
77/F5 Bernina (mts.), It., Swi.
77/G5 Bernina, Passo del (pass), Swi.
77/F5 Bernina, Piz (peak), Swi.
68/C3 Bernissart, Belg.
69/G4 Bernkastel-Kues, Ger.
133/H8 Beroroha, Madg.
71/H3 Beroun, Czh.
71/H3 Berounka (riv.), Czh.
82/F5 Berovo, Macd.
72/F5 Berre (lag.), Fr.
55/K7 Berriedale, Sc,UK
58/C1 Berriew, Wal,UK
123/S15 Berrouaghia, Alg.
150/B1 Berry (isls.), Bahm.
72/D3 Berry (hist. reg.), Fr.
165/K9 Berryessa (lake), Ca,US
165/K9 Berryessa (peak), Ca,US
58/C6 Berry Head (pt.), Wal,UK
166/A2 Berry Mountain (ridge), Pa,US
162/E2 Berryville, Ar,US
140/C2 Bertolínia, Braz.
124/H7 Bertoua, Camr.
143/J7 Bertrand (peak), Arg.
69/E4 Bertrix, Belg.
79/F3 Bertuzzi, Valli (lag.), It.
120/G5 Beru (atoll), Kiri.
110/D3 Beruit (isl.), Malay.
54/D3 Bervie Water (riv.), Sc,UK
119/G5 Berwick, Austl.
161/H2 Berwick, NB,Can
166/B1 Berwick, Pa,US
54/D5 Berwick-upon-Tweed, Eng,UK
56/E6 Berwyn (mts.), Wal,UK
165/Q16 Berwyn, Il,US
166/C3 Berwyn-Devon, Pa,US
72/E4 Bès (riv.), Fr.
133/H7 Besalampy, Madg.
76/C3 Besançon, Fr.
111/E4 Besar (peak), Indo.
72/E3 Besbre (riv.), Fr.
88/F6 Beshahr, Iran
82/E3 Beška, Yugo.
65/K4 Beskids (mts.), Pol.
87/H4 Beslan, Rus.
82/F4 Besna Kobila (peak), Yugo.
157/G2 Besnard (lake), Sk,Can
92/D2 Besni, Turk.
78/B1 Besozzo, It.
57/G4 Bessacarr, Eng,UK
53/S9 Bessancourt, Fr.
83/J2 Bessarabia (reg.), Mol.
56/B3 Bessbrook, NI,UK
163/G3 Bessemer, Al,US
160/B2 Bessemer, Mi,US
165/D2 Bessemer (mtn.), Wa,US
87/K3 Besshoky, Gora (peak), Kaz.
66/C6 Best, Neth.
67/F6 Bestwig, Ger.
74/A1 Betanzos, Sp.
123/M14 Beth (riv.), Mor.
91/G6 Beth Alpha Synagogue Nat'l Park, Isr.
165/L11 Bethany (res.), Ca,US
159/J2 Bethany, Mo,US
168/A3 Bethel, Ct,US
168/G7 Bethel Park, Pa,US
56/D5 Bethesda, Wal,UK
166/A6 Bethesda, Md,US
132/E3 Bethlehem, SAfr.
166/C2 Bethlehem, Pa,US
91/D4 Bethlehem (Bayt Laḩm), WBnk.
76/C2 Bethoncourt, Fr.
167/E2 Bethpage, NY,US
157/G3 Béthune, Sk,Can
68/B2 Béthune, Fr.
68/A4 Béthune (riv.), Fr.
141/C1 Betim, Braz.
133/H8 Betioky, Madg.
102/A2 Betpak-Dala (des.), Kaz.
69/G6 Betschdorf, Fr.
91/D3 Bet She'an, Isr.
91/F8 Bet Shemesh, Isr.
161/G1 Betsiamites (riv.), Qu,Can
133/H7 Betsiboka (riv.), Madg.
125/J3 Bette (peak), Libya
69/F4 Bettembourg, Lux.
106/D2 Bettiah, India
106/C3 Betūl, India
66/C5 Betuwe (reg.), Neth.
56/E5 Betws-y-Coed, Wal,UK
69/G2 Betzdorf, Ger.
157/H4 Beulah, ND,US
165/P14 Beulah (lake), Wi,US
66/D3 Beulakerwijde (lake), Neth.
59/G4 Beult (riv.), Eng,UK
66/C5 Beuningen, Neth.
72/D3 Beuvron (riv.), Fr.
53/U10 Beuvronne (riv.), Fr.
68/B2 Beuvry, Fr.
67/H2 Bevensen, Ger.
67/E4 Bever (riv.), Ger.
68/D1 Beveren, Belg.
77/F4 Beverin, Piz (peak), Swi.
57/H4 Beverley, Eng,UK
164/B2 Beverly Hills, Ca,US
165/F6 Beverly Hills, Mi,US
67/G5 Beverungen, Ger.
66/B4 Beverwijk, Neth.
57/F1 Bewcastle, Eng,UK
58/D2 Bewdley, Eng,UK
59/G4 Bewl Bridge (res.), Eng,UK
69/G5 Bexbach, Ger.
59/G5 Bexhill, Eng,UK
53/P7 Bexley (bor.), Eng,UK
83/J5 Beykoz, Turk.
93/N6 Beylerbeyi Palace, Turk.
69/E2 Beyne-Heusay, Belg.
93/M6 Beyoğlu, Turk.
83/K5 Beypazarı, Turk.
108/E3 Beypore, India
108/F3 Beypore (riv.), India
92/B2 Beyşehir, Turk.
92/B2 Beyşehir (lake), Turk.
82/D3 Bezdan, Yugo.
71/H1 Bezděz (peak), Czh.
71/H4 Bezdrev (lake), Czh.
84/H4 Bezhetsk, Rus.
72/E5 Béziers, Fr.
106/D2 Bhabua, India
108/C2 Bhadaur, India
106/E3 Bhadrak, India
106/C5 Bhadrāvati, India
106/A3 Bhadreswar, India
106/E2 Bhāgalpur, India
108/B2 Bhāi Pheru, Pak.
108/A2 Bhakkar, Pak.
108/D2 Bhākra (dam), India
106/E2 Bhaktapur, Nepal
108/B1 Bhalwāl, Pak.
104/C3 Bhamo, Burma
106/C2 Bharatpur, India
104/B3 Bhareli (riv.), India
106/B3 Bharuch, India
106/D3 Bhātāpāra, India
108/C2 Bhatinda, India
106/B5 Bhatkal, India
106/E3 Bhātpāra, India
108/F3 Bhavāni, India
108/F3 Bhavāni (riv.), India
106/B3 Bhavnagar, India
108/B2 Bhawāna, Pak.
106/C3 Bhawāni Mandi, India
106/D4 Bhawānipatna, India
108/B1 Bhera, Pak.
106/D3 Bhilai, India
106/B2 Bhīlwāra, India
106/C4 Bhīma (riv.), India
106/D4 Bhīmavaram, India
106/D4 Bhimunipatnam, India
106/C2 Bhind, India
106/B3 Bhīnmāl, India
106/B4 Bhiwandi, India
106/E2 Bhojpur, Nepal
106/C3 Bhopāl, India
106/B4 Bhor, India
54/A1 Bhraoin, Loch (lake), Sc,UK
106/E3 Bhuban, India
106/E3 Bhubaneswar, India
106/A3 Bhūj, India
109/B2 Bhumibol (dam), Thai.
106/C3 Bhusawal, India
106/E2 Bhutan
108/G3 Bhuvanagiri, India
102/F5 Bi (riv.), China
136/E4 Biá (riv.), Braz.
128/E5 Bia (riv.), Gui., IvC.
130/A2 Biaboye, Zaire
68/B3 Biache-Saint-Vaast, Fr.
124/G7 Biafra (bight), Afr.
111/J4 Biak (isl.), Indo.
65/M2 Biała Podlaska, Pol.
65/M3 Biała Podlaska (prov.), Pol.
65/L3 Białobrzegi, Pol.
65/J2 Białogard, Pol.
65/K4 Białowieski Nat'l Park, Pol.
65/M2 Białystok, Pol.
65/M2 Białystok (prov.), Pol.
73/J3 Bianca (peak), It.
80/D4 Biancavilla, It.
125/L7 Biaro, Zaire
72/C5 Biarritz, Fr.
127/B2 Bibā, Egypt
100/B2 Bibai, Japan
70/C6 Biberach an der Riss, Ger.
76/D3 Biberist, Swi.
104/A3 Bibiyana (riv.), Bang., India
138/B5 Biblián, Ecu.
70/B3 Biblis, Ger.
141/K6 Bicas, Braz.
83/H2 Bicaz, Rom.
59/E3 Bicester, Eng,UK
114/F2 Bickerton (isl.), Austl.
116/L7 Bickley (brook), Austl.
82/D2 Bicske, Hun.
112/B4 Bidadari, Tanjong (cape), Malay.
128/D5 Bidaga (rapids), IvC.
106/C4 Bīdar, India
161/G3 Biddeford, Me,US
57/F5 Biddulph, Eng,UK
54/A3 Bidean nam Bian (mtn.), Sc,UK
58/B4 Bideford, Eng,UK
58/B4 Bideford (Barnstaple) (bay), Eng,UK
79/F4 Bidente (riv.), It.
59/E2 Bidford on Avon, Eng,UK
109/E3 Bi Doup (peak), Viet.
75/E1 Bidouze (riv.), Fr.
126/B4 Bié (plat.), Ang.
70/B3 Biebesheim am Rhein, Ger.
65/M2 Biebrza (riv.), Pol.
76/D3 Biel, Swi.
65/J3 Bielawa, Pol.
54/D2 Bieldside, Sc,UK
67/F4 Bielefeld, Ger.
153/J1 Bieler (lake), NW,Can
76/D3 Bieler (lake), Swi.
78/B1 Biella, It.
65/K4 Bielsko (prov.), Pol.
65/K4 Bielsko-Biała, Pol.
65/M2 Bielsk Podlaski, Pol.
109/D4 Bien Hoa, Viet.
76/B5 Bienne (riv.), Fr.
109/D1 Bien Son, Viet.
153/J3 Bienville (lake), Qu,Can
66/B5 Biesbosch (reg.), Neth.
66/D5 Biesme (riv.), Fr.
76/D5 Bietschhorn (peak), Swi.
53/S10 Bièvre (riv.), Fr.
53/S10 Bièvres, Fr.
80/D2 Biferno (riv.), It.
119/B2 Big (des.), Austl.
152/D1 Big (isl.), NW,Can
152/D1 Big (riv.), NW,Can
165/E6 Big (lake), Mi,US
83/H5 Biga, Turk.
92/B2 Bigadiç, Turk.
156/F4 Big Belt (mts.), Mt,US
162/C4 Big Bend Nat'l Park, Tx,US
159/K4 Big Black (riv.), Ms,US
159/H2 Big Blue (riv.), Ks, Ne,US
58/C6 Bigbury (bay), Eng,UK
151/D2 Big Diomede (isl.), Rus.
166/D1 Big Flat (brook), NJ,US
157/K4 Big Fork (riv.), Mn,US
156/G2 Biggar, Sk,Can
54/C5 Biggar, Sc,UK
69/G1 Biggasee (lake), Ger.
114/D2 Bigge (isl.), Austl.
67/E6 Bigge (riv.), Ger.
67/E6 Biggesee (res.), Ger.
53/P8 Biggin Hill, Eng,UK
59/F2 Biggleswade, Eng,UK
132/D3 Big Hole, SAfr.
156/E4 Big Hole (riv.), Mt,US
156/F4 Bighorn (lake), Mt, Wy,US
156/G4 Bighorn (mts.), Mt, Wy,US
156/G4 Bighorn (riv.), Mt, Wy,US
158/E1 Bighorn (basin), Wy,US
152/F4 Bighorn Canyon Nat'l Rec. Area, Mt,US
150/C1 Bight, The, Bahm.
162/C4 Big Lake, Tx,US
158/D2 Big Lost (riv.), Id,US
165/P14 Big Muskego (lake), Wi,US
128/A3 Bignona, Sen.
166/C1 Big Pine (hill), Pa,US
166/A4 Big Pipe (cr.), Md,US
160/C3 Big Rapids, Mi,US
156/G2 Big River, Sk,Can
165/N16 Big Rock (cr.), Il,US
163/H4 Big Saltilla (cr.), Ga,US
159/G3 Big Sandy (cr.), Co,US
163/F2 Big Sandy (riv.), Tn,US
158/E2 Big Sandy (riv.), Wy,US
157/J5 Big Sioux (riv.), Ia, SD,US
162/C3 Big Spring, Tx,US
157/J4 Big Stone (lake), Mn, SD,US
160/D4 Big Stone Gap, Va,US
156/F4 Big Timber, Mt,US
152/H3 Big Trout (lake), On,Can
164/B2 Big Tujunga (canyon), Ca,US
141/B3 Biguaçu, Braz.
158/D2 Big Wood (riv.), Id,US
82/B3 Bihać, Yugo.
106/E2 Bihār, India
106/D3 Bihār (state), India
130/A3 Biharamulo, Tanz.
130/A3 Biharamulo Game Rsv., Tanz.
82/F2 Bihor (co.), Rom.
68/A4 Bihorel, Fr.
100/D2 Bihoro, Japan
128/A4 Bijagós (isls.), GBis.
106/C4 Bijāpur, India
93/F3 Bījār, Iran
82/D3 Bijeljina, Bosn.
82/D4 Bijelo Polje, Yugo.
105/H3 Bijia (mtn.), China
104/C3 Bijiang, China
104/E3 Bijie, China
106/C2 Bijnor, India
106/B2 Bīkaner, India
120/G3 Bikar (atoll), Mrsh.
97/L2 Bikin, Rus.
97/M2 Bikin (riv.), Rus.
120/F3 Bikini (atoll), Mrsh.
131/C4 Bikita, Zim.
126/C4 Bikuar Nat'l Park, Moz.
109/B3 Bilauktaung (range), Burma, Thai.
114/G5 Bilba Morea Claypan (lake), Austl.
74/D1 Bilbao, Sp.
91/B4 Bilbays, Egypt
82/D4 Bileća, Bosn.
92/B1 Bilecik, Turk.
83/K5 Bilecik (prov.), Turk.
65/M3 Biłgoraj, Pol.
89/S3 Bilibino, Rus.
131/D2 Bilila, Malw.
109/B2 Bilin (riv.), Burma
71/G1 Bílina, Czh.
71/G2 Bílina (riv.), Czh.
112/D3 Biliran (isl.), Phil.
101/B3 Biliu (riv.), China
119/C2 Billabong (cr.), Austl.
67/H1 Bille (riv.), Ger.
67/E5 Billerbeck, Ger.
72/C5 Billère, Fr.
59/G3 Billericay, Eng,UK
117/J5 Billiat Consv. Park, Austl.
57/F5 Billinge, Eng,UK
57/G2 Billingham, Eng,UK
156/F4 Billings, Mt,US
59/F4 Billingshurst, Eng,UK
90/K10 Billiton (isl.), Indo.
158/D4 Bill Williams (riv.), Az,US
124/H4 Bilma, Niger
118/C4 Biloela, Austl.
163/F4 Biloxi, Ms,US
117/H3 Bilpa Morea (claypan), Austl.
92/B4 Bilqās Qism Awwal, Egypt
106/C2 Bilsi, India
125/K5 Biltine, Chad
69/E2 Bilzen, Belg.
111/E5 Bima, Indo.
119/D2 Bimberi (peak), Austl.
125/J7 Bimbo, CAfr.
150/B1 Bimini (isls.), Bahm.
71/F6 Bina (riv.), Ger.
106/C3 Bina-Etāwa, India
123/X17 Bin 'Arūs (gov.), Tun.
161/Q9 Binbrook, On,Can
57/H5 Binbrook, Eng,UK
68/D3 Binche, Belg.
104/D3 Binchuan, China
96/G2 Binder, Mong.
106/D2 Bindki, India
112/C3 Bindoy, Phil.
126/C2 Bindu, Zaire
131/C3 Bindura, Zim.
75/F2 Binéfar, Sp.
59/F4 Binfield, Eng,UK
131/D3 Binga (mtn.), Moz.
131/B3 Binga, Zim.
70/A3 Bingen, Ger.
128/E5 Bingerville, IvC.
57/H6 Bingham, Eng,UK
160/F3 Binghamton, NY,US
57/G4 Bingley, Eng,UK
92/E2 Bingöl, Turk.
92/E2 Bingöl (prov.), Turk.
103/D4 Binhai, China
109/D4 Binh Chanh, Viet.
109/D4 Binh Chau, Viet.
104/B5 Binhon (peak), Burma
109/E3 Binh Son, Viet.
110/A3 Binjai, Indo.
76/D2 Binningen, Swi.
111/F5 Binongko (isl.), Indo.
110/B2 Bintang (peak), Malay.
105/F4 Binyang, China
103/D3 Binzhou, China
142/B3 Bío-Bío (reg.), Chile
142/B3 Bío-Bío (riv.), Chile
82/B4 Biograd, Cro.
82/D4 Biogradska Nat'l Park, Yugo.
124/G7 Bioko (isl.), EqG.
106/C4 Bīr, India
124/H2 Birāk, Libya
124/H2 Bi'r al Ghuzayyil (well), Libya
125/K2 Bi'r al Ḩarash (well), Libya
149/G1 Birama (pt.), Cuba
125/K5 Birao, CAfr.
106/E2 Birātnagar, Nepal
100/C2 Biratori, Japan
152/E3 Birch (mts.), Ab,Can
131/D3 Birchenough Bridge, Zim.
157/G2 Birch Hills, Sk,Can
157/H2 Birch River, Mb,Can
113/X Bird (isl.), Ant.
115/K4 Bird Islet (isl.), Austl.
119/D2 Birds Rock (peak), Austl.
92/D2 Birecik, Turk.
141/B2 Birigui, Braz.
141/G8 Biritiba-Mirim, Braz.
95/G2 Bīrjand, Iran
70/B3 Birkenau, Ger.
120/G4 Birkenebeu, Kiri.
57/E5 Birkenhead, Eng,UK
54/B5 Birkenshaw, Sc,UK
63/T9 Birkerød, Den.
77/H3 Birkkarspitze (peak), Aus.
83/H2 Bîrlad, Rom.
83/H2 Bîrlad (riv.), Rom.
102/B3 Birlik, Kaz.
59/E2 Birmingham, Eng,UK
163/G3 Birmingham, Al,US
165/F6 Birmingham, Mi,US
54/C3 Birnam, Sc,UK
73/K3 Birnhorn (peak), Aus.
121/H5 Birnie (isl.), Kiri.
129/G3 Birni Nkonni, Niger
97/L2 Birobidzhan, Rus.
124/E3 Bîr Ounâne (well), Mali
60/A2 Birreencorragh (mtn.), Ire.
76/D3 Birs (riv.), Swi.
76/D3 Birse (riv.), Swi.
76/D2 Birsfelden, Swi.
85/M5 Birsk, Rus.
70/C2 Birstein, Ger.
96/C5 Biru, China
63/L3 Biržai, Lith.
83/F4 Bis (lake), Rom.
99/M9 Bisai, Japan
130/C2 Bisa-Nadi Nat'l Rsv., Kenya
158/E5 Bisbee, Az,US
72/C4 Biscarrosse, Fr.
72/C4 Biscarrosse (lag.), Fr.
72/B4 Biscay (bay), Eur.
150/A1 Biscayne (bay), Fl,US
163/H5 Biscayne Nat'l Park, Fl,US
80/E2 Bisceglie, It.
76/D1 Bischheim, Fr.
70/B3 Bischofsheim, Ger.
73/K3 Bischofshofen, Aus.
69/G6 Bischwiller, Fr.
113/V Biscoe (isls.), Ant.
79/F5 Biscubio (riv.), It.
138/D2 Biscucuy, Ven.
94/D4 Bīshah (dry riv.), SAr.
102/B3 Bishkek (cap.), Kyr.
158/C3 Bishop, Ca,US
57/G2 Bishop Auckland, Eng,UK
54/B5 Bishopbriggs, Sc,UK
58/D2 Bishops Castle, Eng,UK
58/D3 Bishops Cleeve, Eng,UK
161/L1 Bishop's Falls, Nf,Can
59/G3 Bishop's Stortford, Eng,UK
59/E5 Bishops Waltham, Eng,UK
54/B5 Bishopton, Sc,UK
57/H4 Bishop Wilton, Eng,UK
70/B6 Bisingen, Ger.
124/G1 Biskra, Alg.
123/T16 Biskra (wilaya), Alg.
65/L2 Biskupiec, Pol.
112/D3 Bislig, Phil.
161/Q9 Bismarck, On,Can
120/D5 Bismarck (arch.), PNG
120/D5 Bismarck (sea), PNG
157/H4 Bismarck (cap.), ND,US
92/E2 Bismil, Turk.
149/F3 Bismuna (lag.), Nic.

130/A2 **Biso,** Ugan.
128/B4 **Bissau** (cap.), GBis.
67/F4 **Bissendorf,** Ger.
157/K3 **Bissett,** Mb,Can
83/G2 **Bistrița,** Rom.
83/G2 **Bistrița-Năsăud** (co.), Rom.
63/T9 **Bistrup,** Den.
138/D3 **Bita** (riv.), Col.
130/A4 **Bitale,** Tanz.
124/H7 **Bitam,** Gabon
69/F4 **Bitburg,** Ger.
69/G5 **Bitche,** Fr.
124/J5 **Bitkin,** Chad
92/E2 **Bitlis,** Turk.
92/E2 **Bitlis** (prov.), Turk.
82/E5 **Bitola,** Macd.
82/C5 **Bitonto,** It.
83/G2 **Bitrița** (riv.), Rom.
76/D2 **Bitschwiller,** Fr.
127/C2 **Bitter** (lakes), Egypt
156/E4 **Bitterroot** (range), Id, Mt,US
111/G3 **Bitung,** Indo.
141/B3 **Bituruna,** Braz.
124/H5 **Biu,** Nga.
99/M9 **Biwa,** Japan
98/E3 **Biwa** (lake), Japan
159/J4 **Bixby,** Ok,US
91/B4 **Biyalā,** Egypt
103/C4 **Biyang,** China
102/E1 **Biysk,** Rus.
161/N7 **Bizard** (isl.), Qu,Can
123/W17 **Bizerte** (Banzart), Tun.
61/M6 **Bjargtangar** (pt.), Ice.
63/U9 **Bjärred,** Swe.
82/C3 **Bjelovar,** Cro.
62/C3 **Bjerringbro,** Den.
62/D2 **Bjørkelangen,** Nor.
63/S7 **Björknäs,** Swe.
62/A1 **Bjørnafjorden** (fjord), Nor.
153/S7 **Bjorne** (pen.), NW,Can
62/E3 **Bjuv,** Swe.
59/E1 **Blaby,** Eng,UK
65/K3 **Blachownia,** Pol.
86/D4 **Black** (sea), Asia, Eur.
160/B1 **Black** (bay), On,Can
157/L2 **Black** (riv.), On,Can
151/M3 **Black** (mtn.), Yk,Can
109/C1 **Black** (riv.), China
86/D4 **Black** (sea), Eur.
76/D2 **Black** (for.), Ger.
132/A2 **Black** (pt.), Namb.
58/A6 **Black** (pt.), Eng,UK
58/C3 **Black** (mtn.), Wal,UK
58/C3 **Black** (mts.), Wal,UK
159/K3 **Black** (riv.), Ar, Mo,US
158/D4 **Black** (mts.), Az,US
158/E4 **Black** (riv.), Az,US
165/L11 **Black** (hills), Ca,US
168/B3 **Black** (pt.), Ct,US
165/G5 **Black** (riv.), Mi,US
158/F4 **Black** (range), NM,US
160/F3 **Black** (riv.), NY,US
168/E5 **Black** (riv.), Oh,US
166/B2 **Black** (cr.), Pa,US
157/H5 **Black** (hills), SD, Wy,US
157/L4 **Black** (riv.), Wi,US
107/H3 **Black** (riv.), Viet.
54/D5 **Blackadder Water** (riv.), Sc,UK
165/P16 **Blackberry** (cr.), Il,US
59/E3 **Black Bourton,** Eng,UK
57/F4 **Blackburn,** Eng,UK
54/C5 **Blackburn,** Sc,UK
54/B6 **Blackcraig** (hill), Sc,UK
109/C1 **Black (Da)** (riv.), Viet.
156/E3 **Black Diamond,** Ab,Can
59/F4 **Blackdown** (hill), Eng,UK
58/C5 **Blackdown** (hills), Eng,UK
118/C3 **Blackdown Tableland Nat'l Park,** Austl.
156/F4 **Black Eagle,** Mt,US
168/E5 **Black, East Branch** (riv.), Oh,US
156/E5 **Blackfoot,** Id,US
156/F5 **Blackfoot** (res.), Id,US
54/C4 **Blackford,** Sc,UK
70/B5 **Black Forest** (Schwarzwald) (uplands), Ger.
168/E6 **Black Fork** (riv.), Oh,US
57/G2 **Blackhall Rocks,** Eng,UK
60/A3 **Black Head** (pt.), Ire.
56/C2 **Black Head** (pt.), NI,UK
54/B1 **Black Isle** (pen.), Sc,UK
158/E3 **Black Mesa** (upland), Az,US
58/B6 **Blackmoor** (upland), Eng,UK
53/P6 **Blackmore,** Eng,UK
118/B1 **Black Mountain Nat'l Park,** Austl.
57/E4 **Blackpool,** Eng,UK
132/A2 **Black Reef** (pt.), Namb.
160/B2 **Black River Falls,** Wi,US
158/C2 **Black Rock** (des.), Nv,US
167/G1 **Black Rock** (pt.), RI,US
57/F4 **Blackrod,** Eng,UK
160/D4 **Blacksburg,** Va,US
163/H3 **Blackshear** (lake), Ga,US
60/D4 **Blackstairs** (mts.), Ire.
168/C1 **Blackstone,** Ma,US
168/C2 **Blackstone** (riv.), RI,US
160/E4 **Blackstone,** Va,US
119/D1 **Black Sugarloaf** (peak), Austl.
118/G8 **Blacktown,** Austl.
161/H2 **Blackville,** NB,Can
128/E4 **Black Volta** (riv.), Afr.
163/G3 **Black Warrior** (riv.), Al,US
118/C3 **Blackwater,** Austl.
60/C5 **Blackwater** (riv.), Ire.
60/D2 **Blackwater** (riv.), Ire.
59/G3 **Blackwater** (riv.), Eng,UK
56/B3 **Blackwater** (riv.), NI,UK
54/B3 **Blackwater** (res.), Sc,UK
159/J3 **Blackwater** (riv.), Mo,US
159/H3 **Blackwell,** Ok,US
168/E5 **Black, West Branch** (riv.), Oh,US
116/B5 **Blackwood** (riv.), Austl.
58/C3 **Blackwood,** Wal,UK
166/B6 **Bladensburg,** Md,US
118/A3 **Bladensburg Nat'l Park,** Austl.
56/D2 **Bladnoch** (riv.), Sc,UK
56/E6 **Blaenau-Ffestiniog,** Wal,UK
58/C3 **Blaenavon,** Wal,UK
72/D5 **Blagnac,** Fr.
83/F4 **Blagoevgrad,** Bul.
97/K1 **Blagoveshchensk,** Rus.
156/G2 **Blaine Lake,** Sk,Can
161/N6 **Blainville,** Qu,Can
159/H2 **Blair,** Ne,US
166/C1 **Blair** (hill), Pa,US
54/C3 **Blair Atholl,** Sc,UK
54/C3 **Blairgowrie,** Sc,UK
156/E3 **Blairmore,** Ab,Can
76/A1 **Blaise** (riv.), Fr.
83/F2 **Blaj,** Rom.
163/G4 **Blakely,** Ga,US
73/G4 **Blanc** (mtn.), Fr.
124/B3 **Blanc** (cape), Mrta.
142/E3 **Blanca** (bay), Arg.
136/C5 **Blanca** (range), Peru
74/E3 **Blanca,** Sp.
75/E4 **Blanca** (coast), Sp.
159/F4 **Blanca** (peak), NM,US
146/B2 **Blanca, Punta** (pt.), Mex.
117/G5 **Blanche** (cape), Austl.
116/D2 **Blanche** (lake), Austl.
117/H4 **Blanche** (lake), Austl.
76/C6 **Blanc, Mont** (mtn.), Fr.
68/A2 **Blanc Nez** (cape), Fr.
143/K6 **Blanco** (riv.), Arg.
143/K8 **Blanco** (lake), Chile
142/C1 **Blanco** (riv.), Chile
149/E4 **Blanco** (cape), CR
136/B4 **Blanco** (cape), Peru
156/B5 **Blanco** (cape), Or,US
159/H5 **Blanco** (riv.), Tx,US
58/D5 **Blandford Forum,** Eng,UK
158/E3 **Blanding,** Ut,US
75/G2 **Blanes,** Sp.
75/G1 **Blanes, Serre de** (mtn.), Fr.
65/G4 **Blanice** (riv.), Czh.
68/C1 **Blankenberge,** Belg.
69/F3 **Blankenheim,** Ger.
150/E5 **Blanquilla** (isl.), Ven.
65/J4 **Blansko,** Czh.
131/D2 **Blantyre,** Malw.
54/B5 **Blantyre,** Sc,UK
72/F3 **Blanzy,** Fr.
66/C4 **Blaricum,** Neth.
60/B6 **Blarney Castle and Stone,** Ire.
77/E4 **Blas, Piz** (peak), Swi.
71/G4 **Blatná,** Czh.
70/C6 **Blau** (riv.), Ger.
70/C6 **Blaubeuren,** Ger.
76/D2 **Blauen** (peak), Ger.
70/C6 **Blaustein,** Ger.
64/E1 **Blåvands Huk** (pt.), Den.
72/B2 **Blavet** (riv.), Fr.
114/D2 **Blaze** (pt.), Austl.
67/H2 **Bleckede,** Ger.
62/C2 **Blefjell** (peak), Nor.
69/E2 **Blégny,** Belg.
68/C2 **Bléharies,** Belg.
82/B2 **Bleiburg,** Aus.
67/H6 **Bleicherode,** Ger.
77/G2 **Bleick, Hohe** (peak), Ger.
66/B4 **Bleiswijk,** Neth.
62/F3 **Blekinge** (co.), Swe.
115/R11 **Blenheim,** NZ
59/E3 **Blenheim Palace,** Eng,UK
73/G4 **Bléone** (riv.), Fr.
68/C4 **Blérancourt,** Fr.
132/C4 **Blesberg** (peak), SAfr.
53/N8 **Bletchingley,** Eng,UK
59/F2 **Bletchley,** Eng,UK
130/A2 **Bleus** (mts.), Zaire
59/E3 **Blewbury,** Eng,UK
123/S15 **Blida,** Alg.
123/S15 **Blida** (wilaya), Alg.
57/G5 **Blidworth,** Eng,UK
71/E2 **Blieloch-Stausee** (res.), Ger.
69/G5 **Blies** (riv.), Fr., Ger.
69/G5 **Bliesbruck,** Fr.
69/G5 **Blieskastel,** Ger.
121/Y18 **Bligh Water** (sound), Fiji
112/D4 **Blik** (mtn.), Phil.
77/E5 **Blinnenhorn** (peak), Swi.
57/G6 **Blithfield** (res.), Eng,UK
113/L **Blizzard** (peak), Ant.
167/G1 **Block** (isl.), RI,US
167/G1 **Block Island** (sound), NY, RI,US
167/G1 **Block Island C. G. Sta.,** RI,US
167/G1 **Block Island Nat'l Wild. Ref.,** RI,US
66/B4 **Bloemendaal,** Neth.
132/D3 **Bloemfontein,** SAfr.
132/D2 **Bloemhofdam** (res.), SAfr.
72/D3 **Blois,** Fr.
66/C3 **Blokker,** Neth.
67/G5 **Blomberg,** Ger.
157/J3 **Bloodvein** (riv.), Mb, On,Can
55/G9 **Bloody Foreland** (pt.), Ire.
160/B2 **Bloomer,** Wi,US
168/B2 **Bloomfield,** Ct,US
167/D2 **Bloomfield,** NJ,US
158/F3 **Bloomfield,** NM,US
165/F6 **Bloomfield Hills,** Mi,US
118/B1 **Bloomfield River Abor. Community,** Austl.
165/P16 **Bloomingdale,** Il,US
167/H7 **Bloomingdale,** NJ,US
164/C2 **Bloomington,** Ca,US
160/B3 **Bloomington,** Il,US
160/C4 **Bloomington,** In,US
157/K4 **Bloomington,** Mn,US
166/B1 **Bloomsburg,** Pa,US
110/D5 **Blora,** Indo.
131/C4 **Blouberg** (peak), SAfr.
163/G4 **Blountstown,** Fl,US
113/L **Blowaway** (peak), Ant.
59/E3 **Bloxham,** Eng,UK
58/E1 **Bloxwich,** Eng,UK
71/G2 **Blšanka** (riv.), Czh.
77/F3 **Bludenz,** Aus.
104/B4 **Blue** (mtn.), India
162/D3 **Blue** (riv.), Ok,US
156/D4 **Blue** (mts.), Or, Wa,US
157/K5 **Blue Earth,** Mn,US
160/D4 **Bluefield,** Va,US
160/D4 **Bluefield,** WV,US
149/F4 **Bluefields,** Nic.
149/F4 **Bluefields** (bay), Nic.
54/C1 **Blue Head** (pt.), Sc,UK
165/Q16 **Blue Island,** Il,US
158/C2 **Bluejoint** (lake), Or,US
131/B2 **Blue Lagoon Nat'l Park,** Zam.
118/D4 **Blue Lake Nat'l Park,** Austl.
166/B3 **Blue Marsh** (lake), Pa,US
158/F3 **Blue Mesa** (res.), Co,US
149/G2 **Blue Mountain** (peak), Jam.
166/B3 **Blue Mountain** (ridge), Pa,US
119/D2 **Blue Mountains Nat'l Park,** Austl.
114/F2 **Blue Mud** (bay), Austl.
125/M5 **Blue Nile** (riv.), Eth., Sudan
152/E2 **Bluenose** (lake), NW,Can
163/G3 **Blue Ridge,** Ga,US
163/H2 **Blue Ridge** (mts.), NC, Va,US
116/C5 **Bluff** (peak), Austl.
116/B3 **Bluff** (pt.), Austl.
115/Q12 **Bluff,** NZ
160/C3 **Bluffton,** In,US
77/E2 **Blumberg,** Ger.
141/B3 **Blumenau,** Braz.
76/D5 **Blümlisalp** (peak), Swi.
78/D1 **Blumone, Cornone di** (peak), It.
57/G1 **Blyth,** Eng,UK
57/G5 **Blyth,** Eng,UK
59/H2 **Blyth** (riv.), Eng,UK
54/C5 **Blyth Bridge,** Sc,UK
57/F6 **Blythe** (riv.), Eng,UK
158/D4 **Blythe,** Ca,US
57/F6 **Blythe Bridge,** Eng,UK
163/F3 **Blytheville,** Ar,US
109/D4 **B'nom M'hai** (peak), Viet.
128/C5 **Bo,** SLeo.
112/C2 **Boac,** Phil.
148/E3 **Boaco,** Nic.
141/C2 **Boa Esperança,** Braz.
140/A2 **Boa Esperança** (res.), Braz.
103/C4 **Bo'ai,** China
111/G4 **Boano** (isl.), Indo.
168/G5 **Boardman,** Oh,US
153/H2 **Boas** (riv.), NW,Can
140/C2 **Boa Viagem,** Braz.
139/F4 **Boa Vista,** Braz.
122/K10 **Boa Vista** (isl.), CpV.
163/G3 **Boaz,** Al,US
105/F4 **Bobai,** China
123/G6 **Bobaomby** (cape), Madg.
106/D4 **Bobbili,** India
70/B3 **Bobenheim-Roxheim,** Ger.
68/B6 **Bobigny,** Fr.
70/D6 **Bobingen,** Ger.
70/C5 **Böblingen,** Ger.
128/D4 **Bobo Dioulasso,** Burk.
131/C4 **Bobonong,** Bots.
82/D4 **Bobotov Kuk** (peak), Yugo.
82/F4 **Bobovdol,** Bul.
65/H3 **Bóbr** (riv.), Pol.
86/G2 **Bobrov,** Rus.
86/D1 **Bobruysk,** Bela.
138/D2 **Bobures,** Ven.
133/H8 **Boby** (peak), Madg.
136/E5 **Boca do Acre,** Braz.
141/J7 **Bocaina** (mts.), Braz.
140/B5 **Bocaiúva,** Braz.
163/H5 **Boca Raton,** Fl,US
149/E3 **Bocay** (riv.), Nic.
131/C4 **Bochem,** SAfr.
65/L4 **Bochnia,** Pol.
69/E1 **Bocholt,** Belg.
66/D5 **Bocholt,** Ger.
67/E6 **Bochum,** Ger.
67/H4 **Bockenem,** Ger.
67/F2 **Bockhorn,** Ger.
59/G3 **Bocking,** Eng,UK
138/D2 **Boconó,** Ven.
69/D3 **Bocq** (riv.), Belg.
124/J7 **Boda,** CAfr.
89/M4 **Bodaybo,** Rus.
54/E2 **Boddam,** Sc,UK
64/F3 **Bode** (riv.), Ger.
158/B3 **Bodega** (bay), Ca,US
66/B4 **Bodegraven,** Neth.
124/J4 **Bodélé** (depr.), Chad
61/G2 **Boden,** Swe.
70/B3 **Bodenheim,** Ger.
77/F2 **Bodensee** (Lake Constance) (lake), Ger., Swi.
60/B2 **Boderg, Lough** (lake), Ire.
106/C4 **Bodhan,** India
108/F3 **Bodināyakkanūr,** India
166/B5 **Bodkin** (pt.), Md,US
58/B6 **Bodmin,** Eng,UK
58/B5 **Bodmin Moor** (upland), Eng,UK
61/E2 **Bodø,** Nor.
140/C2 **Bodocó,** Braz.
96/C2 **Bodonchiyn** (riv.), Mong.
82/E1 **Bodrog** (riv.), Hun.
92/A2 **Bodrum,** Turk.
109/D4 **Bo Duc,** Viet.
132/A2 **Boegoeberg** (peak), Namb.
66/C5 **Boekel,** Neth.
126/D1 **Boende,** Zaire
159/K4 **Boeuf** (riv.), Ar, La,US
130/A2 **Boga,** Zaire
163/F4 **Bogalusa,** La,US
119/C1 **Bogan** (riv.), Austl.
129/E3 **Bogandé,** Burk.
82/D3 **Bogatić,** Yugo.
65/H3 **Bogatynia,** Pol.
92/C1 **Boğazkale-Alacahöyük Nat'l Park,** Turk.
92/C2 **Boğazlıyan,** Turk.
102/E5 **Bogcang** (riv.), China
96/E2 **Bogd,** Mong.
96/B3 **Bogda** (mts.), China
102/E3 **Bogda Feng** (peak), China
71/F5 **Bogen,** Ger.
63/S7 **Bogesundslandet** (reg. park), Swe.
60/A5 **Boggerragh** (mts.), Ire.
150/F3 **Boggy** (peak), Anti.
59/F5 **Bognor Regis,** Eng,UK
69/D4 **Bogny-sur-Meuse,** Fr.
112/D3 **Bogo,** Phil.
119/C3 **Bogong** (peak), Austl.
119/C3 **Bogong Nat'l Park,** Austl.
110/C5 **Bogor,** Indo.
130/A2 **Bogoro,** Zaire
138/C3 **Bogotá** (cap.), Col.
167/J8 **Bogota,** NJ,US
82/E5 **Bogovinje,** Macd.
106/E3 **Bogra,** Bang.
56/E1 **Bogrie** (hill), Sc,UK
128/B2 **Bogué,** Mrta.
103/D3 **Bohai** (bay), China
103/E3 **Bohai** (str.), China
103/D3 **Bo Hai** (Chihli) (gulf), China
68/C4 **Bohain-en-Vermandois,** Fr.
71/G3 **Bohemia** (reg.), Czh.
71/G4 **Bohemian Forest** (uplands), Ger.
70/B4 **Böhl-Iggelheim,** Ger.
67/G3 **Böhme** (riv.), Ger.
67/F4 **Bohmte,** Ger.
112/C3 **Bohol** (isl.), Phil.
112/C3 **Bohol** (str.), Phil.
104/E5 **Bo Ho Su,** Viet.
102/E3 **Bohu,** China
80/D2 **Boiano,** It.
104/B4 **Boinu** (riv.), Burma, India
140/C4 **Boipeda** (isl.), Braz.
74/A1 **Boiro,** Sp.
141/B1 **Bois** (riv.), Braz.
53/S10 **Bois-d'Arcy,** Fr.
156/D5 **Boise** (cap.), Id,US
156/E5 **Boise** (riv.), Id,US
159/G3 **Boise City,** Ok,US
68/A5 **Bois-Guillaume,** Fr.
157/H3 **Boissevain,** Mb,Can
53/S9 **Boissy-l'Aillerie,** Fr.
53/T10 **Boissy-Saint-Léger,** Fr.
67/H2 **Boizenburg,** Ger.
124/C2 **Bojador** (cape), WSah.
112/C1 **Bojeador** (cape), Phil.
130/D2 **Boji** (plain), Kenya
65/J4 **Bojkovice,** Czh.
93/J2 **Bojnūrd,** Iran
106/E3 **Bokaro Steel City,** India
128/B4 **Boké** (comm.), Gui.
126/D1 **Bokele,** Zaire
130/C2 **Bokhol** (plain), Kenya
62/A2 **Boknafjorden** (fjord), Nor.
130/C2 **Bokol** (peak), Kenya
124/J5 **Bokoro,** Chad
132/E2 **Boksburg,** SAfr.
163/H5 **Bok Tower Gardens,** Fl,US
124/H5 **Bol,** Chad
128/B4 **Bolama,** GBis.
95/J3 **Bolān** (pass), Pak.
146/E4 **Bolaños,** Mex.
74/D3 **Bolaños de Calatrava,** Sp.
72/D2 **Bolbec,** Fr.
83/H3 **Boldești-Scăeni,** Rom.
57/G2 **Boldon,** Eng,UK
102/D3 **Bole,** China
129/E4 **Bole,** Gha.
65/H3 **Bolesławiec,** Pol.
129/E4 **Bolgatanga,** Gha.
97/L2 **Boli,** China
112/B1 **Bolinao,** Phil.
112/B1 **Bolinao** (cape), Phil.
165/P16 **Bolingbrook,** Il,US
142/E3 **Bolívar,** Arg.
138/B3 **Bolívar,** Col.
138/C2 **Bolívar** (dept.), Col.
138/B5 **Bolívar** (prov.), Ecu.
159/J3 **Bolivar,** Mo,US
160/B5 **Bolivar,** Tn,US
139/E3 **Bolívar** (state), Ven.
139/F3 **Bolívar, Cerro** (mtn.), Ven.
138/D2 **Bolívar, Pico** (mtn.), Ven.
136/F7 **Bolivia**
78/C1 **Bollate,** It.
69/F4 **Bollendorf,** Ger.
72/F4 **Bollène,** Fr.
76/D4 **Bolligen,** Swi.
57/F5 **Bollin** (riv.), Eng,UK
57/F5 **Bollington,** Eng,UK
63/S7 **Bollmora,** Swe.
62/G1 **Bollnäs,** Swe.
74/B4 **Bollullos Par del Condado,** Sp.
62/E3 **Bolmen** (lake), Swe.
59/F5 **Bolney,** Eng,UK
126/C1 **Bolobo,** Zaire
79/E4 **Bologna,** It.
79/E3 **Bologna** (prov.), It.
84/G4 **Bologoye,** Rus.
125/J7 **Bolomba,** Zaire
97/M2 **Bolon'** (lake), Rus.
126/C2 **Bolongongo,** Ang.
109/D3 **Bolovens** (plat.), Laos
80/B1 **Bolsena** (lake), It.
87/K2 **Bol'shaya Khobda** (riv.), Kaz.
87/K1 **Bol'shaya Kinel'** (riv.), Rus.
85/P2 **Bol'shaya Rogovaya** (riv.), Rus.
85/N2 **Bol'shaya Synya** (riv.), Rus.
97/L2 **Bol'shaya Ussurka** (riv.), Rus.
89/L2 **Bol'shevik** (isl.), Rus.
85/M2 **Bol'shezemel'skaya** (tundra), Rus.
88/F2 **Bol'shoy Bolvanskiy Nos** (pt.), Rus.
87/H2 **Bol'shoy Irgiz** (riv.), Rus.
89/Q2 **Bol'shoy Lyakhovskiy** (isl.), Rus.
87/J2 **Bol'shoy Uzen'** (riv.), Kaz., Rus.
96/D1 **Bol'shoy Yenisey** (riv.), Rus.
57/G5 **Bolsover,** Eng,UK
66/C2 **Bolsward,** Neth.
58/C6 **Bolt Head** (pt.), Wal,UK
161/Q8 **Bolton,** On,Can
57/F4 **Bolton,** Eng,UK
57/G4 **Bolton Abbey,** Eng,UK
83/K5 **Bolu,** Turk.
83/K5 **Bolu** (prov.), Turk.
54/F11 **Bolus Head** (pt.), Ire.
92/B2 **Bolvadin,** Turk.
77/H5 **Bolzano** (Bozen), It.
77/H4 **Bolzano-Bozen** (prov.), It.
126/B2 **Boma,** Zaire
119/D2 **Bomaderry,** Austl.
106/B4 **Bombay,** India
166/C5 **Bombay Hook Nat'l Wild. Ref.,** De,US
111/H4 **Bomberai** (pen.), Indo.
130/B2 **Bombo,** Ugan.
140/C3 **Bom Conselho,** Braz.
141/C1 **Bom Despacho,** Braz.
104/B2 **Bomi,** China
140/A1 **Bom Jardim,** Braz.
141/J6 **Bom Jardin de Minas,** Braz.
140/A3 **Bom Jesus,** Braz.
141/B4 **Bom Jesus,** Braz.
140/B3 **Bom Jesus da Gurguéia** (mts.), Braz.
140/B4 **Bom Jesus da Lapa,** Braz.
141/B1 **Bom Jesus de Goiás,** Braz.
141/D2 **Bom Jesus do Itabapoana,** Braz.
141/G8 **Bom Jesus dos Perdões,** Braz.
67/G3 **Bomlitz,** Ger.
62/A2 **Bømlo** (isl.), Nor.
141/B3 **Bom Retiro,** Braz.
125/L6 **Bomu** (riv.), Zaire
123/X17 **Bon** (cape), Tun.
151/K3 **Bona** (mtn.), Ak,US
150/D4 **Bonaire** (isl.), NAnt.
148/D2 **Bonampak** (ruins), Mex.
150/D3 **Bonao,** DRep.
114/C2 **Bonaparte** (arch.), Austl.
151/F3 **Bonasila** (mtn.), Ak,US
161/H1 **Bonaventure,** Qu,Can
161/H1 **Bonaventure** (riv.), Qu,Can
161/L1 **Bonavista** (bay), Nf,Can
161/L1 **Bonavista** (cape), Nf,Can
54/D6 **Bonchester Bridge,** Sc,UK
79/E3 **Bondeno,** It.
118/H8 **Bondi,** Austl.
125/K7 **Bondo,** Zaire
112/C2 **Bondoc** (pen.), Phil.
128/E4 **Bondoukou,** IvC.
110/D5 **Bondowoso,** Indo.
111/F4 **Bone** (gulf), Indo.
67/E5 **Bönen,** Ger.
111/F5 **Bonerate** (isls.), Indo.
54/C4 **Bo'ness,** Sc,UK
102/F5 **Bong** (lake), China
128/C5 **Bong** (co.), Libr.
128/C5 **Bong** (range), Libr.
112/C2 **Bongabong,** Phil.
125/K7 **Bongandanga,** Zaire
111/E2 **Bongao,** Phil.
112/B4 **Bonggaw,** Phil.
110/E2 **Bonggi** (isl.), Malay.
112/B4 **Bonggi** (isl.), Malay.
111/F4 **Bongka** (riv.), Indo.
133/H7 **Bongolava** (uplands), Madg.
124/J5 **Bongor,** Chad
125/K6 **Bongos** (mts.), CAfr.
109/E3 **Bong Son,** Viet.
162/D3 **Bonham,** Tx,US
68/D1 **Bonheiden,** Belg.
54/B5 **Bonhill,** Sc,UK
76/D1 **Bonhomme, Col du** (pass), Fr.
80/A2 **Bonifacio** (str.), Fr., It.
163/G4 **Bonifay,** Fl,US
120/D2 **Bonin** (isls.), Japan
130/D3 **Boni Nat'l Rsv.,** Kenya
164/C5 **Bonita,** Ca,US
163/H5 **Bonita Springs,** Fl,US
148/E3 **Bonito** (peak), Hon.
140/C2 **Bonito de Santa Fé,** Braz.
69/G2 **Bonn,** Ger.
53/S11 **Bonnelles,** Fr.
156/D3 **Bonners Ferry,** Id,US
156/E4 **Bonner-West Riverside,** Mt,US
157/K3 **Bonnet** (lake), Mb,Can
53/T10 **Bonneuil-sur-Marne,** Fr.
76/C5 **Bonneville,** Fr.
156/C4 **Bonneville** (dam), Or, Wa,US
165/C3 **Bonney Lake,** Wa,US
70/C4 **Bönnigheim,** Ger.
54/C5 **Bonnybridge,** Sc,UK
54/C5 **Bonnyrigg,** Sc,UK
156/F2 **Bonnyville,** Ab,Can
132/C4 **Bontberg** (peak), SAfr.
132/C4 **Bontebok Nat'l Park,** SAfr.
111/E5 **Bonthain,** Indo.
128/B5 **Bonthe,** SLeo.
105/J5 **Bontoc,** Phil.
82/D2 **Bonyhád,** Hun.
113/J **Bonzare** (coast), Ant.
68/D1 **Boom,** Belg.
157/K5 **Boone,** Ia,US
163/H2 **Boone,** NC,US
163/F3 **Booneville,** Ms,US
166/D2 **Boonton,** NJ,US
96/D2 **Bööntsagaan** (lake), Mong.
160/C4 **Boonville,** In,US
116/D4 **Boorabbin Nat'l Park,** Austl.
125/P6 **Boorama,** Som.
119/C1 **Booroondara** (peak), Austl.
68/A5 **Boos,** Fr.
161/G3 **Boothbay Harbor,** Me,US
113/D **Boothby** (cape), Ant.
152/G1 **Boothia** (gulf), NW,Can
152/G1 **Boothia** (pen.), NW,Can
57/E5 **Bootle,** Eng,UK
124/H8 **Booué,** Gabon
70/D5 **Bopfingen,** Ger.
132/D2 **Bophuthatswana** (ind. (homeland), SAfr.
69/G3 **Boppard,** Ger.
119/C1 **Boppy** (peak), Austl.
140/B3 **Boqueirão** (mts.), Braz.
142/C4 **Boquete** (peak), Arg.
146/D3 **Boquilla** (res.), Mex.
140/B4 **Boquira,** Braz.
125/N7 **Bor** (dry riv.), Kenya
85/K4 **Bor,** Rus.
125/M6 **Bor,** Sudan
92/C2 **Bor,** Turk.
82/F3 **Bor,** Yugo.
121/K6 **Bora Bora** (isl.), FrPol.
156/E4 **Borah** (peak), Id,US
62/E3 **Borås,** Swe.
93/G4 **Borāzjān,** Iran
136/G4 **Borba,** Braz.
78/B3 **Borbera** (riv.), It.
72/D3 **Borbonnais** (hist. reg.), Fr.
78/B3 **Borbore** (riv.), It.
140/C2 **Borborema** (plat.), Braz.
82/E3 **Borča,** Yugo.
67/F5 **Borchen,** Ger.
113/M **Borchgrevink** (coast), Ant.
87/G4 **Borçka,** Turk.
66/D4 **Borculo,** Neth.
117/H5 **Borda** (cape), Austl.
141/G7 **Borda da Mata,** Braz.
72/C4 **Bordeaux,** Fr.
153/R7 **Borden** (isl.), NW,Can
153/H2 **Borden** (pen.), NW,Can
54/C6 **Borders** (reg.), Sc,UK
78/A5 **Bordighera,** It.
123/T15 **Bordj Bou Arreridj,** Alg.
123/T15 **Bordj Bou Arreridj** (wilaya), Alg.
75/G4 **Bordj el Bahri** (cape), Alg.
123/S15 **Bordj el Kiffan,** Alg.
123/S15 **Bordj Manaïel,** Alg.
124/G2 **Bordj Omar Driss,** Alg.
59/F4 **Bordon,** Eng,UK
53/N7 **Borehamwood,** Eng,UK
63/L1 **Borgä** (Porvoo), Fin.
78/A2 **Borgaro Torinese,** It.
61/E2 **Børgefjell Nat'l Park,** Nor.
67/G5 **Borgentreich,** Ger.
66/D3 **Borger,** Neth.
162/C3 **Borger,** Tx,US
68/D1 **Borgerhout,** Belg.
62/G3 **Borgholm,** Swe.
67/F4 **Borgholzhausen,** Ger.
67/E4 **Borghorst,** Ger.
76/D5 **Borgne** (riv.), Swi.
78/B1 **Borgomanero,** It.
73/G4 **Borgo San Dalmazzo,** It.
79/E5 **Borgo San Lorenzo,** It
78/D2 **Borgosatollo,** It.
78/B1 **Borgosesia,** It.
129/F4 **Borgou** (prov.), Ben.
129/F4 **Borgu Game Rsv.,** Nga.
62/B1 **Borgund,** Nor.
86/B2 **Borislav,** Ukr.
87/G2 **Borisoglebsk,** Rus.
84/F5 **Borisov,** Bela.
133/H6 **Boriziny,** Madg.
66/D5 **Borken,** Ger.
66/D1 **Borkum** (isl.), Ger.
62/F1 **Borlänge,** Swe.
78/B3 **Bormida** (riv.), It.
78/B3 **Bormida di Millesimo** (riv.), It.
78/B4 **Bormida di Spigno** (riv.), It.
66/C6 **Born,** Neth.
64/G3 **Borna,** Ger.
66/C2 **Borndiep** (chan.), Neth.
76/C6 **Borne** (riv.), Fr.
66/D4 **Borne,** Neth.
68/D1 **Bornem,** Belg.
110/E3 **Borneo** (isl.), Asia
69/F2 **Bornheim,** Ger.
62/F4 **Bornholm** (co.), Den.
62/F4 **Bornholm** (isl.), Den.
65/H1 **Bornholmsgat** (chan.), Swe.
129/H3 **Borno** (state), Nga.
74/C4 **Bornos,** Sp.
124/H5 **Bornu** (plains), Nga.
125/L6 **Boro** (riv.), Sudan
102/D3 **Borohoro** (mts.), China, Kaz.
112/D3 **Borongan,** Phil.
57/G3 **Boroughbridge,** Eng,UK
84/G4 **Borovichi,** Rus.
82/D3 **Borovo,** Cro.
62/D2 **Borre,** Nor.
86/B3 **Borşa,** Rom.
97/H1 **Borshchovochnyy** (mts.), Rus.
82/E1 **Borsod-Abaúj-Zemplén** (co.), Hun.
66/A6 **Borssele,** Neth.
102/D3 **Bortala** (riv.), China
58/B2 **Borth,** Wal,UK
93/G3 **Borūjen,** Iran
93/G3 **Borūjerd,** Iran
96/D3 **Bor Ul** (mts.), China
96/H1 **Borzya,** Rus.
80/A2 **Bosa,** It.
82/C3 **Bosanska Dubica,** Bosn.
82/C3 **Bosanska Gradiška,** Bosn.
82/C3 **Bosanska Kostajnica,** Bosn.
82/C3 **Bosanska Krupa,** Bosn.
82/D3 **Bosanski Brod,** Bosn.
82/C3 **Bosanski Petrovac,** Bosn.
82/D3 **Bosanski Šamac,** Bosn.
125/Q5 **Bosaso** (Bender Cassim), Som.
58/B5 **Boscastle,** Eng,UK
104/E4 **Bose,** China
59/F5 **Bosham,** Eng,UK
66/B4 **Boskoop,** Neth.
65/J4 **Boskovice,** Czh.
82/D3 **Bosna** (riv.), Bosn.
82/C3 **Bosnia and Hercegovina**
99/G3 **Bōsō** (pen.), Japan
125/J7 **Bosobolo,** Zaire
83/J5 **Bosporus** (str.), Turk.
158/F4 **Bosque Farms,** NM,US
143/K6 **Bosques Petrificados Natural Mon.,** Arg.
124/J6 **Bossangoa,** CAfr.
162/E3 **Bossier City,** La,US
102/E3 **Bosten** (lake), China
57/H6 **Boston,** Eng,UK
162/E3 **Boston** (mts.), Ar,US
161/G3 **Boston** (cap.), Ma,US
162/E3 **Boston,** Tx,US
168/C1 **Boston Common,** Ma,US
167/F1 **Bostwick** (pt.), NY,US
82/D3 **Bosut** (riv.), Cro.
106/B3 **Botād,** India
118/H8 **Botany** (bay), Austl.
163/H3 **Boteler** (peak), NC,US
133/F2 **Botelerpunt** (pt.), SAfr.
141/G6 **Botelhos,** Braz.
81/J1 **Botev** (peak), Bul.
83/F4 **Botevgrad,** Bul.
133/E2 **Bothaspas** (pass), SAfr.
57/E2 **Bothel,** Eng,UK
165/C2 **Bothell,** Wa,US
58/D5 **Bothenhampton,** Eng,UK
84/C3 **Bothnia** (gulf), Fin., Swe.
63/R7 **Botkyrka,** Swe.
131/A4 **Botletle** (riv.), Bots.
86/C3 **Botoşani,** Rom.
83/H2 **Botoşani** (co.), Rom.
103/D3 **Botou,** China
109/D2 **Bo Trach,** Viet.
69/F3 **Botrange** (mtn.), Belg.
131/A4 **Botswana**
80/E3 **Botte Donato** (peak), It.
57/H4 **Bottesford,** Eng,UK
57/H6 **Bottesford,** Eng,UK
78/D1 **Botticino,** It.
157/H3 **Bottineau,** ND,US
66/D5 **Bottrop,** Ger.
141/B2 **Botucatu,** Braz.
161/L1 **Botwood,** Nf,Can
128/D4 **Bou** (riv.), IvC.
128/D5 **Bouaflé,** IvC.
128/D5 **Bouaké,** IvC.
124/J6 **Bouar,** CAfr.
71/G5 **Boubín** (peak), Czh.
125/J6 **Bouca,** CAfr.
161/P6 **Boucherville,** Qu,Can
128/C3 **Boucle du Baoulé Nat'l Park,** Mali
124/E1 **Boudenib,** Mor.
129/E2 **Boû Djébéha** (well), Mali
123/S15 **Boufarik,** Alg.
53/S9 **Bouffémont,** Fr.
118/B1 **Bougainville** (reef), Austl.
143/N7 **Bougainville** (cape), Falk.
120/E5 **Bougainville** (isl.), PNG
123/S15 **Bougara,** Alg.
123/V17 **Bougar'oûn** (cape), Alg.
128/D4 **Bougouni,** Mali
128/E4 **Bougouriba** (prov.), Burk.
72/C3 **Bouguenais,** Fr.
123/M13 **Bouhalla** (peak), Mor.
123/V17 **Bou Hamdane** (riv.), Alg.
123/S15 **Bouira,** Alg.
123/S15 **Bouira** (wilaya), Alg.
123/S15 **Bou Ismaïl,** Alg.
123/R15 **Bou Kadir,** Alg.
120/B8 **Boulder,** Austl.
159/F2 **Boulder,** Co,US
156/E4 **Boulder,** Mt,US
158/D4 **Boulder City,** Nv,US
165/P16 **Boulder Hill,** Il,US
129/E4 **Boulgo** (prov.), Burk.
129/E3 **Boulkiemde** (prov.), Burk.
72/C3 **Boulogne** (riv.), Fr.
53/S10 **Boulogne-Billancourt,** Fr.
68/A2 **Boulogne-sur-Mer,** Fr.
57/F4 **Boulsworth** (hill), Eng,UK
123/S15 **Boumerdas,** Alg.
123/S15 **Boumerdas** (wilaya), Alg.
75/F1 **Boumort** (mtn.), Sp.
151/K3 **Boundary,** Yk,Can
158/C3 **Boundary** (peak), Nv,US
166/D2 **Bound Brook,** NJ,US
128/D4 **Boundiali,** IvC.
158/E2 **Bountiful,** Ut,US
51/T8 **Bounty** (isls.), NZ
164/B1 **Bouquet** (canyon), Ca,US
164/B1 **Bouquet** (res.), Ca,US
76/C3 **Bourbet, Rochers du** (mtn.), Fr.
160/C3 **Bourbonnais,** Il,US
68/B2 **Bourbourg,** Fr.
123/L14 **Bou Regreg** (riv.), Mor.
129/F2 **Bouressa** (wadi), Mali
76/B5 **Bourg-en-Bresse,** Fr.
72/E3 **Bourges,** Fr.
72/F4 **Bourg-lès-Valence,** Fr.
72/B3 **Bourgneuf** (bay), Fr.
68/D5 **Bourgogne,** Fr.
76/B3 **Bourgogne** (can.), Fr.
72/E3 **Bourgogne** (reg.), Fr.
72/F4 **Bourgoin-Jallieu,** Fr.
59/F1 **Bourne,** Eng,UK
53/M8 **Bourne** (riv.), Eng,UK
59/F3 **Bourne End,** Eng,UK
59/E5 **Bournemouth,** Eng,UK
59/E2 **Bournville,** Eng,UK

178

Bourn – Burit

60/A5 **Bourn-Vincent Mem. Nat'l Park,** Ire.
67/E3 **Bourtanger Moor** (reg.), Ger.
59/E3 **Bourton on the Water,** Eng,UK
123/T15 **Bou Sellam** (riv.), Alg.
124/J5 **Bousso,** Chad
128/B2 **Boutilimit,** Mrta.
116/B5 **Bouvard** (cape), Austl.
51/K8 **Bouvet** (isl.), Nor.
68/C5 **Bouzy,** Fr.
67/G5 **Bovenden,** Ger.
139/H4 **Boven Tapanahoni** (riv.), Sur.
66/D3 **Bovenwijde** (lake), Neth.
58/C5 **Bovey Tracey,** Eng,UK
78/D1 **Bovezzo,** It.
53/M6 **Bovingdon,** Eng,UK
93/G4 **Bovīr Aḩmadi and Kohkīlūyeh** (gov.), Iran
79/E2 **Bovolone,** It.
156/E3 **Bow** (riv.), Ab,Can
157/J4 **Bowdle,** SD,US
57/F5 **Bowdon,** Eng,UK
118/C3 **Bowen,** Austl.
66/C5 **Bowen Merwede** (can.), Neth.
57/G3 **Bowes,** Eng,UK
158/E4 **Bowie,** Az,US
166/B6 **Bowie,** Md,US
156/F3 **Bow Island,** Ab,Can
118/B2 **Bowling Green** (cape), Austl.
160/C4 **Bowling Green,** Ky,US
159/K3 **Bowling Green,** Mo,US
160/D3 **Bowling Green,** Oh,US
118/B2 **Bowling Green Bay Nat'l Park,** Austl.
113/G **Bowman** (isl.), Ant.
153/J2 **Bowman** (bay), NW,Can
157/H4 **Bowman,** ND,US
161/S8 **Bowmanville,** Nf,Can
55/H9 **Bowmore,** Sc,UK
57/E2 **Bowness-on-Solway,** Eng,UK
111/F4 **Bowokan** (isls.), Indo.
119/D2 **Bowral,** Austl.
156/C2 **Bowron** (riv.), BC,Can
131/B3 **Bowwood,** Zam.
70/C4 **Boxberg,** Ger.
157/H4 **Box Elder,** SD,US
119/C3 **Box Hill,** Austl.
119/G5 **Box Hill,** Austl.
103/D3 **Boxing,** China
66/C5 **Boxmeer,** Neth.
66/C5 **Boxtel,** Neth.
92/C1 **Boyabat,** Turk.
138/C3 **Boyacá** (dept.), Col.
93/M6 **Boyalik,** Turk.
119/D2 **Boyd-Konangra Nat'l Park,** Austl.
103/C3 **Boye,** China
157/K5 **Boyer** (riv.), Ia,US
156/E2 **Boyle,** Ab,Can
60/D2 **Boyne** (riv.), Ire.
160/C2 **Boyne City,** Mi,US
163/H5 **Boynton Beach,** Fl,US
156/F5 **Boysen** (res.), Wy,US
92/B1 **Boz** (pt.), Turk.
81/J3 **Bozcaada** (isl.), Turk.
92/B2 **Bozdoğan,** Turk.
156/F4 **Bozeman,** Mt,US
77/H5 **Bozen** (Bolzano), It.
92/C2 **Bozkir,** Turk.
124/J6 **Bozoum,** CAfr.
92/D2 **Bozova,** Turk.
92/B2 **Bozüyük,** Turk.
91/C1 **Bozyazı,** Turk.
78/A3 **Bra,** It.
54/C3 **Braan** (riv.), Sc,UK
68/D2 **Brabant** (prov.), Belg.
59/G4 **Brabourne Lees,** Eng,UK
82/C4 **Brač** (isl.), Cro.
80/B1 **Bracciano** (lake), It.
160/E2 **Bracebridge,** On,Can
84/B3 **Bräcke,** Swe.
70/C4 **Brackenheim,** Ger.
162/C4 **Brackettville,** Tx,US
59/E2 **Brackley,** Eng,UK
59/F4 **Bracknell,** Eng,UK
141/B4 **Braço do Norte,** Braz.
82/F2 **Brad,** Rom.
80/D2 **Bradano** (riv.), It.
56/D3 **Bradda Head** (pt.), IM,UK
163/H5 **Bradenton,** Fl,US
57/G4 **Bradford,** Eng,UK
160/E3 **Bradford,** Pa,US
58/D4 **Bradford on Avon,** Eng,UK
59/E5 **Brading,** Eng,UK
58/C5 **Bradninch,** Eng,UK
162/D4 **Brady,** Tx,US
55/P12 **Brae,** Sc,UK
151/L3 **Braeburn,** Yk,Can
54/C2 **Braemar,** Sc,UK
54/C2 **Braemar** (dist.), Sc,UK
54/C2 **Braeriach** (mtn.), Sc,UK
74/A2 **Braga,** Port.
74/A2 **Braga** (dist.), Port.
142/E2 **Bragado,** Arg.
137/J4 **Bragança,** Braz.
74/B2 **Bragança,** Port.
74/B2 **Bragança** (dist.), Port.
141/G7 **Bragança Paulista,** Braz.
107/F2 **Brahmaputra** (riv.), Asia
56/D6 **Braich-y-Pwll** (pt.), Wal,UK
56/B2 **Braid** (riv.), NI,UK
83/H3 **Brăila,** Rom.
83/H3 **Brăila** (co.), Rom.
68/D2 **Braine-l'Alleud,** Belg.
68/D2 **Braine-le-Comte,** Belg.
157/K4 **Brainerd,** Mn,US
59/G3 **Braintree,** Eng,UK
168/D1 **Braintree,** Ma,US
132/C3 **Brak** (riv.), SAfr.
67/F2 **Brake,** Ger.
68/C2 **Brakel,** Belg.
67/G5 **Brakel,** Ger.
128/B2 **Brakna** (reg.), Mrta.
161/Q8 **Bramalea,** On,Can
57/G4 **Bramhope,** Eng,UK
161/Q8 **Brampton,** On,Can
57/F2 **Brampton,** Eng,UK
67/E4 **Bramsche,** Ger.
54/A1 **Bran** (riv.), Sc,UK
139/F5 **Branco** (riv.), Braz.
126/B5 **Brandberg** (peak), Namb.
64/G2 **Brandenburg,** Ger.
64/G2 **Brandenburg** (state), Ger.
54/C1 **Branderburgh,** Sc,UK
54/A4 **Brander, Pass of** (pass), Sc,UK
57/H4 **Brandesburton,** Eng,UK
78/A2 **Brandizzo,** It.
157/J3 **Brandon,** Mb,Can
60/D4 **Brandon** (mtn.), Ire.
59/G2 **Brandon,** Eng,UK
163/H5 **Brandon,** Fl,US
163/F3 **Brandon,** Ms,US
142/F2 **Brandsen,** Arg.
71/H2 **Brandýs nad Labem,** Czh.
166/C4 **Brandywine** (cr.), De, Pa,US
166/C3 **Brandywine, East Branch** (cr.), Pa,US
166/C4 **Brandywine, West Branch** (cr.), Pa,US
65/K1 **Braniewo,** Pol.
59/E5 **Bransgore,** Eng,UK
54/D5 **Branxton,** Eng,UK
77/H5 **Branzoll** (Bronzolo), It.
161/J2 **Bras d'Or** (lake), NS,Can
136/E6 **Brasiléia,** Braz.
140/A4 **Brasília** (cap.), Braz.
140/A5 **Brasília de Minas,** Braz.
140/A4 **Brasília Nat'l Park,** Braz.
141/D1 **Brasil, Planalto do** (plat.), Braz.
83/G3 **Braşov,** Rom.
83/G3 **Braşov** (co.), Rom.
66/B6 **Brasschaat,** Belg.
117/G2 **Brassey** (peak), Austl.
163/H3 **Brasstown Bald** (peak), Ga,US
65/J4 **Bratislava** (cap.), Slvk.
65/J4 **Bratislava** (reg.), Slvk.
89/L4 **Bratsk,** Rus.
161/F3 **Brattleboro,** Vt,US
149/F4 **Braulio Carrillo Nat'l Park,** CR
71/G6 **Braunau am Inn,** Aus.
70/B1 **Braunfels,** Ger.
67/H5 **Braunlage,** Ger.
67/H4 **Braunschweig** (Brunswick), Ger.
58/B4 **Braunton,** Eng,UK
122/J11 **Brava** (isl.), CpV.
75/G2 **Brava** (coast), Sp.
143/T12 **Brava** (pt.), Uru.
62/G2 **Bråviken** (inlet), Swe.
136/F7 **Bravo** (peak), Bol.
144/B2 **Bravo** (peak), Peru
138/C2 **Bravo** (riv.), Ven.
158/D4 **Brawley,** Ca,US
153/J2 **Bray** (isl.), NW,Can
60/D3 **Bray,** Ire.
72/D3 **Braye** (riv.), Fr.
56/B5 **Bray Head** (pt.), Ire.
68/B4 **Bray-sur-Somme,** Fr.
134/D3 **Brazil**
160/C4 **Brazil,** In,US
134/E4 **Brazilian** (plat.), Braz.
139/E4 **Brazo Casiquare** (riv.), Ven.
141/H7 **Brazópolis,** Braz.
162/D4 **Brazos** (riv.), Tx,US
159/H4 **Brazos, Clear Fork** (riv.), Tx,US
159/G4 **Brazos, Double Mtn. Fork** (riv.), Tx,US
143/K7 **Brazo Sur** (riv.), Arg.
126/C1 **Brazzaville** (cap.), Congo
82/D3 **Brčko,** Bosn.
64/J2 **Brda** (riv.), Pol.
71/G3 **Brdy** (mts.), Czh.
164/C3 **Brea,** Ca,US
54/B4 **Breadalbane** (dist.), Sc,UK
58/D3 **Bream,** Eng,UK
54/E6 **Breamish** (riv.), Eng,UK
83/G3 **Breaza,** Rom.
70/B2 **Brechen,** Ger.
54/D3 **Brechin,** Sc,UK
66/B6 **Brecht,** Belg.
157/J4 **Breckenridge,** Mn,US
67/E6 **Breckerfeld,** Ger.
59/G2 **Breckland** (reg.), Eng,UK
143/K8 **Brecknock** (pen.), Chile
168/F5 **Brecksville,** Oh,US
65/J4 **Břeclav,** Czh.
58/C3 **Brecon,** Wal,UK
58/C3 **Brecon Beacons** (mts.), Wal,UK
58/C3 **Brecon Beacons Nat'l Park,** Wal,UK
66/B5 **Breda,** Neth.
68/B1 **Bredene,** Belg.
69/E1 **Bree,** Belg.
132/L10 **Breë** (riv.), SAfr.
77/E1 **Breg** (riv.), Ger.
77/F5 **Bregagno, Monte** (peak), It.
82/F5 **Bregalinca** (riv.), Macd.
77/F2 **Bregenz,** Aus.
77/F3 **Bregenzer Ache** (riv.), Aus.
61/M6 **Breidhafjördhur** (bay), Ice.
76/D1 **Breisach,** Ger.
71/G5 **Breitenauriegel** (peak), Ger.
76/D5 **Breithorn** (peak), Swi.
76/D6 **Breithorn** (peak), Swi., It.
140/B1 **Brejo,** Braz.
140/C2 **Brejo do Cruz,** Braz.
140/B3 **Brejões,** Braz.
140/C2 **Brejo Santo,** Braz.
78/C1 **Brembo** (riv.), It.
67/F2 **Bremen,** Ger.
67/F1 **Bremen** (state), Ger.
67/F2 **Bremen** (state), Ger.
118/E7 **Bremer** (riv.), Austl.
67/F1 **Bremerhaven,** Ger.
165/B2 **Bremerton,** Wa,US
67/G2 **Bremervörde,** Ger.
62/A2 **Bremnes,** Nor.
70/D2 **Brend** (riv.), Ger.
165/E6 **Brendel** (lake), Mi,US
58/C4 **Brendon** (hills), Eng,UK
162/D4 **Brenham,** Tx,US
56/E5 **Brenig, Llyn** (lake), Wal,UK
76/B4 **Brenne** (riv.), Fr.
117/N9 **Brenner** (riv.), Austl.
77/H4 **Brenner** (Brennerpass) (pass), Aus.
77/E4 **Brenno** (riv.), Swi.
53/N7 **Brent** (bor.), Eng,UK
53/N7 **Brent** (res.), Eng,UK
53/N7 **Brent** (riv.), Eng,UK
79/F2 **Brenta** (riv.), It.
77/G5 **Brenta, Cima** (peak), It.
53/P7 **Brentwood,** Eng,UK
165/L11 **Brentwood,** Ca,US
167/E2 **Brentwood,** NY,US
168/H7 **Brentwood,** Pa,US
70/D5 **Brenz** (riv.), Ger.
78/D1 **Brescia,** It.
78/D1 **Brescia** (prov.), It.
68/A4 **Bresle** (riv.), Fr.
73/J3 **Bressanone,** It.
55/P12 **Bressay** (isl.), Sc,UK
72/C3 **Bressuire,** Fr.
65/M2 **Brest,** Bela.
72/A2 **Brest,** Fr.
65/M2 **Brest Obl.,** Bela.
72/B2 **Bretagne** (mts.), Fr.
72/B2 **Bretagne** (reg.), Fr.
133/R15 **Bretagne** (pt.), Reun.
53/S11 **Brétigny-sur-Orge,** Fr.
156/E2 **Breton,** Ab,Can
161/K2 **Breton** (cape), NS,Can
115/R10 **Brett** (cape), NZ
70/C4 **Brettach** (riv.), Ger.
70/B4 **Bretten,** Ger.
70/C3 **Breuberg,** Ger.
53/S11 **Breuillet,** Fr.
66/B4 **Breukelen,** Neth.
137/H4 **Breves,** Braz.
63/S7 **Brevik,** Swe.
153/K2 **Brevoort** (isl.), NW,Can
161/G2 **Brewer,** Me,US
58/D1 **Brewood,** Eng,UK
159/H2 **Brewster,** Ne,US
156/D3 **Brewster,** Wa,US
163/G4 **Brewton,** Al,US
82/B3 **Brežice,** Slov.
83/G3 **Brezoi,** Rom.
125/K6 **Bria,** CAfr.
73/G4 **Briançon,** Fr.
58/C2 **Brianne, Lyn** (res.), Wal,UK
167/D3 **Brick,** NJ,US
53/M6 **Bricket Wood,** Eng,UK
60/B5 **Bride** (riv.), Ire.
56/D3 **Bride,** IM,UK
162/E4 **Bridge City,** Tx,US
58/C4 **Bridgend,** Wal,UK
54/C4 **Bridge of Allan,** Sc,UK
54/D2 **Bridge of Don,** Sc,UK
54/B5 **Bridge of Weir,** Sc,UK
158/C3 **Bridgeport,** Ca,US
168/A3 **Bridgeport,** Ct,US
159/G2 **Bridgeport,** Ne,US
160/D4 **Bridgeport,** WV,US
156/F4 **Bridger,** Mt,US
166/C5 **Bridgeton,** NJ,US
150/G4 **Bridgetown** (cap.), Bar.
119/C4 **Bridgewater,** Austl.
161/H2 **Bridgewater,** NS,Can
168/D2 **Bridgewater,** Ma,US
160/E4 **Bridgewater,** Va,US
58/D1 **Bridgnorth,** Eng,UK
161/G2 **Bridgton,** Me,US
58/D4 **Bridgwater,** Eng,UK
58/C4 **Bridgwater** (bay), Eng,UK
57/H3 **Bridlington,** Eng,UK
57/H3 **Bridlington** (bay), Eng,UK
58/D5 **Bridport,** Eng,UK
53/U10 **Brie** (reg.), Fr.
53/T10 **Brie-Comte-Robert,** Fr.
65/J3 **Brieg Brzeg,** Pol.
66/B5 **Brielle,** Neth.
76/D4 **Brienzersee** (lake), Swi.
163/H3 **Brier** (cr.), Ga,US
57/F4 **Brierfield,** Eng,UK
73/G3 **Brig,** Swi.
77/E1 **Brigach** (riv.), Ger.
167/D5 **Brigantine,** NJ,US
57/H4 **Brigg,** Eng,UK
76/D5 **Brig-Glis,** Swi.
158/D2 **Brigham City,** Ut,US
57/G4 **Brighouse,** Eng,UK
59/E5 **Brighstone,** Eng,UK
59/H3 **Brightlingsea,** Eng,UK
117/M9 **Brighton,** Austl.
118/F6 **Brighton,** Austl.
119/F5 **Brighton,** Austl.
59/F5 **Brighton,** Eng,UK
159/F3 **Brighton,** Co,US
54/C5 **Brightons,** Sc,UK
72/F4 **Brignais,** Fr.
72/G5 **Brignoles,** Fr.
108/G3 **Brihadeshwara Temple,** India
53/S11 **Briis-sous-Forges,** Fr.
79/G3 **Brijuni,** Cro.
128/A3 **Brikama,** Gam.
59/E3 **Brill,** Eng,UK
137/H8 **Brillante** (riv.), Braz.
67/F6 **Brilon,** Ger.
57/G5 **Brimington,** Eng,UK
150/F3 **Brimstone Hill Nat'l Park,** StK.
81/E2 **Brindisi,** It.
58/E3 **Brinkworth,** Eng,UK
74/A1 **Brion,** Sp.
165/K11 **Briones** (res.), Ca,US
118/E6 **Brisbane,** Austl.
118/F6 **Brisbane** (riv.), Austl.
118/E6 **Brisbane For. Park,** Austl.
118/D4 **Brisbane** (inset), Austl.
119/C3 **Brisbane Ranges Nat'l Park,** Austl.
119/D2 **Brisbane Waters Nat'l Park,** Austl.
58/B4 **Bristol** (chan.), UK
58/D4 **Bristol,** Eng,UK
151/F4 **Bristol** (bay), Ak,US
168/B2 **Bristol,** Ct,US
168/C2 **Bristol** (co.), Ma,US
166/D3 **Bristol,** Pa,US
168/C2 **Bristol,** RI,US
168/C2 **Bristol** (co.), RI,US
163/H2 **Bristol,** Tn,US
159/H4 **Bristow,** Ok,US
151/K2 **British** (mts.), Yk,Can, Ak,US
152/D3 **British Columbia** (prov.), Can.
153/S6 **British Empire** (range), NW,Can
90/G10 **British Indian Ocean Terr.**
53/N7 **British Museum,** Eng,UK
150/E3 **British Virgin Islands**
132/P12 **Brits,** SAfr.
72/B2 **Brittany** (reg.), Fr.
157/J4 **Britton,** SD,US
72/D4 **Brive-la-Gaillarde,** Fr.
58/C6 **Brixham,** Eng,UK
59/F2 **Brixworth,** Eng,UK
65/J4 **Brno,** Czh.
63/R6 **Bro,** Swe.
118/C3 **Broad** (sound), Austl.
151/J3 **Broad** (pass), Ak,US
163/H3 **Broad** (riv.), NC, SC,US
160/E1 **Broadback** (riv.), Qu,Can
166/C6 **Broadkill** (riv.), De,US
54/C6 **Broad Law** (mtn.), Sc,UK
119/F5 **Broadmeadows,** Austl.
118/C3 **Broad Sound** (chan.), Austl.
59/H4 **Broadstairs,** Eng,UK
59/E5 **Broadstone,** Eng,UK
157/G4 **Broadus,** Mt,US
168/F5 **Broadview Heights,** Oh,US
119/E1 **Broadwater Nat'l Park,** Austl.
59/E2 **Broadway,** Eng,UK
59/E2 **Broadway** (hill), Eng,UK
58/D5 **Broadwindsor,** Eng,UK
149/F1 **Broa, Ensenada de la** (bay), Cuba
153/R7 **Brock** (isl.), NW,Can
67/H5 **Brocken** (peak), Ger.
59/E5 **Brockenhurst,** Eng,UK
116/C2 **Brockman** (peak), Austl.
168/C1 **Brockton,** Ma,US
160/F2 **Brockville,** On,Can
152/G1 **Brodeur** (pen.), NW,Can
166/C1 **Brodhead** (cr.), Pa,US
54/A5 **Brodick,** Sc,UK
65/K2 **Brodnica,** Pol.
66/B3 **Broek Op Langedijk,** Neth.
119/D2 **Broken** (bay), Austl.
159/J3 **Broken Arrow,** Ok,US
159/H2 **Broken Bow,** Ne,US
159/J4 **Broken Bow,** Ok,US
159/J4 **Broken Bow** (lake), Ok,US
117/J4 **Broken Hill,** Austl.
162/B3 **Brokeoff** (mts.), NM,US
139/H3 **Brokopondo** (dist.), Sur.
53/P7 **Bromley,** Eng,UK
53/P7 **Bromley** (bor.), Eng,UK
131/C3 **Bromley,** Zim.
53/P7 **Bromley Common,** Eng,UK
63/R7 **Bromma,** Swe.
62/F3 **Bromölla,** Swe.
58/D2 **Bromsgrove,** Eng,UK
58/D2 **Bromyard,** Eng,UK
72/F4 **Bron,** Fr.
63/T9 **Brøndby,** Den.
62/C3 **Brønderslev,** Den.
129/E5 **Brong-Ahafo** (reg.), Gha.
78/C2 **Broni,** It.
58/C3 **Bronllys,** Wal,UK
61/E2 **Brønnøysund,** Nor.
161/Q9 **Bronte,** On,Can
80/D4 **Bronte,** It.
167/E2 **Bronx** (co.), NY,US
167/E2 **Bronx** (riv.), NY,US
167/K8 **Bronxville,** NY,US
167/E2 **Bronx Zoo,** NY,US
112/B3 **Brookes Point,** Phil.
168/A3 **Brookfield,** Ct,US
165/Q16 **Brookfield,** Il,US
159/J3 **Brookfield,** Mo,US
165/P13 **Brookfield,** Wi,US
163/F4 **Brookhaven,** Ms,US
167/F2 **Brookhaven,** NY,US
157/J4 **Brookings,** SD,US
168/C1 **Brookline,** Ma,US
168/C2 **Brooklyn,** Ct,US
168/F5 **Brooklyn,** Oh,US
167/K9 **Brooklyn** (Kings) (co.), NY,US
166/B5 **Brooklyn Park,** Md,US
53/N6 **Brookmans Park,** Eng,UK
168/F5 **Brook Park,** Oh,US
156/F3 **Brooks,** Ab,Can
151/E2 **Brooks** (mtn.), Ak,US
151/F2 **Brooks** (range), Ak,US
162/D4 **Brooks A.F.B.,** Tx,US
166/C4 **Brookside,** De,US
163/H4 **Brooksville,** Fl,US
166/C4 **Broomall,** Pa,US
60/C3 **Brosna** (riv.), Ire.
161/P7 **Brossard,** Qu,Can
57/H2 **Brotton,** Eng,UK
57/F2 **Brough,** Eng,UK
161/R8 **Brougham,** On,Can
55/N13 **Brough Head** (pt.), Sc,UK
56/B2 **Broughshane,** NI,UK
59/F2 **Broughton,** Eng,UK
54/C5 **Broughton,** Sc,UK
57/E3 **Broughton in Furness,** Eng,UK
59/G4 **Broughton Street,** Eng,UK
66/A5 **Brouwersdam** (dam), Neth.
117/H5 **Brown** (peak), Austl.
117/G5 **Brown** (pt.), Austl.
58/D2 **Brown Clee** (hill), Eng,UK
162/C3 **Brownfield,** Tx,US
59/E1 **Brownhills,** Eng,UK
156/E3 **Browning,** Mt,US
59/E5 **Brownsea** (isl.), Eng,UK
166/D4 **Browns Mills,** NJ,US
167/K9 **Brownsville,** NY,US
163/F3 **Brownsville,** Tn,US
162/D5 **Brownsville,** Tx,US
58/B5 **Brown Willy** (hill), Eng,UK
162/D4 **Brownwood,** Tx,US
53/N6 **Broxbourne,** Eng,UK
54/C5 **Broxburn,** Sc,UK
76/C4 **Broye** (riv.), Swi.
68/B3 **Bruay-en-Artois,** Fr.
68/C3 **Bruay-sur-l'Escaut,** Fr.
116/C2 **Bruce** (peak), Austl.
160/D2 **Bruce** (pen.), On,Can
76/D1 **Bruche** (riv.), Fr.
70/B2 **Bruchköbel,** Ger.
69/G5 **Bruchmühlbach-Miesau,** Ger.
70/B4 **Bruchsal,** Ger.
67/G5 **Brucht** (riv.), Ger.
73/K3 **Bruck an der Grossglockner-strasse,** Aus.
82/C1 **Bruck an der Leitha,** Aus.
73/L3 **Bruck an der Mur,** Aus.
64/F5 **Bruckmühl,** Ger.
58/D4 **Brue** (riv.), Eng,UK
68/C1 **Bruges** (Brugge), Belg.
68/C1 **Brugge** (Bruges), Belg.
66/D6 **Brüggen,** Ger.
69/F2 **Brühl,** Ger.
132/B2 **Brukkaros** (peak), Namb.
140/B4 **Brumado,** Braz.
69/G6 **Brumath,** Fr.
66/D4 **Brummen,** Neth.
62/D1 **Brumunddal,** Nor.
80/A2 **Bruncu Spina** (peak), It.
59/H1 **Brundall,** Eng,UK
68/D4 **Brune** (riv.), Fr.
158/D2 **Bruneau** (riv.), Id, Nv,US
112/A4 **Brunei**
112/A4 **Brunei** (bay), Bru.
75/M9 **Brunete,** Sp.
73/J3 **Brunico,** It.
76/E4 **Brünigpass** (pass), Swi.
63/R6 **Brunna,** Swe.
77/E4 **Brunnen,** Swi.
53/T10 **Brunoy,** Fr.
67/G1 **Brunsbüttel,** Ger.
69/E2 **Brunssum,** Neth.
119/F5 **Brunswick,** Austl.
143/J8 **Brunswick** (pen.), Chile
163/H4 **Brunswick,** Ga,US
161/G3 **Brunswick,** Me,US
168/F5 **Brunswick,** Oh,US
67/H4 **Brunswick** (Braunschweig), Ger.
149/E3 **Brus** (lag.), Hon.
168/G6 **Brush** (cr.), Pa,US
141/B3 **Brusque,** Braz.
68/D2 **Brussels** (Bruxelles) (cap.), Belg.
58/D4 **Bruton,** Eng,UK
68/D2 **Bruxelles** (Brussels) (cap.), Belg.
53/S11 **Bruyères-le-Châtel,** Fr.
53/S9 **Bruyères-sur-Oise,** Fr.
72/C2 **Bruz,** Fr.
113/U **Bryan** (coast), Ant.
117/H5 **Bryan** (peak), Austl.
160/C3 **Bryan,** Oh,US
162/D4 **Bryan,** Tx,US
86/E1 **Bryansk,** Rus.
86/E1 **Bryansk Obl.,** Rus.
158/D3 **Bryce Canyon Nat'l Park,** Ut,US
57/E5 **Brymbo,** Wal,UK
58/C2 **Bryn Brawd** (mtn.), Wal,UK
62/A2 **Bryne,** Nor.
58/C3 **Brynithel,** Wal,UK
58/C3 **Brynmawr,** Wal,UK
65/J3 **Brzeg Dolny,** Pol.
65/L4 **Brzesko,** Pol.
65/M4 **Brzozów,** Pol.
131/D2 **Bua** (riv.), Malw.
109/C3 **Bua Yai,** Thai.
128/B4 **Buba,** GBis.
130/A3 **Bubanza,** Buru.
128/B4 **Bubaque,** GBis.
93/G4 **Būbiyan** (isl.), Kuw.
130/B4 **Bubu** (riv.), Tanz.
131/C4 **Bubye** (riv.), Zim.
53/S10 **Buc,** Fr.
92/B2 **Bucak,** Turk.
138/C3 **Bucaramanga,** Col.
112/D3 **Bucas Grande** (isl.), Phil.
112/C1 **Bucay,** Phil.
75/P10 **Bucelas,** Port.
153/J1 **Buchan** (gulf), NW,Can
54/D1 **Buchan** (dist.), Sc,UK
128/C5 **Buchanan,** Libr.
159/H5 **Buchanan** (lake), Tx,US
55/L8 **Buchan Ness** (pt.), Sc,UK
161/K1 **Buchans,** Nf,Can
83/H3 **Bucharest** (Bucureşti) (cap.), Rom.
70/C3 **Buchen,** Ger.
130/B3 **Buchenzi,** Tanz.
67/G2 **Buchholz in der Nordheide,** Ger.
70/D6 **Buchloe,** Ger.
54/B4 **Buchlyvie,** Sc,UK
158/B4 **Buchon** (pt.), Ca,US
77/F3 **Buchs,** Swi.
57/F3 **Buckden Pike** (mtn.), Eng,UK
67/G4 **Bückeburg,** Ger.
58/C6 **Buckfastleigh,** Eng,UK
160/D4 **Buckhannon,** WV,US
54/C4 **Buckhaven,** Sc,UK
53/P7 **Buckhurst Hill,** Eng,UK
54/D1 **Buckie,** Sc,UK
160/F2 **Buckingham,** Qu,Can
59/F3 **Buckingham,** Eng,UK
53/N7 **Buckingham Palace,** Eng,UK
59/F3 **Buckinghamshire** (co.), Eng,UK
57/E5 **Buckley,** Wal,UK
58/D2 **Bucknell,** Eng,UK
166/C3 **Bucks** (co.), Pa,US
54/D2 **Bucksburn,** Sc,UK
54/D2 **Buck, The** (mtn.), Sc,UK
161/H2 **Buctouche,** NB,Can
83/H3 **Bucureşti** (Bucharest) (cap.), Rom.
160/D3 **Bucyrus,** Oh,US
130/B2 **Budaka,** Ugan.
82/D2 **Budaörs,** Hun.
82/D2 **Budapest** (cap.), Hun.
106/C2 **Budaun,** India
113/H **Budd** (coast), Ant.
165/B3 **Budd** (inlet), Wa,US
166/D2 **Budd Lake,** NJ,US
54/D4 **Buddon Ness** (pt.), Sc,UK
58/B5 **Bude,** Eng,UK
58/B5 **Bude** (bay), Eng,UK
66/C6 **Budel,** Neth.
64/E1 **Büdelsdorf,** Ger.
70/C2 **Büdingen,** Ger.
125/J7 **Budjala,** Zaire
58/C5 **Budleigh Salterton,** Eng,UK
79/E3 **Budrio,** It.
82/D4 **Budva,** Yugo.
83/J2 **Budzhak** (reg.), Mol., Ukr.
124/G7 **Buea,** Camr.
138/B5 **Buena Fe,** Ecu.
164/C3 **Buena Park,** Ca,US
138/B4 **Buenaventura,** Col.
146/E5 **Buenavista,** Mex.
159/F3 **Buena Vista,** Co,US
160/E4 **Buena Vista,** Va,US
142/B4 **Bueno** (riv.), Chile
141/G7 **Bueno Brandão,** Braz.
141/C1 **Buenópolis,** Braz.
142/F2 **Buenos Aires** (cap.), Arg.
142/C5 **Buenos Aires** (lake), Arg.
142/E3 **Buenos Aires** (prov.), Arg.
143/S12 **Buenos Aires** (inset) (cap.), Arg.
140/C4 **Buerarema,** Braz.
76/C5 **Buet** (mtn.), Fr.
74/A1 **Bueu,** Sp.
119/C3 **Buffalo** (peak), Austl.
156/E2 **Buffalo** (lake), Ab,Can
133/E2 **Buffalo** (riv.), SAfr.
162/E2 **Buffalo** (riv.), Ar,US
157/K4 **Buffalo,** Mn,US
159/J3 **Buffalo,** Mo,US
161/S10 **Buffalo,** NY,US
159/H3 **Buffalo,** Ok,US
166/A2 **Buffalo** (cr.), Pa,US
166/A3 **Buffalo** (cr.), Pa,US
168/H6 **Buffalo** (cr.), Pa,US
157/H4 **Buffalo,** SD,US
163/G3 **Buffalo** (riv.), Tn,US
156/G4 **Buffalo,** Wy,US
165/Q15 **Buffalo Grove,** Il,US
156/F2 **Buffalo Narrows,** Sk,Can
119/B1 **Buffalo Riv. Overflow** (swamp), Austl.
130/C2 **Buffalo Springs Nat'l Rsv.,** Kenya
168/B2 **Buff Cap** (hill), Ct,US
132/B3 **Buffelsrivier** (dry riv.), SAfr.
163/G3 **Buford,** Ga,US
83/G3 **Buftea,** Rom.
86/B1 **Bug** (riv.), Eur.
83/K2 **Bug** (estuary), Ukr.
138/B4 **Buga,** Col.
149/F4 **Bugaba,** Pan.
130/B3 **Bugala** (isl.), Ugan.
72/E5 **Bugarach, Pic de** (peak), Fr.
130/A3 **Bugarama,** Rwa.
130/A3 **Bugaza,** Zaire
59/E2 **Bugbrooke,** Eng,UK
110/D5 **Bugel** (pt.), Indo.
130/A3 **Bugene,** Tanz.
68/D1 **Buggenhout,** Belg.
130/B2 **Bugiri,** Ugan.
82/C3 **Bugojno,** Bosn.
112/B3 **Bugsuk** (isl.), Phil.
85/M5 **Bugul'ma,** Rus.
87/K1 **Buguruslan,** Rus.
96/D4 **Buh** (riv.), China
92/D2 **Buhayrat al Asad** (lake), Syria
92/B4 **Buhayrat al Manzilah** (lake), Egypt
93/E3 **Buḩayrat ath Tharthār** (lake), Iraq
130/B3 **Buhemba,** Tanz.
131/C3 **Buhera,** Zim.
77/E2 **Bühl,** Ger.
156/E5 **Buhl,** Id,US
70/C4 **Bühler** (riv.), Ger.
83/H2 **Buhuşi,** Rom.
129/E4 **Bui** (dam), Gha.
129/E4 **Bui Gorge** (res.), Gha.
58/C2 **Builth Wells,** Wal,UK
142/Q9 **Buin,** Chile
77/G4 **Buin, Piz** (peak), Swi.
140/C3 **Buíque,** Braz.
74/C4 **Bujalance,** Sp.
82/E4 **Bujanovac,** Yugo.
79/G2 **Buje,** Cro.
83/H3 **Bujor,** Rom.
130/A3 **Bujumbura** (cap.), Buru.
65/J2 **Buk,** Pol.
120/E5 **Buka** (isl.), PNG
96/H1 **Bukachacha,** Rus.
102/F4 **Bukadaban Feng** (peak), China
130/B3 **Bukakata,** Ugan.
93/F2 **Būkān,** Iran
130/B3 **Bukasa** (isl.), Ugan.
130/A3 **Bukavu,** Zaire
130/B4 **Bukene,** Tanz.
109/C5 **Buket Bubat** (peak), Malay.
88/G6 **Bukhara,** Uzb.
96/A2 **Bukhtarma** (riv.), Kaz.
130/B3 **Bukima,** Tanz.
110/B4 **Bukittinggi,** Indo.
82/E1 **Bükki Nat'l Park,** Hun.
130/A3 **Bukoba,** Tanz.
130/B3 **Bukonyo,** Tanz.
110/B4 **Buku** (cape), Indo.
112/E6 **Bulacan,** Phil.
112/E6 **Bulacan** (prov.), Phil.
77/E2 **Bülach,** Swi.
112/C2 **Bulalakao,** Phil.
112/C2 **Bulan,** Phil.
92/D1 **Bulancak,** Turk.
106/C2 **Bulandshahr,** India
92/E2 **Bulanık,** Turk.
111/F3 **Bulawa** (peak), Indo.
131/C4 **Bulawayo,** Zim.
92/B2 **Buldan,** Turk.
151/B5 **Buldir** (isl.), Ak,US
96/C2 **Bulgan,** Mong.
96/C2 **Bulgan** (riv.), Mong.
83/G4 **Bulgaria**
80/D2 **Bulgheria** (peak), It.
112/B3 **Buliluyan** (cape), Phil.
118/F7 **Bulimba** (cr.), Austl.
62/D4 **Bülk** (pt.), Ger.
59/E2 **Bulkington,** Eng,UK
156/B2 **Bulkley** (riv.), BC,Can
56/B1 **Bull** (pt.), NI,UK
74/E3 **Bullas,** Sp.
76/D4 **Bulle,** Swi.
119/C3 **Buller** (peak), Austl.
158/D4 **Bullhead City,** Az,US
69/F3 **Büllingen,** Belg.
53/R11 **Bullion,** Fr.
118/A5 **Bulloo** (riv.), Austl.
118/A5 **Bulloo Riv. Overflow** (swamp), Austl.
159/J3 **Bull Shoals** (lake), Ar, Mo,US
68/B3 **Bully-les-Mines,** Fr.
96/D2 **Bulnayn** (mts.), Mong.
142/B3 **Bulnes,** Chile
120/D5 **Bulolo,** PNG
53/Q7 **Bulphan,** Eng,UK
112/D4 **Buluan,** Phil.
111/F5 **Bulukumba,** Indo.
126/D2 **Bulungu,** Zaire
130/B4 **Bulungwa,** Tanz.
125/K7 **Bumba,** Zaire
112/B4 **Bum Bum** (isl.), Malay.
104/C3 **Bumhpa** (peak), Burma
130/C2 **Buna,** Kenya
99/L9 **Bunaga-take** (peak), Japan
112/D3 **Bunawan,** Phil.
130/A3 **Bunazi,** Tanz.
116/B5 **Bunbury,** Austl.
118/D4 **Bundaberg,** Austl.
67/E2 **Bünde,** Ger.
67/F4 **Bünde,** Ger.
106/C2 **Būndi,** India
112/D2 **Bunga** (pt.), Phil.
59/H2 **Bungay,** Eng,UK
130/B2 **Bungoma,** Kenya
110/C3 **Bunguran** (isl.), Indo.
130/A2 **Bunia,** Zaire
63/T9 **Bunkeflo Strand,** Swe.
163/H4 **Bunnell,** Fl,US
66/C4 **Bunnik,** Neth.
75/E3 **Buñol,** Sp.
66/C4 **Bunschoten,** Neth.
59/F3 **Buntingford,** Eng,UK
130/B2 **Bunyala,** Kenya
118/C4 **Bunya Mountains Nat'l Park,** Austl.
92/C2 **Bünyan,** Turk.
118/E6 **Bunya Park,** Austl.
112/B5 **Bunyu** (isl.), Indo.
109/E3 **Buon Me Thuot,** Viet.
109/E3 **Buon Mrong,** Viet.
140/C3 **Buquim,** Braz.
130/C3 **Bura,** Kenya
125/L5 **Buram,** Sudan
102/D5 **Burang,** China
125/M7 **Buranga** (pass), Ugan.
79/F5 **Burano** (riv.), It.
125/Q6 **Burao,** Som.
163/F4 **Buras-Triumph,** La,US
112/D3 **Burauen,** Phil.
94/D3 **Buraydah,** SAr.
69/H2 **Burbach,** Ger.
164/B2 **Burbank,** Ca,US
165/Q16 **Burbank,** Il,US
125/Q6 **Burco** (Burao), Som.
118/B3 **Burdekin** (riv.), Austl.
165/J10 **Burdell** (mtn.), Ca,US
92/B2 **Burdur,** Turk.
92/B2 **Burdur** (lake), Turk.
92/B2 **Burdur** (prov.), Turk.
106/E3 **Burdwān,** India
59/H1 **Bure** (riv.), Eng,UK
67/F5 **Büren,** Ger.
66/C5 **Buren,** Neth.
96/E2 **Bürengiyn** (mts.), Mong.
53/S10 **Bures-sur-Yvette,** Fr.
108/B2 **Būrewāla,** Pak.
97/L1 **Bureya** (mts.), Rus.
97/L1 **Bureya** (riv.), Rus.
59/E3 **Burford,** Eng,UK
64/F2 **Burg,** Ger.
83/H4 **Burgas,** Bul.
83/H4 **Burgas** (bay), Bul.
83/H4 **Burgas** (reg.), Bul.
70/D6 **Burgau,** Ger.
67/H4 **Burgdorf,** Ger.
76/D3 **Burgdorf,** Swi.
73/M3 **Burgenland** (prov.), Aus.
161/K2 **Burgeo,** Nf,Can
132/D3 **Burgersdorp,** SAfr.
116/D4 **Burges** (peak), Austl.
152/C2 **Burgess** (mtn.), NW,Can
151/L2 **Burgess** (mtn.), Yk,Can
59/F5 **Burgess Hill,** Eng,UK
61/E2 **Burgfjället** (peak), Swe.
71/F6 **Burghausen,** Ger.
54/C1 **Burghead,** Sc,UK
54/C1 **Burghead** (bay), Sc,UK
57/J5 **Burgh le Marsh,** Eng,UK
71/F6 **Burgkirchen an der Alz,** Ger.
70/E2 **Burgkunstadt,** Ger.
71/F4 **Burglengenfeld,** Ger.
74/D1 **Burgos,** Sp.
77/H4 **Burgstall** (Postal), It.
67/E4 **Burgsteinfurt,** Ger.
72/F3 **Burgundy** (hist. reg.), Fr.
67/G3 **Burgwedel,** Ger.
96/D4 **Burhan Budai** (mts.), China
92/A2 **Burhaniye,** Turk.
106/C3 **Burhānpur,** India
104/B3 **Burhi Dihing** (riv.), India
112/C2 **Burias** (isl.), Phil.
149/F4 **Burica** (pen.), CR, Pan.
149/F4 **Burica** (pt.), Pan.
165/C3 **Burien,** Wa,US
161/L2 **Burin,** Nf,Can
161/K2 **Burin** (pen.), Nf,Can
109/C3 **Buriram,** Thai.
141/B2 **Buritama,** Braz.
140/B1 **Buriti,** Braz.
141/B1 **Buriti Alegre,** Braz.
140/B2 **Buriti Bravo,** Braz.

179
Burit – Capit

140/B1 Buriti dos Lopes, Braz.
140/A4 Buritis, Braz.
141/C1 Buritizeiro, Braz.
75/E3 Burjasot, Sp.
70/D2 Burkardroth, Ger.
162/D3 Burkburnett, Tx,US
113/S Burke (isl.), Ant.
166/A6 Burke, Va,US
156/B2 Burke Channel (inlet), BC,Can
77/G4 Bürkelkopf (peak), Aus.
129/E3 Burkina Faso
70/C6 Burladingen, Ger.
156/E5 Burley, Id,US
165/K11 Burlingame, Ca,US
161/Q9 Burlington, On,Can
159/G3 Burlington, Co,US
168/B2 Burlington, Ct,US
157/L5 Burlington, Ia,US
159/J3 Burlington, Ks,US
163/J2 Burlington, NC,US
166/D3 Burlington, NJ,US
166/D4 Burlington (co.), NJ,US
161/F2 Burlington, Vt,US
165/P14 Burlington, Wi,US
107/G2 Burma (Myanmar)
83/K3 Burnas (lake), Ukr.
162/D4 Burnet, Tx,US
143/J8 Burney (peak), Chile
158/B2 Burney, Ca,US
59/G3 Burnham on Crouch, Eng,UK
58/D4 Burnham on Sea, Eng,UK
119/C4 Burnie-Somerset, Austl.
57/F4 Burnley, Eng,UK
54/D5 Burnmouth, Sc,UK
156/D5 Burns, Or,US
152/E2 Burnside (riv.), NW,Can
156/B2 Burns Lake, BC,Can
54/C4 Burntisland, Sc,UK
157/J2 Burntwood (riv.), Mb,Can
59/E1 Burntwood, Eng,UK
119/B2 Buronga, Austl.
96/B2 Burqin, China
96/B2 Burqin (riv.), China
115/H6 Burragorang (lake), Austl.
81/G2 Burrel, Alb.
119/D2 Burrendong (res.), Austl.
60/A3 Burren, The (reg.), Ire.
119/D2 Burrewarra (pt.), Austl.
75/E3 Burriana, Sp.
119/D2 Burrinjuck (res.), Austl.
146/E2 Burro, Serranías del (mts.), Mex.
118/A2 Burrowes (pt.), Austl.
56/D2 Burrow Head (pt.), Sc,UK
165/Q16 Burr Ridge, Il,US
118/D4 Burrum River Nat'l Park, Austl.
58/B3 Burry (inlet), Wal,UK
58/B3 Burry Port, Wal,UK
83/J5 Bursa, Turk.
83/J5 Bursa (prov.), Turk.
127/C3 Būr Safājah, Egypt
91/C4 Būr Sa'īd (gov.), Egypt
91/C4 Būr Sa'īd (Port Said), Egypt
67/E6 Burscheid, Ger.
57/F4 Burscough Bridge, Eng,UK
70/B3 Bürstadt, Ger.
127/D5 Būr Sūdān (Port Sudan), Sudan
161/S9 Burt, NY,US
127/C2 Būr Tawfīq, Egypt
59/E5 Burton, Eng,UK
165/E6 Burton, Mi,US
59/F2 Burton Latimer, Eng,UK
59/E1 Burton upon Trent, Eng,UK
111/G4 Buru (isl.), Indo.
91/B4 Burullus, Buḩayrat al (lag.), Egypt
112/C2 Buruncan (pt.), Phil.
130/A2 Burundi
96/F2 Burun Shibertuy (peak), Rus.
130/A3 Bururi, Buru.
140/A2 Buruticupu (riv.), Braz.
151/L3 Burwash Landing, Yk,Can
59/G2 Burwell, Eng,UK
159/H2 Burwell, Ne,US
59/F5 Bury, Eng,UK
89/M4 Buryat Aut. Rep., Rus.
87/J3 Burynshyk (pt.), Kaz.
59/G2 Bury Saint Edmunds, Eng,UK
112/D4 Busa (mtn.), Phil.
78/B3 Busalla, It.
163/H4 Busch Gardens, Fl,US
130/B2 Busembatia, Ugan.
56/B1 Bush (riv.), NI,UK
166/B5 Bush (riv.), Md,US
96/C2 Bus Hayrhan (peak), Mong.
93/G4 Būshehr, Iran
93/G4 Būshehr (gov.), Iran
53/M7 Bushey, Eng,UK
166/C1 Bushkill (falls), Pa,US
166/C1 Bush Kill (riv.), Pa,US
132/B3 Bushmanland (reg.), SAfr.
131/B4 Bushman Pits, Bots.
56/B1 Bushmills, NI,UK
130/B2 Busia, Kenya
125/K7 Businga, Zaire
62/C1 Buskerud (co.), Nor.
65/L3 Busko-Zdrój, Pol.
130/B2 Busoga (prov.), Ugan.
116/B5 Busselton, Austl.
125/L6 Busseri (riv.), Sudan
79/D2 Bussolengo, It.
66/C4 Bussum, Neth.
143/K7 Bustamente (pt.), Arg.
118/C4 Bustard (pt.), Austl.
83/G3 Buşteni, Rom.
78/B1 Busto Arsizio, It.
78/B1 Busto Garolfo, It.
125/K7 Buta, Zaire
130/A3 Butare, Rwa.
120/G4 Butaritari (atoll), Kiri.
156/B3 Bute (inlet), BC,Can
54/A5 Bute (isl.), Sc,UK
54/A5 Bute (sound), Sc,UK
96/E2 Büteeliyn (mts.), Mong.
130/C2 Bute Helu, Kenya
130/A2 Butembo, Zaire
141/B4 Butiá, Braz.
130/A2 Butiaba, Ugan.
167/H8 Butler, NJ,US
168/H6 Butler, Pa,US
168/H6 Butler (co.), Pa,US
111/F5 Buton (isl.), Indo.
53/S9 Butry-sur-Oise, Fr.
76/D4 Bütschelegg (peak), Swi.
156/E4 Butte, Mt,US
70/B3 Büttelborn, Ger.
110/B2 Butterworth, Malay.
112/D3 Butuan City, Phil.
111/F5 Butung (isl.), Indo.
87/G2 Buturlinovka, Rus.
70/B2 Butzbach, Ger.
64/F2 Bützow, Ger.
125/Q7 Buulo Berde, Som.
125/P7 Buur Hakaba, Som.
130/B2 Buvuma (isl.), Ugan.
67/G2 Buxtehude, Ger.
57/G5 Buxton, Eng,UK
84/J4 Buy, Rus.
87/H4 Buynaksk, Rus.
128/D5 Buyo, Barrage de (dam), IvC.
97/H2 Buyr (lake), Mong.
104/D4 Buyuan (riv.), China
93/N7 Büyükada (isl.), Turk.
83/J5 Büyükçekmece, Turk.
93/M6 Büyükçekmece (lake), Turk.
130/C4 Buyuni (pt.), Tanz.
103/E2 Buyun Shan (peak), China
87/J3 Buzachi (pen.), Kaz.
83/H3 Buzău, Rom.
83/H3 Buzău (co.), Rom.
83/H3 Buzău (riv.), Rom.
79/G2 Buzet, Cro.
131/D3 Búzi (riv.), Moz.
82/E3 Buziaş, Rom.
141/H8 Búzios (isl.), Braz.
87/K1 Buzuluk, Rus.
168/C3 Buzzards (bay), Ma,US
60/B5 Bweeng (mtn.), Ire.
83/G4 Byala, Bul.
83/F4 Byala Slatina, Bul.
153/R7 Byam Martin (chan.), NW,Can
153/R7 Byam Martin (isl.), NW,Can
65/J2 Bydgoszcz, Pol.
65/J2 Bydgoszcz (prov.), Pol.
59/E2 Byfield, Eng,UK
53/M8 Byfleet, Eng,UK
116/L7 Byford, Austl.
86/D1 Bykhov, Bela.
56/E5 Bylchau, Wal,UK
153/J1 Bylot (isl.), NW,Can
166/B4 Bynum (run), Md,US
93/F2 Byoyuk-Kirs (peak), Azer.
167/E2 Byram (pt.), Ct,US
167/E1 Byram (riv.), Ct, NY,US
167/L7 Byram (lake), NY,US
113/U Byrd (cape), Ant.
113/L Byrd (glac.), Ant.
143/J6 Byron (isl.), Chile
88/K2 Byrranga (mts.), Rus.
71/F2 Bystice (riv.), Czh.
65/K4 Bystrá (peak), Slvk.
89/N3 Bytantay (riv.), Rus.
65/K3 Bytom, Pol.
65/J1 Bytów, Pol.
93/M6 Büyükçekmece, Turk.

C

109/D2 Ca (riv.), Viet.
126/C3 Caála, Ang.
140/B2 Caatingas (reg.), Braz.
135/E2 Caazapá, Par.
112/D3 Cabadbaran, Phil.
149/G1 Cabaiguán, Cuba
158/F4 Caballo (res.), NM,US
74/C1 Cabañaquinta, Sp.
112/C2 Cabanatuan City, Phil.
58/C2 Caban Coch (res.), Wal,UK
161/G2 Cabano, Qu,Can
112/C1 Cabarroquis, Phil.
112/C3 Cabatuan, Phil.
140/D2 Cabedelo, Braz.
72/E5 Cabestany, Fr.
74/C3 Cabeza del Buey, Sp.
144/B3 Cabeza Lagarto (pt.), Peru
74/C1 Cabezón de la Sal, Sp.
138/D2 Cabimas, Ven.
126/B2 Cabinda, Ang.
140/D3 Cabo, Braz.
124/C2 Cabo Bojador, WSah.
130/C5 Cabo Delgado (prov.), Moz.
141/D2 Cabo Frio, Braz.
160/E2 Cabonga (res.), Qu,Can
118/D4 Caboolture, Austl.
137/H3 Cabo Orange Nat'l Park, Braz.
131/D2 Cabora Bassa (dam), Moz.
131/C2 Cabora Bassa (lake), Moz.
161/J2 Cabot (str.), Nf, NS,Can
141/G6 Cabo Verde, Braz.
74/C4 Cabra, Sp.
140/A5 Cabral (mts.), Braz.
150/D3 Cabral, DRep.
118/G8 Cabramatta, Austl.
80/A3 Cabras, It.
75/G3 Cabrera (isl.), Sp.
156/F3 Cabri, Sk,Can
74/E3 Cabriel (riv.), Sp.
140/C3 Cabrobó, Braz.
138/D2 Cabudare, Ven.
112/C1 Cabugao, Phil.
141/B3 Caçador, Braz.
82/E4 Čačak, Yugo.
141/H8 Caçapava, Braz.
80/A2 Caccia (cape), It.
136/G7 Cáceres, Braz.
138/C3 Cáceres, Col.
74/B3 Cáceres, Sp.
53/S10 Cachan, Fr.
142/Q10 Cachapoal (riv.), Chile
158/B3 Cache (cr.), Ca,US
165/L10 Cache (slough), Ca,US
156/E5 Cache (peak), Id,US
156/C3 Cache Creek, BC,Can
128/A3 Cacheu, GBis.
135/C2 Cachí, Arg.
137/G5 Cachimbo (mts.), Braz.
141/H7 Cachoeira de Minas, Braz.
141/A4 Cachoeira do Sul, Braz.
141/J7 Cachoeira Paulista, Braz.
141/L7 Cachoeiras de Macacu, Braz.
141/B4 Cachoeirinha, Braz.
141/D2 Cachoeiro de Itapemirim, Braz.
141/G6 Caconde, Braz.
141/B1 Caçu, Braz.
126/B3 Cacula, Ang.
140/B4 Caculé, Braz.
75/G1 Cadaques, Sp.
65/K4 Čadca, Slvk.
162/E3 Caddo (mts.), Ar,US
77/F5 Cadelle, Monte (peak), It.
58/C1 Cader Idris (mtn.), Wal,UK
117/G4 Cadibarrawirracanna (lake), Austl.
160/C2 Cadillac, Mi,US
112/C3 Cadiz, Phil.
74/B4 Cádiz, Sp.
74/B4 Cádiz (gulf), Sp.
160/C4 Cadiz, Ky,US
59/E5 Cadnam, Eng,UK
70/D4 Cadolzburg, Ger.
79/D1 Cadria, Monte (peak), It.
72/C2 Caen, Fr.
72/C2 Caen (har.), Fr.
58/D3 Caerleon, Wal,UK
56/D5 Caernafon Castle, Wal,UK
56/D5 Caernarfon, Wal,UK
56/D5 Caernarfon (bay), Wal,UK
58/C3 Caerphilly, Wal,UK
58/C1 Caersws, Wal,UK
91/F6 Caesarea Nat'l Park, Isr.
68/B2 Caëstre, Fr.
140/B4 Caetité, Braz.
140/B3 Cafarnaum, Braz.
126/C3 Cafayate, Arg.
112/C3 Cagayan (isls.), Phil.
112/D3 Cagayan de Oro City, Phil.
112/B4 Cagayan Sulu (isl.), Phil.
80/A3 Cagliari, It.
80/A3 Cagliari (gulf), It.
73/G5 Cagnes-sur-Mer, Fr.
112/C1 Cagoyan (riv.), Phil.
112/C1 Cagua (mtn.), Phil.
138/C4 Caguán (riv.), Col.
150/E3 Caguas, PR
60/A6 Caha (mts.), Ire.
126/B4 Cahama, Ang.
60/A5 Caherbarnagh (mtn.), Ire.
54/F11 Cahirsiveen (Cahirciveen), Ire.
60/D4 Cahore (pt.), Ire.
72/D4 Cahors, Fr.
138/D5 Cahuinari (riv.), Col.
149/F4 Cahuita (pt.), CR
149/F4 Cahuita Nat'l Park, CR
141/B4 Cai (riv.), Braz.
131/D3 Caia, Moz.
131/A1 Caianda, Ang.
137/H7 Caiapó (mts.), Braz.
137/H7 Caiapó (riv.), Braz.
149/G1 Caibarién, Cuba
139/F2 Caicara, Ven.
139/E3 Caicara de Orinoco, Ven.
138/C3 Caicedonia, Col.
140/C2 Caicó, Braz.
150/C2 Caicos (passg.), Bahm., Trks.
150/C2 Caicos (isls.), Trks.
141/G8 Caieiras, Braz.
68/A4 Cailly (riv.), Fr.
112/B2 Caiman (pt.), Phil.
112/F6 Cainta, Phil.
109/D4 Cai Nuoc, Viet.
78/D4 Caio, Monte (peak), It.
113/Y Caird (coast), Ant.
151/G3 Cairn (mtn.), Ak,US
119/B3 Cairn Curran (dam), Austl.
54/B4 Cairndow, Sc,UK
54/C2 Cairn Gorm (mtn.), Sc,UK
54/C2 Cairngorm (mts.), Sc,UK
56/C2 Cairn Pat (hill), Sc,UK
56/C2 Cairnryan, Sc,UK
118/B2 Cairns, Austl.
117/G2 Cairns (peak), Austl.
54/B6 Cairnsmore of Carsphairn (mtn.), Sc,UK
54/B6 Cairn Table (mtn.), Sc,UK
54/C2 Cairn Toul (mtn.), Sc,UK
163/G4 Cairo, Ga,US
160/B4 Cairo, Il,US
91/B4 Cairo (Al Qāhirah) (cap.), Egypt
78/B4 Cairo Montenotte, It.
59/H1 Caister on Sea, Eng,UK
57/H5 Caistor, Eng,UK
161/Q9 Caistor Centre, On,Can
161/Q9 Caistorville, On,Can
126/B3 Caitou, Ang.
126/C4 Caiundo, Ang.
103/C5 Caizi (lake), China
138/B5 Cajabamba, Ecu.
144/B2 Cajabamba, Peru
144/B2 Cajamarca (ruins), Peru
140/A1 Cajari, Braz.
140/C2 Cajazeiras, Braz.
112/C2 Cajidiocan, Phil.
149/E1 Cajón (pt.), Cuba
140/B1 Caju (isl.), Braz.
129/H5 Calabar, Nga.
139/E2 Calabozo, Ven.
80/E3 Calabria (reg.), It.
80/D3 Calabria Nat'l Park, It.
80/E3 Calabria Nat'l Park, It.
74/C4 Calaburras, Punta de (pt.), Sp.
82/F4 Calafat, Rom.
112/C2 Calagua (isls.), Phil.
74/E1 Calahorra, Sp.
68/A2 Calais, Fr.
161/H2 Calais, Me,US
68/A2 Calais, Canal de (can.), Fr.
135/C2 Calalaste (mts.), Arg.
135/C1 Calama, Chile
112/B2 Calamian (isls.), Phil.
82/F3 Călan, Rom.
112/C2 Calapan, Phil.
83/H3 Călăraşi, Rom.
83/H3 Călăraşi (co.), Rom.
138/C3 Calarca, Col.
74/E3 Calasparra, Sp.
74/E2 Calatayud, Sp.
112/C2 Calauag, Phil.
165/L12 Calaveras (res.), Ca,US
112/C2 Calavite (cape), Phil.
112/C2 Calavite (mtn.), Phil.
112/C1 Calayan, Phil.
112/C1 Calayan (isl.), Phil.
112/D2 Calbayog City, Phil.
112/D3 Calbiga, Phil.
142/B4 Calbuco, Chile
144/D4 Calca, Peru
140/D2 Calcanhar, Ponta do (pt.), Braz.
162/E4 Calcasieu (riv.), La,US
138/A5 Calceta, Ecu.
160/F2 Calcium, NY,US
137/H3 Calçoene, Braz.
106/E3 Calcutta, India
141/G6 Caldas, Braz.
138/C3 Caldas (dept.), Col.
74/A3 Caldas da Rainha, Port.
141/B1 Caldas Novas, Braz.
57/E2 Caldbeck, Eng,UK
67/G6 Calden, Ger.
57/G4 Calder (riv.), Eng,UK
151/M4 Calder (mtn.), Ak,US
54/C5 Caldercruix, Sc,UK
75/L6 Caldes de Montbui, Sp.
57/F2 Caldew (riv.), Eng,UK
58/D3 Caldicot, Wal,UK
156/D5 Caldwell, Id,US
167/H6 Caldwell, NJ,US
162/D4 Caldwell, Tx,US
58/B3 Caldy (isl.), Wal,UK
132/D3 Caledon (riv.), Les., SAfr.
161/Q8 Caledon East, On,Can
161/H2 Caledonia (hills), NB,Can
54/B2 Caledonian (can.), Sc,UK
75/G2 Calella, Sp.
79/E5 Calenzano, It.
142/Q9 Calera de Tango, Chile
149/H1 Caleta (pt.), Cuba
142/D5 Caleta Olivia, Arg.
158/D4 Calexico, Ca,US
55/N13 Calfsound, Sc,UK
57/F3 Calf, The (mtn.), Eng,UK
156/E3 Calgary, Ab,Can
75/S12 Calheta, Azor.,Port.
75/U15 Calheta, Madr.,Port.
163/G3 Calhoun, Ga,US
160/C4 Calhoun, Ky,US
138/B4 Cali, Col.
74/E4 Calida, Costa (coast), Sp.
158/D3 Caliente, Nv,US
158/B3 California (state), US
164/C2 California (aqueduct), Ca,US
160/E4 California, Md,US
159/J3 California, Mo,US
135/D1 Calilegua Nat'l Park, Arg.
83/G3 Călimăneşti, Rom.
108/G3 Calimere (pt.), India
147/H4 Calkiní, Mex.
117/J4 Callabonna (lake), Austl.
54/B4 Callander, Sc,UK
144/B4 Callao, Peru
60/B4 Callaun (mtn.), Ire.
163/G4 Callaway, Fl,US
142/Q9 Calle Larga, Chile
58/B6 Callington, Eng,UK
75/E3 Callosa de Ensarriá, Sp.
75/E3 Callosa de Segura, Sp.
58/D4 Calne, Eng,UK
78/C1 Calolziocorte, It.
68/B3 Calonne-Ricouart, Fr.
112/E6 Caloocan, Phil.
80/D2 Calore (riv.), It.
147/H4 Calotmul, Mex.
118/D4 Caloundra, Austl.
75/F3 Calpe, Sp.
147/L7 Calpulálpan, Mex.
58/B6 Calstock, Eng,UK
80/D4 Caltagirone, It.
80/D4 Caltanissetta, It.
72/F4 Caluire-et-Cuire, Fr.
165/Q16 Calumet (riv.), Il,US
165/Q16 Calumet City, Il,US
165/Q16 Calumet Sag (chan.), Il,US
126/B3 Caluquembe, Ang.
156/A3 Calvert (isl.), BC,Can
57/G5 Calverton, Eng,UK
166/B5 Calverton, Md,US
167/F2 Calverton, NY,US
75/G3 Calviá, Sp.
146/E4 Calvillo, Mex.
79/E4 Calvi, Monte (peak), It.
132/B3 Calvinia, SAfr.
74/C2 Calvitero (mtn.), Sp.
70/B5 Calw, Ger.
59/G2 Cam (riv.), Eng,UK
140/C4 Camaçari, Braz.
126/C3 Camacupa, Ang.
149/G1 Camagüey, Cuba
149/G1 Camagüey (arch.), Cuba
78/D5 Camaiore, It.
149/G1 Camajuaní, Cuba
140/C4 Camamu, Braz.
140/C4 Camamu (bay), Braz.
144/C5 Camaná, Peru
141/G7 Camanducaia, Braz.
141/B4 Camaquã, Braz.
141/A4 Camaquã (riv.), Braz.
75/V15 Câmara de Lobos, Madr.,Port.
73/G5 Camarat (cape), Fr.
79/D1 Camargo, Sp.
164/A2 Camarillo, Ca,US
74/A1 Camariñas, Sp.
149/E3 Camarón (cape), Hon.
142/D5 Camarones (bay), Arg.
74/B4 Camas, Sp.
109/D4 Ca Mau, Viet.
109/D4 Ca Mau (cape), Viet.
148/D3 Camayagua (mts.), Hon.
74/A1 Cambados, Sp.
141/B2 Cambará, Braz.
106/B3 Cambay, India
106/B3 Cambay (gulf), India
141/B2 Cambé, Braz.
59/F4 Camberley Frimley, Eng,UK
53/N7 Camberwell, Eng,UK
109/D3 Cambodia
141/C3 Camboriú, Ponta do (pt.), Braz.
58/A6 Camborne, Eng,UK
68/C3 Cambrai, Fr.
58/C2 Cambrian (mts.), Wal,UK
160/D3 Cambridge, On,Can
115/S10 Cambridge, NZ
59/G2 Cambridge, Eng,UK
168/C1 Cambridge, Ma,US
160/E4 Cambridge, Md,US
157/K4 Cambridge, Mn,US
160/D3 Cambridge, Oh,US
59/G2 Cambridgeshire (co.), Eng,UK
75/F2 Cambrils, Sp.
141/G7 Cambuí, Braz.
141/H6 Cambuquira, Braz.
54/B5 Cambuslang, Sc,UK
149/F5 Cambutal (mtn.), Pan.
119/D2 Camden, Austl.
53/N7 Camden (bor.), Eng,UK
163/G4 Camden, Al,US
162/E3 Camden, Ar,US
161/G2 Camden, Me,US
166/C4 Camden, NJ,US
166/D4 Camden (co.), NJ,US
163/H3 Camden, SC,US
159/J3 Camdenton, Mo,US
126/B3 Cameia Nat'l Park, Ang.
58/B6 Camel (riv.), Eng,UK
166/C1 Camelback (mtn.), Pa,US
58/B5 Camelford, Eng,UK
78/B2 Cameri, It.
153/R7 Cameron (isl.), NW,Can
158/E4 Cameron, Az,US
162/E4 Cameron, La,US
159/J3 Cameron, Mo,US
162/D4 Cameron, Tx,US
129/H5 Cameroon
137/J4 Cametá, Braz.
68/A2 Camiers, Fr.
112/D3 Camiguin (isl.), Phil.
112/C2 Camiling, Phil.
163/G4 Camilla, Ga,US
136/F8 Camiri, Bol.
92/C1 Çamlıdere, Turk.
92/C2 Çamlık Nat'l Park, Turk.
60/C2 Camlin (riv.), Ire.
91/D1 Çamlıyayla, Turk.
131/D4 Camo-Camo, Moz.
140/B1 Camocim, Braz.
107/F6 Camorta (isl.), India
112/D3 Camotes (sea), Phil.
68/A3 Campagne, Fr.
142/F2 Campana, Arg.
143/J7 Campana (isl.), Chile
142/C2 Campanario (peak), Arg.
80/D2 Campanella (cape), It.
141/H6 Campanha, Braz.
80/D2 Campania (reg.), It.
51/T8 Campbell (isl.), NZ
165/L12 Campbell, Ca,US
168/G5 Campbell, Oh,US
156/A2 Campbell Island, BC,Can
156/B3 Campbell River, BC,Can
160/C4 Campbellsville, Ky,US
161/H2 Campbellton, NB,Can
118/G9 Campbelltown, Austl.
161/Q9 Campbellville, On,Can
55/J9 Campbeltown, Sc,UK
161/R9 Campden, On,Can
147/H5 Campeche, Mex.
147/G4 Campeche (bay), Mex.
147/H5 Campeche (state), Mex.
157/H3 Camperville, Mb,Can
141/G6 Campestre, Braz.
109/D1 Cam Pha, Viet.
166/B3 Camp Hill, Pa,US
79/E5 Campi Bisenzio, It.
80/A3 Campidano (range), It.
74/C4 Campillos, Sp.
140/D2 Campina Grande, Braz.
141/F7 Campinas, Braz.
141/B1 Campina Verde, Braz.
138/C4 Campoalegre, Col.
80/D2 Campobasso, It.
141/C2 Campo Belo, Braz.
74/D3 Campo de Criptana, Sp.
78/B1 Campo dei Fiori (peak), It.
138/C2 Campo de la Cruz, Col.
140/B3 Campo Formoso, Braz.
137/H8 Campo Grande, Braz.
135/G2 Campo Largo, Braz.
141/G8 Campo Limpo Paulista, Braz.
140/B2 Campo Maior, Braz.
74/B3 Campo Maior, Port.
78/B4 Campomorone, It.
141/A3 Campo Mourão, Braz.
140/C2 Campo Redondo, Braz.
74/C1 Camporredondo (res.), Sp.
141/D2 Campos, Braz.
140/A4 Campos (reg.), Braz.
141/C1 Campos Altos, Braz.
140/A4 Campos Belos, Braz.
75/G3 Campos del Puerto, Sp.
141/H7 Campos do Jordão, Braz.
141/C2 Campos Gerais, Braz.
141/B3 Campos Novos, Braz.
140/B2 Campos Sales, Braz.
77/E5 Campo Tencia, Pizzo (peak), Swi.
164/C4 Camp Pendleton Marine Corps Base, Ca,US
54/B4 Campsie Fells (hills), Sc,UK
166/B6 Camp Springs, Md,US
162/E4 Campti, La,US
109/E4 Cam Ranh, Viet.
156/E2 Camrose, Ab,Can
109/D1 Cam Thuy, Viet.
83/H5 Çan, Turk.
139/G5 Canaçari (lake), Braz.
152/E2 Canada
142/E2 Cañada de Gómez, Arg.
159/H4 Canadian (riv.), US
162/C3 Canadian, Tx,US
142/C5 Cañadon Grande (mts.), Arg.
138/D2 Canagua, Ven.
139/F3 Canaima Nat'l Park, Ven.
83/H5 Çanakkale, Turk.
83/H5 Çanakkale (prov.), Turk.
121/U12 Canala, NCal.
79/E2 Canalbianco (riv.), It.
142/E3 Canal No. 1 (can.), Arg.
142/F3 Canal No. 11 (can.), Arg.
143/F3 Canal No. 2 (riv.), Arg.
143/F3 Canal No. 5 (riv.), Arg.
142/F3 Canal No. 9 (can.), Arg.
142/E2 Canals, Arg.
75/E3 Canals, Sp.
160/E3 Canandaigua, NY,US
146/C2 Cananea, Mex.
141/C3 Cananéia, Braz.
141/B1 Canápolis, Braz.
144/B1 Cañar, Ecu.
138/B5 Cañar (prov.), Ecu.
165/G7 Canard (riv.), On,Can
149/F1 Canarreos (arch.), Cuba
167/K9 Canarsie, NY,US
75/X16 Canary Is. (aut. comm.), Sp.
149/E4 Cañas, CR
78/D3 Canassa, It.
163/H4 Canaveral (cape), Fl,US
140/C4 Canavieiras, Braz.
119/D2 Canberra (cap.), Austl.
68/A3 Canche (riv.), Fr.
148/E1 Cancún, Mex.
92/A2 Çandarlı (gulf), Turk.
74/C1 Candás, Sp.
140/C4 Candeias, Braz.
147/H5 Candelaria (riv.), Mex.
78/B1 Candelo, It.
161/N7 Candiac, Qu,Can
140/B4 Candiba, Braz.
141/B2 Candido Mota, Braz.
110/D5 Canding (cape), Indo.
92/C2 Çandır, Turk.
157/G2 Candle (lake), Sk,Can
168/A2 Candlewood (res.), Ct,US
167/D3 Candlewood, NJ,US
157/J3 Cando, ND,US
112/C1 Candon, Phil.
78/B2 Canegrate, It.
141/B4 Canela, Braz.
78/B3 Canelli, It.
143/F2 Canelones, Uru.
143/F2 Canelones (dept.), Uru.
144/B4 Canete (riv.), Peru
74/A1 Cangas, Sp.
74/B1 Cangas de Narcea, Sp.
74/C1 Cangas de Onís, Sp.
110/C5 Cangkuang (cape), Indo.
132/C4 Cango Caves, SAfr.
126/D3 Cangombe, Ang.
143/J7 Cangrejo (peak), Arg.
103/D4 Cangshan, China
140/D2 Canguaretama, Braz.
141/A4 Canguçu, Braz.
107/K3 Cangwu, China
104/C4 Cangyuan Vazu Zizhixian (Cangyuan), China
103/D3 Cangzhou, China
109/D1 Canh Cuoc (isl.), Viet.
126/B3 Canhoca, Ang.
118/C4 Cania Gorge Nat'l Park, Austl.
153/K3 Caniapiscau (lake), Qu,Can
153/K3 Caniapiscau (riv.), Qu,Can
80/C4 Canicatti, It.
72/E5 Canigou, Pic de (peak), Fr.
92/C1 Canik (mts.), Turk.
74/D4 Caniles, Sp.
140/C2 Canindé, Braz.
140/B2 Canindé (riv.), Braz.
167/H7 Canistear (res.), NJ,US
92/C1 Çankırı, Turk.
92/C1 Çankırı (prov.), Turk.
112/C3 Canlaon (vol.), Phil.
156/E3 Canmore, Ab,Can
55/H8 Canna (isl.), Sc,UK
108/E3 Cannanore, India
80/E2 Canne (ruins), It.
69/F5 Canner (riv.), Fr.
73/G5 Cannes, Fr.
54/B2 Cannich, Sc,UK
54/B2 Cannich (riv.), Sc,UK
116/C4 Canning (peak), Austl.
116/L7 Canning (res.), Austl.
116/K7 Canning (riv.), Austl.
58/D1 Cannock, Eng,UK
159/G4 Cannon A.F.B., NM,US
157/H4 Cannonball (riv.), ND,US
157/K4 Cannon Falls, Mn,US
141/B4 Canoas, Braz.
141/B3 Canoas (riv.), Braz.
119/D2 Canobolas (peak), Austl.
156/F2 Canoe (lake), Sk,Can
164/E7 Canoga Park, Ca,US
138/D3 Caño Guaritico (riv.), Ven.
141/B3 Canoinhas, Braz.
57/F1 Canonbie, Sc,UK
159/F3 Canon City, Co,US
148/C2 Cañon del Sumidero Nat'l Park, Mex.
147/M8 Cañon de Río Blanco Nat'l Park, Mex.
149/E4 Caño Negro Nat'l Wild. Ref., CR
157/H3 Canora, Sk,Can
150/F4 Canouan (isl.), StV.
140/C3 Cansanção, Braz.
161/J2 Canso (cape), Can.
74/C1 Cantabria (aut. comm.), Sp.
72/E4 Cantal (plat.), Fr.
140/A1 Cantanhede, Braz.
74/A2 Cantanhede, Port.
139/E2 Cantaura, Ven.
118/H8 Canterbury, Austl.
115/R11 Canterbury (bight), NZ
59/H4 Canterbury, Eng,UK
59/H4 Canterbury Cathedral, Eng,UK
109/D4 Can Tho, Viet.
112/D3 Cantilan, Phil.
74/C4 Cantillana, Sp.
140/B3 Canto do Buriti, Braz.
168/B2 Canton, Ct,US
160/B3 Canton, Il,US
168/C1 Canton, Ma,US
165/E7 Canton, Mi,US
163/F3 Canton, Ms,US
160/F2 Canton, NY,US
168/F6 Canton, Oh,US
159/H3 Canton, Ok,US
157/J5 Canton, SD,US
162/E3 Canton, Tx,US
121/H5 Canton (Abariringa) (atoll), Kiri.
105/G4 Canton (Guangzhou), China
78/C1 Cantù, It.
142/F2 Cañuelas, Arg.
119/B3 Canunda Nat'l Park, Austl.
59/G3 Canvey Island, Eng,UK
156/G2 Canwood, Sk,Can
162/C3 Canyon, Tx,US
158/E3 Canyon de Chelly Nat'l Mon., Az,US
158/E3 Canyonlands Nat'l Park, Ut,US
101/C2 Cao (riv.), China
109/D1 Cao Bang, Viet.
105/E3 Caodu (riv.), China
105/J2 Cao'e (riv.), China
54/A3 Caol, Sc,UK
109/D4 Cao Lanh, Viet.
79/F1 Caorle, It.
103/C4 Cao Xian, China
112/B4 Cap (isl.), Phil.
112/C2 Capalonga, Phil.
138/D3 Capanaparo (riv.), Ven.
137/J4 Capanema, Braz.
80/B1 Capanne (peak), It.
78/D5 Capannori, It.
141/B3 Capão Bonito, Braz.
141/D2 Caparaó Nat'l Park, Braz.
74/A3 Caparica, Port.
138/D3 Caparo (riv.), Ven.
161/H1 Cap-Chat, Qu,Can
161/F2 Cap-de-la-Madeleine, Qu,Can
118/B3 Cape (riv.), Austl.
132/C3 Cape (prov.), SAfr.
116/D5 Cape Arid Nat'l Park, Austl.
119/D4 Cape Barren (isl.), Austl.
161/J2 Cape Breton (highlands), NS,Can
161/J2 Cape Breton (isl.), NS,Can
161/J2 Cape Breton Highlands Nat'l Park, NS,Can
118/B2 Cape Cleveland Nat'l Park, Austl.
129/E5 Cape Coast, Gha.
161/G3 Cape Cod Nat'l Seashore, Ma,US
163/H5 Cape Coral, Fl,US
163/J3 Cape Fear (riv.), NC,US
159/K3 Cape Girardeau, Mo,US
163/K3 Cape Hatteras Nat'l Seashore, NC,US
151/E2 Cape Krusenstern Nat'l Mon., Ak,US
53/Q8 Capel, Eng,UK
140/C3 Capela, Braz.
56/E5 Capel-Curig, Wal,UK
116/D5 Cape Le Grande Nat'l Park, Austl.
141/D1 Capelinha, Braz.
75/K6 Capellades, Sp.
59/H4 Capel le Ferne, Eng,UK
163/J3 Cape Lookout Nat'l Seashore, NC,US
59/H2 Capel Saint Mary, Eng,UK
166/D5 Cape May (co.), NJ,US
166/D6 Cape May Lighthouse, NJ,US
118/B1 Cape Melville Nat'l Park, Austl.
118/C3 Cape Palmerston Nat'l Park, Austl.
116/B2 Cape Range Nat'l Park, Austl.
166/B5 Cape Saint Claire, Md,US
132/B4 Cape Town (cap.), SAfr.
118/B2 Cape Tribulation Nat'l Park, Austl.
118/B2 Cape Upstart Nat'l Park, Austl.
122/K9 Cape Verde
118/A1 Cape York (pen.), Austl.
149/H2 Cap-Haïtien, Haiti
80/A2 Capicciola (pt.), Fr.
137/J4 Capim (riv.), Braz.
140/D2 Capina, Braz.
141/B1 Capinópolis, Braz.
141/B2 Capirara (res.), Braz.
140/C2 Capistrano, Braz.
162/B3 Capitan (mts.), NM,US
140/B2 Capitão de Campos, Braz.
137/J4 Capitão Poco, Braz.

180

Capit – Chalf

158/E3 Capitol Reef Nat'l Park, Ut,US
140/A4 Capivara (mts.), Braz.
137/H8 Capivara (res.), Braz.
141/J6 Capivari (riv.), Braz.
82/C4 Čapljina, Bosn.
78/D1 Caplone, Monte (peak), It.
131/D2 Capoche (riv.), Moz.
80/D3 Capo d'Orlando, It.
80/A3 Capoterra, It.
112/D2 Capotoan (mtn.), Phil.
80/A1 Capraia (isl.), It.
160/D2 Capreol, On,Can
80/D2 Capri, It.
118/C3 Capricorn (cape), Austl.
118/C3 Capricorn (chan.), Austl.
78/C1 Capriolo, It.
131/A3 Caprivi Strip (reg.), Namb.
162/C3 Cap Rock Escarpment (cliffs), Tx,US
162/C3 Caprock, The (cliffs), NM,US
161/G2 Cap-Rouge, Qu,Can
73/G5 Cap Roux, Pointe du (pt.), Fr.
167/L7 Captain (har.), Ct,US
147/K7 Capulhuac de Mirafuentes, Mex.
159/G3 Capulin Volcano Nat'l Mon., NM,US
138/C4 Caquetá (dept.), Col.
138/D5 Caquetá (riv.), Col.
75/N9 Carabanchel (nrbhd.), Sp.
138/D2 Carabobo (state), Ven.
83/G3 Caracal, Rom.
139/E2 Caracas (cap.), Ven.
140/B3 Caracol, Braz.
58/B5 Caradon (hill), Eng,UK
112/D4 Caraga, Phil.
141/H8 Caraguatatuba, Braz.
141/H8 Caraguatatuba (bay), Braz.
142/B3 Carahue, Chile
137/H5 Carajás (mts.), Braz.
112/C2 Caramoan, Phil.
112/D2 Caramoran, Phil.
136/E7 Caranavi, Bol.
141/D2 Carandaí, Braz.
141/D2 Carangola, Braz.
82/F3 Caransebeş, Rom.
80/D2 Carapelle (riv.), It.
141/G8 Carapicuíba, Braz.
117/H5 Carappee Hill (peak), Austl.
161/H2 Caraquet, NB,Can
82/E3 Caraş-Severin (co.), Rom.
149/F3 Caratasca (lag.), Hon.
78/C1 Carate Brianza, It.
141/D1 Caratinga, Braz.
136/E4 Carauari, Braz.
140/C2 Caraúbas, Braz.
74/E3 Caravaca de la Cruz, Sp.
78/C2 Caravaggio, It.
128/A4 Caravela (isl.), GBis.
140/C5 Caravelas, Braz.
135/F2 Carazinho, Braz.
74/A1 Carballino, Sp.
74/A1 Carballo, Sp.
157/J3 Carberry, Mb,Can
123/U17 Carbon (cape), Alg.
166/C2 Carbon (co.), Pa,US
165/C3 Carbon (riv.), Wa,US
80/A3 Carbonara (cape), It.
80/D4 Carbonara, Pizzo (peak), It.
160/B4 Carbondale, Il,US
160/F3 Carbondale, Pa,US
80/A3 Carbonia, It.
55/H8 Carbost, Sc,UK
75/E3 Carcagente, Sp.
112/C3 Carcar, Phil.
142/E2 Carcaraña, Arg.
72/E5 Carcassonne, Fr.
75/P10 Carcavelos, Port.
74/E3 Carche (mtn.), Sp.
138/B4 Carchi (prov.), Ecu.
152/C2 Carcross, Yt,Can
108/F4 Cardamon (hills), India
75/L6 Cardedeu, Sp.
149/F1 Cárdenas, Cuba
147/F4 Cárdenas, Mex.
148/C2 Cárdenas, Mex.
54/C4 Cardenden, Sc,UK
143/K7 Cardiel (lake), Arg.
58/C4 Cardiff (cap.), Wal,UK
58/B2 Cardigan, Wal,UK
75/F2 Cardona, Sp.
141/B2 Cardoso, Braz.
156/E3 Cardston, Ab,Can
141/H7 Careaçu, Braz.
77/G5 Care Alto, Monte (peak), It.
82/F2 Carei, Rom.
72/C2 Carentan, Fr.
82/F4 Carev vrh (peak), Macd.
116/D4 Carey (lake), Austl.
72/B2 Carhaix-Plouguer, Fr.
142/E3 Carhué, Arg.
141/D2 Cariacica, Braz.
139/F2 Cariaco, Ven.
144/B2 Cariamanga, Ecu.
80/E3 Cariati, It.
145/K8 Caribbean (sea), NAm., SAm.
156/C2 Cariboo (mts.), BC,Can
152/E3 Caribou (mts.), Ab,Can
160/B1 Caribou (lake), On,Can
151/L3 Caribou, Yk,Can
156/F5 Caribou (range), Id,US
161/G2 Caribou, Me,US
112/D3 Carigara, Phil.
78/A3 Carignano, It.
140/B4 Carinhanha, Braz.
140/A4 Carinhanha (riv.), Braz.
80/C3 Carini, It.
73/K3 Carinthia (prov.), Aus.
139/F2 Caripito, Ven.
140/C2 Caririaçu, Braz.
140/B2 Cariri Novos (mts.), Braz.
159/G3 Carizzo (cr.), NM, Tx,US
159/G3 Carizzo (creek), NM, Tx,US
75/E3 Carlet, Sp.
161/H2 Carleton (peak), NB,Can
161/H2 Carleton (riv.), NS,Can
161/H1 Carleton, Qu,Can
160/E2 Carleton Place, On,Can
132/D2 Carletonville, SAfr.
158/C2 Carlin, Nv,US
116/C2 Carlindie Abor. Land, Austl.
118/H8 Carlingford, Austl.
60/D1 Carlingford (mtn.), Ire.
56/B3 Carlingford Lough (inlet), Ire.
160/B4 Carlinville, Il,US
161/Q9 Carlisle, On,Can
57/F2 Carlisle, Eng,UK
166/A3 Carlisle, Pa,US
166/A3 Carlisle Barracks, Pa,US
72/D5 Carlit (peak), Fr.
142/E2 Carlos Casares, Arg.
141/D1 Carlos Chagas, Braz.
149/G1 Carlos M. De Cespedes, Cuba
60/D4 Carlow, Ire.
60/D4 Carlow (co.), Ire.
55/H7 Carloway, Sc,UK
164/C4 Carlsbad, Ca,US
159/F4 Carlsbad, NM,US
159/F4 Carlsbad Caverns Nat'l Park, NM,US
57/G6 Carlton, Eng,UK
157/K4 Carlton, Mn,US
161/Q9 Carluke, On,Can
54/C5 Carluke, Sc,UK
157/H3 Carlyle, Sk,Can
159/K3 Carlyle (lake), Il,US
152/C2 Carmacks, Yk,Can
78/A3 Carmagnola, It.
157/J3 Carman, Mb,Can
58/B3 Carmarthen, Wal,UK
58/B3 Carmarthen (bay), Wal,UK
72/E4 Carmaux, Fr.
91/D3 Carmel (mtn.), Isr.
160/C4 Carmel, In,US
56/D5 Carmel Head (pt.), Wal,UK
91/D3 Carmel, Mount (Har Karmel) (mtn.), Isr.
142/F2 Carmelo, Uru.
146/C3 Carmen (isl.), Mex.
160/B4 Carmi, Il,US
165/M9 Carmichael, Ca,US
141/L6 Carmo, Braz.
141/H6 Carmo da Cachoeira, Braz.
141/H7 Carmo de Minas, Braz.
141/C1 Carmo do Paranaíba, Braz.
141/C2 Carmo do Rio Claro, Braz.
78/B4 Carmo, Monte (peak), It.
74/C4 Carmona, Sp.
56/B1 Carnanmore (mtn.), NI,UK
114/A4 Carnarvon, Austl.
132/C3 Carnarvonleegte (dry riv.), SAfr.
118/B4 Carnarvon Nat'l Park, Austl.
75/P10 Carnaxide, Port.
54/B2 Carn Ban (mtn.), Sc,UK
56/C2 Carncastle, NI,UK
157/H3 Carnduff, Sk,Can
54/B2 Carn Easgann Bàna (mtn.), Sc,UK
56/D5 Carnedd Dafydd (mtn.), Wal,UK
56/E5 Carnedd Llewelyn (mtn.), Wal,UK
116/D3 Carnegie (lake), Austl.
168/G7 Carnegie, Pa,US
54/A2 Càrn Eige (mtn.), Sc,UK
113/S Carney (isl.), Ant.
57/F3 Carnforth, Eng,UK
54/C2 Carn Glas-choire (mtn.), Sc,UK
68/C3 Carnières, Fr.
54/C2 Carn Kitty (hill), Sc,UK
56/B2 Carnlough, NI,UK
54/B3 Carn Mairg (mtn.), Sc,UK
54/C2 Carn Mór (mtn.), Sc,UK
54/C1 Carn na Cailliche (hill), Sc,UK
54/B2 Carn na Saobhaidhe (mtn.), Sc,UK
140/C2 Carnoió, Braz.
117/G5 Carnot (cape), Austl.
124/J7 Carnot, CAfr.
74/A1 Carnota, Sp.
168/G6 Carnot-Moon, Pa,US
54/D4 Carnoustie, Sc,UK
60/D5 Carnsore (pt.), Ire.
152/D2 Carnwath (riv.), NW,Can
54/C5 Carnwath, Sc,UK
160/D3 Caro, Mi,US
140/A2 Carolina, Braz.
150/E3 Carolina, PR
121/K5 Caroline (isl.), Kiri.
120/D4 Caroline (isls.), Micr.
166/C6 Caroline (co.), Md,US
165/P16 Carol Stream, Il,US
139/F3 Caroní (riv.), Ven.
138/D2 Carora, Ven.
76/C5 Carouge, Swi.
86/B2 Carpathian (mts.), Eur.
79/F5 Carpegna, Monte (peak), It.
78/D2 Carpenedolo, It.
114/F2 Carpentaria (gulf), Austl.
165/P15 Carpentersville, Il,US
72/F4 Carpentras, Fr.
79/D3 Carpi, It.
164/A2 Carpinteria, Ca,US
165/B3 Carr (inlet), Wa,US
163/G4 Carrabelle, Fl,US
60/A2 Carra, Lough (lake), Ire.
60/A6 Carran (mtn.), Ire.
60/A5 Carrantuohill (mtn.), Ire.
148/C2 Carranza, Mex.
78/D4 Carrara, It.
54/C2 Carrbridge, Sc,UK
56/D6 Carreg Ddu (pt.), Wal,UK
150/F4 Carriacou (isl.), Gren.
54/B6 Carrick (dist.), Sc,UK
56/C2 Carrickfergus, NI,UK
56/C2 Carrickfergus (dist.), NI,UK
56/A2 Carrickmore, NI,UK
53/S10 Carrières-sous-Poissy, Fr.
56/B3 Carrigatuke (mtn.), NI,UK
60/B6 Carrigtohill, Ire.
157/J4 Carrington, ND,US
74/C1 Carrión (riv.), Sp.
154/E4 Carrizo (mts.), Az,US
162/C2 Carrizo (cr.), NM,US
162/D4 Carrizo Springs, Tx,US
158/E4 Carrizo Wash (dry riv.), Az, NM,US
159/F4 Carrizozo, NM,US
166/A5 Carroll (co.), Md,US
168/F6 Carroll (co.), Oh,US
163/G3 Carrollton, Ga,US
160/C4 Carrollton, Ky,US
159/J3 Carrollton, Mo,US
54/A2 Carron (riv.), Sc,UK
54/A2 Carron, Loch (inlet), Sc,UK
157/H2 Carrot (riv.), Sk,Can
157/H2 Carrot River, Sk,Can
56/C2 Carrowdore, NI,UK
119/G6 Carrum Downs, Austl.
56/C2 Carryduff, NI,UK
92/D1 Çarşamba, Turk.
164/B3 Carson, Ca,US
158/C3 Carson (riv.), Nv,US
158/C3 Carson (sink), Nv,US
158/C3 Carson City (cap.), Nv,US
56/D1 Carsphairn, Sc,UK
156/E3 Carstairs, Ab,Can
54/C5 Carstairs Junction, Sc,UK
162/D3 Carswell A.F.B., Tx,US
142/Q9 Cartagena, Chile
138/C2 Cartagena, Col.
75/E4 Cartagena, Sp.
138/C3 Cartago, Col.
149/F4 Cartago, CR
74/C4 Cártama, Sp.
74/A3 Cartaxo, Port.
74/B4 Cartaya, Sp.
118/A1 Carter (peak), Austl.
54/D6 Carter Bar (hill), Eng,UK
167/D2 Carteret, NJ,US
163/G3 Cartersville, Ga,US
59/E3 Carterton, Eng,UK
80/B4 Carthage (ruins), Tun.
159/J3 Carthage, Mo,US
163/F3 Carthage, Ms,US
163/G2 Carthage, Tn,US
162/E3 Carthage, Tx,US
149/G4 Cartí (mtn.), Pan.
114/C2 Cartier Islet (isl.), Austl.
153/L3 Cartwright, Nf,Can
140/D3 Caruaru, Braz.
136/F1 Carúpano, Ven.
159/K3 Caruthersville, Mo,US
168/D2 Carver, Ma,US
68/B2 Carvin, Fr.
74/A3 Carvoeiro (cape), Port.
165/P15 Cary, Il,US
163/J3 Cary, NC,US
123/L14 Casablanca, Mor.
141/F6 Casa Branca, Braz.
158/E4 Casa Grande, Az,US
158/E4 Casa Grande Nat'l Mon., Az,US
80/D2 Casal di Principe, It.
79/E4 Casalecchio di Reno, It.
78/B2 Casale Monferrato, It.
78/D3 Casalmaggiore, It.
78/C2 Casalpusterlengo, It.
128/A3 Casamance (riv.), Sen.
138/C3 Casanare (inten.), Col.
138/D3 Casanare (riv.), Col.
140/B3 Casa Nova, Braz.
81/F3 Casarano, It.
79/F1 Casarsa della Delizia, It.
146/C2 Casas Grandes (ruins), Mex.
146/C2 Cascada de Bassaseachic Nat'l Park, Mex.
156/C5 Cascade (range), Can., US
156/D4 Cascade (res.), Id,US
165/C3 Cascade-Fairwood, Wa,US
133/R15 Cascades (pt.), Reun.
75/P10 Cascais, Port.
161/H1 Cascapédia (riv.), Qu,Can
140/C2 Cascavel, Braz.
78/D5 Cascina-Navacchio, It.
165/B3 Case (inlet), Wa,US
78/A2 Caselle Torinese, It.
79/E5 Casentino (val.), It.
80/D2 Caserta, It.
113/H Casey, Ant.
113/D Casey (bay), Ant.
123/H3 Caseyr (cape), Som.
131/D3 Cashel, Zim.
60/B3 Cashlaundrumlahan (mtn.), Ire.
156/C4 Cashmere, Wa,US
112/C1 Casiguran, Phil.
112/D2 Casiguran, Phil.
142/E2 Casilda, Arg.
149/F1 Casilda (pt.), Cuba
146/D5 Casimiro Castillo, Mex.
77/G4 Casina, Cima la (Piz Murtaröl) (peak), It.
119/E1 Casino, Austl.
164/A2 Casitas (lake), Ca,US
144/B3 Casma, Peru
75/E2 Caspe, Sp.
157/G5 Casper, Wy,US
88/F6 Caspian (sea), Eur., Asia
165/F6 Cass (lake), Mi,US
75/G2 Cassà de la Selva, Sp.
126/D3 Cassai (riv.), Ang.
126/D3 Cassamba, Ang.
80/E3 Cassano allo Ionio, It.
78/C1 Cassano d'Adda, It.
160/D3 Cass City, Mi,US
141/C2 Cássia, Braz.
152/C3 Cassiar (mts.), BC,Can
141/B1 Cassilândia, Braz.
80/C2 Cassino, It.
159/J3 Cassville, Mo,US
164/B1 Castaic (lake), Ca,US
75/E3 Castalla, Sp.
137/J4 Castanhal, Braz.
148/E3 Castañones (pt.), Nic.
78/C2 Casteggio, It.
80/D4 Castelbuono, It.
79/G6 Castelfidardo, It.
79/D5 Castelfiorentino, It.
79/E3 Castelfranco Emilia, It.
79/E1 Castelfranco Veneto, It.
80/C3 Castellammare (gulf), It.
80/D2 Castellammare di Stabia, It.
78/A2 Castellamonte, It.
78/B1 Castellanza, It.
75/G2 Castellar del Vallès, Sp.
75/K7 Castelldefels, Sp.
75/L7 Castell de Montjuic, Sp.
78/C2 Castelleone, It.
79/G1 Castello di Miramare, It.
80/D4 Castello Eurialo (ruins), It.
79/E5 Castello, Monte il (peak), It.
75/E3 Castellón de la Plana, Sp.
91/G8 Castel Nat'l Park, Isr.
72/D5 Castelnaudary, Fr.
72/E5 Castelnau-le-Lez, Fr.
74/B3 Castelo Branco, Port.
74/B2 Castelo Branco (dist.), Port.
140/B2 Castelo do Piauí, Braz.
78/C2 Castel San Giovanni, It.
79/E4 Castel San Pietro Terme, It.
72/D4 Castelsarrasin, Fr.
80/C4 Castelvetrano, It.
79/E4 Castenaso, It.
78/D2 Castiglione delle Stiviere, It.
141/B2 Castilho, Braz.
144/A2 Castilla, Peru
74/C2 Castille and León (aut. comm.), Sp.
74/D3 Castille-La Mancha (aut. comm.), Sp.
142/C4 Castillo (peak), Arg.
148/D3 Castillo de San Felipe, Guat.
163/H4 Castillo de San Marcos Nat'l Mon., Fl,US
143/G2 Castillos, Uru.
59/G1 Castle Acre, Eng,UK
158/B3 Castle A.F.B., Ca,US
60/A2 Castlebar, Ire.
55/H8 Castlebay, Sc,UK
58/D4 Castle Cary, Eng,UK
56/B3 Castlecaulfield, NI,UK
58/D4 Castle Combe, Eng,UK
158/E3 Castle Dale, Ut,US
56/B2 Castledawson, NI,UK
57/G6 Castle Donnington, Eng,UK
56/E2 Castle Douglas, Sc,UK
57/G4 Castleford, Eng,UK
156/D3 Castlegar, BC,Can
118/H8 Castle Hill, Austl.
168/C3 Castle Hill C. G. Sta., RI,US
161/L2 Castle Hill Nat'l Hist. Park, Nf,Can
56/D2 Castle Kennedy, Sc,UK
119/C3 Castlemaine, Austl.
118/G8 Castlereagh, Austl.
56/B1 Castlerock, NI,UK
159/F3 Castle Rock, Co,US
157/L5 Castle Rock (lake), Wi,US
168/G7 Castle Shannon, Pa,US
118/C4 Castle Tower Nat'l Park, Austl.
56/D3 Castletown, IM,UK
60/A6 Castletownshend, Ire.
56/C3 Castlewellan, NI,UK
156/F2 Castor, Ab,Can
124/D6 Castos (riv.), Libr.
72/E5 Castres, Fr.
66/B3 Castricum, Neth.
150/F4 Castries (cap.), StL.
141/B3 Castro, Braz.
142/B4 Castro, Chile
141/B4 Castro Alves, Braz.
74/C4 Castro del Río, Sp.
74/B1 Castro de Rey, Sp.
67/E5 Castrop-Rauxel, Ger.
74/D1 Castro-Urdiales, Sp.
165/K11 Castro Valley, Ca,US
80/E3 Castrovillari, It.
74/C3 Castuera, Sp.
150/C1 Cat (isl.), Bahm.
157/K3 Cat (lake), On,Can
148/E3 Catacamas, Hon.
144/A2 Catacaos, Peru
144/B2 Catacocha, Ecu.
120/B3 Catanduanes (isl.), Phil.
141/L6 Cataguases, Braz.
111/F1 Cataiñgan, Phil.
83/K5 Çatalağzı, Turk.
141/C1 Catalão, Braz.
83/J5 Çatalca, Turk.
158/E4 Catalina, Az,US
75/F2 Catalonia (aut. comm.), Sp.
135/C2 Catamarca, Arg.
144/B1 Catamayo, Ecu.
112/C2 Catanauan, Phil.
131/D3 Catandica, Moz.
112/D2 Catanduanes (isl.), Phil.
141/B2 Catanduva, Braz.
80/D4 Catania, It.
80/D4 Catania (gulf), It.
80/E3 Catanzaro, It.
111/F1 Catarman, Indo.
112/D2 Catarman, Phil.
112/D3 Catarman, Phil.
112/D4 Catarman (pt.), Phil.
75/E3 Catarroja, Sp.
117/G5 Catastrophe (cape), Austl.
138/C2 Catatumbo (riv.), Col., Ven.
112/D4 Catatungan (mtn.), Phil.
163/H3 Catawba (riv.), NC, SC,US
105/E4 Cat Ba (isl.), Viet.
112/D3 Catbalogan, Phil.
105/E4 Cat Ba Nat'l Park, Viet.
143/G2 Catedral (peak), Uru.
112/D4 Cateel, Phil.
148/C2 Catemaco (lake), Mex.
140/D3 Catende, Braz.
53/N8 Caterham, Eng,UK
59/F4 Caterham and Warlingham, Eng,UK
127/C2 Catherine, Mount (Jabal Katrīnah) (mtn.), Egypt
149/G4 Cativá, Pan.
54/C3 Cat Law (mtn.), Sc,UK
160/D4 Catlettsburg, Ky,US
112/D3 Catmon, Phil.
115/K4 Cato (isl.), Austl.
147/J4 Catoche, Cabo (cape), Mex.
140/C2 Catolé do Rocha, Braz.
166/B5 Catonsville, Md,US
73/K5 Catria (peak), It.
79/F6 Catria, Monte (peak), It.
139/F4 Catrimani (riv.), Braz.
54/B6 Catrine, Sc,UK
58/D2 Catshill, Eng,UK
160/F3 Catskill (mts.), NY,US
166/B2 Cattawissa (cr.), Pa,US
69/F5 Cattenom, Fr.
57/G3 Catterick, Eng,UK
79/F5 Cattolica, It.
140/C4 Catu, Braz.
112/D2 Catubig, Phil.
112/C1 Cauayan, Phil.
112/C3 Cauayan, Phil.
138/B4 Cauca (dept.), Col.
138/C2 Cauca (riv.), Col.
140/C3 Caucaia, Braz.
138/C3 Caucasia, Col.
86/G4 Caucasus (mts.), Eur.
75/E3 Caudete, Sp.
68/C3 Caudry, Fr.
131/C2 Cauese (mts.), Moz.
54/D6 Cauldcleuch (mtn.), Sc,UK
142/B2 Cauquenes, Chile
139/E3 Caura (riv.), Ven.
131/D3 Cauresi (riv.), Moz.
72/D4 Caussade, Fr.
149/G1 Cauto (riv.), Cuba
108/F3 Cauvery (riv.), India
80/D4 Cava d'Ispica (ruins), It.
74/B2 Cávado (riv.), Port.
72/F5 Cavaillon, Fr.
157/J3 Cavalier, ND,US
124/D6 Cavalla (riv.), IvC., Libr.
128/D5 Cavalla (Cavally) (riv.), IvC., Libr.
80/A1 Cavallo, Capo al (cape), Fr.
128/C5 Cavally (Cavalla) (riv.), IvC., Libr.
60/C2 Cavan (co.), Ire.
79/F2 Cavarzere, It.
158/E4 Cave Creek, Az,US
137/J3 Caviana, Braz.
112/E7 Cavite (prov.), Phil.
83/F2 Cavnic, Rom.
78/B2 Cavour (can.), It.
112/C3 Cawayan, Phil.
54/C1 Cawdor, Sc,UK
119/B2 Cawndilla (lake), Austl.
57/G4 Cawood, Eng,UK
59/H1 Cawston, Eng,UK
141/J6 Caxambu, Braz.
140/B2 Caxias, Braz.
141/B4 Caxias do Sul, Braz.
148/E2 Caxinas (pt.), Hon.
126/B2 Caxito, Ang.
92/B2 Çay, Turk.
93/N6 Çayağzi (riv.), Turk.
138/B4 Cayambe, Ecu.
138/B4 Cayambe (vol.), Ecu.
163/H3 Cayce, SC,US
83/L5 Çaycuma, Turk.
92/E1 Çayeli, Turk.
137/H3 Cayenne (cap.), FrG.
149/F2 Cayman (isls.), UK
149/G2 Cayman Brac (isl.), Cay.
149/F2 Cayman Islands (dpcy.), UK
161/S10 Cayuga (cr.), NY,US
82/B3 Cazin, Bosn.
148/B1 Cazones (riv.), Mex.
74/D4 Cazorla, Sp.
131/D2 Cazula, Moz.
78/D1 Cazzago San Martino, It.
74/C1 Cea (riv.), Sp.
60/D2 Ceanannus Mór (Kells), Ire.
140/C3 Ceará (state), Braz.
140/D2 Ceará-Mirim, Braz.
149/F5 Cébaco (isl.), Pan.
143/G2 Cebollatí (riv.), Uru.
112/C3 Cebu (isl.), Phil.
112/C3 Cebu City, Phil.
80/C2 Ceccano, It.
166/C4 Cecil (co.), Md,US
133/E2 Cecil Macks (pass), Swaz.
116/D3 Cecil Rhodes (peak), Austl.
78/D6 Cecina, It.
79/D6 Cecina (riv.), It.
80/E3 Cecita (lake), It.
157/H2 Cedar (lake), Mb,Can
160/E2 Cedar (lake), On,Can
165/L11 Cedar (mtn.), Ca,US
157/L5 Cedar (riv.), Ia,US
167/D4 Cedar (cr.), NJ,US
165/C3 Cedar (riv.), Wa,US
118/B1 Cedar Bay Nat'l Park, Austl.
159/G3 Cedar Bluff (res.), Ks,US
158/D3 Cedar Breaks Nat'l Mon., Ut,US
158/D3 Cedar City, Ut,US
162/D3 Cedar Creek (res.), Tx,US
157/K5 Cedar Falls, Ia,US
165/D3 Cedar Falls (dam), Wa,US
167/D2 Cedar Grove, NJ,US
163/H4 Cedar Key, Fl,US
157/L5 Cedar Rapids, Ia,US
163/G3 Cedartown, Ga,US
158/B2 Cedarville, Ca,US
74/A1 Cedeira, Sp.
140/C2 Cedro, Braz.
146/B2 Cedros (isl.), Mex.
74/A1 Cee, Sp.
125/Q7 Ceel Dheere, Som.
125/Q5 Ceerigaabo (Erigabo), Som.
80/D3 Cefalù, It.
56/D5 Cefni (riv.), Wal,UK
57/E6 Cefn-mawr, Wal,UK
74/C2 Cega (riv.), Sp.
82/D2 Cegléd, Hun.
74/E3 Cehegín, Sp.
104/E3 Ceheng Bouyeizu Zizhixian, China
83/F2 Cehu Silvaniei, Rom.
57/E6 Ceiriog (riv.), Wal,UK
92/C1 Çekerek, Turk.
86/F4 Çekerek (riv.), Turk.
71/H2 Čelákovice, Czh.
74/B1 Celanova, Sp.
148/E1 Celarain, Punta (pt.), Mex.
147/E4 Celaya, Mex.
60/D3 Celbridge, Ire.
111/F3 Celebes (sea), Asia
111/E4 Celebes (Sulawesi) (isl.), Indo.
144/B2 Celendín, Peru
144/B2 Celica, Ecu.
92/D2 Çelikhan, Turk.
160/C3 Celina, Oh,US
82/B2 Celje, Slov.
82/C2 Celldömölk, Hun.
72/E2 Celle (riv.), Fr.
67/H3 Celle, Ger.
58/A4 Celtic (sea), Eur.
58/B2 Cemaes Head (pt.), Wal,UK
110/D3 Cemaru (peak), Indo.
74/E3 Cenajo (res.), Sp.
111/H4 Cenderawasih (bay), Indo.
144/B1 Cenepa (riv.), Peru
107/J2 Cengong, China
78/C3 Ceno (riv.), It.
135/C4 Centenario, Arg.
141/B2 Centenario do Sul, Braz.
158/D4 Centennial (wash), Az,US
156/E4 Centennial (mts.), Id,US
157/H4 Center, ND,US
162/E4 Center, Tx,US
167/E2 Centereach, NY,US
165/F7 Center Line, Mi,US
163/G3 Center Point, Al,US
163/G3 Centerville, Tn,US
162/E4 Centerville, Tx,US
146/E2 Centinela, Pichaco del (peak), Mex.
79/E3 Cento, It.
78/C4 Cento Croci, Passo di (pass), It.
142/C4 Central (peak), Arg.
131/B4 Central (dist.), Bots.
140/B3 Central, Braz.
129/E5 Central (reg.), Gha.
91/D3 Central (dist.), Isr.
130/C3 Central (prov.), Kenya
131/D2 Central (reg.), Malw.
112/C1 Central (mts.), Phil.
130/B2 Central (prov.), Ugan.
54/B4 Central (reg.), Sc,UK
131/C2 Central (prov.), Zam.
125/J6 Central African Republic
117/F2 Central Australia Abor. Rsv., Austl.
117/E3 Central Australia (Warburton) Abor. Rsv., Austl.
156/G3 Central Butte, Sk,Can
159/H2 Central City, Ne,US
112/C1 Central, Cordillera (mts.), Phil.
136/C5 Central, Cordillera (range), SAm.
117/F2 Central Desert Abor. Land, Austl.
168/C2 Central Falls, RI,US
160/B4 Centralia, Il,US
156/C4 Centralia, Wa,US
166/A6 Central Intelligence Agency, Va,US
130/C2 Central Island Nat'l Park, Kenya
167/E2 Central Islip, NY,US
131/A4 Central Kalahari Game Rsv., Bots.
95/H3 Central Makrān (range), Pak.
72/E4 Central, Massif (plat.), Fr.
117/G2 Central Mount Stuart (peak), Austl.
117/F2 Central Mount Wedge (peak), Austl.
167/K8 Central Park, New York City, NY,US
137/J7 Central, Planalto (plat.), Braz.
156/C5 Central Point, Or,US
89/L3 Central Siberian (plat.), Rus.
85/N4 Central Ural (mts.), Rus.
72/D3 Centre (reg.), Fr.
123/L14 Centre (reg.), Mor.
166/A2 Centre (co.), Pa,US
123/M13 Centre Nord (reg.), Mor.
123/M14 Centre Sud (reg.), Mor.
163/G3 Centreville, Al,US
104/E3 Cenwanglao (mtn.), China
107/K3 Cenxi, China
72/D4 Céou (riv.), Fr.
82/D3 Čepin, Cro.
111/G4 Ceram (isl.), Indo.
111/G4 Ceram (sea), Indo.
78/B2 Cerano, It.
80/A2 Ceraso (cape), It.
139/E3 Cerbatana (mts.), Ven.
71/F4 Čerchov (peak), Czh.
75/L7 Cerdanyola del Vallès, Sp.
72/D4 Cère (riv.), Fr.
79/E2 Cerea, It.
135/D2 Ceres, Arg.
137/J7 Ceres, Braz.
132/B4 Ceres, SAfr.
138/C2 Cereté, Col.
79/E6 Cerfone (riv.), It.
53/S9 Cergy, Fr.
80/D2 Cerignola, It.
92/C1 Çerkeş, Turk.
83/J5 Çerkezköy, Turk.
92/D2 Çermik, Turk.
71/G5 Černá (peak), Czh.
71/H5 Černá (riv.), Czh.
83/J3 Cernavodă, Rom.
76/D2 Cernay, Fr.
53/R10 Cernay-la-Ville, Fr.
58/D5 Cerne Abbas, Eng,UK
146/C3 Cerralvo (isl.), Mex.
78/D4 Cerreto, Passo del (pass), It.
56/E5 Cerrig-y-Druidion, Wal,UK
81/F2 Cërrik, Alb.
147/E4 Cerritos, Mex.
164/F8 Cerritos, Ca,US
147/F4 Cerro Azul, Mex.
142/C3 Cerro Colorados (res.), Arg.
139/F2 Cerro El Copey Nat'l Park, Ven.
143/G2 Cerro Largo (dept.), Uru.
78/B1 Cerro Maggiore, It.
144/A2 Cerros de Amotape Nat'l Park, Peru
79/E5 Certaldo, It.
78/C2 Certosa di Pavia, It.
78/D5 Certosa di Pisa, It.
80/D2 Cervaro (riv.), It.
80/D2 Cervati (peak), It.
78/D3 Cervellino, Monte (peak), It.
75/F2 Cervera, Sp.
79/F4 Cervia, It.
80/D2 Cervialto (peak), It.
79/G1 Cervignano del Friuli, It.
77/H4 Cervina, Punta (peak), It.
141/H7 Cervo (hills), Braz.
78/B1 Cervo (riv.), It.
74/B1 Cervo, Sp.
78/C1 Cesano Maderno, It.
138/C2 César (riv.), Col.
79/F4 Cesena, It.
79/F4 Cesenatico, It.
79/F1 Cesen, Monte (peak), It.
63/L3 Cēsis, Lat.
71/H5 České Budějovice, Czh.
71/G2 České Středohoří (mts.), Czh.
65/H4 Českomoravská Vysočina (upland), Czh.
71/H2 Český Brod, Czh.
71/H5 Český Krumlov, Czh.
71/F3 Český Les (mts.), Czh.
82/C3 Česma (riv.), Cro.
81/K3 Çeşme, Turk.
149/G1 Céspedes, Cuba
53/T11 Cesson, Fr.
72/C2 Cesson-Sévigné, Fr.
128/C5 Cestos (riv.), Libr.
82/C4 Cetina (riv), Cro.
82/D4 Cetinje, Yugo.
74/D2 Ceurda del Pozo (res.), Sp.
74/C5 Ceuta, Sp.
77/G5 Cevedale, Monte (peak), It.
72/E5 Cévennes (mts.), Fr.
72/E4 Cévennes Nat'l Park, Fr.
91/D1 Ceyhan, Turk.
91/D1 Ceyhan (riv.), Turk.
92/E2 Ceylânpınar, Turk.
108/H4 Ceylon (isl.), SrL.
72/F4 Cèze (riv.), Fr.
72/C5 Chabarrou (peak), Fr.
116/B2 Chabjuwardoo (bay), Austl.
142/E2 Chacabuco, Arg.
144/D5 Chachani (peak), Peru
144/B2 Chachapoyas, Peru
109/C3 Chachoengsao, Thai.
144/B3 Chaclacayo, Peru
158/F3 Chaco (dry riv.), NM,US
162/B3 Chaco (mesa), NM,US
135/D2 Chaco Austral (plain), Arg.
136/G8 Chaco Boreal (plain), Par.
135/D1 Chaco Central (plain), Arg.
135/E2 Chaco Nat'l Park, Arg.
148/D3 Chacujal (ruins), Guat.
125/J4 Chad
124/H5 Chad (lake), Afr.
109/E4 Cha Da (cape), Viet.
131/D2 Chadiza, Zam.
59/E3 Chadlington, Eng,UK
159/G2 Chadron, Ne,US
83/J2 Chadyr-Lunga, Mol.
123/N13 Chafarinas (isls.), Sp.
101/D2 Chagang-do (prov.), NKor.
102/D5 Chagdo Kangri (peak), China
90/G10 Chagos (arch.), BrIn.
168/F5 Chagrin (riv.), Oh,US
150/F5 Chaguanas, Trin.
144/B1 Chaguarpamba, Ecu.
93/G4 Chahār Maḩāll and Bakhtīārī (gov.), Iran
95/H3 Chāh Behār (Bandar Beheshtī), Iran
109/C3 Chainat, Thai.
135/B5 Chaitén, Chile
109/C3 Chaiyaphum, Thai.
131/C3 Chakari, Zim.
130/C4 Chake Chake, Tanz.
108/B1 Chakwāl, Pak.
76/B4 Chalain (lake), Fr.
108/F3 Chālakudi, India
76/B5 Chalamont, Fr.
76/A5 Chalaronne (riv.), Fr.
148/D3 Chalatenango, ESal.
130/C2 Chalbi (des.), Kenya
97/H2 Chalchyn (riv.), Mong.
147/R10 Chalco, Mex.
147/F5 Chalco de Díaz Covarrubias, Mex.
130/C4 Chale (pt.), Kenya
161/H2 Chaleur (bay), NB, Qu,Can
53/M7 Chalfont Saint Giles, Eng,UK

181

Chalf – Chris

53/M7 Chalfont Saint Peter, Eng,UK
59/E3 Chalgrove, Eng,UK
53/U10 Chalifert (can.), Fr.
130/C4 Chalinze, Tanz.
162/C4 Chalk (mts.), Tx,US
147/F1 Chalk Mountain, Tx,US
72/C3 Challans, Fr.
136/E7 Challapata, Bol.
153/T6 Challenger (mtn.), NW,Can
69/D5 Challerange, Fr.
156/E4 Challis, Id,US
59/G4 Challock, Eng,UK
68/D6 Châlons-sur-Marne, Fr.
76/A4 Chalon-sur-Saône, Fr.
93/G2 Chālūs, Iran
71/F4 Cham, Ger.
71/F4 Cham (riv.), Ger.
77/E3 Cham, Swi.
158/F3 Chama (riv.), Co, NM,US
131/D1 Chama, Zam.
110/B2 Chamah (peak), Malay.
95/J2 Chaman, Pak.
108/D1 Chamba, India
106/C2 Chambal (riv.), India
72/F4 Chambaran (plat.), Fr.
161/G2 Chamberlain (lake), Me,US
157/J5 Chamberlain, SD,US
151/K2 Chamberlin (mtn.), Ak,US
160/E4 Chambersburg, Pa,US
72/F4 Chambéry, Fr.
131/C1 Chambeshi, Zam.
131/C1 Chambeshi (riv.), Zam.
131/C2 Chambishi, Zam.
161/P7 Chambly, Qu,Can
53/S9 Chambly, Fr.
53/S10 Chambourcy, Fr.
93/F3 Chamchamāl, Iraq
149/G4 Chame (pt.), Pan.
72/F4 Chamechaude (mtn.), Fr.
135/C3 Chamical, Arg.
76/C6 Chamonix-Mont-Blanc, Fr.
151/L3 Champagne, Yk,Can
68/C6 Champagne (reg.), Fr.
72/F2 Champagne-Ardennes (reg.), Fr.
53/S9 Champagne-sur-Oise, Fr.
76/B4 Champagnole, Fr.
160/B3 Champaign, Il,US
142/D1 Champaqui (peak), Arg.
69/F6 Champigneulles, Fr.
53/T10 Champigny-sur-Marne, Fr.
160/F2 Champlain (lake), Can., US
147/H5 Champotón, Mex.
147/H5 Champotón (riv.), Mex.
68/B6 Champs-sur-Marne, Fr.
108/F3 Chāmrājnagar, India
135/B2 Chañaral, Chile
74/B4 Chança (riv.), Port.
144/B3 Chancay, Peru
144/B3 Chan Chan (ruins), Peru
142/B2 Chanco, Chile
151/J2 Chandalar (riv.), Ak,US
151/J2 Chandalar, East Fork (riv.), Ak,US
106/C2 Chandausi, India
106/C3 Chanderi, India
108/D2 Chandigarh, India
108/D2 Chandigarh (terr.), India
161/H1 Chandler, Qu,Can
151/H2 Chandler (riv.), Ak,US
162/D3 Chandler, Ok,US
144/D3 Chandless (riv.), Braz., Peru
96/D2 Chandmanĭ, Mong.
106/C4 Chandrapur, India
138/A5 Chanduy, Ecu.
103/C5 Chang (lake), China
103/L8 Chang (riv.), China
109/C3 Chang (isl.), Thai.
108/F4 Changanācheri, India
131/D4 Changane (riv.), Moz.
131/D3 Changara, Moz.
101/E2 Changbai (peak), China
101/D2 Changbai (mts.), China, NKor.
101/E2 Changbai Chaoxianzu Zizhixian, China
103/F2 Changchun, China
103/D5 Changdang (lake), China
103/E3 Changdao, China
105/F2 Changde, China
103/D4 Changfeng, China
103/C4 Changge, China
98/A2 Changgi-ap (cape), SKor.
101/B3 Changhai, China
105/J3 Changhua, Tai.
101/D5 Changhŭng, SKor.
105/F5 Changjiang, China
105/G2 Changjiang Zhongxiayou (plain), China
101/D2 Changjin (lake), NKor.
101/D2 Changjin (res.), NKor.
103/D3 Changle, China
103/D3 Changli, China
103/E1 Changling, China
104/E2 Changning, China
103/D2 Changping, China
103/H6 Changping, China
103/D3 Changqing, China
101/C3 Changsan-got (cape), NKor.
105/G2 Changsha, China
101/B3 Changshan (arch.), China
103/E5 Changshu, China
103/L8 Changshu, China
104/E3 Changshun, China
101/D5 Changsŏng, SKor.
103/F2 Changtu, China
149/F4 Changuinola, Pan.
101/E5 Ch'angwŏn, SKor.
96/F4 Changwu, China
103/K8 Changxing, China
103/E3 Changxing (isl.), China
103/B5 Changyang, China
103/D5 Chang (Yangtze) (riv.), China
103/D3 Changyi, China
103/C4 Changyuan, China
103/C3 Changzhi, China
103/D5 Changzhou, China
108/G4 Chankanai, SrL.
130/C2 Chanlers (falls), Kenya
109/E2 Chan May Dong (cape), Viet.
72/B4 Channel (isls.), UK
158/C4 Channel (isls.), Ca,US
118/A4 Channel Country (plain), Austl.
72/B2 Channel Islands, UK
158/B4 Channel Islands Nat'l Park, Ca,US
161/K2 Channel-Port aux Basques, Nf,Can
59/H4 Channel Tunnel, UK, Fr.
74/B1 Chantada, Sp.
53/S10 Chanteloup-les-Vignes, Fr.
109/C3 Chanthaburi, Thai.
68/B5 Chantilly, Fr.
152/G2 Chantrey (inlet), NW,Can
159/J3 Chanute, Ks,US
103/D5 Chao (lake), China
103/D2 Chao (riv.), China
97/H4 Chaobai (riv.), China
109/C3 Chao Phraya (riv.), Thai.
97/J2 Chaor (riv.), China
105/H4 Chaoyang, China
105/H4 Chaozhou, China
140/B4 Chapada Diamantina Nat'l Park, Braz.
140/A4 Chapada dos Veadeiros Nat'l Park, Braz.
140/B1 Chapadinha, Braz.
160/F1 Chapais, Qu,Can
146/E4 Chapala, Mex.
146/E4 Chapala (lake), Mex.
138/C4 Chaparral, Col.
87/J1 Chapayevsk, Rus.
141/A3 Chapecó, Braz.
57/G5 Chapel en le Frith, Eng,UK
57/F2 Chapelfell Top (mtn.), Eng,UK
163/J3 Chapel Hill, NC,US
68/D3 Chapelle-Lez-Herlaimont, Belg.
54/D4 Chapel Ness (pt.), Sc,UK
57/J5 Chapel Saint Leonards, Eng,UK
57/G5 Chapeltown, Eng,UK
165/D2 Chaplain (lake), Wa,US
109/D2 Chap Le, Viet.
160/D2 Chapleau, On,Can
156/G3 Chaplin, Sk,Can
159/G2 Chappell, Ne,US
147/Q10 Chapultepec Park, Mex.
89/M4 Chara (riv.), Rus.
138/B3 Charambirá (pt.), Col.
81/L6 Charandra (riv.), Gre.
135/D2 Charata, Arg.
147/E4 Charcas, Mex.
113/U Charcot (isl.), Ant.
58/D5 Chard, Eng,UK
88/G6 Chardzhou, Trkm.
123/N14 Charef, Oued (riv.), Mor.
72/C4 Charente (riv.), Fr.
53/T10 Charenton-le-Pont, Fr.
124/J5 Chari (riv.), Chad
95/J1 Chārīkār, Afg.
59/G4 Charing, Eng,UK
159/J2 Chariton (riv.), Ia, Mo,US
59/E3 Charlbury, Eng,UK
56/B3 Charlemont, NI,UK
68/D3 Charleroi, Belg.
68/D2 Charleroi à Bruxelles, Canal de (can.), Belg.
116/C3 Charles (peak), Austl.
116/D5 Charles (peak), Austl.
153/J2 Charles (isl.), NW,Can
168/C1 Charles (riv.), Ma,US
160/F4 Charles (cape), Va,US
157/K5 Charles City, Ia,US
168/E6 Charles Mill (dam), Oh,US
168/E6 Charles Mill (res.), Oh,US
160/B4 Charleston, Il,US
159/K3 Charleston, Mo,US
163/F3 Charleston, Ms,US
158/D2 Charleston, Nv,US
163/J3 Charleston, SC,US
160/D4 Charleston (cap.), WV,US
168/C3 Charlestown, RI,US
69/D4 Charleville-Mézières, Fr.
160/C2 Charlevoix, Mi,US
156/B2 Charlotte (lake), BC,Can
160/C3 Charlotte, Mi,US
163/H3 Charlotte, NC,US
150/E3 Charlotte Amalie, USVI
160/E4 Charlottesville, Va,US
161/J2 Charlottetown (cap.), PE,Can
153/H3 Charlton (isl.), NW,Can
168/C1 Charlton, Ma,US
58/D3 Charlton Kings, Eng,UK
53/N8 Charlwood, Eng,UK
76/B2 Charmes (res.), Fr.
72/F3 Charolais (mts.), Fr.
53/R9 Chars, Fr.
102/D2 Charsk, Kaz.
118/B3 Charters Towers, Austl.
72/D2 Chartres, Fr.
102/C3 Charyn (riv.), Kaz.
102/D1 Charysh (riv.), Rus.
77/G4 Chaschauna, Piz (peak), Swi.
142/F2 Chascomús, Arg.
156/D3 Chase, BC,Can
72/F4 Chassezac (riv.), Fr.
72/C3 Chassiron, Pointe de (pt.), Fr.
72/C3 Châteaubriant, Fr.
76/D5 Château-d'Oex, Swi.
72/C3 Château-d'Olonne, Fr.
72/D2 Châteaudun, Fr.
161/N7 Châteauguay, Qu,Can
161/N7 Châteauguay (co.), Qu,Can
72/F5 Châteaurenard-Provence, Fr.
72/D3 Château-Renault, Fr.
72/D3 Châteauroux, Fr.
68/C5 Château-Thierry, Fr.
68/D3 Châtelet, Belg.
72/D3 Châtellerault, Fr.
53/S10 Châtenay-Malabry, Fr.
76/D1 Châtenois, Fr.
159/J2 Chatfield, Mn,US
161/H2 Chatham, NB,Can
160/D3 Chatham, On,Can
143/J7 Chatham (isl.), Chile
59/G4 Chatham, Eng,UK
166/D2 Chatham, NJ,US
53/S10 Châtillon, Fr.
72/F3 Châtillon-sur-Seine, Fr.
53/S10 Chatou, Fr.
106/D4 Chatrapur, India
118/H8 Chatswood, Austl.
164/E7 Chatsworth, Ca,US
164/B2 Chatsworth (res.), Ca,US
163/G3 Chatsworth, Ga,US
131/C3 Chatsworth, Zim.
163/G4 Chattahoochee, Fl,US
163/G4 Chattahoochee (riv.), Fl, Ga,US
163/G3 Chattanooga, Tn,US
59/G2 Chatteris, Eng,UK
72/C2 Chausey (isls.), Fr.
69/E2 Chaudfontaine, Belg.
161/G2 Chaudière (riv.), Qu,Can
109/D4 Chau Doc, Viet.
104/B4 Chauk, Burma
104/C3 Chaukan (pass), India
68/B4 Chaulnes, Fr.
53/U10 Chaumes-en-Brie, Fr.
76/B1 Chaumont, Fr.
68/A5 Chaumont-en-Vexin, Fr.
68/D4 Chaumont-Porcien, Fr.
89/T3 Chaunskaya (bay), Rus.
68/C4 Chauny, Fr.
160/E3 Chautauqua (lake), NY,US
72/D3 Chauvigny, Fr.
108/H4 Chavakachcheri, SrL.
130/B2 Chavakali, Kenya
108/F3 Chavakkad, India
140/B1 Chaval, Braz.
74/B2 Chaves, Port.
144/B3 Chavín de Huantar (ruins), Peru
109/D1 Chay (riv.), Viet.
136/E7 Chayana (riv.), Bol.
85/M4 Chaykovskiy, Rus.
57/G6 Cheadle, Eng,UK
163/G3 Cheaha (peak), Al,US
71/F2 Cheb, Czh.
85/K4 Cheboksary, Rus.
85/K4 Cheboksary (res.), Rus.
160/C2 Cheboygan, Mi,US
123/M13 Chechaouene, Mor.
87/H4 Chechen' (isl.), Rus.
87/H4 Chechen-Ingush Aut. Rep., Rus.
124/D3 Chech, 'Erg (des.), Afr.
101/E4 Chech'ŏn, SKor.
159/J4 Checotah, Ok,US
161/J2 Chedabucto (bay), NS,Can
58/D4 Cheddar, Eng,UK
104/B5 Cheduba (isl.), Burma
104/B5 Cheduba (str.), Burma
161/S10 Cheektowaga, NY,US
160/D1 Cheepash (riv.), On,Can
160/D1 Cheepay (riv.), On,Can
97/L1 Chegdomyn, Rus.
131/C3 Chegutu, Zim.
156/C4 Chehalis, Wa,US
73/G5 Cheiron, Cime du (peak), Fr.
97/K5 Cheju, SKor.
97/K5 Cheju (isl.), SKor.
97/K5 Cheju (str.), SKor.
156/C4 Chelan, Wa,US
156/C4 Chelan (lake), Wa,US
57/F5 Chelford, Eng,UK
123/V17 Chelghoum El Aïd, Alg.
87/L3 Chelkar, Kaz.
53/T10 Chelles, Fr.
65/M3 Chełm, Pol.
65/M3 Chełm (prov.), Pol.
59/G3 Chelmer (riv.), Eng,UK
65/K2 Chełmno, Pol.
59/G3 Chelmsford, Eng,UK
65/K2 Chełmża, Pol.
119/G6 Chelsea, Austl.
53/N7 Chelsea, Eng,UK
168/C1 Chelsea, Ma,US
53/N7 Chelsea & Kensington (bor.), Eng,UK
161/Q8 Cheltenham, On,Can
58/D3 Cheltenham, Eng,UK
85/P5 Chelyabinsk, Rus.
85/P5 Chelyabinsk Obl., Rus.
89/L2 Chelyuskina (cape), Rus.
131/D3 Chemba, Moz.
131/C1 Chembe, Zam.
64/G3 Chemnitz, Ger.
105/F3 Chen (riv.), China
108/A2 Chenāb (riv.), India, Pak.
124/E2 Chenachane (well), Alg.
148/C2 Chenalhó, Mex.
97/H2 Chen Baraq Qi, China
156/D4 Cheney, Wa,US
104/D3 Cheng (lake), China
108/F4 Chengannūr, India
103/C3 Cheng'anpu, China
105/F3 Chengbu Miaozu Zizhixian, China
103/D2 Chengde, China
104/E2 Chengdu, China
105/F2 Chengkou, China
105/F5 Chengmai, China
101/B4 Chengshan (cape), China
103/E3 Chengshan Jiao (cape), China
103/C4 Chengwu, China
53/T10 Chennevières-sur-Marne, Fr.
76/A3 Chenôve, Fr.
107/K2 Chenxi, China
105/G3 Chenzhou, China
83/G5 Chepelare, Bul.
144/B2 Chepén, Peru
121/V12 Chépénéhé, NCal.
135/C3 Chepes, Arg.
142/C2 Chépica, Chile
149/G4 Chepigana, Pan.
130/B2 Cheploske, Kenya
58/D3 Chepstow, Wal,UK
85/M4 Cheptsa (riv.), Rus.
72/D3 Cher (riv.), Fr.
163/J3 Cheraw, SC,US
72/C2 Cherbourg, Fr.
123/S15 Cherchell, Alg.
96/E1 Cheremkhovo, Rus.
84/H4 Cherepovets, Rus.
123/V17 Cherf (riv.), Alg.
123/S16 Chergui (lake), Alg.
123/V18 Cheria, Alg.
86/E2 Cherkassy, Ukr.
86/D2 Cherkassy Obl., Ukr.
87/G3 Cherkessk, Rus.
118/E6 Chermside, Austl.
85/M2 Chernaya (riv.), Rus.
86/D2 Chernigov, Ukr.
86/D2 Chernigov Obl., Ukr.
83/H4 Cherni Lom (riv.), Bul.
83/F4 Cherni Vrŭkh (peak), Bul.
86/C2 Chernovtsy, Ukr.
86/C2 Chernovtsy Obl., Ukr.
85/N4 Chernushka, Rus.
96/H1 Chernyshevsk, Rus.
159/H3 Cherokee, Ok,US
162/E2 Cherokees (lake), Ok,US
107/F2 Cherrapunjee, India
158/D3 Cherry Creek, Nv,US
166/C4 Cherry Hill, NJ,US
89/Q3 Cherskiy (range), Rus.
53/M7 Chertsey, Eng,UK
83/G4 Cherven Bryag, Bul.
86/C2 Chervonograd, Ukr.
59/E3 Cherwell (riv.), Eng,UK
160/C3 Chesaning, Mi,US
160/E4 Chesapeake (bay), Md, Va,US
166/C5 Chesapeake & Delaware (can.), De, Md,US
166/B6 Chesapeake Bay Maritime Museum, Md,US
59/F3 Chesham, Eng,UK
57/F5 Cheshire (co.), Eng,UK
57/F5 Cheshire (plain), Eng,UK
85/K2 Cheshskaya (bay), Rus.
53/N6 Cheshunt, Eng,UK
57/F5 Chester, Eng,UK
158/B2 Chester, Ca,US
166/B5 Chester (riv.), De, Md,US
166/B5 Chester (riv.), Md, De,US
156/F3 Chester, Mt,US
166/C4 Chester, Pa,US
166/C4 Chester (co.), Pa,US
166/C4 Chester (cr.), Pa,US
163/H3 Chester, SC,US
152/G2 Chesterfield (inlet), NW,Can
120/E7 Chesterfield (isls.), NCal.
57/G5 Chesterfield, Eng,UK
133/H7 Chesterfield, Nosy (isl.), Madg.
57/G2 Chester-le-Street, Eng,UK
165/D3 Chester Morse (lake), Wa,US
118/B3 Chesterton (range), Austl.
161/G2 Chesuncook (lake), Me,US
148/D2 Chetumal (bay), Belz., Mex.
147/H5 Chetumal, Mex.
156/C2 Chetwynd, BC,Can
149/H2 Cheval Blanc, Pointe du (pt.), Haiti
76/B3 Chevigny-Saint-Sauveur, Fr.
53/T10 Chevilly-Larue, Fr.
54/D6 Cheviot (hills), Eng, Sc,UK
53/S10 Chevreuse, Fr.
53/T10 Chevry-Cossigny, Fr.
58/D4 Chew (riv.), Eng,UK
156/D3 Chewelah, Wa,US
131/C2 Chewore Game Rsv., Zim.
58/D4 Chew Valley (lake), Eng,UK
159/H4 Cheyenne, Ok,US
157/H4 Cheyenne (riv.), SD, Wy,US
157/G5 Cheyenne (cap.), Wy,US
159/F2 Cheyenne, Dry Fork (riv.), Wy,US
159/G3 Cheyenne Wells, Co,US
106/C3 Chhatarpur, India
106/C3 Chhindwāra, India
109/D3 Chhlong, Camb.
103/D4 Chi (riv.), China
109/C2 Chi (riv.), Thai.
138/C3 Chía, Col.
101/E4 Ch'iak-san Nat'l Park, SKor.
79/E1 Chiampo, It.
109/B2 Chiang Dao (caves), Thai.
104/C5 Chiang Dao Caves, Thai.
109/B2 Chiang Mai, Thai.
109/B2 Chiang Rai, Thai.
80/C1 Chiani (riv.), It.
79/E6 Chianti (mts.), It.
79/E6 Chianti (reg.), It.
147/G5 Chiapas (state), Mex.
78/C4 Chiappa, Punta (pt.), It.
79/G5 Chiaravalle, It.
78/C1 Chiari, It.
77/F6 Chiasso, Swi.
87/G4 Chiatura, Geo.
78/C4 Chiavari, It.
77/F5 Chiavenna, It.
131/C2 Chiawa, Zam.
105/J4 Chiayi, Tai.
99/G3 Chiba, Japan
99/G3 Chiba (pref.), Japan
131/D4 Chibabava, Moz.
131/C4 Chibi, Zim.
160/F1 Chibougamau, Qu,Can
160/F1 Chibougamau (lake), Qu,Can
160/F1 Chibougamau (riv.), Qu,Can
151/D3 Chibukak (pt.), Ak,US
131/D5 Chibuto, Moz.
131/C2 Chibwe, Zam.
165/Q16 Chicago, Il,US
165/Q16 Chicago Heights, Il,US
165/Q16 Chicago, North Branch (riv.), Il,US
165/Q16 Chicago Ridge, Il,US
165/Q16 Chicago Sanitary & Ship (can.), Il,US
144/B2 Chicama, Peru
131/D3 Chicamba Real (dam), Moz.
151/L4 Chichagof (isl.), Ak,US
108/B2 Chīchāwatni, Pak.
103/C2 Chicheng, China
147/H4 Chichén Itzá (ruins), Mex.
116/C2 Chichester (range), Austl.
59/F5 Chichester, Eng,UK
116/C2 Chichester-Millstream Nat'l Park, Austl.
99/F3 Chichibu, Japan
99/F3 Chichibu-Tama Nat'l Park, Japan
148/D3 Chichicastenango, Guat.
148/E3 Chichigalpa, Nic.
120/D2 Chichishima (isls.), Japan
131/D4 Chichocane, Moz.
163/G3 Chickamauga (lake), Tn,US
159/H4 Chickasha, Ok,US
58/D5 Chickerell, Eng,UK
166/B3 Chickies (cr.), Pa,US
74/B4 Chiclana de la Frontera, Sp.
144/B2 Chiclayo, Peru
142/C4 Chico (riv.), Arg.
142/D5 Chico (riv.), Arg.
112/C1 Chico (riv.), Phil.
158/B3 Chico, Ca,US
131/D5 Chicomo, Moz.
146/E4 Chicomostoc (ruins), Mex.
168/B1 Chicopee, Ma,US
126/D4 Chicote, Ang.
161/G1 Chicoutimi, Qu,Can
131/C4 Chicualacuala, Moz.
108/G3 Chidambaram, India
53/P8 Chiddingstone, Eng,UK
131/D5 Chidenguele, Moz.
153/K2 Chidley (cape), Nf,Can
163/H4 Chiefland, Fl,US
109/D1 Chiem Hoa, Viet.
71/F7 Chiemsee (lake), Ger.
80/C1 Chienti (riv.), It.
109/B4 Chieo Lan (res.), Thai.
78/A2 Chieri, It.
69/E5 Chiers (riv.), Fr.
78/D2 Chiese (riv.), It.
80/D1 Chieti, It.
59/E4 Chieveley, Eng,UK
97/H3 Chifeng, China
140/B5 Chifre (mts.), Braz.
99/F3 Chigasaki, Japan
151/G4 Chiginagak (mtn.), Ak,US
147/L7 Chignahuapan, Mex.
161/H2 Chignecto (bay), NB,Can
131/D4 Chigubo, Moz.
53/P7 Chigwell, Eng,UK
99/L10 Chihayaakasaka, Japan
103/D3 Chihli (Bo Hai) (gulf), China
159/H3 Chikaskia (riv.), Ks,US
106/C5 Chikballāpur, India
106/C3 Chikhli, India
106/C5 Chikmagalūr, India
96/G1 Chikoy (riv.), Rus.
98/B4 Chikugo (riv.), Japan
99/F2 Chikuma (riv.), Japan
99/H8 Chikura, Japan
131/D1 Chikwa, Zam.
131/D3 Chikwawa, Malw.
105/J3 Chilaichu (mtn.), Tai.
106/D4 Chilakalūrupet, India
131/C2 Chilanga, Zam.
148/B2 Chilapa, Mex.
106/C6 Chilaw, SrL.
101/E2 Chilbo-san (mtn.), NKor.
147/M7 Chilchotla, Mex.
156/C3 Chilcotin (riv.), BC,Can
163/G3 Childersburg, Al,US
162/C3 Childress, Tx,US
134/B6 Chile
135/C2 Chilecito, Arg.
131/C2 Chilembwe, Zam.
101/D4 Ch'ilgap-san Nat'l Park, SKor.
131/B2 Chililabombwe, Zam.
106/E4 Chilka (lake), India
156/C3 Chilko (lake), BC,Can
151/L4 Chilkoot (pass), BC,Can, Ak,US
142/B3 Chillán, Chile
144/B1 Chillanes, Ecu.
117/F2 Chilla Well Abor. Land, Austl.
160/B3 Chillicothe, Il,US
159/J3 Chillicothe, Mo,US
160/D4 Chillicothe, Oh,US
166/B2 Chillisquaque (cr.), Pa,US
156/C3 Chilliwack, BC,Can
76/C5 Chillon, Swi.
53/S10 Chilly-Mazarin, Fr.
142/B4 Chiloé (isl.), Chile
142/B4 Chiloé Nat'l Park, Chile
156/C5 Chiloquin, Or,US
147/F5 Chilpancingo, Mex.
59/F3 Chiltern (hills), Eng,UK
130/B5 Chilumba, Malw.
131/D2 Chilwa (lake), Malw.
131/D1 Chimaliro (hill), Malw.
148/D3 Chimaltenango, Guat.
131/D3 Chimanimani, Zim.
131/D3 Chimanimani Nat'l Park, Zim.
139/F3 Chimantá-Tepuí (peak), Ven.
68/D3 Chimay, Belg.
88/F5 Chimbay, Uzb.
138/B5 Chimborazo (prov.), Ecu.
138/B5 Chimborazo (vol.), Ecu.
144/B3 Chimbote, Peru
138/C2 Chimichaqua, Col.
102/A3 Chimkent, Kaz.
131/D3 Chimoio, Moz.
131/D3 Chimoio (plat.), Moz.
104/B4 Chin (hills), Burma
104/B4 Chin (state), Burma
101/D5 Chin (isl.), SKor.
90/J6 China
147/F3 China, Mex.
131/B3 Chinamba (hills), Bots.
148/E3 Chinandega, Nic.
162/B4 Chinati (mts.), Tx,US
144/B4 Chincha Alta, Peru
152/E3 Chinchaga (riv.), Ab,Can
138/C3 Chinchiná, Col.
148/E2 Chinchorro, Banco (reef), Mex.
160/F4 Chincoteague, Va,US
126/G4 Chinde, Moz.
96/D4 Chindu, China
104/B4 Chindwin (riv.), Burma
104/E4 Chi Ne, Viet.
138/C3 Chingaza Nat'l Park, Col.
53/P7 Chingford, Eng,UK
106/C5 Chingleput, India
131/B2 Chingola, Zam.
128/B1 Chinguetti, Dhar de (hills), Mrta.
101/E5 Chinhae, SKor.
131/C3 Chinhoyi, Zim.
131/C3 Chinhoyi Caves, Zim.
151/H4 Chiniak (cape), Ak,US
108/B2 Chiniot, Pak.
109/D3 Chinit (riv.), Camb.
101/E5 Chinju, SKor.
125/K6 Chinko (riv.), CAfr.
158/E3 Chinle (dry riv.), Az, Ut,US
108/F3 Chinnalappatti, India
108/F4 Chinnamanūr, India
59/F3 Chinnor, Eng,UK
99/F3 Chino, Japan
164/C2 Chino, Ca,US
164/G8 Chino (hills), Ca,US
156/F3 Chinook, Mt,US
130/B5 Chinsali, Zam.
131/D1 Chintheche, Malw.
138/C2 Chinú, Col.
130/C5 Chinunje, Tanz.
131/D2 Chipata, Zam.
103/D3 Chiping, China
131/D4 Chipinge, Zim.
74/B4 Chipiona, Sp.
163/G4 Chipley, Fl,US
106/B4 Chiplūn, India
130/C4 Chipogolo, Tanz.
131/D2 Chipoka, Malw.
163/G4 Chipola (riv.), Fl,US
131/D2 Chiponde, Malw.
58/D4 Chippenham, Eng,UK
157/K4 Chippewa (riv.), Mn,US
168/F6 Chippewa (cr.), Oh,US
160/B2 Chippewa (riv.), Wi,US
160/B2 Chippewa Falls, Wi,US
168/F5 Chippewa Lake (Chippewa-on-the-Lake), Oh,US
59/E2 Chipping Campden, Eng,UK
59/E3 Chipping Norton, Eng,UK
53/P6 Chipping Ongar, Eng,UK
58/D3 Chipping Sodbury, Eng,UK
53/N8 Chipstead, Eng,UK
161/H2 Chiputneticook (lakes), NB,Can, Me,US
148/D3 Chiquimula, Guat.
148/D3 Chiquimulilla, Guat.
138/C3 Chiquinquirá, Col.
134/C6 Chiquita, Mar (lake), Arg.
134/A3 Chira (riv.), Peru
147/C1 Chiracahua Nat'l Mon., Az,US
131/D2 Chiradzulu, Malw.
106/D4 Chīrāla, India
102/A3 Chirchik, Uzb.
131/D3 Chire (riv.), Moz.
131/C4 Chiredzi, Zim.
124/H3 Chirfa, Niger
158/E4 Chiricahua Nat'l Mon., Az,US
138/C2 Chiriguaná, Col.
151/G4 Chirikof (isl.), Ak,US
149/E4 Chiripa (mtn.), Nic.
100/E1 Chirip Gora (mtn.), Rus.
149/F4 Chiriquí (gulf), Pan.
149/F4 Chiriquí (lag.), Pan.
101/D5 Chiri-san (mtn.), SKor.
101/D5 Chiri-san Nat'l Park, SKor.
57/E6 Chirk, Eng,UK
54/D5 Chirnside, Sc,UK
131/D3 Chiromo, Malw.
83/G4 Chirpan, Bul.
149/F4 Chirripó Grande (mtn.), CR
149/F4 Chirripó Nat'l Park, CR
131/C3 Chirundu, Zim.
99/M10 Chiryu, Japan
131/C2 Chisamba, Zam.
131/B2 Chisasa, Zam.
153/J3 Chisasibi (Fort-George), Qu,Can
59/E3 Chiseldon, Eng,UK
130/B5 Chisenga, Malw.
160/A2 Chisholm, Mn,US
95/K3 Chishtiān Mandi, Pak.
104/E3 Chishui (riv.), China
125/P8 Chisimayu, Som.
130/A5 Chisimba (falls), Zam.
82/E2 Chişineu Criş, Rom.
131/C2 Chisomo, Zam.
85/L5 Chistopol', Rus.
53/M6 Chiswell Green, Eng,UK
53/N7 Chiswick, Eng,UK
99/M10 Chita, Japan
99/M10 Chita (bay), Japan
99/M10 Chita (pen.), Japan
96/G1 Chita, Rus.
126/B4 Chitado, Ang.
130/B5 Chitipa, Malw.
131/D4 Chitobiço, Moz.
131/B3 Chitongo, Zam.
106/B3 Chitorgarh, India
100/B2 Chitose, Japan
106/C5 Chitradurga, India
106/D2 Chitrakut, India
149/F5 Chitré, Pan.
107/F3 Chittagong, Bang.
106/C5 Chittoor, India
108/F3 Chittūr, India
126/D4 Chiume, Ang.
131/C2 Chiundaponde, Zam.
78/A1 Chiusella (riv.), It.
138/D2 Chivacoa, Ven.
78/A2 Chivasso, It.
131/C3 Chivhu, Zim.
142/E2 Chivilcoy, Arg.
130/B5 Chiwanda, Tanz.
148/D3 Chixoy (riv.), Guat., Mex.
131/B3 Chizarira (hills), Zim.
131/B3 Chizarira Nat'l Park, Zim.
131/B2 Chizela, Zam.
123/R15 Chlef, Alg.
123/R15 Chlef (riv.), Alg.
123/R15 Chlef (wilaya), Alg.
71/H5 Chlum (peak), Czh.
54/B3 Chno Dearg (mtn.), Sc,UK
104/C2 Cho (pass), China
101/C3 Ch'o (isl.), NKor.
109/D3 Choam Khsant, Camb.
142/C1 Choapa (riv.), Chile
131/B3 Chobe (dist.), Bots.
131/B3 Chobe (riv.), Bots., Namb.
131/B3 Chobe Nat'l Park, Bots.
65/K4 Choč (peak), Slvk.
65/J4 Choceň, Czh.
101/D4 Choch'iwŏn, SKor.
65/H3 Chocianów, Pol.
138/B3 Chocó (dept.), Col.
158/D4 Chocolate (mts.), Ca,US
144/B2 Chocope, Peru
71/F2 Chodov, Czh.
65/J2 Chodzież, Pol.
99/F3 Chōfu, Japan
99/H7 Chōfu, Japan
120/E5 Choiseul (isl.), Sol.
53/T10 Choisy-le-Roi, Fr.
65/H2 Chojna, Pol.
65/J2 Chojnice, Pol.
65/H3 Chojnów, Pol.
100/B4 Chokai-san (mtn.), Japan
162/D4 Choke Canyon (res.), Tx,US
131/D5 Chokwe, Moz.
96/D5 Chola (mts.), China
72/C3 Cholet, Fr.
101/D5 Chŏlla-Bukto (prov.), SKor.
101/D5 Chŏlla-Namdo (prov.), SKor.
59/E3 Cholsey, Eng,UK
147/L7 Cholula de Rivadabia, Mex.
148/E3 Choluteca, Hon.
148/E3 Choluteca (riv.), Hon., Nic.
131/B3 Choma, Zam.
101/E4 Chŏmch'on, SKor.
106/E2 Chomo Lhāri (mtn.), Bhu.
71/G2 Chomutov, Czh.
71/G2 Chomutovka (riv.), Czh.
99/J7 Chōnan, Japan
101/D4 Ch'ŏnan, SKor.
109/C3 Chon Buri, Thai.
142/B4 Chonchi, Chile
138/A5 Chone, Ecu.
101/D2 Ch'ongch'ŏn (riv.), NKor.
101/E2 Ch'ŏngjin, NKor.
101/E2 Ch'ŏngjin-Si, NKor.
101/E2 Ch'ŏngjin-Si (prov.), NKor.
101/D4 Ch'ŏngju, SKor.
109/C3 Chong Kal, Camb.
103/C2 Chongli, China
103/L8 Chongming (isl.), China
101/G6 Chongmyo Shrine, SKor.
131/B3 Chongo, Zam.
144/B2 Chongoyape, Peru
104/E2 Chongqing, China
105/H3 Chongren, China
101/E4 Ch'ŏngsong, SKor.
131/C2 Chongwe, Zam.
103/C5 Chongyang, China
107/K2 Chongyi, China
105/E4 Chongzuo, China
101/D5 Chŏnju, SKor.
101/G6 Ch'ŏnmasan (mtn.), SKor.
142/A5 Chonos (arch.), Chile
135/A6 Chonos (isls.), Chile
109/D4 Chon Thanh, Viet.
166/C6 Choptank (riv.), Md,US
149/F4 Chorcha (mtn.), Pan.
57/F4 Chorley, Eng,UK
53/M7 Chorleywood, Eng,UK
86/C2 Chortkov, Ukr.
101/D3 Ch'ŏrwŏn, SKor.
65/K3 Chorzów, Pol.
99/G3 Chōshi, Japan
105/J4 Choshui (riv.), Tai.
65/H2 Choszczno, Pol.
144/B2 Chota, Peru
156/E4 Choteau, Mt,US
71/H3 Chotýšanka (riv.), Czh.
132/A2 Chowagasberg (peak), Namb.
163/J2 Chowan (riv.), NC,US
96/G2 Choybalsan, Mong.
115/R11 Christchurch, NZ
59/E5 Christchurch, Eng,UK
59/E5 Christchurch (bay), Eng,UK
151/L4 Christian (sound), Ak,US
149/G2 Christiana, Jam.
132/D2 Christiana, SAfr.
160/D4 Christiansburg, Va,US
166/C4 Christina (riv.), De,US

182

Chris – Coon

156/F2 Christine (riv.), Ab,Can
90/K11 Christmas (isl.), Austl.
121/K4 Christmas (Kiritimati) (atoll), Kiri.
65/H4 Chrudim, Czh.
54/B5 Chryston, Sc,UK
65/K3 Chrzanów, Pol.
105/H2 Chu (riv.), China
102/B3 Chu (riv.), Kaz.
109/D2 Chu (riv.), Viet.
103/E4 Chuanchang (riv.), China
103/E5 Chuansha, China
156/E5 Chubbuck, Id,US
100/A4 Chūbu (dist.), Japan
99/F2 Chūbu (prov.), Japan
142/C4 Chubut (prov.), Arg.
142/D4 Chubut (riv.), Arg.
149/G4 Chucanti (mtn.), Pan.
98/C3 Chūgoku (mts.), Japan
98/C3 Chūgoku (prov.), Japan
108/B2 Chūhar Kāna, Pak.
110/B3 Chukai, Malay.
97/M1 Chukchagirskoye (lake), Rus.
89/U3 Chukchi (pen.), Rus.
89/S3 Chukchi Aut. Okr., Rus.
151/D3 Chukotskiy, Mys (pt.), Rus.
164/C5 Chula Vista, Ca,US
144/A2 Chulucanas, Peru
88/J4 Chulym (riv.), Rus.
102/E1 Chulyshman (riv.), Rus.
83/G4 Chumerna (peak), Bul.
109/B4 Chumphon, Thai.
88/K4 Chuna (riv.), Rus.
101/D4 Ch'unch'ŏn, SKor.
101/D4 Ch'ungch'ong-Bukto (prov.), SKor.
101/D4 Ch'ungch'ŏng-Namdo (prov.), SKor.
101/D4 Ch'ungju, SKor.
101/D4 Ch'ungju-ho (lake), SKor.
101/C2 Ch'ungman (riv.), NKor.
101/E5 Ch'ungmu, SKor.
101/G6 Chungnang, SKor.
130/A5 Chungu, Zam.
108/B2 Chūniān, Pak.
108/G4 Chunnakam, SrL.
89/L3 Chunya (riv.), Rus.
130/B5 Chunya, Tanz.
135/C1 Chuquicamata, Chile
77/F4 Chur, Swi.
104/B3 Churachandpur, India
57/F4 Church, Eng,UK
152/D3 Churchill (peak), BC,Can
152/G3 Churchill, Mb,Can
152/G3 Churchill (cape), Mb,Can
152/G3 Churchill (riv.), Mb, Sk,Can
153/K3 Churchill (riv.), Nf,Can
156/F1 Churchill (lake), Sk,Can
152/G3 Churchill (riv.), Mb, Sk,Can
119/G5 Churchill Nat'l Park, Austl.
58/D1 Church Stretton, Eng,UK
57/G6 Churnet (riv.), Eng,UK
106/B2 Churu, India
138/D2 Churuguara, Ven.
158/E3 Chuska (mts.), Az, NM,US
85/N4 Chusovaya (riv.), Rus.
85/N4 Chusovoy, Rus.
85/K5 Chuvash Aut. Rep., Rus.
101/E4 Chuwang-san Nat'l Park, SKor.
104/D3 Chuxiong, China
96/B1 Chuya (riv.), Rus.
109/E3 Chu Yang Sin (peak), Viet.
105/H1 Chuzhou, China
99/M9 Chūzu, Japan
110/C5 Ciamis, Indo.
80/C2 Ciampino, It.
110/C5 Cianjur, Indo.
165/Q16 Cicero, Il,US
140/C3 Cícero Dantas, Braz.
80/C2 Cicero Nat'l Park, It.
92/C1 Cide, Turk.
65/L2 Ciechanów, Pol.
65/K2 Ciechanów (prov.), Pol.
65/K2 Ciechocinek, Pol.
149/G1 Ciego de Ávila, Cuba
138/C2 Ciénaga, Col.
138/C2 Ciénaga de Oro, Col.
149/F1 Cienfuegos, Cuba
65/H3 Cieplice Śląskie Zdrój, Pol.
65/K4 Cieszyn, Pol.
74/E3 Cieza, Sp.
92/B2 Çifteler, Turk.
149/F1 Cifuentes, Cuba
74/D3 Cigüela (riv.), Sp.
92/C2 Cihanbeyli, Turk.
146/D5 Cihuatlán, Mex.
74/C3 Cijara (res.), Sp.
110/C5 Cijulang, Indo.
110/C5 Cilacap, Indo.
93/E1 Çıldır (lake), Turk.
58/C2 Cilfaesty (hill), Wal,UK
159/G3 Cimarron, Ks,US
159/H3 Cimarron (riv.), Ks, Ok,US
162/B2 Cimarron (range), NM,US
79/D4 Cimone, Monte (peak), It.
82/F2 Cîmpeni, Rom.
83/F2 Cîmpia Turzii, Rom.
83/G3 Cîmpina, Rom.
83/G3 Cîmpulung, Rom.
83/G2 Cîmpulung Moldovenesc, Rom.
138/D3 Cinaruco (riv.), Ven.
75/F1 Cinca (riv.), Sp.
82/C4 Cincar (peak), Bosn.
160/C4 Cincinnati, Oh,US
142/C3 Cinco Saltos, Arg.
58/D3 Cinderford, Eng,UK
83/F3 Cîndrelu (peak), Rom.
92/B2 Çine, Turk.
69/E3 Ciney, Belg.
78/C1 Cinisello Balsamo, It.
166/D4 Cinnaminson, NJ,US
148/C2 Cintalapa, Mex.
80/A1 Cinto (mtn.), Fr.
82/C4 Čiovo (isl.), Cro.
140/C3 Cipó, Braz.
142/D3 Cipolletti, Arg.
157/G4 Circle, Mt,US
160/D4 Circleville, Oh,US
110/C5 Cirebon, Indo.
58/E3 Cirencester, Eng,UK
78/A2 Ciriè, It.
80/E3 Cirò Marina, It.
72/C4 Ciron (riv.), Fr.
132/D4 Ciskei (ind. homeland), SAfr.
83/G3 Cisnădie, Rom.
138/C3 Cisneros, Col.
142/B5 Cisnes (riv.), Chile
72/D3 Cisse (riv.), Fr.
80/C2 Cisterna di Latina, It.
148/B2 Citlaltépetl (vol.), Mex.
165/M9 Citrus Heights, Ca,US
78/C1 Cittadella, It.
79/F6 Città di Castello, It.
80/E3 Cittanova, It.
167/K8 City (isl.), NY,US
116/K6 City Beach, Austl.
139/F2 Ciudad Bolívar, Ven.
147/H5 Ciudad del Carmen, Mex.
75/G3 Ciudadela, Sp.
139/F2 Ciudad Guayana, Ven.
146/E5 Ciudad Guzmán, Mex.
147/E5 Ciudad Hidalgo, Mex.
146/E3 Ciudad Lerdo, Mex.
147/F4 Ciudad Madero, Mex.
147/F4 Ciudad Mante, Mex.
147/M8 Ciudad Mendoza, Mex.
146/C3 Ciudad Obregón, Mex.
138/D2 Ciudad Ojeda, Ven.
74/D3 Ciudad Real, Sp.
74/B2 Ciudad-Rodrigo, Sp.
147/M8 Ciudad Serdán, Mex.
147/F4 Ciudad Valles, Mex.
147/F4 Ciudad Victoria, Mex.
92/D1 Civa (pt.), Turk.
86/F4 Civa Burnu (pt.), Turk.
79/G1 Cividale del Friuli, It.
80/C1 Civita Castellana, It.
80/B1 Civitavecchia, It.
92/B2 Çivril, Turk.
103/L9 Cixi, China
103/C3 Ci Xian, China
92/E2 Cizre, Turk.
92/E2 Cizre (dam), Turk.
74/E1 Cizur, Sp.
54/C4 Clackmannan, Sc,UK
59/H3 Clacton on Sea, Eng,UK
58/C2 Claerwen (res.), Wal,UK
72/D3 Clain (riv.), Fr.
152/E3 Claire (lake), Ab,Can
158/B2 Clair Engle (lake), Ca,US
72/D3 Claise (riv.), Fr.
165/A2 Clallam (co.), Wa,US
53/S10 Clamart, Fr.
59/F5 Clanfield, Eng,UK
163/G3 Clanton, Al,US
54/A5 Claonig, Sc,UK
161/Q9 Clappison's Corners, On,Can
142/D4 Clara (pt.), Arg.
60/B4 Clare (co.), Ire.
54/F10 Clare (isl.), Ire.
60/B3 Clare (riv.), Ire.
160/C3 Clare, Mi,US
164/C2 Claremont, Ca,US
161/F3 Claremont, NH,US
159/J3 Claremore, Ok,US
119/E1 Clarence (riv.), Austl.
114/E2 Clarence (str.), Austl.
153/T7 Clarence (pt.), NW,Can
115/R11 Clarence, NZ
161/S9 Clarence, NY,US
162/C3 Clarendon, Tx,US
156/E3 Claresholm, BC,Can
113/J3 Clarie (coast), Ant.
146/B5 Clarion (isl.), Mex.
167/H9 Clark, NJ,US
166/B3 Clark (cr.), Pa,US
157/J4 Clark, SD,US
119/D4 Clarke (isl.), Austl.
118/B3 Clarke (range), Austl.
166/B4 Clarke (lake), Pa,US
156/E3 Clark Fork (riv.), Id, Mt,US
163/H3 Clark Hill (lake), Ga, SC,US
160/D4 Clarksburg, WV,US
163/F3 Clarksdale, Ms,US
161/Q8 Clarkson, On,Can
165/F6 Clarkston, Mi,US
165/D4 Clarkston, Wa,US
162/E3 Clarksville, Ar,US
163/G2 Clarksville, Tn,US
162/E3 Clarksville, Tx,US
141/B1 Claro (riv.), Braz.
68/C3 Clary, Fr.
56/D1 Clatteringshaws Loch (lake), Sc,UK
56/A2 Claudy, NI,UK
67/H5 Clausthal-Zellerfeld, Ger.
112/D3 Claver, Phil.
112/C1 Claveria, Phil.
112/D3 Claveria, Phil.
165/F6 Clawson, Mi,US
159/H3 Clay Center, Ks,US
57/G5 Clay Cross, Eng,UK
59/H2 Claydon, Eng,UK
53/U10 Claye-Souilly, Fr.
53/M7 Claygate, Eng,UK
56/D3 Clay Head (pt.), IM,UK
166/C4 Claymont, De,US
165/L11 Clayton, Ca,US
163/H3 Clayton, Ga,US
166/C4 Clayton, NJ,US
159/G3 Clayton, NM,US
159/J4 Clayton, Ok,US
57/F4 Clayton-le-Moors, Eng,UK
143/S11 Clé (stream), Arg.
152/E3 Clear (hills), Ab,Can
55/G11 Clear (cape), Ire.
158/B3 Clear (lake), Ca,US
151/J4 Cleare (cape), Ak,US
147/E1 Clear Fork (riv.), Tx,US
157/J4 Clear Lake, SD,US
156/C3 Clearwater, BC,Can
163/H5 Clearwater, Fl,US
156/D4 Clearwater (mts.), Id,US
157/K4 Clearwater (riv.), Mn,US
56/E2 Cleator Moor, Eng,UK
162/D3 Cleburne, Tx,US
57/H4 Cleethorpes, Eng,UK
58/D3 Cleeve (hill), Eng,UK
117/M8 Cleland Rec. Area, Austl.
163/H3 Clemson, SC,US
58/D2 Cleobury Mortimer, Eng,UK
112/B3 Cleopatra Needle (mtn.), Phil.
68/A4 Clères, Fr.
69/E3 Clerf (riv.), Belg., Lux.
68/B5 Clermont, Fr.
58/D4 Clevedon, Eng,UK
118/B2 Cleveland (cape), Austl.
57/G2 Cleveland (co.), Eng,UK
57/^3 Cleveland (hills), Eng,UK
163/F3 Cleveland, Ms,US
156/E3 Cleveland (peak), Mt,US
168/F4 Cleveland, Oh,US
163/G3 Cleveland, Tn,US
162/E4 Cleveland, Tx,US
168/F5 Cleveland Heights, Oh,US
141/A3 Clevelândia, Braz.
164/C3 Cleveland Nat'l For., Ca,US
60/A2 Clew (bay), Ire.
163/H5 Clewiston, Fl,US
68/B6 Clichy, Fr.
53/T10 Clichy-sous-Bois, Fr.
167/K8 Cliffside Park, NJ,US
58/D4 Clifton, Eng,UK
158/E4 Clifton, Az,US
167/D2 Clifton, NJ,US
162/D4 Clifton, Tx,US
163/J2 Clifton Forge, Va,US
58/D2 Clifton upon Teme, Eng,UK
68/C5 Clignon (riv.), Fr.
163/H3 Clingmans (mtn.), Tn,US
156/C3 Clinton, BC,Can
157/L5 Clinton, Ia,US
160/B3 Clinton, Il,US
163/F4 Clinton, La,US
168/C1 Clinton, Ma,US
165/G6 Clinton, Mi,US
165/F6 Clinton (riv.), Mi,US
159/J3 Clinton, Mo,US
163/F3 Clinton, Ms,US
163/J3 Clinton, NC,US
166/D1 Clinton (res.), NJ,US
159/H4 Clinton, Ok,US
166/A1 Clinton (co.), Pa,US
163/H3 Clinton, SC,US
152/F2 Clinton-Colden (lake), NW,Can
152/B2 Clinton Creek, Yk,Can
165/G6 Clinton, Middle Branch (riv.), Mi,US
165/G6 Clinton, North Branch (riv.), Mi,US
166/B6 Clinton (Surrattsville), Md,US
54/D5 Clints Dod (hill), Sc,UK
160/D3 Clio, Mi,US
50/D5 Clipperton (isl.), Fr.
59/F2 Clipston, Eng,UK
57/F4 Clitheroe, Eng,UK
116/B2 Cloates (pt.), Austl.
55/H10 Clogher, Ire.
60/D2 Clogherhead, Ire.
60/D2 Clogher Head (pt.), Ire.
56/C3 Cloghy, NI,UK
60/B6 Clonakilty (bay), Ire.
60/C5 Clonmel, Ire.
67/F3 Cloppenburg, Ger.
157/K4 Cloquet, Mn,US
135/E2 Clorinda, Arg.
56/E1 Closeburn, Sc,UK
167/K8 Closter, NJ,US
156/G4 Cloud (peak), Wy,US
162/B3 Cloudcroft, NM,US
151/G3 Cloudy (mtn.), Ak,US
56/B2 Cloughmills, NI,UK
57/H3 Cloughton, Eng,UK
58/B4 Clovelly, Eng,UK
158/B3 Cloverdale, Ca,US
158/C3 Clovis, Ca,US
159/G4 Clovis, NM,US
54/A3 Clovullin, Sc,UK
57/G5 Clowne, Eng,UK
54/A2 Cluanie, Loch (lake), Sc,UK
83/F2 Cluj (co.), Rom.
83/F2 Cluj-Napoca, Rom.
58/C2 Clun, Eng,UK
58/B3 Clunderwen, Wal,UK
76/C5 Cluses, Fr.
78/C1 Clusone, It.
56/E5 Clwyd (co.), Wal,UK
57/E5 Clwyd (riv.), Wal,UK
57/E5 Clwydian (range), Wal,UK
58/C3 Clydach, Wal,UK
161/H2 Clyde (riv.), NS,Can
156/E2 Clyde, NW,Can
54/B5 Clyde (riv.), Sc,UK
54/B5 Clydebank, Sc,UK
54/B6 Clyde, Firth of (inlet), Sc,UK
54/C5 Clydesdale (val.), Sc,UK
55/K10 Clywd (riv.), Wal,UK
58/C2 Clywedog (riv.), Wal,UK
161/R8 CN Tower, On,Can
74/B2 Côa (riv.), Port.
158/C4 Coachella, Ca,US
56/B2 Coagh, NI,UK
146/E3 Coahuila (state), Mex.
54/C5 Coalburn, Sc,UK
156/E3 Coaldale, Ab,Can
159/H4 Coalgate, Ok,US
156/E3 Coalhurst, Ab,Can
56/B2 Coalisland, NI,UK
59/E1 Coalville, Eng,UK
158/E2 Coalville, Ut,US
140/C4 Coaraci, Braz.
136/F4 Coari, Braz.
136/F5 Coari (riv.), Braz.
152/C2 Coast (mts.), BC, Yk,Can
130/C3 Coast (prov.), Kenya
154/B4 Coast (ranges), Ca,US
163/H4 Coastal (plain), US
54/B5 Coatbridge, Sc,UK
147/F5 Coatepec, Mex.
147/F5 Coatepec Harinas, Mex.
166/C4 Coatesville, Pa,US
147/K8 Coatetelco, Mex.
161/G2 Coaticook, Qu,Can
153/H2 Coats (isl.), NW,Can
113/Y Coats Land (reg.), Ant.
147/G5 Coatzacoalcos, Mex.
148/C2 Coatzacoalcos (riv.), Mex.
147/L8 Coatzingo, Mex.
147/M6 Coatzintla, Mex.
147/J4 Coba (ruins), Mex.
74/B1 Coba de Serpe, Sierra de (mtn.), Sp.
148/D3 Cobán, Guat.
119/D3 Cobberas (peak), Austl.
168/B1 Cobble Mountain (res.), Ma,US
164/B1 Cobblestone (mtn.), Ca,US
60/B6 Cóbh, Ire.
157/K2 Cobham (riv.), Mb, On,Can
53/M8 Cobham, Eng,UK
136/E6 Cobija, Bol.
114/E2 Cobourg (pen.), Austl.
160/E3 Cobourg, On,Can
142/B3 Cobquecura, Chile
131/D2 Cóbuè, Moz.
119/F5 Coburg, Austl.
153/T7 Coburg (isl.), NW,Can
70/D2 Coburg, Ger.
138/B5 Coca, Ecu.
138/B5 Coca (riv.), Ecu.
140/B1 Cocal, Braz.
166/B3 Cocalico (cr.), Pa,US
77/G5 Coca, Pizzo di (peak), It.
75/E3 Cocentaina, Sp.
136/E7 Cochabamba, Bol.
139/F2 Coche (isl.), Ven.
108/F4 Cochin, India
168/C1 Cochituate, Ma,US
163/H3 Cochran, Ga,US
156/E3 Cochrane, Ab,Can
160/D1 Cochrane, On,Can
168/B3 Cockaponset Saint For., Ct,US
119/G5 Cockatoo, Austl.
116/K7 Cockburn (sound), Austl.
143/J8 Cockburn (chan.), Chile
54/D5 Cockburnspath, Sc,UK
54/D3 Cock Cairn (mtn.), Sc,UK
54/D5 Cockenzie, Sc,UK
57/E2 Cockermouth, Eng,UK
166/B5 Cockeysville, Md,US
132/D4 Cockscomb (peak), SAfr.
136/A2 Coco (isl.), CR
149/G1 Coco (cay), Cuba
149/F3 Coco (riv.), Hon., Nic.
163/H4 Cocoa, Fl,US
158/D4 Coconino (plat.), Az,US
119/C2 Cocoparra Nat'l Park, Austl.
90/J11 Cocos (isls.), Austl.
140/A4 Côcos, Braz.
149/G4 Cocos (pt.), Pan.
153/K3 Cod (isl.), Nf,Can
136/F4 Codajás, Braz.
57/G3 Cod Beck (riv.), Eng,UK
142/C2 Codegua, Chile
139/E2 Codera (cape), Ven.
79/F3 Codigoro, It.
83/G3 Codlea, Rom.
140/B2 Codó, Braz.
78/C2 Codogno, It.
166/B4 Codorus (cr.), Pa,US
79/F1 Codroipo, It.
58/D1 Codsall, Eng,UK
156/F4 Cody, Wy,US
140/B2 Coelho Neto, Braz.
67/E5 Coesfeld, Ger.
51/M6 Coetivy (isl.), Sey.
156/D4 Coeur d'Alene, Id,US
156/D4 Coeur d'Alene (lake), Id,US
66/D3 Coevorden, Neth.
159/J3 Coffeyville, Ks,US
117/G5 Coffin Bay Nat'l Park, Austl.
119/E1 Coffs Harbour, Austl.
147/F5 Cofre de Perote Nat'l Park, Mex.
59/G3 Coggeshall, Eng,UK
80/A2 Coghinas (lake), It.
72/C4 Cognac, Fr.
78/B4 Cogoleto, It.
166/C5 Cohansey (riv.), NJ,US
168/D1 Cohasset, Ma,US
116/L7 Cohunu Nat'l Park, Austl.
149/F5 Coiba (isl.), Pan.
143/K7 Coig (riv.), Arg.
142/B5 Coihaique, Chile
142/C3 Coihueco, Chile
108/F3 Coimbatore, India
74/A2 Coimbra, Port.
74/A2 Coimbra (dist.), Port.
74/C4 Coín, Sp.
75/P10 Coina (riv.), Port.
72/F4 Coise (riv.), Fr.
136/E2 Cojedes (riv.), Ven.
138/D2 Cojedes (state), Ven.
138/A4 Cojimíes, Ecu.
142/C5 Cojudo Blanco (peak), Arg.
148/D3 Cojutepeque, ESal.
156/F5 Cokeville, Wy,US
119/B3 Colac, Austl.
159/H2 Colamus (riv.), Ne,US
75/P10 Colares, Port.
141/D1 Colatina, Braz.
113/P Colbeck (cape), Ant.
142/C2 Colbún, Chile
159/G3 Colby, Ks,US
144/D4 Colca (riv.), Peru
59/G3 Colchester, Eng,UK
168/B2 Colchester, Ct,US
156/F2 Cold (lake), Ab, Sk,Can
57/F2 Cold Fell (mtn.), Eng,UK
54/D5 Coldingham, Sc,UK
156/F2 Cold Lake, Ab,Can
157/K4 Cold Spring, Mn,US
162/E4 Coldspring, Tx,US
54/D5 Coldstream, Sc,UK
159/H3 Coldwater, Ks,US
160/C3 Coldwater, Mi,US
59/E3 Cole (riv.), Eng,UK
58/D3 Coleford, Eng,UK
162/D4 Coleman, Tx,US
93/E2 Çölemerik, Turk.
56/B1 Coleraine, NI,UK
56/B1 Coleraine (dist.), NI,UK
108/G3 Coleroon (riv.), India
132/D3 Colesberg, SAfr.
59/E2 Coleshill, Eng,UK
166/A5 Colesville, Md,US
156/D4 Colfax, Wa,US
153/S6 Colgate (cape), NW,Can
142/C5 Colhué Huapí (lake), Arg.
109/D2 Co Lieu, Viet.
146/E5 Colima, Mex.
146/D5 Colima (state), Mex.
146/E5 Colima, de Nevado (peak), Mex.
142/C2 Colina, Chile
140/A2 Colinas, Braz.
164/F7 Coliseum, Los Angeles, Ca,US
63/Q1 Colkhov (riv.), Rus.
55/H8 Coll (isl.), Sc,UK
74/D2 Collado-Villalba, Sp.
78/D3 Collecchio, It.
131/C4 Colleen Bawn, Zim.
151/J3 College, Ak,US
166/B6 College Park, Md,US
162/D4 College Station, Tx,US
78/A2 Collegno, It.
116/C5 Collie, Austl.
114/C3 Collier (bay), Austl.
116/C3 Collier (range), Austl.
57/G2 Collier Law (hill), Eng,UK
116/C3 Collier Range Nat'l Park, Austl.
163/F3 Collierville, Tn,US
58/B6 Collifford (res.), Eng,UK
57/G4 Collingham, Eng,UK
160/D2 Collingwood, On,Can
115/R11 Collingwood, NZ
163/F4 Collins, Ms,US
159/J3 Collinsville, Ok,US
160/E4 Collinsville, Va,US
123/V17 Collo, Alg.
76/D1 Colmar, Fr.
74/D2 Colmenar Viejo, Sp.
143/J7 Colmillo (cape), Chile
56/D1 Colmonell, Sc,UK
59/E3 Coln (riv.), Eng,UK
57/F4 Colne, Eng,UK
59/G3 Colne (riv.), Eng,UK
146/A2 Colnett, Punta (pt.), Mex.
53/N6 Colney Heath, Eng,UK
109/D1 Co Loa Citadel, Viet.
69/F2 Cologne (Köln), Ger.
78/C1 Cologno Monzese, It.
53/S10 Colombes, Fr.
76/A1 Colombey-les-Deux-Eglises, Fr.
136/D3 Colombia
78/D1 Colombine, Monte (peak), It.
141/B3 Colombo, Braz.
106/C6 Colombo (cap.), SrL.
78/A2 Colombo, Monte (peak), It.
72/D5 Colomiers, Fr.
142/E2 Colón, Arg.
142/F2 Colón, Arg.
149/F1 Colón, Cuba
149/E3 Colón (mts.), Hon.
149/G4 Colón, Pan.
144/A1 Colonche, Ecu.
120/C4 Colonia, Micro.
143/F2 Colonia (dept.), Uru.
167/D2 Colonia, NJ,US
143/F2 Colonia Del Sacramento, Uru.
140/D3 Colônia Leopoldina, Braz.
166/B3 Colonial Park, Pa,US
55/H8 Colonsay (isl.), Sc,UK
143/K7 Colorado (peak), Arg.
142/D3 Colorado (riv.), Arg.
141/B2 Colorado, Braz.
158/D4 Colorado (riv.), Mex., US
158/E3 Colorado (plat.), US
158/F3 Colorado (state), US
162/D4 Colorado (riv.), Tx,US
159/F3 Colorado City, Co,US
162/C3 Colorado City, Tx,US
158/E3 Colorado Nat'l Mon., Co,US
164/C3 Colorado River (aqueduct), Ca,US
135/C2 Colorados, Desagües de los (marsh), Arg.
159/F3 Colorado Springs, Co,US
146/E4 Colotlán, Mex.
148/B2 Colotlipa, Mex.
136/E7 Colquiri, Bol.
148/D2 Colson (pt.), Belz.
156/G4 Colstrip, Mt,US
56/D1 Colt (hill), Sc,UK
142/C2 Coltauco, Chile
59/H1 Coltishall, Eng,UK
164/C2 Colton, Ca,US
134/D4 Coluene (riv.), Braz.
144/B1 Columbe, Ecu.
152/E3 Columbia (mtn.), Ab,Can
156/C2 Columbia (mts.), BC,Can
153/T6 Columbia (cape), NW,Can
156/C4 Columbia (riv.), Can., US
156/D4 Columbia (plat.), US
160/C4 Columbia, Ky,US
162/E3 Columbia, La,US
166/B5 Columbia, Md,US
159/J3 Columbia, Mo,US
163/F4 Columbia, Ms,US
152/E4 Columbia (plat.), Or,US
166/B3 Columbia, Pa,US
163/H3 Columbia (cap.), SC,US
163/G3 Columbia, Tn,US
156/E3 Columbia Falls, Mt,US
168/G6 Columbiana (co.), Oh,US
132/B4 Columbine (cape), SAfr.
163/G3 Columbus, Ga,US
160/C4 Columbus, In,US
163/F3 Columbus, Ms,US
156/F4 Columbus, Mt,US
159/H2 Columbus, Ne,US
158/F5 Columbus, NM,US
160/D4 Columbus (cap.), Oh,US
162/D4 Columbus, Tx,US
163/F3 Columbus A.F.B., Ms,US
158/B3 Colusa, Ca,US
152/D2 Colville (lake), NW,Can
151/H2 Colville (riv.), Ak,US
156/D3 Colville, Wa,US
165/B3 Colvos (passg.), Wa,US
58/D2 Colwall, Eng,UK
58/C4 Colwinston, Wal,UK
56/E5 Colwyn Bay, Wal,UK
79/F3 Comacchio, It.
79/F3 Comacchio, Valli di (lag.), It.
107/F2 Comai, China
147/G5 Comalcalco, Mex.
162/D4 Comanche, Tx,US
142/F3 Comandante Nicanor Otamendi, Arg.
83/H2 Comănești, Rom.
83/G3 Comarnic, Rom.
144/B3 Comas, Peru
148/E3 Comayagua, Hon.
135/B3 Combarbalá, Chile
58/B4 Combe Martin, Eng,UK
56/C2 Comber, NI,UK
104/B5 Combermere (bay), Burma
53/T11 Combs-la-Ville, Fr.
118/C4 Comet (riv.), Austl.
107/F3 Comilla, Bang.
68/B2 Comines, Belg.
68/C2 Comines, Fr.
148/C2 Comitán, Mex.
167/E2 Commack, NY,US
72/E3 Commentry, Fr.
164/B2 Commerce, Ca,US
69/E6 Commercy, Fr.
139/H3 Commewijne (dist.), Sur.
153/H2 Committee (bay), NW,Can
102/B4 Communism (Kommunizma) (peak), Taj.
78/C1 Como, It.
77/F5 Como (lake), It.
78/C1 Como (prov.), It.
165/P14 Como (lake), Wi,US
142/D5 Comodoro Rivadavia, Arg.
128/D4 Comoé (prov.), Burk.
128/E4 Comoé Nat'l Park, IvC.
108/F4 Comorin (cape), India
133/G5 Comoros
156/B3 Comox, BC,Can
68/B5 Compiègne, Fr.
146/D4 Compostela, Mex.
164/B3 Compton, Ca,US
54/C4 Comrie, Sc,UK
162/C4 Comstock, Tx,US
107/F2 Cona, China
104/A2 Co Nag (lake), China
128/B4 Conakry (cap.), Gui.
128/B4 Conakry (comm.), Gui.
138/B5 Conambo (riv.), Ecu.
79/F5 Conca (riv.), It.
72/B3 Concarneau, Fr.
141/E1 Conceição da Barra, Braz.
141/B1 Conceição das Alagoas, Braz.
137/J5 Conceição do Araguaia, Braz.
140/C3 Conceição do Coité, Braz.
141/D1 Conceição do Mato Dentro, Braz.
141/H6 Conceição do Rio Verde, Braz.
141/H7 Conceição dos Ouros, Braz.
135/C2 Concepción, Arg.
136/E6 Concepción, Bol.
136/F7 Concepción (lake), Bol.
142/B3 Concepción, Chile
146/C3 Concepción (bay), Mex.
135/E1 Concepción, Par.
136/C6 Concepción, Peru
147/E3 Concepción del Oro, Mex.
142/F2 Concepción del Uruguay, Arg.
146/C3 Concepción, Punta (pt.), Mex.
158/B4 Conception (pt.), Ca,US
78/D1 Concesio, It.
131/C3 Concession, Zim.
141/F7 Conchal, Braz.
159/F4 Conchas (lake), NM,US
53/U10 Conches, Fr.
159/G5 Concho (riv.), Tx,US
165/K11 Concord, Ca,US
163/H3 Concord, NC,US
161/G3 Concord (cap.), NH,US
135/E3 Concordia, Arg.
141/A3 Concórdia, Braz.
159/H3 Concordia, Ks,US
79/F1 Concordia Sagittaria, It.
168/C1 Concord Museum, Ma,US
156/C3 Concrete, Wa,US
148/D3 Concuen (riv.), Guat.
109/D2 Con Cuong, Viet.
149/G1 Condado, Cuba
115/J5 Condamine (riv.), Austl.
140/C3 Conde, Braz.
68/C3 Condé-sur-L'Escaut, Fr.
72/C2 Condé-sur-Noireau, Fr.
140/B4 Condeúba, Braz.
118/C4 Condomine (riv.), Austl.
156/C4 Condon, Or,US
69/D3 Condroz (plat.), Belg.
163/G4 Conecuh (riv.), Al,US
79/F1 Conegliano, It.
162/B2 Conejos, Co,US
166/B3 Conestoga (riv.), Pa,US
166/B3 Conewago (cr.), Pa,US
166/B3 Conewago (lake), Pa,US
167/K9 Coney Island, NY,US
53/S10 Conflans-Sainte-Honorine, Fr.
167/E1 Congers, NY,US
105/G4 Conghua, China
105/F3 Congjiang, China
57/F5 Congleton, Eng,UK
126/B1 Congo
125/K7 Congo (basin), Afr.
126/C1 Congo (riv.), Afr.
141/G7 Congonhal, Braz.
141/D2 Congonhas, Braz.
122/E5 Congo (Zaire)
142/C3 Conguillio Parque Nacional, Chile
54/B4 Conic (hill), Sc,UK
142/C4 Cónico, Cerro (peak), Arg.
142/C4 Cónico, Cerro Nevado (peak), Chile
74/B4 Conil de la Frontera, Sp.
57/H5 Coningsby, Eng,UK
57/G5 Conisbrough, Eng,UK
57/E3 Coniston, Eng,UK
57/E3 Coniston Water (lake), Eng,UK
56/C2 Conlig, NI,UK
153/J1 Conn (lake), NW,Can
60/B2 Connacht (prov.), Ire.
57/E5 Connah's Quay, Wal,UK
160/D3 Conneaut, Oh,US
161/G2 Connecticut (riv.), US
161/F3 Connecticut (state), US
54/A4 Connel, Sc,UK
160/E3 Connellsville, Pa,US
60/A2 Connemara (dist.), Ire.
55/G10 Connemara Nat'l Park, Ire.
112/C1 Conner, Phil.
160/C4 Connersville, In,US
60/A1 Conn, Lough (lake), Ire.
138/B5 Conocoto, Ecu.
166/B3 Conodoguinet (cr.), Pa,US
143/K7 Cono Grande (peak), Arg.
54/B1 Cononbridge, Sc,UK
118/D4 Conondale Nat'l Park, Austl.
54/B1 Conon, Falls of (falls), Sc,UK
168/F6 Conotton (cr.), Oh,US
166/B4 Conowingo (dam), Md,US
72/E4 Conques, Fr.
156/F3 Conrad, Mt,US
162/E4 Conroe, Tx,US
167/F2 Conscience Point Nat'l Wild. Ref., NY,US
141/D2 Conselheiro Lafaiete, Braz.
141/D1 Conselheiro Pena, Braz.
57/G2 Consett, Eng,UK
166/C3 Conshohocken, Pa,US
149/F1 Consolación del Sur, Cuba
109/D4 Con Son (isl.), Viet.
77/F2 Constance (Bodensee) (lake), Ger., Swi.
150/F4 Constant (mtn.), Guad.
83/J3 Constanța, Rom.
83/J3 Constanța (co.), Rom.
75/F2 Constantí, Sp.
74/C4 Constantina, Sp.
123/V17 Constantine, Alg.
123/V17 Constantine (gov.), Alg.
151/G4 Constantine (cape), Ak,US
150/D3 Constanza, DRep.
142/B2 Constitución, Chile
143/T11 Constitución (res.), Uru.
146/B2 Constitución de 1857 Nat'l Park, Mex.
74/D3 Consuegra, Sp.
106/E3 Contai, India
79/F2 Contarina, It.
140/B4 Contas (riv.), Braz.
141/C1 Contegem, Braz.
68/B4 Contigny, Fr.
156/C2 Continental (ranges), Ab, BC,Can
148/E1 Contoy (isl.), Mex.
165/L11 Contra Costa (can.), Ca,US
165/L11 Contra Costa (co.), Ca,US
74/E3 Contreras (res.), Sp.
151/J3 Controller (bay), Ak,US
142/B3 Contulmo, Chile
152/E2 Contwoyto (lake), NW,Can
68/B4 Conty, Fr.
138/C2 Convención, Col.
80/E2 Conversano, It.
118/C3 Conway (cape), Austl.
162/E3 Conway, Ar,US
161/G3 Conway, NH,US
163/J3 Conway, SC,US
118/C3 Conway Range Nat'l Park, Austl.
56/E5 Conway, Vale of (val.), Wal,UK
56/E5 Conwy, Wal,UK
56/D5 Conwy (bay), Wal,UK
56/E5 Conwy (riv.), Wal,UK
106/E2 Cooch Behār, India
118/F7 Coochiemudlo (isl.), Austl.
143/K8 Cook (bay), Chile
115/R11 Cook (str.), NZ
151/H3 Cook (inlet), Ak,US
165/Q16 Cook (co.), Il,US
116/C5 Cooke (peak), Austl.
163/G2 Cookeville, Tn,US
113/L Cook Ice Shelf, Ant.
121/J6 Cook Islands (terr.), NZ
115/R11 Cook, Mount (peak), NZ
56/B2 Cookstown, NI,UK
56/B2 Cookstown (dist.), NI,UK
119/B3 Coola Coola (swamp), Austl.
60/D2 Cooley (pt.), Ire.
118/D4 Cooloola Nat'l Park, Austl.
116/K7 Cooloongup (lake), Austl.
119/D3 Cooma, Austl.
60/A6 Coomhola (riv.), Ire.
165/N15 Coon (cr.), Il,US
165/G6 Coon (cr.), Mi,US

183

Coona – Dafen

116/D4 **Coonana Abor. Land**, Austl.
106/B5 **Coondapoor**, India
165/G6 **Coon, East Branch** (cr.), Mi,US
116/C2 **Coongan Abor. Land**, Austl.
108/F3 **Coonoor**, India
114/F5 **Cooper** (cr.), Austl.
162/E3 **Cooper**, Tx,US
157/J4 **Cooperstown**, ND,US
116/C3 **Coordewandy** (peak), Austl.
119/A3 **Coorong Nat'l Park**, Austl.
163/G3 **Coosa** (riv.), Al,US
156/B5 **Coos Bay**, Or,US
119/D2 **Cootamundra**, Austl.
138/C3 **Copacabana**, Col.
142/C3 **Copahué** (vol.), Chile
148/D3 **Copán** (ruins), Hon.
74/E4 **Cope** (cape), Sp.
56/C2 **Copeland** (isl.), NI,UK
62/E4 **Copenhagen** (København) (cap.), Den.
81/F2 **Copertino**, It.
119/D1 **Copeton** (dam), Austl.
167/E2 **Copiague**, NY,US
135/B2 **Copiapó**, Chile
79/E3 **Copparo**, It.
139/G3 **Coppename** (riv.), Sur.
67/G4 **Coppenbrügge**, Ger.
162/D4 **Copperas Cove**, Tx,US
131/B2 **Copperbelt** (prov.), Zam.
152/E2 **Coppermine** (riv.), NW,Can
57/F4 **Coppull**, Eng,UK
83/G2 **Copşa Mică**, Rom.
102/E5 **Coqên**, China
57/F1 **Coquet** (riv.), Eng,UK
57/G1 **Coquet Dale** (val.), Eng,UK
135/B2 **Coquimbo**, Chile
142/C1 **Coquimbo** (reg.), Chile
83/G4 **Corabia**, Rom.
140/A5 **Coração de Jesus**, Braz.
118/C1 **Coral** (sea), Austl.
138/C2 **Corales del Rosario Nat'l Park**, Col.
163/H5 **Coral Gables**, Fl,US
115/J2 **Coral Sea Is.** (terr.), Austl.
163/H5 **Coral Springs**, Fl,US
167/F2 **Coram**, NY,US
168/G6 **Coraopolis**, Pa,US
72/E2 **Corbeil-Essonnes**, Fr.
123/T15 **Corbelin** (cape), Alg.
77/F5 **Corbet, Piz** (peak), Swi.
78/B2 **Corbetta**, It.
68/B4 **Corbie**, Fr.
72/E5 **Corbieres** (mts.), Fr.
160/C4 **Corbin**, Ky,US
57/F2 **Corbridge**, Eng,UK
59/F2 **Corby**, Eng,UK
141/K7 **Corcovado** (mon.), Braz.
142/B4 **Corcovado** (gulf), Chile
142/B4 **Corcovado** (vol.), Chile
149/F4 **Corcovado Nat'l Park**, CR
141/D2 **Cordeiro**, Braz.
163/H4 **Cordele**, Ga,US
159/H4 **Cordell** (New Cordell), Ok,US
73/K4 **Cordenons**, It.
112/C1 **Cordillera Central** (mts.), Phil.
138/C4 **Cordillera de los Picachos Nat'l Park**, Col.
141/C1 **Cordisburgo**, Braz.
135/D3 **Córdoba**, Arg.
135/D3 **Córdoba** (mts.), Arg.
142/E2 **Córdoba** (prov.), Arg.
138/C2 **Córdoba** (dept.), Col.
147/F5 **Córdoba**, Mex.
74/C4 **Córdoba**, Sp.
151/J3 **Cordova** (peak), Ak,US
140/B1 **Coreaú**, Braz.
74/E1 **Corella**, Sp.
140/C2 **Coremas**, Braz.
136/G3 **Corentyne** (riv.), Guy.
81/F3 **Corfu** (Kérkira) (isl.), Gre.
74/B3 **Coria**, Sp.
74/B4 **Coria del Río**, Sp.
140/A4 **Coribe**, Braz.
119/D2 **Coricudgy** (peak), Austl.
80/E3 **Corigliano Calabro**, It.
115/J3 **Coringa Islets** (isls.), Austl.
81/H3 **Corinth** (gulf), Gre.
81/H4 **Corinth** (ruins), Gre.
163/F3 **Corinth**, Ms,US
81/H4 **Corinth** (Kórinthos), Gre.
141/C1 **Corinto**, Braz.
148/E3 **Corinto**, Nic.
74/A1 **Coristanco**, Sp.
60/B6 **Cork**, Ire.
60/B6 **Cork** (co.), Ire.
60/B6 **Cork** (har.), Ire.
80/C4 **Corleone**, It.
83/H5 **Çorlu**, Turk.
68/D5 **Cormontreuil**, Fr.
157/H2 **Cormorant**, Mb,Can
157/H2 **Cormorant** (lake), Mb,Can
58/C1 **Corndon** (hill), Wal,UK
141/B2 **Cornélio Procópio**, Braz.
153/K2 **Cornelius Grinnel** (bay), NW,Can
75/L7 **Cornella**, Sp.
119/C3 **Corner** (inlet), Austl.
161/K1 **Corner Brook**, Nf,Can
77/H6 **Cornetto** (peak), It.
168/B3 **Cornfield** (pt.), Ct,US
54/D1 **Cornhill**, Sc,UK
160/E3 **Corning**, NY,US
118/B3 **Cornish** (cr.), Austl.
79/D4 **Corno alle Scale** (peak), It.
78/D1 **Cornone di Blumone** (peak), It.
143/L8 **Cornú** (peak), Arg.
153/S7 **Cornwall** (isl.), NW,Can
160/F2 **Cornwall**, On,Can
161/J2 **Cornwall**, PE,Can
55/J11 **Cornwall** (cape), Eng,UK
58/B6 **Cornwall** (co.), Eng,UK
153/S7 **Cornwallis** (isl.), NW,Can
117/H5 **Corny** (pt.), Austl.
138/D2 **Coro**, Ven.
122/J9 **Coroa** (mtn.), CpV.
140/A2 **Coroatá**, Braz.
136/F7 **Corocoro**, Bol.
141/C1 **Coromandel**, Braz.
106/D5 **Coromandel** (coast), India
115/S10 **Coromandel**, NZ
115/S10 **Coromandel** (pen.), NZ
112/C2 **Coron**, Phil.
112/C3 **Coron** (isl.), Phil.
164/C3 **Corona**, Ca,US
159/F4 **Corona**, NM,US
164/G8 **Corona del Mar**, Ca,US
149/E4 **Coronado** (bay), CR
164/C5 **Coronado**, Ca,US
156/F2 **Coronation**, Ab,Can
152/E2 **Coronation** (gulf), NW,Can
142/E1 **Coronda**, Arg.
142/B3 **Coronel**, Chile
142/E3 **Coronel Dorrego**, Arg.
141/D1 **Coronel Fabriciano**, Braz.
142/D2 **Coronel Moldes**, Arg.
140/B5 **Coronel Murta**, Braz.
135/E2 **Coronel Oviedo**, Par.
142/E3 **Coronel Pringles**, Arg.
142/E3 **Coronel Suárez**, Arg.
141/A3 **Coronel Vivida**, Braz.
139/G3 **Coronie** (dist.), Sur.
144/C4 **Coropuna** (peak), Peru
148/D2 **Corozal**, Belz.
138/C2 **Corozal**, Col.
54/A3 **Corpach**, Sc,UK
162/D5 **Corpus Christi**, Tx,US
74/D3 **Corral de Almaguer**, Sp.
142/E2 **Corral de Bustos**, Arg.
75/Y16 **Corralejo**, Canl.
149/F1 **Corralillo**, Cuba
119/B3 **Corrangamite** (lake), Austl.
149/F4 **Corredor**, CR
79/D3 **Correggio**, It.
140/A3 **Corrente**, Braz.
140/A4 **Corrente** (riv.), Braz.
141/B1 **Corrente** (riv.), Braz.
131/D5 **Correntes, Cabo das** (cape), Moz.
140/A4 **Correntina**, Braz.
60/A3 **Corrib, Lough** (lake), Ire.
54/A5 **Corrie**, Sc,UK
135/E2 **Corrientes**, Arg.
138/B3 **Corrientes** (cape), Col.
149/E1 **Corrientes** (cape), Cuba
144/C1 **Corrientes** (riv.), Ecu., Peru
146/D4 **Corrientes, Cabo** (cape), Mex.
58/C1 **Corris**, Wal,UK
139/G3 **Corriverton**, Guy.
54/C2 **Corryhabbie** (mtn.), Sc,UK
80/A1 **Corse** (cape), Fr.
80/A1 **Corse** (reg.), Fr.
54/B5 **Corse** (hill), Sc,UK
56/D1 **Corserine** (mtn.), Sc,UK
56/C1 **Corsewall** (pt.), Sc,UK
58/D4 **Corsham**, Eng,UK
80/A1 **Corsica** (isl.), Fr.
162/D3 **Corsicana**, Tx,US
78/C3 **Corsico**, It.
166/D5 **Corsons** (inlet), NJ,US
80/A1 **Corte**, Fr.
112/D3 **Cortes**, Phil.
158/E3 **Cortez**, Co,US
73/K3 **Cortina d'Ampezzo**, It.
160/E3 **Cortland**, NY,US
128/B4 **Corubal** (riv.), GBis.
74/A3 **Coruche**, Port.
87/G4 **Çoruh** (riv.), Turk.
92/C1 **Çorum**, Turk.
92/C1 **Çorum** (prov.), Turk.
136/G7 **Corumbá**, Braz.
141/B1 **Corumbá** (riv.), Braz.
140/C5 **Corumbaú** (pt.), Braz.
140/C3 **Coruripe**, Braz.
156/C4 **Corvallis**, Or,US
58/D2 **Corve** (riv.), Eng,UK
75/R12 **Corvo** (isl.), Azor.
80/C1 **Corvo** (peak), It.
57/E6 **Corwen**, Wal,UK
147/G5 **Cosamaloapan**, Mex.
147/P8 **Cosamaloapan de Carpio**, Mex.
147/N7 **Cosautlán de Carvajal**, Mex.
147/M7 **Coscomatepec de Bravo**, Mex.
80/E3 **Cosenza**, It.
160/D3 **Coshocton**, Oh,US
168/E7 **Coshocton** (co.), Oh,US
148/E3 **Cosigüina** (pt.), Nic.
74/D2 **Coslada**, Sp.
116/D3 **Cosmo Newberry Abor. Rsv.**, Austl.
141/F7 **Cosmópolis**, Braz.
72/E3 **Cosne-Cours-sur-Loire**, Fr.
147/N8 **Cosolapa**, Mex.
147/G5 **Cosoleacaque**, Mex.
74/B1 **Cospeito**, Sp.
135/D3 **Cosquín**, Arg.
78/B1 **Cossato**, It.
72/D3 **Cosson** (riv.), Fr.
75/P10 **Costa da Caparica**, Port.
75/C4 **Costa del Sol** (coast), Sp.
164/C3 **Costa Mesa**, Ca,US
149/F4 **Costa Rica**
146/D3 **Costa Rica**, Mex.
78/D1 **Costa Volpino**, It.
59/H1 **Costessey**, Eng,UK
83/G3 **Costeşti**, Rom.
165/M10 **Cosumnes** (riv.), Ca,US
112/D4 **Cotabato City**, Phil.
138/B4 **Cotacachi** (peak), Ecu.
149/H4 **Cotatumbo** (riv.), Col., Ven.
128/D5 **Côte d'Ivoire** (Ivory Coast)
76/A3 **Côte-d'Or** (dept.), Fr.
72/F3 **Côte d'Or** (uplands), Fr.
140/A4 **Cotegipe**, Braz.
72/C2 **Cotentin** (pen.), Fr.
161/N7 **Côte-Saint-Luc**, Qu,Can
58/B3 **Cothi** (riv.), Wal,UK
141/G8 **Cotia**, Braz.
129/F5 **Cotonou**, Ben.
138/B5 **Cotopaxi** (prov.), Ecu.
138/B5 **Cotopaxi** (vol.), Ecu.
138/B5 **Cotopaxi Nat'l Park**, Ecu.
58/D4 **Cotswolds** (hills), Eng,UK
156/C5 **Cottage Grove**, Or,US
65/H3 **Cottbus**, Ger.
59/G2 **Cottenham**, Eng,UK
158/D4 **Cottonwood**, Az,US
162/D2 **Cottonwood** (riv.), Ks,US
159/F5 **Cottonwood** (dry riv.), Tx,US
116/K6 **Cottsloe**, Austl.
150/D3 **Cotuí**, DRep.
162/D4 **Cotulla**, Tx,US
53/U10 **Coubert**, Fr.
72/C4 **Coubre, Pointe de la** (pt.), Fr.
76/C5 **Cou, Col de** (pass), Fr.
68/C5 **Coucy-le-Château-Auffrique**, Fr.
68/B1 **Coudekerque-Branche**, Fr.
72/E5 **Couguille, Pic de** (peak), Fr.
72/D2 **Coulaines**, Fr.
156/D4 **Coulee City**, Wa,US
113/M **Coulman** (isl.), Ant.
68/C6 **Coulommiers**, Fr.
160/E2 **Coulonge** (riv.), Qu,Can
72/D4 **Coulounieix-Chamiers**, Fr.
53/N8 **Coulsdon**, Eng,UK
60/C5 **Coumfea** (mtn.), Ire.
156/D4 **Council**, Id,US
157/K5 **Council Bluffs**, Ia,US
159/H3 **Council Grove**, Ks,US
54/C3 **Coupar Angus**, Sc,UK
53/U10 **Coupvray**, Fr.
139/G3 **Courantyne** (riv.), Sur.
53/S10 **Courbevoie**, Fr.
68/D3 **Courcelles**, Belg.
69/F5 **Courcelles-Chaussy**, Fr.
53/T11 **Courcouronnes**, Fr.
72/E4 **Cournon-d'Auvergne**, Fr.
152/D4 **Courtenay**, BC,Can
161/S8 **Courtice**, On,Can
60/B6 **Courtmacsherry** (bay), Ire.
68/C2 **Courtrai** (Kortrijk), Belg.
53/T10 **Courtry**, Fr.
60/A6 **Cousane Gap** (pass), Ire.
72/C2 **Coutances**, Fr.
156/F3 **Coutts**, Ab,Can
68/D3 **Couvin**, Belg.
75/P10 **Cova da Piedade**, Port.
74/C1 **Covadonga Nat'l Park**, Sp.
83/H3 **Covasna**, Rom.
82/G3 **Covasna** (co.), Rom.
54/B5 **Cove**, Sc,UK
54/D2 **Cove Bay**, Sc,UK
59/E2 **Coventry**, Eng,UK
59/E1 **Coventry** (can.), Eng,UK
168/B2 **Coventry**, Ct,US
93/M7 **Covered Market**, Turk.
74/B2 **Covilhã**, Port.
164/C2 **Covina**, Ca,US
163/H3 **Covington**, Ga,US
160/C4 **Covington**, Ky,US
163/F3 **Covington**, Tn,US
160/E4 **Covington**, Va,US
54/A4 **Cowal** (dist.), Sc,UK
118/H8 **Cowan**, Austl.
116/D4 **Cowan** (lake), Austl.
58/C4 **Cowbridge**, Wal,UK
54/C4 **Cowdenbeath**, Sc,UK
59/E5 **Cowes**, Eng,UK
57/F2 **Cow Green** (res.), Eng,UK
54/C4 **Cowie**, Sc,UK
156/C4 **Cowlitz** (riv.), Wa,US
163/H3 **Cowpens Nat'l Bfld.**, SC,US
119/D2 **Cowra**, Austl.
57/G2 **Coxhoe**, Eng,UK
137/H7 **Coxim**, Braz.
53/T9 **Coye-la-Forêt**, Fr.
147/Q10 **Coyoacán**, Mex.
165/L12 **Coyote** (cr.), Ca,US
147/K7 **Coyotepec**, Mex.
147/E5 **Coyuca**, Mex.
148/A2 **Coyuca de Benítez**, Mex.
147/M6 **Coyutla**, Mex.
159/H2 **Cozad**, Ne,US
148/E1 **Cozumel** (isl.), Mex.
119/C4 **Cradle** (peak), Austl.
119/C4 **Cradle Mountain-Lake Saint Clair Nat'l Park**, Austl.
132/D4 **Cradock**, SAfr.
168/G7 **Crafton**, Pa,US
151/K3 **Crag** (mtn.), Yk,Can
57/F3 **Crag** (hill), Eng,UK
158/F2 **Craig**, Co,US
56/C2 **Craigavad**, NI,UK
56/B3 **Craigavon**, NI,UK
56/B3 **Craigavon** (dist.), NI,UK
54/C2 **Craigellachie**, Sc,UK
119/F5 **Craigieburn**, Austl.
157/G3 **Craik**, Sk,Can
54/D4 **Crail**, Sc,UK
70/D4 **Crailsheim**, Ger.
83/F3 **Craiova**, Rom.
77/E5 **Cramalina, Pizzo** (peak), Swi.
57/G1 **Cramlington**, Eng,UK
56/A1 **Crana** (riv.), Ire.
157/H2 **Cranberry Portage**, Mb,Can
58/D5 **Cranborne Chase** (for.), Eng,UK
119/C3 **Cranbourne**, Austl.
156/E3 **Cranbrook**, BC,Can
59/G4 **Cranbrook**, Eng,UK
162/C4 **Crane**, Tx,US
167/E2 **Crane Neck** (pt.), NY,US
157/J3 **Crane River**, Mb,Can
167/D2 **Cranford**, NJ,US
76/C6 **Cran-Gevrier**, Fr.
59/F4 **Cranleigh**, Eng,UK
168/C2 **Cranston**, RI,US
68/C5 **Craonne**, Fr.
83/F2 **Crasna** (riv.), Rom.
55/L9 **Craster**, Eng,UK
156/C5 **Crater** (lake), Or,US
156/C5 **Crater Lake Nat'l Park**, Or,US
156/E5 **Craters of the Moon Nat'l Mon.**, Id,US
140/B2 **Crateús**, Braz.
80/E3 **Crati** (riv.), It.
140/C2 **Crato**, Braz.
141/C2 **Cravinhos**, Braz.
54/C6 **Crawford**, Sc,UK
168/G4 **Crawford** (co.), Pa,US
160/C3 **Crawfordsville**, In,US
163/G4 **Crawfordville**, Fl,US
59/F4 **Crawley**, Eng,UK
53/P7 **Cray** (riv.), Eng,UK
53/P7 **Crayford**, Eng,UK
156/F4 **Crazy** (mts.), Mt,US
54/B3 **Creag Meagaidh** (mtn.), Sc,UK
166/B1 **Creasy** (Mifflinville), Pa,US
79/F2 **Creazzo**, It.
68/A3 **Crécy-en-Ponthieu**, Fr.
58/D2 **Credenhill**, Eng,UK
161/Q8 **Credit** (riv.), On,Can
58/C5 **Crediton**, Eng,UK
152/F3 **Cree** (lake), Sk,Can
152/F3 **Cree** (riv.), Sk,Can
56/D2 **Cree** (riv.), Sc,UK
146/D3 **Creel**, Mex.
56/D2 **Creetown**, Sc,UK
53/U10 **Crégy-lès-Meaux**, Fr.
157/H2 **Creighton**, Sk,Can
68/B5 **Creil**, Fr.
78/C2 **Crema**, It.
67/H4 **Cremlingen**, Ger.
78/D2 **Cremona**, It.
78/C2 **Cremona** (prov.), It.
68/B5 **Crépy-en-Valois**, Fr.
54/A3 **Creran, Loch** (inlet), Sc,UK
82/B3 **Cres** (isl.), Cro.
158/A2 **Crescent City**, Ca,US
105/F5 **Crescent Group** (isls.), China
142/E2 **Crespo**, Arg.
167/K8 **Cresskill**, NJ,US
72/F4 **Crest**, Fr.
165/P16 **Crest Hill**, Il,US
164/C2 **Crestline**, Ca,US
156/D3 **Creston**, BC,Can
157/K5 **Creston**, Ia,US
163/G4 **Crestview**, Fl,US
57/G5 **Creswell**, Eng,UK
76/B5 **Crêt de la Neige** (mtn.), Fr.
76/B5 **Crêt du Nu** (mtn.), Fr.
81/J5 **Crete** (isl.), Gre.
81/J5 **Crete** (sea), Gre.
159/H2 **Crete**, Ne,US
53/T10 **Créteil**, Fr.
54/B5 **Creuch** (hill), Sc,UK
75/G1 **Creus** (cape), Sp.
72/D3 **Creuse** (riv.), Fr.
71/E3 **Creussen** (riv.), Ger.
69/F5 **Creutzwald-la-Croix**, Fr.
79/E3 **Crevalcore**, It.
75/E3 **Crevillente**, Sp.
57/F5 **Crewe**, Eng,UK
58/D5 **Crewkerne**, Eng,UK
54/B4 **Crianlarich**, Sc,UK
56/D6 **Criccieth**, Wal,UK
141/B4 **Criciúma**, Braz.
58/C3 **Crickhowell**, Wal,UK
59/E3 **Cricklade**, Eng,UK
54/C4 **Crieff**, Sc,UK
68/A3 **Criel-sur-Mer**, Fr.
56/E2 **Criffell** (hill), Eng,UK
86/E3 **Crimean** (pen.), Ukr.
86/E3 **Crimean Obl.**, Ukr.
54/E1 **Crimond**, Sc,UK
124/H7 **Cristal** (mts.), Gabon
140/A5 **Cristalina**, Braz.
141/H7 **Cristina**, Braz.
140/A3 **Cristino Castro**, Braz.
144/J7 **Cristóbal** (pt.), Ecu.
138/C2 **Cristóbal Colón** (peak), Col.
82/F2 **Criştul Alb** (riv.), Rom.
83/G2 **Cristuru Secuiesc**, Rom.
82/E2 **Crişul Negru** (riv.), Rom.
137/H6 **Crixás-Açu** (riv.), Braz.
81/G2 **Crna Reka** (riv.), Macd.
60/A2 **Croaghmoyle** (mtn.), Ire.
119/D3 **Croajingolong Nat'l Park**, Austl.
82/B3 **Croatia**
77/H5 **Croce, Monte** (peak), It.
77/H4 **Croce, Pico di** (peak), It.
161/F2 **Croche** (riv.), Qu,Can
76/C6 **Croche, Aiguille** (peak), Fr.
144/J7 **Crocker** (peak), Ecu.
112/A4 **Crocker** (range), Malay.
56/E1 **Crocketford**, Sc,UK
162/E4 **Crockett**, Tx,US
119/D2 **Crocodile** (pt.), Austl.
166/B5 **Crofton**, Md,US
58/B3 **Crofty**, Wal,UK
60/D4 **Croghan** (mtn.), Ire.
60/A6 **Crohane** (mtn.), Ire.
72/F5 **Croisette** (cape), Fr.
53/T10 **Croissy-Beaubourg**, Fr.
157/L3 **Croix** (lake), Can., US
76/B5 **Croix de la Serra, Col de la** (pass), Fr.
114/E2 **Croker** (isl.), Austl.
54/B1 **Cromarty**, Sc,UK
54/B1 **Cromarty** (firth), Sc,UK
117/F3 **Crombie** (peak), Austl.
54/C2 **Cromdale**, Sc,UK
54/C2 **Cromdale** (hills), Sc,UK
59/H1 **Cromer**, Eng,UK
115/Q12 **Cromwell**, NZ
168/B2 **Cromwell**, Ct,US
109/E3 **Crong A Na** (riv.), Viet.
118/H9 **Cronulla**, Austl.
57/G2 **Crook**, Eng,UK
150/C2 **Crooked** (isl.), Bahm.
150/C2 **Crooked Island** (passg.), Bahm.
157/J4 **Crookston**, Mn,US
57/E5 **Crosby**, Eng,UK
157/H3 **Crosby**, ND,US
162/C3 **Crosbyton**, Tx,US
53/T10 **Crosne**, Fr.
129/H5 **Cross** (riv.), Camr., Nga.
157/J2 **Cross** (lake), Mb,Can
163/H4 **Cross City**, Fl,US
162/F3 **Crossett**, Ar,US
57/F2 **Cross Fell** (mtn.), Eng,UK
156/E3 **Crossfield**, Ab,Can
54/C4 **Crossford**, Sc,UK
56/C3 **Crossgar**, NI,UK
58/C2 **Crossgates**, Wal,UK
54/B6 **Crosshill**, Sc,UK
54/B5 **Crosshouse**, Sc,UK
58/C3 **Crosskeys**, Wal,UK
56/B3 **Crossmaglen**, NI,UK
56/E2 **Crossmichael**, Sc,UK
129/H5 **Cross River** (state), Nga.
167/E1 **Cross River** (res.), NY,US
163/G3 **Crossville**, Tn,US
166/D3 **Crosswicks** (cr.), NJ,US
78/D3 **Crostolo** (riv.), It.
57/F4 **Croston**, Eng,UK
80/E3 **Crotone**, It.
167/E1 **Croton-Harmon** (Croton-on-Hudson), NY,US
167/E1 **Croton-on-Hudson** (Croton-Harmon), NY,US
59/G3 **Crouch** (riv.), Eng,UK
68/C5 **Crouy-sur-Ourq**, Fr.
156/G4 **Crow Agency**, Mt,US
59/G4 **Crowborough**, Eng,UK
119/E1 **Crowdy Bay Nat'l Park**, Austl.
160/E2 **Crowe** (riv.), On,Can
156/F5 **Crowheart**, Wy,US
59/F1 **Crowland**, Eng,UK
57/H4 **Crowle**, Eng,UK
162/E4 **Crowley**, La,US
163/F3 **Crowley's** (ridge), Ar,US
157/K4 **Crow, North Fork** (riv.), Mn,US
160/C3 **Crown Point**, In,US
158/E4 **Crownpoint**, NM,US
153/H1 **Crown Prince Frederik** (isl.), NW,Can
118/D4 **Crows Nest Falls Nat'l Park**, Austl.
59/F4 **Crowthorne**, Eng,UK
53/M7 **Croxley Green**, Eng,UK
119/G5 **Croydon**, Austl.
53/N7 **Croydon**, Eng,UK
53/N7 **Croydon** (bor.), Eng,UK
166/D3 **Croydon**, Pa,US
51/M8 **Crozet** (isls.), FrAnt.
113/M **Crozier** (cape), Ant.
72/A2 **Crozon**, Fr.
54/A4 **Cruach Mhór** (mtn.), Sc,UK
54/A5 **Cruach nan Capull** (mtn.), Sc,UK
149/G1 **Crucero Contramaestre**, Cuba
54/E2 **Cruden Bay**, Sc,UK
54/D3 **Cruick Water** (riv.), Sc,UK
56/B2 **Crumlin**, NI,UK
57/E2 **Crummock Water** (lake), Eng,UK
69/E5 **Crusnes** (riv.), Fr.
149/G2 **Cruz** (cape), Cuba
142/E2 **Cruz Alta**, Arg.
135/F2 **Cruz Alta**, Braz.
75/P10 **Cruz Alta** (mtn.), Port.
140/C4 **Cruz das Almas**, Braz.
135/D3 **Cruz del Eje**, Arg.
141/J7 **Cruzeiro**, Braz.
144/C2 **Cruzeiro do Sul**, Braz.
140/C2 **Cruzeta**, Braz.
141/J6 **Cruzília**, Braz.
82/D3 **Crvenka**, Yugo.
57/E5 **Cryn-y-Brain** (mtn.), Wal,UK
166/C1 **Crystal** (lake), Pa,US
158/C3 **Crystal Bay**, Nv,US
166/C2 **Crystal Cave**, Pa,US
162/D4 **Crystal City**, Tx,US
160/B2 **Crystal Falls**, Mi,US
165/P15 **Crystal Lake**, Il,US
165/K11 **Crystal Springs** (res.), Ca,US
82/E2 **Csongrád**, Hun.
82/E2 **Csongrád** (co.), Hun.
82/C2 **Csorna**, Hun.
82/E2 **Csorvás**, Hun.
82/D2 **Csóványos** (peak), Hun.
93/F3 **Ctesiphon** (ruins), Iraq
126/G3 **Cuamba**, Moz.
126/D4 **Cuando** (riv.), Ang.
126/C4 **Cuangar**, Ang.
126/C2 **Cuango** (riv.), Ang.
126/B2 **Cuanza** (riv.), Ang.
75/E3 **Cuart de Poblet**, Sp.
142/D2 **Cuarto** (riv.), Arg.
146/E3 **Cuatrociénagas**, Mex.
146/D2 **Cuauhtémoc**, Mex.
147/L6 **Cuautepec de Hinojosa**, Mex.
147/Q9 **Cuautitlán**, Mex.
147/Q9 **Cuautitlán** (riv.), Mex.
147/F5 **Cuautla**, Mex.
148/B2 **Cuautla**, Mex.
149/F1 **Cuba**
159/K3 **Cuba**, Mo,US
139/E2 **Cubagua** (isl.), Ven.
126/C4 **Cubango** (riv.), Ang.
141/G8 **Cubatão**, Braz.
140/C2 **Cubati**, Braz.
92/C1 **Çubuk**, Turk.
164/C2 **Cucamonga** (Rancho Cucamonga), Ca,US
164/C2 **Cucamonga Wilderness**, Ca,US
139/E3 **Cuchivero** (riv.), Ven.
148/D3 **Cuchumatanes, Sierra los** (range), Guat.
59/F4 **Cuckfield**, Eng,UK
59/G5 **Cuckmere** (riv.), Eng,UK
109/D1 **Cuc Phuong Nat'l Park**, Viet.
139/E4 **Cucuí**, Braz.
138/C3 **Cúcuta**, Col.
164/F8 **Cudahy**, Ca,US
165/Q14 **Cudahy**, Wi,US
108/G3 **Cuddalore**, India
106/C5 **Cuddapah**, India
57/F5 **Cuddington**, Eng,UK
74/B1 **Cudillero**, Sp.
57/G4 **Cudworth**, Eng,UK
74/C2 **Cuéllar**, Sp.
138/B5 **Cuenca**, Ecu.
74/D2 **Cuenca**, Sp.
74/E2 **Cuenca** (range), Sp.
146/E3 **Cuencamé**, Mex.
147/E5 **Cueramo**, Mex.
147/F5 **Cuernavaca**, Mex.
162/D4 **Cuero**, Tx,US
72/G5 **Cuers**, Fr.
149/H1 **Cueto**, Cuba
138/D2 **Cueva de la Quebrada del Toro Nat'l Park**, Ven.
138/B4 **Cueva de los Guarcharos Nat'l Park**, Col.
74/E4 **Cuevas del Almanzora**, Sp.
53/N6 **Cuffley**, Eng,UK
83/F3 **Cugir**, Rom.
72/D5 **Cugnaux-Vingtcasses**, Fr.
137/G7 **Cuiabá**, Braz.
137/G7 **Cuiabá** (riv.), Braz.
138/D2 **Cuicas**, Ven.
66/C5 **Cuijk**, Neth.
148/D3 **Cuilapa**, Guat.
60/C1 **Cuilcagh** (mtn.), Wal,UK
148/C3 **Cuilco** (riv.), Guat., Mex.
55/H8 **Cuillin** (sound), Sc,UK
126/C2 **Cuilo** (riv.), Ang.
126/C3 **Cuima**, Ang.
76/B4 **Cuisance** (riv.), Fr.
140/C2 **Cuité**, Braz.
147/N8 **Cuitlahuac**, Mex.
126/C4 **Cuito** (riv.), Ang.
126/C4 **Cuito-Cuanavale**, Ang.
139/E5 **Cuiuni** (riv.), Braz.
105/G3 **Cuiwei** (mtn.), China
147/Q10 **Cujimalpa**, Mex.
109/E4 **Cu Lao** (isl.), Viet.
112/C3 **Culasi**, Phil.
56/A1 **Culdaff** (riv.), Ire.
66/C5 **Culemborg**, Neth.
137/H6 **Culene** (riv.), Braz.
119/C1 **Culgoa** (riv.), Austl.
146/D3 **Culiacán**, Mex.
112/B3 **Culion** (isl.), Phil.
112/C3 **Culion Res.**, Phil.
74/D4 **Cúllar Baza**, Sp.
54/D1 **Cullen**, Sc,UK
60/A4 **Cullenagh** (riv.), Ire.
75/E3 **Cullera**, Sp.
74/A1 **Culleredo**, Sp.
60/A2 **Cullin** (lake), Ire.
163/G3 **Cullman**, Al,US
54/B2 **Culloden Battlesite** (1746), Sc,UK
58/C5 **Cullompton**, Eng,UK
56/B2 **Cullybackey**, NI,UK
165/D2 **Culmback** (dam), Wa,US
56/A1 **Culmore**, NI,UK
118/B5 **Culoga** (riv.), Austl.
160/E4 **Culpeper**, Va,US
54/C4 **Culross**, Sc,UK
60/B3 **Cultra, Lough** (lake), Ire.
54/D2 **Cults**, Sc,UK
116/E5 **Culver** (pt.), Austl.
164/B2 **Culver City**, Ca,US
166/D1 **Culvers** (lake), NJ,US
139/E2 **Cumaná**, Ven.
141/B1 **Cumari**, Braz.
138/B4 **Cumbal, Nevado de** (peak), Col.
153/K2 **Cumberland** (pen.), NW,Can
153/K2 **Cumberland** (sound), NW,Can
157/H2 **Cumberland** (delta), Sk,Can
157/H2 **Cumberland** (lake), Sk,Can
163/G3 **Cumberland** (plat.), US
163/H4 **Cumberland** (isl.), Ga,US
163/G2 **Cumberland** (falls), Ky,US
160/C4 **Cumberland** (lake), Ky,US
163/G2 **Cumberland** (riv.), Ky, Tn,US
160/E4 **Cumberland**, Md,US
166/C5 **Cumberland** (co.), NJ,US
166/A3 **Cumberland** (co.), Pa,US
160/D4 **Cumberland Gap Nat'l Hist. Park**, Tn,US
168/C2 **Cumberland Hill**, RI,US
157/H2 **Cumberland House**, Sk,Can
54/C5 **Cumbernauld**, Sc,UK
147/G5 **Cumbres Bastonal, Cerro** (mtn.), Mex.
147/E3 **Cumbres de Monterrey Nat'l Park**, Mex.
57/F2 **Cumbria** (co.), Eng,UK
57/E3 **Cumbrian** (mts.), Eng,UK
106/C4 **Cumbum**, India
54/B6 **Cumnock**, Sc,UK
92/C2 **Çumra**, Turk.
151/M5 **Cumshewa** (pt.), BC,Can
142/B3 **Cunco**, Chile
116/D4 **Cundeelee Abor. Rsv.**, Austl.
138/C3 **Cundinamarca** (dept.), Col.
126/B4 **Cunene** (riv.), Ang.
78/A4 **Cuneo**, It.
78/A3 **Cuneo** (prov.), It.
109/E3 **Cung Son**, Viet.
141/J8 **Cunha**, Braz.
54/B5 **Cunninghame** (dist.), Sc,UK
61/H1 **Čuokkaraš'ša** (peak), Nor.
78/A2 **Cuorgnè**, It.
54/C4 **Cupar**, Sc,UK
165/K12 **Cupertino**, Ca,US
82/E4 **Ćuprija**, Yugo.
139/F3 **Cuquenán** (riv.), Ven.
140/C3 **Curaçá**, Braz.
150/D4 **Curaçao** (isl.), NAnt.
142/C3 **Curacautín**, Chile
142/B3 **Curanilahue**, Chile
138/C5 **Curaray** (riv.), Ecu., Peru
142/Q9 **Curaumilla** (pt.), Chile
82/F2 **Curcubăta** (peak), Rom.
72/E3 **Cure** (riv.), Fr.
133/S15 **Curepipe**, Mrts.
142/B2 **Curepto**, Chile
142/C2 **Curicó**, Chile
140/A3 **Curimatá**, Braz.
141/B3 **Curitiba**, Braz.
141/B3 **Curitibanos**, Braz.
78/B3 **Curone** (riv.), It.
60/D3 **Curragh, The**, Ire.
140/C2 **Currais Novos**, Braz.
159/K3 **Current** (riv.), Ar, Mo,US
54/C5 **Currie**, Sc,UK
158/D2 **Currie**, Nv,US
83/G3 **Curtea de Argeş**, Rom.
82/E2 **Curtici**, Rom.
118/C3 **Curtis** (isl.), Austl.
120/H8 **Curtis** (isl.), NZ
166/B6 **Curtis** (pt.), Md,US
139/H5 **Curuá** (riv.), Braz.
139/H5 **Curuá Una** (riv.), Braz.
144/C2 **Curuçú** (riv.), Braz.
149/E4 **Curú Nat'l Wild. Ref.**, CR
110/B4 **Curup**, Indo.
137/K4 **Cururupu**, Braz.
135/E2 **Curuzú Cuatiá**, Arg.
141/C1 **Curvelo**, Braz.
155/J2 **Curwood** (mtn.), Mi,US
144/D4 **Cusco**, Peru
56/B1 **Cushendall**, NI,UK
56/B3 **Cusher** (riv.), NI,UK
54/D6 **Cushet Law** (mtn.), Eng,UK
159/H4 **Cushing**, Ok,US
78/D4 **Cusna, Monte** (peak), It.
72/E3 **Cusset**, Fr.
163/G3 **Cusseta**, Ga,US
156/G4 **Custer**, Mt,US
157/H5 **Custer**, SD,US
140/C3 **Custódia**, Braz.
58/C5 **Cut** (hill), Eng,UK
156/E3 **Cut Bank**, Mt,US
144/B2 **Cutervo**, Peru
163/G4 **Cuthbert**, Ga,US
156/F2 **Cut Knife**, Sk,Can
142/C3 **Cutral-Có**, Arg.
106/E3 **Cuttack**, India
116/B3 **Cuvier** (cape), Austl.
67/F1 **Cuxhaven**, Ger.
168/F5 **Cuyahoga** (co.), Oh,US
168/F5 **Cuyahoga** (riv.), Oh,US
168/F5 **Cuyahoga Falls**, Oh,US
168/F5 **Cuyahoga Valley Nat'l Rec. Area**, Oh,US
158/C4 **Cuyama** (riv.), Ca,US
112/C3 **Cuyo**, Phil.
112/C3 **Cuyo** (isls.), Phil.
112/C3 **Cuyo East** (chan.), Phil.
112/C3 **Cuyo West** (chan.), Phil.
139/G3 **Cuyuni** (riv.), Guy., Ven.
139/F3 **Cuyuni-Mazaruni** (reg.), Guy.
144/D4 **Cuzco** (ruins), Peru
58/C3 **Cwm**, Wal,UK
58/C3 **Cwmafan**, Wal,UK
58/C3 **Cwmbran**, Wal,UK
157/H5 **C.W. McConaughy** (lake), Ne,US
130/A3 **Cyangugu**, Rwa.
81/J4 **Cyclades** (isls.), Gre.
160/C4 **Cynthiana**, Ky,US
58/B3 **Cynwyl Elfed**, Wal,UK
156/F3 **Cypress** (hills), Ab, Sk,Can
164/B3 **Cypress**, Ca,US
91/C2 **Cyprus**
125/K1 **Cyrenaica** (reg.), Libya
58/B3 **Cywyn** (riv.), Wal,UK
65/J2 **Czaplinek**, Pol.
65/M2 **Czarna Białostocka**, Pol.
65/J2 **Czarnków**, Pol.
65/H4 **Czech Republic**
65/K3 **Częstochowa**, Pol.
65/K3 **Częstochowa** (prov.), Pol.
65/J2 **Człuchów**, Pol.

D

105/J2 **Da** (riv.), China
97/J2 **Da'an**, China
103/B4 **Daba** (mts.), China
130/B5 **Dabaga**, Tanz.
82/D2 **Dabas**, Hun.
92/C5 **Dabbāgh, Jabal** (mtn.), SAr.
138/B3 **Dabeiba**, Col.
106/B3 **Dabhoi**, India
105/G2 **Dabie** (mts.), China
109/D1 **Da** (Black) (riv.), Viet.
165/B2 **Dabob** (bay), Wa,US
125/Q6 **Daborow**, Som.
128/D5 **Dabou**, IvC.
106/C2 **Dabra**, India
65/M2 **Dąbrowa Białostocka**, Pol.
65/K3 **Dąbrowa Górnicza**, Pol.
103/H7 **Dachang Huizu Zizhixian**, China
71/E6 **Dachau**, Ger.
109/D3 **Dac Sut**, Viet.
109/D3 **Dac To**, Viet.
163/H4 **Dade City**, Fl,US
111/H4 **Dadi** (cape), Indo.
106/B4 **Dadra & Nagar Haveli** (terr.), India
104/D2 **Dadu** (riv.), China
95/J3 **Dādu**, Pak.
106/D6 **Daduru** (riv.), SrL.
109/B4 **Daen Noi** (peak), Thai.
112/C2 **Daet**, Phil.
104/E3 **Dafang**, China
103/E4 **Dafeng**, China

104/D2 Dafu, China
128/B2 Dagana, Sen.
87/H3 Dagestan Aut. Rep., Rus.
132/D4 Daggaboersnek (pass), SAfr.
118/B2 Dagmar Range Nat'l Park, Austl.
104/D3 Daguan, China
118/E6 D'Aguilar (mtn.), Austl.
118/E6 D'Aguilar (range), Austl.
97/K2 Daguokui (peak), China
112/C1 Dagupan City, Phil.
102/E5 Dagzê (lake), China
103/C2 Dahaituo Shan (mtn.), China
90/D7 Dahana (des.), SAr.
106/B4 Dāhānu, India
106/A2 Daharki, Pak.
103/B2 Dahei (riv.), China
97/K2 Daheiding (peak), China
97/J2 Da Hinggang (mts.), China
125/N4 Dahlak (arch.), Erit.
163/H3 Dahlonega, Ga,US
65/G3 Dahme (riv.), Ger.
109/D4 Da Hoa, Viet.
103/C5 Dahong (mtn.), China
93/E2 Dahūk, Iraq
93/E2 Dahūk (gov.), Iraq
101/C2 Dahuofang (res.), China
105/J2 Dai (isl.), China
103/C2 Dai (lake), China
99/M9 Daian, Japan
103/D3 Daicheng, China
99/G2 Daigo, Japan
106/D2 Dailekh, Nepal
54/B6 Dailly, Sc,UK
109/E3 Dai Loc, Viet.
103/D3 Daimiao, China
74/D3 Daimiel, Sp.
162/E3 Daingerfield, Tx,US
118/B2 Daintree Nat'l Park, Austl.
99/E3 Daiō-zaki (pt.), Japan
149/H2 Daiquirí, Cuba
108/A2 Dāira Dīn Panāh, Pak.
142/E3 Daireaux, Arg.
117/N8 Dairy (cr.), Austl.
100/B3 Dai-Segen-dake (mtn.), Japan
98/C3 Dai-sen (mtn.), Japan
98/C2 Daisen-Oki Nat'l Park, Japan
98/C3 Daisen-Oki Nat'l Park, Japan
100/C2 Daisetsuzan Nat'l Park, Japan
99/L10 Daitō, Japan
120/C2 Daito (isls.), Japan
103/C3 Dai Xian, China
105/H3 Daiyun (peak), China
150/D3 Dajabón, DRep.
128/A3 Dakar (cap.), Sen.
128/A3 Dakar (reg.), Sen.
127/B3 Dākhilah, Wāḩāt ad (oasis), Egypt
124/B3 Dakhla, WSah.
128/A1 Dakhlet Nouadhibou (reg.), Mrta.
109/D3 Dak Nhe, Viet.
129/G3 Dakoro, Niger
159/H2 Dakota City, Ne,US
82/E4 Đakovica, Yugo.
82/D3 Đakovo, Yugo.
113/A Dakshin Gangotri, Ant.
52/E2 Dal (riv.), Swe.
103/B2 Dalad Qi, China
96/H3 Dalai (salt lake), China
92/B2 Dalaman, Turk.
96/E3 Dalandzadgad, Mong.
96/F2 Dalanjargalan, Mong.
62/E1 Dalarna (reg.), Swe.
63/S7 Dalarö, Swe.
109/E4 Da Lat, Viet.
61/Q6 Dalatangi (pt.), Ice.
54/A4 Dalavich, Sc,UK
56/E2 Dalbeattie, Sc,UK
118/C4 Dalby, Austl.
127/B4 Dal Cataract (falls), Sudan
66/D4 Dalfsen, Neth.
60/B2 Dalgan (riv.), Ire.
116/C3 Dalgaranger (mtn.), Austl.
162/C2 Dalhart, Tx,US
161/H1 Dalhousie, NB,Can
151/N1 Dalhousie (cape), NW,Can
103/B4 Dali, China
104/D3 Dali, China
103/B3 Dali (riv.), China
101/A3 Dalian, China
101/A3 Dalian (bay), China
74/D4 Dalías, Sp.
55/H8 Daliburgh, Sc,UK
93/F2 Dalidag (peak), Azer.
101/A2 Daling (riv.), China
82/D3 Dalj, Cro.
54/C5 Dalkeith, Sc,UK
151/M4 Dall (isl.), Ak,US
151/F3 Dall (lake), Ak,US
54/C1 Dallas, Sc,UK
162/D3 Dallas, Tx,US
156/C4 Dalles, The, Or,US
129/F3 Dallol Bosso (wadi), Mali, Niger
54/B4 Dalmally, Sc,UK
82/C4 Dalmatia (reg.), Cro.
54/B6 Dalmellington, Sc,UK
78/C1 Dalmine, It.
97/M3 Dal'negorsk, Rus.
97/L2 Dal'nerechensk, Rus.
128/D5 Daloa, IvC.
127/B4 Dalqū, Sudan
54/B5 Dalry, Sc,UK
118/B3 Dalrymple (lake), Austl.
54/B6 Dalrymple, Sc,UK
163/G3 Dalton, Ga,US
106/D3 Daltonganj, India
57/E3 Dalton-in-Furness, Eng,UK
105/G4 Daluo (peak), China
112/C1 Dalupiri (isl.), Phil.
54/B3 Dalwhinnie, Sc,UK
114/E2 Daly (riv.), Austl.
152/H2 Daly (bay), NW,Can
165/K11 Daly City, Ca,US
102/F5 Dam (riv.), China
93/J5 Damāgheh-ye Kūh (pt.), Iran
106/B3 Damān, India
106/B3 Damān & Diu (terr.), India
91/B4 Damanhūr, Egypt
105/H2 Damao (mtn.), China
111/G5 Damar (isl.), Indo.
166/A5 Damascus, Md,US
91/E3 Damascus (Dimashq) (cap.), Syria
124/H5 Damaturu, Nga.
93/H3 Damāvand (mtn.), Iran
109/D4 Dam Doi, Viet.
149/H2 Dame Marie (cape), Haiti
59/E5 Damerham, Eng,UK
93/H2 Dāmghān, Iran
91/B4 Damietta (Dumyāţ), Egypt
103/C3 Daming, China
105/F4 Daming (mtn.), China
69/D4 Damion (mtn.), Fr.
53/U9 Dammartin-en-Goële, Fr.
77/E4 Dammastock (peak), Swi.
68/C1 Damme, Belg.
67/F3 Damme, Ger.
106/C3 Damoh, India
129/E4 Damongo, Gha.
116/C2 Dampier (arch.), Austl.
111/H4 Dampier (str.), Indo.
53/R10 Dampierre, Fr.
109/C4 Damrei (mts.), Camb.
66/D2 Damsterdiep (riv.), Neth.
105/H3 Damuzhi (mtn.), China
69/E5 Damvillers, Fr.
102/F5 Damxung, China
103/B4 Dan (riv.), China
163/H2 Dan (riv.), NC,US
125/P5 Danakil (reg.), Djib.
128/C5 Danané, IvC.
109/E2 Da Nang, Viet.
112/D3 Danao, Phil.
164/C4 Dana Point, Ca,US
104/D2 Danba, China
59/G3 Danbury, Eng,UK
168/A3 Danbury, Ct,US
103/C4 Dancheng, China
119/G5 Dandenong, Austl.
119/G5 Dandenong (cr.), Austl.
119/G5 Dandenong (mtn.), Austl.
54/C5 Danderhall, Sc,UK
63/S7 Danderyd, Swe.
101/C2 Dandong, China
57/F5 Dane (riv.), Eng,UK
96/D4 Dang (riv.), China
105/J5 Dangayos (pt.), Phil.
132/B4 Danger (pt.), SAfr.
117/H5 Danggali Consv. Park, Austl.
125/N5 Dangila, Eth.
103/D4 Dangshan, China
103/D5 Dangtu, China
103/B5 Dangyang, China
84/J4 Danilov, Rus.
103/B3 Daning, China
103/B4 Danjiangkou, China
103/B4 Danjiangkou (res.), China
86/F1 Dankov, Rus.
102/C3 Dankova, Pik (peak), Kyr.
104/D2 Danleng, China
148/E3 Danlí, Hon.
163/G3 Dannelly (res.), Al,US
64/F2 Dannenberg, Ger.
115/S11 Dannevirke, NZ
52/F4 Danube (riv.), Eur.
83/J3 Danube (delta), Rom.
83/H3 Danube, Borcea Branch (riv.), Rom.
83/J3 Danube, Mouths of the, Rom.
83/J3 Danube, Sfîntu Gheorghe Branch (riv.), Rom.
83/J3 Danube, Sulina Branch (riv.), Rom.
165/L11 Danville, Ca,US
160/C3 Danville, Il,US
160/C4 Danville, Ky,US
160/E4 Danville, Va,US
105/F5 Dan Xian, China
105/F3 Dao Xian, China
105/E2 Daozhen, China
112/D3 Dapa, Phil.
129/F4 Dapaong, Togo
163/G4 Daphne, Al,US
112/C3 Dapitan, Phil.
97/K2 Daqing, China
103/H7 Daqing (riv.), China
95/H2 Daqq-e Patargān (lake), Afg., Iran
105/J2 Daqu (isl.), China
91/E3 Dar'ā, Syria
92/C3 Dar'ā (prov.), Syria
93/H4 Dārāb, Iran
83/H1 Darabani, Rom.
112/C2 Daraga, Phil.
112/D3 Daram, Phil.
82/E4 Đaravica (peak), Yugo.
91/E3 Dārayyā, Syria
106/E2 Darbhanga, India
151/F3 Darby (cape), Ak,US
166/C4 Darby, Pa,US
82/D3 Darda, Cro.
159/J4 Dardanelle (lake), Ar,US
92/A2 Dardanelles (str.), Turk.
119/G5 Darebin (cr.), Austl.
92/D2 Darende, Turk.
53/P8 Darent (riv.), Eng,UK
130/C4 Dar es Salaam (cap.), Tanz.
130/C4 Dar es Salaam (prov.), Tanz.
115/R11 Darfield, NZ
78/D1 Darfo, It.
115/R10 Dargaville, NZ
56/B5 Dargle (riv.), Ire.
96/F2 Darhan, Mong.
96/F2 Darhan (peak), Mong.
125/Q6 Darie (hills), Som.
138/B2 Darién (mts.), Col., Pan.
167/E1 Darien, Ct,US
163/H4 Darien, Ga,US
165/Q16 Darien, Il,US
149/G5 Darién Nat'l Park, Pan.
96/G2 Dariganga, Mong.
149/G4 Darién (range), Pan.
106/E2 Darjiling, India
96/D5 Darlag, China
116/L6 Darling (range), Austl.
119/B2 Darling (riv.), Austl.
118/C4 Darling Downs (upland), Austl.
57/G2 Darlington, Eng,UK
163/J3 Darlington, SC,US
65/J1 Darłowo, Pol.
70/B3 Darmstadt, Ger.
125/K1 Darnah, Libya
123/W18 Darnāya, Tun.
68/A5 Darnétal, Fr.
113/E Darnley (cape), Ant.
152/D2 Darnley (bay), NW,Can
57/G1 Darras Hall, Eng,UK
93/J2 Darreh Gaz, Iran
125/K6 Dar Rounga (reg.), CAfr.
62/E4 Darsser (cape), Ger.
113/R Dart (cape), Ant.
58/C6 Dart (riv.), Eng,UK
53/P7 Dartford, Eng,UK
58/C6 Dartington, Eng,UK
58/B5 Dartmoor (upland), Eng,UK
58/C5 Dartmoor Nat'l Park, Eng,UK
119/C3 Dartmouth (dam), Austl.
119/C3 Dartmouth (res.), Austl.
161/J2 Dartmouth, NS,Can
58/C6 Dartmouth, Eng,UK
168/C2 Dartmouth, Ma,US
57/G4 Darton, Eng,UK
75/G3 Dartuch (cape), Sp.
120/D5 Daru, PNG
82/C3 Daruvar, Cro.
112/B4 Darvel (bay), Malay.
54/B5 Darvel, Sc,UK
57/F4 Darwen, Eng,UK
131/C3 Darwendale, Zim.
114/E2 Darwin, Austl.
142/B5 Darwin (bay), Chile
143/K8 Darwin (mts.), Chile
144/J6 Darwin (isl.), Ecu.
144/J7 Darwin (vol.), Ecu.
95/H2 Daryācheh-ye Sīstān (lake), Iran
108/A2 Darya Khan, Pak.
97/H3 Dashengtang (peak), China
103/B5 Dashennongjia (peak), China
125/N5 Dashen, Ras (peak), Eth.
168/G6 Dashields (dam), Pa,US
93/H3 Dasht-e Kavīr (des.), Iran
93/J4 Dasht-e Lūt (des.), Iran
95/H2 Dasht-e Mārgow (des.), Afg.
95/H3 Dasht Kaur (riv.), Pak.
108/C1 Daska, Pak.
67/G5 Dassel, Ger.
132/B4 Dasseneiland (isl.), SAfr.
108/C2 Dasūya, India
53/M7 Datchet, Eng,UK
109/D4 Dat Do, Viet.
100/B2 Date, Japan
106/C2 Datia, India
105/F4 Datian (peak), China
158/F4 Datil, NM,US
103/C2 Datong, China
96/D4 Datong (mts.), China
96/D4 Datong (riv.), China
67/E5 Datteln, Ger.
110/C3 Datu (cape), Malay.
110/B3 Datuk (cape), Indo.
61/H4 Daugava (riv.), Lat.
63/L3 Daugava (riv.), Lat.
63/M4 Daugavpils, Lat.
138/B5 Daule, Ecu.
138/B5 Daule (riv.), Ecu.
69/F3 Daun, Ger.
109/B3 Daung (isl.), Burma
157/H3 Dauphin, Mb,Can
157/J3 Dauphin (lake), Mb,Can
166/B3 Dauphin (co.), Pa,US
106/C5 Dāvangere, India
112/D4 Davao (gulf), Phil.
112/D4 Davao City, Phil.
117/F2 Davenport (peak), Austl.
117/G2 Davenport (range), Austl.
157/L5 Davenport, Ia,US
156/D4 Davenport, Wa,US
59/E2 Daventry, Eng,UK
153/T6 Davgaard-Jensen (reg.), Grld.
149/F4 David, Pan.
159/H2 David City, Ne,US
157/G3 Davidson, Sk,Can
165/K11 Davidson (mtn.), Ca,US
117/F3 Davies (peak), Austl.
54/D2 Daviot, Sc,UK
113/F Davis (sea), Ant.
113/F Davis (sta.), Ant.
145/M3 Davis (str.), Can., Grld.
165/L9 Davis, Ca,US
165/E7 Davis (cr.), Mi,US
160/E4 Davis (peak), Pa,US
162/B4 Davis (mts.), Tx,US
85/M5 Davlekanovo, Rus.
128/D5 Davo (riv.), IvC.
77/F4 Davos, Swi.
96/C1 Davst, Mong.
101/B2 Dawa, China
105/H3 Dawang (mtn.), China
125/N7 Dawa Wenz (riv.), Afr.
103/D4 Dawen (riv.), China
58/C5 Dawlish, Eng,UK
118/C4 Dawson (riv.), Austl.
151/L3 Dawson, Yk,Can
143/K8 Dawson (isl.), Chile
163/G4 Dawson, Ga,US
156/C2 Dawson Creek, BC,Can
104/D2 Dawu, China
105/G2 Dawu, China
105/G2 Dawu (mtn.), China
103/C5 Dawu Shan (mtn.), China
94/G4 Dawwah, Oman
72/C5 Dax, Fr.
105/E2 Daxian, China
109/D1 Daxin, China
103/D3 Daxing, China
103/D2 Daxue (mts.), China
104/C4 Daxue (peak), China
101/B2 Dayang (riv.), China
104/D3 Dayao, China
103/C5 Daye, China
104/D2 Dayi, China
104/C3 Daying (riv.), China
143/F1 Dayman (riv.), Uru.
105/F2 Dayong, China
91/D4 Dayr al Balaḩ, Gaza
92/E3 Dayr az Zawr, Syria
92/E3 Dayr Az Zawr (prov.), Syria
127/B3 Dayrūt, Egypt
156/E2 Daysland, Ab,Can
160/C4 Dayton, Oh,US
163/G3 Dayton, Tn,US
156/D4 Dayton, Wa,US
163/H4 Daytona Beach, Fl,US
105/G3 Dayu, China
105/J3 Dayu (isl.), China
105/G4 Dayunwu (mtn.), China
105/E2 Dazhu, China
132/D3 De Aar, SAfr.
60/B4 Dead (riv.), Ire.
91/D4 Dead (sea), Isr., Jor.
116/C2 Deadman (peak), Austl.
157/H4 Deadwood, SD,US
119/C3 Deal (isl.), Austl.
59/H4 Deal, Eng,UK
156/B2 Dean (riv.), BC,Can
156/B2 Dean Channel (inlet), BC,Can
58/D3 Dean, Forest of (for.), Eng,UK
135/D3 Deán Funes, Arg.
165/F7 Dearborn, Mi,US
165/F7 Dearborn Heights, Mi,US
57/G4 Dearne, Eng,UK
57/G4 Dearne (riv.), Eng,UK
151/N4 Dease (riv.), BC,Can
152/F2 Dease (str.), NW,Can
158/C3 Death Valley, Ca,US
158/C3 Death Valley Nat'l Mon., Ca, Nv,US
93/F1 Deavgay (peak), Rus.
82/E5 Debar, Macd.
151/G3 Debauch (mtn.), Ak,US
59/H2 Deben (riv.), Eng,UK
59/H2 Debenham, Eng,UK
65/L3 Dębica, Pol.
66/C4 De Bilt, Neth.
65/L3 Dęblin, Pol.
65/H2 Dębno, Pol.
151/J3 Deborah (mtn.), Ak,US
125/N6 Debre Birhan, Eth.
82/E2 Debrecen, Hun.
125/N5 Debre Mark'os, Eth.
125/N5 Debre Tabor, Eth.
125/N6 Debre Zeyit, Eth.
163/G3 Decatur, Al,US
163/G3 Decatur, Ga,US
160/B4 Decatur, Il,US
160/C3 Decatur, In,US
162/D3 Decatur, Tx,US
72/E4 Decazeville, Fr.
106/C5 Deccan (plat.), India
104/D3 Dechang, China
65/H3 Děčín, Czh.
72/E3 Decize, Fr.
59/E3 Deddington, Eng,UK
66/D3 Dedemsvaart, Neth.
168/C1 Dedham, Ma,US
142/C5 Dedo (peak), Arg.
128/E3 Dédougou, Burk.
97/K2 Dedu, China
131/D2 Dedza, Malw.
60/D2 Dee (riv.), Ire.
55/K10 Dee (riv.), NI,UK
54/D2 Dee (riv.), Sc,UK
57/E5 Dee (riv.), Wal,UK
60/A1 Deel (riv.), Ire.
60/B5 Deel (riv.), Ire.
60/C2 Deel (riv.), Ire.
117/M8 Deep (cr.), Austl.
166/C6 Deep (cr.), De,US
59/F1 Deeping Saint James, Eng,UK
160/E2 Deep River, On,Can
166/C5 Deepwater (pt.), De,US
60/A4 Deer (isl.), Ire.
151/F5 Deer (isl.), Ak,US
166/B4 Deer (cr.), Md, Pa,US
165/Q15 Deerfield, Il,US
161/K1 Deer Lake, Nf,Can
68/C2 Deerlijk, Belg.
156/E4 Deer Lodge, Mt,US
167/E2 Deer Park, NY,US
156/D4 Deer Park, Wa,US
106/B3 Deesa, India
54/D2 Deeside (val.), Sc,UK
118/H8 Dee Why, Austl.
125/Q6 Deex Nugaaleed (dry river), Som.
136/F8 Defensores del Chaco Nat'l Park, Par.
160/C3 Defiance, Oh,US
167/K7 DeForest (lake), NY,US
163/G4 De Funiak Springs, Fl,US
56/E5 Deganwy, Wal,UK
125/P6 Degeh Bur, Eth.
161/G2 Dégelis, Qu,Can
62/F2 Degerfors, Swe.
71/F5 Deggendorf, Ger.
116/C2 De Grey (riv.), Austl.
68/C1 De Haan, Belg.
125/P4 Dehalak (isl.), Erit.
125/P4 Dehalak Marine Nat'l Park, Erit.
166/B3 De Hart (res.), Pa,US
95/L2 Dehra Dūn, India
106/D3 Dehri, India
105/H3 Dehua, China
97/K3 Dehui, China
68/C2 Deinze, Belg.
67/G4 Deister (mts.), Ger.
83/F2 Dej, Rom.
105/F2 Dejiang, China
160/B3 De Kalb, Il,US
165/N16 De Kalb (co.), Il,US
125/N4 Dek'emhāre, Erit.
163/H4 De Land, Fl,US
158/C4 Delano, Ca,US
95/H2 Delārām, Afg.
156/G2 Delarode (lake), Sk,Can
165/N14 Delavan, Wi,US
165/N14 Delavan (lake), Wi,US
160/F3 Delaware (riv.), US
160/F4 Delaware (state), US
166/C5 Delaware (bay), De, NJ,US
160/D3 Delaware, Oh,US
166/C4 Delaware (co.), Pa,US
166/C2 Delaware Water Gap (pass), Pa,US
166/D1 Delaware Water Gap Nat'l Rec. Area, NJ, Pa,US
67/F5 Delbrück, Ger.
142/D2 Del Campillo, Arg.
82/F5 Delčevo, Macd.
66/D4 Delden, Neth.
66/D2 De Leijen (lake), Neth.
76/D3 Delémont, Swi.
66/B4 Delft, Neth.
108/G4 Delft (isl.), SrL.
66/D2 Delfzijl, Neth.
142/E4 Delgada (pt.), Arg.
130/D5 Delgado (cape), Moz.
96/D2 Delger (riv.), Mong.
96/F2 Delgerhaan, Mong.
96/E2 Delgerhangay, Mong.
106/C2 Delhi, India
86/E5 Delice (riv.), Turk.
146/D2 Delicias, Mex.
66/B5 De Lier, Neth.
80/D5 Delimara, Ponta Ta' (pt.), Malta
156/G3 Delisle, Sk,Can
67/G5 Delligsen, Ger.
157/J5 Dell Rapids, SD,US
132/Q13 Delmas, SAfr.
69/F6 Delme, Fr.
67/F3 Delme (riv.), Ger.
67/F2 Delmenhorst, Ger.
140/C3 Delmiro Gouveia, Braz.
159/F3 Del Norte, Co,US
157/H3 Deloraine, Mb,Can
81/J4 Delos (ruins), Gre.
81/H3 Delphi (ruins), Gre.
160/C3 Delphos, Oh,US
165/M12 Del Puerto (cr.), Ca,US
166/D3 Delran, NJ,US
163/H5 Delray Beach, Fl,US
162/C4 Del Rio, Tx,US
158/E3 Delta, Co,US
158/D3 Delta, Ut,US
139/F2 Delta Amacuro (terr.), Ven.
143/T12 Delta del Tigre, Uru.
165/M11 Delta-Mendota (can.), Ca,US
163/H4 Deltona, Fl,US
96/C2 Delüün, Mong.
165/L11 Del Valle (lake), Ca,US
85/M5 Dëma (riv.), Rus.
74/D1 Demanda (range), Sp.
151/K2 Demarcation (pt.), Ak,US
126/D2 Demba, Zaire
125/M6 Dembī Dolo, Eth.
66/B7 Demer (riv.), Belg.
139/G3 Demerara (riv.), Guy.
139/G3 Demerara-Mahaica (reg.), Guy.
140/B2 Demerval Lobão, Braz.
76/A4 Demigny, Fr.
158/F4 Deming, NM,US
139/F4 Demini (riv.), Braz.
92/B2 Demirci, Turk.
92/C2 Demirkazık (peak), Turk.
64/G2 Demmin, Ger.
163/G3 Demopolis, Al,US
110/B4 Dempo (peak), Indo.
116/D5 Dempster (pt.), Austl.
68/C3 Denain, Fr.
125/P5 Denakil (reg.), Eth.
151/H3 Denali Nat'l Park & Prsv., Ak,US
157/H2 Denare Beach, Sk,Can
57/E5 Denbigh, Wal,UK
66/B2 Den Burg, Neth.
57/G4 Denby Dale, Eng,UK
68/D2 Dender (riv.), Belg.
68/D2 Denderleeuw, Belg.
68/D1 Dendermonde, Belg.
131/C4 Dendron, SAfr.
66/D4 Denekamp, Neth.
103/C4 Dengfeng, China
96/F3 Dengkou, China
105/G3 Dengta, China
103/C4 Deng Xian, China
116/B3 Denham (sound), Austl.
66/D4 Den Ham, Neth.
53/M7 Denham, Eng,UK
66/B3 Den Helder, Neth.
57/G4 Denholme, Eng,UK
75/F3 Denia, Sp.
119/C2 Deniliquin, Austl.
158/C2 Denio, Nv,US
151/H4 Denison (mtn.), Ak,US
157/K5 Denison, Ia,US
162/D3 Denison, Tx,US
92/B2 Denizli, Turk.
92/B2 Denizli (prov.), Turk.
113/G Denman (glac.), Ant.
62/C4 Denmark
145/Q3 Denmark (str.), NAm
54/C4 Denny, Sc,UK
110/E5 Denpasar, Indo.
76/D5 Dent Blanche (peak), Swi.
76/C4 Dent de Lys (peak), Swi.
76/D6 Dent d'Hérens (peak), It., Swi.
68/C2 Dentergem, Belg.
59/G5 Denton, Eng,UK
162/D3 Denton, Tx,US
116/B5 D'Entrecasteaux (pt.), Austl.
120/D5 D'Entrecasteaux (isls.), PNG
76/C5 Dents du Midi (peak), Swi., It.
159/F3 Denver (cap.), Co,US
160/D2 Denville, NJ,US
70/A6 Denzlingen, Ger.
106/C2 Deoband, India
106/D3 Deogarh, India
106/E3 Deoghar, India
106/B4 Deolāli, India
106/C2 Deoli, India
72/D3 Déols, Fr.
106/D2 Deoria, India
68/B1 De Panne, Belg.
66/C6 De Peel (reg.), Neth.
139/E1 Dependencias Federales (terr.), Ven.
161/S10 Depew, NY,US
68/C2 De Pinte, Belg.
53/N7 Deptford, Eng,UK
103/J9 Deqing, China
125/P7 Dera (dry riv.), Som.
130/A2 Dera, Zaire
108/A2 Dera Ghāzi Khān, Pak.
108/A2 Dera Ismā'īl Khān, Pak.
87/J4 Derbent, Rus.
57/G6 Derby, Eng,UK
168/A3 Derby, Ct,US
159/H3 Derby, Ks,US
57/G6 Derbyshire (co.), Eng,UK
83/F3 Đerdap Nat'l Park, Yugo.
82/E2 Derecske, Hun.
93/M6 Dereköy (riv.), Turk.
96/F2 Deren, Mong.
60/B4 Derg, Lough (lake), Ire.
162/E4 De Ridder, La,US
92/E2 Derik, Turk.
92/C2 Derinkuyu, Turk.
72/B2 Déroute (passg.), Fr., Chl,UK
60/C2 Derravaragh, Lough (lake), Ire.
60/D4 Derreen (riv.), Ire.
60/D4 Derry (riv.), Ire.
161/G3 Derry, NH,US
56/C3 Derryboy, NI,UK
56/C3 Derrylin, NI,UK
60/A6 Derrynasaggart (mts.), Ire.
59/G1 Dersingham, Eng,UK
55/H8 Dervaig, Sc,UK
82/C3 Derventa, Bosn.
56/B1 Dervock, NI,UK
119/C4 Derwent (riv.), Austl.
57/F2 Derwent (res.), Eng,UK
57/E2 Derwent (riv.), Eng,UK
57/G5 Derwent (riv.), Eng,UK
57/H4 Derwent (riv.), Eng,UK
56/E2 Derwent Water (lake), Eng,UK
142/D2 Desaguadero (riv.), Arg.
136/E7 Desaguadero (riv.), Bol.
147/Q9 Desagüe, Gran Canal de (can.), Mex.
59/F2 Desborough, Eng,UK
142/C2 Descabezado Grande (vol.), Chile
141/C2 Descalvado, Braz.
148/E4 Descartes (pt.), CR
157/H2 Deschambault (lake), Sk,Can
157/H2 Deschambault Lake, Sk,Can
158/B2 Deschutes (riv.), Or,US
149/H2 Desdunes, Haiti
125/N5 Desē, Eth.
135/C6 Deseado (riv.), Arg.
143/J8 Deseado (cape), Chile
143/L7 Desengaño (pt.), Arg.
78/D2 Desenzano del Garda, It.
75/V15 Desertas (isl.), Madr.,Port.
103/B4 Deshengpu, China
147/Q10 Desierto de Los Leones Nat'l Park, Mex.
78/C1 Desio, It.
157/J4 De Smet, SD,US
157/K5 Des Moines (cap.), Ia,US
157/K5 Des Moines (riv.), Ia, Mo,US
165/C3 Des Moines, Wa,US
86/D2 Desna (riv.), Rus., Ukr.
143/J8 Desolación (isl.), Chile
112/D3 Desolation (pt.), Phil.
132/D4 Desolation, Valley of (val.), SAfr.
140/A2 Desordem (mts.), Braz.
159/K3 De Soto, Mo,US
132/D4 Despatch, SAfr.
165/Q15 Des Plaines, Il,US
165/P16 Des Plaines (riv.), Il,US
64/G3 Dessau, Ger.
69/E1 Dessel, Belg.
76/C3 Dessoubre (riv.), Fr.
68/C1 Destelbergen, Belg.
151/L3 Destruction Bay, Yk,Can
82/E3 Deta, Rom.
131/B3 Dete, Zim.
67/F5 Detmold, Ger.
165/F7 Detroit, Mi,US
165/F7 Detroit (riv.), On,Can, Mi,US
157/K4 Detroit Lakes, Mn,US
70/D3 Dettelbach, Ger.
61/P6 Dettifoss (falls), Ice.
119/D2 Deua Nat'l Park, Austl.
53/S10 Deuil-la-Barre, Fr.
68/B2 Deûle (riv.), Fr.
66/B6 Deurne, Belg.
66/C6 Deurne, Neth.
73/L3 Deutschlandsberg, Aus.
161/N6 Deux-Montagnes, Qu,Can
161/M6 Deux-Montagnes (co.), Qu,Can
161/M7 Deux-Montagnes (lake), Qu,Can
82/F3 Deva, Rom.
108/G4 Devakottai, India
82/E2 Dévaványa, Hun.
92/E2 Devegeçidi (dam), Turk.
92/C2 Develi, Turk.
66/D4 Deventer, Neth.
54/D1 Deveron (riv.), Sc,UK
137/H2 Devil's (isl.), FrG.
108/H4 Devil's (pt.), SrL.
159/G5 Devils (riv.), Tx,US
60/C4 Devilsbit (mtn.), Ire.
54/C3 Devil's Elbow (pass), Sc,UK
157/J3 Devils Lake, ND,US
151/M4 Devils Paw (mtn.), BC,Can, Ak,US
158/C3 Devils Postpile Nat'l Mon., Ca,US
157/G4 Devils Tower Nat'l Mon., Wy,US
83/G5 Devin, Bul.
162/D4 Devine, Tx,US
59/E4 Devizes, Eng,UK
83/H4 Devnya, Bul.
81/G2 Devoll (riv.), Alb.
156/E2 Devon, Ab,Can
153/S7 Devon (isl.), NW,Can
58/C5 Devon (co.), Eng,UK
54/C4 Devon (riv.), Sc,UK
119/C4 Devonport, Austl.
83/K5 Devrek, Turk.
86/D4 Devrek (riv.), Turk.
86/E4 Devrez (riv.), Turk.
131/C3 Devure (riv.), Zim.
110/A3 Dewa (pt.), Indo.
100/B4 Dewa (mts.), Japan
106/C3 Dewās, India
162/E2 Dewey, Ok,US
159/H2 De Witt, Ne,US
57/G4 Dewsbury, Eng,UK
161/G2 Dexter, Me,US
104/E2 Deyang, China
117/F4 Dey-Dey (lake), Austl.
93/G3 Dez (riv.), Iran
93/G3 Dezfūl, Iran
151/E2 Dezhneva, Mys (pt.), Rus.
103/D3 Dezhou, China
127/C2 Dhahab, Egypt
106/F3 Dhākā (Dacca) (cap.), Bang.
104/B4 Dhaleswari (riv.), India
106/D3 Dhamtari, India
108/C2 Dhanaula, India
106/E3 Dhānbād, India
106/E2 Dhankuta, Nepal
106/B3 Dharampur, India
108/F3 Dhārāpuram, India
106/B3 Dhāri, India
108/C2 Dhāriwāl, India
106/C5 Dharmapuri, India
106/C5 Dharmavaram, India
108/D1 Dharmsāla, India
106/D2 Dhaulāgiri (peak), Nepal
81/H3 Dhelfoí (Delphi) (ruins), Gre.
106/E3 Dhenkānāl, India
76/A4 Dheune (riv.), Fr.
81/K2 Dhidhimótikhon, Gre.
93/F4 Dhī Qār (gov.), Iraq
81/H3 Dhírfis (peak), Gre.
131/C3 Dhlo Dhlo (ruins), Zim.
94/F5 Dhofar (reg.), Oman
106/B3 Dholka, India
106/C2 Dholpur, India
106/B4 Dhond, India
81/J4 Dhonoúsa (isl.), Gre.
106/B3 Dhorāji, India
81/J2 Dhráma, Gre.
69/F4 Dhronbach (riv.), Ger.
106/E2 Dhubri, India
106/B3 Dhūlia, India
106/E3 Dhuliān, India
106/E2 Dhupgāri, India
108/C2 Dhūri, India
81/J5 Dia (isl.), Gre.
73/G4 Diable, Cime du (peak), Fr.
151/H4 Diablo (mtn.), Ak,US
165/L11 Diablo (mtn.), Ca,US
158/B3 Diablo (range), Ca,US
162/B4 Diablo (plat.), Tx,US
143/G2 Diablo, Punta del (pt.), Uru.
150/F4 Diablotin (peak), Dom.
141/G8 Diadema, Braz.
142/E2 Diamante, Arg.
142/D2 Diamante (riv.), Arg.
117/J3 Diamantina (riv.), Austl.
141/D1 Diamantina, Braz.
140/B3 Diamantina (mts.), Braz.
137/G6 Diamantino, Braz.
119/G5 Diamond (cr.), Austl.
156/E4 Diamond (peak), Id,US
164/C3 Diamond Bar, Ca,US
154/W13 Diamond Head (crater), Hi,US
154/W13 Diamond Head Saint Mon., Hi,US
104/D3 Dian (lake), China
105/F4 Dianbai, China
104/D3 Diancang (mtn.), China
105/E2 Dianjiang, China
78/B5 Diano Marina, It.
103/L8 Dianshan (lake), China
129/F3 Diapaga, Burk.
77/F5 Diavolezza (peak), Swi.
113/J Dibble Iceberg Tongue, Ant.
131/B4 Dibete, Bots.
127/B4 Dibis, Bīr (well), Egypt
162/E4 Diboll, Tx,US
104/B3 Dibrugarh, India
167/G1 Dickens (pt.), RI,US
162/C3 Dickens, Tx,US
157/H4 Dickinson, ND,US
163/G2 Dickson, Tn,US
66/D5 Didam, Neth.
59/E3 Didcot, Eng,UK
156/E3 Didsbury, Ab,Can
95/K3 Didwāna, India
92/A2 Didyma (ruins), Turk.
133/E2 Die Berg (peak), SAfr.
128/E4 Diébougou, Burk.
70/B3 Dieburg, Ger.
152/F3 Diefenbaker (lake), Sk,Can
143/J7 Diego de Almagro (isl.), Chile
90/G10 Diego Garcia (isl.), BrIn.
69/E4 Diekirch (dist.), Lux.
67/F5 Diemel (riv.), Ger.
66/B4 Diemen, Neth.
109/C1 Dien Bien Phu, Viet.
109/D2 Dien Chau, Viet.
109/E3 Dien Khanh, Viet.
69/E2 Diepenbeek, Belg.
66/D4 Diepenveen, Neth.
67/F3 Diepholz, Ger.
68/A4 Dieppe, Fr.
77/H2 Diessen am Ammersee, Ger.
69/E2 Diest, Belg.
77/E3 Dietikon, Swi.
77/G2 Dietmannsried, Ger.
70/B2 Dietzenbach, Ger.
70/B2 Diez, Ger.
130/D2 Dif, Kenya
124/H5 Diffa, Niger
129/H3 Diffa (dept.), Niger
69/E4 Differdange, Lux.
119/B3 Difficult (peak), Austl.
104/B3 Digboi, India
161/H2 Digby, NS,Can

185
Digne – Eagle

73/G4 Digne, Fr.
72/E3 Digoin, Fr.
112/D4 Digos, Phil.
106/C3 Digras, India
104/B2 Dihang (riv.), India
68/D2 Dijle (Dyle) (riv.), Belg.
76/A3 Dijon, Fr.
125/P5 Dikhil, Djib.
91/B4 Dikirnis, Egypt
87/H4 Diklosmta, Gora (peak), Geo.
68/B1 Diksmuide, Belg.
124/H5 Dikwa, Nga.
125/N6 Dīla, Eth.
68/D2 Dilbeek, Belg.
92/A2 Dilek Yarımadası Nat'l Park, Turk.
111/G5 Dili, Indo.
70/B1 Dill (riv.), Ger.
69/H2 Dillenburg, Ger.
125/L5 Dilling, Sudan
69/F5 Dillingen, Ger.
70/D5 Dillingen an der Donau, Ger.
154/V12 Dillingham A.F.B., Hi,US
163/J3 Dillon, SC,US
126/D3 Dilolo, Zaire
69/E1 Dilsen, Belg.
104/B3 Dimāpur, India
92/D3 Dimashq (prov.), Syria
91/E3 Dimashq (Damascus) (cap.), Syria
112/C4 Dimataling, Phil.
128/D5 Dimbokro, IvC.
83/G3 Dîmbovița (co.), Rom.
89/P2 Dimitriya Lapteva (str.), Rus.
83/G4 Dimitrovgrad, Bul.
87/J1 Dimitrovgrad, Rus.
82/F4 Dimitrovgrad, Yugo.
124/H6 Dimlang (peak), Nga.
91/D4 Dimona, Isr.
91/D4 Dimona, Hare (mtn.), Isr.
108/B1 Dina, Pak.
112/D3 Dinagat, Phil.
112/D3 Dinagat (isl.), Phil.
106/E2 Dinājpur, Bang.
72/B2 Dinan, Fr.
108/C1 Dīnānagar, India
69/D3 Dinant, Belg.
92/B2 Dinar, Turk.
72/B2 Dinard, Fr.
81/E1 Dinaric Alps (range), Bosn., Cro.
58/B2 Dinas (pt.), Wal,UK
58/C4 Dinas Powys, Wal,UK
125/N5 Dinder Nat'l Park, Eth.
108/F3 Dindigul, India
108/B1 Dinga, Pak.
105/F5 Ding'an, China
96/F4 Dingbian, China
106/E2 Dinggyê, China
54/F10 Dingle (bay), Ire.
71/F5 Dingolfing, Ger.
112/C1 Dingras, Phil.
103/C4 Dingtao, China
54/B1 Dingwall, Sc,UK
96/E4 Dingxi, China
103/C3 Dingxiang, China
103/C3 Dingxing, China
103/G7 Dingxing, China
103/D4 Dingyuan, China
109/D1 Dinh Lap, Viet.
67/E5 Dinkel (riv.), Ger.
70/D4 Dinkelsbühl, Ger.
77/G1 Dinkelscherben, Ger.
67/F3 Dinklage, Ger.
57/G1 Dinnington, Eng,UK
131/B4 Dinokwe, Bots.
158/E2 Dinosaur, Co,US
158/E2 Dinosaur Nat'l Mon., Co, Ut,US
66/D5 Dinslaken, Ger.
156/G3 Dinsmore, Sk,Can
66/B5 Dintel Mark (riv.), Neth.
158/C3 Dinuba, Ca,US
66/D5 Dinxperlo, Neth.
128/C4 Dion (riv.), Gui.
128/A3 Diourbel, Sen.
128/A3 Diourbel (reg.), Sen.
108/B2 Dīpālpur, Pak.
104/B3 Diphu, India
104/C2 Diphu (pass), India
95/J4 Diplo, Pak.
92/E2 Dipni (dam), Turk.
112/C3 Dipolog, Phil.
118/C3 Dipperu Nat'l Park, Austl.
149/H4 Dique (can.), Col.
128/E2 Diré, Mali
115/G2 Direction (cape), Austl.
125/P6 Dirē Dawa, Eth.
148/E4 Diriamba, Nic.
116/B3 Dirk Hartog (isl.), Austl.
124/H4 Dirkou, Niger
66/B5 Dirksland, Neth.
54/D5 Dirrington Great Law (hill), Sc,UK
158/E3 Dirty Devil (riv.), Ut,US
116/D2 Disappointment (lake), Austl.
121/L6 Disappointment (isls.), FrPol.
119/B3 Discovery (bay), Austl.
77/F5 Disgrazi, Monte (peak), It.
127/C3 Dishnā, Egypt
153/L2 Disko (isl.), Grld.
57/F5 Disley, Eng,UK
164/C3 Disneyland, Ca,US
69/E2 Dison, Belg.
106/F2 Dispur, India
161/G2 Disraëli, Qu,Can
59/H2 Diss, Eng,UK
67/F4 Dissen am Teutoburger Wald, Ger.
56/E2 Distington, Eng,UK
166/A6 District of Columbia (cap.), US
138/C3 Distrito Especial (fed. dist.), Col.
143/S12 Distrito Federal (fed. dist.), Arg.
140/A4 Distrito Federal (fed. dist.), Braz.
147/F5 Distrito Federal (fed. dist.), Mex.
139/E2 Distrito Federal (fed. dist.), Ven.
91/B4 Disūq, Egypt
59/F5 Ditchling Beacon (hill), Eng,UK
80/D4 Dittaino (riv.), It.
70/D2 Dittelbrunn, Ger.
70/C5 Ditzingen, Ger.
95/K4 Diu (isl.), India
112/D3 Diuata (mts.), Phil.
106/B3 Diu, Damān and (terr.), India
82/D4 Diva (riv.), Yugo.
72/D3 Dive (riv.), Fr.
141/G6 Divinolândia, Braz.
141/C2 Divinópolis, Braz.
56/B2 Divis (mtn.), NI,UK
141/G6 Divisa Nova, Braz.
144/C2 Divisor (mts.), Braz.
128/D5 Divo, IvC.
92/D2 Divriği, Turk.
76/D5 Dix (lake), Swi.
151/M4 Dixon (chan.), Ak,US
165/L10 Dixon, Ca,US
160/B3 Dixon, Il,US
152/C3 Dixon Entrance (chan.), BC,Can
93/E2 Diyadin, Turk.
93/F3 Diyālá (gov.), Iraq
92/E2 Diyarbakır, Turk.
92/E2 Diyarbakir (prov.), Turk.
91/B4 Diyarb Najm, Egypt
124/H3 Djado, Niger
124/H3 Djado (plat.), Niger
124/G1 Djamaa, Alg.
126/B1 Djambala, Congo
130/A2 Djamu, Zaire
124/G3 Djanet, Alg.
123/S16 Djelfa, Alg.
123/S16 Djelfa (wilaya), Alg.
125/L6 Djema, CAfr.
123/U17 Djemila (ruins), Alg.
128/D3 Djénné, Mali
129/E3 Djibo, Burk.
125/P5 Djibouti
125/P5 Djibouti (cap.), Djib.
60/D3 Djouce (mtn.), Ire.
129/F4 Djougou, Ben.
130/A2 Djugu, Zaire
52/G3 Dnepr (riv.), Eur.
86/E2 Dneprodzerzhinsk, Ukr.
86/E2 Dnepropetrovsk, Ukr.
86/E2 Dnepropetrovsk Obl., Ukr.
86/D3 Dnestr (riv.), Eur.
96/E5 Do (riv.), China
129/E3 Do (lake), Mali
131/D3 Doa, Moz.
124/J6 Doba, Chad
167/E1 Dobbs Ferry, NY,US
63/K3 Dobele, Lat.
64/G3 Döbeln, Ger.
111/H4 Doberai (pen.), Indo.
82/D3 Doboj, Bosn.
71/E2 Döbra (hill), Ger.
65/L2 Dobre Miasto, Pol.
71/H3 Dobříš, Czh.
83/H4 Dobruja (reg.), Bul., Rom.
86/D1 Dobrush, Bela.
85/N4 Dobryanka, Rus.
141/D1 Doce (riv.), Braz.
54/B4 Dochart (riv.), Sc,UK
59/G1 Docking, Eng,UK
163/H4 Dock Junction, Ga,US
135/D1 Doctor Pedro P. Peña, Par.
82/F2 Doctor Petru Groza, Rom.
160/F1 Doda (lake), Qu,Can
108/F3 Doda Betta (mtn.), India
56/B5 Dodder (riv.), Ire.
53/P7 Doddinghurst, Eng,UK
159/G3 Dodge City, Ks,US
164/F7 Dodger Stadium, Los Angles, Ca,US
160/B3 Dodgeville, Wi,US
58/B6 Dodman (pt.), Wal,UK
130/B4 Dodoma, Tanz.
130/B4 Dodoma (prov.), Tanz.
81/G3 Dodoni (ruins), Gre.
130/D3 Dodori Nat'l Rsv., Kenya
156/F3 Dodsland, Sk,Can
57/G4 Dodworth, Eng,UK
66/D4 Doesburg, Neth.
66/D5 Doetinchem, Neth.
102/E5 Dogai Coring (lake), China
92/B2 Doğanhisar, Turk.
92/D1 Doğankent (riv.), Turk.
92/D2 Doğanşehir, Turk.
98/C2 Dōgo (isl.), Japan
129/G3 Dogondoutchi, Niger
93/F2 Doğubayazıt, Turk.
92/D1 Doğukaradeniz (mts.), Turk.
94/F3 Doha (Ad Dawḩah) (cap.), Qatar
106/B3 Dohad, India
109/B2 Doi Inthanon Nat'l Park, Thai.
109/B2 Doi Khun Tan Nat'l Park, Thai.
106/F1 Doilungdêqên, China
74/B1 Doiras (res.)
140/B3 Dois Irmãos (mts.), Braz.
109/B2 Doi Suthep-Pui Nat'l Park, Thai.
62/D1 Dokka, Nor.
66/D2 Dokkum, Neth.
66/C2 Dokkumer Ee (riv.), Neth.
161/F1 Dolbeau, Qu,Can
76/B3 Dôle, Fr.
76/D6 Dolent, Mont (peak), Swi.
58/C1 Dolgellau, Wal,UK
80/A3 Dolianova, It.
97/N2 Dolinsk, Rus.
83/F3 Dolj (co.), Rom.
54/C4 Dollar, Sc,UK
161/N7 Dollard-des-Ormeaux, Qu,Can
67/E2 Dollard (Dollart) (bay), Neth.
54/C5 Dollar Law (mtn.), Sc,UK
67/E2 Dollart (Dollard) (bay), Ger.
64/D5 Doller (riv.), Fr.
93/N6 Dolmançe Palace, Turk.
70/D1 Dolmar (peak), Ger.
82/C5 Dolmen (ruins), It.
125/P7 Dolo, Eth.
78/D4 Dolo (riv.), It.
73/J3 Dolomite Alps (Alpi Dolomitiche) (range), It.
73/J3 Dolomitiche, Alpi (Dolomite Alps) (range), It.
143/F3 Dolores, Arg.
148/D2 Dolores, Guat.
112/D2 Dolores, Phil.
75/E3 Dolores, Sp.
142/F2 Dolores, Uru.
158/E3 Dolores, Co,US
158/E3 Dolores (riv.), Co, Ut,US
147/E4 Dolores Hidalgo, Mex.
143/N7 Dolphin (cape), Falk.
132/A2 Dolphin (pt.), Namb.
152/E1 Dolphin and Union (str.), NW,Can
57/F4 Dolphinholme, Eng,UK
58/B5 Dolton, Eng,UK
165/Q16 Dolton, Il,US
109/D2 Do Luong, Viet.
111/J4 Dom (peak), Indo.
76/D5 Dom (peak), Swi.
131/C3 Doma, Zim.
131/D2 Domasi, Malw.
77/F4 Domat-Ems, Swi.
71/F4 Domažlice, Czh.
73/G2 Dombasle-sur-Meurthe, Fr.
87/G4 Dombay-Ul'gen, Gora (peak), Geo.
76/B5 Dombes (reg.), Fr.
131/C3 Domboshawa, Zim.
82/D2 Dombóvár, Hun.
82/E1 Dombrád, Hun.
131/D4 Dom Carlos (pt.), Moz.
113/J Dome C (sta.), Ant.
72/E3 Domérat, Fr.
135/C1 Domeyko (mts.), Chile
150/F4 Dominica
150/F4 Dominica (passg.), West Indies
150/D3 Dominican Republic
66/C6 Dommel (riv.), Belg., Neth.
109/D3 Dom Noi (res.), Thai.
85/X9 Domodedovo, Rus.
77/E5 Domodossola, It.
53/S9 Domont, Fr.
135/F3 Dom Pedrito, Braz.
140/A2 Dom Pedro, Braz.
111/E5 Dompu, Indo.
82/D2 Dömsöd, Hun.
80/A3 Domusnovas, It.
142/C3 Domuyo (vol.), Arg.
118/C5 Domvilk (peak), Austl.
82/B2 Domžale, Slov.
72/C3 Don (riv.), Fr.
87/G2 Don (ridge), Rus.
87/G3 Don (riv.), Rus.
57/F5 Don (riv.), Eng,UK
54/D2 Don (riv.), Sc,UK
131/D3 Dona Ana, Moz.
56/C2 Donaghadee, NI,UK
56/B2 Donaghmore, NI,UK
163/F4 Donaldsonville, La,US
74/B4 Doñana Nat'l Park, Sp.
72/E5 Dona, Pic de la (peak), Fr.
65/H4 Donau (Danube) (riv.), Aus., Ger.
77/E2 Donaueschingen, Ger.
70/D5 Donauwörth, Ger.
74/C3 Don Benito, Sp.
119/G5 Doncaster, Austl.
57/G4 Doncaster, Eng,UK
126/B2 Dondo, Ang.
131/D3 Dondo, Moz.
106/D6 Dondra Head (pt.), SrL.
55/G9 Donegal (bay), Ire.
56/A1 Donegal (co.), Ire.
87/G3 Donets (riv.), Rus., Ukr.
86/F3 Donetsk, Ukr.
86/F3 Donetsk Obl., Ukr.
104/E2 Dong (riv.), China
105/G4 Dong (riv.), China
107/J5 Dong (riv.), Viet.
129/H5 Donga (riv.), Camr., Nga.
101/B2 Dongbei (plain), China
104/D3 Dongchuan, China
107/J3 Dong Dang, Viet.
103/E5 Dongdongting Shan (mtn.), China
103/D3 Dong'e, China
66/B5 Dongen, Neth.
105/F5 Dongfang, China
117/J5 Donggali Consv. Park, Austl.
101/C3 Donggou, China
105/G4 Dongguan, China
103/D3 Dongguang, China
109/D2 Dong Ha, Viet.
103/D4 Donghai, China
109/D2 Donghen, Laos
109/D2 Dong Hoi, Viet.
105/G2 Dongjing (riv.), China
103/E2 Dongliao (riv.), China
103/C4 Dongming, China
105/F4 Dongnan (mts.), China
109/D4 Dong Noi (riv.), Viet.
130/B4 Dongobesh, Tanz.
103/D4 Dongping, China
103/D3 Dongping (lake), China
105/H4 Dongshan (isl.), China
105/H4 Dongsha (Pratas) (isl.), China
103/B3 Dongsheng, China
103/E4 Dongtai, China
103/L9 Dongtaio (riv.), China
109/D2 Dong Tau, Viet.
105/G2 Dongting (lake), China
103/D3 Dongying, China
103/D5 Dongzhi, China
142/Q10 Donihue, Chile
57/H6 Donington, Eng,UK
152/C2 Donjek (riv.), Yk,Can
82/C3 Donji Vakuf, Bosn.
70/A3 Donnersberg (peak), Ger.
76/D1 Donon (mtn.), Fr.
112/C2 Donsol, Phil.
104/B5 Donyan (riv.), Burma
70/C5 Donzdorf, Ger.
116/C2 Dooleena (peak), Austl.
54/B6 Doon (riv.), Sc,UK
60/A4 Doonbeg (riv.), Ire.
151/H2 Doonerak (mtn.), Ak,US
54/B6 Doon, Loch (lake), Sc,UK
160/C2 Door (pen.), Wi,US
66/C4 Doorn, Neth.
132/B3 Doorn (riv.), SAfr.
78/D1 Doppo, Monte (peak), It.
116/D2 Dora (lake), Austl.
78/A2 Dora Baltea (riv.), It.
75/F2 Dorada (coast), Sp.
95/K1 Do Rāh (pass), Afg.
102/B4 Dorāh Ān (pass), Pak.
73/G4 Dora Riparia (riv.), It.
161/H2 Dorchester, NB,Can
153/J2 Dorchester (cape), NW,Can
58/D5 Dorchester, Eng,UK
72/D4 Dordogne (riv.), Fr.
66/B5 Dordrecht, Neth.
156/G2 Dore (lake), Sk,Can
72/E4 Dore (mts.), Fr.
72/E4 Dore (riv.), Fr.
54/B2 Dores, Sc,UK
141/C1 Dores do Indaiá, Braz.
71/F6 Dorfen, Ger.
71/E6 Dorfen (riv.), Ger.
80/A2 Dorgali, It.
96/C2 Dörgön (lake), Mong.
129/E3 Dori, Burk.
161/M7 Dorion, Qu,Can
53/N8 Dorking, Eng,UK
66/D6 Dormagen, Ger.
53/P8 Dormans Land, Eng,UK
168/G7 Dormont, Pa,US
54/C2 Dornbach Burn (riv.), Sc,UK
77/F3 Dornbirn, Aus.
166/C2 Dorney Park/Wildwater Kingdom, Pa,US
54/B1 Dornoch, Sc,UK
55/K8 Dornoch Firth (inlet), Sc,UK
70/C6 Dornstadt, Ger.
70/B6 Dornstetten, Ger.
82/D2 Dorog, Hun.
83/H2 Dorohoi, Rom.
131/C3 Dorowa Mining Lease, Zim.
116/B3 Dorre (isl.), Austl.
59/E2 Dorridge, Eng,UK
119/E1 Dorrigo Nat'l Park, Austl.
58/D1 Dorrington, Eng,UK
158/B2 Dorris, Ca,US
123/W17 Dorsale (mts.), Tun.
70/B2 Dorsbach (riv.), Ger.
58/D5 Dorset (co.), Eng,UK
66/D5 Dorsten, Ger.
67/E5 Dortmund, Ger.
67/E4 Dortmund-Ems (can.), Ger.
91/E1 Dörtyol, Turk.
161/N7 Dorval, Qu,Can
67/G3 Dörverden, Ger.
142/D5 Dos Bahias (cape), Arg.
165/A2 Dosewallips (riv.), Wa,US
74/C4 Dos Hermanas, Sp.
99/H7 Dōshi (riv.), Japan
109/D1 Do Son, Viet.
146/B2 Dos Picachos, Cerro (mtn.), Mex.
138/C3 Dos Quebradas, Col.
64/G2 Dosse (riv.), Ger.
129/F3 Dosso, Niger
129/F3 Dosso (dept.), Niger
87/K3 Dossor, Kaz.
163/G4 Dothan, Al,US
68/C3 Douai, Fr.
124/G7 Douala, Camr.
72/A2 Douarnenez, Fr.
72/A2 Douarnenez (bay), Fr.
118/D4 Double I. (pt.), Austl.
76/C3 Doubs (dept.), Fr.
76/B4 Doubs (riv.), Fr.
116/C5 Doubtful I. (bay), Austl.
68/C3 Douchy-les-Mines, Fr.
72/C3 Doué-la-Fontaine, Fr.
128/E3 Douentza, Mali
123/W17 Dougga (ruins), Tun.
168/F7 Doughty (cr.), Oh,US
56/D3 Douglas, IM,UK
54/C5 Douglas, Sc,UK
151/H4 Douglas (mtn.), Ak,US
158/E5 Douglas, Az,US
163/H4 Douglas, Ga,US
157/G5 Douglas, Wy,US
68/B3 Doullens, Fr.
55/N13 Dounby, Sc,UK
54/B4 Doune, Sc,UK
54/B4 Doune (mtn.), Sc,UK
71/G2 Doupovské Hory (mts.), Czh.
68/C3 Dour, Belg.
137/H8 Dourados, Braz.
53/S11 Dourdan, Fr.
72/E4 Dourdou (riv.), Fr.
74/B2 Douro (riv.), Port.
72/F4 Doux (riv.), Fr.
72/C4 Douze (riv.), Fr.
57/G6 Dove (riv.), Eng,UK
57/H3 Dove (riv.), Eng,UK
59/H2 Dove (riv.), Eng,UK
158/E3 Dove Creek, Co,US
116/E5 Dover (pt.), Austl.
68/A2 Dover (str.), Fr., UK
59/H4 Dover, Eng,UK
166/C5 Dover (cape), De,US
161/G3 Dover, NH,US
166/D2 Dover, NJ,US
168/F6 Dover, Oh,US
166/C5 Dover A.F.B., De,US
161/G2 Dover-Foxcroft, Me,US
57/G6 Doveridge, Eng,UK
93/J2 Dowghā'ī, Iran
56/C3 Down (dist.), NI,UK
165/P16 Downers Grove, Il,US
164/B3 Downey, Ca,US
59/G1 Downham Market, Eng,UK
158/B3 Downieville, Ca,US
166/C3 Downingtown, Pa,US
56/C3 Downpatrick, NI,UK
59/H4 Downs, The (har.), Eng,UK
59/E4 Downton, Eng,UK
166/C3 Doylestown, Pa,US
98/C3 Dōzen (isl.), Japan
160/E2 Dozois (res.), Qu,Can
124/D2 Drâa (plat.), Alg., Mor.
124/D2 Drâa (wadi), Alg., Mor.
72/F4 Drac (riv.), Fr.
141/B2 Dracena, Braz.
66/D2 Drachten, Neth.
83/G3 Drăgănești-Olt, Rom.
83/G3 Drăgășani, Rom.
139/F2 Dragon's Mouth (str.), Trin., Ven.
62/C4 Dragør, Den.
73/G5 Draguignan, Fr.
143/L8 Drake (passage), Arg., Chile
126/E6 Drakensberg (range), Afr.
130/A2 Dramba, Zaire
62/D2 Drammen, Nor.
76/D5 Drance (riv.), Swi.
53/T10 Drancy, Fr.
76/C5 Dranse (riv.), Fr.
56/B2 Draperstown, NI,UK
73/L3 Drau (riv.), Aus.
82/C3 Drava (riv.), Eur.
68/B6 Draveil, Fr.
65/H2 Drawa (riv.), Pol.
65/H2 Drawsko Pomorskie, Pol.
157/J3 Drayton, ND,US
156/E2 Drayton Valley, Ab,Can
54/B5 Dreghorn, Sc,UK
71/G5 Dreiesselberg (peak), Ger.
76/D2 Dreisam (riv.), Ger.
111/K4 Drei Zinnen (peak), PNG
67/E5 Drensteinfurt, Ger.
66/D3 Drenthe (prov.), Neth.
66/D3 Drentse Hoofdvaart (can.), Neth.
65/G3 Dresden, Ger.
68/A6 Dreux, Fr.
65/H2 Drezdenko, Pol.
66/C4 Driebergen, Neth.
156/F5 Driggs, Id,US
95/J4 Drigh Road, Pak.
81/F2 Drin (gulf), Alb.
81/F1 Drin (riv.), Alb.
82/D3 Drina (riv.), Bosn., Yugo.
82/E5 Drinizi (riv.), Alb.
62/D2 Drøbak, Nor.
82/F3 Drobeta-Turnu Severin, Rom.
67/G1 Drochtersen, Ger.
60/D2 Drogheda, Ire.
86/B2 Drogobych, Ukr.
58/D2 Droitwich, Eng,UK
69/G6 Drolingen, Fr.
67/E6 Drolshagen, Ger.
72/F4 Drôme (riv.), Fr.
56/A3 Dromore (riv.), Ire.
56/B3 Dromore, NI,UK
57/G5 Dronfield, Eng,UK
54/B6 Drongan, Sc,UK
72/D4 Dronne (riv.), Fr.
66/C3 Dronten, Neth.
72/D4 Dropt (riv.), Fr.
63/R7 Drottningholm Palace, Swe.
68/A6 Drouette (riv.), Fr.
160/C1 Drowning (riv.), On,Can
78/A2 Druento, It.
56/C3 Drumaness, NI,UK
56/C2 Drumbeg, NI,UK
156/E3 Drumheller, Ab,Can
60/D3 Drumleck (pt.), Ire.
118/B4 Drummond (peak), Austl.
117/G5 Drummond (pt.), Austl.
118/B4 Drummond (range), Austl.
161/F2 Drummondville, Qu,Can
56/D2 Drummore, Sc,UK
54/B2 Drumnadrochit, Sc,UK
56/A2 Drumnakilly, NI,UK
54/B3 Drumochter, Pass of (pass), Sc,UK
66/C5 Drunen, Neth.
57/G1 Druridge (bay), Eng,UK
63/K4 Druskininkai, Lith.
66/C5 Druten, Neth.
82/C3 Drvar, Bosn.
65/K2 Drwęca (riv.), Pol.
165/M10 Dry (cr.), Ca,US
83/G4 Dryanovo, Bul.
151/K3 Dry Creek, Yk,Can
160/A1 Dryden, On,Can
162/C4 Dryden, Tx,US
58/C2 Drygarn Fawr (mtn.), Wal,UK
54/B4 Drymen, Sc,UK
129/H5 Dschang, Camr.
103/B4 Du (riv.), China
58/B3 Duad (riv.), Wal,UK
150/D3 Duarte (peak), DRep.
164/G7 Duarte, Ca,US
152/F2 Dubawnt (lake), NW,Can
152/F2 Dubawnt (riv.), NW,Can
95/G3 Dubayy, UAE
119/D2 Dubbo, Austl.
130/A2 Dubele, Zaire
77/E3 Dübendorf, Swi.
60/D3 Dublin (bay), Ire.
60/D3 Dublin (cap.), Ire.
60/D3 Dublin (co.), Ire.
165/L11 Dublin, Ca,US
163/H3 Dublin, Ga,US
84/H4 Dubna, Rus.
65/K4 Dubnica nad Váhom, Slvk.
86/C2 Dubno, Ukr.
160/E3 Du Bois, Pa,US
156/F5 Dubois, Wy,US
83/J2 Dubossary (res.), Mol.
82/D4 Dubrovnik, Cro.
157/L5 Dubuque, Ia,US
71/G1 Duchcov, Czh.
158/E2 Duchesne, Ut,US
158/E2 Duchesne (riv.), Ut,US
121/N7 Ducie (atoll), Pitc.
165/E6 Duck (lake), Mi,US
163/G3 Duck (riv.), Tn,US
165/A2 Duckabush (riv.), Wa,US
157/G2 Duck Lake, Sk,Can
158/D3 Duckwater, Nv,US
109/D3 Duc Lap, Viet.
109/E3 Duc Pho, Viet.
109/D4 Duc Phong, Viet.
138/C4 Duda (riv.), Col.
57/E3 Dudden (riv.), Eng,UK
69/F5 Dudelange, Lux.
67/H5 Duderstadt, Ger.
88/J3 Dudinka, Rus.
58/D2 Dudley, Eng,UK
168/C1 Dudley, Ma,US
74/C2 Duero (Douro) (riv.), Sp.
130/C3 Dufaja (riv.), Kenya
113/W Dufek Massive (mtn.), Ant.
120/F5 Duff (isl.), Sol.
68/D1 Duffel, Belg.
57/G6 Duffield, Eng,UK
54/C2 Dufftown, Sc,UK
78/A1 Dufour, Punta (Dufourspitze) (peak), It., Swi.
78/A1 Dufourspitze (Punta Dufour) (peak), It., Swi.
82/B3 Dugi Otok (isl.), Cro.
158/D2 Dugway, Ut,US
54/A2 Duich, Loch (inlet), Sc,UK
139/E4 Duida (peak), Ven.
139/E4 Duida Marahuaca Nat'l Park, Ven.
115/G2 Duifken (pt.), Austl.
66/D6 Duisburg, Ger.
138/C3 Duitama, Col.
66/D5 Duiven, Neth.
121/L7 Duke of Gloucester (isls.), FrPol.
54/B4 Duke's (pass), Sc,UK
168/D3 Dukes (co.), Ma,US
65/L4 Dukielska, Przełęcz (Dukla) (pass), Pol.
65/L4 Dukla (Przełęcz Dukielska) (pass), Pol.
96/D4 Dulan China
135/D2 Dulce (riv.), Arg.
149/F4 Dulce (gulf), CR
158/F3 Dulce, NM,US
105/F3 Duliu (riv.), China
108/A2 Dullewāla, Pak.
67/E5 Dülmen, Ger.
54/C2 Dulnain (riv.), Sc,UK
157/K4 Duluth, Mn,US
58/C4 Dulverton, Eng,UK
104/B3 Dulong (pass), China
83/H4 Dulovo, Bul.
112/C4 Dulunguin (pt.), Phil.
91/E3 Dūmā, Syria
112/C4 Dumagasa (pt.), Phil.
112/C3 Dumaguete City, Phil.
112/C4 Dumalinao, Phil.
112/C3 Dumanjug, Phil.
112/B3 Dumaran, Phil.
112/B3 Dumaran (isl.), Phil.
119/D1 Dumaresq (riv.), Austl.
162/F3 Dumas, Ar,US
162/C3 Dumas, Tx,US
54/B5 Dumbarton, Sc,UK
65/K4 Ďumbier (peak), Slvk.
126/C3 Dumbo, Ang.
83/G2 Dumbrăveni, Rom.
164/B2 Dume (pt.), Ca,US
56/E1 Dumfries, Sc,UK
54/C6 Dumfries & Galloway (reg.), Sc,UK
67/F3 Dümmer (lake), Ger.
160/E2 Dumoine (lake), Qu,Can
160/E2 Dumoine (riv.), Qu,Can
167/E2 Dumont, NJ,US
113/K Dumont d'Urville, Ant.
91/B4 Dumyāţ (gov.), Egypt
91/B4 Dumyāţ (Damietta), Egypt
65/K5 Duna (Danube) (riv.), Hun.
82/D2 Dunaföldvár, Hun.
82/D2 Dunaharaszti, Hun.
65/K5 Dunaj (Danube) (riv.), Slvk.
65/L4 Dunajec (riv.), Pol.
65/K5 Dunakeszi, Hun.
60/D2 Dunany (pt.), Ire.
82/D2 Dunaújváros, Hun.
82/D2 Dunavecse, Hun.
54/D5 Dunbar, Sc,UK
54/C4 Dunblane, Sc,UK
158/E4 Duncan, Az,US
159/H4 Duncan, Ok,US
55/K7 Duncansby Head (pt.), Sc,UK
162/D3 Duncanville, Tx,US
60/D2 Dundalk, Ire.
60/D2 Dundalk (bay), Ire.
166/B5 Dundalk, Md,US
116/D5 Dundas (lake), Austl.
114/E2 Dundas (str.), Austl.
153/R7 Dundas (pen.), NW,Can
161/Q9 Dundas, On,Can
133/E3 Dundee, SAfr.
54/D4 Dundee, Sc,UK
54/B5 Dundonald, Sc,UK
56/C3 Dundrum, NI,UK
56/C3 Dundrum (bay), NI,UK
156/G3 Dundurn, Sk,Can
115/R12 Dunedin, NZ
163/H4 Dunedin, Fl,US
167/H9 Dunellen, NJ,US
54/C4 Dunfermline, Sc,UK
56/B2 Dungannon, NI,UK
56/B3 Dungannon (dist.), NI,UK
106/B3 Dungarpur, India
60/C5 Dungarvan, Ire.
60/C5 Dungarvan (har.), Ire.
71/F5 Dungau (reg.), Ger.
143/K8 Dungeness (pt.), Arg.
59/G5 Dungeness (pt.), Eng,UK
56/B2 Dungiven, NI,UK
130/A2 Dungu, Zaire
130/A2 Dungu (riv.), Zaire
97/K3 Dunhua, China
96/C3 Dunhuang, China
54/C3 Dunkeld, Sc,UK
60/B3 Dunkellin (riv.), Ire.
68/B1 Dunkerque (Dunkirk), Fr.
58/C4 Dunkery (hill), Eng,UK
68/B1 Dunkirk (Dunkerque), Fr.
129/E5 Dunkwa, Gha.
60/D3 Dún Laoghaire, Ire.
56/B2 Dunloy, NI,UK
60/A6 Dunmanus (bay), Ire.
56/B2 Dunmurry, NI,UK
163/J3 Dunn, NC,US
56/A2 Dunnamanagh, NI,UK
56/B2 Dunnamore, NI,UK
76/D3 Dünnern (riv.), Swi.
55/N13 Dunnet Head (pt.), Sc,UK
54/C4 Dunning, Sc,UK
57/H4 Dunnington, Eng,UK
161/Q10 Dunnville, On,Can
54/B5 Dunoon, Sc,UK
127/B5 Dunqulah, Sudan
56/D2 Dunragit, Sc,UK
54/C5 Dun Rig (mtn.), Sc,UK
54/D5 Duns, Sc,UK
56/E1 Dunscore, Sc,UK
157/H3 Dunseith, ND,US
56/B1 Dunseverick, NI,UK
158/B2 Dunsmuir, Ca,US
59/F3 Dunstable, Eng,UK
69/E5 Dun-sur-Meuse, Fr.
54/B5 Duntocher, Sc,UK
54/B6 Dunure, Sc,UK
97/J1 Duobukur (riv.), China
96/H3 Duolun, China
165/P16 Du Page (co.), Il,US
165/P16 Du Page (riv.), Il,US
165/P16 Du Page, East Branch (riv.), Il,US
157/H4 Dupree, SD,US
116/B2 Dupuy (cape), Austl.
141/K7 Duque de Caxias, Braz.
143/J7 Duque de York (isl.), Chile
168/H7 Duquesne, Pa,US
160/B4 Du Quoin, Il,US
114/D3 Durack (range), Austl.
92/C1 Durağan, Turk.
72/F5 Durance (riv.), Fr.
146/D3 Durango, Mex.
74/D1 Durango, Sp.
158/F3 Durango, Co,US
159/H4 Durant, Ok,US
143/F2 Durazno, Uru.
143/F2 Durazno (dept.), Uru.
133/E3 Durban, SAfr.
132/L10 Durbanville, SAfr.
76/C1 Durbion (riv.), Fr.
69/E3 Durbuy, Belg.
82/C2 Đurđevac, Cro.
82/E3 Đurđevo, Yugo.
69/F2 Düren, Ger.
106/D3 Durg, India
106/E3 Durgāpur, India
161/S8 Durham (co.), On,Can
57/G2 Durham, Eng,UK
57/F2 Durham (co.), Eng,UK
163/J3 Durham, NC,US
161/G3 Durham, NH,US
59/E5 Durlston Head (pt.), Eng,UK
68/D1 Durme (riv.), Belg.
82/D4 Durmitor Nat'l Park, Yugo.
54/A5 Duror, Sc,UK
81/F2 Durrës, Alb.
59/E4 Durrington, Eng,UK
58/D3 Dursley, Eng,UK
92/B2 Dursunbey, Turk.
93/M6 Durusu, Turk.
93/M6 Durusu (lake), Turk.
111/J4 D'Urville (cape), Indo.
160/C1 Dusey (riv.), On,Can
105/E3 Dushan, China
103/D2 Du Shan (peak), China
88/G6 Dushanbe (cap.), Taj.
105/E3 Dushui (riv.), China
66/D6 Düsseldorf, Ger.
57/H4 Dutch (riv.), Eng,UK
166/B3 Dutch Wonderland, Pa,US
67/F4 Düte (riv.), Ger.
131/A4 Dutlwe, Bots.
132/L10 Dutoitspiek (peak), SAfr.
105/E3 Duyun, China
83/K5 Düzce, Turk.
92/D2 Düzici, Turk.
84/H2 Dvina (bay), Rus.
85/J3 Dvina, Northern (riv.), Rus.
84/F5 Dvina, Western (riv.), Bel., Rus.
71/H4 Dvořiště (lake), Czh.
106/A3 Dwārka, India
156/D4 Dworshak (res.), Id,US
56/D6 Dwyfor (riv.), Wal,UK
132/C4 Dwyka (riv.), SAfr.
86/E1 Dyat'kovo, Rus.
153/K2 Dyer (cape), NW,Can
143/J7 Dyer (cape), Chile
160/C3 Dyer, In,US
163/F2 Dyersburg, Tn,US
162/D3 Dyess A.F.B., Tx,US
58/B3 Dyfed (co.), Wal,UK
56/D6 Dyffryn, Wal,UK
58/C1 Dyfi (riv.), Wal,UK
65/J4 Dyje (riv.), Czh.
87/G4 Dykh-tau, Gora (peak), Rus.
68/D2 Dyle (Dijle) (riv.), Belg.
71/F3 Dyleň (peak), Czh.
65/K2 Dylewska Gora (peak), Pol.
59/G4 Dymchurch, Eng,UK
87/H4 Dyul'tydag, Gora (peak), Rus.
131/D2 Dzalanyama (range), Malw., Moz.
133/H6 Dzaoudzi (cap.), May.
96/C2 Dzavhan (riv.), Mong.
86/F3 Dzenzik, Mys (pt.), Ukr.
96/C2 Dzereg, Mong.
84/J4 Dzerzhinsk, Rus.
102/B3 Dzhalal-Abad, Kyr.
102/B3 Dzhambul, Kaz.
86/E3 Dzhankoy, Ukr.
87/M1 Dzhetygara, Kaz.
102/A2 Dzhezkazgan, Kaz.
88/G5 Dzhizak, Uzb.
89/P4 Dzhugdzhur (range), Rus.
65/L2 Działdowo, Pol.
147/H4 Dzibilchaltún (ruins), Mex.
147/H4 Dzidzantún, Mex.
65/J3 Dzierżoniów, Pol.
96/B3 Dzungarian (basin), China
102/D3 Dzungarian Gate (pass), China
96/E2 Dzüünbayan-Ulaan, Mong.
102/F2 Dzüüngovĭ, Mong.
96/D2 Dzüünhangay, Mong.
96/F2 Dzüünharaa, Mong.

E

159/G3 Eads, Co,US
153/L3 Eagle (riv.), Nf,Can
160/A1 Eagle (lake), On,Can
156/F3 Eagle (riv.), Sk,Can
60/A5 Eagle (mtn.), Ire.
158/B2 Eagle (lake), Ca,US
158/F3 Eagle, Co,US
157/L4 Eagle (peak), Mn,US

Eagle – Ereğl

187

Eremo – Fishe

79/E5 Eremo di Camaldoli, It.
102/D3 Erenhaberga (mts.), China
96/G3 Erenhot, China
83/K5 Erenler, Turk.
139/H5 Erepecu (lake), Braz.
74/C2 Eresma (riv.), Sp.
70/C3 Erfa (riv.), Ger.
124/E1 Erfoud, Mor.
69/F1 Erft (riv.), Ger.
69/F2 Erftstadt, Ger.
64/F3 Erfurt, Ger.
92/D2 Ergani, Turk.
124/D3 'Erg Chech (des.), Afr.
124/H4 'Erg du Ténéré (des.), Niger
83/H5 Ergene Nehri (riv.), Turk.
124/D2 'Erg Iguidi (des.), Afr.
124/J5 Erguig (riv.), Chad
97/H1 Ergun (riv.), China, Rus.
97/J1 Ergun Youqi, China
97/J1 Ergun Zuoqi, China
80/C3 Erice, It.
54/B3 Ericht (riv.), Sc,UK
54/C3 Ericht (riv.), Sc,UK
54/B3 Ericht, Loch (lake), Sc,UK
156/D3 Erickson, BC,Can
157/J3 Erickson, Mb,Can
160/D3 Erie (lake), Can., US
161/S9 Erie (can.), NY,US
161/S10 Erie (co.), NY,US
168/H5 Erie (co.), Oh,US
160/D3 Erie, Pa,US
168/H4 Erie Nat'l Wild. Ref., Pa,US
125/Q5 Erigabo, Som.
157/J3 Eriksdale, Mb,Can
120/F4 Erikub (atoll), Mrsh.
130/B2 Erima, Ugan.
81/G4 Erimanthos (peak), Gre.
100/C2 Erimo, Japan
100/C3 Erimo-misaki (cape), Japan
125/N4 Eritrea
66/D6 Erkelenz, Ger.
63/H1 Erken (isl.), Swe.
60/C4 Erkina (riv.), Ire.
65/G2 Erkner, Ger.
66/D6 Erkrath, Ger.
104/D2 Erlang (peak), China
70/E3 Erlangen, Ger.
71/G5 Erlau (riv.), Ger.
70/B4 Erlenbach (riv.), Ger.
76/D4 Erlenbach, Swi.
70/C3 Erlenbach am Main, Ger.
76/D3 Erlinsbach, Swi.
103/F2 Erlongshan (res.), China
58/C6 Erme (riv.), Eng,UK
66/C4 Ermelo, Neth.
133/E2 Ermelo, SAfr.
91/C1 Ermenek, Turk.
91/C1 Ermenek (riv.), Turk.
53/U9 Ermenonville, Fr.
53/S10 Ermont, Fr.
81/J4 Ermoúpolis, Gre.
70/C6 Erms (riv.), Ger.
69/H2 Erndtebrück, Ger.
72/C2 Ernée (riv.), Fr.
55/H9 Erne, Lower Lough (lake), NI,UK
60/C1 Erne, Upper Lough (lake), NI,UK
108/F3 Erode, India
68/D3 Erquelinnes, Belg.
124/E1 Er Rachidia, Mor.
123/M13 Er Rif (mts.), Mor.
55/G9 Errigal (mtn.), Ire.
54/G9 Erris Head (pt.), Ire.
78/B4 Erro (riv.), It.
54/B3 Errochty, Loch (lake), Sc,UK
54/C4 Errol, Sc,UK
120/F6 Erromango (isl.), Van.
77/F4 Err, Piz d' (peak), Swi.
67/H4 Erse (riv.), Ger.
76/D1 Erstein, Fr.
96/B2 Ertix (riv.), China
141/B3 Erval d'Oeste, Braz.
160/D4 Erwin, Tn,US
67/F5 Erwitte, Ger.
104/C3 Eryuan, China
81/F2 Erzen (riv.), Alb.
71/F2 Erzgebirge (Krušné Hory) (mts.), Czh., Ger.
70/B3 Erzhausen, Ger.
92/D2 Erzincan, Turk.
92/D2 Erzincan (prov.), Turk.
92/E2 Erzurum, Turk.
92/E1 Erzurum (prov.), Turk.
120/D5 Esa'ala, PNG
126/D1 Esambo, Zaire
100/B3 Esan-misaki (cape), Japan
100/B3 Esashi, Japan
100/B4 Esashi, Japan
100/C1 Esashi, Japan
92/D1 Esbiye, Turk.
62/C4 Esbjerg, Den.
53/U10 Esbly, Fr.
63/L1 Esbo (Espoo), Fin.
140/D3 Escada, Braz.
158/E3 Escalante (riv.), Ut,US
163/G4 Escambia (riv.), Fl,US
160/C2 Escanaba, Mi,US
112/C1 Escarpada (pt.), Phil.
68/C3 Escaudain, Fr.
68/C3 Escaut (riv.), Belg., Fr.
69/E6 Esch (riv.), Fr.
77/E1 Eschach (riv.), Ger.
77/G2 Eschach (riv.), Ger.
76/D1 Eschau, Fr.
68/B5 Esches (riv.), Fr.
70/A4 Eschkopf (mtn.), Ger.
69/E5 Esch-sur-Alzette, Lux.
67/H6 Eschwege, Ger.
69/F2 Eschweiler, Ger.
164/C4 Escondido, Ca,US
164/C4 Escondido (cr.), Ca,US
146/D4 Escuinapa, Mex.
148/D3 Escuintla, Guat.
91/G6 Esdraelon, Plain of (plain), Isr.
124/H7 Eséka, Camr.
92/D2 Esence (peak), Turk.
67/E1 Esens, Ger.
75/F1 Esera (riv.), Sp.
93/G3 Eşfahān, Iran
93/H3 Eşfahān (gov.), Iran
58/C1 Esgair Ddu (mtn.), Wal,UK
57/G2 Esh, Eng,UK
55/P12 Esha Ness (pt.), Sc,UK
104/D3 Eshan Yizu Zizhixian, China
53/M7 Esher, Eng,UK
126/D2 Eshimba, Zaire
57/G2 Esh Winning, Eng,UK
79/G5 Esina (riv.), It.
57/E2 Esk (riv.), Eng,UK
57/H3 Esk (riv.), Eng,UK
55/K9 Esk (riv.), Sc,UK
57/E1 Eskdale (val.), Sc,UK
92/C2 Eskil, Turk.
62/G2 Eskilstuna, Swe.
92/D2 Eskimalatya, Turk.
151/M2 Eskimo (lakes), NW,Can
92/C1 Eskipazar, Turk.
92/B2 Eskişehir, Turk.
92/B2 Eskişehir (prov.), Turk.
74/C1 Esla (riv.), Sp.
93/F3 Eslāmābād, Iran
67/F6 Eslohe, Ger.
62/E4 Eslöv, Swe.
92/B2 Eşme, Turk.
149/G1 Esmeralda, Cuba
138/B4 Esmeraldas, Ecu.
138/B4 Esmeraldas (prov.), Ecu.
69/E2 Esneux, Belg.
138/D1 Espada (pt.), Col.
160/D2 Espanola, On,Can
144/K7 Española (isl.), Ecu.
159/F4 Española, NM,US
75/K6 Esparreguera, Sp.
67/F4 Espelkamp, Ger.
140/D2 Esperança, Braz.
116/D5 Esperance, Austl.
116/D5 Esperance (bay), Austl.
140/B1 Esperantina, Braz.
140/A2 Esperantinópolis, Braz.
156/B3 Esperanza (inlet), BC,Can
150/D3 Esperanza, DRep.
146/C3 Esperanza, Mex.
147/M8 Esperanza, Mex.
74/A3 Espichel (cape), Port.
138/C3 Espinal, Col.
147/M6 Espinal, Mex.
144/D4 Espinar, Peru
140/B5 Espinhaço (mts.), Braz.
74/A2 Espinho, Port.
143/F2 Espinillo (pt.), Uru.
140/B4 Espinosa, Braz.
141/D1 Espírito Santo (state), Braz.
141/G7 Espírito Santo do Pinhal, Braz.
148/E2 Espíritu Santo (bay), Mex.
146/C3 Espíritu Santo (isl.), Mex.
112/D2 Espiritu Santo (cape), Phil.
120/F6 Espiritu Santo (isl.), Van.
140/C3 Esplanada, Braz.
75/L7 Espluges, Sp.
63/L1 Espoo (Esbo), Fin.
131/D4 Espungabera, Moz.
142/C4 Esquel, Arg.
135/E3 Esquina, Arg.
63/T8 Esrum Sø (lake), Den.
124/D1 Essaouira, Mor.
67/G5 Esse (riv.), Ger.
66/B6 Essen, Belg.
66/E6 Essen, Ger.
71/F5 Essenbach, Ger.
119/F5 Essendon, Austl.
116/D3 Essendon (peak), Austl.
139/G3 Essequibo (riv.), Guy.
139/G3 Essequibo Island-West Demerara (reg.), Guy.
165/G7 Essex, On,Can
165/G7 Essex (co.), On,Can
53/P6 Essex (co.), Eng,UK
166/B5 Essex, Md,US
167/D2 Essex (co.), NJ,US
70/C5 Esslingen, Ger.
53/S11 Essonne (dept.), Fr.
53/T11 Essonne (riv.), Fr.
76/C1 Est (can.), Fr.
146/B1 Estación Coatiuila, Mex.
143/L8 Estados (isl.), Arg.
93/H4 Eşţahbān, Iran
140/C3 Estância, Braz.
143/L8 Estancia La Carmen, Arg.
143/L8 Estancia La Sera, Arg.
147/F4 Estancia Tamuín, Mex.
75/F1 Estats, Pico de (peak), Sp.
133/E3 Estcourt, SAfr.
67/G2 Este (riv.), Ger.
79/E2 Este, It.
141/B4 Esteio, Braz.
148/E3 Estelí, Nic.
74/D1 Estella, Sp.
164/C3 Estelle (mtn.), Ca,US
150/D3 Este Nat'l Park, DRep.
74/C4 Estepa, Sp.
74/C4 Estepona, Sp.
143/G2 Este, Punta del, Uru.
157/H3 Esterhazy, Sk,Can
124/G7 Esterias (cape), Gabon
71/G5 Esternberg, Aus.
73/G5 Estéron (riv.), Fr.
157/H3 Estevan, Sk,Can
68/D3 Estinnes-Au-Mont, Belg.
57/G2 Eston, Eng,UK
63/L2 Estonia
74/A3 Estoril, Port.
74/B2 Estrela, Serra da (mtn.), Port.
74/A3 Estrela, Serra da (range), Port.
146/B2 Estrella, Punta (pt.), Mex.
140/B3 Estrelto (mts.), Braz.
74/B3 Estremadura (aut. comm.), Sp.
74/B3 Estremoz, Port.
137/J5 Estrondo (mts.), Braz.
82/D2 Esztergom, Hun.
120/E4 Etal (atoll), Micr.
54/D5 Etal, Eng,UK
68/A2 Étaples, Fr.
106/C2 Etāwah, India
157/H3 Ethelbert, Mb,Can
125/N5 Ethiopia
125/N6 Ethiopian (plat.), Eth.
99/M9 Eti (riv.), Japan
53/T11 Étiolles, Fr.
54/A4 Etive, Loch (inlet), Sc,UK
80/D4 Etna, Monte (Mount Etna) (vol.), It.
161/Q8 Etobicoke, On,Can
131/B1 Etoile, Zaire
151/E3 Etolin (str.), Ak,US
100/E1 Etorofu (isl.), Rus.
126/C4 Etosha Nat'l Park, Namb.
126/C4 Etosha Pan (salt pan), Namb.
83/G4 Etropole, Bul.
77/G4 Etsch (Adige) (riv.), It.
99/F2 Etsu-Joshin Kogen Nat'l Park, Japan
91/F7 Et Taiyiba, Isr.
69/F4 Ettelbruck, Lux.
76/D1 Ettenheim, Ger.
66/B5 Etten-Leur, Neth.
80/D2 Etterbeek, Belg.
166/B3 Etters (Goldsboro), Pa,US
91/F7 Et Tīra, Isr.
70/B5 Ettlingen, Ger.
54/C6 Ettrick, Sc,UK
54/C6 Ettrick Pen (mtn.), Sc,UK
54/C5 Ettrick Water (riv.), Sc,UK
68/A3 Eu, Fr.
121/H7 Eua (isl.), Tonga
118/B2 Eubenangee Swamp Nat'l Park, Austl.
117/F4 Eucla Motel, Austl.
168/F4 Euclid, Oh,US
140/C3 Euclides da Cuhna, Braz.
115/H7 Eucumbene (lake), Austl.
163/F3 Eudora, Ar,US
163/G4 Eufaula, Al,US
159/J4 Eufaula, Ok,US
159/H4 Eufaula (lake), Ok,US
156/C4 Eugene, Or,US
146/B3 Eugenia, Punta (pt.), Mex.
74/B1 Eume (lake), Sp.
118/C3 Eungella Nat'l Park, Austl.
162/E4 Eunice, La,US
159/G4 Eunice, NM,US
69/F2 Eupen, Belg.
93/F4 Euphrates (riv.), Asia
63/K1 Eura, Fin.
72/D2 Eure (riv.), Fr.
153/S6 Eureka, NW,Can
153/S7 Eureka (sound), NW,Can
158/A2 Eureka, Ca,US
156/E3 Eureka, Mt,US
158/D3 Eureka, Nv,US
157/J4 Eureka, SD,US
68/B6 Eurodisney, Fr.
76/C1 Euron (riv.), Fr.
123/M12 Europa (pt.), Gib.
126/G5 Europa (isl.), Reun.
77/H3 Europabrücke, Aus.
52/* Europe
66/B5 Europoort, Neth.
69/F2 Euskirchen, Ger.
163/H4 Eustis, Fl,US
64/F1 Eutin, Ger.
131/D1 Eutini, Malw.
156/B2 Eutsuk (lake), BC,Can
57/F4 Euxton, Eng,UK
160/E1 Évain, Qu,Can
153/H2 Evans (str.), NW,Can
160/E1 Evans (lake), Qu,Can
159/F2 Evans, Co,US
159/F3 Evans (mtn.), Co,US
165/Q15 Evanston, Il,US
156/F5 Evanston, Wy,US
160/C4 Evansville, In,US
159/F2 Evansville, Wy,US
54/B1 Evanton, Sc,UK
156/E5 Evaporation (basin), Ut,US
160/C3 Evart, Mi,US
132/D2 Evaton, SAfr.
93/H5 Evaz, Iran
157/K4 Eveleth, Mn,US
89/L3 Evenki Aut. Okr., Rus.
59/E3 Evenlode (riv.), Eng,UK
119/D3 Everard (cape), Austl.
117/G4 Everard (lake), Austl.
117/G3 Everard (peak), Austl.
58/D4 Evercreech, Eng,UK
106/E2 Everest (mt.), China, Nep.
168/C1 Everett, Ma,US
168/A1 Everett (mtn.), Ma,US
165/C2 Everett, Wa,US
68/C1 Evergem, Belg.
163/H5 Everglades (swamp), Fl,US
163/H5 Everglades Nat'l Park, Fl,US
163/G4 Evergreen, Al,US
165/Q16 Evergreen Park, Il,US
59/F3 Eversholt, Eng,UK
67/E5 Everswinkel, Ger.
59/E2 Evesham, Eng,UK
76/C5 Évian-les-Bains, Fr.
81/G3 Évinos (riv.), Gre.
74/B3 Évora, Port.
74/A3 Évora (dist.), Port.
68/A5 Évreux, Fr.
72/C2 Évron, Fr.
81/H4 Evrótas (riv.), Gre.
53/T11 Évry, Fr.
81/H3 Évvoia (gulf), Gre.
81/H3 Évvoia (isl.), Gre.
154/V13 Ewa, Hi,US
154/V13 Ewa Beach, Hi,US
149/G2 Ewarton, Jam.
130/B3 Ewaso Ngiro (riv.), Kenya
130/C2 Ewaso Ng'iro (riv.), Kenya
53/N7 Ewell, Eng,UK
97/H2 Ewenkizu Zizhiqi, China
166/D3 Ewing, NJ,US
159/J3 Excelsior Springs, Mo,US
58/C5 Exe (riv.), Eng,UK
58/C5 Exeter, Eng,UK
161/G3 Exeter, NH,US
58/C5 Exminster, Eng,UK
58/C4 Exmoor (upland), Eng,UK
58/C4 Exmoor Nat'l Park, Eng,UK
160/F4 Exmore, Va,US
116/B2 Exmouth (gulf), Austl.
143/J7 Exmouth (pen.), Chile
58/C5 Exmouth, Eng,UK
153/L4 Exploits (riv.), Nf,Can
141/G7 Extrema, Braz.
140/C2 Exu, Braz.
150/B1 Exuma (sound), Bahm.
70/B6 Eyach (riv.), Ger.
57/G5 Eyam, Eng,UK
130/B3 Eyasi (lake), Tanz.
70/C5 Eyb (riv.), Ger.
62/C2 Eydehamn, Nor.
59/H2 Eye, Eng,UK
59/F1 Eye (brook), Eng,UK
54/D5 Eyemouth, Sc,UK
91/G8 Eyn Hemed Nat'l Park, Isr.
53/P7 Eynsford, Eng,UK
117/G5 Eyre (pen.), Austl.
117/H4 Eyre North (lake), Austl.
117/H4 Eyre South (lake), Austl.
93/M6 Eyüp, Turk.
93/M6 Eyüp Mosque, Turk.
53/T9 Ézanville, Fr.
81/K3 Ezine, Turk.
124/H3 Ezzane (well), Alg.

F

121/L6 Faaa, FrPol.
130/D2 Faafaxdhuun, Som.
162/B4 Fabens, Tx,US
74/B1 Fabero, Sp.
62/D4 Fåborg, Den.
79/F6 Fabriano, It.
138/C3 Facatativá, Col.
68/C2 Faches-Thumesnil, Fr.
125/K4 Fada, Chad
54/A1 Fada, Lochan (lake), Sc,UK
129/F3 Fada-N'Gourma, Burk.
79/E4 Faenza, It.
125/J6 Fafa (riv.), CAfr.
74/A2 Fafe, Port.
125/P6 Fafen Shet' (riv.), Eth.
83/G3 Făgăraş, Rom.
62/F2 Fagersta, Swe.
79/E4 Faggiola, Monte (peak), It.
143/L8 Fagnano (lake), Arg.
128/D2 Faguibine (lake), Mali
124/F1 Fahl (well), Alg.
75/S12 Faial (isl.), Azor.,Port.
57/F4 Failsworth, Eng,UK
55/P13 Fair (isl.), Sc,UK
151/J3 Fairbanks, Ak,US
165/J11 Fairfax, Ca,US
166/A6 Fairfax, Va,US
166/A6 Fairfax (co.), Va,US
118/G8 Fairfield, Austl.
165/K10 Fairfield, Ca,US
167/E1 Fairfield, Ct,US
168/A3 Fairfield (co.), Ct,US
156/F4 Fairfield, Mt,US
167/H8 Fairfield, NJ,US
160/C4 Fairfield, Oh,US
162/D4 Fairfield, Tx,US
59/E3 Fairford, Eng,UK
168/D2 Fairhaven, Ma,US
161/F3 Fair Haven, Vt,US
56/B1 Fair Head (pt.), NI,UK
55/P13 Fair Isle (isl.), Sc,UK
166/B5 Fairland, Md,US
167/D2 Fair Lawn, NJ,US
166/D3 Fairless Hills, Pa,US
54/B5 Fairlie, Sc,UK
59/G5 Fairlight, Eng,UK
157/K5 Fairmont, Mn,US
160/D4 Fairmont, WV,US
165/M9 Fair Oaks, Ca,US
162/B2 Fairplay, Co,US
156/D1 Fairview, Ab,Can
167/K8 Fairview, NJ,US
159/H3 Fairview, Ok,US
131/D3 Fairview (peak), Zim.
168/F5 Fairview Park, Oh,US
151/L4 Fairweather (cape), Ak,US
151/L4 Fairweather (mtn.), BC,Can, Ak,US
165/C3 Fairwood-Cascade, Wa,US
108/B2 Faisalabad, Pak.
81/J5 Faistós (ruins), Gre.
106/D2 Faizābād, India
150/E3 Fajardo, PR
121/M6 Fakahina (isl.), FrPol.
121/H5 Fakaofo (atoll), Tok.
121/L6 Fakarava (atoll), FrPol.
59/G1 Fakenham, Eng,UK
124/G7 Fako (peak), Camr.
62/E4 Fakse Bugt (bay), Den.
103/E2 Faku, China
58/B6 Fal (riv.), Eng,UK
104/B4 Falam, Burma
123/Q16 Falcon (cape), Alg.
162/D5 Falcon (res.), Mex., US
138/D2 Falcón (state), Ven.
79/G5 Falconara Marittima, It.
128/C3 Falémé (riv.), Mali, Sen.
121/S9 Faleolo, WSam.
162/D5 Falfurrias, Tx,US
156/D2 Falher, Ab,Can
62/E3 Falkenberg, Swe.
59/H2 Falkenham, Eng,UK
71/F2 Falkenstein, Ger.
54/C5 Falkirk, Sc,UK
143/M8 Falkland (sound), Falk.
54/C4 Falkland, Sc,UK
143/M8 Falkland Islands (Islas Malvinas) (dpcy.), UK
62/E2 Falköping, Swe.
164/C4 Fallbrook, Ca,US
76/D6 Fallere, Monte (peak), It.
67/G3 Fallingbostel, Ger.
158/C3 Fallon, Nv,US
168/C2 Fall River, Ma,US
166/A6 Falls Church, Va,US
159/J2 Falls City, Ne,US
58/A6 Falmouth, Eng,UK
58/A6 Falmouth (bay), Eng,UK
62/C4 Falshöft (pt.), Ger.
149/J2 Falso, Cabo (cape), DRep.
149/F3 Falso, Cabo (cape), Hon.
146/C4 Falso, Cabo (cape), Mex.
143/K8 Falso Cabo de Hornos (cape), Chile
62/E4 Falster (isl.), Den.
79/E5 Falterona, Monte (peak), It.
83/H2 Fălticeni, Rom.
62/F1 Falun, Swe.
91/C2 Famagusta, Cyp.
91/C2 Famagusta (bay), Cyp.
91/C2 Famagusta (dist.), Cyp.
69/F5 Fameck, Fr.
69/E3 Famenne (reg.), Belg.
103/D5 Fanchang, China
123/G7 Fandriana, Madg.
60/D2 Fane (riv.), Ire.
121/L6 Fangatau (isl.), FrPol.
121/L7 Fangataufa (isl.), FrPol.
103/C4 Fangcheng, China
109/E1 Fangcheng, China
107/J3 Fangcheng Gezu Zizhixian, China
105/E2 Fangdou (mts.), China
103/B3 Fangshan, China
103/B4 Fang Xian, China
105/F3 Fanjing (peak), China
54/A1 Fannich, Loch (lake), Sc,UK
121/K4 Fanning (Tabuaeran) (atoll), Kiri.
62/C4 Fanø (isl.), Den.
79/G5 Fano, It.
103/C3 Fanshi, China
109/C1 Fan Si Pan (peak), Viet.
167/H9 Fanwood, NJ,US
91/B4 Fāqūs, Egypt
130/A2 Faradje, Zaire
123/G7 Faradofay, Madg.
123/G7 Farafangana, Madg.
127/A3 Farāfirah, Wāḩāt al (oasis), Egypt
88/G6 Farāh, Afg.
95/H2 Farāh (riv.), Afg.
91/G7 Fa'rah, Wādī (dry riv.), WBnk.
158/B3 Farallon (isls.), Ca,US
139/E2 Farallon Centinela (isl.), Ven.
120/D3 Farallon de Medinilla (isl.), NMar.
120/D2 Farallon de Pajaros (isl.), NMar.
138/B4 Farallones de Cali Nat'l Park, Col.
128/C4 Faranah (comm.), Gui.
133/H8 Faraony (riv.), Madg.
120/D4 Faraulep (atoll), Micr.
68/D3 Farciennes, Belg.
59/E5 Fareham, Eng,UK
54/D2 Fare, Hill of (hill), Sc,UK
63/R7 Farentuna, Swe.
115/R11 Farewell (cape), NZ
157/J4 Fargo, ND,US
157/K4 Faribault, Mn,US
106/C2 Farīdābād, India
108/C2 Farīdkot, India
106/E3 Farīdpur, Bang.
59/E3 Faringdon, Eng,UK
91/B4 Fāriskūr, Egypt
130/B4 Farkwa, Tanz.
167/M9 Farmingdale, NY,US
168/B2 Farmington, Ct,US
161/G2 Farmington, Me,US
165/F7 Farmington, Mi,US
159/K3 Farmington, Mo,US
158/E3 Farmington, NM,US
165/F7 Farmington Hills, Mi,US
160/E4 Farmville, Va,US
59/F4 Farnborough, Eng,UK
55/L9 Farne (isls.), Eng,UK
59/F4 Farnham, Eng,UK
53/P7 Farningham, Eng,UK
57/F4 Farnworth, Eng,UK
152/C2 Faro, Yk,Can
74/B4 Faro, Port.
74/A4 Faro (dist.), Port.
52/D2 Faroe (isls.), Den.
61/F4 Fårön (isl.), Swe.
124/H6 Faro Nat'l Park, Camr.
116/B2 Farquhar (cape), Austl.
123/H5 Farquhar (isls.), Sey.
54/B2 Farrar (riv.), Sc,UK
168/G5 Farrell, Pa,US
167/K9 Far Rockaway, NY,US
141/B4 Farroupilha, Braz.
106/C2 Farrukhābād, India
93/H4 Fars (gov.), Iran
81/H3 Fársala, Gre.
156/F5 Farson, Wy,US
62/B2 Farsund, Nor.
94/F5 Fartak, Ra's (pt.), Yem.
63/T9 Farum, Den.
145/N4 Farvel (cape), Grld.
113/T Farwell (isl.), Ant.
93/H4 Fasā, Iran
80/E2 Fasano, It.
91/C1 Faşıkan (pass), Turk.
67/H3 Fassberg, Ger.
54/D5 Fast Castle (pt.), Sc,UK
86/D2 Fastov, Ukr.
111/H4 Fatagar Tuting (cape), Indo.
108/B1 Fatahjang, Pak.
51/T6 Fataka (isl.), Sol.
106/B2 Fatehpur, India
106/D2 Fatehpur, India
128/A3 Fatick (reg.), Sen.
74/A3 Fátima, Port.
94/C4 Fāţimah (dry riv.), SAr.
92/D1 Fatsa, Turk.
121/M6 Fatu Hiva (isl.), FrPol.
76/C5 Faucille, Col de la (pass), Fr.
76/B1 Faucilles (mts.), Fr.
56/A2 Faughan (riv.), NI,UK
54/C5 Fauldhouse, Sc,UK
157/J4 Faulkton, SD,US
116/B3 Faure (isl.), Austl.
61/E2 Fauske, Nor.
79/F6 Favalto, Monte (peak), It.
80/C4 Favara, It.
76/D1 Fave (riv.), Fr.
59/G4 Faversham, Eng,UK
59/E5 Fawley, Eng,UK
152/H3 Fawn (riv.), On,Can
61/M7 Faxaflói (bay), Ice.
141/B2 Faxinal, Braz.
125/J4 Faya-Largeau, Chad
163/G3 Fayette, Al,US
159/J3 Fayette, Mo,US
163/F4 Fayette, Ms,US
162/E2 Fayetteville, Ar,US
163/G3 Fayetteville, Ga,US
163/J3 Fayetteville, NC,US
163/G3 Fayetteville, Tn,US
79/G3 Fažana, Cro.
129/F4 Fazao (mts.), Gha., Togo
129/F4 Fazao Nat'l Park, Togo
156/D3 F.D.R. (Franklin D. Roosevelt) (lake), Wa,US
60/A5 Feale (riv.), Ire.
163/J3 Fear (cape), NC,US
55/K8 Fearn, Hill of (hill), Sc,UK
166/D3 Feasterville-Trevose, Pa,US
158/B3 Feather (riv.), Ca,US
57/G4 Featherstone, Eng,UK
131/C3 Featherstone, Zim.
72/D2 Fécamp, Fr.
76/D1 Fecht (riv.), Fr.
108/A1 Fed. Admin. Tribal Areas (terr.), Pak.
167/K9 Federal Hall Nat'l Mem., NY,US
165/C3 Federal Way, Wa,US
70/C6 Federsee (lake), Ger.
56/A2 Feeny, NI,UK
82/F2 Fehérgyarmat, Hun.
64/F1 Fehmarn (isl.), Ger.
64/F1 Fehmarn Belt (str.), Ger., Den.
103/D4 Fei (riv.), China
141/D2 Feia (lake), Braz.
103/D3 Feicheng, China
103/D5 Feidong, China
68/C3 Feignies, Fr.
103/D4 Fei Huang (riv.), China
140/C4 Feira de Santana, Braz.
73/L3 Feistritz (riv.), Aus.
103/D5 Feixi, China
103/D4 Fei Xian, China
82/D2 Fejér (co.), Hun.
62/D4 Fejø (isl.), Den.
75/G3 Felanitx, Sp.
71/H6 Feldaist (riv.), Aus.
76/E2 Feldberg (peak), Ger.
77/F3 Feldkirch, Aus.
73/L3 Feldkirchen in Kärnten, Aus.
79/G1 Feletto Umberto, It.
131/C3 Felixburg, Zim.
141/C1 Felixlândia, Braz.
59/H3 Felixstowe, Eng,UK
71/E5 Fellbach, Ger.
57/G2 Felling, Eng,UK
67/G6 Felsberg, Ger.
53/M7 Feltham, Eng,UK
59/G2 Feltwell, Eng,UK
62/D4 Femø (isl.), Den.
103/C4 Fen (riv.), China
74/A1 Fene, Sp.
91/D1 Fener (pt.), Turk.
69/G6 Fénétrange, Fr.
81/J2 Fengári (peak), Gre.
101/C2 Fengcheng, China
105/G3 Fengchuihudie (peak), China
105/G2 Fengding (mtn.), China
103/B5 Fengjie, China
103/D5 Fengle (riv.), China
103/D2 Fengnan, China
103/D2 Fengning, China
104/C3 Fengqing, China
103/C4 Fengqiu, China
103/D3 Fengrun, China
105/G3 Fengshuba (res.), China
97/J1 Fengshui (peak), China
103/H7 Fengtai, China
103/D4 Feng Xian, China
103/E5 Fengxian, China
103/B3 Fengyang, China
103/D4 Fengyang, China
103/C2 Fengzhen, China
151/C5 Fenimore (passg.), Ak,US
133/J7 Fenoarivo Atsinanana, Madg.
105/H3 Fenshui (pass), China
105/H4 Fenshui Guan (pass), China
71/F4 Fensterbach (riv.), Ger.
59/G2 Fens, The (reg.), Eng,UK
165/E6 Fenton, Mi,US
165/E6 Fenton (lake), Mi,US
103/B3 Fenxi, China
86/E3 Feodosiya, Ukr.
123/V17 Fer, Cap de (cape), Alg.
93/J3 Ferdows, Iran
80/C2 Ferentino, It.
80/C1 Ferento (ruins), It.
102/B3 Fergana, Uzb.
60/B4 Fergus (riv.), Ire.
157/J4 Fergus Falls, Mn,US
152/F2 Ferguson (lake), NW,Can
128/D4 Ferkéssédougou, IvC.
73/L3 Ferlach, Aus.
124/C4 Ferlo (reg.), Sen.
128/B3 Ferlo, Vallée du (wadi), Sen.
56/A3 Fermanagh (dist.), NI,UK
164/B3 Fermin (pt.), Ca,US
165/P16 Fermi Nat'l Accelerator Lab., Il,US
80/C1 Fermo, It.
147/F4 Fernández, Mex.
144/J7 Fernandina (isl.), Ecu.
163/H4 Fernandina Beach, Fl,US
137/M4 Fernando de Noronha, Braz.
134/F3 Fernando de Noronha (isl.), Braz.
141/B2 Fernandópolis, Braz.
74/C4 Fernán-Núñez, Sp.
166/B6 Ferndale, Md,US
165/F7 Ferndale, Mi,US
59/E5 Ferndown, Eng,UK
54/C2 Ferness, Sc,UK
76/C5 Ferney-Voltaire, Fr.
156/E3 Fernie, BC,Can
77/G3 Fernpass (pass), Aus.
119/G5 Ferntree Gully Nat'l Park, Austl.
108/E3 Feroke, India
80/E2 Ferrandina, It.
79/E3 Ferrara, It.
79/E3 Ferrara (prov.), It.
74/A3 Ferreira do Alentejo, Port.
144/B2 Ferreñafe, Peru
72/C4 Ferret (cape), Fr.
162/F4 Ferriday, La,US
163/F4 Ferriday, La,US
54/D3 Ferryden, Sc,UK
57/G2 Ferryhill, Eng,UK
58/B3 Ferryside, Wal,UK
73/M3 Fertő (Neusiedler See) (lake), Aus., Hun.
66/C2 Ferwerd, Neth.
123/M13 Fès, Mor.
126/C2 Feshi, Zaire
54/C2 Feshie (riv.), Sc,UK
117/M8 Festival Centre, Austl.
163/F2 Festus, Mo,US
53/M8 Fetcham, Eng,UK
83/H3 Feteşti, Rom.
55/P12 Fethaland (pt.), Sc,UK
92/B2 Fethiye, Turk.
53/R10 Feucherolles, Fr.
70/E4 Feucht, Ger.
70/D4 Feuchtwangen, Ger.
153/J3 Feuilles (lake), Qu,Can
153/J3 Feuilles (riv.), Qu,Can
72/F4 Feurs, Fr.
95/K1 Feyzābād, Afg.
124/H2 Fezzan (reg.), Libya
56/E6 Ffestiniog, Wal,UK
123/G7 Fianarantsoa, Madg.
133/H8 Fianarantsoa (prov.), Madg.
124/J6 Fianga, Chad
71/F2 Fichtelberg (peak), Ger.
71/E2 Fichtelgebirge (mts.), Ger.
71/E3 Fichtelnaab (riv.), Ger.
132/D3 Ficksburg, SAfr.
78/D3 Fidenza, It.
128/C4 Fié (riv.), Gui., Mali
117/M9 Field (riv.), Austl.
83/G3 Fieni, Rom.
81/F2 Fier, Alb.
76/B6 Fier (riv.), Fr.
81/G1 Fierzë (lake), Alb.
54/D4 Fife (reg.), Sc,UK
54/D4 Fife Ness (pt.), Sc,UK
127/C5 Fifth Cataract (falls), Sudan
123/Q16 Figalo (cape), Alg.
72/E4 Figeac, Fr.
117/G2 Figg (peak), Austl.
79/E5 Figline Valdarno, It.
131/C4 Figtree, Zim.
74/A2 Figueira da Foz, Port.
75/G1 Figueres, Sp.
124/E1 Figuig, Mor.
133/G8 Fiherenana (riv.), Madg.
120/G6 Fiji
131/C4 Filabusi, Zim.
135/D1 Filadelfia, Par.
113/X Filchner Ice Shelf, Ant.
57/H3 Filey, Eng,UK
57/H3 Filey (bay), Eng,UK
83/F3 Filiaşi, Rom.
80/D3 Filicudi (isl.), It.
76/C6 Filière (riv.), Fr.
129/F3 Filingué, Niger
81/J2 Filippoi (ruins), Gre.
62/F2 Filipstad, Swe.
164/B2 Fillmore, Ca,US
158/D3 Fillmore, Ut,US
121/S9 Filo (peak), WSam.
147/H5 Filomena Mata, Mex.
70/C5 Fils (riv.), Ger.
58/D3 Filton, Eng,UK
113/Z Fimbul Ice Shelf, Ant.
124/J8 Fimi (riv.), Zaire
79/E3 Finale Emilia, It.
78/B4 Finale Ligure, It.
128/C3 Fina Rsv., Mali
53/N7 Finchley, Eng,UK
54/C1 Findhorn, Sc,UK
54/C1 Findhorn (riv.), Sc,UK
160/D3 Findlay, Oh,US
54/D1 Findochty, Sc,UK
119/D4 Fingal, Austl.
153/K2 Finger (lake), On,Can
160/E3 Finger (lakes), NY,US
131/C2 Fingoè, Moz.
72/E4 Finiels, Sommet de (peak), Fr.
91/B1 Finike, Turk.
74/A1 Finisterre (cape), Sp.
117/G3 Finke (riv.), Austl.
117/G3 Finke Gorge Nat'l Park, Austl.
73/K3 Finkenstein, Aus.
61/H2 Finland
63/L2 Finland (gulf), Eur.
152/D3 Finlay (riv.), BC,Can
162/B4 Finlay (mts.), Tx,US
55/H9 Finn (riv.), Ire.
67/E6 Finnentrop, Ger.
165/C2 Finn Hill-Inglewood, Wa,US
118/B1 Finnigan (peak), Austl.
117/G5 Finnis (cape), Austl.
61/G1 Finnmark (co.), Nor.
78/C1 Fino Mornasco, It.
62/F2 Finspång, Swe.
76/E4 Finsteraarhorn (peak), Swi.
55/N13 Finstown, Sc,UK
56/A3 Fintona, NI,UK
54/A1 Fionn Loch (lake), Sc,UK
80/B1 Fiora (riv.), It.
79/D3 Fiorano, It.
78/C3 Fiorenzuola d'Arda, It.
165/C2 Fircrest-Silver Lake, Wa,US
167/E2 Fire Island Nat'l Seash., NY,US
79/E5 Firenze (prov.), It.
79/E5 Firenze (Florence), It.
142/E2 Firmat, Arg.
72/F4 Firminy, Fr.
106/C2 Fīrozābād, India
108/C2 Fīrozpur, India
127/C3 First Cataract (falls), Egypt
93/H4 Fīrūzābād, Iran
73/L3 Fischbacher (mts.), Aus.
131/C2 Fisenge, Zam.
132/B2 Fish (riv.), Namb.
132/C3 Fish (riv.), SAfr.
57/G2 Fishburn, Eng,UK
113/E Fisher (glac.), Ant.

Fishe – Galil

157/J3 Fisher (bay), Mb,Can
153/H2 Fisher (str.), NW,Can
157/J3 Fisher Branch, Mb,Can
118/F6 Fisherman (isl.), Austl.
167/G1 Fishers (isl.), NY,US
58/B3 Fishguard, Wal,UK
166/A1 Fishing (cr.), Pa,US
166/B1 Fishing (cr.), Pa,US
86/F4 Fisht, Gora (peak), Rus.
57/J6 Fishtoft, Eng,UK
63/S7 Fisksätra, Swe.
55/P13 Fitful Head (pt.), Sc,UK
121/S8 Fito (peak), WSam.
63/R7 Fittja, Swe.
151/L2 Fitton (mtn.), Yk,Can
163/H4 Fitzgerald, Ga,US
116/C5 Fitzgerald River Nat'l Park, Austl.
156/B3 Fitz Hugo (sound), BC,Can
143/J7 Fitzroy (peak), Arg.
118/C3 Fitzroy (riv.), Austl.
153/R7 Fitzwilliam (str.), NW,Can
80/C2 Fiumicino, It.
56/A3 Fivemiletown, NI,UK
54/A2 Five Sisters (mtn.), Sc,UK
130/A4 Fizi, Zaire
62/A1 Fjell, Nor.
59/F3 Flackwell Heath, Eng,UK
159/G3 Flagler, Co,US
163/H4 Flagler Beach, Fl,US
158/E4 Flagstaff, Az,US
160/B2 Flambeau (riv.), Wi,US
161/Q9 Flamborough, On,Can
57/H3 Flamborough, Eng,UK
57/H3 Flamborough Head (pt.), Eng,UK
64/G2 Fläming (hills), Ger.
156/F5 Flaming Gorge (res.), Ut, Wy,US
156/F5 Flaming Gorge Nat'l Rec. Area, Ut, Wy,US
157/K2 Flanagan (riv.), On,Can
68/B2 Flanders (reg.), Belg., Fr.
157/J4 Flandreau, SD,US
167/K9 Flatbush, NY,US
151/L3 Flat Creek, Yk,Can
156/E4 Flathead (lake), Mt,US
156/E4 Flathead (riv.), Mt,US
156/E4 Flathead, South Fork (riv.), Mt,US
58/C4 Flat Holm (isl.), Eng,UK
159/K3 Flat River, Mo,US
165/F7 Flat Rock, Mi,US
118/B1 Flattery (cape), Austl.
156/B3 Flattery (cape), Wa,US
138/B5 Flavio Alfaro, Ecu.
77/F3 Flawil, Swi.
59/F4 Fleet, Eng,UK
57/E4 Fleetwood, Eng,UK
62/B2 Flekkefjord, Nor.
119/F5 Flemington Racecourse, Austl.
62/G2 Flen, Swe.
64/E1 Flensburg, Ger.
69/E2 Fleron, Belg.
72/C2 Flers, Fr.
60/A5 Flesk (riv.), Ire.
76/D5 Fletschhorn (peak), Swi.
68/D3 Fleurus, Belg.
72/D3 Fleury-les-Aubrais, Fr.
66/C4 Flevoland (prov.), Neth.
77/G3 Flexenpass (pass), Aus.
70/C2 Flieden, Ger.
70/C2 Flieden (riv.), Ger.
56/E2 Flimby, Eng,UK
116/B5 Flinders (bay), Austl.
117/G5 Flinders (isl.), Austl.
119/D3 Flinders (isl.), Austl.
117/H5 Flinders (range), Austl.
118/C2 Flinders (reefs), Austl.
118/A2 Flinders (riv.), Austl.
117/H5 Flinders Chase Nat'l Park, Austl.
117/H4 Flinders Ranges Nat'l Park, Austl.
157/J3 Flindt (riv.), On,Can
157/H2 Flin Flon, Mb,Can
153/J2 Flint (lake), NW,Can
121/K6 Flint (isl.), Kiri.
57/E5 Flint, Wal,UK
163/G4 Flint (riv.), Ga,US
159/H3 Flint (hills), Ks,US
165/E5 Flint, Mi,US
62/D4 Flintbek, Ger.
164/B2 Flintridge-La Cañada, Ca,US
165/F6 Flint, South Branch (riv.), Mi,US
62/E1 Flisa, Nor.
59/F3 Flitwick, Eng,UK
147/Q10 Floating Gardens, Mex.
62/E3 Floda, Swe.
54/D5 Flodden, Eng,UK
67/F1 Flögelner See (lake), Ger.
65/G3 Flöha (riv.), Ger.
116/C2 Flora (peak), Austl.
112/C1 Flora, Phil.
160/B4 Flora, Il,US
167/E2 Floral Park, NY,US
69/F5 Florange, Fr.
140/C2 Florânia, Braz.
69/D3 Floreffe, Belg.
163/G3 Florence, Al,US
158/E4 Florence, Az,US
159/F3 Florence, Co,US
163/J3 Florence, SC,US
79/E5 Florence (Firenze), It.
164/F8 Florence-Graham, Ca,US
138/C4 Florencia, Col.
68/D3 Florennes, Belg.
142/E3 Flores (riv.), Arg.
156/B3 Flores (isl.), BC,Can
148/D2 Flores, Guat.
111/F5 Flores (isl.), Indo.
111/E5 Flores (sea), Indo.
75/R12 Flores (isl.), Azor.,Port.
143/F2 Flores (dept.), Uru.
140/B2 Flores do Piauí, Braz.
140/C3 Floresta, Braz.
162/D4 Floresville, Tx,US
166/D2 Florham Park, NJ,US
140/B2 Floriano, Braz.
141/B3 Florianópolis, Braz.
138/B4 Florida, Col.
149/G1 Florida, Cuba
155/K7 Florida (str.), Cuba, US
143/F2 Florida, Uru.
143/F2 Florida (dept.), Uru.
163/H4 Florida (state), US
163/H5 Florida (bay), Fl,US
138/C3 Floridablanca, Col.
163/H5 Florida Keys (isls.), Fl,US
80/D4 Floridia, It.
165/M10 Florin, Ca,US
81/G2 Flórina, Gre.
159/K3 Florissant, Mo,US
61/C3 Florø, Nor.
70/B2 Flörsheim am Main, Ger.
70/B2 Florstadt, Ger.
162/C3 Floydada, Tx,US
77/G4 Fluchthorn (peak), Aus.
77/F4 Flüelapass (pass), Swi.
66/C3 Fluessen (lake), Neth.
80/A3 Flumendosa (riv.), It.
160/D3 Flushing, Mi,US
167/K8 Flushing, NY,US
66/A6 Flushing (Vlissingen), Neth.
120/D5 Fly (riv.), PNG
113/T Flying Fish (cape), Ant.
61/P6 Fnjóská (riv.), Ice.
157/H3 Foam Lake, Sk,Can
82/D4 Foča, Bosn.
54/C1 Fochabers, Sc,UK
83/H3 Focşani, Rom.
107/K3 Fogang, China
80/D2 Foggia, It.
79/F5 Foglia (riv.), It.
63/J2 Föglö (isl.), Fin.
122/J10 Fogo (isl.), CpV.
73/L3 Fohnsdorf, Aus.
64/E1 Föhr (isl.), Ger.
72/D5 Foix, Fr.
62/B1 Folarskardnuten (peak), Nor.
61/D2 Folda (fjord), Nor.
81/J4 Folégandros (isl.), Gre.
153/J2 Foley (isl.), NW,Can
80/C1 Foligno, It.
59/H4 Folkestone, Eng,UK
163/H4 Folkston, Ga,US
80/B1 Follonica (gulf), It.
152/F3 Fond du Lac (riv.), Sk,Can
160/B3 Fond du Lac, Wi,US
80/C2 Fondi, It.
61/D3 Fongen (peak), Nor.
74/B1 Fonsagrada, Sp.
138/C2 Fonseca, Col.
148/E3 Fonseca (gulf), NAm.
72/F4 Fontaine, Fr.
72/E2 Fontainebleau, Fr.
76/A3 Fontaine-lès-Dijon, Fr.
68/D3 Fontaine-L'Evêque, Belg.
164/C2 Fontana, Ca,US
72/C3 Fontenay-le-Comte, Fr.
53/S10 Fontenay-le-Fleury, Fr.
53/S11 Fontenay-les-Briis, Fr.
53/T10 Fontenay-sous-Bois, Fr.
53/U10 Fontenay-Trésigny, Fr.
156/F5 Fontenelle (res.), Wy,US
73/G4 Font Sancte, Pic de la (peak), Fr.
61/P6 Fontur (pt.), Ice.
119/F5 Footscray, Austl.
96/F5 Foping, China
151/H3 Foraker (mtn.), Ak,US
69/F5 Forbach, Fr.
70/B5 Forbach, Ger.
119/D2 Forbes, Austl.
74/A1 Forcarey, Sp.
70/E3 Forchheim, Ger.
76/D5 Forclaz, Col de la (pass), Swi.
54/D5 Ford, Eng,UK
165/E7 Ford (lake), Mi,US
167/K8 Fordham, NY,US
59/E5 Fordingbridge, Eng,UK
167/D2 Fords, NJ,US
162/E3 Fordyce, Ar,US
58/C4 Foreland (pt.), Eng,UK
59/E5 Foreland, The (pt.), Eng,UK
156/F3 Foremost, Ab,Can
59/H4 Foreness (pt.), Eng,UK
163/F3 Forest, Ms,US
167/K9 Forest Hills, NY,US
119/D4 Forestier (cape), Austl.
161/G1 Forestville, Qu,Can
166/B6 Forestville, Md,US
72/E4 Forez (mts.), Fr.
54/D3 Forfar, Sc,UK
53/S11 Forges-les-Bains, Fr.
77/G2 Forggensee (lake), Ger.
161/H1 Forillon Nat'l Park, Qu,Can
56/B3 Forkill, NI,UK
79/F4 Forlì, It.
79/F4 Forlì (prov.), It.
79/F4 Forlimpopoli, It.
54/D2 Formartine (dist.), Sc,UK
57/E4 Formby, Eng,UK
57/E4 Formby (pt.), Eng,UK
75/F3 Formentera (isl.), Sp.
75/G3 Formentor, Cabo de (cape), Sp.
80/C2 Formia, It.
141/C2 Formiga, Braz.
79/D3 Formigine, It.
135/E2 Formosa, Arg.
140/A4 Formosa, Braz.
137/G6 Formosa (mts.), Braz.
128/A4 Formosa (isl.), GBis.
132/C4 Formosa (bay), SAfr.
140/A3 Formosa do Rio Prêto, Braz.
140/A4 Formoso (riv.), Braz.
79/E5 Fornacelle, It.
62/D3 Fornæs (cape), Den.
54/C1 Forres, Sc,UK
163/F3 Forrest City, Ar,US
62/E2 Forshaga, Swe.
63/K1 Forssa, Fin.
118/A3 Forsyth (range), Austl.
163/H3 Forsyth, Ga,US
156/G4 Forsyth, Mt,US
167/D5 Forsythe Nat'l Wild. Ref., NJ,US
95/K3 Fort Abbās, Pak.
140/C1 Fortaleza, Braz.
140/A2 Fortaleza dos Nogueiras, Braz.
143/G2 Fortaleza Santa Teresa, Uru.
54/B2 Fort Augustus, Sc,UK
132/D4 Fort Beaufort, SAfr.
161/H2 Fort Beauséjour Nat'l Hist. Park, NB,Can
166/A6 Fort Belvoir (mil. res.), Va,US
156/F4 Fort Benton, Mt,US
158/B3 Fort Bragg, Ca,US
161/F2 Fort Chambly Nat'l Hist. Park, Qu,Can
159/H4 Fort Cobb (res.), Ok,US
159/F2 Fort Collins, Co,US
162/C4 Fort Davis, Tx,US
69/E5 Fort de Douaumont, Fr.
150/F4 Fort-de-France, Mart.
150/F4 Fort Desaix, Mart.
69/E5 Fort de Vaux, Fr.
166/D3 Fort Dix (mil. res.), NJ,US
157/K5 Fort Dodge, Ia,US
126/D3 Forte Cameia, Ang.
78/D5 Forte dei Marmi, It.
161/S10 Fort Erie, On,Can
116/C2 Fortescue (riv.), Austl.
160/A1 Fort Frances, On,Can
163/F4 Fort Gaines, Al,US
161/R9 Fort George, On,Can
153/J3 Fort-George (Chisasibi), Qu,Can
159/J4 Fort Gibson, Ok,US
162/E2 Fort Gibson (lake), Ok,US
124/C3 Fort-Gouraud, Mrta.
60/D5 Forth (mtn.), Ire.
54/C5 Forth, Sc,UK
54/C4 Forth (riv.), Sc,UK
167/D2 Fort Hamilton (mil. res.), NY,US
167/D3 Fort Hancock (mil. res.), NJ,US
54/B4 Forth, Carse of (plain), Sc,UK
54/D4 Forth, Firth of (inlet), Sc,UK
147/N8 Fortín de las Flores, Mex.
166/B3 Fort Indiantown Gap (mil. res.), Pa,US
161/G2 Fort Kent, Me,US
163/H5 Fort Lauderdale, Fl,US
167/E2 Fort Lee, NJ,US
165/B3 Fort Lewis (mil. res.), Wa,US
159/F2 Fort Lupton, Co,US
156/E3 Fort Macleod, Ab,Can
157/L5 Fort Madison, Ia,US
165/F7 Fort Malden Nat'l Hist. Park, On,Can
163/H4 Fort Matanzas Nat'l Mon., Fl,US
166/B5 Fort McHenry Nat'l Mon. & Hist. Site, Md,US
152/E3 Fort McMurray, Ab,Can
166/B5 Fort Meade (mil. res.), Md,US
160/C2 Fort Michilimackinac, Mi,US
167/D3 Fort Monmouth (mil. res.), NJ,US
159/G2 Fort Morgan, Co,US
163/J3 Fort Moultrie, SC,US
163/H5 Fort Myers, Fl,US
152/D3 Fort Nelson (riv.), BC,Can
57/F4 Forton, Eng,UK
80/D2 Fortore (riv.), It.
163/G3 Fort Payne, Al,US
157/G4 Fort Peck (dam), Mt,US
156/G4 Fort Peck (lake), Mt,US
163/H5 Fort Pierce, Fl,US
157/H4 Fort Pierre, SD,US
130/A2 Fort Portal, Ugan.
157/H3 Fort Qu'Appelle, Sk,Can
163/K3 Fort Raleigh Nat'l Hist. Site, NC,US
157/J5 Fort Randall (dam), SD,US
161/J2 Fortress of Louisbourg Nat'l Hist. Park, NS,Can
131/C4 Fort Rixon, Zim.
54/B1 Fortrose, Sc,UK
156/B2 Fort Saint James, BC,Can
152/D3 Fort Saint John, BC,Can
156/E2 Fort Saskatchewan, Ab,Can
159/J3 Fort Scott, Ks,US
87/J3 Fort-Shevchenko, Kaz.
162/E3 Fort Smith, Ar,US
162/C4 Fort Stockton, Tx,US
159/F4 Fort Sumner, NM,US
167/E2 Fort Tilden (mil. res.), NY,US
157/J4 Fort Totten, ND,US
140/A2 Fortuna, Braz.
161/L2 Fortune, Nf,Can
161/L2 Fortune (bay), Nf,Can
150/C2 Fortune (Long Cay) (cay), Bahm.
58/D5 Fortuneswell, Eng,UK
159/F4 Fort Union Nat'l Mon., NM,US
167/D2 Fort Wadsworth (mil. res.), NY,US
163/G4 Fort Walton Beach, Fl,US
166/A6 Fort Washington Park, Md,US
160/C3 Fort Wayne, In,US
160/F2 Fort Wellington Nat'l Hist. Park, On,Can
54/A3 Fort William, Sc,UK
162/D3 Fort Worth, Tx,US
157/H4 Fort Yates, ND,US
118/B2 Forty Mile Scrub Nat'l Park, Austl.
93/H5 Forūr (isl.), Iran
105/G4 Foshan, China
153/S7 Fosheim (pen.), NW,Can
57/G3 Foss (riv.), Eng,UK
78/A3 Fossano, It.
53/T9 Fosses, Fr.
69/D3 Fosses-la-Ville, Belg.
156/C4 Fossil, Or,US
156/F5 Fossil Butte Nat'l Mon., Wy,US
79/F5 Fossombrone, It.
160/D3 Fostoria, Oh,US
72/C2 Fougères, Fr.
125/N3 Foul (bay), Egypt, Sudan
108/H4 Foul (pt.), SrL.
55/N12 Foula (isl.), Sc,UK
59/G3 Foulness (isl.), Eng,UK
59/G3 Foulness (pt.), Eng,UK
57/H4 Foulness (riv.), Eng,UK
59/H1 Foulsham, Eng,UK
129/H5 Foumban, Camr.
159/F3 Fountain, Co,US
57/G3 Fountains Abbey, Eng,UK
164/C3 Fountain Valley, Ca,US
162/E3 Fourche La Fave (riv.), Ar,US
59/E4 Four Marks, Eng,UK
68/D4 Fourmies, Fr.
151/D5 Four Mountains (isls.), Ak,US
133/R15 Fournaise, Piton de la (peak), Reun.
127/C5 Fourth Cataract (falls), Sudan
128/B4 Fouta Djallon (reg.), Gha.
115/Q12 Foveaux (str.), NZ
58/B6 Fowey, Eng,UK
58/B6 Fowey (riv.), Eng,UK
119/B1 Fowlers Gap, Austl.
93/G2 Fowman, Iran
151/M3 Fox (mtn.), Yk,Can
151/E5 Fox (isls.), Ak,US
165/P15 Fox (lake), Il,US
160/B3 Fox (riv.), Il, Wi,US
165/B3 Fox (isl.), Wa,US
156/D2 Fox Creek, Ab,Can
153/H2 Foxe (chan.), NW,Can
153/J2 Foxe (pen.), NW,Can
153/J2 Foxe Basin (sound), NW,Can
62/D2 Foxen (lake), Swe.
115/R11 Fox Glacier, NZ
165/P15 Fox Lake, Il,US
59/G2 Foxton, Eng,UK
156/F3 Fox Valley, Sk,Can
54/B2 Foyers, Sc,UK
56/A2 Foyle (riv.), NI,UK
56/A1 Foyle, Lough (inlet), Ire., NI,UK
74/B1 Foz, Sp.
126/B4 Foz do Cunene, Ang.
135/F2 Foz do Iguaçu, Braz.
75/F2 Fraga, Sp.
149/G1 Fragosa (cay), Cuba
141/B3 Fraiburgo, Braz.
136/E7 Frailes (range), Bol.
68/C3 Frameries, Belg.
168/C1 Framingham, Ma,US
59/H2 Framlingham, Eng,UK
141/C2 Franca, Braz.
81/E2 Francavilla Fontana, It.
72/D3 France
53/T9 France, Pays de (plain), Fr.
72/E5 France, Roc de (mtn.), Fr.
152/C2 Frances (lake), Yk,Can
149/F1 Frances (cape), Cuba
126/B1 Franceville, Gabon
76/C3 Franche-Comté (hist. reg.), Fr.
73/G3 Franche-Comté (reg.), Fr.
157/J5 Francis Case (lake), SD,US
147/H5 Francisco Escárcega, Mex.
146/E3 Francisco I. Madero, Mex.
131/B4 Francistown, Bots.
141/G8 Franco da Rocha, Braz.
156/B2 Francois (lake), BC,Can
53/S10 Franconville, Fr.
66/C2 Franeker, Neth.
67/F6 Frankenberg-Eder, Ger.
70/D4 Frankenhöhe (mts.), Ger.
160/D3 Frankenmuth, Mi,US
70/B3 Frankenthal, Ger.
71/E2 Franken Wald (for.), Ger.
160/C3 Frankfort, In,US
160/C4 Frankfort (cap.), Ky,US
65/H2 Frankfurt, Ger.
70/B2 Frankfurt am Main, Ger.
116/D5 Frank Hann Nat'l Park, Austl.
70/E3 Fränkische Alb (mts.), Ger.
70/D4 Fränkische Rezat (riv.), Ger.
70/C2 Fränkische Saale (riv.), Ger.
70/E2 Fränkische Schweiz (reg.), Ger.
119/C3 Frankland (cape), Austl.
113/M Franklin (isl.), Ant.
151/N1 Franklin (bay), NW,Can
152/D2 Franklin (mts.), NW,Can
151/G1 Franklin (pt.), Ak,US
160/C4 Franklin, In,US
160/C4 Franklin, Ky,US
168/C1 Franklin, Ma,US
163/H3 Franklin, NC,US
168/H5 Franklin, Pa,US
163/G3 Franklin, Tn,US
162/D4 Franklin, Tx,US
160/E4 Franklin, Va,US
165/P14 Franklin, Wi,US
160/E4 Franklin, WV,US
156/D3 Franklin D. Roosevelt (lake), Wa,US
167/D1 Franklin Lakes, NJ,US
119/C4 Franklin-Lower Gordon Wild Rivers Nat'l Park, Austl.
166/D1 Franklin Mineral Museum, NJ,US
165/Q16 Franklin Park, Il,US
168/G6 Franklin Park, Pa,US
167/E2 Franklin Square, NY,US
135/F2 Fransisco Beltrão, Braz.
141/G8 Fransisco Morato, Braz.
140/B5 Fransisco Sá, Braz.
88/F2 Franz Josef Land (arch.), Rus.
118/D4 Fraser (isl.), Austl.
116/C3 Fraser (peak), Austl.
156/B2 Fraser (lake), BC,Can
156/C3 Fraser (riv.), BC,Can
165/G6 Fraser, Mi,US
54/D1 Fraserburgh, Sc,UK
156/B2 Fraser Lake, BC,Can
119/C3 Fraser Nat'l Park, Austl.
79/E2 Frassine (riv.), It.
79/F5 Frati, Monte dei (peak), It.
77/E2 Frauenfeld, Swi.
142/F2 Fray Bentos, Uru.
158/C4 Frazier Park, Ca,US
69/F2 Frechen, Ger.
114/A5 Frecinet (estuary), Austl.
132/E3 Fred (mtn.), SAfr.
63/T9 Fredensborg, Den.
62/C4 Fredericia, Den.
115/J4 Frederick (reef), Austl.
160/E4 Frederick, Md,US
166/A5 Frederick (co.), Md,US
159/H4 Frederick, Ok,US
162/D4 Fredericksburg, Tx,US
160/E4 Fredericksburg, Va,US
161/H2 Fredericton (cap.), NB,Can
63/T9 Frederiksberg, Den.
63/T9 Frederiksborg (co.), Den.
62/E4 Frederiksborg Castle, Den.
62/D3 Frederikshavn, Den.
63/T9 Frederikssund, Den.
139/G4 Frederik Willem IV (falls), Sur.
158/D3 Fredonia, Az,US
159/J3 Fredonia, Ks,US
160/E3 Fredonia, NY,US
62/D2 Fredrikstad, Nor.
159/H3 Freedom, Ok,US
167/D3 Freehold, NJ,US
117/G2 Freeling (peak), Austl.
117/H4 Freeling Heights (peak), Austl.
150/B1 Freeport, Bahm.
160/B3 Freeport, Il,US
167/E2 Freeport, NY,US
162/E4 Freeport, Tx,US
162/D5 Freer, Tx,US
128/B4 Freetown (cap.), SLeo.
168/C2 Freetown-Fall River Saint For., Ma,US
72/B2 Fréhel (cape), Fr.
64/G3 Freib (riv.), Ger.
65/G3 Freiberg, Ger.
64/G3 Freiberger Mulde (riv.), Ger.
76/D2 Freiburg, Ger.
77/E3 Freienbach, Swi.
141/D1 Frei Inocêncio, Braz.
71/F7 Freilassing, Ger.
142/B3 Freire, Chile
69/G4 Freisen, Ger.
71/E6 Freising, Ger.
71/H6 Freistadt, Aus.
65/G3 Freital, Ger.
73/G5 Fréjus, Fr.
116/K7 Fremantle, Austl.
58/B4 Fremington, Eng,UK
165/L11 Fremont, Ca,US
160/C3 Fremont, Mi,US
159/H2 Fremont, Ne,US
160/D3 Fremont, Oh,US
158/E3 Fremont (riv.), Ut,US
156/F5 Fremont (peak), Wy,US
160/D2 French (riv.), On,Can
166/C3 French (cr.), Pa,US
168/H5 French (cr.), Pa,US
166/C3 French Creek Saint Park, Pa,US
121/J2 French Frigate (shoals), Hi,US
134/D2 French Guiana (dpcy.), Fr.
156/G3 Frenchman (riv.), Can., US
159/G2 Frenchman (cr.), Ne,US
161/R8 Frenchman's (bay), On,Can
119/C4 Frenchmans Cap (peak), Austl.
121/M6 French Polynesia (terr.), Fr.
123/R16 Frenda, Alg.
53/S9 Frépillon, Fr.
137/H5 Fresco (riv.), Braz.
59/E5 Freshwater, Eng,UK
142/B4 Fresia, Chile
53/S10 Fresnes, Fr.
146/E4 Fresnillo, Mex.
158/C3 Fresno, Ca,US
63/R6 Frestaby, Swe.
54/C3 Freuchie, Loch (lake), Sc,UK
69/G2 Freudenberg, Ger.
70/B6 Freudenstadt, Ger.
116/B3 Freycinet (har.), Austl.
119/D4 Freycinet Nat'l Park, Austl.
69/F5 Freyming-Merlebach, Fr.
71/E4 Freystadt, Ger.
71/G5 Freyung, Ger.
126/B4 Fria (cape), Namb.
135/C2 Frías, Arg.
76/D4 Fribourg, Swi.
76/D4 Fribourg (canton), Swi.
70/B2 Friedberg, Ger.
70/D6 Friedberg, Ger.
67/E2 Friedeburg, Ger.
70/B2 Friedrichsdorf, Ger.
77/F2 Friedrichshafen, Ger.
69/G5 Friedrichsthal, Ger.
67/G7 Frielendorf, Ger.
70/A6 Friesenheim, Ger.
66/C2 Friesland (prov.), Neth.
67/E2 Friesoythe, Ger.
59/F4 Frimley, Eng,UK
59/H3 Frinton, Eng,UK
50/G7 Frio (cape), Braz.
159/H5 Frio (riv.), Tx,US
54/D3 Friockheim, Sc,UK
168/A1 Frissel (mtn.), Ct,US
67/G6 Fritzlar, Ger.
73/K3 Friuli-Venezia Giula (reg.), It.
56/E2 Frizington, Eng,UK
153/K2 Frobisher (bay), NW,Can
156/F1 Frobisher (lake), Sk,Can
57/F5 Frodsham, Eng,UK
61/D3 Frohavet (bay), Nor.
68/D3 Froidchapelle, Belg.
87/G2 Frolovo, Rus.
117/J4 Frome (lake), Austl.
117/H4 Frome (riv.), Austl.
58/D4 Frome, Eng,UK
58/D2 Frome (riv.), Eng,UK
58/D5 Frome (riv.), Eng,UK
159/F2 Front (range), Co,US
140/B2 Fronteiras, Braz.
147/E3 Frontera, Mex.
147/G5 Frontera, Mex.
72/E5 Frontignan, Fr.
160/E4 Front Royal, Va,US
80/C2 Frosinone, It.
61/E3 Frösö, Swe.
113/J Frost (glac.), Ant.
69/F6 Frouard, Fr.
60/B6 Frower (pt.), Ire.
61/D3 Frøya (isl.), Nor.
153/H2 Frozen (str.), NW,Can
161/Q9 Fruitland, On,Can
82/D3 Fruška Gora Nat'l Park, Yugo.
141/B2 Frutal, Braz.
142/B4 Frutillar, Chile
65/K4 Frýdek-Místek, Czh.
103/C5 Fu (riv.), China
105/H3 Fu'an, China
79/D5 Fucecchio, It.
103/D3 Fucheng, China
64/E3 Fuchskaute (peak), Ger.
69/H2 Fuchskauten (peak), Ger.
98/C3 Fuchū, Japan
103/D5 Fuchun (riv.), China
111/H4 Fudi (mtn.), Indo.
105/J3 Fuding, China
74/C4 Fuengirola, Sp.
74/D2 Fuenlabrada, Sp.
75/N8 Fuente, Sp.
75/E4 Fuente-Álamo, Sp.
74/B3 Fuente del Maestre, Sp.
74/C3 Fuente Obejuna, Sp.
74/E1 Fuenterrabiá, Sp.
74/C4 Fuentes de Andalucía, Sp.
146/C3 Fuerte (riv.), Mex.
136/G8 Fuerte Olimpo, Par.
112/C1 Fuga (isl.), Phil.
107/G2 Fugong, China
103/C4 Fugou, China
96/B2 Fuhai, China
64/F3 Fuhne (riv.), Ger.
67/H4 Fuhse (riv.), Ger.
99/F3 Fuji, Japan
99/F3 Fuji (riv.), Japan
105/H3 Fujian (prov.), China
99/F3 Fujieda, Japan
99/F3 Fuji-Hakone-Izu Nat'l Park, Japan
99/L10 Fujiidera, Japan
99/H7 Fujimi, Japan
99/H7 Fujino, Japan
99/F3 Fujinomiya, Japan
99/F2 Fujioka, Japan
99/F3 Fujisawa, Japan
99/J7 Fujishiro, Japan
99/M9 Fujiwara, Japan
99/F3 Fujiyama (mtn.), Japan
99/F3 Fujiyoshida, Japan
100/C2 Fukagawa, Japan
102/E3 Fukang, China
98/D3 Fukuchiyama, Japan
98/A4 Fukue, Japan
98/A4 Fukue (isl.), Japan
98/E2 Fukui, Japan
98/E3 Fukui (pref.), Japan
98/B4 Fukuoka, Japan
98/B4 Fukuoka (pref.), Japan
99/E3 Fukuroi, Japan
113/C Fukushima (peak), Ant.
100/B3 Fukushima, Japan
99/G2 Fukushima, Japan
99/F2 Fukushima (pref.), Japan
98/C3 Fukuyama, Japan
95/J2 Fūlādī (mtn.), Afg.
59/G2 Fulbourn, Eng,UK
70/C1 Fulda, Ger.
70/C2 Fulda (riv.), Ger.
57/G4 Fulford, Eng,UK
105/E2 Fuling, China
164/C3 Fullerton, Ca,US
166/C2 Fullerton (Whitehall), Pa,US
161/Q9 Fulton, On,Can
160/B4 Fulton, Ky,US
159/K3 Fulton, Mo,US
160/E3 Fulton, NY,US
62/E1 Fulufjället (peak), Swe.
57/F4 Fulwood, Eng,UK
79/F5 Fumaiolo, Monte (peak), It.
72/D4 Fumel, Fr.
104/D3 Fumin, China
99/H7 Funabashi, Japan
120/G5 Funafuti (atoll), Tuv.
103/C4 Funan, China
138/C2 Fundación, Col.
161/H2 Fundy (bay), NB, NS,Can
161/H2 Fundy Nat'l Park, NB,Can
131/D4 Funhalouro, Moz.
103/D4 Funing, China
104/E4 Funing, China
60/B5 Funshion (riv.), Ire.
77/G4 Fuorn (Ofenpass) (pass), Swi.
103/C3 Fuping, China
107/J2 Fuquan, China
101/C2 Fur (riv.), China
76/B6 Furan (riv.), Fr.
131/D2 Furancungo, Moz.
100/C2 Furano, Japan
63/T9 Furesø (lake), Den.
84/J4 Furmanov, Rus.
54/A4 Furnace, Sc,UK
141/B6 Furnas (res.), Braz.
119/C4 Furneaux Group (isls.), Austl.
67/E3 Fürstenau, Ger.
82/C2 Fürstenfeld, Aus.
70/E6 Fürstenfeldbruck, Ger.
65/H2 Fürstenwalde, Ger.
70/D4 Fürth, Ger.
71/F4 Furth im Wald, Ger.
70/B6 Furtwangen im Schwarzwald, Ger.
100/B4 Furukawa, Japan
153/H2 Fury and Hecla (str.), NW,Can
138/C3 Fusagasugá, Col.
103/B4 Fushan, China
103/E3 Fushan, China
101/B2 Fushun, China
99/M9 Fuso, Japan
101/D1 Fusong, China
99/H7 Fussa, Japan
77/G2 Füssen, Ger.
109/D1 Fusui, China
99/M10 Futami, Japan
82/D3 Futog, Yugo.
142/B4 Futrono, Chile
99/F3 Futtsu, Japan
120/H6 Futuna (isl.), Wall.
91/B4 Fuwah, Egypt
103/B3 Fu Xian, China
104/D3 Fuxian (lake), China
101/A1 Fuxin, China
101/A1 Fuxin Monggolzu Zizhixian, China
103/C4 Fuyang, China
105/F3 Fuyi (riv.), China
97/J2 Fuyu, China
104/E3 Fuyuan, China
96/B2 Fuyun, China
65/L5 Füzesabony, Hun.
105/H3 Fuzhou, China
53/P6 Fyfield, Eng,UK
62/D4 Fyn (co.), Den.
61/D5 Fyn (isl.), Den.
54/A4 Fyne, Loch (inlet), Sc,UK
63/R6 Fysingen (lake), Swe.
54/D2 Fyvie, Sc,UK

G

125/Q6 Gaalkacyo (Galcaio), Som.
66/D5 Gaanderen, Neth.
66/C2 Gaast, Neth.
72/C5 Gabas (riv.), Fr.
158/C3 Gabbs, Nv,US
126/B3 Gabela, Ang.
124/H1 Gabes (gulf), Tun.
124/H7 Gabon
131/B5 Gaborone (cap.), Bots.
60/A6 Gabriel (mtn.), Ire.
83/G4 Gabrovo, Bul.
82/D4 Gacko, Bosn.
106/C4 Gadag-Betgeri, India
163/G3 Gadsden, Al,US
63/T9 Gadstrup, Den.
131/C3 Gadzema, Zim.
83/G3 Găeşti, Rom.
80/C2 Gaeta, It.
80/C2 Gaeta (gulf), It.
163/H3 Gaffney, SC,US
84/G5 Gagarin, Rus.
70/B5 Gaggenau, Ger.
128/D5 Gagnoa, IvC.
161/G1 Gagnon, Qu,Can
53/T10 Gagny, Fr.
86/G4 Gagra, Geo.
77/G3 Gaichtpass (pass), Aus.
82/A2 Gail (riv.), Aus.
70/C5 Gaildorf, Ger.
72/D5 Gaillac, Fr.
168/B3 Gaillard (lake), Ct,US
73/K3 Gailtaler Alps (mts.), Aus.
142/D4 Gaiman, Arg.
71/E5 Gaimersheim, Ger.
163/H4 Gainesville, Fl,US
163/H3 Gainesville, Ga,US
159/J3 Gainesville, Mo,US
162/D3 Gainesville, Tx,US
57/G2 Gainford, Eng,UK
57/H5 Gainsborough, Eng,UK
117/G4 Gairdner (lake), Austl.
131/C3 Gairezi (riv.), Zim.
54/C2 Gairn (riv.), Sc,UK
166/A5 Gaithersburg, Md,US
101/B2 Gai Xian, China
63/L3 Gaizina Kalns (peak), Lat.
132/C2 Gakarosa (peak), SAfr.
130/C3 Galana (riv.), Kenya
74/D2 Galapagar, Sp.
144/J6 Galápagos (isls.), Ecu.
144/J7 Galápagos (prov.), Ecu.
144/J7 Galápagos Nat'l Park, Ecu.
54/D5 Galashiels, Sc,UK
83/J3 Galaţi, Rom.
83/H3 Galaţi (co.), Rom.
81/F2 Galatina, It.
81/F2 Galatone, It.
160/D4 Galax, Va,US
81/H3 Galaxidhiou, Gre.
111/G3 Galela, Indo.
160/B3 Galena, Il,US
142/B3 Galera (pt.), Chile
138/A4 Galera (pt.), Ecu.
150/F5 Galera (pt.), Trin.
160/B3 Galesburg, Il,US
60/A5 Galey (riv.), Ire.
56/B2 Galgorm, NI,UK
84/J4 Galich, Rus.
65/L3 Galicia (reg.), Pol., Ukr.
74/A1 Galicia (aut. comm.), Sp.
82/E5 Galičica Nat'l Park, Macd.
168/C3 Galilee, RI,US
91/D3 Galilee, Sea of (Tiberias) (lake), Isr.
141/D1 Galiléia, Braz.

189

Galin – Gokwe

77/F3 **Galinakopf** (peak), Aus.
160/D3 **Galion**, Oh,US
55/H7 **Gallan Head** (pt.), Sc,UK
78/B1 **Gallarate**, It.
163/G2 **Gallatin**, Tn,US
106/D6 **Galle**, SrL.
143/K7 **Gallegos** (riv.), Arg.
60/B6 **Galley Head** (pt.), Ire.
78/B2 **Galliate**, It.
138/D1 **Gallinas** (pt.), Col.
162/B3 **Gallinas** (mts.), NM,US
81/E2 **Gallipoli**, It.
83/H5 **Gallipoli** (pen.), Turk.
83/H5 **Gallipoli** (Gelibolu), Turk.
160/D4 **Gallipolis**, Oh,US
61/G2 **Gällivare**, Swe.
80/C3 **Gallo** (cape), It.
77/G4 **Gallo** (lake), It.
56/D2 **Galloway, Mull of** (pt.), Sc,UK
158/E4 **Gallup**, NM,US
53/R10 **Gally** (riv.), Fr.
118/H8 **Galston**, Austl.
54/B5 **Galston**, Sc,UK
96/D2 **Galt**, Mong.
165/M10 **Galt**, Ca,US
60/B5 **Galty** (mts.), Ire.
60/B5 **Galtymore** (mtn.), Ire.
96/E2 **Galuut**, Mong.
142/B3 **Galvarino**, Chile
162/E4 **Galveston**, Tx,US
162/E4 **Galveston** (bay), Tx,US
162/E4 **Galveston** (isl.), Tx,US
142/E2 **Gálvez**, Arg.
60/A3 **Galway**, Ire.
60/A3 **Galway** (bay), Ire.
60/B3 **Galway** (co.), Ire.
109/D1 **Gam** (riv.), Viet.
132/C2 **Gamagara** (dry riv.), SAfr.
99/E3 **Gamagōri**, Japan
112/D2 **Gamay**, Phil.
106/E2 **Gamba**, China
129/E4 **Gambaga Scarp** (escarp.), Gha., Togo
106/A2 **Gambat**, Pak.
125/M6 **Gambēla**, Eth.
125/M6 **Gambela Nat'l Park**, Eth.
79/F4 **Gambettola**, It.
128/B3 **Gambia**
128/A3 **Gambia (Gambie)** (riv.), Afr.
128/B3 **Gambie (Gambia)** (riv.), Afr.
121/M7 **Gambier** (isls.), FrPol.
161/L1 **Gambo**, Nf,Can
126/C1 **Gamboma**, Congo
132/C4 **Gamka** (riv.), SAfr.
132/B3 **Gamkab** (dry riv.), Namb.
59/F2 **Gamlingay**, Eng,UK
84/D2 **Gammelstad**, Swe.
70/C6 **Gammertingen**, Ger.
117/H4 **Gammon Ranges Nat'l Park**, Austl.
99/M9 **Gamo**, Japan
65/G5 **Gamsfeld** (peak), Aus.
130/C1 **Gamud** (peak), Eth.
105/G2 **Gan** (riv.), China
160/E2 **Gananoque**, On,Can
93/G4 **Ganāveh**, Iran
126/B3 **Ganda**, Ang.
126/D2 **Gandajika**, Zaire
112/D2 **Gandara**, Phil.
161/L1 **Gander**, Nf,Can
161/L1 **Gander** (lake), Nf,Can
67/F2 **Ganderkesee**, Ger.
106/B3 **Gāndhī Dhām**, India
106/B3 **Gandhinagar**, India
106/B3 **Gāndhi Sāgar** (res.), India
75/E3 **Gandía**, Sp.
130/A3 **Gandjo**, Zaire
149/F4 **Gandoca-Manzanillo Nat'l Wild. Ref.**, CR
140/C4 **Gandu**, Braz.
124/C4 **Ganeb** (well), Mrta.
106/C2 **Gangāpur**, India
106/E2 **Gangārāmpur**, India
96/E4 **Gangca**, China
102/D5 **Gangdisê** (mts.), China
69/F2 **Gangelt**, Ger.
106/E3 **Ganges** (riv.), India
80/D4 **Gangi**, It.
71/F6 **Gangkofen**, Ger.
106/E2 **Gangtok**, India
91/G7 **Gan Hashlosha Nat'l Park**, Isr.
63/T9 **Ganløse**, Den.
107/H2 **Ganluo**, China
97/J2 **Gannan**, China
156/F5 **Gannett** (peak), Wy,US
103/B3 **Ganquan**, China
102/F4 **Gansu** (prov.), China
76/D4 **Gantrisch** (peak), Swi.
112/B3 **Gantung** (mtn.), Phil.
124/H6 **Ganye**, Nga.
103/D4 **Ganyu**, China
105/G3 **Ganzhou**, China
129/E3 **Ganzourgou** (prov.), Burk.
105/G3 **Gao** (mtn.), China
129/E2 **Gao**, Mali
129/E2 **Gao** (reg.), Mali
105/G2 **Gao'an**, China
103/C3 **Gaocheng**, China
103/D5 **Gaochun**, China
96/E4 **Gaolan**, China
105/G4 **Gaolan** (isl.), China
104/C3 **Gaoligong** (mts.), China
103/D3 **Gaomi**, China
103/C4 **Gaoping**, China
103/D3 **Gaoqing**, China
54/A3 **Gaor Bheinn** (Gulvain) (mtn.), Sc,UK
96/D4 **Gaotai**, China
103/D3 **Gaotang**, China
128/E4 **Gaoua**, Burk.
103/C3 **Gaoyang**, China
103/C3 **Gaoyi**, China
103/D4 **Gaoyou**, China
103/D4 **Gaoyou** (lake), China
105/F4 **Gaozhou**, China
73/G4 **Gap**, Fr.
60/C5 **Gap, The** (pass), Ire.
102/C5 **Gar**, China
96/D5 **Gar** (riv.), China
149/G4 **Garachiné** (pt.), Pan.
106/E3 **Garai** (riv.), Bang.
60/B2 **Gara, Lough** (lake), Ire.
130/A2 **Garamba Nat'l Park**, Zaire
140/C3 **Garanhuns**, Braz.
130/C2 **Garba Tula**, Kenya
64/E2 **Garbsen**, Ger.
141/B2 **Garça**, Braz.
140/B3 **Garças** (riv.), Braz.
53/S10 **Garches**, Fr.
71/F6 **Garching an der Alz**, Ger.
74/C3 **Garcia de Sota** (res.), Sp.
72/F5 **Gard** (riv.), Fr.
78/D1 **Garda** (lake), It.
123/V17 **Garde, Cap de** (cape), Alg.
64/F2 **Gardelegen**, Ger.
116/K7 **Garden** (isl.), Austl.
164/B3 **Gardena**, Ca,US
163/H3 **Garden City**, Ga,US
159/G3 **Garden City**, Ks,US
165/F7 **Garden City**, Mi,US
167/E2 **Garden City**, NY,US
156/A2 **Gardener Canal** (inlet), BC,Can
164/C3 **Garden Grove**, Ca,US
167/D3 **Garden State Arts Ctr.**, NJ,US
54/D1 **Gardenstown**, Sc,UK
95/J2 **Gardēz**, Afg.
161/G2 **Gardiner**, Me,US
156/F4 **Gardiner**, Mt,US
167/F1 **Gardiners** (bay), NY,US
167/F1 **Gardiners** (isl.), NY,US
168/B2 **Gardner** (lake), Ct,US
121/H5 **Gardner** (Nikumaroro) (atoll), Kiri.
78/D1 **Gardone val Trompia**, It.
54/B4 **Gare Loch** (inlet), Sc,UK
54/B4 **Garelochhead**, Sc,UK
124/G2 **Garet el Djenoun** (peak), Alg.
156/E4 **Garfield** (peak), Mt,US
167/D2 **Garfield**, NJ,US
168/F5 **Garfield Heights**, Oh,US
57/G4 **Garforth**, Eng,UK
72/D4 **Gargan** (mtn.), Fr.
53/T10 **Garges-lès-Gonesse**, Fr.
57/F4 **Gargrave**, Eng,UK
106/C3 **Garhākotā**, India
108/A2 **Garh Mahārāja**, Pak.
141/B4 **Garibaldi**, Braz.
54/D2 **Garioch** (dist.), Sc,UK
130/C3 **Garissa**, Kenya
162/D3 **Garland**, Tx,US
78/B2 **Garlasco**, It.
56/D2 **Garlieston**, Sc,UK
77/H3 **Garmisch-Partenkirchen**, Ger.
54/C1 **Garmouth**, Sc,UK
168/A1 **Garnet** (hill), Ma,US
131/C2 **Garneton**, Zam.
163/J3 **Garnett**, Ks,US
119/B2 **Garnpung** (lake), Austl.
63/S6 **Garnsviken** (lake), Swe.
72/D4 **Garonne** (riv.), Fr.
141/B4 **Garopaba**, Braz.
129/E2 **Garou** (lake), Mali
124/H6 **Garoua**, Camr.
124/H6 **Garoua Boulaï**, Camr.
75/K7 **Garraf** (range), Sp.
56/D6 **Garreg**, Wal,UK
67/F3 **Garrel**, Ger.
157/H4 **Garrison**, ND,US
157/H4 **Garrison** (dam), ND,US
56/C1 **Garron** (pt.), NI,UK
153/H2 **Garry** (bay), NW,Can
152/F2 **Garry** (lake), NW,Can
54/A2 **Garry** (riv.), Sc,UK
54/B3 **Garry** (riv.), Sc,UK
54/B2 **Garry, Loch** (lake), Sc,UK
130/D3 **Garsen**, Kenya
57/F4 **Garstang**, Eng,UK
71/H6 **Garsten**, Aus.
67/H6 **Garte** (riv.), Ger.
72/D3 **Gartempe** (riv.), Fr.
58/C2 **Garth**, Wal,UK
54/B4 **Gartmore**, Sc,UK
70/B5 **Gärtringen**, Ger.
110/C5 **Garut**, Indo.
56/B2 **Garvagh**, NI,UK
65/L3 **Garwolin**, Pol.
165/R16 **Gary**, In,US
104/D2 **Garzê**, China
138/C4 **Garzón**, Col.
102/F4 **Gas** (lake), China
61/P6 **Gæsafjöll** (peak), Ice.
112/C2 **Gasan**, Phil.
160/C3 **Gas City**, In,US
159/J3 **Gasconade** (riv.), Mo,US
72/C5 **Gascony** (reg.), Fr.
116/C3 **Gascoyne** (peak), Austl.
116/C3 **Gascoyne** (riv.), Austl.
141/B3 **Gaspar**, Braz.
110/C4 **Gaspar** (riv.), Indo.
161/H1 **Gaspé**, Qu,Can
161/H1 **Gaspé** (pen.), Qu,Can
161/H1 **Gaspé, Cap de** (cape), Qu,Can
161/S9 **Gasport**, NY,US
100/B4 **Gas-san** (mtn.), Japan
78/A2 **Gassino Torinese**, It.
163/J2 **Gaston** (lake), NC, Va,US
163/H3 **Gastonia**, NC,US
91/C2 **Gata** (cape), Cyp.
74/B2 **Gata** (range), Sp.
74/D4 **Gata, Cabo de** (cape), Sp.
63/P2 **Gatchina**, Rus.
56/D2 **Gatehouse-of-Fleet**, Sc,UK
152/F1 **Gateshead** (isl.), NW,Can
57/G2 **Gateshead**, Eng,UK
151/H2 **Gates of the Arctic Nat'l Pk. & Prsv.**, Ak,US
162/D4 **Gatesville**, Tx,US
167/E3 **Gateway Nat'l Rec. Area**, NJ, NY,US
131/C4 **Gaths Mine**, Zim.
72/C3 **Gâtine** (hills), Fr.
160/F2 **Gatineau**, Qu,Can
160/F2 **Gatineau** (riv.), Qu,Can
78/B1 **Gattinara**, It.
149/G4 **Gatun** (dam), Pan.
149/G4 **Gatún** (lake), Pan.
69/H4 **Gau-Bickelheim**, Ger.
107/F2 **Gauhāti**, India
63/L3 **Gauja** (riv.), Lat.
57/G2 **Gaunless** (riv.), Eng,UK
54/B3 **Gaur** (riv.), Sc,UK
106/E2 **Gaurīpur**, India
106/E2 **Gauri Sankar** (mtn.), Nepal
62/C2 **Gausta** (peak), Nor.
71/E6 **Gauting**, Ger.
63/L3 **Gauya Nat'l Park**, Lat.
75/G2 **Gavà**, Sp.
81/J5 **Gávdhos** (isl.), Gre.
74/E1 **Gave de Pau** (riv.), Fr.
68/C2 **Gavere**, Belg.
78/B1 **Gavirate**, It.
62/G1 **Gävle**, Swe.
62/G1 **Gävleborg** (co.), Swe.
117/H5 **Gawler**, Austl.
117/G5 **Gawler** (ranges), Austl.
96/D3 **Gaxun** (lake), China
87/L2 **Gay**, Rus.
160/D4 **Gay** (peak), WV,US
97/K3 **Gaya** (riv.), China
106/E3 **Gayā**, India
129/F4 **Gaya**, Niger
130/A3 **Gayaza**, Ugan.
168/D3 **Gay Head** (pt.), Ma,US
160/C2 **Gaylord**, Mi,US
86/D2 **Gaysin**, Ukr.
131/D4 **Gaza** (prov.), Moz.
91/D4 **Gaza** (Ghazzah), Gaza
91/C4 **Gaza Strip**
91/E1 **Gaziantep**, Turk.
91/E1 **Gaziantep** (prov.), Turk.
97/H1 **Gazimur** (riv.), Rus.
91/C1 **Gazipaşa**, Turk.
76/D1 **Gazon de Faing** (peak), Fr.
125/K7 **Gbadolite**, Zaire
128/C5 **Gbarnga**, Libr.
65/K1 **Gdańsk**, Pol.
65/K1 **Gdańsk** (prov.), Pol.
65/K1 **Gdańsk** (gulf), Pol., Rus.
65/K1 **Gdynia**, Pol.
103/D5 **Ge** (lake), China
54/A3 **Geal Charn** (mtn.), Sc,UK
54/C2 **Geal Charn** (mtn.), Sc,UK
168/F5 **Geauga** (co.), Oh,US
70/D1 **Gebaberg** (peak), Ger.
111/G3 **Gebe** (isl.), Indo.
127/D4 **Gebeit Mine**, Sudan
83/J5 **Gebze**, Turk.
110/C5 **Gede** (peak), Indo.
130/D3 **Gede**, Kenya
91/F8 **Gedera**, Isr.
70/C2 **Gedern**, Ger.
130/D3 **Gedi Ruins Nat'l Mon.**, Kenya
92/B2 **Gediz**, Turk.
92/A2 **Gediz** (riv.), Turk.
62/D4 **Gedser** (cape), Den.
69/E1 **Geel**, Belg.
119/C3 **Geelong**, Austl.
116/B4 **Geelvink** (chan.), Austl.
67/E3 **Geeste**, Ger.
67/F2 **Geeste** (riv.), Ger.
67/H2 **Geesthacht**, Ger.
102/D5 **Gê'gyai**, China
67/G4 **Gehrden**, Ger.
58/C2 **Geifas** (mtn.), Wal,UK
77/G3 **Geige, Hohe** (peak), Aus.
152/F3 **Geikie** (riv.), Sk,Can
69/F2 **Geilenkirchen**, Ger.
99/M10 **Geinō**, Japan
71/E5 **Geisenfeld**, Ger.
70/A3 **Geisenheim**, Ger.
70/B6 **Geislingen**, Ger.
70/C5 **Geislingen an der Steige**, Ger.
130/B3 **Geita**, Tanz.
104/D4 **Gejiu**, China
125/L6 **Gel** (riv.), Sudan
80/D4 **Gela**, It.
80/D4 **Gela** (gulf), It.
125/Q6 **Geladī**, Eth.
130/C3 **Gelai** (peak), Tanz.
77/E5 **Gelato** (mtn.), It.
66/C4 **Gelderland** (prov.), Neth.
66/C5 **Geldermalsen**, Neth.
66/D5 **Geldern**, Ger.
66/C6 **Geldrop**, Neth.
69/E2 **Geleen**, Neth.
92/B2 **Gelendost**, Turk.
86/F3 **Gelendzhik**, Rus.
83/H5 **Gelibolu** (Gallipoli), Turk.
86/C4 **Gelibolu Yarımadas Nat'l Park**, Turk.
93/E2 **Gelincik** (peak), Turk.
58/C3 **Gelligaer**, Wal,UK
70/C2 **Gelnhausen**, Ger.
66/E5 **Gelsenkirchen**, Ger.
69/D2 **Gembloux**, Belg.
125/J7 **Gemena**, Zaire
66/C5 **Gemert**, Neth.
83/J5 **Gemlik**, Turk.
83/J5 **Gemlik** (gulf), Turk.
73/K3 **Gemona del Friuli**, It.
132/C2 **Gemsbok-Kalahari Nat'l Park**, SAfr.
132/C2 **Gemsbok Nat'l Park**, Bots.
151/G3 **Gemuk** (mtn.), Ak,US
70/C2 **Gemünden am Main**, Ger.
97/J1 **Gen** (riv.), China
125/N6 **Genalē Wenz** (riv.), Eth.
68/D2 **Genappe**, Belg.
80/A3 **Genargentu** (mts.), It.
92/E2 **Genç**, Turk.
66/D5 **Gendringen**, Neth.
66/C5 **Gendt**, Neth.
66/D3 **Genemuiden**, Neth.
142/D3 **General Acha**, Arg.
142/D2 **General Alvear**, Arg.
142/F2 **General Belgrano**, Arg.
142/E2 **General Cabrera**, Arg.
142/B5 **General Carrera** (lake), Chile
167/K8 **General Grant Nat'l Mem.**, NY,US
147/F5 **General Juan Álvarez**, Mex.
148/B2 **General Juan Álvarez Nat'l Park**, Mex.
143/F3 **General Juan Madariaga**, Arg.
143/S12 **General Las Heras**, Arg.
135/C1 **General Martín Miguel de Güemes**, Arg.
142/E2 **General Pico**, Arg.
135/D2 **General Pinedo**, Arg.
142/D3 **General Roca**, Arg.
143/S12 **General San Martín**, Arg.
112/D4 **General Santos**, Phil.
83/J4 **General-Toshevo**, Bul.
112/E7 **General Trias**, Phil.
142/E2 **General Viamonte**, Arg.
142/E2 **General Villegas**, Arg.
77/F6 **Generoso, Monte** (peak), Swi.
165/E6 **Genesee** (co.), Mi,US
160/E3 **Genesee** (riv.), NY,US
157/L5 **Geneseo**, Il,US
160/E3 **Geneseo**, NY,US
163/G4 **Geneva**, Al,US
165/P16 **Geneva**, Il,US
159/H2 **Geneva**, Ne,US
160/E3 **Geneva**, NY,US
165/P14 **Geneva** (lake), Wi,US
76/C5 **Geneva** (Genève), Swi.
76/C5 **Geneva** (Léman) (lake), Fr., Swi.
76/C5 **Genève** (canton), Swi.
76/C5 **Genève** (Geneva), Swi.
105/E3 **Gengding** (mtn.), China
70/B6 **Gengenbach**, Ger.
104/C4 **Gengma Daizu Vazu Zizhixian**, China
86/E3 **Genichesk**, Ukr.
74/C4 **Genil** (riv.), Sp.
69/E2 **Genk**, Belg.
70/D6 **Gennach** (riv.), Ger.
66/C5 **Gennep**, Neth.
53/S10 **Gennevilliers**, Fr.
78/B4 **Genoa** (Genova), It.
78/B4 **Genova** (gulf), It.
78/C4 **Genova** (prov.), It.
78/B4 **Genova** (Genoa), It.
144/K6 **Genovesa** (isl.), Ecu.
68/C1 **Gent-Brugge** (can.), Belg.
110/C5 **Genteng** (cape), Indo.
68/C1 **Gent** (Ghent), Belg.
63/T9 **Gentofte**, Den.
116/B5 **Geographe** (bay), Austl.
118/B3 **Geographe** (chan.), Austl.
116/D2 **George** (lake), Austl.
119/D2 **George** (lake), Austl.
118/C3 **George** (pt.), Austl.
153/K3 **George** (riv.), Qu,Can
132/C4 **George**, SAfr.
130/A3 **George** (lake), Ugan.
163/H4 **George** (lake), Fl,US
88/E1 **George Land** (isl.), Rus.
118/G9 **Georges** (riv.), Austl.
161/Q8 **Georgetown**, On,Can
149/F2 **George Town**, Cay.
139/G3 **Georgetown** (cap.), Guy.
163/H4 **Georgetown**, Ga,US
160/C4 **Georgetown**, Ky,US
163/J3 **Georgetown**, SC,US
162/D4 **Georgetown**, Tx,US
113/L **George V** (coast), Ant.
113/V **George VI** (sound), Ant.
162/D4 **George West**, Tx,US
87/G4 **Georgia**
156/B3 **Georgia** (str.), Can., US
163/G3 **Georgia** (state), US
160/D2 **Georgian** (bay), On,Can
160/D2 **Georgian Bay Islands Nat'l Park**, On,Can
117/H2 **Georgina** (riv.), Austl.
83/H4 **Georgi Traykov**, Bul.
67/F4 **Georgsmarienhütte**, Ger.
64/G3 **Gera**, Ger.
68/C2 **Geraardsbergen**, Belg.
140/A3 **Geral** (mts.), Braz.
140/A4 **Geral de Goiás** (Espigão Mestre) (range), Braz.
115/R11 **Geraldine**, NZ
116/B4 **Geraldton**, Austl.
160/C1 **Geraldton**, On,Can
76/C1 **Gérardmer**, Fr.
72/F4 **Gerbier de Jonc** (mtn.), Fr.
67/H3 **Gerdau** (riv.), Ger.
151/H3 **Gerdine** (mtn.), Ak,US
83/L5 **Gerede**, Turk.
95/H2 **Gereshk**, Afg.
77/H2 **Geretsried**, Ger.
158/C2 **Gerlach**, Nv,US
65/L4 **Gerlachovský Štít** (peak), Slvk.
166/A5 **Germantown**, Md,US
163/F3 **Germantown**, Tn,US
64/E3 **Germany**
71/E6 **Germering**, Ger.
70/B4 **Germersheim**, Ger.
132/E2 **Germiston**, SAfr.
70/B5 **Gernsbach**, Ger.
69/F3 **Gerolstein**, Ger.
70/D3 **Gerolzhofen**, Ger.
75/G2 **Gerona** (Girona), Sp.
75/E1 **Ger, Pic du** (peak), Fr.
68/D3 **Gerpinnes**, Belg.
53/M7 **Gerrards Cross**, Eng,UK
72/D5 **Gers** (riv.), Fr.
69/G5 **Gersheim**, Ger.
70/B3 **Gerspenz** (riv.), Ger.
70/E5 **Gerstetten**, Ger.
70/D6 **Gersthofen**, Ger.
102/D5 **Gêrzê**, China
92/C1 **Gerze**, Turk.
66/E5 **Gescher**, Ger.
67/F5 **Geseke**, Ger.
125/P6 **Gestro Wenz** (riv.), Eth.
74/D2 **Getafe**, Sp.
103/B5 **Getai**, China
69/E2 **Gete** (riv.), Belg.
166/A4 **Gettysburg**, Pa,US
157/J4 **Gettysburg**, SD,US
166/A4 **Gettysburg Nat'l Mil. Park**, Pa,US
141/A3 **Getúlio Vargas**, Braz.
113/S **Getz Ice Shelf**, Ant.
69/E2 **Geul** (riv.), Belg., Neth.
110/A3 **Geureudong** (peak), Indo.
93/E2 **Gevaş**, Turk.
67/E6 **Gevelsberg**, Ger.
82/F5 **Gevgelija**, Macd.
125/P5 **Gewanē**, Eth.
70/C3 **Geyersberg** (peak), Ger.
133/H6 **Geyser** (reef), Madg.
83/K5 **Geyve**, Turk.
102/B4 **Gez** (riv.), China
124/G1 **Ghadāmis**, Libya
127/C3 **Ghadir, Bi'r** (well), Egypt
108/D2 **Ghaggar** (riv.), India
129/E4 **Ghana**
126/D5 **Ghanzi**, Bots.
131/A4 **Ghanzi** (dist.), Bots.
127/B5 **Gharb Binna**, Sudan
124/F1 **Ghardaïa**, Alg.
124/H1 **Gharyān**, Libya
124/H3 **Ghāt**, Libya
124/J5 **Ghazal** (riv.), Chad
123/P13 **Ghazaouet**, Alg.
106/C2 **Ghaziābād**, India
95/J2 **Ghaznī**, Afg.
91/D4 **Ghazzah** (Gaza), Gaza
78/D2 **Ghedi**, It.
96/G2 **Ghengis Khan Wall** (ruins), Mong.
68/C1 **Ghent** (Gent), Belg.
83/H2 **Gheorghe Gheorghiu-Dej**, Rom.
83/G2 **Gheorgheni**, Rom.
83/F2 **Gherla**, Rom.
142/C5 **Ghio** (lake), Arg.
106/A2 **Ghotki**, Pak.
95/H2 **Ghūrīān**, Afg.
109/D4 **Gia Nghia**, Viet.
132/E3 **Giant's Castle** (peak), SAfr.
56/B1 **Giant's Causeway**, NI,UK
80/D4 **Giarre**, It.
109/E3 **Gia Vuc**, Viet.
156/E2 **Gibbons**, Ab,Can
76/D4 **Gibloux, Mont** (peak), Swi.
74/B4 **Gibraleón**, Sp.
74/B4 **Gibraltar** (str.), Afr., Eur.
161/R8 **Gibraltar** (pt.), On,Can
74/C4 **Gibraltar** (dpcy.), UK
55/M10 **Gibraltar** (pt.), UK
164/A1 **Gibraltar** (res.), Ca,US
165/F7 **Gibraltar**, Mi,US
119/E1 **Gibraltar Range Nat'l Park**, Austl.
116/E2 **Gibson** (des.), Austl.
116/E3 **Gibson Desert Nature Rsv.**, Austl.
108/C2 **Giddarbāha**, India
162/D4 **Giddings**, Tx,US
91/C4 **Gidi** (Mamarr al Jady) (pass), Egypt
125/N6 **Gīdolē**, Eth.
72/E3 **Gien**, Fr.
70/D5 **Giengen an der Brenz**, Ger.
72/F4 **Gier** (riv.), Fr.
76/E4 **Giessbachfälle** (falls), Swi.
76/D1 **Giessen** (riv.), Fr.
70/B1 **Giessen**, Ger.
66/B5 **Giessendam**, Neth.
68/B6 **Gif**, Fr.
153/H1 **Gifford** (riv.), NW,Can
54/D5 **Gifford**, Sc,UK
163/H5 **Gifford**, Fl,US
76/C5 **Giffre** (riv.), Fr.
67/H4 **Gifhorn**, Ger.
53/S10 **Gif-sur-Yvette**, Fr.
99/E3 **Gifu**, Japan
99/E3 **Gifu** (pref.), Japan
146/C3 **Giganta, Sierra de la** (mts.), Mex.
148/E4 **Gigante** (pt.), Nic.
57/F3 **Giggleswick**, Eng,UK
80/B1 **Giglio** (isl.), It.
74/C1 **Gijón**, Sp.
130/A3 **Gikongoro**, Rwa.
158/D4 **Gila** (riv.), Az, NM,US
158/D4 **Gila Bend**, Az,US
158/E4 **Gila Cliff Dwellings Nat'l Mon.**, NM,US
93/G2 **Gīlān** (gov.), Iran
57/H4 **Gilberdyke Newport**, Eng,UK
118/A2 **Gilbert** (riv.), Austl.
120/G5 **Gilbert** (isls.), Kiri.
160/A2 **Gilbert**, Mn,US
140/A3 **Gilbués**, Braz.
70/E6 **Gilching**, Ger.
142/C2 **Gil de Vilches Nat'l Park**, Chile
58/C3 **Gilfach Goch**, Wal,UK
56/B3 **Gilford**, NI,UK
167/D4 **Gilford Park**, NJ,US
130/C3 **Gilgil**, Kenya
95/K1 **Gilgit** (riv.), Pak.
63/T8 **Gilleleje**, Den.
117/H5 **Gilles** (lake), Austl.
157/G4 **Gillette**, Wy,US
76/C3 **Gilley**, Fr.
156/B3 **Gillies Bay**, BC,Can
58/D4 **Gillingham**, Eng,UK
59/G4 **Gillingham**, Eng,UK
60/B1 **Gill, Lough** (lake), Ire.
162/E3 **Gilmer**, Tx,US
95/K1 **Gilqit** (riv.), Pak.
97/K1 **Gilyuy** (riv.), Rus.
66/B5 **Gilze**, Neth.
125/N6 **Gīmbī**, Eth.
150/F4 **Gimie** (mtn.), StL.
157/J3 **Gimli**, Mb,Can
75/F1 **Gimone** (riv.), Fr.
99/M9 **Ginan**, Japan
69/E2 **Gingelom**, Belg.
130/C1 **Gingero**, Eth.
112/D3 **Gingoog**, Phil.
80/E2 **Ginosa**, It.
100/J7 **Ginowan**, Japan
74/B1 **Ginzo de Limia**, Sp.
125/Q7 **Giohar**, Som.
80/D3 **Gioia** (gulf), It.
80/E2 **Gioia del Colle**, It.
80/D3 **Gioia Tauro**, It.
81/J3 **Gioūra** (isl.), Gre.
77/G4 **Gioveretto** (peak), It.
79/E5 **Giovi, Monte** (peak), It.
59/G2 **Gipping** (riv.), Eng,UK
168/G5 **Girard**, Oh,US
138/C3 **Girardot**, Col.
126/B4 **Giraul**, Ang.
122/D6 **Giraul de Cima**, Ang.
54/D2 **Girdle Head** (pt.), Sc,UK
55/K8 **Girdle Ness** (pt.), Sc,UK
92/D1 **Giresun**, Turk.
92/D1 **Giresun** (prov.), Turk.
106/E3 **Girīdīh**, India
80/E3 **Girifalco**, It.
53/N7 **Girling** (res.), Eng,UK
138/C3 **Girón**, Col.
138/B5 **Girón**, Ecu.
75/G2 **Girona** (Gerona), Sp.
72/C4 **Gironde** (riv.), Fr.
119/D1 **Girraween Nat'l Park**, Austl.
59/G2 **Girton**, Eng,UK
56/D1 **Girvan**, Sc,UK
56/D1 **Girvan, Water of** (riv.), Sc,UK
115/S10 **Gisborne**, NZ
130/A3 **Gisenyi**, Rwa.
62/E3 **Gislaved**, Swe.
68/A5 **Gisors**, Fr.
68/B1 **Gistel**, Belg.
130/A3 **Gitarama**, Rwa.
130/A3 **Gitega**, Buru.
84/B2 **Gittsfjället** (peak), Swe.
77/F5 **Giubiasco**, Swi.
80/C1 **Giulianova**, It.
83/G4 **Giurgiu**, Rom.
83/G4 **Giurgiu** (co.), Rom.
78/C1 **Giussano**, It.
91/F7 **Giv'atayim**, Isr.
69/D3 **Givet**, Fr.
72/F4 **Givors**, Fr.
76/C5 **Givrine, Col de la** (pass), Swi.
69/D6 **Givry-en-Argonne**, Fr.
131/C4 **Giyani**, SAfr.
125/N6 **Giyon**, Eth.
91/B5 **Giza, Pyramids of** (Ahrāmāt al Jīzah), Egypt
89/R3 **Gizhiga** (bay), Rus.
65/L1 **Giżycko**, Pol.
81/G2 **Gjirokastër**, Alb.
62/D1 **Gjøvik**, Nor.
81/F2 **Gjuhëzës, Kep i** (cape), Alb.
161/K2 **Glace Bay**, NS,Can
156/D3 **Glacier**, BC,Can
156/C3 **Glacier** (peak), Wa,US
151/L4 **Glacier Bay Nat'l Park & Prsv.**, Ak,US
156/D3 **Glacier Nat'l Park**, Can., US
66/D5 **Gladbeck**, Ger.
63/T9 **Gladsakse**, Den.
118/C3 **Gladstone**, Austl.
160/C3 **Gladwin**, Mi,US
62/D2 **Glafsfjorden** (lake), Swe.
57/H3 **Glaisdale**, Eng,UK
52/E2 **Glåma** (riv.), Nor.
54/D3 **Glamis**, Sc,UK
69/G4 **Glan** (riv.), Ger.
112/D4 **Glan**, Phil.
58/C3 **Glanamman**, Wal,UK
60/A5 **Glanaruddery** (mts.), Ire.
68/D4 **Gland** (riv.), Fr.
77/E3 **Glärnisch** (range), Swi.
77/F4 **Glarus** (canton), Swi.
77/F4 **Glarus Alps** (range), Swi.
58/C2 **Glasbury**, Wal,UK
54/B5 **Glasgow**, Sc,UK
160/C4 **Glasgow**, Ky,US
156/G3 **Glasgow**, Mt,US
56/D6 **Glaslyn** (riv.), Wal,UK
54/C3 **Glas Maol** (mtn.), Sc,UK
56/D3 **Glass** (riv.), IM,UK
54/B2 **Glass** (riv.), Sc,UK
162/D2 **Glass** (mts.), Ok,US
162/C4 **Glass** (mts.), Tx,US
166/C4 **Glassboro**, NJ,US
54/B1 **Glass, Loch** (lake), Sc,UK
166/B6 **Glassmanor-Oxon Hill**, Md,US
58/D4 **Glastonbury**, Eng,UK
168/B2 **Glastonbury**, Ct,US
70/B6 **Glatt** (riv.), Ger.
77/E2 **Glatt** (riv.), Swi.
85/M4 **Glazov**, Rus.
70/C5 **Glems** (riv.), Ger.
59/G2 **Glemsford**, Eng,UK
57/H6 **Glen** (riv.), Eng,UK
119/C3 **Glenaladale Nat'l Park**, Austl.
160/E4 **Glen Allen**, Va,US
56/C2 **Glenarm**, NI,UK
56/C2 **Glenarm** (riv.), NI,UK
56/B2 **Glenavy**, NI,UK
119/D2 **Glenbawn** (dam), Austl.
157/J3 **Glenboro**, Mb,Can
118/G8 **Glenbrook**, Austl.
166/B5 **Glen Burnie**, Md,US
158/E3 **Glen Canyon** (dam), Az,US
158/E3 **Glen Canyon Nat'l Rec. Area**, Az, Ut,US
56/E1 **Glencaple**, Sc,UK
131/C3 **Glenclova**, Zim.
133/E3 **Glencoe**, SAfr.
54/A3 **Glencoe**, Sc,UK
54/B3 **Glen Coe** (pass), Sc,UK
165/Q15 **Glencoe**, Il,US
167/E2 **Glen Cove**, NY,US
158/D4 **Glendale**, Az,US
164/B2 **Glendale**, Ca,US
156/C5 **Glendale**, Or,US
131/C3 **Glendale**, Zim.
165/P16 **Glendale Heights**, Il,US
157/G4 **Glendive**, Mt,US
159/F2 **Glendo** (res.), Wy,US
164/C2 **Glendora**, Ca,US
56/B1 **Glendun** (riv.), NI,UK
166/A6 **Glen Echo**, Md,US
117/M8 **Glenelg**, Austl.
119/B3 **Glenelg** (riv.), Austl.
55/J8 **Glenelg**, Sc.,UK
56/A2 **Glenelly** (riv.), NI,UK
116/C3 **Glengarry** (range), Austl.
56/D2 **Glenluce**, Sc,UK
167/D1 **Glenmere** (lake), NY,US
54/B2 **Glen Mòr** (val.), Sc,UK
166/C4 **Glenolden**, Pa,US
151/M4 **Glenora**, BC,Can
118/H8 **Glenorie**, Austl.
159/H4 **Glenpool**, Ok,US
167/J8 **Glen Ridge**, NJ,US
167/D2 **Glen Rock**, NJ,US
162/D3 **Glen Rose**, Tx,US
54/C4 **Glenrothes**, Sc,UK
160/F3 **Glens Falls**, NY,US
56/B2 **Glenshane** (pass), NI,UK
166/C3 **Glenside**, Pa,US
56/D1 **Glentrool**, Sc,UK
157/H4 **Glen Ullin**, ND,US
55/H9 **Glenveagh Nat'l Park**, Ire.
165/Q15 **Glenview**, Il,US
165/Q15 **Glenview Nav. Air Sta.**, Il,US
161/Q8 **Glen Williams**, On,Can
158/F3 **Glenwood Springs**, Co,US
54/A2 **Gleouraich** (mtn.), Sc,UK
81/L7 **Glifáhda**, Gre.
67/H1 **Glinde**, Ger.
61/D3 **Glittertinden** (peak), Nor.
65/K3 **Gliwice**, Pol.
158/E4 **Globe**, Az,US
77/G4 **Glockturm** (peak), Aus.
65/H5 **Gloggnitz**, Aus.
65/J3 **Głogów**, Pol.
65/J3 **Głogówek**, Pol.
70/E6 **Glonn** (riv.), Ger.
149/G1 **Gloria** (bay), Cuba
133/H5 **Glorieuses, Iles** (isls.), Reun.
118/E6 **Glorious** (mtn.), Austl.
151/D3 **Glory of Russia** (cape), Ak,US
57/G5 **Glossop**, Eng,UK
63/T9 **Glostrup**, Den.
160/F2 **Gloucester**, On,Can
58/D3 **Gloucester**, Eng,UK
166/C4 **Gloucester** (co.), NJ,US
166/C4 **Gloucester City**, NJ,US
58/D3 **Gloucestershire** (co.), Eng,UK
58/D3 **Gloucester, Vale of** (val.), Eng,UK
148/E2 **Glovers** (reef), Belz.
161/L1 **Glovertown**, Nf,Can
65/K3 **Głowno**, Pol.
65/J3 **Głubczyce**, Pol.
65/J3 **Głuchołazy**, Pol.
64/E1 **Glücksburg**, Ger.
67/G1 **Glückstadt**, Ger.
86/E2 **Glukhov**, Ukr.
63/T9 **Glumslöv**, Swe.
60/D2 **Glyde** (riv.), Ire.
58/C3 **Glyncorrwg**, Wal,UK
56/C2 **Glynn**, NI,UK
58/C3 **Glyn Neath**, Wal,UK
65/H4 **Gmünd**, Aus.
129/E3 **Gnagna** (prov.), Burk.
67/G2 **Gnarrenburg**, Ger.
63/H5 **Gniew**, Pol.
65/J2 **Gniezno**, Pol.
82/E4 **Gnjilane**, Yugo.
58/D1 **Gnosall**, Eng,UK
98/C3 **Gō** (riv.), Japan
106/B4 **Goa** (state), India
106/F2 **Goālpāra**, India
54/A5 **Goat Fell** (mtn.), Sc,UK
57/H3 **Goathland**, Eng,UK
125/N6 **Goba**, Eth.
131/D5 **Goba**, Moz.
126/C5 **Gobabeb**, Namb.
126/C5 **Gobabis**, Namb.
96/E3 **Gobi** (des.), China, Mong.
71/G6 **Göblberg** (peak), Aus.
98/D4 **Gobō**, Japan
57/E6 **Gobowen**, Eng,UK
66/D5 **Goch**, Ger.
70/D2 **Gochsheim**, Ger.
109/D4 **Go Cong**, Viet.
59/F4 **Godalming**, Eng,UK
109/D4 **Go Dau Ha**, Viet.
106/D4 **Godāvari** (riv.), India
125/P6 **Godē**, Eth.
82/F3 **Godeanu** (peak), Rom.
160/D3 **Goderich**, On,Can
106/B3 **Godhra**, India
59/F2 **Godmanchester**, Eng,UK
111/F4 **Godo** (mtn.), Indo.
99/M9 **Gōdo**, Japan
82/D2 **Gödöllő**, Hun.
58/A6 **Godolphin Cross**, Eng,UK
142/C2 **Godoy Cruz**, Arg.
157/K2 **Gods** (lake), Mb,Can
157/K2 **Gods** (riv.), Mb,Can
153/H2 **Gods Mercy** (bay), NW,Can
53/N8 **Godstone**, Eng,UK
145/M3 **Godthåb** (Nuuk), Grld.
102/C4 **Godwin Austen** (K2) (peak), China, Pak.
160/E1 **Goéland** (lake), Qu,Can
66/A5 **Goerce**, Neth.
66/A6 **Goes**, Neth.
160/B2 **Gogebic** (range), Mi,US
63/M1 **Gogland** (isl.), Rus.
106/D2 **Gogra** (riv.), India
67/G3 **Gohbach** (riv.), Ger.
140/D2 **Goiana**, Braz.
141/B1 **Goiandira**, Braz.
137/J7 **Goiânia**, Braz.
140/D2 **Goianinha**, Braz.
137/H7 **Goiás**, Braz.
140/A4 **Goiás** (state), Braz.
141/B1 **Goiás** (state), Braz.
141/B1 **Goiatuba**, Braz.
54/B4 **Goil, Loch** (inlet), Sc,UK
66/C5 **Goirle**, Neth.
98/D3 **Gojō**, Japan
100/B4 **Gojōme**, Japan
108/B2 **Gojra**, Pak.
86/E4 **Gok** (riv.), Turk.
98/B4 **Gokase** (riv.), Japan
99/M9 **Gokashō**, Japan
83/G5 **Gökçeada** (isl.), Turk.
91/C1 **Göksu** (riv.), Turk.
92/D2 **Göksun**, Turk.
131/C3 **Gokwe**, Zim.

190

Golan – Gross

91/D3 Golan Heights (reg.), Syria
92/C2 Gölbaşı, Turk.
92/D2 Gölbaşı, Turk.
76/C1 Golbey, Fr.
57/F5 Golborne, Eng,UK
83/J5 Gölcük, Turk.
165/B2 Gold (mtn.), Wa,US
77/F3 Goldach, Swi.
65/M1 Gołdap, Pol.
70/C3 Goldbach, Ger.
156/B5 Gold Beach, Or,US
118/D4 Gold Coast, Austl.
129/E5 Gold Coast (reg.), Gha.
156/D3 Golden, BC,Can
60/B5 Golden, Ire.
159/F3 Golden, Co,US
156/C4 Goldendale, Wa,US
64/F3 Goldene Aue (reg.), Ger.
165/J11 Golden Gate (chan.), Ca,US
132/E3 Golden Gate Highlands Nat'l Park, SAfr.
165/J11 Golden Gate Nat'l Rec. Area, Ca,US
156/B3 Golden Hinde (peak), BC,Can
67/F3 Goldenstedt, Ger.
108/C2 Golden Temple, India
60/B4 Golden Vale (plain), Ire.
131/C3 Golden Valley, Zim.
158/C3 Goldfield, Nv,US
156/B3 Gold River, BC,Can
163/J3 Goldsboro, NC,US
162/D4 Goldthwaite, Tx,US
92/E1 Göle, Turk.
65/H2 Goleniów, Pol.
149/F4 Golfito Nat'l Wild. Ref., CR
91/A1 Gölhısar, Turk.
162/D4 Goliad, Tx,US
92/D1 Gölköy, Turk.
70/D3 Gollach (riv.), Ger.
92/A2 Gölmarmara, Turk.
96/C4 Golmud, China
131/D2 Golomoti Station, Malw.
100/D2 Golovnina Gora (mtn.), Rus.
100/D2 Golovnino, Rus.
93/G3 Golpāyegān, Iran
83/K5 Gölpazarı, Turk.
65/K2 Golub-Dobrzyń, Pol.
83/H4 Golyama Kamchiya (riv.), Bul.
83/G5 Golyama Syutkya (peak), Bul.
83/G5 Golyam Perelik (peak), Bul.
130/A3 Goma, Zaire
112/B4 Gomantong Caves, Malay.
70/C6 Gomaringen, Ger.
130/A2 Gombari, Zaire
130/A4 Gombe (riv.), Tanz.
130/A4 Gombe Nat'l Park, Tanz.
86/D1 Gomel', Bela.
86/C2 Gomel' Obl., Bela.
53/S10 Gometz-le-Châtel, Fr.
146/E3 Gómez Palacio, Mex.
64/F2 Gommern, Ger.
77/F3 Goms, Swi.
76/E5 Goms (val.), Swi.
59/F4 Gomshall, Eng,UK
93/J3 Gonābād, Iran
149/H2 Gonaïves, Haiti
131/C4 Gonarezhou Nat'l Park, Zim.
149/H2 Gonâve (gulf), Haiti
149/H2 Gonâve (isl.), Haiti
93/H2 Gonbad-e Qābūs, Iran
140/A2 Gonçalves Dias, Braz.
106/D2 Gondā, India
106/B3 Gondal, India
125/N5 Gonder, Eth.
106/D3 Gondia, India
74/A2 Gondomar, Port.
74/A1 Gondomar, Sp.
83/H5 Gönen, Turk.
53/T10 Gonesse, Fr.
105/F3 Gong'an, China
107/F2 Gongbo'gyamda, China
104/D2 Gongga (peak), China
106/F2 Gonggar, China
96/E4 Gonghe, China
102/D3 Gongliu, China
129/H4 Gongola (riv.), Nga.
129/H4 Gongola (state), Nga.
119/C1 Gongolgon, Austl.
107/G2 Gongshan Drungzu Nuzu Zizhixian, China
104/D3 Gongwang (mts.), China
103/C4 Gong Xian, China
103/F2 Gongzhuling, China
130/C4 Gonja, Tanz.
104/C2 Gonjo, China
100/B3 Gonohe, Japan
82/C2 Gönyű, Hun.
112/C1 Gonzaga, Phil.
162/D4 Gonzales, Tx,US
147/F4 González, Mex.
113/J Goodenough (cape), Ant.
162/C4 Goodfellow A.F.B., Tx,US
131/B5 Goodhope, Bots.
132/B4 Good Hope, Cape of (cape), SAfr.
156/E5 Gooding, Id,US
159/G3 Goodland, Ks,US
118/E7 Goodna, Austl.
58/B3 Goodwick, Wal,UK
132/B4 Goodwood, SAfr.
66/C4 Gooimeer (lake), Neth.
57/H4 Goole, Eng,UK
116/D4 Goongarrie Nat'l Park, Austl.
66/D4 Goor, Neth.
157/H2 Goose (lake), Mb,Can
154/B3 Goose (lake), Ca, Or,US
166/C5 Goose (pt.), De,US
153/K3 Goose Bay-Happy Valley, Nf,Can
57/F5 Goostrey, Eng,UK
108/F3 Gopichettipālaiyam, India
70/C5 Göppingen, Ger.
109/D4 Go Quao, Viet.
65/J3 Góra, Pol.
65/L3 Góra Kalwaria, Pol.
106/D2 Gorakhpur, India
82/D4 Goražde, Bosn.
149/F1 Gorda (pt.), Cuba
149/F3 Gorda (pt.), Nic.
149/F4 Gorda (pt.), Nic.
158/A2 Gorda (pt.), Ca,US
92/B2 Gördes, Turk.
119/C4 Gordon (lake), Austl.
54/D5 Gordon, Sc,UK
124/J6 Goré, Chad
125/N6 Gorē, Eth.
115/Q12 Gore, NZ
59/G1 Gore (pt.), Eng,UK
151/H4 Gore (pt.), Ak,US
54/C5 Gorebridge, Sc,UK
92/D1 Görele, Turk.
72/B2 Gorey, Chl,UK
93/H2 Gorgān, Iran
93/H2 Gorgān (riv.), Iran
69/F4 Gorge du Loup, Lux.
128/B3 Gorgol (reg.), Mrta.
128/B2 Gorgol (riv.), Mrta.
78/C6 Gorgona (isl.), It.
78/C1 Gorgonzola, It.
87/H4 Gori, Geo.
66/B5 Gorinchem, Neth.
59/E3 Goring, Eng,UK
59/F5 Goring by Sea, Eng,UK
79/G1 Gorizia, It.
79/G1 Gorizia (prov.), It.
83/F3 Gorj (co.), Rom.
86/D1 Gorki, Bela.
84/J4 Gor'kiy (res.), Rus.
85/K4 Gor'kiy (Nizhniy Novgorod), Rus.
65/L4 Gorlice, Pol.
65/H3 Görlitz, Ger.
58/C2 Gorllwyn (mtn.), Wal,UK
86/F2 Gorlovka, Ukr.
60/D2 Gormanston, Ire.
161/R8 Gormley, On,Can
83/G4 Gorna Oryakhovitsa, Bul.
76/D6 Gorner (glac.), It., Swi.
82/E3 Gornji Milanovac, Yugo.
82/C4 Gornji Vakuf, Bosn.
88/J4 Gorno-Altay Aut. Obl., Rus.
102/E1 Gorno-Altaysk, Rus.
88/H6 Gorno-Badakhstan Aut. Obl., Taj.
85/J4 Gorodets, Rus.
120/D5 Goroka, PNG
131/C3 Goromonzi, Zim.
111/H4 Gorong (isl.), Indo.
131/D3 Gorongosa, Serra da (peak), Moz.
131/D3 Gorongoza, Moz.
131/D3 Gorongoza Nat'l Park, Moz.
111/F3 Gorontalo, Indo.
79/F3 Goro, Po di (riv.), It.
58/B3 Gorseinon, Wal,UK
66/D4 Gorssel, Neth.
56/A2 Gortin, NI,UK
86/C2 Goryn' (riv.), Bela., Ukr.
65/H2 Gorzów (prov.), Pol.
65/H2 Gorzów Wielkopolski, Pol.
98/D3 Gōse, Japan
99/F2 Gosen, Japan
57/G2 Gosforth, Eng,UK
100/B3 Goshogawara, Japan
67/H5 Goslar, Ger.
82/B3 Gospić, Cro.
59/E5 Gosport, Eng,UK
77/F3 Gossau, Swi.
77/H4 Gossenass (Colle Isarco), It.
82/E5 Gostivar, Macd.
65/J3 Gostyń, Pol.
65/K2 Gostynin, Pol.
62/G2 Göta (can.), Swe.
62/E3 Götaland (reg.), Swe.
62/D3 Göteborg, Swe.
62/D2 Göteborg och Bohus (co.), Swe.
124/H6 Gotel (mts.), Camr., Nga.
99/F3 Gotemba, Japan
67/H7 Gotha, Ger.
159/G2 Gothenburg, Ne,US
62/G3 Gotland (co.), Swe.
62/G3 Gotland (isl.), Swe.
98/A4 Gotō (isls.), Japan
83/F5 Gotse Delchev, Bul.
63/H2 Gotska Sandön (isl.), Swe.
63/H2 Gotska Sandön Nat'l Park, Swe.
98/C3 Gōtsu, Japan
67/G5 Göttingen, Ger.
77/E2 Gottmadingen, Ger.
66/B4 Gouda, Neth.
50/J8 Gough (isl.), StH.
160/F1 Gouin (res.), Qu,Can
160/C2 Goulais (riv.), On,Can
119/D2 Goulburn, Austl.
114/E2 Goulburn (isls.), Austl.
119/D2 Goulburn (riv.), Austl.
113/P Gould (coast), Ant.
116/C3 Gould (peak), Austl.
162/F3 Gould, Ar,US
105/F4 Goulou (mts.), China
104/E3 Goulou (peak), China
128/E2 Goundam, Mali
129/H3 Gouré, Niger
132/C4 Gourits (riv.), SAfr.
129/F3 Gourma (prov.), Burk.
129/F3 Gourma (reg.), Burk.
129/E2 Gourma-Rharous, Mali
68/A5 Gournay-en-Bray, Fr.
125/J4 Gouro, Chad
54/B5 Gourock, Sc,UK
53/T9 Goussainville, Fr.
141/D1 Gouvêa, Braz.
68/B5 Gouvieux, Fr.
86/C2 Goverla (peak), Ukr.
140/A2 Governador Archer, Braz.
140/C2 Governador Dix-Sept Rosado, Braz.
141/D1 Governador Valadares, Braz.
112/D4 Governor Generoso, Phil.
167/J9 Governors (isl.), NY,US
96/D3 Govĭ Altayn (mts.), Mong.
108/D2 Govind Sāgar (res.), India
95/H3 Gowd-e-Zereh (lake), Afg.
58/B3 Gower (pen.), Wal,UK
60/C2 Gowna, Lough (lake), Ire.
54/C4 Gowrie, Carse of (plain), Sc,UK
57/H4 Goxhill, Eng,UK
135/E2 Goya, Arg.
57/F5 Goyt (riv.), Eng,UK
99/M9 Gozaisho-yama (peak), Japan
102/D4 Gozha (lake), China
80/D4 Gozo (isl.), Malta
132/D4 Graaff-Reinet, SAfr.
66/D4 Graafschap (reg.), Neth.
132/B2 Graberberg (peak), Namb.
64/F2 Grabow, Ger.
140/A2 Graça Aranha, Braz.
82/B3 Gračac, Cro.
82/D3 Gračanica, Bosn.
163/G4 Graceville, Fl,US
149/F3 Gracias a Dios (cape), Nic.
75/S12 Graciosa (isl.), Azor.,Port.
82/D3 Gradačac, Bosn.
137/H5 Gradaús, Braz.
79/G1 Gradisca d'Isonzo, It.
79/G1 Grado, It.
74/B1 Grado, Sp.
71/E6 Gräfelfing, Ger.
71/E3 Grafenwöhr, Ger.
59/F2 Grafham Water (lake), Eng,UK
71/E6 Grafing bei München, Ger.
62/C1 Gråfjell (peak), Nor.
119/E1 Grafton, Austl.
118/B2 Grafton (passg.), Austl.
168/C1 Grafton, Ma,US
157/J3 Grafton, ND,US
160/D4 Grafton, WV,US
152/C3 Graham (isl.), BC,Can
153/S7 Graham (isl.), NW,Can
162/D3 Graham, Tx,US
165/C3 Graham, Wa,US
88/G1 Graham Bell (isl.), Rus.
164/F8 Graham-Florence, Ca,US
113/V Graham Land (reg.), Ant.
132/D4 Grahamstown, SAfr.
59/G4 Grain, Eng,UK
128/C5 Grain Coast (reg.), Libr.
140/A2 Grajaú, Braz.
137/J4 Grajaú (riv.), Braz.
65/M2 Grajewo, Pol.
72/D4 Gramat (plat.), Fr.
54/B3 Grampian (mts.), Sc,UK
54/D2 Grampian (reg.), Sc,UK
119/B3 Grampians Nat'l Park, Austl.
66/D3 Gramsbergen, Neth.
62/D1 Gran, Nor.
138/C4 Granada, Col.
148/E4 Granada, Nic.
74/D4 Granada, Sp.
143/K7 Gran Altiplanicie Central (plat.), Arg.
143/K7 Gran Bajo de San Julián (val.), Arg.
142/C5 Gran Bajo Oriental (val.), Arg.
162/D3 Granbury, Tx,US
159/F2 Granby, Co,US
168/B2 Granby, Ct,US
134/C5 Gran Chaco (plain), SAm.
144/B3 Gran Chavin (dept.), Peru
161/H2 Grand (lake), NB,Can
161/K1 Grand (lake), Nf,Can
161/Q9 Grand (riv.), On,Can
153/J3 Grand (riv.), Qu,Can
103/D4 Grand (can.), China
56/B5 Grand (can.), Ire.
130/C3 Grand (falls), Kenya
158/D3 Grand (canyon), Az,US
159/J3 Grand (riv.), Ia, Mo,US
159/J5 Grand (lake), La,US
160/C2 Grand (isl.), Mi,US
162/E2 Grand (riv.), Mo,US
161/S9 Grand (isl.), NY,US
168/G5 Grand (riv.), Oh,US
157/H4 Grand (riv.), SD,US
76/D2 Grand Alsace (can.), Fr.
150/B1 Grand Bahama (isl.), Bahm.
161/L2 Grand Bank, Nf,Can
128/C5 Grand Bassa (co.), Libr.
128/E5 Grand-Bassam, IvC.
161/H2 Grand Bay, NB,Can
165/E6 Grand Blanc, Mi,US
158/D3 Grand Canyon Nat'l Park, Az,US
128/C5 Grand Cape Mount (co.), Libr.
149/F2 Grand Cayman (isl.), Cay.
156/F2 Grand Centre, Ab,Can
76/C2 Grand-Charmont, Fr.
76/B6 Grand Colombier (mtn.), Fr.
76/D6 Grand Combin (peak), Swi.
156/D4 Grand Coulee, Wa,US
156/D4 Grand Coulee (dam), Wa,US
76/C2 Grand Drumont (mtn.), Fr.
143/K7 Grande (bay), Arg.
143/K8 Grande (riv.), Arg.
136/F7 Grande (riv.), Bol.
141/K8 Grande (isl.), Braz.
139/H5 Grande (lake), Braz.
139/F4 Grande (mts.), Braz.
141/J7 Grande (riv.), Braz.
147/Q9 Grande (riv.), Mex.
149/G4 Grande (pt.), Pan.
143/T11 Grande (stream), Uru.
156/D2 Grande Cache, Ab,Can
133/G5 Grande Comore (isl.), Com.
80/C1 Grande, Corno (peak), It.
137/H4 Grande de Gurupá, Braz.
139/F5 Grande de Manacapurú (lake), Braz.
149/E3 Grande de Matagalpa (riv.), Nic.
76/D5 Grande Dixence, Barrage de la (dam), Swi.
139/G5 Grande do Curuaí (lake), Braz.
80/C4 Grande, Monte (peak), It.
156/D2 Grande Prairie, Ab,Can
124/H4 Grand 'Erg de Bilma (des.), Niger
124/E1 Grand Erg Occidental (des.), Alg.
124/G1 Grand Erg Oriental (des.), Alg.
162/C4 Grande, Rio (riv.), Mex., US
150/C3 Grande Rivière du Nord, Haiti
76/D6 Grandes Jorasses (peak), It.
68/B1 Grande-Synthe, Fr.
150/F3 Grande-Terre (isl.), Guad.
161/H2 Grand Falls, NB,Can
161/L1 Grand Falls, Nf,Can
156/D3 Grand Forks, BC,Can
157/J4 Grand Forks, ND,US
68/B2 Grand-Fort-Philippe, Fr.
160/C3 Grand Haven, Mi,US
159/H2 Grand Island, Ne,US
163/F4 Grand Isle, La,US
128/D5 Grand Jide (co.), Libr.
158/E3 Grand Junction, Co,US
159/J3 Grand Lake O'The Cherokees (lake), Ok,US
161/H2 Grand Manan (isl.), NB,Can
157/L4 Grand Marais, Mn,US
68/C6 Grand Marin (riv.), Fr.
161/F2 Grand-Mère, Qu,Can
161/K2 Grand Miquelon (isl.), StP.
76/C5 Grand Mont Ruan (mtn.), Fr.
76/D5 Grand Muveran (peak), Swi.
74/A3 Grândola, Port.
157/L4 Grand Portage Nat'l Mon., Mn,US
69/D5 Grandpré, Fr.
161/H2 Grand Pré Nat'l Hist. Park, NS,Can
157/J2 Grand Rapids, Mb,Can
160/C3 Grand Rapids, Mi,US
157/K4 Grand Rapids, Mn,US
72/F5 Grand Rhône (riv.), Fr.
76/C4 Grand Taureau (mtn.), Fr.
156/F5 Grand Teton (peak), Wy,US
156/F5 Grand Teton Nat'l Park, Wy,US
53/M6 Grand Union (can.), Eng,UK
157/H3 Grandview, Mb,Can
156/D4 Grandview, Wa,US
142/C2 Graneros, Chile
62/E1 Granfjället (peak), Swe.
117/M8 Grange, Austl.
60/B2 Grange (riv.), Ire.
57/F3 Grange, Eng,UK
76/C5 Grange, Mont de (mtn.), Fr.
54/C4 Grangemouth, Sc,UK
151/L3 Granger (mtn.), Yk,Can
156/D4 Grangeville, Id,US
156/B2 Granisle, BC,Can
156/F4 Granite (peak), Mt,US
160/B4 Granite City, Il,US
140/B1 Granja, Braz.
142/D5 Gran Laguna Salada (lake), Arg.
75/G2 Granollers, Sp.
78/A1 Gran Paradiso Nat'l Park, It.
149/H2 Gran Piedra (hill), Cuba
73/J3 Gran Pilastro (peak), It.
139/F3 Gran Sabana, La (plain), Ven.
75/Y16 Gran Tarajal, Canl.,Sp.
57/H6 Grantham, Eng,UK
54/C2 Grantown-on-Spey, Sc,UK
158/F4 Grants, NM,US
160/A2 Grantsburg, Wi,US
156/C5 Grants Pass, Or,US
144/B2 Gran Vilaya (ruins), Peru
157/H1 Granville (lake), Mb,Can
72/C2 Granville, Fr.
140/B5 Grão Mogol, Braz.
165/B3 Grapeview-Allyn, Wa,US
67/F2 Grasberg, Ger.
70/B3 Grasellenbach, Ger.
57/E3 Grasmere, Eng,UK
62/H1 Grasö (isl.), Swe.
165/P15 Grass (lake), Il,US
73/G5 Grasse, Fr.
161/Q9 Grassie, On,Can
57/G3 Grassington, Eng,UK
156/G3 Grasslands Nat'l Park, Sk,Can
63/T8 Græsted, Den.
82/B2 Gratkorn, Aus.
144/A2 Grau (dept.), Peru
77/F4 Graubünden (canton), Swi.
72/E5 Graulhet, Fr.
140/D3 Gravatá, Braz.
66/C5 Grave, Neth.
156/G3 Gravelbourg, Sk,Can
68/B2 Gravelines, Fr.
78/B1 Gravellona Toce, It.
131/C4 Gravelotte, SAfr.
160/E2 Gravenhurst, On,Can
53/Q7 Gravesend, Eng,UK
68/A5 Gravigny, Fr.
80/E2 Gravina di Puglia, It.
149/H2 Gravois, Pointe à (pt.), Haiti
76/B3 Gray, Fr.
160/C2 Grayling, Mi,US
53/P7 Grays, Eng,UK
156/F5 Grays (lake), Id,US
156/B4 Grays (har.), Wa,US
165/P15 Grayslake, Il,US
157/H3 Grayson, Sk,Can
73/L3 Graz, Aus.
119/C4 Great (lake), Austl.
157/G3 Great (plains), Can., US
60/B6 Great (isl.), Ire.
50/E3 Great (lakes), NAm.
158/C2 Great (basin), US
167/D4 Great (bay), NJ,US
167/J8 Great (falls), NJ,US
150/B1 Great Abaco (isl.), Bahm.
65/L5 Great Alföld (plain), Hun.
116/E5 Great Australian (bight), Austl.
150/B1 Great Bahama (bank), Bahm.
59/F2 Great Barford, Eng,UK
118/B1 Great Barrier (reef), Austl.
115/S10 Great Barrier (isl.), NZ
118/B2 Great Barrier Reef Marine Park, Austl.
59/G2 Great Barton, Eng,UK
158/D3 Great Basin Nat'l Park, Nv,US
152/D2 Great Bear (lake), NW,Can
159/H3 Great Bend, Ks,US
91/C4 Great Bitter (lake), Egypt
53/M8 Great Bookham, Eng,UK
132/C3 Great Brak (riv.), SAfr.
55/L9 Great Britain (isl.), UK
166/D5 Great Cedar (swamp), NJ,US
51/P5 Great Coco (isl.), Burma
59/G2 Great Cornard, Eng,UK
54/B5 Great Cumbrae (isl.), Sc,UK
156/F5 Great Divide (basin), Wyo,US
115/H7 Great Dividing (range), Austl.
57/H4 Great Driffield, Eng,UK
59/G3 Great Dunmow, Eng,UK
166/D5 Great Egg (har.), NJ,US
166/D4 Great Egg Harbor (riv.), NJ,US
129/F5 Greater Accra (reg.), Gha.
87/L3 Greater Barsuki (des.), Kaz.
53/P7 Greater London (co.), Eng,UK
57/F5 Greater Manchester (co.), Eng,UK
110/C4 Greater Sunda (isls.), Indo.
150/C2 Great Exuma (isl.), Bahm.
156/F4 Great Falls, Mt,US
132/D4 Great Fish (pt.), SAfr.
132/D4 Great Fish (riv.), SAfr.
59/F2 Great Gransden, Eng,UK
150/B1 Great Guana (cay), Bahm.
57/G2 Greatham, Eng,UK
57/F4 Great Harwood, Eng,UK
106/D2 Great Himalaya (range), Asia
150/C2 Great Inagua (isl.), Bahm.
106/A2 Great Indian (des.), India, Pak.
132/C3 Great Karoo (reg.), SAfr.
132/D4 Great Kei (riv.), SAfr.
165/Q15 Great Lakes Nav. Trng. Ctr., Il,US
58/D2 Great Malvern, Eng,UK
59/E3 Great Milton, Eng,UK
58/B5 Great Mis Tor (hill), Eng,UK
167/E2 Great Neck, NY,US
107/F6 Great Nicobar (isl.), India
59/G1 Great Ouse (riv.), Eng,UK
119/C4 Great Oyster (bay), Austl.
167/F2 Great Peconic (bay), NY,US
163/J3 Great Pee Dee (riv.), SC,US
167/H8 Great Piece (meadows), NJ,US
130/B4 Great Rift (val.), Afr.
130/B4 Great Ruaha (riv.), Tanz.
76/D6 Great Saint Bernard (pass), Swi., It.
150/B1 Great Sale (cay), Bahm.
158/D2 Great Salt (lake), Ut,US
158/D2 Great Salt Lake (des.), Ut,US
159/F3 Great Sand Dunes Nat'l Mon., Co,US
127/A3 Great Sand Sea (des.), Egypt, Libya
116/D2 Great Sandy (des.), Austl.
158/B2 Great Sandy (des.), Or,US
118/D4 Great Sandy Nat'l Park, Austl.
128/B4 Great Scarcies (riv.), Gui., SLeo.
59/G2 Great Shelford, Eng,UK
57/F3 Great Shunner Fell (mtn.), Eng,UK
152/E2 Great Slave (lake), NW,Can
163/H3 Great Smoky Mts. Nat'l Park, NC, Tn,US
167/E2 Great South (bay), NY,US
59/G4 Great Stour (riv.), Eng,UK
166/D2 Great Swamp Nat'l Wild. Ref., NJ,US
109/B3 Great Tenasserim (riv.), Burma
58/B5 Great Torrington, Eng,UK
117/F3 Great Victoria (des.), Austl.
117/E4 Great Victoria Desert Nature Rsv., Austl.
103/B3 Great Wall (ruins), China
53/P7 Great Warley, Eng,UK
119/C4 Great Western Tiers (mts.), Austl.
132/B4 Great Winterhoek (peak), SAfr.
58/D2 Great Witley, Eng,UK
59/H1 Great Yarmouth, Eng,UK
93/E2 Great Zab (riv.), Iraq
131/C4 Great Zimbabwe (ruins), Zim.
129/H2 Grébon (peak), Niger
91/D2 Greco (cape), Cyp.
80/D2 Greco (peak), It.
71/E4 Greding, Ger.
74/C2 Gredos (range), Sp.
81/G3 Greece
159/F2 Greeley, Co,US
153/S6 Greely (fjord), NW,Can
119/D3 Green (cape), Austl.
160/C4 Green (riv.), Ky,US
157/M4 Green (bay), Mi, Wi,US
158/E3 Green (riv.), Ut, Wy,US
161/G3 Green (mts.), Vt,US
165/D3 Green (riv.), Wa,US
160/B2 Green Bay, Wi,US
166/B5 Greenbelt, Md,US
166/B6 Greenbelt Park, Md,US
160/C4 Greencastle, In,US
163/H4 Green Cove Springs, Fl,US
165/Q14 Greendale, Wi,US
163/H2 Greeneville, Tn,US
160/C4 Greenfield, In,US
161/F3 Greenfield, Ma,US
165/P14 Greenfield, Wi,US
161/P7 Greenfield Park, Qu,Can
166/B5 Green Haven, Md,US
56/C2 Greenisland, NI,UK
145/R2 Greenland (sea)
145/N2 Greenland (Kalaallit Nunaat) (dpcy.), Den.
166/C3 Green Lane (res.), Pa,US
54/D5 Greenlaw, Sc,UK
54/C6 Green Lowther (mtn.), Sc,UK
54/B5 Greenock, Sc,UK
60/D5 Greenore (pt.), Ire.
116/B4 Greenough (riv.), Austl.
151/K2 Greenough (mtn.), Ak,US
167/H8 Green Pond (lake), NJ,US
161/R8 Green River, On,Can
158/E3 Green River, Ut,US
156/F5 Green River, Wy,US
163/G3 Greensboro, Al,US
163/J2 Greensboro, NC,US
160/C4 Greensburg, In,US
160/E3 Greensburg, Pa,US
161/Q9 Greensville, On,Can
158/E5 Green Valley, Az,US
166/A5 Green Valley, Md,US
128/C5 Greenville, Libr.
163/G4 Greenville, Al,US
158/B2 Greenville, Ca,US
160/C4 Greenville, Ky,US
160/C3 Greenville, Mi,US
163/F3 Greenville, Ms,US
163/J3 Greenville, NC,US
160/C3 Greenville, Oh,US
168/G5 Greenville, Pa,US
168/C2 Greenville, RI,US
163/H3 Greenville, SC,US
162/D3 Greenville, Tx,US
165/D3 Greenwater (riv.), Wa,US
53/P7 Greenwich (bor.), Eng,UK
167/E1 Greenwich, Ct,US
167/L8 Greenwich (pt.), Ct,US
53/P7 Greenwich Observatory, Eng,UK
167/K9 Greenwich Village, NY,US
161/R8 Greenwood, On,Can
163/F3 Greenwood, Ms,US
167/D1 Greenwood (lake), NJ, NY,US
163/H3 Greenwood, SC,US
163/H3 Greenwood (lake), SC,US
159/J4 Greers Ferry (lake), Ar,US
60/D4 Greese (riv.), Ire.
66/D6 Grefrath, Ger.
144/D2 Gregório (riv.), Braz.
116/C3 Gregory (lake), Austl.
117/E2 Gregory (lake), Austl.
117/H4 Gregory (lake), Austl.
118/A2 Gregory (range), Austl.
157/J5 Gregory, SD,US
116/E2 Gregory Lake Abor. Land, Austl.
65/G1 Greifswald, Ger.
65/G1 Greifswalder Bodden (bay), Ger.
82/B2 Greimberg (peak), Aus.
64/G3 Greiz, Ger.
85/N4 Gremyachinsk, Rus.
62/D3 Grenå, Den.
150/F5 Grenada
163/F3 Grenada, Ms,US
76/D3 Grenchen, Swi.
157/H3 Grenfell, Sk,Can
72/F4 Grenoble, Fr.
114/G2 Grenville (cape), Austl.
76/D2 Grenzach-Wyhlen, Ger.
61/E2 Gressåmoen Nat'l Park, Nor.
57/E2 Greta (riv.), Eng,UK
57/F3 Greta (riv.), Eng,UK
157/J3 Gretna, Mb,Can
57/E2 Gretna, Sc,UK
163/F4 Gretna, La,US
59/F1 Gretton, Eng,UK
53/U10 Gretz-Armainvilliers, Fr.
63/T9 Greve, Den.
79/E5 Greve (riv.), It.
66/B5 Grevelingendam (dam), Neth.
67/E4 Greven, Ger.
81/G2 Grevená, Gre.
66/D6 Grevenbroich, Ger.
69/F4 Grevenmacher (dist.), Lux.
64/F2 Grevesmühlen, Ger.
66/A5 Grevlingen (chan.), Neth.
114/F2 Grey (cape), Austl.
118/A5 Grey (range), Austl.
161/K2 Grey (riv.), Nf,Can
56/C2 Grey (pt.), NI,UK
56/C2 Grey Abbey, NI,UK
156/F4 Greybull, Wy,US
151/L3 Grey Hunter (peak), Yk,Can
115/R11 Greymouth, NZ
118/B2 Grey Peaks Nat'l Park, Austl.
57/F2 Greystoke, Eng,UK
60/D3 Greystones, Ire.
133/E3 Greytown, SAfr.
69/D2 Grez-Doiceau, Belg.
58/B6 Gribbin (pt.), Eng,UK
77/E5 Gridone (Monte Limidario) (peak), It.
77/E3 Griefensee (lake), Swi.
66/C2 Griend (isl.), Neth.
70/B3 Griesheim, Ger.
77/H3 Griesskogel (peak), Aus.
163/G3 Griffin, Ga,US
119/C2 Griffith, Austl.
165/R16 Griffith, In,US
164/F7 Griffith Park, Los Angeles, Ca,US
78/C1 Grigna (peak), It.
68/B6 Grigny, Fr.
148/C2 Grijalva (riv.), Mex.
119/C4 Grim (cape), Austl.
68/D2 Grimbergen, Belg.
58/D2 Grimley, Eng,UK
64/G1 Grimmen, Ger.
161/Q9 Grimsby, On,Can
57/H4 Grimsby, Eng,UK
77/E4 Grimselpass (pass), Swi.
61/N6 Grimsey (isl.), Ice.
62/C2 Grimstad, Nor.
62/C4 Grindsted, Den.
153/S7 Grinnel (pen.), NW,Can
82/B2 Grintavec (peak), Slov.
132/E3 Griqualand East (reg.), SAfr.
132/C2 Griqualand West (reg.), SAfr.
68/A2 Gris Nez (cape), Fr.
53/U10 Grisy-Suisnes, Fr.
165/K10 Grizzly (bay), Ca,US
82/C3 Grmeč (mtn.), Bosn.
140/B1 Groaíras, Braz.
69/D1 Grobbendonk, Belg.
71/E6 Gröbenzell, Ger.
65/J3 Grodków, Pol.
63/K5 Grodno, Bela.
63/L5 Grodno Obl., Bela.
65/J2 Grodzisk Wielkopolski, Pol.
66/D4 Groenlo, Neth.
162/D4 Groesbeck, Tx,US
66/C5 Groesbeek, Neth.
72/B3 Groix (isl.), Fr.
65/L3 Grójec, Pol.
64/F1 Grömitz, Ger.
66/E4 Gronau, Ger.
66/D2 Groningen, Neth.
66/D2 Groningen (prov.), Neth.
77/H5 Gronlait (peak), It.
132/C4 Groot (riv.), SAfr.
132/Q13 Grootdraaidam (res.), SAfr.
114/F2 Groote Eylandt (isl.), Austl.
66/D2 Grootegast, Neth.
126/C4 Grootfontein, Namb.
131/B4 Grootgeluk, SAfr.
131/C4 Groot-Letabarivier (riv.), SAfr.
132/D2 Groot-Marico (riv.), SAfr.
132/C3 Grootvloer (salt pan), SAfr.
150/F4 Gros Islet, StL.
161/K1 Gros Morne (peak), Nf,Can
161/K1 Gros Morne Nat'l Park, Nf,Can
72/F3 Grosne (riv.), Fr.
67/G6 Grossalmerode, Ger.
70/C5 Grossbottwar, Ger.
67/E3 Grosse Aa (riv.), Ger.
165/F7 Grosse Ile, Mi,US
165/F7 Grosse Ile (isl.), Mi,US
71/F5 Grosse Laber (riv.), Ger.
70/C6 Grosse Lauter (riv.), Ger.
71/G6 Grosse Mühl (riv.), Aus.
132/A2 Grosse Münzenberg (peak), Namb.
69/G2 Grosse Nister (riv.), Ger.
67/F3 Grossenkneten, Ger.
70/C1 Grossenlüder, Ger.
165/G7 Grosse Pointe, Mi,US
165/G7 Grosse Pointe Farms, Mi,US
165/G7 Grosse Pointe Park, Mi,US
165/G7 Grosse Pointe Shores, Mi,US
165/G7 Grosse Pointe Woods, Mi,US
76/D5 Grosser Aletsch (glac.), Swi.
71/G4 Grosser Arber (peak), Ger.
67/G3 Grosser Aue (riv.), Ger.
64/F3 Grosser Beer-Berg (peak), Ger.
73/L3 Grosser Bösenstein (peak), Aus.
77/G3 Grosser Daumen (peak), Ger.
70/B2 Grosser Feldberg (peak), Ger.
70/D2 Grosser Gleichberg (peak), Ger.
70/B6 Grosser Heuberg (mts.), Ger.

191

Gross – Harli

67/F1 **Grosser Knechtsand** (isl.), Ger.
71/H6 **Grosse Rodl** (riv.), Aus.
65/H4 **Grosser Peilstein** (peak), Aus.
73/L3 **Grosser Priel** (peak), Aus.
65/H5 **Grosser Pyhrgas** (peak), Aus.
71/G5 **Grosser Rachel** (peak), Ger.
67/E2 **Grosses Meer** (lake), Ger.
82/A2 **Grosses Wiesbachhorn** (peak), Aus.
80/B1 **Grosseto,** It.
70/B3 **Grossgerau,** Ger.
73/K3 **Grossglockner** (peak), Aus.
67/H1 **Grosshansdorf,** Ger.
73/H5 **Grosso** (cape), Fr.
140/C2 **Grossos,** Braz.
69/F5 **Grossrosseln,** Ger.
70/B3 **Gross Unstadt,** Ger.
70/B3 **Gross-Zimmern,** Ger.
69/E2 **Grote Gete** (riv.), Belg.
69/D1 **Grote Nete** (riv.), Belg.
168/B3 **Groton,** Ct,US
157/J4 **Groton,** SD,US
79/G1 **Grotta Gigante,** It.
80/E2 **Grottaglie,** It.
69/E3 **Grotte de Han,** Belg.
75/E1 **Grottes de Bétharram,** Fr.
123/L14 **Grou** (riv.), Mor.
156/D2 **Grouard Mission,** Ab,Can
160/D1 **Groundhog** (riv.), On,Can
66/C2 **Grouw,** Neth.
59/E3 **Grove,** Eng,UK
166/B5 **Grove** (pt.), Md,US
159/J3 **Grove,** Ok,US
168/G5 **Grove City,** Pa,US
158/B4 **Grover City,** Ca,US
162/E4 **Groves,** Tx,US
166/A6 **Groveton,** Va,US
87/H4 **Groznyy,** Rus.
83/H4 **Grudovo,** Bul.
65/K2 **Grudziądz,** Pol.
78/A2 **Grugliasco,** It.
130/B3 **Grumeti** (riv.), Tanz.
62/E2 **Grums,** Swe.
70/C2 **Gründau,** Ger.
57/E2 **Grune** (pt.), Eng,UK
70/B3 **Grünstadt,** Ger.
71/E6 **Grünwald,** Ger.
76/D4 **Gruyère** (lake), Swi.
86/F1 **Gryazi,** Rus.
65/H2 **Gryfice,** Pol.
65/H2 **Gryfino,** Pol.
105/H3 **Gu** (mtn.), China
142/B4 **Guabun** (pt.), Chile
149/G1 **Guacanayabo** (gulf), Cuba
138/E2 **Guacara,** Ven.
139/E2 **Guacharo Nat'l Park,** Ven.
141/D2 **Guaçuí,** Braz.
146/E4 **Guadalajara,** Mex.
74/D2 **Guadalajara,** Sp.
120/E6 **Guadalcanal** (isl.), Sol.
74/E4 **Guadalentín** (riv.), Sp.
74/D3 **Guadalimlar** (riv.), Sp.
75/N8 **Guadalix** (riv.), Sp.
75/E2 **Guadalope** (riv.), Sp.
74/D4 **Guadalquivir** (riv.), Sp.
140/B2 **Guadalupe,** Braz.
146/E4 **Guadalupe,** Mex.
147/Q9 **Guadalupe** (res.), Mex.
149/G4 **Guadalupe,** Pan.
144/B2 **Guadalupe,** Peru
144/C4 **Guadalupe,** Peru
74/C3 **Guadalupe** (range), Sp.
162/B3 **Guadalupe** (mts.), NM, Tx,US
162/B4 **Guadalupe** (peak), Tx,US
162/D4 **Guadalupe** (riv.), Tx,US
162/B4 **Guadalupe Mts. Nat'l Park,** Tx,US
146/D3 **Guadalupe Victoria,** Mex.
147/M7 **Guadalupe Victoria,** Mex.
75/M8 **Guadarrama** (pass), Sp.
74/C2 **Guadarrama** (range), Sp.
74/C3 **Guadarrama** (riv.), Sp.
150/F3 **Guadeloupe** (dept.), Fr.
150/F3 **Guadeloupe** (passg.), NAm.
150/F3 **Guadeloupe Nat'l Park,** Guad.
147/Q9 **Guadelupe, Basilica of,** Mex.
74/B4 **Guadiana** (riv.), Sp., Port.
74/D4 **Guadiana Menor** (riv.), Sp.
74/D4 **Guadix,** Sp.
142/B4 **Guafo** (chan.), Chile
142/B4 **Guafo** (isl.), Chile
138/B5 **Guagua Pichincha** (peak), Ecu.
141/B4 **Guaíba,** Braz.
141/B4 **Guaiba** (riv.), Braz.
149/G1 **Guaicanamar,** Cuba
149/G1 **Guáimaro,** Cuba
138/D4 **Guainía** (comm.), Col.
138/D4 **Guainía** (riv.), Col., Ven.
139/F3 **Guaiquinima** (peak), Ven.
141/B2 **Guaíra,** Braz.
142/B4 **Guaiteca** (isl.), Chile
136/E6 **Guajará-Mirim,** Braz.
138/D1 **Guajira** (pen.), Col., Ven.
138/B5 **Gualaceo,** Ecu.
158/B3 **Gualala,** Ca,US
148/D3 **Gualán,** Guat.
80/C1 **Gualdo Tadino,** It.
142/F2 **Gualeguay,** Arg.
142/F2 **Gualeguay** (riv.), Arg.
142/F2 **Gualeguaychú,** Arg.
142/D4 **Gualicho** (val.), Arg.
120/D3 **Guam** (isl.), PacUS
142/B5 **Guamblin** (isl.), Chile
144/B1 **Guamote,** Ecu.
146/D3 **Guamuchil,** Mex.
103/D3 **Gu'an,** China
103/H7 **Gu'an,** China
149/F1 **Guanabacoa,** Cuba
141/K7 **Guanabara** (bay), Braz.
149/E1 **Guanahacabibes** (gulf), Cuba
149/E1 **Guanahacabibes** (pen.), Cuba
148/E2 **Guanaja** (isl.), Hon.
149/F1 **Guanajay,** Cuba
147/E4 **Guanajuato,** Mex.
147/E4 **Guanajuato** (state), Mex.
139/F3 **Guanajuña,** Ven.
140/B4 **Guanambi,** Braz.
138/D2 **Guanare,** Ven.
138/D2 **Guanare** (riv.), Ven.
139/E3 **Guanay** (peak), Ven.
103/C3 **Guancen Shan** (mtn.), China
103/B3 **Guandi Shan** (mtn.), China
103/B5 **Guandu,** China
149/E1 **Guane,** Cuba
105/H3 **Guangchang,** China
103/D5 **Guangde,** China
105/G3 **Guangdong** (prov.), China
103/C3 **Guangling,** China
101/B3 **Guanglu** (isl.), China
104/D3 **Guangmao** (mtn.), China
103/D5 **Guangming Ding** (peak), China
104/E3 **Guangnan,** China
103/C3 **Guangping,** China
105/H3 **Guangping,** China
103/D3 **Guangrao,** China
103/C4 **Guangshan,** China
105/F4 **Guangxi Zhuangzu Zizhiqu** (aut. reg.), China
104/E1 **Guangyuan,** China
105/H3 **Guangze,** China
105/G4 **Guangzhou** (Canton), China
141/D1 **Guanhães,** Braz.
139/F2 **Guanipa** (riv.), Ven.
105/F2 **Guanmian** (mts.), China
103/D4 **Guannan,** China
149/H1 **Guantánamo,** Cuba
149/H2 **Guantánamo Bay U.S. Nav. Base,** Cuba
103/C3 **Guantao,** China
103/G6 **Guanting** (res.), China
138/B5 **Guanujo,** Ecu.
103/C3 **Guan Xian,** China
104/D2 **Guan Xian,** China
103/D4 **Guanyun,** China
138/B3 **Guapa,** Col.
141/B4 **Guaporé,** Braz.
136/F6 **Guaporé** (riv.), Braz.
140/A4 **Guara** (riv.), Braz.
75/E1 **Guara** (peak), Sp.
140/D2 **Guarabira,** Braz.
141/B2 **Guaraci,** Braz.
140/B2 **Guaraciaba do Norte,** Braz.
137/J5 **Guaraí,** Braz.
141/B3 **Guaramirim,** Braz.
138/B5 **Guaranda,** Ecu.
141/K6 **Guarani,** Braz.
141/D2 **Guarapari,** Braz.
141/B3 **Guarapuava,** Braz.
141/K6 **Guarará,** Braz.
141/B2 **Guararapes,** Braz.
141/G8 **Guararema,** Braz.
140/C5 **Guaratinga,** Braz.
141/H7 **Guaratinguetá,** Braz.
141/B3 **Guaratuba,** Braz.
74/B2 **Guarda,** Port.
74/B2 **Guarda** (dist.), Port.
77/H4 **Guardia Alta** (peak), It.
74/B3 **Guareña,** Sp.
149/H1 **Guarico** (pt.), Cuba
139/E2 **Guárico** (res.), Ven.
139/E2 **Guárico** (riv.), Ven.
139/E2 **Guárico** (state), Ven.
141/G9 **Guarujá,** Braz.
141/G8 **Guarulhos,** Braz.
146/C3 **Guasave,** Mex.
138/D3 **Guasdualito,** Ven.
78/D3 **Guastalla,** It.
148/D3 **Guatemala**
148/D3 **Guatemala** (cap.), Guat.
138/C3 **Guateque,** Col.
138/C4 **Guaviare** (comm.), Col.
138/D4 **Guaviare** (riv.), Col.
141/G6 **Guaxupé,** Braz.
138/C4 **Guayabero** (riv.), Col.
149/G1 **Guayabo** (cay), Cuba
147/F4 **Guayalejo** (riv.), Mex.
150/E3 **Guayama,** PR
148/E3 **Guayape** (riv.), Hon.
138/B5 **Guayaquil,** Ecu.
144/A1 **Guayaquil** (gulf), Ecu.
136/E6 **Guayaramerín,** Bol.
138/C4 **Guayas** (riv.), Col.
138/B5 **Guayas,** Ecu.
138/A5 **Guayas** (prov.), Ecu.
146/C3 **Guaymas,** Mex.
85/N4 **Gubakha,** Rus.
79/F6 **Gubbio,** It.
65/H3 **Guben,** Ger.
65/H3 **Gubin,** Pol.
86/F2 **Gubkin,** Rus.
103/B4 **Gucheng,** China
103/C3 **Gucheng,** China
105/F1 **Gucheng,** China
96/E2 **Guchin-Us,** Mong.
108/F3 **Gūdalūr,** India
108/F4 **Gūdalūr,** India
75/E2 **Gúdar** (range), Sp.
62/D3 **Gudenå** (riv.), Den.
67/G6 **Gudensberg,** Ger.
87/H4 **Gudermes,** Rus.
106/D4 **Gudivāda,** India
105/G4 **Gudou** (peak), China
106/C5 **Gūdūr,** India
76/D2 **Guebwiller,** Fr.
74/D1 **Guecho,** Sp.
128/B1 **Guelb Azefal** (mts.), Mrta.
123/V17 **Guelma,** Alg.
123/V17 **Guelma** (wilaya), Alg.
160/D3 **Guelph,** On,Can
124/C2 **Guelta Zemmur,** WSah.
69/F5 **Guénange,** Fr.
72/B3 **Guérande,** Fr.
72/D3 **Guéret,** Fr.
74/D1 **Guernica y Luno,** Sp.
72/B2 **Guernsey** (isl.), Chl,UK
147/E5 **Guerrero** (state), Mex.
72/F3 **Gueugnon,** Fr.
129/H3 **Guézaoua,** Niger
125/N6 **Gugē** (peak), Eth.
120/D3 **Guguan** (isl.), NMar.
105/F4 **Gui** (riv.), China
75/X16 **Guía de Isora,** Sp.
136/F2 **Guiana Highlands** (mts.), SAm.
103/D5 **Guichi,** China
148/C2 **Guichicovi,** Mex.
124/H6 **Guidder,** Camr.
128/B3 **Guidimaka** (reg.), Mrta.
107/J2 **Guiding,** China
107/K2 **Guidong,** China
80/C2 **Guidonia,** It.
128/D5 **Guiglo,** IvC.
53/U11 **Guignes,** Fr.
68/C5 **Guignicourt,** Fr.
138/E2 **Güigüe,** Ven.
112/E6 **Guiguinto,** Phil.
112/C3 **Guihulñgan,** Phil.
131/D5 **Guija,** Moz.
53/M8 **Guildford,** Eng,UK
72/F4 **Guilherand,** Fr.
105/F3 **Guilin,** China
153/J3 **Guillaume-Delisle** (lake), Qu,Can
74/B4 **Guillena,** Sp.
58/C1 **Guilsfield,** Wal,UK
140/A1 **Guimarães,** Braz.
74/A2 **Guimarães,** Port.
112/C3 **Guimaras** (isl.), Phil.
112/C2 **Guimba,** Phil.
103/D4 **Guimeng Ding** (mtn.), China
96/E4 **Guinan,** China
54/A1 **Guinard** (riv.), Sc,UK
112/D3 **Guindulman,** Phil.
128/C4 **Guinea**
124/F7 **Guinea** (gulf), Afr.
128/B3 **Guinea-Bissau**
72/B2 **Guingamp,** Fr.
112/C2 **Guintinguintin** (mtn.), Phil.
148/E4 **Guiones** (pt.), CR
72/A2 **Guipavas,** Fr.
137/H7 **Guiratinga,** Braz.
139/F2 **Güiria,** Ven.
57/G2 **Guisborough,** Eng,UK
68/C4 **Guise,** Fr.
57/G4 **Guiseley,** Eng,UK
74/B1 **Guitiriz,** Sp.
112/D3 **Guiuan,** Phil.
105/F4 **Gui Xian,** China
104/E3 **Guiyang,** China
105/G3 **Guiyang,** China
138/B4 **Güiza** (riv.), Col.
104/E3 **Guizhou** (prov.), China
72/C4 **Gujan-Mestras,** Fr.
106/B3 **Gujarāt** (state), India
108/B1 **Gūjar Khān,** Pak.
108/C1 **Gujrānwāla,** Pak.
108/C1 **Gujrāt,** Pak.
86/F2 **Gukovo,** Rus.
96/E4 **Gulang,** China
106/C4 **Gulbarga,** India
69/G3 **Guldenbach** (riv.), Ger.
163/F4 **Gulf Islands Nat'l Seashore,** US
163/F4 **Gulfport,** Ms,US
163/G4 **Gulf Shores,** Al,US
88/G5 **Gulistan,** Uzb.
97/J2 **Guliya** (peak), China
56/B2 **Gulladuff,** NI,UK
54/D4 **Gullane,** Sc,UK
54/D4 **Gullane Head** (pt.), Sc,UK
156/F3 **Gull Lake,** Sk,Can
92/B2 **Güllükdağı** (Termessos) Nat'l Park, Turk.
91/C1 **Gülnar,** Turk.
69/E2 **Gulpen,** Neth.
92/C2 **Gülşehir,** Turk.
130/B2 **Gulu,** Ugan.
83/G4 **Gŭlŭbovo,** Bul.
54/A3 **Gulvain** (Gaor Bheinn) (mtn.), Sc.,UK
108/A2 **Gumal** (riv.), Pak.
126/D4 **Gumare,** Bots.
130/B5 **Gumbiro,** Tanz.
99/F2 **Gumma** (pref.), Japan
67/E6 **Gummersbach,** Ger.
86/E4 **Gümüşhacıköy,** Turk.
92/D1 **Gümüşhane,** Turk.
92/D1 **Gümüşhane** (prov.), Turk.
125/N5 **Guna** (peak), Eth.
106/C3 **Guna,** India
70/A6 **Gundelfingen,** Ger.
70/D5 **Gundelfingen an der Donau,** Ger.
70/C4 **Gundelsheim,** Ger.
108/F3 **Gundlupet,** India
92/B2 **Güney,** Turk.
92/D2 **Güneydogu Toroslar** (mts.), Turk.
157/J2 **Gunisao** (lake), Mb,Can
157/J2 **Gunisao** (riv.), Mb,Can
119/D1 **Gunnedah,** Austl.
158/F3 **Gunnison,** Co,US
158/F3 **Gunnison** (riv.), Co,US
158/E3 **Gunnison,** Ut,US
166/B5 **Gunpowder** (riv.), Md,US
102/B4 **Gunt** (riv.), Taj.
163/G3 **Guntersville,** Al,US
163/G3 **Guntersville** (dam), Al,US
163/G3 **Guntersville** (lake), Al,US
106/D4 **Guntūr,** India
112/A5 **Gunung Mulu Nat'l Park,** Malay.
70/D6 **Günz** (riv.), Ger.
70/D6 **Günzburg,** Ger.
70/D4 **Gunzenhausen,** Ger.
103/C4 **Guo** (riv.), China
103/D4 **Guoyang,** China
125/N6 **Guragē** (peak), Eth.
83/G2 **Gura Humorului,** Rom.
135/F2 **Gural** (mts.), Braz.
96/B2 **Gurbantünggut** (des.), China
108/C1 **Gurdāspur,** India
92/D1 **Gürgentepe,** Turk.
140/B3 **Gurguéia** (riv.), Braz.
139/F3 **Guri** (res.), Ven.
73/L3 **Gurk** (riv.), Aus.
73/K3 **Gurkthaler** (mts.), Aus.
165/Q15 **Gurnee,** Il,US
131/D3 **Guro,** Moz.
92/E2 **Güroymak,** Turk.
93/M7 **Gürpinar,** Turk.
83/J5 **Gürsu,** Turk.
92/D2 **Gürün,** Turk.
137/J6 **Gurupi,** Braz.
137/J4 **Gurupi** (mts.), Braz.
140/A1 **Gurupi** (riv.), Braz.
106/B3 **Guru Sikhar** (mtn.), India
131/C3 **Guruve,** Zim.
96/G2 **Gurvandzagal,** Mong.
87/J3 **Gur'yev,** Kaz.
87/J3 **Gur'yev Obl.,** Kaz.
103/C4 **Gushi,** China
100/J7 **Gushikawa,** Japan
84/J5 **Gus'-Khrustal'nyy,** Rus.
80/A3 **Guspini,** It.
63/S7 **Gustausberg,** Swe.
147/Q10 **Gustavo A. Marrero,** Mex.
64/G2 **Güstrow,** Ger.
67/F5 **Gütersloh,** Ger.
159/H4 **Guthrie,** Ok,US
159/G4 **Guthrie,** Tx,US
147/F4 **Gutiérrez Zamora,** Mex.
167/J8 **Guttenberg,** NJ,US
61/E3 **Gutulia Nat'l Park,** Nor.
103/B3 **Guxian,** China
139/G3 **Guyana**
53/S10 **Guyancourt,** Fr.
163/H2 **Guyandotte** (riv.), WV,US
103/B2 **Guyang,** China
72/C4 **Guyenne** (reg.), Fr.
119/E1 **Guy Fawkes Riv. Nat'l Park,** Austl.
59/G1 **Guyhirn,** Eng,UK
159/G3 **Guymon,** Ok,US
96/F4 **Guyuan,** China
96/H3 **Guyuan,** China
107/J2 **Guzhang,** China
103/D4 **Guzhen,** China
146/D2 **Guzman** (lake), Mex.
131/B3 **Gwaai,** Zim.
95/H3 **Gwādar,** Pak.
131/B3 **Gwai** (riv.), Zim.
106/C2 **Gwalior,** India
131/C4 **Gwanda,** Zim.
59/F1 **Gwash** (riv.), Eng,UK
58/C2 **Gwaunceste** (mtn.), Wal,UK
159/J3 **G. W. Carver Nat'l Mon.,** Mo,US
65/J2 **Gwda** (riv.), Pol.
58/A6 **Gweek,** Eng,UK
131/B3 **Gwembe,** Zam.
58/D3 **Gwent** (co.), Wal,UK
57/E5 **Gwersyllt,** Wal,UK
131/C3 **Gweru,** Zim.
119/D1 **Gwydir** (riv.), Austl.
56/D5 **Gwynedd** (co.), Wal,UK
107/F2 **Gyaca,** China
87/H4 **Gyandzhe,** Azer.
106/E2 **Gyangzê,** China
97/D5 **Gyaring** (lake), China
129/F5 **Gyasikan,** Gha.
88/H2 **Gyda** (pen.), Rus.
62/D4 **Gyldenløveshøj** (peak), Den.
118/D4 **Gympie,** Austl.
104/B5 **Gyobingauk,** Burma
82/E2 **Gyoma,** Hun.
82/D2 **Gyöngyös,** Hun.
82/C2 **Győr,** Hun.
82/C2 **Győr-Sopron** (co.), Hun.
82/E2 **Gyula,** Hun.

H

68/D2 **Haacht,** Belg.
66/D4 **Haaksbergen,** Neth.
68/D2 **Haaltert,** Belg.
66/E6 **Haan,** Ger.
121/H6 **Ha'apai Group** (isls.), Tonga
61/H2 **Haapavesi,** Fin.
63/K2 **Haapsalu,** Est.
71/E6 **Haar,** Ger.
70/A4 **Haardt** (mts.), Ger.
66/B4 **Haarlem,** Neth.
115/Q11 **Haast,** NZ
117/F2 **Haasts Bluff Abor. Land,** Austl.
95/J3 **Hab** (riv.), Pak.
96/B2 **Habahe,** China
71/F2 **Habartov,** Czh.
130/C2 **Habaswein,** Kenya
69/E4 **Habay,** Belg.
93/E3 **Habbānīyah,** Iraq
77/H3 **Habicht** (peak), Aus.
107/F3 **Habiganj,** Bang.
99/L10 **Habikino,** Japan
100/D2 **Habomai** (isls.), Rus.
100/B1 **Haboro,** Japan
139/F3 **Hacha** (falls), Ven.
67/F3 **Hache** (riv.), Ger.
97/N5 **Hachijō** (isl.), Japan
100/B3 **Hachimantai-Towada Nat'l Park,** Japan
100/A3 **Hachimori,** Japan
100/B3 **Hachinohe,** Japan
99/F3 **Hachiōji,** Japan
92/C2 **Hacıbektaş,** Turk.
164/C3 **Hacienda Heights,** Ca,US
92/C2 **Hacılar,** Turk.
117/H4 **Hack** (peak), Austl.
167/D2 **Hackensack,** NJ,US
167/J8 **Hackensack** (riv.), NJ, NY,US
166/D2 **Hackettstown,** NJ,US
53/N7 **Hackney** (bor.), Eng,UK
109/D1 **Ha Coi,** Viet.
108/B1 **Hadāli,** Pak.
70/B2 **Hadamar,** Ger.
99/F3 **Hadano,** Japan
127/D4 **Hadarba, Ras** (cape), Sudan
125/J4 **Haddad** (wadi), Chad
168/B3 **Haddam,** Ct,US
59/F3 **Haddenham,** Eng,UK
54/D5 **Haddington,** Sc,UK
166/C4 **Haddonfield,** NJ,US
166/C4 **Haddon** (Westmont), NJ,US
95/G4 **Ḩadd, Ra's al** (pt.), Ōman
129/H3 **Hadejia** (riv.), Nga.
67/F1 **Hadelner** (can.), Ger.
91/D3 **Ḩadera,** Isr.
62/C4 **Haderslev,** Den.
94/G5 **Hadhramaut** (region), Yem.
91/C1 **Hadım,** Turk.
123/S15 **Hadjout,** Alg.
82/E2 **Hadjú-Bihar** (co.), Hun.
152/F1 **Hadley** (bay), NW,Can
53/Q8 **Hadlow,** Eng,UK
57/F1 **Hadrian's Wall** (ruins), Eng,UK
61/E1 **Hadselfjorden** (fjord), Nor.
101/C3 **Haeju,** NKor.
101/C4 **Haeju** (bay), NKor.
154/S9 **Haena** (pt.), Hi,US
131/C4 **Haenertsburg,** SAfr.
92/D2 **Hafik,** Turk.
108/B1 **Hāfizābād,** Pak.
61/N7 **Hafnarfjördhur,** Ice.
94/E3 **Ḩafr al Bāṭin,** SAr.
93/G4 **Ḩaft Gel,** Iran
123/H3 **Hafun, Ras** (pt.), Som.
151/F4 **Hagemeister** (isl.), Ak,US
67/E6 **Hagen,** Ger.
67/E4 **Hagen am Teutoburger Wald,** Ger.
64/F2 **Hagenow,** Ger.
159/F4 **Hagerman,** NM,US
160/E4 **Hagerstown,** Md,US
62/E1 **Hagfors,** Swe.
98/B3 **Hagi,** Japan
109/D1 **Ha Giang,** Viet.
58/D2 **Hagley,** Eng,UK
69/F5 **Hagondange,** Fr.
60/A4 **Hags Head** (pt.), Ire.
157/G2 **Hague,** Sk,Can
72/C2 **Hague, Cap de la** (cape), Fr.
69/G6 **Haguenau,** Fr.
66/B4 **Hague, The** ('s-Gravenhage) (cap.), Neth.
120/D2 **Hahashima** (isl.), Jap.
67/H6 **Hahle** (riv.), Ger.
117/M9 **Hahndorf,** Austl.
69/G3 **Hahnenbach** (riv.), Ger.
103/D3 **Hai** (riv.), China
103/E4 **Hai'an,** China
99/L10 **Haibara,** Japan
101/B2 **Haicheng,** China
71/E3 **Haidenaab** (riv.), Ger.
109/D1 **Hai Duong,** Viet.
91/D3 **Haifa** (dist.), Isr.
91/D3 **Haifa** (Ḩefa), Isr.
105/G4 **Haifeng,** China
69/H2 **Haiger,** Ger.
70/B6 **Haigerloch,** Ger.
109/D1 **Hai Hau,** Viet.
105/F4 **Haikou,** China
97/H2 **Hailar,** China
97/J2 **Hailar** (riv.), China
160/E2 **Haileybury,** On,Can
105/F4 **Hailing** (isl.), China
59/G5 **Hailsham,** Eng,UK
97/K2 **Hailun,** China
103/E5 **Haimen,** China
105/F5 **Hainan** (isl.), China
105/F5 **Hainan** (prov.), China
105/F4 **Hainan** (str.), China
68/B2 **Hainaut** (prov.), Belg.
70/C1 **Hainburg,** Ger.
163/H4 **Haines City,** Fl,US
151/L3 **Haines Junction,** Yk,Can
67/H6 **Hainich** (mts.), Ger.
103/L9 **Haining,** China
109/D1 **Haiphong** (Hai Phong), Viet.
105/H3 **Haitan** (isl.), China
149/H2 **Haiti**
109/E2 **Hai Van** (pass), Viet.
107/K3 **Haixia** (str.), China
103/D3 **Haixing,** China
103/E3 **Haiyang,** China
101/B3 **Haiyang** (isl.), China
96/F4 **Haiyuan,** China
103/D4 **Haizhou** (bay), China
71/F2 **Háj** (peak), Czh.
65/L5 **Hajdú-Bihar** (co.), Hun.
82/E2 **Hajdúboszormény,** Hun.
82/E2 **Hajdúdorog,** Hun.
82/E2 **Hajdúhadház,** Hun.
82/E2 **Hajdúnánás,** Hun.
82/E2 **Hajdúszoboszló,** Hun.
99/F1 **Hajiki-zaki** (pt.), Japan
65/M2 **Hajnówka,** Pol.
107/F2 **Hājo,** India
121/L5 **Hakahau,** Fr.Pol.
117/G3 **Hakee** (peak), Austl.
93/E2 **Hakkâri** (prov.), Turk.
98/D3 **Hakken-san** (mtn.), Japan
100/B3 **Hakkōda-san** (mtn.), Japan
100/B3 **Hakodate,** Japan
99/H7 **Hakone,** Japan
99/H8 **Hakone-Fuji-Izu Nat'l Park,** Japan
99/E2 **Hakui,** Japan
99/M10 **Hakusan,** Japan
99/E2 **Haku-san** (mtn.), Japan
99/E2 **Hakusan Nat'l Park,** Japan
95/J3 **Hāla,** Pak.
92/D3 **Ḩalab** (prov.), Syria
91/E1 **Ḩalab** (Aleppo), Syria
93/F3 **Ḩalabjah,** Iraq
147/M6 **Halachó,** Mex.
127/D4 **Ḩalā'ib,** Sudan
112/C2 **Halcon** (mtn.), Phil.
62/D2 **Halden,** Nor.
64/F2 **Haldensleben,** Ger.
161/Q10 **Haldimand,** On,Can
96/G2 **Haldzan,** Mong.
116/C3 **Hale** (peak), Austl.
130/C4 **Hale,** Tanz.
57/F5 **Hale,** Eng,UK
154/T10 **Haleakala Nat'l Park,** Hi,US
167/J8 **Haledon,** NJ,US
69/E2 **Halen,** Belg.
165/P14 **Hales Corners,** Wi,US
58/D2 **Halesowen,** Eng,UK
59/H2 **Halesworth,** Eng,UK
163/G3 **Haleyville,** Al,US
128/E5 **Half Assini,** Gha.
166/A3 **Half Falls** (mtn.), Pa,US
165/K12 **Half Moon Bay,** Ca,US
91/D4 **Ḩalḩūl,** WBnk.
160/E2 **Haliburton** (hills), On,Can
118/B2 **Halifax** (bay), Austl.
161/J2 **Halifax** (cap.), NS,Can
57/G4 **Halifax,** Eng,UK
168/D2 **Halifax,** Ma,US
63/K1 **Halikko,** Fin.
93/J4 **Halīl** (riv.), Iran
63/T9 **Häljarp,** Swe.
151/H1 **Halkett** (cape), Ak,US
153/K2 **Hall** (pen.), NW,Can
120/E4 **Hall** (isls.), Micr.
151/D3 **Hall** (isl.), Ak,US
55/K7 **Halladale** (riv.), Sc,UK
166/B3 **Hallam** (Hellam), Pa,US
62/E3 **Halland** (co.), Swe.
97/K5 **Halla-san** (mtn.), SKor.
68/D2 **Halle,** Belg.
67/F4 **Halle,** Ger.
61/E4 **Hällefors,** Swe.
73/K3 **Hallein,** Aus.
68/A4 **Hallencourt,** Fr.
64/F3 **Halle-Neustadt,** Ger.
71/E5 **Hallertau** (reg.), Ger.
113/M **Hallett** (cape), Ant.
162/D4 **Hallettsville,** Tx,US
62/C1 **Hallingdalselvi** (riv.), Nor.
157/J3 **Hallock,** Mn,US
62/F2 **Hallsberg,** Swe.
63/R7 **Hallsfjärden** (lake), Swe.
70/D3 **Hallstadt,** Ger.
62/G2 **Hallstahammar,** Swe.
64/B4 **Hallu** (riv.), Fr.
68/B3 **Hallue** (riv.), Fr.
68/C2 **Halluin,** Fr.
76/E3 **Hallwilersee** (lake), Swi.
101/E5 **Hallyŏ Haesang Nat'l Park,** SKor.
111/G3 **Halmahera** (isl.), Indo.
111/G4 **Halmahera** (sea), Indo.
62/E3 **Halmstad,** Swe.
123/X17 **Ḩalq al Wādī,** Tun.
62/E3 **Hälsingborg,** Swe.
59/G3 **Halstead,** Eng,UK
66/B5 **Halsteren,** Neth.
96/C4 **Haltang** (riv.), China
57/H4 **Haltemprice,** Eng,UK
67/E5 **Haltern,** Ger.
161/Q8 **Halton** (co.), On,Can
161/Q8 **Halton Hills,** On,Can
57/F2 **Haltwhistle,** Eng,UK
67/E6 **Halver,** Ger.
67/E3 **Halverder Aa** (riv.), Ger.
68/C4 **Ham,** Fr.
98/C3 **Hamada,** Japan
93/G3 **Hamadān,** Iran
93/G3 **Hamadān** (gov.), Iran
91/E2 **Ḩamāh,** Syria
92/D3 **Ḩamāh** (prov.), Syria
99/M10 **Hamajima,** Japan
99/E3 **Hamakita,** Japan
99/E3 **Hamamatsu,** Japan
100/D2 **Hamanaka,** Japan
62/D1 **Hamar,** Nor.
127/C3 **Ḩamāṭah, Jabal** (mtn.), Egypt
100/C1 **Hamatombetsu,** Japan
106/D6 **Hambantota,** SrL.
59/E5 **Hamble,** Eng,UK
57/G3 **Hambleton** (hills), Eng,UK
67/G3 **Hambühren,** Ger.
67/G1 **Hamburg,** Ger.
67/H1 **Hamburg** (state), Ger.
162/F3 **Hamburg,** Ar,US
160/E3 **Hamburg,** NY,US
168/B3 **Hamden,** Ct,US
63/K1 **Häme** (prov.), Fin.
63/K1 **Hämeenkyrö,** Fin.
63/L1 **Hämeenlinna,** Fin.
116/B3 **Hamelin,** Austl.
116/B3 **Hamelin Pool** (bay), Austl.
67/G4 **Hameln,** Ger.
116/C2 **Hamersley** (range), Austl.
116/C2 **Hamersley Range Nat'l Park,** Austl.
59/H3 **Hamford Water** (inlet), Eng,UK
101/E2 **Hamgyŏng** (mts.), NKor.
101/D2 **Hamgyŏng-Namdo** (prov.), NKor.
101/D3 **Hamhŭng,** NKor.
101/D3 **Hamhŭng-Si** (prov.), NKor.
96/C3 **Hami,** China
112/D4 **Hamiguitan** (mtn.), Phil.
119/B3 **Hamilton,** Austl.
153/L3 **Hamilton** (inlet), Nf,Can
161/Q9 **Hamilton,** On,Can
161/Q9 **Hamilton** (har.), On,Can
115/S10 **Hamilton,** NZ
54/B5 **Hamilton,** Sc,UK
163/G3 **Hamilton,** Al,US
165/L12 **Hamilton** (mtn.), Ca,US
156/E4 **Hamilton,** Mt,US
160/C4 **Hamilton,** Oh,US
162/D4 **Hamilton,** Tx,US
167/K8 **Hamilton Grange Mem.,** NY,US
166/D3 **Hamilton Square-Mercerville,** NJ,US
63/M1 **Hamina,** Fin.
108/D2 **Hamīrpur,** India
67/E5 **Hamm,** Ger.
123/V17 **Hamma-Bouziane,** Alg.
123/X17 **Hammāmāt** (gulf), Tun.
123/Q16 **Hamman, Oued el** (riv.), Alg.
62/E2 **Hammarön** (isl.), Swe.
68/D1 **Hamme,** Belg.
67/F2 **Hamme** (riv.), Ger.
70/C2 **Hammelburg,** Ger.
166/B3 **Hammer** (cr.), Pa,US
61/G1 **Hammerfest,** Nor.
62/F4 **Hammershus,** Den.
53/N7 **Hammersmith & Fulham** (bor.), Eng,UK
66/D5 **Hamminkeln,** Ger.
168/B3 **Hammonasset** (pt.), Ct,US
165/R16 **Hammond,** In,US
163/F4 **Hammond,** La,US
53/N6 **Hammond Street,** Eng,UK
166/D4 **Hammonton,** NJ,US
55/P12 **Hamnavoe,** Sc,UK
69/E1 **Hamont-Achel,** Belg.
168/B1 **Hampden** (co.), Ma,US
59/E4 **Hampshire** (co.), Eng,UK
168/B1 **Hampshire** (co.), Ma,US
59/E4 **Hampshire Downs** (hills), Eng,UK
53/N7 **Hampstead,** Eng,UK
160/E4 **Hampton,** Va,US
167/F2 **Hampton Bays,** NY,US
53/M7 **Hampton Court,** Eng,UK
166/B5 **Hampton Nat'l Hist. Site,** Md,US
119/G6 **Hampton Park,** Austl.
124/H1 **Ḩamrā** (upland), Libya
165/F7 **Hamtramck,** Mi,US
99/H7 **Hamura,** Japan
101/E2 **Hamyŏng-Bukto** (prov.), NKor.
103/C5 **Han** (riv.), China
101/D4 **Han** (riv.), SKor.
100/B4 **Hanamaki,** Japan
154/U11 **Hanamalo** (pt.), Hi,US
97/M5 **Hanamatsu,** Japan
130/B4 **Hanang** (peak), Tanz.
70/B2 **Hanau,** Ger.
103/C5 **Hanchuan,** China
160/B2 **Hancock,** Mi,US
168/G6 **Hancock** (co.), WV,US
168/A1 **Hancock Shaker Village,** Ma,US
99/M10 **Handa,** Japan
103/C3 **Handan,** China
63/S7 **Handen,** Swe.
130/C4 **Handeni,** Tanz.
59/E1 **Handsworth,** Eng,UK
158/C3 **Hanford,** Ca,US
96/D2 **Hangayn** (mts.), Mong.
103/B3 **Hanggin Qi,** China
58/C5 **Hangingstone** (hill), Eng,UK
132/L11 **Hangklip** (cape), SAfr.
63/K2 **Hangö** (Hanko), Fin.
108/A1 **Hangu,** Pak.
103/L9 **Hangzhou,** China
96/C2 **Hanhöhiy** (mts.), Mong.
92/E2 **Hani,** Turk.
157/J4 **Hankinson,** ND,US
63/K2 **Hanko** (Hangö), Fin.
157/G3 **Hanley,** Sk,Can
156/F3 **Hanna,** Ab,Can
156/G5 **Hanna,** Wy,US
99/L10 **Hannan,** Japan
159/K3 **Hannibal,** Mo,US
99/H7 **Hannō,** Japan
67/G4 **Hannover,** Ger.
69/E2 **Hannut,** Belg.
62/F4 **Hanöbukten** (bay), Swe.
109/D1 **Hanoi** (Ha Noi) (cap.), Viet.
160/D2 **Hanover,** On,Can
143/J7 **Hanover** (isl.), Chile
168/D1 **Hanover,** Ma,US
161/F3 **Hanover,** NH,US
166/B4 **Hanover,** Pa,US
165/P16 **Hanover Park,** Il,US
164/B2 **Hansen** (dam), Ca,US
164/F7 **Hansen Dam Rec. Area,** Ca,US
103/D5 **Hanshan,** China
106/C2 **Hānsi,** India
168/D1 **Hanson,** Ma,US
102/D3 **Hantengri Feng** (peak), China
153/J2 **Hantzsch** (riv.), NW,Can
106/B2 **Hanumāngarh,** India
96/E2 **Hanuy** (riv.), Mong.
104/D2 **Hanyuan,** China
96/F5 **Hanzhong,** China
121/L6 **Hao** (atoll), FrPol.
61/H2 **Haparanda,** Swe.
117/M9 **Happy Valley** (res.), Austl.
153/K3 **Happy Valley-Goose Bay,** Nf,Can
96/D4 **Har** (lake), China
96/C2 **Har** (lake), Mong.
96/F2 **Haraa** (riv.), Mong.
99/G2 **Haramachi,** Japan
108/B2 **Harappa** (ruins), Pak.
131/C3 **Harare** (cap.), Zim.
96/F2 **Har-Ayrag,** Mong.
128/C5 **Harbel,** Libr.
97/K2 **Harbin,** China
91/E1 **Harbiye,** Turk.
161/L2 **Harbour Breton,** Nf,Can
59/E2 **Harbury,** Eng,UK
77/F3 **Hard,** Aus.
106/C3 **Hardā,** India
62/B1 **Hardangervidda Nat'l Park,** Nor.
132/B2 **Hardap** (dam), Namb.
67/H3 **Hardau** (riv.), Ger.
67/G5 **Hardegsen,** Ger.
66/D3 **Hardenberg,** Neth.
66/C4 **Harderwijk,** Neth.
70/C3 **Hardheim,** Ger.
156/G4 **Hardin,** Mt,US
95/L3 **Hardwār,** India
143/K8 **Hardy** (pen.), Chile
161/L1 **Hare** (bay), Nf,Can
68/C2 **Harelbeke,** Belg.
67/E3 **Haren,** Ger.
66/D2 **Haren,** Neth.
125/P6 **Hārer,** Eth.
91/G7 **Har Eval** (Jabal 'Aybāl) (mtn.), WBnk.
166/B4 **Harford** (co.), Md,US
125/P6 **Hargeysa,** Som.
83/G2 **Harghita** (co.), Rom.
83/G2 **Harghita** (peak), Rom.
63/K2 **Hari** (str.), Est.
110/B4 **Hari** (riv.), Indo.
106/C5 **Harihar,** India
98/D3 **Harima** (sound), Japan
66/B5 **Haringvliet** (chan.), Neth.
66/B5 **Haringvlietdam** (dam), Neth.
108/F4 **Haripād,** India
95/H2 **Harīrūd** (riv.), Afg.
63/K1 **Harjavalta,** Fin.
160/D4 **Harlan,** Ky,US
56/D6 **Harlech,** Wal,UK
167/K8 **Harlem,** NY,US
59/H2 **Harleston,** Eng,UK
66/C2 **Harlingen,** Neth.
162/D5 **Harlingen,** Tx,US

192

Harli – Hogar

59/F3 Harlington, Eng,UK
53/P6 Harlow, Eng,UK
156/F4 Harlowton, Mt,US
66/B4 Harmelen, Neth.
68/B3 Harnes, Fr.
156/D5 Harney (lake), Or,US
156/D5 Harney (val.), Or,US
157/H5 Harney (peak), SD,US
108/A1 Harnoli, Pak.
61/F3 Härnösand, Swe.
74/D1 Haro, Sp.
146/C3 Haro, Cabo (pt.), Mex.
59/F3 Harpenden, Eng,UK
151/L3 Harper (mtn.), Yk,Can
128/D5 Harper, Libr.
151/K3 Harper (mtn.), Ak,US
162/D2 Harper, Ks,US
160/E4 Harpers Ferry Nat'l Hist. Park, WV,US
165/G7 Harper Woods, Mi,US
97/H3 Harqin Qi, China
103/D2 Harqin Zuoyi Monggolzu Zizhixian, China
160/E1 Harricana (riv.), Qu,Can
163/G3 Harriman, Tn,US
167/D1 Harriman Saint Park, NY,US
117/G4 Harris (lake), Austl.
117/F3 Harris (peak), Austl.
55/H8 Harris (reg.), Sc,UK
160/B4 Harrisburg, Il,US
159/G2 Harrisburg, Ne,US
166/B3 Harrisburg (cap.), Pa,US
64/E1 Harrislee, Ger.
132/E3 Harrismith, SAfr.
156/C3 Harrison (lake), BC,Can
153/L3 Harrison (cape), Nf,Can
151/H1 Harrison (bay), Ak,US
162/E2 Harrison, Ar,US
159/G2 Harrison, Ne,US
167/J9 Harrison, NJ,US
167/E2 Harrison, NY,US
168/F7 Harrison (co.), Oh,US
160/E4 Harrisonburg, Va,US
160/C4 Harrodsburg, Ky,US
57/G4 Harrogate, Eng,UK
53/N7 Harrow, Eng,UK
53/M7 Harrow (bor.), Eng,UK
159/J3 Harry S Truman (res.), Mo,US
67/G2 Harsefeld, Ger.
67/F5 Harsewinkel, Ger.
61/F1 Harstad, Nor.
152/C2 Hart (riv.), Yk,Can
167/K8 Hart (isl.), NY,US
158/C2 Hart (lake), Or,US
132/C3 Hartbeesrivier (dry riv.), SAfr.
62/B1 Hårteigen (peak), Nor.
66/B5 Hartelkanaal (can.), Neth.
54/C6 Hart Fell (mtn.), Sc,UK
168/B2 Hartford (cap.), Ct,US
168/B2 Hartford (co.), Ct,US
160/C3 Hartford City, In,US
54/C5 Harthill, Sc,UK
159/H2 Hartington, Ne,US
58/B5 Hartland, Eng,UK
58/B4 Hartland (pt.), Eng,UK
58/D2 Hartlebury, Eng,UK
57/G2 Hartlepool, Eng,UK
53/P7 Hartley, Eng,UK
157/H3 Hartney, Mb,Can
132/D3 Harts (riv.), SAfr.
167/E1 Hartsdale, NY,US
163/G3 Hartselle, Al,US
59/E1 Hartshill, Eng,UK
165/B3 Hartstene (isl.), Wa,US
163/H3 Hartwell, Ga,US
163/H3 Hartwell (lake), Ga, SC,US
119/C4 Hartz Mtn. Nat'l Park, Austl.
69/G6 Hartzviller, Fr.
95/K3 Hārūnābād, Pak.
111/E3 Harun, Bukit (peak), Indo.
102/F2 Har Us (lake), Mong.
96/D2 Har-Us (riv.), Mong.
95/H2 Hārūt (riv.), Afg.
165/Q16 Harvey, Il,US
157/J4 Harvey, ND,US
166/B1 Harveys (lake), Pa,US
59/H3 Harwich, Eng,UK
57/G5 Harworth, Eng,UK
106/C2 Haryana (state), India
67/H5 Harz (mts.), Ger.
92/C2 Hasan (peak), Turk.
167/D2 Hasbrouck Heights, NJ,US
67/E3 Hase (riv.), Ger.
70/D1 Hasel (riv.), Ger.
67/E3 Haselünne, Ger.
76/D3 Hasenmalt (mtn.), Swi.
99/M9 Hashima, Japan
98/D3 Hashimoto, Japan
124/D2 Hasi el Farsia (well), WSah.
95/K3 Hāsilpur, Pak.
162/D3 Haskell, Tx,US
70/B6 Haslach im Kinzigtal, Ger.
59/F4 Haslemere, Eng,UK
165/F6 Hasler (cr.), Mi,US
57/F4 Haslingden, Eng,UK
57/F5 Haslington, Eng,UK
91/E1 Hassa, Turk.
106/C5 Hassan, India
70/D2 Hassberge (hills), Ger.
153/S7 Hassel (sound), NW,Can
69/E2 Hasselt, Belg.
66/D3 Hasselt, Neth.
70/D2 Hassfurt, Ger.
123/S16 Hassi Bahbah, Alg.
124/G1 Hassi Messaoud, Alg.
62/E3 Hässleholm, Swe.
70/B4 Hassloch, Ger.
115/S10 Hastings, NZ
55/M11 Hastings, UK
59/G5 Hastings, Eng,UK
160/C3 Hastings, Mi,US
157/K4 Hastings, Mn,US
159/H2 Hastings, Ne,US
59/G5 Hastings Battlesite, Eng,UK
167/E1 Hastings-on-Hudson, NY,US
99/H7 Hasuda, Japan
123/W18 Ḩaṭab (riv.), Tun.
99/M9 Hatashō, Japan
91/E1 Hatay (prov.), Turk.
166/C3 Hatboro, Pa,US
158/F4 Hatch, NM,US
109/B5 Hat Chao Mai Nat'l Park, Thai.
143/J7 Hatcher (peak), Arg.
82/F3 Haţeg, Rom.
53/N6 Hatfield, Eng,UK
119/E1 Hat Head Nat'l Park, Austl.
57/G5 Hathersage, Eng,UK
106/C2 Hāthras, India
94/C4 Ḩāţibah, Ra's (pt.), SAr.
109/D4 Ha Tien, Viet.
109/D2 Ha Tinh, Viet.
109/B5 Hat Nai Yang Nat'l Park, Thai.
99/H7 Hatogaya, Japan
150/D3 Hato Mayor, DRep.
99/H7 Hatoyama, Japan
106/C3 Hatta, India
119/B2 Hattah-Kulkyne Nat'l Park, Austl.
68/D4 Hattem, Neth.
67/F2 Hatten, Ger.
163/K3 Hatteras (cape), NC,US
70/B2 Hattersheim am Mein, Ger.
163/F4 Hattiesburg, Ms,US
67/E6 Hattingen, Ger.
57/G6 Hatton, Eng,UK
54/E2 Hatton, Sc,UK
63/L1 Hattula, Fin.
82/D2 Hatvan, Hun.
109/C5 Hat Yai, Thai.
67/F6 Hatzfeld, Ger.
109/E3 Hau Bon, Viet.
68/B2 Haubourdin, Fr.
125/Q6 Haud (reg.), Eth., Som.
62/A2 Haugesund, Nor.
109/D4 Hau Giang (riv.), Viet.
61/H2 Haukipudas, Fin.
70/C1 Haune (riv.), Ger.
71/F7 Haunsberg (peak), Aus.
167/E2 Hauppauge, NY,US
115/S10 Hauraki (gulf), NZ
62/A1 Haus, Nor.
63/L1 Hausjärvi, Fin.
75/E1 Hauskoa (mtn.), Fr.
77/F4 Hausstock (peak), Swi.
124/D1 Haut Atlas (mts.), Mor.
76/B1 Haute-Marne (dept.), Fr.
72/D2 Haute-Normandie (reg.), Fr.
161/G1 Hauterive, Qu,Can
76/B2 Haute-Saône (dept.), Fr.
76/C5 Haute-Savoie (dept.), Fr.
69/E3 Hautes Fagnes (uplands), Belg.
68/C3 Hautmont, Fr.
76/B1 Hautmont, Côte de (hill), Fr.
76/D2 Haut-Rhin (dept.), Fr.
53/S10 Hauts-de-Seine (dept.), Fr.
130/A2 Haut-Zaire (reg.), Zaire
149/F1 Havana (La Habana) (cap.), Cuba
121/V13 Havannah (chan.), NCal.
59/F5 Havant, Eng,UK
158/D4 Havasu (lake), Az, Ca,US
65/G2 Havel (riv.), Ger.
64/G2 Havelland (reg.), Ger.
163/J3 Havelock, NC,US
115/S10 Havelock North, NZ
59/G3 Havengore (isl.), Eng,UK
58/B3 Haverfordwest, Wal,UK
59/G2 Haverhill, Eng,UK
161/G3 Haverhill, Ma,US
53/P7 Havering (bor.), Eng,UK
167/E1 Haverstraw, NY,US
65/K4 Havířov, Czh.
67/E5 Havixbeck, Ger.
65/H4 Havlíčkův Brod, Czh.
156/F3 Havre, Mt,US
166/B4 Havre de Grace, Md,US
161/J1 Havre-Saint-Pierre, Qu,Can
83/H5 Havsa, Turk.
92/C1 Havza, Turk.
154/S10 Hawaii (state), US
154/U11 Hawaii (isl.), Hi,US
121/H2 Hawaiian (isls.), Hi,US
164/F8 Hawaiian Gardens, Ca,US
154/U11 Hawaii Volcanoes Nat'l Park, Hi,US
93/G4 Ḩawallī, Kuw.
57/E5 Hawarden, Wal,UK
157/J5 Hawarden, Ia,US
115/R10 Hawera, NZ
57/F3 Hawes, Eng,UK
57/F2 Haweswater (res.), Eng,UK
54/D6 Hawick, Sc,UK
119/E2 Hawke (cape), Austl.
115/S10 Hawke (bay), NZ
118/G8 Hawkesbury (riv.), Austl.
156/A2 Hawkesbury (isl.), BC,Can
160/F2 Hawkesbury, On,Can
150/C1 Hawks Nest (pt.), Bahm.
93/F4 Hawr al Ḩammār (lake), Iraq
91/B4 Ḩawsh 'Īsá, Egypt
164/B3 Hawthorne, Ca,US
167/J8 Hawthorne, NJ,US
158/C3 Hawthorne, Nv,US
57/G3 Haxby, Eng,UK
118/C3 Hay (pt.), Austl.
117/H3 Hay (riv.), Austl.
152/E3 Hay (riv.), Ab, NW,Can
100/B4 Hayachine-san (mtn.), Japan
99/H7 Hayama, Japan
69/F5 Hayange, Fr.
57/F5 Haydock, Eng,UK
57/F2 Haydon Bridge, Eng,UK
152/G3 Hayes (riv.), Mb,Can
152/G2 Hayes (riv.), NW,Can
153/T7 Hayes (pen.), Grld.
53/M7 Hayes, Eng,UK
151/J3 Hayes (mtn.), Ak,US
58/A6 Hayle, Eng,UK
58/A6 Hayle (riv.), Eng,UK
59/F5 Hayling (isl.), Eng,UK
92/C2 Haymana, Turk.
162/E3 Haynesville, La,US
58/C2 Hay on Wye, Wal,UK
83/H5 Hayrabolu, Turk.
159/H3 Hays, Ks,US
159/H3 Haysville, Ks,US
165/K11 Hayward, Ca,US
160/B2 Hayward, Wi,US
59/F5 Haywards Heath, Eng,UK
93/J4 Hazār (mtn.), Iran
160/D4 Hazard, Ky,US
106/E3 Hazāribag, India
68/B2 Hazebrouck, Fr.
57/F5 Hazel Grove, Eng,UK
165/F7 Hazel Park, Mi,US
153/R7 Hazen (str.), NW,Can
151/E3 Hazen (bay), Ak,US
66/B4 Hazerswoude-Dorp, Neth.
163/F4 Hazlehurst, Ms,US
59/F3 Hazlemere, Eng,UK
167/D3 Hazlet, NJ,US
156/B2 Hazleton (mts.), BC,Can
166/C2 Hazleton, Pa,US
117/F2 Hazlett (lake), Austl.
99/N10 Hazu, Japan
105/G3 He (riv.), China
59/G1 Heacham, Eng,UK
59/G4 Headcorn, Eng,UK
57/G4 Headingley, Eng,UK
131/D3 Headlands, Zim.
158/B3 Healdsburg, Ca,US
119/G5 Healesville, Austl.
57/G6 Heanor, Eng,UK
131/C4 Heany Junction, Zim.
51/P8 Heard (isl.), Austl.
162/D4 Hearne, Tx,US
113/V Hearst (isl.), Ant.
160/D1 Hearst, On,Can
157/H4 Heart (riv.), ND,US
54/D5 Heart Law (hill), Sc,UK
161/J1 Heath (pt.), Qu,Can
118/G9 Heathcote Nat'l Park, Austl.
59/G5 Heathfield, Eng,UK
162/D5 Hebbronville, Tx,US
57/F4 Hebden Bridge, Eng,UK
103/G6 Hebei (prov.), China
162/E3 Heber Springs, Ar,US
103/C4 Hebi, China
52/C3 Hebrides (isls.), Sc,UK
55/H8 Hebrides (sea), Sc,UK
55/H8 Hebrides, Inner (isls.), Sc,UK
55/G8 Hebrides, Outer (isls.), Sc,UK
168/B2 Hebron, Ct,US
159/H2 Hebron, Ne,US
91/D4 Hebron (Al Khalīl), WBnk.
151/M5 Hecate (str.), BC,Can
105/F3 Hechi, China
70/B6 Hechingen, Ger.
69/E1 Hechtel, Belg.
104/E2 Hechuan, China
57/H6 Heckington, Eng,UK
157/J4 Hecla, SD,US
153/R7 Hecla and Griper (bay), NW,Can
156/D3 Hector (peak), Ab,Can
62/C2 Heddal, Nor.
62/F1 Hedemora, Swe.
105/F4 Hedi (res.), China
62/D1 Hedmark (co.), Nor.
100/K7 Hedo-misaki (cape), Japan
57/H4 Hedon, Eng,UK
67/E4 Heek, Ger.
66/B3 Heemskerk, Neth.
66/B4 Heemstede, Neth.
66/D4 Heerde, Neth.
66/C3 Heerenveen, Neth.
66/B3 Heerhugowaard, Neth.
69/E2 Heerlen, Neth.
69/E2 Heers, Belg.
66/C5 Heesch, Neth.
66/C6 Heeze, Neth.
91/D3 Ḩefa (Haifa), Isr.
103/D5 Hefei, China
103/B5 Hefeng Tujiazu Zizhixian, China
97/L2 Hegang, China
77/E2 Hegau (reg.), Ger.
99/L10 Heguri, Japan
96/D4 Hei (riv.), China
100/B4 Hei (riv.), Japan
103/B3 Heicha Shan (mtn.), China
64/E1 Heide, Ger.
119/G5 Heidelberg, Austl.
70/B4 Heidelberg, Ger.
133/E2 Heidelberg, SAfr.
163/F4 Heidelberg, Ms,US
66/D5 Heiden, Ger.
70/D5 Heidenheim, Ger.
97/K1 Heihe, China
64/F1 Heikendorf, Ger.
132/D2 Heilbron, SAfr.
70/C4 Heilbronn, Ger.
70/D4 Heilbronn, Ger.
64/F1 Heiligenhafen, Ger.
66/D6 Heiligenhaus, Ger.
67/H6 Heiligenstadt, Ger.
97/L2 Heilong (Amur) (riv.), China
66/B3 Heiloo, Neth.
70/D4 Heilsbronn, Ger.
61/N7 Heimaey (isl.), Ice.
154/V12 Heimano (stream), Hi,US
66/D4 Heino, Neth.
63/M1 Heinola, Fin.
66/D6 Heinsberg, Ger.
101/B2 Heishan, China
103/C3 Heituo Shan (mtn.), China
99/M9 Heiwa, Japan
103/D3 Hejian, China
103/B4 Hejin, China
102/E3 Hejing, China
92/D2 Hekimhan, Turk.
99/M10 Hekinan, Japan
61/N7 Hekla (vol.), Ice.
107/H3 Hekou, China
96/F4 Helan (mts.), China
70/D2 Heldburg, Ger.
66/D6 Helden, Neth.
116/L6 Helena (brook), Austl.
163/F3 Helena, Ar,US
156/E4 Helena (cap.), Mt,US
54/B4 Helensburgh, Sc,UK
62/F3 Helgasjön (lake), Swe.
64/D1 Helgoland (isl.), Ger.
64/D1 Helgoländer Bucht (bay), Ger.
141/H7 Heliodora, Braz.
63/T8 Hellebæk, Den.
93/G4 Ḩelleh (riv.), Iran
66/D4 Hellendoorn, Neth.
69/F3 Hellenthal, Ger.
66/B5 Hellevoetsluis, Neth.
74/E3 Hellín, Sp.
156/D4 Hells (canyon), Id, Or,US
156/D4 Hells Canyon Nat'l Rec. Area, Id, Or,US
130/C3 Hell's Gate Nat'l Park, Kenya
95/H2 Helmand (riv.), Afg.
71/E2 Helmbrechts, Ger.
64/F3 Helme (riv.), Ger.
151/K2 Helmet (mtn.), Ak,US
66/C6 Helmond, Neth.
57/G3 Helmsley, Eng,UK
64/F2 Helmstedt, Ger.
97/K3 Helong, China
158/E3 Helper, Ut,US
71/G6 Helpfau-Uttendorf, Aus.
57/F5 Helsby, Eng,UK
76/E5 Helsenhorn (peak), Swi.
63/T8 Helsinge, Den.
63/L1 Helsingfors (Helsinki) (cap.), Fin.
63/T8 Helsingør, Den.
63/L1 Helsinki (Helsingfors) (cap.), Fin.
58/A6 Helston, Eng,UK
61/G3 Helvetinjärven Nat'l Park, Fin.
60/C5 Helvick (pt.), Ire.
68/C2 Hem, Fr.
68/B2 Hem (riv.), Fr.
71/E4 Hemau, Ger.
53/M6 Hemel Hempstead, Eng,UK
67/E6 Hemer, Ger.
164/D3 Hemet, Ca,US
67/G4 Hemmingen, Ger.
67/G1 Hemmoor, Ger.
162/E4 Hemphill, Tx,US
167/E2 Hempstead, NY,US
167/L8 Hempstead (har.), NY,US
59/H1 Hemsby, Eng,UK
57/G4 Hemsworth, Eng,UK
103/B4 Henan (prov.), China
74/D2 Henares (riv.), Sp.
100/A3 Henashi-zaki (pt.), Japan
72/C5 Hendaye, Fr.
83/K5 Hendek, Turk.
142/E3 Henderson, Arg.
121/N7 Henderson (isl.), Pitc.
160/C4 Henderson, Ky,US
163/J2 Henderson, NC,US
158/D3 Henderson, Nv,US
163/F3 Henderson, Tn,US
162/E3 Henderson, Tx,US
165/B3 Henderson (bay), Wa,US
163/H3 Hendersonville, NC,US
163/G2 Hendersonville, Tn,US
53/N7 Hendon, Eng,UK
66/B5 Hendrik-Ido-Ambacht, Neth.
139/G3 Hendrik Top (peak), Sur.
132/D3 Hendrik Verwoerdam (res.), SAfr.
59/F5 Henfield, Eng,UK
103/L8 Heng (isl.), China
105/G3 Heng (peak), China
104/D3 Heng (riv.), China
107/K2 Hengdong, China
104/C2 Hengduan (mts.), China
66/D4 Hengelo, Neth.
71/G5 Hengersberg, Ger.
103/B4 Hengku, China
103/B3 Hengshan, China
103/C3 Heng Shan (mtn.), China
103/C3 Hengshui, China
105/F4 Heng Xian, China
105/G3 Hengyang, China
68/B3 Hénin-Beaumont, Fr.
117/M8 Henley Beach, Austl.
59/F3 Henley-on-Thames, Eng,UK
166/C6 Henlopen (cape), De,US
59/E2 Henly-in-Arden, Eng,UK
72/B3 Hennebont, Fr.
69/G2 Hennef, Ger.
69/E2 Henri-Chapelle, Belg.
162/D3 Henrietta, Tx,US
153/H3 Henrietta Maria (cape), On,Can
139/E2 Henri Pittier Nat'l Park, Ven.
151/M5 Henry (cape), BC,Can
158/E3 Henry (mts.), Ut,US
159/J4 Henryetta, Ok,US
165/F7 Henry Ford Museum & Greenfield Vill., Mi,US
68/C3 Hensies, Belg.
96/F2 Hentiyn (mts.), Mong.
104/B5 Henzada, Burma
70/B3 Heppenheim an der Bergstrasse, Ger.
105/F4 Hepu, China
104/D3 Heqing, China
103/B3 Hequ, China
61/N6 Heradhsvötn (riv.), Ice.
95/H2 Herāt, Afg.
75/G1 Hérault (riv.), Fr.
118/B2 Herbert (riv.), Austl.
156/G3 Herbert, Sk,Can
118/B2 Herbert Riv. (falls), Austl.
118/B2 Herbert Riv. Falls Nat'l Park, Austl.
53/S10 Herblay, Fr.
76/D1 Herbolzheim, Ger.
70/D5 Herbrechtingen, Ger.
82/D4 Hercegnovi, Yugo.
165/K10 Hercules, Ca,US
67/E6 Herdecke, Ger.
69/G2 Herdorf, Ger.
149/E4 Heredia, CR
58/D2 Hereford, Eng,UK
166/D5 Hereford (inlet), NJ,US
162/C3 Hereford, Tx,US
58/D2 Hereford & Worcester (co.), Eng,UK
121/L6 Hereheretue (isl.), FrPol.
83/J5 Hereke, Turk.
74/C3 Herencia, Sp.
69/D1 Herentals, Belg.
67/F4 Herford, Ger.
76/C2 Héricourt, Fr.
159/H3 Herington, Ks,US
77/F3 Herisau, Swi.
69/E2 Herk (riv.), Belg.
69/E2 Herk-de-Stad, Belg.
96/G2 Herlen (riv.), Mong.
63/T9 Herlev, Den.
55/P12 Herma Ness (pt.), Sc,UK
67/F2 Hermann, Mo,US
67/H3 Hermannsburg, Ger.
117/G2 Hermannsburg Abor. Land, Austl.
68/B5 Hermes, Fr.
156/D4 Hermiston, Or,US
168/G5 Hermitage, Pa,US
91/D3 Hermon (mtn.), Leb., Syria
164/B3 Hermosa Beach, Ca,US
146/C2 Hermosillo, Mex.
142/E2 Hernando, Arg.
163/F3 Hernando, Ms,US
74/E1 Hernani, Sp.
68/D2 Herne, Belg.
67/E5 Herne, Ger.
59/H4 Herne Bay, Eng,UK
62/C3 Herning, Den.
91/G8 Herodian (ruins), WBnk.
91/G8 Herodion Nat'l Park, WBnk.
146/B2 Heroica Caborca, Mex.
70/E3 Heroldsberg, Ger.
70/D1 Herpf (riv.), Ger.
70/B5 Herrenberg, Ger.
147/J5 Herrero (pt.), Mex.
70/D4 Herrieden, Ger.
77/H2 Herrsching am Ammersee, Ger.
72/D5 Hers (riv.), Fr.
71/E3 Hersbruck, Ger.
67/E6 Herscheid, Ger.
151/L2 Herschel, Yk,Can
69/D1 Herselt, Belg.
166/B3 Hershey, Pa,US
69/E2 Herstal, Belg.
59/G5 Herstmonceux, Eng,UK
67/E5 Herten, Ger.
59/F3 Hertford, Eng,UK
53/N6 Hertfordshire (co.), Eng,UK
69/E2 Herve, Belg.
118/D4 Hervey (bay), Austl.
118/D4 Hervey Bay, Austl.
70/B4 Herxheim bei Landau, Ger.
67/H5 Herzberg am Harz, Ger.
67/F5 Herzebrock-Clarholz, Ger.
68/C2 Herzele, Belg.
91/F7 Herzliyya, Isr.
70/D3 Herzogenaurach, Ger.
82/B1 Herzogenburg, Aus.
69/F2 Herzogenrath, Ger.
69/D3 Hesbaye (plat.), Belg.
105/F4 Heshan, China
96/F4 Heshui, China
103/C3 Heshun, China
69/F4 Hesperange, Lux.
164/C2 Hesperia, Ca,US
151/M3 Hess (riv.), Yk,Can
67/G6 Hesse (state), Ger.
67/F5 Hessel (riv.), Ger.
67/G6 Hessisch Lichtenau, Ger.
67/G4 Hessisch Oldendorf, Ger.
57/H4 Hessle, Eng,UK
57/E5 Heswall, Eng,UK
165/L11 Hetch Hetchy (aqueduct), Ca,US
157/H4 Hettinger, ND,US
57/G2 Hetton-le-Hole, Eng,UK
70/C5 Heubach, Ger.
67/E5 Heubach (riv.), Ger.
70/B1 Heuchelheim, Ger.
65/H5 Heukuppe (peak), Aus.
69/E1 Heusden-Zolder, Belg.
70/B2 Heusenstamm, Ger.
69/F5 Heusweiler, Ger.
72/D2 Hève, Cap de la (cape), Fr.
82/E2 Heves, Hun.
65/L5 Heves (co.), Hun.
167/L9 Hewlett, NY,US
167/E2 Hewlett (pt.), NY,US
77/G3 Hexenkopf (peak), Aus.
57/F2 Hexham, Eng,UK
103/D5 He Xian, China
97/H3 Hexigten, China
97/H3 Hexigten Qi, China
132/L10 Hex River (mts.), SAfr.
132/L10 Hex River (pass), SAfr.
93/N7 Heybeli (isl.), Turk.
57/F3 Heysham, Eng,UK
66/C6 Heythuysen, Neth.
57/F4 Heywood, Eng,UK
103/C4 Heze, China
104/E3 Hezhang, China
163/H5 Hialeah, Fl,US
159/J3 Hiawatha, Ks,US
157/K4 Hibbing, Mn,US
119/C4 Hibbs (pt.), Austl.
149/F1 Hicacos (pt.), Cuba
154/W13 Hickam A.F.B., Hi,US
151/M4 Hickman (mtn.), BC,Can
160/B4 Hickman, Ky,US
165/Q16 Hickory (cr.), Il,US
163/H3 Hickory, NC,US
166/C1 Hickory Run Saint Park, Pa,US
167/E2 Hicksville, NY,US
99/E3 Hida (riv.), Japan
100/C2 Hidaka, Japan
99/H7 Hidaka, Japan
100/C2 Hidaka (mts.), Japan
98/D4 Hidaka (riv.), Japan
147/E3 Hidalgo, Mex.
148/B1 Hidalgo (state), Mex.
67/F4 Hiddenhausen, Ger.
140/B2 Hidrolândia, Braz.
92/B2 Hierapolis (ruins), Turk.
67/E2 Hieve (lake), Ger.
99/H7 Higashikurume, Japan
99/H7 Higashimurayama, Japan
99/G1 Higashine, Japan
99/L10 Higashi-Ōsaka, Japan
99/K10 Higashiura, Japan
99/H7 Higashiyamato, Japan
99/L10 Higashiyoshino, Japan
156/C5 High (des.), Or,US
166/C1 High (hill), Pa,US
59/F2 Higham Ferrers, Eng,UK
58/D4 Highbridge, Eng,UK
162/E4 High Island, Tx,US
54/B2 Highland (reg.), Sc,UK
164/C2 Highland, Ca,US
150/A1 Highland (pt.), Fl,US
165/R16 Highland, In,US
165/Q15 Highland Park, Il,US
165/F7 Highland Park, Mi,US
166/D3 Highland Park, NJ,US
58/D2 Highley, Eng,UK
157/J4 Highmore, SD,US
112/C2 High Park (mtn.), Phil.
163/H3 High Point, NC,US
166/D1 High Point (peak), NJ,US
166/D2 High Point Saint Park, NJ,US
156/D2 High Prairie, Ab,Can
157/H2 Highrock (lake), Mb,Can
57/F3 High Street (mtn.), Eng,UK
57/E4 Hightown, Eng,UK
58/B5 High Willhays (hill), Eng,UK
59/E3 Highworth, Eng,UK
59/F3 High Wycombe, Eng,UK
150/D3 Higüey, DRep.
91/B4 Hihyā, Egypt
61/J3 Hiidenportin Nat'l Park, Fin.
63/K2 Hiiumaa (isl.), Est.
94/C3 Hijāz, Jabal al (mts.), SAr.
98/B4 Hiji, Japan
142/Q9 Hijuelas de Conchalí, Chile
99/L9 Hikami, Japan
98/E3 Hikone, Japan
121/L6 Hikueru (atoll), FrPol.
115/S10 Hikurangi (peak), NZ
69/H2 Hilchenbach, Ger.
70/D2 Hildburghausen, Ger.
66/D6 Hilden, Ger.
67/G4 Hildesheim, Ger.
166/B3 Hill (isl.), Pa,US
150/G4 Hillaby (mtn.), Bar.
113/L Hillary (coast), Ant.
159/H3 Hill City, Ks,US
167/D1 Hillcrest, NY,US
67/F4 Hille, Ger.
66/B4 Hillegom, Neth.
62/E4 Hillerød, Den.
56/B2 Hillhall, NI,UK
53/M7 Hillingdon (bor.), Eng,UK
54/C1 Hill of Fearn, Sc,UK
157/J4 Hillsboro, ND,US
158/F4 Hillsboro, NM,US
160/D4 Hillsboro, Oh,US
156/C4 Hillsboro, Or,US
162/D3 Hillsboro, Tx,US
118/C3 Hillsborough (chan.), Austl.
56/B3 Hillsborough, NI,UK
165/K11 Hillsborough, Ca,US
166/D3 Hillsborough, NJ,US
160/C3 Hillsdale, Mi,US
167/D1 Hillsdale, NJ,US
54/D3 Hillside, Sc,UK
167/D2 Hillside, NJ,US
55/P12 Hillswick, Sc,UK
56/B3 Hilltown, NI,UK
154/U11 Hilo, Hi,US
112/D3 Hilonghilong (mtn.), Phil.
70/E4 Hilpoltstein, Ger.
57/E3 Hilpsford (pt.), Eng,UK
163/H3 Hilton Head (isl.), SC,US
163/H3 Hilton Head Island, SC,US
66/C6 Hilvarenbeek, Neth.
66/C4 Hilversum, Neth.
77/E2 Hilzingen, Ger.
108/D2 Himachal Pradesh (state), India
106/D2 Himalaya, Great (range), Asia
112/C3 Himamaylan, Phil.
98/D3 Himeji, Japan
98/D3 Himeji Castle, Japan
99/E2 Himi, Japan
125/N5 Himora, Eth.
91/E2 Ḩimş, Syria
92/D3 Ḩimş (prov.), Syria
112/D3 Hinatuan, Phil.
149/H2 Hinche, Haiti
115/H3 Hinchinbrook (isl.), Austl.
151/J3 Hinchinbrook (chan.), Ak,US
118/B2 Hinchinbrook I. Nat'l Park, Austl.
59/E1 Hinckley, Eng,UK
117/G5 Hincks Consv. Park, Austl.
57/H2 Hinderwell, Eng,UK
57/F4 Hindley, Eng,UK
119/B2 Hindmarsh (lake), Austl.
95/J1 Hindu Kush (mts.), Afg., Pak.
106/C5 Hindupur, India
163/H4 Hinesville, Ga,US
106/C3 Hinganghāt, India
95/J3 Hingol (riv.), Pak.
106/C4 Hingoli, India
95/J3 Hingorja, Pak.
92/E2 Hınıs, Turk.
99/H7 Hino, Japan
99/M9 Hino (riv.), Japan
99/H7 Hinode, Japan
99/H7 Hinohara, Japan
74/C3 Hinojosa del Duque, Sp.
98/C3 Hino-misaki (cape), Japan
165/Q16 Hinsdale, Il,US
57/F6 Hinstock, Eng,UK
67/E2 Hinte, Ger.
77/F4 Hinterrhein (riv.), Swi.
77/F3 Hinterrugg (peak), Swi.
156/D2 Hinton, Ab,Can
160/D4 Hinton, WV,US
112/D3 Hinunangan, Phil.
77/E3 Hinwil, Swi.
57/G3 Hipswell, Eng,UK
99/L9 Hira (mts.), Japan
98/A4 Hirado, Japan
98/D3 Hirakata, Japan
106/D3 Hirakud (res.), India
130/C3 Hiraman (riv.), Kenya
100/B3 Hiranai, Japan
100/H8 Hirara, Japan
98/C3 Hirata, Japan
99/H7 Hiratsuka, Japan
92/C2 Hirfanlı (dam), Turk.
83/H2 Hîrlău, Rom.
100/C2 Hiro'o, Japan
100/B3 Hirosaki, Japan
98/C3 Hiroshima, Japan
98/C3 Hiroshima (pref.), Japan
70/E3 Hirschaid, Ger.
71/E3 Hirschau, Ger.
68/D4 Hirson, Fr.
83/H3 Hîrşova, Rom.
62/C3 Hirtshals, Den.
58/C3 Hirwaun, Wal,UK
98/E3 Hisai, Japan
106/C2 Hisār, India
92/E2 Hishig-Öndör, Mong.
150/C2 Hispaniola (isl.), DRep., Haiti
93/E3 Hīt, Iraq
99/G2 Hitachi, Japan
99/G2 Hitachi-ōta, Japan
59/F3 Hitchin, Eng,UK
98/B4 Hitoyoshi, Japan
61/C3 Hitra (isl.), Nor.
63/T8 Hittarp, Swe.
121/M5 Hiva Oa (isl.), FrPol.
99/L9 Hiyoshi, Japan
62/F2 Hjälmaren (lake), Swe.
84/B2 Hjartfjellet (peak), Nor.
63/U9 Hjärup, Swe.
62/F2 Hjo, Swe.
62/C3 Hjørring, Den.
109/B1 Hka (riv.), Burma
104/C2 Hkakabo (peak), Burma
65/J4 Hlohovec, Slvk.
118/G8 Hmas-Nirimba, Austl.
104/C5 Hmawbi, Burma
129/F5 Ho, Gha.
109/D1 Hoa Bin, Viet.
109/E4 Hoa Da, Viet.
109/C1 Hoang Lien (mts.), Viet.
153/K2 Hoare (bay), NW,Can
99/G2 Hobara, Japan
119/C4 Hobart, Austl.
159/H4 Hobart, Ok,US
113/Q Hobbs (coast), Ant.
159/G4 Hobbs, NM,US
68/D1 Hoboken, Belg.
167/D2 Hoboken, NJ,US
102/E2 Hoboksar Monggol Zizhixian (Hoboksar), China
62/C3 Hobro, Den.
125/Q6 Hobyo, Som.
82/A2 Hochalmspitze (peak), Aus.
70/C3 Höchberg, Ger.
77/F3 Hochfinsler (peak), Swi.
77/G3 Hochgrat (peak), Ger.
70/B2 Hochheim am Main, Ger.
109/D4 Ho Chi Minh City (Saigon), Viet.
104/E4 Ho Chi Minh Mausoleum, Viet.
73/K3 Hochkönig (peak), Aus.
101/D2 Hŏch'ŏn (riv.), NKor.
73/L3 Hochschwab (peak), Aus.
69/G3 Hochsimmer (peak), Ger.
70/D3 Höchstadt an der Aisch, Ger.
70/B3 Höchst im Odenwald, Ger.
77/G3 Hochvogel (peak), Aus.
77/F4 Hochwang (peak), Swi.
70/B4 Hockenheim, Ger.
59/G3 Hockley, Eng,UK
57/F4 Hodder (riv.), Eng,UK
53/N6 Hoddesdon, Eng,UK
164/C4 Hodges (lake), Ca,US
156/G3 Hodgeville, Sk,Can
128/C2 Hodh (reg.), Mrta.
91/F7 Hod HaSharon, Isr.
128/D2 Hodh ech Chargui (reg.), Mrta.
128/C2 Hodh el Gharbi (reg.), Mrta.
82/E2 Hódmezővásárhely, Hun.
123/T16 Hodna, Chott el (salt lake), Alg.
57/F6 Hodnet, Eng,UK
65/J4 Hodonín, Czh.
69/E2 Hoegnel (riv.), Belg.
66/B5 Hoekse Waard (polder), Neth.
69/G6 Hoenheim, Fr.
69/E2 Hoensbroek, Neth.
69/E2 Hoeselt, Belg.
66/C4 Hoevelaken, Neth.
66/B5 Hoeven, Neth.
130/B2 Hoeys Bridge, Kenya
71/E2 Hof, Ger.
165/P15 Hoffman Estates, Il,US
67/G6 Hofgeismar, Ger.
103/B3 Hofong Qagan (salt lake), China
62/G1 Hofors, Swe.
61/P6 Hofsá (riv.), Ice.
61/N7 Hofsjökull (glac.), Ice.
98/B3 Hōfu, Japan
117/H2 Hogarth (peak), Austl.

66/C4 Hoge Veluwe Nat'l Park, Neth.
130/C4 Hogoro, Tanz.
67/G6 Hohegrass (peak), Ger.
71/E6 Hohenbrunn, Ger.
77/F3 Hohenems, Aus.
67/H4 Hohenhameln, Ger.
70/C4 Hohenloher Ebene (plain), Ger.
71/E1 Hohenwarte-Stausee (res.), Ger.
73/K3 Hoher Dachstein (peak), Aus.
73/K3 Hohe Tauern (mts.), Aus.
73/K3 Hohe Tauern Nat'l Park, Aus.
76/D4 Hohgant (peak), Swi.
103/B2 Hohhot, China
76/D1 Hohneck (mtn.), Fr.
69/G3 Höhr-Grenzhausen, Ger.
102/F4 Hoh Sai (lake), China
102/F4 Hoh Xil (lake), China
102/E4 Hoh Xil (mts.), China
109/E3 Hoi An, Viet.
130/A2 Hoima, Ugan.
162/D2 Hoisington, Ks,US
109/D1 Hoi Xuan, Viet.
98/C4 Hōjō, Japan
115/R11 Hokitika, NZ
100/C2 Hokkaidō (dept.), Japan
100/B2 Hokkaidō (isl.), Japan
62/C2 Hokksund, Nor.
99/G2 Hokota, Japan
99/K10 Hokudan, Japan
99/M9 Hokusei, Japan
130/D3 Hola, Kenya
62/D4 Holbaek, Den.
57/J6 Holbeach, Eng,UK
59/H3 Holbrook, Eng,UK
158/E4 Holbrook, Az,US
168/C1 Holbrook, Ma,US
168/C1 Holden, Ma,US
159/H4 Holdenville, Ok,US
57/H4 Holderness (pen.), Eng,UK
159/H2 Holdrege, Ne,US
149/G1 Holguín, Cuba
151/G3 Holitna (riv.), Ak,US
166/B6 Holland (pt.), Md,US
160/C3 Holland, Mi,US
163/F3 Hollandale, Ms,US
66/B4 Hollandse IJssel (riv.), Neth.
55/N13 Hollandstoun, Sc,UK
59/H2 Hollesley, Eng,UK
159/H4 Hollis, Ok,US
116/B2 Hollister (peak), Austl.
158/B3 Hollister, Ca,US
168/C1 Holliston, Ma,US
69/E2 Hollogne-aux-Pierres, Belg.
63/L1 Hollola, Fin.
159/F4 Holloman A.F.B., NM,US
62/E4 Höllviksnäs, Swe.
163/F3 Holly Springs, Ms,US
164/F7 Hollywood, Ca,US
163/H5 Hollywood, Fl,US
164/F7 Hollywood Bowl, Los Angeles, Ca,US
61/F3 Holm, Swe.
152/E1 Holman, NW,Can
167/D3 Holmdel, NJ,US
118/C2 Holmes (reefs), Austl.
168/F6 Holmes (co.), Oh,US
155/F4 Holmes (peak), Wy,US
57/F5 Holmes Chapel, Eng,UK
53/N8 Holmesdale (val.), Eng,UK
62/D2 Holmestrand, Nor.
57/H4 Holme upon Spalding Moor, Eng,UK
57/G4 Holmfirth, Eng,UK
54/B6 Holmhead, Sc,UK
113/C Holm-Lützow (bay), Ant.
61/F3 Holmsjön (lake), Swe.
91/D3 Ḥolon, Isr.
62/C3 Holstebro, Den.
163/H2 Holston (riv.), Tn,US
58/B5 Holsworthy, Eng,UK
59/H1 Holt, Eng,UK
66/D4 Holten, Neth.
159/J3 Holton, Ks,US
167/E2 Holtsville, NY,US
56/D5 Holy (isl.), Wal,UK
56/D5 Holyhead, Wal,UK
56/D5 Holyhead (mtn.), Wal,UK
54/E5 Holy (Lindisfarne) (isl.), Eng,UK
159/G2 Holyoke, Co,US
168/B1 Holyoke, Ma,US
57/E5 Holywell, Wal,UK
56/C2 Holywood, NI,UK
64/F5 Holzkirchen, Ger.
67/G5 Holzminden, Ger.
67/E6 Holzwickede, Ger.
132/B3 Hom (dry riv.), Namb.
130/B3 Homa Bay, Kenya
66/D6 Homberg, Ger.
67/G6 Homberg, Ger.
129/E3 Hombori Tondo (peak), Mali
69/F5 Hombourg-Haut, Fr.
69/G5 Homburg, Ger.
153/K2 Home (bay), NW,Can
69/E5 Homécourt, Fr.
162/E3 Homer, La,US
163/H5 Homestead, Fl,US
163/H5 Homestead A.F.B., Fl,US
163/G3 Homewood, Al,US
165/Q16 Homewood, Il,US
163/F4 Homochitto (riv.), Ms,US
131/D4 Homoíne, Moz.
112/D3 Homonhon (isl.), Phil.
106/B5 Honāvar, India
100/C2 Honbetsu, Japan
109/D4 Hon Chong, Viet.
138/C3 Honda, Col.
58/C3 Honddu (riv.), Wal,UK
148/D2 Hondo (riv.), Belz., Mex.
98/B4 Hondo, Japan
165/L12 Hondo (arroyo), Ca,US
159/F4 Hondo (dry riv.), NM,US
162/D4 Hondo, Tx,US
147/Q9 Hondo de Tepotzotlán (riv.), Mex.
66/D3 Hondsrug (reg.), Neth.
148/E3 Honduras
148/D2 Honduras (gulf), NAm.
147/L6 Honey, Mex.
158/B2 Honey (lake), Ca,US
165/P14 Honey (cr.), Wi,US
59/E2 Honeybourne, Eng,UK
105/G2 Hong (lake), China
103/C4 Hong (riv.), China
103/C5 Hong'an, China
101/D4 Hongch'ŏn, SKor.
107/J2 Hongdu (riv.), China
109/D1 Hong Gai, Viet.
103/C5 Honghu, China
105/F3 Hongjiang, China
105/G4 Hong Kong (dpcy.), UK
103/B3 Hongliu (riv.), China
105/H2 Hongmiao (mtn.), China
109/C1 Hong (Red) (riv.), Viet.
76/D5 Hongrin (lake), Swi.
105/H3 Hongshan (mtn.), China
105/E4 Hongshui (riv.), China
101/D4 Hongsŏng, SKor.
103/C3 Hongtao Shan (mtn.), China
103/B3 Hongtong, China
161/H1 Honguedo (passg.), Qu,Can
104/D2 Hongya, China
103/B5 Hongyan, China
96/E5 Hongyuan, China
103/D4 Hongze, China
103/D4 Hongze (lake), China
120/E5 Honiara (cap.), Sol.
58/C5 Honiton, Eng,UK
100/B4 Honjō, Japan
154/T10 Honolulu (cap.), Hi,US
154/V13 Honolulu (co.), Hi,US
109/D4 Hon Quan, Viet.
97/M5 Honshu (isl.), Japan
116/C5 Hood (pt.), Austl.
165/J10 Hood (mtn.), Ca,US
156/C4 Hood (mtn.), Or,US
156/C4 Hood Canal (inlet), Wa,US
66/B4 Hoofddorp, Neth.
66/C6 Hoogeloon, Neth.
66/B6 Hoogerheide, Neth.
66/D3 Hoogeveen, Neth.
66/D3 Hoogeveense Vaart (can.), Neth.
66/D2 Hoogezand, Neth.
106/E3 Hooghly-Chinsura, India
62/C2 Hooglede, Belg.
66/B6 Hoogstraten, Belg.
118/C3 Hook (isl.), Austl.
59/F4 Hook, Eng,UK
60/D5 Hook Head (pt.), Ire.
160/C3 Hoopeston, Il,US
66/C3 Hoorn, Neth.
66/C3 Hoornse Hop (bay), Neth.
158/D3 Hoover (dam), Az,US
92/E1 Hopa, Turk.
166/D2 Hopatcong, NJ,US
166/D2 Hopatcong (lake), NJ,US
116/D5 Hope (lake), Austl.
156/C3 Hope, BC,Can
57/E5 Hope, Wal,UK
162/E3 Hope, Ar,US
54/C1 Hopeman, Sc,UK
153/K2 Hopes Advance (cape), Qu,Can
58/C6 Hope's Nose (pt.), Eng,UK
58/D2 Hope under Dinmore, Eng,UK
118/B1 Hope Vale Abor. Community, Austl.
118/B1 Hope Vale Abor. Land, Austl.
160/E4 Hopewell, Va,US
166/C3 Hopewell Furnace Nat'l Hist. Site, Pa,US
117/F3 Hopkins (lake), Austl.
119/B3 Hopkins (riv.), Austl.
160/C4 Hopkinsville, Ky,US
168/C3 Hopkinton, RI,US
67/F6 Hoppecke (riv.), Ger.
164/B2 Hopper Mountain Nat'l Wild. Ref., Ca,US
67/E4 Hopsten, Ger.
156/C4 Hoquiam, Wa,US
151/J2 Horace (mtn.), Ak,US
99/L9 Hōrai-san (peak), Japan
92/E1 Horasan, Turk.
71/G4 Horažďovice, Czh.
70/B6 Horb am Neckar, Ger.
91/D3 Ḥorbat Qesari (ruins), Isr.
57/G4 Horbury, Eng,UK
62/A1 Hordaland (co.), Nor.
57/G2 Horden, Eng,UK
83/G3 Horezu, Rom.
77/E3 Horgen, Swi.
96/F3 Hörh (peak), Mong.
51/S6 Horiara (cap.), Sol.
103/B2 Horinger, China
53/N8 Horley, Eng,UK
113/R Horlick Ice Stream, Ant.
150/E3 Hormigüeros, PR
93/H5 Hormozgān (gov.), Iran
93/H5 Hormuz (str.), Iran, Oman
73/L2 Horn, Aus.
61/M6 Horn (pt.), Ice.
65/L4 Hornád (riv.), Slvk.
61/E2 Hornavan (lake), Swe.
67/F5 Horn-Bad Meinberg, Ger.
63/T8 Hornbæk, Den.
161/Q8 Hornby, On,Can
57/H5 Horncastle, Eng,UK
53/P7 Hornchurch, Eng,UK
160/E3 Hornell, NY,US
160/C1 Hornepayne, On,Can
143/L8 Horn (Hornos) (cape), Chile
70/B5 Hornisgrinde (peak), Ger.
71/F2 Horní Slavkov, Czh.
143/L8 Hornos (Horn) (cape), Chile
143/L8 Hornos Nat'l Park, Cabo de, Chile
68/A4 Hornoy-le-Bourg, Fr.
118/H8 Hornsby, Austl.
57/H4 Hornsea, Eng,UK
62/C4 Hörnum (cape), Ger.
64/E1 Hornum Odde (cape), Ger.
100/C2 Horoshiri-dake (mtn.), Japan
103/E1 Horqin Youyi Zhongqi, China
103/E2 Horqin Zuoyi Houqi, China
103/E1 Horqin Zuoyi Zhongqi, China
58/B6 Horrabridge, Eng,UK
159/F2 Horse (cr.), Ne, Wy,US
160/C4 Horse Cave, Ky,US
156/C2 Horsefly (lake), BC,Can
62/C4 Horsens, Den.
59/H3 Horsey (isl.), Eng,UK
57/G4 Horsforth, Eng,UK
119/B3 Horsham, Austl.
59/F4 Horsham, Eng,UK
166/C3 Horsham, Pa,US
62/G1 Horslandet (pen.), Swe.
66/D6 Horst, Neth.
67/E4 Hörstel, Ger.
67/E4 Horstmar, Ger.
75/S12 Horta, Azor.,Port.
75/N9 Hortaleza, Sp.
62/D2 Horten, Nor.
82/E2 Hortobágyi Nat'l Park, Hun.
151/N2 Horton (riv.), NW,Can
167/F1 Horton (pt.), NY,US
53/P7 Horton Kirby, Eng,UK
71/H4 Horusický Rybník (lake), Czh.
91/D4 Ḥorvot 'Avedat (ruins), Isr.
91/D4 Ḥorvot Meẕada (Masada) (ruins), Isr.
77/E3 Horw, Swi.
57/F4 Horwich, Eng,UK
160/D2 Horwood (lake), On,Can
70/C2 Hösbach, Ger.
106/C3 Hoshangābād, India
108/C2 Hoshiārpur, India
106/C4 Hospet, India
143/K8 Hoste (isl.), Chile
55/P12 Hoswick, Sc,UK
99/E2 Hotaka, Japan
99/E2 Hotaka-dake (mtn.), Japan
102/C4 Hotan, China
102/C4 Hotan (riv.), China
157/H5 Hot Springs, SD,US
162/E3 Hot Springs Nat'l Park, Ar,US
162/E3 Hot Springs Village, Ar,US
152/E2 Hottah (lake), NW,Can
132/A2 Hottentot (bay), Namb.
132/A2 Hottentots (pt.), Namb.
105/E2 Hou (riv.), China
68/B3 Houdain, Fr.
128/D4 Houet (prov.), Burk.
160/B2 Houghton, Mi,US
160/C2 Houghton Lake, Mi,US
57/G2 Houghton-le-Spring, Eng,UK
53/S10 Houilles, Fr.
161/H2 Houlton, Me,US
103/B4 Houma, China
163/F4 Houma, La,US
53/M7 Hounslow (bor.), Eng,UK
68/B2 Houplines, Fr.
68/A3 Hourdel, Pointe du (pt.), Fr.
54/A2 Hourn, Loch (inlet), Sc,UK
168/A3 Housatonic (riv.), Ct, Ma,US
168/A2 Housatonic Saint For., Ct,US
158/D3 House (range), Ut,US
57/F1 Housesteads Roman Fort, Eng,UK
156/B2 Houston, BC,Can
159/K3 Houston, Mo,US
163/F3 Houston, Ms,US
162/E4 Houston, Tx,US
66/C4 Houten, Neth.
68/B2 Houthulst, Belg.
116/B4 Houtman Abrolhos (isls.), Austl.
66/C3 Houtribdijk (dam), Neth.
63/J1 Houtskär (isl.), Fin.
62/D1 Hov, Nor.
96/C2 Hovd, Mong.
63/T9 Hove (riv.), Den.
59/F5 Hove, Eng,UK
67/F5 Hövelhof, Ger.
158/E3 Hovenweep Nat'l Mon., Co,US
59/H1 Hoveton, Eng,UK
62/E1 Hovfjället (peak), Swe.
57/H3 Hovingham, Eng,UK
96/E1 Hövsgöl (lake), Mong.
151/H2 Howard (hill), Ak,US
151/G2 Howard (pass), Ak,US
166/B5 Howard (co.), Md,US
167/K9 Howard Beach, NY,US
165/D3 Howard Hanson (dam), Wa,US
165/D3 Howard Hanson (res.), Wa,US
57/H4 Howden, Eng,UK
119/D3 Howe (cape), Austl.
109/D3 Howell, Mi,US
167/D3 Howell, NJ,US
133/E3 Howick, SAfr.
121/H4 Howland (isl.), PacUS
55/H8 Howmore, Sc,UK
106/E3 Howrah, India
64/E3 Höxter, Ger.
102/E3 Hoxud, China
55/N13 Hoy (isl.), Sc,UK
65/H3 Hoyerswerda, Ger.
57/E5 Hoylake, Eng,UK
57/G5 Hoyland Nether, Eng,UK
75/N8 Hoyo-de-Manzanares, Sp.
69/E3 Hoyoux (riv.), Belg.
96/E2 Hoyt Tamir (riv.), Mong.
99/M9 Hozumi, Japan
71/G3 Hracholusky, Údolní nádrž (res.), Czh.
65/H3 Hradec Králové, Czh.
71/G2 Hradiště (peak), Czh.
84/D2 Hrasnica, Bosn.
82/B2 Hrastnik, Slov.
79/G1 Hrastovlje, Slov.
61/M6 Hrolleifsborg (peak), Ice.
65/K4 Hron (riv.), Slvk.
82/D1 Hron (riv.), Slvk.
65/J3 Hronov, Czh.
65/M3 Hrubieszów, Pol.
65/J3 Hrubý Jeseník (mts.), Czh.
61/P6 Hrútafjöll (peak), Ice.
105/J4 Hsiukulan (mtn.), Tai.
105/J3 Hsüeh (peak), Tai.
96/G5 Hua (peak), China
96/F4 Huachi, China
144/B3 Huacho, Peru
97/L2 Huachuan, China
96/G3 Huade, China
97/K3 Huadian, China
105/J2 Huading (mtn.), China
109/B3 Hua Hin, Thai.
121/K6 Huahine (isl.), FrPol.
103/C4 Huai (riv.), China
103/D4 Huai'an, China
96/H5 Huaibei, China
103/C4 Huaibin, China
105/F3 Huaihua, China
105/G4 Huaiji, China
103/C2 Huailai, China
103/D4 Huainan, China
103/D5 Huaining, China
103/C3 Huairen, China
103/C2 Huairou, China
103/C4 Huaiyang, China
103/D4 Huaiyin, China
103/D4 Huaiyuan, China
147/F5 Huajuapan de León, Mex.
142/C2 Hualañé, Chile
144/B2 Huallaga (riv.), Peru
144/B2 Huamachuco, Peru
147/F5 Huamantla, Mex.
126/C3 Huambo, Ang.
148/C2 Huamelula, Mex.
105/G2 Huan (riv.), China
97/L2 Huanan, China
144/C4 Huancavelica, Peru
144/C4 Huancayo, Peru
136/E8 Huanchaca (peak), Bol.
109/C2 Huang (riv.), Laos, Thai.
103/C4 Huangchuan, China
103/C5 Huanggang, China
105/H3 Huanggang (peak), China
103/D3 Huanghua, China
105/H3 Huangjinkenggang (mtn.), China
103/B4 Huangling, China
103/B4 Huanglong, China
103/B4 Huanglongtan, China
105/H3 Huangmao (peak), China
103/C5 Huangmei, China
103/C5 Huangpi, China
107/J2 Huangping, China
103/D5 Huangshan, China
103/C5 Huangshi, China
103/C5 Huangtang (lake), China
103/B4 Huangtu (plat.), China
107/H4 Huang (Yellow) (riv.), China
103/B4 Huangyunpu, China
96/E4 Huangzhong, China
107/J3 Huanjiang, China
101/C2 Huanren, China
144/C4 Huanta, Peru
103/D3 Huantai, China
144/B3 Huánuco, Peru
136/E7 Huanuni, Bol.
96/F4 Huan Xian, China
149/E3 Huapi (mts.), Nic.
147/F5 Huaquechula, Mex.
144/A1 Huaquillas, Ecu.
144/B3 Huaral, Peru
144/B3 Huaráz, Peru
144/B3 Huarmey, Peru
144/B3 Huascarán (peak), Peru
144/B3 Huascarán Nat'l Park, Peru
103/B4 Hua Shan (peak), China
105/G3 Huashi (mts.), China
146/C3 Huatabampo, Mex.
136/E6 Huatunas (lake), Bol.
148/B2 Huatusco, Mex.
147/F4 Huauchinango, Mex.
144/B3 Huaura, Peru
147/F5 Huautla, Mex.
103/C4 Hua Xian, China
104/E2 Huaying, China
144/B3 Huayllay, Peru
107/K3 Huazhou, China
151/L3 Hubbard (mtn.), Ak,US, Yk,Can
168/G5 Hubbard, Oh,US
159/H4 Hubbard Creek (res.), Tx,US
103/C5 Hubei (prov.), China
103/B4 Hubei Kou (pass), China
106/C4 Hubli-Dhārwār, India
66/D6 Hückelhoven, Ger.
67/E6 Hückeswagen, Ger.
57/G5 Hucknall Torkard, Eng,UK
68/A2 Hucqueliers, Fr.
57/G4 Huddersfield, Eng,UK
63/R7 Huddinge, Swe.
67/F2 Hude, Ger.
62/G1 Hudiksvall, Swe.
113/L Hudson (cape), Ant.
153/H2 Hudson (bay), Can.
153/J2 Hudson (str.), NW, Qu,Can
161/M7 Hudson, Qu,Can
168/C1 Hudson, Ma,US
167/J9 Hudson (co.), NJ,US
160/F3 Hudson (riv.), NJ, NY,US
160/F3 Hudson, NY,US
157/H2 Hudson Bay, Sk,Can
152/D3 Hudson's Hope, BC,Can
109/D2 Hue, Viet.
82/F2 Huedin, Rom.
148/D3 Huehuetenango, Guat.
147/L6 Huehuetla, Mex.
147/L8 Huehuetlán el Chico, Mex.
147/L7 Huejotzingo, Mex.
147/F4 Huejutla, Mex.
74/B4 Huelva, Sp.
74/B3 Huelva (riv.), Sp.
142/B4 Huequi (vol.), Chile
74/E4 Huércal-Overa, Sp.
159/F3 Huerfano (riv.), Co,US
75/E1 Huesca, Sp.
74/D4 Huéscar, Sp.
142/F3 Huesos (riv.), Arg.
147/E5 Huetamo, Mex.
148/C2 Hueyapan de Ocampo, Mex.
77/E2 Hüfingen, Ger.
106/E3 Hugli (riv.), India
159/G3 Hugo, Co,US
159/J4 Hugo, Ok,US
159/G3 Hugoton, Ks,US
103/C3 Huguan, China
96/H2 Hui (riv.), China
132/B2 Huib-Hoch (plat.), Namb.
147/K6 Huichapan, Mex.
126/B4 Huíla (plat.), Ang.
138/C4 Huila (dept.), Col.
138/C4 Huila, Nevado del (peak), Col.
107/H2 Huili, China
147/G5 Huimanguillo, Mex.
103/D3 Huimin, China
97/K3 Huinan, China
142/D2 Huinca Renancó, Arg.
96/F4 Huining, China
101/D2 Hŭisaek-pong (mtn.), NKor.
103/E5 Hui Shan (mtn.), China
107/J2 Huishui, China
72/D2 Huisne (riv.), Fr.
66/C5 Huissen, Neth.
107/J2 Huitong, China
63/K1 Huittinen, Fin.
147/M7 Huitzilan, Mex.
147/F5 Huitzuco, Mex.
103/C4 Hui Xian, China
148/C3 Huixtla, Mex.
104/D3 Huize, China
66/C4 Huizen, Neth.
105/G4 Huizhou, China
108/B2 Hujra, Pak.
101/C5 Hŭksan (arch.), SKor.
97/K2 Hulan, China
96/K2 Hulan (riv.), China
96/F2 Huld, Mong.
157/G4 Hulett, Wy,US
160/F2 Hull, Qu,Can
57/H4 Hull, Eng,UK
57/H4 Hull (riv.), Eng,UK
168/D1 Hull, Ma,US
67/F4 Hüllhorst, Ger.
121/H5 Hull (Orona) (atoll), Kiri.
66/B6 Hulst, Neth.
103/B3 Hulu (riv.), China
96/H2 Hulun (lake), China
97/K1 Huma, China
97/K1 Huma (riv.), China
135/C1 Humahuaca, Arg.
136/F5 Humaitá, Braz.
126/B4 Humbe, Ang.
161/K2 Humber (riv.), Nf,Can
161/R8 Humber (bay), On,Can
161/Q8 Humber (riv.), On,Can
57/H4 Humber (riv.), Eng,UK
57/H4 Humberside (co.), Eng,UK
57/H4 Humberston, Eng,UK
140/B1 Humberto de Campos, Braz.
162/E4 Humble, Tx,US
146/E1 Humble City, NM,US
157/G2 Humboldt, Sk,Can
149/G5 Humboldt (bay), Col.
120/F7 Humboldt (peak), NCal.
158/C2 Humboldt (range), Nv,US
158/D2 Humboldt (riv.), Nv,US
163/F3 Humboldt, Tn,US
119/C2 Hume (lake), Austl.
65/L4 Humenné, Slvk.
63/T9 Humlebæk, Den.
151/K2 Humphrey (pt.), Ak,US
158/E4 Humphreys (peak), Az,US
57/F1 Humshaugh, Eng,UK
101/C2 Hun (riv.), China
124/J2 Hūn, Libya
61/N6 Húnaflói (bay), Ice.
105/F2 Hunan (prov.), China
97/L3 Hunchun, China
82/F3 Hunedoara, Rom.
82/F2 Hunedoara (co.), Rom.
64/E3 Hünfeld, Ger.
82/D2 Hungary
70/B2 Hungen, Ger.
59/E4 Hungerford, Eng,UK
96/C2 Hüngüy (riv.), Mong.
109/D1 Hung Yen, Viet.
101/D2 Hunjiang, China
57/H3 Hunmanby, Eng,UK
69/G1 Hunspach, Fr.
69/G4 Hunsrück (mts.), Ger.
59/G1 Hunstanton, Eng,UK
67/F2 Hunte (riv.), Ger.
119/C4 Hunter (isl.), Austl.
119/D2 Hunter (riv.), Austl.
156/A3 Hunter (isl.), BC,Can
151/H3 Hunter (mtn.), Ak,US
166/D2 Hunterdon (co.), NJ,US
160/C4 Huntingburg, In,US
59/F2 Huntingdon, Eng,UK
57/G4 Huntington, Eng,UK
160/C3 Huntington, In,US
167/E2 Huntington, NY,US
167/M8 Huntington (bay), NY,US
166/B1 Huntington (cr.), Pa,US
160/D4 Huntington, WV,US
164/C3 Huntington Beach, Ca,US
164/B3 Huntington Park, Ca,US
167/M8 Huntington Station, NY,US
165/F7 Huntington Woods, Mi,US
115/S10 Huntly, NZ
54/D2 Huntly, Sc,UK
151/M4 Hunts Inlet, BC,Can
160/E2 Huntsville, On,Can
163/G3 Huntsville, Al,US
166/B1 Huntsville (res.), Pa,US
162/E4 Huntsville, Tx,US
147/H4 Hunucmá, Mex.
66/D5 Hünxe, Ger.
103/C3 Hunyuan, China
105/H2 Huo (mtn.), China
102/D3 Huocheng, China
103/C4 Huojia, China
97/H2 Huolin Gol, China
109/D2 Huong Hoa, Viet.
109/D2 Huong Khe, Viet.
109/D2 Huong Son, Viet.
107/J4 Huong Thuy, Viet.
103/D4 Huoqiu, China
103/C5 Huoshan, China
103/B3 Huo Shan (mtn.), China
103/B3 Huo Xian, China
125/R5 Hurdiyo, Som.
53/S11 Hurepoix (reg.), Fr.
103/E2 Hure Qi, China
158/E4 Hurley, NM,US
54/B5 Hurlford, Sc,UK
160/D2 Huron (lake), Can., US
165/G6 Huron (pt.), Mi,US
165/F7 Huron (riv.), Mi,US
168/E5 Huron, Oh,US
168/E5 Huron (co.), Oh,US
168/E5 Huron (riv.), Oh,US
157/J4 Huron, SD,US
160/D4 Hurricane, WV,US
59/F5 Hurstpierpoint, Eng,UK
68/D4 Hurtaut (riv.), Fr.
69/F2 Hürth, Ger.
57/G3 Hurworth, Eng,UK
106/D3 Husainābād, India
59/E2 Husbands Bosworth, Eng,UK
83/J2 Huşi, Rom.
64/E1 Husum, Ger.
159/H3 Hutchinson, Ks,US
157/K4 Hutchinson, Mn,US
104/D3 Hutiaoxia, China
57/J5 Huttoft, Eng,UK
118/C4 Hutton (peak), Austl.
53/Q7 Hutton, Eng,UK
57/H4 Hutton Cranswick, Eng,UK
57/G3 Hutton Rudby, Eng,UK
161/Q8 Huttonville, On,Can
96/B3 Hutubi, China
103/C3 Hutuo (riv.), China
103/B4 Hu Xian, China
103/E5 Huzhou, China
69/E2 Huy, Belg.
57/F5 Huyton-with-Roby, Eng,UK
61/P7 Hvannadalshnúkur (peak), Ice.
82/C4 Hvar (isl.), Cro.
63/T9 Hvidovre, Den.
61/N7 Hvítá (riv.), Ice.
131/B3 Hwange, Zim.
131/B3 Hwange (Wankie) Nat'l Park, Zim.
101/D3 Hwanghae-Bukto (prov.), NKor.
101/C3 Hwanghae-Namdo (prov.), NKor.
101/D3 Hwangju (riv.), NKor.
142/B5 Hyades (peak), Chile
96/C2 Hyargas, Mong.
96/C2 Hyargas (lake), Mong.
166/B6 Hyattsville, Md,US
57/F5 Hyde, Eng,UK
53/N7 Hyde Park, Eng,UK
106/C4 Hyderābād, India
95/J3 Hyderābād, Pak.
73/G5 Hyères, Fr.
73/G5 Hyères (isls.), Fr.
152/D2 Hyland (riv.), Yk,Can
160/D4 Hylton (hill), Ky,US
98/D3 Hyōgo (pref.), Japan
101/G6 Hyŏndŭngsan (mtn.), SKor.
98/D3 Hyō-no-sen (mtn.), Japan
158/E2 Hyrum, Ut,US
59/E5 Hythe, Eng,UK
59/H4 Hythe, Eng,UK
98/B4 Hyūga, Japan
63/L1 Hyvinkää, Fin.

I

141/B2 Iacanga, Braz.
140/A4 Iaciara, Braz.
144/D3 Iaco (riv.), Braz., Peru
140/B4 Iaçu, Braz.
82/A2 Iâf di Montasio (peak), It.
83/H3 Ialomiţa (riv.), Rom.
141/D1 Iapu, Braz.
83/H2 Iaşi, Rom.
83/H2 Iaşi (co.), Rom.
112/B3 Iba, Phil.
129/F5 Ibadan, Nga.
138/C3 Ibagué, Col.
141/B2 Ibaiti, Braz.
112/C3 Ibajay, Phil.
130/A3 Ibanda, Ugan.
149/E3 Ibans (lag.), Hon.
158/D2 Ibapah, Ut,US
82/E4 Ibar (riv.), Yugo.
98/C3 Ibara, Japan
99/L10 Ibaraki, Japan
99/F2 Ibaraki (pref.), Japan
138/B4 Ibarra, Ecu.
135/E2 Ibarreta, Arg.
125/L6 Ibba (riv.), Sudan
67/E4 Ibbenbüren, Ger.
129/F2 Ibdekhene (wadi), Mali
135/E2 Ibera, Esteros de (marshes), Arg.
74/D2 Ibérico, Sistema (range), Sp.
161/P7 Iberville, Qu,Can
98/E3 Ibi (riv.), Japan
75/E3 Ibi, Sp.
141/C1 Ibiá, Braz.
140/B2 Ibiapaba (mts.), Braz.
140/B1 Ibiapina, Braz.
140/C4 Ibicaraí, Braz.
140/C3 Ibimirim, Braz.
141/D1 Ibiraçu, Braz.
140/B5 Ibirapuã, Braz.
141/B2 Ibitinga, Braz.
141/F8 Ibiúna, Braz.
75/F3 Ibiza, Sp.
75/F3 Ibiza (isl.), Sp.
98/D3 Ibo (riv.), Japan
126/H3 Ibo, Moz.
140/B4 Ibotirama, Braz.
124/H8 Iboundji (peak), Gabon
65/L4 Ibrány, Hun.
91/B5 Ibshawāy, Egypt
59/E1 Ibstock, Eng,UK
111/G3 Ibu (mtn.), Indo.
99/M9 Ibuki, Japan
99/M9 Ibuki-yama (peak), Japan
138/D5 Içá (riv.), Braz.
144/C4 Ica, Peru
139/E4 Içana, Braz.
138/D4 Içana (riv.), Braz., Col.
91/C1 İçel (prov.), Turk.
61/N7 Iceland
141/B2 Icém, Braz.
106/B4 Ichalkaranji, India
106/D4 Ichchāpuram, India
70/D6 Ichenhausen, Ger.
99/J7 Ichihara, Japan
99/L9 Ichijima, Japan
99/H7 Ichikawa, Japan
100/B3 Ichinohe, Japan
99/M9 Ichinomiya, Japan
100/B4 Ichinoseki, Japan
99/M10 Ichishi, Japan
68/C1 Ichtegem, Belg.
140/C2 Icó, Braz.
151/K4 Icy (bay), Ak,US
151/F1 Icy (cape), Ak,US
151/L4 Icy (str.), Ak,US
159/J4 Idabel, Ok,US
156/E5 Idaho (state), US
156/E5 Idaho Falls, Id,US
108/F3 Idāppādi, India
106/B3 Idar, India
69/G4 Idarkopf (peak), Ger.
69/G4 Idar-Oberstein, Ger.
99/L10 Ide, Japan
124/G3 Ideles, Alg.
96/D2 Ider (riv.), Mong.
127/C3 Idfū, Egypt
81/J5 Idhi (peak), Gre.
79/E3 Idice (riv.), It.
92/E2 Idil, Turk.
130/A3 Idjwe (isl.), Zaire
91/B4 Idkū, Egypt
57/H5 Idle (riv.), Eng,UK
91/E2 Idlib, Syria
91/E2 Idlib (prov.), Syria
82/B3 Idrija, Slov.
123/M13 Idriss I (dam), Mor.
123/M13 Idriss I (res.), Mor.
78/D1 Idro (lake), It.
70/B2 Idstein, Ger.
100/J7 Ie (isl.), Japan
68/B2 Ieper, Belg.
81/J5 Ierápetra, Gre.
130/C5 Ifakara, Tanz.
120/D4 Ifalik (isl.), Micr.
133/H8 Ifanadiana, Madg.
129/G5 Ife, Nga.
77/G3 Ifen, Hoher (peak), Ger., Aus.
99/M10 Iga, Japan
99/M10 Iga (riv.), Japan
130/B4 Igalula, Tanz.
130/B2 Iganga, Ugan.
140/B4 Igaporã, Braz.
138/C5 Igara Paraná (riv.), Col.
141/C2 Igarapava, Braz.
137/J4 Igarapé-Miri, Braz.
140/D2 Igarassu, Braz.
141/G8 Igaratá, Braz.
88/J3 Igarka, Rus.
106/B4 Igatpuri, India
130/B5 Igawa, Tanz.
93/F2 Iğdır, Turk.
53/P8 Ightham, Eng,UK
151/H2 Igikpak (mtn.), Ak,US
80/A3 Iglesias, It.
160/B1 Ignace, On,Can
147/P8 Ignacio de la Llave, Mex.
83/J5 Iğneada (cape), Turk.
76/A2 Ignon (riv.), Fr.
53/S10 Igny, Fr.
130/B3 Igombe, Tanz.
130/B4 Igombe (riv.), Tanz.
144/C1 Igora Paraná (riv.), Col.
85/M4 Igra, Rus.
141/B3 Iguaçu (riv.), Braz.
135/F2 Iguaçu Nat'l Park, Braz.
140/B4 Iguaí, Braz.
148/B2 Iguala, Mex.
75/F2 Igualada, Sp.
147/F5 Iguala de la Independencia, Mex.
135/F2 Iguapa (riv.), Braz.
141/C3 Iguape, Braz.
141/C3 Iguape (riv.), Braz.
140/C2 Iguatu, Braz.
134/D5 Iguazú (falls), Braz.
135/F2 Iguazu Nat'l Park, Arg.
130/B4 Igugunu, Tanz.
124/D2 Iguidi, 'Erg (des.), Afr.
100/J7 Iheya (isl.), Japan
133/H8 Ihosy, Madg.
133/G8 Ihotry (lake), Madg.
88/C3 Ii (riv.), Fin.
99/E3 Iida, Japan
99/F2 Iide-san (mtn.), Japan
84/E2 Iijoki (riv.), Fin.
99/M10 Iinan, Japan
61/H3 Iisalmi, Fin.
99/M10 Iitaka, Japan
63/M1 Iitti, Fin.
99/F2 Iiyama, Japan
98/B4 Iizuka, Japan
130/D3 Ijara, Kenya
124/C3 Ijill (peak), Mrta.
66/C4 IJmeer (bay), Neth.
66/B4 IJmuiden, Neth.
128/B2 Ijnaoun (well), Mrta.
61/H2 Ijoki (riv.), Fin.
66/C4 IJssel (riv.), Neth.
66/C3 IJsselmeer (lake), Neth.
66/C2 IJsselmeer (Afsluitdijk) (dam), Neth.
66/C3 IJsselmuiden, Neth.
66/C4 IJsselstein, Neth.
135/F2 Ijuí, Braz.
98/B5 Ijūin, Japan
68/B2 Ijzer (riv.), Belg.
85/M5 Ik (riv.), Rus.
133/H7 Ikahavo (plat.), Madg.
130/A4 Ikamba, Tanz.
81/J4 Ikaría (isl.), Gre.
130/B4 Ikasi, Tanz.
62/C3 Ikast, Den.
98/C3 Ikeda, Japan
126/D1 Ikela, Zaire
99/M10 Ikenokoya-yama (peak), Japan
83/F4 Ikhtiman, Bul.
98/A4 Iki (chan.), Japan
98/A4 Iki (isl.), Japan
92/C2 Ikizce, Turk.
99/L10 Ikoma, Japan
130/B3 Ikoma, Tanz.
133/H7 Ikopa (riv.), Madg.
130/B4 Ikungi, Tanz.
130/B4 Ikungu, Tanz.
144/D5 Ilabaya, Peru
130/A4 Ilagala, Tanz.
112/C1 Ilagan, Phil.
108/G4 Ilaiyānkudi, India
93/F3 Īlām, Iran

93/F3 Īlām (gov.), Iran
106/E2 Ilam, Nepal
130/B4 Ilangali, Tanz.
144/D5 Ilave, Peru
65/K2 Iława, Pol.
125/M4 'Ilay, Sudan
79/E5 Il Castello, Monte (peak), It.
58/D4 Ilchester, Eng,UK
156/G2 Ile-à-la-Crosse, Sk,Can
157/G2 Ile-a-la-Crosse (lake), Sk,Can
126/D1 Ilebo, Zaire
72/E2 Ile-de-France (reg.), Fr.
161/N6 Ile-de-Montréal (co.), Qu,Can
161/N6 Ile-Jésus (co.), Qu,Can
87/K2 Ilek (riv.), Kaz., Rus.
60/A6 Ilen (riv.), Ire.
161/N7 Ile-Perrot, Qu,Can
128/E5 Iles Ehotilés Nat'l Park, IvC.
129/G5 Ilesha, Nga.
76/D4 Ilfis (riv.), Swi.
53/P7 Ilford, Eng,UK
118/B3 Ilfracombe, Austl.
58/B4 Ilfracombe, Eng,UK
86/E4 Ilgaz, Turk.
92/C1 Ilgazdağı Nat'l Park, Turk.
92/B2 Ilgın, Turk.
141/H8 Ilhabela, Braz.
141/J8 Ilha Grande (bay), Braz.
141/B1 Ilha Solteira (res.), Braz.
74/A2 Ílhavo, Port.
140/C4 Ilhéus, Braz.
102/C3 Ili (riv.), China, Kaz.
151/G4 Iliamna (lake), Ak,US
151/H3 Iliamna (vol.), Ak,US
92/E2 Ilıca, Turk.
112/C3 Iligan (bay), Phil.
112/D3 Iligan City, Phil.
138/B5 Ilíniza (peak), Ecu.
92/E2 Ilisu (res.), Turk.
83/H6 Ilium (Troy) (ruins), Turk.
57/G6 Ilkeston, Eng,UK
57/G4 Ilkley, Eng,UK
77/F3 Ill (riv.), Aus.
76/D1 Ill (riv.), Fr.
142/C1 Illapel, Chile
79/E1 Illasi (riv.), It.
117/G3 Illbillee (peak), Austl.
129/G3 Illéla, Niger
70/D6 Iller (riv.), Ger.
70/D6 Illertissen, Ger.
74/D2 Illescas, Sp.
136/E7 Illimani (peak), Bol.
69/G5 Illingen, Ger.
160/B4 Illinois (state), US
160/B3 Illinois (riv.), Il,US
124/G2 Illizi, Alg.
76/D1 Illkirch-Graffenstaden, Fr.
77/E3 Illnau, Swi.
58/A6 Illogan, Eng,UK
74/D4 Illora, Sp.
76/D2 Illzach, Fr.
71/E5 Ilm (riv.), Ger.
61/G3 Ilmajoki, Fin.
67/G5 Ilme (riv.), Ger.
84/F4 Il'men' (lake), Rus.
64/F3 Ilmenau, Ger.
67/H2 Ilmenau (riv.), Ger.
58/D5 Ilminster, Eng,UK
144/D5 Ilo, Peru
112/C3 Iloilo City, Phil.
130/B4 Ilongero, Tanz.
129/G4 Ilorin, Nga.
87/H2 Ilovlya (riv.), Rus.
67/H4 Ilse (riv.), Ger.
67/H4 Ilsede, Ger.
67/H5 Ilsenburg, Ger.
70/C4 Ilsfeld, Ger.
83/H5 Ilyas (pt.), Turk.
85/N3 Ilych (riv.), Rus.
71/G5 Ilz (riv.), Ger.
98/C3 Imabari, Japan
99/F2 Imaichi, Japan
133/H8 Imaloto (riv.), Madg.
92/C2 İmamoğlu, Turk.
84/F2 Imandra (lake), Rus.
98/A4 Imari, Japan
63/N1 Imatra, Fin.
98/E3 Imazu, Japan
99/J7 Imba, Japan
138/B4 Imbabura (prov.), Ecu.
141/B4 Imbituba, Braz.
141/B3 Imbituva, Braz.
125/P6 Īmī, Eth.
87/J5 Imishli, Azer.
81/L7 Imittós (mtn.), Gre.
101/C5 Imja (isl.), SKor.
101/D3 Imjin (riv.), NKor., SKor.
158/C2 Imlay, Nv,US
67/G6 Immenhausen, Ger.
77/G2 Immenstadt im Allgäu, Ger.
57/H4 Immingham, Eng,UK
163/H5 Immokalee, Fl,US
151/J2 Imnavait (mtn.), Ak,US
129/G5 Imo (state), Nga.
79/E4 Imola, It.
140/A2 Imperatriz, Braz.
78/B5 Imperia, It.
78/A5 Imperia (prov.), It.
157/G3 Imperial, Sk,Can
144/B4 Imperial, Peru
159/G2 Imperial, Ne,US
164/C5 Imperial Beach, Ca,US
99/H7 Imperial Palace, Japan
78/A5 Impero (riv.), It.
124/J7 Impfondo, Congo
104/B3 Imphāl, India
83/J5 İmrali (isl.), Turk.
92/D2 İmranlı, Turk.
77/G3 Imst, Aus.
112/E7 Imus, Phil.
112/E7 Imus (riv.), Phil.
131/A3 Imusho, Zam.
99/E3 Ina, Japan
99/L10 Ina (riv.), Japan
65/H2 Ina (riv.), Pol.
112/D3 Inabanga, Phil.
99/M9 Inabe, Japan
113/E Inaccessability, Pole of, Ant.
99/L10 Inagawa, Japan
99/H7 Inagi, Japan
140/C3 Inajá, Braz.
144/D4 Inambari (riv.), Peru
124/G2 I-n-Amenas, Alg.
99/K10 Inami, Japan
123/M13 Inaouene (riv.), Mor.
61/H1 Inari (lake), Fin.
83/G2 Inău (peak), Rom.
99/G2 Inawashiro (lake), Japan
99/M9 Inazawa, Japan
144/D4 Inca (dept.), Peru
75/G3 Inca, Sp.
91/C1 Incekum (pt.), Turk.
129/F2 I-n-Chaouâg (wadi), Mali
54/D4 Inchcape (Bell Rock) (isl.), Sc,UK
54/B5 Inchinnan, Sc,UK
128/B2 Inchiri (reg.), Mrta.
54/C4 Inchkeith (isl.), Sc,UK
55/J7 Inchnadamph, Sc,UK
101/D4 Inch'ŏn, SKor.
101/D4 Inch'ŏn-Jikhalsi, SKor.
131/D3 Inchope, Moz.
92/A2 Inciriova, Turk.
131/D5 Incomati (riv.), Moz.
141/G7 Inconfidentes, Braz.
124/E3 I-n-Dagouber (well), Mali
141/C1 Indaiá (riv.), Braz.
141/C2 Indaiatuba, Braz.
112/C4 Indanan, Phil.
104/B3 Indawgyi (lake), Burma
69/F2 Inde (riv.), Ger.
69/F2 Inden, Ger.
158/C3 Independence, Ca,US
159/J3 Independence, Ks,US
159/J3 Independence, Mo,US
158/C2 Independence (mts.), Nv,US
166/C4 Independence Nat'l Hist. Park, Pa,US
140/B2 Independência, Braz.
87/J2 Inder (lake), Kaz.
106/C3 India
51/N6 Indian (ocean)
160/C3 Indiana (state), US
160/E3 Indiana, Pa,US
165/R16 Indiana Dunes Nat'l Lakesh., In,US
160/C4 Indianapolis (cap.), In,US
166/B3 Indian Echo Caverns, Pa,US
157/H3 Indian Head, Sk,Can
163/F3 Indianola, Ms,US
163/H5 Indiantown, Fl,US
141/B1 Indiaporã, Braz.
89/Q3 Indigirka (riv.), Rus.
82/E3 Indija, Yugo.
158/C4 Indio, Ca,US
109/C1 Indochina (reg.), Asia
111/E4 Indonesia
118/E6 Indooroopilly, Austl.
106/C3 Indore, India
110/B4 Indragiri (riv.), Indo.
110/C5 Indramayu (cape), Indo.
106/D4 Indrāvati (riv.), India
72/D3 Indre (riv.), Fr.
72/D3 Indrois (riv.), Fr.
78/B1 Induno Olona, It.
90/F7 Indus (riv.), Asia
95/J4 Indus, Mouths of the, Pak.
92/C1 İnebolu, Turk.
129/E1 I-n-Echaï (well), Mali
92/B1 İnegöl, Turk.
82/E2 Ineu, Rom.
124/D1 Inezgane, Mor.
132/C4 Infanta (cape), SAfr.
146/E5 Infiernillo (res.), Mex.
74/C1 Infiesto, Sp.
140/D2 Ingá, Braz.
138/B5 Ingapirca, Ecu.
138/B5 Ingapirca (ruins), Ecu.
63/S7 Ingarö, Swe.
63/S7 Ingarö (isl.), Swe.
57/G7 Ingatestone, Eng,UK
68/C2 Ingelmunster, Belg.
118/G8 Ingleburn, Austl.
70/B2 Ingleheim, Ger.
57/G2 Ingleton, Eng,UK
161/Q8 Inglewood, On,Can
164/B3 Inglewood, Ca,US
165/C2 Inglewood-Finn Hill, Wa,US
163/H4 Inglis, Fl,US
96/G1 Ingoda (riv.), Rus.
57/J5 Ingoldmells, Eng,UK
71/E5 Ingolstadt, Ger.
53/Q7 Ingrave, Eng,UK
113/E Ingrid Christianson (coast), Ant.
129/G2 I-n-Guezzâm, Alg.
86/E3 Ingulets (riv.), Ukr.
87/G4 Inguri (riv.), Geo.
131/D4 Inhambane, Moz.
131/D4 Inhambane (prov.), Moz.
140/C3 Inhambupe, Braz.
131/D3 Inhaminga, Moz.
131/D5 Inharrime, Moz.
131/D4 Inhassoro, Moz.
140/B2 Inhuma, Braz.
137/J7 Inhumas, Braz.
139/H4 Inini (riv.), FrG.
138/D4 Inírida (riv.), Col.
54/F10 Inishbofin (isl.), Ire.
60/A6 Inishcarra (res.), Ire.
56/A1 Inishowen (pen.), Ire.
56/B1 Inishowen Head (pt.), Ire.
165/F7 Inkster, Mi,US
98/C3 Inland (sea), Japan
104/C4 Inle (lake), Burma
129/E2 I-n-Milach (well), Mali
73/K2 Inn (riv.), Eur.
71/H6 Innbach (riv.), Aus.
54/B5 Innellan, Sc,UK
148/D2 Inner (chan.), Belz.
55/J8 Inner (sound), Sc,UK
54/C4 Innerdouny (hill), Sc,UK
55/H8 Inner Hebrides (isls.), Sc,UK
77/F3 Innerhoden (demi-canton), Swi.
54/C5 Innerleithen, Sc,UK
96/G3 Inner Mongolia (reg.), China
67/H4 Innerste (riv.), Ger.
117/H5 Innes Nat'l Park, Austl.
73/K3 Innichen (San Candido), It.
118/B2 Innisfail, Austl.
156/E2 Innisfail, Ab,Can
151/G3 Innoko (riv.), Ak,US
151/G3 Innoko Nat'l Wild. Ref., Ak,US
77/H3 Innsbruck, Aus.
71/G6 Innviertel (reg.), Aus.
60/C2 Inny (riv.), Ire.
58/B5 Inny (riv.), Eng,UK
98/C4 Ino, Japan
141/B1 Inocência, Braz.
126/C1 Inongo, Zaire
65/K4 Inovec (peak), Slvk.
65/K2 Inowrocław, Pol.
129/E1 I-n-Sâkâne, Erg (des.), Mali
124/F2 I-n-Salah, Alg.
54/D2 Insch, Sc,UK
116/B3 Inscription (cape), Austl.
104/C5 Insein, Burma
156/A2 Inside (passg.), BC,Can
131/C3 Insiza, Zim.
85/P2 Inta, Rus.
129/F2 I-n-Tassik (well), Mali
156/B2 Interior (plat.), BC,Can
157/K3 International Falls, Mn,US
157/H3 International Peace Garden, Can., US
109/B2 Inthanon (peak), Thai.
83/H3 Întorsura Buzăului, Rom.
99/G3 Inubō-zaki (pt.), Japan
153/J3 Inukjuak, Qu,Can
143/K8 Inútil (bay), Chile
99/E3 Inuyama, Japan
54/C1 Inver (bay), Sc,UK
54/A4 Inveraray, Sc,UK
54/D3 Inverbervie, Sc,UK
115/Q12 Invercargill, NZ
119/D1 Inverell, Austl.
54/B2 Invergarry, Sc,UK
54/B1 Invergordon, Sc,UK
54/C4 Invergowrie, Sc,UK
55/J8 Inverie, Sc,UK
54/D3 Inverkeilor, Sc,UK
54/C4 Inverkeithing, Sc,UK
157/H3 Invermay, Sk,Can
161/J2 Inverness, NS,Can
54/B2 Inverness, Sc,UK
163/G3 Inverness, Al,US
163/H4 Inverness, Fl,US
78/B1 Inveruno, It.
54/D2 Inverurie, Sc,UK
117/H5 Investigator (str.), Austl.
167/L9 Inwood, NY,US
131/D3 Inyanga, Zim.
131/D3 Inyangani (peak), Zim.
131/C3 Inyati, Zim.
151/D2 Inymney, Gora (mtn.), Rus.
158/C3 Inyo (mts.), Ca,US
130/B4 Inyonga, Tanz.
87/H1 Inza, Rus.
78/C1 Inzago, It.
99/J7 Inzai, Japan
81/G3 Ioánnina, Gre.
159/J3 Iola, Ks,US
95/H1 Iolotan', Trkm.
55/H8 Iona (isl.), Sc,UK
126/B4 Iona Nat'l Park, Ang.
160/C3 Ionia, Mi,US
81/F3 Ionian (sea), Eur.
81/F3 Ionian (isls.), Gre.
81/J4 Íos (isl.), Gre.
128/A2 Iouîk (cape), Mrta.
157/K5 Iowa (state), US
157/L5 Iowa (riv.), Ia,US
157/L5 Iowa City, Ia,US
157/K5 Iowa Falls, Ia,US
141/B1 Ipameri, Braz.
142/B5 Ipan (isl.), Chile
141/D1 Ipanema, Braz.
141/D1 Ipatinga, Braz.
65/K4 Ipel' (Ipoly) (riv.), Hun., Slvk.
138/B4 Ipiales, Col.
140/C4 Ipiaú, Braz.
140/C4 Ipirá, Braz.
141/B3 Ipiranga, Braz.
110/B3 Ipoh, Malay.
130/B4 Ipole, Tanz.
65/K4 Ipoly (Ipel') (riv.), Hun., Slvk.
137/H7 Iporá, Braz.
81/K2 Ipsala, Turk.
118/E7 Ipswich, Austl.
59/H2 Ipswich, Eng,UK
157/J4 Ipswich, SD,US
140/B2 Ipu, Braz.
141/B2 Ipuã, Braz.
140/B2 Ipubi, Braz.
140/B2 Ipueiras, Braz.
141/G7 Ipuiúna, Braz.
130/A4 Ipumba (hill), Tanz.
140/B3 Ipupiara, Braz.
136/D8 Iquique, Chile
144/C1 Iquitos, Peru
99/M10 Irago (chan.), Japan
99/E3 Irago-misaki (cape), Japan
81/J4 Iráklia (isl.), Gre.
81/J5 Iráklion, Gre.
140/B4 Iramaia, Braz.
130/B3 Iramba, Tanz.
94/F2 Iran
110/D3 Iran (mts.), Indo., Malay.
95/H3 Irānshahr, Iran
147/E4 Irapuato, Mex.
92/E3 Iraq
140/C4 Irará, Braz.
141/B3 Irati, Braz.
111/H4 Irau (mtn.), Indo.
140/C1 Irauçuba, Braz.
91/D3 Irbid, Jor.
91/E3 Irbid (gov.), Jor.
93/F2 Irbīl, Iraq
93/E3 Irbīl (gov.), Iraq
140/B3 Irecê, Braz.
55/G10 Ireland
60/D3 Ireland's Eye (isl.), Ire.
85/N5 Iremel', Gora (peak), Rus.
141/A3 Iretama, Braz.
58/C3 Irfon (riv.), Wal,UK
129/G2 Irhazer Oua-n-Agadez (wadi), Niger
101/D5 Iri, SKor.
111/H4 Irian Jaya (reg.), Indo.
139/G4 Iricoumé (mts.), Braz.
128/D2 Irîgui (reg.), Mali, Mrta.
87/L2 Iriklinskiy (res.), Rus.
130/B4 Iringa, Tanz.
130/B5 Iringa (prov.), Tanz.
108/F3 Irinjālakuda, India
100/G8 Iriomote (isl.), Japan
137/H4 Iriri (riv.), Braz.
56/C4 Irish (sea), Ire., UK
96/E1 Irkut (riv.), Rus.
96/E1 Irkutsk, Rus.
57/F5 Irlam, Eng,UK
167/J9 Ironbound, NJ,US
58/D1 Iron Bridge, Eng,UK
82/F3 Iron Gate (gorge), Rom.
160/B2 Iron Mountain, Mi,US
160/B2 Iron River, Mi,US
160/D4 Ironton, Oh,US
160/B2 Ironwood, Mi,US
160/D1 Iroquois Falls, On,Can
99/F3 Irō-zaki (pt.), Japan
86/E1 Irput' (riv.), Bela., Rus.
104/B5 Irrawaddy (riv.), Burma
104/B5 Irrawaddy (Ayeyarwady) (div.), Burma
104/B5 Irrawaddy, Mouths of the, Burma
69/F4 Irrel, Ger.
69/F3 Irsen (riv.), Ger.
57/E3 Irt (riv.), Eng,UK
57/F1 Irthing (riv.), Eng,UK
59/F2 Irthlingborough, Eng,UK
88/G4 Irtysh (riv.), Kaz., Rus.
99/H7 Iruma, Japan
130/A2 Irumu, Zaire
74/E1 Irún, Sp.
54/B5 Irvine, Sc,UK
54/B5 Irvine (bay), Sc,UK
54/B5 Irvine (riv.), Sc,UK
164/C3 Irvine, Ca,US
162/D3 Irving, Tx,US
167/D2 Irvington, NJ,US
167/E1 Irvington, NY,US
118/C3 Isaac (riv.), Austl.
144/J7 Isabela (isl.), Ecu.
112/C4 Isabela, Phil.
150/E3 Isabela, PR
148/E3 Isabelia, Cordillera (range), Nic.
153/K2 Isabella (bay), NW,Can
153/R7 Isachsen (cape), NW,Can
61/M6 Ísafjardhardjúp (fjord), Ice.
98/B4 Isahaya, Japan
133/H8 Isalo Nat'l Park, Madg.
133/H8 Isalo Ruiniform, Massif (plat.), Madg.
133/E3 Isandhlwana Battlesite, SAfr.
131/C1 Isangano Nat'l Park, Zam.
130/A3 Isango-Isoro, Zaire
64/G4 Isar (riv.), Aus., Ger.
73/J3 Isarco (Eisack) (riv.), It.
80/C2 Ischia, It.
67/H3 Ise (riv.), Ger.
99/E3 Ise, Japan
99/M10 Ise (bay), Japan
59/F2 Ise (riv.), Eng,UK
99/F3 Isehara, Japan
167/D2 Iselin, NJ,US
71/F6 Isen (riv.), Ger.
130/B5 Isenyela, Tanz.
78/D1 Iseo (lake), It.
130/B4 Iseramagazi, Tanz.
72/F4 Isère (riv.), Fr.
67/E6 Iserlohn, Ger.
80/D2 Isernia, It.
99/F2 Isesaki, Japan
99/E3 Ise-Shima Nat'l Park, Japan
85/Q4 Iset' (riv.), Rus.
129/F5 Iseyin, Nga.
99/L10 Ishi (riv.), Japan
99/F2 Ishibashi, Japan
99/M9 Ishibe, Japan
100/B4 Ishidoriya, Japan
100/H8 Ishigaki, Japan
100/G8 Ishigaki (isl.), Japan
99/F2 Ishige, Japan
100/B2 Ishikari, Japan
100/B2 Ishikari (bay), Japan
100/C2 Ishikari (mts.), Japan
99/G2 Ishikawa, Japan
99/E2 Ishikawa (pref.), Japan
99/N10 Ishiki, Japan
88/H4 Ishim (riv.), Kaz., Rus.
85/R4 Ishim, Rus.
87/L1 Ishimbay, Rus.
99/G1 Ishinomaki, Japan
99/G2 Ishioka, Japan
98/C4 Ishizuchi-san (mtn.), Japan
63/T9 Ishøj, Den.
160/C2 Ishpeming, Mi,US
136/E7 Isiboro Securé Nat'l Park, Bol.
143/G1 Isidoro, Uru.
88/H4 Isil'kul', Rus.
130/C2 Isiolo, Kenya
125/L7 Isiro, Zaire
127/C4 Is, Jabal (peak), Sudan
91/E1 İskenderun, Turk.
91/D1 İskenderun (gulf), Turk.
92/C1 İskilip, Turk.
81/H1 Iskŭr (res.), Bul.
81/H1 Iskŭr (riv.), Bul.
147/F5 Isla, Mex.
54/C2 Isla (riv.), Sc,UK
54/C3 Isla (riv.), Sc,UK
147/H5 Isla Aguada, Mex.
150/D3 Isla Cabritos Nat'l Park, DRep.
74/B4 Isla Cristina, Sp.
142/Q9 Isla de Maipo, Chile
138/C2 Isla de Salamanca Nat'l Park, Col.
118/C4 Isla Gorge Nat'l Park, Austl.
92/E1 İslâhiye, Turk.
146/D4 Isla Isabela Nat'l Park, Mex.
108/B1 Islāmābād (cap.), Pak.
108/B1 Islāmābād Cap. Terr. (terr.), Pak.
142/B5 Isla Magdalena Nat'l Park, Chile
106/E2 Islāmpur, India
117/H4 Island (lag.), Austl.
157/K2 Island (lake), Mb,Can
165/C2 Island (co.), Wa,US
167/D4 Island Beach Saint Park, NJ,US
157/K2 Island Lake, Mb,Can
161/K1 Islands (bay), Nf,Can
55/J9 Islay (isl.), Sc,UK
72/D4 Isle (riv.), Fr.
57/G2 Isleham, Eng,UK
56/D3 Isle of Man, UK
56/D2 Isle of Whithorn, Sc,UK
160/B1 Isle Royale (isl.), Mi,US
160/B2 Isle Royale Nat'l Park, Mi,US
53/N7 Islington (bor.), Eng,UK
167/E2 Islip, NY,US
91/C4 Ismailia (Al Ismā'īlīyah), Egypt
85/X9 Izmailovo Park, Rus.
71/E6 Ismaning, Ger.
127/C3 Isnā, Egypt
77/G2 Isny, Ger.
99/M10 Isobe, Japan
63/L1 Isojärven Nat'l Park, Fin.
63/J1 Isojärvi (lake), Fin.
130/B5 Isoka, Zam.
79/E2 Isola Della Scala, It.
80/C2 Isola del Liri, It.
80/E3 Isola di Capo Rizzuto, It.
79/G1 Isonzo (riv.), It.
92/B2 Isparta, Turk.
92/B2 Isparta (prov.), Turk.
72/C5 Ispéguy, Col d' (pass), Fr.
83/H4 Isperikh, Bul.
92/E1 İspir, Turk.
91/C3 Israel
139/G3 Issano, Guy.
165/C2 Issaquah, Wa,US
165/C2 Issaquah (cr.), Wa,US
66/D5 Issel (riv.), Ger.
66/D5 Isselburg, Ger.
128/D5 Issia, IvC.
72/E4 Issoire, Fr.
72/E3 Issoudun, Fr.
66/D5 Issum, Ger.
130/B4 Issuna, Tanz.
102/C3 Issyk-Kul' (lake), Kyr.
68/B6 Issy-les-Moulineaux, Fr.
82/E1 Istállós-kő (peak), Hun.
92/B1 İstanbul, Turk.
83/J5 İstanbul (prov.), Turk.
93/M6 İstanbul (inset), Turk.
79/G2 Istarske Toplice, Cro.
83/H5 Istranca (mts.), Turk.
72/F5 Istres, Fr.
82/A3 Istria (pen.), Cro.
112/D4 Isulan, Phil.
140/C3 Itabaiana, Braz.
140/D2 Itabaiana, Braz.
140/C3 Itabaianinha, Braz.
141/D2 Itabapoana (riv.), Braz.
140/B4 Itaberaba, Braz.
141/D1 Itabira, Braz.
141/D2 Itabirito, Braz.
141/L7 Itaboraí, Braz.
140/C4 Itabuna, Braz.
137/H5 Itacaiunas (riv.), Braz.
140/A4 Itacarambi, Braz.
139/G5 Itacoatiara, Braz.
144/D2 Itacuaí (riv.), Braz.
140/C3 Itacuruba, Braz.
140/B4 Itaeté, Braz.
101/G6 It'aewŏn, SKor.
130/B4 Itaga, Tanz.
140/C4 Itagibá, Braz.
141/K7 Itaguaí, Braz.
141/C2 Itaguara, Braz.
138/C3 Itagüí, Col.
141/B2 Itaí, Braz.
140/C3 Itaíba, Braz.
140/C2 Itaiçaba, Braz.
140/B2 Itainópolis, Braz.
141/B3 Itaiópolis, Braz.
135/F1 Itaipu (res.), Braz., Par.
135/F2 Itaipú (dam), Par.
137/G4 Itaituba, Braz.
141/B1 Itajá, Braz.
141/B3 Itajaí, Braz.
141/B3 Itajaí (riv.), Braz.
141/H7 Itajubá, Braz.
140/C4 Itajuípe, Braz.
99/G3 Itako, Japan
52/E4 Italy
140/C5 Itamaraju, Braz.
141/D1 Itamarandiba, Braz.
141/D1 Itambacuri, Braz.
140/B4 Itambé, Braz.
141/D1 Itambé (peak), Braz.
99/L10 Itami, Japan
141/J7 Itamonte, Braz.
104/B3 Itanagar, India
141/G9 Itanhaém, Braz.
141/C2 Itanhandu, Braz.
140/B5 Itanhém, Braz.
141/D1 Itanhém (riv.), Braz.
141/D1 Itanhomi, Braz.
140/B5 Itaobim, Braz.
141/D2 Itaocara, Braz.
140/C1 Itapagé, Braz.
140/C4 Itaparica (isl.), Braz.
140/C4 Itapebi, Braz.
141/C2 Itapecerica, Braz.
140/A1 Itapecuru-Mirim, Braz.
141/D2 Itapemirim, Braz.
141/D2 Itaperuna, Braz.
140/B4 Itapetinga, Braz.
141/B2 Itapetininga, Braz.
141/B2 Itapeva, Braz.
141/B2 Itapevi, Braz.
140/C3 Itapicuru (riv.), Braz.
140/A1 Itapicuru (riv.), Braz.
140/C1 Itapipoca, Braz.
141/G7 Itapira, Braz.
140/C4 Itapitanga, Braz.
141/B2 Itaporanga, Braz.
141/G8 Itaquaquecetuba, Braz.
140/B4 Itarantim, Braz.
141/B3 Itararé, Braz.
141/F9 Itariri, Braz.
106/C3 Itārsi, India
140/B4 Itaruçu, Braz.
141/C2 Itatiaia Nat'l Park, Braz.
141/G8 Itatiba, Braz.
141/C2 Itatinga (res.), Braz.
140/B2 Itaueira, Braz.
140/B3 Itaueira (riv.), Braz.
141/C2 Itaúna, Braz.
100/B3 Itayanagi, Japan
105/J4 Itbayat (isl.), Phil.
59/E4 Itchen (riv.), Eng,UK
125/K7 Itembiri (riv.), Zaire
136/F6 Iténez (riv.), Bol.
126/E4 Itezhi-Tezhi (dam), Zam.
160/E3 Ithaca, NY,US
81/G3 Ithaca (Itháki) (isl.), Gre.
81/G3 Itháki (Ithaca) (isl.), Gre.
67/G5 Ith Hils (ridge), Ger.
58/C2 Ithon (riv.), Wal,UK
130/B4 Itigi, Tanz.
140/B5 Itinga, Braz.
99/F3 Itō, Japan
130/B4 Itobo, Tanz.
99/E2 Itoigawa, Japan
100/J7 Itoman, Japan
72/D2 Iton (riv.), Fr.
140/B4 Itororó, Braz.
77/F5 I Tre Signori, Pizzo dei (peak), It.
99/H7 Itsukaichi, Japan
67/F6 Itter (riv.), Ger.
80/A2 Ittiri, It.
141/C2 Itu, Braz.
140/C4 Ituberá, Braz.
144/D2 Ituí (riv.), Braz.
141/B1 Ituiutaba, Braz.
141/B1 Itumbiara, Braz.
141/B1 Itumbiara (res.), Braz.
141/J6 Itumirim, Braz.
157/H3 Ituna, Sk,Can
130/B5 Itungi Port, Tanz.
137/J5 Itupiranga, Braz.
141/B3 Ituporanga, Braz.
141/B1 Iturama, Braz.
141/J6 Itutinga (res.), Braz.
136/E5 Ituxi (riv.), Braz.
141/C2 Ituverava, Braz.
143/F2 Ituzaingó, Uru.
91/B4 Ityāy al Bārūd, Egypt
70/E2 Itz (riv.), Ger.
64/E2 Itzehoe, Ger.
151/C2 Iul'tin, Gora (mtn.), Rus.
141/D2 Iuna, Braz.
141/B2 Ivaí (riv.), Braz.
141/B3 Ivaiporã, Braz.
61/H1 Ivalo, Fin.
61/H1 Ivalojoki (riv.), Fin.
73/M2 Ivančice, Czh.
82/D4 Ivangrad, Yugo.
160/D1 Ivanhoe (riv.), On,Can
82/E4 Ivanjica, Yugo.
86/C2 Ivano-Frankovsk, Ukr.
86/C2 Ivano-Frankovsk Obl., Ukr.
84/J4 Ivanovo, Rus.
85/J4 Ivanovo Obl., Rus.
81/J2 Ivaylovgrad (res.), Bul.
85/P3 Ivdel, Rus.
53/M7 Iver, Eng,UK
54/G11 Iveragh (pen.), Ire.
53/M7 Iver Heath, Eng,UK
127/H7 Ivindo (riv.), Gabon
133/H8 Ivohibe, Madg.
133/J7 Ivondro (riv.), Madg.
128/D5 Ivory Coast (reg.), IvC.
128/D5 Ivory Coast (Côte d'Ivoire)
62/F3 Ivösjön (lake), Swe.
78/A2 Ivrea, It.
68/B6 Ivry-sur-Seine, Fr.
58/C6 Ivybridge, Eng,UK
99/F2 Iwai, Japan
100/B4 Iwaizumi, Japan
99/G2 Iwaki, Japan
100/B3 Iwaki-san (mtn.), Japan
98/C3 Iwakuni, Japan
99/M9 Iwakura, Japan
98/D3 Iwami, Japan
100/B2 Iwamizawa, Japan
100/B2 Iwanai, Japan
99/G1 Iwanuma, Japan
99/E3 Iwata, Japan
100/B4 Iwate, Japan
100/B4 Iwate (dept.), Japan
100/B4 Iwate-san (mtn.), Japan
99/H7 Iwatsuki, Japan
129/G5 Iwo, Nga.
120/D2 Iwo Jima (isl.), Japan
148/D3 Ixcán (riv.), Guat., Mex.
64/C3 Ixelles, Belg.
147/F4 Ixmiquilpan, Mex.
147/L7 Ixtaccihuatl-Popotzteco Nat'l Park, Mex.
147/Q10 Ixtapalapa, Mex.
147/K8 Ixtapan de la Sal, Mex.
146/D4 Ixtlán del Río, Mex.
59/G2 Ixworth, Eng,UK
96/D1 Iya (riv.), Rus.
98/C4 Iyo, Japan
98/C4 Iyo (sea), Japan
148/D3 Izabal (lake), Guat.
147/H4 Izamal, Mex.
87/H4 Izberbash, Rus.
68/C2 Izegem, Belg.
151/F4 Izembek Nat'l Wild. Ref., Ak,US
85/M4 Izhevsk, Rus.
85/M2 Izhma (riv.), Rus.
151/E5 Izigan (cape), Ak,US
95/G4 Izkī, Oman
83/J3 Izmail, Ukr.
92/A2 İzmir, Turk.
92/A2 İzmir (prov.), Turk.
83/J5 İzmit, Turk.
83/J5 İzmit (gulf), Turk.
74/C4 Iznájar, Sp.
83/J5 İznik, Turk.
83/H5 İznik (lake), Turk.
79/G1 Izola, Slov.
148/E3 Izopo (pt.), Hon.
91/E3 Izra', Syria
82/D2 Izsák, Hun.
97/M5 Izu (isls.), Japan
99/F3 Izu (pen.), Japan
147/F5 Izúcar de Matamoros, Mex.
99/H8 Izu-Fuji-Hakone Nat'l Park, Japan
98/A3 Izuhara, Japan
98/B4 Izumi, Japan
98/D3 Izumi, Japan
99/L10 Izumi-ōtsu, Japan
98/D3 Izumi-Sano, Japan
98/C3 Izumo, Japan
86/F2 Izyum, Ukr.

J

63/M1 Jääsjarvi (lake), Fin.
127/B5 Jabal Abyad (plat.), Sudan
149/F5 Jabalí (pt.), Pan.
91/D2 Jabal Lubnān (gov.), Leb.
74/D3 Jabalón (riv.), Sp.
106/C3 Jabalpur, India
91/D4 Jabālyah, Gaza
68/C1 Jabbeke, Belg.
92/D3 Jabbūl, Sabkhat al (lake), Syria
127/C4 Jabjabah, Wādī (dry riv.), Egypt, Sudan
91/D2 Jablah, Syria
81/G2 Jablanica (mts.), Alb.
65/H3 Jablonec nad Nisou, Czh.
140/D3 Jaboatão, Braz.
141/B2 Jaboticabal, Braz.
82/E3 Jabuka, Yugo.
110/B4 Jabung (cape), Indo.
75/E1 Jaca, Sp.
140/B3 Jacaré (riv.), Braz.
141/C2 Jacareí, Braz.
125/Q5 Jaceel (riv.), Som.
140/B5 Jacinto, Braz.
161/G2 Jackman, Me,US
158/D2 Jackpot, Nv,US
162/D3 Jacksboro, Tx,US
166/A2 Jacks Mountain (ridge), Pa,US
163/G4 Jackson, Al,US
158/B3 Jackson, Ca,US
160/C3 Jackson, Mi,US
157/K5 Jackson, Mn,US
159/K3 Jackson, Mo,US
163/F3 Jackson (cap.), Ms,US
156/D5 Jackson (mts.), Nv,US
160/D4 Jackson, Oh,US
163/F3 Jackson, Tn,US
156/F5 Jackson, Wy,US
156/F4 Jackson (lake), Wy,US
167/K9 Jackson Heights, NY,US
163/G3 Jacksonville, Al,US
162/E3 Jacksonville, Ar,US
163/H4 Jacksonville, Fl,US
160/B4 Jacksonville, Il,US
163/J3 Jacksonville, NC,US
162/E4 Jacksonville, Tx,US
163/H4 Jacksonville Beach, Fl,US
149/H2 Jacmel, Haiti
146/E3 Jaco, Mex.
95/J3 Jacobābād, Pak.
140/B3 Jacobina, Braz.
146/E5 Jacona de Plancarte, Mex.
161/H1 Jacques-Cartier (mtn.), Qu,Can
161/G2 Jacques-Cartier (riv.), Qu,Can
135/F2 Jacuí (riv.), Braz.
140/C3 Jacuipe (riv.), Braz.
141/C3 Jacupiranga, Braz.
138/D2 Jacūra, Ven.
95/H3 Jaddi (pt.), Pak.
64/E2 Jade (bay), Ger.
67/F2 Jade (riv.), Ger.
67/F2 Jadebusen (bay), Ger.
144/B2 Jaén, Peru
112/C2 Jaen, Phil.
74/D4 Jaén, Sp.
119/A3 Jaffa (cape), Austl.
108/H4 Jaffna, SrL.
108/H4 Jaffna (dist.), SrL.
108/D2 Jagādhri, India
106/D4 Jagdalpur, India
106/D2 Jagdīspur, India
112/D3 Jagna, Phil.
108/C2 Jagraon, India
70/C4 Jagst (riv.), Ger.
106/C4 Jagtiāl, India
140/C4 Jaguaquara, Braz.
143/G2 Jaguarão, Braz.
143/G2 Jaguarão (riv.), Braz.
140/B3 Jaguarari, Braz.
141/B2 Jaguaretama, Braz.
141/G7 Jaguari (riv.), Braz.
141/B3 Jaguariaíva, Braz.
140/C2 Jaguaribe, Braz.
140/C2 Jaguaribe (riv.), Braz.
141/G7 Jaguariúna, Braz.
140/C2 Jaguaruana, Braz.
119/D3 Jagungal (peak), Austl.
93/H4 Jahrom, Iran
139/H4 Jai (cr.), Sur.
140/B2 Jaicós, Braz.
111/G3 Jailolo, Indo.
96/E4 Jainca, China
106/C2 Jaipur, India
106/B2 Jaisalmer, India
82/C3 Jajce, Bosn.
106/E3 Jājpur, India
110/C5 Jakarta (cap.), Indo.
61/G3 Jakobstad, Fin.
159/G4 Jal, NM,US
147/M7 Jalacingo, Mex.
97/J2 Jalaid Qi, China
95/K2 Jalālābād, Afg.
108/C2 Jalālābād, India
148/D3 Jalapa, Guat.
147/N7 Jalapa Enríquez, Mex.
61/G3 Jalasjärvi, Fin.
141/B2 Jales, Braz.
106/C3 Jālgaon, India
93/F4 Jalīb ash Shuyūkh, Kuw.
124/H6 Jalingo, Nga.
146/D4 Jalisco (state), Mex.
80/A4 Jāliṭah, Jazīrat (isl.), Tun.
76/C6 Jallouvre, Pic de (peak), Fr.
106/C4 Jālna, India
74/E2 Jalon (riv.), Sp.
106/B2 Jālor, India
146/E4 Jalpa, Mex.
106/E2 Jalpaiguri, India
148/C2 Jaltepec (riv.), Mex.
147/G5 Jáltipan, Mex.
125/K2 Jālū, Libya
120/F4 Jaluit (atoll), Mrsh.
93/F3 Jalūlā', Iraq
125/P7 Jamaame, Som.
129/H4 Jamaare (riv.), Nga.
149/G2 Jamaica
149/F2 Jamaica (chan.), Haiti, Jam.
167/K9 Jamaica, NY,US
167/E3 Jamaica (bay), NY,US
106/E3 Jamālpur, Bang.
106/E2 Jamālpur, India

195
Jaman – Kalug

150/D4 Jamanota (peak), Aru.
137/G5 Jamanxim (riv.), Braz.
147/N7 Jamapa, Mex.
136/F5 Jamari (riv.), Braz.
110/B4 Jambi, Indo.
112/B4 Jambongan (isl.), Malay.
110/A2 Jambuair (cape), Indo.
155/K1 James (lake), On,Can
153/H3 James (bay), On, Qu,Can
142/B5 James (pt.), Chile
157/J4 James (riv.), ND, SD,US
160/E4 James (riv.), Va,US
154/V12 James Campbell Nat'l Wild. Ref., Hi,US
167/F2 Jamesport, NY,US
152/G1 James Ross (str.), NW,Can
157/J4 Jamestown, ND,US
160/E3 Jamestown, NY,US
163/G2 Jamestown, Tn,US
148/B2 Jamiltepec, Mex.
62/C3 Jammerbugt (bay), Den.
102/B5 Jammu, India
102/C5 Jammu and Kashmīr (state), India
106/B3 Jāmnagar, India
95/K3 Jāmpur, Pak.
61/H3 Jämsä, Fin.
106/E3 Jamshedpur, India
61/E3 Jämtland (co.), Swe.
106/E3 Jamūi, India
157/H2 Jan (lake), Sk,Can
63/L1 Janakkala, Fin.
140/B4 Janaúba, Braz.
137/J3 Janaucu (isl.), Braz.
141/B2 Jandaia do Sul, Braz.
74/C4 Jándula (riv.), Sp.
116/L6 Jane (brook), Austl.
160/B3 Janesville, Wi,US
131/D5 Jangamo, Moz.
106/C4 Jangaon, India
106/E3 Jangipur, India
65/K2 Janikowo, Pol.
91/D3 Janīn, WBnk.
82/D3 Janja, Bosn.
52/D1 Jan Mayen (isl.), Nor.
146/C2 Janos, Mex.
82/D2 Jánoshalma, Hun.
65/M3 Janów Lubelski, Pol.
140/A4 Januária, Braz.
91/C5 Janūb Sīnā' (gov.), Egypt
106/C3 Jaora, India
97/M4 Japan
97/L4 Japan (sea), Asia
99/E3 Japanese Alps (range), Japan
99/E2 Japanese Alps Nat'l Park, Japan
139/E5 Japurá (riv.), Braz.
150/D3 Jarabacoa, DRep.
74/C2 Jaraíz de la Vera, Sp.
108/B2 Jarānwāla, Pak.
91/D3 Jarash, Jor.
124/H1 Jarbah (isl.), Tun.
140/C2 Jardim, Braz.
140/C2 Jardim do Seridó, Braz.
135/E2 Jardín América, Arg.
149/G1 Jardines de la Reina (arch.), Cuba
141/C2 Jardinópolis, Braz.
63/R7 Jarfalla, Swe.
137/H3 Jari (riv.), Braz.
106/E3 Jaridih, India
124/H1 Jarjīs, Tun.
62/G2 Järna, Swe.
69/E5 Jarny, Fr.
112/D3 Jaro, Phil.
65/J3 Jarocin, Pol.
65/H3 Jaroměř, Czh.
65/M3 Jarosław, Pol.
57/G2 Jarrow, Eng,UK
109/C2 Jars (plain), Laos
103/E1 Jarud Qi, China
63/L1 Järvenpää, Fin.
69/F6 Jarville-la-Malgrange, Fr.
121/J5 Jarvis (isl.), PacUS
65/L4 Jasło, Pol.
156/D2 Jasper, Ab,Can
163/G3 Jasper, Al,US
163/H4 Jasper, Fl,US
163/G3 Jasper, Ga,US
160/C4 Jasper, In,US
162/E4 Jasper, Tx,US
156/D2 Jasper Nat'l Park, Ab, BC,Can
106/C2 Jaspur, India
70/C2 Jassa (riv.), Ger.
65/J2 Jastrowie, Pol.
65/K4 Jastrzębie Zdroj, Pol.
82/E2 Jászapáti, Hun.
82/D2 Jászárokszállás, Hun.
82/D2 Jászberény, Hun.
82/E2 Jászladány, Hun.
82/E2 Jász-Nagykun-Szolnok (co.), Hun.
141/B1 Jataí, Braz.
139/G5 Jatapu (riv.), Braz.
148/D2 Jatate (riv.), Mex.
140/C2 Jati, Braz.
149/G1 Jatibonico, Cuba
75/E3 Játiva, Sp.
141/B2 Jaú, Braz.
139/F5 Jaú (riv.), Braz.
139/E5 Jauaperi (riv.), Braz.
139/F5 Jauaperi (riv.), Braz.
139/H5 Jauaru (mts.), Braz.
139/F3 Jaua Sarisarinama Nat'l Park, Ven.
108/B1 Jauharābād, Pak.
144/C3 Jauja, Peru
76/D4 Jaunpass (pass), Swi.
110/C5 Java (isl.), Indo.
110/D5 Java (sea), Indo.
144/C2 Javari (riv.), Braz.
75/F3 Jávea, Sp.
143/J6 Javier (isl.), Chile
82/D1 Javorie (peak), Slvk.
71/G2 Javornice (riv.), Czh.
71/G4 Javorník (peak), Czh.
71/H3 Javorová Skála (peak), Czh.
125/Q7 Jawhar (Giohar), Som.
65/J3 Jawor, Pol.
111/J4 Jaya (peak), Indo.
144/B2 Jayanca, Peru
111/K4 Jayapura, Indo.
162/C3 Jayton, Tx,US
59/H3 Jaywick, Eng,UK
94/D5 Jazā'ir Farasān (isls.), SAr.
54/D6 Jedburgh, Sc,UK
65/L3 Jędrzejów, Pol.
54/D6 Jed Water (riv.), Sc,UK
64/F2 Jeetze (riv.), Ger.
168/G7 Jefferson (co.), Oh,US
156/C4 Jefferson (peak), Or,US
162/E3 Jefferson, Tx,US
165/B2 Jefferson (co.), Wa,US
165/N14 Jefferson (co.), Wi,US
159/J3 Jefferson City (cap.), Mo,US
160/C4 Jeffersonville, In,US
156/G5 Jeffrey City, Wy,US
71/G2 Jehličná (mtn.), Czh.
142/B5 Jeinemeni (peak), Chile
63/L3 Jēkabpils, Lat.
65/J3 Jelcz-Laskowice, Pol.
65/H3 Jelenia Góra, Pol.
65/H3 Jelenia Góra (prov.), Pol.
106/E2 Jelep (pass), China
63/K3 Jelgava, Lat.
68/C3 Jemappes, Belg.
110/D5 Jember, Indo.
130/C4 Jembiani, Tanz.
158/F4 Jemez Pueblo, NM,US
96/B2 Jeminay, China
111/E4 Jempang (riv.), Indo.
127/C3 Jemsa, Egypt
64/F3 Jena, Ger.
162/E4 Jena, La,US
111/E5 Jeneponto, Indo.
162/E4 Jennings, La,US
152/F2 Jenny Lind (isl.), NW,Can
153/H2 Jens Muck (isl.), NW,Can
140/B4 Jequié, Braz.
140/A5 Jequitaí, Braz.
140/B5 Jequitinhonha, Braz.
140/C5 Jequitinhonha (riv.), Braz.
123/N13 Jerada, Mor.
149/H2 Jérémie, Haiti
140/C3 Jeremoabo, Braz.
146/E4 Jerez, Mex.
74/B4 Jerez de la Frontera, Sp.
74/B3 Jerez de los Caballeros, Sp.
167/E2 Jericho, NY,US
91/D4 Jericho (Arīḩā), WBnk.
168/C2 Jerimoth (hill), RI,US
156/E5 Jerome, Id,US
168/E6 Jerome Fork (riv.), Oh,US
72/B2 Jersey (isl.), ChI,UK
167/D2 Jersey City, NJ,US
167/H8 Jersey City (res.), NJ,US
160/B4 Jerseyville, Il,US
94/B2 Jerusalem (cap.), Isr.
91/F8 Jerusalem (dist.), Isr.
91/G8 Jerusalem Walls Nat'l Park, Isr.
91/D4 Jerusalem (Yerushalayim) (cap.), Isr.
156/C3 Jervis (inlet), BC,Can
67/G6 Jesberg, Ger.
82/B2 Jesenice, Slov.
71/F2 Jesenice, Udolní nádrž (res.), Czh.
79/G5 Jesi, It.
62/D1 Jessheim, Nor.
106/E3 Jessore, Bang.
141/H7 Jesuâna, Braz.
163/H4 Jesup, Ga,US
161/N6 Jésus (isl.), Qu,Can
135/D3 Jesús María, Arg.
149/G1 Jesús Menéndez, Cuba
128/A4 Jeta (isl.), GBis.
159/H3 Jetmore, Ks,US
106/B3 Jetpur, India
68/D3 Jeumont, Fr.
67/E1 Jever, Ger.
157/G5 Jewel Cave Nat'l Mon., SD,US
106/D4 Jeypore, India
81/F2 Jezerce (peak), Alb.
71/G4 Jezerní Stěna (peak), Czh.
65/K2 Jeziorák (lake), Pol.
106/E3 Jhā Jhā, India
106/C3 Jhālawār, India
108/B2 Jhang Sadar, Pak.
106/C2 Jhānsi, India
106/D3 Jhārsuguda, India
108/B1 Jhawāriān, Pak.
108/B1 Jhelum (riv.), India, Pak.
108/B1 Jhelum, Pak.
108/B2 Jhumra, Pak.
104/B1 Ji (riv.), China
103/L8 Jiading, China
106/E3 Jiāganj, India
107/K2 Jiahe, China
96/F5 Jialing (riv.), China
103/C4 Jialu (riv.), China
97/L2 Jiamusi, China
105/F4 Jian (riv.), China
105/H3 Jian (riv.), China
104/E2 Jiancheng, China
109/E1 Jiang (riv.), China
107/J2 Jiang'an, China
104/C3 Jiangao (mtn.), China
104/D4 Jiangcheng Hanizu Yizu Zizhixian (Jiangcheng), China
104/D3 Jiangchuan, China
103/D4 Jiangdu, China
105/F3 Jianghua Yaozu Zizhixian, China
104/E2 Jiangjin, China
103/C5 Jiangling, China
105/G4 Jiangmen, China
103/D5 Jiangning, China
103/D4 Jiangsu (prov.), China
105/G3 Jiangxi (prov.), China
103/B4 Jiang Xian, China
103/E5 Jiangyin, China
105/F3 Jiangyong, China
104/E2 Jiangyou, China
107/J2 Jianhe, China
103/D4 Jianhu, China
103/C5 Jianli, China
105/H3 Jian'ou, China
97/H3 Jianping, China
103/B5 Jianshi, China
104/D4 Jianshui, China
105/H3 Jianyang, China
103/C3 Jiaocheng, China
97/K3 Jiaohe, China
105/J2 Jiaojiang, China
103/C5 Jiaokou, China
97/J3 Jiaolai (riv.), China
103/D4 Jiaonan, China
103/C4 Jiaozuo, China
103/D4 Jiashan, China
103/L9 Jiashan, China
102/C4 Jiashi, China
103/B3 Jia Xian, China
103/D4 Jiaxiang, China
103/L9 Jiaxing, China
97/L2 Jiayin, China
103/C5 Jiayu, China
96/D4 Jiayuguan, China
83/F2 Jibou, Rom.
95/G4 Jibsh, Ra's (pt.), Oman
147/N8 Jicaro, Mex.
149/F5 Jicarón (isl.), Pan.
65/H3 Jičín, Czh.
147/F5 Jico, Mex.
97/L2 Jidong, China
103/C4 Jieshou, China
103/B3 Jiexiu, China
105/H4 Jieyang, China
116/D2 Jigalong Abor. Land, Austl.
149/G1 Jiguaní, Cuba
96/E5 Jigzhi, China
71/H4 Jihlava, Czh.
71/H4 Jihočeský (reg.), Czh.
65/J4 Jihomoravský (reg.), Czh.
123/U17 Jijel, Alg.
123/U17 Jijel (gov.), Alg.
83/H2 Jijia (riv.), Rom.
125/P6 Jijiga, Eth.
75/E3 Jijona, Sp.
127/A4 Jilf al Kabīr, Hadabat al (upland), Egypt
141/B2 Jilhá (res.), Braz.
65/J4 Jihlava (riv.), Czh.
102/E2 Jili (lake), China
125/P7 Jilib, Som.
97/K3 Jilin, China
101/D1 Jilin (prov.), China
97/J1 Jiliu (riv.), China
75/E2 Jiloca (riv.), Sp.
125/N6 Jīma, Eth.
131/A1 Jimbe, Ang.
82/E3 Jimbolia, Rom.
74/C4 Jimena de la Frontera, Sp.
146/D3 Jiménez, Mex.
103/E3 Jimo, China
96/B3 Jimsar, China
105/G2 Jin (riv.), China
105/H3 Jin (riv.), China
103/J3 Jinan, China
96/E4 Jinchang, China
103/C3 Jincheng, China
106/C2 Jīnd, India
119/D3 Jindabyne (dam), Austl.
65/H4 Jindřichuv Hradec, Czh.
105/E2 Jinfo (mtn.), China
103/B4 Jing (riv.), China
103/D4 Jingbian, China
103/D5 Jingde, China
105/H2 Jingdezhen, China
107/H3 Jingdong, China
105/G3 Jinggangshan, China
103/D3 Jinghai, China
102/D3 Jinghe, China
104/D4 Jinghong, China
103/E4 Jingjiang, China
103/D3 Jingle, China
103/C5 Jingmen, China
96/F4 Jingning, China
104/D3 Jingping (mts.), China
103/C5 Jingshan, China
104/E4 Jingxi, China
103/D5 Jing Xian, China
105/F3 Jing Xian, China
101/D1 Jingyu, China
96/E4 Jingyuan, China
103/D4 Jinhu, China
105/H2 Jinhua, China
103/C2 Jining, China
103/D4 Jining, China
130/B2 Jinja, Ugan.
107/H2 Jinkouhe, China
105/H3 Jinmen (isl.), China
148/E3 Jinotega, Nic.
148/E4 Jinotepe, Nic.
104/D4 Jinping, China
105/F3 Jinping, China
103/B4 Jinqian (riv.), China
103/E5 Jinshan, China
104/D3 Jinsha (Yangtze) (riv.), China
107/K2 Jinshi, China
103/D5 Jintan, China
112/C2 Jintotolo (chan.), Phil.
106/C4 Jintūr, India
103/E2 Jinxi, China
105/H3 Jinxi, China
103/D4 Jinxiang, China
107/K3 Jinxiu Yaozu Zizhixian, China
105/J2 Jinyun, China
103/C5 Jinzhai, China
103/E2 Jinzhou, China
101/A3 Jinzhou (bay), China
136/F6 Ji-Paraná, Braz.
136/F5 Jiparaná (riv.), Braz.
138/A5 Jipijapa, Ecu.
146/E5 Jiquilpan de Juárez, Mex.
147/Q9 Jiquipilco, Mex.
127/B3 Jirgā, Egypt
71/G2 Jiřkov, Czh.
103/B4 Jishan, China
105/F2 Jishou, China
91/E2 Jisr ash Shughūr, Syria
83/F4 Jiu (riv.), Rom.
104/D2 Jiuding (mtn.), China
105/G2 Jiugong (mtn.), China
105/H2 Jiuhua (mtn.), China
103/C5 Jiujiang, China
105/G2 Jiuling (mts.), China
104/D2 Jiulong, China
97/K3 Jiutai, China
105/E3 Jiuwan (mts.), China
105/H2 Jixi, China
103/C4 Ji Xian, China
103/D2 Ji Xian, China
97/L2 Jixian, China
103/D3 Jiyang, China
103/C4 Jiyuan, China
91/B5 Jīzah, Ahrāmāt al (Pyramids of Giza) (ruins), Egypt
103/C3 Jize, China
71/H2 Jizera (riv.), Czh.
98/C3 Jizō-zaki (pt.), Japan
104/D3 Jizu (mtn.), China
94/F5 Jiz', Wādī al (dry riv.), Yem.
141/B3 Joaçaba, Braz.
147/N8 Joachín, Mex.
140/B5 Joaíma, Braz.
140/D2 João Câmara, Braz.
140/A2 João Lisboa, Braz.
141/D1 João Monlevade, Braz.
140/D2 João Pessoa, Braz.
141/C1 João Pinheiro, Braz.
135/D2 Joaquín V. González, Arg.
149/G1 Jobabo, Cuba
70/B4 Jockgrim, Ger.
74/D4 Jódar, Sp.
106/B2 Jodhpur, India
69/D2 Jodoigne, Belg.
61/J3 Joensuu, Fin.
99/F2 Jōetsu, Japan
69/F5 Joeuf, Fr.
132/E2 Johannesburg, SAfr.
158/C4 Johannesburg, Ca,US
71/F2 Johanngeorgenstadt, Ger.
156/D4 John Day, Or,US
156/C4 John Day (riv.), Or,US
156/C4 John Day Fossil Beds Nat'l Mon., Or,US
156/D4 John Day, Middle Fork (riv.), Or,US
156/D4 John Day, North Fork (riv.), Or,US
116/C4 John Forrest Nat'l Park, Austl.
160/E4 John H. Kerr (dam), Va,US
162/C2 John Martin (res.), Co,US
55/K7 John O'Groats, Sc,UK
54/D3 Johnshaven, Sc,UK
161/S9 Johnson (cr.), NY,US
163/H2 Johnson City, Tn,US
162/D4 Johnson City, Tx,US
159/G3 Johnson (Johnson City), Ks,US
151/M3 Johnsons Crossing, Yk,Can
116/D5 Johnston (lake), Austl.
121/J3 Johnston (atoll), PacUS
58/B3 Johnston, Wal,UK
130/A5 Johnston (falls), Zam.
54/B5 Johnstone, Sc,UK
160/E3 Johnstown, Pa,US
110/B3 Johor Baharu, Malay.
72/E3 Joigny, Fr.
141/B3 Joinville, Braz.
113/W Joinville (isl.), Ant.
147/F5 Jojutla, Mex.
147/K8 Jojutla de Juárez, Mex.
125/M6 Jokau, Sudan
61/F2 Jokkmokk, Swe.
61/P6 Jökulsargljufur Nat'l Park, Ice.
165/P16 Joliet, Il,US
160/F2 Joliette, Qu,Can
162/D4 Jollyville, Tx,US
112/C4 Jolo, Phil.
112/C4 Jolo (isl.), Phil.
112/C2 Jomalig (isl.), Phil.
110/D5 Jombang, Indo.
104/C2 Jomda, China
130/B3 Jomu, Tanz.
77/E3 Jona, Swi.
147/L8 Jonacatepec
63/L4 Jonava, Lith.
153/S7 Jones (sound), NW,Can
167/L9 Jones (inlet), NY,US
166/A2 Jones (mtn.), Pa,US
167/L9 Jones Beach Saint Park, NY,US
163/F3 Jonesboro, Ar,US
162/E3 Jonesboro, La,US
56/B3 Jonesborough, NI,UK
62/F3 Jönköping, Swe.
62/F3 Jönköping (co.), Swe.
161/G1 Jonquière, Qu,Can
116/K6 Joondalup (lake), Austl.
159/J3 Joplin, Mo,US
166/B5 Joppa (Joppatowne), Md,US
92/D4 Jordan
161/R9 Jordan, On,Can
91/D4 Jordan (riv.), Jor., WBnk.
156/G4 Jordan, Mt,US
166/C2 Jordan (cr.), Pa,US
158/E2 Jordan (riv.), Ut,US
140/B4 Jordânia, Braz.
161/R9 Jordan Station, On,Can
156/D5 Jordan Valley, Or,US
63/S7 Jordbro, Swe.
143/J7 Jorge (cape), Chile
104/B3 Jorhāt, India
67/G1 Jork, Ger.
162/B3 Jornada del Muerto (val.), NM,US
62/B2 Jørpeland, Nor.
129/H4 Jos (plat.), Nga.
112/D4 Jose Abad Santos, Phil.
141/B2 José Bonifacio, Braz.
147/N7 José Cardel, Mex.
140/B2 José de Freitas, Braz.
135/B5 José de San Martín, Arg.
112/C2 Jose Pañganiban, Phil.
114/D2 Joseph Bonaparte (gulf), Austl.
99/F2 Joshin-Etsu Kogen Nat'l Park, Japan
168/B3 Joshua (pt.), Ct,US
158/D4 Joshua Tree Nat'l Mon., Ca,US
62/C1 Jotunheimen Nat'l Park, Nor.
72/C2 Jouanne (riv.), Fr.
68/C6 Jouarre, Fr.
72/D3 Joué-lès-Tours, Fr.
118/B2 Jourama Falls Nat'l Park, Austl.
162/D4 Jourdanton, Tx,US
66/C3 Joure, Neth.
63/N1 Joutseno, Fin.
76/C4 Joux (lake), Fr.
53/S10 Jouy-en-Josas, Fr.
53/S9 Jouy-le-Moutier, Fr.
149/F1 Jovellanos, Cuba
93/J2 Joveyn (riv.), Iran
107/F2 Jowai, India
151/M3 Joy (mtn.), Yk,Can
60/A2 Joyce's Country (dist.), Ire.
99/L10 Jōyō, Japan
100/B2 Jozankei Spa, Japan
164/E7 J. Paul Getty Museum, Ca,US
128/A2 Jreïda, Mrta.
105/F2 Ju (riv.), China
146/E3 Juan Aldama, Mex.
103/C4 Juancheng, China
156/B3 Juan de Fuca (str.), Can., US
133/G7 Juan de Nova (isl.), Reun.
134/A6 Juan Fernández (isls.), Chile
139/F2 Juangriego, Ven.
144/B2 Juanjuí, Peru
143/T12 Juan L. Lacaze, Uru.
142/F3 Juárez, Arg.
141/J8 Juatinga (pt.), Braz.
140/B3 Juazeiro, Braz.
140/C2 Juazeiro do Norte, Braz.
125/M7 Juba, Sudan
125/P7 Jubba (riv.), Eth., Som.
144/B1 Jubones (riv.), Ecu.
75/Y17 Juby (cape), Mor.
74/D3 Júcar (riv.), Sp.
140/C2 Jucás, Braz.
66/D6 Jüchen, Ger.
146/E4 Juchipila, Mex.
147/N7 Juchique de Ferrer, Mex.
148/C2 Juchitán, Mex.
140/B5 Jucurucu (riv.), Braz.
140/C2 Jucurutu, Braz.
91/G8 Judaea (reg.), WBnk.
149/E4 Judas (pt.), CR
73/L3 Judenburg, Aus.
156/F4 Judith (riv.), Mt,US
127/B3 Juhaynah, Egypt
105/F3 Juicai (mtn.), China
149/E3 Juigalpa, Nic.
53/U9 Juilly, Fr.
105/H2 Juilong (mtn.), China
72/E2 Juine (riv.), Fr.
66/D1 Juist (isl.), Ger.
141/K6 Juiz de Fora, Braz.
159/G2 Julesburg, Co,US
144/D4 Juliaca, Peru
73/K3 Julian Alps (mts.), It., Slov.
139/G4 Juliana Top (peak), Sur.
69/F2 Jülich, Ger.
77/F5 Julierpass (pass)
108/C2 Jullundur, India
103/C3 Julu, China
103/C3 Juma (riv.), China
131/C3 Jumbo, Zim.
74/E3 Jumilla, Sp.
123/W17 Jūmīn (riv.), Tun.
63/L2 Juminda (pt.), Est.
106/D2 Jumla, Nepal
67/E2 Jümme (riv.), Ger.
100/B4 Jūmonji, Japan
105/G2 Jun (mtn.), China
106/B3 Junāgadh, India
103/D4 Junan, China
142/C2 Juncal (peak), Arg., Chile
162/D4 Junction, Tx,US
158/D3 Junction, Ut,US
159/H3 Junction City, Ks,US
156/C4 Junction City, Or,US
141/G8 Jundiaí, Braz.
103/H6 Jundu (mts.), China
123/W17 Jundūbah, Tun.
123/W17 Jundūbah (gov.), Tun.
151/M4 Juneau (cap.), Ak,US
103/B3 Jungar Qi, China
76/D4 Jungfrau (peak), Swi.
76/D4 Jungfraujoch, Swi.
63/S7 Jungfrufjärden (bay), Swe.
166/A2 Juniata (co.), Pa,US
166/A2 Juniata (riv.), Pa,US
142/E2 Junín, Arg.
138/A5 Junín, Ecu.
144/C3 Junín, Peru
135/B4 Junín de los Andes, Arg.
68/D5 Juniville, Fr.
103/C3 Junji Guan (pass), China
104/E2 Junlian, China
163/H5 Juno Beach, Fl,US
141/B2 Junqueirópolis, Braz.
141/E1 Juparanã (lake), Braz.
161/J1 Jupiter (riv.), Qu,Can
163/H5 Jupiter, Fl,US
165/J2 Jupiter (mtn.), Wa,US
141/C3 Juquiá, Braz.
141/F8 Juquitiba, Braz.
125/L6 Jur (riv.), Sudan
76/C4 Jura (mts.), Eur.
76/B4 Jura (dept.), Fr.
76/D3 Jura (canton), Swi.
55/H9 Jura (isl.), Sc,UK
55/J9 Jura (sound), Sc,UK
72/C5 Jurançon, Fr.
68/C2 Jurbise, Belg.
56/D3 Jurby Head (pt.), IM,UK
63/K3 Jūrmala, Lat.
139/E5 Juruá (riv.), Braz.
136/G6 Juruena (riv.), Braz.
137/G4 Juruti, Braz.
99/M9 Jushiyama, Japan
142/D2 Justo Daract, Arg.
136/E5 Jutaí, Braz.
139/E5 Jutaí (riv.), Braz.
148/D3 Jutiapa, Guat.
148/E3 Juticalpa, Hon.
61/D4 Jutland (pen.), Den.
61/H3 Juva, Fin.
149/K7 Juventud (isl.), Cuba
53/T10 Juvisy-sur-Orge, Fr.
103/D4 Ju Xian, China
103/D4 Juye, China
103/C5 Juzhang (riv.), China
82/E4 Južna Morava (riv.), Yugo.
131/B5 Jwaneng, Bots.
63/T9 Jyllinge, Den.
61/H3 Jyväskylä, Fin.

K

102/C4 K2 (Godwin Austen) (mtn.), China, Pak.
124/F5 Ka (riv.), Nga.
101/C3 Ka (isl.), NKor.
130/B2 Kaabong, Ugan.
132/C3 Kaap (plat.), SAfr.
63/K1 Kaarina, Fin.
66/D6 Kaarst, Ger.
82/E2 Kaba, Hun.
111/F5 Kabaena (isl.), Indo.
147/H4 Kabah (ruins), Mex.
130/A3 Kabale, Ugan.
130/A2 Kabalega (falls), Ugan.
130/A2 Kabalega Nat'l Park, Ugan.
126/E2 Kabalo, Zaire
126/E2 Kabamba (lake), Zaire
112/C3 Kabankalan, Phil.
87/G4 Kabardin-Balkar Aut. Rep., Rus.
130/A3 Kabare, Zaire
108/F3 Kabbani (riv.), India
130/B2 Kaberamaido, Ugan.
160/C1 Kabinakagami (lake), On,Can
126/D2 Kabinda, Zaire
123/V17 Kabīr (riv.), Alg.
92/F3 Kabīr Kūh (mts.), Syria
108/A2 Kabīrwāla, Pak.
80/A5 Kabīyah (lag.), Tun.
95/J2 Kābol (Kābul) (cap.), Afg.
131/B2 Kabompo, Zam.
131/A2 Kabompo (riv.), Zam.
126/E2 Kabongo, Zaire
95/J2 Kabul (riv.), Afg.
95/J2 Kābul (Kābol) (cap.), Afg.
131/C2 Kabunda, Zaire
112/D5 Kaburuang (isl.), Indo.
131/C2 Kabwe, Zam.
82/E4 Kačanik, Yugo.
131/C2 Kachalola, Zam.
151/H4 Kachemak (bay), Ak,US
131/B3 Kachikau, Bots.
104/C3 Kachin (state), Burma
92/E1 Kaçkar (peak), Turk.
108/F4 Kadaianallur, India
130/B2 Kadam (peak), Ugan.
109/B3 Kadan (isl.), Burma
71/G2 Kadaň, Czh.
120/G6 Kadavu (isl.), Fiji
124/J7 Kadeï (riv.), CAfr., Congo
83/H5 Kadıköy, Turk.
93/N7 Kadiköy, Turk.
131/B1 Kadilo, Zaire
92/C2 Kadınhanı, Turk.
129/E3 Kadiogo (prov.), Burk.
106/C5 Kadiri, India
92/D2 Kadirli, Turk.
157/H5 Kadoka, SD,US
99/L10 Kadoma, Japan
131/C3 Kadoma, Zim.
129/G4 Kaduna, Nga.
129/G4 Kaduna (riv.), Nga.
129/G4 Kaduna (state), Nga.
125/L5 Kāduqli, Sudan
128/B2 Kaédi, Mrta.
124/H5 Kaélé, Camr.
154/V12 Kaena (pt.), Hi,US
109/C2 Kaeng Khlo, Thai.
109/B3 Kaeng Krachan Nat'l Park, Thai.
101/D3 Kaesŏng, NKor.
101/D4 Kaesŏng-Si, NKor.
87/H5 Kafan, Arm.
95/J2 Kafar Jar Ghar (mts.), Afg.
132/D4 Kaffraria (reg.), SAfr.
128/B3 Kaffrine, Sen.
125/K6 Kafia Kingi, Sudan
81/J3 Kafirévs, Akra (cape), Gre.
91/B4 Kafr ad Dawwār, Egypt
91/B4 Kafr ash Shaykh, Egypt
91/B4 Kafr ash Shaykh (gov.), Egypt
91/B4 Kafr az Zayyāt, Egypt
91/G7 Kafr Qari', Isr.
91/F7 Kafr Qāsim, Isr.
130/A2 Kafu (riv.), Ugan.
131/B1 Kafubu (riv.), Zaire
131/C2 Kafue, Zam.
131/C2 Kafue (dam), Zam.
131/C2 Kafue (riv.), Zam.
131/B2 Kafue Flats (swamp), Zam.
131/B2 Kafue Nat'l Park, Zam.
131/D1 Kafukule, Malw.
130/A5 Kafulwe, Zam.
98/E2 Kaga, Japan
124/J6 Kaga Bandoro, CAfr.
88/G6 Kagan, Uzb.
98/D3 Kagawa (pref.), Japan
130/A3 Kagera (riv.), Rwa., Tanz.
130/A4 Kagera, Tanz.
63/G8 Kågeröd, Swe.
83/J5 Kağıthane, Turk.
83/J5 Kağıthane (riv.), Turk.
93/E1 Kağızman, Turk.
98/B5 Kagoshima, Japan
98/B5 Kagoshima (bay), Japan
98/B5 Kagoshima (pref.), Japan
83/J3 Kagul, Mol.
130/B3 Kahama, Tanz.
154/W12 Kahana, Hi,US
110/D4 Kahayan (riv.), Indo.
130/C3 Kahe, Tanz.
126/C2 Kahemba, Zaire
130/C5 Kahindi, Tanz.
154/T10 Kahiu (pt.), Hi,US
96/D1 Kahmsara (riv.), Rus.
108/C2 Kāhna, Pak.
159/K2 Kahoka, Mo,US
154/T10 Kahoolawe (isl.), Hi,US
61/G1 Kahperusvaara (peak), Fin.
92/D2 Kahramanmaraş, Turk.
92/D2 Kahraman Maraş (prov.), Turk.
95/K3 Kahror Pakka, Pak.
92/D2 Kâhta, Turk.
154/T10 Kahuku (pt.), Hi,US
154/T10 Kahului, Hi,US
126/E1 Kahuzi-Biega Nat'l Park, Zaire
111/H5 Kai (isls.), Indo.
115/R11 Kaiapoi, NZ
158/D3 Kaibab (plat.), Az,US
99/L9 Kaibara, Japan
111/H5 Kai Besar (isl.), Indo.
102/E3 Kaidu (riv.), China
139/G3 Kaieteur (falls), Guy.
139/G3 Kaieteur Nat'l Park, Guy.
96/G5 Kaifeng, China
98/D4 Kaifu, Japan
105/E2 Kaijiang, China
111/H5 Kai Kecil (isl.), Indo.
115/R10 Kaikohe, NZ
115/R11 Kaikoura, NZ
105/E3 Kaili, China
103/E2 Kailu, China
154/U11 Kailua, Hi,US
132/B2 Kainab (dry riv.), Namb.
82/B2 Kainach (riv.), Aus.
98/D3 Kainan, Japan
131/B2 Kaindu, Zam.
129/G4 Kainji (dam), Nga.
129/G4 Kainji (lake), Nga.
115/R10 Kaipara (har.), NZ
99/H7 Kaisei, Japan
76/D4 Kaiseregg (peak), Swi.
69/G5 Kaiserslautern, Ger.
76/D1 Kaiserstuhl (peak), Ger.
115/R10 Kaitaia, NZ
117/G2 Kaitej Abor. Land, Austl.
102/C6 Kaithal, India
130/B3 Kaiti, Tanz.
154/T10 Kaiwi (chan.), Hi,US
107/J2 Kaiyang, China
103/F2 Kaiyuan, China
104/D4 Kaiyuan, China
99/M9 Kaizu, Japan
99/L10 Kaizuka, Japan
52/F2 Kajaani, Fin.
130/C3 Kajiado, Kenya
101/E5 Kaji-san (mtn.), SKor.
130/A2 Kajo-Kaji, Sudan
125/M5 Kākā, Sudan
61/G3 Kakaanpää, Fin.
130/B2 Kakamega, Kenya
99/E3 Kakamigahara, Japan
82/D3 Kakanj, Bosn.
151/M4 Kaketsa (mtn.), BC,Can
86/E3 Kakhovka, Ukr.
86/E3 Kakhovka (res.), Ukr.
131/C2 Kakielo, Zaire
106/D4 Kākināda, India
130/B2 Kakiri, Ugan.
99/L9 Kako (riv.), Japan
131/A2 Kakonga, Zam.
130/A3 Kakonko, Tanz.
128/B4 Kakrima (riv.), Gui.
99/G2 Kakuda, Japan
130/B2 Kakuma, Kenya
131/C2 Kakumbi, Zam.
100/B4 Kakunodate, Japan
130/A3 Kakuto, Ugan.
130/C3 Kakya, Kenya
108/H4 Kala (riv.), SrL.
123/X18 Kalaa-Kebira, Tun.
145/N2 Kalaallit Nunaat (Greenland) (dpcy.), Den.
108/A1 Kālābāgh, Pak.
126/D3 Kalabo, Zam.
87/G2 Kalach, Rus.
88/H4 Kalachinsk, Rus.
87/G2 Kalach-na-Donu, Rus.
107/F3 Kaladan (riv.), Burma
154/U11 Ka Lae (cape), Hi,US
126/D5 Kalahari (des.), Afr.
132/C2 Kalahari-Gemsbok Nat'l Park, SAfr.
81/L7 Kalamáki, Gre.
124/H5 Kalamaloué Nat'l Park, Camr.
131/B4 Kalamare, Bots.
81/H2 Kalamariá, Gre.
81/H4 Kalamáta, Gre.
160/C3 Kalamazoo, Mi,US
130/B4 Kalangali, Tanz.
109/C2 Kalasin, Thai.
95/J3 Kalāt, Pak.
116/B3 Kalbarri Nat'l Park, Austl.
123/X18 Kalbīyah (lake), Tun.
61/N7 Kaldakvísl (riv.), Ice.
92/C1 Kalecik, Turk.
67/H5 Kalefeld, Ger.
130/A3 Kalehe, Zaire
130/A4 Kalemie, Zaire
131/B1 Kalene Hill, Zam.
93/J2 Kāl-e Shūr (riv.), Iran
65/K3 Kalety, Pol.
131/B2 Kaleya, Zam.
116/D4 Kalgoorlie-Boulder, Austl.
63/R7 Kalhall, Swe.
83/J4 Kaliakra, Nos (pt.), Bul.
110/C5 Kalianda, Indo.
112/C3 Kalibo, Phil.
126/E1 Kalima, Zaire
110/D4 Kalimantan (reg.), Indo.
63/J4 Kaliningrad, Rus.
63/H4 Kaliningrad (lag.), Rus.
63/J4 Kaliningrad Obl., Rus.
87/H2 Kalininsk, Rus.
86/D1 Kalinkovichi, Bela.
130/B2 Kaliro, Ugan.
130/A3 Kalisizo, Ugan.
156/E3 Kalispell, Mt,US
65/K3 Kalisz, Pol.
65/J3 Kalisz (prov.), Pol.
130/A4 Kaliua, Tanz.
61/G2 Kalix, Swe.
61/G2 Kalixälv (riv.), Swe.
106/E2 Kāliyāganj, India
160/C2 Kalkaska, Mi,US
108/G3 Kallakkurichichi, India
108/F4 Kallidaikurichchi, India
62/F3 Kallinge, Swe.
81/L7 Kallithea, Gre.
61/E3 Kallsjön (lake), Swe.
62/G3 Kalmar, Swe.
62/G3 Kalmar (co.), Swe.
62/G3 Kalmarsund (sound), Swe.
70/B4 Kalmit (mtn.), Ger.
66/B6 Kalmthout, Belg.
87/H3 Kalmyk Aut. Rep., Rus.
82/D2 Kalocsa, Hun.
154/T10 Kalohi (chan.), Hi,US
106/B3 Kālol, India
131/B3 Kalomo, Zam.
130/B2 Kalongo, Ugan.
106/C2 Kālpi, India
102/C3 Kalpin, China
64/E2 Kaltenkirchen, Ger.
77/H5 Kaltern (Caldaro), It.
106/D6 Kalu (riv.), SrL.
84/H5 Kaluga, Rus.
84/G5 Kaluga Obl., Rus.

196

Kalul – Khaba

131/C2 **Kalulushi,** Zam.
62/D4 **Kalundborg,** Den.
130/A3 **Kalungu,** Ugan.
130/A5 **Kalungwishi** (riv.), Zam.
108/A1 **Kalūr Kot,** Pak.
86/C2 **Kalush,** Ukr.
106/C6 **Kalutara,** SrL.
131/C2 **Kalwelwe,** Zam.
106/B4 **Kalyān,** India
85/M4 **Kama** (res.), Rus.
85/M3 **Kama** (riv.), Rus.
126/E1 **Kama,** Zaire
130/A3 **Kamachumu,** Tanz.
99/J7 **Kamagaya,** Japan
100/B4 **Kamaishi,** Japan
154/T10 **Kamakou** (peak), Hi,US
99/H7 **Kamakura,** Japan
130/A4 **Kamalampaka,** Tanz.
108/B2 **Kamālia,** Pak.
92/C2 **Kaman,** Turk.
130/A3 **Kamande,** Zaire
128/E2 **Kamango** (lake), Mali
130/A2 **Kamango,** Zaire
126/B4 **Kamanjab,** Namb.
130/A3 **Kamanyola,** Zaire
106/C4 **Kāmāreddi,** India
106/E3 **Kāmārhāti,** India
139/G3 **Kamaria** (falls), Guy.
131/B3 **Kamativi,** Zim.
108/F4 **Kambam,** India
106/A2 **Kambar,** Pak.
131/B1 **Kambove,** Zaire
111/F4 **Kambuno** (peak), Indo.
89/R4 **Kamchatka** (pen.), Rus.
89/R4 **Kamchatka Obl.,** Rus.
83/H4 **Kamchiya** (riv.), Bul.
67/E5 **Kamen,** Ger.
86/C2 **Kamenets-Podol'skiy,** Ukr.
82/A3 **Kamenjak, Rt** (cape), Cro.
87/H1 **Kamenka,** Rus.
102/D1 **Kamen'-na-Obi,** Rus.
86/G2 **Kamensk-Shakhtinskiy,** Rus.
85/P4 **Kamensk-Ural'skiy,** Rus.
98/D3 **Kameoka,** Japan
54/A5 **Kames,** Sc,UK
99/M10 **Kameyama,** Japan
99/K9 **Kami,** Japan
156/D4 **Kamiah,** Id,US
65/H2 **Kamień Pomorski,** Pol.
99/H7 **Kamifukuoka,** Japan
100/B3 **Kamiisco,** Japan
99/M9 **Kamiishizu,** Japan
100/C2 **Kamikawa,** Japan
154/U11 **Kamilo** (pt.), Hi,US
126/E2 **Kamina,** Zaire
99/G1 **Kaminoyama,** Japan
151/H4 **Kamishak** (bay), Ak,US
98/B5 **Kamiyaku,** Japan
156/C3 **Kamloops,** BC,Can
109/C4 **Kamlot,** Camb.
99/L10 **Kammaki,** Japan
70/D6 **Kammlach** (riv.), Ger.
82/B2 **Kamnik,** Slov.
99/F2 **Kamo,** Japan
99/J7 **Kamo** (riv.), Japan
99/G3 **Kamogawa,** Japan
98/D3 **Kamojima,** Japan
108/C2 **Kāmoke,** Pak.
73/L2 **Kamp** (riv.), Aus.
130/B2 **Kampala** (cap.), Ugan.
112/D4 **Kampalili** (mtn.), Phil.
110/B3 **Kampar** (riv.), Indo.
110/B3 **Kampar,** Malay.
66/C3 **Kampen,** Neth.
109/B2 **Kamphaeng Phet,** Thai.
109/B2 **Kamphaeng Phet** (ruins), Thai.
65/L2 **Kampinoski Nat'l Park,** Pol.
66/D6 **Kamp-Lintfort,** Ger.
109/D4 **Kampong Cham,** Camb.
109/D3 **Kampong Chhnang,** Camb.
109/D3 **Kampong Khleang,** Camb.
109/C4 **Kampong Saom,** Camb.
109/C4 **Kampong Saom** (bay), Camb.
109/D4 **Kampong Spoe,** Camb.
109/D3 **Kampong Thum,** Camb.
109/D4 **Kampong Trabek,** Camb.
109/D4 **Kampot,** Camb.
111/H4 **Kamrau** (bay), Indo.
157/H3 **Kamsack,** Sk,Can
157/H1 **Kamuchawie** (lake), Sk,Can
100/B2 **Kamui-misaki** (cape), Japan
149/F4 **Kámuk** (mtn.), CR
130/B2 **Kamuli,** Ugan.
87/H2 **Kamyshin,** Rus.
153/J3 **Kanaaupscow** (riv.), Qu,Can
158/D3 **Kanab** (riv.), Az, Ut,US
158/D3 **Kanab,** Ut,US
151/C6 **Kanaga** (isl.), Ak,US
151/C6 **Kanaga** (vol.), Ak,US
99/F3 **Kanagawa** (pref.), Japan
153/K3 **Kanairiktok** (riv.), Nf,Can
99/L10 **Kanan,** Japan
126/D2 **Kananga,** Zaire
85/K5 **Kanash,** Rus.
161/N7 **Kanawake Ind. Res.,** Qu,Can
160/D4 **Kanawha** (riv.), WV,US
99/E2 **Kanazawa,** Japan
130/A3 **Kanazi,** Tanz.
109/B3 **Kanchanaburi,** Thai.
106/C5 **Kānchīpuram,** India
84/G2 **Kandalaksha,** Rus.
84/G2 **Kandalaksha** (gulf), Rus.
121/Y18 **Kandavu** (passg.), Fiji
70/B4 **Kandel,** Ger.
70/B6 **Kandel** (peak), Ger.
76/D4 **Kander** (riv.), Swi.
76/D2 **Kandern,** Ger.
95/J3 **Kandhkot,** Pak.
106/E3 **Kāndi,** India
111/F3 **Kandi** (cape), Indo.
83/K5 **Kandıra,** Turk.
106/C4 **Kandukūr,** India
106/D6 **Kandy,** SrL.
165/P16 **Kane** (co.), Il,US
153/T7 **Kane Basin** (sound), NW,Can
124/H5 **Kanem** (reg.), Chad
154/W13 **Kaneohe,** Hi,US
154/W13 **Kaneohe** (bay), Hi,US
154/W13 **Kaneohe Marine Air Sta.,** Hi,US
100/B4 **Kaneyama,** Japan
126/D5 **Kang,** Bots.
130/C4 **Kanga,** Tanz.
130/A2 **Kanga,** Zaire
92/D2 **Kangal,** Turk.
116/C2 **Kangan Abor. Land,** Austl.
110/B2 **Kangar,** Malay.
117/G5 **Kangaroo** (isl.), Austl.
63/L1 **Kangasala,** Fin.
93/F3 **Kangāvar,** Iran
96/G3 **Kangbao,** China
104/D2 **Kangding,** China
111/E5 **Kangean** (isls.), Indo.
101/D4 **Kanghwa** (isl.), SKor.
153/K3 **Kangiqsualujjuaq,** Qu,Can
153/J2 **Kangiqsujuaq,** Qu,Can
153/J2 **Kangirsuk,** Qu,Can
106/E2 **Kangmar,** China
101/C2 **Kangnam** (mts.), NKor.
101/G6 **Kangnam,** SKor.
101/E4 **Kangnŭng,** SKor.
130/C3 **Kangondi,** Kenya
103/E2 **Kangping,** China
102/D5 **Kangrinboqê Feng** (peak), China
101/F6 **Kangsŏ,** SKor.
104/B3 **Kangto** (peak), China
101/D3 **Kangwŏn-do** (prov.), NKor.
101/E4 **Kangwŏn-do** (prov.), SKor.
106/C3 **Kanhān** (riv.), India
99/N9 **Kani,** Japan
99/M9 **Kanie,** Japan
85/K2 **Kanin** (pen.), Rus.
130/C3 **Kaningo,** Kenya
52/H2 **Kanin Nos** (pt.), Rus.
108/F4 **Kanjirapalli,** India
82/E2 **Kanjiža,** Yugo.
160/C3 **Kankakee,** Il,US
160/C3 **Kankakee** (riv.), Il, In,Us
128/C4 **Kankan,** Gui.
128/C4 **Kankan** (comm.), Gui.
106/D3 **Kānker,** India
108/H4 **Kankesanturai,** SrL.
98/C3 **Kanmuri-yama** (mtn.), Japan
163/H3 **Kannapolis,** NC,US
106/C2 **Kannauj,** India
108/F4 **Kanniyākumāri,** India
99/H7 **Kannon-zaki** (pt.), Japan
129/H4 **Kano,** Nga.
129/H3 **Kano** (state), Nga.
131/C2 **Kanona,** Zam.
98/C3 **Kan'onji,** Japan
167/H7 **Kanouse** (mtn.), NJ,US
98/B5 **Kanoya,** Japan
106/D2 **Kānpur,** India
130/C3 **Kansarokana** (riv.), Kenya
159/H3 **Kansas** (state), US
159/H3 **Kansas** (riv.), Ks,US
159/J3 **Kansas City,** Ks,US
159/J3 **Kansas City,** Mo,US
88/K4 **Kansk,** Rus.
106/D3 **Kantābānji,** India
99/F2 **Kantō** (prov.), Japan
139/G4 **Kanuku** (mts.), Guy.
99/F2 **Kanuma,** Japan
151/H2 **Kanuti Nat'l Wild. Ref.,** Ak,US
132/D2 **Kanye,** Bots.
131/B2 **Kanyilombi,** Zam.
109/D3 **Kaoh Nhek,** Camb.
105/J4 **Kaohsiung,** Tai.
126/B4 **Kaokoveld** (reg.), Namb.
128/A3 **Kaolack,** Sen.
128/B3 **Kaolack** (reg.), Sen.
131/B2 **Kaoma,** Zam.
154/S9 **Kapaa,** Hi,US
131/C2 **Kapalala,** Zam.
112/D4 **Kapalong,** Phil.
126/D2 **Kapanga,** Zaire
82/E4 **Kapaonik** (upland), Yugo.
102/C3 **Kapchagay,** Kaz.
102/C3 **Kapchagay** (res.), Kaz.
130/B2 **Kapchorwa,** Ugan.
130/C2 **Kapedo,** Kenya
66/B6 **Kapellen,** Belg.
130/B2 **Kapenguria,** Kenya
131/C2 **Kapengwe,** Zam.
73/L3 **Kapfenberg,** Aus.
83/H5 **Kapidaği** (pen.), Turk.
120/E4 **Kapingamarangi** (isl.), Micr.
131/C2 **Kapiri Mposhi,** Zam.
153/H3 **Kapiskau** (riv.), On,Can
125/M7 **Kapoeta,** Sudan
130/A4 **Kapona,** Zaire
130/B5 **Kaporo,** Malw.
82/C2 **Kapos** (riv.), Hun.
82/C2 **Kaposvár,** Hun.
130/B2 **Kapsabet,** Kenya
63/K4 **Kapsukas,** Lith.
110/C4 **Kapuas** (riv.), Indo.
110/D3 **Kapuas Hulu** (mts.), Indo., Malay.
108/C2 **Kapūrthala,** India
160/D1 **Kapuskasing,** On,Can
160/D1 **Kapuskasing** (riv.), On,Can
130/A5 **Kaputa,** Zam.
82/C2 **Kapuvár,** Hun.
87/H5 **Kapydzhik, Gora** (peak), Azer.
85/Q1 **Kara** (riv.), Rus.
88/G2 **Kara** (sea), Rus.
87/K4 **Kara-Bogaz-Gol** (gulf), Trkm.
111/H4 **Karabra** (riv.), Indo.
92/C1 **Karabük,** Turk.
92/D2 **Karaca** (peak), Turk.
92/B1 **Karacabey,** Turk.
91/C1 **Karaçal** (peak), Turk.
87/G4 **Karachay-Cherkass Aut. Obl.,** Rus.
86/E1 **Karachev,** Rus.
95/J4 **Karāchi,** Pak.
106/B4 **Karād,** India
102/B2 **Karaganda,** Kaz.
90/R4 **Karaginskiy** (isl.), Rus.
102/E1 **Karagoš** (peak), Rus.
108/G3 **Kāraikkudi,** India
92/C2 **Karaisalı,** Turk.
108/G4 **Karaitivu** (isl.), SrL.
93/G3 **Karaj,** Iran
87/L3 **Karakalpak Aut. Rep.,** Uzb.
102/C4 **Karakax** (riv.), China
92/D2 **Karakaya** (dam), Turk.
112/D4 **Karakelong** (isl.), Indo.
96/E3 **Karakhoto** (ruins), China
92/E2 **Karakoçan,** Turk.
102/C4 **Karakoram** (range), Asia
102/C4 **Karakoram** (pass), China, India
128/C3 **Karakoro** (riv.), Mali, Mrta.
96/E2 **Karakorum** (ruins), Mong.
93/E2 **Karaköse,** Turk.
102/B4 **Karakul'** (lake), Taj.
87/L5 **Karakumy** (des.), Trkm.
87/K4 **Karakyon, Gora** (peak), Trkm.
95/H1 **Karakyr** (peak), Trkm.
111/E4 **Karam** (riv.), Indo.
92/C2 **Karaman,** Turk.
91/C1 **Karaman** (prov.), Turk.
102/D2 **Karamay,** China
130/A3 **Karambi,** Tanz.
115/R11 **Karamea,** NZ
115/R11 **Karamea** (bight), NZ
102/D4 **Karamiran** (riv.), China
102/E4 **Karamiran Shankou** (pass), China
130/B2 **Karamoja** (prov.), Ugan.
83/J5 **Karamürsel,** Turk.
107/G4 **Karan** (state), Burma
111/E5 **Karangasem,** Indo.
89/S4 **Karanginskiy** (bay), Rus.
89/S4 **Karanginskiy** (isl.), Rus.
106/C3 **Kāranja,** India
109/B2 **Karan** (Kayin) (state), Burma
92/C2 **Karapınar,** Turk.
98/A3 **Kara-saki** (pt.), Japan
99/M10 **Karasu,** Japan
83/K5 **Karasu,** Turk.
102/C1 **Karasuk,** Rus.
149/F3 **Karatá** (lag.), Nic.
102/C2 **Karatal** (riv.), Kaz.
91/D1 **Karataş,** Turk.
102/B3 **Karatau,** Kaz.
102/A3 **Karatau** (mts.), Kaz.
98/A4 **Karatsu,** Japan
81/G3 **Karáva** (peak), Gre.
102/B2 **Karazhal,** Kaz.
127/C5 **Karbaka,** Sudan
93/F3 **Karbalā',** Iraq
93/E3 **Karbalā'** (gov.), Iraq
70/B2 **Karben,** Ger.
82/E2 **Karcag,** Hun.
81/G3 **Kardhítsa,** Gre.
88/D3 **Karelian Aut. Rep.,** Rus.
130/A4 **Karema,** Tanz.
96/H1 **Karenga** (riv.), Rus.
63/K1 **Karhijärvi** (lake), Fin.
131/C3 **Kariba** (dam), Zam., Zim.
131/B3 **Kariba** (lake), Zam., Zim.
131/C3 **Kariba,** Zim.
100/A2 **Kariba-yama** (mtn.), Japan
126/C5 **Karibib,** Namb.
130/A2 **Karibumba,** Zaire
108/G3 **Karikal,** India
110/C4 **Karimata** (isl.), Indo.
110/C4 **Karimata** (str.), Indo.
106/C4 **Karīmnagar,** India
130/A3 **Karisimbi** (vol.), Rwa.
99/M10 **Kariya,** Japan
125/Q6 **Karkaar** (mts.), Som.
106/B5 **Kārkāl,** India
120/D5 **Karkar** (isl.), PNG
86/E3 **Karkinitsk** (gulf), Ukr.
63/L1 **Karkkila,** Fin.
102/B4 **Karla Marksa, Pik** (peak), Taj.
92/E2 **Karlıova,** Turk.
82/B3 **Karlovac,** Slov.
83/G4 **Karlovo,** Bul.
71/F2 **Karlovy Vary** (Karlsbad), Czh.
71/F2 **Karlsbad** (Karlovy Vary), Czh.
70/B4 **Karlsdorf-Neuthard,** Ger.
71/E6 **Karlsfeld,** Ger.
62/F3 **Karlshamn,** Swe.
62/F2 **Karlskoga,** Swe.
62/F3 **Karlskrona,** Swe.
63/T9 **Karlslunde Strand,** Den.
70/B4 **Karlsruhe,** Ger.
62/E2 **Karlstad,** Swe.
70/C3 **Karlstadt,** Ger.
70/C2 **Karlstein am Main,** Ger.
127/B5 **Karmah,** Sudan
106/C4 **Karmāla,** India
91/D3 **Karmel, Har** (Mount Carmel) (mtn.), Isr.
106/C2 **Karnāl,** India
108/F3 **Karnataka** (state), India
162/D4 **Karnes City,** Tx,US
83/H4 **Karnobat,** Bul.
82/A2 **Kärnten** (prov.), Aus.
131/C3 **Karoi,** Zim.
112/C4 **Karomatan,** Phil.
130/B5 **Karonga,** Malw.
132/C4 **Karoo Nat'l Park,** SAfr.
108/A2 **Karor,** Pak.
111/E5 **Karoso** (cape), Indo.
116/C2 **Karratha,** Austl.
132/M11 **Kars** (riv.), SAfr.
93/E1 **Kars,** Turk.
92/E1 **Kars** (prov.), Turk.
87/G4 **Kars** (riv.), Turk.
88/G6 **Karshi,** Uzb.
87/M1 **Kartaly,** Rus.
108/C2 **Kartārpur,** India
83/L3 **Kartinitsk** (gulf), Ukr.
65/K1 **Kartuzy,** Pol.
130/B2 **Karuma** (falls), Ugan.
93/G4 **Kārūn** (riv.), Iran
108/G3 **Karūr,** India
65/K4 **Karviná,** Czh.
106/B5 **Karwar,** India
157/L2 **Kasabonika** (lake), On,Can
99/L10 **Kasagi,** Japan
106/E3 **Kāsai** (riv.), India
98/D3 **Kasai,** Japan
126/C1 **Kasai** (riv.), Zaire
130/A5 **Kasakalawe,** Zam.
131/B2 **Kasalu,** Zam.
99/G2 **Kasama,** Japan
130/A5 **Kasama,** Zam.
99/M9 **Kasamatsu,** Japan
131/B3 **Kasane,** Bots.
130/A5 **Kasanga,** Tanz.
131/B3 **Kasanga** (falls), Zam.
131/C2 **Kasanka Nat'l Park,** Zam.
98/C3 **Kasaoka,** Japan
106/C5 **Kāsaragod,** India
127/D5 **Kasar, Ras** (cape), Sudan
99/M10 **Kasartori-yama** (peak), Japan
152/F2 **Kasba** (lake), NW,Can
98/B5 **Kaseda,** Japan
131/B1 **Kaseke,** Zaire
130/C5 **Kasembe,** Tanz.
131/B2 **Kasempa,** Zam.
130/A2 **Kasenyi,** Zaire
130/A2 **Kasese,** Ugan.
106/C2 **Kāsganj,** India
95/H1 **Kashaf** (riv.), Iran
93/G3 **Kāshān,** Iran
102/C4 **Kashi,** China
99/L10 **Kashiba,** Japan
130/A5 **Kashiba,** Zam.
98/D3 **Kashihara,** Japan
98/B4 **Kashima,** Japan
99/G3 **Kashima,** Japan
84/H4 **Kashin,** Rus.
99/H7 **Kashiwa,** Japan
99/L10 **Kashiwara,** Japan
99/F2 **Kashiwazaki,** Japan
93/J3 **Kāshmar,** Iran
106/A2 **Kashmor,** Pak.
93/J2 **Kashof** (riv.), Iran
130/A3 **Kashofu,** Zaire
130/C3 **Kasigau** (peak), Kenya
84/J5 **Kasimov,** Rus.
130/A2 **Kasindi,** Zaire
111/G4 **Kasiruta** (isl.), Indo.
111/H4 **Kasiui** (isl.), Indo.
131/D2 **Kasiya,** Malw.
160/B4 **Kaskaskia** (riv.), Il,US
156/D3 **Kaslo,** BC,Can
126/E1 **Kasongo,** Zaire
126/C2 **Kasongo-Lunda,** Zaire
87/H4 **Kaspiysk,** Rus.
125/N4 **Kassala,** Sudan
81/H3 **Kassándra** (pen.), Gre.
67/G6 **Kassel,** Ger.
139/G4 **Kassikaityu** (riv.), Guy.
157/K4 **Kasson,** Mn,US
92/C1 **Kastamonu,** Turk.
92/C1 **Kastamonu** (prov.), Turk.
69/D1 **Kasterlee,** Belg.
81/G2 **Kastoría,** Gre.
81/G3 **Kastrakíou** (lake), Gre.
99/L9 **Kasuga,** Japan
99/E3 **Kasugai,** Japan
99/F3 **Kasukabe,** Japan
130/A4 **Kasulu,** Tanz.
99/G2 **Kasumiga** (lake), Japan
131/D2 **Kasungu,** Malw.
131/D2 **Kasungu Nat'l Park,** Malw.
131/D2 **Kasupe,** Malw.
108/C2 **Kasūr,** Pak.
131/B3 **Kataba,** Zam.
161/G2 **Katahdin** (mtn.), Me,US
130/A3 **Katale,** Zaire
130/A3 **Katanda,** Zaire
126/E2 **Katanga** (reg.), Zaire
99/L10 **Katano,** Japan
130/A4 **Katavi Nat'l Park,** Tanz.
107/F6 **Katchall** (isl.), India
126/D2 **Katea,** Zaire
126/E2 **Katea,** Zaire
130/B3 **Katebo,** Ugan.
81/H2 **Kateríni,** Gre.
130/B4 **Katesh,** Tanz.
151/M4 **Kates Needle** (mtn.), Ak,US
131/D2 **Katete,** Malw.
131/D2 **Katete,** Zam.
104/C3 **Katha,** Burma
106/C2 **Kāthgodām,** India
95/K4 **Kathiawar** (pen.), India
117/G2 **Kathleen** (peak), Austl.
106/E2 **Kāthmāndu** (cap.), Nepal
108/C1 **Kathua,** India
128/C3 **Kati,** Mali
128/D4 **Katiola,** IvC.
67/H5 **Katlenburg-Lindau,** Ger.
151/H4 **Katmai** (vol.), Ak,US
151/G4 **Katmai Nat'l Park & Prsv.,** Ak,US
130/A4 **Katoba,** Tanz.
130/A2 **Katonga** (riv.), Ugan.
65/K3 **Katowice,** Pol.
65/K3 **Katowice** (prov.), Pol.
125/M2 **Kātrīnā, Jabal** (Mt. Catherine) (peak), Egypt
62/G2 **Katrineholm,** Swe.
54/B4 **Katrine, Loch** (lake), Sc,UK
129/G3 **Katsina,** Nga.
129/G3 **Katsina** (state), Nga.
129/H5 **Katsina Ala** (riv.), Camr., Nga.
99/L9 **Katsura** (riv.), Japan
98/D3 **Katsuragi,** Japan
99/L10 **Katsuragi-san** (peak), Japan
99/G2 **Katsuta,** Japan
99/G3 **Katsuura,** Japan
98/E2 **Katsuyama,** Japan
160/E1 **Kattawagami** (riv.), On,Can
62/D3 **Kattegat** (str.), Den., Swe.
131/D1 **Katumbi,** Malw.
102/E1 **Katun'** (riv.), Rus.
102/E1 **Katun'chuya** (riv.), Rus.
131/B3 **Katundu,** Zam.
131/C1 **Katuta Kampemba,** Zam.
130/A3 **Katwe,** Ugan.
66/B4 **Katwijk aan Zee,** Neth.
70/B4 **Katzenbach** (riv.), Ger.
70/C4 **Katzenbuckel** (peak), Ger.
154/S10 **Kauai** (chan.), Hi,US
154/S9 **Kauai** (isl.), Hi,US
77/G2 **Kaufbeuren,** Ger.
70/D6 **Kaufering,** Ger.
162/D3 **Kaufman,** Tx,US
67/G6 **Kaufungen,** Ger.
61/G3 **Kauhajoki,** Fin.
61/G3 **Kauhanevan-Pohjankankaan Nat'l Park,** Fin.
61/G3 **Kauhava,** Fin.
154/U10 **Kauhola** (pt.), Hi,US
154/U10 **Kauiki Head** (pt.), Hi,US
126/C5 **Kaukaveld** (mts.), Namb.
121/L6 **Kaukura** (atoll), FrPol.
154/R9 **Kaulakahi** (chan.), Hi,US
131/C2 **Kaulashishi** (hill), Zam.
154/U11 **Kauna** (pt.), Hi,US
63/K4 **Kaunas,** Lith.
63/L4 **Kaunas** (res.), Lith.
130/C2 **Kauro,** Kenya
109/B4 **Kau-ye** (isl.), Burma
82/F5 **Kavadarci,** Macd.
81/F2 **Kavajë,** Alb.
81/J2 **Kavála,** Gre.
97/M3 **Kavalerovo,** Rus.
106/C5 **Kāvali,** India
120/C4 **Kavangel** (isls.), Palau
106/B5 **Kavaratti,** India
83/J4 **Kavarna,** Bul.
120/E5 **Kavieng,** PNG
131/B3 **Kavimba,** Bots.
93/H4 **Kavīr-e Bāfq** (salt depr.), Iran
93/J3 **Kavīr-e Namak** (salt depr.), Iran
63/U9 **Kävlinge,** Swe.
162/D2 **Kaw** (lake), Ok,US
127/B5 **Kawa** (ruins), Sudan
100/B4 **Kawabe,** Japan
99/J7 **Kawachi,** Japan
99/L10 **Kawachi-Nagano,** Japan
99/M10 **Kawage,** Japan
99/F3 **Kawagoe,** Japan
99/M9 **Kawagoe,** Japan
99/F3 **Kawaguchi,** Japan
154/R10 **Kawaihoa** (pt.), Hi,US
154/S9 **Kawaikini** (peak), Hi,US
99/H7 **Kawajima,** Japan
99/L10 **Kawakami,** Japan
99/G2 **Kawamata,** Japan
130/A5 **Kawambwa,** Zam.
131/B2 **Kawana,** Zam.
99/L10 **Kawanishi,** Japan
106/D3 **Kawardha,** India
160/E2 **Kawartha** (lakes), On,Can
99/F3 **Kawasaki,** Japan
99/M9 **Kawashima,** Japan
154/V12 **Kawela Bay** (Kawela), Hi,US
115/S10 **Kawerau,** NZ
127/C3 **Kawm Umbū,** Egypt
102/D3 **Kax** (riv.), China
102/C3 **Kaxgar** (riv.), China
151/L2 **Kay** (pt.), Yk,Can
129/E4 **Kaya,** Burk.
124/J6 **Kayagangiri** (peak), CAfr.
109/B2 **Kayah** (state), Burma
108/G4 **Kāyalpatnam,** India
131/B2 **Kayamba** (hills), Zam.
111/E3 **Kayan** (riv.), Indo.
128/B3 **Kayanga** (riv.), Sen.
108/F4 **Kāyankulam,** India
101/D4 **Kaya-san** (mtn.), SKor.
101/E5 **Kaya-san Nat'l Park,** SKor.
156/G5 **Kaycee,** Wy,US
158/E3 **Kayenta,** Az,US
128/C3 **Kayes,** Mali
128/C3 **Kayes** (reg.), Mali
109/B2 **Kayin** (Karan) (state), Burma
69/F5 **Kayl,** Lux.
111/G3 **Kayoa** (isl.), Indo.
139/G4 **Kayser** (mts.), Sur.
92/E2 **Kayser** (dam), Turk.
92/C2 **Kayseri,** Turk.
92/C2 **Kayseri** (prov.), Turk.
117/G2 **Kaytej Abor. Land,** Austl.
110/B4 **Kayuagung,** Indo.
102/B2 **Kazakh** (uplands), Kaz.
88/G5 **Kazakhstan**
152/F2 **Kazan** (riv.), NW,Can
85/L5 **Kazan',** Rus.
83/G4 **Kazanlŭk,** Bul.
86/D2 **Kazatin,** Ukr.
87/H4 **Kazbek** (peak), Geo.
93/G4 **Kāzerūn,** Iran
65/L3 **Kazimierza Wielka,** Pol.
82/E1 **Kazincbarcika,** Hun.
104/B3 **Kaziranga Nat'l Park,** India
131/A1 **Kaziza,** Zaire
63/K4 **Kazlų Rūda,** Lith.
131/B3 **Kazuma Pan Nat'l Park,** Zim.
100/B3 **Kazuno,** Japan
81/J4 **Kéa** (isl.), Gre.
56/B3 **Keady,** NI,UK
154/T11 **Keahole** (pt.), Hi,US
154/T10 **Keanapapa** (pt.), Hi,US
167/D3 **Keansburg,** NJ,US
159/H2 **Kearney,** Ne,US
56/C3 **Kearny** (pt.), NI,UK
167/D2 **Kearny,** NJ,US
165/E6 **Kearsley** (cr.), Mi,US
154/U11 **Keawekaheka** (pt.), Hi,US
92/D2 **Keban** (dam), Turk.
61/F2 **Kebnekaise** (peak), Swe.
125/P6 **K'ebri Dehar,** Eth.
110/C5 **Kebumen,** Indo.
82/D2 **Kecel,** Hun.
92/B2 **Keçiborlu,** Turk.
82/D2 **Kecskemét,** Hun.
63/K4 **Kėdainiai,** Lith.
69/F5 **Kédange-sur Canner,** Fr.
110/D5 **Kediri,** Indo.
97/K2 **Kedong,** China
128/B3 **Kédougou,** Sen.
65/K3 **Kędzierzyn-Koźle,** Pol.
165/F6 **Keego Harbor,** Mi,US
152/D2 **Keele** (riv.), NW,Can
152/C2 **Keele** (peak), Yk,Cán
105/J3 **Keelung,** Tai.
54/D3 **Keen** (mtn.), Sc,UK
161/F3 **Keene,** NH,US
119/D1 **Keepit** (dam), Austl.
118/A1 **Keer-weer** (cape), Austl.
132/B2 **Keetmanshoop,** Namb.
81/G3 **Kefallinía** (isl.), Gre.
91/F7 **Kefar Sava,** Isr.
61/M7 **Keflavík,** Ice.
107/J5 **Ke Ga** (cape), Viet.
106/D6 **Kegalla,** SrL.
57/G6 **Kegworth,** Eng,UK
69/G6 **Kehl,** Ger.
57/G4 **Keighley,** Eng,UK
99/L9 **Keihoku,** Japan
119/F5 **Keilor,** Austl.
60/A6 **Keimaneigh** (pass), Ire.
125/J6 **Kéita** (riv.), Chad
54/D1 **Keith,** Sc,UK
161/H2 **Kejimkujik Nat'l Park,** NS,Can
82/D2 **Kékes** (peak), Hun.
103/B3 **Kelan,** China
111/G4 **Kelang** (isl.), Indo.
110/B3 **Kelang,** Malay.
129/H3 **Kélé-Kélé,** Niger
130/B1 **Kelem,** Eth.
71/E5 **Kelheim,** Ger.
70/B2 **Kelkheim,** Ger.
92/D1 **Kelkit,** Turk.
92/D1 **Kelkıt** (riv.), Turk.
152/D2 **Keller** (lake), NW,Can
164/C2 **Keller** (peak), Ca,US
152/D1 **Kellett** (cape), NW,Can
156/D4 **Kellogg,** Id,US
56/B2 **Kells,** NI,UK
60/D2 **Kells** (Ceanannus Mór), Ire.
162/D4 **Kelly A.F.B.,** Tx,US
124/J6 **Kélo,** Chad
156/D3 **Kelowna,** BC,Can
57/F5 **Kelsall,** Eng,UK
58/A6 **Kelsey Head** (pt.), UK
54/D5 **Kelso,** Sc,UK
156/C4 **Kelso,** Wa,US
70/B2 **Kelsterbach,** Ger.
110/B3 **Keluang,** Malay.
59/G3 **Kelvedon,** Eng,UK
157/H2 **Kelvington,** Sk,Can
84/G2 **Kem',** Rus.
84/G2 **Kem'** (riv.), Rus.
92/E1 **Kemalpaşa,** Turk.
58/D3 **Kemble,** Eng,UK
110/D3 **Kemena** (riv.), Malay.
93/M6 **Kemerburgaz,** Turk.
92/C2 **Kemerhisar,** Turk.
88/J4 **Kemerovo,** Rus.
61/H2 **Kemi,** Fin.
61/H2 **Kemijärvi,** Fin.
61/H2 **Kemijoki** (riv.), Fin.
68/B2 **Kemmel,** Belg.
156/F5 **Kemmerer,** Wy,US
54/D2 **Kemnay,** Sc,UK
113/W **Kemp** (pen.), Ant.
159/H4 **Kemp** (lake), Tx,US
61/H2 **Kempele,** Fin.
66/D6 **Kempen,** Ger.
66/C6 **Kempenland** (reg.), Belg.
66/B6 **Kempisch** (can.), Belg.
119/E1 **Kempsey,** Austl.
59/F2 **Kempston,** Eng,UK
160/F2 **Kempt** (lake), Qu,Can
77/G2 **Kempten,** Ger.
132/E2 **Kempton Park,** SAfr.
111/E3 **Kemul** (peak), Indo.
151/H3 **Kenai,** Ak,US
151/J3 **Kenai Fjords Nat'l Park,** Ak,US
151/H3 **Kenai Nat'l Wild. Ref.,** Ak,US
123/V18 **Kenchela** (gov.), Alg.
57/F3 **Kendal,** Eng,UK
163/H5 **Kendall,** Fl,US
165/P16 **Kendall** (co.), Il,US
166/D3 **Kendall Park,** NJ,US
160/C3 **Kendallville,** In,US
111/F4 **Kendari,** Indo.
66/D5 **Kendel** (riv.), Neth., Ger.
106/E3 **Kendrāpāra,** India
128/D4 **Kénédougou** (prov.), Burk.
128/C5 **Kenema,** SLeo.
104/E5 **Keng Deng,** Laos
126/C1 **Kenge,** Zaire
109/B1 **Kēng Tung,** Burma
128/C3 **Kenié-Baoulé Rsv.,** Mali
59/E2 **Kenilworth,** Eng,UK
167/H9 **Kenilworth,** NJ,US
123/L13 **Kenitra,** Mor.
103/D3 **Kenli,** China
56/D1 **Ken, Loch** (lake), Sc,UK
60/A6 **Kenmare** (riv.), Ire.
157/H3 **Kenmare,** ND,US
54/C3 **Kenmore,** Sc,UK
161/S10 **Kenmore,** NY,US
165/C2 **Kenmore,** Wa,US
115/K4 **Kenn** (reef), Austl.
161/G2 **Kennebec** (riv.), Me,US
161/G3 **Kennebunk,** Me,US
116/B3 **Kennedy** (range), Austl.
153/T6 **Kennedy** (chan.), NW,Can
151/H4 **Kennedy** (str.), Ak,US
66/B4 **Kennemerduinen Nat'l Park,** Neth.
163/F4 **Kenner,** La,US
58/D4 **Kennet** (can.), Eng,UK
59/E4 **Kennet** (riv.), Eng,UK
160/B4 **Kennett,** Mo,US
156/D4 **Kennewick,** Wa,US
160/C1 **Kenogami** (riv.), On,Can
151/L3 **Keno Hill,** Yk,Can
160/A1 **Kenora,** On,Can
165/Q14 **Kenosha,** Wi,US
165/P14 **Kenosha** (co.), Wi,US
167/K7 **Kensico** (res.), NY,US
168/B2 **Kensington,** Ct,US
53/N7 **Kensington & Chelsea** (bor.), Eng,UK
152/F2 **Kent** (pen.), NW,Can
165/H7 **Kent** (co.), On,Can
53/P8 **Kent** (co.), Eng,UK
57/F3 **Kent** (riv.), Eng,UK
166/C5 **Kent** (co.), De,US
166/C5 **Kent** (co.), Md,US
166/B6 **Kent** (isl.), Md,US
166/B6 **Kent** (pt.), Md,US
165/E6 **Kent** (lake), Mi,US
168/F5 **Kent,** Oh,US
168/C2 **Kent** (co.), RI,US
165/C3 **Kent,** Wa,US
102/A3 **Kentau,** Kaz.
119/C3 **Kent Group** (isls.), Austl.
105/J4 **Kenting Nat'l Park,** Tai.
160/D3 **Kenton,** Oh,US
160/C4 **Kentucky** (state), US
160/C4 **Kentucky** (riv.), Ky,US
163/F2 **Kentucky** (lake), Ky, Tn,US
59/G4 **Kent, Vale of** (val.), Eng,UK
161/H2 **Kentville,** NS,Can
56/D1 **Ken, Water of** (riv.), Sc,UK
130/C1 **Kenya**
125/M8 **Kenya** (mtn.), Kenya
99/H7 **Ken-zaki** (pt.), Japan
76/D1 **Kenzingen,** Ger.
157/L5 **Keokuk,** Ia,US
106/E3 **Keonjhar,** India
65/J3 **Kępno,** Pol.
108/F3 **Kerala** (state), India
129/F4 **Kéran Nat'l Park,** Togo
81/H4 **Keratéa,** Gre.
86/F3 **Kerch'** (str.), Rus., Ukr.
86/F3 **Kerch',** Ukr.
156/D3 **Keremeos,** BC,Can
92/C1 **Kerempe Burnu** (pt.), Turk.
125/N4 **Keren,** Erit.
84/G2 **Keret'** (lake), Rus.
51/N8 **Kerguélen** (isl.), FrAnt.
130/B3 **Kericho,** Kenya
115/R9 **Kerikeri** (cape), NZ
110/B4 **Kerinci** (peak), Indo.
130/C2 **Kerio** (riv.), Kenya
130/B2 **Kerio Valley Nat'l Rsv.,** Kenya
102/D4 **Keriya** (riv.), China
102/D4 **Keriya Shankou** (pass), China
66/C5 **Kerkdriel,** Neth.
66/D6 **Kerken,** Ger.
88/G6 **Kerki,** Trkm.
81/H2 **Kerkínis** (lake), Gre.
81/F3 **Kérkira** (Corfu), Gre.
81/F3 **Kérkira** (Corfu) (isl.), Gre.
69/F2 **Kerkrade,** Neth.
66/C5 **Kerkwijk,** Neth.
120/G7 **Kermadec** (isls.), NZ
93/J4 **Kermān,** Iran
93/J4 **Kermān** (gov.), Iran
162/C4 **Kermit,** Tx,US
158/C4 **Kern** (riv.), Ca,US
158/C4 **Kern, South Fork** (riv.), Ca,US
81/J4 **Kéros** (isl.), Gre.
163/J2 **Kerr** (res.), NC, Va,US
159/J4 **Kerr** (lake), Ok,US
156/F3 **Kerrobert,** Sk,Can
162/D4 **Kerrville,** Tx,US
60/A5 **Kerry** (co.), Ire.
58/C2 **Kerry,** Wal,UK
123/N13 **Kert** (riv.), Mor.
96/G2 **Kerulen** (riv.), China, Mong.
124/E2 **Kerzaz,** Alg.
160/D1 **Kesagami** (riv.), On,Can
83/H5 **Keşan,** Turk.
77/F4 **Kesch, Piz** (peak), Swi.
100/B4 **Kesen'numa,** Japan
59/H2 **Kesgrave,** Eng,UK
97/K2 **Keshan,** China
106/B3 **Keshod,** India
92/C2 **Keskin,** Turk.
61/H3 **Keski-Suomi** (prov.), Fin.
70/D5 **Kesselbach** (riv.), Ger.
59/H2 **Kessingland,** Eng,UK
92/B1 **Kestel,** Turk.
66/C5 **Kesteren,** Neth.
57/E2 **Keswick,** Eng,UK
82/C2 **Keszthely,** Hun.
88/J4 **Ket'** (riv.), Rus.
129/F5 **Keta,** Gha.
88/K2 **Keta** (riv.), Rus.
151/M4 **Ketchikan,** Ak,US
156/E5 **Ketchum,** Id,US
129/E5 **Kete Krachi,** Gha.
66/C3 **Ketelmeer** (lake), Neth.
65/L1 **Kętrzyn,** Pol.
70/B4 **Ketsch,** Ger.
59/F2 **Kettering,** Eng,UK
160/C4 **Kettering,** Oh,US
156/D3 **Kettle** (riv.), Can., US
157/K4 **Kettle** (riv.), Mn,US
165/P14 **Kettle Moraine Saint Park,** Wi,US
57/F3 **Kettlewell,** Eng,UK
66/B4 **Keukenhof,** Neth.
61/H3 **Keuruu,** Fin.
66/D5 **Kevelaer,** Ger.
160/B2 **Keweenaw** (bay), Mi,US
160/B2 **Keweenaw** (pen.), Mi,US
160/C2 **Keweenaw** (pt.), Mi,US
53/N7 **Kew Gardens,** Eng,UK
163/H5 **Key Largo,** Fl,US
60/B1 **Key, Lough** (lake), Ire.
58/D4 **Keynsham,** Eng,UK
167/D3 **Keyport,** NJ,US
160/E4 **Keyser,** WV,US
162/D2 **Keystone** (lake), Ok,US
163/H5 **Key West,** Fl,US
57/G6 **Keyworth,** Eng,UK
131/C4 **Kezi,** Zim.
65/L4 **Kežmarok,** Slvk.
131/A5 **Kgalagadi** (dist.), Bots.
131/B5 **Kgatleng** (dist.), Bots.
131/A4 **Kgwebe** (hills), Bots.
125/Q5 **Khaanziir** (cape), Som.
97/M2 **Khabarovsk,** Rus.

197
Khach – Kōnan

87/J4 **Khachmas**, Azer.
104/B5 **Khadaungnge** (peak), Burma
94/E3 **Khafjī, Ra's al**, SAr.
106/D2 **Khairābād**, India
95/J3 **Khairpur**, Pak.
131/A5 **Khakhea**, Bots.
81/H3 **Khalándrion**, Gre.
81/H2 **Khalkhidhikhi** (pen.), Gre.
81/H3 **Khalkís**, Gre.
96/E1 **Khamar-Daban** (mts.), Rus.
106/D3 **Khamaria**, India
95/J4 **Khambaliya**, India
106/C3 **Khāmgaon**, India
94/D5 **Khamīs Mushayţ**, SAr.
106/D4 **Khammam**, India
95/J1 **Khānābād**, Afg.
93/F3 **Khānaqīn**, Iraq
106/C3 **Khandwa**, India
124/F1 **Khanem** (well), Alg.
108/A2 **Khānewāl**, Pak.
108/B2 **Khāngāh Dogrān**, Pak.
81/J5 **Khaniá**, Gre.
97/L3 **Khanka** (lake), Rus.
96/E1 **Khankh**, Mong.
108/D2 **Khanna**, India
95/K3 **Khānpur**, Pak.
88/G3 **Khanty-Mansiysk**, Rus.
88/G3 **Khanty-Mansiysk Aut. Okr.**, Rus.
91/D4 **Khān Yūnus**, Gaza
109/C3 **Khao Chamao-Khao Wong Nat'l Park**, Thai.
109/C3 **Khao Khitchakut Nat'l Park**, Thai.
109/B3 **Khao Laem** (res.), Thai.
109/B3 **Khao Sam Roi Yot Nat'l Park**, Thai.
109/C3 **Khao Yai Nat'l Park**, Thai.
106/E3 **Kharagpur**, India
108/A1 **Kharak**, Pak.
95/J3 **Khārān**, Pak.
108/D2 **Kharar**, India
106/C3 **Khargon**, India
108/B1 **Khāriān**, Pak.
127/B3 **Khārijah, Al Wāḩāt al** (oasis), Egypt
127/C3 **Kharīt, Wādī al** (dry riv.), Egypt
93/G4 **Khārk** (isl.), Iran
86/F2 **Khar'kov**, Ukr.
86/F2 **Khar'kov Obl.**, Ukr.
83/G5 **Kharmanli**, Bul.
84/J4 **Kharovsk**, Rus.
123/M13 **Kharrour** (riv.), Mor.
125/M4 **Khartoum** (cap.), Sudan
125/M4 **Khartoum North**, Sudan
125/M4 **Kharţūm** (Khartoum) (cap.), Sudan
130/B3 **Kharumwa**, Tanz.
87/H4 **Khasavyurt**, Rus.
95/H2 **Khāsh** (riv.), Afg.
95/H3 **Khāsh**, Iran
87/G4 **Khashuri**, Geo.
83/G5 **Khaskovo**, Bul.
83/G5 **Khaskovo** (reg.), Bul.
89/L2 **Khatanga** (gulf), Rus.
89/L2 **Khatanga** (riv.), Rus.
91/C4 **Khatmia** (pass), Egypt
95/G3 **Khaymah, Ra's al**, UAE
93/F3 **Khazzān Darbandīkhān** (res.), Iraq
93/F3 **Khazzān Dūkān** (res.), Iraq
125/M4 **Khazzān Jabal Al Awliyā** (dam), Sudan
123/S15 **Khemis el Khechna**, Alg.
123/S15 **Khemis Miliana**, Alg.
123/V18 **Khenchela**, Alg.
124/D1 **Khenifra**, Mor.
93/G4 **Khersān** (riv.), Iran
86/E3 **Kherson**, Ukr.
86/E3 **Kherson Obl.**, Ukr.
96/G1 **Khilok**, Rus.
96/F1 **Khilok** (riv.), Rus.
81/K3 **Khíos**, Gre.
81/J3 **Khíos** (isl.), Gre.
83/G4 **Khisarya**, Bul.
88/G5 **Khiva**, Uzb.
86/C2 **Khmel'nitskiy**, Ukr.
95/J2 **Khojak** (pass), Pak.
109/C3 **Khok Samrong**, Thai.
95/J1 **Kholm**, Afg.
97/N2 **Kholmsk**, Rus.
131/D2 **Kholombidzo** (falls), Malw.
93/G3 **Khomeynīshahr**, Iran
109/C2 **Khon Kaen**, Thai.
87/G2 **Khopēr** (riv.), Rus.
97/M2 **Khor** (riv.), Rus.
93/J3 **Khorāsān** (gov.), Iran
126/C5 **Khorixas**, Namb.
130/D2 **Khorof Harar**, Kenya
102/B4 **Khorog**, Taj.
93/G3 **Khorramābād**, Iran
93/G4 **Khorramshahr**, Iran
109/C2 **Kho Sawai** (plat.), Thai.
151/G3 **Khotol** (mtn.), Ak,US
124/D1 **Khouribga**, Mor.
107/F3 **Khowai**, India
95/J2 **Khowst**, Afg.
81/J2 **Khrisoúpolis**, Gre.
87/L2 **Khromtau**, Kaz.
81/J5 **Khrysi** (isl.), Gre.
109/C2 **Khuan Ubon Ratana** (res.), Thai.
108/C2 **Khudiān**, Pak.
131/B4 **Khudumelapye**, Bots.
102/A3 **Khudzhand**, Taj.
106/E3 **Khulna**, Bang.
95/L1 **Khūnjerāb** (pass), Pak.
106/C3 **Khurai**, India
106/E3 **Khurda**, India
106/C2 **Khurja**, India
108/B1 **Khushāb**, Pak.
86/B2 **Khust**, Ukr.
95/J3 **Khuzdār**, Pak.
93/G4 **Khūzestān** (gov.), Iran
93/G4 **Khūzestān, Jolgeh-ye** (plain), Iran
97/L3 **Khvalynka**, Rus.
93/G3 **Khvonsār**, Iran
93/F2 **Khvoy**, Iran
102/B5 **Khyber** (pass), Afg., Pak.
119/D2 **Kiama**, Austl.
112/D4 **Kiamba**, Phil.
162/E3 **Kiamichi** (mts.), Ok,US
112/C1 **Kiangan**, Phil.
130/A2 **Kibali** (riv.), Zaire
130/A4 **Kibanga**, Zaire
130/B3 **Kibara**, Tanz.
130/B5 **Kibau**, Tanz.
112/D4 **Kibawe**, Phil.
130/C4 **Kibaya**, Tanz.
57/G2 **Kibblesworth**, Eng,UK
130/C4 **Kiberege**, Tanz.
61/J1 **Kibergneset** (pt.), Nor.
130/C4 **Kibindu**, Tanz.
130/C4 **Kibiti**, Tanz.
130/A2 **Kiboga**, Ugan.
130/C3 **Kiboko**, Kenya
130/A3 **Kibondo**, Tanz.
56/B2 **Kibongoto**, Tanz.
130/A3 **Kibungo**, Rwa.
130/A3 **Kibuye**, Rwa.
130/A4 **Kibwesa**, Tanz.
130/C3 **Kibwezi**, Kenya
82/E5 **Kičevo**, Macd.
60/A6 **Kid** (mtn.), Ire.
111/G2 **Kidapawan**, Phil.
58/D2 **Kidderminster**, Eng,UK
125/M7 **Kidepo Valley Nat'l Park**, Ugan.
130/C4 **Kidete**, Tanz.
130/C4 **Kidodi**, Tanz.
57/F5 **Kidsgrove**, Eng,UK
130/C4 **Kidugallo**, Tanz.
58/B3 **Kidwelly**, Wal,UK
64/F1 **Kiel** (bay), Den., Ger.
64/F1 **Kiel**, Ger.
65/L3 **Kielce**, Pol.
65/L3 **Kielce** (prov.), Pol.
57/F1 **Kielder**, Eng,UK
57/F1 **Kielder** (res.), Eng,UK
131/B1 **Kiembe**, Zaire
109/D1 **Kien An**, Viet.
109/D4 **Kien Duc**, Viet.
109/D4 **Kien Thanh**, Viet.
67/E6 **Kierspe**, Ger.
86/D2 **Kiev** (Kiyev) (cap.), Ukr.
86/D2 **Kiev Obl.**, Ukr.
128/C2 **Kiffa**, Mrta.
81/L6 **Kifisiá**, Gre.
93/F3 **Kifrī**, Iraq
130/A3 **Kigali** (cap.), Rwa.
130/B4 **Kiganga**, Tanz.
130/A4 **Kigoma**, Tanz.
130/A4 **Kigoma** (prov.), Tanz.
154/T10 **Kihei**, Hi,US
63/L2 **Kihnu** (isl.), Est.
63/J1 **Kihti** (str.), Fin.
130/C5 **Kihundo**, Tanz.
130/C4 **Kihurio**, Tanz.
98/D4 **Kii** (chan.), Japan
98/D4 **Kii** (mts.), Japan
102/D3 **Kiines** (riv.), China
130/C4 **Kijungu**, Tanz.
100/L6 **Kikai** (isl.), Japan
130/A3 **Kikarara**, Ugan.
154/R9 **Kikepa** (pt.), Hi,US
151/H2 **Kikiktat** (mtn.), Ak,US
82/E3 **Kikinda**, Yugo.
130/B4 **Kikombo**, Tanz.
100/B3 **Kikonai**, Japan
126/C2 **Kikwit**, Zaire
62/E2 **Kil**, Swe.
130/C3 **Kilaguni**, Kenya
108/G4 **Kilakarai**, India
130/B3 **Kilalo**, Tanz.
148/E3 **Kilambe** (mtn.), Nic.
54/B5 **Kilbarchan**, Sc,UK
54/B5 **Kilbirnie**, Sc,UK
54/A6 **Kilbrannan** (sound), Sc,UK
161/Q9 **Kilbride**, On,Can
55/H8 **Kilchoan**, Sc,UK
60/A3 **Kilcolgan** (pt.), Ire.
54/B5 **Kilcreggan**, Sc,UK
60/B3 **Kilcrow** (riv.), Ire.
60/D3 **Kildare** (co.), Ire.
84/G1 **Kil'din** (isl.), Rus.
130/B2 **Kildepo Valley Nat'l Park**, Ugan.
131/C3 **Kildonan**, Zim.
130/A2 **Kilembe**, Ugan.
162/E3 **Kilgore**, Tx,US
130/B3 **Kilgoris**, Kenya
57/H3 **Kilham**, Eng,UK
153/R7 **Kilian** (isl.), NW,Can
130/C3 **Kilifi**, Kenya
108/F4 **Kilikollūr**, India
130/C3 **Kilimanjaro** (mtn.), Tanz.
130/C3 **Kilimanjaro Nat'l Park**, Tanz.
130/B4 **Kilimatinde**, Tanz.
83/K5 **Kilimli**, Turk.
130/C4 **Kilindoni**, Tanz.
108/H4 **Kilinochchi** (dist.), SrL.
91/E1 **Kilis**, Turk.
86/D3 **Kiliya**, Ukr.
56/B3 **Kilkeel**, NI,UK
60/C4 **Kilkenny**, Ire.
60/C4 **Kilkenny** (co.), Ire.
81/H2 **Kilkís**, Gre.
60/A1 **Killala** (bay), Ire.
156/F2 **Killam**, Ab,Can
57/G5 **Killamarsh**, Eng,UK
118/H8 **Killara**, Austl.
157/J3 **Killarney**, Mb,Can
60/A5 **Killarney**, Ire.
168/F6 **Killbuck** (cr.), Oh,US
157/H4 **Killdeer**, ND,US
54/B4 **Killearn**, Sc,UK
162/D4 **Killeen**, Tx,US
54/C3 **Killiecrankie** (pass), Sc,UK
54/B4 **Killin**, Sc,UK
56/C3 **Killinchy**, NI,UK
153/K2 **Killinek** (isl.), NW,Can
81/H4 **Killíni** (peak), Gre.
56/C3 **Killough**, NI,UK
167/K8 **Kill Van Kull** (str.), NJ, NY,US
56/A2 **Killyclogher**, NI,UK
56/C3 **Killyleagh**, NI,UK
60/D3 **Kilmacanoge**, Ire.
54/B5 **Kilmacolm**, Sc,UK
54/B5 **Kilmarnock**, Sc,UK
58/B5 **Kilmar Tor** (hill), Eng,UK
54/B5 **Kilmaurs**, Sc,UK
60/D4 **Kilmichael** (pt.), Ire.
55/J8 **Kilninver**, Sc,UK
130/C5 **Kilombero** (riv.), Tanz.
130/A2 **Kilomines**, Zaire
130/C4 **Kilosa**, Tanz.
56/B1 **Kilraghts**, NI,UK
56/B2 **Kilrea**, NI,UK
54/D4 **Kilrenny**, Sc,UK
54/B5 **Kilsyth**, Sc,UK
130/A5 **Kilwa** (isl.), Zam.
130/C5 **Kilwa Kivinje**, Tanz.
130/C5 **Kilwa Masoko**, Tanz.
56/C2 **Kilwaughter**, NI,UK
54/B5 **Kilwinning**, Sc,UK
130/B3 **Kimali**, Tanz.
130/C4 **Kimamba**, Tanz.
157/H5 **Kimball**, Ne,US
157/J5 **Kimball**, SD,US
120/E5 **Kimbe**, PNG
118/B2 **Kimberley** (cape), Austl.
114/D3 **Kimberley** (plat.), Austl.
156/E3 **Kimberley**, BC,Can
132/D3 **Kimberley**, SAfr.
101/E2 **Kimch'aek**, NKor.
101/E4 **Kimch'ŏn**, SKor.
101/E5 **Kimhae**, SKor.
63/K1 **Kimito** (isl.), Fin.
99/F3 **Kimitsu**, Japan
101/D5 **Kimje**, SKor.
101/G7 **Kimnyangjang-ni**, SKor.
81/J4 **Kímolos** (isl.), Gre.
130/B2 **Kimoset**, Kenya
86/F1 **Kimovsk**, Rus.
126/D2 **Kimpanga**, Zaire
84/H4 **Kimry**, Rus.
111/E2 **Kinabalu, Gunung** (peak), Malay.
112/B4 **Kinabalu Nat'l Park**, Malay.
111/E2 **Kinabatangan** (riv.), Malay.
130/C4 **Kinango**, Kenya
156/D2 **Kinbasket** (lake), BC,Can
55/K7 **Kinbrace**, Sc,UK
156/G3 **Kincaid**, Sk,Can
160/D2 **Kincardine**, On,Can
54/C4 **Kincardine**, Sc,UK
119/B2 **Kinchega Nat'l Park**, Austl.
54/C2 **Kincraig**, Sc,UK
126/D2 **Kindambi**, Zaire
73/L3 **Kindberg**, Aus.
57/G5 **Kinder Scout** (mtn.), Eng,UK
128/B4 **Kindia**, Gui.
128/B4 **Kindia** (comm.), Gui.
126/E1 **Kindu**, Zaire
87/J1 **Kinel'**, Rus.
84/J4 **Kineshma**, Rus.
59/E2 **Kineton**, Eng,UK
119/C3 **King** (isl.), Austl.
116/C5 **King** (lake), Austl.
118/B4 **King** (peak), Austl.
114/C3 **King** (sound), Austl.
156/B2 **King** (isl.), BC,Can
151/N4 **King** (mtn.), BC,Can
151/K3 **King** (peak), Yk,Can
146/E2 **King** (mtn.), Tx,US
165/D2 **King** (co.), Wa,US
118/C4 **Kingaroy**, Austl.
153/R7 **King Christian** (isl.), NW,Can
145/P3 **King Christian IX Land** (reg.), Grld.
145/Q2 **King Christian X Land** (reg.), Grld.
161/Q8 **King City**, On,Can
158/B3 **King City**, Ca,US
159/H4 **Kingfisher**, Ok,US
145/N3 **King Frederik VI Coast** (reg.), Grld.
145/Q2 **King Frederik VIII Land** (reg.), Grld.
121/L6 **King George** (isl.), FrPol.
160/E4 **King George**, Va,US
53/N7 **King George's** (res.), Eng,UK
54/C4 **Kinghorn**, Sc,UK
119/C3 **Kinglake Nat'l Park**, Austl.
114/D3 **King Leopold** (ranges), Austl.
121/J4 **Kingman** (reef), PacUS
158/D4 **Kingman**, Az,US
159/H3 **Kingman**, Ks,US
166/C3 **King of Prussia**, Pa,US
158/C3 **Kings** (riv.), Ca,US
158/E2 **Kings** (peak), Ut,US
58/C6 **Kingsbridge**, Eng,UK
167/K9 **Kings** (Brooklyn) (co.), NY,US
158/C3 **Kings Canyon Nat'l Park**, Ca,US
59/E4 **Kingsclere**, Eng,UK
59/F1 **King's Cliffe**, Eng,UK
58/D2 **Kingsland**, Eng,UK
53/M6 **Kings Langley**, Eng,UK
59/G1 **King's Lynn**, Eng,UK
116/K6 **Kings Park**, Austl.
163/H2 **Kingsport**, Tn,US
54/C4 **King's Seat** (hill), Sc,UK
59/E2 **Kings Sutton**, Eng,UK
58/C5 **Kingsteignton**, Eng,UK
119/C4 **Kingston**, Austl.
160/E2 **Kingston**, On,Can
149/G2 **Kingston** (cap.), Jam.
120/F7 **Kingston**, Norfl.
168/D2 **Kingston**, Ma,US
160/F3 **Kingston**, NY,US
166/C1 **Kingston**, Pa,US
168/G3 **Kingston**, RI,US
119/A3 **Kingston South East**, Austl.
59/F4 **Kingston upon Thames**, Eng,UK
53/N7 **Kingston upon Thames** (bor.), Eng,UK
150/F4 **Kingstown** (cap.), StV.
163/J3 **Kingstree**, SC,US
127/C3 **Kings, Valley of the**, Egypt
162/D5 **Kingsville**, Tx,US
58/D2 **Kingswinford**, Eng,UK
58/D4 **Kingswood**, Eng,UK
91/D3 **King Ţalāl** (dam), Jor.
58/C2 **Kington**, Eng,UK
54/B2 **Kingussie**, Sc,UK
152/G2 **King William** (isl.), NW,Can
132/D4 **King William's Town**, SAfr.
131/C1 **Kiniama**, Zaire
92/A2 **Kınık**, Turk.
151/L4 **Kinkaid** (mtn.), Ak,US
126/B1 **Kinkala**, Congo
98/D3 **Kinki** (prov.), Japan
128/B4 **Kinkon, Chutes de** (falls), Gui.
54/A1 **Kinlochewe**, Sc,UK
54/B3 **Kinlochleven**, Sc,UK
54/B3 **Kinloch Rannoch**, Sc,UK
54/C1 **Kinloss**, Sc,UK
56/E5 **Kinmel**, Wal,UK
62/E3 **Kinna**, Swe.
54/D1 **Kinnairds Head** (pt.), Sc,UK
166/D2 **Kinnelon**, NJ,US
167/H8 **Kinnelon** (lake), NJ,US
91/F8 **Kinneret-Negev Conduit**, Isr.
108/H4 **Kinniya**, SrL.
98/D3 **Kino** (riv.), Japan
160/D1 **Kinoje** (riv.), On,Can
69/E1 **Kinrooi**, Belg.
54/C4 **Kinross**, Sc,UK
71/F4 **Kinsach** (riv.), Ger.
161/R8 **Kinsale**, On,Can
60/B6 **Kinsale** (har.), Ire.
126/C1 **Kinshasa** (cap.), Zaire
159/H3 **Kinsley**, Ks,US
163/J3 **Kinston**, NC,US
129/E4 **Kintampo**, Gha.
130/B4 **Kintinku**, Tanz.
54/D2 **Kintore**, Sc,UK
55/J9 **Kintyre** (pen.), Sc,UK
56/C1 **Kintyre, Mull of** (pt.), Sc,UK
99/F2 **Kinu** (riv.), Japan
130/B4 **Kinyangiri**, Tanz.
125/M7 **Kinyeti** (peak), Sudan
70/B6 **Kinzig** (riv.), Ger.
70/C2 **Kinzig** (riv.), Ger.
130/B4 **Kiomboi**, Tanz.
81/G4 **Kiparissia** (gulf), Gre.
160/E2 **Kipawa** (lake), Qu,Can
130/A4 **Kipili**, Tanz.
131/C2 **Kipilingu**, Zaire
130/D3 **Kipini**, Kenya
130/B2 **Kipkarren** (riv.), Kenya
157/H3 **Kipling**, Sk,Can
54/B4 **Kippen**, Sc,UK
60/D3 **Kippure** (mtn.), Ire.
131/B1 **Kipushi**, Zaire
99/N10 **Kira**, Japan
81/H3 **Kira Panayía** (isl.), Gre.
71/F1 **Kirchberg**, Ger.
70/B3 **Kirchheimbolanden**, Ger.
70/C5 **Kirchheim unter Teck**, Ger.
67/F6 **Kirchhundem**, Ger.
67/F4 **Kirchlengern**, Ger.
67/G3 **Kirchlinteln**, Ger.
77/H2 **Kirchsee** (lake), Ger.
71/E6 **Kirchseeon**, Ger.
70/A7 **Kirchzarten**, Ger.
56/C3 **Kircubbin**, NI,UK
56/D2 **Kircudbright** (bay), Sc,UK
89/L4 **Kirensk**, Rus.
102/B3 **Kirgizskiy** (mts.), Kyr.
88/F5 **Kirgiz Steppe** (grsld.), Kaz., Rus.
120/H5 **Kiribati**
91/E1 **Kırıkhan**, Turk.
92/C2 **Kırıkkale**, Turk.
92/C2 **Kirikkale** (prov.), Turk.
96/C3 **Kirikkuduk**, China
63/Q2 **Kirishi**, Rus.
98/B5 **Kirishima-Yaku Nat'l Park**, Japan
98/B5 **Kirishima-yama** (mtn.), Japan
121/K4 **Kiritimati** (Christmas) (atoll), Kiri.
92/A2 **Kırkağaç**, Turk.
57/G4 **Kirkburton**, Eng,UK
57/F5 **Kirkby**, Eng,UK
57/G5 **Kirkby in Ashfield**, Eng,UK
57/F3 **Kirkby Lonsdale**, Eng,UK
57/H3 **Kirkbymoorside**, Eng,UK
57/F3 **Kirkby Stephen**, Eng,UK
54/C4 **Kirkcaldy**, Sc,UK
56/C2 **Kirkcolm**, Sc,UK
54/C6 **Kirkconnel**, Sc,UK
56/D2 **Kirkcowan**, Sc,UK
56/D2 **Kirkcudbright**, Sc,UK
106/B4 **Kirkee**, India
62/E1 **Kirkenær**, Nor.
61/J1 **Kirkenes**, Nor.
57/F4 **Kirkham**, Eng,UK
54/B2 **Kirkhill**, Sc,UK
56/D2 **Kirkinner**, Sc,UK
54/B5 **Kirkintilloch**, Sc,UK
63/L1 **Kirkkonummi** (Kyrkslätt), Fin.
161/N7 **Kirkland**, Qu,Can
54/C6 **Kirkland** (hill), Sc,UK
165/C2 **Kirkland**, Wa,US
160/D1 **Kirkland Lake**, On,Can
92/A2 **Kırklar** (peak), Turk.
83/H5 **Kırklareli**, Turk.
83/H5 **Kırklareli** (prov.), Turk.
54/C5 **Kirkliston**, Sc,UK
56/D3 **Kirkmichael**, IM,UK
54/C5 **Kirkmuirhill**, Sc,UK
83/L2 **Kirkovgrad Obl.**, Ukr.
113/M **Kirkpatrick** (mtn.), Ant.
159/J2 **Kirksville**, Mo,US
54/C3 **Kirkton of Glenisla**, Sc,UK
93/F3 **Kirkūk**, Iraq
55/N13 **Kirkwall**, Sc,UK
69/G4 **Kirn**, Ger.
130/C4 **Kirongwe**, Tanz.
130/B5 **Kiropa**, Tanz.
86/E1 **Kirov**, Rus.
87/H4 **Kirovakan**, Arm.
85/L4 **Kirovo-Chepetsk**, Rus.
86/E2 **Kirovograd**, Ukr.
86/D2 **Kirovograd Obl.**, Ukr.
54/D3 **Kirriemuir**, Sc,UK
87/G1 **Kirsanov**, Rus.
92/C2 **Kırşehir**, Turk.
92/C2 **Kırsehir** (prov.), Turk.
57/H6 **Kirton**, Eng,UK
57/H5 **Kirton in Lindsey**, Eng,UK
61/G2 **Kiruna**, Swe.
168/F4 **Kirwan** (res.), Oh,US
99/F2 **Kiryū**, Japan
100/A4 **Kisakata**, Japan
125/L7 **Kisangani**, Zaire
130/C4 **Kisarawe**, Tanz.
99/F3 **Kisarazu**, Japan
65/K5 **Kisbér**, Hun.
88/J4 **Kiselevsk**, Rus.
130/B3 **Kisesa**, Tanz.
130/B3 **Kisessa**, Tanz.
93/H5 **Kīsh** (isl.), Iran
130/A3 **Kishanda**, Tanz.
106/E2 **Kishanganj**, India
106/B2 **Kishangarh**, India
83/J2 **Kishinëv** (cap.), Mol.
100/D2 **Kishiro-Shitsugen Nat'l Park**, Japan
98/D3 **Kishiwada**, Japan
106/F3 **Kishorganj**, Bang.
108/C1 **Kishtwar**, India
165/N15 **Kishwaukee** (riv.), Il,US
130/B4 **Kisigo** (riv.), Tanz.
130/B3 **Kisii**, Kenya
130/C4 **Kisiju**, Tanz.
130/C4 **Kisiwani**, Tanz.
151/B6 **Kiska** (isl.), Ak,US
151/B5 **Kiska** (vol.), Ak,US
156/C2 **Kiskatinaw** (riv.), BC,Can
157/J2 **Kiskitto** (lake), Mb,Can
82/D2 **Kiskőrös**, Hun.
82/D2 **Kiskunfélegyháza**, Hun.
82/D2 **Kiskunhalas**, Hun.
82/D2 **Kiskunmajsa**, Hun.
82/D2 **Kiskunsági Nat'l Park**, Hun.
87/G4 **Kislovodsk**, Rus.
125/P8 **Kismaayo** (Chisimayu), Som.
99/E3 **Kiso** (riv.), Japan
99/M9 **Kisogawa**, Japan
99/M9 **Kisozaki**, Japan
163/H4 **Kissimmee**, Fl,US
163/H4 **Kissimmee** (lake), Fl,US
70/D6 **Kissing**, Ger.
157/H2 **Kississing** (lake), Mb,Can
77/F2 **Kisslegg**, Ger.
82/E2 **Kisújszállás**, Hun.
130/B3 **Kisumu**, Kenya
82/F1 **Kisvárda**, Hun.
130/C5 **Kiswere**, Tanz.
99/G2 **Kita** (inlet), Japan
128/C3 **Kita**, Mali
99/M9 **Kitagata**, Japan
99/G2 **Kita-Ibaraki**, Japan
100/B4 **Kitakami**, Japan
100/B4 **Kitakami** (mts.), Japan
99/F2 **Kitakata**, Japan
98/B4 **Kitakyūshū**, Japan
130/B2 **Kitale**, Kenya
100/C2 **Kitami**, Japan
100/C1 **Kitami** (mts.), Japan
99/H6 **Kitamoto**, Japan
130/C5 **Kitangari**, Tanz.
130/B4 **Kitangiri** (lake), Tanz.
160/D3 **Kitchener**, On,Can
61/J3 **Kitee**, Fin.
130/A4 **Kitendwe**, Zaire
130/B2 **Kitgum**, Ugan.
81/H4 **Kíthira** (isl.), Gre.
81/J4 **Kíthnos** (isl.), Gre.
156/A2 **Kitimat**, BC,Can
156/A2 **Kitimat Arm** (inlet), BC,Can
165/B3 **Kitsap** (co.), Wa,US
165/B2 **Kitsap Lake-Erlands Point**, Wa,US
166/C1 **Kittatinny** (mts.), NJ, Pa,US
161/G3 **Kittery**, Me,US
130/C3 **Kitui**, Kenya
130/C3 **Kitumbeine** (peak), Tanz.
130/C5 **Kitumbini**, Tanz.
130/B4 **Kitunda**, Tanz.
130/D5 **Kitunguli**, Tanz.
131/C2 **Kitwe**, Zam.
73/K3 **Kitzbühel**, Aus.
70/D3 **Kitzingen**, Ger.
130/D3 **Kiunga**, Kenya
130/D3 **Kiunga Marine Nat'l Rsv.**, Kenya
61/H3 **Kiuruvesi**, Fin.
130/C4 **Kiuyu** (pt.), Tanz.
61/H2 **Kivalo** (mts.), Fin.
63/M1 **Kivijärvi** (lake), Fin.
63/M2 **Kiviõli**, Est.
130/A3 **Kivu** (lake), Rwa., Zaire
130/A3 **Kivu** (reg.), Zaire
130/B5 **Kiwira**, Tanz.
86/D2 **Kiyev** (res.), Ukr.
86/D2 **Kiyev** (Kiev) (cap.), Ukr.
99/H7 **Kiyokawa**, Japan
99/H7 **Kiyose**, Japan
99/M9 **Kiyosu**, Japan
126/C2 **Kizamba**, Zaire
85/N4 **Kizel**, Rus.
102/B4 **Kizil** (riv.), China
92/C1 **Kızılcahamam**, Turk.
92/B2 **Kızıldag Nat'l Park**, Turk.
92/B2 **Kızılhisar**, Turk.
92/C1 **Kızılırmak** (riv.), Turk.
92/E2 **Kızıltepe**, Turk.
130/C5 **Kizimbani**, Tanz.
130/C4 **Kizimkazi**, Tanz.
87/H4 **Kizlyar**, Rus.
99/L10 **Kizu**, Japan
98/E3 **Kizu** (riv.), Japan
100/B3 **Kizukuri**, Japan
87/L5 **Kizyl-Arvat**, Trkm.
84/C1 **Kjerkestinden** (peak), Nor.
61/E2 **Kjølen** (Kölen) (mts.), Nor., Swe.
71/G3 **Klabava** (riv.), Czh.
82/D3 **Kladanj**, Bosn.
71/H2 **Kladno**, Czh.
82/F3 **Kladovo**, Yugo.
73/L3 **Klagenfurt**, Aus.
63/J4 **Klaipėda**, Lith.
156/C5 **Klamath** (mts.), Ca, Or,US
156/C5 **Klamath** (riv.), Ca, Or,US
156/C5 **Klamath Falls**, Or,US
88/B3 **Klar** (riv.), Swe.
61/E3 **Klarälven** (riv.), Swe.
71/G4 **Klatovy**, Czh.
77/H4 **Klausen** (Chiusa), It.
77/E4 **Klausenpass** (pass), Swi.
151/L3 **Klaza** (mtn.), Yk,Can
66/E3 **Klazienaveen**, Neth.
69/G5 **Kleinblittersdorf**, Ger.
161/Q8 **Kleinburg**, On,Can
65/G3 **Kleine Elster** (riv.), Ger.
76/E4 **Kleine Emme** (riv.), Swi.
69/E2 **Kleine Gete** (riv.), Belg.
71/F5 **Kleine Laber** (riv.), Ger.
66/B6 **Kleine Nete** (riv.), Belg.
131/C4 **Klein-Letabarivier** (riv.), SAfr.
132/Q12 **Kleinolifants** (riv.), SAfr.
62/A1 **Kleppestø**, Nor.
132/D2 **Klerksdorp**, SAfr.
71/H5 **Kleť** (peak), Czh.
66/D5 **Kleve**, Ger.
70/C3 **Klingenberg am Main**, Ger.
71/F2 **Klingenthal**, Ger.
71/F2 **Klínovec** (peak), Czh.
86/E1 **Klintsy**, Rus.
132/E2 **Klip** (riv.), SAfr.
62/E3 **Klippan**, Swe.
82/C3 **Ključ**, Bosn.
65/K2 **Kłodawa**, Pol.
65/J3 **Kłodzko**, Pol.
77/E3 **Klöntalersee** (lake), Swi.
67/F3 **Klosterbach** (riv.), Ger.
73/M2 **Klosterneuburg**, Aus.
73/L3 **Klosterwappen** (peak), Aus.
77/E3 **Kloten**, Swi.
64/F2 **Klötze**, Ger.
151/L3 **Kluane**, Yk,Can
151/K3 **Kluane Nat'l Park**, Yk,Can
65/K3 **Kluczbork**, Pol.
151/L3 **Klukshu**, Yk,Can
66/B5 **Klundert**, Neth.
67/E3 **Klüstenkanal** (can.), Ger.
84/J4 **Klyaz'ma** (riv.), Rus.
89/S4 **Klyuchevskaya** (peak), Rus.
57/G3 **Knaresborough**, Eng,UK
59/F3 **Knebworth**, Eng,UK
157/K2 **Knee** (lake), Mb,Can
83/G4 **Knezha**, Bul.
156/B3 **Knight** (inlet), BC,Can
58/C2 **Knighton**, Wal,UK
82/C3 **Knin**, Cro.
73/L3 **Knittelfeld**, Aus.
70/B4 **Knittlingen**, Ger.
71/H5 **Knížecí Stolec** (peak), Czh.
71/F3 **Knížecí Strom** (peak), Czh.
82/F4 **Knjaževac**, Yugo.
116/C5 **Knob** (cape), Austl.
112/C2 **Knob** (peak), Phil.
116/B4 **Knobby** (pt.), Austl.
54/D1 **Knoch** (hill), Sc,UK
60/C6 **Knockadoon Head** (pt.), Ire.
60/B1 **Knockalongy** (mtn.), Ire.
60/C5 **Knockanaffrin** (mtn.), Ire.
60/A6 **Knockboy** (mtn.), Ire.
56/B2 **Knockcloghrim**, NI,UK
60/A6 **Knockeirke** (mtn.), Ire.
56/B1 **Knocklayd** (mtn.), NI,UK
60/C5 **Knockmealdown** (mtn.), Ire.
60/B5 **Knockmealdown** (mts.), Ire.
60/B5 **Knockshanahullion** (mtn.), Ire.
68/C1 **Knokke-Heist**, Belg.
132/A2 **Knoll** (pt.), Namb.
62/D3 **Knøsen** (peak), Den.
62/E4 **Knösen** (pt.), Swe.
81/J5 **Knosós** (Knossos) (ruins), Gre.
57/F4 **Knott End**, Eng,UK
57/G4 **Knottingley**, Eng,UK
164/G8 **Knott's Berry Farm**, Ca,US
113/G **Knox** (coast), Ant.
119/G5 **Knox**, Austl.
151/M4 **Knox** (cape), BC,Can
168/E7 **Knox** (co.), Oh,US
168/E6 **Knox** (lake), Oh,US
163/H3 **Knoxville**, Tn,US
57/F5 **Knutsford**, Eng,UK
132/C4 **Knysna**, SAfr.
97/M2 **Ko** (peak), Rus.
130/C4 **Koani**, Tanz.
98/B5 **Kobayashi**, Japan
98/D3 **Kōbe**, Japan
63/T9 **København** (co.), Den.
62/E4 **København** (Copenhagen) (cap.), Den.
63/T9 **København** (Copenhagen) (inset) (cap.), Den.
111/G4 **Kobipato** (peak), Indo.
69/G3 **Koblenz**, Ger.
65/N2 **Kobrin**, Bela.
151/G2 **Kobuk** (riv.), Ak,US
151/G2 **Kobuk Valley Nat'l Park**, Ak,US
99/F3 **Kobushi-ga-take** (mtn.), Japan
71/H3 **Kocába** (riv.), Czh.
83/J5 **Kocaeli** (prov.), Turk.
92/D2 **Koçali**, Turk.
82/F5 **Kočani**, Macd.
82/B3 **Kočevje**, Slov.
153/J2 **Koch** (isl.), NW,Can
101/D5 **Koch'ang**, SKor.
77/H2 **Kochelsee** (lake), Ger.
70/C4 **Kocher** (riv.), Ger.
98/C4 **Kōchi**, Japan
98/C4 **Kōchi** (pref.), Japan
151/H4 **Kodiak**, Ak,US
151/H4 **Kodiak** (isl.), Ak,US
151/H4 **Kodiak Nat'l Wild. Ref.**, Ak,US
106/B3 **Kodinār**, India
125/M6 **Kodok**, Sudan
100/B3 **Kodomari**, Japan
83/H2 **Kodry** (hills), Mol.
68/B1 **Koekelare**, Belg.
106/D3 **Koel** (riv.), India
69/F5 **Koenigsmacker**, Fr.
139/G4 **Koetari** (riv.), Guy., Sur.
158/D4 **Kofa** (mts.), Az,US
111/G4 **Kofiau** (isl.), Indo.
129/E5 **Koforidua**, Gha.
99/F3 **Kōfu**, Japan
102/D3 **Koga**, China
99/F2 **Koga**, Japan
130/B4 **Koga**, Tanz.
99/H7 **Koganei**, Japan
62/E4 **Køge**, Den.
62/E4 **Køge Bugt** (bay), Den.
128/B4 **Kogon** (riv.), Gui.
101/D5 **Kŏgum** (isl.), SKor.
108/A1 **Kohāt**, Pak.
104/B3 **Kohīma**, India
93/G4 **Kohkīlūyeh and Bovīr Aḩmadi** (gov.), Iran
71/H5 **Kohout** (peak), Czh.
63/M2 **Kohtla-Järve**, Est.
101/D5 **Kohŭng**, SKor.
147/H5 **Kohunlich** (ruins), Mex.
132/A2 **Koichab** (dry riv.), Namb.
151/K3 **Koidern**, Yk,Can
99/H7 **Koito** (riv.), Japan
130/C3 **Koito**, Kenya
63/M3 **Koiva** (riv.), Est.
101/E5 **Kŏje** (isl.), SKor.
65/L4 **Kojšovská Hol'a** (peak), Slvk.
109/B1 **Kok** (riv.), Burma
99/M10 **Kōka**, Japan
99/J7 **Kokai** (riv.), Japan
102/B3 **Kokand**, Uzb.
63/J2 **Kökar** (isl.), Fin.
102/A1 **Kokchetav**, Kaz.
63/J1 **Kokemäenjoki** (riv.), Fin.
61/G3 **Kokkola**, Fin.
128/C3 **Kokofata**, Mali
154/W13 **Koko Head** (crater), Hi,US
130/A2 **Kokola**, Zaire
160/C3 **Kokomo**, In,US
131/A5 **Kokong**, Bots.
106/F2 **Kokrajhar**, India
102/C3 **Kokshaal-Tau** (mts.), Kyr.
68/B1 **Koksijde**, Belg.
153/K3 **Koksoak** (riv.), Qu,Can
132/E3 **Kokstad**, SAfr.
98/B5 **Kokubu**, Japan
84/H1 **Kola** (pen.), Rus.
84/G1 **Kola** (riv.), Rus.
108/F4 **Kolachel**, India
111/F4 **Kolaka**, Indo.
106/C5 **Kolār**, India
82/D4 **Kolašin**, Yugo.
64/G5 **Kolbermoor**, Ger.
130/D3 **Kolbio**, Kenya
65/L3 **Kolbuszowa**, Pol.
128/B3 **Kolda**, Sen.
128/B3 **Kolda** (reg.), Sen.
62/C4 **Kolding**, Den.
61/E2 **Kölen** (Kjølen) (mts.), Nor., Swe.
120/C5 **Kolepom** (isl.), Indo.
63/N2 **Kolgompya** (cape), Rus.
85/K1 **Kolguyev** (isl.), Rus.
106/B4 **Kolhāpur**, India
128/B3 **Koliba** (riv.), Gui.
65/H3 **Kolín**, Czh.
63/K3 **Kolkasrags** (pt.), Lat.
71/F5 **Kollbach** (riv.), Ger.
66/D2 **Kollum**, Neth.
66/D7 **Köln** (Cologne), Ger.
65/L2 **Kolno**, Pol.
86/A1 **Koło**, Pol.
130/B4 **Kolo**, Tanz.
65/H1 **Kołobrzeg**, Pol.
128/C3 **Kolokani**, Mali
86/F1 **Kolomna**, Rus.
86/C2 **Kolomyya**, Ukr.
106/C6 **Kolonnawa**, SrL.
128/D3 **Kolossa** (riv.), Mali
88/J4 **Kolpashevo**, Rus.
63/P2 **Kolpino**, Rus.
82/E3 **Kolubara** (riv.), Yugo
65/K3 **Koluszki**, Pol.
102/A1 **Koluton** (riv.), Kaz.
85/N2 **Kolva** (riv.), Rus.
131/B1 **Kolwezi**, Zaire
89/R2 **Kolyma** (lowland), Rus.
89/R3 **Kolyma** (range), Rus.
89/R3 **Kolyma** (riv.), Rus.
82/F4 **Kom** (peak), Bul.
99/H7 **Koma** (riv.), Japan
82/E2 **Komádi**, Hun.
129/H4 **Komadugu Gana** (riv.), Nga.
129/H3 **Komadugu Yobé** (riv.), Nga.
99/H7 **Komae**, Japan
99/E3 **Komagane**, Japan
99/M9 **Komaki**, Japan
130/A2 **Komanda**, Zaire
89/S4 **Komandorskiye** (isls.), Rus.
65/K5 **Komárno**, Slvk.
82/D2 **Komárom**, Hun.
82/D2 **Komárom-Esztergom** (co.), Hun.
132/R12 **Komatirivier** (riv.), SAfr.
98/E2 **Komatsu**, Japan
98/D4 **Komatsushima**, Japan
130/B3 **Kome** (isl.), Tanz.
130/B3 **Kome** (isl.), Ugan.
79/G1 **Komen**, Slov.
85/L2 **Komi Aut. Rep.**, Rus.
85/M3 **Komi-Permyak Aut. Okr.**, Rus.
82/D2 **Komló**, Hun.
86/F2 **Kommunarsk**, Ukr.
102/B4 **Kommunizma** (Communism) (peak), Taj.
111/E5 **Komodo** (isl.), Indo.
111/E5 **Komodo I. Nat'l Park**, Indo.
128/E5 **Komoé** (riv.), IvC.
98/E3 **Komono**, Japan
81/J2 **Komotiní**, Gre.
132/D3 **Kompasberg** (peak), SAfr.
83/J2 **Komrat**, Mol.
89/L1 **Komsomolets** (isl.), Rus.
85/P2 **Komsomol'skiy**, Rus.
97/M1 **Komsomol'sk-na-Amure**, Rus.
71/K3 **Kōmūr** (pt.), Turk.
102/A2 **Kon** (riv.), Kaz.
84/H4 **Konakovo**, Rus.
99/M10 **Kōnan**, Japan
99/M9 **Kōnan**, Japan

198

Konan – Ladys

119/D2 **Konangra-Boyd Nat'l Park,** Austl.
111/F4 **Konaweha** (riv.), Indo.
99/L10 **Konda,** Japan
96/G1 **Konda** (riv.), Rus.
130/B4 **Kondoa,** Tanz.
84/G3 **Kondopoga,** Rus.
95/J1 **Kondūz,** Afg.
109/C4 **Kong** (isl.), Camb.
109/D3 **Kong** (riv.), Laos
101/D4 **Kongju,** SKor.
103/D4 **Kong Miao,** China
101/F6 **Kongnŭng** (riv.), SKor.
131/A3 **Kongola,** Namb.
126/E2 **Kongolo,** Zaire
99/L10 **Kongō-zan** (peak), Japan
62/C2 **Kongsberg,** Nor.
62/E1 **Kongsvinger,** Nor.
102/C4 **Kongur Shan** (peak), China
130/C4 **Kongwa,** Tanz.
65/K3 **Koniecpol,** Pol.
70/B5 **Königsberg-Stein,** Ger.
70/D5 **Königsbronn,** Ger.
70/D6 **Königsbrunn,** Ger.
77/G2 **Königschlösser,** Ger.
67/H4 **Königslutter am Elm,** Ger.
70/B2 **Königstein im Taunus,** Ger.
69/G2 **Königswinter,** Ger.
65/G2 **Königs Wusterhausen,** Ger.
65/K2 **Konin,** Pol.
65/K2 **Konin** (prov.), Pol.
76/D4 **Köniz,** Swi.
82/C4 **Konjic,** Bosn.
132/B2 **Konkiep** (dry riv.), Namb.
131/B2 **Konkola,** Zam.
128/B4 **Konkouré** (riv.), Gui.
86/E2 **Konotop,** Ukr.
102/E3 **Konqi** (riv.), China
100/D2 **Konsen** (plat.), Japan
65/L3 **Końskie,** Pol.
65/L2 **Konstancin-Jeziorna,** Pol.
86/F2 **Konstantinovka,** Ukr.
65/K3 **Konstantynów Łódzki,** Pol.
77/F2 **Konstanz,** Ger.
68/D1 **Kontich,** Belg.
61/J3 **Kontiolahti,** Fin.
109/E3 **Kon Tum,** Viet.
92/C2 **Konya,** Turk.
91/C1 **Konya** (prov.), Turk.
69/F4 **Konz,** Ger.
130/C3 **Konza,** Kenya
156/E3 **Koocanusa** (lake), Can., US
156/D3 **Kootenai** (riv.), Id, Mt,US
156/D3 **Kootenay** (lake), BC,Can
156/D3 **Kootenay Nat'l Park,** BC,Can
92/E1 **Kop** (pass), Turk.
106/B4 **Kopargaon,** India
61/N7 **Kópavogur,** Ice.
128/D5 **Kope** (peak), IvC.
65/G2 **Köpenick,** Ger.
79/G1 **Koper,** Slov.
85/P5 **Kopeysk,** Rus.
86/G4 **Kop Gecidi** (pass), Turk.
125/K7 **Kopia,** Zaire
104/B3 **Kopili** (riv.), India
62/G2 **Köping,** Swe.
111/F5 **Kopondei** (cape), Indo.
63/N2 **Koporskiy** (bay), Rus.
62/E1 **Kopparberg** (co.), Swe.
97/M2 **Koppi** (riv.), Rus.
82/C2 **Koprivnica,** Cro.
91/B1 **Köprü** (riv.), Turk.
92/B2 **Köprülü Kanyon Nat'l Park,** Turk.
93/H4 **Kor** (riv.), Iran
99/M9 **Kōra,** Japan
81/G2 **Korab** (peak), Alb.
71/G4 **Koráb** (peak), Czh.
98/C3 **Korakuen Garden,** Japan
153/K3 **Koraluk** (riv.), Nf,Can
73/L4 **Korana** (riv.), Bosn., Cro.
130/C2 **Kora Nat'l Park,** Kenya
106/D4 **Koraput,** India
106/D3 **Korba,** India
67/F6 **Korbach,** Ger.
81/G2 **Korçë,** Alb.
82/C4 **Korčula** (isl.), Cro.
82/C4 **Korčulanski** (chan.), Cro.
93/F3 **Kordestān** (gov.), Iran
93/H2 **Kord Kūy,** Iran
101/B3 **Korea** (bay), China, NKor.
98/A4 **Korea** (str.), Japan, SKor.
101/D4 **Korean Folk Vill.,** SKor.
101/D2 **Korea, North**
101/D4 **Korea, South**
86/F3 **Korenovsk,** Rus.
92/D1 **Korgan,** Turk.
128/D4 **Korhogo,** IvC.
81/H4 **Kórinthos** (Corinth), Gre.
82/C2 **Kőris-hegy** (peak), Hun.
99/G2 **Kōriyama,** Japan
124/J3 **Korizo, Passe de** (pass), Chad
89/R3 **Korkodon** (riv.), Rus.
91/B1 **Korkuteli,** Turk.
102/E3 **Korla,** China
91/C2 **Kormakiti** (cape), Cyp.
82/B4 **Kornat** (isl.), Cro.
73/L5 **Kornot** (isl.), Cro.
70/C5 **Korntal-Münchingen,** Ger.
70/C5 **Kornwestheim,** Ger.
121/Z18 **Koro** (isl.), Fiji
120/G6 **Koro** (sea), Fiji
83/K5 **Köroğlu** (peak), Turk.
130/C4 **Korogwe,** Tanz.
111/G2 **Koronadal,** Phil.
81/H2 **Korónia** (lake), Gre.
65/J2 **Koronowo,** Pol.
81/L7 **Koropí,** Gre.
120/C4 **Koror** (cap.), Palau
82/E2 **Körös** (riv.), Hun.
86/D2 **Korosten',** Ukr.
86/D2 **Korostyshev,** Ukr.
85/P1 **Korotaikha** (riv.), Rus.
124/J4 **Koro Toro,** Chad
151/D5 **Korovin** (vol.), Ak,US
63/J1 **Korpo,** Fin.
97/N2 **Korsakov,** Rus.
66/D6 **Korschenbroich,** Ger.
62/D4 **Korsør,** Den.
68/C1 **Kortemark,** Belg.
69/E2 **Kortenaken,** Belg.
68/D2 **Kortenberg,** Belg.
69/E2 **Kortessem,** Belg.
68/C2 **Kortrijk,** Belg.
129/H5 **Korup Nat'l Park,** Camr.
90/R3 **Koryak** (range), Rus.
89/S3 **Koryak Aut. Okr.,** Rus.
85/K3 **Koryazhma,** Rus.
99/L10 **Kōryō,** Japan
99/E3 **Kosai,** Japan
98/A3 **Ko-saki** (pt.), Japan
109/C3 **Ko Samut Nat'l Park,** Thai.
71/E5 **Kösching,** Ger.
65/J2 **Kościan,** Pol.
65/J1 **Kościerzyna,** Pol.
119/D3 **Kosciusko** (mtn.), Austl.
163/F3 **Kosciusko,** Ms,US
119/D3 **Kosciusko Nat'l Park,** Austl.
92/D1 **Köse,** Turk.
99/M10 **Kosei,** Japan
127/B4 **Kosha,** Sudan
99/F3 **Koshigaya,** Japan
100/K5 **Koshiki** (isl.), Japan
95/H2 **Koshk,** Afg.
106/E2 **Kosi** (riv.), India
65/L4 **Košice,** Slvk.
102/C2 **Kosoba, Gora** (peak), Kaz.
82/E4 **Kosovo** (aut. reg.), Yugo.
82/E4 **Kosovo Polje,** Yugo.
82/E4 **Kosovska Mitrovica,** Yugo.
71/F3 **Kosový** (riv.), Czh.
120/F4 **Kosrae** (isl.), Micr.
128/D3 **Kossi** (prov.), Burk.
128/D5 **Kossou** (lake), IvC.
128/D5 **Kossou, Barrage de** (dam), IvC.
83/F4 **Kostinbrod,** Bul.
86/C2 **Kostopol',** Ukr.
84/J4 **Kostroma,** Rus.
84/J4 **Kostroma** (riv.), Rus.
84/J4 **Kostroma Obl.,** Rus.
65/H2 **Kostrzyn,** Pol.
65/J2 **Kostrzyn,** Pol.
85/N4 **Kos'va** (riv.), Rus.
85/N2 **Kos'yu** (riv.), Rus.
65/J1 **Koszalin,** Pol.
65/H2 **Koszalin** (prov.), Pol.
106/C2 **Kota,** India
99/N10 **Kōta,** Japan
110/B5 **Kotaagung,** Indo.
110/B2 **Kota Baharu,** Malay.
111/E4 **Kotabaru,** Indo.
110/C4 **Kotabumi,** Indo.
108/A2 **Kot Addu,** Pak.
108/F3 **Kotagiri,** India
83/H4 **Kotel,** Bul.
85/L4 **Kotel'nich,** Rus.
87/G3 **Kotel'nikovo,** Rus.
89/P2 **Kotel'nyy** (isl.), Rus.
64/F3 **Köthen,** Ger.
130/B2 **Kotido,** Ugan.
63/M1 **Kotka,** Fin.
108/C2 **Kot Kapūra,** India
85/K3 **Kotlas,** Rus.
99/M9 **Kotō,** Japan
82/D4 **Kotor,** Yugo.
87/H2 **Kotovo,** Rus.
87/G1 **Kotovsk,** Rus.
95/J3 **Kotri,** Pak.
106/D4 **Kottagūdem,** India
108/F4 **Kottai Malai** (mtn.), India
108/F4 **Kottayam,** India
106/C6 **Kotte,** SrL.
125/K6 **Kotto** (riv.), CAfr.
89/L3 **Kotuy** (riv.), Rus.
151/E2 **Kotzebue** (sound), Ak,US
71/F4 **Kötzting,** Ger.
161/H2 **Kouchibouguac Nat'l Park,** NB,Can
129/E3 **Koudougou,** Burk.
81/J5 **Koufonísion** (isl.), Gre.
151/E2 **Kougarok** (mtn.), Ak,US
153/J2 **Koukdjuak** (riv.), NW,Can
126/B1 **Koula-Moutou,** Gabon
128/D3 **Koulikoro,** Mali
128/B3 **Koulountou** (riv.), Gui., Sen.
128/D3 **Koumbi Saleh** (ruins), Mrta.
124/J6 **Koumra,** Chad
102/C2 **Kounradskiy,** Kaz.
162/E4 **Kountze,** Tx,US
129/H5 **Koupé** (peak), Camr.
129/E3 **Koupela,** Burk.
129/E3 **Kouritenga** (prov.), Burk.
137/H2 **Kourou,** FrG.
124/J4 **Koussi** (peak), Chad
128/D3 **Koutiala,** Mali
63/M1 **Kouvola,** Fin.
82/E3 **Kovačica,** Yugo.
92/B2 **Kovada Gölü Nat'l Park,** Turk.
108/F4 **Kovalam,** India
84/F2 **Kovdozero** (lake), Rus.
86/C2 **Kovel',** Ukr.
108/F4 **Kovilpatti,** India
84/J4 **Kovrov,** Rus.
106/C5 **Kovūr,** India
87/G1 **Kovylkino,** Rus.
118/A1 **Kowanyama Abor. Community,** Austl.
118/A1 **Kowanyama Abor. Land,** Austl.
95/J1 **Kowkcheh** (riv.), Afg.
95/H2 **Kowl-e Namaksār** (lake), Afg., Iran
105/G4 **Kowloon,** HK
98/B5 **Kōyama,** Japan
83/G4 **Koynare,** Bul.
151/H2 **Koyukuk** (riv.), Ak,US
151/G2 **Koyukuk Nat'l Wild. Ref.,** Ak,US
151/H2 **Koyukuk, North Fork** (riv.), Ak,US
151/H2 **Koyukuk, South Fork** (riv.), Ak,US
99/N10 **Kozakai,** Japan
92/C2 **Kozaklı,** Turk.
92/C2 **Kozan,** Turk.
81/G2 **Kozáni,** Gre.
82/C3 **Kozara Nat'l Park,** Bosn.
108/E3 **Kozhikode,** India
84/H3 **Kozhozero** (lake), Rus.
85/M2 **Kozhva** (riv.), Rus.
65/L3 **Kozienice,** Pol.
83/F4 **Kozloduy,** Bul.
83/K5 **Kozlu,** Turk.
92/E2 **Kozluk,** Turk.
65/J3 **Koźmin,** Pol.
83/F4 **Koznitsa** (peak), Bul.
65/H3 **Kożuchów,** Pol.
129/F5 **Kpalimé,** Togo
129/F5 **Kpandu,** Gha.
109/B4 **Kra** (isth.), Burma, Thai.
132/D3 **Kraai** (riv.), SAfr.
132/L10 **Kraaifontein,** SAfr.
109/B4 **Krabi,** Thai.
109/D3 **Kracheh,** Camb.
62/C2 **Kragerø,** Nor.
82/E3 **Kragujevac,** Yugo.
70/B4 **Kraichbach** (riv.), Ger.
70/B4 **Kraichgau** (reg.), Ger.
71/E6 **Krailling,** Ger.
110/C5 **Krakatoa** (vol.), Indo.
109/D3 **Krakor,** Camb.
65/K3 **Kraków,** Pol.
65/K3 **Kraków** (prov.), Pol.
109/C3 **Kralanh,** Camb.
150/D4 **Kralendijk,** NAnt.
82/E4 **Kraljevo,** Yugo.
71/H2 **Kralupy nad Vltavou,** Czh.
86/F2 **Kramatorsk,** Ukr.
61/F3 **Kramfors,** Swe.
66/B5 **Krammer** (chan.), Neth.
66/D5 **Kranenburg,** Ger.
82/B2 **Kranj,** Slov.
65/J3 **Krapkowice,** Pol.
71/F2 **Kraslice,** Czh.
65/M3 **Kraśnik,** Pol.
65/M3 **Kraśnik Fabryczny,** Pol.
87/H2 **Krasnoarmeysk,** Rus.
86/F3 **Krasnodar,** Rus.
86/F3 **Krasnodar Kray,** Rus.
86/F1 **Krasnogorsk,** Rus.
86/E2 **Krasnograd,** Ukr.
97/H1 **Krasnokamensk,** Rus.
85/M4 **Krasnokamsk,** Rus.
87/H2 **Krasnoslobodsk,** Rus.
88/G4 **Krasnotur'insk,** Rus.
85/P4 **Krasnoural'sk,** Rus.
87/K5 **Krasnovodsk,** Trkm.
88/K4 **Krasnoyarsk,** Rus.
65/M3 **Krasnystaw,** Pol.
87/H2 **Krasnyy Kut,** Rus.
86/F2 **Krasnyy Luch,** Ukr.
86/G3 **Krasnyy Sulin,** Rus.
109/C4 **Kravanh** (mts.), Camb.
110/C5 **Krawang,** Indo.
70/D2 **Kreck** (riv.), Ger.
66/D6 **Krefeld,** Ger.
67/G5 **Kreiensen,** Ger.
81/G3 **Kremastón** (lake), Gre.
71/G4 **Křemelna** (riv.), Czh.
86/E2 **Kremenchug,** Ukr.
86/E2 **Kremenchug** (res.), Ukr.
158/F2 **Kremmling,** Co,US
73/L2 **Krems an der Donau,** Aus.
77/F2 **Kressbronn am Bodensee,** Ger.
89/T3 **Kresta** (gulf), Rus.
63/J4 **Kretinga,** Lith.
69/F2 **Kreuzau,** Ger.
70/C2 **Kreuzberg** (peak), Ger.
77/F2 **Kreuzlingen,** Swi.
69/G2 **Kreuztal,** Ger.
124/G7 **Kribi,** Camr.
86/D1 **Krichev,** Bela.
77/E3 **Kriens,** Swi.
100/C1 **Kril'on,** Rus.
100/B1 **Kril'on** (pen.), Rus.
97/N2 **Kril'on, Mys** (cape), Rus.
66/B5 **Krimpen aan de IJssel,** Neth.
106/D4 **Krishna** (riv.), India
106/C5 **Krishnagiri,** India
62/B2 **Kristiansand,** Nor.
62/F3 **Kristianstad,** Swe.
62/E3 **Kristianstad** (co.), Swe.
61/C3 **Kristiansund,** Nor.
62/F2 **Kristinehamn,** Swe.
82/F4 **Kriva Palanka,** Macd.
86/E3 **Krivoy Rog,** Ukr.
82/B3 **Krk,** Cro.
82/B3 **Krk** (isl.), Cro.
82/C3 **Krka** (riv.), Cro.
65/J3 **Krnov,** Czh.
133/E2 **Krokodil** (riv.), SAfr.
132/D2 **Krokodilrivier** (riv.), SAfr.
66/C4 **Kröller Müller Museum,** Neth.
86/E2 **Krolovets,** Ukr.
65/J4 **Kroměříž,** Czh.
71/E2 **Kronach,** Ger.
70/B2 **Kronberg im Taunus,** Ger.
109/C4 **Krong Kaoh Kong,** Camb.
109/D4 **Krong Keb,** Camb.
62/F3 **Kronoberg** (co.), Swe.
63/N2 **Kronshtadt,** Rus.
118/C4 **Kroombit Tops Nat'l Park,** Austl.
132/D2 **Kroonstad,** SAfr.
87/G3 **Kropotkin,** Rus.
65/L4 **Krosno,** Pol.
65/L4 **Krosno** (prov.), Pol.
65/H2 **Krosno Odrzańskie,** Pol.
65/J3 **Krotoszyn,** Pol.
77/G3 **Krottenkopf, Grat** (peak), Aus.
82/B3 **Krško,** Slov.
67/G1 **Kruckau** (riv.), Ger.
131/C4 **Kruger Nat'l Park,** SAfr.
132/P13 **Krugersdorp,** SAfr.
85/N5 **Kruglitsa, Gora** (peak), Rus.
151/A5 **Krugloi** (pt.), Ak,US
66/B6 **Kruibeke,** Belg.
82/D5 **Krujë,** Alb.
70/D6 **Krumbach,** Ger.
83/G5 **Krumovgrad,** Bul.
109/C3 **Krung Thep** (Bangkok) (cap.), Thai.
65/K4 **Krupina,** Slvk.
151/F2 **Krusenstern** (cape), Ak,US
82/E4 **Kruševac,** Yugo.
71/F2 **Krušné Hory** (Erzgebirge) (mts.), Czh., Ger.
65/K2 **Kruszwica,** Pol.
151/L4 **Kruzof** (isl.), Ak,US
86/F3 **Krymsk,** Rus.
65/L4 **Krynica,** Pol.
65/M3 **Krzna** (riv.), Pol.
65/J2 **Krzyż,** Pol.
123/M13 **Ksar el Kebir,** Mor.
103/D4 **Kuai** (riv.), China
112/A4 **Kuala Belait,** Bru.
110/B3 **Kuala Dungun,** Malay.
110/B3 **Kuala Lipis,** Malay.
110/B3 **Kuala Lumpur** (cap.), Malay.
110/B3 **Kuala Pilah,** Malay.
110/B2 **Kuala Terengganu,** Malay.
105/J4 **Kuan** (peak), Tai.
103/D2 **Kuancheng,** China
101/C2 **Kuandian,** China
110/B3 **Kuantan,** Malay.
87/J4 **Kuba,** Azer.
86/E3 **Kuban'** (riv.), Rus.
86/F3 **Kuban'** (riv.), Rus.
84/H4 **Kubenskoye** (lake), Rus.
98/C4 **Kubokawa,** Japan
83/H4 **Kubrat,** Bul.
77/G3 **Kuchen** (peak), Aus.
110/D3 **Kuching,** Malay.
100/L6 **Kuchino** (isl.), Japan
81/F2 **Kuçovë,** Alb.
93/M6 **Küçükcekmece** (lake), Turk.
98/B4 **Kudamatsu,** Japan
108/G4 **Kudremalai** (pt.), SrL.
110/D5 **Kudus,** Indo.
85/M4 **Kudymkar,** Rus.
125/K3 **Kufrah** (oasis), Libya
91/D3 **Kufrinjah,** Jor.
73/K3 **Kufstein,** Aus.
61/J2 **Kuhmo,** Fin.
66/D3 **Kuinder of Tjonger** (riv.), Neth.
105/F4 **Kuishan** (mtn.), China
126/C3 **Kuito,** Ang.
151/M4 **Kuiu** (isl.), Ak,US
129/E5 **Kujani Game Rsv.,** Gha.
65/K2 **Kujawy** (reg.), Pol.
100/B3 **Kuji,** Japan
98/B4 **Kujū-san** (mtn.), Japan
149/E3 **Kukalaya** (riv.), Nic.
104/C3 **Kuke** (riv.), China
81/G1 **Kukës,** Alb.
99/F2 **Kuki,** Japan
99/J7 **Kukizaki,** Japan
63/L1 **Kukkia** (lake), Fin.
93/H5 **Kūl** (riv.), Iran
92/B2 **Kula,** Turk.
82/D3 **Kula,** Yugo.
108/A2 **Kulachi,** Pak.
110/B3 **Kulai,** Malay.
130/C2 **Kulal** (peak), Kenya
87/J3 **Kulaly** (isl.), Kaz.
87/K4 **Kulandag** (mts.), Trkm.
108/G4 **Kulasekharapatnam,** India
63/J3 **Kuldīga,** Lat.
84/J5 **Kulebaki,** Rus.
109/D3 **Kulen,** Camb.
108/G3 **Kulittalai,** India
119/B2 **Kulkyne-Hattah Nat'l Park,** Austl.
62/E3 **Kullen** (cape), Swe.
95/L2 **Kullu,** India
71/E2 **Kulmbach,** Ger.
85/J2 **Kuloy** (riv.), Rus.
87/K3 **Kul'sary,** Kaz.
108/D2 **Kulu,** India
92/C2 **Kulu,** Turk.
88/H4 **Kulunda,** Rus.
102/C1 **Kulunda** (lake), Rus.
102/D1 **Kulunda** (riv.), Rus.
102/C1 **Kulunda Steppe** (grsld.), Kaz., Rus.
95/J1 **Kulyab,** Taj.
101/D4 **Kŭm** (riv.), SKor.
87/H3 **Kuma** (riv.), Rus.
99/F2 **Kumagaya,** Japan
100/A2 **Kumaishi,** Japan
98/B4 **Kumamoto,** Japan
98/B4 **Kumamoto** (pref.), Japan
98/E4 **Kumano,** Japan
98/D4 **Kumano** (riv.), Japan
82/E4 **Kumanovo,** Macd.
129/E5 **Kumasi,** Gha.
99/L10 **Kumatori,** Japan
87/G4 **Kumayri,** Arm.
129/H5 **Kumba,** Camr.
108/G3 **Kumbakonam,** India
129/H5 **Kumbo,** Camr.
87/K5 **Kum-Dag,** Trkm.
100/J7 **Kumé** (isl.), Japan
87/K1 **Kumertau,** Rus.
101/E3 **Kumgang-san** (mtn.), NKor.
101/E5 **Kŭmho** (riv.), SKor.
101/E4 **Kumi,** SKor.
130/B2 **Kumi,** Ugan.
99/L10 **Kumiyama,** Japan
104/C3 **Kumjawng** (pass), India
62/F2 **Kumla,** Swe.
91/B1 **Kumluca,** Turk.
71/E4 **Kümmersbruck,** Ger.
52/F2 **Kumo** (riv.), Fin.
104/C3 **Kumon** (range), Burma
130/A3 **Kumsenga,** Tanz.
106/B5 **Kumta,** India
154/U11 **Kumukahi** (cape), Hi,US
100/E2 **Kunashiri** (isl.), Rus.
106/C2 **Kūnch,** India
108/F4 **Kundara,** India
131/B1 **Kundelungu Nat'l Park,** Zaire
108/A1 **Kundiān,** Pak.
106/B3 **Kundla,** India
130/C4 **Kunduchi,** Tanz.
62/D3 **Kungälv,** Swe.
63/R7 **Kungsängen,** Swe.
62/E3 **Kungsbacka,** Swe.
125/J7 **Kungu,** Zaire
130/A5 **Kungu,** Zam.
85/N4 **Kungur,** Rus.
130/B5 **Kungutas,** Tanz.
82/E2 **Kunhegyes,** Hun.
98/B4 **Kunimi-dake** (mtn.), Japan
110/C5 **Kuningan,** Indo.
99/H7 **Kunitachi,** Japan
102/C4 **Kunjirap Daban** (pass), China
102/C4 **Kunlun** (mts.), China
105/F4 **Kunlun** (pass), China
82/E2 **Kunmadaras,** Hun.
104/D3 **Kunming,** China
108/E3 **Kunnamangalam,** India
108/F3 **Kunnamkulam,** India
101/D5 **Kunsan,** SKor.
103/E5 **Kunshan,** China
82/E2 **Kunszentmárton,** Hun.
103/E3 **Kunyu Shan** (mtn.), China
70/C1 **Künzell,** Ger.
71/G5 **Kunžvartské** (pass), Czh.
105/J2 **Kuocang** (peak), China
63/L1 **Kuohijärvi** (lake), Fin.
63/M1 **Kuolimo** (lake), Fin.
61/H3 **Kuopio,** Fin.
61/H3 **Kuopio** (prov.), Fin.
82/B3 **Kupa** (riv.), Cro., Slov.
111/F6 **Kupang,** Indo.
88/H4 **Kupino,** Rus.
70/B5 **Kuppenheim,** Ger.
151/M4 **Kupreanof** (isl.), Ak,US
86/F2 **Kupyansk,** Ukr.
89/M5 **Kuqa,** China
97/L1 **Kur** (riv.), Rus.
87/J5 **Kura** (riv.), Azer., Geo.
108/D2 **Kūrālī,** India
99/L9 **Kurama-yama** (peak), Japan
98/C3 **Kurashiki,** Japan
127/B5 **Kuraymah,** Sudan
98/C3 **Kurayoshi,** Japan
93/E2 **Kurdistan** (reg.), Asia
83/G5 **Kŭrdzhali,** Bul.
81/J2 **Kŭrdzhali** (res.), Bul.
98/C3 **Kure,** Japan
92/C1 **Küre** (mts.), Turk.
120/H2 **Kure** (isl.), Hi,US
63/K2 **Kuressaare,** Est.
88/K3 **Kureyka** (riv.), Rus.
85/Q5 **Kurgan,** Rus.
85/Q5 **Kurgan Obl.,** Rus.
95/J1 **Kurgan-Tyube,** Taj.
101/G6 **Kuri,** SKor.
120/G4 **Kuria** (isl.), Kiri.
94/G5 **Kuria Muria** (isls.), Oman
100/B4 **Kurikoma-yama** (mtn.), Japan
89/Q5 **Kuril** (isls.), Rus.
100/E1 **Kuril'sk,** Rus.
118/H8 **Ku-Ring-Gai Nat'l Park,** Austl.
108/F3 **Kurinjippādi,** India
149/E3 **Kurinwas** (riv.), Nic.
100/B2 **Kurisawa,** Japan
100/B2 **Kuriyama,** Japan
125/M5 **Kurmuk,** Sudan
106/C4 **Kurnool,** India
101/F7 **Kuro,** SKor.
99/K9 **Kurodashō,** Japan
100/B3 **Kuroishi,** Japan
99/G2 **Kuroiso,** Japan
71/F2 **Kurort Oberwiessenthal,** Ger.
99/M10 **Kuroso-yama** (peak), Japan
108/A1 **Kurram** (riv.), Pak.
63/K4 **Kuršėnai,** Lith.
106/E2 **Kurseong,** India
86/F2 **Kursk,** Rus.
63/J4 **Kurskaya** (spit), Lith., Rus.
63/J4 **Kurskiy** (lag.), Rus.
86/E2 **Kursk Obl.,** Rus.
82/E4 **Kuršumlija,** Yugo.
92/C1 **Kurşunlu,** Turk.
92/E2 **Kurtalan,** Turk.
67/E6 **Kürten,** Ger.
127/B5 **Kūrtī,** Sudan
93/N7 **Kurtköy,** Turk.
125/L6 **Kuru** (riv.), Sudan
92/E2 **Kuruca** (pass), Turk.
87/G4 **Kuruçay** (riv.), Turk.
102/E3 **Kuruktag** (mts.), China
132/C2 **Kurumanrivier** (dry riv.), SAfr.
98/B4 **Kurume,** Japan
106/D6 **Kurunegala,** SrL.
127/B4 **Kurur, Jabal** (peak), Sudan
118/E6 **Kurwongbah** (lake), Austl.
101/C3 **Kuryong** (riv.), NKor.
92/A2 **Kuşadası,** Turk.
125/M7 **Kusania** (lake), Ugan.
109/C2 **Ku Sathan** (peak), Thai.
99/L9 **Kusatsu,** Japan
99/M9 **Kusatsu,** Japan
92/B1 **Kuş Cenneti Nat'l Park,** Turk.
99/M10 **Kushida** (riv.), Japan
99/N9 **Kushihara,** Japan
98/B5 **Kushikino,** Japan
98/B5 **Kushima,** Japan
98/D4 **Kushimoto,** Japan
100/D2 **Kushiro,** Japan
100/D2 **Kushiro** (riv.), Japan
85/Q5 **Kushmurun** (lake), Kaz.
96/F4 **Kushui** (riv.), China
87/J2 **Kushum** (riv.), Kaz.
151/F4 **Kuskokwim** (bay), Ak,US
151/G3 **Kuskokwim** (mts.), Ak,US
151/F3 **Kuskokwim** (riv.), Ak,US
151/H3 **Kuskokwim, North Fork** (riv.), Ak,US
151/H3 **Kuskokwim, South Fork** (riv.), Ak,US
77/E3 **Küsnacht,** Swi.
100/C2 **Kussharo** (lake), Japan
77/E3 **Küssnacht am Rigi,** Swi.
87/M1 **Kustanay,** Kaz.
87/M2 **Kustanay Obl.,** Kaz.
70/C5 **Kusterdingen,** Ger.
125/M5 **Kūstī,** Sudan
99/M10 **Kusu,** Japan
109/C4 **Kut** (isl.), Thai.
92/B2 **Kütahya,** Turk.
92/B2 **Kütahya** (prov.), Turk.
87/G4 **Kutaisi,** Geo.
106/A3 **Kutch** (gulf), India
106/A3 **Kutch** (reg.), India
100/B2 **Kutchan,** Japan
100/C1 **Kutcharo** (lake), Japan
95/J4 **Kutch, Rann of** (swamp), India, Pak.
65/H4 **Kutná Hora,** Czh.
65/K2 **Kutno,** Pol.
131/A4 **Kutse Game Rsv.,** Bots.
99/L9 **Kutsuki,** Japan
126/C1 **Kutu,** Zaire
125/K5 **Kutum,** Sudan
152/E1 **Kuujjua** (riv.), NW,Can
153/K3 **Kuujjuaq** (Fort-Chimo), Qu,Can
153/J3 **Kuujjuarapik,** Qu,Can
61/J2 **Kuusamo,** Fin.
63/M1 **Kuusankoski,** Fin.
63/M2 **Kuutse Mägi** (hill), Est.
87/L2 **Kuvandyk,** Rus.
93/F4 **Kuwait**
93/F4 **Kuwait** (Al Kuwait) (cap.), Kuw.
106/D2 **Kuwānā** (riv.), India
98/E3 **Kuwana,** Japan
85/L5 **Kuybyshev** (res.), Rus.
103/B3 **Kuye** (riv.), China
93/F2 **Kūysanjaq,** Iraq
84/F2 **Kuyto** (lake), Rus.
102/E3 **Kuytun,** China
102/D2 **Kuytun** (riv.), China
139/G4 **Kuyuwini** (riv.), Guy.
108/F4 **Kuzhittura,** India
151/E2 **Kuzitrin** (riv.), Ak,US
87/H1 **Kuznetsk,** Rus.
100/B3 **Kuzumaki,** Japan
61/F1 **Kvaløy** (isl.), Nor.
82/B3 **Kvarerić** (chan.), Cro.
82/B3 **Kvarner** (chan.), Cro.
73/L4 **Kvarnerić** (chan.), Cro.
61/E2 **Kvigtinden** (peak), Nor.
62/B2 **Kvinnherad,** Nor.
126/C1 **Kwa** (riv.), Zaire
101/G7 **Kwach'ŏn,** SKor.
109/B3 **Kwai, River** (bridge), Thai.
120/F4 **Kwajelein** (atoll), Mrsh.
130/C4 **Kwale,** Kenya
130/B4 **Kwa Mtoro,** Tanz.
132/Q12 **Kwandebele** (homeland), SAfr.
131/A3 **Kwando** (riv.), Bots., Namb.
101/D5 **Kwangju,** SKor.
101/G7 **Kwangju,** SKor.
101/D5 **Kwangju-Jikhalsi,** SKor.
126/C1 **Kwango** (riv.), Zaire
101/F7 **Kwangsan** (mtn.), SKor.
130/C4 **Kwangwazi,** Tanz.
130/B2 **Kwania** (lake), Ugan.
129/G4 **Kwara** (state), Nga.
130/B4 **Kwaraha** (peak), Tanz.
160/D1 **Kwataboahegan** (riv.), On,Can
131/C3 **Kwekwe,** Zim.
131/B4 **Kweneng** (dist.), Bots.
65/K2 **Kwidzyn,** Pol.
125/N5 **Kwīha,** Eth.
122/D5 **Kwilu** (riv.), Zaire
116/B5 **Kwinana,** Austl.
124/J6 **Kyabé,** Chad
109/B2 **Kyaikkami,** Burma
109/B2 **Kyaiktiyo Pagoda,** Burma
104/C5 **Kyaikto,** Burma
130/A3 **Kyaka,** Tanz.
96/F1 **Kyakhta,** Rus.
104/B5 **Kyangin,** Burma
109/D2 **Ky Anh,** Viet.
100/J7 **Kyan-zaki** (cape), Japan
104/C4 **Kyaukme,** Burma
104/B5 **Kyaukpyu,** Burma
104/C4 **Kyaukse,** Burma
130/A2 **Kyegegwa,** Ugan.
130/A2 **Kyenjojo,** Ugan.
101/D4 **Kyeryong-san Nat'l Park,** SKor.
65/J4 **Kyjov,** Czh.
156/F3 **Kyle,** Sk,Can
54/B5 **Kyle** (dist.), Sc,UK
131/C4 **Kyle Nat'l Park,** Zim.
69/F3 **Kyll** (riv.), Ger.
69/F3 **Kyllburg,** Ger.
59/F2 **Kym** (riv.), Eng,UK
63/M1 **Kymi** (prov.), Fin.
63/M1 **Kymijoki** (riv.), Fin.
106/C3 **Kymore,** India
71/F2 **Kynšperk nad Ohří,** Czh.
130/B2 **Kyoga** (lake), Ugan.
98/D3 **Kyōga-misaki** (cape), Japan
99/F3 **Kyonan,** Japan
101/G7 **Kyŏngan,** SKor.
101/F6 **Kyongbok Palace,** SKor.
101/C4 **Kyŏnggi** (bay), SKor.
101/D4 **Kyŏnggi-do** (prov.), SKor.
101/E5 **Kyŏngju,** SKor.
101/E5 **Kyŏngju Nat'l Park,** SKor.
101/E4 **Kyŏngsang-bukto** (prov.), SKor.
101/E5 **Kyŏngsang-namdo** (prov.), SKor.
98/D3 **Kyōto,** Japan
98/D3 **Kyōto** (pref.), Japan
99/L10 **Kyōto Imperial Palace,** Japan
91/C2 **Kyrenia** (dist.), Cyp.
102/B3 **Kyrgyzstan**
64/G2 **Kyritz,** Ger.
63/L1 **Kyrkslätt** (Kirkkonummi), Fin.
63/K1 **Kyrösjärvi** (lake), Fin.
104/E5 **Ky Son,** Viet.
98/B5 **Kyūshū** (isl.), Japan
98/B4 **Kyūshū** (mts.), Japan
98/B4 **Kyūshū** (prov.), Japan
82/F4 **Kyustendil,** Bul.
102/F1 **Kyzyl,** Rus.
88/G5 **Kyzylkum** (des.), Kaz.,Uzb.
88/G5 **Kzyl-Orda,** Kaz.

L

64/G2 **Laage,** Ger.
149/H4 **La Aguja, Cabo de** (pt.), Col.
71/G7 **Laakirchen,** Aus.
74/B4 **La Algaba,** Sp.
149/F4 **La Amistad Int'l Park,** CR
147/N7 **La Antigua Veracruz,** Mex.
142/B3 **La Araucanía** (reg.), Chile
68/C1 **Laarne,** Belg.
125/Q6 **Laas Caanood,** Som.
77/G4 **Laas** (Lasa), It.
125/Q5 **Laas Qoray,** Som.
67/G4 **Laatzen,** Ger.
124/C2 **Laayoune,** WSah.
161/G1 **La Baie,** Qu,Can
74/A1 **La Baña,** Sp.
135/D2 **La Banda,** Arg.
74/C1 **La Bañeza,** Sp.
146/E4 **La Barca,** Mex.
112/C3 **Labason,** Phil.
68/B2 **La Bassée,** Fr.
72/B3 **La Baule-Escoublac,** Fr.
80/B1 **Labbro** (peak), It.
124/H1 **Labdah** (Leptis Magna) (ruins), Libya
128/B4 **Labé,** Gui.
128/B4 **Labé** (comm.), Gui.
65/H3 **Labe** (Elbe) (riv.), Czh.
163/H5 **La Belle,** Fl,US
112/B4 **Labian, Tanjong** (cape), Malay.
82/B3 **Labin,** Cro.
87/G3 **Labinsk,** Rus.
75/G2 **La Bisbal,** Sp.
139/E2 **La Blanquilla** (isl.), Ven.
147/H4 **Labná** (ruins), Mex.
112/C2 **Labo,** Phil.
65/L4 **Laborec** (riv.), Slvk.
142/E2 **Laboulaye,** Arg.
153/K3 **Labrador** (reg.), Nf,Can
145/M4 **Labrador** (sea), Can., Grld.
153/K3 **Labrador City,** Nf,Can
136/F5 **Lábrea,** Braz.
112/A4 **Labuan** (terr.), Malay.
111/E2 **Labuk** (bay), Malay.
111/E2 **Labuk** (riv.), Malay.
107/F4 **Labutta,** Burma
81/F2 **Laç,** Alb.
130/C2 **Lac Afwein** (riv.), Kenya
142/C2 **La Calera,** Chile
161/N6 **Lac-Alouette,** Qu,Can
142/C2 **La Campana Nat'l Park,** Chile
164/B2 **La Cañada-Flintridge,** Ca,US
148/D2 **Lacantum** (riv.), Mex.
142/E2 **La Carlota,** Arg.
74/C4 **La Carlota,** Sp.
74/D3 **La Carolina,** Sp.
147/Q9 **La Catedral** (mtn.), Mex.
106/B5 **Laccadive** (sea), India
157/J3 **Lac du Bonnet,** Mb,Can
148/E3 **La Ceiba,** Hon.
53/S10 **La Celle-Saint-Cloud,** Fr.
119/A3 **Lacepede** (bay), Austl.
131/D3 **Lacerdónia,** Moz.
165/B3 **Lacey,** Wa,US
84/H3 **Lacha** (lake), Rus.
68/A5 **Lachapelle-aux-Pots,** Fr.
72/F2 **La Chapelle-Saint-Luc,** Fr.
72/C3 **La Chapelle-sur-Erdre,** Fr.
76/C3 **La Chaux-de-Fonds,** Swi.
144/B3 **Lachay** (pt.), Peru
161/N6 **Lachenaie,** Qu,Can
108/A1 **Lāchi,** Pak.
161/N7 **Lachine,** Qu,Can
119/C2 **Lachlan** (riv.), Austl.
149/G4 **La Chorrera,** Pan.
67/H3 **Lachte** (riv.), Ger.
159/F4 **La Cienega,** NM,US
74/A1 **La Ciñiza,** Sp.
72/F5 **La Ciotat,** Fr.
161/S10 **Lackawanna,** NY,US
166/C1 **Lackawanna** (co.), Pa,US
62/E2 **Läckö,** Swe.
156/F2 **Lac La Biche,** Ab,Can
161/G2 **Lac-Mégantic,** Qu,Can
105/J5 **Lacob ti-Duyong** (mtn.), Phil.
58/D4 **Lacock,** Eng,UK
156/E2 **Lacombe,** Ab,Can
147/Q9 **La Concepción** (res.), Mex.
148/E4 **La Concepción,** Nic.
149/F4 **La Concepción,** Pan.
138/D2 **La Concepcíon,** Ven.
148/C2 **La Concordia,** Mex.
161/G3 **Laconia,** NH,US
74/A1 **La Coruña,** Sp.
53/T10 **La Courneuve,** Fr.
72/D4 **La Couronne,** Fr.
157/L5 **La Crescent,** Mn,US
164/B2 **La Crescenta-Montrose,** Ca,US
160/B3 **La Crosse,** Wi,US
142/Q9 **La Cruz,** Chile
109/D1 **Lac Son,** Viet.
110/C1 **Lac Thien,** Viet.
144/J7 **La Cumbre** (vol.), Ecu.
141/D1 **Ladainha,** Braz.
95/L2 **Ladakh** (mts.), Pak., India
54/C2 **Ladder** (hills), Sc,UK
119/B3 **Laddon** (riv.), Austl.
65/J3 **Lądek-Zdrój,** Pol.
164/F8 **Ladera Heights,** Ca,US
80/C2 **Ladispoli,** It.
84/F3 **Ladoga** (lake), Rus.
76/C5 **La Dôle** (peak), Swi.
138/C3 **La Dorada,** Col.
143/J8 **Ladrillero** (mtn.), Chile
149/G1 **Ladrillo** (pt.), Cuba
54/B5 **Lady** (isl.), Sc,UK
54/C4 **Ladybank,** Sc,UK
57/G5 **Ladybower** (res.), Eng,UK
132/D3 **Ladybrand,** SAfr.
109/D4 **Lady Chua Xu, Temple of,** Viet.
133/E3 **Ladysmith,** SAfr.
160/B2 **Ladysmith,** Wi,US

120/F4 **Lae** (atoll), Mrsh.
120/D5 **Lae**, PNG
62/D3 **Laesø** (isl.), Den.
148/E3 **La Esperanza**, Sierra (range), Hon.
74/B1 **La Estaca de Bares, Punta de** (cape), Sp.
74/A1 **La Estrada**, Sp.
135/D3 **La Falda**, Arg.
165/K11 **Lafayette**, Ca,US
163/G3 **La Fayette**, Ga,US
160/C3 **Lafayette**, In,US
162/E4 **Lafayette**, La,US
72/D2 **La Ferté-Bernard**, Fr.
72/C2 **La Ferté-Macé**, Fr.
68/C6 **La Ferté-sous-Jouarre**, Fr.
160/E1 **Laflamme** (riv.), Qu,Can
72/C3 **La Flèche**, Fr.
73/L3 **Lafnitz** (riv.), Aus.
161/M6 **Lafontaine**, Qu,Can
73/G4 **La Font Sancte, Pic de** (peak), Fr.
138/C2 **La Fría**, Ven.
107/F6 **Lāfūl**, India
130/C2 **Laga Balal** (riv.), Kenya
130/C2 **Laga Mado Gali** (riv.), Kenya
130/C2 **Laga Merille** (riv.), Kenya
62/E3 **Lagan** (riv.), Swe.
56/B3 **Lagan** (riv.), NI,UK
53/S10 **La Garenne-Colombes**, Fr.
79/D2 **Lagarina** (val.), It.
162/B2 **La Garita** (mts.), Co,US
75/L6 **La Garriga**, Sp.
140/C3 **Lagarto**, Braz.
130/D2 **Laga Sure** (riv.), Kenya
112/C1 **Lagawe**, Phil.
130/A2 **Lagbo**, Zaire
124/H6 **Lagdo** (riv.), Camr.
124/H6 **Lagdo, Barrage de** (dam), Camr.
67/F5 **Lage**, Ger.
62/C1 **Lågen** (riv.), Nor.
62/D1 **Lågen** (riv.), Nor.
141/B3 **Lages**, Braz.
66/C4 **Lage Vaart** (can.), Neth.
54/B2 **Laggan**, Sc,UK
54/B3 **Laggan, Loch** (lake), Sc,UK
130/C2 **Lagh Bogal** (riv.), Kenya
130/C2 **Lagh Bor** (riv.), Kenya
130/D2 **Lagh Kutula** (riv.), Kenya
124/F1 **Laghouat**, Alg.
60/C5 **Laghtnafrankee** (mtn.), Ire.
53/U9 **Lagny-le-Sec**, Fr.
53/U10 **Lagny-sur-Marne**, Fr.
141/C2 **Lagoa da Prata**, Braz.
141/C1 **Lagoa Formosa**, Braz.
141/B4 **Lagoa Vermelha**, Braz.
140/A2 **Lago da Pedra**, Braz.
148/D3 **Lago de Atitlán Nat'l Park**, Guat.
77/E5 **Lago Gelato, Pizzo di** (peak), It.
142/C4 **Lago Puelo Nat'l Park**, Arg.
129/F5 **Lagos**, Nga.
129/F5 **Lagos** (state), Nga.
74/A4 **Lagos**, Port.
146/E4 **Lagos de Moreno**, Mex.
145/K4 **La Grande** (riv.), Can.
156/D4 **La Grande**, Or,US
73/G4 **La Grande Ruine** (mtn.), Fr.
163/G3 **La Grange**, Ga,US
160/C4 **La Grange**, Ky,US
162/D4 **La Grange**, Tx,US
139/F3 **La Gran Sabana** (plain), Ven.
149/J4 **La Grita**, Ven.
138/C2 **La Guajira** (dept.), Col.
74/A2 **La Guardia**, Sp.
142/D3 **La Guerra** (peak), Arg.
141/B4 **Laguna**, Braz.
165/M10 **Laguna** (cr.), Ca,US
164/C3 **Laguna Beach**, Ca,US
142/C3 **Laguna Blanca Nat'l Park**, Arg.
164/C3 **Laguna Hills**, Ca,US
143/J6 **Laguna San Rafael Nat'l Park**, Chile
148/B2 **Lagunas de Chacahua Nat'l Park**, Mex.
146/D4 **Lagunillas**, Mex.
138/D2 **Lagunillas**, Ven.
149/E3 **Laguntara** (lag.), Hon.
149/F1 **La Habana** (Havana) (cap.), Cuba
164/C3 **La Habra**, Ca,US
110/B4 **Lahat**, Indo.
161/H2 **La Have** (riv.), NS,Can
135/B2 **La Higuera**, Chile
93/G2 **Lāhījān**, Iran
64/E3 **Lahn** (riv.), Ger.
69/G3 **Lahnstein**, Ger.
62/E3 **Laholm**, Swe.
62/E3 **Laholmsbukten** (bay), Swe.
108/C2 **Lahore**, Pak.
70/A4 **Lahr**, Ger.
63/L1 **Lahti**, Fin.

124/J6 **Laï**, Chad
103/D4 **Lai'an**, China
79/D6 **Laiatico**, It.
107/J3 **Laibin**, China
109/C1 **Lai Chau**, Viet.
70/C6 **Laichingen**, Ger.
54/B3 **Laidon, Loch** (lake), Sc,UK
103/B5 **Laifeng**, China
72/D2 **L'Aigle**, Fr.
61/G3 **Laihia**, Fin.
78/C1 **Lainate**, It.
61/G2 **Lainioälven** (riv.), Swe.
130/C2 **Laisamis**, Kenya
103/C3 **Laishui**, China
63/J1 **Laitila**, Fin.
77/H5 **Laives** (Leifers), It.
103/D3 **Laiwu**, China
103/E3 **Laixi**, China
103/E3 **Laiyang**, China
103/C3 **Laiyuan**, China
103/D3 **Laizhou** (bay), China
142/C3 **Laja** (lake), Chile
140/B3 **Laje**, Braz.
141/B4 **Lajeado**, Braz.
140/C3 **Lajedo**, Braz.
75/S12 **Lajes do Pico**, Azor.,Port.
141/D2 **Lajinha**, Braz.
82/D2 **Lajosmizse**, Hun.
138/B5 **La Joya de los Sachas**, Ecu.
159/G3 **La Junta**, Co,US
130/A3 **L'Akagera Nat'l Park**, Rwa.
165/J9 **Lake** (co.), Ca,US
165/P15 **Lake** (co.), Il,US
165/R16 **Lake** (co.), In,US
168/F4 **Lake** (co.), Oh,US
168/E5 **Lake** (plains), Oh,US
117/F3 **Lake Amadeus Abor. Land**, Austl.
157/J5 **Lake Andes**, SD,US
164/C2 **Lake Arrowhead**, Ca,US
148/D3 **Lake Atitlán Nat'l Park**, Guat.
130/C2 **Lake Bogoria Nat'l Rsv.**, Kenya
162/E4 **Lake Charles**, La,US
158/F3 **Lake City**, Co,US
163/H4 **Lake City**, Fl,US
157/K4 **Lake City**, Mn,US
151/H3 **Lake Clark Nat'l Park & Prsv.**, Ak,US
57/E2 **Lake District Nat'l Park**, Eng,UK
164/C3 **Lake Elsinore**, Ca,US
117/H4 **Lake Eyre Nat'l Park**, Austl.
118/B1 **Lakefield Nat'l Park**, Austl.
165/Q15 **Lake Forest**, Il,US
168/E6 **Lake Fork** (riv.), Oh,US
162/E3 **Lake Fork** (res.), Tx,US
158/D4 **Lake Havasu City**, Az,US
167/D3 **Lakehurst Nav. Air Eng. Ctr.**, NJ,US
162/E4 **Lake Jackson**, Tx,US
163/H4 **Lakeland**, Fl,US
156/D3 **Lake Louise**, Ab,Can
117/F2 **Lake Mackay Abor. Land**, Austl.
131/D2 **Lake Malawi Nat'l Park**, Malw.
130/B3 **Lake Manyara Nat'l Park**, Tanz.
130/A3 **Lake Mburo Nat'l Park**, Ugan.
158/D4 **Lake Mead Nat'l Rec. Area**, Az, Nv,US
81/G2 **Lake Mikri Prespa Nat'l Park**, Gre.
166/D1 **Lake Mohawk**, NJ,US
130/C3 **Lake Nakuru Nat'l Park**, Kenya
59/G2 **Lakenheath**, Eng,UK
159/J3 **Lake of the Ozarks** (lake), Mo,US
157/K3 **Lake of the Woods** (lake), Can.,US
165/F6 **Lake Orion**, Mi,US
70/B3 **Lakenperthaim**, Ger.
58/B2 **Lake Perris Saint Rec. Area**, Ca,US
58/B3 **Lakenheim**, Wal,UK
109/B2 **Lamphun**, Thai.
157/H3 **Lampman**, Sk,Can
130/C3 **Lamu**, Kenya
130/D3 **Lamu** (isl.), Kenya
149/F4 **La Muerte, Cerro** (mtn.), CR
130/B2 **Lamwa** (peak), Ugan.
105/J4 **Lan** (isl.), Tai.
154/T10 **Lanai** (isl.), Hi,US
154/T10 **Lanaihale** (peak), Hi,US
69/E2 **Lanaken**, Belg.
112/D4 **Lanao** (lake), Phil.
75/F3 **La Nao, Cabo de** (cape), Sp.
148/C2 **Lana, Rio de la** (riv.), Mex.
166/C3 **Lansdale**, Pa,US
166/C4 **Lansdowne**, Pa,US
166/B5 **Lansdowne-Baltimore Highlands**, Md,US
160/B2 **L'Anse**, Mi,US
161/L1 **L'Anse aux Meadows Nat'l Hist. Park**, Nf,Can
105/G3 **Lanshan**, China
151/M3 **Lansing**, Yk,Can
165/Q16 **Lansing**, Il,US
57/F3 **Lancaster**, Eng,UK
158/C4 **Lancaster**, Ca,US
168/C1 **Lancaster**, Ma,US
161/S10 **Lancaster**, NY,US
168/D4 **Lancaster**, Oh,US

81/H4 **Lakonía** (gulf), Gre.
106/B5 **Lakshadweep** (isls.), India
106/B6 **Lakshadweep** (terr.), India
112/C4 **Lala**, Phil.
130/B3 **Lalago**, Tanz.
108/B1 **Lāla Mūsa**, Pak.
133/H8 **Lalana** (riv.), Madg.
110/B4 **Lalang** (riv.), Indo.
106/E3 **Lālgola**, India
78/C1 **Lalinate**, It.
125/N5 **Lalī́bela**, Eth.
138/A5 **La Libertad**, Ecu.
148/D2 **La Libertad**, Guat.
142/C2 **La Ligua**, Chile
117/C2 **Lander** (riv.), Austl.
156/F5 **Lander**, Wy,US
72/A2 **Landerneau**, Fr.
72/C4 **Landes** (reg.), Fr.
72/B3 **Landes de Lanvaux** (reg.), Fr.
156/F1 **Landis**, Sk,Can
166/B3 **Landisville Valley Museum**, Pa,US
166/B3 **Landisville-Salunga**, Pa,US
72/A2 **Landivisiau**, Fr.
67/G1 **Land Kehdingen** (reg.), Ger.
140/B2 **Landri Sales**, Braz.
70/D6 **Landsberg**, Ger.
118/B3 **Landsborough** (cr.), Austl.
58/A4 **Land's End** (pt.), Eng,UK
71/F5 **Landshut**, Ger.
62/E4 **Landskrona**, Swe.
66/B4 **Landsmeer**, Neth.
69/G5 **Landstuhl**, Ger.
72/B2 **Lamballe**, Fr.
135/E2 **Lambaré**, Par.
126/B1 **Lambaréné**, Gabon
141/H6 **Lambari**, Braz.
60/D3 **Lambay** (isl.), Ire.
144/B2 **Lambayeque**, Peru
138/B5 **Lambeg**, NI,UK
128/C3 **Lambé Koba** (riv.), Mali
113/E **Lambert** (glac.), Ant.
160/D3 **Lambertville**, Mi,US
53/N7 **Lambeth** (bor.), Eng,UK
59/E3 **Lambourn**, Eng,UK
78/C1 **Lambro** (riv.), It.
165/H6 **Lambton** (co.), On,Can
74/B2 **Lamego**, Port.
138/C4 **La Mensura** (peak), Col.
161/H2 **Lamèque** (isl.), NB,Can
74/D3 **La Merced**, Peru
72/F3 **La Mère Boitier, Signal de** (mtn.), Fr.
164/C5 **La Mesa**, Ca,US
162/C3 **Lamesa**, Tx,US
81/H3 **Lamía**, Gre.
166/D2 **Lamington** (riv.), NJ,US
118/D5 **Lamington Nat'l Park**, Austl.
110/A2 **Langkawi** (isl.), Malay.
109/B4 **Lang Kha Tuk** (peak), Thai.
53/M7 **Langley**, Eng,UK
76/D4 **Langnau im Emmental**, Swi.
59/G5 **Langney** (pt.), UK
61/E1 **Langøya** (isl.), Nor.
102/C5 **Langqên** (riv.), China
76/B2 **Langres**, Fr.
76/B2 **Langres, Plateau de** (plat.), Fr.
110/A3 **Langsa**, Indo.
109/D1 **Lang Son**, Viet.
161/R8 **Langstaff**, On,Can
162/C4 **Langtry**, Tx,US
75/G1 **Languedoc** (hist. reg.), Fr.
72/E5 **Languedoc-Roussillon** (reg.), Fr.
67/G3 **Langwedel**, Ger.
77/I1 **Langweid am Lech**, Ger.
103/C3 **Langxi**, China
103/C3 **Langya Shan** (mtn.), China
166/B3 **Lanham-Seabrook**, Md,US
157/G3 **Lanigan**, Sk,Can
154/W12 **Laniloa** (pt.), Hi,US
142/C3 **Lanín** (vol.), Chile
142/C3 **Lanín Nat'l Park**, Arg.
72/B3 **Lannemezan**, Fr.
72/B3 **Lannemezan** (plat.), Fr.
58/A4 **Lanner**, Eng,UK
72/B2 **Lannion**, Fr.
72/B2 **Lannion** (bay), Fr.
53/S11 **La Norville**, Fr.
109/B2 **Lan Sang Nat'l Park**, Thai.
74/D1 **Laredo**, Sp.
144/B3 **Laredo**, Peru
162/D5 **Laredo**, Tx,US
66/C4 **Laren**, Neth.
149/F1 **Largo** (cay), Cuba
54/B3 **Largo** (bay), Sc,UK
163/H5 **Largo**, Fl,US
54/B5 **Largs**, Sc,UK
76/D2 **Largue** (riv.), Fr.
81/H3 **Lárisa**, Gre.
65/L4 **Latorica** (riv.), Slvk.
59/G2 **Lark** (riv.), Eng,UK
95/J3 **Lārkāna**, Pak.

166/B3 **Lancaster**, Pa,US
166/B4 **Lancaster** (co.), Pa,US
163/H3 **Lancaster**, SC,US
160/B3 **Lancaster**, Wi,US
57/G2 **Lancaster**, Eng,UK
80/D1 **Lanciano**, It.
65/M3 **Lańcut**, Pol.
76/C5 **Lancy**, Swi.
71/F5 **Landau an der Isar**, Ger.
70/B4 **Landau in der Pfalz**, Ger.
77/M3 **Landeck**, Aus.
69/E2 **Landen**, Belg.
70/B4 **Landenburg**, Ger.
105/H2 **Lanxi**, China
96/E4 **Lanzhou**, China
101/D2 **Lao** (mts.), China
105/G2 **Lao** (riv.), China
112/C1 **Laoag**, Phil.
109/C1 **Lao Cai**, Viet.
105/G2 **Laodao** (riv.), China
97/H3 **Laoha** (riv.), China
103/B4 **Laohekou**, China
60/C4 **Laois** (Leix) (co.), Ire.
103/B4 **Laojun Shan** (mtn.), China
68/C4 **Laon**, Fr.
139/E2 **La Orchila** (isl.), Ven.
144/C3 **La Oroya**, Peru
109/C2 **Laos**
103/E3 **Laoshan**, China
103/E3 **Lao Shan** (peak), China
103/E3 **Laotie Shan** (mtn.), China
103/F2 **Laotuding Shan** (peak), China
123/M13 **Laou** (riv.), Mor.
75/G1 **Laouzas, Barrage de** (dam), Fr.
141/B3 **Lapa**, Braz.
129/G4 **Lapai**, Nga.
146/D3 **La Palma**, Mex.
142/D3 **La Pampa** (prov.), Arg.
136/E7 **La Paz** (cap.), Bol.
144/D4 **La Paz** (dept.), Bol.
148/E3 **La Paz**, Hon.
146/C3 **La Paz**, Mex.
146/C3 **La Paz** (bay), Mex.
112/D3 **La Paz**, Phil.
143/F2 **La Paz**, Uru.
160/F2 **La Pêche**, Qu,Can
84/F3 **Lapeenranta**, Fin.
165/F5 **Lapeer**, Mi,US
165/F6 **Lapeer** (co.), Mi,US
149/F4 **La Peña**, Pan.
100/B1 **La Pérouse** (str.), Japan, Rus.
76/D1 **La Petite-Raon**, Fr.
61/H3 **Lapinlahti**, Fin.
61/F1 **Lapland** (reg.), Eur.
143/F2 **La Plata**, Arg.
138/C4 **La Plata**, Col.
162/B2 **La Plata** (peak), Co,US
72/F5 **La Plata**, Fr.
160/E4 **La Plata**, Md,US
143/T12 **La Plata, Rio de** (est.), Arg.,Urg.
143/F2 **Las Flores**, Arg.
165/F5 **Lapeer**, Mi,US
147/E4 **Las Campanas Nat'l Park, Cerro de**, Mex.
142/C2 **Las Cabras**, Chile
143/J6 **Lascano**, Uru.
143/G5 **Las Choapas**, Mex.
161/L1 **La Scie**, Nf,Can
158/F4 **Las Cruces**, NM,US
156/F4 **Laurel**, Mt,US
166/B3 **Laurel** (co.), Pa,US
163/G2 **Laurens**, SC,US
160/D4 **Laurel**, Va,US
166/C5 **Lebanon-Rising Sun**, De,US
68/D2 **Lebbeke**, Belg.
86/E2 **Lebedin**, Ukr.
160/E1 **Lebel-sur-Quévillon**, Qu,Can
123/M13 **Lebene** (riv.), Mor.
56/D2 **Laurieston**, Sc,UK
163/J3 **Laurinburg**, NC,US
160/B2 **Laurium**, Mi,US
54/A4 **Lausanne**, Swi.
111/E4 **Laut** (isl.), Indo.
131/C5 **Lebombo** (mts.), Moz., SAfr.
65/J1 **Lębork**, Pol.
132/Q12 **Lebowa** (homeland), SAfr.
74/B4 **Lebrija**, Sp.
135/B4 **Lebu**, Chile
74/A2 **Leça da Palmeira**, Port.
73/G5 **Le Cannet**, Fr.
68/C3 **Le Cateau**, Fr.
81/F2 **Lecce**, It.
78/C1 **Lecco** (lake), It.
78/C1 **Lecco**, It.
77/G1 **Lech** (riv.), Aus., Ger.
107/K2 **Lechang**, China
76/D3 **Le Chasseral** (peak), Swi.
76/C4 **Le Chasseron** (peak), Swi.
149/G1 **Leche** (lag.), Cuba
53/S10 **Le Chesnay**, Fr.
76/C5 **Le Cheval Blanc** (mtn.), Fr.
59/E3 **Lechlade**, Eng,UK
77/G3 **Lechtaler Alps** (mts.), Aus.
64/E1 **Leck**, Ger.
60/A3 **Leckavrea** (mtn.), Ire.
73/J5 **Le Cornate** (peak), It.
75/G1 **Le Crès**, Fr.
72/F3 **Le Creusot**, Fr.
65/M3 **Łęczna**, Pol.
70/E1 **Leda** (riv.), Ger.
110/B3 **Ledang** (peak), Malay.
58/D2 **Ledbury**, Eng,UK
68/C2 **Lede**, Belg.
140/C2 **Lavras da Mangabeira**, Braz.
105/F5 **Ledong**, China
81/J4 **Lávrion**, Gre.
79/D1 **Ledro** (lake), It.
156/E2 **Leduc**, Ab,Can
77/F5 **Leduc, Pizzo** (peak), It.
60/B6 **Lee** (riv.), Ire.
166/B1 **Lee** (riv.), Fy., Sur.
157/K4 **Leech** (lake), Mn,US
57/G4 **Leeds**, Eng,UK
57/G4 **Leeds and Liverpool** (can.), Eng,UK
66/D2 **Leek**, Neth.
57/F5 **Leek**, Eng,UK
53/N7 **Lee** (Lea) (riv.), Eng,UK
66/D2 **Leer**, Ger.
66/C5 **Leerdam**, Neth.
66/C4 **Leersum**, Neth.
163/H4 **Leesburg**, Fl,US
160/E4 **Leesburg**, Va,US
72/E4 **Leesville**, La,US
118/F7 **Leesville** (dam), Oh,US
168/F7 **Leesville** (res.), Oh,US
117/D2 **Leeton**, Austl.
132/L10 **Leeu** (riv.), SAfr.
66/C2 **Leeuwarden**, Neth.
116/B5 **Leeuwin** (cape), Austl.
116/B5 **Leeuwin-Naturaliste Nat'l Park**, Austl.
158/C3 **Lee Vining**, Ca,US

200

Leewa – Lizar

150/F3 Leeward Islands (isls.), West Indies
72/B2 Leff (riv.), Fr.
129/H5 Lefo (peak), Camr.
116/D4 Lefroy (lake), Austl.
74/D2 Leganés, Sp.
112/C2 Legazpi, Phil.
74/D1 Legazpia, Sp.
119/C4 Legges Tor (peak), Austl.
65/L2 Legionowo, Pol.
79/E2 Legnago, It.
78/B1 Legnano, It.
65/J3 Legnica, Pol.
65/H3 Legnica (prov.), Pol.
77/F5 Legnone, Monte (peak), It.
76/C5 Le Grammont (peak), Swi.
76/D2 Le Grand Ballon (mtn.), Fr.
116/D5 Le Grande (cape), Austl.
102/C5 Leh, India
72/D2 Le Havre, Fr.
166/C2 Lehigh (co.), Pa,US
166/C2 Lehigh (riv.), Pa,US
163/H5 Lehigh Acres, Fl,US
67/G4 Lehrte, Ger.
105/G3 Lei (riv.), China
108/A2 Leiah, Pak.
73/L3 Leibnitz, Aus.
107/H2 Leibo, China
59/E1 Leicester, Eng,UK
168/C1 Leicester, Ma,US
59/E1 Leicestershire (co.), Eng,UK
117/H2 Leichhardt (dam), Austl.
118/B3 Leichhardt (mts.), Austl.
114/F3 Leichhardt (riv.), Austl.
66/E6 Leichlingen, Ger.
66/B4 Leiden, Neth.
66/B4 Leiderdorp, Neth.
66/B4 Leidschendam, Neth.
66/A7 Leie (riv.), Belg.
77/H5 Leifers (Laives), It.
53/N8 Leigh, Eng,UK
53/P8 Leigh, Eng,UK
59/F3 Leighton Buzzard, Eng,UK
105/F3 Leigong (mtn.), China
70/C5 Lein (riv.), Ger.
67/G5 Leine (riv.), Ger.
67/H6 Leinefelde, Ger.
70/C5 Leinfelden-Echterdingen, Ger.
60/D4 Leinster (mtn.), Ire.
60/C3 Leinster (prov.), Ire.
58/D2 Leintwardine, Eng,UK
166/C5 Leipsic (riv.), De,US
64/G3 Leipzig, Ger.
68/C2 Leir (riv.), Belg.
62/C1 Leira, Nor.
74/A3 Leiria, Port.
74/A3 Leiria (dist.), Port.
117/F2 Leisler (peak), Austl.
59/H2 Leiston cum Sizewell, Eng,UK
160/C4 Leitchfield, Ky,US
59/F4 Leith (hill), Eng,UK
54/C5 Leith, Sc,UK
82/C2 Leitha (riv.), Aus.
60/C2 Leitrim (co.), Ire.
60/C4 Leix (Laois) (co.), Ire.
60/D3 Leixlip, Ire.
105/G3 Leiyang, China
103/B4 Leiyuanzhen, China
105/F4 Leizhou (pen.), China
66/B5 Lek (riv.), Neth.
66/B5 Lekkerkerk, Neth.
129/G5 Lekki (lag.), Nga.
62/F1 Leksands-Noret, Swe.
84/F3 Leksozero (lake), Rus.
111/G3 Lelai (cape), Indo.
163/F3 Leland, Ms,US
62/E2 Lelång (lake), Swe.
103/D3 Leling, China
76/C3 Le Locle, Swi.
120/F4 Lelu, Micro.
73/G5 Le Luc, Fr.
66/C3 Lelystad, Neth.
143/L8 Le Maire (str.), Arg.
77/E5 Lema, Monte (peak), It.
76/C5 Léman (Geneva) (lake), Fr., Swi.
72/D3 Le Mans, Fr.
157/J5 Le Mars, Ia,US
69/G5 Lembach, Fr.
70/B6 Lemberg (peak), Ger.
110/A3 Lembu (peak), Indo.
141/C2 Leme, Braz.
53/T11 Le Mée-sur-Seine, Fr.
61/H1 Lemenjoen Nat'l Park, Fin.
53/S10 Le Mesnil-le-Roi, Fr.
53/R10 Le Mesnil-Saint-Denis, Fr.
67/F4 Lemgo, Ger.
63/H2 Lemland (isl.), Fin.
66/C3 Lemmer, Neth.
157/H4 Lemmon, SD,US
76/C5 Le Môle (mtn.), Fr.
164/C5 Lemon Grove, Ca,US
76/C4 Le Morond (mtn.), Fr.
72/E4 Le Moure de la Gardille (mtn.), Fr.
148/D3 Lempa (riv.), NAm.
63/K1 Lempäälä, Fin.
72/E4 Lempdes, Fr.
104/B4 Lemro (riv.), Burma
80/E2 Le Murge (upland), It.
85/P2 Lemva (riv.), Rus.
62/C3 Lemvig, Den.
67/F2 Lemwerder, Ger.
62/D1 Lena, Nor.
89/N3 Lena (riv.), Rus.
166/D5 Lenape (lake), NJ,US
140/B1 Lençóis Maranhenses Nat'l Park, Braz.
141/B2 Lençóis Paulista, Braz.
79/E2 Lendinara, It.
60/C2 Lene, Lough (lake), Ire.
67/H4 Lengede, Ger.
71/F1 Lengenfeld, Ger.
67/E4 Lengerich, Ger.
77/H2 Lenggries, Ger.
105/F3 Lengshuijiang, China
105/F3 Lengshuitan, China
135/B3 Lengua de Vaca (pt.), Chile
131/D3 Lengwe Nat'l Park, Malw.
130/C1 Lenia, Eth.
102/B4 Lenina, Pik (peak), Kyr.
84/F4 Leningrad (Saint Petersburg), Rus.
85/V7 Leningrad (Saint Petersburg) (inset), Rus.
113/L Leningradskaya, Ant.
102/D1 Leninogorsk, Kaz.
85/M5 Leninogorsk, Rus.
88/J4 Leninsk-Kuznetskiy, Rus.
82/E2 Leninváros, Hun.
53/H5 Lenkoran', Azer.
67/E6 Lenne (riv.), Ger.
67/F6 Lennestadt, Ger.
70/C5 Lenningen, Ger.
143/L8 Lennox (isl.), Chile
54/B5 Lennox (hills), Sc,UK
164/F8 Lennox, Ca,US
54/B5 Lennoxtown, Sc,UK
78/D2 Leno, It.
163/H3 Lenoir, NC,US
163/G3 Lenoir City, Tn,US
76/C4 Le Noirmont (mtn.), Fr.
76/C5 Le Noirmont (peak), Swi.
68/B3 Lens, Fr.
89/M3 Lensk, Rus.
61/F1 Lenvik, Nor.
54/B4 Leny, Pass of (pass), Sc,UK
76/E3 Lenzburg, Swi.
129/E4 Léo, Burk.
73/L3 Leoben, Aus.
68/B2 Leoberghe, Fr.
79/E1 Leogra (riv.), It.
157/J4 Leola, SD,US
166/B3 Leola-Leacock-Bareville, Pa,US
58/D2 Leominster, Eng,UK
72/C4 Leon (lag.), Fr.
147/E4 León, Mex.
148/E3 León, Nic.
74/C1 León, Sp.
162/D3 Leon (riv.), Tx,US
165/F6 Leonard, Mi,US
70/C5 Leonberg, Ger.
71/H6 Leonding, Aus.
76/E5 Leone, Monte (peak), It.
142/E2 Leones, Arg.
80/D4 Leonforte, It.
167/K8 Leonia, NJ,US
147/F2 Leon Valley, Tx,US
113/F Leopold and Astrid (coast), Ant.
141/L6 Leopoldina, Braz.
68/C1 Leopoldkanaal (can.), Belg.
69/E1 Leopoldsburg, Belg.
67/F4 Leopoldshöhe, Ger.
159/G3 Leoti, Ks,US
156/G2 Leoville, Sk,Can
72/D4 Le Passage, Fr.
74/B4 Lepe, Sp.
53/S10 Le Pecq, Fr.
82/F3 Lepenski Vir, Yugo.
76/D2 Le Petit Ballon (mtn.), Fr.
131/B4 Lephepe, Bots.
105/H2 Leping, China
53/U9 Le Plessis-Belleville, Fr.
53/T10 Le Plessis-Trévise, Fr.
77/E5 Lepontine Alps (mts.), It., Swi.
133/R15 Le Port, Reun.
68/A2 Le Portel, Fr.
61/H3 Leppävirta, Fin.
102/C2 Lepsy (riv.), Kaz.
75/F1 Le Puech (mtn.), Fr.
72/E4 Le Puy, Fr.
128/D4 Léraba (riv.), Burk., IvC.
53/T10 Le Raincy, Fr.
78/A2 Lera, Monte (peak), It.
80/C4 Lercara Friddi, It.
147/P8 Lerdo de Tejada, Mex.
78/C4 Lerici, It.
75/F2 Lérida (Lleida), Sp.
147/K7 Lerma (riv.), Mex.
132/D3 Le Rouxdam, P. K. (res.), SAfr.
62/E3 Lerum, Swe.
55/P12 Lerwick, Sc,UK
68/A5 Les Andelys, Fr.
149/H2 Les Cayes, Haiti
161/M7 Les Cèdres, Qu,Can
53/R10 Les Clayes-sous-Bois, Fr.
76/D5 Les Diablerets (range), Swi.
76/D5 Le Sépey, Swi.
104/D2 Leshan, China
72/C3 Les Herbiers, Fr.
53/T10 Lésigny, Fr.
78/C3 Lesima, Monte (peak), It.
82/E4 Leskovac, Yugo.
54/C4 Leslie, Sc,UK
53/T10 Les Lilas, Fr.
54/C5 Lesmahagow, Sc,UK
53/S10 Les Molières, Fr.
68/A6 Les Mureaux, Fr.
72/A2 Lesneven, Fr.
133/D3 Lesotho
97/L2 Lesozavodsk, Rus.
75/G1 L'Espinouse, Sommet de (peak), Fr.
72/C3 Les Sables-d'Olonne, Fr.
69/E4 Lesse (riv.), Belg.
62/F3 Lessebo, Swe.
150/E3 Lesser Antilles (isls.), NAm.
87/G4 Lesser Kavkaz (mts.), Eur.
156/D2 Lesser Slave (lake), Ab,Can
111/E5 Lesser Sunda (isls.), Indo.
68/C2 Lessines, Belg.
69/E5 L'Est, Canal de (can.), Fr.
76/C4 Le Suchet (peak), Swi.
68/B6 Les Ulis, Fr.
110/D3 Lesung (peak), Indo.
81/J3 Lésvos (isl.), Gre.
56/C2 Leswalt, Sc,UK
65/J3 Leszno, Pol.
65/J3 Leszno (prov.), Pol.
131/C4 Letaba, SAfr.
133/R15 Le Tampon, Reun.
53/S10 L'Étang-la-Ville, Fr.
59/F3 Letchworth, Eng,UK
54/D3 Letham, Sc,UK
156/E3 Lethbridge, Ab,Can
67/F2 Lethe (riv.), Ger.
111/G5 Leti (isls.), Indo.
144/D2 Leticia, Col.
103/D3 Leting, China
131/B4 Letlhakane, Bots.
131/B5 Letlhakeng, Bots.
104/B5 Letpadan, Burma
68/A3 Le Tréport, Fr.
109/B4 Letsôk-Aw (isl.), Burma
55/H9 Letterkenny, Ire.
54/D4 Leuchars, Sc,UK
55/H7 Leurbost, Sc,UK
66/C4 Leusden-Zuid, Neth.
110/A3 Leuser (peak), Indo.
70/D4 Leutershausen, Ger.
77/G2 Leutkirch im Allgäu, Ger.
69/D2 Leuven (Louvain), Belg.
68/C2 Leuze-en-Hainaut, Belg.
81/H3 Levádhia, Gre.
53/S10 Levallois-Perret, Fr.
61/D3 Levanger, Nor.
78/C4 Levante (coast), It.
142/B5 Level (isl.), Chile
162/C3 Levelland, Tx,US
133/F2 Leven (pt.), SAfr.
57/H4 Leven, Eng,UK
57/F3 Leven (riv.), Eng,UK
57/G3 Leven (riv.), Eng,UK
54/D4 Leven, Sc,UK
54/C4 Leven (riv.), Sc,UK
54/A3 Leven, Loch (inlet), Sc,UK
54/C4 Leven, Loch (lake), Sc,UK
77/E5 Leventina (Prato), It.
114/C3 Leveque (cape), Austl.
66/D6 Leverkusen, Ger.
53/S10 Le Vésinet, Fr.
65/K4 Levice, Slvk.
115/S11 Levin, NZ
161/G2 Lévis, Qu,Can
53/R10 Lévis-Saint-Nom, Fr.
167/E2 Levittown, NY,US
166/D3 Levittown, Pa,US
81/G3 Levkás, Gre.
81/G3 Levkás (isl.), Gre.
65/L4 Levoča, Slvk.
83/G4 Levski, Bul.
59/G5 Lewes, Eng,UK
161/K1 Lewis (hills), Nf,Can
115/R11 Lewis (pass), NZ
55/H7 Lewis (isl.), Sc,UK
156/E3 Lewis (range), Mt,US
156/C4 Lewis (riv.), Wa,US
157/J5 Lewis & Clark (lake), Ne, SD,US
163/G3 Lewisburg, Tn,US
160/D4 Lewisburg, WV,US
55/H7 Lewis, Butt of (promontory), Sc,UK
53/N7 Lewisham (bor.), Eng,UK
161/L1 Lewisporte, Nf,Can
163/G3 Lewis Smith (lake), Al,US
156/D4 Lewiston, Id,US
161/G2 Lewiston, Me,US
161/R9 Lewiston, NY,US
156/F4 Lewistown, Mt,US
160/E3 Lewistown, Pa,US
111/F5 Lewotobi (peak), Indo.
160/C4 Lexington, Ky,US
168/C1 Lexington, Ma,US
163/H3 Lexington, NC,US
159/H2 Lexington, Ne,US
163/H3 Lexington, SC,US
163/F3 Lexington, Tn,US
160/E4 Lexington, Va,US
160/E4 Lexington Park, Md,US
57/G3 Leyburn, Eng,UK
104/E3 Leye, China
57/F4 Leyland, Eng,UK
112/D3 Leyte, Phil.
112/D3 Leyte (gulf), Phil.
112/D3 Leyte (isl.), Phil.
53/N7 Leyton, Eng,UK
72/F4 Lez (riv.), Fr.
65/M3 Leżajsk, Pol.
81/F2 Lezhë, Alb.
104/E2 Lezhi, China
72/E5 Lézignan-Corbières, Fr.
86/E2 L'gov, Rus.
54/C1 Lhanbyrd, Sc,UK
104/B2 Lhari, China
106/F2 Lhasa, China
106/E2 Lhazê, China
104/C2 Lhorong, China
75/G2 L'Hospitalet, Sp.
106/F2 Lhozhag, China
107/G2 Lhünzê, China
103/B5 Li (riv.), China
103/C4 Li (riv.), China
105/F3 Li (riv.), China
104/E3 Lian (riv.), China
105/G3 Lian (riv.), China
105/H3 Liancheng, China
68/B5 Liancourt, Fr.
98/B2 Liancourt (rocks), Japan, SKor.
103/C2 Liangcheng, China
110/D3 Liangpran (peak), Indo.
103/D4 Liang Shan (mtn.), China
104/D3 Liangwan (mts.), Laos
103/B3 Liangzhen, China
103/C3 Liangzi (lake), China
107/K2 Lianhua, China
104/D3 Lianhua (mts.), China
105/H3 Lianjiang, China
105/G3 Liannan Yaozu Zizhixian, China
103/D4 Lianshui, China
105/G3 Lian Xian, China
105/G3 Lianyuan (peak), China
103/D4 Lianyungang, China
101/A2 Liao (riv.), China
103/C3 Liaocheng, China
101/A2 Liaodong (gulf), China
101/B3 Liaodong (pen.), China
101/B2 Liaoning (prov.), China
101/B2 Liaoyang, China
103/E2 Liaoyuan, China
101/B2 Liaozhong, China
95/K3 Liāquatpur, Pak.
152/D2 Liard (riv.), Can.
112/C3 Libacao, Phil.
156/E3 Libby, Mt,US
125/J7 Libenge, Zaire
159/G3 Liberal, Ks,US
68/C3 Libercourt, Fr.
141/J7 Liberdade, Braz.
137/H6 Liberdade (riv.), Braz.
65/H3 Liberec, Czh.
128/C5 Liberia
149/E4 Liberia, CR
143/F2 Libertad, Uru.
135/D1 Libertador General San Martín, Arg.
163/G2 Liberty, Ky,US
166/B5 Liberty (res.), Md,US
162/E2 Liberty, Mo,US
163/F4 Liberty, Ms,US
162/E4 Liberty, Tx,US
165/Q15 Libertyville, Il,US
112/C2 Libmanan, Phil.
105/E3 Libo, China
111/G4 Libobo (cape), Indo.
71/G2 Liboc (riv.), Czh.
112/C2 Libon, Phil.
147/M7 Libres, Mex.
124/G7 Libreville (cap.), Gabon
125/J2 Libya
125/K2 Libyan (des.), Afr.
125/K1 Libyan (plat.), Libya
142/C2 Licantén, Chile
80/C4 Licata, It.
92/E2 Lice, Turk.
70/B1 Lich, Ger.
103/C3 Licheng, China
59/E1 Lichfield, Eng,UK
131/D2 Lichinga, Moz.
131/D2 Lichinga (plat.), Moz.
67/F5 Lichtenau, Ger.
72/E2 Lichtenfels, Ger.
66/D5 Lichtenvoorde, Neth.
68/C1 Lichtervelde, Belg.
105/F2 Lichuan, China
105/H3 Lichuan, China
140/B4 Licinio de Almeida, Braz.
160/C4 Licking (riv.), Ky,US
165/L12 Lick Observatory, Ca,US
80/D2 Licosa (cape), It.
63/L5 Lida, Bela.
57/F1 Liddell Water (riv.), Sc,UK
153/R7 Liddon (gulf), NW,Can
62/H2 Lidingö, Swe.
62/E2 Lidköping, Swe.
59/F2 Lidlington, Eng,UK
79/F2 Lido, It.
79/F1 Lido di Iesolo, It.
80/C2 Lido di Ostia, It.
65/K2 Lidzbark, Pol.
65/L1 Lidzbark Warmiński, Pol.
132/E2 Liebenbergsvlei (riv.), SAfr.
117/F2 Liebig (peak), Austl.
146/B3 Liebre (bay), Mex.
77/F3 Liechtenstein
68/D2 Liedekerke, Belg.
69/E2 Liège, Belg.
69/E3 Liège (prov.), Belg.
61/J3 Lieksa, Fin.
66/C5 Lienden, Neth.
67/E4 Lienen, Ger.
73/K3 Lienz, Aus.
63/J3 Liepāja, Lat.
68/D1 Lier, Belg.
72/E1 Lies (riv.), Belg.
69/F3 Lieser (riv.), Ger.
63/K1 Liesjärven Nat'l Park, Fin.
76/D3 Liestal, Swi.
63/K1 Lieto, Fin.
68/B3 Liévin, Fr.
160/F2 Lièvre (riv.), Qu,Can
76/B2 Liez (lake), Fr.
73/L3 Liezen, Aus.
60/D3 Liffey (riv.), Ire.
121/V12 Lifou (isl.), NCal.
58/B5 Lifton, Eng,UK
130/B5 Liganga, Tanz.
111/F1 Ligao, Phil.
77/F5 Ligoncio, Pizzo (peak), It.
78/B3 Ligure, Appennino (mts.), It.
78/C4 Liguria (reg.), It.
73/H5 Ligurian (sea), Eur.
115/J3 Lihou (reef), Austl.
107/H2 Lijiang (Lijiang Naxizu Zizhixian), China
103/D3 Lijin, China
105/H2 Liju (mtn.), China
131/B1 Likasi, Zaire
156/C2 Likely, BC,Can
131/D2 Likoma (isl.), Malw.
124/J8 Likouala (riv.), Congo
80/A1 L'Ile-Rousse, Fr.
53/T10 L'Ile-Saint-Denis, Fr.
67/F2 Lilienthal, Ger.
107/K2 Liling, China
69/D1 Lille, Belg.
68/C2 Lille, Fr.
62/C4 Lille Bælt (chan.), Den.
62/D1 Lillehammer, Nor.
63/T9 Lillerød, Den.
68/B2 Lillers, Fr.
62/C2 Lillesand, Nor.
62/D2 Lillestrøm, Nor.
113/L Lillie Marleen Hütte, Ant.
54/D5 Lilliesleaf, Sc,UK
156/C3 Lillooet, BC,Can
156/C3 Lillooet (riv.), BC,Can
131/D2 Lilongwe (cap.), Malw.
112/C3 Liloy, Phil.
119/G5 Lilydale, Austl.
84/D2 Lim (riv.), Yugo.
144/B4 Lima (cap.), Peru
144/B3 Lima (dept.), Peru
74/A2 Lima (riv.), Port.
157/L4 Lima (peak), Mn,US
160/C3 Lima, Oh,US
142/D9 Limache, Chile
77/E5 Limadario, Monte (Gridone) (peak), It.
141/K6 Lima Duarte, Braz.
65/L4 Limanowa, Pol.
91/C2 Limassol, Cyp.
91/C2 Limassol (dist.), Cyp.
56/B1 Limavady, NI,UK
56/A2 Limavady (dist.), NI,UK
142/C4 Limay (riv.), Arg.
68/A6 Limay, Fr.
112/A4 Limbang (riv.), Malay.
80/A2 Limbara (peak), It.
106/B3 Limbdi, India
149/H2 Limbé, Haiti
131/D2 Limbe, Malw.
78/C1 Limbiate, It.
69/E2 Limburg (prov.), Belg.
69/E1 Limburg (prov.), Neth.
70/B2 Limburg an der Lahn, Ger.
70/B4 Limburgerhof, Ger.
161/Q8 Limehouse, On,Can
53/T10 Limeil-Brévannes, Fr.
141/C2 Limeira, Braz.
54/C4 Limekilns, Sc,UK
60/B4 Limerick, Ire.
60/B5 Limerick (co.), Ire.
62/C3 Limfjorden (chan.), Den.
74/B2 Limia (riv.), Sp.
114/F2 Limmen (bight), Austl.
81/J3 Límnos (isl.), Gre.
140/D2 Limoeiro, Braz.
140/C2 Limoeiro do Norte, Braz.
72/D4 Limoges, Fr.
72/D4 Limogne (plat.), Fr.
149/F4 Limón, CR
159/G3 Limon, Co,US
53/S11 Limours, Fr.
72/D4 Limousin (mts.), Fr.
72/D4 Limousin (reg.), Fr.
72/E5 Limoux, Fr.
126/F5 Limpopo (riv.), Afr.
53/P8 Limpsfield, Eng,UK
105/F5 Limu (mtn.), China
131/A2 Limulunga, Zam.
130/C3 Limuru, Kenya
112/C4 Linao (pt.), Phil.
112/B3 Linapacan (isl.), Phil.
77/G4 Linard, Piz (peak), Swi.
142/C2 Linares, Chile
147/F3 Linares, Mex.
74/D3 Linares, Sp.
104/D4 Lincang, China
103/C3 Lincheng, China
105/H3 Linchuan, China
142/E2 Lincoln, Arg.
161/R9 Lincoln, On,Can
145/L1 Lincoln (sea), Can., Grld.
57/H5 Lincoln, Eng,UK
160/B3 Lincoln, Il,US
168/C1 Lincoln, Ma,US
161/G2 Lincoln, Me,US
159/H2 Lincoln (cap.), Ne,US
156/B4 Lincoln Beach, Or,US
156/B4 Lincoln City, Or,US
57/H5 Lincoln Heath (woodl.), Eng,UK
117/G5 Lincoln Nat'l Park, Austl.
165/F7 Lincoln Park, Mi,US
167/D2 Lincoln Park, NJ,US
57/H5 Lincolnshire (co.), Eng,UK
57/H5 Lincolnshire Wolds (hills), Eng,UK
163/H3 Lincolnton, NC,US
167/D3 Lincroft, NJ,US
80/A2 L'Incudine, Mont (mtn.), Fr.
77/F2 Lindau, Ger.
66/D3 Linde (riv.), Neth.
118/C3 Lindeman (isl.), Austl.
70/B1 Linden, Ger.
139/G3 Linden, Guy.
163/G3 Linden, Al,US
167/D2 Linden, NJ,US
77/F2 Lindenberg im Allgäu, Ger.
165/P15 Lindenhurst, Il,US
167/E2 Lindenhurst, NY,US
166/D4 Lindenwold, NJ,US
62/F2 Lindesberg, Swe.
62/B3 Lindesnes (cape), Nor.
130/C5 Lindi, Tanz.
130/C5 Lindi (prov.), Tanz.
97/J2 Lindian, China
54/E5 Lindisfarne (Holy) (isl.), Eng,UK
67/E6 Lindlar, Ger.
119/D3 Lind Nat'l Park, Austl.
62/E3 Lindome, Swe.
116/F3 Lindsay (mtn.), Austl.
117/C5 Lindsay (mtn.), Austl.
160/E2 Lindsay, On,Can
158/C3 Lindsay, Ca,US
162/D2 Lindsborg, Ks,US
121/K4 Line (isls.), Kiri.
166/B2 Line Mountain (ridge), Pa,US
103/B3 Linfen, China
54/A2 Ling (riv.), Sc,UK
166/A5 Linganore (cr.), Md,US
105/F5 Lingao, China
112/C1 Lingayen, Phil.
112/C1 Lingayen (gulf), Phil.
103/B4 Lingbao, China
103/D4 Lingbi, China
103/C4 Lingchuan, China
66/C5 Linge (riv.), Neth.
67/E3 Lingen, Ger.
53/N8 Lingfield, Eng,UK
110/B3 Lingga (isls.), Indo.
69/G6 Lingolsheim, Fr.
103/C3 Lingqiu, China
103/C3 Lingshan, China
105/F4 Lingshan, China
103/B3 Lingshi, China
105/F5 Lingshui, China
128/B3 Linguère, Sen.
103/D3 Ling Xian, China
103/E5 Lingyang Shan (mtn.), China
103/L8 Lingyen Shan (mtn.), China
103/E5 Lingyin Si, China
103/D2 Lingyuan, China
107/J3 Lingyun, China
105/J2 Linhai, China
141/D1 Linhares, Braz.
103/A2 Linhe, China
62/F2 Linköping, Swe.
54/C5 Linlithgow, Sc,UK
103/C3 Linliu Shan (mtn.), China
77/E3 Linmat (riv.), Swi.
61/J3 Linnansaaren Nat'l Park, Fin.
58/A3 Linney Head (pt.), Wal,UK
54/A3 Linnhe, Loch (inlet), Sc,UK
69/F2 Linnich, Ger.
80/C5 Linosa (isl.), It.
103/C3 Linqing, China
103/D3 Linqu, China
103/C4 Linquan, China
103/C4 Linru, China
141/B2 Lins, Braz.
103/D4 Linshu, China
149/G2 Linstead, Jam.
133/H9 Linta (riv.), Madg.
77/E4 Linth (riv.), Swi.
59/G2 Linton, Eng,UK
160/C4 Linton, In,US
157/H4 Linton, ND,US
57/H5 Linwood, Eng,UK
107/K2 Linwu, China
103/C3 Linxi, China
103/C3 Lin Xian, China
131/A3 Linyanti (swamp), Bots., Namb.
103/B4 Linyi, China
103/D3 Linyi, China
103/D4 Linyi, China
103/C4 Linying, China
71/H6 Linz, Aus.
96/E4 Linze, China
103/C3 Linzhang, China
72/E5 Lions (gulf), Fr.
131/C3 Lions Den, Zim.
80/D3 Lipari (isl.), It.
80/D3 Lipari (isls.), It.
61/J3 Liperi, Fin.
86/F1 Lipetsk, Rus.
86/F1 Lipetsk Obl., Rus.
136/E8 Lípez (range), Bol.
136/E8 Lípez (riv.), Bol.
59/F4 Liphook, Eng,UK
105/F3 Liping, China
82/E4 Lipljan, Yugo.
65/K2 Lipno, Pol.
71/H5 Lipno, Údolní nádrž (res.), Czh.
131/D1 Lipoche, Moz.
82/E2 Lipova, Rom.
66/E5 Lippe (riv.), Ger.
67/F5 Lippetal, Ger.
67/F5 Lippstadt, Ger.
65/K4 Liptovský Mikuláš, Slvk.
119/C3 Liptrap (cape), Austl.
105/F3 Lipu, China
102/D5 Lipu La (pass), India
102/D5 Lipu Lehk Shankou (pass), China
130/B2 Lira, Ugan.
126/C1 Liranga, Congo
131/D2 Lirangwe, Malw.
80/C2 Liri (riv.), It.
75/E3 Liria, Sp.
77/F5 Liro (riv.), It.
125/K7 Lisala, Zaire
74/A3 Lisboa (dist.), Port.
74/A3 Lisboa (Lisbon) (cap.), Port.
161/G2 Lisbon, Me,US
157/J4 Lisbon, ND,US
74/A3 Lisbon (Lisboa) (cap.), Port.
75/P10 Lisbon (Lisboa) (inset) (cap.), Port.
56/B2 Lisburn, NI,UK
56/B3 Lisburn (dist.), NI,UK
151/E2 Lisburne (cape), Ak,US
103/B4 Li Shan (mtn.), China
104/D3 Lishe (riv.), China
103/F2 Lishu, China
105/H2 Lishui, China
121/H2 Lisianski (isl.), Hi,US
86/F2 Lisichansk, Ukr.
72/D2 Lisieux, Fr.
58/B6 Liskeard, Eng,UK
165/P16 Lisle, Il,US
68/B5 L'Isle-Adam, Fr.
72/F5 L'Isle-sur-la-Sorgue, Fr.
119/E1 Lismore, Austl.
56/B3 Lisnacree, NI,UK
60/C1 Lisnaskea, NI,UK
59/F4 Liss, Eng,UK
66/B4 Lisse, Neth.
53/T11 Lisses, Fr.
67/E6 Lister (riv.), Ger.
160/D3 Listowel, On,Can
104/D2 Litang, China
104/D2 Litang (riv.), China
91/D3 Līṭanī (riv.), Leb.
71/G3 Litavka (riv.), Czh.
168/A2 Litchfield, Ct,US
168/A2 Litchfield (co.), Ct,US
160/B4 Litchfield, Il,US
157/K4 Litchfield, Mn,US
131/C2 Liteta, Zam.
66/C5 Lith, Neth.
57/F5 Litherland, Eng,UK
119/D2 Lithgow, Austl.
63/K4 Lithuania
166/B3 Lititz, Pa,US
71/H1 Litoměřice, Czh.
130/C5 Litoo, Tanz.
63/M4 Litovskiy Nat'l Park, Lith.
118/D4 Littabella Nat'l Park, Austl.
77/E3 Littau, Swi.
163/H4 Little (riv.), Ga,US
163/J4 Little (riv.), La,US
163/J3 Little (riv.), NC,US
159/J4 Little (riv.), Ok,US
162/D4 Little (riv.), Tx,US
160/D1 Little Abitibi (riv.), On,Can
65/J5 Little Alföld (plain), Hun.
107/F5 Little Andaman (isl.), India
168/G6 Little Beaver, Middle Fork (cr.), Oh,US
168/G6 Little Beaver, North Fork (cr.), Oh,US
168/G6 Little Beaver, West Fork (cr.), Oh,US
156/F4 Little Belt (mts.), Mt,US
53/N6 Little Berkhamstead, Eng,UK
156/G4 Little Bighorn Nat'l Mon., Mt,US
91/C4 Little Bitter (lake), Egypt
159/H2 Little Blue (riv.), Ks, Ne,US
57/F4 Littleborough, Eng,UK
165/Q16 Little Calumet (riv.), Il,US
149/F2 Little Cayman (isl.), Cay.
53/M7 Little Chalfont, Eng,UK
158/E4 Little Colorado (riv.), Az,US
54/B5 Little Cumbrae (isl.), Sc,UK
160/D2 Little Current, On,Can
160/C1 Little Current (riv.), On,Can
58/C5 Little Dart (riv.), Eng,UK
119/B3 Little Desert Nat'l Park, Austl.
151/E2 Little Diomede (isl.), Ak,US
167/D4 Little Egg (har.), NJ,US
157/K4 Little Falls, Mn,US
167/J8 Little Falls, NJ,US
162/C3 Littlefield, Tx,US
166/B1 Little Fishing (cr.), Pa,US
157/K4 Little Fork (riv.), Mn,US
59/F5 Littlehampton, Eng,UK
150/C2 Little Inagua (isl.), Bahm.
132/C4 Little Karoo (reg.), SAfr.
166/C2 Little Lehigh (riv.), Pa,US
55/H8 Little Minch (sound), Sc,UK
161/K2 Little Miquelon (isl.), StP.
159/J4 Little Missouri (riv.), Ar,US
157/H4 Little Missouri (riv.), ND, SD,US
166/B1 Little Muncy (cr.), Pa,US
167/K8 Little Neck (bay), NY,US
107/F6 Little Nicobar (isl.), India
59/G2 Little Ouse (riv.), Eng,UK
117/M8 Little Para (res.), Austl.
117/M8 Little Para (riv.), Austl.
166/B5 Little Patuxent (riv.), Md,US
167/F2 Little Peconic (bay), NY,US
59/G2 Littleport, Eng,UK
159/J4 Little Red (riv.), Ar,US
162/E3 Little Rock (cap.), Ar,US
165/N16 Little Rock (cr.), Il,US
148/D2 Little Rocky (pt.), Belz.
151/L3 Little Salmon, Yk,Can
128/B4 Little Scarcies (riv.), Gui., SLeo.
166/C2 Little Schuylkill (riv.), Pa,US
168/G5 Little Shenango (riv.), Pa,US
157/K5 Little Sioux (riv.), Ia,US
151/B5 Little Sitkin (isl.), Ak,US
156/D2 Little Smoky (riv.), Ab,Can
158/E2 Little Snake (riv.), Co, Wy,US
59/G4 Little Stour (riv.), Eng,UK
59/F2 Little Stukeley, Eng,UK
166/B3 Little Swatara (cr.), Pa,US
161/G2 Littleton, NH,US
160/B4 Little Wabash (riv.), Il,US
159/G2 Little White (riv.), SD,US
156/E5 Little Wood (riv.), Id,US
93/E3 Little Zab (riv.), Iraq
71/G1 Litvínov, Czh.
101/C1 Liu (riv.), China
96/F5 Liuba, China
107/J3 Liucheng, China
101/C2 Liuhe, China
105/J2 Liuheng (isl.), China
130/B5 Liuli, Tanz.
103/B3 Liulin, China
126/D3 Liuwa Pan Nat'l Park, Zam.
105/G4 Liuxi (riv.), China
107/K2 Liuyang, China
105/G2 Liuyang (riv.), China
105/F3 Liuzhou, China
79/G2 Livade, Cro.
79/F1 Livenza (riv.), It.
163/H4 Live Oak, Fl,US
69/F6 Liverdun, Fr.
165/L11 Livermore, Ca,US
162/B4 Livermore (peak), Tx,US
118/G8 Liverpool, Austl.
161/H2 Liverpool, NS,Can
151/M2 Liverpool (bay), NW,Can
153/J1 Liverpool (cape), NW,Can
57/F5 Liverpool, Eng,UK
57/E5 Liverpool (bay), Eng,UK
57/H2 Liverton, Eng,UK
148/D3 Livingston, Guat.
54/C5 Livingston, Sc,UK
165/E6 Livingston (co.), Mi,US
156/F4 Livingston, Mt,US
167/D2 Livingston, NJ,US
162/E4 Livingston, Tx,US
159/J5 Livingston (lake), Tx,US
156/E3 Livingstone (range), Ab,Can
131/B3 Livingstone, Zam.
126/B1 Livingstone, Chutes de (Livingstone) (falls), Congo
131/C2 Livingstone Mem., Zam.
131/D1 Livingstonia, Malw.
82/C4 Livno, Bosn.
86/F1 Livny, Rus.
61/H2 Livojoki (riv.), Fin.
165/F7 Livonia, Mi,US
78/D5 Livorno, It.
78/D6 Livorno (prov.), It.
140/B4 Livramento do Brumado, Braz.
72/F4 Livron-sur-Drôme, Fr.
68/B6 Livry-Gargan, Fr.
130/C5 Liwale, Tanz.
131/D2 Liwonde, Malw.
131/D2 Liwonde Nat'l Park, Malw.
105/F2 Li Xian, China
103/D4 Lixin, China
103/D5 Liyang, China
58/A7 Lizard, Eng,UK
58/A7 Lizard (pt.), Eng,UK

201
Lizar – Luzho

58/A6 **Lizard, The** (pen.), Eng,UK
82/B2 **Ljubljana** (cap.), Slov.
82/C4 **Ljubuški**, Cro.
61/F3 **Ljungan** (riv.), Swe.
62/E3 **Ljungby**, Swe.
84/C3 **Ljusdal**, Swe.
62/G1 **Ljusnan** (riv.), Swe.
62/H2 **Ljusterø** (isl.), Swe.
142/C2 **Llaillay**, Chile
142/C3 **Llaima** (vol.), Chile
136/E7 **Llallagua**, Bol.
58/B2 **Llanarth**, Wal,UK
56/D5 **Llanberis**, Wal,UK
56/D5 **Llanberis, Pass of** (pass), Wal,UK
142/C2 **Llancañelo** (lake), Arg.
58/C3 **Llandeilo**, Wal,UK
58/D3 **Llandogo**, Wal,UK
58/C3 **Llandovery**, Wal,UK
56/E6 **Llandrillo**, Wal,UK
58/C2 **Llandrindod Wells**, Wal,UK
56/E5 **Llandudno**, Wal,UK
58/C3 **Llandybie**, Wal,UK
58/B2 **Llandyssul**, Wal,UK
58/B3 **Llanelli**, Wal,UK
58/C1 **Llanelltyd**, Wal,UK
56/D6 **Llanenddwyn**, Wal,UK
56/D5 **Llanerchymedd**, Wal,UK
74/C1 **Llanes**, Sp.
58/C1 **Llanfair Caereinion**, Wal,UK
56/E5 **Llanfairfechan**, Wal,UK
56/D5 **Llanfair-Pwllgwyngyll**, Wal,UK
58/C1 **Llanfyllin**, Wal,UK
58/C2 **Llangammarch Wells**, Wal,UK
58/C3 **Llangattock**, Wal,UK
57/E6 **Llangollen**, Wal,UK
58/C2 **Llangurig**, Wal,UK
58/C2 **Llanidloes**, Wal,UK
56/D5 **Llanllyfni**, Wal,UK
58/B3 **Llannon**, Wal,UK
162/D4 **Llano**, Tx,US
159/H5 **Llano** (riv.), Tx,US
158/G4 **Llano Estacado** (plain), NM, Tx,US
58/B2 **Llanon**, Wal,UK
138/D3 **Llanos** (plain), Col., Ven.
142/B4 **Llanquihue** (lake), Chile
57/E5 **Llanrhaeadr**, Wal,UK
58/B2 **Llanrhystyd**, Wal,UK
58/A3 **Llanrian**, Wal,UK
56/E5 **Llanrwst**, Wal,UK
58/C3 **Llanthony**, Wal,UK
58/C3 **Llantrisant**, Wal,UK
58/C4 **Llantwit Major**, Wal,UK
56/E6 **Llanuwchllyn**, Wal,UK
58/C1 **Llanwnog**, Wal,UK
58/C2 **Llanwrtyd Wells**, Wal,UK
57/E5 **Llay**, Wal,UK
58/C2 **Lledrod**, Wal,UK
75/F2 **Lleida** (Lérida), Sp.
56/D6 **Lleyn** (pen.), Wal,UK
75/F1 **Llobregat** (riv.), Sp.
74/D1 **Llodio**, Sp.
112/D3 **Llorente**, Phil.
75/G2 **Lloret de Mar**, Sp.
167/E2 **Lloyd** (pt.), NY,US
156/F2 **Lloydminster**, Ab, Sk,Can
161/K1 **Lloyds** (riv.), Nf,Can
75/G3 **Lluchmayor**, Sp.
135/C1 **Llullaillaco** (vol.), Chile
58/C3 **Llynfi** (riv.), Wal,UK
104/E4 **Lo** (riv.), Viet.
135/C1 **Loa** (riv.), Chile
158/E3 **Loa**, Ut,US
54/C5 **Loanhead**, Sc,UK
78/B4 **Loano**, It.
75/N8 **Loaoya** (can.), Sp.
130/A3 **Loashi**, Zaire
132/D2 **Lobatse**, Bots.
117/M8 **Lobenthal**, Austl.
142/F3 **Lobería**, Arg.
126/B3 **Lobito**, Ang.
128/D5 **Lobo** (riv.), IvC.
142/F2 **Lobos**, Arg.
136/B5 **Lobos de Tierra** (isl.), Peru
142/B2 **Lobos, Punta de** (pt.), Chile
77/E5 **Locarno**, Swi.
54/B3 **Lochaber** (dist.), Sc,UK
56/D2 **Lochans**, Sc,UK
56/E1 **Locharbriggs**, Sc,UK
54/A4 **Lochawe**, Sc,UK
55/H8 **Lochboisdale**, Sc,UK
54/B4 **Lochearnhead**, Sc,UK
66/D4 **Lochem**, Neth.
54/B2 **Lochend**, Sc,UK
54/C4 **Lochgelly**, Sc,UK
54/A4 **Lochgilphead**, Sc,UK
54/B4 **Lochgoilhead**, Sc,UK
54/C2 **Lochindorb** (lake), Sc,UK
131/B2 **Lochinvar Nat'l Park**, Zam.
55/J7 **Lochinver**, Sc,UK
56/E1 **Lochmaben**, Sc,UK
55/H8 **Lochmaddy**, Sc,UK
54/A5 **Lochranza**, Sc,UK
166/B5 **Loch Raven** (res.), Md,US
68/C1 **Lochristi**, Belg.
54/B5 **Lochwinnoch**, Sc,UK
54/B3 **Lochy** (riv.), Sc,UK
54/B3 **Lochy, Loch** (lake), Sc,UK
57/E1 **Lockerbie**, Sc,UK
162/D4 **Lockhart**, Tx,US
118/A1 **Lockhart Abor. Land**, Austl.
160/E3 **Lock Haven**, Pa,US
119/C3 **Lockington**, Austl.
165/P16 **Lockport**, Il,US
161/S9 **Lockport**, NY,US
53/N7 **Lockwood** (res.), Eng,UK
109/D4 **Loc Ninh**, Viet.
80/E3 **Locri**, It.
159/J3 **Locust** (cr.), Ia, Mo,US
163/G3 **Locust Fork** (riv.), Al,US
91/F8 **Lod**, Isr.
63/U9 **Lodde** (riv.), Swe.
63/U9 **Löddeköpinge**, Swe.
115/G7 **Loddon** (riv.), Austl.
59/H1 **Loddon**, Eng,UK
59/E4 **Loddon** (riv.), Eng,UK
71/H2 **Lodenice** (riv.), Czh.
72/E5 **Lodève**, Fr.
84/G3 **Lodeynoye Pole**, Rus.
156/F3 **Lodge** (cr.), Mt,US
159/G2 **Lodgepole** (cr.), Ne, Wy,US
78/C2 **Lodi**, It.
165/M10 **Lodi**, Ca,US
167/D2 **Lodi**, NJ,US
126/D1 **Lodja**, Zaire
130/B2 **Lodwar**, Kenya
65/K3 **Łódź**, Pol.
65/K3 **Łódź** (prov.), Pol.
75/N9 **Loeches**, Sp.
109/C2 **Loei**, Thai.
66/C4 **Loenen**, Neth.
128/C5 **Lofa** (co.), Libr.
128/C5 **Lofa** (riv.), Libr.
77/E2 **Löffingen**, Ger.
61/D2 **Lofoten** (isls.), Nor.
57/H2 **Loftus**, Eng,UK
117/M8 **Lofty** (mtn.), Austl.
116/C3 **Lofty** (range), Austl.
119/C4 **Lofty** (range), Austl.
118/F7 **Logan**, Austl.
151/K3 **Logan** (mtn.), Yk,Can
159/G4 **Logan**, NM,US
160/D4 **Logan**, Oh,US
158/E2 **Logan**, Ut,US
160/D4 **Logan**, WV,US
56/D2 **Logan, Mull of** (pt.), Sc,UK
160/C3 **Logansport**, In,US
124/J6 **Logone** (riv.), Camr., Chad
74/D1 **Logroño**, Sp.
67/G6 **Lohfelden**, Ger.
63/L1 **Lohja**, Fin.
63/K1 **Lohjanjärvi** (lake), Fin.
69/G2 **Lohmar**, Ger.
64/E2 **Lohne**, Ger.
67/F3 **Löhne**, Ger.
70/C3 **Lohr**, Ger.
104/C4 **Loi Lun** (range), Burma, China
63/K1 **Loimaa**, Fin.
72/E2 **Loing** (riv.), Fr.
72/C3 **Loir** (riv.), Fr.
72/C3 **Loire** (riv.), Fr.
69/E5 **Loisin** (riv.), Fr.
104/C4 **Loi Song** (mtn.), Burma
130/B3 **Loita** (hills), Kenya
144/B2 **Loja**, Ecu.
144/B2 **Loja** (prov.), Ecu.
74/C4 **Loja**, Sp.
68/D1 **Lokeren**, Belg.
130/B2 **Lokichar**, Kenya
130/B1 **Lokichokio**, Kenya
130/B1 **Lokitaung**, Kenya
126/D1 **Lokolia**, Zaire
125/K8 **Lokolo** (riv.), Zaire
130/B2 **Lokopo**, Ugan.
130/C2 **Lokori**, Kenya
125/J8 **Lokoro** (riv.), Zaire
153/K2 **Loks** (isl.), NW,Can
130/B2 **Lokwakangole**, Kenya
125/L6 **Lol** (riv.), Sudan
130/B2 **Lolelia**, Ugan.
130/B3 **Lolgorien**, Kenya
130/B3 **Loliondo**, Tanz.
130/C3 **Lolkisale**, Tanz.
62/D4 **Lolland** (isl.), Den.
156/E4 **Lolo** (peak), Mt,US
126/E1 **Lolo**, Zaire
147/F4 **Lolotla**, Mex.
120/G5 **Lolua**, Tuv.
130/B3 **Lolui** (isl.), Ugan.
83/F4 **Lom**, Bul.
71/G3 **Lom** (hill), Czh.
128/C4 **Loma** (mts.), Gui., SLeo.
164/C5 **Loma** (pt.), Ca,US
147/G5 **Loma Bonita**, Mex.
164/C2 **Loma Linda**, Ca,US
128/C4 **Loma Mansa** (peak), SLeo.
125/K8 **Lomami** (riv.), Zaire
143/S12 **Lomas de Zamora**, Arg.
78/C1 **Lomazzo**, It.
165/P16 **Lombard**, Il,US
137/H3 **Lombarda** (mts.), Braz.
73/J4 **Lombardy** (reg.), It.
111/F5 **Lomblen** (isl.), Indo.
111/E5 **Lombok** (isl.), Indo.
129/F5 **Lomé** (cap.), Togo
126/D1 **Lomela**, Zaire
125/K8 **Lomela** (riv.), Zaire
164/B3 **Lomita**, Ca,US
62/E4 **Lomma**, Swe.
63/T9 **Lommabukten** (bay), Swe.
72/E1 **Lomme**, Fr.
69/E1 **Lommel**, Belg.
71/G4 **Lomnice** (riv.), Czh.
54/C4 **Lomond** (hills), Sc,UK
54/B4 **Lomond, Loch** (lake), Sc,UK
79/E4 **Lomone** (riv.), It.
63/N2 **Lomonosov**, Rus.
111/E5 **Lompobatang** (peak), Indo.
158/B4 **Lompoc**, Ca,US
109/C2 **Lom Sak**, Thai.
65/M2 **Łomża**, Pol.
65/M2 **Łomża** (prov.), Pol.
106/B4 **Lonāvale**, India
142/B3 **Loncoche**, Chile
68/D2 **Londerzeel**, Belg.
130/B3 **Londiani**, Kenya
68/A4 **Londinières**, Fr.
160/D3 **London**, On,Can
149/F3 **London** (reef), Nic.
59/F3 **London** (cap.), Eng,UK
160/C4 **London**, Ky,US
53/N7 **London, City of** (bor.), Eng,UK
53/N6 **London Colney**, Eng,UK
114/D2 **Londonderry** (cape), Austl.
143/J8 **Londonderry** (isl.), Chile
56/A2 **Londonderry**, NI,UK
56/A2 **Londonderry** (dist.), NI,UK
141/B2 **Londrina**, Braz.
70/D5 **Lone** (riv.), Ger.
159/H4 **Lone Grove**, Ok,US
118/E7 **Lone Pine Sanct.**, Austl.
118/C4 **Lonesome Nat'l Park**, Austl.
150/C2 **Long** (isl.), Bahm.
157/J2 **Long** (pt.), Mb,Can
160/C1 **Long** (lake), On,Can
105/F3 **Long** (riv.), China
75/F1 **Long** (peak), Fr.
60/A6 **Long** (isl.), Ire.
89/T2 **Long** (str.), Rus.
58/C1 **Long** (mtn.), Wal,UK
168/D2 **Long** (pond), Ma,US
167/E2 **Long** (isl.), NY,US
140/B1 **Longá** (riv.), Braz.
107/J3 **Long'an**, China
142/C2 **Longaví**, Chile
161/R10 **Long Beach**, On,Can
164/B3 **Long Beach**, Ca,US
167/D4 **Long Beach** (isl.), NJ,US
167/E2 **Long Beach**, NY,US
164/B3 **Long Beach Nav. Shipyard**, Ca,US
57/G1 **Longbenton**, Eng,UK
163/H5 **Longboat Key**, Fl,US
167/E3 **Long Branch**, NJ,US
59/E2 **Long Buckby**, Eng,UK
104/E2 **Longchang**, China
109/D1 **Long Chau**, Viet.
104/C3 **Longchuan** (riv.), Burma, China
105/G3 **Longchuan**, China
54/E6 **Long Crag** (hill), Eng,UK
59/F3 **Long Crendon**, Eng,UK
96/F4 **Longde**, China
57/N7 **Long Ditton**, Eng,UK
57/G6 **Long Eaton**, Eng,UK
69/E5 **Longeau** (riv.), Fr.
161/G2 **Longfellow** (mts.), Me,US
53/P7 **Longfield**, Eng,UK
60/C2 **Longford**, Ire.
150/C2 **Long** (Fortune I.) (cay), Bahm.
103/D2 **Longhua**, China
105/F3 **Longhua** (pass), China
105/F3 **Longhui**, China
130/D3 **Longido**, Tanz.
167/E2 **Long Island** (sound), Ct, NY,US
97/J2 **Longjiang**, China
53/S10 **Longjumeau**, Fr.
103/E3 **Longkou**, China
160/C1 **Longlac**, On,Can
58/D4 **Longleat House**, Eng,UK
107/J2 **Longli**, China
54/A2 **Long, Loch** (inlet), Sc,UK
54/B4 **Long, Loch** (inlet), Sc,UK
168/B1 **Longmeadow**, Ma,US
103/C4 **Longmen**, China
104/D3 **Longmen** (Dragon Gate), China
103/B4 **Longmen Shan** (mtn.), China
103/C4 **Longmen Shiyao** (caves), China
159/F2 **Longmont**, Co,US
58/D1 **Long Mynd, The** (hill), Eng,UK
105/G3 **Longnan**, China
167/E1 **Long Neck** (pt.), Ct,US
54/D5 **Longniddry**, Sc,UK
57/G5 **Longnor**, Eng,UK
109/D4 **Long Phu**, Viet.
53/S11 **Longpont-sur-Orge**, Fr.
105/H2 **Longquan**, China
161/K2 **Long Range** (mts.), Nf,Can
57/F4 **Longridge**, Eng,UK
105/F2 **Longshan**, China
96/E4 **Longshou** (mts.), China
57/J6 **Long Sutton**, Eng,UK
57/F2 **Longtown**, Eng,UK
68/B2 **Longuenesse**, Fr.
161/N6 **Longueuil**, Qu,Can
69/E5 **Longuyon**, Fr.
76/B3 **Longvic**, Fr.
162/E3 **Longview**, Tx,US
156/C4 **Longview**, Wa,US
166/C4 **Longwood Gardens**, Pa,US
69/E4 **Longwy**, Fr.
96/E4 **Longxi**, China
109/D4 **Long Xuyen**, Viet.
105/H3 **Longyan**, China
105/H2 **Longyou**, China
109/D1 **Longzhou**, China
79/E2 **Lonigo**, It.
67/E3 **Löningen**, Ger.
72/C5 **Lons**, Fr.
76/B4 **Lons-le-Saunier**, Fr.
69/E2 **Lontzen**, Belg.
76/D5 **Lonza** (riv.), Swi.
112/C2 **Looc**, Phil.
58/B6 **Looe**, Eng,UK
58/B6 **Looe** (isl.), Eng,UK
118/B1 **Lookout** (pt.), Austl.
163/J3 **Lookout** (cape), NC,US
130/B3 **Loolmalasin** (peak), Tanz.
156/F2 **Loon Lake**, Sk,Can
66/C5 **Loon op Zand**, Neth.
54/G10 **Loop Head** (pt.), Ire.
68/C2 **Loos**, Fr.
102/F3 **Lop** (lake), China
89/R4 **Lopatka, Mys** (cape), Rus.
109/C3 **Lop Buri**, Thai.
124/G8 **Lopez** (cape), Gabon
112/C2 **Lopez**, Phil.
66/B5 **Lopik**, Neth.
125/K7 **Lopori** (riv.), Zaire
61/G1 **Lopphavet** (bay), Nor.
63/L1 **Loppi**, Fin.
117/G4 **Lora** (cr.), Austl.
95/J3 **Lora** (riv.), Pak.
74/C4 **Lora del Río**, Sp.
95/J3 **Lora, Hāmūn-i-** (lake), Pak.
168/E5 **Lorain**, Oh,US
168/E5 **Lorain** (co.), Oh,US
95/J2 **Loralai**, Pak.
75/E4 **Lorca**, Sp.
115/K6 **Lord Howe** (isl.), Austl.
158/E4 **Lordsburg**, NM,US
69/G3 **Lorelei** (cliff), Ger.
141/H7 **Lorena**, Braz.
62/D2 **Lørenskog**, Nor.
111/J5 **Lorentz** (riv.), Indo.
66/C2 **Lorentzsluizen** (dam), Neth.
93/G3 **Lorestān** (gov.), Iran
140/A2 **Loreto**, Braz.
79/G6 **Loreto**, It.
157/J3 **Lorette**, Mb,Can
125/N7 **Lorian** (swamp), Kenya
138/C2 **Lorica**, Col.
72/B3 **Lorient**, Fr.
123/N13 **L'Oriental** (reg.), Mor.
152/G2 **Lorillard** (riv.), NW,Can
82/D2 **Lorinci**, Hun.
161/Q8 **Lorne Park**, On,Can
55/H8 **Lorn, Firth of** (inlet), Sc,UK
130/B2 **Lorosuk** (peak), Kenya
76/D2 **Lörrach**, Ger.
69/F6 **Lorrain** (plat.), Fr.
161/N6 **Lorraine**, Qu,Can
73/G2 **Lorraine** (reg.), Fr.
70/B3 **Lorsch**, Ger.
57/E2 **Lorton**, Eng,UK
166/A6 **Lorton**, Va,US
130/C2 **Loruk**, Kenya
130/C2 **Losai Nat'l Rsv.**, Kenya
164/B3 **Los Alamitos**, Ca,US
158/B4 **Los Alamos**, Ca,US
159/F4 **Los Alamos**, NM,US
142/C4 **Los Alerces Nat'l Park**, Arg.
165/K12 **Los Altos**, Ca,US
148/D3 **Los Amates**, Guat.
142/C2 **Los Andes**, Chile
142/B3 **Los Angeles**, Chile
164/B2 **Los Angeles**, Ca,US
164/B1 **Los Angeles** (aqueduct), Ca,US
164/B2 **Los Angeles** (co.), Ca,US
164/B2 **Los Angeles** (riv.), Ca,US
164/F7 **Los Angeles** (inset), Ca,US
164/F8 **Los Angeles Outer** (har.), Ca,US
158/B3 **Los Banos**, Ca,US
74/C4 **Los Barrios**, Sp.
134/B7 **Los Chonos** (arch.), Chile
74/C1 **Los Corrales de Buelna**, Sp.
143/J7 **Los Glaciares Nat'l Park**, Arg.
150/D3 **Los Haitises Nat'l Park**, DRep.
69/F4 **Losheim**, Ger.
65/M2 **Łosice**, Pol.
149/F1 **Los Indios** (can.), Cuba
82/B3 **Lošinj** (isl.), Cro.
138/B3 **Los Katios Nat'l Park**, Col.
142/B3 **Los Lagos**, Chile
142/B4 **Los Lagos** (reg.), Chile
144/C4 **Los Libertadores-Wari** (dept.), Peru
158/F4 **Los Lunas**, NM,US
147/F4 **Los Mármoles Nat'l Park**, Mex.
146/C3 **Los Mochis**, Mex.
142/B4 **Los Muermos**, Chile
144/A2 **Los Órganos**, Peru
138/B3 **Los Orquideas Nat'l Park**, Col.
164/A1 **Los Padres Nat'l For.**, Ca,US
74/C4 **Los Palacios y Villafranca**, Sp.
143/J8 **Los Pingüinos Nat'l Park**, Chile
146/C4 **Los Planes**, Mex.
146/C2 **Los Pocitos**, Mex.
146/E5 **Los Reyes**, Mex.
138/B5 **Los Ríos** (prov.), Ecu.
139/E2 **Los Roques** (isls.), Ven.
74/B3 **Los Santos de Maimona**, Sp.
142/B3 **Los Sauces**, Chile
66/E4 **Losser**, Neth.
54/C1 **Lossie** (riv.), Sc,UK
54/C1 **Lossiemouth**, Sc,UK
71/F1 **Lössnitz**, Ger.
130/C4 **Lossoganeu** (hill), Tanz.
139/E2 **Los Teques**, Ven.
139/F2 **Los Testigos** (isls.), Ven.
158/D1 **Lost River** (range), Id,US
166/C2 **Lost River Caverns**, Pa,US
58/B6 **Lostwithiel**, Eng,UK
142/C1 **Los Vilos**, Chile
74/D3 **Los Yébenes**, Sp.
72/D4 **Lot** (riv.), Fr.
142/B3 **Lota**, Chile
62/D1 **Løten**, Nor.
95/G1 **Lotfābād**, Trkm.
130/B2 **Lothaa**, Ugan.
54/C5 **Lothian** (reg.), Sc,UK
131/B4 **Lotsane** (dry riv.), Bots.
67/E4 **Lotte**, Ger.
130/B1 **Lotuke** (peak), Sudan
103/B5 **Lou** (riv.), China
109/C2 **Louangphrabang**, Laos
126/B1 **Loubomo**, Congo
72/B2 **Loudéac**, Fr.
105/F3 **Loudi**, China
72/D3 **Loudun**, Fr.
76/B3 **Loue** (riv.), Fr.
103/B3 **Loufan**, China
128/A3 **Louga**, Sen.
128/B3 **Louga** (reg.), Sen.
57/G6 **Loughborough**, Eng,UK
56/B3 **Loughbrickland**, NI,UK
153/R7 **Loughheed** (isl.), NW,Can
56/B3 **Loughgall**, NI,UK
53/P7 **Loughton**, Eng,UK
76/B4 **Louhans**, Fr.
160/E4 **Louisa**, Va,US
120/E6 **Louisiade** (arch.), PNG
162/E4 **Louisiana** (state), US
131/C4 **Louis Trichardt**, SAfr.
160/C4 **Louisville**, Ky,US
163/F3 **Louisville**, Ms,US
168/F6 **Louisville**, Oh,US
153/J3 **Louis XIV** (pt.), Qu,Can
123/M13 **Loukkos** (riv.), Mor.
74/A4 **Loulé**, Port.
71/G2 **Louny**, Czh.
159/H2 **Loup** (riv.), Ne,US
56/B2 **Loup, The**, NI,UK
53/U10 **L'Ourcq** (can.), Fr.
72/C5 **Lourdes**, Fr.
75/P10 **Loures**, Port.
74/A3 **Louriçal**, Port.
74/A3 **Lourinhã**, Port.
74/A2 **Lousã**, Port.
75/P10 **Lousa**, Port.
105/E2 **Loushan** (pass), China
60/D2 **Louth** (co.), Ire.
57/H5 **Louth**, Eng,UK
81/H4 **Loutrákion**, Gre.
75/E1 **Louts** (riv.), Fr.
69/D2 **Louvain** (Leuven), Belg.
141/G8 **Louveira**, Braz.
68/A5 **Louviers**, Fr.
53/T9 **Louvres**, Fr.
68/C3 **Louvroil**, Fr.
68/B2 **Lovaart** (can.), Belg.
84/F4 **Lovat'** (riv.), Bela., Rus.
82/D4 **Lovćen Nat'l Park**, Yugo.
83/G4 **Lovech**, Bul.
83/G4 **Lovech** (reg.), Bul.
159/F2 **Loveland**, Co,US
156/F4 **Lovell**, Wy,US
158/C2 **Lovelock**, Nv,US
78/D1 **Lovere**, It.
159/F4 **Loving**, NM,US
159/G4 **Lovington**, NM,US
63/M1 **Lovisa**, Fin.
82/C2 **Lövő**, Hun.
63/R7 **Lovön** (isl.), Swe.
71/H1 **Lovosice**, Czh.
84/G2 **Lovozero** (lake), Rus.
153/H2 **Low** (cape), NW,Can
125/L8 **Lowa** (riv.), Zaire
147/E2 **Lowake**, Tx,US
57/H6 **Lowdham**, Eng,UK
161/G3 **Lowell**, Ma,US
132/B2 **Löwen** (dry riv.), Namb.
167/D2 **Lower** (bay), NY,US
165/D3 **Lower** (dam), Wa,US
156/D3 **Lower Arrow** (lake), BC,Can
73/L2 **Lower Austria** (prov.), Aus.
59/E2 **Lower Brailes**, Eng,UK
168/H6 **Lower Burrell**, Pa,US
77/G4 **Lower Engadine** (vall.), Swi.
119/B3 **Lower Glenelg Nat'l Park**, Austl.
119/C4 **Lower Gordon-Franklin Wild Rivers Nat'l Park**, Austl.
59/E3 **Lower Heyford**, Eng,UK
115/R11 **Lower Hutt**, NZ
55/H9 **Lower Lough Erne** (lake), NI,UK
53/P6 **Lower Nazeing**, Eng,UK
164/D5 **Lower Otay** (lake), Ca,US
157/K4 **Lower Red** (lake), Mn,US
165/E7 **Lower Rouge** (riv.), Mi,US
64/E2 **Lower Saxony** (state), Ger.
88/K3 **Lower Tunguska** (riv.), Rus.
131/C2 **Lower Zambezi Nat'l Park**, Zam.
59/H2 **Lowestoft**, Eng,UK
126/F1 **Lowi** (riv.), Zaire
54/E5 **Lowick**, Eng,UK
65/K2 **Łowicz**, Pol.
54/C6 **Lowther** (hills), Sc,UK
161/Q9 **Lowville**, On,Can
148/B3 **Loxicha**, Mex.
67/F2 **Loxstedt**, Ger.
130/B4 **Loya**, Tanz.
121/V12 **Loyalty** (isls.), NCal.
54/A2 **Loyne, Loch** (lake), Sc,UK
130/B2 **Loyoro**, Ugan.
82/D3 **Loznica**, Yugo.
86/F2 **Lozovaya**, Ukr.
82/E3 **Lozovik**, Yugo.
105/G2 **Lu** (peak), China
105/G2 **Lu** (riv.), China
105/J4 **Lü** (isl.), Tai.
131/E3 **Luabo**, Moz.
126/D2 **Luachimo**, Ang.
131/B1 **Lualaba** (riv.), Zaire
103/J6 **Luam** (riv.), China
154/T10 **Lua Makika** (crater), Hi,US
131/B2 **Luampa**, Zam.
131/B2 **Luampa** (riv.), Zam.
103/D5 **Lu'an**, China
103/D2 **Luan** (riv.), China
149/G2 **Luana** (pt.), Jam.
103/B4 **Luanchuan**, China
74/C1 **Luanco**, Sp.
126/B2 **Luanda** (cap.), Ang.
130/B2 **Luanda**, Kenya
109/C5 **Luang** (lag.), Thai.
109/B4 **Luang** (peak), Thai.
109/C2 **Luang Prabang** (range), Laos
126/F3 **Luangwa** (riv.), Moz., Zam.
130/A5 **Luangwe** (riv.), Zam.
103/D2 **Luanping**, China
131/C2 **Luanshya**, Zam.
103/D3 **Luan Xian**, China
126/D3 **Luao**, Ang.
131/C1 **Luapula** (riv.), Zaire, Zam.
130/A5 **Luapula** (prov.), Zam.
131/C1 **Luapula** (prov.), Zam.
74/B1 **Luarca**, Sp.
131/A1 **Luashi**, Zaire
131/C2 **Luatize** (riv.), Moz.
124/G7 **Luba**, EqG.
112/D4 **Lubaantun** (ruins), Belz.
65/M3 **Lubaczów**, Pol.
65/H3 **Lubań**, Pol.
112/C2 **Lubang**, Phil.
112/B2 **Lubang** (isl.), Phil.
126/B3 **Lubango**, Ang.
130/A5 **Lubansenshi** (riv.), Zam.
65/M3 **Lubartów**, Pol.
65/K2 **Lubawa**, Pol.
67/F4 **Lübbecke**, Ger.
69/D2 **Lubbeek**, Belg.
162/C3 **Lubbock**, Tx,US
64/F2 **Lübeck**, Ger.
126/D1 **Lubefu**, Zaire
65/M3 **Lubelska** (upland), Pol.
130/A3 **Lubero**, Zaire
130/A2 **Lubero** (riv.), Zaire
130/A4 **Lubika**, Zaire
65/J3 **Lubin**, Pol.
65/M3 **Lublin**, Pol.
65/M3 **Lublin** (prov.), Pol.
65/K3 **Lubliniec**, Pol.
54/B4 **Lubnaig, Loch** (lake), Sc,UK
86/E2 **Lubny**, Ukr.
65/J2 **Luboń**, Pol.
65/H3 **Lubsko**, Pol.
112/C1 **Lubuagan**, Phil.
126/E2 **Lubudi**, Zaire
131/B1 **Lubudi** (riv.), Zaire
110/B4 **Lubuklinggau**, Indo.
110/B3 **Lubuksikaping**, Indo.
131/B1 **Lubumbashi**, Zaire
126/E2 **Lubunda**, Zaire
131/C1 **Lubwe**, Zam.
126/C2 **Lucala**, Ang.
60/D3 **Lucan**, Ire.
109/D1 **Luc An Chau**, Viet.
151/K3 **Lucania** (mtn.), Yk,Can
126/D2 **Lucapa**, Ang.
78/D5 **Lucca**, It.
78/D5 **Lucca** (prov.), It.
56/D2 **Luce** (bay), Sc,UK
163/F4 **Lucedale**, Ms,US
141/B2 **Lucélia**, Braz.
112/C2 **Lucena**, Phil.
74/C4 **Lucena**, Sp.
65/K4 **Lučenec**, Slvk.
164/C1 **Lucerne** (lake),Ca,US
77/E3 **Lucerne** (Luzern), Swi.
77/E3 **Lucerne** (Vierwaldstättensee) (lake), Swi.
103/C3 **Lucheng**, China
131/D2 **Lucheringo** (riv.), Moz.
64/F2 **Lüchow**, Ger.
107/K3 **Luchuan**, China
65/G2 **Luckenwalde**, Ger.
106/D2 **Lucknow**, India
156/G3 **Lucky Lake**, Sk,Can
77/E4 **Lucomagno, Passo del** (pass), It., Swi.
149/H1 **Lucrecia** (cape), Cuba
126/D3 **Lucusse**, Ang.
83/H4 **Luda Kamchiya** (riv.), Bul.
67/E6 **Lüdenscheid**, Ger.
132/A2 **Lüderitz**, Namb.
59/E4 **Ludgershall**, Eng,UK
108/C2 **Ludhiāna**, India
107/H2 **Ludian**, China
104/D2 **Luding**, China
67/E5 **Ludinghausen**, Ger.
160/C3 **Ludington**, Mi,US
58/D2 **Ludlow**, Eng,UK
168/B1 **Ludlow**, Ma,US
83/H4 **Ludogorie** (reg.), Bul.
83/G2 **Luduş**, Rom.
62/F1 **Ludvika**, Swe.
71/E4 **Ludwigs** (can.), Ger.
70/C5 **Ludwigsburg**, Ger.
65/G2 **Ludwigsfelde**, Ger.
70/B4 **Ludwigshafen**, Ger.
64/F2 **Ludwigslust**, Ger.
126/D2 **Luebo**, Zaire
130/A3 **Luemba**, Zaire
126/C3 **Luena**, Ang.
131/A2 **Luena Flats** (swamp), Zam.
131/D3 **Luenha** (riv.), Moz.
105/G4 **Lufeng**, China
162/E4 **Lufkin**, Tx,US
131/B2 **Lufupa** (riv.), Zam.
84/F4 **Luga**, Rus.
63/N2 **Luga** (bay), Rus.
63/N2 **Luga** (riv.), Rus.
130/A2 **Luga**, Zaire
77/E6 **Lugano** (lake), It., Swi.
77/E6 **Lugano**, Swi.
86/F2 **Lugansk**, Ukr.
86/F2 **Lugansk Obl.**, Ukr.
130/C3 **Lugards** (falls), Kenya
67/G5 **Lügde**, Ger.
126/G3 **Lugenda** (riv.), Moz.
58/D2 **Lugg** (riv.), Eng,UK
60/D4 **Lugnaquillia** (mtn.), Ire.
79/E4 **Lugo**, It.
74/B1 **Lugo**, Sp.
130/B2 **Lugogo** (riv.), Ugan.
82/E3 **Lugoj**, Rom.
130/C4 **Lugunga** (peak), Tanz.
130/C5 **Luguruka**, Tanz.
103/D4 **Luhe**, China
67/H2 **Lühe** (riv.), Ger.
71/F3 **Lühe** (riv.), Ger.
104/C3 **Luhit** (riv.), India
130/C4 **Luhombero** (peak), Tanz.
130/B3 **Luhumbo**, Tanz.
104/D2 **Luhuo**, China
131/A2 **Lui** (riv.), Zam.
131/D2 **Luia** (riv.), Moz.
131/D3 **Luia** (riv.), Moz.
126/D4 **Luiana**, Ang.
54/B1 **Luichart, Loch** (lake), Sc,UK
77/E6 **Luino**, It.
140/B1 **Luís Correia**, Braz.
131/B1 **Luishia**, Zaire
113/X **Luitpold** (coast), Ant.
143/S12 **Luján**, Arg.
103/D5 **Lujiang**, China
131/B2 **Lukanga** (swamp), Zam.
82/D3 **Lukavac**, Bosn.
116/C3 **Luke** (peak), Austl.
126/C1 **Lukenie** (riv.), Zaire
83/G4 **Lukovit**, Bul.
65/M3 **Łuków**, Pol.
130/A4 **Lukuga** (riv.), Zaire
131/A2 **Lukulu**, Zam.
130/A5 **Lukulu** (riv.), Zam.
120/E4 **Lukunor** (atoll), Micr.
131/C2 **Lukusashi** (riv.), Zam.
131/D2 **Lukusuzi Nat'l Park**, Zam.
130/A5 **Lukwesa**, Zam.
61/G2 **Luleå**, Swe.
61/G2 **Luleälv** (riv.), Swe.
83/H5 **Lüleburgaz**, Turk.
107/H2 **Luliang**, China
130/A4 **Lulimba**, Zaire
103/B4 **Luling Guan** (pass), China
103/D3 **Lulong**, China
122/E4 **Lulonga** (riv.), Zaire
120/G5 **Lulua**, Tuv.
131/A1 **Lulua** (riv.), Zaire
126/D3 **Lumai**, Ang.
102/D5 **Lumajamgdong** (lake), China
130/A5 **Lumangwe** (falls), Zam.
131/A2 **Lumbala N'guimbo**, Ang.
131/A3 **Lumbe** (riv.), Zam.
163/J3 **Lumberton**, NC,US
162/E4 **Lumberton**, Tx,US
126/H4 **Lumbo**, Moz.
156/D3 **Lumby**, BC,Can
104/B3 **Lumding**, India
141/J6 **Luminárias**, Braz.
69/E2 **Lummen**, Belg.
109/D3 **Lumphat**, Camb.
157/G3 **Lumsden**, Sk,Can
115/Q12 **Lumsden**, NZ
54/D2 **Lumsden**, Sc,UK
112/C1 **Luna**, Phil.
164/C2 **Luna** (mtn.), Ca,US
126/D3 **Lunache**, Ang.
104/D3 **Lunan** (mts.), China
54/C4 **Luncarty**, Sc,UK
62/E4 **Lund**, Swe.
158/D3 **Lund**, Nv,US
131/D2 **Lundazi**, Zam.
131/C4 **Lundi** (riv.), Zim.
131/D1 **Lundu**, Zam.
58/B4 **Lundy** (isl.), Eng,UK
67/F2 **Lune** (riv.), Ger.
57/F2 **Lune** (riv.), Eng,UK
57/F3 **Lune** (riv.), Eng,UK
67/H2 **Lüneburg**, Ger.
67/G2 **Lüneburger Heide** (reg.), Ger.
72/F5 **Lunel**, Fr.
67/E5 **Lünen**, Ger.
161/H2 **Lunenburg**, NS,Can
60/B2 **Lung** (riv.), Ire.
131/B2 **Lunga** (riv.), Zam.
130/C4 **Lunga-Lunga**, Kenya
104/B4 **Lunglei**, India
126/D3 **Lungue-Bungo** (riv.), Ang.
106/B3 **Luni** (riv.), India
102/D3 **Luntai**, China
131/D2 **Lunzu**, Malw.
103/B3 **Luo** (riv.), China
103/B4 **Luo** (riv.), China
97/L2 **Luobei**, China
105/H3 **Luobo** (mtn.), China
105/F3 **Luocheng**, China
104/E3 **Luodian**, China
105/F4 **Luoding**, China
105/G4 **Luofu** (peak), China
105/H3 **Luohan** (mtn.), China
103/C4 **Luohe**, China
103/D4 **Luoma** (lake), China
109/C1 **Luong** (mts.), Viet.
130/A5 **Luongo** (riv.), Zam.
103/B4 **Luoning**, China
104/E3 **Luoping**, China
105/F3 **Luoqing** (riv.), China
103/C4 **Luoshan**, China
105/F2 **Luoshuikan**, China
103/C5 **Luotian**, China
103/C4 **Luoyang**, China
103/B3 **Luoyukou**, China
126/B1 **Luozi**, Zaire
130/B5 **Lupa Market**, Tanz.
131/B3 **Lupane**, Zim.
104/E3 **Lupanshui**, China
83/F3 **Lupeni**, Rom.
130/C5 **Lupiro**, Tanz.
112/D4 **Lupon**, Phil.
96/E5 **Luqu**, China
104/D3 **Luquan**, China
95/J2 **Lūrah** (riv.), Afg.
160/E4 **Luray**, Va,US
76/C2 **Lure**, Fr.
56/B3 **Lurgan**, NI,UK
144/B4 **Lurín**, Peru
126/H3 **Lúrio**, Moz.
126/G3 **Lúrio** (riv.), Moz.
130/A3 **Lusahunga**, Tanz.
131/C2 **Lusaka** (cap.), Zam.
131/C2 **Lusaka** (prov.), Zam.
126/E1 **Lusamba**, Zaire
126/D1 **Lusambo**, Zaire
131/C2 **Lusemfwa** (riv.), Zam.
71/G5 **Lusen** (peak), Ger.
130/A5 **Lusenga Nat'l Park**, Zam.
103/C4 **Lushan**, China
103/D3 **Lu Shan** (mtn.), China
103/C5 **Lu Shan** (peak), China
103/B4 **Lushi**, China
81/F2 **Lushnje**, Alb.
130/C4 **Lushoto**, Tanz.
104/C3 **Lushui**, China
157/G5 **Lusk**, Wy,US
54/B4 **Luss**, Sc,UK
77/F3 **Lustenau**, Aus.
125/J7 **Lutanga** (riv.), Zaire
166/B5 **Lutherville**, Md,US
131/A4 **Luthle**, Bots.
66/D1 **Lütjehorn** (isl.), Ger.
59/F3 **Luton**, Eng,UK
76/C5 **Lutry**, Swi.
86/C2 **Lutsk**, Ukr.
67/F5 **Lutter** (riv.), Ger.
77/F3 **Lutz** (riv.), Aus.
113/C **Lützow-Holm** (bay), Ant.
125/P7 **Luuq**, Som.
157/J5 **Luverne**, Mn,US
130/A5 **Luvua** (riv.), Zaire
130/C5 **Luwegu** (riv.), Tanz.
131/C2 **Luwembe**, Zam.
130/B2 **Luwero**, Ugan.
130/A5 **Luwingu**, Zam.
69/E4 **Luxembourg**
69/E4 **Luxembourg** (prov.), Belg.
69/F4 **Luxembourg** (cap.), Lux.
69/F4 **Luxembourg** (dist.), Lux.
76/C2 **Luxeuil-les-Bains**, Fr.
104/C3 **Luxi**, China
104/D3 **Luxi**, China
107/J2 **Lu Xian**, China
127/C3 **Luxor** (Al Uqşur), Egypt
72/C5 **Luy** (riv.), Fr.
103/B3 **Luya Shan** (mtn.), China
103/C4 **Luyi**, China
141/C1 **Luz**, Braz.
85/L3 **Luza** (riv.), Rus.
76/E3 **Luzern** (canton), Swi.
166/B1 **Luzerne** (co.), Pa,US
77/E3 **Luzern** (Lucerne), Swi.
107/J3 **Luzhai**, China
104/E3 **Luzhi**, China
104/D3 **Lüzhi** (riv.), China
104/E2 **Luzhou**, China

202

Luziâ – Manga

140/A5 Luziânia, Braz.
140/B1 Luzilândia, Braz.
130/B2 Luzinga, Ugan.
71/H4 Lužnice (riv.), Czh.
120/B2 Luzon (str.)
112/C1 Luzon (isl.), Phil.
86/C2 L'viv, Ukr.
86/B2 L'viv Obl., Ukr.
130/B2 Lwala (peak), Ugan.
130/A5 Lwena Mission, Zam.
109/C1 Lwi (riv.), Burma
130/A3 Lyantonde, Ugan.
85/P3 Lyapin (riv.), Rus.
83/G4 Lyaskovets, Bul.
61/F2 Lycksele, Swe.
166/A1 Lycoming (co.), Pa,US
59/G5 Lydd, Eng,UK
113/Y Lyddan (isl.), Ant.
133/E2 Lydenburg, SAfr.
58/D3 Lydney, Eng,UK
117/F2 Lyell Brown (peak), Austl.
156/F5 Lyman, Wy,US
58/C5 Lyme (bay), Eng,UK
58/D5 Lyme Regis, Eng,UK
59/E5 Lymington, Eng,UK
57/F5 Lymm, Eng,UK
65/L1 Lyna (riv.), Pol.
56/D5 Lynas (pt.), Wal,UK
167/E2 Lynbrook, NY,US
160/E4 Lynchburg, Va,US
163/H3 Lynches (riv.), SC,US
118/A2 Lynd (riv.), Austl.
59/E5 Lyndhurst, Eng,UK
167/D2 Lyndhurst, NJ,US
168/F4 Lyndhurst, Oh,US
168/H6 Lyndora, Pa,US
57/F1 Lyne (riv.), Eng,UK
55/N13 Lyness, Sc,UK
63/T9 Lyngby-Tårbæk, Den.
62/B2 Lyngdal, Nor.
63/T9 Lynge, Den.
61/G1 Lyngen (fjord), Nor.
161/G3 Lynn, Ma,US
163/G4 Lynn Haven, Fl,US
165/C2 Lynnwood, Wa,US
58/C4 Lynton, Eng,UK
164/B3 Lynwood, Ca,US
152/F2 Lynx (lake), NW,Can
72/F4 Lyon, Fr.
54/B3 Lyon (riv.), Sc,UK
54/B3 Lyon, Loch (lake), Sc,UK
116/C2 Lyons (riv.), Austl.
159/H3 Lyons, Ks,US
58/C4 Lype (hill), Eng,UK
120/E5 Lyra (reef), PNG
68/B2 Lys (riv.), Fr.
78/A1 Lys (riv.), It.
65/K4 Lysá (peak), Czh.
62/D2 Lysaker, Nor.
71/H2 Lysá nad Labem, Czh.
84/E5 Lysaya, Gora (hill), Bela.
62/D2 Lysekil, Swe.
65/L3 Lysica (peak), Pol.
71/F2 Lysina (peak), Czh.
68/C2 Lys-lez-Lannoy, Fr.
76/D3 Lyss, Swi.
62/D3 Lystrup, Den.
85/N4 Lys'va, Rus.
58/D5 Lytchett Matravers, Eng,UK
57/E4 Lytham Saint Anne's, Eng,UK
85/X9 Lytkarino, Rus.
164/C2 Lytle (cr.), Ca,US
156/C3 Lytton, BC,Can
86/F1 Lyubertsy, Rus.
83/H5 Lyubimets, Bul.
86/E2 Lyubotin, Ukr.
86/E1 Lyudinovo, Rus.
58/C3 Lywd (riv.), Wal,UK

M

109/C1 Ma (riv.), Laos, Viet.
91/D3 Ma'alot, Isr.
91/D4 Ma'ān, Jor.
91/E5 Ma'ān (gov.), Jor.
84/F2 Maanselkä (mts.), Fin.
103/D5 Ma'anshan, China
66/C6 Maarheeze, Neth.
91/E2 Ma'arrat an Nu'mān, Syria
66/C4 Maarssen, Neth.
64/D3 Maas (riv.), Eur.
66/C6 Maasbracht, Neth.
66/D6 Maasbree, Neth.
69/E1 Maaseik, Belg.
112/D3 Maasin, Phil.
69/E2 Maasmechelen, Belg.
66/B5 Maassluis, Neth.
131/C4 Maasstroom, SAfr.
69/E2 Maastricht, Neth.
131/D4 Maave, Moz.
91/G6 Ma'ayan Harod Nat'l Park, Isr.
131/A3 Mababe (depr.), Bots.
112/D3 Mabaho (mtn.), Phil.
112/C2 Mabalacat, Phil.
131/D4 Mabalane, Moz.
100/B3 Mabechi (riv.), Japan
107/H2 Mabian, China
112/C3 Mabinay, Phil.
112/D3 Mabini, Phil.
57/J5 Mablethorpe, Eng,UK
131/D4 Mabote, Moz.
132/C2 Mabuasehube Game Rsv., Bots.
130/B3 Mabuki, Tanz.
131/B5 Mabuli, Bots.
142/B5 Macá (peak), Chile
141/D2 Macaé, Braz.
140/D2 Macaíba, Braz.
131/D2 Macaloge, Moz.
137/H3 Macapá, Braz.
144/B2 Macará, Ecu.
140/B4 Macarani, Braz.
138/B5 Macas, Ecu.
140/C2 Macau, Braz.
105/G4 Macau (cap.), Macau
105/G4 Macau (dpcy.), Port.
140/B4 Macaúbas, Braz.
120/H7 Macauley (isl.), NZ
138/C4 Macaya (riv.), Col.
149/H2 Macaya, Pic de (peak), Haiti
163/H4 Macclenny, Fl,US
57/F5 Macclesfield, Eng,UK
57/F5 Macclesfield (can.), Eng,UK
132/D3 Macdhui (peak), SAfr.
163/H5 MacDill A.F.B., Fl,US
117/F2 MacDonald (lake), Austl.
117/G2 Macdonnell (ranges), Austl.
54/D1 Macduff, Sc,UK
81/G2 Macedonia
81/G2 Macedonia (reg.), Gre., Macd.
168/F5 Macedonia, Oh,US
140/D3 Maceió, Braz.
140/C2 Maceió (pt.), Braz.
80/C1 Macerata, It.
79/G6 Macerata (prov.), It.
113/E Macey (peak), Ant.
117/H5 Macfarlane (lake), Austl.
60/A6 Macgillycuddy's Reeks (mts.), Ire.
140/B5 Machacalis, Braz.
136/E7 Machacamarca, Bol.
132/D3 Machache (peak), Les.
138/B5 Machachi, Ecu.
141/H6 Machado, Braz.
149/H4 Machado, Ciénaga de (lake), Col.
131/D4 Machaíla, Moz.
130/C3 Machakos, Kenya
144/B1 Machala, Ecu.
138/A5 Machalilla Nat'l Park, Ecu.
131/D4 Machanga, Moz.
148/D2 Machaquilá (riv.), Guat.
56/D2 Machars, The (pen.), Sc,UK
117/H3 Machattie (lake), Austl.
131/D4 Machaze, Moz.
138/C2 Machedo (lake), Col.
131/C3 Macheke, Zim.
131/C4 Machemma (ruins), SAfr.
58/C3 Machen, Wal,UK
103/C5 Macheng, China
161/H2 Machias, Me,US
74/D1 Machichaco (cape), Sp.
75/V15 Machico, Madr.,Port.
99/H7 Machida, Japan
131/B3 Machili (riv.), Zam.
106/D4 Machilipatnam, India
138/C2 Machiques, Ven.
159/F4 Macho (dry riv.), NM,US
131/B3 Machobani, Zam.
71/H1 Machovo Jezero (res.), Czh.
144/C4 Machu Picchu (ruins), Peru
136/F6 Machupo (riv.), Bol.
58/C1 Machynlleth, Wal,UK
131/D5 Macia, Moz.
83/J3 Măcin, Rom.
128/D3 Macina (reg.), Mali
119/D1 Macintyre (riv.), Austl.
158/E3 Mack, Co,US
118/C3 Mackay, Austl.
117/F2 Mackay (lake), Austl.
113/E MacKenzie (bay), Ant.
118/C3 Mackenzie (riv.), Austl.
156/C2 Mackenzie, BC,Can
151/N2 Mackenzie (riv.), NW,Can
153/C2 Mackenzie (bay), NW, Yk,Can
152/C2 Mackenzie (mts.), NW, Yk,Can
153/R7 Mackenzie King (isl.), NW,Can
160/C2 Mackinac Island, Mi,US
163/F1 Mackinaw (riv.), Il,US
160/C2 Mackinaw City, Mi,US
130/C3 Mackinnon Road, Kenya
156/F2 Macklin, Sk,Can
118/F7 Macleay (isl.), Austl.
116/B3 Macleod (lake), Austl.
151/L3 Macmillan (riv.), Yk,Can
165/G6 Macomb (co.), Mi,US
80/A2 Macomer, It.
76/A5 Mâcon, Fr.
159/K4 Macon (bayou), Ar, La,US
163/H3 Macon, Ga,US
165/E7 Macon (cr.), Mi,US
159/J3 Macon, Mo,US
130/C5 Macondes (plat.), Moz.
131/A2 Macondo, Ang.
131/A2 Macondo (riv.), Ang.
165/E7 Macon, North Branch (cr.), Mi,US
56/B1 Macosquin, NI,UK
131/D4 Macovane (pt.), Moz.
119/C4 Macquarie (har.), Austl.
51/S8 Macquarie (isl.), Austl.
119/C1 Macquarie (riv.), Austl.
119/C4 Macquarie (riv.), Austl.
115/G8 Macquarie Harbour (bay), Austl.
113/D Mac-Robertson Land (reg.), Ant.
136/F5 Macuim (riv.), Braz.
138/D1 Macuira Nat'l Park, Col.
144/B1 Macuma (riv.), Ecu.
117/H3 Macumba (riv.), Austl.
147/G5 Macuspana, Mex.
146/C3 Macuzari (res.), Mex.
156/C5 Mad (riv.), Ca,US
91/D4 Ma'dabā, Jor.
133/H8 Madagascar
124/H3 Madama, Niger
83/G5 Madan, Bul.
106/C5 Madanapalle, India
120/D5 Madang, PNG
124/H1 Madanīyīn, Tun.
129/G3 Madaoua, Niger
106/F3 Mādārīpur, Bang.
160/E2 Madawaska (riv.), On,Can
161/G2 Madawaska, Me,US
149/G4 Madden (dam), Pan.
136/F5 Madeira (riv.), Braz.
75/V15 Madeira (isl.), Madr., Port.
75/U14 Madeira (aut. reg.), Port.
77/G3 Mädelegabel (peak), Ger., Aus.
157/L4 Madelin (isl.), Wi,US
92/D2 Maden, Turk.
146/C2 Madera, Mex.
149/E4 Madera (vol.), Nic.
146/E2 Madera (mtn.), Tx,US
106/E2 Madhipura, India
106/C3 Madhya Pradesh (state), India
130/B3 Madiany, Kenya
130/B5 Madibura, Tanz.
136/E6 Madidi (riv.), Bol.
159/H4 Madill, Ok,US
126/B1 Madingo-Kayes, Congo
130/B2 Madi Opei, Ugan.
163/G3 Madison, Al,US
163/H4 Madison, Fl,US
160/C4 Madison, In,US
163/F3 Madison, Ms,US
156/F4 Madison (riv.), Mt,US
159/H2 Madison, Ne,US
166/D2 Madison, NJ,US
157/J4 Madison, SD,US
160/B3 Madison (cap.), Wi,US
160/D4 Madison, WV,US
165/F6 Madison Heights, Mi,US
160/C4 Madisonville, Ky,US
162/E4 Madisonville, Tx,US
110/D5 Madiun, Indo.
130/C2 Mado Gashi, Kenya
96/D5 Madoi, China
76/C1 Madon (riv.), Fr.
80/C4 Madonie Nebrodi (mts.), It.
77/G5 Madonna di Campiglio, It.
95/G5 Madrakah, Ra's al (pt.), Oman
106/D5 Madras, India
156/C4 Madras, Or,US
147/F3 Madre (bay), Mex.
112/C1 Madre (mts.), Phil.
162/D5 Madre (lag.), Tx,US
141/J6 Madre de Deus de Minas, Braz.
134/C4 Madre de Dios (riv.), Bol., Peru
143/J7 Madre de Dios (isl.), Chile
147/E5 Madre del Sur, Sierra (mts.), Mex.
146/C2 Madre Occidental, Sierra (mts.), Mex.
72/E5 Madrès (mtn.), Fr.
148/C3 Madre, Sierra (mts.), Mex.
112/C1 Madre, Sierra (mts.), Phil.
138/C3 Madrid, Col.
74/C2 Madrid (aut. comm.), Sp.
74/D2 Madrid (cap.), Sp.
74/D3 Madridejos, Sp.
75/N9 Madrid (inset) (cap.), Sp.
77/F4 Madrisahorn (peak), Swi.
106/D4 Madugula, India
130/B3 Madukani, Tanz.
108/F3 Madukkarai, India
110/D5 Madura (Isl.), Indo.
108/G4 Madurai, India
99/F2 Maebashi, Japan
109/C2 Mae Charim, Thai.
109/B2 Mae Ping Nat'l Park, Thai.
58/C3 Maesteg, Wal,UK
149/G2 Maestra, Sierra (range), Cuba
109/B2 Mae Tho (peak), Thai.
120/F6 Maewo (isl.), Van.
109/B2 Mae Ya (mtn.), Thai.
130/C5 Mafia (chan.), Tanz.
130/C4 Mafia (isl.), Tanz.
132/D2 Mafikeng, SAfr.
128/C4 Mafou (riv.), Gui.
141/B3 Mafra, Braz.
74/A3 Mafra, Port.
131/C3 Mafungabusi (plat.), Zim.
89/R4 Magadan, Rus.
130/C3 Magadi, Kenya
132/P12 Magalies Berg (range), SAfr.
112/C2 Magallanes, Phil.
143/K8 Magallanes (Magellan) (str.), Arg., Chile
143/K8 Magallanes y Antártica Chilena (reg.), Chile
138/C2 Magangué, Col.
112/D4 Maganoy, Phil.
129/H3 Magaria, Niger
112/C1 Magat (riv.), Phil.
159/J4 Magazine (peak), Ar,US
97/K1 Magdagachi, Rus.
161/J2 Magdalen (isls.), Qu,Can
143/T12 Magdalena, Arg.
136/F6 Magdalena, Bol.
138/C2 Magdalena (dept.), Col.
138/C3 Magdalena (riv.), Col.
146/C2 Magdalena, Mex.
111/E3 Magdalena, Gunung (peak), Malay.
64/F2 Magdeburg, Ger.
64/F2 Magdeburger Börde (plain), Ger.
115/J3 Magdelaine (cays), Austl.
141/K7 Magé, Braz.
163/F4 Magee, Ms,US
56/C2 Magee, Island (pen.), NI,UK
110/C5 Magelang, Indo.
143/K8 Magellan (Magallanes) (str.), Arg., Chile
116/C5 Magenta (lake), Austl.
78/B2 Magenta, It.
61/H1 Magerøya (isl.), Nor.
77/E5 Maggia (riv.), Swi.
79/E6 Maggio, Monte (peak), It.
78/C3 Maggiorasca, Monte (peak), It.
77/E6 Maggiore (lake), It., Swi.
79/E5 Maggiore, Monte (peak), It.
127/B2 Maghāghah, Egypt
60/B4 Maghera (mtn.), Ire.
56/B2 Maghera, NI,UK
56/B2 Magherafelt, NI,UK
56/B2 Magherafelt (dist.), NI,UK
123/W18 Maghīla (peak), Tun.
123/P13 Maghnia, Alg.
57/F4 Maghull, Eng,UK
56/B1 Magilligan, NI,UK
56/B1 Magilligan (pt.), NI,UK
82/D3 Maglaj, Bosn.
82/D4 Maglić (peak), Yugo.
81/F2 Maglie, It.
160/D2 Magnetawan (riv.), On,Can
118/B2 Magnetic (passg.), Austl.
118/B2 Magnetic I. Nat'l Park, Austl.
85/N5 Magnitogorsk, Rus.
162/E3 Magnolia, Ar,US
166/D4 Magnolia-Elwood, NJ,US
53/S10 Magny-les-Hameaux, Fr.
131/C2 Mágoè, Moz.
161/F2 Magog, Qu,Can
125/N6 Mago Nat'l Park, Eth.
58/D3 Magor, Wal,UK
131/B3 Magoye, Zam.
161/H1 Magpie (lake), Qu,Can
161/H1 Magpie (riv.), Qu,Can
161/H1 Magpie Ouest (riv.), Qu,Can
78/C4 Magra (riv.), It.
112/D3 Magsaysay, Phil.
109/D1 Maguan, China
131/D5 Magude, Moz.
125/L7 Maguerite (peak), Zaire
104/B4 Magwe, Burma
104/B5 Magwe (div.), Burma
93/F2 Mahābād, Iran
106/B4 Mahād, India
121/X15 Mahaena, FrPol.
130/A2 Mahagi, Zaire
130/A2 Mahagi-Port, Zaire
139/G3 Mahaica, Guy.
139/G3 Mahaica-Berbice (reg.), Guy.
133/H6 Mahajamba (bay), Madg.
133/H7 Mahajamba (riv.), Madg.
133/H6 Mahajanga (prov.), Madg.
133/H7 Mahajilo (riv.), Madg.
111/E3 Mahakam (riv.), Indo.
131/B4 Mahalapye, Bots.
93/G3 Mahallāt, Iran
93/J4 Māhān, Iran
106/D3 Mahānadī (riv.), India
128/D4 Mahandiabani (riv.), IvC.
130/B5 Mahanje, Tanz.
166/B2 Mahanoy (cr.), Pa,US
166/B2 Mahantango (cr.), Pa,US
166/B2 Mahantango Mtn. (ridge), Pa,US
106/C2 Mahārajpur, India
106/B4 Mahārāshtra (state), India
106/D3 Mahāsamund, India
109/C2 Maha Sarakham, Thai.
133/H7 Mahavavy (riv.), Madg.
108/H4 Mahaweli (riv.), SrL.
106/C4 Mahbubnagar, India
108/E3 Mahe, India
123/H5 Mahé (isl.), Sey.
133/S15 Mahébourg, Mrts.
130/C5 Mahenge, Tanz.
115/S10 Mahia (pen.), NZ
104/B4 Mahlaing, Burma
123/V18 Mahmel (peak), Alg.
106/C2 Mahoba, India
60/C5 Mahon (riv.), Ire.
75/H3 Mahón, Sp.
168/G6 Mahoning (co.), Oh,US
168/G5 Mahoning (riv.), Oh, Pa,US
131/C3 Mahusekwa, Zim.
130/C5 Mahuta, Tanz.
106/B3 Mahuva, India
167/D1 Mahwah, NJ,US
118/E6 Maiala Nat'l Park, Austl.
120/G4 Maiana (atoll), Kiri.
121/W15 Maiao (isl.), FrPol.
138/C2 Maicao, Col.
139/H5 Maicuru (riv.), Braz.
166/C2 Maiden (cr.), Pa,US
59/F3 Maidenhead, Eng,UK
58/D5 Maiden Newton, Eng,UK
54/B6 Maidens, Sc,UK
165/G7 Maidstone, On,Can
156/F2 Maidstone, Sk,Can
59/G4 Maidstone, Eng,UK
124/H5 Maiduguri, Nga.
130/A2 Maie, Zaire
68/B4 Maignelay-Montigny, Fr.
60/B4 Maigue (riv.), Ire.
106/D3 Maihar, India
98/E3 Maihara, Japan
125/L8 Maiko Nat'l Park, Zaire
154/V13 Maili, Hi,US
95/K3 Mailsi, Pak.
70/B2 Main (riv.), Ger.
56/B2 Main (riv.), NI,UK
114/G6 Main Barrier (range), Austl.
53/U11 Maincy, Fr.
126/C1 Mai-Ndombe (lake), Zaire
70/E4 Main-Donau (can.), Ger.
161/G3 Maine (gulf), Can., US
57/C2 Maine (hills), Fr.
60/A5 Maine (riv.), Ire.
161/G2 Maine (state), US
124/H5 Maïné-Soroa, Niger
70/B2 Mainhausen, Ger.
112/D3 Mainit, Phil.
55/N13 Mainland (isl.), Sc,UK
55/P12 Mainland (isl.), Sc,UK
104/B2 Mainling, China
118/C5 Main Range Nat'l Park, Austl.
70/B3 Mainz, Ger.
122/K10 Maio (isl.), CpV.
142/C2 Maipo (vol.), Arg., Chile
142/Q9 Maipo (riv.), Chile
142/F3 Maipú, Arg.
142/C2 Maipú, Chile
139/E2 Maiquetía, Ven.
78/A3 Maira (riv.), It.
140/B3 Mairi, Braz.
141/G8 Mairiporã, Braz.
70/E6 Maisach, Ger.
130/B3 Maisome (isl.), Tanz.
53/T10 Maisons-Alfort, Fr.
53/S10 Maisons-Laffitte, Fr.
131/B4 Maitengwe, Bots.
119/D2 Maitland, Austl.
160/D3 Maitland (riv.), On,Can
112/D4 Maitum, Phil.
149/F3 Maiz Grande (isl.), Nic.
102/F6 Maizhokunggar, China
69/F5 Maizières-lès-Metz, Fr.
149/F3 Maiz Pequeña (isl.), Nic.
98/D3 Maizuru, Japan
75/N9 Majadahonda, Sp.
81/G2 Maja e Zezë (peak), Alb.
123/W17 Majardah (mts.), Alg., Tun.
123/W17 Majardah (riv.), Tun.
82/E3 Majdanpek, Yugo.
124/J2 Majdūl, Libya
111/E4 Majene, Indo.
125/N6 Majī, Eth.
103/D3 Maji (riv.), China
130/B3 Maji Moto, Tanz.
77/F5 Majolapass (pass), Swi.
75/G3 Majorca (Mallorca) (isl.), Sp.
120/G4 Majuro (atoll), Mrsh.
126/B1 Makabana, Congo
154/V13 Makaha, Hi,US
154/V13 Makakilo City, Hi,US
131/A4 Makalamabedi, Bots.
130/B5 Makampi, Tanz.
154/W13 Makapuu (pt.), Hi,US
97/N2 Makarov, Rus.
82/C4 Makarska, Cro.
130/A5 Makasa, Zam.
110/E4 Makassar (str.), Indo.
121/L6 Makatea (isl.), FrPol.
112/F6 Makati, Phil.
133/H8 Makay (massif), Madg.
121/L6 Makemo (atoll), FrPol.
128/B4 Makeni, SLeo.
86/F2 Makeyevka, Ukr.
131/B4 Makgadikgadi Pans (salt pans), Bots.
131/B4 Makgadikgadi Pans Game Rsv., Bots.
87/H4 Makhachkala, Rus.
108/B2 Makhdūmpur, Pak.
111/G3 Makian (isl.), Indo.
120/G4 Makin (atoll), Kiri.
102/B1 Makinsk, Kaz.
94/C4 Makkah (Mecca), SAr.
82/E2 Makó, Hun.
130/A2 Makofi, Zaire
124/H7 Makokou, Gabon
130/B5 Makonde, Tanz.
130/C5 Makonde (plat.), Tanz.
130/B5 Makongolosi, Tanz.
130/A3 Makota, Ugan.
65/L2 Maków Mazowiecki, Pol.
95/G4 Makran (coast), Iran, Pak.
95/H3 Makran (reg.), Iran, Pak.
95/K3 Makrāna, India
93/F2 Mākū, Iran
130/B5 Makumbako, Tanz.
131/B3 Makunka, Zam.
98/B5 Makurazaki, Japan
151/E5 Makushin (vol.), Ak,US
130/B2 Makutano, Kenya
130/C3 Makuyuni, Tanz.
131/C3 Makwiro, Zim.
148/E4 Mala (pt.), CR
149/G5 Mala (pt.), Pan.
144/B4 Mala, Peru
112/D4 Malabang, Phil.
106/B5 Malabar (coast), India
108/E3 Malabar Coast (reg.), India
123/M13 Malabata (pt.), Mor.
79/E3 Malabergo, It.
124/G7 Malabo (cap.), EqG.
112/E6 Malabon, Phil.
141/D1 Malacacheta, Braz.
112/F6 Malacanang Palace, Phil.
109/B5 Malacca (str.), Malay., Thai.
65/J4 Malacky, Slvk.
156/E5 Malad City, Id,US
74/C4 Málaga, Sp.
164/F8 Malaga (cove), Ca,US
130/A4 Malagarasi, Tanz.
130/A4 Malagarasi (riv.), Tanz.
74/D3 Malagón, Sp.
149/G1 Malagueta (bay), Cuba
60/D3 Malahide, Ire.
120/F5 Malaita (isl.), Sol.
125/M6 Malakāl, Sudan
106/D4 Malakangiri, India
108/B1 Malakwāl, Pak.
138/C2 Malambo, Col.
110/D5 Malang, Indo.
126/C2 Malange, Ang.
112/D4 Malapatan, Phil.
108/F3 Malappuram, India
63/R7 Mälaren (lake), Swe.
142/C2 Malargüe, Arg.
160/E1 Malartic, Qu,Can
111/E5 Malasoro (pt.), Indo.
92/D2 Malatya, Turk.
92/D2 Malatya (prov.), Turk.
108/C2 Malaut, India
112/B4 Malawali (isl.), Malay.
131/D2 Malawi
131/D2 Malawi (Nyasa) (lake), Afr.
109/B5 Malay (pen.), Malay.
84/G4 Malaya Vishera, Rus.
112/D3 Malaybalay, Phil.
93/G3 Malāyer, Iran
110/C2 Malaysia
85/L2 Malazemel'skaya (tundra), Rus.
92/E2 Malazgirt, Turk.
161/G2 Malbaie (riv.), Qu,Can
129/G3 Malbaza-Usine, Niger
65/K1 Malbork, Pol.
72/D5 Malcaras, Pic de (peak), Fr.
64/G2 Malchin, Ger.
96/C2 Malchin, Mong.
117/M8 Malcolm (cr.), Austl.
68/C1 Maldegem, Belg.
121/K5 Malden (isl.), Kiri.
168/C1 Malden, Ma,US
160/B4 Malden, Mo,US
106/B6 Maldive (isls.), Mald.
90/G9 Maldives
59/G3 Maldon, Eng,UK
143/G2 Maldonado, Uru.
143/G2 Maldonado (dept.), Uru.
90/G9 Male (cap.), Mald.
51/N5 Male (isl.), Mald.
81/H4 Maléa, Ákra (cape), Gre.
106/B3 Mālegaon, India
120/F6 Malekula (isl.), Van.
72/D4 Malemort-sur-Corrèze, Fr.
64/F1 Malente, Ger.
108/C2 Māler Kotla, India
130/C2 Malgis (riv.), Kenya
87/H4 Malgobek, Rus.
75/G2 Malgrat de Mar, Sp.
125/L4 Malha Wells, Sudan
156/D5 Malheur (lake), Or,US
156/D5 Malheur (riv.), Or,US
133/S14 Malheureux (cape), Mrts.
128/E2 Mali
109/B3 Mali (isl.), Burma
96/F4 Malian (riv.), China
125/L4 Malik (wadi), Sudan
86/D2 Malin, Ukr.
112/B5 Malinau, Indo.
112/C3 Malindang (mtn.), Phil.
130/D3 Malindi, Kenya
68/D1 Malines (Mechelen), Belg.
103/C3 Maling Guan (pass), China
55/H9 Malin Head (pt.), Ire.
130/C5 Malinyi, Tanz.
133/H8 Malio (riv.), Madg.
109/D1 Malipo, China
95/J4 Malīr Cantonment, Pak.
112/D4 Malita, Phil.
125/P7 Malka Mari Nat'l Park, Kenya
83/H5 Malkara, Turk.
55/J8 Mallaig, Sc,UK
129/H3 Mallammaduri, Nga.
123/W17 Mallāq, Wādī (riv.), Tun.
63/K1 Mallasvesi (lake), Fin.
127/B3 Mallawī, Egypt
119/B2 Mallee Cliffs Nat'l Park, Austl.
77/F5 Mallero (riv.), It.
71/F5 Mallersdorf-Pfaffenberg, Ger.
142/Q10 Malloa, Chile
75/G3 Mallorca (Majorca) (isl.), Sp.
60/B5 Mallow, Ire.
61/G2 Malmberget, Swe.
69/F3 Malmédy, Belg.
132/B4 Malmesbury, SAfr.
58/D3 Malmesbury, Eng,UK
62/E4 Malmö, Swe.
62/E4 Malmöhus (co.), Swe.
150/D4 Malmok (peak), NAnt.
85/L4 Malmyzh, Rus.
78/B1 Malnate, It.
79/E1 Malo, It.
137/H5 Maloca, Braz.
120/G4 Maloelap (atoll), Mrsh.
112/E6 Malolos, Phil.
131/D2 Malombe (lake), Malw.
78/A2 Malone (riv.), It.
160/F2 Malone, NY,US
104/D3 Malong, China
130/A5 Malonje (peak), Tanz.
65/L3 Małopolska (upland), Pol.
61/C3 Måløy, Nor.
57/F5 Malpas, Eng,UK
136/B3 Malpelo (isl.), Col.
74/A1 Malpica, Sp.
71/H5 Malsch (riv.), Aus.
70/B5 Malsch, Ger.
71/H5 Malše (riv.), Czh.
77/G4 Mals (Malles), It.
80/D5 Malta
140/C2 Malta, Braz.
80/D5 Malta (isl.), Malta
156/G3 Malta, Mt,US
57/G2 Maltby, Eng,UK
57/G5 Maltby, Eng,UK
92/B1 Maltepe, Turk.
161/Q8 Malton, On,Can
57/H3 Malton, Eng,UK
126/C1 Maluku, Zaire
62/E1 Malung, Swe.
112/C4 Maluso, Phil.
106/B4 Malvan, India
75/P10 Malveira, Port.
119/G5 Malvern, Austl.
162/E3 Malvern, Ar,US
167/L9 Malverne, NY,US
58/D2 Malvern (Great Malvern), Eng,UK
143/M8 Malvinas, Islas (Falkland Islands) (dpcy.), UK
87/J2 Malyy Uzen' (riv.), Kaz.
96/D1 Malyy Yenisey (riv.), Rus.
69/F6 Malzéville, Fr.
140/D2 Mamanguape, Braz.
167/E2 Mamaroneck, NY,US
91/C4 Mamarr al Jady (Gidi) (pass), Egypt
91/C4 Mamarr Mitlah (Mitla) (pass), Egypt
131/B3 Mamba, Zam.
112/D3 Mambajao, Phil.
130/B4 Mambali, Tanz.
130/A2 Mambasa, Zaire
111/J4 Mamberamo (riv.), Indo.
124/J6 Mambéré (riv.), CAfr.
92/D2 Mambij, Syria
131/B3 Mambova, Zam.
130/D3 Mambrui, Kenya
112/C2 Mamburao, Phil.
69/F4 Mamer, Lux.
72/D2 Mamers, Fr.
68/B2 Mametz, Fr.
129/F5 Mamfé, Camr.
76/C3 Mamirolle, Fr.
160/C4 Mammoth Cave Nat'l Park, Ky,US
163/F2 Mammoth Spring, Ar,US
136/E6 Mamoré (riv.), Bol.
129/E5 Mampong, Gha.
63/J4 Mamry (lake), Pol.
111/E4 Mamuju, Indo.
126/D5 Mamuno, Bots.
137/G4 Mamuri (riv.), Braz.
130/C4 Mamwera (peak), Tanz.
103/C5 Man (riv.), China
128/D5 Man, IvC.
55/J9 Man (isl.), UK
139/H3 Mana (riv.), FrG.
138/A5 Manabí (prov.), Ecu.
148/D3 Manabique, Punta de (pt.), Hon.
136/F4 Manacapuru, Braz.
58/A6 Manacle (pt.), UK
75/G3 Manacor, Sp.
111/F3 Manado, Indo.
148/E3 Managua (cap.), Nic.
148/E3 Managua (lake), Nic.
133/J8 Manakara, Madg.
166/D3 Manalapan, NJ,US
94/F3 Manama (Al Manāmah) (cap.), Bahr.
108/G4 Mānāmadurai, India
133/H7 Manambaho (riv.), Madg.
133/H7 Manambolo (riv.), Madg.
133/H8 Mananantanana (riv.), Madg.
133/J7 Mananara, Madg.
133/H8 Mananara (riv.), Madg.
133/J7 Mananara (riv.), Madg.
133/J8 Mananjary, Madg.
133/H8 Mananjary (riv.), Madg.
131/C2 Mana Pools Nat'l Park, Zim.
108/G3 Manappārai, India
78/C4 Manara, Punta (pt.), It.
102/E3 Manas, China
102/D2 Manas (lake), China
102/E3 Manas (riv.), China
106/D2 Manāslu (mtn.), Nepal
167/D3 Manasquan (riv.), NJ,US
159/F3 Manassa, Co,US
160/E4 Manassas, Va,US
81/G1 Manastir Dečani, Yugo.
81/G1 Manastir Gračanica, Yugo.
81/G1 Manastir Sopoćani, Yugo.
99/H7 Manatsuru, Japan
139/F5 Manaus, Braz.
91/B1 Manavgat, Turk.
157/H2 Manawan (lake), Sk,Can
112/D4 Manay, Phil.
99/H7 Manazuru-misaki (cape), Japan
56/D3 Man, Calf of (isl.), IM,UK
76/B2 Mance (riv.), Fr.
74/D4 Mancha Real, Sp.
103/C3 Mancheng, China
106/C4 Mancherāl, India
118/E6 Manchester (lake), Austl.
57/F5 Manchester, Eng,UK
168/B2 Manchester, Ct,US
160/D4 Manchester, Ky,US
161/G3 Manchester, NH,US
163/G3 Manchester, Tn,US
101/B2 Manchuria (reg.), China
93/H4 Mand (riv.), Iran
130/B4 Manda, Tanz.
130/B5 Manda, Tanz.
141/B2 Mandaguari, Braz.
62/B2 Mandal, Nor.
111/K4 Mandala (peak), Indo.
104/C4 Mandalay, Burma
109/A1 Mandalay (div.), Burma
104/C4 Mandalay Palace, Burma
89/L5 Mandalgovĭ, Mong.
93/F3 Mandalī, Iraq
112/E6 Mandaluyong, Phil.
157/H4 Mandan, ND,US
125/J6 Manda Nat'l Park, Chad
103/D4 Mandang Shan (mtn.), China
111/F5 Mandasavu (peak), Indo.
112/C3 Mandaue, Phil.
123/G3 Mandeb, BAb el (str.), Afr., Asia
78/C1 Mandello del Lario, It.
125/P7 Mandera, Kenya
130/C4 Mandera, Tanz.
69/F3 Manderscheid, Ger.
76/C3 Mandeure, Fr.
149/G2 Mandeville, Jam.
108/D2 Mandi, India
131/D3 Mandié, Moz.
131/D2 Mandimba, Moz.
111/G4 Mandiola (isl.), Indo.
108/B2 Mandi Sādiqganj, Pak.
130/A4 Mandje, Zaire
106/D3 Mandla, India
62/C4 Mandø (isl.), Den.
81/L6 Mándra, Gre.
133/H9 Mandrare (riv.), Madg.
133/J6 Mandritsara, Madg.
106/C3 Mandsaur, India
116/B5 Mandurah, Austl.
81/E2 Manduria, It.
106/A3 Māndvi, India
106/C5 Mandya, India
106/D2 Mane (pass), Nepal
59/G2 Manea, Eng,UK
106/D3 Manendragarh, India
129/H5 Manéngouba, Massif du (peak), Camr.
78/D2 Manerbio, It.
92/B5 Manfalūt, Egypt
80/D2 Manfredonia, It.
80/E2 Manfredonia (gulf), It.
103/B4 Mang (riv.), China
140/B4 Manga, Braz.

203
Manga – Mays

140/A3 Mangabeiras (hills), Braz.
126/C1 Mangai, Zaire
121/K7 Mangaia (isl.), Cookls.
107/F2 Mangaldai, India
112/C1 Mangaldan, Phil.
83/J4 Mangalia, Rom.
130/C4 Mangalisa (peak), Tanz.
106/B5 Mangalore, India
141/J7 Mangaratiba, Braz.
121/M7 Mangareva (isl.), FrPol.
105/E3 Mangchang, China
60/A6 Mangerton (mtn.), Ire.
104/B4 Mangin (range), Burma
87/K4 Mangistau Obl., Kaz.
111/E3 Mangkalihat (cape), Indo.
108/B1 Mangla, Pak.
108/B1 Mangla (dam), Pak.
108/B1 Mangla (res.), Pak.
144/A1 Manglaralto, Ecu.
138/B4 Manglares (pt.), Col.
116/K7 Mangles (bay), Austl.
129/F4 Mango, Togo
131/D2 Mangoche, Malw.
133/H8 Mangoky (riv.), Madg.
111/G4 Mangole (isl.), Indo.
133/J7 Mangoro (riv.), Madg.
58/D4 Mangotsfield, Eng,UK
106/B3 Māngrol, India
143/G2 Mangueira (lake), Braz.
159/H4 Mangum, Ok,US
130/A2 Manguredjipa, Zaire
131/C4 Mangwe, Zim.
87/J3 Mangyshlak (pen.), Kaz.
87/K4 Mangyshlak (plat.), Kaz.
96/C2 Manhan, Mong.
167/L8 Manhasset, NY,US
167/L8 Manhasset (bay), NY,US
159/H3 Manhattan, Ks,US
156/F4 Manhattan, Mt,US
167/J9 Manhattan (isl.), NY,US
164/B3 Manhattan Beach, Ca,US
131/D5 Manhiça, Moz.
141/D2 Manhuaçu, Braz.
141/D2 Manhumirim, Braz.
81/H4 Máni (pen.), Gre.
133/H7 Mania (riv.), Madg.
131/D2 Maniamba, Moz.
131/D3 Manica, Moz.
131/D3 Manica (prov.), Moz.
131/C3 Manicaland (prov.), Zim.
136/F5 Manicoré, Braz.
136/F5 Manicoré (riv.), Braz.
157/J3 Manicouagan, Mb,Can
161/G1 Manicouagan (res.), Qu,Can
161/G1 Manicouagan (riv.), Qu,Can
161/H1 Manicouagan, Petit Lac (lake), Qu,Can
118/C3 Manifold (cape), Austl.
121/L6 Manihi (isl.), FrPol.
121/J6 Manihiki (atoll), Cookls.
112/C2 Manila (cap.), Phil.
158/E2 Manila, Ut,US
112/E6 Manila (inset) (cap.), Phil.
133/J7 Maningory (riv.), Madg.
111/G4 Manipa (str.), Indo.
104/B3 Manipur (state), India
92/A2 Manisa, Turk.
92/B2 Manisa (prov.), Turk.
56/D3 Man, Isle of (isl.), UK
160/C2 Manistee, Mi,US
160/C2 Manistee (riv.), Mi,US
152/G3 Manitoba (prov.), Can.
157/J3 Manitoba (lake), Mb,Can
161/H1 Manitou (riv.), Qu,Can
160/D2 Manitoulin (isl.), On,Can
162/B2 Manitou Springs, Co,US
160/C1 Manitouwadge, On,Can
160/C2 Manitowoc, Wi,US
160/F2 Maniwaki, Qu,Can
138/C3 Manizales, Col.
131/D5 Manjacaze, Moz.
108/F3 Manjeri, India
106/C4 Manjlegaon, India
95/L5 Mānjra (riv.), India
157/K4 Mankato, Mn,US
131/C5 Mankayane, Swaz.
128/D4 Mankono, IvC.
108/H4 Mankulam, SrL.
96/F3 Manlay, Mong.
74/D2 Manlleu, Sp.
118/H8 Manly, Austl.
106/B3 Manmād, India
105/J5 Manmanoc (mtn.), Phil.
109/B4 Man Mia (peak), Thai.
108/G4 Mannar (gulf), India, SrL.
108/G4 Mannar, SrL.
108/H4 Mannar (dist.), SrL.
108/G4 Mannar (isl.), SrL.
108/G3 Mannārgudi, India
77/E3 Männedorf, Swi.
132/C4 Mannetjiesberg (peak), SAfr.
70/B4 Mannheim, Ger.
153/Q7 Manning (cape), NW,Can
163/H3 Manning, SC,US
166/C4 Mannington Meadow (lake), NJ,US
59/H3 Manningtree, Eng,UK
76/D4 Männlifluh (peak), Swi.
80/A2 Mannu (riv.), It.
80/A3 Mannu (riv.), It.
128/C5 Mano (riv.), Libr., SLeo.
126/E2 Manono, Zaire
167/F2 Manorville, NY,US
72/F5 Manosque, Fr.
161/G1 Manouane (lake), Qu,Can
161/G1 Manouane (riv.), Qu,Can
121/H5 Manra (Sydney) (atoll), Kiri.
75/F2 Manresa, Sp.
131/C1 Mansa, Zam.
128/B3 Mansa Konko, Gam.
112/C2 Mansalay, Phil.
153/H2 Mansel (isl.), NW,Can
57/G5 Mansfield, Eng,UK
162/E3 Mansfield, La,US
168/C1 Mansfield, Ma,US
168/E6 Mansfield, Oh,US
168/B2 Mansfield Hollow (dam), Ct,US
57/G5 Mansfield Woodhouse, Eng,UK
138/A5 Manta, Ecu.
112/B3 Mantalingajan (mtn.), Phil.
130/B3 Mantare, Tanz.
144/C3 Mantaro (riv.), Peru
158/B3 Manteca, Ca,US
141/D1 Mantena, Braz.
68/A6 Mantes-la-Jolie, Fr.
68/A6 Mantes-la-Ville, Fr.
106/C4 Manthani, India
158/E3 Manti, Ut,US
141/C2 Mantiquiera (range), Braz.
103/C3 Mantou Shan (mtn.), China
79/D2 Mantova, It.
78/D2 Mantova (prov.), It.
63/L1 Mäntsälä, Fin.
149/E1 Mantua, Cuba
85/K4 Manturovo, Rus.
63/M1 Mäntyharju, Fin.
144/D3 Manú (riv.), Peru
121/J6 Manua (isls.), ASam.
121/K6 Manuae (atoll), Cookls.
154/W13 Manuawili, Hi,US
137/J6 Manuel Alves (riv.), Braz.
110/C5 Manuk (riv.), Indo.
112/C3 Manukan, Phil.
115/R10 Manukau, NZ
166/D5 Manumuskin (riv.), NJ,US
144/C3 Manú Nat'l Park, Peru
136/E6 Manuripe (riv.), Bol.
120/D5 Manus (isl.), PNG
166/D2 Manville, NJ,US
162/E4 Many, La,US
131/C3 Manyame (riv.), Zim.
130/B3 Manyara (lake), Tanz.
87/G3 Manych (riv.), Rus.
87/G3 Manych-Gudilo (lake), Rus.
158/E3 Many Farms, Az,US
130/B4 Manyoni, Tanz.
74/D3 Manzanares, Sp.
75/N8 Manzanares (riv.), Sp.
149/G1 Manzanillo, Cuba
146/D5 Manzanillo, Mex.
149/F4 Manzanillo-Gandoca Nat'l Wild. Ref., CR
162/B3 Manzano (mts.), NM,US
130/A4 Manzanza, Zaire
97/H2 Manzhouli, China
76/A5 Manziat, Fr.
127/C2 Manzilah, Buḩayat al (lake), Egypt
123/W17 Manzil bū Ruqaybah, Tun.
123/X17 Manzil Tamīn, Tun.
133/E2 Manzini, Swaz.
124/J5 Mao, Chad
150/D3 Mao, DRep.
111/J4 Maoke (mts.), Indo.
105/F4 Maoming, China
104/D3 Maotou (peak), China
131/C4 Mapai, Moz.
102/D5 Mapam (lake), China
146/D3 Mapimí (depr.), Mex.
161/Q8 Maple, On,Can
157/K5 Maple (riv.), Ia,US
157/J4 Maple (riv.), ND,US
157/H3 Maple Creek, Sk,Can
168/F5 Maple Heights, Oh,US
166/D4 Maple Shade, NJ,US
167/D2 Maplewood, NJ,US
101/F6 Map'o, SKor.
114/G2 Mapoon Mission Sta., Austl.
139/G5 Mapuera (riv.), Braz.
106/B4 Mapusa, India
131/D5 Maputo (cap.), Moz.
131/D5 Maputo (prov.), Moz.
131/D5 Maputo (riv.), Moz.
127/D5 Maqdam, Ras (cape), Sudan
95/J2 Maqor, Afg.
102/D5 Maquan (riv.), China
126/C2 Maquela do Zombo, Ang.
159/K2 Maquoketa (riv.), Ia,US
141/B3 Mar (range), Braz.
104/D1 Mar (riv.), China
54/D2 Mar (dist.), Sc,UK
130/B3 Mara (prov.), Tanz.
130/B3 Mara (riv.), Tanz.
137/J5 Marabá, Braz.
137/J3 Maracá (isl.), Braz.
138/D2 Maracaibo, Ven.
138/D2 Maracaibo (lake), Ven.
137/H7 Maracaju (mts.), Braz.
140/B4 Maracás, Braz.
140/B4 Maracás (hills), Braz.
139/E2 Maracay, Ven.
74/D4 Maracena, Sp.
124/J2 Marādah, Libya
129/G3 Maradi, Niger
129/G3 Maradi (dept.), Niger
93/F2 Marāgheh, Iran
139/E4 Marahuaca (peak), Ven.
112/C1 Maraira (pt.), Phil.
159/J3 Marais des Cygnes (riv.), Ks, Mo,US
137/J4 Marajó, Braz.
137/J4 Marajó (bay), Braz.
134/D3 Marajó (isl.), Braz.
130/C2 Maralal, Kenya
117/F4 Maralinga-Tjarutja Abor. Land, Austl.
112/D4 Maramag, Phil.
141/K8 Marambaia (isl.), Braz.
163/F2 Maramec (riv.), Mo,US
83/F2 Maramureş (co.), Rom.
158/E4 Marana, Az,US
93/F2 Marand, Iran
140/C1 Maranguape, Braz.
140/A4 Maranhão (riv.), Braz.
140/A2 Maranhão (state), Braz.
79/G1 Marano (lag.), It.
118/C4 Maranoa (riv.), Austl.
136/C4 Marañón (riv.), Peru
79/E1 Marano Vicentino, It.
128/D5 Maraoue Nat'l Park, IvC.
110/B4 Marapi (peak), Indo.
110/C4 Maras (peak), Indo.
83/H3 Mărăşeşti, Rom.
160/C1 Marathon, On,Can
163/H5 Marathon, Fl,US
162/C4 Marathon, Tx,US
141/A4 Marau, Braz.
159/G5 Maravillas (cr.), Tx,US
112/D3 Marawi, Phil.
127/B5 Marawī, Sudan
58/A6 Marazion, Eng,UK
70/C5 Marbach am Neckar, Ger.
74/C4 Marbella, Sp.
156/F5 Marbleton, Wy,US
64/E3 Marburg, Ger.
166/B4 Marburg (lake), Pa,US
82/C2 Marcali, Hun.
126/B4 Marca, Ponta da (pt.), Ang.
59/G1 March, Eng,UK
164/C3 March A.F.B., Ca,US
72/D3 Marche (mts.), Fr.
79/F5 Marche (reg.), It.
69/E3 Marche-en-Famenne, Belg.
144/J6 Marchena (isl.), Ecu.
74/C4 Marchena, Sp.
135/D3 Mar Chiquita (lake), Arg.
71/H6 Marchtrenk, Aus.
76/B3 Marcilly-sur-Tille, Fr.
68/A2 Marck, Fr.
140/B1 Marco, Braz.
163/H5 Marco, Fl,US
144/C4 Marcona, Peru
156/E3 Marconi (peak), BC,Can
142/E2 Marcos Juárez, Arg.
68/C2 Marcq-en-Baroeul, Fr.
151/J3 Marcus Baker (mtn.), Ak,US
160/F2 Marcy (peak), NY,US
95/K2 Mardān, Pak.
143/F3 Mar del Plata, Arg.
59/G4 Marden, Eng,UK
92/E2 Mardin, Turk.
92/E2 Mardin (prov.), Turk.
121/W12 Maré (isl.), NCal.
79/F5 Marecchia (riv.), It.
118/B2 Mareeba, Austl.
54/A1 Maree, Loch (lake), Sc,UK
57/H5 Mareham le Fen, Eng,UK
59/G5 Maresfield, Eng,UK
162/B4 Marfa, Tx,US
108/B1 Margalla Hills Nat'l Park, Pak.
58/C3 Margam, Wal,UK
86/E3 Marganets, Ukr.
106/B4 Margao, India
116/C2 Margaret (peak), Austl.
164/C4 Margarita (peak), Ca,US
139/F2 Margarita (isl.), Ven.
59/H4 Margate, Eng,UK
166/D5 Margate City, NJ,US
72/E4 Margeride (mts.), Fr.
130/A2 Margherita (peak), Ugan.
82/F2 Marghita, Rom.
102/B3 Margilan, Uzb.
102/E5 Margog Caka (lake), China
112/C4 Margosatubig, Phil.
69/E2 Margraten, Neth.
113/V Marguerite (bay), Ant.
119/D4 Maria (peak), Austl.
121/K7 Maria (isl.), FrPol.
112/C2 Maria Aurora, Phil.
146/D4 María Cleófas (isl.), Mex.
141/H7 Maria da Fé, Braz.
119/D4 Maria Island Nat'l Park, Austl.
130/C3 Mariakani, Kenya
146/D4 María Madre (isl.), Mex.
146/D4 María Magdalena (isl.), Mex.
149/F1 Marianao, Cuba
163/F3 Marianna, Ar,US
163/G4 Marianna, Fl,US
78/C1 Mariano Comense, It.
71/F3 Mariánské Lázně (Marienbad), Czh.
156/F3 Marias (riv.), Mt,US
149/F5 Mariato (pt.), Pan.
82/B2 Maribor, Slov.
141/L7 Maricá, Braz.
139/E5 Marié (riv.), Braz.
113/S Marie Byrd Land (reg.), Ant.
150/F4 Marie-Galante (isl.), Guad.
63/H1 Mariehamn, Fin.
63/U9 Marieholm, Swe.
149/F1 Mariel, Cuba
71/F3 Marienbad (Mariánské Lázně), Czh.
67/E6 Marienheide, Ger.
62/E2 Mariestad, Swe.
163/G3 Marietta, Ga,US
160/D4 Marietta, Oh,US
130/B2 Marigat, Kenya
72/F5 Marignane, Fr.
112/D3 Marihatag, Phil.
112/F6 Marikina, Phil.
112/F6 Marikina (riv.), Phil.
112/E6 Marilao, Phil.
141/B2 Marília, Braz.
74/A1 Marín, Sp.
165/J10 Marin (co.), Ca,US
164/B3 Marina del Rey, Ca,US
164/F8 Marina del Rey (har.), Ca,US
112/C2 Marinduque (isl.), Phil.
117/M8 Marineland, Austl.
130/D3 Marine Nat'l Rsv., Kenya
53/R9 Marines, Fr.
160/C2 Marinette, Wi,US
165/K10 Marine World (Africa USA), Ca,US
141/B2 Maringá, Braz.
131/D3 Maríngué, Moz.
74/A3 Marinha Grande, Port.
115/J3 Marion (reef), Austl.
163/G3 Marion, Al,US
160/B4 Marion, Il,US
160/C3 Marion, In,US
160/B4 Marion, Ky,US
160/C2 Marion, Mi,US
160/D3 Marion, Oh,US
163/H3 Marion (lake), SC,US
160/D4 Marion, Va,US
158/C3 Mariposa, Ca,US
136/F8 Mariscal Estigarribia, Par.
83/H5 Maritsa (riv.), Bul., Turk.
86/F3 Mariupol', Ukr.
85/K4 Mariy Aut. Rep., Rus.
91/D3 Marj 'Uyūn, Leb.
66/B6 Mark (riv.), Belg.
96/B2 Markakol (lake), Kaz.
104/C2 Markam, China
125/P7 Marka (Merca), Som.
62/E3 Markaryd, Swe.
93/G3 Markazī (gov.), Iran
77/F2 Markdorf, Ger.
66/C4 Marken (isl.), Neth.
66/C4 Markerwaard (polder), Neth.
59/E1 Market Bosworth, Eng,UK
59/F1 Market Deeping, Eng,UK
57/F6 Market Drayton, Eng,UK
59/F2 Market Harborough, Eng,UK
56/B3 Markethill, NI,UK
57/H5 Market Rasen, Eng,UK
57/H4 Market Weighton, Eng,UK
70/C5 Markgroningen, Ger.
153/J2 Markham (bay), NW,Can
161/R8 Markham, On,Can
65/L2 Marki, Pol.
54/C4 Markinch, Sc,UK
102/C4 Markit, China
158/C3 Markleeville, Ca,US
71/F2 Markneukirchen, Ger.
81/L7 Markópoulon, Gre.
87/H2 Marks, Rus.
162/E4 Marksville, La,US
70/C3 Marktheidenfeld, Ger.
71/E6 Markt Indersdorf, Ger.
77/G2 Marktoberdorf, Ger.
71/F3 Marktredwitz, Ger.
71/E6 Markt Schwaben, Ger.
159/J3 Mark Twain (lake), Mo,US
67/E5 Marl, Ger.
167/D3 Marlboro, NJ,US
59/E4 Marlborough, Eng,UK
168/C1 Marlborough, Ma,US
68/B3 Marles-les-Mines, Fr.
77/H4 Marling (Marlengo), It.
59/F3 Marlow, Eng,UK
166/D4 Marlton, NJ,US
68/C3 Marly, Fr.
53/T9 Marly-la-Ville, Fr.
53/S10 Marly-le-Roi, Fr.
69/F5 Marly-sur-Seille, Fr.
72/D4 Marmande, Fr.
83/H5 Marmara (isl.), Turk.
53/F4 Marmara (sea), Turk.
92/B2 Marmaris, Turk.
136/F5 Marmelos (riv.), Braz.
116/D4 Marmion (lake), Austl.
160/A1 Marmion (lake), On,Can
73/J3 Marmolada (peak), It.
74/C3 Marmolejo, Sp.
77/F5 Marmontana, Monte (peak), It.
68/C6 Marne (dept.), Fr.
72/E2 Marne (riv.), Fr.
76/B3 Marne à la Saône (can.), Fr.
69/D6 Marne au Rhin, Canal de la (can.), Fr.
58/D5 Marnhull, Eng,UK
124/J6 Maro, Chad
121/H2 Maro (reef), Hi,US
133/J6 Maroantsetra, Madg.
121/L6 Marokau (atoll), FrPol.
123/G7 Marolambo, Madg.
53/S11 Marolles-en-Hurepoix, Fr.
133/J6 Maromokotro (peak), Madg.
131/C3 Marondera, Zim.
139/H3 Maroni (riv.), FrG., Sur.
118/D4 Maroochydore-Mooloolaba, Austl.
79/E1 Marostica, It.
124/H5 Maroua, Camr.
139/H4 Marouni (riv.), FrG.
133/H7 Marovoay, Madg.
139/H3 Marowijne (dist.), Sur.
69/G5 Marpingen, Ger.
57/F5 Marple, Eng,UK
96/D5 Marqên Gangri (peak), China
120/D8 Marquarie (riv.), Austl.
121/M5 Marquesas (isls.), FrPol.
160/C2 Marquette, Mi,US
131/D5 Marracuene, Moz.
125/K5 Marrah (mts.), Sudan
125/K5 Marrah (peak), Sudan
124/D1 Marrakech, Mor.
131/D3 Marromeu, Moz.
126/G3 Marrupa, Moz.
124/J1 Marsá al Burayqah, Libya
130/C2 Marsabit, Kenya
80/C4 Marsala, It.
125/L1 Marsá Matrūḩ, Egypt
53/U10 Marsange (riv.), Fr.
67/F6 Marsberg, Ger.
80/C1 Marsciano, It.
57/G4 Marsden, Eng,UK
66/B3 Marsdiep (chan.), Neth.
72/F5 Marseille, Fr.
162/E4 Marsh (isl.), La,US
165/F7 Marsh (cr.), Mi,US
166/A4 Marsh (cr.), Pa,US
117/H2 Marshall (riv.), Austl.
156/F2 Marshall, Sk,Can
157/K4 Marshall, Mn,US
159/J3 Marshall, Mo,US
162/E3 Marshall, Tx,US
120/G3 Marshall Islands
157/K5 Marshalltown, Ia,US
159/J3 Marshfield, Mo,US
160/B2 Marshfield, Wi,US
59/E3 Marsh Gibbon, Eng,UK
166/C6 Marshyhope (cr.), De, Md,US
57/G2 Marske-by-the-Sea, Eng,UK
78/A1 Mars, Monte (peak), It.
62/G2 Märsta, Swe.
109/B2 Martaban (gulf), Burma
156/G2 Martensville, Sk,Can
168/D3 Martha's Vineyard (isl.), Ma,US
76/D5 Martigny, Swi.
72/F5 Martigues, Fr.
113/S Martin (pen.), Ant.
65/K4 Martin, Slvk.
163/G3 Martin (lake), Al,US
157/H5 Martin, SD,US
163/F2 Martin, Tn,US
80/E2 Martina Franca, It.
78/C1 Martinengo, It.
74/F4 Martínez, Mex.
165/K10 Martinez, Ca,US
163/H3 Martinez, Ga,US
147/M6 Martínez de la Torre, Mex.
141/C1 Martinho Campos, Braz.
150/F4 Martinique (isl.), Fr.
150/F4 Martinique (passg.), West Indies
140/B1 Martinópole, Braz.
141/B2 Martinópolis, Braz.
140/C2 Martins, Braz.
160/E4 Martinsburg, WV,US
160/C4 Martinsville, In,US
160/E4 Martinsville, Va,US
137/N8 Martin Vaz (isls.), Braz.
58/D2 Martley, Eng,UK
58/D5 Martock, Eng,UK
75/F2 Martorell, Sp.
74/D4 Martos, Sp.
160/F1 Martre (riv.), Qu,Can
157/J5 Marty, SD,US
98/C3 Marugame, Japan
99/F2 Maruko, Japan
66/D2 Marum, Neth.
130/C5 Marumba, Tanz.
98/E2 Maruoka, Japan
121/M7 Marutea (atoll), FrPol.
99/H7 Maruyama, Japan
93/H4 Marv Dasht, Iran
118/D4 Mary (riv.), Austl.
95/H1 Mary, Trkm.
116/B2 Mary Anne (passg.), Austl.
118/D4 Maryborough, Austl.
119/B3 Maryborough, Austl.
163/G4 Mary Esther, Fl,US
157/H3 Maryfield, Sk,Can
54/D3 Marykirk, Sc,UK
128/C5 Maryland (co.), Libr.
160/E4 Maryland (state), US
166/B5 Maryland City, Md,US
131/C3 Maryland Junction, Zim.
56/E2 Maryport, Eng,UK
161/L2 Marystown, Nf,Can
159/H3 Marysville, Ks,US
165/H6 Marysville, Mi,US
165/C1 Marysville, Wa,US
159/J2 Maryville, Mo,US
163/H3 Maryville, Tn,US
80/D2 Marzano (peak), It.
138/B3 Marzo (pt.), Col.
147/F3 Marzo, 18 de, Mex.
124/H2 Marzūq, Libya
124/H3 Marzūq, Şaḩrā (des.), Libya
130/C2 Masabit Nat'l Rsv., Kenya
91/D4 Masada (Horvot Mezada) (ruins), Isr.
130/B3 Masai Mara Nat'l Reserve, Kenya
130/C4 Masai Steppe (grsld.), Tanz.
130/A3 Masaka, Ugan.
123/X18 Masākin, Tun.
75/E3 Masamagrell, Sp.
111/F4 Masamba, Indo.
101/E5 Masan, SKor.
130/A4 Masangwe (hill), Tanz.
101/F7 Masan-ni, SKor.
130/C5 Masasi, Tanz.
148/E4 Masaya, Nic.
112/B2 Masbate, Phil.
112/C2 Masbate (isl.), Phil.
123/R16 Mascara, Alg.
123/R16 Mascara (wilaya), Alg.
133/S15 Mascarene (isls.), Mrts., Reun.
161/N6 Mascouche, Qu,Can
130/A3 Masereka, Zaire
132/D3 Maseru (cap.), Les.
131/C4 Mashaba, Zim.
90/E6 Mashad, Iran
57/G3 Masham, Eng,UK
107/J3 Mashan, China
95/G1 Mashhad, Iran
100/B2 Mashike, Japan
95/H3 Māshkel, Hāmūn-i- (lake), Pak.
95/H3 Māshkīd (riv.), Iran
131/C3 Mashonaland Central (prov.), Zim.
131/C3 Mashonaland East (prov.), Zim.
131/C3 Mashonaland West (prov.), Zim.
91/B4 Mashtūl as Sūq, Egypt
100/D2 Mashū (lake), Japan
87/L1 Masim (peak), Rus.
130/A2 Masindi, Ugan.
130/B2 Masindi Port, Ugan.
112/B2 Masinloc, Phil.
95/G5 Masira (gulf), Oman
95/G4 Maşīrah (isl.), Oman
130/A3 Masisi, Zaire
93/G4 Masjed-e Soleymān, Iran
148/D2 Maskall, Belz.
60/A2 Mask, Lough (lake), Ire.
63/R7 Måsnaren (lake), Swe.
133/J6 Masoala (cape), Madg.
133/J6 Masoala (pen.), Madg.
160/C3 Mason, Mi,US
162/D4 Mason, Tx,US
165/A3 Mason (co.), Wa,US
165/A3 Mason (lake), Wa,US
157/K5 Mason City, Ia,US
75/X17 Maspalomas, Canl.,Sp.
75/K6 Masquefa, Sp.
78/D4 Massa, It.
78/D4 Massa-Carrara (prov.), It.
161/F3 Massachusetts (state), US
161/G3 Massachusetts (bay), Ma,US
78/D5 Massaciuccoli (lake), It.
80/E2 Massafra, It.
79/E4 Massa Lombarda, It.
131/D4 Massangena, Moz.
140/B1 Massapê, Braz.
167/E2 Massapequa, NY,US
167/M9 Massapequa Park, NY,US
78/D5 Massarosa, It.
160/F2 Massena, NY,US
153/S7 Massey (sound), NW,Can
126/D3 Massibi, Ang.
72/E4 Massif Central (plat.), Fr.
168/F6 Massillon, Oh,US
131/D4 Massinga, Moz.
131/D4 Massingir, Moz.
113/G Masson (isl.), Ant.
53/S10 Massy, Fr.
115/S11 Masterton, NZ
66/B5 Mastgat (chan.), Neth.
167/F2 Mastic, NY,US
167/F2 Mastic Beach, NY,US
71/H3 Mastník (riv.), Czh.
95/J3 Mastung, Pak.
98/B3 Masuda, Japan
130/C5 Masuguru, Tanz.
110/B4 Masurai (peak), Indo.
131/C4 Masvingo, Zim.
131/C4 Masvingo (prov.), Zim.
130/B3 Maswa Game Rsv., Tanz.
91/E2 Maşyāf, Syria
81/F2 Mat (riv.), Alb.
131/B3 Matabeleland North (prov.), Zim.
131/C4 Matabeleland South (prov.), Zim.
126/B2 Matadi, Zaire
162/C3 Matador, Tx,US
148/E3 Matagalpa, Nic.
149/E3 Matagalpa, Rio Grande de (riv.), Nic.
160/E1 Matagami (lake), Qu,Can
162/D4 Matagorda (bay), Tx,US
162/D4 Matagorda (isl.), Tx,US
106/D6 Matale, SrL.
128/B3 Matam, Sen.
147/F3 Matamoros, Mex.
125/K3 Ma'ţan as Sarra (well), Libya
131/C1 Matanda, Zam.
130/C5 Matandu (riv.), Tanz.
161/H1 Matane, Qu,Can
161/H1 Matane (riv.), Qu,Can
149/F1 Matanzas, Cuba
141/B2 Matão, Braz.
146/C2 Matape (riv.), Mex.
161/H1 Matapedia (riv.), Qu,Can
139/F2 Mata, Punta de, Ven.
142/C2 Mataquito (riv.), Chile
94/C6 Matara (ruins), Egypt
106/D6 Matara, SrL.
111/E5 Mataram, Indo.
75/G2 Mataró, Sp.
121/L7 Mataura, FrPol.
120/H6 Mata Utu (cap.), Wall.
167/D3 Matawan, NJ,US
147/E4 Matehuala, Mex.
131/C4 Mateke (hills), Zim.
80/E2 Matera, It.
82/F2 Mátészalka, Hun.
131/B3 Matetsi, Zim.
130/B2 Matheniko Game Rsv., Kenya
130/C2 Mathew's (peak), Kenya
162/C3 Mathews (lake), Ca,US
162/D4 Mathis, Tx,US
106/C2 Mathurā, India
112/D4 Mati, Phil.
141/K6 Matias Barbosa, Braz.
148/C2 Matías Romero, Mex.
149/E3 Matiguás, Nic.
164/A2 Matilija (dam), Ca,US
130/B5 Matimbuka, Tanz.
141/B3 Matinhos, Braz.
167/E2 Matinicock (pt.), NY,US
123/W17 Mātir, Tun.
138/D3 Matiyuri (riv.), Ven.
57/G5 Matlock, Eng,UK
131/C4 Matobo (Matopos) Nat'l Park, Zim.
136/G7 Mato Grosso, Braz.
137/J7 Mato Grosso (plat.), Braz.
141/A1 Mato Grosso do Sul (state), Braz.
131/D5 Matolo-Rio, Moz.
130/C4 Matombo, Tanz.
131/C4 Matopos, Zim.
131/C4 Matopos (Matobo) Nat'l Park, Zim.
74/A2 Matosinhos, Port.
140/B4 Mato Verde, Braz.
95/G4 Maţraḩ, Oman
140/D3 Matriz de Camaragibe, Braz.
132/B4 Matroosberg (peak), SAfr.
127/A2 Maţrūḩ, Egypt
127/B2 Maţrūḩ (gov.), Egypt
63/K2 Matsalu (str.), Est.
133/H8 Matsiatra (riv.), Madg.
99/L10 Matsubara, Japan
99/H7 Matsubushi, Japan
99/H7 Matsuda, Japan
99/H7 Matsudo, Japan
98/C3 Matsue, Japan
100/B3 Matsumae, Japan
99/E2 Matsumoto, Japan
98/E3 Matsusaka, Japan
99/G1 Matsushima, Japan
98/E2 Matsutō, Japan
98/C4 Matsuyama, Japan
160/D1 Mattagami (riv.), On,Can
108/F4 Mattancherry Palace, India
160/E2 Mattawa, On,Can
76/D6 Matterhorn (peak), It., Swi.
76/D5 Mattertal (val.), Swi.
165/Q16 Matteson, Il,US
151/H2 Matthews (mtn.), Ak,US
71/G6 Mattig (riv.), Aus.
76/E5 Mattmarksee (lake), Swi.
98/E2 Mattō, Japan
56/B4 Mattock (riv.), Ire.
160/B4 Mattoon, Il,US
131/D3 Matundwe (range), Malw., Moz.
139/F2 Maturín, Ven.
131/C3 Matusadona Nat'l Park, Zim.
112/D4 Matutum (mtn.), Phil.
139/G3 Maú (riv.), Braz., Guy.
130/B3 Mau (peak), Kenya
141/C2 Mauá, Braz.
68/C3 Maubeuge, Fr.
104/B5 Ma-ubin, Burma
54/B5 Mauchline, Sc,UK
116/B2 Maud (pt.), Austl.
54/D1 Maud, Sc,UK
106/D2 Maudaha, India
131/D5 Mau-é-Ele, Moz.
136/G4 Maués, Braz.
136/G4 Maués Açu (riv.), Braz.
120/D3 Maug (isls.), NMar.
56/D3 Maughold, IM,UK
56/D3 Maughold Head (pt.), IM,UK
72/F5 Mauguio, Fr.
60/B4 Mauherslieve (mtn.), Ire.
154/T10 Maui (isl.), Hi,US
121/K7 Mauke (isl.), Cookls.
70/B5 Maulbronn, Ger.
68/A6 Mauldre (riv.), Fr.
142/B2 Maule (reg.), Chile
142/C1 Maule (riv.), Chile
72/C3 Mauléon, Fr.
142/B4 Maullín, Chile
160/C3 Maumee (riv.), In, Oh,US
60/A2 Maumtrasna (mtn.), Ire.
131/A3 Maun, Bots.
154/U11 Mauna Kea (vol.), Hi,US
154/U11 Mauna Loa (vol.), Hi,US
131/B4 Maunatlala, Bots.
121/K6 Maupiti (isl.), FrPol.
77/E3 Maur, Swi.
106/C2 Mau Rānīpur, India
53/S10 Maurecourt, Fr.
68/A6 Maurepas, Fr.
117/F4 Maurice (lake), Austl.
166/C5 Maurice (riv.), NJ,US
161/F2 Mauricie Nat'l Park, Qu,Can
141/B1 Maurilândia, Braz.
128/B2 Mauritania
140/C2 Mauriti, Braz.
123/H6 Mauritius
130/C4 Maurui, Tanz.
160/B3 Mauston, Wi,US
76/D6 Mauvoisin, Barrage de (dam), Swi.
108/F4 Māvelikara, India
82/E5 Mavrovo Nat'l Park, Macd.
131/C3 Mavuradonha (mts.), Zim.
109/B4 Maw Daung (pass), Thai.
113/E Mawson, Ant.
113/D Mawson (coast), Ant.
147/H4 Maxcanú, Mex.
69/F6 Maxéville, Fr.
71/F4 Maxhütte-Haidhof, Ger.
131/D4 Maxixe, Moz.
54/D4 May (isl.), Sc,UK
160/F4 May (cape), NJ,US
148/D2 Maya (mts.), Belz., Guat.
110/C4 Maya (isl.), Indo.
89/P4 Maya (riv.), Rus.
150/C2 Mayaguana (isl.), Bahm.
150/C2 Mayaguana (passg.), Bahm.
150/E3 Mayagüez, PR
95/K1 Mayakovskogo (peak), Taj.
102/B4 Mayakovskogo, Pik (peak), Taj.
107/J2 Mayang, China
149/H1 Mayarí, Cuba
99/L10 Maya-san (peak), Japan
54/B6 Maybole, Sc,UK
125/N5 Maych'ew, Eth.
112/D3 Maydolong, Phil.
69/G3 Mayen, Ger.
72/C2 Mayenne, Fr.
72/C3 Mayenne (riv.), Fr.
156/E2 Mayerthorpe, Ab,Can
54/C5 Mayfield, Sc,UK
160/B4 Mayfield, Ky,US
168/F4 Mayfield Heights, Oh,US
86/G3 Maykop, Rus.
59/G3 Mayland, Eng,UK
104/C4 Maymyo, Burma
168/C1 Maynard, Ma,US
142/C5 Mayo (riv.), Arg.
151/L3 Mayo, Yk,Can
60/A2 Mayo, Ire.
60/A2 Mayo (co.), Ire.
146/C3 Mayo (riv.), Mex.
112/C2 Mayon (vol.), Phil.
74/D1 Mayor (cape), Sp.
122/G6 Mayotte (isl.), Fr.
133/H6 Mayotte (terr.), Fr.
112/C1 Mayoyao, Phil.
149/G2 May Pen, Jam.
93/F4 Maysān (gov.), Iraq

Maysv – Millp

160/D4 Maysville, Ky,US
131/C1 Mayuka, Zam.
108/G3 Mayuram, India
157/J4 Mayville, ND,US
164/F8 Maywood, Ca,US
165/Q16 Maywood, Il,US
167/J8 Maywood, NJ,US
131/B2 Mazabuka, Zam.
137/H4 Mazagão, Braz.
72/E5 Mazamet, Fr.
93/H2 Māzandarān (gov.), Iran
80/C4 Mazara (val.), It.
80/C4 Mazara del Vallo, It.
95/J1 Mazār-e Sharīf, Afg.
74/A1 Mazaricos, Sp.
74/E4 Mazarrón, Sp.
139/G3 Mazaruni (riv.), Guy.
146/C2 Mazatán, Mex.
148/D3 Mazatenango, Guat.
146/D4 Mazatlán, Mex.
63/K3 Mažeikiai, Lith.
118/B3 Mazeppa Nat'l Park, Austl.
56/B3 Mazetown, NI,UK
92/D2 Mazıkıran (pass), Turk.
68/B3 Mazingarbe, Fr.
126/C2 Mazingu, Zaire
131/D3 Mazoe (riv.), Moz.
131/C3 Mazoe, Zim.
96/D3 Mazong (peak), China
131/C3 Mazowe (riv.), Zim.
131/C4 Mazunga, Zim.
65/L2 Mazury (reg.), Pol.
131/B3 Mbabala, Zam.
130/A5 Mbabala (isl.), Zam.
133/E2 Mbabane (cap.), Swaz.
124/H6 Mbabo (peak), Camr.
124/J7 Mbaïki, CAfr.
125/H6 Mbakaou (lake), Camr.
130/A5 Mbala, Zam.
131/C4 Mbalabala, Zim.
124/H7 Mbalam, Camr.
130/C3 Mbalambala, Kenya
130/B2 Mbale, Ugan.
124/H7 Mbalmayo, Camr.
129/H5 Mbam (riv.), Camr.
131/D1 Mbamba Bay, Tanz.
129/H5 Mbam, Massif du (peak), Camr.
125/J7 Mbandaka, Zaire
130/C5 Mbaranganda (riv.), Tanz.
130/C5 Mbarangandu, Tanz.
130/A3 Mbarara, Ugan.
125/J7 Mbata, CAfr.
121/Y18 Mbengga (isl.), Fiji
131/C4 Mberengwa, Zim.
130/A5 Mbereshi Mission, Zam.
130/B5 Mbeya, Tanz.
130/B5 Mbeya (peak), Tanz.
130/B4 Mbeya (prov.), Tanz.
130/B5 Mbeya (range), Tanz.
131/D1 Mbeya, Zam.
126/B1 M'Bigou, Gabon
124/G7 Mbini, EqG.
124/H7 Mbini (riv.), EqG.
130/A4 Mbirira, Tanz.
130/A3 Mbirizi, Ugan.
131/C4 Mbizi, Zim.
130/B4 Mbogo, Tanz.
130/A3 Mboko, Zaire
131/C2 Mboloma, Zam.
125/L6 Mbomou (riv.), CAfr.
128/B3 Mboune, Vallée du (wadi), Sen.
128/A3 M'Bour, Sen.
126/D2 Mbuji-Mayi, Zaire
130/B3 Mbulu, Tanz.
130/C3 Mbuvu, Kenya
131/D2 Mbuzi, Zam.
130/C5 Mbwemburu (riv.), Tanz.
130/B4 Mbwikwe, Tanz.
159/J4 McAlester, Ok,US
162/D5 McAllen, Tx,US
156/C2 McBride, BC,Can
156/D4 McCall, Id,US
162/C4 McCamey, Tx,US
165/C3 McChord A.F.B., Wa,US
165/M9 McClellan A.F.B., Ca,US
157/H4 McClusky, ND,US
163/F4 McComb, Ms,US
159/G2 McConaughy (lake), Ne,US
159/H3 McConnell A.F.B., Ks,US
159/G2 McCook, Ne,US
163/H3 McCormick, SC,US
157/J3 McCreary, Mb,Can
158/C2 McDermitt, Nv,US
51/N8 McDonald (isls.), Austl.
151/F3 McDonald (mtn.), Ak,US
117/H5 McDonnell (peak), Austl.
151/L2 McDougall (pass), NW, Yk,Can
162/F3 McGehee, Ar,US
163/F3 McGehee, Ar,US
156/C2 McGregor (riv.), BC,Can
165/G7 McGregor, On,Can
166/D3 McGuire A.F.B., NJ,US
165/P15 McHenry, Il,US
165/N15 McHenry (co.), Il,US
130/C5 Mchinga, Tanz.
131/D2 Mchinji, Malw.
121/H5 McKean (atoll), Kiri.
153/K2 McKeand (riv.), NW,Can
168/H7 McKeesport, Pa,US
168/G7 McKees Rocks, Pa,US
163/F2 McKenzie, Tn,US
151/H3 McKinley (mtn.), Ak,US
151/J3 McKinley Park, Ak,US
156/B5 McKinleyville, Ca,US
162/D3 McKinney, Tx,US
117/G2 McLaren Creek Abor. Land, Austl.
157/H4 McLaughlin, SD,US
166/A6 McLean, Va,US
156/D2 McLennan, Ab,Can
114/A4 McLeod (lake), Austl.
156/D2 McLeod (riv.), Ab,Can
152/E2 McLeod (bay), NW,Can
156/C2 McLeod Lake, BC,Can
152/F1 M'Clintock (chan.), NW,Can
153/Q7 M'Clure (str.), NW,Can
156/C4 McMinnville, Or,US
163/G3 McMinnville, Tn,US
113/M McMurdo, Ant.
165/B3 McNeil (isl.), Wa,US
131/D2 Mcocha, Malw.
159/H3 McPherson, Ks,US
130/B4 Mdabulo, Tanz.
130/B4 Mdaburo, Tanz.
130/B5 Mdandu, Tanz.
96/E5 Mê (riv.), China
158/D3 Mead (lake), Az, Nv,US
151/G2 Meade (riv.), Ak,US
156/F2 Meadow Lake, Sk,Can
167/J8 Meadowlands Sports Complex, NJ,US
161/Q8 Meadowvale, On,Can
158/D3 Meadow Valley (riv.), Nv,US
163/F4 Meadville, Ms,US
160/D3 Meadville, Pa,US
100/C2 Me-akan-dake (mtn.), Japan
60/A6 Mealagh (riv.), Ire.
54/B3 Meall a' Bhuiridh (mtn.), Sc,UK
54/B3 Meall Buidhe (mtn.), Sc,UK
54/C3 Meall Dearg (mtn.), Sc,UK
54/B2 Meall Dubh (mtn.), Sc,UK
54/C4 Meall nam Fuaran (mtn.), Sc,UK
54/C3 Meall Tairneachan (mtn.), Sc,UK
168/G5 Meander Creek (res.), Oh,US
140/A1 Mearim (riv.), Braz.
54/D3 Mearns, Howe of the (dist.), Sc,UK
59/E1 Measham, Eng,UK
151/F2 Meat (mtn.), Ak,US
60/D2 Meath (co.), Ire.
157/G2 Meath Park, Sk,Can
53/U10 Meaux, Fr.
147/M6 Mecapalapa, Mex.
94/C4 Mecca (Makkah), SAr.
166/A3 Mechanicsburg, Pa,US
166/B3 Mechanicsburg Nav. Supply Dep., Pa,US
68/D1 Mechelen (Malines), Belg.
92/C1 Mecitözü, Turk.
77/F2 Meckenbeuren, Ger.
69/G2 Meckenheim, Ger.
62/D4 Mecklenburg (bay), Ger.
64/F1 Mecklenburger Bucht (bay), Ger.
64/F2 Mecklenburg-Western Pomerania (state), Ger.
131/D2 Mecuia (peak), Moz.
78/C1 Meda, It.
106/C4 Medak, India
110/A3 Medan, Indo.
143/L7 Medanosa (pt.), Arg.
138/D2 Medanos de Coro Nat'l Park, Ven.
59/F1 Medbourne, Eng,UK
123/S15 Médéa, Alg.
123/S15 Médéa (wilaya), Alg.
75/G4 Medea (wilaya), Alg.
67/F6 Medebach, Ger.
140/B5 Medeiros Neto, Braz.
138/C3 Medellín, Col.
78/B2 Mede Lomellina, It.
77/E4 Medel, Piz (peak), Swi.
66/C3 Medemblik, Neth.
57/G5 Meden (riv.), Eng,UK
92/C2 Medetsiz (peak), Turk.
168/C1 Medford, Ma,US
167/F2 Medford, NY,US
156/C5 Medford, Or,US
160/B2 Medford, Wi,US
83/J3 Medgidia, Rom.
83/G2 Mediaş, Rom.
156/D4 Medical Lake, Wa,US
158/F2 Medicine Bow (range), Co, Wy,US
157/G5 Medicine Bow, Wy,US
156/F3 Medicine Hat, Ab,Can
140/B5 Medina, Braz.
59/E5 Medina (riv.), Eng,UK
157/J4 Medina, ND,US
168/F5 Medina, Oh,US
168/F5 Medina (co.), Oh,US
159/H5 Medina, Tx,US
94/C4 Medina (Al Madīnah), SAr.
74/C2 Medina del Campo, Sp.
74/C4 Medina-Sidonia, Sp.
51/K4 Mediterranean (sea)
156/F2 Medley, Ab,Can
87/L2 Mednogorsk, Rus.
87/H2 Medveditsa, Gora (riv.), Rus.
89/S2 Medvezh'i (isls.), Rus.
84/G3 Medvezh'yegorsk, Rus.
53/P8 Medway (riv.), Eng,UK
168/C1 Medway, Ma,US
158/F2 Meeker, Co,US
67/G3 Meerbach (riv.), Ger.
66/D6 Meerbusch, Ger.
69/E1 Meerhout, Belg.
69/E2 Meerssen, Neth.
106/C2 Meerut, India
59/E1 Meese (riv.), Eng,UK
156/F4 Meeteetse, Wy,US
125/N7 Mēga, Eth.
125/P6 Megalo, Eth.
161/G2 Megantic (peak), Qu,Can
81/H3 Mégara, Gre.
107/F2 Meghalaya (state), India
91/G6 Megiddo (ruins), Isr.
160/E1 Mégiscane (lake), Qu,Can
160/E1 Mégiscane (riv.), Qu,Can
91/A1 Megista (isl.), Gre.
131/C4 Meguzalala, Moz.
69/E2 Mehaigne (riv.), Belg.
116/C2 Meharry (mtn.), Austl.
123/R16 Mehdia, Alg.
67/G1 Mehe (riv.), Ger.
106/C3 Mehkar, India
93/H5 Mehrān (riv.), Iran
93/H4 Mehriz, Iran
106/B3 Mehsāna, India
105/G4 Mei (riv.), China
130/B4 Meia Meia, Tanz.
141/B1 Meia Ponte (riv.), Braz.
124/H6 Meiganga, Camr.
153/R6 Meighen (isl.), NW,Can
54/C3 Meigle, Sc,UK
107/H2 Meigu, China
97/K3 Meihekou, China
54/B4 Meikle Bin (mtn.), Sc,UK
54/D5 Meikle Says Law (mtn.), Sc,UK
104/B4 Meiktila, Burma
77/E3 Meilen, Swi.
67/H4 Meine, Ger.
67/E6 Meinerzhagen, Ger.
70/D1 Meiningen, Ger.
103/D5 Meishan, China
104/D2 Meishan, China
103/C5 Meishan (res.), China
65/G3 Meissen, Ger.
67/G6 Meissner (peak), Ger.
70/D5 Meitingen, Ger.
99/M10 Meiwa, Japan
105/H3 Meizhou, China
79/E2 Mejaniga, It.
124/H7 Mekambo, Gabon
125/N5 Mek'elē, Eth.
123/M14 Meknès, Mor.
109/D4 Mekong (riv.), Asia
111/F4 Mekongga (peak), Indo.
104/D4 Mekong (Lancang) (riv.), China
109/D4 Mekong, Mouths of the, Viet.
110/B3 Melaka, Malay.
120/E5 Melanesia (reg.)
108/F4 Melappālaiyam, India
110/D4 Melawi (riv.), Indo.
59/G2 Melbourn, Eng,UK
119/C3 Melbourne, Austl.
152/F5 Melbourne (isl.), NW,Can
57/G6 Melbourne, Eng,UK
163/H4 Melbourne, Fl,US
119/F5 Melbourne (inset), Austl.
142/B5 Melchor (isl.), Chile
148/D2 Melchor de Mencos, Guat.
58/D5 Melcombe Regis, Eng,UK
79/F4 Meldola, It.
64/E1 Meldorf, Ger.
78/B5 Mele, Capo (cape), It.
78/C2 Melegnano, It.
82/E3 Melenci, Yugo.
84/J5 Melenki, Rus.
87/K1 Meleuz, Rus.
153/J3 Mélèzes (riv.), Qu,Can
77/E5 Melezza (riv.), It.
124/J5 Melfi, Chad
80/D2 Melfi, It.
157/G2 Melfort, Sk,Can
61/D3 Melhus, Nor.
70/B3 Melibocus (peak), Ger.
130/C3 Melili (peak), Kenya
123/N13 Melilla, Sp.
142/B5 Melimoyu (peak), Chile
142/Q9 Melipilla, Chile
81/F3 Melissano, It.
157/H3 Melita, Mb,Can
80/D4 Melito di Porto Salvo, It.
86/E3 Melitopol', Ukr.
73/L2 Melk, Aus.
125/P7 Melka Meri, Eth.
58/D4 Melksham, Eng,UK
78/D2 Mella (riv.), It.
62/E2 Mellan Fryken (lake), Swe.
68/C2 Melle, Belg.
67/F4 Melle, Ger.
123/W17 Mellègue (riv.), Alg.
62/E2 Mellerud, Swe.
74/B1 Mellid, Sp.
57/F3 Melling, Eng,UK
115/K3 Mellish (reef), Austl.
143/J7 Mellizo Sur (peak), Chile
70/D2 Mellrichstadt, Ger.
67/F1 Mellum (isl.), Ger.
71/H2 Mělník, Czh.
143/G2 Melo, Uru.
54/D5 Melrose, Sc,UK
54/D5 Melrose Abbey, Sc,UK
165/Q16 Melrose Park, Il,US
77/F3 Mels, Swi.
67/G6 Melsungen, Ger.
57/G4 Meltham, Eng,UK
119/C3 Melton, Austl.
57/H6 Melton Mowbray, Eng,UK
53/T11 Melun, Fr.
108/G3 Melūr, India
116/K7 Melville, Austl.
114/F2 Melville (bay), Austl.
118/B1 Melville (cape), Austl.
114/E2 Melville (isl.), Austl.
153/L3 Melville (lake), Nf,Can
153/R7 Melville (isl.), NW,Can
153/H2 Melville (pen.), NW,Can
157/H3 Melville, Sk,Can
112/B4 Melville (cape), Phil.
167/E2 Melville, NY,US
165/F7 Melvindale, Mi,US
82/D2 Mélykút, Hun.
78/C2 Melzo, It.
102/D5 Mêmar (lake), China
66/D1 Memmert (isl.), Ger.
77/G2 Memmingen, Ger.
109/D4 Memot, Camb.
91/B5 Memphis (ruins), Egypt
165/G6 Memphis, Mi,US
159/J2 Memphis, Mo,US
163/F3 Memphis, Tn,US
162/C3 Memphis, Tx,US
162/E3 Mena, Ar,US
56/D5 Menai (str.), Wal,UK
56/D5 Menai Bridge, Wal,UK
66/C2 Menaldum, Neth.
133/H9 Menarandra (riv.), Madg.
162/D4 Menard, Tx,US
160/B2 Menasha, Wi,US
133/H7 Menavava (riv.), Madg.
110/D4 Mendawai (riv.), Indo.
72/E4 Mende, Fr.
67/E6 Menden, Ger.
151/E4 Mendenhall (cape), Ak,US
141/K7 Mendes, Braz.
125/N6 Mendī, Eth.
69/G3 Mendig, Ger.
58/D4 Mendip (hills), Eng,UK
158/B3 Mendocino, Ca,US
154/B3 Mendocino (cape), Ca,US
165/M11 Mendota-Delta (can.), Ca,US
142/C2 Mendoza, Arg.
142/C2 Mendoza (prov.), Arg.
133/H9 Mendrare (riv.), Madg.
77/E6 Mendrisio, Swi.
82/F3 Menedinţi (co.), Rom.
78/C3 Menegosa, Monte (peak), It.
138/D2 Mene Grande, Ven.
92/A2 Menemen, Turk.
68/C2 Menen, Belg.
130/C3 Menengai Crater, Kenya
96/H2 Menengiyn (plain), Mong.
80/C4 Menfi, It.
103/D4 Mengcheng, China
70/C6 Mengen, Ger.
110/C4 Menggala, Indo.
109/C1 Menghai, China
74/D4 Mengibar, Sp.
109/C1 Mengla, China
104/C4 Menglian Daizu Lahuzu Vazu Zizhixian, China
103/D4 Menglianggu (mtn.), China
105/F3 Mengshan, China
103/C4 Meng Xian, China
103/D4 Mengyin, China
104/D4 Mengzi, China
119/B2 Menindee (dam), Austl.
119/B2 Menindee (lake), Austl.
142/B5 Menlolat (peak), Chile
165/K12 Menlo Park, Ca,US
53/T11 Mennecy, Fr.
160/C2 Menominee, Mi,US
160/B3 Menomonee Falls, Wi,US
160/B2 Menomonie, Wi,US
126/C3 Menongue, Ang.
75/H3 Menorca (Minorca) (isl.), Sp.
110/A4 Mentawai (isls.), Indo.
110/A4 Mentawai (str.), Indo.
162/C4 Mentone, Tx,US
160/D3 Mentor, Oh,US
76/C4 Mentue (riv.), Swi.
53/R9 Menucourt, Fr.
111/E3 Menyapa (peak), Indo.
96/E4 Menyuan, China
123/W17 Menzel Bourguiba, Tun.
151/M3 Menzie (mtn.), Yk,Can
59/E5 Meon (riv.), Eng,UK
53/Q7 Meopham, Eng,UK
111/H4 Meos Waar (isl.), Indo.
126/B2 Mepala, Ang.
87/G4 Mepistskaro (peak), Geo.
66/D3 Meppel, Neth.
67/E3 Meppen, Ger.
75/E2 Mequinenzo (res.), Sp.
77/F5 Mera (riv.), It., Swi.
159/K3 Meramec (riv.), Mo,US
77/H4 Merano, It.
110/D4 Meratus (mts.), Indo.
120/D5 Merauke, Indo.
125/P7 Merca, Som.
73/G4 Mercantour Nat'l Park, Fr.
158/B3 Merced, Ca,US
158/C3 Merced (riv.), Ca,US
142/C1 Mercedario (peak), Arg.
142/D2 Mercedes, Arg.
142/F2 Mercedes, Arg.
143/F2 Mercedes, Uru.
166/D3 Mercer (co.), NJ,US
168/G5 Mercer (co.), Pa,US
165/C2 Mercer (isl.), Wa,US
165/C2 Mercer Island, Wa,US
166/D3 Mercerville-Hamilton Square, NJ,US
68/D2 Merchtem, Belg.
161/N7 Mercier, Qu,Can
156/D2 Mercoal, Ab,Can
158/D3 Mercury, Nv,US
153/K2 Mercy (cape), Yk,Can
72/E5 Merdellou (mtn.), Fr.
58/D4 Mere, Eng,UK
143/M8 Meredith (cape), Falk.
162/C3 Meredith (lake), Tx,US
86/F2 Merefa, Ukr.
68/C2 Merelbeke, Belg.
109/D3 Mereuch, Camb.
53/Q8 Mereworth, Eng,UK
97/J2 Mergel (riv.), China
109/B3 Mergui, Burma
109/B4 Mergui (arch.), Burma
68/B3 Méricourt, Fr.
147/H4 Mérida, Mex.
74/B3 Mérida, Sp.
138/D2 Mérida, Ven.
138/D3 Mérida (mts.), Ven.
138/D2 Mérida (state), Ven.
168/B2 Meriden, Ct,US
163/F3 Meridian, Ms,US
162/D4 Meridian, Tx,US
165/C2 Meridian-East Hill, Wa,US
72/C4 Mérignac, Fr.
70/D6 Mering, Ger.
68/D1 Merksem, Belg.
69/B6 Merksplas, Belg.
143/S12 Merlo, Arg.
125/M4 Meroe (ruins), Sudan
91/D3 Meron, Har (mtn.), Isr.
119/F5 Merri (cr.), Austl.
55/J9 Merrick (mtn.), UK
167/E2 Merrick, NY,US
160/B2 Merrill, Wi,US
166/C2 Merrill Creek (res.), NJ,US
161/G3 Merrimack, NH,US
58/D5 Merriott, Eng,UK
156/C3 Merritt, BC,Can
163/H4 Merritt Island, Fl,US
54/D5 Merse (dist.), Sc,UK
57/F5 Mersey (riv.), Eng,UK
57/F5 Merseyside (co.), Eng,UK
91/D1 Mersin, Turk.
110/B3 Mersing, Malay.
53/N8 Merstham, Eng,UK
69/F5 Merten, Fr.
58/C3 Merthyr Tydfil, Wal,UK
53/N7 Merton (bor.), Eng,UK
113/K Mertz (glac.), Ant.
162/C4 Mertzon, Tx,US
68/B5 Méru, Fr.
130/C2 Meru, Kenya
130/C3 Meru (peak), Tanz.
130/C2 Meru Nat'l Park, Kenya
68/B2 Merville, Fr.
66/C5 Merwedekanaal (can.), Neth.
53/S9 Méry-sur-Oise, Fr.
69/F2 Merzenich, Ger.
92/C1 Merzifon, Turk.
69/F5 Merzig, Ger.
143/K7 Mesa (peak), Arg.
151/G3 Mesa (mtn.), Ak,US
158/E4 Mesa, Az,US
157/K4 Mesabi (range), Mn,US
81/E2 Mesagne, It.
81/J5 Mesarás (gulf), Gre.
158/E3 Mesa Verde Nat'l Park, Co,US
162/C3 Mescalero (ridge), NM,US
67/F6 Meschede, Ger.
79/F5 Mescolino, Monte (peak), It.
78/C4 Mesco, Punta di (pt.), It.
160/F1 Mesgouez (lake), Qu,Can
168/B2 Meshomasic Saint For., Ct,US
81/G3 Mesolóngion, Gre.
142/F2 Mesopotamia (reg.), Arg.
93/E3 Mesopotamia (reg.), Iraq
80/E3 Mesoraca, It.
162/D3 Mesquite, Tx,US
124/E1 Mesrouh (peak), Mor.
124/F1 Messaad, Alg.
143/J7 Messier (chan.), Chile
80/D3 Messina, It.
80/D4 Messina (str.), It.
131/C4 Messina, SAfr.
131/D2 Messinge (riv.), Moz.
81/H4 Messíni, Gre.
81/H4 Messini (gulf), Gre.
70/C7 Messkirch, Ger.
70/B6 Messstetten, Ger.
53/U10 Messy, Fr.
83/F5 Mesta (riv.), Bul.
79/F2 Mestre, It.
130/C4 Mesumba (peak), Tanz.
128/C5 Mesurado (cape), Libr.
138/C4 Meta (dept.), Col.
138/D3 Meta (riv.), Col., Ven.
161/G1 Métabetchouan, Qu,Can
161/G1 Métabetchouane (riv.), Qu,Can
153/K2 Meta Incognita (pen.), NW,Can
163/F4 Metairie, La,US
79/D6 Metallifere (mts.), It.
135/D2 Metán, Arg.
131/D2 Metangula, Moz.
80/E2 Metapontum (ruins), It.
79/F5 Metauro (riv.), It.
81/G3 Metéora, Gre.
57/H5 Metheringham, Eng,UK
54/C4 Methil, Sc,UK
54/D2 Methlick, Sc,UK
81/G4 Methóni, Gre.
54/C4 Methven, Sc,UK
138/C4 Metica (riv.), Col.
82/C4 Metković, Cro.
160/B4 Metropolis, Il,US
161/R8 Metro Toronto Zoo, On,Can
69/D3 Mettet, Belg.
67/E4 Mettingen, Ger.
69/F5 Mettlach, Ger.
66/D6 Mettmann, Ger.
108/F3 Mettupālaiyam, India
108/F3 Mettūr, India
125/N6 Metu, Eth.
167/D2 Metuchen, NJ,US
69/F5 Metz, Fr.
70/C5 Metzingen, Ger.
53/S10 Meudon, Fr.
68/C2 Meulebeke, Belg.
76/C1 Meurthe (riv.), Fr.
69/E6 Meurthe-et-Moselle (dept.), Fr.
69/E3 Meuse (riv.), Belg., Fr.
68/E6 Meuse (dept.), Fr.
72/F2 Meuse (uplands), Fr.
69/E5 Meuse, Cotes de (uplands), Fr.
76/A3 Meuzin (riv.), Fr.
91/G8 Mevasseret Ẕiyyon, Isr.
57/G5 Mexborough, Eng,UK
162/D4 Mexia, Tx,US
137/J3 Mexiana, Braz.
145/G7 México
147/E5 México (state), Mex.
154/H6 Mexico (gulf), NAm
159/K3 Mexico, Mo,US
147/K7 Mexico City (cap.), Mex.
147/Q10 Mexico City (inset) (cap.), Mex.
93/H3 Meybod, Iran
112/F6 Meycauayan, Phil.
93/H4 Meydān-e Gel (lake), Iran
132/Q13 Meyerton, SAfr.
95/H1 Meymaneh, Afg.
76/C5 Meyrin, Swi.
72/E3 Meythet, Fr.
91/D4 Meẕada, Horvot (Masada) (ruins), Isr.
83/F4 Mezdra, Bul.
84/J2 Mezen' (bay), Rus.
53/H2 Mezen' (riv.), Rus.
63/P4 Mezha (riv.), Rus.
88/J4 Mezhdurechensk, Rus.
88/E2 Mezhdusharskiy (isl.), Rus.
82/E2 Mezőberény, Hun.
82/E2 Mezőkovácsháza, Hun.
82/E2 Mezőkövesd, Hun.
82/E2 Mezőtúr, Hun.
77/G5 Mezzana, Cima (peak), It.
130/B3 Mfangano (isl.), Ugan.
130/B5 Mfrika, Tanz.
130/C4 Mgambo, Tanz.
130/C4 Mgera, Tanz.
130/C5 Mgeta, Tanz.
130/B4 Mgori, Tanz.
54/B2 Mhòr, Loch (lake), Sc,UK
106/C3 Mhow, India
130/B3 Mhunze, Tanz.
103/D3 Mi (riv.), China
148/B2 Miahuatlán, Mex.
74/C3 Miajadas, Sp.
158/E4 Miami, Az,US
163/H5 Miami, Fl,US
159/J3 Miami, Ok,US
163/H5 Miami Beach, Fl,US
108/B2 Miān Channūn, Pak.
103/B4 Mianchi, China
93/F2 Mīāndoāb, Iran
133/H7 Miandrivazo, Madg.
93/F2 Mīāneh, Iran
108/B1 Miāni, Pak.
104/D2 Mianmian (mts.), China
104/D2 Mianning, China
167/E1 Mianus (riv.), Ct,US
108/A1 Miānwāli, Pak.
104/E2 Mianyang, China
104/E2 Mianzhu, China
103/E3 Miaodao (isls.), China
105/F3 Miao'er (peak), China
103/H6 Miaofeng Shan (mtn.), China
85/P5 Miass, Rus.
85/Q5 Miass (riv.), Rus.
65/J2 Miastko, Pol.
127/C5 Miberika, Sudan
156/D2 Mica Creek, BC,Can
65/L4 Michalovce, Slvk.
151/K2 Michelson (mtn.), Ak,US
70/C3 Michelstadt, Ger.
150/D3 Miches, DRep.
160/C3 Michigan (lake), Can., US
160/C2 Michigan (state), US
160/C3 Michigan City, In,US
160/C2 Michipicoten (isl.), On,Can
147/E5 Michoacán (state), Mex.
87/G1 Michurinsk, Rus.
57/F2 Mickle Fell (mtn.), Eng,UK
57/F2 Mickleton, Eng,UK
149/E3 Mico (riv.), Nic.
150/F4 Micoud, StL.
120/E3 Micronesia (reg.)
120/D4 Micronesia, Fed. States of
129/G2 Midal (well), Niger
157/H3 Midale, Sk,Can
66/A6 Middelburg, Neth.
132/D3 Middelburg, SAfr.
133/E2 Middelburg, SAfr.
64/E1 Middelfart, Den.
66/B5 Middelharnis, Neth.
68/B1 Middelkerke, Belg.
165/M11 Middle (riv.), Ca,US
167/L9 Middle (bay), NY,US
166/A2 Middle (cr.), Pa,US
158/C2 Middle Alkali (lake), Ca,US
107/F5 Middle Andaman (isl.), India
168/D2 Middleboro, Ma,US
168/F5 Middleburg Heights, Oh,US
168/A2 Middlebury, Ct,US
161/F2 Middlebury, Vt,US
150/D2 Middle Caicos (isl.), Trks.
162/C4 Middle Concho (riv.), Tx,US
57/G3 Middleham, Eng,UK
159/G2 Middle Loup (riv.), Ne,US
159/J2 Middle Raccoon (riv.), Ia,US
166/B5 Middle River, Md,US
165/F7 Middle Rouge (riv.), Mi,US
160/D4 Middlesboro, Ky,US
57/G2 Middlesbrough, Eng,UK
59/F4 Middlesex (reg.), Eng,UK
168/B2 Middlesex (co.), Ct,US
168/C1 Middlesex (co.), Ma,US
166/D2 Middlesex, NJ,US
166/D3 Middlesex (co.), NJ,US
156/C4 Middle Sister (peak), Or,US
57/F4 Middleton, Eng,UK
59/E2 Middleton Cheney, Eng,UK
57/F2 Middleton-in-Teesdale, Eng,UK
56/B3 Middletown, NI,UK
168/B2 Middletown, Ct,US
167/D3 Middletown, NJ,US
166/B3 Middletown, Pa,US
168/C2 Middletown, RI,US
57/F5 Middlewich, Eng,UK
58/C3 Mid Glamorgan (co.), Wal,UK
59/F5 Midhurst, Eng,UK
72/D5 Midi (can.), Fr.
72/D4 Midi-Pyrénées (reg.), Fr.
116/L6 Midland, Austl.
160/E2 Midland, On,Can
160/C3 Midland, Mi,US
162/C4 Midland, Tx,US
167/J8 Midland Park, NJ,US
131/C3 Midlands (prov.), Zim.
165/Q16 Midlothian, Il,US
114/G6 Midona (lake), Austl.
72/C5 Midou (riv.), Fr.
112/D4 Midsayap, Phil.
58/D4 Midsomer Norton, Eng,UK
107/H2 Midu, China
120/H2 Midway (isls.), PacUS
119/C4 Midway Point-Sorell, Austl.
159/H4 Midwest City, Ok,US
92/C5 Midyan (reg.), SAr.
92/E2 Midyat, Turk.
55/P12 Mid Yell, Sc,UK
86/B4 Midzhur (peak), Bul.
82/F4 Midžor (peak), Yugo.
98/B4 Mie, Japan
98/E3 Mie (pref.), Japan
65/H2 Międzychód, Pol.
65/M3 Międzyrzec Podlaski, Pol.
65/H2 Międzyrzecz, Pol.
65/L3 Mielec, Pol.
124/J7 Mièle I, Congo
83/G2 Miercurea Ciuc, Rom.
74/C1 Mieres, Sp.
73/J3 Miesbach, Ger.
125/P6 Mī'ēso, Eth.
72/E3 Migennes, Fr.
130/B3 Migori, Kenya
130/B3 Migori (riv.), Kenya
147/N8 Miguel Aleman (res.), Mex.
140/B2 Miguel Alves, Braz.
146/E3 Miguel Auza, Mex.
140/B3 Miguel Calmon, Braz.
147/Q10 Miguel Hidalgo, Mex.
146/C3 Miguel Hidalgo (res.), Mex.
141/B2 Miguelópolis, Braz.
141/K7 Miguel Pereira, Braz.
74/D3 Miguelturra, Sp.
98/D3 Mihama, Japan
98/C3 Mihara, Japan
99/G2 Miharu, Japan
108/H4 Mihintale (ruins), SrL.
95/J3 Mihrābpur, Pak.
75/E2 Mijares (riv.), Sp.
74/C4 Mijas, Sp.
66/B4 Mijdrecht, Neth.
100/B2 Mikasa, Japan
99/N10 Mikawa (bay), Japan
99/N9 Mikawa-Mino (mts.), Japan
130/C4 Mikese, Tanz.
83/F4 Mikhaylovgrad, Bul.
82/F4 Mikhaylovgrad (reg.), Bul.
87/G2 Mikhaylovka, Rus.
99/K10 Miki, Japan
130/D5 Mikindani, Tanz.
61/H3 Mikkeli, Fin.
63/L1 Mikkeli (prov.), Fin.
81/J4 Míkonos (isl.), Gre.
81/G2 Mikri Prespa (lake), Gre.
99/M10 Mikuma, Japan
130/C4 Mikumi, Tanz.
130/C4 Mikumi Nat'l Park, Tanz.
98/E2 Mikuni, Japan
99/F2 Mikuni-tōge (pass), Japan
123/V17 Mila, Alg.
123/U17 Mila (gov.), Alg.
140/C2 Milagres, Braz.
138/B5 Milagro, Ecu.
52/D4 Milan, It.
131/D3 Milange, Moz.
78/C2 Milan (Milano), It.
78/C2 Milano (prov.), It.
78/C2 Milano (Milan), It.
92/A2 Milas, Turk.
80/D3 Milazzo, It.
58/D5 Milborne Port, Eng,UK
59/G2 Mildenhall, Eng,UK
119/B2 Mildura, Austl.
104/D3 Mile, China
130/A5 Milepa, Tanz.
162/C4 Miles, Tx,US
157/G4 Miles City, Mt,US
71/G1 Milešovka (peak), Czh.
157/G3 Milestone, Sk,Can
80/D2 Miletto (peak), It.
71/H4 Milevsko, Czh.
59/F4 Milford, Eng,UK
56/B3 Milford, NI,UK
168/A3 Milford, Ct,US
166/C6 Milford, De,US
162/D2 Milford (lake), Ks,US
168/C1 Milford, Ma,US
158/D3 Milford, Ut,US
58/A3 Milford Haven, Wal,UK
58/A3 Milford Haven (inlet), Wal,UK
59/E5 Milford on Sea, Eng,UK
120/G4 Mili (atoll), Mrsh.
123/S15 Miliana, Alg.
65/J3 Milicz, Pol.
154/V13 Mililani Town, Hi,US
156/F3 Milk (riv.), Can., US
59/E4 Milk (hill), Eng,UK
156/E3 Milk River, Ab,Can
113/G Mill (isl.), Ant.
153/J2 Mill (isl.), NW,Can
165/G5 Mill (cr.), Mi,US
168/F7 Mill (cr.), Oh,US
168/G5 Mill (cr.), Oh,US
72/E4 Millau, Fr.
165/K11 Millbrae, Ca,US
117/M8 Millbrook (res.), Austl.
58/B6 Millbrook, Eng,UK
167/H9 Millburn, NJ,US
168/C1 Millbury, Ma,US
163/H3 Milledgeville, Ga,US
161/N6 Mille Iles (riv.), Qu,Can
160/B1 Mille Lacs (lake), On,Can
157/K4 Mille Lacs (lake), Mn,US
157/J4 Miller, SD,US
87/G2 Millerovo, Rus.
163/G3 Millers Ferry (dam), Al,US
166/B4 Millersville, Pa,US
56/C1 Milleur (pt.), Sc,UK
72/D4 Millevaches (plat.), Fr.
161/Q9 Millgrove, On,Can
161/R8 Milliken, On,Can
162/G2 Millinocket, Me,US
168/C1 Millis, Ma,US
56/C2 Millisle, NI,UK
57/E3 Millom, Eng,UK
54/B5 Millport, Sc,UK

157/G5 Mills, Wy,US
167/F1 Millstone (pt.), Ct,US
166/D3 Millstone (riv.), NJ,US
116/C2 Millstream-Chichester Nat'l Park, Austl.
57/F3 Millthrop, Eng,UK
167/H10 Milltown, NJ,US
165/J11 Mill Valley, Ca,US
166/C5 Millville, NJ,US
162/E3 Millwood (lake), Ar,US
120/E5 Milne (bay), PNG
54/B5 Milngavie, Sc,UK
57/F4 Milnrow, Eng,UK
128/C4 Milo (riv.), Gui.
161/G2 Milo, Me,US
81/J4 Milos (isl.), Gre.
147/Q10 Milpa Alta, Mex.
165/L12 Milpitas, Ca,US
70/C1 Milseburg (peak), Ger.
70/C3 Miltenberg, Ger.
161/Q8 Milton, On,Can
115/Q12 Milton, NZ
57/F2 Milton, Eng,UK
59/G4 Milton, Eng,UK
163/G4 Milton, Fl,US
168/C1 Milton, Ma,US
161/G3 Milton, NH,US
168/F5 Milton (res.), Oh,US
166/B1 Milton, Pa,US
156/D4 Milton-Freewater, Or,US
161/Q8 Milton Heights, On,Can
59/F2 Milton Keynes, Eng,UK
54/D3 Milton Ness (pt.), Sc,UK
54/B5 Milton of Campsie, Sc,UK
55/G10 Miltown Malbay, Ire.
105/G2 Miluo (riv.), China
58/C4 Milverton, Eng,UK
165/Q13 Milwaukee, Wi,US
165/Q14 Milwaukee (co.), Wi,US
70/D2 Milz (riv.), Ger.
98/B4 Mimi (riv.), Japan
72/C4 Mimizan, Fr.
100/B3 Mimmaya, Japan
104/D2 Min (riv.), China
105/H3 Min (riv.), China
123/R16 Mina (riv.), Alg.
158/C3 Mina, Nv,US
111/F3 Minahasa (pen.), Indo.
99/M10 Minakuchi, Japan
98/D4 Minamata, Japan
99/F3 Minami-Alps Nat'l Park, Japan
99/M10 Minamichita, Japan
120/D2 Minamiiō (isl.), Japan
100/B3 Minamikayabe, Japan
120/E2 Minami-Tori-Shima (isl.), Japan
99/L10 Minamiyamashiro, Japan
149/G2 Minas, Cuba
138/B5 Minas (peak), Ecu.
143/G2 Minas, Uru.
149/F1 Minas de Matahambre, Cuba
74/B4 Minas de Riotinto, Sp.
141/H6 Minas Gerais (state), Braz.
140/B5 Minas Novas, Braz.
147/G5 Minatitlán, Mex.
104/B4 Minbu, Burma
142/C1 Mincha, Chile
108/B2 Minchinābād, Pak.
58/D3 Minchinhampton, Eng,UK
142/B4 Minchinmávida (vol.), Chile
55/H8 Minch, The (sound), Sc,UK
79/D2 Mincio (riv.), It.
112/C4 Mindanao (isl.), Phil.
112/C3 Mindanao (sea), Phil.
70/D6 Mindel (riv.), Ger.
70/D6 Mindelheim, Ger.
122/J10 Mindelo, CpV.
67/F4 Minden, Ger.
162/E3 Minden, La,US
159/H2 Minden, Ne,US
112/C2 Mindoro (isl.), Phil.
112/C2 Mindoro (str.), Phil.
60/C5 Mine Head (pt.), Ire.
58/C4 Minehead, Eng,UK
137/H7 Mineiros, Braz.
167/E2 Mineola, NY,US
147/L6 Mineral del Monte, Mex.
87/G3 Mineral'nye Vody, Rus.
162/D3 Mineral Wells, Tx,US
73/H5 Minerbio (riv.), Fr.
102/D4 Minfeng, China
103/C3 Ming (riv.), China
131/B1 Minga, Zaire
161/J1 Mingan (riv.), Qu,Can
95/K2 Mingāora, Pak.
87/H4 Mingechaur, Azer.
87/H4 Mingechaur (res.), Azer.
104/B4 Mingin, Burma
130/C5 Mingoyo, Tanz.
104/D2 Mingshan, China
97/K2 Mingshui, China
109/A1 Mingun, Ancient City of (ruins), Burma
96/E4 Minhe, China
74/B1 Minho (riv.), Sp.
116/D4 Minigwal (lake), Austl.
157/L3 Miniss (lake), On,Can
157/H2 Minitonas, Mb,Can

96/E4 Minle, China
157/K4 Minneapolis, Mn,US
157/J3 Minnedosa, Mb,Can
157/K4 Minnesota (state), US
157/K4 Minnesota (riv.), Mn,US
56/D2 Minnigaff, Sc,UK
160/B1 Minnis (lake), On,Can
160/A1 Minnitaki (lake), On,Can
99/E3 Mino, Japan
99/F3 Minobu, Japan
99/N9 Mino-Mikawa (mts.), Japan
99/L10 Mino'o, Japan
99/L10 Mino'o (riv.), Japan
75/G3 Minorca (Menorca) (isl.), Sp.
157/H3 Minot, ND,US
96/E4 Minqin, China
105/H3 Minqing, China
103/C4 Minquan, China
67/F1 Minsener Oog (isl.), Ger.
86/C1 Minsk (cap.), Bela.
65/L2 Mińsk Mazowiecki, Pol.
86/C1 Minsk Obl., Bela.
59/G4 Minster, Eng,UK
102/B4 Mintaka (pass), China
54/E1 Mintlaw, Sc,UK
161/H2 Minto, NB,Can
152/E1 Minto (inlet), NW,Can
151/L3 Minto, Yk,Can
80/C2 Minturno, It.
91/B4 Minūf, Egypt
88/K4 Minusinsk, Rus.
96/E5 Min Xian, China
91/B4 Minyā al Qamḥ, Egypt
102/E3 Miquan, China
161/K2 Miquelon, StP.
138/B4 Mira (riv.), Col., Ecu.
74/A2 Mira, Port.
74/A4 Mira (riv.), Port.
161/M6 Mirabel, Qu,Can
140/A5 Mirabela, Braz.
141/D2 Miracema, Braz.
137/J3 Miracema do Norte, Braz.
140/A2 Mirador, Braz.
142/C4 Mirador (pass), Chile
106/B4 Miraj, India
164/C2 Mira Loma, Ca,US
142/F3 Miramar, Arg.
164/C5 Miramar Nav. Air Sta., Ca,US
81/J5 Mirambéllou (gulf), Gre.
164/A3 Mira Monte, Ca,US
137/G8 Miranda (riv.), Braz.
139/E2 Miranda (state), Ven.
74/D1 Miranda de Ebro, Sp.
79/E3 Mirandola, It.
141/B2 Mirandópolis, Braz.
79/F2 Mirano, It.
141/B2 Mirante do Paranapanema, Braz.
141/B2 Mirassol, Braz.
79/F2 Mira Taglio, It.
149/E4 Miravalles (vol.), CR
74/B1 Miravalles (mtn.), Sp.
76/C1 Mirecourt, Fr.
57/G4 Mirfield, Eng,UK
86/E2 Mirgorod, Ukr.
143/G2 Mirim (lake), Braz., Uru.
140/A1 Mirinzal, Braz.
138/D5 Miritiparaná (riv.), Col.
95/H3 Mirjāveh, Iran
79/G2 Mirna (riv.), Cro.
113/G Mirnyy, Ant.
89/M3 Mirnyy, Rus.
157/H2 Mirond (lake), Sk,Can
147/B2 Mixteco (riv.), Mex.
81/H4 Mirtóōn (sea), Gre.
101/E5 Miryang, SKor.
106/D2 Mirzāpur, India
79/G5 Misa (riv.), It.
125/M7 Misa, Zaire
127/A4 Misāha, Bīr (well), Egypt
98/D3 Misaki, Japan
147/F5 Misantla, Mex.
130/C4 Misasa, Tanz.
100/B3 Misawa, Japan
97/L2 Mishan, China
168/D2 Mishaum (pt.), Ma,US
99/F3 Mishima, Japan
146/B2 Misión de San Fernando, Mex.
135/F2 Misiones (mts.), Arg.
149/F3 Miskitos (cay), Nic.
82/E1 Miskolc, Hun.
99/M10 Misono, Japan
111/H4 Misool (isl.), Indo.
157/L4 Misquah (hills), Mn,US
124/J3 Mişrātah, Libya
125/L1 Mişrātah (pt.), Libya
140/C2 Missão Velha, Braz.
160/D1 Missinaibi (lake), On,Can
160/D1 Missinaibi (riv.), On,Can
164/C5 Mission (bay), Ca,US
162/D5 Mission, Tx,US
164/C4 Mission Ind. Res., Ca,US
164/C3 Mission Viejo, Ca,US
157/M2 Missisa (lake), On,Can
160/E1 Missisicabi (riv.), On,Can
161/Q8 Mississauga, On,Can
116/D5 Mississippi (pt.), Austl.

155/J6 Mississippi (delta), US
155/H5 Mississippi (riv.), US
163/F3 Mississippi (state), US
120/C5 Missol (isl.), Indo.
156/N4 Missoula, Mt,US
155/G3 Missouri (riv.), US
159/J3 Missouri (state), US
162/E4 Missouri City, Tx,US
157/H3 Missouri, Coteau du (upland), Can., US
130/B3 Missungwi, Tanz.
118/B3 Mistake (cr.), Austl.
161/L2 Mistaken (pt.), Can.
161/F1 Mistassibi (riv.), Qu,Can
161/G1 Mistassibi Nord Est (riv.), Qu,Can
160/F1 Mistassini, Qu,Can
160/F1 Mistassini (lake), Qu,Can
161/F1 Mistassini (riv.), Qu,Can
65/J4 Mistelbach an der Zaya, Aus.
163/H4 Mistley, Eng,UK
81/H4 Mistrás (ruins), Gre.
90/D4 Mistretta, It.
151/M4 Misty Fjords Nat'l Mon., Ak,US
99/M10 Misugi, Japan
131/C2 Miswa, Zam.
99/H7 Mitaka, Japan
99/N9 Mitake, Japan
146/D4 Mita, Punta de (pt.), Mex.
117/M9 Mitcham, Austl.
58/D3 Mitcheldean, Eng,UK
118/A1 Mitchell (riv.), Austl.
163/H3 Mitchell (mtn.), NC,US
159/G4 Mitchell, Ne,US
157/J5 Mitchell, SD,US
118/A1 Mitchell & Alice Rivers Nat'l Park, Austl.
91/B4 Mit Ghamr, Egypt
106/B2 Mithankot, Pak.
95/J4 Mithi, Pak.
121/K6 Mitiaro (isl.), CookIs.
81/K3 Mitilini, Gre.
148/B2 Mitla (ruins), Mex.
91/C4 Mitla (Mamarr Mitlah) (pass), Egypt
99/J6 Mitō, Japan
124/G7 Mitra (peak), EqG.
143/L8 Mitre (pen.), Arg.
82/D3 Mitrovica, Bosn.
133/H7 Mitsinjo, Madg.
133/J6 Mitsio, Nosy (isl.), Madg.
125/N4 Mits'iwa, Erit.
99/M10 Mitsue, Japan
99/F2 Mitsukaidō, Japan
99/F2 Mitsuke, Japan
77/F3 Mittagspitze (mtn.), Aus.
67/F4 Mittelland (can.), Ger.
67/E3 Mittelradde (riv.), Ger.
71/H3 Mittenwald, Ger.
71/F3 Mitterteich, Ger.
71/E6 Mittlere-Isar (can.), Ger.
64/G3 Mittweida, Ger.
130/A4 Mitumba (mts.), Zaire
126/E2 Mitwaba, Zaire
99/H7 Miura, Japan
99/H7 Miura (pen.), Japan
148/D3 Mixco Viejo (ruins), Guat.
103/C4 Mi Xian, China
99/M10 Miyagawa, Japan
99/G1 Miyagi (pref.), Japan
100/B4 Miyako, Japan
99/H8 Miyako (isls.), Japan
99/B5 Miyakonojō, Japan
99/L9 Miyama, Japan
98/B4 Miyanojō, Japan
99/H6 Miyashiro, Japan
98/B5 Miyazaki, Japan
98/B4 Miyazaki (pref.), Japan
98/D3 Miyazu, Japan
97/H2 Miyi, China
99/E3 Miyoshi, Japan
103/D2 Miyun, China
103/D2 Miyun (res.), China
56/B6 Mizen Head (pt.), Ire.
83/H3 Mizil, Rom.
104/B4 Mizoram (state), India
99/M11 Mizunami, Japan
100/B4 Mizusawa, Japan
62/F2 Mjøndalen, Nor.
62/E3 Mjörn (lake), Swe.
62/D1 Mjøsa (lake), Nor.
130/C4 Mkalama, Tanz.
130/C4 Mkata (plain), Tanz.
130/C4 Mkoani, Tanz.
130/C4 Mkokotoni, Tanz.
130/C4 Mkomazi Game Rsv., Tanz.
130/C4 Mkombo (riv.), Tanz.
124/D1 Mkondoa (riv.), Tanz.
130/C4 Mkorn (peak), Mor.
130/C4 Mkumbi (pt.), Tanz.
131/C2 Mkushi, Zam.
131/C2 Mkushi (riv.), Zam.
133/F2 Mkuze (riv.), SAfr.
71/H2 Mladá Boleslav, Czh.
130/B4 Mladenovac, Yugo.
130/B4 Mlala (hills), Tanz.
65/L2 Mława, Pol.

82/C4 Mljet (isl.), Cro.
82/C4 Mljet Nat'l Park, Cro.
131/D2 Mlolo, Zam.
131/B4 Mmadinare, Bots.
131/B4 Mmamabula, Bots.
131/B5 Mmathethe, Bots.
130/D3 Mnazini, Kenya
71/H3 Mníšek, Czh.
130/B5 Mnyera (riv.), Tanz.
61/E2 Mo, Nor.
149/H1 Moa, Cuba
111/G5 Moa (isl.), Indo.
128/C5 Moa (riv.), Libr., SLeo.
130/C4 Moa, Tanz.
120/H6 Moala Group (isls.), Fiji
119/C3 Moama, Austl.
131/D5 Moamba, Moz.
74/A1 Moaña, Sp.
126/A1 Moanda, Gabon
93/G3 Mobārakeh, Iran
125/K7 Mobaye, CAfr.
159/J3 Moberly, Mo,US
156/C2 Moberly Lake, BC,Can
163/H4 Mobile, Al,US
157/H4 Mobridge, SD,US
150/D3 Moca, DRep.
91/C1 Moca (pass), Turk.
138/B5 Mocache, Ecu.
137/J4 Mocajuba, Braz.
126/H4 Moçambique, Moz.
126/H4 Moçâmedes, Ang.
104/E4 Moc Chau, Viet.
144/B3 Moche (ruins), Peru
139/E2 Mochima Nat'l Park, Ven.
109/D4 Moc Hoa, Viet.
131/B5 Mochudi, Bots.
130/D5 Mocímboa da Praia, Moz.
62/E3 Möckeln (lake), Swe.
70/C4 Möckmühl, Ger.
138/B4 Mocoa, Col.
141/G6 Mococa, Braz.
126/G4 Mocuba, Moz.
106/B3 Modāsa, India
58/C6 Modbury, Eng,UK
132/D3 Modderrivier (riv.), SAfr.
79/D3 Modena, It.
79/D4 Modena (prov.), It.
73/G2 Moder (riv.), Fr., Ger.
73/G5 Modesto, Ca,US
80/D4 Modica, It.
124/H4 Modjigo (riv.), Niger
65/J4 Mödling, Aus.
82/D3 Modriča, Bosn.
109/E3 Mo Duc, Viet.
80/E2 Modugno, It.
119/C3 Moe, Austl.
132/A2 Moeb (bay), Namb.
72/B3 Moëlan-sur-Mer, Fr.
57/E5 Moel Fammau (mtn.), Wal,UK
57/E6 Moel Ffrena (mtn.), Wal,UK
58/C2 Moel Hywel (mtn.), Wal,UK
57/E6 Moel Sych (mtn.), Wal,UK
58/C2 Moel y Llyn (mtn.), UK
120/E4 Moen, Micr.
158/E3 Moenkopi (dry riv.), Az,US
121/K7 Moerai, FrPol.
66/D6 Moers, Ger.
68/C1 Moervaart (can.), Belg.
77/F5 Moesa (riv.), Swi.
54/C6 Moffat, Sc,UK
165/K12 Moffett Field Nav. Air Sta., Ca,US
108/C2 Moga, India
125/Q7 Mogadishu (cap.), Som.
100/B4 Mogami, Japan
99/G1 Mogami (riv.), Japan
131/B4 Mogapinyana, Bots.
75/L6 Mogent (riv.), Sp.
141/G8 Mogi das Cruzes, Braz.
141/F7 Mogi-Guaçu, Braz.
141/G7 Mogi-Guaçu (riv.), Braz.
86/D1 Mogilëv, Bela.
86/D1 Mogilëv Obl., Bela.
86/C2 Mogilev-Podol'skiy, Ukr.
65/J2 Mogilno, Pol.
141/F7 Mogi-Mirim, Braz.
79/F1 Mogliano Veneto, It.
97/H1 Mogocha, Rus.
104/C4 Mogok, Burma
131/B4 Mogolrivier (riv.), SAfr.
143/F3 Mogotes (pt.), Arg.
130/D3 Mogotio, Kenya
148/E3 Mogotón (peak), Nic.
74/B4 Moguer, Sp.
82/D3 Mohács, Hun.
157/H3 Mohall, ND,US
123/N13 Mohamed V (dam), Mor.
123/N13 Mohamed V (res.), Mor.
123/H16 Mohammadia, Alg.
123/L14 Mohammedia, Mor.
166/D1 Mohawk (lake), NJ,US
168/F6 Mohawk (lake), Oh,US
133/G6 Mohéli (isl.), Com.
126/D4 Mohembo, Bots.
151/E2 Mohican (cape), Ire.
168/E7 Mohican (riv.), Oh,US
168/E6 Mohican Saint Pk., Oh,US
76/D2 Möhlin, Swi.
67/F6 Möhne (riv.), Ger.

67/F6 Möhnestausee (res.), Ger.
130/C5 Mohoro, Tanz.
83/H2 Moineşti, Rom.
102/A3 Moinkum (des.), Kaz.
129/E5 Moinsi (hills), Gha.
160/E2 Moira (riv.), On,Can
72/F4 Moirans, Fr.
72/D4 Moissac, Fr.
75/Q10 Moita, Port.
158/C4 Mojave (des.), Ca,US
158/C4 Mojave (dry riv.), Ca,US
104/D4 Mojiang Hanizu Zizhixian, China
141/G7 Moji-Guaçu (riv.), Braz.
157/L3 Mojikit (lake), On,Can
136/E6 Mojos (plain), Bol.
137/J4 Moju (riv.), Braz.
99/F2 Mōka, Japan
165/M11 Mokelumne (aqueduct), Ca,US
158/B3 Mokelumne (riv.), Ca,US
165/Q16 Mokena, Il,US
120/F4 Mokil (atoll), Micr.
109/B3 Mokochu (peak), Thai.
104/B3 Mokokchūng, India
124/H5 Mokolo, Camr.
101/D5 Mokp'o, SKor.
82/E3 Mokrin, Yugo.
87/G1 Moksha (riv.), Rus.
69/E1 Mol, Belg.
82/E3 Mol, Yugo.
79/G1 Molat (isl.), Cro.
82/B3 Molat (isl.), Cro.
74/E3 Molatón (mtn.), Sp.
57/E5 Mold, Wal,UK
83/H2 Moldavia (reg.), Rom.
83/G2 Moldavian Carpathians (range), Rom.
61/C3 Molde, Nor.
86/C3 Moldova
83/H2 Moldova, Rom.
83/G3 Moldova Nouă, Rom.
83/G3 Moldoveanu (peak), Rom.
53/M7 Mole (riv.), Eng,UK
149/H2 Môle, Cap du (cape), Haiti
129/E4 Mole Game Rsv., Gha.
131/B5 Molepolole, Bots.
80/E2 Molfetta, It.
103/F2 Molihong Shan (peak), China
142/C2 Molina, Chile
74/E3 Molina de Segura, Sp.
160/B3 Moline, Il,US
79/E3 Molinella, It.
147/L7 Molino de Flores Nat'l Park, Mex.
165/M2 Moliro, Zaire
80/D2 Molise (reg.), It.
73/K3 Möll (riv.), Aus.
61/D5 Mollebjerg (peak), Den.
144/C5 Mollendo, Peru
76/C4 Mollendruz, Col du (pass), Swi.
75/F2 Mollerussa, Sp.
142/C2 Molles (pt.), Chile
75/L6 Mollet del Vallès, Sp.
75/L7 Mollins de Rei, Sp.
64/F2 Mölln, Ger.
62/E3 Mölndal, Swe.
62/E3 Mölnlycke, Swe.
130/B3 Molo, Kenya
63/M4 Molodechno, Bela.
113/D Molodezhnaya, Ant.
84/H4 Mologa (riv.), Rus.
154/T10 Molokai (isl.), Hi,US
85/L4 Moloma (riv.), Rus.
132/C2 Molopo (dry riv.), Bots.
132/C2 Moloporivier (dry riv.), SAfr.
124/J7 Moloundou, Camr.
76/D1 Molsheim, Fr.
157/J2 Molson (lake), Mb,Can
111/H5 Molu (isl.), Indo.
111/G4 Molucca (sea), Indo.
111/G3 Moluccas (isls.), Indo.
77/G5 Molveno (lake), It.
140/C2 Mombaça, Braz.
130/C4 Mombasa, Kenya
100/C1 Mombetsu, Japan
100/C2 Mombetsu, Japan
130/C4 Mombo, Tanz.
70/C2 Mömbris, Ger.
83/G5 Momchilgrad, Bul.
111/H4 Momfafa (cape), Indo.
100/B3 Momoishi, Japan
138/C2 Mompós, Col.
104/B4 Mon (riv.), Burma
104/C5 Mon (state), Burma
61/E4 Møn (isl.), Den.
150/D3 Mona (passg.), NAm.
150/E2 Mona (isl.), PR
73/G5 Monaco
73/G5 Monaco (cap.)
54/B2 Monadhliath (mts.), Sc,UK
139/F2 Monagas (state), Ven.
60/D1 Monaghan, Ire.
60/D1 Monaghan (co.), Ire.
149/F5 Monagrillo, Pan.

149/F4 Monagrillo (ruins), Pan.
162/C2 Monahans, Tx,US
54/A2 Monar, Loch (lake), Sc,UK
156/D3 Monashee (mts.), BC,Can
118/H8 Mona Vale, Austl.
75/E3 Moncada, Sp.
78/A3 Moncalieri, It.
74/D2 Moncayo (range), Sp.
76/E4 Mönch (peak), Swi.
84/G2 Monchegorsk, Rus.
66/D6 Mönchengladbach, Ger.
74/A4 Monchique, Port.
74/A4 Monchique (range), Port.
163/H3 Moncks Corner, SC,US
161/H2 Moncton, NB,Can
74/A2 Mondego (cape), Port.
74/A2 Mondego (riv.), Port.
78/A4 Mondovì, It.
74/D1 Mondragón, Sp.
80/C2 Mondragone, It.
71/G7 Mondsee (lake), Aus.
130/C3 Monduli, Tanz.
74/B3 Monesterio, Sp.
159/J3 Monett, Mo,US
56/C2 Money Head (pt.), Sc,UK
56/B2 Moneymore, NI,UK
56/C2 Moneyreagh, NI,UK
79/G1 Monfalcone, It.
78/B3 Monferrato (reg.), It.
74/B1 Monforte, Sp.
130/C5 Monga, Tanz.
141/G9 Mongaguá, Braz.
109/D1 Mong Cai, Viet.
116/C4 Mongers (lake), Austl.
106/F2 Monghyr, India
125/J5 Mongo, Chad
128/C4 Mongo (riv.), Gui., SLeo.
96/D2 Mongolia
125/K5 Mongororo, Chad
126/B1 Mongoungou, Gabon
131/A2 Mongu, Zam.
66/D6 Monheim, Ger.
102/F2 Mönh Hayrhan Uul (peak), Mong.
96/E1 Mönh Sarĭdag (peak), Mong.
112/D4 Monkayo, Phil.
131/D4 Monkey Bay, Malw.
116/B3 Monkey Mia, Austl.
65/M2 Mońki, Pol.
126/D1 Monkoto, Zaire
164/B5 Monks (isl.), Md,US
58/D3 Monmouth, Wal,UK
160/B3 Monmouth, Il,US
166/D3 Monmouth (co.), NJ,US
156/C4 Monmouth, Or,US
58/D2 Monmow (riv.), UK
66/C4 Monnickendam, Neth.
129/F5 Mono (prov.), Ben.
149/F4 Mono (pt.), Nic.
164/A1 Mono (cr.), Ca,US
158/B3 Mono (lake), Ca,US
166/A4 Monocacy (riv.), Md, Pa,US
80/E2 Monopoli, It.
82/D2 Monor, Hun.
161/Q8 Mono Road, On,Can
75/E3 Monóvar, Sp.
80/C3 Monreale, It.
168/A3 Monroe, Ct,US
163/H3 Monroe, Ga,US
162/E3 Monroe, La,US
160/D3 Monroe, Mi,US
165/K7 Monroe (co.), Mi,US
163/H3 Monroe, NC,US
167/D1 Monroe, NY,US
166/C1 Monroe (co.), Pa,US
158/D3 Monroe, Ut,US
160/B3 Monroe, Wi,US
163/G4 Monroeville, Al,US
168/H7 Monroeville, Pa,US
128/C5 Monrovia (cap.), Libr.
164/C2 Monrovia, Ca,US
69/F2 Mons, Belg.
69/F2 Monschau, Ger.
144/B2 Monsefú, Peru
79/E2 Monselice, It.
140/B2 Monsenhor Hipólito, Braz.
140/B2 Monsenhor Tabosa, Braz.
167/D1 Monsey, NY,US
161/D1 Monson, Ma,US
63/S10 Mönsterås, Swe.
66/B4 Monster, Neth.
79/D5 Monsummano Terme, It.
70/A2 Montabaur, Ger.
77/E3 Montafon (val.), Aus.
79/E2 Montagnana, It.
133/J6 Montagne d'Ambre Nat'l Park, Madg.
53/U9 Montagny-Sainte-Félicité, Fr.
151/L3 Montague, Yk,Can
151/J4 Montague (isl.), Ak,US

151/J4 Montague (str.), Ak,US
162/D3 Montague, Tx,US
80/E2 Montalbano Jonico, It.
156/F4 Montana (state), US
144/C3 Montaña, La (reg.), Peru
141/D1 Montanha, Braz.
72/D4 Montargis, Fr.
72/D4 Montauban, Fr.
75/F1 Montaud, Pic de (peak), Fr.
167/G1 Montauk (pt.), NY,US
126/E6 Mont aux Sources (peak), Les.
72/F3 Montbard, Fr.
76/C2 Montbéliard, Fr.
75/L7 Montcada i Reixac, Sp.
72/F3 Montceau-les-Mines, Fr.
164/C2 Montclair, Ca,US
167/J8 Montclair, NJ,US
72/C5 Mont-de-Marsan, Fr.
68/B4 Montdidier, Fr.
148/B2 Monte Albán (ruins), Mex.
139/H5 Monte Alegre, Braz.
140/D2 Monte Alegre, Braz.
141/B1 Monte Alegre de Minas, Braz.
140/A3 Monte Alegre do Piauí, Braz.
140/B4 Monte Alto, Braz.
140/B4 Monte Azul, Braz.
116/B2 Montebello (isls.), Austl.
164/B2 Montebello, Ca,US
79/F1 Montebelluna, It.
135/F2 Montecarlo, Arg.
141/C1 Monte Carmelo, Braz.
138/D2 Monte Carmelo, Ven.
135/E3 Monte Caseros, Arg.
79/D5 Montecatini Terme, It.
149/G2 Monte Cristi, DRep.
80/B1 Montecristo (isl.), It.
148/D3 Montecristo Nat'l Park, ESal.
148/E3 Monte el Chile (mtn.), Hon.
79/F5 Montefeltro (reg.), It.
74/C4 Montefrío, Sp.
149/G2 Montego Bay, Jam.
79/E2 Montegrotto Terme, It.
140/C2 Monteiro, Braz.
75/P10 Montelavar, Port.
72/F4 Montélimar, Fr.
74/C4 Montellano, Sp.
79/E5 Montelupo Fiorentino, It.
142/D3 Montemayor (plat.), Arg.
147/F3 Montemorelos, Mex.
74/A3 Montemor-o-Novo, Port.
74/A2 Montemuro (range), Port.
141/B4 Montenegro, Braz.
82/D4 Montenegro (rep.), Yugo.
80/D2 Montenero di Bisaccia, It.
64/D3 Montenoison, Butte de (mtn.), Fr.
140/E4 Monte Pascoal Nat'l Park, Braz.
150/D3 Monte Plata, DRep.
72/E2 Montereau-faut-Yonne, Fr.
158/B3 Monterey (bay), Ca,US
158/B3 Monterey, Ca,US
164/B2 Monterey Park, Ca,US
138/C2 Montería, Col.
135/C2 Monteros, Arg.
76/D6 Monte Rosa (mtn.), It., Swi.
77/G4 Monterosso (peak), It.
80/C1 Monterotondo, It.
147/E3 Monterrey, Mex.
140/A2 Montes Altos, Braz.
80/D2 Monte Sant'Angelo, It.
80/E2 Montescaglioso, It.
140/B5 Montes Claros, Braz.
80/D1 Montesilvano Marina, It.
53/S10 Montesson, Fr.
79/E5 Montevarchi, It.
143/F2 Montevideo (cap.), Uru.
157/K4 Montevideo, Mn,US
53/U10 Montévrain, Fr.
165/L10 Montezuma (slough), Ca,US
69/E5 Montfaucon, Fr.
66/B4 Montfoort, Neth.
53/T10 Montgeron, Fr.
58/C2 Montgomery, Wal,UK
163/G3 Montgomery (cap.), Al,US
166/A5 Montgomery (co.), Md,US
166/C3 Montgomery (co.), Oh,US
168/G6 Montgomery (dam), Pa,US
160/D3 Montgomery, WV,US
166/A5 Montgomery Village, Md,US

166/C3 Montgomeryville, Pa,US
72/E3 Montgrand (mtn.), Fr.
76/C5 Monthey, Swi.
53/U9 Monthyon, Fr.
162/F3 Monticello, Ar,US
165/K9 Monticello (dam), Ca,US
163/H4 Monticello, Fl,US
160/C3 Monticello, In,US
159/K2 Monticello, Ky,US
159/K2 Monticello, Mo,US
158/E3 Monticello, Ut,US
160/E4 Monticello, Va,US
78/D2 Montichiari, It.
68/B3 Montigny-en-Gohelle, Fr.
53/S10 Montigny-le-Bretonneux, Fr.
53/S10 Montigny-lès-Cormeilles, Fr.
69/F5 Montigny-lès-Metz, Fr.
68/D3 Montigny-le-Tilleul, Belg.
74/A3 Montijo, Port.
74/B3 Montijo, Sp.
74/C4 Montilla, Sp.
72/D2 Montivilliers, Fr.
161/G1 Mont-Joli, Qu,Can
160/F2 Mont-Laurier, Qu,Can
53/S11 Monthléry, Fr.
72/E3 Montluçon, Fr.
161/G2 Montmagny, Qu,Can
53/S10 Montmorency, Fr.
72/D3 Montmorillon, Fr.
79/F4 Montone (riv.), It.
74/C3 Montoro, Sp.
166/B2 Montour (ridge), Pa,US
128/D3 Mont Peko Nat'l Park, IvC.
149/G2 Montpelier, Jam.
156/F5 Montpelier, Id,US
167/L2 Montpelier (cap.), Vt,US
72/E5 Montpellier, Fr.
160/C2 Montreal (riv.), On,Can
161/N7 Montréal, Qu,Can
157/G2 Montreal (lake), Sk,Can
157/G2 Montreal Lake, Sk,Can
161/N6 Montréal-Nord, Qu,Can
72/F4 Montreuil, Fr.
68/A3 Montreuil, Fr.
76/C5 Montreux, Swi.
54/D3 Montrose, Sc,UK
158/F3 Montrose, Co,US
54/D3 Montrose Basin (lag.), Sc,UK
164/B2 Montrose-La Crescenta, Ca,US
53/S10 Montrouge, Fr.
161/N6 Mont-Royal, Qu,Can
53/U10 Montry, Fr.
161/P6 Mont-Saint-Hilaire, Qu,Can
69/E4 Mont-Saint-Martin, Fr.
160/F2 Mont-Saint-Michel, Qu,Can
72/C2 Mont-Saint-Michel, Fr.
72/C2 Mont-Saint-Michel (bay), Fr.
128/D4 Mont Sangbé Nat'l Park, IvC.
75/L6 Montseny Nat'l Park, Sp.
128/C5 Montserrado (co.), Libr.
75/F2 Montserrat (mtn.), Sp.
150/F3 Montserrat (isl.), UK
53/S9 Montsoult, Fr.
167/J7 Montvale, NJ,US
167/J7 Montville, NJ,US
159/G4 Monument Draw (cr.), NM, Tx,US
104/B4 Monywa, Burma
78/C1 Monza, It.
131/B3 Monze, Zam.
75/F2 Monzón, Sp.
131/B4 Mookane, Bots.
132/P13 Mooi (riv.), SAfr.
118/C2 Mooloolaba-Maroochydore, Austl.
119/G5 Moorabbin, Austl.
157/H4 Moorcroft, Wy,US
116/C4 Moore (lake), Austl.
161/R8 Moore (pt.), On,Can
159/H4 Moore, Ok,US
121/K6 Moorea (isl.), FrPol.
163/H5 Moore Haven, Fl,US
116/B4 Moore River Nat'l Park, Austl.
150/B1 Moore's (isl.), Bahm.
166/D4 Moorestown, NJ,US
163/H3 Mooresville, NC,US
54/C5 Moorfoot (hills), Sc,UK
157/J4 Moorhead, Mn,US
164/B2 Moorpark, Ca,US
71/E6 Moosburg, Ger.
160/D1 Moose (riv.), On,Can
157/H3 Moose (mtn.), Sk,Can
160/D1 Moose Factory, On,Can
161/G2 Moosehead (lake), Me,US
165/P16 Mooseheart, Il,US
157/J4 Moose Jaw, Sk,Can
157/H3 Moosomin, Sk,Can
160/D1 Moosonee, On,Can
131/D3 Mopeia, Moz.

206

Mopi – Mwen

131/B4 **Mopipi**, Bots.
128/D3 **Mopti**, Mali
128/E3 **Mopti** (reg.), Mali
144/D5 **Moquegua**, Peru
144/D4 **Moquegua-Tacna-Puno** (reg.), Peru
82/D2 **Mór**, Hun.
124/H5 **Mora**, Camr.
74/D3 **Mora**, Sp.
62/F1 **Mora**, Swe.
159/F4 **Mora**, NM,US
159/F4 **Mora** (riv.), NM,US
81/F1 **Morača** (riv.), Yugo.
106/C2 **Morādābād**, India
140/C2 **Morada Nova**, Braz.
141/C1 **Morada Nova de Mina**, Braz.
142/C2 **Morado Nat'l Park**, Chile
133/H7 **Morafenobe**, Madg.
65/K2 **Morąg**, Pol.
165/K11 **Moraga**, Ca,US
168/H6 **Moraine Saint Pk.**, Pa,US
53/R10 **Morainvilliers**, Fr.
142/B5 **Moraleda** (chan.), Chile
74/B2 **Moraleja**, Sp.
148/D3 **Morales**, Guat.
133/J7 **Moramanga**, Madg.
158/E2 **Moran**, Wy,US
118/C3 **Moranbah**, Austl.
121/M7 **Morane** (isl.), FrPol.
53/T10 **Morangis**, Fr.
149/G2 **Morant Bay**, Jam.
55/J8 **Morar, Loch** (lake), Sc,UK
76/D4 **Morat** (lake), Swi.
74/E3 **Moratalla**, Sp.
65/J4 **Morava** (riv.), Czh.
81/G1 **Morava** (riv.), Yugo.
65/J4 **Moravia** (reg.), Czh.
65/J4 **Moravská Třebová**, Czh.
65/H4 **Moravské Budějovice**, Czh.
136/G2 **Morawhanna**, Guy.
54/C1 **Moray** (firth), Sc,UK
69/G4 **Morbach**, Ger.
68/B2 **Morbecque**, Fr.
77/F5 **Morbegno**, It.
62/G3 **Mörbylanga**, Swe.
76/C5 **Morclan, Pic de** (mtn.), Fr.
76/C5 **Morclan, Pic de** (peak), Fr.
157/J3 **Morden**, Mb,Can
53/N7 **Morden**, Eng,UK
119/G6 **Mordialloc**, Austl.
87/G1 **Mordvian Aut. Rep.**, Rus.
157/H4 **Moreau** (riv.), SD,US
54/D5 **Morebattle**, Sc,UK
57/F3 **Morecambe**, Eng,UK
57/E3 **Morecambe** (bay), Eng,UK
119/D1 **Moree**, Austl.
160/D4 **Morehead**, Ky,US
163/J3 **Morehead City**, NC,US
147/E5 **Morelia**, Mex.
148/B2 **Morelos** (state), Mex.
131/A3 **Moremi Wild. Rsv.**, Bots.
106/C2 **Morena**, India
74/C3 **Morena** (range), Sp.
83/G3 **Moreni**, Rom.
164/C3 **Moreno Valley**, Ca,US
61/C3 **Møre og Romsdal** (co.), Nor.
152/C3 **Moresby** (isl.), BC,Can
118/F6 **Moreton** (bay), Austl.
118/D4 **Moreton** (cape), Austl.
118/D4 **Moreton** (isl.), Austl.
53/P6 **Moreton**, Eng,UK
58/C5 **Moretonhampstead**, Eng,UK
118/D4 **Moreton I. Nat'l Park**, Austl.
59/E3 **Moreton in Marsh**, Eng,UK
85/N2 **Moreyu** (riv.), Rus.
76/C4 **Morez**, Fr.
167/F1 **Morgan** (pt.), Ct,US
163/F4 **Morgan City**, La,US
160/C4 **Morganfield**, Ky,US
80/D4 **Morgantina** (ruins), It.
163/H3 **Morganton**, NC,US
160/C4 **Morgantown**, Ky,US
160/E4 **Morgantown**, WV,US
72/E3 **Morge** (riv.), Fr.
76/C4 **Morges**, Swi.
95/H1 **Morghāb** (riv.), Afg.
76/C5 **Morgins, Pas de** (pass), Fr., Swi.
142/B3 **Morguilla** (pt.), Chile
96/C3 **Mori**, China
79/D1 **Mori**, It.
100/B2 **Mori**, Japan
117/M8 **Morialta Consv. Park**, Austl.
159/F4 **Moriarty**, NM,US
156/B2 **Morice** (lake), BC,Can
54/B1 **Morie, Loch** (lake), Sc,UK
99/L10 **Moriguchi**, Japan
102/F3 **Mori Kazak Zizhixian** (Mori), China
97/J2 **Morin Dawa**, China
67/G5 **Moringen**, Ger.
156/E2 **Morinville**, Ab,Can
100/B4 **Morioka**, Japan
54/B2 **Moriston** (riv.), Sc,UK
99/H7 **Moriya**, Japan
98/D3 **Moriyama**, Japan
72/B2 **Morlaix**, Fr.
68/D3 **Morlanwelz**, Belg.
70/B3 **Mörlenbach**, Ger.
57/G4 **Morley**, Eng,UK
54/D1 **Mormond** (hill), Sc,UK
106/B4 **Mormugao**, India
118/F6 **Morningside**, Austl.
60/B5 **Morningstar** (riv.), Ire.
114/F3 **Mornington** (isl.), Austl.
143/J7 **Mornington** (isl.), Chile
95/J3 **Moro**, Pak.
123/M13 **Morocco**
144/B3 **Morococha**, Peru
130/C4 **Morogoro**, Tanz.
130/C4 **Morogoro** (prov.), Tanz.
119/C3 **Moroka-Wonnangatta Nat'l Park**, Austl.
147/E4 **Moroleón**, Mex.
133/G8 **Morombe**, Madg.
142/F2 **Morón**, Arg.
149/G1 **Morón**, Cuba
96/E2 **Mörön**, Mong.
138/D2 **Morón**, Ven.
144/B1 **Morona** (riv.), Ecu., Peru
138/B5 **Morona-Santiago** (prov.), Ecu.
133/H8 **Morondava** (riv.), Madg.
133/H8 **Morondava**, Madg.
74/C4 **Morón de la Frontera**, Sp.
133/G5 **Moroni** (cap.), Com.
111/G3 **Morotai** (isl.), Indo.
111/G3 **Morotai** (str.), Indo.
130/B2 **Moroto**, Ugan.
130/B2 **Moroto** (peak), Ugan.
99/H7 **Moroyama**, Japan
87/G2 **Morozovsk**, Rus.
140/B3 **Morpará**, Braz.
57/G1 **Morpeth**, Eng,UK
91/C2 **Morphou**, Cyp.
91/C2 **Morphou** (bay), Cyp.
66/C3 **Morra** (lake), Neth.
159/G2 **Morrill**, Ne,US
140/B1 **Morrinhos**, Braz.
141/B1 **Morrinhos**, Braz.
117/F3 **Morris** (peak), Austl.
157/J3 **Morris**, Mb,Can
164/C2 **Morris** (res.), Ca,US
160/B3 **Morris**, Il,US
157/K4 **Morris**, Mn,US
166/D2 **Morris** (co.), NJ,US
145/P1 **Morris Jesup** (cape), Grld.
58/C3 **Morriston**, Wal,UK
166/D2 **Morristown**, NJ,US
163/H2 **Morristown**, Tn,US
166/D2 **Morristown Nat'l Mil. Park**, NJ,US
166/D3 **Morrisville**, Pa,US
118/A2 **Morr Morr Abor. Land**, Austl.
158/B4 **Morro Bay**, Ca,US
138/D2 **Morrocoy Nat'l Park**, Ven.
126/C3 **Morro de Môco** (peak), Ang.
149/F5 **Morro de Puercos** (pt.), Pan.
141/B3 **Morro do Capão Doce** (hill), Braz.
140/B3 **Morro do Chapéu**, Braz.
144/B2 **Morropón**, Peru
147/F5 **Morro, Punta del** (pt.), Mex.
140/A1 **Morros**, Braz.
149/G4 **Morrosquillo** (gulf), Col.
131/D3 **Morrumbala**, Moz.
131/D4 **Morrumbene**, Moz.
62/C3 **Mørs** (isl.), Den.
53/T11 **Morsang-sur-Orge**, Fr.
69/G2 **Morsbach**, Ger.
87/G1 **Morshansk**, Rus.
87/J3 **Morskoy** (isl.), Kaz.
76/C1 **Mortagne** (riv.), Fr.
78/B2 **Mortara**, It.
76/B3 **Morte** (riv.), Fr.
58/B4 **Morte** (pt.), UK
76/C3 **Morteau**, Fr.
137/H6 **Mortes** (riv.), Braz.
59/E4 **Mortimer**, Eng,UK
58/D2 **Mortimers Cross**, Eng,UK
160/B3 **Morton**, Il,US
165/Q15 **Morton Grove**, Il,US
119/D2 **Morton Nat'l Park**, Austl.
167/F1 **Morton Nat'l Wild. Ref.**, NY,US
68/D1 **Mortsel**, Belg.
141/G7 **Morungaba**, Braz.
72/E3 **Morvan** (plat.), Fr.
54/C2 **Morven** (mtn.), Sc,UK
106/B3 **Morvi**, India
119/C3 **Morwell**, Austl.
74/A1 **Mos**, Sp.
70/C4 **Mosbach**, Ger.
75/P10 **Moscavide**, Port.
84/G5 **Moscow** (upland), Rus.
156/D4 **Moscow**, Id,US
84/H5 **Moscow** (Moskva) (cap.), Rus.
85/X9 **Moscow** (Moskva) (inset) (cap.), Rus.
84/H5 **Moscow Obl.**, Rus.
113/H **Moscow Univ. Ice Shelf**, Ant.
69/F4 **Mosel** (riv.), Ger.
131/B5 **Moselebe** (dry riv.), Bots.
68/F5 **Moselle** (dept.), Fr.
69/F5 **Moselle** (riv.), Fr.
76/C2 **Moselotte** (riv.), Fr.
156/D4 **Moses Lake**, Wa,US
131/B4 **Mosetse**, Bots.
115/R12 **Mosgiel**, NZ
132/C2 **Moshaweng** (dry riv.), SAfr.
63/M2 **Moshchnyy** (isl.), Rus.
130/C3 **Moshi**, Tanz.
131/B5 **Moshupa**, Bots.
65/J2 **Mosina**, Pol.
131/B3 **Mosi-oa-Tunya Nat'l Park**, Zam.
131/B3 **Mosi-oa-Tunya** (Victoria) (falls), Zam.
61/E2 **Mosjøen**, Nor.
84/G5 **Moskva** (riv.), Rus.
84/H5 **Moskva** (Moscow) (cap.), Rus.
85/X9 **Moskva** (Moscow) (inset) (cap.), Rus.
131/B5 **Mosomane**, Bots.
82/C2 **Mosonmagyaróvár**, Hun.
159/G4 **Mosquero**, NM,US
149/E3 **Mosquitia** (reg.), Hon.
149/G4 **Mosquito** (pt.), Pan.
168/G5 **Mosquito Creek** (res.), Oh,US
149/F4 **Mosquitos** (gulf), Pan.
149/E4 **Mosquitos, Costa de** (reg.), Nic.
62/D2 **Moss**, Nor.
76/D5 **Mosses, Col des** (pass), Swi.
128/E4 **Mossi Highlands** (upland), Burk.
70/C6 **Mössingen**, Ger.
57/F4 **Mossley**, Eng,UK
56/C2 **Mossley**, NI,UK
140/C2 **Mossoró**, Braz.
163/F4 **Moss Point**, Ms,US
56/B1 **Moss-side**, NI,UK
71/G1 **Most**, Czh.
123/R16 **Mostaganem**, Alg.
123/R15 **Mostaganem** (wilaya), Alg.
82/C4 **Mostar**, Bosn.
141/B4 **Mostardas**, Braz.
74/D2 **Móstoles**, Sp.
57/E5 **Mostyn**, Wal,UK
93/E2 **Mosul** (Al Mawşil), Iraq
62/B2 **Møsvatnet** (lake), Nor.
148/D3 **Motagua** (riv.), Guat.
62/F2 **Motala**, Swe.
148/D2 **Mother** (pt.), Belz.
54/C5 **Motherwell**, Sc,UK
101/B2 **Motian** (mtn.), China
103/E2 **Motian Ling** (mtn.), China
106/D2 **Motīhāri**, India
131/B4 **Motloutse**, Bots.
131/B4 **Motloutse** (riv.), Bots.
130/A2 **Moto**, Zaire
100/J7 **Motobu**, Japan
131/A5 **Motokwe**, Bots.
99/G2 **Motomiya**, Japan
99/J7 **Motono**, Japan
61/K1 **Motovskiy** (gulf), Rus.
79/G2 **Motovun**, Cro.
100/B4 **Motoyoshi**, Japan
74/D4 **Motril**, Sp.
100/A2 **Motsuta-misaki** (cape), Japan
157/H4 **Mott**, ND,US
78/B1 **Mottarone** (peak), It.
115/R11 **Motueka**, NZ
147/H4 **Motul de Felipe Carrillo Puerto**, Mex.
88/K4 **Motygino**, Rus.
149/J1 **Mouchoir** (passg.), Trks.
128/B2 **Mougris** (well), Mrta.
128/E3 **Mouhoun** (prov.), Burk.
126/B1 **Mouila**, Gabon
124/H4 **Moul** (well), Niger
119/C2 **Moulamein** (riv.), Austl.
57/F5 **Mouldsworth**, Eng,UK
72/E3 **Moulins**, Fr.
104/C5 **Moulmein**, Burma
123/N13 **Moulouya** (riv.), Mor.
59/G2 **Moulton**, Eng,UK
163/H4 **Moultrie**, Ga,US
163/H3 **Moultrie** (lake), SC,US
159/J3 **Mound City**, Ks,US
124/J6 **Moundou**, Chad
160/D4 **Moundsville**, WV,US
109/C3 **Moung Roessei**, Camb.
109/D3 **Mounlapamok**, Laos
75/E1 **Moun Né** (mtn.), Fr.
118/B3 **Mount Aberdeen Nat'l Park**, Austl.
106/B3 **Mount Abu**, India
152/D2 **Mountain** (riv.), NW,Can
166/A3 **Mountain** (cr.), Pa,US
58/C3 **Mountain Ash**, Wal,UK
163/G3 **Mountain Brook**, Al,US
159/J3 **Mountain Grove**, Mo,US
162/E2 **Mountain Home**, Ar,US
156/E5 **Mountain Home**, Id,US
167/H9 **Mountainside**, NJ,US
162/E3 **Mountain View**, Ar,US
165/K12 **Mountain View**, Ca,US
132/D4 **Mountain Zebra Nat'l Park**, SAfr.
163/H2 **Mount Airy**, NC,US
117/G2 **Mount Allan Abor. Land**, Austl.
112/D4 **Mount Apo Nat'l Park**, Phil.
112/C2 **Mount Arayat Nat'l Park**, Phil.
165/D3 **Mount Baker-Snoqualmie Nat'l For.**, Wa,US
117/M9 **Mount Barker**, Austl.
117/G2 **Mount Barkly Abor. Land**, Austl.
118/C5 **Mount Barney Nat'l Park**, Austl.
117/M9 **Mount Bold** (res.), Austl.
119/C3 **Mount Buffalo Nat'l Park**, Austl.
160/C4 **Mount Carmel**, Il,US
166/B2 **Mount Carmel**, Pa,US
125/M2 **Mount Catherine** (peak), Egypt
165/G6 **Mount Clemens**, Mi,US
118/E6 **Mount Coot'tha**, Austl.
126/F4 **Mount Darwin**, Zim.
165/L11 **Mount Diablo Saint Park**, Ca,US
119/B3 **Mount Eccles Nat'l Park**, Austl.
130/B2 **Mount Elgon Nat'l Park**, Kenya
118/B2 **Mount Elliot Nat'l Park**, Austl.
119/B3 **Mount Emu** (cr.), Austl.
119/C4 **Mount Field Nat'l Park**, Austl.
119/B3 **Mount Gambier**, Austl.
120/D5 **Mount Hagen**, PNG
166/D4 **Mount Holly**, NJ,US
161/Q9 **Mount Hope**, On,Can
119/D3 **Mount Imlay Nat'l Park**, Austl.
117/H2 **Mount Isa**, Austl.
166/B3 **Mount Joy**, Pa,US
119/D1 **Mount Kaputar Nat'l Park**, Austl.
130/C3 **Mount Kenya Nat'l Park**, Kenya
167/E1 **Mount Kisco**, NY,US
165/C2 **Mountlake Terrace**, Wa,US
166/D4 **Mount Laurel**, NJ,US
168/G7 **Mount Lebanon**, Pa,US
117/M9 **Mount Lofty** (ranges), Austl.
115/S10 **Mount Maunganui**, NZ
118/D4 **Mount Mistake Nat'l Park**, Austl.
160/D3 **Mount Morris**, Mi,US
118/E6 **Mount Nebo**, Austl.
53/Q7 **Mountnessing**, Eng,UK
163/J3 **Mount Olive**, NC,US
81/H3 **Mount Parnes Nat'l Park**, Gre.
161/L2 **Mount Pearl**, Nf,Can
157/L5 **Mount Pleasant**, Ia,US
160/C3 **Mount Pleasant**, Mi,US
162/E3 **Mount Pleasant**, Tx,US
158/E3 **Mount Pleasant**, Ut,US
165/Q15 **Mount Prospect**, Il,US
166/B6 **Mount Rainier**, Md,US
156/C4 **Mount Rainier Nat'l Park**, Wa,US
117/H5 **Mount Remarkable Nat'l Park**, Austl.
156/D3 **Mount Revelstoke Nat'l Park**, BC,Can
119/B3 **Mount Richmond Nat'l Park**, Austl.
159/G2 **Mount Rushmore Nat'l Mem.**, SD,US
58/A6 **Mount's** (bay), Eng,UK
131/D4 **Mount Selinda**, Zim.
118/B2 **Mount Spec Nat'l Park**, Austl.
160/D4 **Mount Sterling**, Ky,US
160/B4 **Mount Vernon**, Il,US
160/C4 **Mount Vernon**, In,US
167/E2 **Mount Vernon**, NY,US
168/E7 **Mount Vernon**, Oh,US
166/A6 **Mount Vernon**, Va,US
156/C3 **Mount Vernon**, Wa,US
118/C4 **Mount Walsh Nat'l Park**, Austl.
119/E1 **Mount Warning Nat'l Park**, Austl.
116/C2 **Mount Welcome Abor. Land**, Austl.
119/D4 **Mount William Nat'l Park**, Austl.
74/B3 **Moura**, Port.
72/C5 **Mourenx**, Fr.
56/B3 **Mourne** (dist.), NI,UK
56/B3 **Mourne** (mts.), NI,UK
68/C2 **Mouscron**, Belg.
124/J5 **Moussoro**, Chad
53/T9 **Moussy-le-Neuf**, Fr.
76/D3 **Moutier**, Swi.
68/C2 **Mouvaux**, Fr.
76/B1 **Mouzon** (riv.), Fr.
140/C3 **Moxotó** (riv.), Braz.
60/B1 **Moy** (riv.), Ire.
56/B3 **Moy**, NI,UK
130/C2 **Moyalē**, Eth.
101/B4 **Moye** (isl.), China
124/D1 **Moyen Atlas** (mts.), Mor.
69/F5 **Moyeuvre-Grande**, Fr.
56/B2 **Moygashel**, NI,UK
56/B1 **Moyle** (dist.), NI,UK
111/E5 **Moyo** (isl.), Indo.
130/A2 **Moyo**, Ugan.
144/B2 **Moyobamba**, Peru
130/A3 **Moyowosi** (riv.), Tanz.
102/C4 **Moyu**, China
148/D3 **Moyuta**, Guat.
131/D3 **Mozambique**
126/G5 **Mozambique** (chan.), Afr.
84/H5 **Mozhaysk**, Rus.
85/M4 **Mozhga**, Rus.
86/D1 **Mozyr'**, Bela.
130/A5 **Mpalapata**, Zam.
130/A4 **Mpanda**, Tanz.
126/C4 **Mpangu**, Namb.
131/B4 **Mphoengs**, Zim.
130/B2 **Mpigi**, Ugan.
131/C1 **Mpika**, Zam.
130/A5 **Mporokoso**, Zam.
129/E5 **Mpraeso**, Gha.
130/A5 **Mpulungu**, Zam.
130/C4 **Mpwapwa**, Tanz.
65/L2 **Mrągowo**, Pol.
82/C3 **Mrkonjić Grad**, Bosn.
130/C4 **Msanga**, Tanz.
123/T16 **M'Sila**, Alg.
123/T16 **M'Sila** (riv.), Alg.
123/T16 **M'Sila** (wilaya), Alg.
131/C2 **Msoro**, Zam.
123/N13 **Msoun** (riv.), Mor.
84/G4 **Msta** (riv.), Rus.
130/A5 **Msumbu Nat'l Park**, Zam.
130/C5 **Mswega**, Tanz.
65/L4 **Mszana Dolna**, Pol.
130/A4 **Mtakuja**, Tanz.
130/C5 **Mtalika**, Tanz.
131/D3 **Mtarazi Falls Nat'l Park**, Zim.
130/C3 **Mtito Andei**, Kenya
130/C4 **Mtondoni**, Tanz.
130/B5 **Mtorwi** (peak), Tanz.
86/F1 **Mtsensk**, Rus.
130/D5 **Mtwara**, Tanz.
130/D5 **Mtwara** (prov.), Tanz.
104/B4 **Mu** (riv.), Burma
126/G4 **Mualama**, Moz.
109/D2 **Muang Gnommarat**, Laos
109/C2 **Muang Kenthao**, Laos
109/D3 **Muang Khong**, Laos
109/D3 **Muang Khongxedon**, Laos
109/D3 **Muang Lakhonpheng**, Laos
109/D1 **Muang Soy**, Laos
109/C2 **Muang Thathom**, Laos
109/D2 **Muang Xamteu**, Laos
109/D2 **Muang Xepon**, Laos
110/B3 **Muar**, Malay.
110/B4 **Muarabungo**, Indo.
95/J4 **Muāri** (pt.), Pak.
131/C3 **Mubayira**, Zim.
130/A2 **Mubende**, Ugan.
124/H5 **Mubi**, Nga.
139/F4 **Mucajaí** (riv.), Braz.
69/G2 **Much**, Ger.
131/C2 **Muchinga** (mts.), Zam.
131/C2 **Muchinga Escarpment** (cliff), Zam.
58/D1 **Much Wenlock**, Eng,UK
55/H8 **Muck** (isl.), Sc,UK
56/B2 **Muckamore Abbey**, NI,UK
165/C3 **Muckleshoot Ind. Res.**, Wa,US
60/D1 **Muckno** (lake), Ire.
126/H3 **Mucojo**, Moz.
148/E3 **Mucupina** (mtn.), Hon.
92/C2 **Mucur**, Turk.
141/D1 **Mucuri** (riv.), Braz.
126/D3 **Mucussueje**, Ang.
97/K3 **Mudanjiang**, China
83/J5 **Mudanya**, Turk.
70/C3 **Mudbach** (riv.), Ger.
97/K2 **Muddan** (riv.), China
61/F2 **Muddas Nat'l Park**, Swe.
166/B4 **Muddy** (cr.), Pa,US
158/E3 **Muddy** (riv.), Ut,US
159/H4 **Muddy Boggy** (cr.), Ok,US
168/E6 **Muddy Fork** (riv.), Oh,US
166/B4 **Muddy Run** (res.), Pa,US
69/G2 **Mudersbach**, Ger.
119/D2 **Mudgee**, Austl.
156/G1 **Mudjatik** (riv.), Sk,Can
165/D3 **Mud Mountain** (dam), Wa,US
165/D3 **Mud Mountain** (lake), Wa,US
109/B2 **Mudon**, Burma
108/F3 **Mudumalai Wild. Sanct.**, India
143/J8 **Muela** (peak), Chile
91/G7 **Mufjir, Nahr** (dry riv.), WBnk.
105/G2 **Mufu** (peak), China
131/C2 **Mufulira**, Zam.
131/C2 **Mufulwe** (hills), Zam.
130/B3 **Mugango**, Tanz.
74/A1 **Mugardos**, Sp.
79/G1 **Muggia**, It.
74/A1 **Mugía**, Sp.
92/B2 **Muğla**, Turk.
91/A1 **Muğla** (prov.), Turk.
87/L2 **Mugodzharskoye** (mts.), Kaz.
130/A4 **Mugombazi**, Tanz.
130/A4 **Muhala**, Zaire
127/D4 **Muḩammad Qawl**, Sudan
127/C3 **Muḩammad, Ra's** (pt.), Egypt
130/A3 **Muhavura** (vol.), Rwa.
130/C4 **Muheza**, Tanz.
131/B1 **Muhila** (mts.), Zaire
70/B5 **Mühlacker**, Ger.
70/A2 **Mühlbach** (riv.), Ger.
71/F6 **Mühldorf**, Ger.
67/H6 **Mühlhausen**, Ger.
70/B2 **Mühlheim am Main**, Ger.
71/G6 **Mühlviertel** (reg.), Aus.
61/H2 **Muhos**, Fin.
94/C2 **Mūḩ, Sabkhat al** (lake), Syria
92/D3 **Mūḩ, Sabkhat al** (riv.), Syria
63/K2 **Muhu** (isl.), Est.
130/A3 **Muhutwe**, Tanz.
66/C4 **Muiden**, Neth.
54/B5 **Muirkirk**, Sc,UK
54/B1 **Muir of Ord**, Sc,UK
166/B2 **Muir-Orwin-Reinerton**, Pa,US
165/J11 **Muir Woods Nat'l Mon.**, Ca,US
101/D5 **Muju**, SKor.
86/B2 **Mukachevo**, Ukr.
100/B2 **Mukawa**, Japan
100/C2 **Mu-kawa** (riv.), Japan
127/D4 **Mukawwar** (isl.), Sudan
108/C2 **Mukeriān**, India
157/M2 **Muketei** (riv.), On,Can
91/E3 **Mukhayyam al Yarmūk**, Syria
165/C2 **Mukilteo**, Wa,US
99/L10 **Mukō**, Japan
130/A3 **Muko**, Ugan.
130/B2 **Mukono**, Ugan.
120/D2 **Mukoshima** (isls.), Japan
109/B4 **Mu Ko Similan Nat'l Park**, Thai.
109/B4 **Mu Ko Surin Nat'l Park**, Thai.
108/C2 **Muktsar**, India
131/C2 **Mukuku**, Zam.
130/A5 **Mukunsa**, Zam.
130/A5 **Mukwakwa**, Zam.
131/C1 **Mukwikile**, Zam.
74/E3 **Mula**, Sp.
97/K2 **Mulan**, China
131/D3 **Mulanje**, Malw.
151/G4 **Mulchatna** (riv.), Ak,US
142/B3 **Mulchén**, Chile
64/G3 **Mulde** (riv.), Ger.
113/D **Mule** (pt.), Ant.
74/D4 **Mulhacén, Cerro de** (mtn.), Sp.
64/F3 **Mülhausen**, Ger.
66/D6 **Mülheim an der Ruhr**, Ger.
76/D2 **Mulhouse**, Fr.
130/B5 **Mulilansolo Mission**, Zam.
103/D3 **Muling** (pass), China
97/L2 **Muling** (riv.), China
121/R9 **Mulinu'u** (cape), WSam.
104/D3 **Muli Zangzu Zizhixian**, China
60/B4 **Mulkear** (riv.), Ire.
95/L2 **Mulkila** (mtn.), India
55/J8 **Mull** (isl.), Sc,UK
54/A1 **Mullach Coire Mhic Fhearchair** (mtn.), Sc,UK
60/A6 **Mullaghanish** (mtn.), Ire.
60/A5 **Mullaghareirk** (mts.), Ire.
60/D3 **Mullaghcleevaun** (mtn.), Ire.
56/B2 **Mullaghmore** (mtn.), NI,UK
108/H4 **Mullaittivu** (dist.), SrL.
54/A2 **Mullardoch, Loch** (lake), Sc,UK
159/G2 **Mullen**, Ne,US
110/D4 **Muller** (mts.), Indo.
76/D2 **Müllheim**, Ger.
166/D5 **Mullica** (riv.), NJ,US
60/C2 **Mullingar**, Ire.
163/J3 **Mullins**, SC,US
58/A6 **Mullion**, Eng,UK
131/B3 **Mulobezi**, Zam.
126/C4 **Mulondo**, Ang.
108/A2 **Multān**, Pak.
60/B4 **Multeen** (riv.), Ire.
156/C3 **Multnomah** (falls), Or,US
110/D3 **Mulu, Gunung** (peak), Malay.
131/C2 **Mulungushi**, Zam.
131/B1 **Mulungwishi**, Zaire
127/B5 **Mulwad**, Sudan
131/C2 **Mumbotuta** (falls), Zaire, Zam.
126/C3 **Mumbué**, Ang.
131/B2 **Mumbwa**, Zam.
131/B1 **Mumena**, Zaire
70/B3 **Mümling** (riv.), Ger.
109/B5 **Mum Nauk** (pt.), Thai.
130/C3 **Mumoni** (peak), Kenya
109/C3 **Mun** (riv.), Thai.
111/F4 **Muna** (isl.), Indo.
63/M3 **Munamägi** (hill), Est.
71/E2 **Münchberg**, Ger.
71/E6 **München** (Munich), Ger.
76/D2 **Münchenstein**, Swi.
138/B4 **Munchique** (peak), Col.
138/B4 **Munchique Nat'l Park**, Col.
160/C3 **Muncie**, In,US
166/B1 **Muncy** (cr.), Pa,US
108/F4 **Mundakāyam**, India
165/P15 **Mundelein**, Il,US
129/H5 **Mundemba**, Camr.
64/E3 **Munden**, Ger.
67/G6 **Münden**, Ger.
59/H1 **Mundesley**, Eng,UK
59/G2 **Mundford**, Eng,UK
116/K7 **Mundijong**, Austl.
140/B3 **Mundo Novo**, Braz.
106/C3 **Mungaolī**, India
119/B2 **Mungo Nat'l Park**, Austl.
102/F1 **Mungun-Tayga, Gora** (peak), Rus.
71/E6 **Munich** (München), Ger.
160/C2 **Munising**, Mi,US
89/L4 **Munku-Sardyk** (peak), Rus.
96/D1 **Munku-Sasan** (peak), Rus.
70/D2 **Münnerstadt**, Ger.
143/J8 **Muñoz Gamero** (pen.), Chile
101/D4 **Munsan**, SKor.
70/C6 **Münsingen**, Ger.
76/D4 **Münsingen**, Swi.
63/R7 **Munsön** (isl.), Swe.
168/F6 **Munson** (hill), Oh,US
67/E5 **Münster**, Ger.
67/H3 **Munster**, Ger.
70/B3 **Münster**, Ger.
60/B5 **Munster** (prov.), Ire.
60/C4 **Munster** (riv.), Ire.
165/Q16 **Munster**, In,US
67/E4 **Münsterland** (reg.), Ger.
83/F2 **Muntele Mare** (peak), Rom.
112/F7 **Muntinglupa**, Phil.
110/C4 **Muntok**, Indo.
76/D3 **Müntschemier**, Swi.
92/D2 **Munzur Vadisi Nat'l Park**, Turk.
109/D1 **Muong Khuong**, Viet.
61/G1 **Muonioälv** (riv.), Swe.
61/G1 **Muoniojoki** (riv.), Fin.
126/C4 **Mupa Nat'l Park**, Moz.
101/A4 **Muping**, China
125/Q7 **Muqdisho** (Mogadishu) (cap.), Som.
73/L3 **Mur** (riv.), Aus.
82/C2 **Mura** (riv.), Slvk.
93/E2 **Muradiye**, Turk.
99/F1 **Murakami**, Japan
143/J7 **Murallón** (peak), Chile
130/A3 **Muramvya**, Buru.
130/C3 **Murang'a**, Kenya
92/B2 **Murat** (peak), Turk.
86/D5 **Murat Daği** (peak), Turk.
92/E2 **Muratlı**, Turk.
100/B4 **Murayama**, Japan
116/C3 **Murchison** (peak), Austl.
116/B3 **Murchison** (riv.), Austl.
115/R11 **Murchison**, NZ
75/E4 **Murcia**, Sp.
74/E4 **Murcia** (aut. comm.), Sp.
166/C6 **Murderkill** (riv.), De,US
161/H1 **Murdochville**, Qu,Can
118/B1 **Murdock** (pt.), Austl.
83/G2 **Mureş** (co.), Rom.
83/G2 **Mureş** (riv.), Rom.
72/D5 **Muret**, Fr.
131/C3 **Murewa**, Zim.
162/E3 **Murfreesboro**, Ar,US
163/G3 **Murfreesboro**, Tn,US
70/B5 **Murg** (riv.), Ger.
95/H1 **Murgab** (riv.), Trkm.
110/D5 **Muria** (peak), Indo.
141/D2 **Muriaé**, Braz.
95/G3 **Mūrī ān, Hāmūn-e Jaz** (lake), Iran
76/D4 **Muri bei Bern**, Swi.
140/D3 **Murici**, Braz.
64/G2 **Müritz See** (lake), Ger.
130/C3 **Murka**, Kenya
125/N6 **Murle**, Eth.
84/G1 **Murmansk**, Rus.
84/G2 **Murmansk Obl.**, Rus.
77/H2 **Murnau**, Ger.
99/M10 **Muro**, Japan
75/G3 **Muro**, Sp.
84/J5 **Murom**, Rus.
130/A3 **Murongo**, Tanz.
100/B2 **Muroran**, Japan
74/A1 **Muros**, Sp.
98/D4 **Muroto**, Japan
98/D4 **Muroto-zaki** (pt.), Japan
65/J2 **Murowana Goślina**, Pol.
163/G3 **Murphy**, NC,US
160/B4 **Murphysboro**, Il,US
70/C5 **Murr** (riv.), Ger.
148/E3 **Murra**, Nic.
119/D2 **Murramarang Nat'l Park**, Austl.
119/A2 **Murray** (riv.), Austl.
120/D5 **Murray** (lake), PNG
160/B4 **Murray**, Ky,US
163/H3 **Murray** (lake), SC,US
117/H5 **Murray Bridge**, Austl.
119/C2 **Murrumbidgee** (riv.), Austl.
168/H7 **Murrysville**, Pa,US
82/C2 **Murska Sobota**, Slov.
77/G4 **Murtaröl, Piz** (Cima la Casina) (peak), Swi.
57/G2 **Murton**, Eng,UK
112/A5 **Murud, Gunung** (peak), Malay.
115/S10 **Murupara**, NZ
121/M7 **Mururoa** (isl.), FrPol.
106/D3 **Murwāra**, India
119/E1 **Murwillumbah**, Austl.
65/H5 **Mürz** (riv.), Aus.
73/L3 **Mürzzuschlag**, Aus.
92/E2 **Muş**, Turk.
92/E2 **Muş** (prov.), Turk.
83/F4 **Musala** (peak), Bul.
93/H5 **Musandam** (pen.), Oman
130/A3 **Musasa**, Tanz.
99/H7 **Musashino**, Japan
95/G4 **Muscat** (Musqaţ) (cap.), Oman
166/C2 **Musconetcong** (riv.), NJ,US
167/E1 **Muscoot** (res.), NY,US
164/C2 **Muscoy**, Ca,US
130/A4 **Muse**, Tanz.
126/E5 **Musekwapoort** (pass), SAfr.
75/N9 **Museo del Prado**, Sp.
165/C2 **Museum of Flight**, Wa,US
117/F3 **Musgrave** (ranges), Austl.
161/L1 **Musgrave Harbour**, Nf,Can
106/E3 **Mushābani**, India
91/G8 **Mushāsh, Wādī** (dry riv.), WBnk.
60/B5 **Musheramore** (mtn.), Ire.
126/C1 **Mushie**, Zaire
110/B4 **Musi** (riv.), Indo.
138/B3 **Musinga** (peak), Col.
165/P14 **Muskego**, Wi,US
160/C3 **Muskegon**, Mi,US
160/C3 **Muskegon** (riv.), Mi,US
160/D4 **Muskingum** (riv.), Oh,US
159/J4 **Muskogee**, Ok,US
160/E2 **Muskoka** (lake), On,Can
131/C2 **Musofu**, Zam.
130/B3 **Musoma**, Tanz.
79/G5 **Musone** (riv.), It.
95/G4 **Musqaţ** (Muscat) (cap.), Oman
161/J1 **Musquaro** (riv.), Qu,Can
120/D5 **Mussau** (isl.), PNG
54/C5 **Musselburgh**, Sc,UK
156/F4 **Musselshell** (riv.), Mt,US
80/C4 **Mussomeli**, It.
108/B2 **Mustafābād**, Pak.
92/B1 **Mustafakemalpaşa**, Turk.
106/D2 **Mustāng**, Nepal
159/H4 **Mustang**, Ok,US
71/G4 **Můstek** (peak), Czh.
142/C5 **Musters** (lake), Arg.
101/E2 **Musu-dan** (pt.), NKor.
149/E3 **Musún** (mtn.), Nic.
119/D2 **Muswellbrook**, Austl.
127/B3 **Mūt**, Egypt
91/C1 **Mut**, Turk.
131/D3 **Mutambara**, Zim.
140/C4 **Mutá, Ponta do** (pt.), Braz.
131/D3 **Mutare**, Zim.
131/C2 **Mutenge**, Zam.
131/C3 **Mutepatepa**, Zim.
54/C4 **Muthill**, Sc,UK
111/F5 **Mutis** (peak), Indo.
131/D3 **Mutoko**, Zim.
133/H6 **Mutsamudu**, Com.
100/B3 **Mutsu**, Japan
100/B3 **Mutsu** (bay), Japan
77/G3 **Muttekopf** (peak), Aus.
76/D2 **Muttenz**, Swi.
70/B4 **Mutterstadt**, Ger.
77/G4 **Muttler** (peak), Swi.
108/G3 **Muttupet**, India
141/D1 **Mutum**, Braz.
108/H4 **Mutur**, SrL.
130/A2 **Mutwanga**, Zaire
108/F4 **Mūvattupula**, India
130/B4 **Muwale**, Tanz.
130/A3 **Muyinga**, Buru.
87/L4 **Muynak**, Uzb.
131/B1 **Muyuya**, Zaire
108/A2 **Muzaffargarh**, Pak.
106/C2 **Muzaffarnagar**, India
106/E2 **Muzaffarpur**, India
141/G6 **Muzambinho**, Braz.
102/D3 **Muzat** (riv.), China
131/B3 **Muzoka**, Zam.
146/E3 **Múzquiz**, Mex.
102/D4 **Muztag** (peak), China
102/E4 **Muztag** (peak), China
102/C4 **Muztagata** (peak), China
130/C4 **Mvomero**, Tanz.
131/C3 **Mvuma**, Zim.
126/C2 **Mwadi-Kalumbu**, Zaire
131/B1 **Mwadingusha**, Zaire
130/B3 **Mwadui**, Tanz.
131/C3 **Mwami**, Zim.
130/D3 **Mwana** (cape), Kenya
131/D2 **Mwanza**, Malw.
130/B3 **Mwanza**, Tanz.
130/B3 **Mwanza** (prov.), Tanz.
131/D2 **Mwase Lundaz**, Zam.
130/C5 **Mwaya**, Tanz.
55/G10 **Mweelrea** (mtn.), Ire.
130/C3 **Mweiga**, Kenya
126/D1 **Mweka**, Zaire
130/A5 **Mwenda**, Zam.
126/D2 **Mwene-Ditu**, Zaire
131/C4 **Mwenezi**, Zim.
131/C4 **Mwenezi** (riv.), Zim.
130/A5 **Mwense**, Zam.
130/B5 **Mwenzo Mission**, Zam.

130/C4 Mwera, Tanz.
130/A5 Mweru (lake), Zaire, Zam.
130/A5 Mweru-Wantipa (lake), Zam.
130/A5 Mweru-Wantipa Nat'l Park, Zam.
130/A4 Mwesi, Tanz.
130/A4 Mwesi (peak), Tanz.
130/A5 Mwimba, Tanz.
131/B1 Mwinilunga, Zam.
130/B4 Mwitikira, Tanz.
131/B2 Mwombezhi (riv.), Zam.
119/E2 Myall Lakes Nat'l Park, Austl.
104/B5 Myanaung, Burma
96/C2 Myangad, Mong.
107/G2 Myanmar (Burma)
104/B5 Myaungmya, Burma
104/B4 Myingyan, Burma
104/B4 Myintha, Burma
104/C2 Myitinge (riv.), Burma
104/C3 Myitkyina, Burma
104/B4 Myittha (riv.), Burma
65/J4 Myjava, Slvk.
58/C2 Mynydd Eppynt (mts.), Wal,UK
58/B2 Mynydd Pencarreg (mtn.), Wal,UK
104/B4 Myohaung, Burma
99/F2 Myōkō-san (mtn.), Japan
163/J3 Myrtle Beach, SC,US
163/J3 Myrtle Beach A.F.B., SC,US
156/C5 Myrtle Creek, Or,US
62/D2 Mysen, Nor.
65/K4 Myślenice, Pol.
65/H2 Myślibórz, Pol.
71/H5 Myslivna (peak), Czh.
109/E3 My Son (ruins), Viet.
106/C5 Mysore, India
165/B1 Mystery Bay Rec. Area, Wa,US
166/D4 Mystic Island, NJ,US
168/C3 Mystic Seaport, Ct,US
65/K3 Myszków, Pol.
109/D4 My Tho, Viet.
84/H5 Mytishchi, Rus.
71/G3 Mže (riv.), Czh.
131/D1 Mzimba, Malw.
131/D1 Mzuzu, Malw.

N

109/C1 Na (riv.), Viet.
71/E4 Naab (riv.), Ger.
66/B5 Naaldwijk, Neth.
63/K1 Naantali, Fin.
66/C4 Naarden, Neth.
71/H6 Naarn (riv.), Aus.
60/D3 Naas, Ire.
132/B3 Nababeep, SAfr.
106/E3 Nabadwīp, India
98/E3 Nabari, Japan
99/M10 Nabari (riv.), Japan
116/D3 Nabberu (lake), Austl.
71/F4 Nabburg, Ger.
130/C4 Naberera, Tanz.
85/M5 Naberezhnye Chelny, Rus.
108/D2 Nābha, India
94/D5 Nabī Shu'ayb, Jabal an (mtn.), Yem.
161/J1 Nabisipi (riv.), Qu,Can
144/B1 Nabón, Ecu.
112/C2 Nabua, Phil.
123/X17 Nābul, Tun.
123/X17 Nābul (gov.), Tun.
91/D3 Nābulus, WBnk.
112/D4 Nabunturan, Phil.
126/H3 Nacala, Moz.
148/E3 Nacaome, Hon.
98/D4 Nachi-Katsuura, Japan
130/C5 Nachingwea, Tanz.
65/J3 Náchod, Czh.
67/E6 Nachrodt-Wiblingwerde, Ger.
142/B3 Nacimiento, Chile
63/S7 Nacka, Swe.
162/E4 Nacogdoches, Tx,US
58/D4 Nadder (riv.), Eng,UK
120/G6 Nadi, Fiji
106/B3 Nadiād, India
82/E2 Nădlac, Rom.
123/N13 Nador, Mor.
101/D5 Naejang-san Nat'l Park, SKor.
57/H3 Nafferton, Eng,UK
95/J3 Nag, Pak.
104/B3 Naga (hills), India
112/C2 Naga City, Phil.
98/C4 Nagahama, Japan
98/E3 Nagahama, Japan
99/G1 Nagai, Japan
107/F2 Nāgāland (state), India
99/F2 Nagano, Japan
99/E3 Nagano (pref.), Japan
100/B2 Naganuma, Japan
99/F2 Nagaoka, Japan
98/D3 Nagaokakyō, Japan
108/G3 Nagappattinam, India
99/J7 Nagara, Japan
99/E3 Nagara (riv.), Japan
99/H7 Nagareyama, Japan
106/B4 Nagar Haveli, Dadrak (terr.), India
106/C4 Nāgārjuna Sāgar (res.), India
106/F2 Nagarzê, China
151/M5 Nagas (pt.), BC,Can
98/A4 Nagasaki, Japan
98/A4 Nagasaki (pref.), Japan
98/A4 Nagasaki Peace Park, Japan
99/M9 Nagashima, Japan
98/B3 Nagato, Japan
106/B2 Nāgaur, India
106/C3 Nāgda, India
108/F4 Nāgercoil, India
60/B5 Nagles (mts.), Ire.
100/J7 Nago, Japan
70/B5 Nagold, Ger.
130/B2 Nagongera, Ugan.
102/F2 Nagoonnuur, Mong.
87/H5 Nagorno-Karabakh Aut. Obl., Azer.
99/E3 Nagoya, Japan
99/M9 Nagoya Castle, Japan
106/C3 Nāgpur, India
104/B2 Nagqu, China
96/C5 Nagqu (riv.), China
63/J1 Nagu, Fin.
150/D3 Nagua, DRep.
99/H7 Naguri, Japan
82/C2 Nagyatád, Hun.
82/E1 Nagyhalász, Hun.
82/E2 Nagykálló, Hun.
82/C2 Nagykanizsa, Hun.
82/D2 Nagykáta, Hun.
82/D2 Nagykőrös, Hun.
82/E1 Nagy-Milic (peak), Hun.
100/J7 Naha, Japan
108/D2 Nāhan, India
152/D2 Nahanni Nat'l Park, NW,Can
91/D3 Nahariyya, Isr.
120/D2 Nahashima (isls.), Japan
93/G3 Nahāvand, Iran
69/G4 Nahe (riv.), Ger.
129/E4 Nahouri (prov.), Burk.
142/B3 Nahuelbuta Nat'l Park, Chile
142/C4 Nahuel Huapí (lake), Arg.
142/C4 Nahuel Huapí Nat'l Park, Arg.
146/D3 Naica, Mex.
96/C4 Naij Gol (riv.), China
98/C3 Naikai-Seto Nat'l Park, Japan
71/E2 Naila, Ger.
58/D4 Nailsea, Eng,UK
58/D3 Nailsworth, Eng,UK
103/E2 Naiman Qi, China
106/D3 Nainpur, India
54/C1 Nairn, Sc,UK
54/B2 Nairn (riv.), Sc,UK
117/M9 Nairne, Austl.
117/M9 Nairne (cr.), Austl.
130/C3 Nairobi (cap.), Kenya
130/C3 Nairobi Nat'l Park, Kenya
130/C3 Naivasha, Kenya
93/G3 Najafābād, Iran
92/E5 Najd (des.), SAr.
74/D1 Nájera, Sp.
106/C2 Najībābād, India
99/K9 Naka, Japan
98/D4 Naka (riv.), Japan
99/G2 Naka (riv.), Japan
99/H7 Nakai, Japan
99/F1 Nakajō, Japan
154/T10 Nakalele (pt.), Hi,US
99/G2 Nakaminato, Japan
98/C4 Nakamura, Japan
99/F2 Nakano, Japan
98/C3 Nakano (lake), Japan
100/B3 Nakasato, Japan
100/D2 Nakashibetsu, Japan
130/B2 Nakasongola, Ugan.
98/B5 Nakatane, Japan
98/B4 Nakatsu, Japan
99/E3 Nakatsugawa, Japan
125/N4 Nak'fa, Erit.
87/H5 Nakhichevan', Azer.
87/H5 Nakhichevan Aut. Rep., Azer.
97/L3 Nakhodka, Rus.
109/C3 Nakhon Nayok, Thai.
109/C3 Nakhon Pathom, Thai.
109/D2 Nakhon Phanom, Thai.
109/C3 Nakhon Ratchasima, Thai.
109/C3 Nakhon Sawan, Thai.
109/B4 Nakhon Si Thammarat, Thai.
63/J1 Nakkila, Fin.
65/J2 Nakł o nad Notecią, Pol.
108/C2 Nakodar, India
130/B5 Nakonde, Zam.
101/E3 Naksan-sa, SKor.
62/D4 Nakskov, Den.
101/E5 Naktong (riv.), SKor.
130/C3 Nakuru, Kenya
156/D3 Nakusp, BC,Can
95/J3 Nāl (riv.), Pak.
96/F2 Nalayh, Mong.
131/D5 Nalázi, Moz.
69/F5 Nalbach, Ger.
107/F2 Nalbāri, India
119/D3 Nalbaugh Nat'l Park, Austl.
87/G4 Nal'chik, Rus.
109/C2 Nale, Laos
106/C4 Nalgonda, India
83/K5 Nallıhan, Turk.
74/B1 Nalón (riv.), Sp.
124/H1 Nālūt, Libya
104/A2 Nam (lake), China
101/D3 Nam (riv.), NKor.
101/D5 Nam (riv.), SKor.
131/D2 Namadzi, Malw.
93/G3 Namak (lake), Iran
108/G3 Nāmakkal, India
95/G2 Namakzār-e Shadād (salt dep.), Iran
130/C3 Namanga, Kenya
102/B3 Namangan, Uzb.
101/G7 Namansansong Prov. Park, SKor.
130/A4 Namanyere, Tanz.
130/C5 Namaputa, Tanz.
132/B3 Namaqualand (reg.), SAfr.
111/J4 Namaripi (cape), Indo.
130/B2 Namasagali, Ugan.
130/C5 Namasakata, Tanz.
130/C5 Nambanje, Tanz.
69/G4 Namborn, Ger.
118/D4 Nambour, Austl.
116/B4 Nambung Nat'l Park, Austl.
109/D4 Nam Can, Viet.
109/C1 Nam Cum, Viet.
101/E2 Namdae (riv.), NKor.
109/D1 Nam Dinh, Viet.
63/S7 Nämdöfjärden (sound), Swe.
160/B2 Namekagon (riv.), Wi,US
129/E3 Namementenga (prov.), Burk.
99/E2 Namerikawa, Japan
126/G4 Nametil, Moz.
101/D5 Namhae (isl.), SKor.
126/B5 Namib (des.), Namb.
132/B2 Namibia
132/A2 Namib-Naukluft Park, Namb.
99/G2 Namie, Japan
100/B3 Namioka, Japan
131/D2 Namitete, Malw.
106/D2 Namja (pass), Nepal
104/B2 Namjagbarwa (peak), China
106/E2 Namling, China
77/G3 Namloser Wetterspitze (peak), Aus.
109/C2 Nam Nao Nat'l Park, Thai.
109/B4 Namnoi (peak), Burma
119/D1 Namoi (riv.), Austl.
120/E4 Namonuito (atoll), Micr.
120/F4 Namorik (atoll), Mrsh.
156/D5 Nampa, Id,US
101/C3 Namp'o, NKor.
126/G4 Nampula, Moz.
102/D6 Namsê Shankou (pass), China
61/D2 Namsos, Nor.
109/B2 Nam Tok Mae Surin Nat'l Park, Thai.
120/F4 Namu (atoll), Mrsh.
109/C2 Nam Un (res.), Thai.
69/D3 Namur, Belg.
69/D3 Namur (prov.), Belg.
131/B2 Namwala, Zam.
101/D5 Namwŏn, SKor.
65/J3 Namysł ów, Pol.
105/G3 Nan (mts.), China
104/E1 Nan (riv.), China
105/F1 Nan (riv.), China
109/C2 Nan, Thai.
109/C2 Nan (riv.), Thai.
147/L7 Nanacamilpa, Mex.
100/B3 Nanae, Japan
156/C3 Nanaimo, BC,Can
154/V13 Nanakuli, Hi,US
105/H4 Nan'ao (isl.), China
99/E2 Nanao, Japan
144/C1 Nanay (riv.), Peru
142/C2 Nancagua, Chile
97/K2 Nancha, China
105/G2 Nanchang, China
104/E2 Nanchong, China
105/E2 Nanchuan, China
69/F6 Nancy, Fr.
148/E4 Nandaime, Nic.
107/J3 Nandan, China
106/C4 Nānded, India
131/C4 Nandi Mill, Zim.
104/C4 Nanding (riv.), China
105/F5 Nandu (riv.), China
108/C3 Nandurbār, India
106/C4 Nandyāl, India
105/H3 Nanfeng, China
105/J4 Nang (isl.), Phil.
95/K1 Nanga Parbat (mtn.), Pak.
110/D4 Nangapinoh, Indo.
101/D2 Nangnim (mts.), NKor.
103/C3 Nangong, China
112/C3 Nangtud (mtn.), Phil.
130/C5 Nangua, Tanz.
104/B2 Nang Xian, China
103/E5 Nanhui, China
104/D3 Nanjian Yizu Zizhixian, China
103/D4 Nanjing, China
104/C4 Nanka (riv.), Burma, China
108/B2 Nankāna Sāhib, Pak.
98/C4 Nankoku, Japan
104/D4 Nanlan (riv.), Burma, China
103/C4 Nanle, China
103/D4 Nanling, China
105/F4 Nanliu (riv.), China
97/K3 Nanlou (peak), China
62/D1 Nannestad, Nor.
105/F4 Nanning, China
99/M9 Nannō, Japan
60/D2 Nanny (riv.), Ire.
104/E3 Nanpan (riv.), China
106/D2 Nanpāra, India
103/D3 Nanpi, China
105/H3 Nanping, China
99/M10 Nansei, Japan
100/J7 Nansei-Shotō (Ryukyu) (isls.), Japan
153/S6 Nansen (sound), NW,Can
130/B3 Nansio, Tanz.
99/F2 Nantai-san (mtn.), Japan
53/S10 Nanterre, Fr.
72/C3 Nantes, Fr.
53/U9 Nanteuil-le-Haudouin, Fr.
160/D3 Nanticoke, On,Can
166/B1 Nanticoke, Pa,US
54/A4 Nant, Loch (lake), Sc,UK
156/E3 Nanton, Ab,Can
103/E4 Nantong, China
161/G3 Nantucket (isl.), MA,US
57/F5 Nantwich, Eng,UK
58/C3 Nantyglo, Wal,UK
167/D1 Nanuet, NY,US
121/Z18 Nanuku (chan.), Fiji
120/G5 Nanumanga (atoll), Tuv.
120/G5 Nanumea (isl.), Tuv.
141/D1 Nanuque, Braz.
103/C4 Nanwon (res.), China
103/B4 Nanwutai (mtn.), China
104/E2 Nanxi, China
130/C5 Nanyamba, Tanz.
103/D4 Nanyang, China
103/D4 Nanyang (lake), China
130/C2 Nanyuki, Kenya
103/B5 Nanzhang, China
103/C4 Nanzhao, China
153/J3 Naococane (lake), Qu,Can
106/A3 Naokot, Pak.
97/L2 Naoli (riv.), China
147/N7 Naolinco de Victoria, Mex.
128/D5 Naoua (falls), IvC.
81/H2 Náousa, Gre.
105/F4 Naozhou (isl.), China
165/K10 Napa, Ca,US
165/K10 Napa (co.), Ca,US
165/K10 Napa (riv.), Ca,US
165/K10 Napa (val.), Ca,US
130/B2 Napak (peak), Ugan.
160/E2 Napanee, On,Can
127/B5 Napata (ruins), Sudan
165/P16 Naperville, Il,US
76/D4 Napf (peak), Swi.
115/S10 Napier, NZ
132/L11 Napier, SAfr.
161/N7 Napierville (co.), Qu,Can
163/H5 Naples, Fl,US
80/D2 Naples (Napoli), It.
107/J3 Napo, China
138/B5 Napo (prov.), Ecu.
138/C5 Napo (riv.), Ecu., Peru
157/J4 Napoleon, ND,US
166/B5 Napoleon, Oh,US
80/D2 Napoli (gulf), It.
80/D2 Napoli (Naples), It.
118/A4 Nappa Merrie, Austl.
59/E2 Napton on the Hill, Eng,UK
121/L6 Napuka (isl.), FrPol.
98/D3 Nara, Japan
98/D3 Nara (pref.), Japan
128/D3 Nara, Mali
95/J4 Nāra (riv.), Pak.
102/D5 Nara Logna (pass), Nepal
138/B5 Naranjal, Ecu.
144/B1 Naranjito, Ecu.
147/E3 Naranjo, Mex.
106/D4 Narasannapeta, India
99/J7 Narashino, Japan
109/C5 Narathiwat, Thai.
106/F3 Nārāyanganj, Bang.
106/C4 Nārāyanpet, India
58/B3 Narberth, Wal,UK
72/E5 Narbonne, Fr.
74/B1 Narcea (riv.), Sp.
81/F2 Nardò, It.
58/B6 Nare (pt.), UK
118/G9 Narellan, Austl.
153/T7 Nares (str.), NW,Can
65/L2 Narew (riv.), Pol.
149/G4 Narganá, Pan.
133/H6 Narinda (bay), Madg.
138/B4 Nariño (dept.), Col.
143/K8 Nariz (peak), Chile
106/D2 Narkatiāganj, India
106/C3 Narmada (riv.), India
87/G4 Narman, Turk.
80/C1 Narni, It.
53/K2 Narodnaya (peak), Rus.
130/B3 Narok, Kenya
130/C3 Naro Moru, Kenya
74/A1 Narón, Sp.
108/C1 Nārowāl, Pak.
61/G3 Närpes, Fin.
112/B3 Narra, Phil.
119/D1 Narrabri, Austl.
168/C2 Narragansett (bay), RI,US
167/J9 Narrows, The (str.), NJ,US
106/C3 Narsimhapur, India
106/C3 Narsinghgarh, India
130/C5 Narungombe, Tanz.
98/D3 Naruto, Japan
63/N2 Narva, Est.
63/M2 Narva (bay), Est., Rus.
63/M2 Narva (res.), Est., Rus.
63/M2 Narva (riv.), Est., Rus.
112/C1 Narvacan, Phil.
61/F1 Narvik, Nor.
85/M2 Nar'yan-Mar, Rus.
102/C3 Naryn, Kyr.
102/B3 Naryn (riv.), Kyr.
91/E2 Naşarī'yah, Jabal an (mts.), Syria
83/G2 Năsăud, Rom.
160/F4 NASA Wallops Space Ctr., Va,US
54/A1 Na Sealga, Loch (lake), Sc,UK
59/F3 Nash, Eng,UK
58/C4 Nash (pt.), Wal,UK
161/G3 Nashua, NH,US
162/E3 Nashville, Ar,US
163/G2 Nashville (cap.), Tn,US
82/D3 Našice, Cro.
65/L2 Nasielsk, Pol.
63/K1 Nasijärvi (lake), Fin.
106/B4 Nāsik, India
125/M6 Nāşir, Sudan
106/B2 Nasīrābād, India
95/J3 Nasīrābād, Pak.
112/C3 Naso (pt.), Phil.
121/Z17 Nasorolevu (peak), Fiji
151/N4 Nass (riv.), BC,Can
70/D2 Nassach (riv.), Ger.
150/B1 Nassau (cap.), Bahm.
143/L8 Nassau (bay), Chile
121/J6 Nassau (isl.), CookIs.
167/E2 Nassau (co.), NY,US
127/C4 Nasser (res.), Egypt
62/F3 Nässjö, Swe.
153/J3 Nastapoka (isls.), NW,Can
63/K1 Nastola, Fin.
62/D4 Næstved, Den.
99/F2 Nasu-dake (mtn.), Japan
112/C2 Nasugbu, Phil.
104/C5 Nat (peak), Burma
131/B4 Nata, Bots.
138/C4 Natagaima, Col.
160/C1 Natagani (riv.), On,Can
140/D2 Natal, Braz.
133/E3 Natal (prov.), SAfr.
108/G3 Nataraja Temple, India
99/L9 Natashō, Japan
161/J1 Natashquan (riv.), Qu,Can
168/B2 Natchaug Saint For., Ct,US
163/F4 Natchez, Ms,US
162/E4 Natchitoches, La,US
76/D5 Naters, Swi.
121/Z17 Natewa (bay), Fiji
168/B2 Nathan Hale Saint Mon., Ct,US
106/B3 Nāthdwāra, India
131/D2 Nathenje, Malw.
168/C1 Natick, Ma,US
147/E3 Natillas, Mex.
156/B2 Nation (riv.), BC,Can
81/L6 National Archaeological Museum, Gre.
164/C5 National City, Ca,US
59/E2 National Exhibition Centre, Eng,UK
166/B5 Nat'l Agriculture Research Ctr., Md,US
166/B5 Nat'l Aquarium, Md,US
166/A5 Nat'l Institutes of Health, Md,US
166/B5 Nat'l Security Agency, Md,US
130/B3 Natron (lake), Tanz.
108/G3 Nattam, India
107/G4 Nattaung (peak), Burma
110/C3 Natuna (isls.), Indo.
158/E3 Natural Bridges Nat'l Mon., Ut,US
116/B5 Naturaliste (cape), Austl.
119/D4 Naturaliste (cape), Austl.
116/B3 Naturaliste (chan.), Austl.
116/B5 Naturaliste-Leeuwin Nat'l Park, Austl.
77/G4 Naturno (Naturns), It.
77/G4 Naturns (Naturno), It.
147/K7 Naucalpan de Juárez, Mex.
132/E3 Naudesnek (pass), SAfr.
168/A3 Naugatuck, Ct,US
168/A2 Naugatuck (riv.), Ct,US
147/M7 Nauhcampatépetl (vol.), Mex.
70/B3 Nauheim, Ger.
112/C2 Naujan, Phil.
63/K3 Naujoji-Akmenė, Lith.
132/A2 Naukluft-Namib Game Rsv., Namb.
120/F5 Nauru
147/N6 Nautla, Mex.
75/N8 Navacarrada (pass), Sp.
78/A4 Nava, Colle di (pass), It.
158/E3 Navajo Nat'l Mon., Az,US
112/D3 Naval, Phil.
75/M9 Navalcarnero, Sp.
74/C3 Navalmoral de la Mata, Sp.
56/B4 Navan, Ire.
89/T3 Navarin (cape), Rus.
143/L8 Navarino (isl.), Chile
74/D1 Navarre (aut. comm.), Sp.
142/F2 Navarro, Arg.
149/H2 Navassa (isl.), USVI
58/A6 Navax (pt.), UK
78/D1 Nave, It.
74/B1 Navia, Sp.
74/B1 Navia (riv.), Sp.
142/C2 Navidad, Chile
137/H8 Naviraí, Braz.
83/J3 Năvodari, Rom.
88/G5 Navoi, Uzb.
146/C3 Navojoa, Mex.
146/D3 Navolato, Mex.
112/E6 Navotas, Phil.
81/G3 Návpaktos, Gre.
81/H4 Návplion, Gre.
106/B3 Navsāri, India
153/H1 Navy Board (inlet), NW,Can
106/E3 Nawābganj, Bang.
106/D2 Nawābganj, India
95/J3 Nawābshāh, Pak.
108/A1 Nawān Jandānwāla, Pak.
108/D2 Nawāshahr, India
95/G5 Nawş, Ra's (pt.), Oman
107/J2 Naxi, China
81/J4 Náxos (isl.), Gre.
146/D4 Nayarit (state), Mex.
59/G3 Nayland, Eng,UK
107/J2 Nayong, China
100/C1 Nayoro, Japan
96/B2 Nayramadlīn (peak), Mong.
102/E2 Nayramadlīn Orgil (peak), Mong.
131/D2 Nayuci, Malw.
102/B4 Nayzatash, Pereval (pass), Taj.
140/C4 Nazaré, Braz.
74/A3 Nazaré, Port.
140/B2 Nazaré do Piauí, Braz.
141/G8 Nazaré Paulista, Braz.
68/C2 Nazareth, Belg.
91/D3 Nazareth (Nazerat), Isr.
146/D3 Nazas (riv.), Mex.
144/C4 Nazca, Peru
144/C4 Nazca Lines, Peru
100/K6 Naze, Japan
91/D3 Nazerat (Nazareth), Isr.
59/H3 Naze, The (pt.), Eng,UK
92/B2 Nazilli, Turk.
125/N6 Nazrēt, Eth.
88/H4 Nazyvayevsk, Rus.
131/B2 Nchanga, Zam.
130/A5 Nchelenge, Zam.
131/D2 Ncheu, Malw.
131/D2 Nchisi, Malw.
131/C2 Ndabala, Zam.
130/B4 Ndala, Tanz.
126/B2 Ndalatando, Ang.
125/K6 Ndele, CAfr.
120/F6 Ndende (isl.), Sol.
131/D1 Ndengu, Tanz.
124/J5 N'Djamena (cap.), Chad
124/H8 N'Djolé, Gabon
131/C2 Ndola, Zam.
130/C3 Ndolo Corner, Kenya
129/H5 Ndop, Camr.
128/B2 Ndrhamcha, Sebkha de (dry lake), Mrta.
130/B4 Nduguti, Tanz.
130/B4 Nduli, Tanz.
130/C5 Ndumbwe, Tanz.
130/C4 Ndungu, Tanz.
72/C4 Né (riv.), Fr.
81/J5 Néa Alikarnassós, Gre.
56/B2 Neagh, Lough (lake), NI,UK
81/H3 Néa Ionía, Gre.
117/F3 Neale (lake), Austl.
83/H2 Neamț (co.), Rom.
151/A6 Near (isls.), Ak,US
58/C3 Neath, Wal,UK
58/C3 Neath (riv.), Wal,UK
56/D3 Neb (riv.), IM,UK
130/A2 Nebbi, Ugan.
77/G3 Nebel-Horn (peak), Ger.
87/K5 Nebit-Dag, Trkm.
139/E4 Neblina, Pico da (peak), Braz.
118/E6 Nebo (mtn.), Austl.
159/G2 Nebraska (state), US
159/J2 Nebraska City, Ne,US
80/C4 Nebrodi, Madonie (mts.), It.
156/B2 Nechako (riv.), BC,Can
162/E4 Neches (riv.), Tx,US
125/N6 Nechisar Nat'l Park, Eth.
71/G2 Nechranice, Údolní nádrž (res.), Czh.
70/B4 Neckar (riv.), Ger.
70/B4 Neckargemünd, Ger.
70/C4 Neckarsulm, Ger.
121/J2 Necker (isl.), Hi,US
142/F3 Necochea, Arg.
138/B2 Necoclí, Col.
80/C1 Necropoli (ruins), It.
74/A1 Neda, Sp.
66/C6 Nederweert, Neth.
116/K6 Nedlands, Austl.
108/F4 Nedumangād, India
66/D4 Neede, Neth.
168/C1 Needham, Ma,US
59/H2 Needham Market, Eng,UK
59/F2 Needingworth, Eng,UK
158/D4 Needles, Ca,US
59/E5 Needles, The (seastacks), UK
160/B2 Neenah, Wi,US
157/J3 Neepawa, Mb,Can
116/K6 Neerabup Nat'l Park, Austl.
69/E1 Neerpelt, Belg.
67/H2 Neetze (riv.), Ger.
69/F2 Neffelbach (riv.), Ger.
85/M4 Neftekamsk, Rus.
90/C7 Nefud (des.), SAr.
56/D6 Nefyn, Wal,UK
131/C2 Nega Nega, Zam.
160/C2 Negaunee, Mi,US
125/N6 Negēlē, Eth.
91/D4 Negev (reg.), Isr.
91/F8 Negev-Kinneret Conduit, Isr.
83/G3 Negoiu (peak), Rom.
130/C5 Negomano, Moz.
106/C6 Negombo, SrL.
82/F3 Negotin, Yugo.
82/F5 Negotino, Macd.
148/D2 Negra (pt.), Belz.
140/A3 Negra (mts.), Braz.
144/A2 Negra (pt.), Peru
107/F4 Negrais (cape), Burma
74/A1 Negreira, Sp.
83/H2 Negrești, Rom.
149/G2 Negril, Jam.
144/A2 Negritos, Peru
142/C3 Negro (peak), Arg.
142/D3 Negro (riv.), Arg.
136/F7 Negro (riv.), Bol.
137/G7 Negro (riv.), Braz.
136/F4 Negro (riv.), Braz., Ven.
143/T11 Negro (stream), Uru.
143/F2 Negro (riv.), Uru., Braz.
112/C3 Negros (isl.), Phil.
95/G2 Nehbandān, Iran
150/D3 Neiba, DRep.
149/J2 Neiba, Sierra de (range), DRep.
133/R15 Neiges, Piton des (peak), Reun.
103/C4 Neihuang, China
104/E2 Neijiang, China
54/B5 Neilston, Sc,UK
103/B2 Nei Monggol (aut. reg.), China
96/G3 Nei Monggol (plat.), China
103/C3 Neiqiu, China
138/C4 Neiva, Col.
103/B4 Neixiang, China
152/G3 Nejanilini (lake), Mb,Can
148/C2 Nejapa, Mex.
71/F2 Nejdek, Czh.
125/N6 Nejo, Eth.
125/N6 Nek'emtē, Eth.
84/G4 Nelidovo, Rus.
159/H2 Neligh, Ne,US
108/G3 Nellikkuppam, India
106/C5 Nellore, India
119/B3 Nelson (cape), Austl.
156/D3 Nelson, BC,Can
152/G3 Nelson (riv.), Mb,Can
143/J7 Nelson (str.), Chile
115/R11 Nelson, NZ
57/F4 Nelson, Eng,UK
58/C3 Nelson, Wal,UK
151/F3 Nelson (isl.), Ak,US
119/E2 Nelson Bay, Austl.
133/E2 Nelspruit, SAfr.
128/D2 Néma, Mrta.
128/D2 Néma, Dhar (hills), Mrta.
63/K4 Neman (Nemunas) (riv.), Eur.
78/C1 Nembro, It.
83/H2 Nemira (peak), Rom.
97/J2 Nemor (riv.), China
72/E2 Nemours, Fr.
63/K4 Nemunas (Neman) (riv.), Eur.
100/D2 Nemuro, Japan
100/D2 Nemuro (pen.), Japan
100/D2 Nemuro (str.), Japan, Rus.
59/F1 Nene (riv.), Eng,UK
85/M2 Nenets Aut. Okr., Rus.
97/K2 Nenjiang, China
159/J3 Neosho (riv.), Ks, Mo,US
159/J3 Neosho, Mo,US
75/F1 Néouville, Pic de (peak), Fr.
147/Q10 Neo Volcanica, Cordillera (range), Mex.
106/D2 Nepal
106/D2 Nepālganj, Nepal
106/C3 Nepanagar, India
118/G8 Nepean (riv.), Austl.
160/F2 Nepean, Can.
144/B3 Nepeña, Peru
165/F5 Nepessina (lake), Mi,US
158/E3 Nephi, Ut,US
60/A1 Nephin (mtn.), Ire.
60/A1 Nephin Beg (mtn.), Ire.
60/A2 Nephin Beg (range), Ire.
161/H2 Nepisiguit (riv.), NB,Can
71/H2 Neratovice, Czh.
96/H1 Nercha (riv.), Rus.
84/J4 Nerekhta, Rus.
70/D5 Neresheim, Ger.
82/D4 Neretva (riv.), Bosn., Cro.
63/L4 Neris (riv.), Lith.
74/D4 Nerja, Sp.
144/A2 Nermete (pt.), Peru
79/F5 Nerone, Monte (peak), It.
70/D6 Nersingen, Ger.
74/B4 Nerva, Sp.
78/A5 Nèrvia (riv.), It.
78/B1 Nerviano, It.
166/C1 Nescopeck (cr.), Pa,US
86/C4 Nesebŭr, Bul.
166/C3 Neshaminy (cr.), Pa,US
168/G5 Neshannock (cr.), Pa,US
53/S9 Nesles-la-Vallée, Fr.
54/B2 Ness (riv.), Sc,UK
159/H3 Ness City, Ks,US
67/H6 Nesse (riv.), Ger.
151/M4 Nesselrode (mtn.), Ak,US
54/B2 Ness, Loch (lake), Sc,UK
57/E5 Neston, Eng,UK
81/J2 Néstos (riv.), Gre.
91/F8 Nes Ziyyona, Isr.
91/D3 Netanya, Isr.
67/G5 Nethe (riv.), Ger.
58/D3 Netherend, Eng,UK
66/B5 Netherlands
150/D5 Netherlands Antilles (isls.), Neth.
54/C2 Nethy Bridge, Sc,UK
59/E5 Netley, Eng,UK
80/E3 Neto (riv.), It.
69/H2 Netphen, Ger.
66/D6 Nette (riv.), Ger.
67/H5 Nette (riv.), Ger.
69/G3 Nettebach (riv.), Ger.
69/F3 Nettersheim, Ger.
66/D6 Nettetal, Ger.
153/J2 Nettilling (lake), NW,Can
57/H5 Nettleham, Eng,UK
80/C2 Nettuno, It.
147/L7 Netzahualcóyotl, Mex.
71/E6 Neubiberg, Ger.
65/G2 Neubrandenburg, Ger.
70/E5 Neuburg an der Donau, Ger.
76/C4 Neuchâtel, Swi.
76/C4 Neuchâtel (canton), Swi.
76/C4 Neuchâtel (lake), Swi.
70/B5 Neuenbürg, Ger.
76/D2 Neuenburg am Rhein, Ger.
70/D4 Neuendettelsau, Ger.
65/G2 Neuenhagen, Ger.
66/D4 Neuenhaus, Ger.
67/E4 Neuenkirchen, Ger.
67/F3 Neuenkirchen, Ger.
67/E6 Neuenrade, Ger.
70/C4 Neuenstadt am Kocher, Ger.
71/E6 Neufahrn bei Freising, Ger.
69/E4 Neufchâteau, Belg.
76/B1 Neufchâteau, Fr.
70/E1 Neuhaus am Rennweg, Ger.
77/E2 Neuhausen am Rheinfall, Swi.
70/C2 Neuhof, Ger.
70/B4 Neuhofen, Ger.
68/B5 Neuilly-en-Thelle, Fr.
68/C5 Neuilly-Saint-Front, Fr.
53/T10 Neuilly-sur-Marne, Fr.
53/S10 Neuilly-sur-Seine, Fr.
70/B2 Neu-Isenburg, Ger.
77/H5 Neumarkt (Egna), It.
71/E4 Neumarkt in der Oberpfalz, Ger.
64/E1 Neumünster, Ger.
82/C2 Neunkirchen, Aus.
69/G5 Neunkirchen, Ger.
69/H2 Neunkirchen, Ger.
69/G2 Neunkirchen-Seelscheid, Ger.
142/C3 Neuquén, Arg.
142/C3 Neuquén (prov.), Arg.
142/C3 Neuquén (riv.), Arg.
64/G2 Neuruppin, Ger.
70/D6 Neusäss, Ger.
163/J3 Neuse (riv.), NC,US
66/D6 Neuss, Ger.
67/G4 Neustadt am Rübenberge, Ger.
70/D3 Neustadt an der Aisch, Ger.
71/E5 Neustadt an der Donau, Ger.
70/B4 Neustadt an der Weinstrasse, Ger.
70/E2 Neustadt bei Coburg, Ger.
64/F1 Neustadt in Holstein, Ger.
64/G2 Neustrelitz, Ger.
71/F5 Neutraubling, Ger.
70/D6 Neu-Ulm, Ger.
72/G2 Neuves-Maisons, Fr.
76/A6 Neuville-sur-Saône, Fr.
67/F1 Neuwerk (isl.), Ger.
69/G3 Neuwied, Ger.
63/P2 Neva (riv.), Rus.
74/D4 Nevada (mts.), Sp.
158/C3 Nevada (state), US
159/J3 Nevada, Mo,US
142/C4 Nevado Cónico (peak), Chile
135/C1 Nevado de Chañi (peak), Arg.
135/C2 Nevado del Candado (peak), Arg.
136/C3 Nevado del Huila (peak), Col.
138/C4 Nevado del Huila Nat'l Park, Col.
147/K7 Nevado de Toluca Nat'l Park, Mex.
142/C2 Nevado, Sierra del (mts.), Arg.
63/N3 Nevel', Rus.
68/C1 Nevele, Belg.
97/N2 Nevel'sk, Rus.
72/E3 Nevers, Fr.
82/D4 Nevesinje, Bosn.
87/G3 Nevinnomyssk, Rus.
150/F3 Nevis (isl.), StK.
150/F3 Nevis (peak), StK.
79/F5 Nevola (riv.), It.
92/C2 Nevşehir, Turk.
92/C2 Nevsehir (prov.), Turk.
139/G4 New (riv.), Guy.
59/E5 New (for.), Eng,UK
160/D4 New (riv.), WV,US
56/E2 New Abbey, Sc,UK
130/C5 Newala, Tanz.
160/C4 New Albany, In,US

New A – North

163/F3 **New Albany**, Ms,US
59/E4 **New Alresford**, Eng,UK
139/G3 **New Amsterdam**, Guy.
57/H5 **New Ancholme** (riv.), Eng,UK
165/K11 **Newark**, Ca,US
166/C4 **Newark**, De,US
167/D2 **Newark**, NJ,US
167/J9 **Newark** (bay), NJ,US
160/D3 **Newark**, Oh,US
57/H5 **Newark-on-Trent**, Eng,UK
165/G6 **New Baltimore**, Mi,US
168/D2 **New Bedford**, Ma,US
165/P14 **New Berlin**, Wi,US
163/J3 **New Bern**, NC,US
160/C2 **Newberry**, Mi,US
163/H3 **Newberry**, SC,US
57/G1 **Newbiggin-by-the-Sea**, Eng,UK
162/D4 **New Braunfels**, Tx,US
58/C2 **Newbridge on Wye**, Wal,UK
168/G6 **New Brighton**, Pa,US
120/D5 **New Britain** (isl.), PNG
168/B2 **New Britain**, Ct,US
161/H2 **New Brunswick** (prov.), Can.
166/D3 **New Brunswick**, NJ,US
56/A2 **New Buildings**, NI,UK
54/C4 **Newburgh**, Sc,UK
54/E2 **Newburgh**, Sc,UK
57/G2 **Newburn**, Eng,UK
59/E4 **Newbury**, Eng,UK
57/F3 **Newby Bridge**, Eng,UK
120/F6 **New Caledonia** (terr.), Fr.
121/U12 **New Caledonia** (isl.), NCal.
167/E1 **New Canaan**, Ct,US
119/D2 **Newcastle**, Austl.
161/H2 **Newcastle**, NB,Can
161/S8 **Newcastle**, On,Can
133/E2 **Newcastle**, SAfr.
56/C3 **Newcastle**, NI,UK
166/C5 **New Castle** (co.), De,US
160/C4 **New Castle**, In,US
168/G5 **New Castle**, Pa,US
157/G5 **Newcastle**, Wy,US
58/B2 **Newcastle Emlyn**, Wal,UK
57/F1 **Newcastleton**, Sc,UK
57/F5 **Newcastle-under-Lyme**, Eng,UK
57/G2 **Newcastle upon Tyne**, Eng,UK
167/E1 **New City**, NY,US
168/G6 **New Cumberland** (dam), Oh,US
166/B3 **New Cumberland**, Pa,US
54/B6 **New Cumnock**, Sc,UK
54/D2 **New Deer**, Sc,UK
106/C2 **New Delhi** (cap.), India
156/D3 **New Denver**, BC,Can
53/N8 **Newdigate**, Eng,UK
167/J9 **New Dorp**, NY,US
119/E1 **New England Nat'l Park**, Austl.
151/F4 **Newenham** (cape), Ak,US
58/D3 **Newent**, Eng,UK
168/A3 **New Fairfield**, Ct,US
161/S9 **Newfane**, NY,US
153/K3 **Newfoundland** (prov.), Can.
161/L1 **Newfoundland** (isl.), Nf,Can
56/D1 **New Galloway**, Sc,UK
120/E5 **New Georgia** (isls.), Sol.
120/E5 **New Georgia** (sound), Sol.
161/J2 **New Glasgow**, NS,Can
161/N6 **New Glasgow**, Qu,Can
120/C5 **New Guinea** (isl.), Indo., PNG
53/P7 **Newham** (bor.), Eng,UK
161/G3 **New Hampshire** (state), US
120/D5 **New Hanover** (isl.), PNG
59/F5 **Newhaven**, Eng,UK
168/B3 **New Haven**, Ct,US
168/B3 **New Haven** (co.), Ct,US
165/G6 **New Haven**, Mi,US
120/F6 **New Hebrides** (isls.), Van.
167/L9 **New Hyde Park**, NY,US
162/F4 **New Iberia**, La,US
59/G5 **Newick**, Eng,UK
168/B2 **Newington**, Ct,US
120/E5 **New Ireland** (isl.), PNG
166/D3 **New Jersey** (state), US
168/H6 **New Kensington**, Pa,US
162/D2 **Newkirk**, Ok,US
165/Q16 **New Lenox**, Il,US
160/E2 **New Liskeard**, On,Can
168/B3 **New London**, Ct,US
168/B2 **New London** (co.), Ct,US
160/B2 **New London**, Wi,US
168/B3 **New London Submarine Base**, Ct,US
58/A6 **Newlyn**, Eng,UK
159/K3 **New Madrid**, Mo,US
54/C5 **Newmains**, Sc,UK
116/C2 **Newman** (peak), Austl.
118/F6 **Newmarket**, Austl.
160/E2 **Newmarket**, On,Can
60/A5 **Newmarket**, Ire.
59/G2 **Newmarket**, Eng,UK
160/D4 **New Martinsville**, WV,US
156/D4 **New Meadows**, Id,US
158/F4 **New Mexico** (state), US
167/D2 **New Milford**, NJ,US
54/D1 **Newmill**, Sc,UK
57/F5 **New Mills**, Eng,UK
163/G3 **Newnan**, Ga,US
58/D3 **Newnham**, Eng,UK
119/C4 **New Norfolk**, Austl.
163/F4 **New Orleans**, La,US
168/F7 **New Philadelphia**, Oh,US
54/D1 **New Pitsligo**, Sc,UK
115/R10 **New Plymouth**, NZ
57/F6 **Newport**, Eng,UK
59/E5 **Newport**, Eng,UK
58/B2 **Newport**, Wal,UK
58/D3 **Newport**, Wal,UK
163/F3 **Newport**, Ar,US
164/C3 **Newport** (bay), Ca,US
160/C4 **Newport**, Ky,US
156/B4 **Newport**, Or,US
168/C3 **Newport**, RI,US
168/C2 **Newport** (co.), RI,US
160/D5 **Newport**, Tn,US
161/F2 **Newport**, Vt,US
156/D3 **Newport**, Wa,US
164/C3 **Newport Beach**, Ca,US
166/C5 **Newport Meadows** (lake), NJ,US
160/E4 **Newport News**, Va,US
54/D4 **Newport-on-Tay**, Sc,UK
59/F2 **Newport Pagnell**, Eng,UK
163/H4 **New Port Richey**, Fl,US
150/B1 **New Providence** (isl.), Bahm.
166/D2 **New Providence**, NJ,US
58/A6 **Newquay**, Eng,UK
58/B2 **New Quay**, Wal,UK
58/C2 **New Radnor**, Wal,UK
161/H1 **New Richmond**, Qu,Can
167/E2 **New Rochelle**, NY,US
157/J4 **New Rockford**, ND,US
59/G5 **New Romney**, Eng,UK
57/G5 **New Rossington**, Eng,UK
56/B3 **Newry**, NI,UK
56/B3 **Newry** (can.), NI,UK
113/Z **New Schwabenland** (reg.), Ant.
54/C4 **New Scone**, Sc,UK
167/G1 **New Shoreham** (Block Island), RI,US
167/D3 **New Shrewsbury** (Tinton Falls), NJ,US
89/P2 **New Siberian** (isls.), Rus.
163/H4 **New Smyrna Beach**, Fl,US
119/C2 **New South Wales** (state), Austl.
58/D2 **Newton**, Eng,UK
57/E1 **Newton**, Sc,UK
159/H3 **Newton**, Ks,US
168/C1 **Newton**, Ma,US
166/D1 **Newton**, NJ,US
162/E4 **Newton**, Tx,US
58/C5 **Newton Abbot**, Eng,UK
57/G2 **Newton Aycliffe**, Eng,UK
58/B6 **Newton Ferrers**, Eng,UK
54/C5 **Newtongrange**, Sc,UK
57/F5 **Newton-le-Willows**, Eng,UK
54/B5 **Newton Mearns**, Sc,UK
54/B2 **Newtonmore**, Sc,UK
57/G1 **Newton on the Moor**, Eng,UK
56/D2 **Newton Stewart**, Sc,UK
54/D5 **Newton Tors** (hill), Eng,UK
119/B3 **Newtown**, Austl.
58/C1 **Newtown**, Wal,UK
168/A3 **Newtown**, Ct,US
157/H4 **New Town**, ND,US
56/C2 **Newtownabbey**, NI,UK
56/C2 **Newtownards**, NI,UK
60/C1 **Newtownbutler**, NI,UK
56/B3 **Newtownhamilton**, NI,UK
54/D5 **Newtown Saint Boswells**, Sc,UK
56/A2 **Newtownstewart**, NI,UK
58/C3 **New Tredegar**, Wal,UK
54/C3 **Newtyle**, Sc,UK
157/K4 **New Ulm**, Mn,US
161/J2 **New Waterford**, NS,Can
156/C3 **New Westminster**, BC,Can
160/F3 **New York** (state), US
167/K9 **New York**, NY,US
167/K8 **New York** (co.), NY,US
115/Q10 **New Zealand**
113/L **New Zealand** (peak), Ant.
99/L10 **Neyagawa**, Japan
58/B3 **Neyland**, Wal,UK
93/H4 **Neyrīz**, Iran
93/J2 **Neyshābūr**, Iran
85/P4 **Neyva** (riv.), Rus.
108/G3 **Neyveli**, India
108/F4 **Neyyāttinkara**, India
86/D2 **Nezhin**, Ukr.
156/D4 **Nezperce**, Id,US
110/C3 **Ngabang**, Indo.
111/H5 **Ngabordamlu** (cape), Indo.
131/D3 **Ngabu**, Malw.
131/B2 **Ngabwe**, Zam.
130/C5 **Ngaga**, Tanz.
130/C3 **Ngai-Npethya Nat'l Rsv.**, Kenya
124/H5 **Ngala**, Nga.
131/B3 **Ngambwe** (rapids), Zam.
131/A3 **Ngamiland** (dist.), Bots.
130/B5 **Nganda** (peak), Malw.
130/D3 **Ngangerabeli** (plain), Kenya
102/D5 **Ngangla Ringco** (lake), China
102/E5 **Ngangzê** (lake), China
124/H6 **Ngaoundéré**, Camr.
130/A3 **Ngara**, Tanz.
119/B2 **Ngarkat Consv. Park**, Austl.
117/F2 **Ngarti Abor. Land**, Austl.
120/E4 **Ngatik** (isl.), Micr.
121/Z18 **Ngau** (isl.), Fiji
115/S10 **Ngauruhoe** (vol.), NZ
130/C4 **Ngerengere**, Tanz.
109/D2 **Nghia Dan**, Viet.
109/D1 **Nghia Lo**, Viet.
126/C4 **Ngiva**, Ang.
126/C1 **Ngo**, Congo
109/E4 **Ngoan Muc** (pass), Viet.
107/J4 **Ngoc Linh** (peak), Viet.
130/B3 **Ngogwa**, Tanz.
131/C4 **Ngomahuru**, Zim.
130/D3 **Ngomeni** (cape), Kenya
130/C3 **Ngong**, Kenya
126/D4 **Ngonye** (falls), Zam.
130/B2 **Ngora**, Ugan.
97/D5 **Ngoring** (lake), China
130/B3 **Ngorongoro Consv. Area**, Tanz.
131/B5 **Ngotwane** (riv.), Bots., SAfr.
124/H8 **Ngounié** (riv.), Gabon
130/B4 **Ngoywa**, Tanz.
130/B2 **Ngozi**, Buru.
130/B2 **Ngozi**, Ugan.
130/B3 **Ngudu**, Tanz.
124/H5 **Nguigmi**, Niger
120/C4 **Ngulu** (atoll), Micr.
109/C2 **Ngum** (riv.), Laos
130/C5 **Ngumbe Sukani** (pt.), Tanz.
131/C4 **Ngundu Halt**, Zim.
130/B3 **Ngunga**, Tanz.
130/C4 **Nguru** (mts.), Tanz.
109/D1 **Nguyen Binh**, Viet.
133/E2 **Ngwenya** (peak), Swaz.
131/C2 **Ngwerere**, Zam.
136/G4 **Nhamundá** (riv.), Braz.
131/D3 **Nhandugue** (riv.), Moz.
109/E3 **Nha Trang**, Viet.
128/E3 **Niafounké**, Mali
161/R9 **Niagara** (co.), On,Can
161/R9 **Niagara** (riv.), Can., US
161/S9 **Niagara** (co.), NY,US
161/R9 **Niagara** (falls), NY,US
161/R9 **Niagara Falls**, On,Can
161/R9 **Niagara Falls**, NY,US
161/R9 **Niagara-on-the-Lake**, On,Can
129/F3 **Niamey** (cap.), Niger
129/F3 **Niamey** (dept.), Niger
128/C4 **Niandan** (riv.), Gui.
125/L7 **Niangara**, Zaire
128/E3 **Niangay** (lake), Mali
103/C3 **Niangzi Guan** (pass), China
110/A3 **Nias** (isl.), Indo.
131/D2 **Niassa** (prov.), Moz.
149/E3 **Nicaragua**
149/E4 **Nicaragua** (lake), Nic.
80/E3 **Nicastro-Sambiase**, It.
73/G5 **Nice**, Fr.
163/G4 **Niceville**, Fl,US
78/A3 **Nichelino**, It.
98/B5 **Nichinan**, Japan
149/F1 **Nicholas** (chan.), Bahm., Cuba
116/C3 **Nicholson** (range), Austl.
139/G3 **Nickerie** (dist.), Sur.
139/G3 **Nickerie** (riv.), Sur.
116/C2 **Nickol** (bay), Austl.
107/F6 **Nicobar** (isls.), India
107/F6 **Nicobar, Car** (isl.), India
161/F2 **Nicolet**, Qu,Can
167/E2 **Nicolls** (pt.), NY,US
91/C2 **Nicosia** (cap.), Cyp.
91/C2 **Nicosia** (dist.), Cyp.
80/D4 **Nicosia**, It.
149/E4 **Nicoya**, CR
149/E4 **Nicoya** (gulf), CR
149/E4 **Nicoya** (pen.), CR
76/D3 **Nidau**, Swi.
57/G4 **Nidd** (riv.), Eng,UK
70/C2 **Nidda**, Ger.
70/B2 **Nidda** (riv.), Ger.
70/B2 **Niddatal**, Ger.
70/C2 **Nidder** (riv.), Ger.
69/F2 **Nideggen**, Ger.
69/G6 **Niderviller**, Fr.
77/E4 **Nidwalden** (demi-canton), Swi.
65/L2 **Nidzica**, Pol.
64/E1 **Niebüll**, Ger.
73/G2 **Nied** (riv.), Fr.
69/F5 **Nied** (riv.), Ger.
73/K3 **Niedere Tauern** (mts.), Aus.
65/G3 **Niederlausitz** (reg.), Ger.
70/B2 **Niedernhausen**, Ger.
69/H4 **Nieder-Olm**, Ger.
67/E1 **Niedersächsisches Wattenmeer Nat'l Park**, Ger.
82/B1 **Niederösterreich** (prov.), Aus.
70/D2 **Niederwerrn**, Ger.
69/F2 **Niederzier**, Ger.
70/B5 **Niefern-Öschelbronn**, Ger.
65/L2 **Niegocin** (lake), Pol.
67/G5 **Nieheim**, Ger.
65/J3 **Niemodlin**, Pol.
67/G3 **Nienburg**, Ger.
128/D5 **Niénokoué** (peak), IvC.
68/B2 **Nieppe**, Fr.
128/B3 **Niéri Ko** (riv.), Sen.
66/D5 **Niers** (riv.), Ger.
70/B3 **Nierstein**, Ger.
109/D4 **Niet Ban Tinh Xa**, Viet.
139/G3 **Nieuw-Amsterdam**, Sur.
66/D5 **Nieuw-Bergen**, Neth.
66/C4 **Nieuwegein**, Neth.
66/B5 **Nieuwerkerk aan de IJssel**, Neth.
66/B4 **Nieuwkoop**, Neth.
66/D3 **Nieuwleusen**, Neth.
66/C4 **Nieuw-Loosdrecht**, Neth.
139/G3 **Nieuw-Nickerie**, Sur.
68/B1 **Nieuwpoort**, Belg.
66/D3 **Nieuw-Schoonebeek**, Neth.
92/C2 **Niğde**, Turk.
92/C2 **Niğde** (prov.), Turk.
132/E2 **Nigel**, SAfr.
129/G2 **Niger**
129/G5 **Niger** (riv.), Afr.
129/G4 **Niger** (state), Nga.
129/G4 **Nigeria**
129/G5 **Niger, Mouths of the** (delta), Nga.
54/B1 **Nigg** (bay), Sc,UK
160/D1 **Nighthawk** (lake), On,Can
74/A1 **Nigrán**, Sp.
81/H2 **Nigríta**, Gre.
121/J2 **Nihoa** (isl.), Hi,US
99/G2 **Nihonmatsu**, Japan
99/F3 **Nii** (isl.), Japan
99/F2 **Niigata**, Japan
99/F2 **Niigata** (pref.), Japan
98/C4 **Niihama**, Japan
154/R10 **Niihau** (isl.), Hi,US
100/C2 **Niikappu** (riv.), Japan
99/C3 **Niimi**, Japan
99/F2 **Niitsu**, Japan
99/H7 **Niiza**, Japan
74/D4 **Níjar**, Sp.
66/C4 **Nijkerk**, Neth.
68/D1 **Nijlen**, Belg.
66/C5 **Nijmegen**, Neth.
84/F1 **Nikel'**, Rus.
99/F2 **Nikkō**, Japan
99/F2 **Nikkō Nat'l Park**, Japan
86/E3 **Nikolayev**, Ukr.
86/D3 **Nikolayev Obl.**, Ukr.
89/Q4 **Nikolayevsk-na-Amure**, Rus.
87/H1 **Nikol'sk**, Rus.
130/A3 **Nikonga** (riv.), Tanz.
86/E3 **Nikopol'**, Ukr.
92/D1 **Niksar**, Turk.
82/D4 **Nikšic**, Yugo.
121/H5 **Nikumaroro** (Gardner) (atoll), Kiri.
120/G5 **Nikunau** (isl.), Kiri.
125/M2 **Nile** (riv.), Afr.
97/B4 **Nile** (delta), Egypt
130/A2 **Nile** (prov.), Ugan.
91/B4 **Nile, Damietta Branch** (riv.), Egypt
91/B4 **Nile, Rosetta Branch** (riv.), Egypt
165/Q15 **Niles**, Il,US
160/C3 **Niles**, Mi,US
168/G5 **Niles**, Oh,US
108/F3 **Nilgiri** (hills), India
141/K7 **Nilópolis**, Braz.
61/J3 **Nilsiä**, Fin.
106/B3 **Nīmach**, India
97/L1 **Niman** (riv.), Rus.
128/C5 **Nimba** (peak), IvC.
128/C5 **Nimba** (co.), Libr.
72/F5 **Nîmes**, Fr.
168/F6 **Nimishillen** (cr.), Oh,US
113/L **Nimrod** (glac.), Ant.
69/F4 **Nimsbach** (riv.), Ger.
130/B2 **Nimule**, Sudan
130/A2 **Nimule Nat'l Park**, Sudan
92/E3 **Nīnawá** (gov.), Iraq
93/E2 **Nineveh** (ruins), Iraq
142/D4 **Ninfas** (pt.), Arg.
97/K3 **Ning'an**, China
105/J2 **Ningbo**, China
105/G3 **Ninggang**, China
103/C3 **Ningjin**, China
103/D3 **Ningjin**, China
104/C2 **Ningjing** (mts.), China
104/D3 **Ninglang Yizu Zizhixian**, China
103/C4 **Ningling**, China
105/E4 **Ningmeng**, China
109/D1 **Ningming**, China
103/C3 **Ningwu**, China
103/B3 **Ningxia Huizu Zizhiqu** (aut. reg.), China
103/D4 **Ningyang**, China
107/K2 **Ningyuan**, China
109/D1 **Ninh Binh**, Viet.
109/E3 **Ninh Hoa**, Viet.
168/C3 **Ninigret Nat'l Wild. Ref.**, RI,US
120/D5 **Niningo** (isl.), PNG
113/K **Ninnis** (glac.), Ant.
100/B3 **Ninohe**, Japan
99/H7 **Ninomiya**, Japan
68/D2 **Ninove**, Belg.
159/G2 **Niobrara** (riv.), Ne,US
128/B3 **Niokolo-Koba Nat'l Park**, Sen.
128/D3 **Niono**, Mali
128/B3 **Nioro-du-Rip**, Sen.
128/C3 **Nioro du Sahel**, Mali
72/C3 **Niort**, Fr.
157/H2 **Nipawin**, Sk,Can
149/H1 **Nipe** (bay), Cuba
160/B1 **Nipigon**, On,Can
160/B1 **Nipigon** (lake), On,Can
160/E2 **Nipissing** (lake), On,Can
165/P15 **Nippersink** (cr.), Il,US
142/C3 **Niquén**, Chile
149/G1 **Niquero**, Cuba
99/F3 **Nirasaki**, Japan
118/H8 **Nirimba-Hmas**, Austl.
106/C4 **Nirmal**, India
82/E4 **Niš**, Yugo.
74/B3 **Nisa**, Port.
81/H1 **Nišava** (riv.), Yugo.
80/D4 **Niscemi**, It.
99/M9 **Nishiharu**, Japan
99/L9 **Nishiki**, Japan
98/C3 **Nishiki** (riv.), Japan
99/L10 **Nishinomiya**, Japan
98/B5 **Nishino'omote**, Japan
99/E3 **Nishio**, Japan
98/D3 **Nishiwaki**, Japan
65/M3 **Nisko**, Pol.
165/B3 **Nisqually** (riv.), Wa,US
165/B3 **Nisqually Ind. Res.**, Wa,US
165/B3 **Nisqually Nat'l Wild. Ref.**, Wa,US
165/B3 **Nisqually Reach** (str.), Wa,US
120/E5 **Nissan** (isl.), PNG
62/E3 **Nissan** (riv.), Swe.
62/C2 **Nisser** (lake), Nor.
99/N9 **Nisshin**, Japan
62/C3 **Nissum** (bay), Den.
157/K4 **Nisswa**, Mn,US
141/K7 **Niterói**, Braz.
56/E1 **Nith** (riv.), Sc,UK
56/E1 **Nithsdale** (val.), Sc,UK
102/C5 **Niti** (pass), India
65/K4 **Nitra**, Slvk.
65/K4 **Nitra** (riv.), Slvk.
85/P4 **Nitsa** (riv.), Rus.
62/D1 **Nittedal**, Nor.
71/F4 **Nittenau**, Ger.
121/H6 **Niuafo'ou** (isl.), Tonga
121/H6 **Niuatoputapu Group** (isls.), Tonga
121/J7 **Niue** (terr.), NZ
120/G6 **Niulakita** (isl.), Tuv.
104/D3 **Niulan** (riv.), China
110/C3 **Niut** (peak), Indo.
120/G5 **Niutau** (isl.), Tuv.
105/J2 **Niutou** (isl.), China
105/H2 **Niutou** (mtn.), China
63/T9 **Nivå**, Den.
63/T9 **Nivå** (bay), Den.
68/D2 **Nivelles**, Belg.
72/E3 **Nivernais** (hills), Fr.
157/J3 **Niverville**, Mb,Can
158/C3 **Nixon**, Nv,US
102/D4 **Niya** (riv.), China
98/C4 **Niyodo** (riv.), Japan
106/C4 **Nizāmābād**, India
85/K4 **Nizhegorod Obl.**, Rus.
85/M4 **Nizhnekama** (res.), Rus.
85/L5 **Nizhnekamsk**, Rus.
89/K4 **Nizhneudinsk**, Rus.
88/H3 **Nizhnevartovsk**, Rus.
87/G1 **Nizhniy Lomov**, Rus.
85/K4 **Nizhniy Novgorod** (Gor'kiy), Rus.
85/N4 **Nizhniy Tagil**, Rus.
92/D2 **Nizip**, Turk.
65/K4 **Nízke Tatry Nat'l Park**, Slvk.
78/B3 **Nizza Monferrato**, It.
130/B5 **Njombe**, Tanz.
130/B4 **Njombe** (riv.), Tanz.
129/H5 **Nkambe**, Camr.
126/B1 **Nkayi**, Congo
131/D1 **Nkhata Bay**, Malw.
131/D2 **Nkhotakota**, Malw.
129/H5 **Nkogam, Massif du** (peak), Camr.
130/A4 **Nkonde**, Tanz.
129/H5 **N'Kongsamba**, Camr.
130/B4 **Nkululu** (riv.), Tanz.
130/A2 **Nkusi** (riv.), Ugan.
104/C3 **Nmai** (riv.), Burma
68/B5 **Noailles**, Fr.
106/F3 **Noākhāli**, Bang.
106/E3 **Noāmundi**, India
151/F2 **Noatak** (riv.), Ak,US
151/F2 **Noatak Nat'l Prsv.**, Ak,US
98/B4 **Nobeoka**, Japan
159/H4 **Noble**, Ok,US
160/C3 **Noblesville**, In,US
161/Q8 **Nobleton**, On,Can
138/A5 **Noboa**, Ecu.
100/B2 **Noboribetsu**, Japan
77/G5 **Noce** (riv.), It.
148/B2 **Nochixtlán**, Mex.
82/C5 **Noci**, It.
166/C3 **Nockamixon Saint Park**, Pa,US
99/H7 **Noda**, Japan
63/T9 **Nødebo**, Den.
123/P13 **Noé** (cape), Alg.
68/B3 **Noeux-les-Mines**, Fr.
147/M8 **Nogales**, Mex.
158/E5 **Nogales**, Az,US
63/H4 **Nogat** (riv.), Pol.
98/B4 **Nogata**, Japan
72/D2 **Nogent-le-Rotrou**, Fr.
53/T10 **Nogent-sur-Marne**, Fr.
68/B5 **Nogent-sur-Oise**, Fr.
84/H5 **Noginsk**, Rus.
118/B4 **Nogoa** (riv.), Austl.
101/D5 **Nogodan-san** (mtn.), SKor.
96/C2 **Nogoonuur**, Mong.
142/F2 **Nogoyá**, Arg.
65/K5 **Nógrád** (co.), Hun.
75/F1 **Noguera Pallarosa** (riv.), Sp.
101/E4 **Nogwak-san** (mtn.), SKor.
106/B2 **Nohar**, India
100/B3 **Noheji**, Japan
69/G4 **Nohfelden**, Ger.
148/E2 **Nohkú** (pt.), Mex.
160/E2 **Noire** (riv.), Qu,Can
72/B2 **Noires** (mts.), Fr.
72/B3 **Noirmoutier** (isl.), Fr.
68/B6 **Noisiel**, Fr.
53/T10 **Noisy-le-Grand**, Fr.
53/S10 **Noisy-le-Roi**, Fr.
68/B6 **Noisy-le-Sec**, Fr.
99/F3 **Nojima-zaki** (pt.), Japan
63/K1 **Nokia**, Fin.
111/F4 **Nokilalaki** (peak), Indo.
95/H3 **Nok Kundi**, Pak.
124/J7 **Nola**, CAfr.
78/B4 **Noli, Capo di** (cape), It.
119/D2 **Nomadgi Nat'l Park**, Austl.
168/D3 **Nomans Land** (isl.), Ma,US
168/D3 **Nomans Land Island Nat'l Wild. Ref.**, Ma,US
148/E3 **Nombre de Dios, Cordillera** (range), Hon.
151/F3 **Nome** (cape), Ak,US
98/B5 **Nomo-misaki** (cape), Japan
98/A4 **Nomo-zaki** (pt.), Japan
96/D2 **Nömrög**, Mong.
152/F2 **Nonacho** (lake), NW,Can
79/E3 **Nonantola**, It.
130/B4 **Nondwa**, Tanz.
78/A3 **None**, It.
68/B5 **Nonette** (riv.), Fr.
103/F1 **Nong'an**, China
109/D2 **Nong Han** (res.), Thai.
109/C2 **Nong Het**, Laos
109/C2 **Nong Khai**, Thai.
109/C2 **Nong Pet**, Laos
69/F4 **Nonnweiler**, Ger.
120/G5 **Nonouti** (atoll), Kiri.
103/E5 **Nonri** (isl.), China
101/D4 **Nonsan**, SKor.
66/A5 **Noordbeveland** (isl.), Neth.
66/B3 **Noorderhaaks** (isl.), Neth.
66/B3 **Noordhollandsch** (can.), Neth.
66/C3 **Noordostpolder** (polder), Neth.
66/B4 **Noordwijk aan Zee**, Neth.
66/B4 **Noordwijkerhout**, Neth.
66/B4 **Noordzeekanaal** (can.), Neth.
118/D4 **Noosa-Tewantin**, Austl.
156/B3 **Nootka** (isl.), BC,Can
156/B3 **Nootka** (sound), BC,Can
97/L1 **Nora** (riv.), Rus.
62/F2 **Nora**, Swe.
112/D4 **Norala**, Phil.
62/F1 **Norberg**, Swe.
164/C3 **Norco**, Ca,US
161/M6 **Nord** (riv.), Qu,Can
68/C3 **Nord** (dept.), Fr.
68/B3 **Nord, Canal du** (can.), Fr.
67/E1 **Norden**, Ger.
67/F2 **Nordenham**, Ger.
88/K2 **Nordenskjöld** (arch.), Rus.
67/E1 **Norderney**, Ger.
67/E1 **Norderney** (isl.), Ger.
67/G1 **Norderstedt**, Ger.
64/F3 **Nordhausen**, Ger.
67/F1 **Nordholz**, Ger.
67/E4 **Nordhorn**, Ger.
62/C3 **Nordjylland** (co.), Den.
61/H1 **Nordkapp** (North) (cape), Nor.
61/H1 **Nordkinn** (pt.), Nor.
67/E5 **Nordkirchen**, Ger.
61/E2 **Nordland** (co.), Nor.
70/D5 **Nördlingen**, Ger.
61/F3 **Nordmaling**, Swe.
64/E1 **Nord-Ostsee** (can.), Ger.
129/H5 **Nord-Ouest** (prov.), Camr.
123/M13 **Nord Ouest** (reg.), Mor.
72/D1 **Nord-Pas-de-Calais** (reg.), Fr.
67/E3 **Nord-Radde** (riv.), Ger.
67/E3 **Nord-Sud** (can.), Ger.
61/E2 **Nord-Trøndelag** (co.), Nor.
67/E4 **Nordwalde**, Ger.
60/C4 **Nore** (riv.), Ire.
72/E5 **Nore, Pic de** (peak), Fr.
115/M5 **Norfolk** (isl.), Austl.
119/C4 **Norfolk** (peak), Austl.
59/G1 **Norfolk** (co.), Eng,UK
168/C1 **Norfolk**, Ma,US
168/C1 **Norfolk** (co.), Ma,US
159/H2 **Norfolk**, Ne,US
160/E4 **Norfolk**, Va,US
59/H1 **Norfolk Broads** (swamp), Eng,UK
159/J3 **Norfork** (lake), Ar, Mo,US
66/D2 **Norg**, Neth.
62/B1 **Norheimsund**, Nor.
99/E2 **Norikura-dake** (mtn.), Japan
88/J3 **Noril'sk**, Rus.
160/B3 **Normal**, Il,US
118/A2 **Norman** (riv.), Austl.
159/H4 **Norman**, Ok,US
120/E6 **Normanby** (isl.), PNG
72/C2 **Normandy** (reg.), Fr.
165/C3 **Normandy Park**, Wa,US
168/A1 **Norman Rockwell Museum**, Ma,US
57/G4 **Normanton**, Eng,UK
144/B2 **Nororiental del Marañon** (dept.), Peru
132/B3 **Norotshama** (peak), Namb.
157/H3 **Norquay**, Sk,Can
63/R6 **Norra Björkfjärden** (bay), Swe.
63/S6 **Norra Ljusterö** (isl.), Swe.
61/F2 **Norrbotten** (co.), Swe.
74/B1 **Norrea** (riv.), Sp.
68/B2 **Norrent-Fontes**, Fr.
165/Q16 **Norridge**, Il,US
163/H2 **Norris** (lake), Tn,US
166/C3 **Norristown**, Pa,US
62/G2 **Norrköping**, Swe.
61/F2 **Norrland** (reg.), Swe.
63/R6 **Norrsunda**, Swe.
63/H2 **Norrtälje**, Swe.
63/R7 **Norrviken** (lake), Swe.
142/E4 **Norte** (pt.), Arg.
143/F3 **Norte** (pt.), Arg.
136/G6 **Norte** (mts.), Braz.
137/J3 **Norte, Cabo do** (cape), Braz.
143/J6 **Norte, Campo de Hielo** (glacier), Chile
138/C2 **Norte de Santander** (dept.), Col.
137/G6 **Nortelândia**, Braz.
67/G5 **Nörten-Hardenberg**, Ger.
116/B4 **North** (pt.), Austl.
119/C3 **North** (pt.), Austl.
119/C4 **North** (pt.), Austl.
160/D2 **North** (chan.), On,Can
161/J2 **North** (cape), PE,Can
60/A3 **North** (sound), Ire.
115/R9 **North** (cape), NZ
115/R10 **North** (isl.), NZ
56/C1 **North** (chan.), UK
52/D3 **North** (sea), Eur.
55/N13 **North** (sound), Sc,UK
151/D5 **North** (cape), Ak,US
151/F3 **North** (peak), Ak,US
166/B5 **North** (pt.), Md,US
82/D4 **North Albanian Alps** (mts.), Alb., Yugo.
57/G3 **Northallerton**, Eng,UK
116/C4 **Northam**, Austl.
58/B4 **Northam**, Eng,UK
168/B1 **North Amherst**, Ma,US
59/F2 **Northampton**, Eng,UK
59/E2 **Northampton** (uplands), Eng,UK
168/B1 **Northampton**, Ma,US
166/C2 **Northampton**, Pa,US
166/C2 **Northampton** (co.), Pa,US
59/F2 **Northamptonshire** (co.), Eng,UK
107/F5 **North Andaman** (isl.), India
167/J8 **North Arlington**, NJ,US
50/H3 **North Atlantic** (ocean)
168/C2 **North Attleboro**, Ma,US
153/K3 **North Aulatsivik** (isl.), Nf,Can
53/N6 **Northaw**, Eng,UK
167/M9 **North Babylon**, NY,US
54/A3 **North Ballachulish**, Sc,UK
56/D3 **North Barrule** (mtn.), IM,UK
156/F2 **North Battleford**, Sk,Can
160/E2 **North Bay**, On,Can
167/L9 **North Bellmore**, NY,US
156/B5 **North Bend**, Or,US
167/D2 **North Bergen**, NJ,US
54/D4 **North Berwick**, Sc,UK
168/C1 **Northborough**, Ma,US
66/C5 **North Brabant** (prov.), Neth.
168/B3 **North Branford**, Ct,US
168/C1 **Northbridge**, Ma,US
165/Q15 **Northbrook**, Il,US
166/D3 **North Brunswick**, NJ,US
130/A2 **North Buganda** (prov.), Ugan.
150/D2 **North Caicos** (isl.), Trks.
167/H8 **North Caldwell**, NJ,US
159/H3 **North Canadian** (riv.), Ok,US
168/F6 **North Canton**, Oh,US
157/L2 **North Caribou** (lake), On,Can
163/H3 **North Carolina** (state), US
156/C3 **North Cascades Nat'l Park**, Wa,US
108/H4 **North Central** (prov.), SrL.
147/F1 **North Central** (plain), Tx,US
163/J3 **North Charleston**, SC,US
165/Q15 **North Chicago**, Il,US
57/H5 **North Collingham**, Eng,UK
156/C3 **North Cowichan**, BC,Can
157/H4 **North Dakota** (state), US
58/D5 **North Dorset Downs** (uplands), Eng,UK
56/C2 **North Down** (dist.), NI,UK
59/F4 **North Downs** (hills), Eng,UK
118/C3 **North East** (pt.), Austl.
150/C2 **Northeast** (pt.), Bahm.
131/B4 **North-East** (dist.), Bots.
149/G2 **Northeast** (pt.), Jam.
151/E3 **Northeast** (cape), Ak,US
160/E3 **North East**, Pa,US
130/D2 **North Eastern** (prov.), Kenya
88/C2 **Northeast Land** (isl.), Sval.
150/B1 **North East Providence** (chan.), Bahm.
67/G5 **Northeim**, Ger.
59/G1 **North Elmham**, Eng,UK
129/E4 **Northern** (reg.), Gha.
91/D3 **Northern** (dist.), Isr.
131/D1 **Northern** (reg.), Malw.
128/B4 **Northern** (prov.), SLeo.
108/H4 **Northern** (prov.), SrL.
127/B4 **Northern** (reg.), Sudan
130/B2 **Northern** (prov.), Ugan.
130/A5 **Northern** (prov.), Zam.
131/C1 **Northern** (prov.), Zam.
102/B4 **Northern Areas** (terr.), Pak.
121/J6 **Northern Cook** (isls.), CookIs.
52/H2 **Northern Dvina** (riv.), Rus.
55/H9 **Northern Ireland**, UK
160/B1 **Northern Light** (lake), On,Can, Mn,US
120/D3 **Northern Marianas**, US
88/G3 **Northern Sos'va** (riv.), Rus.
81/J3 **Northern Sporades** (isls.), Gre.
117/G2 **Northern Territory** (terr.), Austl.
85/N3 **Northern Ural** (mts.), Rus.
85/K4 **Northern Uval** (hills), Rus.
88/E4 **Northern Wals** (upland), Rus.
151/K2 **Northern Yukon Nat'l Park**, Yk,Can
54/C5 **North Esk** (riv.), Sc,UK
54/D3 **North Esk** (riv.), Sc,UK
157/K4 **Northfield**, Mn,US
53/P7 **Northfleet**, Eng,UK
59/H4 **North Foreland** (pt.), Eng,UK
163/H5 **North Fort Myers**, Fl,US
160/D1 **North French** (riv.), On,Can
64/E1 **North Frisian** (isls.), Den., Ger.
167/J8 **North Haledon**, NJ,US
168/B3 **North Haven**, Ct,US
161/F2 **North Hero**, Vt,US
165/M9 **North Highlands**, Ca,US
165/C3 **North Hill-Edgewood**, Wa,US
66/B3 **North Holland** (prov.), Neth.
164/F7 **North Hollywood**, Ca,US
130/C2 **North Horr**, Kenya

209
North – Olima

57/H5 North Hykeham, Eng,UK
85/Q5 North Kazakhstan Obl., Rus.
130/C3 North Kitui Nat'l Rsv., Kenya
101/D2 North Korea
104/B3 North Lakhimpur, India
158/D3 North Las Vegas, Nv,US
167/M9 North Lindenhurst, NY,US
162/E3 North Little Rock, Ar,US
164/F8 North Long Beach, Ca,US
159/G2 North Loup (riv.), Ne,US
131/D1 North Luangwa Nat'l Park, Zam.
153/R7 North Magnetic Pole, NAm
55/H8 North Minch (The Minch) (sound), Sc,UK
157/J2 North Moose (lake), Mb,Can
166/B1 North Mtn. (ridge), Pa,US
163/J3 North Myrtle Beach, SC,US
61/H1 North (Nordkapp) (cape), Nor.
168/F5 North Olmsted, Oh,US
87/G4 North Ossetian Aut. Rep., Rus.
120/F3 North Pacific (ocean)
161/R9 North Pelham, On,Can
58/C4 North Petherton, Eng,UK
118/E6 North Pine (riv.), Austl.
166/D2 North Plainfield, NJ,US
159/G2 North Platte (riv.), US
159/G2 North Platte, Ne,US
163/G3 Northport, Al,US
167/E2 Northport (Old Northport), NY,US
166/A5 North Potomac, Md,US
168/C2 North Providence, RI,US
157/K5 North Raccoon (riv.), Ia,US
64/E3 North Rhine-Westphalia (state), Ger.
164/E7 Northridge, Ca,US
168/E5 North Ridgeville, Oh,US
158/D3 North Rim, Az,US
55/N13 North Ronaldsay (isl.), Sc,UK
168/F5 North Royalton, Oh,US
156/F2 North Saskatchewan (riv.), Ab, Sk,Can
57/G2 North Shields, Eng,UK
88/K2 North Siberian (plain), Rus.
159/J2 North Skunk (riv.), Ia,US
57/J5 North Somercotes, Eng,UK
118/D4 North Stradbroke (isl.), Austl.
115/R10 North Taranaki (bight), NZ
167/E1 North Tarrytown, NY,US
57/H5 North Thoresby, Eng,UK
59/E4 North Tidworth, Eng,UK
55/H7 North Tolsta, Sc,UK
161/S9 North Tonawanda, NY,US
57/F1 North Tyne (riv.), Eng,UK
55/H8 North Uist (isl.), Sc,UK
161/J2 Northumberland (str.), Can.
57/F1 Northumberland (co.), Eng,UK
166/B2 Northumberland (co.), Pa,US
57/F1 Northumberland Nat'l Park, Eng,UK
158/B2 North Umpqua (riv.), Or,US
152/D4 North Vancouver, BC,Can
165/F7 Northville, Mi,US
59/H1 North Walsham, Eng,UK
53/P6 North Weald Bassett, Eng,UK
116/B2 North West (cape), Austl.
149/G2 Northwest (pt.), Jam.
108/H4 North Western (prov.), SrL.
131/B2 North-Western (prov.), Zam.
102/B4 Northwest Frontier (prov.), Pak.
161/L1 North West Gander (riv.), Nf,Can
54/A2 North West Highlands (mts.), Sc,UK
150/B1 North West Providence (chan.), Bahm.
152/E2 Northwest Territories (terr.), Can.
57/H5 North Wheatley, Eng,UK
57/F5 Northwich, Eng,UK
162/D3 North Wichita (riv.), Tx,US
57/G5 North Wingfield, Eng,UK
157/J4 Northwood, ND,US
161/R8 North York, On,Can
57/H3 North York Moors Nat'l Park, Eng,UK
57/G3 North Yorkshire (co.), Eng,UK
151/F3 Norton (bay), Ak,US
151/E3 Norton (sound), Ak,US
159/H3 Norton, Ks,US
168/F5 Norton, Oh,US
160/D4 Norton, Va,US
131/C3 Norton, Zim.
57/F6 Norton Bridge, Eng,UK
160/C3 Norton Shores, Mi,US
64/E1 Nortorf, Ger.
161/Q8 Norval, On,Can
113/Z Norvegia (cape), Ant.
69/F2 Nörvenich, Ger.
164/B3 Norwalk, Ca,US
167/E1 Norwalk, Ct,US
167/M7 Norwalk (riv.), Ct,US
160/D3 Norwalk, Oh,US
61/B3 Norway
157/J2 Norway House, Mb,Can
153/S7 Norwegian (bay), NW,Can
52/C2 Norwegian (sea), Eur.
168/D1 Norwell, Ma,US
59/H1 Norwich, Eng,UK
168/B2 Norwich, Ct,US
160/F3 Norwich, NY,US
168/C1 Norwood, Ma,US
100/D2 Nosappu-misaki (cape), Japan
99/L10 Nose, Japan
100/B1 Noshappu-misaki (cape), Japan
95/K1 Noshaq (mtn.), Pak.
100/B3 Noshiro, Japan
83/H4 Nos Maslen Nos (pt.), Bul.
110/E2 Nosong (cape), Malay.
112/A4 Nosong, Tanjong (cape), Malay.
132/C2 Nosop (dry riv.), Bots.
86/D2 Nosovka, Ukr.
95/G3 Noşratābād, Iran
140/C3 Nossa Senhora da Glória, Braz.
140/C3 Nossa Senhora das Dores, Braz.
55/K7 Noss Head (pt.), Sc,UK
132/B2 Nossob (dry riv.), Namb.
132/C2 Nossobrivier (dry riv.), SAfr.
143/J7 Notch (cape), Chile
65/J2 Notec (riv.), Pol.
80/D4 Noto, It.
80/D4 Noto (gulf), It.
80/D4 Noto (val.), It.
99/E2 Noto (pen.), Japan
80/D4 Noto Antica (ruins), It.
62/C2 Notodden, Nor.
99/M9 Notogawa, Japan
100/C1 Notoro (lake), Japan
161/L1 Notre Dame (bay), Nf,Can
161/G1 Notre Dame (mts.), Qu,Can
53/T10 Notre Dame, Fr.
161/N7 Notre-Dame-de-l'Ile-Perrot, Qu,Can
117/G5 Nott (peak), Austl.
160/E1 Nottaway (riv.), Qu,Can
62/D2 Nøtterøy, Nor.
153/H2 Nottingham (isl.), NW,Can
57/G6 Nottingham, Eng,UK
57/H5 Nottinghamshire (co.), Eng,UK
67/E5 Nottuln, Ger.
122/A2 Nouadhibou, Mrta.
128/B2 Nouakchott (cap.), Mrta.
75/F1 Noue (riv.), Fr.
121/V13 Nouméa (cap.), NCal.
132/D3 Noupoort, SAfr.
68/A3 Nouvion, Fr.
69/D4 Nouzonville, Fr.
137/H8 Nova Andradina, Braz.
83/F3 Novaci, Rom.
140/D2 Nova Cruz, Braz.
65/K4 Nová Dubnica, Slvk.
141/L7 Nova Friburgo, Braz.
79/G1 Nova Gorica, Slov.
82/C3 Nova Gradiška, Cro.
141/K7 Nova Iguaçu, Braz.
112/F6 Novaliches (res.), Phil.
131/D3 Nova Lusitânia, Moz.
131/D4 Nova Mambone, Moz.
140/C2 Nova Olinda, Braz.
136/G4 Nova Olinda do Norte, Braz.
82/E3 Nova Pazova, Yugo.
141/B4 Nova Prata, Braz.
78/B2 Novara, It.
78/B1 Novara (prov.), It.
140/B2 Nova Russas, Braz.
161/J2 Nova Scotia (prov.), Can.
131/D4 Nova Sofala, Moz.
140/C3 Nova Soure, Braz.
165/J10 Novato, Ca,US
82/D4 Nova Varoš, Yugo.
141/D1 Nova Venécia, Braz.
137/H6 Nova Xavantina, Braz.
86/E3 Novaya Kakhovka, Ukr.
89/R2 Novaya Sibir' (isl.), Rus.
88/E2 Novaya Zemlya (isl.), Rus.
83/H4 Nova Zagora, Bul.
75/E3 Novelda, Sp.
79/D3 Novellara, It.
65/J4 Nové Mesto nad Váhom, Slvk.
79/E2 Noventa Vicentina, It.
65/K5 Nové Zámky, Slvk.
84/F4 Novgorod, Rus.
63/P2 Novgorod Obl., Rus.
165/F7 Novi, Mi,US
82/E3 Novi Bečej, Yugo.
79/G2 Novigrad, Cro.
83/F4 Novi Iskŭr, Bul.
78/B3 Novi Ligure, It.
83/H4 Novi Pazar, Bul.
82/E4 Novi Pazar, Yugo.
82/D3 Novi Sad, Yugo.
141/K6 Novo (riv.), Braz.
87/G2 Novoanninskiy, Rus.
136/F5 Novo Aripuanã, Braz.
85/K4 Novocheboksarsk, Rus.
86/G3 Novocherkassk, Rus.
86/C2 Novograd-Volynskiy, Ukr.
63/L5 Novogrudok, Bela.
141/B4 Novo Hamburgo, Braz.
141/B2 Novo Horizonte, Braz.
71/H5 Novohradské Hory (mts.), Czh.
88/G5 Novokazalinsk, Kaz.
87/J1 Novokuybyshevsk, Rus.
88/J4 Novokuznetsk, Rus.
63/P1 Novoladozhskiy (can.), Rus.
113/A Novolazarevskaya, Ant.
82/B3 Novo Mesto, Slov.
82/E3 Novo Miloševo, Yugo.
86/F1 Novomoskovsk, Rus.
86/E3 Novomoskovsk, Ukr.
140/B2 Novo Oriente, Braz.
63/N4 Novopolotsk, Bela.
86/F3 Novorossiysk, Rus.
86/F3 Novoshakhtinsk, Rus.
88/J4 Novosibirsk, Rus.
87/L2 Novotroitsk, Rus.
86/D2 Novoukrainka, Ukr.
86/C2 Novovolynsk, Ukr.
85/L4 Novovyatsk, Rus.
86/D1 Novozybkov, Rus.
82/C3 Novska, Cro.
65/K4 Nový Jičín, Czh.
87/K4 Novyy Uzen', Kaz.
65/J3 Nowa Dęba, Pol.
65/J3 Nowa Ruda, Pol.
65/M3 Nowa Sarzyna, Pol.
65/H3 Nowa Sól, Pol.
159/J3 Nowata, Ok,US
65/K2 Nowe, Pol.
65/K2 Nowe Miasto Lubawskie, Pol.
60/A6 Nowen (mtn.), Ire.
106/C2 Nowgong, India
107/F2 Nowgong, India
151/H3 Nowitna (riv.), Ak,US
151/H3 Nowitna Nat'l Wild. Ref., Ak,US
65/H2 Nowogard, Pol.
158/F1 Nowood (riv.), Wy,US
95/K2 Nowshera, Pak.
65/K1 Nowy Dwór Gdański, Pol.
65/L4 Nowy Sącz, Pol.
65/L4 Nowy Sącz (prov.), Pol.
65/L4 Nowy Targ, Pol.
65/J2 Nowy Tomyśl, Pol.
74/A1 Noya, Sp.
68/B5 Noye (riv.), Fr.
108/F3 Noyil (riv.), India
68/C4 Noyon, Fr.
131/D3 Nsanje, Malw.
129/E5 Nsawam, Gha.
130/G5 Nsumba Nat'l Park, Zam.
130/A2 Ntoroko, Ugan.
130/A3 Ntungamo, Ugan.
130/A2 Ntusi, Ugan.
131/B4 Ntwetwe Pan (salt pan), Bots.
104/C3 Nu (mts.), China
96/D5 Nu (riv.), China
125/M5 Nūbah (mts.), Sudan
104/B2 Nubgang (pass), China
127/C4 Nubian (des.), Sudan
125/E3 Nucla, Co,US
162/D4 Nueces (riv.), Tx,US
152/G2 Nueltin (lake), NW,Can
66/C6 Nuenen, Neth.
103/E2 Nü'er (riv.), China
148/D2 Nueva Coahuila Nat'l Cap. Park, Mex.
148/D3 Nueva Concepción, Guat.
139/E2 Nueva Esparta (state), Ven.
149/F1 Nueva Gerona, Cuba
143/F2 Nueva Helvecia, Uru.
142/B3 Nueva Imperial, Chile
136/C3 Nueva Loja, Ecu.
138/B4 Nueva Loja (Lago Agrio), Ecu.
148/D3 Nueva Ocotepéque, Hon.
143/S11 Nueva Palmira, Uru.
147/N8 Nueva Patria, Mex.
142/E2 Nueve de Julio, Arg.
149/G1 Nuevitas, Cuba
142/D4 Nuevo (gulf), Arg.
146/D2 Nuevo Casas Grandes, Mex.
147/F3 Nuevo León (state), Mex.
143/S11 Nuevo Palmira, Uru.
77/E5 Nufenenpass (pass), Swi.
120/E5 Nuguria (isls.), PNG
121/J2 Nuhau (isl.), Hi,US
67/F6 Nuhne (riv.), Ger.
120/G5 Nui (atoll), Tuv.
99/N10 Nukata, Japan
151/F4 Nuklunek (mtn.), Ak,US
121/H7 Nuku'alofa (cap.), Tonga
120/G5 Nukufetau (atoll), Tuv.
121/L5 Nuku Hiva (isl.), FrPol.
120/H5 Nukulaelae (isl.), Tuv.
120/F5 Nukumanu (atoll), PNG
121/H5 Nukunonu (atoll), Tok.
120/E4 Nukuoro (isl.), Micr.
88/F5 Nukus, Uzb.
121/M6 Nukutavake (isl.), FrPol.
75/E3 Nules, Sp.
116/E5 Nullarbor (plain), Austl.
117/F4 Nullarbor Nat'l Park, Austl.
124/H6 Numan, Nga.
66/B5 Numansdorp, Neth.
99/F2 Numata, Japan
99/F3 Numazu, Japan
130/A3 Numbi, Zaire
69/G2 Nümbrecht, Ger.
111/H4 Numfoor (isl.), Indo.
119/G5 Nunawading, Austl.
59/E1 Nuneaton, Eng,UK
119/D3 Nungatta Nat'l Park, Austl.
130/B3 Nungwe, Tanz.
151/E4 Nunivak (isl.), Ak,US
66/C4 Nunspeet, Neth.
57/G2 Nunthorpe, Eng,UK
97/J1 Nuomin (riv.), China
128/C5 Nuon (riv.), IvC., Libr.
80/A2 Nuoro, It.
138/B3 Nuqui, Col.
91/E1 Nur (mts.), Turk.
102/B2 Nura (riv.), Kaz.
69/F3 Nürburgring, Ger.
78/C3 Nure (riv.), It.
92/D2 Nurhak, Turk.
127/B5 Nuri (ruins), Sudan
63/L1 Nurmijärvi, Fin.
70/E4 Nürnberg, Ger.
119/C1 Nurri (peak), Austl.
70/C5 Nürtingen, Ger.
104/C2 Nu (Salween) (riv.), China
92/D2 Nusaybin, Turk.
151/G4 Nushagak (riv.), Ak,US
95/J3 Nushki, Pak.
54/C5 Nutberry (hill), Sc,UK
69/E2 Nuth, Neth.
167/D2 Nutley, NJ,US
145/M3 Nuuk (Godthåb), Grld.
121/X15 Nuupere (pt.), FrPol.
127/C2 Nuwaybi', Egypt
132/L10 Nuy (riv.), SAfr.
131/D3 Nuza (peak), Zim.
131/B3 Nxai Pan (salt pan), Bots.
131/B3 Nxai Pan Nat'l Park, Bots.
130/A3 Nyabisindu, Rwa.
167/E1 Nyack, NY,US
130/B4 Nyahua, Tanz.
130/C2 Nyahururu Falls, Kenya
104/B2 Nyainqêntanglha (mts.), China
102/F5 Nyainqêntanglha Feng (peak), China
104/B1 Nyainrong, China
130/B3 Nyakabindi, Tanz.
130/A3 Nyakanyasi, Tanz.
131/D1 Nyaki Nat'l Park, Malw.
131/A2 Nyakulenga, Zam.
125/K5 Nyala, Sudan
106/E2 Nyalam, China
130/B3 Nyalikungu, Tanz.
131/C3 Nyamandhlovu, Zim.
131/D3 Nyamapande, Zim.
130/B3 Nyambiti, Tanz.
125/L6 Nyamlell, Sudan
130/C5 Nyamtumbo, Tanz.
84/J3 Nyandoma, Rus.
131/D3 Nyangui (peak), Zim.
131/D3 Nyanyadzi, Zim.
130/B3 Nyanza (prov.), Kenya
130/A4 Nyanza-Lac, Buru.
130/C4 Nyanzwa, Tanz.
130/A3 Nyaruonga, Tanz.
131/D2 Nyasa (Malawi) (lake), Afr.
131/D3 Nyazura, Zim.
64/F1 Nyborg, Den.
62/F3 Nybro, Swe.
106/F2 Nyêmo, China
130/C3 Nyeri, Kenya
104/D1 Nyikog (riv.), China
102/E5 Nyima, China
131/C2 Nyimba, Zam.
65/L5 Nyíradony, Hun.
82/F2 Nyírbátor, Hun.
82/E2 Nyíregyháza, Hun.
130/C2 Nyiru (peak), Kenya
62/C3 Nykøbing, Den.
62/D4 Nykøbing, Den.
62/G2 Nyköping, Swe.
63/R7 Nykvarn, Swe.
131/C5 Nylrivier (riv.), SAfr.
132/E2 Nylstroom, SAfr.
62/G2 Nynäshamn, Swe.
76/C5 Nyon, Swi.
71/G3 Nýřany, Czh.
71/G4 Nýrsko, Údolní nádrž (res.), Czh.
65/J3 Nysa, Pol.
156/D5 Nyssa, Or,US
100/A4 Nyūdo-zaki (pt.), Japan
84/F2 Nyuk (lake), Rus.
126/E2 Nyunzu, Zaire
99/E2 Nyūzen, Japan
130/B4 Nzega, Tanz.
128/C5 Nzérékoré, Gui.
128/C4 Nzérékoré (comm.), Gui.
128/D5 Nzi (riv.), IvC.

O

100/A3 Ō (isl.), Japan
59/E1 Oadby, Eng,UK
157/H4 Oahe (lake), ND, SD,US
157/H4 Oahe (dam), SD,US
154/V13 Oahu (isl.), Hi,US
157/J3 Oakbank, Mb,Can
165/Q14 Oak Creek, Wi,US
157/J4 Oakes, ND,US
165/Q16 Oak Forest, Il,US
59/F1 Oakham, Eng,UK
160/D4 Oak Hill, WV,US
158/C3 Oakhurst, Ca,US
165/K11 Oakland, Ca,US
165/F6 Oakland (co.), Mi,US
165/F6 Oakland (lake), Mi,US
167/D1 Oakland, NJ,US
165/A3 Oakland (bay), Wa,US
165/Q16 Oak Lawn, Il,US
59/E3 Oakley, Eng,UK
59/F2 Oakley, Eng,UK
165/L11 Oakley, Ca,US
159/G3 Oakley, Ks,US
168/H6 Oakmont, Pa,US
116/D2 Oakover (riv.), Austl.
165/Q16 Oak Park, Il,US
165/F7 Oak Park, Mi,US
156/C5 Oakridge, Or,US
160/C4 Oak Ridge, Tn,US
161/R8 Oak Ridges, On,Can
58/D3 Oaksey, Eng,UK
164/B1 Oaks, The, Ca,US
161/Q9 Oakville, On,Can
168/A2 Oakville, Ct,US
115/R12 Oamaru, NZ
55/H9 Oa, Mull of (pt.), Sc,UK
164/B2 Oat (mtn.), Ca,US
148/B2 Oaxaca, Mex.
148/B2 Oaxaca (state), Mex.
88/H3 Ob' (gulf), Rus.
88/G3 Ob' (riv.), Rus.
120/F6 Oba (isl.), Van.
160/D2 Obabika (lake), On,Can
98/D3 Obama, Japan
129/H5 Oban (hills), Camr., Nga.
115/Q12 Oban, NZ
55/J8 Oban, Sc,UK
100/B4 Obanazawa, Japan
99/N9 Obara, Japan
160/D1 Obasatika (riv.), On,Can
99/M10 Obata, Japan
135/E2 Oberá, Arg.
77/E4 Oberalppass (pass), Swi.
77/E4 Oberalpstock (peak), Swi.
70/D4 Oberasbach, Ger.
70/B4 Oberderdingen, Ger.
71/E6 Oberhaching, Ger.
66/D6 Oberhausen, Ger.
70/B5 Oberkirch, Ger.
70/D5 Oberkochen, Ger.
65/H3 Oberlausitz (reg.), Ger.
159/G3 Oberlin, Ks,US
168/E5 Oberlin, Oh,US
76/D1 Obernai, Fr.
70/C3 Obernburg am Main, Ger.
70/B6 Oberndorf am Neckar, Ger.
67/G4 Obernkirchen, Ger.
71/F3 Oberpfälzer Wald (for.), Ger.
70/B3 Ober Ramstadt, Ger.
77/F3 Oberriet, Swi.
71/E6 Oberschleissheim, Ger.
77/E3 Obersiggenthal, Swi.
77/G2 Oberstaufen, Ger.
77/G3 Oberstdorf, Ger.
69/G4 Oberthal, Ger.
70/B2 Obertshausen, Ger.
70/B2 Oberursel, Ger.
73/L3 Oberwölz, Aus.
111/G4 Obi (isl.), Indo.
111/G4 Obi (isls.), Indo.
111/G4 Obi (str.), Indo.
139/H5 Óbidos, Braz.
100/C2 Obihiro, Japan
82/E4 Obilić, Yugo.
100/B1 Obira, Japan
99/J7 Obitsu (riv.), Japan
109/B2 Ob Luang Gorge, Thai.
97/L2 Obluch'ye, Rus.
84/H5 Obninsk, Rus.
125/L6 Obo, CAfr.
125/P5 Obock, Djib.
65/J2 Oborniki, Pol.
65/J3 Oborniki Śląskie, Pol.
65/J2 Obra (riv.), Pol.
82/E3 Obrenovac, Yugo.
71/G7 Obtrumer See (lake), Aus.
99/M10 Ōbu, Japan
129/E5 Obuasi, Gha.
77/E4 Obwalden (demi-canton), Swi.
163/H4 Ocala, Fl,US
138/C2 Ocaña, Col.
72/C5 Occabe, Sommet d' (peak), Fr.
136/E7 Occidental, Cordillera (range), SAm.
151/L4 Ocean (cape), Ak,US
166/D4 Ocean (co.), NJ,US
160/F4 Ocean City, Md,US
166/D5 Ocean City, NJ,US
156/B2 Ocean Falls, BC,Can
120/* Oceania
164/C4 Oceanside, Ca,US
167/E2 Oceanside, NY,US
109/D4 Oc-Eo, Ancient City of (ruins), Viet.
87/G4 Ochamchira, Geo.
100/D2 Ochiishi-misaki (cape), Japan
54/C4 Ochil (hills), Sc,UK
149/G2 Ocho Rios, Jam.
70/D3 Ochsenfurt, Ger.
70/C6 Ochsenhausen, Ger.
77/F3 Ochsenkopf (peak), Aus.
67/E4 Ochtrup, Ger.
67/F2 Ochtum (riv.), Ger.
59/E3 Ock (riv.), Eng,UK
62/G1 Ockelbo, Swe.
163/H4 Ocmulgee (riv.), Ga,US
83/F2 Ocna Mureş, Rom.
144/C4 Ocoña (riv.), Peru
163/H3 Oconee (lake), Ga,US
163/H3 Oconee (riv.), Ga,US
150/D3 Ocos (bay), DRep.
148/E3 Ocotal, Nic.
166/B4 Octararo (cr.), Pa,US
72/C2 Octeville, Fr.
168/A1 October Mtn. Saint For., Ma,US
89/L1 October Revolution (isl.), Rus.
139/E2 Ocumare del Tuy, Ven.
129/E5 Oda, Gha.
98/C3 Oda, Japan
94/C4 Oda (peak), Sudan
61/P7 Ódádhahraun (lava flow), Ice.
101/E4 Odaesan Nat'l Park, SKor.
99/M10 Ōdai, Japan
98/E3 Ōdaigahara-san (mtn.), Japan
127/D4 Oda, Jabal (peak), Sudan
63/T8 Ödåkra, Swe.
100/B3 Ōdate, Japan
99/F3 Odawara, Japan
62/B1 Odda, Nor.
62/D4 Odder, Den.
125/P7 Oddur, Som.
67/F6 Odeborn (riv.), Ger.
74/A4 Odemira, Port.
92/A2 Ödemiş, Turk.
132/D2 Odendaalsrus, SAfr.
62/D4 Odense, Den.
67/E6 Odenthal, Ger.
166/B5 Odenton, Md,US
65/H2 Oderhaff (lag.), Ger., Pol.
65/H2 Oder (Odra) (riv.), Ger., Pol.
79/F1 Oderzo, It.
86/D3 Odessa, Ukr.
162/C4 Odessa, Tx,US
156/D4 Odessa, Wa,US
166/C5 Odessa, Hist. Homes of, De,US
83/J2 Odessa Obl., Ukr.
72/B2 Odet (riv.), Fr.
128/D4 Odienné, IvC.
84/H5 Odintsovo, Rus.
112/C2 Odioñgan, Phil.
75/P10 Odivelas, Port.
83/H3 Odobeşti, Rom.
72/C2 Odon (riv.), Fr.
109/D4 Ŏdŏngk, Camb.
66/D3 Odoorn, Neth.
83/G2 Odorheiu Secuiesc, Rom.
65/H2 Odra (Oder) (riv.), Ger., Pol.
82/D3 Odžaci, Yugo.
124/J7 Odzala Nat'l Park, Congo
131/D3 Odzi, Zim.
131/D3 Odzi (riv.), Zim.
99/L9 Ōe, Japan
66/B4 Oegstgeest, Neth.
140/B2 Oeiras, Braz.
67/F5 Oelde, Ger.
71/F2 Oelsnitz, Ger.
121/M7 Oeno (atoll), Pitc.,UK
67/E5 Oer-Erkenschwick, Ger.
70/D2 Oerlenbach, Ger.
69/E4 Oesling (mts.), Lux.
66/B6 Oesterdam (dam), Neth.
70/B3 Oestrich-Winkel, Ger.
81/H3 Oeta Nat'l Park, Gre.
92/E1 Of, Turk.
80/D2 Ofanto (riv.), It.
91/D4 Ofaqim, Isr.
77/E5 Ofenhorn (Punta d'Arbola) (peak), Swi.
77/G4 Ofenpass (Fuorn) (pass), Swi.
60/C3 Offaly (co.), Ire.
70/B2 Offenbach, Ger.
70/A6 Offenburg, Ger.
70/B4 Oftersheim, Ger.
73/G3 Oftringen, Swi.
100/B4 Ōfunato, Japan
100/A4 Oga, Japan
100/A4 Oga (pen.), Japan
100/B4 Ogachi, Japan
125/P6 Ogadēn (reg.), Eth.
98/E3 Ōgaki, Japan
159/G2 Ogallala, Ne,US
120/D2 Ogasawara, Japan
100/A3 Ōgata, Japan
100/B4 Ogatsu, Japan
100/B3 Ogawara (lake), Japan
129/G4 Ogbomosho, Nga.
158/E2 Ogden, Ut,US
160/F2 Ogdensburg, NY,US
163/H3 Ogeechee (riv.), Ga,US
78/C1 Oggiono, It.
160/D2 Ogidaki (mtn.), On,Can
151/L3 Ogilvie (mts.), Yk,Can
152/C2 Ogilvie (riv.), Yk,Can
78/D2 Oglio (riv.), It.
58/C4 Ogmore by Sea, Wal,UK
76/B3 Ognon (riv.), Fr.
111/F3 Ogoamas (peak), Indo.
157/M3 Ogoki (lake), On,Can
157/L3 Ogoki (res.), On,Can
157/M3 Ogoki (riv.), On,Can
124/G8 Ogooué (riv.), Gabon
99/H7 Ogose, Japan
83/F4 Ogosta (riv.), Bul.
63/L3 Ogre, Lat.
99/M9 Oguchi, Japan
82/B3 Ogulin, Cro.
129/F5 Ogun (riv.), Nga.
129/F5 Ogun (state), Nga.
87/K5 Ogurchinskiy (isl.), Trkm.
124/G2 Ohanet, Alg.
118/G8 O'Hares (cr.), Austl.
100/B3 Ōhata, Japan
67/E2 Ohe (riv.), Ger.
143/J7 O'Higgins (lake), Chile
160/B4 Ohio (riv.), US
160/D3 Ohio (state), US
70/C1 Ohm (riv.), Ger.
57/F1 Oh Me Edge (hill), Eng,UK
163/H3 Ohoopee (riv.), Ga,US
71/H2 Ohře (riv.), Czh.
64/F2 Ohre (riv.), Ger.
82/E5 Ohrid (lake), Alb., Macd.
82/E5 Ohrid, Macd.
104/C2 Oi (riv.), China
99/H7 Ōi, Japan
99/F3 Ōi (riv.), Japan
137/H3 Oiapoque, Braz.
137/H3 Oiapoque (riv.), Braz.
54/B2 Oich, Loch (lake), Sc,UK
75/P10 Oieras, Port.
68/B3 Oignies, Fr.
76/B5 Oignin (riv.), Fr.
168/H4 Oil (cr.), Pa,US
168/H5 Oil City, Pa,US
168/H4 Oil Creek Saint Pk., Pa,US
66/C5 Oirschot, Neth.
68/B5 Oise (dept.), Fr.
68/B5 Oise (riv.), Fr.
68/C5 Oise à l'Aisne, Canal de (can.), Fr.
68/A4 Oisemont, Fr.
99/H7 Ōiso, Japan
66/C5 Oisterwijk, Neth.
68/C3 Oisy-le-Verger, Fr.
98/B4 Ōita, Japan
98/B4 Ōita (pref.), Japan
98/B4 Ōita (riv.), Japan
164/A2 Ojai, Ca,US
65/K3 Ojcowski Nat'l Park, Pol.
99/L10 Ōji, Japan
99/F2 Ojiya, Japan
146/E4 Ojocaliente, Mex.
146/B3 Ojo de Liebre (lag.), Mex.
149/G2 Ojo del Toro (peak), Cuba
135/C2 Ojos del Salado (peak), Arg., Chile
85/J4 Oka (riv.), Rus.
126/C5 Okahandja, Namb.
161/M6 Oka Ind. Res., Qu,Can
153/K3 Okak (isl.), Nf,Can
156/C3 Okanagan (lake), BC,Can
156/D3 Okanagan Falls, BC,Can
126/B1 Okanda Nat'l Park, Gabon
156/D3 Okanogan, Wa,US
156/D3 Okanogan (riv.), Wa,US
108/B2 Okāra, Pak.
126/C4 Okaukuejo, Namb.
131/A3 Okavango Delta (reg.), Bots.
98/B4 Ōkawa, Japan
99/F2 Okaya, Japan
98/C3 Okayama, Japan
98/C3 Okayama (pref.), Japan
99/E3 Okazaki, Japan
163/H5 Okeechobee, Fl,US
163/H5 Okeechobee (lake), Fl,US
99/H7 Okegawa, Japan
58/C5 Okehampton, Eng,UK
58/B5 Okement (riv.), Eng,UK
67/H4 Oker (riv.), Ger.
89/M4 Okha, Rus.
81/J3 Ókhi (peak), Gre.
89/Q4 Okhotsk (sea), Japan, Rus.
98/C2 Oki (isls.), Japan
98/C2 Oki-Daisen Nat'l Park, Japan
100/K7 Okinawa (isl.), Japan
100/J7 Okinawa (isls.), Japan
100/J8 Okinawa (pref.), Japan
100/K7 Okinoerabu (isl.), Japan
120/C2 Okino-Tori-Shima (Parece Vela) (isl.), Japan
107/G4 Okkan, Burma
159/H4 Oklahoma (state), US
159/H4 Oklahoma City (cap.), Ok,US
163/H4 Oklawaha (riv.), Fl,US
159/J4 Okmulgee, Ok,US
157/K5 Okoboji (lakes), Ia,US
130/B2 Okok (riv.), Ugan.
163/F3 Okolona, Ms,US
100/C1 Okoppe, Japan
156/E3 Okotoks, Ab,Can
122/E6 Okovango (riv.), Afr.
127/C4 Oko, Wādī (dry riv.), Sudan
61/E2 Oksskolten (peak), Nor.
87/J1 Oktyabr'sk, Rus.
85/M5 Oktyabr'skiy, Rus.
98/B4 Ōkuchi, Japan
84/G4 Okulovka, Rus.
100/A2 Okushiri, Japan
100/A2 Okushiri (isl.), Japan
99/H7 Okutama, Japan
126/D5 Okwa (riv.), Bots.
158/C3 Olancha, Ca,US
148/E3 Olanchito, Hon.
62/G3 Öland (isl.), Swe.
62/G3 Ölands norra udde (pt.), Swe.
62/G3 Ölands södra udde (pt.), Swe.
73/G4 Olan, Pic d' (peak), Fr.
80/D2 Olanto (riv.), It.
158/F3 Olathe, Co,US
159/J3 Olathe, Ks,US
142/E3 Olavarría, Arg.
65/J3 Oława, Pol.
67/F5 Ölbach (riv.), Ger.
80/A2 Olbia, It.
77/H1 Olching, Ger.
161/S9 Olcott, NY,US
165/L11 Old (riv.), Ca,US
149/G1 Old Bahama (chan.), Bahm., Cuba
165/D3 Old Baldy (mtn.), Wa,US
59/G2 Old Bedford (can.), Eng,UK
167/D3 Old Bridge, NJ,US
91/G8 Old City, Isr.
151/L2 Old Crow, Yk,Can
130/B3 Oldeani, Tanz.
130/B3 Oldeani (peak), Tanz.
66/C4 Oldebroek, Neth.
67/F2 Oldenburg, Ger.
70/B3 Oldenwald (for.), Ger.
66/D4 Oldenzaal, Neth.
156/F4 Old Faithful (geyser), Wy,US
167/E2 Old Field (pt.), NY,US
161/R9 Old Fort Niagara, NY,US
57/F4 Oldham, Eng,UK
168/B3 Old Lyme, Ct,US
156/E3 Oldman (riv.), Ab,Can
56/E3 Old Man of Coolston, The (mtn.), Eng,UK
55/N13 Old Man of Hoy, Sc,UK
166/C4 Oldmans (cr.), NJ,US
54/D2 Oldmeldrum, Sc,UK
59/F2 Old Nene (riv.), Eng,UK
167/E2 Old Northport (Northport), NY,US
130/C3 Ol-Doinyo Sabuk Nat'l Park, Kenya
67/F1 Oldoog (isl.), Ger.
66/B4 Old Rhine (riv.), Neth.
168/B1 Old Sturbridge Village, Ma,US
161/G2 Old Town, Me,US
130/B3 Olduvai Gorge, Tanz.
53/M7 Old Windsor, Eng,UK
157/G3 Old Wives (lake), Sk,Can
160/E3 Olean, NY,US
65/M1 Olecko, Pol.
78/B1 Oleggio, It.
74/A1 Oleiros, Sp.
89/N4 Olekma (riv.), Rus.
165/B2 Olele (pt.), Wa,US
139/H4 Olemari (riv.), Sur.
84/G1 Olenegorsk, Rus.
89/N2 Olenek (bay), Rus.
89/N2 Olenëk (riv.), Rus.
102/B1 Olenty (riv.), Kaz.
72/C4 Oléron (isl.), Fr.
75/K6 Olesa de Montserrat, Sp.
65/J3 Oleśnica, Pol.
65/K3 Olesno, Pol.
67/E5 Olfen, Ger.
117/F3 Olga (peak), Austl.
78/C1 Olginate, It.
96/B2 Ölgiy, Mong.
74/B4 Olhão, Port.
140/C3 Olho d'Água dos Flores, Braz.
73/L4 Olib (isl.), Cro.
80/A2 Oliena, It.
132/B2 Olifants (dry riv.), Namb.
132/B3 Olifants (riv.), SAfr.
132/E2 Olifantsrivier (riv.), SAfr.
120/D4 Olimarao (atoll), Micr.

210
Ólimb – Pakan

81/H2 Ólimbos (Mount Olympus) (peak), Gre.
141/B2 Olimpia, Braz.
92/B2 Olimpos Beydağları Nat'l Park, Turk.
140/D3 Olinda, Braz.
140/C3 Olindina, Braz.
142/E2 Oliva, Arg.
75/E3 Oliva, Sp.
74/B3 Oliva de la Frontera, Sp.
74/A3 Olivais, Port.
141/C2 Oliveira, Braz.
74/B3 Olivenza, Sp.
156/D3 Oliver, BC,Can
72/D3 Olivet, Fr.
136/E8 Ollagüe (vol.), Bol.
53/S11 Ollainville, Fr.
75/E3 Olleria, Sp.
108/F3 Ollūr, India
130/B3 Olmesutye, Kenya
144/B2 Olmos, Peru
168/F5 Olmsted Falls, Oh,US
142/Q9 Olmué, Chile
59/F2 Olney, Eng,UK
160/B4 Olney, Il,US
166/A5 Olney, Md,US
62/F3 Olofström, Swe.
130/C3 Oloitokitok, Kenya
161/J1 Olomane (riv.), Qu,Can
65/J4 Olomouc, Czh.
112/C2 Olongapo, Phil.
72/C3 Olonne-sur-Mer, Fr.
130/C3 Olorgasailie Nat'l Mon., Kenya
72/C5 Oloron-Sainte-Marie, Fr.
75/G1 Olot, Sp.
89/S3 Oloy (range), Rus.
67/E6 Olpe, Ger.
67/F6 Olsberg, Ger.
66/D4 Olst, Neth.
65/L2 Olsztyn, Pol.
65/L2 Olsztyn (prov.), Pol.
65/L2 Olsztynek, Pol.
83/G3 Olt (co.), Rom.
83/G4 Olt (riv.), Rom.
142/C4 Olte (mts.), Arg.
76/D3 Olten, Swi.
83/H3 Oltenița, Rom.
130/C3 Oltepesi, Kenya
83/F3 Olteț (riv.), Rom.
92/E1 Oltu, Turk.
92/E1 Oltu (riv.), Turk.
105/J4 Oluan Pi (cape), Tai.
112/C4 Olutanga (isl.), Phil.
74/C4 Olvera, Sp.
81/G4 Olympia (ruins), Gre.
165/B3 Olympia (cap.), Wa,US
81/G4 Olympia (Olimbía) (ruins), Gre.
156/B4 Olympic (mts.), Wa,US
165/A1 Olympic Game Farm, Wa,US
165/A2 Olympic Nat'l For., Wa,US
156/B4 Olympic Nat'l Park, Wa,US
91/C2 Olympus (mtn.), Cyp.
156/C4 Olympus (peak), Wa,US
81/H2 Olympus, Mount (Ólimbos) (peak), Gre.
81/H2 Olympus Nat'l Park, Gre.
89/S3 Olyutorskiy (bay), Rus.
100/B3 Ōma, Japan
85/K2 Oma (riv.), Rus.
99/E2 Ōmachi, Japan
99/F3 Omae-zaki (pt.), Japan
100/B4 Ōmagari, Japan
56/A2 Omagh, NI,UK
56/A2 Omagh (dist.), NI,UK
159/J2 Omaha, Ne,US
156/D3 Omak, Wa,US
108/G3 Omalūr, India
95/G4 Oman
95/G4 Oman (gulf), Asia
126/C5 Omaruru, Namb.
126/C4 Omatako (riv.), Namb.
100/B3 Ōma-zaki (pt.), Japan
111/F5 Ombai (str.), Indo.
58/D2 Ombersley, Eng,UK
126/B4 Ombombo, Namb.
126/A1 Omboué, Gabon
80/B1 Ombrone (riv.), It.
125/M4 Omdurman, Sudan
99/H7 Ōme, Japan
78/B1 Omegna, It.
92/E2 Ömerli, Turk.
92/B1 Ömerli (dam), Turk.
93/N7 Ömerli (res.), Turk.
148/E4 Ometepe (isl.), Nic.
148/B2 Ometepec, Mex.
99/M9 Ōmi, Japan
99/M9 Ōmihachiman, Japan
80/E1 Omiš, Cro.
148/B2 Omitlán (riv.), Mex.
99/G2 Ōmiya, Japan
152/C3 Ommancy (cape), Ak,US
151/M4 Ommaney (cape), Ak,US
66/D3 Ommen, Neth.
96/F2 Ömnödelger, Mong.
96/C2 Ömnögovĭ, Mong.
80/A2 Omodeo (lake), It.
90/Q3 Omolon (riv.), Rus.
125/N6 Omo Nat'l Park, Eth.
100/B4 Omono (riv.), Japan
125/N6 Omo Wenz (riv.), Eth.
88/H4 Omsk, Rus.
100/C1 Ōmu, Japan
130/A2 Omugo, Ugan.
83/G3 Omul (peak), Rom.
98/A4 Ōmura, Japan
83/H4 Omurtag, Bul.
98/B4 Ōmuta, Japan
85/M4 Omutninsk, Rus.
99/G1 Onagawa, Japan
159/J5 Onalaska, Tx,US
74/D1 Oñate, Sp.
160/C2 Onaway, Mi,US
142/E1 Oncativo, Arg.
56/D3 Onchan, IM,UK
126/B4 Oncocúa, Ang.
75/E3 Onda, Sp.
126/C4 Ondangua, Namb.
65/L4 Ondava (riv.), Slvk.
126/C4 Ondjiva, Ang.
129/G5 Ondo (state), Nga.
96/G2 Öndörhaan, Mong.
96/C2 Öndorhangay, Mong.
84/H3 Onega, Rus.
84/H2 Onega (bay), Rus.
84/G3 Onega (lake), Rus.
84/H2 Onega (pen.), Rus.
84/H3 Onega (riv.), Rus.
156/C3 One Hundred Mile House, BC,Can
160/F3 Oneida, NY,US
159/H2 O'Neill, Ne,US
160/F3 Oneonta, NY,US
76/C5 Onex, Swi.
96/E2 Ongiyn (riv.), Mong.
130/C3 Ongobit, Kenya
106/D4 Ongole, India
157/H4 Onida, SD,US
75/E3 Onil, Sp.
136/G8 Onilahy (riv.), Madg.
129/G5 Onitsha, Nga.
133/H7 Onive (riv.), Madg.
117/M8 Onkaparinga (riv.), Austl.
68/C3 Onnaing, Fr.
58/D2 Onny (riv.), Eng,UK
98/D3 Ono, Japan
98/E3 Ōno, Japan
98/B4 Onoda, Japan
98/C3 Onomichi, Japan
96/G1 Onon (riv.), Mong., Rus.
120/G5 Onotoa (atoll), Kiri.
99/E3 Ontake-san (mtn.), Japan
152/H3 Ontario (prov.), Can.
160/E3 Ontario (lake), Can., US
164/C2 Ontario, Ca,US
156/D4 Ontario, Or,US
166/C3 Ontelaunee (lake), Pa,US
75/E3 Onteniente, Sp.
160/B2 Ontonagon, Mi,US
120/F5 Ontong Java (isl.), Sol.
101/D4 Onyang, SKor.
162/E2 Oologan (lake), Ok,US
66/A6 Oostburg, Neth.
66/C4 Oostelijk Flevoland (polder), Neth.
68/B1 Oostende, Belg.
66/B5 Oosterhout, Neth.
66/A5 Oosterschelde (chan.), Neth.
64/B3 Oosterschelde (estuary), Neth.
66/A5 Oosterscheldedam (dam), Neth.
68/C2 Oosterzele, Belg.
68/C1 Oostkamp, Belg.
66/C4 Oostvaarderplassen (lake), Neth.
66/B4 Oostzaan, Neth.
108/F3 Ootacamund, India
157/B2 Ootsa (lake), BC,Can
154/V12 Opaeula (stream), Hi,US
126/D1 Opala, Zaire
65/J2 Opalenica, Pol.
82/B3 Opatija, Cro.
65/L3 Opatów, Pol.
65/J4 Opava, Czh.
163/G3 Opelika, Al,US
162/E4 Opelousas, La,US
160/E2 Opeongo (lake), On,Can
78/C2 Opera, It.
69/E1 Opglabbeek, Belg.
116/C2 Ophthalmia (range), Austl.
67/C5 Oploo, Neth.
66/B3 Opmeer, Neth.
65/L3 Opoczno, Pol.
65/J3 Opole, Pol.
65/J3 Opole (prov.), Pol.
65/L3 Opole Lubelskie, Pol.
163/G4 Opp, Al,US
61/D3 Oppdal, Nor.
62/C1 Oppland (co.), Nor.
156/D4 Opportunity, Wa,US
68/D2 Opwijk, Belg.
146/D3 Ora (riv.), Mex.
82/E2 Oradea, Rom.
167/J8 Oradell, NJ,US
167/J8 Oradell (res.), NJ,US
82/E4 Orahovac, Yugo.
106/C2 Orai, India
76/B4 Orain (riv.), Fr.
123/Q16 Oran, Alg.
123/Q16 Oran (wilaya), Alg.
101/E2 Orang (riv.), NKor.
132/B3 Orange (riv.), Afr.
119/D2 Orange, Austl.
72/F4 Orange, Fr.
139/H4 Orange (mts.), Sur.
164/C3 Orange, Ca,US
164/C3 Orange (co.), Ca,US
168/A3 Orange, Ct,US
167/D2 Orange, NJ,US
166/D1 Orange (co.), NY,US
162/E4 Orange, Tx,US
160/E4 Orange, Va,US
163/H3 Orangeburg, SC,US
132/D3 Orange Free State (prov.), SAfr.
163/H4 Orange Park, Fl,US
160/D3 Orangeville, On,Can
148/D2 Orange Walk, Belz.
128/A4 Orango (isl.), GBis.
65/G2 Oranienburg, Ger.
66/D3 Oranjekanaal (can.), Neth.
150/D4 Oranjestad, Aru.
123/Q16 Oran, Sebkha d' (lake), Alg.
131/B4 Orapa, Bots.
91/F7 Or 'Aqiva, Isr.
112/D2 Oras, Phil.
83/F3 Orăștie, Rom.
82/E3 Oravița, Rom.
72/E5 Orb (riv.), Fr.
78/B3 Orba (riv.), It.
78/A2 Orbassano, It.
76/C4 Orbe (riv.), Swi.
74/C1 Órbigo (riv.), Sp.
165/F6 Orchard (lake), Mi,US
162/B2 Orchard City, Co,US
156/E4 Orchard Homes, Mt,US
165/F6 Orchard Lake Village, Mi,US
54/B4 Orchy (riv.), Sc,UK
78/A2 Orco (riv.), It.
72/F3 Or, Côte d' (uplands), Fr.
159/H2 Ord, Ne,US
74/A1 Ordenes, Sp.
75/F1 Ordesa y Monte Perdido Nat'l Park, Sp.
103/B3 Ordos (des.), China
92/D1 Ordu, Turk.
92/D1 Ordu (prov.), Turk.
159/G3 Ordway, Co,US
62/F2 Örebro, Swe.
62/F2 Örebro (co.), Swe.
156/C4 Oregon (state), US
158/B2 Oregon Caves Nat'l Mon., Or,US
156/C4 Oregon City, Or,US
86/F1 Orël, Rus.
86/E2 Orel' (riv.), Ukr.
86/E1 Orel Obl., Rus.
158/E2 Orem, Ut,US
87/K2 Orenburg, Rus.
87/K1 Orenburg Obl., Rus.
74/B1 Orense, Sp.
81/K2 Orestiás, Gre.
62/E4 Øresund (sound), Den., Swe.
59/H2 Orford, Eng,UK
59/H2 Orford Ness (pt.), UK
158/D4 Organ Pipe Cactus Nat'l Mon., Az,US
141/L7 Órgãos (mts.), Braz.
53/S11 Orge (riv.), Fr.
53/R10 Orgeval, Fr.
83/J2 Orgeyev, Mol.
86/D5 Orhaneli, Turk.
83/J5 Orhangazi, Turk.
96/F2 Orhon (riv.), Mong.
72/C5 Orhy, Pic d' (peak), Fr.
60/D2 Oriel (mtn.), Ire.
167/F1 Orient (pt.), NY,US
135/C6 Oriental (val.), Arg.
147/M7 Oriental, Mex.
136/D6 Oriental, Cordillera (range), SAm.
75/E3 Orihuela, Sp.
160/E2 Orillia, On,Can
63/L1 Orimattila, Fin.
165/K11 Orinda, Ca,US
139/F2 Orinoco (riv.), Col., Ven.
139/F2 Orinoco (delta), Ven.
112/C2 Orion, Phil.
165/F6 Orion (lake), Mi,US
106/D3 Orissa (state), India
80/A3 Oristano, It.
80/A3 Oristano (gulf), It.
63/L1 Orivesi, Fin.
139/H5 Oriximiná, Braz.
147/F5 Orizaba, Mex.
147/K6 Orizabita, Mex.
82/D4 Orjen (peak), Yugo.
67/F6 Orke (riv.), Ger.
55/N13 Orkney (isls.), Sc,UK
162/C4 Orla, Tx,US
141/C2 Orlândia, Braz.
163/H4 Orlando, Fl,US
80/D3 Orlando, Capo d' (cape), It.
165/Q16 Orland Park, Il,US
63/R7 Orlången (lake), Swe.
72/D2 Orléanais (hist. reg.), Fr.
72/D3 Orléans, Fr.
158/B2 Orleans, Ca,US
71/H3 Orlík, Údolní nádrž (res.), Czh.
65/K4 Orlová, Czh.
53/T10 Orly, Fr.
54/D5 Ormiston, Sc,UK
112/D3 Ormoc City, Phil.
163/H4 Ormond Beach, Fl,US
76/C4 Or, Mont d' (mtn.), Fr.
57/F4 Ormskirk, Eng,UK
72/F2 Ornain (riv.), Fr.
69/F5 Orne (riv.), Fr.
61/E2 Ørnes, Nor.
65/L1 Orneta, Pol.
61/F3 Örnsköldsvik, Swe.
77/F5 Orobie, Alpi (range), It.
140/C3 Orocó, Braz.
128/D4 Orodara, Burk.
75/E1 Oroel (peak), Sp.
156/D4 Orofino, Id,US
121/L6 Orohena (peak), FrPol.
79/E1 Orolo (riv.), It.
120/E4 Oroluk (atoll), Micr.
161/H2 Oromocto, NB,Can
80/A1 Oro, Monte d' (mtn.), Fr.
121/H5 Orona (Hull) (atoll), Kiri.
161/G2 Orono, Me,US
91/E2 Orontes (riv.), Asia
130/B2 Oropoi, Kenya
97/J1 Oroqen Zizhiqi, China
112/C3 Oroquieta, Phil.
140/C2 Orós, Braz.
140/C2 Orós (res.), Braz.
80/A2 Orosei (gulf), It.
82/E2 Orosháza, Hun.
82/D2 Oroszlány, Hun.
158/C2 Orovada, Nv,US
158/E4 Oro Valley, Az,US
158/B3 Oroville, Ca,US
156/D3 Oroville, Wa,US
53/P7 Orpington, Eng,UK
57/F4 Orrell, Eng,UK
54/B2 Orrin (res.), Sc,UK
54/B2 Orrin (riv.), Sc,UK
168/F6 Orrville, Oh,US
53/T9 Orry-la-Ville, Fr.
62/F1 Orsa, Swe.
53/S10 Orsay, Fr.
53/Q7 Orsett, Eng,UK
84/F5 Orsha, Bela.
87/L2 Orsk, Rus.
82/F3 Orșova, Rom.
61/C3 Ørsta, Nor.
78/B1 Orta (lake), It.
92/B2 Ortaca, Turk.
92/C1 Ortaköy, Turk.
80/D2 Orta Nova, It.
74/B1 Ortegal (cape), Sp.
70/C2 Ortenberg, Ger.
72/C5 Orthez, Fr.
77/H5 Ortigara, Monte (peak), It.
74/B1 Ortigueira, Sp.
77/G4 Ortles (peak), It.
77/G5 Ortles (mts.), It., Swi.
136/E6 Ortón (riv.), Bol.
97/H2 Orton (riv.), China
80/D1 Ortona, It.
165/F6 Ortonville, Mi,US
157/J4 Ortonville, Mn,US
67/H3 Örtze (riv.), Ger.
93/F2 Orūmīyeh, Iran
136/E7 Oruro, Bol.
62/D2 Orust (isl.), Swe.
80/C1 Orvieto, It.
113/V Orville (coast), Ant.
57/H1 Orwell (riv.), Eng,UK
166/B2 Orwin-Reinerton-Muir, Pa,US
96/E1 Orxon (riv.), China
83/F4 Oryakhovo, Bul.
91/F7 Or Yehuda, Isr.
78/C2 Orzinuovi, It.
62/A1 Os, Nor.
149/F4 Osa (pen.), CR
85/M4 Osa, Rus.
159/J3 Osage (riv.), Mo,US
159/J3 Osage Beach, Mo,US
98/D3 Ōsaka, Japan
99/L10 Ōsaka (bay), Japan
98/D3 Ōsaka (pref.), Japan
99/L10 Ōsaka Castle, Japan
98/L10 Ōsaka (inset), Japan
101/D4 Osan, SKor.
141/G8 Osasco, Braz.
151/E3 Osborn (mtn.), Ak,US
159/H3 Osborne, Ks,US
62/E3 Osby, Swe.
163/F3 Osceola, Ar,US
64/F2 Oschersleben, Ger.
162/B3 Oscura (mts.), NM,US
102/B3 Osh, Kyr.
126/C4 Oshakati, Namb.
100/B2 Oshamambe, Japan
161/S8 Oshawa, On,Can
100/B4 Oshika (pen.), Japan
100/A2 Oshima (pen.), Japan
126/C4 Oshivelo, Namb.
157/H5 Oshkosh, Ne,US
160/B2 Oshkosh, Wi,US
129/G5 Oshogbo, Nga.
126/C1 Oshwe, Zaire
82/D3 Osijek, Cro.
79/G6 Osimo, It.
78/C1 Osio Sotto, It.
86/D1 Osipovichi, Bela.
157/K5 Oskaloosa, Ia,US
62/G3 Oskarshamn, Swe.
86/F2 Oskol (riv.), Rus., Ukr.
62/D2 Oslo (cap.), Nor.
62/D2 Oslofjord (fjord), Nor.
106/C4 Osmānābād, India
92/C1 Osmancık, Turk.
83/K5 Osmaneli, Turk.
91/E1 Osmaniye, Turk.
67/F4 Osnabrück, Ger.
53/S9 Osny, Fr.
165/M11 Oso (mtn.), Ca,US
130/A3 Oso (riv.), Zaire
141/B4 Osório, Braz.
142/B4 Osorno, Chile
156/D3 Osoyoos, BC,Can
78/D1 Ospitaletto, It.
118/B1 Osprey (reef), Austl.
66/C5 Oss, Neth.
119/C4 Ossa (peak), Austl.
81/H3 Ossa (mtn.), Gre.
74/B3 Ossa (range), Port.
129/G5 Osse (riv.), Nga.
57/G4 Ossett, Eng,UK
167/E1 Ossining, NY,US
84/G4 Ostashkov, Rus.
67/E4 Ostbevern, Ger.
67/G1 Oste (riv.), Ger.
68/B1 Ostend (Oostende), Belg.
64/F2 Osterburg, Ger.
67/F4 Ostercappeln, Ger.
62/E1 Österdalälven (riv.), Swe.
66/D1 Osterems (chan.), Neth.
62/F2 Östergötland (co.), Swe.
71/G5 Osterhofen, Ger.
67/F2 Osterholz-Scharmbeck, Ger.
67/H5 Osterode, Ger.
64/F3 Osterode am Harz, Ger.
61/E3 Östersund, Swe.
70/C5 Ostfildern, Ger.
62/D2 Østfold (co.), Nor.
67/E2 Ostfriesland (reg.), Ger.
62/H1 Östhammar, Swe.
76/D1 Ostheim, Fr.
70/B3 Osthofen, Ger.
80/C2 Ostia Antica (ruins), It.
79/E2 Ostiglia, It.
148/E4 Ostional Nat'l Wild. Ref., CR
77/F2 Ostrach (riv.), Ger.
62/E2 Östra Silen (lake), Swe.
65/K4 Ostrava, Czh.
67/E2 Ostrhauderfehn, Ger.
68/C3 Ostricourt, Fr.
70/B4 Östringen, Ger.
82/D4 Oštri Rt (cape), Yugo.
65/K2 Ostróda, Pol.
86/F2 Ostrogozhsk, Rus.
65/L2 Ostrołęka, Pol.
65/L2 Ostrołęka (prov.), Pol.
71/F2 Ostrov, Czh.
63/N3 Ostrov, Rus.
65/L3 Ostrowiec Świętokrzyski, Pol.
65/L2 Ostrów Mazowiecka, Pol.
65/J3 Ostrów Wielkopolski, Pol.
65/J3 Ostrzeszów, Pol.
62/E4 Ostseebad Binz, Ger.
67/H1 Oststeinbek, Ger.
80/E2 Ostuni, It.
81/G2 Osum (riv.), Alb.
83/G4 Osŭm (riv.), Bul.
98/B5 Ōsumi (isls.), Japan
98/B5 Ōsumi (pen.), Japan
98/B5 Ōsumi (str.), Japan
74/C4 Osuna, Sp.
141/B2 Osvaldo Cruz, Braz.
57/G3 Oswaldkirk, Eng,UK
57/F4 Oswaldtwistle, Eng,UK
166/D4 Oswego (riv.), NJ,US
160/E3 Oswego, NY,US
57/E6 Oswestry, Eng,UK
65/K3 Oświęcim (Auschwitz), Pol.
98/F2 Ōta, Japan
98/C3 Ōta (riv.), Japan
98/C3 Ōtake, Japan
99/G3 Ōtaki, Japan
99/G2 Ōtakine-yama (mtn.), Japan
100/B2 Otaru, Japan
71/H4 Otava (riv.), Czh.
138/B4 Otavalo, Ecu.
126/C4 Otavi, Namb.
99/G2 Ōtawara, Japan
82/F3 Oțelu Roșu, Rom.
121/L6 Otepa, FrPol.
146/C3 Oteros (riv.), Mex.
96/D2 Otgon, Mong.
96/D2 Otgon Tenger (peak), Mong.
156/D4 Othello, Wa,US
53/U9 Othis, Fr.
81/F3 Othonoí (isl.), Gre.
129/F4 Oti (riv.), Gui.
115/R11 Otira, NZ
168/A1 Otis (res.), Ma,US
126/C5 Otjikango, Namb.
126/C5 Otjinene, Namb.
126/B4 Otjokavare, Namb.
57/G4 Otley, Eng,UK
100/C2 Otofuke, Japan
103/A3 Otog Qi, China
96/F4 Otog Qianqi, China
157/L3 Otoskwin (riv.), On,Can
99/N10 Otowa, Japan
62/B2 Otra (riv.), Nor.
87/J1 Otradnyy, Rus.
81/F2 Otranto (str.), Alb., It.
81/F2 Otranto, It.
65/J4 Otrokovice, Czh.
98/D3 Ōtsu, Japan
100/B4 Ōtsuchi, Japan
61/D3 Otta, Nor.
160/F2 Ottawa (cap.), Can.
153/H3 Ottawa (isls.), NW,Can
160/E2 Ottawa (riv.), On, Qu,Can
160/B3 Ottawa, Il,US
159/J3 Ottawa, Ks,US
160/C3 Ottawa, Oh,US
58/C5 Otter (riv.), Eng,UK
168/G5 Otter (cr.), Pa,US
57/F1 Otterburn, Eng,UK
67/F1 Otterndorf, Ger.
67/G2 Ottersberg, Ger.
53/M7 Ottershaw, Eng,UK
58/C5 Ottery Saint Mary, Eng,UK
68/D2 Ottignies-Louvain-La-Neuve, Belg.
77/G2 Ottobeuren, Ger.
71/E6 Ottobrunn, Ger.
157/K5 Ottumwa, Ia,US
69/G5 Ottweiler, Ger.
147/L7 Otumba de Gómez Farías, Mex.
119/B3 Otway (cape), Austl.
143/J8 Otway (bay), Chile
143/K8 Otway (sound), Chile
119/B3 Otway Nat'l Park, Austl.
65/L2 Otwock, Pol.
77/G4 Ötztal Alps (mts.), Aus., It.
77/G3 Ötztaler Ache (riv.), Aus.
100/B4 Ou (mts.), Japan
109/C1 Ou (riv.), Laos
162/E3 Ouachita (riv.), Ar, La,US
159/J4 Ouachita (mts.), Ar, Ok,US
124/C3 Ouadane, Mrta.
125/K6 Ouadda, CAfr.
125/J5 Ouaddaï (reg.), Chad
129/E3 Ouagadougou (cap.), Burk.
125/K6 Ouaka (riv.), CAfr.
128/D2 Oualâta, Dhar (hills), Mrta.
125/K6 Ouanda Djalle, CAfr.
72/E3 Ouanne (riv.), Fr.
124/C3 Ouarane (reg.), Mrta.
124/G1 Ouargla, Alg.
124/D1 Ouarzazate, Mor.
161/F1 Ouasiemsca (riv.), Qu,Can
123/S16 Ouassel, Nahr (riv.), Alg.
125/J6 Oubangui (riv.), CAfr.
129/E3 Oubritenga (prov.), Burk.
76/B3 Ouche (riv.), Fr.
99/L10 Ōuda, Japan
129/E3 Oudalan (prov.), Burk.
66/B5 Oud-Beijerland, Neth.
66/A5 Ouddorp, Neth.
66/D5 Oude IJssel (riv.), Neth.
68/C2 Oudenaarde, Belg.
66/B5 Oudenbosch, Neth.
68/B1 Oudenburg, Belg.
66/E2 Oude Pekela, Neth.
66/D2 Oude Westereems (chan.), Neth.
72/C3 Oudon (riv.), Fr.
132/C4 Oudtshoorn, SAfr.
66/B6 Oud-Turnhout, Belg.
128/E2 Oued el Hadjar (well), Mali
123/R16 Oued Rhiou, Alg.
124/D1 Oued Zem, Mor.
129/F5 Ouémé (prov.), Ben.
129/F4 Ouémé (riv.), Ben.
121/V13 Ouen (isl.), NCal.
123/W18 Ouenza, Alg.
123/M13 Ouerrha (riv.), Mor.
72/A2 Ouessant (isl.), Fr.
124/J7 Ouesso, Congo
129/H5 Ouest (prov.), Camr.
149/H1 Ouest (pt.), Haiti
149/H2 Ouest (pt.), Haiti
123/M13 Ouezzane, Mor.
60/C2 Oughter, Lough (lake), Ire.
125/J6 Ouham (riv.), CAfr., Chad
68/C5 Ouichy-le-Château, Fr.
123/P13 Oujda, Mor.
61/J2 Oulangan Nat'l Park, Fin.
117/H5 Oulnina (peak), Austl.
61/H2 Oulu, Fin.
61/H2 Oulu (prov.), Fin.
61/H2 Oulujärvi (lake), Fin.
123/V18 Oum El Bouaghi, Alg.
123/V18 Oum El Bouaghi (gov.), Alg.
75/J5 Oum El Bouaghi (wilaya), Alg.
124/D1 Oum er Rhia (riv.), Mor.
125/J5 Oum Hadjer, Chad
84/E2 Ounasjoki (riv.), Fin.
59/F2 Oundle, Eng,UK
125/K4 OuniangaKebir, Chad
69/E2 Oupeye, Belg.
69/E4 Our (riv.), Belg.
69/F4 Our (riv.), Eur.
76/A2 Ource (riv.), Fr.
68/C5 Ourcq (riv.), Fr.
61/H1 Øure Anarjokka Nat'l Park, Nor.
61/F1 Øure Dividal Nat'l Park, Nor.
125/J3 Ouri, Chad
140/B2 Ouricuri, Braz.
141/B2 Ourinhos, Braz.
129/H3 Ourofané, Niger
141/G7 Ouro Fino, Braz.
131/D5 Ouro, Ponta do (pt.), Moz.
141/D2 Ouro Preto, Braz.
69/E3 Ourthe (riv.), Belg.
69/E3 Ourthe Occidentale (riv.), Belg.
69/E3 Ourthe Oriental (riv.), Belg.
57/H4 Ouse (riv.), Eng,UK
59/G5 Ouse (riv.), Eng,UK
72/B3 Oust (riv.), Fr.
75/Q11 Outão, Port.
160/E2 Outaouais (riv.), Qu,Can
161/G1 Outardes (riv.), Qu,Can
161/G1 Outardes Quatre (res.), Qu,Can
128/D2 Outeid Arkas (well), Mali
55/G8 Outer Hebrides (isls.), Sc,UK
74/A1 Outes, Sp.
126/C5 Outjo, Namb.
156/G3 Outlook, Sk,Can
68/A2 Outreau, Fr.
161/N6 Outremont, Qu,Can
121/V12 Ouvéa (atoll), NCal.
121/V12 Ouvéa (lag.), NCal.
78/B3 Ovada, It.
121/Y18 Ovalau (isl.), Fiji
135/B3 Ovalle, Chile
139/E3 Ovana (peak), Ven.
74/A2 Ovar, Port.
69/G2 Overath, Ger.
66/B5 Overflakkee (isl.), Neth.
68/D2 Overijse, Belg.
66/D3 Overijssel (prov.), Neth.
66/D4 Overijssels (can.), Neth.
159/J3 Overland Park, Ks,US
166/B5 Overlea, Md,US
142/C5 Overo (peak), Arg.
69/E1 Overpelt, Belg.
59/E1 Overseal, Eng,UK
59/H1 Overstrand, Eng,UK
59/E4 Overton, Eng,UK
57/F6 Overton, Wal,UK
158/D3 Overton, Nv,US
61/G2 Övertorneå, Swe.
74/C1 Oviedo, Sp.
62/E1 Övre Fryken (lake), Swe.
61/J1 Øvre Pasvik Nat'l Park, Nor.
126/C1 Owando, Congo
100/B3 Ōwani, Japan
99/N9 Owariasahi, Japan
98/E3 Owase, Japan
166/D1 Owassa (lake), NJ,US
159/J3 Owasso, Ok,US
157/K4 Owatonna, Mn,US
160/E3 Owego, NY,US
60/C3 Owel, Lough (lake), Ire.
115/R11 Owen (peak), NZ
130/B2 Owen Falls (dam), Ugan.
60/A1 Oweniny (riv.), Ire.
56/A2 Owenkillew (riv.), NI,UK
158/C3 Owens (riv.), Ca,US
160/C4 Owensboro, Ky,US
160/D2 Owen Sound, On,Can
158/C2 Owhyee (mts.), Id,US
166/B5 Owings Mills, Md,US
156/F4 Owl Creek (mts.), Wy,US
160/C3 Owosso, Mi,US
156/D5 Owyhee (riv.), Id, Or,US
158/C2 Owyhee, Nv,US
158/C2 Owyhee (lake), Or,US
156/D5 Owyhee, South Fork (riv.), Id, Nv,US
94/E1 Owzan (riv.), Iran
157/H3 Oxbow, Sk,Can
165/F6 Oxbow (lake), Mi,US
62/G2 Oxelösund, Swe.
157/K2 Oxford (lake), Mb,Can
59/E3 Oxford, Eng,UK
59/E3 Oxford (co.), Eng,UK
168/A3 Oxford, Ct,US
165/F6 Oxford, Mi,US
163/F3 Oxford, Ms,US
160/C4 Oxford, Oh,US
59/E3 Oxfordshire (co.), Eng,UK
53/M7 Oxhey, Eng,UK
147/H4 Oxkutzcab, Mex.
118/E7 Oxley (cr.), Austl.
164/A2 Oxnard, Ca,US
166/A6 Oxon Hill Farm, Md,US
166/B6 Oxon Hill-Glassmanor, Md,US
53/M8 Oxshott, Eng,UK
60/B1 Ox (Slieve Gamph) (mts.), Ire.
53/N8 Oxted, Eng,UK
54/D5 Oxton, Sc,UK
99/E2 Oyabe, Japan
99/E2 Oyama, Japan
99/M10 Ōyamada, Japan
99/L10 Ōyamazaki, Japan
137/H3 Oyapock (riv.), FrG.
124/H7 Oyem, Gabon
156/F3 Oyen, Ab,Can
55/J7 Oykell (riv.), Sc,UK
129/F5 Oyo, Nga.
129/F4 Oyo (state), Nga.
99/L10 Ōyodo, Japan
98/B5 Ōyodo (riv.), Japan
144/B3 Oyón, Peru
76/B5 Oyonnax, Fr.
167/E2 Oyster Bay, NY,US
167/L8 Oyster Bay (har.), NY,US
167/E2 Oyster Bay Nat'l Wild. Ref., NY,US
67/G2 Oyten, Ger.
130/B3 Oyugis, Kenya
112/C3 Ozamiz City, Phil.
72/D2 Ozanne (riv.), Fr.
159/J3 Ozark (plat.), US
163/G4 Ozark, Al,US
162/E3 Ozark, Ar,US
162/E3 Ozark (mts.), Ar, Mo,US
159/J3 Ozarks, Lake of the (lake), Mo,US
82/E1 Ózd, Hun.
89/S4 Ozernoy (cape), Rus.
156/B3 Ozette (lake), Wa,US
157/L3 Ozhiski (lake), On,Can
80/A2 Ozieri, It.
65/K3 Ozimek, Pol.
53/U10 Ozoir-la-Ferrière, Fr.
162/C4 Ozona, Tx,US
167/K9 Ozone Park, NY,US
65/K3 Ozorków, Pol.
53/U11 Ozouer-le-Voulgis, Fr.
98/C4 Ōzu, Japan
147/L7 Ozumba de Alzate, Mex.

P

70/E5 Paar (riv.), Ger.
132/B4 Paarl, SAfr.
63/T8 Påarp, Swe.
65/K3 Pabianice, Pol.
106/E3 Pābna, Bang.
136/F6 Pacaás Novos (mts.), Braz.
136/F6 Pacaás Novos Nat'l Park, Braz.
137/H4 Pacajá (riv.), Braz.
140/C2 Pacajus, Braz.
139/F4 Pacaraimã (mts.), Braz., Ven.
144/B2 Pacasmayo, Peru
140/C1 Pacatuba, Braz.
144/C2 Pacaya Samiria Nat'l Rsv., Peru
80/C4 Paceco, It.
144/B4 Pachacamac (ruins), Peru
144/C4 Pachamarca (riv.), Peru
168/C2 Pachaug (pond), Ct,US
168/C2 Pachaug Saint For., Ct,US
80/D4 Pachino, It.
144/C3 Pachitea (riv.), Peru
106/C3 Pachmarhī, India
148/B1 Pachuca, Mex.
147/F4 Pachuca de Soto, Mex.
130/A2 Pachwa, Ugan.
50/B4 Pacific (ocean)
156/B3 Pacific (ranges), BC,Can
144/J8 Pacific (ocean), Ecu.
165/K11 Pacifica, Ca,US
164/B2 Pacifico (mtn.), Ca,US
164/E7 Pacific Palisades, Ca,US
152/D4 Pacific Rim Nat'l Park, BC,Can
110/D5 Pacinan (cape), Indo.
110/D5 Pacitan, Indo.
75/P10 Paço de Arcos, Port.
112/D4 Padada, Phil.
110/B4 Padang, Indo.
110/B4 Padangpanjang, Indo.
110/A3 Padangsidempuan, Indo.
112/A4 Padas (riv.), Malay.
53/N7 Paddington, Eng,UK
59/G4 Paddock Wood, Eng,UK
67/F5 Paderborn, Ger.
130/B2 Padibe, Ugan.
95/J3 Pad Īdan, Pak.
57/F4 Padiham, Eng,UK
136/F7 Padilla, Bol.
82/E3 Padina, Yugo.
61/E2 Padjelanta Nat'l Park, Swe.
108/F4 Padmanābhapuram, India
79/E2 Padova (prov.), It.
79/E2 Padova (Padua), It.
126/B2 Padrão, Ponta do (pt.), Ang.
162/D5 Padre (isl.), Tx,US
162/D5 Padre Island Nat'l Seashore, Tx,US
74/A1 Padrón, Sp.
132/D4 Padrone (cape), SAfr.
58/B5 Padstow, Eng,UK
79/E2 Padua (Padova), It.
160/B4 Paducah, Ky,US
162/C3 Paducah, Tx,US
101/E4 Paektŏk-san (mtn.), SKor.
101/E2 Paektu-San (mtn.), NKor.
101/C4 Paengnyŏng (isl.), SKor.
79/F1 Paese, It.
131/C4 Pafúri, Moz.
82/B3 Pag, Cro.
82/B3 Pag (isl.), Cro.
112/C4 Pagadian, Phil.
110/B4 Pagai Selatan (isl.), Indo.
110/A4 Pagai Utara (isl.), Indo.
120/D3 Pagan (isl.), NMar.
158/E3 Page, Az,US
130/B2 Pager (riv.), Ugan.
112/A4 Pagon, Bukit (mtn.), Malay.
121/H6 Pago Pago (cap.), ASam.
158/F3 Pagosa Springs, Co,US
160/C1 Pagwachuan (riv.), On,Can
110/B3 Pahang (riv.), Malay.
149/F3 Páhara (lag.), Nic.
158/D3 Pahrump, Nv,US
147/L6 Pahuatlán de Valle, Mex.
158/C3 Pahute Mesa (upland), Nv,US
103/C5 Pai (lake), China
81/L7 Paiania, Gre.
58/C6 Paignton, Eng,UK
144/B2 Paiján, Peru
63/L1 Päijänne (lake), Fin.
109/C3 Pailin, Camb.
154/T10 Pailolo (chan.), Hi,US
63/K1 Paimio, Fin.
142/C2 Paine, Chile
143/J7 Paine (peak), Chile
160/D3 Painesville, Oh,US
58/C2 Painscastle, Wal,UK
157/J2 Paint (lake), Mb,Can
158/E4 Painted (des.), Az,US
162/D4 Paint Rock, Tx,US
160/D4 Paintsville, Ky,US
54/B5 Paisley, Sc,UK
144/A2 Paita, Peru
106/C4 Paithan, India
61/G2 Pajala, Swe.
138/A5 Paján, Ecu.
65/K3 Pajęczno, Pol.
140/C3 Pajeú (riv.), Braz.
149/F4 Pajonal Abajo, Pan.
110/B3 Pakanbaru, Indo.

211

Pakar – Peram

139/F3 **Pakaraima** (mts.), Guy.
119/G6 **Pakenham,** Austl.
143/J7 **Pakenham** (cape), Chile
81/J5 **Pákhnes** (peak), Gre.
85/X9 **Pakhra** (riv.), Rus.
95/H3 **Pakistan**
82/B3 **Paklenica Nat'l Park,** Cro.
104/B4 **Pakokku,** Burma
156/F3 **Pakowki** (lake), Ab,Can
108/B2 **Pākpattan,** Pak.
107/H6 **Pak Phanang,** Thai.
82/C3 **Pakrac,** Cro.
82/D2 **Paks,** Hun.
130/A2 **Pakwach,** Ugan.
109/D3 **Pakxe,** Laos
124/H6 **Pala,** Chad
75/N9 **Palacio Real,** Sp.
75/G2 **Palafrugell,** Sp.
80/D4 **Palagonia,** It.
80/E1 **Palagruža** (isls.), Cro.
108/F4 **Palai,** India
164/C4 **Pala Ind. Res.,** Ca,US
81/F3 **Palaiokastritsa,** Gre.
53/S10 **Palaiseau,** Fr.
106/D4 **Pālakolla,** India
131/C4 **Palalarivier** (riv.), SAfr.
75/G2 **Palamós,** Sp.
112/C1 **Palanan,** Phil.
112/C1 **Palanan** (mtn.), Phil.
112/C1 **Palanan** (pt.), Phil.
112/C2 **Palanas,** Phil.
110/D4 **Palangkaraya,** Indo.
106/B3 **Pālanpur,** India
154/T10 **Palaoa** (pt.), Hi,US
131/B4 **Palapye,** Bots.
106/C5 **Palar** (riv.), India
74/B1 **Palas de Rey,** Sp.
165/P15 **Palatine,** Il,US
163/H4 **Palatka,** Fl,US
120/C4 **Palau** (terr.), US
112/B3 **Palawan** (chan.), Phil.
112/B3 **Palawan** (isl.), Phil.
112/C2 **Palayan,** Phil.
108/F4 **Pālayankottai,** India
80/D4 **Palazzolo Acreide,** It.
124/G8 **Palé,** EqG.
111/F3 **Paleleh,** Indo.
110/B4 **Palembang,** Indo.
142/B4 **Palena** (riv.), Chile
74/C1 **Palencia,** Sp.
147/H5 **Palenque Nat'l Park,** Mex.
161/Q9 **Palermo,** On,Can
80/C3 **Palermo,** It.
162/E4 **Palestine,** Tx,US
162/E3 **Palestine** (lake), Tx,US
95/K5 **Pālghar,** India
108/F3 **Pālghāt,** India
101/D5 **P'algong-san** (mtn.), SKor.
101/E4 **P'algong-san** (mtn.), SKor.
116/B2 **Palgrave** (peak), Austl.
140/C2 **Palhano,** Braz.
141/B3 **Palhoça,** Braz.
106/B2 **Pāli,** India
143/K8 **Pali Aike Nat'l Park,** Chile
82/D2 **Palić,** Yugo.
154/V13 **Palikea** (peak), Hi,US
81/H3 **Palioúrion, Ákra** (cape), Gre.
167/K8 **Palisades** (bluff), NJ,US
167/D1 **Palisades Intst. Park,** NJ, NY,US
167/E2 **Palisades Park,** NJ,US
106/B3 **Pālitāna,** India
82/C3 **Paljenik** (peak), Bosn.
108/G4 **Palk** (str.), India, SrL.
108/G4 **Palk** (bay), SrL.
77/G4 **Palla Blanca** (Weisskugel) (mtn.), It.
61/H1 **Pallas-Ounastunturin Nat'l Park,** Fin.
61/H1 **Pallastunturi** (peak), Fin.
130/B2 **Pallisa,** Ugan.
115/S11 **Palliser** (cape), NZ
115/H3 **Palm** (isls.), Austl.
140/A4 **Palma** (riv.), Braz.
130/D5 **Palma,** Moz.
75/G3 **Palma,** Sp.
140/C2 **Palmácia,** Braz.
74/C4 **Palma del Río,** Sp.
80/C4 **Palma di Montechiaro,** It.
149/H4 **Palmar** (riv.), Ven.
140/D3 **Palmares,** Braz.
141/B3 **Palmas,** Braz.
128/D5 **Palmas** (cape), Libr.
149/H1 **Palma Soriano,** Cuba
163/H4 **Palm Bay,** Fl,US
118/H8 **Palm Beach,** Austl.
164/B1 **Palmdale,** Ca,US
141/B3 **Palmeira,** Braz.
140/C3 **Palmeira dos Índios,** Braz.
140/B4 **Palmeiras,** Braz.
140/A3 **Palmeiras** (riv.), Braz.
126/B2 **Palmeirinhas, Ponta das** (pt.), Ang.
75/Q10 **Palmela,** Port.
113/V **Palmer** (arch.), Ant.
168/B1 **Palmer,** Ma,US
113/V **Palmer Land** (reg.), Ant.
118/C3 **Palmerston** (cape), Austl.
121/J6 **Palmerston** (atoll), CookIs.
115/R12 **Palmerston,** NZ
118/B2 **Palmerston Nat'l Park,** Austl.
115/S11 **Palmerston North,** NZ
163/H5 **Palmetto,** Fl,US
163/H4 **Palm Harbor,** Fl,US
80/D3 **Palmi,** It.
118/B2 **Palm I. Abor. Settlement,** Austl.
142/C2 **Palmilla,** Chile
149/F1 **Palmillas** (pt.), Cuba
138/B4 **Palmira,** Col.
141/B2 **Palmital,** Braz.
158/C4 **Palm Springs,** Ca,US
121/J4 **Palmyra** (isl.), PacUS
92/D3 **Palmyra** (ruins), Syria
166/B3 **Palmyra,** Pa,US
106/E3 **Palmyras** (pt.), India
56/E2 **Palnackie,** Sc,UK
108/F3 **Palni,** India
108/F3 **Palni** (hills), India
112/D3 **Palo,** Phil.
165/K12 **Palo Alto,** Ca,US
159/G3 **Palo Duro** (cr.), Ok, Tx,US
139/H4 **Palomeu** (riv.), Sur.
73/J4 **Palon** (peak), It.
79/E1 **Palon, Cima** (peak), It.
162/D3 **Palo Pinto,** Tx,US
75/E4 **Palos, Cabo de** (cape), Sp.
165/Q16 **Palos Hills,** Il,US
164/F8 **Palos Verdes** (hills), Ca,US
164/F8 **Palos Verdes** (pt.), Ca,US
164/B3 **Palos Verdes Estates,** Ca,US
149/E4 **Palo Verde Nat'l Park,** CR
106/D2 **Pālpa,** Nepal
135/C1 **Palpalá,** Arg.
111/G4 **Palpetu** (cape), Indo.
92/D2 **Palu,** Turk.
112/C2 **Paluan,** Phil.
110/C3 **Pamangkat,** Indo.
72/D5 **Pamiers,** Fr.
102/B4 **Pamir** (riv.), Afg., Taj.
102/B4 **Pamir** (reg.), China, Taj.
163/J3 **Pamlico** (riv.), NC,US
163/J3 **Pamlico** (sound), NC,US
162/C3 **Pampa,** Tx,US
142/E2 **Pampa Humida** (plain), Arg.
142/E3 **Pampas** (plain), Arg.
144/C4 **Pampas** (riv.), Peru
142/D3 **Pampa Seca** (plain), Arg.
138/C3 **Pamplona,** Col.
74/E1 **Pamplona,** Sp.
83/K5 **Pamukova,** Turk.
112/D4 **Panabo,** Phil.
158/D3 **Panaca,** Nv,US
106/C6 **Panadura,** SrL.
83/G4 **Panagyurishte,** Bul.
110/B5 **Panaitan** (isl.), Indo.
106/B4 **Pānāji,** India
149/F4 **Panama**
149/G4 **Panamá** (bay), Pan.
149/F4 **Panama** (can.), Pan.
149/G4 **Panamá** (cap.), Pan.
149/G4 **Panama** (gulf), Pan.
149/G4 **Panama** (isth.), Pan.
163/G4 **Panama City,** Fl,US
158/C3 **Panamint** (range), Ca,US
112/D3 **Panaon** (isl.), Phil.
79/E3 **Panaro** (riv.), It.
112/C3 **Panay** (gulf), Phil.
112/C3 **Panay** (isl.), Phil.
158/C3 **Pancake** (range), Nv,US
82/E3 **Pančevo,** Yugo.
82/E4 **Pančicev vrh** (peak), Yugo.
83/H3 **Panciu,** Rom.
131/D5 **Panda,** Moz.
131/B1 **Panda,** Zaire
108/E3 **Pandalayini,** India
131/B3 **Pandamatenga,** Bots.
112/C3 **Pandan,** Phil.
112/D2 **Pandan,** Phil.
135/B2 **Pan de Azúcar Nat'l Park,** Chile
106/C4 **Pandharpur,** India
117/H3 **Pandie Pandie,** Austl.
143/G2 **Pando,** Uru.
107/F2 **Pandu,** India
63/L4 **Panevėžys,** Lith.
102/D3 **Panfilov,** Kaz.
104/C4 **Pang** (riv.), Burma
121/H7 **Pangai,** Tonga
81/J2 **Pangaíon** (peak), Gre.
130/C4 **Pangani,** Tanz.
130/C4 **Pangani** (riv.), Tanz.
59/E4 **Pangbourne,** Eng,UK
110/A3 **Pangkalanberandan,** Indo.
111/F4 **Pangkalaseang** (cape), Indo.
110/C4 **Pangkalpinang,** Indo.
104/C3 **Pangsau** (pass), India
158/D3 **Panguitch,** Ut,US
112/C4 **Pangutaran,** Phil.
112/C4 **Pangutaran** (isl.), Phil.
112/B4 **Pangutaran** (isls.), Phil.
162/C3 **Panhandle,** Tx,US
111/J4 **Paniai** (lake), Indo.
154/R10 **Paniau** (peak), Hi,US
120/F7 **Panié** (peak), NCal.
106/C2 **Pānīpat,** India
112/C3 **Panitan,** Phil.
95/K1 **Panj** (Pyandzh) (riv.), Afg., Taj.
106/D3 **Panna,** India
118/F7 **Pannikin** (isl.), Austl.
141/B2 **Panorama,** Braz.
108/G3 **Panruti,** India
97/K3 **Panshi,** China
57/E6 **Pant,** Eng,UK
59/G3 **Pant** (riv.), Eng,UK
137/G7 **Pantanal** (marsh), Braz.
137/G7 **Pantanal Matogrossense Nat'l Park,** Braz.
80/B4 **Pantelleria** (isl.), It.
53/T10 **Pantin,** Fr.
74/B1 **Pantón,** Sp.
112/D4 **Pantukan,** Phil.
147/F4 **Pánuco,** Mex.
147/F4 **Pánuco** (riv.), Mex.
104/D3 **Panzhihua,** China
148/D3 **Panzós,** Guat.
140/C3 **Pão de Açúcar,** Braz.
80/E3 **Paola,** It.
159/J3 **Paola,** Ks,US
158/F3 **Paonia,** Co,US
124/J6 **Paoua,** CAfr.
109/C3 **Paoy Pet,** Camb.
82/C2 **Pápa,** Hun.
148/E4 **Papagayo** (gulf), CR
108/G3 **Papanāsam,** India
141/B3 **Papanduva,** Braz.
147/F4 **Papantla,** Mex.
147/M6 **Papantla de Olarte,** Mex.
121/X15 **Papara,** FrPol.
55/N13 **Papa Westray** (isl.), Sc,UK
121/L6 **Papeete,** FrPol.
121/X15 **Papeete** (cap.), FrPol.
67/E2 **Papenburg,** Ger.
66/B5 **Papendrecht,** Neth.
121/X15 **Papenoo,** FrPol.
121/X15 **Papetoai,** FrPol.
91/C2 **Paphos,** Cyp.
91/C2 **Paphos** (dist.), Cyp.
159/H2 **Papillion,** Ne,US
81/G2 **Papingut, Maj'e** (peak), Alb.
111/H4 **Papisoi** (cape), Indo.
60/A5 **Paps, The** (mtn.), Ire.
120/D5 **Papua** (gulf), PNG
120/D5 **Papua New Guinea**
141/C1 **Pará** (riv.), Braz.
139/G5 **Pará** (state), Braz.
140/A1 **Pará** (state), Braz.
139/H3 **Para** (dist.), Sur.
139/E3 **Pará** (falls), Ven.
112/C2 **Paracale,** Phil.
141/K7 **Paracambi,** Braz.
144/B4 **Paracas** (pen.), Peru
144/B4 **Paracas Nat'l Rsv.,** Peru
140/A5 **Paracatu,** Braz.
140/A5 **Paracatu** (riv.), Braz.
105/F5 **Paracel** (isls.), China
90/N7 **Parace Vela** (Okino-Tori-Shima) (isl.), Japan
82/E4 **Paraćin,** Yugo.
75/N8 **Paracuellos,** Sp.
140/C1 **Paracuru,** Braz.
141/C1 **Pará de Minas,** Braz.
139/G4 **Para de Oeste** (riv.), Braz.
106/E3 **Paradip,** India
156/F2 **Paradise Hill,** Sk,Can
140/A1 **Paragominas,** Braz.
163/F2 **Paragould,** Ar,US
136/F6 **Paraguá** (riv.), Bol.
139/F3 **Paragua** (riv.), Ven.
141/H6 **Paraguaçu,** Braz.
140/B4 **Paraguaçu** (riv.), Braz.
141/B2 **Paraguaçu Paulista,** Braz.
137/G6 **Paraguai** (riv.), Braz.
138/D1 **Paraguaná** (pen.), Ven.
135/E2 **Paraguarí,** Par.
134/D5 **Paraguay**
140/C2 **Paraíba** (state), Braz.
141/D2 **Paraíba do Sul** (riv.), Braz.
140/A2 **Paraibano,** Braz.
141/H8 **Paraibuna** (riv.), Braz.
141/K6 **Paraibuna** (riv.), Braz.
140/A3 **Paraim** (riv.), Braz.
63/K1 **Parainen** (Pargas), Fin.
149/F4 **Paraíso,** CR
147/G5 **Paraíso,** Mex.
137/J6 **Paraíso do Norte de Goiás,** Braz.
141/G7 **Paraisópolis,** Braz.
129/F4 **Parakou,** Ben.
108/G4 **Paramagudi,** India
139/H3 **Paramaribo** (cap.), Sur.
139/H3 **Paramaribo** (dist.), Sur.
140/B2 **Parambu,** Braz.
138/C3 **Paramillo** (peak), Col.
138/B3 **Paramillo Nat'l Park,** Col.
140/B4 **Paramirim,** Braz.
140/B4 **Paramirim** (riv.), Braz.
164/B3 **Paramount,** Ca,US
167/D2 **Paramus,** NJ,US
89/R4 **Paramushir** (isl.), Rus.
141/B3 **Paraná** (state), Braz.
134/D5 **Paraná** (riv.), SAm.
141/B3 **Paranaguá,** Braz.
141/B3 **Paranaguá** (bay), Braz.
141/B1 **Paranaíba,** Braz.
134/E3 **Paranaíba** (riv.), Braz.
141/B1 **Paranaiba** (riv.), Braz.
143/S11 **Paraná Ibicuy** (riv.), Arg.
141/B2 **Paranapanema** (riv.), Braz.
141/B3 **Paranapiacaba** (range), Braz.
112/E6 **Parañaque,** Phil.
134/D4 **Paranatinga** (riv.), Braz.
139/G5 **Paraná Urariá** (riv.), Braz.
137/H8 **Paranavai,** Braz.
112/C4 **Parang,** Phil.
108/H4 **Parangi** (riv.), SrL.
141/C1 **Paraopeba,** Braz.
137/J8 **Parapanema** (riv.), Braz.
115/S11 **Paraparaumu,** NZ
136/F7 **Parapetí** (riv.), Bol.
141/J8 **Parati,** Braz.
140/B4 **Paratinga,** Braz.
141/H8 **Paratinga** (riv.), Braz.
53/T10 **Paray-Vieille-Poste,** Fr.
106/C4 **Parbhani,** India
64/F2 **Parchim,** Ger.
65/M3 **Parczew,** Pol.
91/D3 **Pardes Hanna,** Isr.
91/F7 **Pardes Hanna-Kardur,** Isr.
106/B3 **Pārdi,** India
141/G6 **Pardo** (riv.), Braz.
65/H3 **Pardubice,** Czh.
110/D5 **Pare,** Indo.
130/C3 **Pare** (mts.), Tanz.
136/F6 **Parecis** (mts.), Braz.
75/P10 **Parede,** Port.
142/C2 **Paredones,** Chile
160/E1 **Parent** (lake), Qu,Can
111/E4 **Parepare,** Indo.
75/L6 **Parets del Vallès,** Sp.
81/G3 **Párga,** Gre.
63/K1 **Pargas** (Parainen), Fin.
139/F2 **Paria** (gulf), Trin., Ven.
158/E3 **Paria** (riv.), Az, Ut,US
136/F1 **Paria** (pen.), Ven.
139/E2 **Pariaguán,** Ven.
110/B4 **Pariaman,** Indo.
139/F4 **Parima** (riv.), Braz.
139/E4 **Parima** (mts.), Braz., Ven.
144/D5 **Parinacota** (peak), Bol.
144/A2 **Pariñas** (pt.), Peru
139/G5 **Parintins,** Braz.
68/B6 **Paris** (cap.), Fr.
162/E3 **Paris,** Ar,US
160/B4 **Paris,** Tn,US
162/E3 **Paris,** Tx,US
53/T10 **Paris** (inset) (cap.), Fr.
149/F4 **Parita** (bay), Pan.
158/F2 **Park** (range), Co,US
167/K8 **Parkchester,** NY,US
158/D4 **Parker,** Az,US
159/F3 **Parker,** Co,US
160/D4 **Parkersburg,** WV,US
119/D2 **Parkes,** Austl.
59/H3 **Parkeston,** Eng,UK
160/B2 **Park Falls,** Wi,US
56/B2 **Parkgate,** NI,UK
58/A5 **Park Head** (pt.), UK
59/E5 **Parkhurst,** Eng,UK
165/C3 **Parkland,** Wa,US
157/K4 **Park Rapids,** Mn,US
165/Q15 **Park Ridge,** Il,US
167/D1 **Park Ridge,** NJ,US
157/J3 **Park River,** ND,US
166/B5 **Parkville,** Md,US
166/B4 **Parkville,** Pa,US
165/L9 **Parkway-Sacramento,** Ca,US
74/D2 **Parla,** Sp.
106/D4 **Parlakhemundi,** India
106/C4 **Parli,** India
78/D3 **Parma,** It.
78/D3 **Parma** (prov.), It.
78/D3 **Parma** (riv.), It.
168/F5 **Parma,** Oh,US
168/F5 **Parma Heights,** Oh,US
53/S9 **Parmain,** Fr.
140/A3 **Parnaguá,** Braz.
140/B1 **Parnaíba,** Braz.
140/B1 **Parnaíba** (riv.), Braz.
140/C3 **Parnamirim,** Braz.
140/B2 **Parnarama,** Braz.
81/H3 **Parnassós** (peak), Gre.
81/H3 **Parnassos Nat'l Park,** Gre.
81/H3 **Párnis** (peak), Gre.
81/H4 **Párnon** (mts.), Gre.
63/L2 **Pärnu,** Est.
63/L2 **Pärnu** (bay), Est.
101/D3 **P'aro-ho** (lake), SKor.
115/G5 **Paroo** (riv.), Austl.
81/J4 **Páros** (isl.), Gre.
132/B4 **Parow,** SAfr.
158/D3 **Parowan,** Ut,US
142/C3 **Parral,** Chile
118/H8 **Parramatta,** Austl.
146/E3 **Parras de la Fuente,** Mex.
58/D4 **Parrett** (riv.), Eng,UK
163/H3 **Parris Island Marine Base,** SC,US
149/E4 **Parrita,** CR
131/B4 **Parr's Halt,** Bots.
153/H2 **Parry** (bay), NW,Can
152/F1 **Parry** (chan.), NW,Can
153/R7 **Parry** (isls.), NW,Can
160/D2 **Parry Sound,** On,Can
77/G3 **Parseierspitze** (peak), Aus.
157/H4 **Parshall,** ND,US
166/D2 **Parsippany,** NJ,US
156/C2 **Parsnip** (riv.), BC,Can
159/J3 **Parsons,** Ks,US
84/C2 **Pårtefjället** (peak), Swe.
72/C3 **Parthenay,** Fr.
62/E3 **Partille,** Swe.
80/C3 **Partinico,** It.
97/L3 **Partizansk,** Rus.
160/D1 **Partridge** (riv.), On,Can
60/A2 **Partry** (mts.), Ire.
106/C4 **Partūr,** India
139/H4 **Paru** (riv.), Braz.
137/G3 **Paru de Oeste** (riv.), Braz.
108/F3 **Parūr,** India
106/D4 **Pārvathīpuram,** India
57/G5 **Parwich,** Eng,UK
132/D2 **Parys,** SAfr.
161/K1 **Pasadena,** Nf,Can
164/B2 **Pasadena,** Ca,US
166/B5 **Pasadena,** Md,US
162/E4 **Pasadena,** Tx,US
138/A5 **Pasado** (cape), Ecu.
144/B1 **Pasaje,** Ecu.
109/C3 **Pa Sak** (riv.), Thai.
110/B3 **Pasaman** (peak), Indo.
112/C2 **Pasay City,** Phil.
163/F4 **Pascagoula,** Ms,US
83/H2 **Paşcani,** Rom.
71/H6 **Pasching,** Aus.
156/D4 **Pasco,** Wa,US
144/B3 **Pasco, Cerro de,** Peru
143/J7 **Pascua** (riv.), Chile
144/B1 **Pascuales,** Ecu.
68/A3 **Pas-de-Calais** (dept.), Fr.
68/B3 **Pas-en-Artois,** Fr.
112/C2 **Pasig,** Phil.
104/B2 **Pāsighāt,** India
92/E2 **Pasinler,** Turk.
148/D2 **Pasión, Río de la** (riv.), Guat.
65/K1 **Pasłęk,** Pol.
65/L2 **Pasłęka** (riv.), Pol.
116/D5 **Pasley** (cape), Austl.
82/B4 **Pašman** (isl.), Cro.
95/H3 **Pasni,** Pak.
147/N8 **Paso del Macho,** Mex.
135/E2 **Paso de Los Libres,** Arg.
142/C2 **Paso del Planchón** (peak), Chile
158/B4 **Paso Robles** (El Paso de Robles), Ca,US
108/C1 **Pasrūr,** Pak.
151/M3 **Pass** (peak), Yk,Can
140/B2 **Passagem Franca,** Braz.
167/D2 **Passaic,** NJ,US
166/D1 **Passaic** (co.), NJ,US
167/D2 **Passaic** (riv.), NJ,US
141/J7 **Passa Quatro,** Braz.
71/G5 **Passau,** Ger.
68/C2 **Passendale,** Belg.
80/D4 **Passero** (pt.), It.
112/C3 **Passi,** Phil.
135/F2 **Passo Fundo,** Braz.
141/A3 **Passo Fundo** (res.), Braz.
129/E3 **Passoré** (prov.), Burk.
141/C2 **Passos,** Braz.
76/D3 **Passwang** (peak), Swi.
73/G4 **Passy,** Fr.
138/B5 **Pastaza** (prov.), Ecu.
136/C4 **Pastaza** (riv.), Ecu., Peru
63/J5 **Pastek** (riv.), Pol.
138/B4 **Pasto,** Col.
151/F3 **Pastol** (bay), Ak,US
140/A2 **Pastos Bons,** Braz.
112/C1 **Pasuquin,** Phil.
110/D5 **Pasuruan,** Indo.
82/D2 **Pásztó,** Hun.
112/C3 **Patag Nat'l Park,** Phil.
142/D4 **Patagonia** (reg.), Arg.
110/B4 **Patah** (peak), Indo.
106/B3 **Pātan,** India
166/B5 **Patapsco** (riv.), Md,US
166/B4 **Patapsco, North Branch** (riv.), Md,US
167/E2 **Patchogue,** NY,US
58/D3 **Patchway,** Eng,UK
130/D3 **Pate** (isl.), Kenya
57/G3 **Pateley Bridge,** Eng,UK
75/E3 **Paterna,** Sp.
80/D4 **Paternò,** It.
167/D2 **Paterson,** NJ,US
108/C1 **Pathānkot,** India
156/G5 **Pathfinder** (res.), Wy,US
110/D5 **Pati,** Indo.
138/B4 **Patía** (riv.), Col.
108/D2 **Patiāla,** India
112/C4 **Patikul,** Phil.
106/E2 **Patna,** India
54/B6 **Patna,** Sc,UK
112/C2 **Patnanongan** (isl.), Phil.
112/C3 **Patnongon,** Phil.
93/E2 **Patnos,** Turk.
141/A3 **Pato Branco,** Braz.
163/G2 **Patoka** (riv.), In,US
81/F2 **Patos,** Alb.
140/C2 **Patos,** Braz.
141/B4 **Patos** (lake), Braz.
141/C1 **Patos de Minas,** Braz.
81/G3 **Pátrai,** Gre.
81/G3 **Patrai** (gulf), Gre.
117/F2 **Patricia** (peak), Austl.
143/J7 **Patricio Lynch** (isl.), Chile
57/H4 **Patrington,** Eng,UK
141/C1 **Patrocínio,** Braz.
163/G4 **Patsaliga** (cr.), Al,US
77/H3 **Patscherkofel** (peak), Aus.
109/C5 **Pattani,** Thai.
109/C3 **Pattaya,** Thai.
67/G4 **Pattensen,** Ger.
108/C2 **Patti,** India
80/D3 **Patti,** It.
58/D1 **Pattingham,** Eng,UK
108/B2 **Pattoki,** Pak.
108/G3 **Pattukkottai,** India
151/N4 **Pattullo** (mtn.), BC,Can
140/C2 **Patu,** Braz.
148/E3 **Patuca** (mts.), Hon.
149/E3 **Patuca** (pt.), Hon.
149/E3 **Patuca** (riv.), Hon.
166/B6 **Patuxent** (riv.), Md,US
166/B5 **Patuxent Nat. Wild. Ref.,** Md,US
166/A5 **Patuxent River Saint Park,** Md,US
147/E5 **Pátzcuaro,** Mex.
72/C5 **Pau,** Fr.
140/C4 **Pau Brasil,** Braz.
140/C2 **Pau dos Ferros,** Braz.
136/E5 **Pauini** (riv.), Braz.
104/B5 **Pauksa** (peak), Burma
149/E3 **Paulaya** (riv.), Hon.
141/F7 **Paulínia,** Braz.
166/D1 **Paulins Kill** (riv.), NJ,US
140/B3 **Paulistana,** Braz.
78/C2 **Paullo,** It.
140/C3 **Paulo Afonso,** Braz.
140/C3 **Paulo Afonso Nat'l Park,** Braz.
140/A2 **Paulo Ramos,** Braz.
166/C4 **Paulsboro,** NJ,US
159/H4 **Pauls Valley,** Ok,US
58/D4 **Paulton,** Eng,UK
104/B5 **Paungde,** Burma
102/C5 **Pauri,** India
141/D1 **Pavão,** Braz.
78/C2 **Pavia,** It.
78/C2 **Pavia** (prov.), It.
83/G4 **Pavlikeni,** Bul.
102/C1 **Pavlodar,** Kaz.
151/F4 **Pavlof** (vol.), Ak,US
86/E2 **Pavlograd,** Ukr.
84/J5 **Pavlovo,** Rus.
79/D4 **Pavullo nel Frignano,** It.
110/D4 **Pawan** (riv.), Indo.
159/H3 **Pawhuska,** Ok,US
104/C4 **Pawn** (riv.), Burma
159/H3 **Pawnee** (riv.), Ks,US
160/C3 **Paw Paw,** Mi,US
168/C2 **Pawtucket,** RI,US
166/B5 **Pawtuxent** (riv.), Md,US
81/F3 **Paxoí** (isl.), Gre.
81/G3 **Paxoí** (Yáios), Gre.
110/B4 **Payakumbuh,** Indo.
142/C3 **Payén, Altiplanicie del** (plat.), Arg.
76/C4 **Payerne,** Swi.
156/D4 **Payette,** Id,US
156/D5 **Payette** (riv.), Id,US
85/P1 **Pay-Khoy** (mts.), Rus.
153/J3 **Payne** (lake), Qu,Can
116/C4 **Paynes Find,** Austl.
143/F2 **Paysandú,** Uru.
143/F1 **Paysandú** (dept.), Uru.
53/T9 **Pays de France** (plain), Fr.
72/C3 **Pays de la Loire** (reg.), Fr.
158/E4 **Payson,** Az,US
158/E2 **Payson,** Ut,US
142/C3 **Payún** (peak), Arg.
148/D3 **Paz** (riv.), ESal., Guat.
92/D1 **Pazar,** Turk.
92/D2 **Pazarcık,** Turk.
83/G4 **Pazardzhik,** Bul.
86/D5 **Pazaryeri,** Turk.
141/A2 **Peabiru,** Braz.
152/E3 **Peace** (riv.), Ab, BC,Can
163/H5 **Peace** (riv.), Fl,US
98/C3 **Peace Mem. Park,** Japan
156/D1 **Peace River,** Ab,Can
156/D3 **Peachland,** BC,Can
163/G3 **Peachtree City,** Ga,US
116/D5 **Peak Charles Nat'l Park,** Austl.
57/G5 **Peak District Nat'l Park,** Eng,UK
60/A6 **Peakeen** (mtn.), Ire.
154/W13 **Pearl** (har.), Hi,US
163/F4 **Pearl** (riv.), La, Ms,US
163/F3 **Pearl,** Ms,US
121/H2 **Pearl and Hermes** (reef), Hi,US
154/W13 **Pearl City,** Hi,US
105/G4 **Pearl River** (estuary), China, HK
167/D1 **Pearl River,** NY,US
162/D4 **Pearsall,** Tx,US
153/R7 **Peary** (chan.), NW,Can
159/H4 **Pease** (riv.), Tx,US
126/G4 **Pebane,** Moz.
144/D1 **Pebas,** Peru
59/E2 **Pebworth,** Eng,UK
82/E4 **Peć,** Yugo.
164/C4 **Pechanga Ind. Res.,** Ca,US
75/G1 **Pech de Guillaument** (mtn.), Fr.
85/N2 **Pechora,** Rus.
85/M1 **Pechora** (bay), Rus.
85/M2 **Pechora** (riv.), Rus.
166/C1 **Pecks** (pond), Pa,US
167/F2 **Peconic** (riv.), NY,US
159/G5 **Pecos** (riv.), NM, Tx,US
162/C4 **Pecos,** Tx,US
159/F4 **Pecos Nat'l Mon.,** NM,US
68/C3 **Pecquencourt,** Fr.
82/D2 **Pécs,** Hun.
119/C4 **Pedder** (lake), Austl.
149/E4 **Pedernal** (pt.), Nic.
150/D3 **Pedernales,** DRep.
141/B2 **Pederneiras,** Braz.
164/C3 **Pedley,** Ca,US
140/B5 **Pedra Azul,** Braz.
141/H7 **Pedralva,** Braz.
141/G7 **Pedreira,** Braz.
140/B2 **Pedreiras,** Braz.
106/D6 **Pedro** (pt.), SrL.
140/C2 **Pedro Avelino,** Braz.
149/F1 **Pedro Betancourt,** Cuba
138/A5 **Pedro Carbo,** Ecu.
136/E3 **Pedro II,** Braz.
139/E4 **Pedro II** (isl.), Braz.
135/E1 **Pedro Juan Caballero,** Par.
141/C1 **Pedro Leopoldo,** Braz.
141/A4 **Pedro Osório,** Braz.
140/B2 **Pedro Segundo,** Braz.
54/C5 **Peebles,** Sc,UK
116/B2 **Peedamulla Abor. Land,** Austl.
167/E1 **Peekskill,** NY,US
116/B5 **Peel** (inlet), Austl.
118/F6 **Peel** (isl.), Austl.
152/G1 **Peel** (sound), NW,Can
161/Q8 **Peel** (co.), On,Can
151/L2 **Peel** (riv.), Yk,Can
56/D3 **Peel,** IM,UK
57/F1 **Peel Fell** (mtn.), Eng,UK
62/E5 **Peene** (riv.), Ger.
69/E1 **Peer,** Belg.
115/R11 **Pegasus** (bay), NZ
71/E3 **Pegnitz,** Ger.
71/E3 **Pegnitz** (riv.), Ger.
75/E3 **Pego,** Sp.
57/G1 **Pegswood,** Eng,UK
104/C5 **Pegu,** Burma
104/B4 **Pegu** (mts.), Burma
104/C5 **Pegu** (riv.), Burma
104/B5 **Pegu** (Bago) (div.), Burma
59/H4 **Pegwell** (bay), Eng,UK
142/E2 **Pehuajó,** Arg.
142/C2 **Pehuenche** (pass), Chile
103/B3 **Peijiachuankou,** China
105/J4 **Peinanchu** (mtn.), Tai.
67/H4 **Peine,** Ger.
63/M2 **Peipus** (lake), Est., Rus.
77/H2 **Peissenburg,** Ger.
105/J4 **Peitawu** (peak), Tai.
77/G2 **Peiting,** Ger.
141/K6 **Peixe** (riv.), Braz.
103/D4 **Pei Xian,** China
141/C2 **Peixoto** (res.), Braz.
110/C5 **Pekalongan,** Indo.
110/B3 **Pekan Nanas,** Malay.
160/B3 **Pekin,** Il,US
142/C5 **Pelada** (plain), Arg.
80/C5 **Pelagie** (isls.), It.
82/F3 **Peleaga, Vîrful** (peak), Rom.
161/D3 **Pelee** (isl.), On,Can
160/D3 **Pelee** (pt.), On,Can
150/F4 **Pelée** (mtn.), Mart.
161/R9 **Pelham,** On,Can
163/G3 **Pelham,** Al,US
167/K8 **Pelham,** NY,US
167/K8 **Pelham Bay Park,** NY,US
65/H4 **Pelhřimov,** Czh.
156/E2 **Pelican** (mts.), Ab,Can
157/H2 **Pelican** (lake), Sk,Can
157/H2 **Pelican Narrows,** Sk,Can
128/A4 **Pelindã, Ponta de** (pt.), GBis.
82/E5 **Pelister** (peak), Macd.
82/E5 **Pelister Nat'l Park,** Macd.
82/C4 **Pelješac** (pen.), Cro.
152/H2 **Pelly** (bay), NW,Can
151/M3 **Pelly** (riv.), Yk,Can
151/L3 **Pelly Crossing,** Yk,Can
81/G3 **Peloponnisos** (reg.), Gre.
80/D3 **Peloritani** (mts.), It.
141/A4 **Pelotas,** Braz.
141/B3 **Pelotas** (riv.), Braz.
65/K2 **Pelplin,** Pol.
111/F4 **Pemali** (cape), Indo.
111/F5 **Pemali** (cape), Indo.
110/A3 **Pematangsiantar,** Indo.
126/H3 **Pemba,** Moz.
123/G5 **Pemba** (isl.), Tanz.
130/C4 **Pemba** (prov.), Tanz.
131/B3 **Pemba,** Zam.
156/C3 **Pemberton,** BC,Can
156/E2 **Pembina** (riv.), Ab,Can
157/J3 **Pembina** (riv.), Can., US
157/J3 **Pembina,** ND,US
160/E2 **Pembroke,** On,Can
58/B3 **Pembroke,** Wal,UK
168/D1 **Pembroke,** Ma,US
58/B3 **Pembroke Dock,** Wal,UK
55/J11 **Pembrokeshire Coast Nat'l Park,** Wal,UK
53/P8 **Pembury,** Eng,UK
142/B3 **Pemuco,** Chile
149/F4 **Peña Blanca** (mtn.), Pan.
74/A2 **Penafiel,** Port.
142/Q9 **Peñaflor,** Chile
74/D2 **Peñalara** (mtn.), Sp.
140/A1 **Penalva,** Braz.
141/B2 **Penápolis,** Braz.
74/C2 **Peñaranda de Bracamonte,** Sp.
75/E2 **Peñarroya** (mtn.), Sp.
74/C3 **Peñarroya-Pueblonuevo,** Sp.
58/C4 **Penarth,** Wal,UK
143/L8 **Peñas** (cape), Arg.
143/J6 **Penas** (gulf), Chile
74/C1 **Peñas** (cape), Sp.
159/F4 **Peñasco** (dry riv.), NM,US
142/B3 **Penco,** Chile
81/L6 **Pendelikón** (mtn.), Gre.
140/C2 **Pendências,** Braz.
93/N7 **Pendik,** Turk.
129/F4 **Pendjari** (riv.), Ben., Burk.
129/F4 **Pendjari Nat'l Park,** Ben.
57/F4 **Pendle** (hill), Eng,UK
156/D4 **Pendleton,** Or,US
156/D4 **Pend Oreille** (lake), Id,US
156/D3 **Pend Oreille** (riv.), Id, Wa,US
74/A2 **Peneda-Gerês Nat'l Park,** Port.
140/C3 **Penedo,** Braz.
58/C1 **Penegoes,** Wal,UK
160/E2 **Penetanguishene,** On,Can
106/C4 **Penganga** (riv.), India
53/N7 **Penge,** Eng,UK
105/H4 **Penghu** (isl.), Tai.
103/E3 **Penglai,** China
104/D2 **Peng Xian,** China
141/B3 **Penha,** Braz.
131/D3 **Penhalonga,** Zim.
156/E2 **Penhold,** Ab,Can
74/C4 **Penibético, Sistema** (range), Sp.
78/C3 **Penice, Monte** (peak), It.
74/A3 **Peniche,** Port.
54/C5 **Penicuik,** Sc,UK
139/F2 **Península de Paria Nat'l Park,** Ven.
140/A3 **Penitente** (mts.), Braz.
147/E4 **Pénjamo,** Mex.
58/D1 **Penkridge,** Eng,UK
56/E5 **Penmaenmawr,** Wal,UK
72/A3 **Penmarch,** Fr.
72/A3 **Penmarc'h, Pointe de** (pt.), Fr.
80/D1 **Penna, Punta della** (cape), It.
82/C5 **Penne** (pt.), It.
106/C5 **Penner** (riv.), India
166/C2 **Penn Forest** (res.), Pa,US
168/H7 **Penn Hills,** Pa,US
76/D6 **Pennine Alps** (mts.), It., Swi.
57/F2 **Pennine Chain** (range), Eng,UK
166/A2 **Penns** (cr.), Pa,US
166/C4 **Pennsauken,** NJ,US
166/A2 **Penns Creek** (mtn.), Pa,US
166/C4 **Pennsville,** NJ,US
160/E3 **Pennsylvania** (state), US
153/S7 **Penny** (str.), NW,Can
160/E3 **Penn Yan,** NY,US
166/C3 **Pennypack** (cr.), Pa,US
160/G2 **Penobscot** (riv.), Me,US
149/F4 **Penonomé,** Pan.
56/E1 **Penpont,** Sc,UK
56/D5 **Penrhyn Mawr** (pt.), Wal,UK
56/D6 **Penrhyn Mawr** (pt.), Wal,UK
121/K5 **Penrhyn** (Tongareva) (atoll), CookIs.
118/G8 **Penrith,** Austl.
57/F2 **Penrith,** Eng,UK
58/A6 **Penryn,** Eng,UK
113/X **Pensacola** (mts.), Ant.
163/G4 **Pensacola,** Fl,US
157/G3 **Pense,** Sk,Can
53/P8 **Penshurst,** Eng,UK
58/B5 **Pensilva,** Eng,UK
166/A6 **Pentagon,** Va,US
120/F6 **Pentecost** (isl.), Van.
140/C1 **Pentecoste,** Braz.
83/H3 **Penteleu** (peak), Rom.
156/D3 **Penticton,** BC,Can
58/B5 **Pentire** (pt.), UK
54/C5 **Pentland** (hills), Sc,UK
55/N13 **Pentland Firth** (inlet), Sc,UK
58/C3 **Pentyrch,** Wal,UK
142/C2 **Peñuelas Nat'l Park,** Chile
58/A6 **Penwith** (pen.), Eng,UK
57/E6 **Pen-y-Cae,** Wal,UK
57/F3 **Pen-y-Ghent** (mtn.), Eng,UK
56/E5 **Pen-y-Gogarth** (pt.), Wal,UK
58/C2 **Pen y Gurnos** (mtn.), Wal,UK
87/H1 **Penza,** Rus.
58/A6 **Penzance,** Eng,UK
87/G1 **Penza Obl.,** Rus.
77/H2 **Penzberg,** Ger.
89/S3 **Penzhina** (bay), Rus.
89/S3 **Penzhina** (riv.), Rus.
160/B3 **Peoria,** Il,US
149/F1 **Pepe** (cape), Cuba
154/U11 **Pepeekeo** (pt.), Hi,US
69/E2 **Pepinster,** Belg.
168/F5 **Pepper Pike,** Oh,US
167/D2 **Pequannock,** NJ,US
166/B4 **Pequea** (cr.), Pa,US
166/D2 **Pequest** (riv.), NJ,US
115/G2 **Pera** (head), Austl.
110/B4 **Perabumulih,** Indo.
75/M9 **Perales** (riv.), Sp.
108/G3 **Perambalūr,** India

212

Percé – Polon

161/H1 Percé, Qu,Can
76/C6 Percée, Pointe (peak), Fr.
72/D2 Perche (hills), Fr.
65/J4 Perchtoldsdorf, Aus.
116/E2 Percival (lakes), Austl.
118/C3 Percy (isls.), Austl.
140/A3 Perdida (riv.), Braz.
75/F1 Perdido (mtn.), Sp.
138/C3 Pereira, Col.
141/B2 Pereira Barreto, Braz.
140/C2 Pereiro, Braz.
142/E2 Pergamino, Arg.
92/A2 Pergamum (ruins), Turk.
77/H5 Pergine Valsugana, It.
79/F5 Pergola, It.
161/G1 Péribonca (lake), Qu,Can
161/G1 Péribonca (riv.), Qu,Can
149/F1 Perico, Cuba
72/D4 Périgueux, Fr.
138/C2 Perijá (mts.), Col., Ven.
94/D6 Perim (isl.), Yem.
81/J3 Peristéra (isl.), Gre.
81/L6 Peristéri, Gre.
143/K6 Perito Moreno Nat'l Park, Arg.
108/F3 Periyakulam, India
108/F3 Periyar (riv.), India
108/F4 Periyar Wild. Sanct., India
166/C3 Perkasie, Pa,US
166/C3 Perkiomen (cr.), Pa,US
69/F5 Perl, Ger.
149/F3 Perlas (lag.), Nic.
149/F3 Perlas (pt.), Nic.
149/G4 Perlas (arch.), Pan.
64/F2 Perleberg, Ger.
85/N4 Perm', Rus.
85/M4 Perm' Obl., Rus.
140/C3 Pernambuco (state), Braz.
72/F4 Pernes-les-Fontaines, Fr.
82/F4 Pernik, Bul.
63/K1 Perniö, Fin.
116/B3 Peron (pen.), Austl.
68/B4 Péronne, Fr.
147/F5 Perote, Mex.
85/X9 Perovo, Rus.
72/E5 Perpignan, Fr.
164/C3 Perris, Ca,US
164/C3 Perris (res.), Ca,US
149/G1 Perros (bay), Cuba
72/B2 Perros-Guirec, Fr.
161/N7 Perrot (isl.), Qu,Can
152/F2 Perry (riv.), NW,Can
163/H4 Perry, Fl,US
163/H3 Perry, Ga,US
159/H3 Perry, Ok,US
166/A3 Perry (co.), Pa,US
166/B5 Perry Hall, Md,US
168/F6 Perry Heights, Oh,US
162/C2 Perryton, Tx,US
159/K3 Perryville, Mo,US
53/S9 Persan, Fr.
94/F3 Persepolis (ruins), Iran
63/R7 Pershagen, Swe.
58/D2 Pershore, Eng,UK
94/E3 Persian (gulf), Asia
116/B4 Perth, Austl.
160/E2 Perth, On,Can
54/C4 Perth, Sc,UK
167/D2 Perth Amboy, NJ,US
116/K6 Perth (inset), Austl.
116/K6 Perth Zoo, Austl.
72/F5 Pertuis, Fr.
72/C3 Pertuis Breton (inlet), Fr.
80/A2 Pertusato (cape), Fr.
144/C3 Peru
160/B3 Peru, Il,US
160/C3 Peru, In,US
82/D4 Perućačko (lake), Bosn.
80/C1 Perugia, It.
141/G9 Peruíbe, Braz.
108/F3 Perumpāvūr, India
68/C2 Péruwelz, Belg.
85/J5 Pervomaysk, Rus.
86/D2 Pervomaysk, Ukr.
85/N4 Pervoural'sk, Rus.
79/E5 Pesa (riv.), It.
110/B4 Pesagi (peak), Indo.
79/F5 Pesaro, It.
79/F5 Pesaro e Urbino (prov.), It.
105/H4 Pescadore (chan.), Tai.
80/D1 Pescara, It.
87/J4 Peschanyy, Mys (cape), Kaz.
79/D5 Pescia, It.
85/L2 Pesha (riv.), Rus.
95/K2 Peshāwar, Pak.
83/G4 Peshtera, Bul.
160/B2 Peshtigo (riv.), Wi,US
140/C3 Pesqueira, Braz.
72/C4 Pessac, Fr.
72/D5 Pessons, Pic dels (peak), And.
82/D2 Pest (co.), Hun.
84/G4 Pestovo, Rus.
91/D3 Petah Tiqwa, Isr.
163/F4 Petal, Ms,US
81/J4 Petalión (gulf), Gre.
165/J10 Petaluma, Ca,US
165/J10 Petaluma (riv.), Ca,US
69/E4 Pétange, Lux.
139/E2 Petare, Ven.
146/D3 Petatlán (riv.), Mex.
131/C2 Petauke, Zam.
160/E2 Petawana (riv.), On,Can
160/E2 Petawawa, On,Can
148/D2 Peten Itzá (lake), Guat.
157/L4 Petenwell (lake), Wi,US
160/E2 Peterborough, On,Can
59/F1 Peterborough, Eng,UK
54/D2 Peterculter, Sc,UK
54/E2 Peterhead, Sc,UK
113/T Peter I (isl.), Ant.
50/E9 Peter I (isl.), Nor.
57/G2 Peterlee, Eng,UK
117/F3 Petermann Abor. Land, Austl.
142/C2 Peteroa (vol.), Arg.
156/F1 Peter Pond (lake), Sk,Can
166/B3 Peters (mtn.), Pa,US
70/C1 Petersberg, Ger.
160/E4 Petersburg, Va,US
59/F5 Petersfield, Eng,UK
67/F4 Petershagen, Ger.
159/F3 Peterson A.F.B., Co,US
80/E3 Petilia Policastro, It.
149/H2 Pétionville, Haiti
161/H2 Petitcodiac, NB,Can
149/H2 Petite Rivière de l'Artibonite, Haiti
69/F5 Petite-Rosselle, Fr.
149/H2 Petit Goâve, Haiti
68/C6 Petit Marin (riv.), Fr.
161/K1 Petit Mécatina (riv.), Qu,Can
68/C6 Petit Morin (riv.), Fr.
53/S9 Petit Rosne (riv.), Fr.
61/J3 Petkeljärven Nat'l Park, Fin.
106/B3 Petlād, India
147/H4 Peto, Mex.
142/C2 Petorca, Chile
160/C2 Petoskey, Mi,US
89/M2 Petra (isls.), Rus.
91/D4 Petra (Baṭrā') (ruins), Jor.
75/E3 Petrel, Sp.
80/C2 Petrella (peak), It.
83/F5 Petrich, Bul.
158/E4 Petrified Forest Nat'l Park, Az,US
83/F3 Petrila, Rom.
63/N2 Petrodvorets, Rus.
83/F4 Petrokhanski Prokhod (pass), Bul.
140/C3 Petrolândia, Braz.
140/B3 Petrolina, Braz.
88/G4 Petropavlovsk, Kaz.
89/R4 Petropavlovsk-Kamchatskiy, Rus.
141/K7 Petrópolis, Braz.
83/F3 Petroşani, Rom.
82/D3 Petrovaradin, Yugo.
87/H1 Petrovsk, Rus.
96/F1 Petrovsk-Zabaykal'skiy, Rus.
84/G3 Petrozavodsk, Rus.
63/P1 Petrozavodsk Obl., Rus.
57/F2 Petterill (riv.), Eng,UK
59/F5 Petworth, Eng,UK
82/A2 Petzeck (peak), Aus.
151/G4 Peulik (mtn.), Ak,US
142/C2 Peumo, Chile
59/G5 Pevensey, Eng,UK
165/P13 Pewaukee (lake), Wi,US
59/E4 Pewsey, Eng,UK
85/K2 Peza (riv.), Rus.
72/E5 Pézenas, Fr.
77/G1 Pfaffenhofen an der Roth, Ger.
77/E3 Pfäffikon, Swi.
71/F4 Pfahl (ridge), Ger.
69/G5 Pfälzer Wald (for.), Ger.
71/F6 Pfarrkirchen, Ger.
71/E5 Pfettrach (riv.), Ger.
67/G6 Pfieffe (riv.), Ger.
70/B5 Pfinztal, Ger.
70/B5 Pforzheim, Ger.
71/F3 Pfreimd (riv.), Ger.
70/B3 Pfrimm (riv.), Ger.
77/G2 Pfronten, Ger.
77/G2 Pfroslkopf (peak), Aus.
77/F2 Pfullendorf, Ger.
70/B3 Pfungstadt, Ger.
108/C2 Phagwāra, India
109/C1 Phak (riv.), Laos
131/C4 Phalaborwa, SAfr.
108/B1 Phālia, Pak.
106/B2 Phalodi, India
131/D2 Phalombe, Malw.
109/C3 Phanat Nikhom, Thai.
109/B4 Phangan (isl.), Thai.
109/C3 Phang Hoei (range), Thai.
109/C3 Phanom Dongrak (mts.), Camb., Thai.
109/E4 Phan Rang, Viet.
109/E4 Phan Thiet, Viet.
162/D5 Pharr, Tx,US
104/E4 Phat Diem, Viet.
109/C5 Phatthalung, Thai.
109/C2 Phaya Fo (peak), Thai.
109/B2 Phayao, Thai.
163/G3 Phenix City, Al,US
132/C2 Phepane (dry riv.), SAfr.
109/B3 Phet Buri, Thai.
109/C2 Phetchabun, Thai.
109/C2 Phichit, Thai.
163/F3 Philadelphia, Ms,US
166/C4 Philadelphia, Pa,US
94/B4 Philae (ruins), Egypt
157/H4 Philip, SD,US
68/D3 Philippeville, Belg.
160/D4 Philippi, WV,US
120/B3 Philippine (sea), Asia
112/* Philippines
70/B4 Philippsburg, Ger.
156/E4 Philipsburg, Mt,US
66/B5 Philipsdam (dam), Neth.
108/C2 Phillaur, India
159/H3 Phillipsburg, Ks,US
166/C2 Phillipsburg, NJ,US
109/C3 Phimai (ruins), Thai.
109/C2 Phitsanulok, Thai.
109/D4 Phnom Penh (Phnum Penh) (cap.), Camb.
109/D3 Phnum Tbeng Meanchey, Camb.
109/C5 Pho (pt.), Thai.
121/H5 Phoenix (isls.), Kiri.
158/D4 Phoenix (cap.), Az,US
163/H2 Phoenix (peak), NC,US
60/D3 Phoenix Park, Ire.
121/H5 Phoenix (Rawaki) (atoll), Kiri.
166/C3 Phoenixville, Pa,US
109/C1 Phongsali, Laos
109/C2 Phou Bia (peak), Laos
109/D2 Phou Huatt (peak), Viet.
109/C1 Phou Loi (peak), Laos
109/D2 Phou Xai Lai Leng (peak), Laos
109/C2 Phrae, Thai.
109/C3 Phra Nakhon Si Ayutthaya, Thai.
109/B4 Phra Thong (isl.), Thai.
109/C4 Phsar Ream, Camb.
109/D2 Phuc Loi, Viet.
104/E4 Phuc Yen, Viet.
109/C2 Phu Hin Rong Kla Nat'l Park, Thai.
109/E4 Phu Hoi, Viet.
109/B5 Phuket, Thai.
109/B5 Phuket (isl.), Thai.
109/C2 Phu Kradung Nat'l Park, Thai.
106/D3 Phulabāni, India
108/B1 Phularwan, Pak.
109/D2 Phu Loc, Viet.
109/D1 Phu Luong, Viet.
109/D1 Phu Luong (peak), Viet.
109/D1 Phu Ly, Viet.
109/D4 Phumi Banam, Camb.
109/D3 Phumi Chhlong, Camb.
109/D4 Phumi Chhuk, Camb.
109/C4 Phumi Choan, Camb.
109/D3 Phumi Kampong Putrea Chas, Camb.
109/D3 Phumi Kampong Trabek, Camb.
109/C3 Phumi Kouk Kduoch, Camb.
109/D4 Phumi Krek, Camb.
109/D3 Phumi Labang Siek, Camb.
109/D3 Phumi Mlu Prey, Camb.
109/D3 Phumi O Pou, Camb.
109/C3 Phumi Phang, Camb.
109/D3 Phumi Phsar, Camb.
109/D3 Phumi Phsa Romeas, Camb.
109/D3 Phumi Prek Kak, Camb.
109/D3 Phumi Prek Preah, Camb.
109/C3 Phumi Samraong, Camb.
109/D3 Phumi Spoe Tbong, Camb.
109/D3 Phumi Sre Ta Chan, Camb.
109/C3 Phumi Ta Krei, Camb.
109/C3 Phumi Thma Pok, Camb.
109/C3 Phumi Toek Sok, Camb.
109/C3 Phumi Veal Renh, Camb.
109/E3 Phu My, Viet.
109/E3 Phu Nhon, Viet.
109/D2 Phu Phan Nat'l Park, Thai.
109/C4 Phu Quoc, Viet.
109/C4 Phu Quoc (isl.), Viet.
109/D4 Phu Rieng Sron, Viet.
109/C2 Phu Rua Nat'l Park, Thai.
109/D1 Phu Tho, Viet.
109/D2 Phu Vang, Viet.
103/D4 Pi (riv.), China
140/C3 Piaçabuçu, Braz.
78/C2 Piacenza, It.
78/C2 Piacenza (prov.), It.
140/C2 Piancó, Braz.
79/F6 Pian di Serra (peak), It.
78/A2 Pianezza, It.
79/E4 Pianoro, It.
80/A1 Pianosa (isl.), It.
65/L2 Piaseczno, Pol.
83/H2 Piatra Neamţ, Rom.
140/B3 Piauí (riv.), Braz.
140/B2 Piauí (state), Braz.
79/F1 Piave (riv.), It.
80/D4 Piazza Armerina, It.
77/G5 Piazzi, Cima de' (peak), It.
125/M6 Pibor Post, Sudan
160/C1 Pic (riv.), On,Can
136/E8 Pica, Chile
72/E2 Picardie (reg.), Fr.
68/B4 Picardy (reg.), Fr.
166/D2 Picatinny Arsenal (mil. res.), NJ,US
163/F4 Picayune, Ms,US
80/E2 Piccolo (lag.), It.
135/D1 Pichanal, Arg.
142/C2 Pichidegua, Chile
142/C2 Pichilemu, Chile
138/B5 Pichincha, Ecu.
138/B4 Pichincha (prov.), Ecu.
161/R8 Pickering, On,Can
57/H3 Pickering, Eng,UK
57/H3 Pickering, Vale of (val.), Eng,UK
157/L3 Pickle Lake, On,Can
75/S12 Pico (isl.), Azor.,Port.
139/E4 Pico da Neblina Nat'l Park, Braz.
147/M7 Pico de Orizaba Nat'l Park, Mex.
164/B3 Pico Rivera, Ca,US
140/B2 Picos, Braz.
142/D5 Pico Truncado, Arg.
68/B4 Picquigny, Fr.
117/G5 Picraman (lake), Austl.
144/B2 Picsi, Peru
160/E3 Picton, On,Can
161/J2 Pictou, NS,Can
58/D5 Piddle (riv.), Eng,UK
106/D6 Pidurutagala (peak), SrL.
141/J6 Piedade do Rio Grande, Braz.
138/C3 Piedecuesta, Col.
78/B2 Piedmont (reg.), It.
165/K11 Piedmont, Ca,US
143/F2 Piedras (pt.), Arg.
144/C3 Piedras (riv.), Peru
147/N8 Piedras Negras, Mex.
65/K3 Piekary Śląskie, Pol.
132/B4 Piekenierskloof (pass), SAfr.
61/H3 Pieksämäki, Fin.
61/J3 Pielinen (lake), Fin.
65/L4 Pieniński Nat'l Park, Pol.
75/K6 Piera, Sp.
159/H2 Pierce, Ne,US
165/C3 Pierce (co.), Wa,US
156/F2 Pierceland, Sk,Can
55/N13 Pierowall, Sc,UK
157/H4 Pierre (cap.), SD,US
53/T10 Pierrefitte-sur-Seine, Fr.
161/N7 Pierrefonds, Qu,Can
68/C5 Pierrefonds, Fr.
72/F4 Pierrelatte, Fr.
53/S9 Pierrelaye, Fr.
133/E3 Pietermaritzburg, SAfr.
131/C4 Pietersburg, SAfr.
78/B4 Pietra Ligure, It.
78/A5 Pietravecchia, Monte (peak), It.
133/E2 Piet Retief, SAfr.
83/G2 Pietrosul (peak), Rom.
86/C3 Pietrosul, Virful (peak), Rom.
78/C2 Pieve Emanuele, It.
163/E2 Pigeon (lake), Ab,Can
157/L3 Pigeon (riv.), Can., US
160/B4 Piggott, Ar,US
149/F1 Pigs (bay), Cuba
142/E3 Pigüé, Arg.
66/B4 Pijnacker, Neth.
148/E3 Pijol (peak), Hon.
166/C1 Pike (co.), Pa,US
120/D4 Pikelot (isl.), Micr.
159/F3 Pikes (peak), Co,US
166/B1 Pikes Creek (res.), Pa,US
166/B5 Pikesville, Md,US
160/D4 Pikeville, Ky,US
112/D4 Pikit, Phil.
65/J2 Piła, Pol.
65/J2 Piła (prov.), Pol.
131/B5 Pilane, Bots.
132/P12 Pilanesberg (range), SAfr.
140/B3 Pilão Arcado, Braz.
142/E1 Pilar, Arg.
140/D3 Pilar, Braz.
135/E2 Pilar, Par.
111/F1 Pilar, Phil.
76/E4 Pilatus (peak), Swi.
136/F8 Pilaya (riv.), Bol.
165/D1 Pilchuck (riv.), Wa,US
134/C5 Pilcomayo (riv.), SAm.
53/P7 Pilgrims Hatch, Eng,UK
112/C2 Pili, Phil.
86/B2 Pilica (riv.), Pol.
81/H3 Pílion (peak), Gre.
82/D2 Pilis, Hun.
82/D2 Pilis (peak), Hun.
65/K5 Pilisvörösvár, Hun.
106/C2 Pilkhua, India
119/C4 Pillar (cape), Austl.
57/E2 Pillar (mtn.), Eng,UK
165/K12 Pillar (pt.), Ca,US
76/D5 Pillon, Col du (pass), Swi.
140/A5 Pilões (mts.), Braz.
163/G2 Pilot (peak), Tn,US
71/G3 Pilsen (Plzeň), Czh.
77/H1 Pilsensee (lake), Ger.
158/E4 Pima, Az,US
106/B4 Pimpri-Chinchwad, India
149/G5 Piña (pt.), Pan.
140/C2 Pinacote, Cerro (mtn.), Mex.
143/J7 Pinaculo (peak), Arg.
112/C2 Pinamalayan, Phil.
109/B5 Pinang (cape), Malay.
110/A2 Pinang (isl.), Malay.
92/D2 Pınarbaşı, Turk.
149/F1 Pinar del Río, Cuba
83/H5 Pınarhisar, Turk.
144/B1 Piñas, Ecu.
112/C2 Pinatubo, Mount (vol.), Phil.
157/K3 Pinawa, Mb,Can
57/H6 Pinchbeck, Eng,UK
156/E3 Pincher Creek, Ab,Can
160/D3 Pinconning, Mi,US
82/E2 Pîncota, Rom.
161/N7 Pincourt, Qu,Can
65/L3 Pińczów, Pol.
141/H7 Pindamonhangaba, Braz.
140/A2 Pindaré (riv.), Braz.
140/A1 Pindaré-Mirim, Braz.
108/B1 Pind Dādan Khān, Pak.
108/B1 Pindi Gheb, Pak.
140/B3 Pindobaçu, Braz.
81/G3 Pindos Nat'l Park, Gre.
81/G2 Pindus (mts.), Gre.
106/B3 Pindwāra, India
165/G6 Pine (riv.), Mi,US
163/F4 Pine (hills), Ms,US
157/G4 Pine (hills), Mt,US
166/A1 Pine (cr.), Pa,US
166/D4 Pine Barrens (reg.), NJ,US
162/E3 Pine Bluff, Ar,US
157/G5 Pine Bluffs, Wy,US
167/H7 Pinecliff (lake), NJ,US
167/E1 Pine Creek (pt.), Ct,US
75/G2 Pineda de Mar, Sp.
156/F5 Pinedale, Wy,US
157/J3 Pine Falls, Mb,Can
84/J2 Pinega (riv.), Rus.
166/D4 Pine Hill, NJ,US
157/L2 Pineimuta (riv.), On,Can
113/T Pine Island (bay), Ant.
160/A2 Pine Island, Mn,US
132/L10 Pinelands, SAfr.
157/H5 Pine Ridge, SD,US
73/G4 Pinerolo, It.
167/D2 Pines (lake), NJ,US
165/G6 Pine, South Branch (riv.), Mi,US
133/E3 Pinetown, SAfr.
109/B2 Ping (riv.), Thai.
104/D4 Pingbian Miaozu Zizhixian, China
105/E2 Pingchang, China
103/C3 Pingding, China
103/C4 Pingdingshan, China
103/D3 Pingdu, China
120/F4 Pingelap (atoll), Micr.
103/D2 Pinggu, China
107/J3 Pingguo, China
103/L9 Pinghu, China
105/G2 Pingjing Guan (pass), China
105/F3 Pingle, China
103/B4 Pingliang, China
103/C3 Pinglu, China
107/K3 Pingnan, China
103/D2 Pingquan, China
103/C3 Pingshan, China
103/C2 Pingshun, China
107/J2 Pingtang, China
105/J4 Pingtung, Tai.
103/C3 Pingxiang, China
104/E4 Pingxiang, China
105/G3 Pingxiang, China
103/C3 Pingxing Guan (pass), China
97/J4 Pingyang, China
103/C3 Pingyao, China
103/D4 Pingyi, China
103/D3 Pingyin, China
103/C4 Pingyu, China
103/D3 Pingyuan, China
141/G7 Pinhal, Braz.
75/Q10 Pinhal Novo, Port.
141/B3 Pinhão, Braz.
140/A1 Pinheiro, Braz.
141/D1 Pinheiros, Braz.
81/G3 Piniós (riv.), Gre.
81/G4 Piniós (riv.), Gre.
116/K6 Pinjar (lake), Austl.
117/G5 Pinkawillinie Consv. Park, Austl.
66/C2 Pinkegat (chan.), Neth.
158/B3 Pinnacles Nat'l Mon., Ca,US
67/G1 Pinnau (riv.), Ger.
67/G1 Pinneberg, Ger.
142/C3 Pino Hachado (pass), Arg.
165/K10 Pinole, Ca,US
158/C4 Pinos (peak), Ca,US
149/F1 Pinos (Juventad) (isl.), Cuba
74/D4 Pinos-Puente, Sp.
148/B2 Pinotepa Nacional, Mex.
111/E4 Pinrang, Indo.
121/V13 Pins (isl.), NCal.
120/F7 Pins, Ile des (isl.), NCal.
86/C1 Pinsk, Bela.
144/J6 Pinta (isl.), Ecu.
142/C3 Pinto, Chile
75/N9 Pinto, Sp.
112/D3 Pintuyan, Phil.
158/D3 Pioche, Nv,US
140/B2 Pio IX, Braz.
80/B1 Piombino, It.
116/L7 Pioneer World, Austl.
88/J2 Pioner (isl.), Rus.
65/L3 Pionki, Pol.
139/F5 Piorini (riv.), Braz.
78/A3 Piossasco, It.
78/B3 Piota (riv.), It.
65/K3 Piotrków (prov.), Pol.
65/K3 Piotrków Trybunalski, Pol.
79/F2 Piove di Sacco, It.
79/E1 Piovene-Rocchette, It.
140/A1 Pio XII, Braz.
106/B2 Pīpār, India
158/D3 Pipe Spring Nat'l Mon., Az,US
157/H3 Pipestone (cr.), Mb, Sk,Can
157/L2 Pipestone (riv.), On,Can
157/J4 Pipestone, Mn,US
157/J4 Pipestone Nat'l Mon., Mn,US
108/A1 Piplān, Pak.
161/G1 Pipmuacan (res.), Qu,Can
116/C2 Pippingarra Abor. Land, Austl.
160/C3 Piqua, Oh,US
141/H7 Piquete, Braz.
141/A3 Piquiri (riv.), Braz.
141/B1 Piracanjuba, Braz.
141/C2 Piracicaba, Braz.
140/B1 Piracuruca, Braz.
101/C2 Pirae-bong (mtn.), NKor.
141/K7 Piraí, Braz.
141/B3 Piraí do Sul, Braz.
81/H4 Piraiévs, Gre.
141/B2 Piraju, Braz.
141/B2 Pirajuí, Braz.
143/J7 Pirámide (peak), Chile
79/G1 Piran, Slov.
135/E2 Pirané, Arg.
141/D2 Piranga (riv.), Braz.
140/C2 Piranhas (riv.), Braz.
140/C2 Piranji (riv.), Braz.
140/A1 Pirapemas, Braz.
141/C1 Pirapora, Braz.
141/B2 Pirapòzinho, Braz.
141/C2 Pirássununga, Braz.
142/C1 Pircas (peak), Arg.
141/B1 Pires do Rio, Braz.
81/G4 Pírgos, Gre.
83/F5 Pirin (mtn.), Bul.
83/F5 Pirin (mts.), Bul.
81/H2 Pirin (peak), Bul.
83/F5 Pirin Nat'l Park, Bul.
140/B2 Piripiri, Braz.
140/B3 Piritiba, Braz.
138/D2 Píritu, Ven.
63/K1 Pirkkala, Fin.
108/B2 Pīr Mahal, Pak.
69/G5 Pirmasens, Ger.
65/G3 Pirna, Ger.
82/F4 Pirot, Yugo.
108/C1 Pir Panjal (range), India
149/G5 Pirre (mtn.), Pan.
164/B1 Piru (cr.), Ca,US
164/B2 Piru (lake), Ca,US
86/E2 Piryatin, Ukr.
78/D5 Pisa, It.
79/D6 Pisa (prov.), It.
78/D4 Pisanino, Monte (peak), It.
111/E2 Pisau, Tanjong (cape), Malay.
138/C3 Pisba Nat'l Park, Col.
166/D2 Piscataway, NJ,US
144/B4 Pisco, Peru
144/C4 Pisco (riv.), Peru
71/H4 Písek, Czh.
71/H3 Písek (peak), Czh.
102/C4 Pishan, China
95/J2 Pishīn, Pak.
77/G4 Pisoc, Piz (peak), Swi.
135/C2 Pissis (peak), Arg.
68/B4 Pissy, Fr.
165/P15 Pistakee (lake), Il,US
80/E2 Pisticci, It.
79/D5 Pistoia, It.
79/D5 Pistoia (prov.), It.
74/C1 Pisuerga (riv.), Sp.
65/L2 Pisz, Pol.
158/B2 Pit (riv.), Ca,US
138/B4 Pitalito, Col.
141/B3 Pitanga, Braz.
121/N7 Pitcairn (isl.), Pitc.
121/N7 Pitcairn Islands (terr.), UK
61/G2 Piteå, Swe.
61/F2 Piteälv (riv.), Swe.
83/G3 Piteşti, Rom.
72/E2 Pithiviers, Fr.
117/F3 Pitjantjatjara Abor. Lands, Austl.
54/C3 Pitlochry, Sc,UK
166/C4 Pitman, NJ,US
54/D2 Pitmedden, Sc,UK
112/C2 Pitogo, Phil.
142/B3 Pitrufquén, Chile
131/B5 Pitsane, Bots.
118/H8 Pitt (lake), Austl.
54/D4 Pittenweem, Sc,UK
149/F4 Pittier (mtn.), CR
165/L10 Pittsburg, Ca,US
159/J3 Pittsburg, Ks,US
162/E3 Pittsburg, Tx,US
168/H7 Pittsburgh, Pa,US
168/A1 Pittsfield, Ma,US
161/G2 Pittsfield, Me,US
166/C1 Pittston, Pa,US
77/G3 Pitzbach (riv.), Aus.
141/C2 Piũí, Braz.
144/A2 Piura, Peru
106/D2 Piuthān, Nepal
81/F1 Piva (riv.), Yugo.
138/C2 Pivijay, Col.
82/D4 Pivsko (lake), Yugo.
104/D2 Pi Xian, China
85/K4 Pizhma (riv.), Rus.
77/F4 Pizol (peak), Swi.
80/E3 Pizzo, It.
80/C1 Pizzuto (peak), It.
132/D3 P. K. Le Rouxdam (res.), SAfr.
148/D2 Placentia (pt.), Belz.
161/L2 Placentia (bay), Nf,Can
164/C3 Placentia, Ca,US
148/E2 Placer, Mex.
112/D3 Placer, Phil.
165/M9 Placer (co.), Ca,US
149/G1 Placetas, Cuba
53/T9 Plailly, Fr.
109/C3 Plai Mat (riv.), Thai.
76/C1 Plaine (riv.), Fr.
166/D2 Plainfield, NJ,US
162/C3 Plains, Tx,US
166/D3 Plainsboro, NJ,US
160/A2 Plainview, Mn,US
167/E2 Plainview, NY,US
162/C3 Plainview, Tx,US
168/B2 Plainville, Ct,US
159/H3 Plainville, Ks,US
168/C1 Plainville, Ma,US
53/R10 Plaisir, Fr.
111/E5 Plampang, Indo.
150/C2 Plana (cays), Bahm.
140/A4 Planaltina, Braz.
141/D1 Planalto do Brasil (plat.), Braz.
138/C2 Planeta Rica, Col.
162/D3 Plano, Tx,US
163/H5 Plantation, Fl,US
163/H4 Plant City, Fl,US
163/F4 Plaquemine, La,US
74/B2 Plasencia, Sp.
135/E4 Plata (estuary), Arg.
80/C4 Platani (riv.), It.
143/F2 Plata, Río de la (estuary), Arg.
129/H4 Plateau (state), Nga.
68/D3 Plate Taile, Barrage de la (dam), Belg.
138/C2 Plato, Col.
159/J2 Platte (riv.), Mo,US
159/H2 Platte (riv.), Ne,US
157/J5 Platte, SD,US
160/B3 Platteville, Wi,US
71/F5 Plattling, Ger.
160/F2 Plattsburgh, NY,US
71/F2 Plauen, Ger.
82/D4 Plav, Yugo.
77/G4 Plavna Dadaint, Piz (peak), Swi.
148/E3 Playa de los Muertos (ruins), Hon.
146/C2 Playa Noriega (lake), Mex.
138/A5 Playas, Ecu.
158/E5 Playas (lake), NM,US
109/E3 Play Cu (Pleiku), Viet.
157/J2 Playgreen (lake), Mb,Can
165/K11 Pleasant Hill, Ca,US
168/E6 Pleasant Hill (dam), Oh,US
168/E6 Pleasant Hill (res.), Oh,US
168/H7 Pleasant Hills, Pa,US
165/L11 Pleasanton, Ca,US
162/D4 Pleasanton, Tx,US
165/Q14 Pleasant Prairie, Wi,US
166/D5 Pleasantville, NJ,US
167/E1 Pleasantville, NY,US
71/G5 Plechý (Plöckenstein) (peak), Czh., Ger.
109/E3 Pleiku (Play Cu), Viet.
70/D4 Pleinfeld, Ger.
64/G3 Pleisse (riv.), Ger.
119/G5 Plenty (riv.), Austl.
115/S10 Plenty (bay), NZ
157/G3 Plentywood, Mt,US
72/B2 Plérin, Fr.
71/F2 Plesná (riv.), Czh.
65/J3 Pleszew, Pol.
161/G1 Plétipi (lake), Qu,Can
67/E6 Plettenberg, Ger.
83/G4 Pleven, Bul.
82/B3 Plitvice Lakes Nat'l Park, Cro.
73/L4 Plitvička Jezera Nat'l Park, Cro.
82/D4 Pljevlja, Yugo.
82/B4 Ploča, Rt (pt.), Yugo.
65/K2 Płock, Pol.
65/K2 Płock (prov.), Pol.
71/G5 Plöckenstein (Plechý) (peak), Ger.
82/C4 Pločno (peak), Bosn.
72/B3 Ploemeur, Fr.
83/H3 Ploieşti, Rom.
76/C2 Plombières-les-Bains, Fr.
64/F1 Plön, Ger.
156/G2 Plonge (lake), Sk,Can
65/L2 Płońsk, Pol.
65/H3 Ploučnice (riv.), Czh.
72/B2 Ploufragan, Fr.
72/A2 Plougastel-Daoulas, Fr.
83/G4 Plovdiv, Bul.
83/G5 Plovdiv (reg.), Bul.
160/B2 Plover, Wi,US
167/F1 Plum (isl.), NY,US
168/H7 Plum, Pa,US
56/A2 Plumbridge, NI,UK
116/E4 Plumridge Lakes Nature Rsv., Austl.
131/B4 Plumtree, Zim.
63/J4 Plungė, Lith.
150/F3 Plymouth (cap.), Monts.
58/B6 Plymouth, Eng,UK
58/B6 Plymouth (sound), Eng,UK
160/C3 Plymouth, In,US
168/D2 Plymouth, Ma,US
168/D2 Plymouth (co.), Ma,US
161/G3 Plymouth, NH,US
166/C1 Plymouth, Pa,US
160/C3 Plymouth, Wi,US
168/D2 Plymouth Rock, Ma,US
58/C2 Plynlimon (mtn.), UK
71/G3 Plzeň (Pilsen), Czh.
65/J2 Pniewy, Pol.
129/E4 Pô, Burk.
79/E3 Po (riv.), It.
78/C2 Po (val.), It.
141/G8 Poá, Braz.
139/E2 Poa (riv.), Ven.
102/D3 Pobedy, Pik (peak), Kyr.
65/J2 Pobiedziska, Pol.
163/F2 Pocahontas, Ar,US
140/A2 Poção de Pedra, Braz.
156/E5 Pocatello, Id,US
86/E1 Pochep, Rus.
148/B3 Pochutla, Mex.
71/G6 Pöcking, Ger.
120/E6 Pocklington (reef), PNG
57/H4 Pocklington, Eng,UK
140/B4 Poções, Braz.
141/H6 Poço Fundo, Braz.
159/J4 Pocola, Ok,US
137/G7 Poconé, Braz.
166/C1 Pocono (cr.), Pa,US
166/C1 Pocono (lake), Pa,US
166/C1 Pocono (mts.), Pa,US
141/G6 Poços de Caldas, Braz.
149/F4 Pocrí, Pan.
65/K3 Poddębice, Pol.
79/F3 Po di Goro (riv.), It.
79/F2 Po di Venezia (riv.), It.
79/E3 Po di Volano (riv.), It.
65/M3 Podlasie (reg.), Pol.
84/H5 Podol'sk, Rus.
128/B2 Podor, Sen.
84/G3 Podporozh'ye, Rus.
82/C3 Podravska Slatina, Cro.
82/E4 Podujevo, Yugo.
79/E6 Poggibonsi, It.
81/G2 Pogradec, Alb.
151/F5 Pogromni (vol.), Ak,US
154/U11 Pohakuloa (mil. res.), Hi,US
101/E4 P'ohang, SKor.
166/C2 Pohatcong (cr.), NJ,US
161/G2 Pohénégamook, Qu,Can
61/G3 Pohjanmaa (reg.), Fin.
120/E4 Pohnpei (isl.), Micr.
166/C2 Pohopoco (cr.), Pa,US
166/C2 Pohopoco Mtn. (ridge), Pa,US
71/E6 Poing, Ger.
113/H Poinsett (cape), Ant.
152/E2 Point (lake), NW,Can
163/F4 Point au Fer (isl.), La,US
150/F3 Pointe-à-Pitre, Guad.
161/N7 Pointe-Claire, Qu,Can
161/F2 Pointe-du-Lac, Qu,Can
126/B1 Pointe-Noire, Congo
75/G4 Pointe Pescade, Cap de la (cape), Alg.
150/F5 Point Fortin, Trin.
168/C3 Point Judith Coast Guard Sta., RI,US
119/E1 Point Lookout (peak), Austl.
164/A2 Point Mugo Nav. Air Sta., Ca,US
164/A2 Point Mugo State Park, Ca,US
108/H4 Point Pedro, SrL.
160/D3 Point Pelee Nat'l Park, On,Can
167/D3 Point Pleasant, NJ,US
160/C4 Point Pleasant, Oh,US
160/D4 Point Pleasant, WV,US
168/G7 Point Saint Park, Pa,US
116/E4 Point Salvation Abor. Rsv., Austl.
116/C1 Poissonnier (pt.), Austl.
53/S10 Poissy, Fr.
72/D3 Poitiers, Fr.
72/C3 Poitou (hist. reg.), Fr.
72/C3 Poitou-Charentes (reg.), Fr.
63/K1 Pojo, Fin.
61/J3 Pojois-Karjala (prov.), Fin.
140/C4 Pojuca, Braz.
106/B2 Pokaran, India
106/D2 Pokhara, Nepal
87/K1 Pokhvistnevo, Rus.
109/E4 Po Klong Garai Cham Towers, Viet.
125/L7 Poko, Zaire
71/H2 Polabská Nížina (reg.), Czh.
74/C1 Pola de Laviana, Sp.
74/C1 Pola de Lena, Sp.
74/C1 Pola de Siero, Sp.
86/A2 Pol'ana (peak), Slvk.
65/K2 Poland
65/L3 Połaniec, Pol.
85/P2 Polar Urals (mts.), Rus.
92/C2 Polatlı, Turk.
65/J2 Połczyn-Zdrój, Pol.
95/J1 Pol-e-Khomri, Afg.
113/E Pole of Inaccessability, Ant.
79/E2 Polesine (reg.), It.
59/E1 Polesworth, Eng,UK
82/E2 Polgár, Hun.
101/D5 Pŏlgyo, SKor.
81/J4 Políaigos (isl.), Gre.
80/D3 Policastro (gulf), It.
65/H2 Police, Pol.
80/E2 Policoro, It.
81/H2 Políkhni, Gre.
112/C2 Polillo, Phil.
112/C2 Polillo (isls.), Phil.
112/C1 Polillo (str.), Phil.
80/E3 Polistena, It.
65/J3 Polkowice, Pol.
108/F3 Pollāchi, India
75/G3 Pollensa, Sp.
148/D3 Polochic (riv.), Guat.
112/D4 Polomolok, Phil.
143/G2 Polonia (cape), Uru.
108/H5 Polonnaruwa, SrL.

213

Polon – Pusan

108/H4 **Polonnaruwa** (dist.), SrL.
86/C2 **Polonnoye,** Ukr.
63/N4 **Polotsk,** Bela.
58/B6 **Polperro,** Eng,UK
83/G4 **Polski Trŭmbesh,** Bul.
156/E4 **Polson,** Mt,US
86/E2 **Poltava,** Ukr.
86/E2 **Poltava Obl.,** Ukr.
71/H5 **Poluška** (peak), Czh.
84/F3 **Polvijärvi,** Fin.
84/G1 **Polyarnyy,** Rus.
121/J3 **Polynesia** (reg.)
141/D2 **Pomba** (riv.), Braz.
140/C2 **Pombal,** Braz.
74/A3 **Pombal,** Port.
65/H2 **Pomerania** (reg.), Pol.
65/H1 **Pomeranian** (bay), Ger., Pol.
141/B3 **Pomerode,** Braz.
139/G3 **Pomeroon-Supernaam** (reg.), Guy.
56/B2 **Pomeroy,** NI,UK
156/D4 **Pomeroy,** Wa,US
120/E5 **Pomio,** PNG
164/C2 **Pomona,** Ca,US
83/H4 **Pomorie,** Bul.
91/C2 **Pomos** (pt.), Cyp.
79/F3 **Po, Mouths of the,** It.
163/H5 **Pompano Beach,** Fl,US
80/D2 **Pompei** (ruins), It.
141/C1 **Pompeu,** Braz.
167/H8 **Pompton** (lakes), NJ,US
167/H8 **Pompton** (riv.), NJ,US
167/D1 **Pompton Lakes,** NJ,US
129/E4 **Pô Nat'l Park,** Burk.
159/H3 **Ponca City,** Ok,US
150/E3 **Ponce,** PR
160/E1 **Poncheville** (lake), Qu,Can
76/B5 **Poncin,** Fr.
153/J1 **Pond** (inlet), NW,Can
168/A3 **Pond** (pt.), Ct,US
108/G3 **Pondicherry,** India
108/G3 **Pondicherry** (terr.), India
78/B5 **Ponente** (coast), It.
74/B1 **Ponferrada,** Sp.
133/E2 **Pongolo** (riv.), SAfr.
130/C4 **Pongwe,** Tanz.
128/E4 **Poni** (prov.), Burk.
65/M3 **Poniatowa,** Pol.
108/G3 **Ponnaiyar** (riv.), India
108/E3 **Ponnani,** India
156/E2 **Ponoka,** Ab,Can
84/H2 **Ponoy** (riv.), Rus.
78/D5 **Ponsacco,** It.
68/D3 **Pont-à-Celles,** Belg.
140/C5 **Ponta da Baleia** (pt.), Braz.
75/S12 **Ponta da Pico** (mtn.), Azor.,Port.
75/T13 **Ponta Delgada,** Azor.,Port.
75/U15 **Ponta do Sol,** Madr.,Port.
141/B3 **Ponta Grossa,** Braz.
141/B1 **Pontalina,** Braz.
69/F6 **Pont-à-Mousson,** Fr.
137/G8 **Ponta Porã,** Braz.
58/C3 **Pontardawe,** Wal,UK
58/B3 **Pontardulais,** Wal,UK
76/C4 **Pontarlier,** Fr.
79/E5 **Pontassieve,** It.
53/T10 **Pontault-Combault,** Fr.
160/E1 **Pontax** (riv.), Qu,Can
53/U10 **Pontcarré,** Fr.
163/F4 **Pontchartrain** (lake), La,US
72/B3 **Pontchâteau,** Fr.
72/E4 **Pont-du-Château,** Fr.
80/C2 **Pontecorvo,** It.
78/D5 **Pontedera,** It.
74/A3 **Ponte de Sor,** Port.
57/G4 **Pontefract,** Eng,UK
57/G1 **Ponteland,** Eng,UK
141/D2 **Ponte Nova,** Braz.
58/C2 **Ponterwyd,** Wal,UK
79/E2 **Ponte San Nicolò,** It.
58/D1 **Pontesbury,** Eng,UK
136/G7 **Pontes e Lacerda,** Braz.
112/C3 **Pontevedra,** Phil.
74/A1 **Pontevedra,** Sp.
160/B3 **Pontiac,** Il,US
165/F6 **Pontiac,** Mi,US
165/F6 **Pontiac** (lake), Mi,US
110/C4 **Pontianak,** Indo.
72/B2 **Pontivy,** Fr.
53/S9 **Pontoise,** Fr.
163/F3 **Pontotoc,** Ms,US
58/C2 **Pontrhydfendigaid,** Wal,UK
58/D3 **Pontrilas,** Eng,UK
68/B5 **Pont-Sainte Maxence,** Fr.
72/F4 **Pont-Saint-Esprit,** Fr.
58/B3 **Pontyates,** Wal,UK
58/C3 **Pontyclun,** Wal,UK
58/C3 **Pont y Cymmer,** Wal,UK
58/C3 **Pontypool,** Wal,UK
58/C3 **Pontypridd,** Wal,UK
80/C2 **Ponziane** (isls.), It.
58/E5 **Poole,** Eng,UK
59/E5 **Poole** (bay), Eng,UK
55/J8 **Poolewe,** Sc,UK
106/B4 **Poona,** India
116/C3 **Poondarrie** (peak), Austl.
117/F3 **Poondinna** (peak), Austl.
136/E7 **Poopó** (lake), Bol.
63/K2 **Põõsapää Neem** (pt.), Est.
167/F2 **Poosepatuck Ind. Res.,** NY,US
104/B4 **Popa** (peak), Burma
138/B4 **Popayán,** Col.
68/B2 **Poperinge,** Belg.
146/C2 **Popigochic** (riv.), Mex.
119/B2 **Popilta** (lake), Austl.
119/B2 **Popio** (lake), Austl.
157/K2 **Poplar** (riv.), Mb, On,Can
166/B6 **Poplar** (isl.), Md,US
157/G3 **Poplar,** Mt,US
157/G3 **Poplar** (riv.), Mt,US
159/K3 **Poplar Bluff,** Mo,US
163/F4 **Poplarville,** Ms,US
124/J6 **Popokabaka,** Zaire
120/D5 **Popondetta,** PNG
83/H4 **Popovo,** Bul.
71/E4 **Poppberg** (peak), Ger.
65/L4 **Poprad,** Slvk.
65/L4 **Poprad** (riv.), Slvk.
140/B2 **Poranga,** Braz.
137/J6 **Porangatu,** Braz.
106/A3 **Porbandar,** India
138/C3 **Porce** (riv.), Col.
79/F1 **Porcia,** It.
74/C4 **Porcuna,** Sp.
151/K2 **Porcupine** (riv.), Yk,Can, Ak,US
118/B3 **Porcupine Gorge Nat'l Park,** Austl.
157/H2 **Porcupine Plain,** Sk,Can
79/F1 **Pordenone,** It.
79/F1 **Pordenone** (prov.), It.
79/G2 **Poreč,** Cro.
63/J1 **Pori,** Fin.
115/R11 **Porirua,** NZ
84/E4 **Porkhov,** Rus.
139/F2 **Porlamar,** Ven.
58/C4 **Porlock,** Eng,UK
118/A1 **Pormpuraaw Abor. Land,** Austl.
97/N2 **Poronaysk,** Rus.
116/C5 **Porongurup Nat'l Park,** Austl.
113/J **Porpoise** (bay), Ant.
76/D3 **Porrentruy,** Swi.
74/A1 **Porriño,** Sp.
61/H1 **Porsangen** (fjord), Nor.
62/C2 **Porsgrunn,** Nor.
92/B2 **Porsuk** (riv.), Turk.
136/F7 **Portachuelo,** Bol.
117/M8 **Port Adelaide,** Austl.
56/B3 **Portadown,** NI,UK
56/C3 **Portaferry,** NI,UK
160/C3 **Portage,** Mi,US
168/F5 **Portage** (co.), Oh,US
168/F6 **Portage** (lakes), Oh,US
160/B3 **Portage,** Wi,US
168/F5 **Portage Lakes,** Oh,US
157/J3 **Portage la Prairie,** Mb,Can
156/B3 **Port Alberni,** BC,Can
74/B3 **Portalegre,** Port.
74/B3 **Portalegre** (dist.), Port.
159/G4 **Portales,** NM,US
132/D4 **Port Alfred,** SAfr.
156/B3 **Port Alice,** BC,Can
156/C3 **Port Angeles,** Wa,US
149/G2 **Port Antonio,** Jam.
54/A3 **Port Appin,** Sc,UK
162/E4 **Port Arthur,** Tx,US
55/H9 **Port Askaig,** Sc,UK
161/K1 **Port au Choix,** Nf,Can
161/K1 **Port au Choix Nat'l Hist. Park,** Nf,Can
117/H5 **Port Augusta,** Austl.
149/H2 **Port-au-Prince** (cap.), Haiti
56/C3 **Portavogie,** NI,UK
67/F4 **Porta Westfalica,** Ger.
54/A5 **Port Bannatyne,** Sc,UK
107/F5 **Port Blair,** India
162/E4 **Port Bolivar,** Tx,US
128/E5 **Port-Bouët,** IvC.
153/K2 **Port Burwell,** Qu,Can
161/H1 **Port-Cartier,** Qu,Can
163/H5 **Port Charlotte,** Fl,US
167/E2 **Port Chester,** NY,US
160/D3 **Port Clinton,** Oh,US
161/R10 **Port Colborne,** On,Can
161/Q8 **Port Credit,** On,Can
161/S8 **Port Darlington,** On,Can
119/C4 **Port Davey** (har.), Austl.
149/H2 **Port-de-Paix,** Haiti
110/B3 **Port Dickson,** Malay.
165/B1 **Port Discovery** (bay), Wa,US
151/M4 **Port Edward,** BC,Can
140/B4 **Porteirinha,** Braz.
137/H4 **Portel,** Braz.
160/D2 **Port Elgin,** Can.
132/D4 **Port Elizabeth,** SAfr.
55/H9 **Port Ellen,** Sc,UK
56/D3 **Port Erin,** IM,UK
166/C1 **Porters** (lake), Pa,US
132/L10 **Porterville,** SAfr.
158/C3 **Porterville,** Ca,US
72/F4 **Portes-lès-Valence,** Fr.
149/J3 **Portete** (bay), Col.
124/B3 **Port-Étienne,** Mrta.
72/D5 **Portet-sur-Garonne,** Fr.
58/B3 **Port Eynon,** Wal,UK
58/B3 **Port Eynon** (pt.), Wal,UK
165/B2 **Port Gamble Ind. Res.,** Wa,US
126/A1 **Port-Gentil,** Gabon
54/B5 **Port Glasgow,** Sc,UK
56/B2 **Portglenone,** NI,UK
54/C1 **Portgordon,** Sc,UK
58/C3 **Porth,** Wal,UK
129/G5 **Port Harcourt,** Nga.
156/B3 **Port Hardy,** BC,Can
161/J2 **Port Hawkesbury,** NS,Can
58/C4 **Porthcawl,** Wal,UK
116/C2 **Port Hedland,** Austl.
58/A6 **Porthleven,** Eng,UK
56/D6 **Porthmadog,** Wal,UK
164/A2 **Port Hueneme,** Ca,US
165/H6 **Port Huron,** Mi,US
74/A4 **Portimão,** Port.
58/B5 **Port Isaac,** Eng,UK
58/B5 **Port Isaac** (bay), Eng,UK
58/D4 **Portishead,** Eng,UK
167/E2 **Port Jefferson,** NY,US
166/D1 **Port Jervis,** NY,US
54/D1 **Portknockie,** Sc,UK
119/B3 **Portland,** Austl.
119/C4 **Portland** (cape), Austl.
149/G2 **Portland** (pt.), Jam.
58/D6 **Portland** (pt.), Eng,UK
151/N4 **Portland** (inlet), BC,Can, Ak,US
160/C3 **Portland,** In,US
161/G3 **Portland,** Me,US
156/C4 **Portland,** Or,US
163/G2 **Portland,** Tn,US
55/K11 **Portland, Bill of** (pt.), Eng,UK
58/D5 **Portland, Isle of** (pen.), Eng,UK
162/D4 **Port Lavaca,** Tx,US
54/D2 **Portlethen,** Sc,UK
117/G5 **Port Lincoln,** Austl.
133/S15 **Port Louis** (cap.), Mrts.
119/E1 **Port Macquarie,** Austl.
165/B2 **Port Madison Ind. Res.,** Wa,US
54/C1 **Portmahomack,** Sc,UK
149/G2 **Port Maria,** Jam.
60/D3 **Portmarnock,** Ire.
156/B3 **Port McNeill,** BC,Can
161/H1 **Port-Menier,** Qu,Can
149/G2 **Portmore,** Jam.
120/D5 **Port Moresby** (cap.), PNG
161/G1 **Portneuf** (riv.), Qu,Can
140/B1 **Pôrto,** Braz.
80/A1 **Porto** (gulf), Fr.
74/A2 **Porto,** Port.
74/A2 **Porto** (dist.), Port.
141/B4 **Pôrto Alegre,** Braz.
126/B3 **Porto Amboim,** Ang.
141/B3 **Pôrto Belo,** Braz.
149/G4 **Portobelo Nat'l Park,** Pan.
140/D3 **Pôrto Calvo,** Braz.
79/G6 **Portocivitanova,** It.
140/C3 **Pôrto da Fôlha,** Braz.
80/C4 **Porto Empedocle,** It.
80/B1 **Portoferraio,** It.
141/C2 **Pôrto Ferreira,** Braz.
55/H7 **Port of Ness,** Sc,UK
140/A2 **Porto Franco,** Braz.
150/F5 **Port-of-Spain** (cap.), Trin.
79/F1 **Portogruaro,** It.
79/E3 **Portomaggiore,** It.
137/J6 **Porto Nacional,** Braz.
129/F5 **Porto-Novo** (cap.), Ben.
108/G3 **Portonovo,** India
163/H4 **Port Orange,** Fl,US
79/G6 **Porto Recanati,** It.
79/G1 **Portorož,** Slov.
80/C1 **Porto San Giorgio,** It.
80/B1 **Porto Santo Stefano,** It.
140/C5 **Porto Seguro,** Braz.
80/A2 **Porto Torres,** It.
141/B3 **Porto União,** Braz.
136/F5 **Porto Velho,** Braz.
138/A5 **Portoviejo,** Ecu.
56/C2 **Portpatrick,** Sc,UK
119/C3 **Port Phillip** (bay), Austl.
117/H5 **Port Pirie,** Austl.
55/H8 **Portree,** Sc,UK
167/J9 **Port Richmond,** NY,US
56/B1 **Portrush,** NI,UK
127/C2 **Port Said** (Būr Sa'īd), Egypt
163/G4 **Port Saint Joe,** Fl,US
72/F5 **Port-Saint-Louis-du-Rhône,** Fr.
163/H5 **Port Saint Lucie,** Fl,US
56/D3 **Port Saint Mary,** IM,UK
59/E5 **Portsea** (isl.), Eng,UK
54/D5 **Port Seton,** Sc,UK
151/M4 **Port Simpson,** BC,Can
59/F5 **Portslade by Sea,** Eng,UK
59/E5 **Portsmouth,** Eng,UK
161/G3 **Portsmouth,** NH,US
160/D4 **Portsmouth,** Oh,US
168/C2 **Portsmouth,** RI,US
160/E4 **Portsmouth,** Va,US
54/D1 **Portsoy,** Sc,UK
119/E2 **Port Stephens** (bay), Austl.
56/B1 **Portstewart,** NI,UK
127/D5 **Port Sudan** (Būr Sūdān), Sudan
58/C3 **Port Talbot,** Wal,UK
156/C3 **Port Townsend,** Wa,US
74/A3 **Portugal**
74/D1 **Portugalete,** Sp.
138/D2 **Portuguesa** (riv.), Ven.
138/D2 **Portuguesa** (state), Ven.
164/F8 **Portuguese Bend,** Ca,US
167/E2 **Port Washington,** NY,US
160/C3 **Port Washington,** Wi,US
56/D2 **Port William,** Sc,UK
63/L1 **Porvoo** (Borgä), Fin.
135/E2 **Posadas,** Arg.
74/C4 **Posadas,** Sp.
82/C3 **Posavina** (val.), Bosn., Cro.
111/F4 **Poso** (lake), Indo.
101/D5 **Posŏng,** SKor.
101/D5 **Posŏng** (bay), SKor.
101/D5 **Posŏng** (riv.), SKor.
138/A5 **Posorja,** Ecu.
140/A4 **Posse,** Braz.
165/C2 **Possession** (pt.), Wa,US
165/C2 **Possession** (sound), Wa,US
162/C3 **Post,** Tx,US
63/M4 **Postavy,** Bela.
124/F3 **Poste Maurice Cortier** (ruins), Alg.
124/F3 **Poste Weygand** (ruins), Alg.
156/D4 **Post Falls,** Id,US
132/C3 **Postmasburg,** SAfr.
82/B3 **Postojna,** Slov.
139/G3 **Potaro-Siparuni** (reg.), Guy.
132/D2 **Potchefstroom,** SAfr.
159/J4 **Poteau,** Ok,US
80/D2 **Potenza,** It.
80/C1 **Potenza** (riv.), It.
131/C5 **Potgietersrus,** SAfr.
156/D4 **Potholes** (res.), Wa,US
140/B2 **Poti** (riv.), Braz.
87/G4 **Poti,** Geo.
79/E6 **Poti, Alpe di** (peak), It.
140/C4 **Potiraguá,** Braz.
166/A5 **Potomac,** Md,US
160/E4 **Potomac** (riv.), Md, Va,US
136/E7 **Potosí,** Bol.
159/K3 **Potosi,** Mo,US
135/C2 **Potrerillos,** Chile
64/G2 **Potsdam,** Ger.
160/F2 **Potsdam,** NY,US
53/N6 **Potters Bar,** Eng,UK
59/F2 **Potterspury,** Eng,UK
59/F2 **Potton,** Eng,UK
166/C3 **Pottstown,** Pa,US
166/B2 **Pottsville,** Pa,US
106/D6 **Pottuvil,** SrL.
160/F3 **Poughkeepsie,** NY,US
60/D3 **Poulaphouca** (res.), Ire.
57/G5 **Poulter** (riv.), Eng,UK
57/F4 **Poulton-le-Fylde,** Eng,UK
73/G4 **Pourri** (mtn.), Fr.
141/H7 **Pouso Alegre,** Braz.
109/C3 **Pouthisat,** Camb.
109/C3 **Pouthisat** (riv.), Camb.
65/K4 **Považská Bystrica,** Slvk.
74/A2 **Póvoa de Varzim,** Port.
87/G2 **Povorino,** Rus.
97/L3 **Povorotnyy, Mys** (cape), Rus.
153/J2 **Povungnituk** (riv.), Qu,Can
164/C5 **Poway,** Ca,US
157/G4 **Powder** (riv.), Mt, Wy,US
150/B1 **Powell** (pt.), Bahm.
158/E3 **Powell** (lake), Az, Ut,US
166/B3 **Powell** (cr.), Pa,US
156/F4 **Powell,** Wy,US
156/B3 **Powell River,** BC,Can
161/R9 **Power** (res.), NY,US
60/B6 **Power Head** (pt.), Ire.
165/P14 **Powers** (lake), Wi,US
58/C2 **Powys** (co.), Wal,UK
58/C1 **Powys, Vale** (vall.), Wal,UK
137/H7 **Poxoréo,** Braz.
105/G2 **Poyang** (lake), China
57/F5 **Poynton,** Eng,UK
74/A1 **Poyo,** Sp.
92/C2 **Pozantı,** Turk.
82/E3 **Požarevac,** Yugo.
147/F4 **Poza Rica,** Mex.
82/E4 **Požega,** Yugo.
65/J2 **Poznań,** Pol.
65/J2 **Poznań** (prov.), Pol.
74/D4 **Pozo Alcón,** Sp.
74/C3 **Pozoblanco,** Sp.
75/N9 **Pozuelo de Alarcón,** Sp.
139/E2 **Pozuelos,** Ven.
80/D4 **Pozzallo,** It.
80/C1 **Pozzoni** (peak), It.
65/K2 **Prabuty,** Pol.
109/B4 **Pracham Hiang** (pt.), Thai.
71/H4 **Prachatice,** Czh.
109/C3 **Prachin Buri,** Thai.
109/C3 **Prachin Buri** (riv.), Thai.
109/B4 **Prachuap Khiri Khan,** Thai.
77/G4 **Prad am Stilfserjoch** (Prato allo Stelvio), It.
65/J3 **Praděd** (peak), Czh.
138/B4 **Pradera,** Col.
140/C5 **Prado,** Braz.
164/C3 **Prado** (dam), Ca,US
164/C3 **Prado Flood Control Basin,** Ca,US
77/E4 **Pragelpass** (pass), Swi.
71/H2 **Prague** (Praha) (cap.), Czh.
71/G3 **Praha** (peak), Czh.
71/H2 **Praha** (reg.), Czh.
71/H2 **Praha** (Prague) (cap.), Czh.
83/G3 **Prahova** (co.), Rom.
122/K11 **Praia** (cap.), CpV.
75/S12 **Praia de Victória,** Azor.,Port.
141/G9 **Praia Grande,** Braz.
159/G4 **Prairie Dog Town Fork** (riv.), Ok, Tx,US
160/B3 **Prairie du Chien,** Wi,US
161/N6 **Prairies** (riv.), Qu,Can
157/J4 **Prairies, Coteau des** (upland), US
162/E4 **Prairie View,** Tx,US
71/G6 **Pram** (riv.), Aus.
109/B3 **Pran Buri** (res.), Thai.
106/D4 **Prānhita** (riv.), India
110/A3 **Prapat,** Indo.
109/D3 **Prasat Preah Vihear,** Camb.
65/K3 **Praszka,** Pol.
140/C2 **Prata,** Braz.
141/B1 **Prata,** Braz.
140/A5 **Prata** (riv.), Braz.
141/B1 **Prata** (riv.), Braz.
105/H4 **Pratas** (reef), China
105/H4 **Pratas** (Dongsha) (isl.), China
77/F4 **Prätlgau** (val.), Swi.
79/E5 **Prato,** It.
80/C1 **Pratola Peligna,** It.
79/E5 **Pratomagno** (mts.), It.
143/J7 **Pratt** (isl.), Chile
159/H3 **Pratt,** Ks,US
76/D2 **Pratteln,** Swi.
163/G3 **Prattville,** Al,US
74/B1 **Pravia,** Sp.
55/K11 **Prawle** (pt.), Eng,UK
111/E5 **Praya,** Indo.
83/G3 **Predeal,** Rom.
157/H3 **Preeceville,** Sk,Can
57/F6 **Prees,** Eng,UK
57/F4 **Preesall,** Eng,UK
64/F1 **Preetz,** Ger.
65/L1 **Pregolya** (riv.), Rus.
160/E1 **Preissac** (lake), On,Can
109/D4 **Prek Pouthi,** Camb.
75/L7 **Premiá de Mar,** Sp.
65/G2 **Prenzlau,** Ger.
65/J4 **Přerov,** Czh.
73/J3 **Presanella** (peak), It.
77/G5 **Presanella, Cima** (peak), It.
57/F5 **Prescot,** Eng,UK
160/F2 **Prescott,** On,Can
158/D4 **Prescott,** Az,US
82/E4 **Preševo,** Yugo.
135/D2 **Presidencia Roque Sáenz Peña,** Arg.
140/A2 **Presidente Dutra,** Braz.
141/A2 **Presidente Epitácio,** Braz.
141/C1 **Presidente Olegário,** Braz.
141/B2 **Presidente Prudente,** Braz.
142/B5 **Presidente Ríos** (lake), Chile
141/B2 **Presidente Venceslau,** Braz.
146/D4 **Presidio** (riv.), Mex.
162/B4 **Presidio,** Tx,US
83/H4 **Preslav,** Bul.
53/U10 **Presles-en-Brie,** Fr.
77/G6 **Presolana, Pizzo della** (peak), It.
65/L4 **Prešov,** Slvk.
81/G2 **Prespa** (lake), Eur.
161/G2 **Presque Isle,** Me,US
57/E5 **Prestatyn,** Wal,UK
129/E5 **Prestea,** Gha.
58/D2 **Presteigne,** Wal,UK
71/G3 **Přeštice,** Czh.
119/G5 **Preston,** Austl.
116/C2 **Preston** (cape), Austl.
57/F4 **Preston,** Eng,UK
58/D5 **Preston,** Eng,UK
54/D5 **Preston,** Sc,UK
156/F5 **Preston,** Id,US
54/D5 **Prestonpans,** Sc,UK
160/D4 **Prestonsburg,** Ky,US
57/F4 **Prestwich,** Eng,UK
54/B6 **Prestwick,** Sc,UK
59/F3 **Prestwood,** Eng,UK
140/A3 **Prêto** (riv.), Braz.
140/A5 **Prêto** (riv.), Braz.
132/E2 **Pretoria** (cap.), SAfr.
166/B4 **Pretty Boy** (res.), Md,US
67/F4 **Preussisch Oldendorf,** Ger.
81/G3 **Préveza,** Gre.
151/D4 **Pribilof** (isls.), Ak,US
82/D4 **Priboj,** Yugo.
71/H3 **Příbram,** Czh.
158/E3 **Price,** Ut,US
158/E3 **Price** (riv.), Ut,US
163/F4 **Prichard,** Al,US
74/C4 **Priego de Córdoba,** Sp.
132/C3 **Prieska,** SAfr.
156/D3 **Priest** (lake), Id,US
156/D3 **Priest River,** Id,US
74/C1 **Prieta** (mtn.), Sp.
65/K4 **Prievidza,** Slvk.
64/F2 **Prignitz** (reg.), Ger.
82/C3 **Prijedor,** Bosn.
82/D4 **Prijepolje,** Yugo.
87/H3 **Prikaspian** (plain), Kaz., Rus.
87/H3 **Prikumsk,** Rus.
82/E5 **Prilep,** Macd.
76/C4 **Prilly,** Swi.
86/E2 **Priluki,** Ukr.
80/C2 **Prima Porta,** It.
166/C6 **Prime Hook Nat'l Wild. Ref.,** De,US
140/B1 **Primeira Cruz,** Braz.
143/J7 **Primero** (cape), Chile
59/E1 **Primethorpe,** Eng,UK
89/P5 **Primorsk Kray,** Rus.
86/F3 **Primorsko-Akhtarsk,** Rus.
156/F2 **Primrose** (lake), Ab, Sk,Can
156/F2 **Primrose** (lake), Ab, Sk,Can
69/F5 **Prims** (riv.), Ger.
152/E1 **Prince Albert** (pen.), NW,Can
152/E1 **Prince Albert** (sound), NW,Can
157/G2 **Prince Albert,** Sk,Can
157/G2 **Prince Albert Nat'l Park,** Sk,Can
152/D1 **Prince Alfred** (cape), NW,Can
153/J2 **Prince Charles** (isl.), NW,Can
51/L8 **Prince Edward** (isls.), SAfr.
161/J2 **Prince Edward Island** (prov.), Can.
161/J2 **Prince Edward Island Nat'l Park,** PE,Can
156/C2 **Prince George,** BC,Can
166/B6 **Prince Georges** (co.), Md,US
153/R7 **Prince Gustav Adolf** (sea), NW,Can
113/C **Prince Harold** (coast), Ant.
152/G1 **Prince Leopold** (isl.), NW,Can
66/C2 **Princenhof** (lake), Neth.
114/G2 **Prince of Wales** (isl.), Austl.
152/G1 **Prince of Wales** (isl.), NW,Can
152/E1 **Prince of Wales** (str.), NW,Can
151/M4 **Prince of Wales** (isl.), Ak,US
113/C **Prince Olav** (coast), Ant.
153/R7 **Prince Patrick** (isl.), NW,Can
152/G1 **Prince Regent** (inlet), NW,Can
151/M4 **Prince Rupert,** BC,Can
140/C2 **Princesa Isabel,** Braz.
59/F3 **Princes Risborough,** Eng,UK
113/A **Princess Astrid** (coast), Ant.
118/A1 **Princess Charlotte** (bay), Austl.
153/S6 **Princess Margaret** (range), NW,Can
113/Z **Princess Martha** (coast), Ant.
113/B **Princess Ragnhild** (coast), Ant.
156/A2 **Princess Royal** (isl.), BC,Can
156/C3 **Princeton,** BC,Can
160/B3 **Princeton,** Il,US
160/C4 **Princeton,** In,US
160/C4 **Princeton,** Ky,US
157/K4 **Princeton,** Mn,US
166/D3 **Princeton,** NJ,US
160/D4 **Princeton,** WV,US
151/J3 **Prince William** (sound), Ak,US
124/G7 **Príncipe** (isl.), SaoT.
151/K3 **Prindle** (vol.), Ak,US
156/C4 **Prineville,** Or,US
66/B5 **Prinsenbeek,** Neth.
66/C2 **Prinses Margriet** (can.), Neth.
149/F3 **Prinzapolka,** Nic.
149/E3 **Prinzapolka** (riv.), Nic.
80/D4 **Priolo di Gargallo,** It.
74/A1 **Prior** (cape), Sp.
63/P1 **Priozersk,** Rus.
86/C2 **Pripet** (marshes), Bela., Ukr.
82/E4 **Priština,** Yugo.
64/G2 **Pritzwalk,** Ger.
72/F4 **Privas,** Fr.
87/H2 **Privolzhskiy,** Rus.
87/K1 **Priyutovo,** Rus.
82/E4 **Prizren,** Yugo.
82/C3 **Prnjavor,** Bosn.
110/D5 **Probolinggo,** Indo.
162/D3 **Proctor** (lake), Tx,US
106/C5 **Proddatūr,** India
147/M7 **Profesor Rafael Ramírez,** Mex.
69/D3 **Profondeville,** Belg.
168/F6 **Pro Football Hall of Fame,** Oh,US
148/D1 **Progreso,** Mex.
149/F4 **Progreso,** Pan.
143/T12 **Progreso,** Uru.
147/K6 **Progreso de Obregon,** Mex.
97/K2 **Progress,** Rus.
79/E3 **Progresso,** It.
87/H4 **Prokhladnyy,** Rus.
102/E1 **Prokop'yevsk,** Rus.
82/E4 **Prokuplje,** Yugo.
104/B5 **Prome,** Burma
166/C1 **Promised Land** (lake), Pa,US
141/B2 **Promissão,** Braz.
141/B2 **Promissão** (res.), Braz.
140/C3 **Propriá,** Braz.
65/J2 **Prosna** (riv.), Pol.
117/M8 **Prospect,** Austl.
168/B2 **Prospect,** Ct,US
151/L3 **Prospector** (mtn.), Yk,Can
112/D3 **Prosperidad,** Phil.
65/J4 **Prostějov,** Czh.
65/L3 **Prószowice,** Pol.
83/H4 **Provadiya,** Bul.
73/G5 **Provence** (mts.), Fr.
72/F5 **Provence** (reg.), Fr.
73/G4 **Provence-Alpes-Côte d'Azur** (reg.), Fr.
168/C2 **Providence** (cap.), RI,US
168/C2 **Providence** (co.), RI,US
136/F6 **Providência** (mts.), Braz.
149/F3 **Providencia** (isl.), Col.
150/C2 **Providenciales** (isl.), Trks.
72/E2 **Provins,** Fr.
158/E2 **Provo,** Ut,US
75/T13 **Provoação,** Azor.,Port.
156/F2 **Provost,** Ab,Can
82/C4 **Prozor,** Bosn.
141/B3 **Prudentópolis,** Braz.
57/G2 **Prudhoe,** Eng,UK
151/J1 **Prudhoe** (bay), Ak,US
65/J3 **Prudnik,** Pol.
69/F3 **Prüm** (riv.), Ger.
65/K1 **Pruszcz Gdański,** Pol.
65/L2 **Pruszków,** Pol.
83/J2 **Prut** (riv.), Eur.
113/F **Prydz** (bay), Ant.
162/E2 **Pryor** (cr.), Ok,US
65/L2 **Przasnysz,** Pol.
65/H3 **Przemków,** Pol.
65/M4 **Przemyśl,** Pol.
65/M4 **Przemyśl** (prov.), Pol.
65/M3 **Przeworsk,** Pol.
102/C3 **Przheval'sk,** Kyr.
84/C5 **Przylądek Rozewie** (cape), Pol.
65/L3 **Przysucha,** Pol.
81/J3 **Psará** (isl.), Gre.
84/F4 **Pskov** (lake), Est., Rus.
84/F4 **Pskov,** Rus.
63/N3 **Pskov Obl.,** Rus.
71/H2 **Pšovka** (riv.), Czh.
65/K4 **Pszczyna,** Pol.
63/M5 **Ptich'** (riv.), Bela.
81/G2 **Ptolemaís,** Gre.
82/B2 **Ptuj,** Slov.
109/C2 **Pua,** Thai.
104/E3 **Pu'an,** China
105/F4 **Pubei,** China
144/C3 **Pucallpa,** Peru
144/B1 **Pucará,** Ecu.
165/G7 **Puce,** On,Can
103/B4 **Pucheng,** China
71/E6 **Puchheim,** Ger.
101/D4 **Puch'on,** SKor.
142/Q9 **Puchuncaví,** Chile
83/G3 **Pucioasa,** Rom.
65/K1 **Puck,** Pol.
59/G3 **Puckeridge,** Eng,UK
142/C3 **Pucón,** Chile
148/D2 **Pucté,** Mex.
61/H2 **Pudasjärvi,** Fin.
58/D5 **Puddletown,** Eng,UK
57/G4 **Pudsey,** Eng,UK
104/D3 **Pudu** (riv.), China
108/G3 **Pudukkottai,** India
147/F5 **Puebla,** Mex.
147/F5 **Puebla** (state), Mex.
74/A1 **Puebla del Caramiñal,** Sp.
147/L7 **Puebla de Zaragoza,** Mex.
138/C2 **Pueblito,** Col.
147/L8 **Pueblo** (state), Mex.
159/F3 **Pueblo,** Co,US
148/E3 **Pueblo Nuevo,** Nic.
148/D3 **Pueblo Nuevo Tiquisate,** Guat.
164/G8 **Puente** (hills), Ca,US
142/C2 **Puente Alto,** Chile
74/A1 **Puenteareas,** Sp.
74/A1 **Puente Caldelas,** Sp.
74/A1 **Puente-Ceso,** Sp.
147/K8 **Puente de Ixtla,** Mex.
142/C2 **Puente del Inca,** Arg.
74/A1 **Puentedeume,** Sp.
74/C4 **Puente-Genil,** Sp.
144/B3 **Puente Piedra,** Peru
74/B1 **Puentes de García Rodríguez,** Sp.
154/R10 **Pueo** (pt.), Hi,US
104/D4 **Pu'er,** China
158/E4 **Puerco** (riv.), Az, NM,US
158/F4 **Puerco** (riv.), NM,US
142/B5 **Puerto Aisén,** Chile
149/F4 **Puerto Armuelles,** Pan.
138/B4 **Puerto Asís,** Col.
139/E3 **Puerto Ayacucho,** Ven.
148/D3 **Puerto Barrios,** Guat.
138/C3 **Puerto Berrío,** Col.
138/D2 **Puerto Cabello,** Ven.
138/D2 **Puerto Cumarebo,** Ven.
146/B2 **Puerto de La Libertad,** Mex.
74/A1 **Puerto del Son,** Sp.
135/F2 **Puerto Iguazú,** Arg.
139/E2 **Puerto La Cruz,** Ven.
74/C3 **Puertollano,** Sp.
74/E4 **Puerto Lumbreras,** Sp.
142/D4 **Puerto Madryn,** Arg.
144/D4 **Puerto Maldonado,** Peru
142/B4 **Puerto Montt,** Chile
143/J7 **Puerto Natales,** Chile
149/G1 **Puerto Padre,** Cuba
146/B2 **Puerto Peñasco,** Mex.
150/D3 **Puerto Plata,** DRep.
112/B3 **Puerto Princesa,** Phil.
142/B4 **Puerto Quellón,** Chile
74/B4 **Puerto Real,** Sp.
150/E3 **Puerto Rico** (commonwealth), US
50/F5 **Puerto Rico** (isl.), US
136/G7 **Puerto Suárez,** Bol.
144/B3 **Puerto Supe,** Peru
138/B4 **Puerto Tejada,** Col.
146/D4 **Puerto Vallarta,** Mex.
142/B4 **Puerto Varas,** Chile
142/C5 **Pueyrredón** (lake), Arg.
56/D5 **Puffin** (isl.), Wal,UK
87/J1 **Pugachev,** Rus.
130/B4 **Puge,** Tanz.
165/C2 **Puget** (sound), Wa,US
80/E2 **Puglia** (reg.), It.
72/E5 **Puigmal** (mtn.), Fr.
75/G1 **Puigsacalm** (mtn.), Sp.
104/D2 **Pujiang,** China
138/B5 **Pujilí,** Ecu.
101/D2 **Pujŏn** (lake), NKor.
110/C5 **Pujut** (cape), Indo.
101/F6 **Puk'ansan** (mtn.), SKor.
101/D4 **Puk'an-san Nat'l Park,** SKor.
121/J6 **Pukapuka** (isl.), CookIs.
121/M6 **Puka Puka** (atoll), FrPol.
121/M6 **Pukarua** (isl.), FrPol.
160/C1 **Pukaskwa Nat'l Park,** On,Can
101/E2 **Pukdae** (riv.), NKor.
101/D4 **Pukhan** (riv.), NKor., SKor.
101/E2 **Pukp'ot'ae-san** (mtn.), NKor.
79/G3 **Pula,** Cro.
136/E8 **Pulacayo,** Bol.
101/A3 **Pulandian** (bay), China
111/F1 **Pulanduta** (pt.), Phil.
112/D3 **Pulangi** (riv.), Phil.
120/D4 **Pulap** (atoll), Micr.
163/G3 **Pulaski,** Tn,US
160/D4 **Pulaski,** Va,US
65/L3 **Puławy,** Pol.
59/F5 **Pulborough,** Eng,UK
101/E5 **Pulguk-sa,** SKor.
66/D7 **Pulheim,** Ger.
111/G3 **Pulisan** (cape), Indo.
108/F4 **Puliyangudi,** India
77/H1 **Pullach im Isartal,** Ger.
156/D4 **Pullman,** Wa,US
76/C5 **Pully,** Swi.
112/C1 **Pulog** (mtn.), Phil.
65/G3 **Pulsnitz** (riv.), Ger.
65/L2 **Pułtusk,** Pol.
120/D4 **Puluwat** (atoll), Micr.
130/B4 **Puma,** Tanz.
58/C2 **Pumpsaint,** Wal,UK
107/F2 **Pumu** (pass), China
144/A1 **Puná** (isl.), Ecu.
121/X15 **Punaauia,** FrPol.
108/F4 **Punalūr,** India
136/E7 **Punata,** Bol.
108/C1 **Pūnch,** India
108/C1 **Punch** (riv.), India
131/C4 **Punda Marie-Ruskamp,** SAfr.
110/B3 **Punggai** (cape), Malay.
131/D3 **Púngoè** (riv.), Moz.
131/D3 **Pungwe** (falls), Zim.
126/E1 **Punia,** Zaire
108/C2 **Punjab** (state), India
108/B2 **Punjab** (plains), Pak.
108/B2 **Punjab** (prov.), Pak.
108/G4 **Punkudutivu** (isl.), SrL.
144/D4 **Puno,** Peru
143/K8 **Punta Arenas,** Chile
138/D2 **Punta Cardón,** Ven.
77/E5 **Punta d'Arbola** (Ofenhorn) (peak), It.
149/F4 **Punta Gorda** (bay), Nic.
163/H5 **Punta Gorda,** Fl,US
149/E4 **Puntarenas,** CR
74/B4 **Punta Umbría,** Sp.
154/S10 **Puolo** (pt.), Hi,US
144/D4 **Pupuya** (peak), Bol.
103/C5 **Puqi,** China
144/C4 **Puquio,** Peru
88/H3 **Pur** (riv.), Rus.
138/B4 **Puracé** (vol.), Col.
138/B4 **Puracé Nat'l Park,** Col.
58/D5 **Purbeck, Isle of** (pen.), Eng,UK
159/H4 **Purcell,** Ok,US
138/D5 **Puré** (riv.), Col.
142/B3 **Purén,** Chile
159/G3 **Purgatoire** (riv.), Co,US
106/D3 **Purī,** India
138/C4 **Purificación,** Col.
63/L2 **Purikari** (pt.), Est.
53/N8 **Purley,** Eng,UK
66/B3 **Purmerend,** Neth.
106/C4 **Pūrna,** India
106/C3 **Pūrna** (riv.), India
135/B5 **Purranque,** Chile
59/E3 **Purton,** Eng,UK
147/E4 **Puruándiro de Calderón,** Mex.
138/D5 **Puruê** (riv.), Braz.
139/F3 **Puruni** (riv.), Guy.
134/C3 **Purus** (riv.), Braz.
136/F4 **Purús** (riv.), Braz.
83/G4 **Pŭrvomay,** Bul.
110/C5 **Purwokerto,** Indo.
106/C4 **Pusad,** India
101/E5 **Pusan,** SKor.
101/E5 **Pusan-Jikhalsi** (prov.), SKor.

110/A2 **Pusat Gayo** (mts.), Indo.
63/P2 **Pushkin**, Rus.
82/E2 **Püspökladány**, Hun.
130/A5 **Puta**, Zam.
142/C2 **Putaendo**, Chile
165/L9 **Putah** (cr.), Ca,US
110/D4 **Puting** (cape), Indo.
148/B2 **Putla**, Mex.
168/C2 **Putnam**, Ct,US
138/C4 **Putomayo** (inten.), Col.
142/B4 **Putomayo** (riv.), Col.
88/K3 **Putorana** (mts.), Rus.
142/C4 **Putrachoique** (peak), Arg.
108/G4 **Puttalam**, SrL.
108/G4 **Puttalam** (dist.), SrL.
68/D1 **Putte**, Belg.
66/C4 **Putten**, Neth.
66/B5 **Putten** (isl.), Neth.
71/E3 **Puttlach** (riv.), Ger.
69/F5 **Püttlingen**, Ger.
128/C5 **Putu** (range), Libr.
136/D4 **Putumayo** (riv.), SAm.
110/D3 **Putussibau**, Indo.
154/T10 **Puu Kukui** (peak), Hi,US
63/M1 **Puula** (lake), Fin.
154/V12 **Puu o Mahuka Heiau Saint Mon.**, Hi,US
68/D1 **Puurs**, Belg.
103/B3 **Pu Xian**, China
165/C3 **Puyallup**, Wa,US
165/C3 **Puyallup** (riv.), Wa,US
165/C3 **Puyallup Ind. Res.**, Wa,US
103/C4 **Puyang**, China
72/E4 **Puy de Barbier** (peak), Fr.
72/E4 **Puy de Sancy** (peak), Fr.
142/B4 **Puyehué** (lake), Chile
142/B4 **Puyehué** (vol.), Chile
142/B4 **Puyehué Nat'l Park**, Chile
72/D5 **Puymorens, Col de** (pass), Fr.
138/B5 **Puyo**, Ecu.
75/E3 **Puzal**, Sp.
130/C4 **Pwani** (prov.), Tanz.
130/A5 **Pweto**, Zaire
56/D6 **Pwllheli**, Wal,UK
104/B5 **Pyamalaw** (riv.), Burma
95/K1 **Pyandzh** (Panj) (riv.), Afg., Taj.
84/F2 **Pyaozero** (lake), Rus.
107/G4 **Pyapon**, Burma
88/J2 **Pyasina** (riv.), Rus.
87/G3 **Pyatigorsk**, Rus.
72/F4 **Pyfara** (mtn.), Fr.
61/H3 **Pyhä-Häkin Nat'l Park**, Fin.
61/H3 **Pyhäjärvi**, Fin.
63/K1 **Pyhäjärvi** (lake), Fin.
63/M1 **Pyhäjärvi** (lake), Fin.
61/H2 **Pyhätunturi** (peak), Fin.
63/M1 **Pyhtää**, Fin.
104/C5 **Pyinmana**, Burma
58/C3 **Pyle**, Wal,UK
168/G4 **Pymatuning** (res.), Oh,US
101/C2 **P'yongan-Bukto** (prov.), NKor.
101/C3 **P'yŏngan-Namdo** (prov.), NKor.
101/D4 **Pyŏngt'aek**, SKor.
101/C3 **P'yŏngyang** (cap.), NKor.
101/C3 **P'yŏngyang-Si**, NKor.
101/D5 **Pyŏnsanbando Nat'l Park**, SKor.
151/M4 **Pyramid** (mtn.), BC,Can
164/B1 **Pyramid** (lake), Ca,US
158/C3 **Pyramid** (lake), Nv,US
75/E1 **Pyrenees** (range), Eur.
72/C5 **Pyrénées Occidentales Nat'l Park**, Fr.
65/H2 **Pyrzyce**, Pol.
85/Q4 **Pyshma** (riv.), Rus.
104/C5 **Pyu**, Burma

Q

91/E4 **Qā'al Jafr** (salt pan), Jor.
91/D3 **Qabātiyah**, WBnk.
124/H1 **Qābis**, Tun.
108/A2 **Qādirpur Rān**, Pak.
93/H2 **Qā'emshahr**, Iran
81/G1 **Qafa e Malit** (pass), Alb.
124/G1 **Qafşah**, Tun.
97/J2 **Qagan** (lake), China
103/C2 **Qahar Youyi Qianqi**, China
96/C4 **Qaidam** (basin), China
91/F7 **Qalansuwa**, Isr.
93/F2 **Qal'at Dizah**, Iraq
93/F4 **Qal'at Sukkar**, Iraq
91/B4 **Qallīn**, Egypt
91/D3 **Qalqīlyah**, WBnk.
91/B4 **Qalyūb**, Egypt
94/F5 **Qamar, Ghubbat al** (bay), Yem.
90/J6 **Qamdo**, China
124/K1 **Qamīnis**, Libya
91/G7 **Qanah, Wādī** (dry riv.), WBnk.
95/J2 **Qandahār**, Afg.
93/F2 **Qarāmqū** (riv.), Iran
123/W17 **Qar'at al Ashkal** (lake), Tun.
125/Q6 **Qardho**, Som.
93/G3 **Qareh Chāy** (riv.), Iran
93/F2 **Qareh Sū** (riv.), Iran
102/F4 **Qarqan** (riv.), China
81/G2 **Qarrit, Qaf'e** (pass), Alb.
80/B4 **Qarţājannah** (ruins), Tun.
127/B2 **Qārūn, Birkat** (lake), Egypt
93/F3 **Qaşr-e-Shīrīn**, Iran
127/A3 **Qaşr Farāfirah**, Egypt
91/E3 **Qaţanā**, Syria
94/F3 **Qatar**
127/A2 **Qattara** (depr.), Egypt
91/E2 **Qaţţīnah** (lake), Syria
106/A2 **Qāzi Ahmad**, Pak.
93/G2 **Qazvīn**, Iran
81/F2 **Qendrevica** (peak), Alb.
93/H5 **Qeshm** (isl.), Iran
94/E1 **Qezel** (riv.), Iran
93/F2 **Qezel Owzan** (riv.), Iran
107/J2 **Qi** (riv.), China
103/D4 **Qian** (can.), China
101/B2 **Qian** (mts.), China
101/B2 **Qian** (peak), China
103/D5 **Qian** (riv.), China
105/F2 **Qian** (riv.), China
97/J3 **Qian'an**, China
105/G2 **Qianjiang**, China
103/D5 **Qianqiu Guan** (pass), China
103/E2 **Qian Shan** (peak), China
97/H3 **Qianxi**, China
104/D3 **Qiaojia**, China
97/J5 **Qidong**, China
102/E4 **Qiemo**, China
103/B5 **Qifeng Guan** (pass), China
103/D3 **Qihe**, China
108/C1 **Qila Dīdār Singh**, Pak.
96/D4 **Qilian** (mts.), China
96/D4 **Qilian** (peak), China
91/G8 **Qilţ, Wādī** (dry riv.), WBnk.
102/F4 **Qimantag** (mts.), China
103/D5 **Qimen**, China
103/B4 **Qin** (mts.), China
103/C4 **Qin** (riv.), China
127/C3 **Qinā**, Egypt
127/C3 **Qinā** (gov.), Egypt
127/C3 **Qinā, Wādī** (dry riv.), Egypt
105/F2 **Qing** (riv.), China
97/K2 **Qing'an**, China
103/E3 **Qingdao**, China
103/C4 **Qingfeng**, China
97/K2 **Qinggang**, China
96/D4 **Qinghai** (lake), China
96/D4 **Qinghai** (mts.), China
104/B1 **Qinghai** (prov.), China
103/C3 **Qinghe**, China
105/G2 **Qingjiang**, China
103/D2 **Qinglong**, China
103/E5 **Qingpu**, China
104/D2 **Qingshen**, China
105/F3 **Qingshui** (riv.), China
103/B3 **Qingshuihe**, China
104/C3 **Qingshuilang** (mts.), China
103/D5 **Qingyang**, China
105/G4 **Qingyuan** (mts.), China
103/D3 **Qingyun**, China
97/H4 **Qingzhou**, China
103/D3 **Qinhuangdao**, China
103/C4 **Qinshui**, China
103/C4 **Qinyang**, China
103/C3 **Qinyuan**, China
105/F4 **Qinzhou**, China
107/K4 **Qionghai**, China
104/D2 **Qionglai**, China
104/D2 **Qionglai** (mts.), China
107/K4 **Qiongshan**, China
109/E2 **Qiongzhong**, China
104/E1 **Qipan** (pass), China
97/J2 **Qiqihar**, China
96/B3 **Qiquanhu**, China
102/D4 **Qira**, China
91/D3 **Qiryat Ata**, Isr.
91/D3 **Qiryat Bialik**, Isr.
91/D4 **Qiryat Gat**, Isr.
91/F8 **Qiryat Mal'akhi**, Isr.
91/D3 **Qiryat Shemona**, Isr.
91/D3 **Qiryat Yam**, Isr.
96/B3 **Qitai**, China
97/L2 **Qitaihe**, China
105/G3 **Qitian** (mtn.), China
103/E3 **Qixia**, China
103/C4 **Qi Xian**, China
104/E3 **Qixing** (pass), China
97/L2 **Qixing** (riv.), China
93/G3 **Qom**, Iran
93/G3 **Qom** (riv.), Iran
106/E2 **Qomolangma** (Everest) (peak), China
95/J1 **Qondūz** (riv.), Afg.
107/F2 **Qonggyai**, China
105/E2 **Qu** (riv.), China
105/H2 **Qu** (riv.), China
168/B1 **Quabbin** (res.), Ma,US
59/F3 **Quainton**, Eng,UK
67/E3 **Quakenbrück**, Ger.
166/C3 **Quakertown**, Pa,US
96/H5 **Quan** (riv.), China
162/D3 **Quanah**, Tx,US
103/B4 **Quanbao Shan** (mtn.), China
109/E3 **Quang Ngai**, Viet.
109/D2 **Quang Trach**, Viet.
109/D2 **Quang Tri**, Viet.
103/D4 **Quanjiao**, China
58/C4 **Quantocks** (hills), Eng,UK
105/F3 **Quanzhou**, China
105/H3 **Quanzhou**, China
157/G3 **Qu'Appelle** (riv.), Mb, Sk,Can
157/H3 **Qu'Appelle**, Sk,Can
157/G3 **Qu'Appelle** (dam), Sk,Can
153/K2 **Quaqtaq**, Qu,Can
68/C3 **Quaregnon**, Belg.
110/E4 **Quarles** (mts.), Indo.
79/D5 **Quarrata**, It.
80/A3 **Quartu Sant'Elena**, It.
164/B1 **Quartz Hill**, Ca,US
77/G4 **Quattervals** (peak), Swi.
123/W17 **Qubāllāt**, Tun.
93/J2 **Qūchān**, Iran
119/D2 **Queanbeyan**, Austl.
153/J3 **Québec** (prov.), Can.
161/G2 **Québec** (cap.), Qu,Can
141/J7 **Quebra-Cangalha** (mts.), Braz.
147/M8 **Quecholac**, Mex.
142/B4 **Quedal** (pt.), Chile
58/D3 **Quedgeley**, Eng,UK
166/C5 **Queen Annes** (co.), Md,US
152/C3 **Queen Charlotte** (isls.), BC,Can
152/C3 **Queen Charlotte** (sound), BC,Can
156/B3 **Queen Charlotte** (str.), BC,Can
162/E3 **Queen City**, Tx,US
153/R7 **Queen Elizabeth** (isls.), NW,Can
113/G **Queen Mary** (coast), Ant.
53/M7 **Queen Mary** (res.), Eng,UK
164/F8 **Queen Mary**, Ca,US
113/P **Queen Maud** (mts.), Ant.
152/F2 **Queen Maud** (gulf), NW,Can
113/Z **Queen Maud Land** (reg.), Ant.
114/D2 **Queens** (chan.), Austl.
153/S7 **Queens** (chan.), NW,Can
167/E2 **Queens** (co.), NY,US
56/E1 **Queensberry** (mtn.), Sc,UK
57/G4 **Queensbury**, Eng,UK
57/E5 **Queensferry**, Wal,UK
118/B3 **Queensland** (state), Austl.
161/R9 **Queenston**, On,Can
115/Q12 **Queenstown**, NZ
132/D3 **Queenstown**, SAfr.
116/D4 **Queen Victoria Spring Nature Rsv.**, Austl.
71/A4 **Queich** (riv.), Ger.
142/B4 **Queilén**, Chile
137/H4 **Queimada**, Braz.
140/C3 **Queimadas**, Braz.
126/G4 **Quelimane**, Moz.
74/A3 **Queluz**, Port.
149/H1 **Quemado, Punta del** (pt.), Cuba
59/E3 **Quenington**, Eng,UK
142/F3 **Quequén**, Arg.
142/F3 **Quequén Grande** (riv.), Arg.
144/A2 **Querecotillo**, Peru
147/E4 **Querétaro**, Mex.
147/F4 **Querétaro** (state), Mex.
149/E4 **Quesada**, CR
74/D4 **Quesada**, Sp.
103/C4 **Queshan**, China
156/C2 **Quesnel**, BC,Can
156/C2 **Quesnel** (lake), BC,Can
109/E3 **Que Son**, Viet.
159/F3 **Questa**, NM,US
76/B3 **Questembert**, Fr.
95/J2 **Quetta**, Pak.
142/B5 **Queulat Nat'l Park**, Chile
136/C4 **Quevedo**, Ecu.
138/B5 **Quevedo** (riv.), Ecu.
148/D3 **Quezaltenango**, Guat.
113/D3 **Quezon**, Phil.
112/D4 **Quezon**, Phil.
112/C2 **Quezon City**, Phil.
112/C2 **Quezon Nat'l Park**, Phil.
103/D4 **Qufu**, China
126/B3 **Quibala**, Ang.
138/B3 **Quibdó**, Col.
72/B3 **Quiberon** (bay), Fr.
138/D2 **Quíbor**, Ven.
126/B2 **Quiçama Nat'l Park**, Ang.
67/G1 **Quickborn**, Ger.
69/G5 **Quierschied**, Ger.
79/D3 **Quiesa**, It.
158/D4 **Quijotoa**, Az,US
142/B4 **Quilán** (cape), Chile
142/Q9 **Quilicura**, Chile
157/G2 **Quill** (lakes), Sk,Can
144/C4 **Quillabamba**, Peru
136/E7 **Quillacollo**, Bol.
142/B4 **Quillagua** (pt.), Chile
142/C3 **Quilleco**, Chile
142/C2 **Quillota**, Chile
108/F4 **Quilon**, India
142/C2 **Quilpué**, Chile
135/D2 **Quimilí**, Arg.
72/A3 **Quimper**, Fr.
163/G4 **Quincy**, Fl,US
160/B4 **Quincy**, Il,US
168/C1 **Quincy**, Ma,US
156/D4 **Quincy**, Wa,US
53/T10 **Quincy-sous-Sénart**, Fr.
138/C3 **Quindío** (dept.), Col.
168/C2 **Quinebaug** (riv.), Ct,US
109/E3 **Qui Nhon**, Viet.
158/C2 **Quinn** (riv.), Nv,US
168/B3 **Quinnipac** (riv.), Ct,US
168/C1 **Quinsigamond** (res.), Ma,US
74/D3 **Quintanar de la Orden**, Sp.
148/D2 **Quintana Roo** (state), Mex.
142/Q9 **Quintero**, Chile
142/D2 **Quinto** (riv.), Arg.
130/D5 **Quionga**, Moz.
140/C3 **Quipapá**, Braz.
142/B3 **Quirihue**, Chile
130/D5 **Quirimba** (arch.), Moz.
141/B1 **Quirinópolis**, Braz.
139/F2 **Quiriquire**, Ven.
144/B3 **Quiruvilca**, Peru
161/H2 **Quispamsis**, NB,Can
131/D5 **Quissico**, Moz.
135/D2 **Quitilipi**, Arg.
163/H4 **Quitman**, Ga,US
163/F3 **Quitman**, Ms,US
162/E3 **Quitman**, Tx,US
138/B5 **Quito** (cap.), Ecu.
140/C2 **Quixadá**, Braz.
140/C2 **Quixeramobim**, Braz.
105/G3 **Qujiang**, China
104/D3 **Qujing**, China
96/C4 **Qumar** (riv.), China
152/G2 **Quoich** (riv.), NW,Can
54/A2 **Quoich, Loch** (lake), Sc,UK
56/C3 **Quoile** (riv.), NI,UK
132/B4 **Quoin** (pt.), SAfr.
91/E2 **Qurnat as Sawdā'** (mtn.), Leb.
127/C3 **Qūş**, Egypt
107/F2 **Qusum**, China
103/B4 **Quwo**, China
96/F4 **Quwu** (mts.), China
103/C3 **Quyang**, China
109/C1 **Quynh Nhai**, Viet.
103/C3 **Quzhou**, China
105/H2 **Quzhou**, China
82/D5 **Qyteti Stalin**, Alb.

R

73/L3 **Raab** (riv.), Aus.
61/H2 **Raahe**, Fin.
66/D4 **Raalte**, Neth.
66/B5 **Raamsdonk**, Neth.
63/T9 **Rååan** (riv.), Swe.
91/F7 **Ra'anana**, Isr.
153/S7 **Raanes** (pen.), NW,Can
130/D3 **Raas Jumbo**, Som.
82/B3 **Rab**, Cro.
82/B3 **Rab** (isl.), Cro.
82/C2 **Rába** (riv.), Hun.
80/D5 **Rabat**, Malta
123/L13 **Rabat** (cap.), Mor.
120/E5 **Rabaul**, PNG
79/E4 **Rabbi** (riv.), It.
118/B3 **RAbbot** (peak), Austl.
148/D3 **Rabinal**, Guat.
77/F4 **Rabiusa** (riv.), Swi.
65/K4 **Rabka**, Pol.
106/C4 **Rabkavi**, India
161/S8 **Raby** (pt.), On,Can
78/A3 **Racconigi**, It.
163/F4 **Raccoon** (pt.), La,US
168/G6 **Raccoon** (cr.), Pa,US
168/G6 **Raccoon Creek Saint Pk.**, Pa,US
153/L4 **Race** (cape), Nf,Can
109/D4 **Rach Gia**, Viet.
109/D4 **Rach Gia** (bay), Viet.
65/K3 **Racibórz**, Pol.
165/Q14 **Racine**, Wi,US
165/P14 **Racine** (co.), Wi,US
76/C3 **Racine, Mont** (peak), Swi.
82/D2 **Ráckeve**, Hun.
83/G2 **Rădăuţi**, Rom.
71/G3 **Radbuza** (riv.), Czh.
57/F4 **Radcliffe**, Eng,UK
57/G6 **Radcliffe on Trent**, Eng,UK
71/G3 **Radeč** (peak), Czh.
82/A2 **Radenthein**, Aus.
67/E6 **Radevormwald**, Ger.
160/D4 **Radford**, Va,US
106/B3 **Rādhanpur**, India
156/G2 **Radisson**, Sk,Can
53/N6 **Radlett**, Eng,UK
83/G4 **Radnevo**, Bul.
77/E2 **Radolfzell**, Ger.
65/L3 **Radom**, Pol.
65/L3 **Radom** (prov.), Pol.
82/F4 **Radomir**, Bul.
65/K3 **Radomsko**, Pol.
82/F5 **Radoviš**, Macd.
62/A1 **Radøy** (isl.), Nor.
58/D4 **Radstock**, Eng,UK
63/K4 **Radviliškis**, Lith.
58/C3 **Radyr**, Wal,UK
65/K2 **Radziejów**, Pol.
65/L2 **Radzymin**, Pol.
65/M3 **Radzyń Podlaski**, Pol.
153/H3 **Rae** (isth.), NW,Can
152/E2 **Rae** (riv.), NW,Can
106/D2 **Rāe Bareli**, India
163/J3 **Raeford**, NC,US
69/F2 **Raeren**, Belg.
66/D5 **Raesfeld**, Ger.
116/D4 **Raeside** (lake), Austl.
101/A2 **Raeyang** (riv.), China
135/D3 **Rafaela**, Arg.
91/D4 **Rafaḩ**, Gaza
125/K7 **Rafai**, CAfr.
93/J4 **Rafsanjān**, Iran
156/E5 **Raft** (riv.), Id, Ut,US
125/L6 **Raga**, Sudan
112/D4 **Ragang** (mtn.), Phil.
112/D2 **Ragay** (gulf), Phil.
116/D5 **Ragged** (peak), Austl.
143/J8 **Ragged** (pt.), Chile
56/A1 **Raghtin More** (mtn.), Ire.
58/D3 **Raglan**, Wal,UK
61/E2 **Rago Nat'l Park**, Nor.
53/P8 **Ragstone** (range), Eng,UK
80/D4 **Ragusa**, It.
67/F4 **Rahden**, Ger.
95/K3 **Rahīmyār Khān**, Pak.
130/C2 **Rahole Nat'l Rsv.**, Kenya
167/D2 **Rahway**, NJ,US
121/K6 **Raiatea** (isl.), FrPol.
106/C4 **Raichūr**, India
106/D3 **Raigarh**, India
164/C3 **Railroad Canyon** (res.), Ca,US
158/E3 **Rainbow Bridge Nat'l Mon.**, Ut,US
57/F4 **Rainford**, Eng,UK
53/P7 **Rainham**, Eng,UK
156/C4 **Rainier** (peak), Wa,US
163/G3 **Rainsville**, Al,US
57/G5 **Rainworth**, Eng,UK
157/K3 **Rainy** (lake), Can., US
157/K3 **Rainy** (riv.), Can., US
160/A1 **Rainy River**, On,Can
106/D3 **Raipur**, India
64/F1 **Raisdorf**, Ger.
165/E8 **Raisin** (riv.), Mi,US
61/G3 **Raisio**, Fin.
68/C3 **Raismes**, Fr.
121/L7 **Raivavae** (isl.), FrPol.
108/C2 **Rāiwind**, Pak.
110/A3 **Raja** (pt.), Indo.
106/D4 **Rājahmundry**, India
106/C5 **Rājapalaiyam**, India
110/D3 **Rajang** (riv.), Malay.
95/K3 **Rājanpur**, Pak.
108/F4 **Rājapālaiyam**, India
106/B4 **Rājāpur**, India
106/B2 **Rājasthān** (state), India
106/C3 **Rājgarh**, India
95/L3 **Rājgarh**, India
106/B3 **Rājkot**, India
106/D3 **Rāj-Nāndagaon**, India
108/D2 **Rājpura**, India
106/E3 **Rājshāhi**, Bang.
106/B3 **Rājula**, India
121/J5 **Rakahanga** (atoll), CookIs.
95/K1 **Rakaposhi** (mtn.), Pak.
104/B5 **Rakhine** (state), Burma
95/H3 **Rakhshān** (riv.), Pak.
62/D2 **Rakkestad**, Nor.
131/B4 **Rakops**, Bots.
71/G2 **Rakovnicky Potok** (riv.), Czh.
71/G2 **Rakovník**, Czh.
83/G4 **Rakovski**, Bul.
63/M2 **Rakvere**, Est.
130/B3 **Rakwaro**, Kenya
71/H2 **Rakytka** (riv.), Czh.
163/J3 **Raleigh** (cap.), NC,US
120/F4 **Ralik Chain** (arch.), Mrsh.
156/F3 **Ralston**, Ab,Can
140/A4 **Ramalho** (mts.), Braz.
91/D4 **Rām Allāh**, WBnk.
108/G4 **Rāmanāthapuram**, India
108/G4 **Ramanathaswamy Temple**, India
167/H7 **Ramapo** (mts.), NJ,US
167/J7 **Ramapo** (riv.), NJ, NY,US
106/B4 **Ramas** (cape), India
91/D3 **Ramat Gan**, Isr.
91/F7 **Ramat HaSharon**, Isr.
131/B5 **Ramatlabama**, Bots.
76/C1 **Rambervillers**, Fr.
121/Z17 **Rambi** (isl.), Fiji
68/A6 **Rambouillet**, Fr.
58/B6 **Rame** (pt.), UK
106/E2 **Rāmechhāp**, Nepal
108/G4 **Rāmeshwaram**, India
60/C6 **Ram Head** (pt.), Ire.
93/G4 **Rāmhormoz**, Iran
91/D4 **Ramla**, Isr.
63/T8 **Ramløse**, Den.
91/D5 **Ramm, Jabal** (mtn.), Jor.
131/B4 **Ramokgwebana**, Bots.
91/D4 **Ramon, Har** (mtn.), Isr.
60/C2 **Ramor, Lough** (lake), Ire.
147/E3 **Ramos Arizpe**, Mex.
131/B5 **Ramotswa**, Bots.
104/B5 **Ramree** (isl.), Burma
94/F1 **Ramsar** (Sakht Sar), Iran
57/F4 **Ramsbottom**, Eng,UK
59/E4 **Ramsbury**, Eng,UK
160/D2 **Ramsey** (lake), On,Can
59/F2 **Ramsey**, Eng,UK
56/D3 **Ramsey**, IM,UK
56/D3 **Ramsey** (bay), IM,UK
58/A3 **Ramsey** (isl.), Wal,UK
167/J7 **Ramsey**, NJ,US
59/H4 **Ramsgate**, Eng,UK
69/G5 **Ramstein-Miesenbach**, Ger.
120/D5 **Ramu** (riv.), PNG
106/E3 **Rānāghāt**, India
142/C2 **Rancagua**, Chile
72/B2 **Rance** (riv.), Fr.
72/E5 **Rance** (riv.), Fr.
141/B2 **Rancharia**, Braz.
138/C2 **Ranchería** (riv.), Col.
156/G4 **Ranchester**, Wy,US
106/E3 **Rānchī**, India
165/M9 **Rancho Cordova**, Ca,US
164/C2 **Rancho Cucamonga** (Cucamonga), Ca,US
164/B3 **Rancho Palos Verdes**, Ca,US
142/B4 **Ranco** (lake), Chile
125/P5 **Randa**, Djib.
62/A2 **Randaberg**, Nor.
166/B5 **Randallstown**, Md,US
56/B2 **Randalstown**, NI,UK
80/D4 **Randazzo**, It.
132/P13 **Randburg**, SAfr.
77/E2 **Randen, Hoher** (peak), Ger.
62/D3 **Randers**, Den.
168/C1 **Randolph**, Ma,US
166/D2 **Randolph**, NJ,US
162/D4 **Randolph A.F.B.**, Tx,US
65/H2 **Randow** (riv.), Ger.
62/D1 **Randsfjorden** (lake), Nor.
118/H8 **Randwick**, Austl.
109/C2 **Rang** (peak), Thai.
104/B4 **Rāngāmāti**, Bang.
108/G3 **Ranganathaswamy Temple**, India
111/E4 **Rangasa** (cape), Indo.
158/E2 **Rangely**, Co,US
162/D3 **Ranger**, Tx,US
115/R11 **Rangiora**, NZ
121/L6 **Rangiroa** (atoll), FrPol.
104/C5 **Rangoon** (div.), Burma
104/C5 **Rangoon** (Yangon) (cap.), Burma
106/E2 **Rangpur**, Bang.
106/C5 **Rānībennur**, India
117/H2 **Ranken** (riv.), Austl.
162/C4 **Rankin**, Tx,US
77/F3 **Rankweil**, Aus.
106/A3 **Rann of Kutch** (swamp), India,Pak.
54/B3 **Rannoch, Loch** (lake), Sc,UK
109/B4 **Ranong**, Thai.
69/G3 **Ransbach-Baumbach**, Ger.
161/S9 **Ransomville**, NY,US
68/D1 **Ranst**, Belg.
111/F4 **Rantekombola** (peak), Indo.
160/B3 **Rantoul**, Il,US
109/D2 **Rao Co** (peak), Laos
76/C1 **Raon-L'Etape**, Fr.
120/H7 **Raoul** (isl.), NZ
103/C3 **Raoyang**, China
121/L7 **Rapa** (isl.), FrPol.
78/C4 **Rapallo**, It.
142/Q10 **Rapel** (lake), Chile
142/B5 **Raper** (cape), Chile
157/H4 **Rapid City**, SD,US
160/E4 **Rappahannock** (riv.), Va,US
106/D2 **Rapti** (riv.), India
167/D3 **Raritan** (bay), NY, NJ,US
166/D2 **Raritan** (riv.), NY, NJ,US
166/D2 **Raritan, North Branch** (riv.), NJ,US
166/D2 **Raritan, South Branch** (riv.), NJ,US
121/L6 **Raroia** (atoll), FrPol.
121/J7 **Rarotonga** (isl.), CookIs.
142/E4 **Rasa** (pt.), Arg.
92/E2 **Ra's al 'Ayn**, Syria
125/J7 **Ra's al Unūf**, Libya
123/Q16 **Râs el Ma**, Alg.
123/T16 **Râs el Oued**, Alg.
127/C2 **Ras Gharib**, Egypt
56/B2 **Rasharkin**, NI,UK
91/D3 **Rashayyā**, Leb.
91/B4 **Rashīd** (Rosetta), Egypt
93/G2 **Rasht**, Iran
108/G3 **Rāsipuram**, India
82/E4 **Raška**, Yugo.
152/G2 **Rasmussen** (basin), NW,Can
75/P10 **Raso** (cape), Port.
116/E4 **Rason** (lake), Austl.
87/G1 **Rasskazovo**, Rus.
70/B5 **Rastatt**, Ger.
67/F2 **Rastede**, Ger.
151/B6 **Rat** (isls.), Ak,US
110/B5 **Rata** (cape), Indo.
106/B2 **Ratangarh**, India
109/B3 **Rat Buri**, Thai.
106/C2 **Rāth**, India
157/K5 **Rathbun** (lake), Ia,US
64/G2 **Rathenow**, Ger.
56/B3 **Rathfriland**, NI,UK
56/B1 **Rathlin** (isl.), NI,UK
56/B1 **Rathlin** (sound), NI,UK
120/F4 **Ratik Chain** (arch.), Mrsh.
66/D6 **Ratingen**, Ger.
106/C3 **Ratlām**, India
106/B4 **Ratnāgiri**, India
106/D6 **Ratnapura**, SrL.
159/F3 **Raton**, NM,US
159/H3 **Rattle Snake** (cr.), Ks,US
54/C3 **Rattray**, Sc,UK
62/F1 **Rättvik**, Swe.
64/F2 **Ratzeburg**, Ger.
110/B3 **Raub**, Malay.
142/F3 **Rauch**, Arg.
61/P6 **Raudhúnúpur** (pt.), Ice.
62/D1 **Raufoss**, Nor.
70/D3 **Rauhe Ebrach** (riv.), Ger.
71/E3 **Rauher Kulm** (hill), Ger.
141/D2 **Raul Soares**, Braz.
63/J1 **Rauma**, Fin.
59/F2 **Raunds**, Eng,UK
115/S10 **Raupehu** (vol.), NZ
106/D3 **Raurkela**, India
100/D1 **Rausu**, Japan
80/C4 **Ravanusa**, It.
66/C6 **Ravels**, Belg.
57/E3 **Ravenglass**, Eng,UK
79/F4 **Ravenna**, It.
79/F4 **Ravenna** (prov.), It.
168/F5 **Ravenna**, Oh,US
168/F5 **Ravenna Arsenal** (mil. res.), Oh,US
77/F2 **Ravensburg**, Ger.
57/G5 **Ravenshead**, Eng,UK
160/D4 **Ravenswood**, WV,US
60/D5 **Raven, The** (pt.), Ire.
108/B2 **Rāvi** (riv.), India, Pak.
82/B2 **Ravne na Koroškem**, Slov.
121/H5 **Rawaki** (Phoenix) (atoll), Kiri.
108/B1 **Rāwalpindi**, Pak.
65/L3 **Rawa Mazowiecka**, Pol.
65/J3 **Rawicz**, Pol.
156/G5 **Rawlins**, Wy,US
117/E3 **Rawlinson** (peak), Austl.
57/G5 **Rawmarsh**, Eng,UK
142/D4 **Rawson**, Arg.
57/F4 **Rawtenstall**, Eng,UK
161/K2 **Ray** (cape), Nf,Can
110/D4 **Raya** (peak), Indo.
106/C5 **Rāyadrug**, India
106/D4 **Rāyagada**, India
97/K2 **Raychikhinsk**, Rus.
59/G3 **Rayleigh**, Eng,UK
156/E3 **Raymond**, Ab,Can
162/D5 **Raymondville**, Tx,US
157/G3 **Raymore**, Sk,Can
168/C2 **Raynham**, Ma,US
109/C3 **Rayong**, Thai.
147/E5 **Rayón Nat'l Park**, Mex.
87/H4 **Razdan**, Arm.
83/J3 **Razelm** (lake), Rom.
83/H4 **Razgrad**, Bul.
81/K1 **Razgrad** (reg.), Bul.
83/F5 **Razlog**, Bul.
72/A2 **Raz, Pointe du** (pt.), Fr.
72/C3 **Ré** (isl.), Fr.
58/D2 **Rea** (riv.), Eng,UK
59/F4 **Reading**, Eng,UK
166/C3 **Reading**, Pa,US
144/C3 **Real, Cordillera** (range), Bol., Peru
60/B3 **Rea, Lough** (lake), Ire.
109/C3 **Reang Kesei**, Camb.
121/M6 **Reao** (atoll), FrPol.
116/D4 **Rebecca** (lake), Austl.
141/B3 **Rebouças**, Braz.
100/B1 **Rebun**, Japan
100/B1 **Rebun** (isl.), Japan
79/G6 **Recanati**, It.
78/C4 **Recco**, It.
116/E5 **Recherche** (arch.), Austl.
69/F6 **Réchicourt-le-Château**, Fr.
86/D1 **Rechitsa**, Bela.
140/D3 **Recife**, Braz.
132/D4 **Recife** (cape), SAfr.
67/E4 **Recke**, Ger.
67/E5 **Recklinghausen**, Ger.
64/G2 **Recknitz** (riv.), Ger.
109/B2 **Reclining Buddha** (Shwethalyaung) (ruins), Burma
135/E2 **Reconquista**, Arg.
94/C4 **Red** (sea), Afr., Asia
104/D4 **Red** (riv.), China, Viet.
56/B1 **Red** (bay), NI,UK
159/J5 **Red** (riv.), US
162/D2 **Red** (hills), Ks,US
65/K1 **Reda**, Pol.
167/D3 **Red Bank**, NJ,US
158/B2 **Red Bluff**, Ca,US
159/G4 **Red Bluff** (lake), NM, Tx,US
59/F3 **Redbourn**, Eng,UK
53/P7 **Redbridge** (bor.), Eng,UK
57/G2 **Redcar**, Eng,UK
156/F3 **Redcliff**, Ab,Can
131/C3 **Redcliff**, Zim.
118/F6 **Redcliffe**, Austl.
116/D4 **Redcliffe** (peak), Austl.
159/H2 **Red Cloud**, Ne,US
156/E2 **Red Deer**, Ab,Can
156/F3 **Red Deer** (riv.), Ab,Can
157/H2 **Red Deer** (lake), Mb,Can
157/H2 **Red Deer** (riv.), Mb, Sk,Can
158/B2 **Redding**, Ca,US
168/A3 **Redding**, Ct,US
59/E2 **Redditch**, Eng,UK
57/F1 **Rede** (riv.), Eng,UK
140/A3 **Redenção do Gurguéia**, Braz.
157/J4 **Redfield**, SD,US
165/F7 **Redford**, Mi,US
53/N8 **Redhill**, Eng,UK
154/T10 **Red Hill** (peak), Hi,US
77/G5 **Re di Castello, Monte** (peak), It.
161/K1 **Red Indian** (lake), Nf,Can
69/G6 **Réding**, Fr.
157/K3 **Red Lake**, On,Can
157/K3 **Red Lake** (riv.), Mn,US
166/A5 **Redland**, Md,US
118/F7 **Redland Bay**, Austl.
164/C2 **Redlands**, Ca,US
166/B4 **Red Lion**, Pa,US
156/F4 **Red Lodge**, Mt,US
156/C4 **Redmond**, Or,US
165/C2 **Redmond**, Wa,US
70/D4 **Rednitz** (riv.), Ger.
159/G4 **Red, North Fork** (riv.), Ok, Tx,US
72/B3 **Redon**, Fr.
74/A1 **Redondela**, Sp.
139/F4 **Redondo** (peak), Braz.
74/B3 **Redondo**, Port.
164/B3 **Redondo Beach**, Ca,US
151/H3 **Redoubt** (vol.), Ak,US
157/J3 **Red** (Red R. of the North) (riv.), Mb,Can
157/J3 **Red River of the North** (riv.), US
157/K5 **Red Rock** (lake), Ia,US
117/E5 **Red Rocks** (pt.), Austl.
58/A6 **Redruth**, Eng,UK
159/G4 **Red, Salt Fork** (riv.), Ok, Tx,US
127/D4 **Red Sea** (hills), Sudan
152/D2 **Redstone** (riv.), NW,Can
157/K2 **Red Sucker** (lake), Mb,Can
157/H3 **Redvers**, Sk,Can
129/E4 **Red Volta** (riv.), Burk., Gui.
156/E2 **Redwater**, Ab,Can
158/B2 **Redway**, Ca,US
159/G2 **Red Willow** (cr.), Ne,US
160/A2 **Red Wing**, Mn,US
165/K12 **Redwood City**, Ca,US
157/K4 **Redwood Falls**, Mn,US
158/A2 **Redwood Nat'l Park**, Ca,US
160/C3 **Reed City**, Mi,US
59/H1 **Reedham**, Eng,UK
158/C3 **Reedley**, Ca,US
166/D5 **Reeds** (bay), NJ,US
160/B3 **Reedsburg**, Wi,US
156/B5 **Reedsport**, Or,US
119/B3 **Reedy** (cr.), Austl.
147/J5 **Reef** (pt.), Belz.
120/F6 **Reef** (isls.), Sol.
115/R11 **Reefton**, NZ
60/B2 **Ree, Lough** (lake), Ire.
59/H1 **Reepham**, Eng,UK
66/D5 **Rees**, Ger.
158/C3 **Reese** (riv.), Nv,US
162/C3 **Reese A.F.B.**, Tx,US
66/D3 **Reest** (riv.), Neth.
57/G3 **Reeth**, Eng,UK
66/B4 **Reeuwijk**, Neth.
92/D2 **Refahiye**, Turk.
162/D4 **Refugio**, Tx,US
65/H2 **Rega** (riv.), Pol.
71/G5 **Regen**, Ger.
71/F4 **Regen** (riv.), Ger.
141/E1 **Regência, Pontal de** (pt.), Braz.
140/B2 **Regeneração**, Braz.
71/F4 **Regensburg**, Ger.
77/E3 **Regensdorf**, Swi.
71/F4 **Regenstauf**, Ger.
118/H8 **Regents Park**, Austl.
53/N7 **Regent's Park**, Eng,UK
124/F2 **Reggane**, Alg.
66/D4 **Regge** (riv.), Neth.
80/D3 **Reggio di Calabria**, It.
78/D3 **Reggio nell'Emilia**, It.
78/D3 **Reggio nell'Emilia** (prov.), It.
83/G2 **Reghin**, Rom.
157/G3 **Regina** (cap.), Sk,Can
137/H3 **Régina**, FrG.
158/F3 **Regina**, NM,US
157/G3 **Regina Beach**, Sk,Can
141/C3 **Registro**, Braz.
70/D3 **Regnitz** (riv.), Ger.
74/B3 **Reguengosde Monsaraz**, Port.
71/F2 **Rehau**, Ger.
67/G4 **Rehburg-Loccum**, Ger.
69/F5 **Rehlingen-Siersburg**, Ger.
126/C5 **Rehoboth**, Namb.
168/C2 **Rehoboth**, Ma,US
91/F8 **Rehovot**, Isr.
70/D3 **Reiche Ebrach** (riv.), Ger.
70/B2 **Reichelsheim**, Ger.
70/B3 **Reichelsheim**, Ger.
71/F1 **Reichenbach**, Ger.
69/G2 **Reichshof**, Ger.
156/F3 **Reid** (lake), Sk,Can
163/J2 **Reidsville**, NC,US
53/N8 **Reigate**, Eng,UK
68/D5 **Reims**, Fr.
68/D5 **Reims, Cathédrale de**, Fr.
143/J7 **Reina Adelaida** (arch.), Chile
76/D3 **Reinach**, Swi.
67/H1 **Reinbek**, Ger.
157/J2 **Reindeer** (isl.), Mb,Can
157/H1 **Reindeer** (lake), Mb, Sk,Can
157/H1 **Reindeer** (riv.), Sk,Can
70/B3 **Reinheim**, Ger.
74/C1 **Reinosa**, Sp.
61/G1 **Reisduoddarhal'di** (peak), Nor.
70/B1 **Reiskirchen**, Ger.
71/F5 **Reissingerbach** (riv.), Ger.
166/B5 **Reisterstown**, Md,US
66/D2 **Reitdiep** (riv.), Neth.
75/H4 **Rejaïa** (wilaya), Alg.
156/F5 **Reliance**, Wy,US
123/R16 **Relizane**, Alg.
123/R16 **Relizane** (wilaya), Alg.
67/G1 **Rellingen**, Ger.
69/G2 **Remagen**, Ger.
140/B3 **Remanso**, Braz.
53/S11 **Remarde** (riv.), Fr.

215

Rema – Roun

117/H5 Remarkable (peak), Austl.
110/D5 Rembang, Indo.
123/Q16 Remchi, Alg.
137/H3 Rémire, FrG.
76/C1 Remiremont, Fr.
70/C5 Rems (riv.), Ger.
67/E6 Remscheid, Ger.
103/B5 Ren (riv.), China
142/C2 Renca, Chile
70/A5 Rench (riv.), Ger.
70/B5 Renchen, Ger.
163/F2 Rend (lake), Il,US
64/E1 Rendsburg, Ger.
76/C4 Renens, Swi.
160/E2 Renfrew, On,Can
54/B5 Renfrew, Sc,UK
110/B4 Rengat, Indo.
142/C2 Rengo, Chile
107/K2 Renhua, China
104/E3 Renhuai, China
86/D3 Reni, Ukr.
66/C5 Renkum, Neth.
120/F6 Rennell (isl.), Sol.
72/C2 Rennes, Fr.
70/B5 Renningen, Ger.
79/F3 Reno (riv.), It.
158/C3 Reno, Nv,US
132/C3 Renoster (riv.), SAfr.
132/D2 Renoster (riv.), SAfr.
103/D3 Renqiu, China
160/C3 Rensselaer, In,US
74/E1 Rentería, Sp.
54/B5 Renton, Sc,UK
165/C3 Renton, Wa,US
161/P6 Repentigny, Qu,Can
57/G6 Repton, Eng,UK
156/D3 Republic, Wa,US
159/H2 Republican (riv.), Ks, Ne,US
118/C3 Repulse (bay), Austl.
139/G4 Repununi (riv.), Guy.
144/C2 Requena, Peru
75/E3 Requena, Sp.
142/C2 Requínoa, Chile
140/B2 Reriutuba, Braz.
92/D1 Reşadiye, Turk.
63/S7 Resarö (isl.), Swe.
77/G4 Reschen (Resia), It.
77/G4 Reschensee (Resia) (lake), It.
142/B5 Rescue (pt.), Chile
164/E7 Reseda, Ca,US
82/E5 Resen, Macd.
141/J7 Resende, Braz.
158/E4 Reserve, NM,US
77/G4 Resia, Passo di (pass), It.
77/G4 Resia (Reschensee) (lake), It.
135/E2 Resistencia, Arg.
82/E3 Reşiţa, Rom.
152/G1 Resolute, NW,Can
153/K2 Resolution (isl.), NW,Can
58/C3 Resolven, Wal,UK
141/D1 Resplendor, Braz.
131/D5 Ressano Garcia, Moz.
68/B4 Ressons-sur-Matz, Fr.
161/H2 Restigouche (riv.), NB,Can
157/H3 Reston, Mb,Can
166/A6 Reston, Va,US
165/C2 Restoration (pt.), Wa,US
148/D3 Retalhuleu, Guat.
68/D4 Rethel, Fr.
81/J5 Réthimnon, Gre.
69/E1 Retie, Belg.
82/F3 Retrezap Nat'l Park, Rom.
133/R15 Réunion (dpcy.), Fr.
75/F2 Reus, Sp.
66/C6 Reusel, Neth.
77/E3 Reuss (riv.), Swi.
64/G2 Reuterstadt Stavenhagen, Ger.
70/C6 Reutlingen, Ger.
84/H5 Reutov, Rus.
53/T10 Reveillon (riv.), Fr.
72/D5 Revel, Fr.
156/D3 Revelstoke, BC,Can
147/F4 Reventadero, Mex.
168/C1 Revere, Ma,US
118/H8 Revesby, Austl.
146/B5 Revillagigedo (isls.), Mex.
68/D4 Revin, Fr.
102/B4 Revolyutsii, Pik (peak), Taj.
61/G1 Revsbotn (fjord), Nor.
131/D2 Revúboè (riv.), Moz.
131/D3 Revuè (riv.), Moz.
139/G4 Rewa (riv.), Guy.
106/D3 Rewa, India
106/C2 Rewāri, India
151/J3 Rex (mtn.), Ak,US
156/F5 Rexburg, Id,US
68/B2 Rexpoëde, Fr.
149/G4 Rey (isl.), Pan.
59/H2 Reydon, Eng,UK
158/B3 Reyes (pt.), Ca,US
147/M6 Reyes de Vallarta, Mex.
91/E1 Reyhanlı, Turk.
52/A2 Reykjanestá (cape), Ice.
61/N7 Reykjavík (cap.), Ice.
76/B5 Reyssouze (riv.), Fr.
72/C3 Rezé, Fr.
63/M3 Rēzekne, Lat.
78/D1 Rezzato, It.
77/F5 Rhaetian Alps (mts.), It., Swi.
77/F3 Rhätikon (mts.), Aus., Swi.
58/C2 Rhayader, Wal,UK
67/F5 Rheda-Wiedenbrück, Ger.
66/D5 Rhede, Ger.
66/D5 Rheden, Neth.
59/F2 Rhee (Cam) (riv.), Eng,UK
69/F2 Rheinbach, Ger.
66/D5 Rheinberg, Ger.
67/E4 Rheine, Ger.
77/E2 Rheinfall, Swi.
76/D2 Rheinfelden, Ger.
64/D3 Rhein (Rhine) (riv.), Ger.
77/F5 Rheinwaldhorn (peak), Swi.
124/E2 Rhemiles (well), Alg.
66/C5 Rhenen, Neth.
64/D3 Rhine (riv.), Eur.
67/E5 Rhine-Herne (can.), Ger.
160/B2 Rhinelander, Wi,US
69/F3 Rhineland-Palatinate (state), Ger.
55/H9 Rhinns (pt.), Sc,UK
130/A2 Rhino Camp, Ugan.
73/G2 Rhin (Rhine) (riv.), Fr.
123/R16 Rhiou (riv.), Alg.
69/D3 Rhisnes, Belg.
58/C1 Rhiw (riv.), Wal,UK
78/C1 Rho, It.
168/C2 Rhode (isl.), RI,US
168/C2 Rhode Island (state), US
168/C3 Rhode Island (sound), RI,US
92/A3 Rhodes (isl.), Gre.
83/F4 Rhodope (mts.), Bul.
70/D1 Rhön (mts.), Ger.
58/C3 Rhondda, Wal,UK
72/F4 Rhône (riv.), Fr., Swi.
77/E4 Rhone (glac.), Swi.
72/F4 Rhône-Alpes (reg.), Fr.
76/B3 Rhône au Rhin (can.), Fr.
68/C3 Rhonelle (riv.), Fr.
57/E6 Rhosllanerchrugog, Wal,UK
58/B3 Rhossili, Wal,UK
56/E5 Rhuddlan, Wal,UK
55/H8 Rhum (isl.), Sc,UK
67/H5 Rhume (riv.), Ger.
123/V17 Rhumel (riv.), Alg.
58/C2 Rhyddhywel (mtn.), Wal,UK
58/B2 Rhydowen, Wal,UK
56/E5 Rhyl, Wal,UK
58/C3 Rhymney, Wal,UK
54/D2 Rhynie, Sc,UK
140/A2 Riachão, Braz.
140/A3 Riachão das Neves, Braz.
140/C3 Riachão do Jacuípe, Braz.
140/B4 Riacho de Santana, Braz.
164/C2 Rialto, Ca,US
74/A1 Rianjo, Sp.
110/B3 Riau (isls.), Indo.
74/A1 Ribadavia, Sp.
74/B1 Ribadeo, Sp.
74/C1 Ribadesella, Sp.
133/H8 Riban'i Manamby (mts.), Madg.
57/F4 Ribble (riv.), Eng,UK
57/F4 Ribblesdale (val.), Eng,UK
62/C4 Ribe, Den.
62/C4 Ribe (co.), Den.
141/B3 Ribeira (riv.), Braz.
140/C3 Ribeira do Pombal, Braz.
75/T13 Ribeira Grande, Azor.
122/J9 Ribeira Grande, CpV.
140/D3 Ribeirão, Braz.
141/B2 Ribeirão do Pinha, Braz.
141/C2 Ribeirão Preto, Braz.
140/A2 Ribeiro Gonçalves, Braz.
68/C4 Ribemont, Fr.
80/C4 Ribera, It.
136/E6 Riberalta, Bol.
64/G1 Ribnitz-Damgarten, Ger.
71/H3 Říčany u Prahy, Czh.
79/F5 Riccione, It.
160/E2 Rice (lake), On,Can
160/B2 Rice Lake, Wi,US
152/C2 Richards (isl.), NW,Can
161/G2 Richardson (lakes), Me,US
116/C5 Riche (cape), Austl.
66/C2 Richel (isl.), Neth.
161/P7 Richelieu (riv.), Qu,Can
158/D3 Richfield, Ut,US
56/B3 Richhill, NI,UK
168/E6 Richland (co.), Oh,US
156/D4 Richland, Wa,US
163/H3 Richland Balsam (peak), NC,US
160/B3 Richland Center, Wi,US
162/D4 Richland Creek (res.), Tx,US
119/D2 Richmond, Austl.
161/F2 Richmond, Qu,Can
57/G3 Richmond, Eng,UK
165/K11 Richmond, Ca,US
160/C4 Richmond, In,US
160/C4 Richmond, Ky,US
167/D2 Richmond (co.), NY,US
162/E4 Richmond, Tx,US
160/E4 Richmond (cap.), Va,US
165/C2 Richmond Beach-Innis Arden, Wa,US
168/F4 Richmond Heights, Oh,US
161/R8 Richmond Hill, On,Can
118/G8 Richmond-Raaf, Austl.
167/J9 Richmond Town, NY,US
53/N7 Richmond upon Thames (bor.), Eng,UK
77/E3 Richterswil, Swi.
53/M7 Rickmansworth, Eng,UK
66/B5 Ridderkerk, Neth.
160/E2 Rideau (lake), On,Can
158/C4 Ridgecrest, Ca,US
168/A3 Ridgefield, Ct,US
167/J8 Ridgefield, NJ,US
167/J8 Ridgefield Park, NJ,US
167/D2 Ridgewood, NJ,US
167/K9 Ridgewood, NY,US
57/G2 Riding Mill, Eng,UK
157/H3 Riding Mtn. Nat'l Park, Mb,Can
54/D6 Ridlees Cairn (hill), Eng,UK
166/C4 Ridley (cr.), Pa,US
138/D3 Riecito (riv.), Col., Ven.
71/G6 Ried im Innkreis, Aus.
76/D2 Riedisheim, Fr.
70/C6 Riedlingen, Ger.
69/F5 Riegelsberg, Ger.
77/H2 Riegsee (lake), Ger.
76/D2 Riehen, Swi.
69/E2 Riemst, Belg.
65/G3 Riesa, Ger.
143/J8 Riesco (isl.), Chile
132/D3 Riet (riv.), SAfr.
67/F5 Rietberg, Ger.
80/C1 Rieti, It.
57/G3 Rievaulx, Eng,UK
156/C4 Riffe (lake), Wa,US
158/F3 Rifle, Co,US
61/N6 Rifsnes (pt.), Ice.
130/B2 Rift Valley (prov.), Kenya
63/K3 Riga (gulf), Est., Lat.
63/L3 Riga (Rīga) (cap.), Lat.
156/F5 Rigby, Id,US
95/H2 Rīgestan (reg.), Afg.
156/D4 Riggins, Id,US
77/E3 Rigi (peak), Swi.
54/C5 Rigside, Sc,UK
106/D3 Rihand Sāgar (res.), India
63/L1 Riihimäki, Fin.
113/C Riiser-Larsen (pen.), Ant.
113/Y Riiser-Larsen Ice Shelf, Ant.
61/J2 Riisitunturin Nat'l Park, Fin.
82/B3 Rijeka, Cro.
66/B4 Rijnsburg, Neth.
66/D4 Rijssen, Neth.
66/B4 Rijswijk, Neth.
167/K8 Rikers (isl.), NY,US
121/M7 Rikitea, FrPol.
100/C4 Rikuchū-Kaigan Nat'l Park, Japan
100/B4 Rikuzentakata, Japan
83/F4 Rila (mts.), Bul.
76/A6 Rillieux-la-Pape, Fr.
81/H1 Rilski Manastir, Bul.
121/K7 Rimatara (isl.), FrPol.
65/L4 Rimavská Sobota, Slvk.
94/D3 Rīma, Wādī (dry riv.), SAr.
70/B3 Rimbach, Ger.
156/E2 Rimbey, Ab,Can
125/J5 Rimé (wadi), Chad
79/F4 Rimini, It.
83/H3 Rîmnicu Sărat, Rom.
83/G3 Rîmnicu Vîlcea, Rom.
161/G1 Rimouski, Qu,Can
70/C3 Rimpar, Ger.
76/D5 Rimpfischhorn (peak), Swi.
96/D1 Rinchinlhümbe, Mong.
149/F4 Rincón (pt.), Pan.
74/C4 Rincón de la Victoria, Sp.
149/E4 Rincón de la Vieja Nat'l Park, CR
146/E4 Rincón de Romos, Mex.
63/S7 Rindö (isl.), Swe.
56/C3 Ringboy (pt.), NI,UK
77/F4 Ringelspitz (peak), Swi.
62/C3 Ringkøbing, Den.
62/B3 Ringkøbing (co.), Den.
62/B3 Ringkøbing Fjord (lag.), Den.
59/G5 Ringmer, Eng,UK
56/B1 Ringsend, NI,UK
62/D4 Ringsted, Den.
66/B4 Ringvaart (can.), Neth.
61/F1 Ringvassøy (isl.), Nor.
119/G5 Ringwood, Austl.
59/E5 Ringwood, Eng,UK
167/D1 Ringwood, NJ,US
167/J7 Ringwood Saint Park, NJ,US
81/J4 Rinia (isl.), Gre.
56/C2 Rinns, The (pen.), Sc,UK
67/G4 Rinteln, Ger.
144/B2 Rio Abiseo Nat'l Park, Peru
141/B3 Rio Azul, Braz.
138/B5 Riobamba, Ecu.
148/B2 Río Blanco, Mex.
141/L7 Rio Bonito, Braz.
136/E5 Rio Branco, Braz.
143/G2 Río Branco, Uru.
141/B3 Rio Branco do Sul, Braz.
142/B4 Río Bueno, Chile
141/D2 Rio Casca, Braz.
149/G1 Río Cauto, Cuba
143/T12 Riochuelo, Uru.
142/C2 Río Clarillo Nat'l Park, Chile
141/J7 Rio Claro, Braz.
142/D3 Río Colorado, Arg.
142/D2 Río Cuarto, Arg.
140/B4 Rio de Contas, Braz.
141/K7 Rio de Janeiro, Braz.
141/K7 Rio de Janeiro (state), Braz.
156/B5 Rio Dell, Ca,US
141/B3 Rio do Sul, Braz.
148/D3 Río Dulce Nat'l Park, Guat.
75/Q10 Rio Frio, Port.
143/K7 Río Gallegos, Arg.
143/L8 Río Grande, Arg.
141/A5 Rio Grande, Braz.
146/E4 Río Grande, Mex.
162/C4 Rio Grande (riv.), Mex., US
147/F3 Rio Grande (plain), Tx,US
162/D5 Rio Grande City, Tx,US
141/G8 Rio Grande da Serra, Braz.
140/C2 Rio Grande do Norte (state), Braz.
140/B2 Rio Grande do Piauí, Braz.
141/A4 Rio Grande do Sul (state), Braz.
138/C2 Riohacha, Col.
149/F4 Río Hato, Pan.
144/B2 Rioja, Peru
139/F5 Rio Jaú Nat'l Park, Braz.
141/B1 Riolândia, Braz.
140/D3 Rio Largo, Braz.
72/E4 Riom, Fr.
74/A3 Rio Maior, Port.
156/D3 Riondel, BC,Can
142/D4 Río Negro (prov.), Arg.
138/C3 Rionegro, Col.
143/F2 Río Negro (dept.), Uru.
143/F2 Río Negro (res.), Uru.
80/D2 Rionero in Vulture, It.
141/C1 Rio Paranaíba, Braz.
141/A4 Rio Pardo, Braz.
135/E2 Río Pilcomayo Nat'l Park, Arg.
140/A5 Rio Prêto (mts.), Braz.
158/F4 Rio Rancho, NM,US
140/C3 Rio Real, Braz.
72/F3 Riorges, Fr.
142/E1 Río Segundo, Arg.
142/B5 Río Simpson Nat'l Park, Chile
138/C3 Riosucio, Col.
142/D2 Río Tercero, Arg.
140/D2 Rio Tinto, Braz.
141/B1 Rio Verde, Braz.
147/F4 Ríoverde, Mex.
137/H7 Rio Verde de Mato Grosso, Braz.
82/E3 Ripanj, Yugo.
53/M8 Ripley, Eng,UK
163/F3 Ripley, Ms,US
163/F3 Ripley, Tn,US
75/G1 Ripoll, Sp.
75/L6 Ripoll (riv.), Sp.
75/L6 Ripollet, Sp.
57/G3 Ripon, Eng,UK
157/L5 Ripon, Wi,US
80/D4 Riposto, It.
57/G4 Ripponden, Eng,UK
167/L7 Rippowam (riv.), Ct,US
138/C3 Risaralda (dept.), Col.
58/C3 Risca, Wal,UK
100/B1 Rishiri, Japan
100/B1 Rishiri (isl.), Japan
100/B1 Rishiri-Rebun-Sarobetsu Nat'l Park, Japan
91/D4 Rishon LeZiyyon, Isr.
72/D2 Risle (riv.), Fr.
166/D5 Risley (Estell Manor), NJ,US
82/B3 Risnjak (peak), Cro.
82/B3 Risnjak Nat'l Park, Cro.
83/G3 Rîşnov, Rom.
162/E3 Rison, Ar,US
62/C2 Risør, Nor.
53/T11 Ris-Orangis, Fr.
77/F1 Riss (riv.), Ger.
76/C5 Risse (riv.), Fr.
138/C3 Ritacuba (peak), Col.
120/E2 Ritaiō (isl.), Japan
79/E5 Ritoio, Monte (peak), It.
67/F2 Ritterhude, Ger.
168/F6 Rittman, Oh,US
99/L9 Rittō, Japan
156/D4 Ritzville, Wa,US
79/D1 Riva, It.
142/E2 Rivadavia, Arg.
78/A2 Rivarolo Canavese, It.
148/E4 Rivas, Nic.
72/F4 Rive-de-Gier, Fr.
142/B5 Rivera (isl.), Chile
135/E3 Rivera, Uru.
143/G1 Rivera (dept.), Uru.
167/K8 Riverdale, NY,US
167/J8 River Edge, NJ,US
167/F2 Riverhead, NY,US
115/H7 Riverina (reg.), Austl.
165/F7 River Rouge, Mi,US
156/B3 Rivers (inlet), BC,Can
157/H3 Rivers, Mb,Can
129/G5 Rivers (state), Nga.
132/C4 Riversdale, SAfr.
164/C3 Riverside, Ca,US
164/C3 Riverside (co.), Ca,US
166/D3 Riverside, NJ,US
118/G8 Riverstone, Austl.
157/J3 Riverton, Mb,Can
115/Q12 Riverton, NZ
156/F5 Riverton, Wy,US
167/J8 River Vale, NJ,US
161/H2 Riverview, NB,Can
165/F7 Riverview, Mi,US
163/H5 Riviera Beach, Fl,US
166/B5 Riviera Beach, Md,US
161/G2 Rivière-du-Loup, Qu,Can
132/L11 Riviersonderendreeks (mts.), SAfr.
78/A2 Rivoli, It.
78/C2 Rivolta d'Adda, It.
68/D2 Rixensart, Belg.
76/D2 Rixheim, Fr.
94/E4 Riyadh (Ar Riyāḑ) (cap.), SAr.
112/F6 Rizal (prov.), Phil.
112/E6 Rizal Park, Phil.
92/E1 Rize, Turk.
92/E1 Rize (prov.), Turk.
103/D4 Rizhao, China
80/E3 Rizzuto (cape), It.
62/C2 Rjukan, Nor.
128/B2 Rkîz (lake), Mrta.
62/D1 Roa, Nor.
59/F2 Roade, Eng,UK
54/D3 Roadside, Sc,UK
150/E3 Road Town (cap.), BVI
158/E3 Roan (plat.), Co,US
57/F1 Roan Fell (hill), Sc,UK
163/H2 Roan High (peak), NC,US
72/F3 Roanne, Fr.
163/G3 Roanoke, Al,US
163/J2 Roanoke (riv.), NC, Va,US
167/F2 Roanoke (pt.), NY,US
160/E4 Roanoke, Va,US
163/J2 Roanoke Rapids, NC,US
166/B2 Roaring (cr.), Pa,US
148/E2 Roatán (isl.), Hon.
119/C4 Robbins (isl.), Austl.
78/B2 Robbio, It.
119/B1 Robe (peak), Austl.
60/A2 Robe (riv.), Ire.
78/D2 Robecco d'Oglia, It.
62/E4 Röbel, Ger.
76/B5 Robert (mtn.), Fr.
69/E6 Robert-Espagne, Fr.
162/C4 Robert Lee, Tx,US
151/E4 Roberts (mtn.), Ak,US
59/G5 Robertsbridge, Eng,UK
61/G2 Robertsfors, Swe.
106/D3 Robertsganj, India
132/B4 Robertson, SAfr.
161/F1 Roberval, Qu,Can
57/H3 Robin Hood's Bay, Eng,UK
116/C3 Robinson (ranges), Austl.
160/C4 Robinson, Il,US
165/C3 Robinson (pt.), Wa,US
134/B6 Robinson Crusoe (isl.), Chile
118/C4 Robinson Gorge Nat'l Park, Austl.
157/H3 Roblin, Mb,Can
136/G7 Roboré, Bol.
156/D2 Robson (peak), BC,Can
162/D5 Robstown, Tx,US
162/C3 Roby, Tx,US
74/A3 Roca, Cabo da (cape), Port.
138/A5 Rocafuerte, Ecu.
72/D4 Rocamadour, Fr.
146/B5 Roca Partida (isl.), Mex.
147/G5 Roca Partida, Punta (pt.), Mex.
137/M4 Rocas, Braz.
73/G4 Rocciamelone (peak), It.
72/E5 Roc de France (mtn.), Fr.
76/D1 Roc du Haut du Faite (mtn.), Fr.
143/G2 Rocha, Uru.
143/G2 Rocha (dept.), Uru.
57/F4 Rochdale, Eng,UK
58/B6 Roche, Eng,UK
72/C4 Rochefort, Fr.
75/J1 Roches Blanches (mtn.), Fr.
59/G4 Rochester, Eng,UK
160/C3 Rochester, In,US
165/F6 Rochester, Mi,US
157/K4 Rochester, Mn,US
161/G3 Rochester, NH,US
160/E3 Rochester, NY,US
165/F6 Rochester Hills, Mi,US
59/G3 Rochford, Eng,UK
160/B3 Rock (riv.), Il, Wi,US
156/C4 Rock (cr.), Or,US
52/B3 Rockall (isl.), UK
166/D2 Rockaway, NJ,US
166/D2 Rockaway (riv.), NJ,US
167/K9 Rockaway (inlet), NY,US
167/E3 Rockaway (pt.), NY,US
167/K9 Rockaway Park, NY,US
151/L3 Rock Creek, Yk,Can
118/H8 Rockdale, Austl.
113/R Rockefeller (plat.), Ant.
160/B3 Rockford, Il,US
161/G2 Rock Forest, Qu,Can
157/G3 Rockglen, Sk,Can
118/C3 Rockhampton, Austl.
163/H3 Rock Hill, SC,US
116/B5 Rockingham, Austl.
163/J3 Rockingham, NC,US
160/B3 Rock Island, Il,US
160/F2 Rockland, On,Can
168/D1 Rockland, Ma,US
161/G2 Rockland, Me,US
167/D1 Rockland (co.), NY,US
119/B3 Rocklands (res.), Austl.
163/H4 Rockledge, Fl,US
162/D4 Rockport, Tx,US
162/C4 Rocksprings, Tx,US
156/F5 Rock Springs, Wy,US
139/G3 Rockstone, Guy.
166/A5 Rockville, Md,US
167/E2 Rockville Centre, NY,US
162/D3 Rockwall, Tx,US
168/F5 Rockwell (lake), Oh,US
163/G3 Rockwood, Tn,US
148/D2 Rocky (pt.), Belz.
145/E4 Rocky (mts.), NAm
160/D4 Rocky (peak), Ky,US
167/F1 Rocky (pt.), NY,US
119/C4 Rocky Cape Nat'l Park, Austl.
161/K1 Rocky Harbour, Nf,Can
168/B2 Rocky Hill, Ct,US
160/D2 Rocky Island (lake), On,Can
163/J3 Rocky Mount, NC,US
160/E4 Rocky Mount, Va,US
156/E2 Rocky Mountain House, Ab,Can
159/F2 Rocky Mountain Nat'l Park, Co,US
167/F2 Rocky Point, NY,US
168/F5 Rocky River, Oh,US
168/F5 Rocky, West Branch (riv.), Oh,US
71/E2 Rodach (riv.), Ger.
70/D2 Rodach bei Coburg, Ger.
69/G5 Rodalben, Ger.
161/K1 Roddickton, Nf,Can
58/D1 Roden (riv.), Eng,UK
70/C2 Rodenbach, Ger.
165/K10 Rodeo, Ca,US
70/B3 Rödermark, Ger.
71/F1 Rodewisch, Ger.
72/E4 Rodez, Fr.
71/F4 Roding, Ger.
53/P7 Roding (riv.), Eng,UK
117/G3 Rodinga (peak), Austl.
67/F4 Rödinghausen, Ger.
81/F2 Rodonit, Kep i (cape), Alb.
63/T9 Rødovre, Den.
51/N6 Rodrigues (isl.), Mrts.
62/E4 Rødvig, Den.
56/B2 Roe (riv.), NI,UK
114/C3 Roebuck (bay), Austl.
131/C5 Roedtan, SAfr.
77/H5 Roen (peak), It.
66/D6 Roer (riv.), Neth.
66/C6 Roermond, Neth.
68/C2 Roeselare, Belg.
165/D2 Roesiger (lake), Wa,US
153/H2 Roes Welcome (sound), NW,Can
86/D1 Rogachev, Bela.
62/A2 Rogaland (co.), Nor.
82/D4 Rogatica, Bosn.
162/E2 Rogers, Ar,US
160/D4 Rogers (peak), Va,US
160/D2 Rogers City, Mi,US
163/H2 Rogersville, Tn,US
168/C2 Roger Williams Nat'l Mem., RI,US
79/D6 Roglio (riv.), It.
76/B1 Rognon (riv.), Fr.
65/J2 Rogoźno, Pol.
158/B2 Rogue (riv.), Or,US
125/L6 Rohl (riv.), Sudan
95/J3 Rohri, Pak.
78/A5 Roia (riv.), It.
109/C2 Roi Et, Thai.
63/L1 Roine (lake), Fin.
68/C4 Roisel, Fr.
53/T10 Roissy, Fr.
53/T9 Roissy-en-France, Fr.
142/E2 Rojas, Arg.
147/F4 Rojo, Cabo (cape), Mex.
150/E3 Rojo, Cabo (cape), PR
130/C3 Roka, Kenya
110/B3 Rokan (riv.), Indo.
118/A1 Rokeby-Croll Creek Nat'l Park, Austl.
128/C4 Rokel (riv.), SLeo.
100/B3 Rokkasho, Japan
99/L10 Rokkō-san (peak), Japan
71/G3 Rokycany, Czh.
141/B2 Rolândia, Braz.
71/F2 Rolava (riv.), Czh.
66/D3 Rolde, Neth.
156/C2 Rolla, BC,Can
159/K3 Rolla, Mo,US
157/J3 Rolla, ND,US
164/F8 Rolling Hills Estates, Ca,US
165/P15 Rolling Meadows, Il,US
130/B2 Rom (peak), Ugan.
118/C4 Roma, Austl.
79/E4 Romagna (reg.), It.
72/E4 Romagnat, Fr.
69/E5 Romagne-sous-Montfaucon, Fr.
163/J3 Romain (cape), SC,US
161/J1 Romaine (riv.), Qu,Can
76/B2 Romaine (riv.), Fr.
83/H2 Roman, Rom.
111/G5 Romang (isl.), Indo.
111/G5 Romang (str.), Indo.
83/F3 Romania
149/G1 Romano (cay), Cuba
78/C1 Romano di Lombardia, It.
77/F2 Romanshorn, Swi.
72/F4 Romans-sur-Isère, Fr.
151/E3 Romanzof (cape), Ak,US
80/C2 Roma (Rome) (cap.), It.
69/F5 Rombas, Fr.
112/C2 Romblon, Phil.
163/G3 Rome, Ga,US
160/F3 Rome, NY,US
165/P16 Romeoville, Il,US
80/C2 Rome (Roma) (cap.), It.
53/P7 Romford, Eng,UK
72/E2 Romilly-sur-Seine, Fr.
66/D6 Rommerskirchen, Ger.
59/G4 Romney Marsh (reg.), Eng,UK
86/E2 Romny, Ukr.
62/C4 Rømø (isl.), Den.
72/D3 Romorantin-Lanthenay, Fr.
59/E5 Romsey, Eng,UK
165/F7 Romulus, Mi,US
77/E3 Ron (riv.), Swi.
109/D2 Ron, Viet.
104/E5 Ron (cape), Viet.
156/E4 Ronan, Mt,US
137/H6 Roncador (mts.), Braz.
79/G1 Ronchi dei Legionari, It.
80/C1 Ronciglione, It.
79/F4 Ronco (riv.), It.
68/C2 Roncq, Fr.
74/C4 Ronda, Sp.
61/D3 Rondane Nat'l Park, Nor.
137/H7 Rondonópolis, Braz.
105/F3 Rong (riv.), China
105/F3 Rong'an, China
101/B4 Rongcheng, China
157/G2 Ronge (lake), Sk,Can
120/F3 Rongelap (atoll), Mrsh.
120/F3 Rongerik (atoll), Mrsh.
105/F3 Rongjiang, China
107/J2 Rongshui Miaozu Zizhixian, China
107/K3 Rong Xian, China
121/X15 Roniu (peak), FrPol.
167/E2 Ronkonkoma, NY,US
62/F4 Rønne, Den.
62/F3 Ronneby, Swe.
113/U Ronne Entrance (inlet), Ant.
113/W Ronne Ice Shelf, Ant.
67/G4 Ronnenberg, Ger.
116/B3 Ronsard (cape), Austl.
68/C2 Ronse, Belg.
137/H6 Ronuro (riv.), Braz.
132/P13 Roodepoort-Maraisburg, SAfr.
132/B2 Rooiberg (peak), Namb.
106/C2 Roorkee, India
66/B5 Roosendaal, Neth.
113/N Roosevelt (isl.), Ant.
136/F6 Roosevelt (riv.), Braz.
152/D3 Roosevelt (mtn.), BC,Can
167/L9 Roosevelt, NY,US
167/K8 Roosevelt (isl.), NY,US
158/E2 Roosevelt, Ut,US
151/L4 Root (mtn.), Ak,US
165/Q14 Root (riv.), Wi,US
165/P14 Root, West Branch (riv.), Wi,US
74/D4 Roquetas de Mar, Sp.
139/F4 Roraima (state), Braz.
136/F2 Roraima (peak), Guy.
139/F3 Roraima (peak), SAm.
133/E3 Rorke's Drift Battlesite, SAfr.
157/J3 Rorketon, Mb,Can
77/F3 Rorschach, Swi.
123/W17 Rosa (cape), Alg.
150/C2 Rosa (lake), Bahm.
79/E1 Rosà, It.
76/D5 Rosablanche (peak), Swi.
78/A1 Rosa, Monte (mts.), It.
77/G3 Rosanna (riv.), Aus.
146/C3 Rosa, Punta (pt.), Mex.
142/E2 Rosario, Arg.
140/A1 Rosário, Braz.
146/D4 Rosario, Mex.
112/C1 Rosario, Phil.
143/F2 Rosario, Uru.
146/A2 Rosario de Arriba, Mex.
135/D2 Rosario de la Frontera, Arg.
143/S11 Rosario del Tala, Arg.
135/F3 Rosário do Sul, Braz.
146/B2 Rosarito, Mex.
75/G1 Rosas (gulf), Sp.
138/B4 Rosa Zárate, Ecu.
60/B2 Roscommon (co.), Ire.
67/G6 Rosdorf, Ger.
121/J6 Rose (isl.), ASam.
151/M4 Rose (pt.), BC,Can
157/J3 Roseau (riv.), Can., US
150/F4 Roseau (cap.), Dom.
157/K3 Roseau, Mn,US
133/S15 Rose Belle, Mrts.
156/C5 Roseburg, Or,US
166/B5 Rosedale, Md,US
163/F3 Rosedale, Ms,US
54/D1 Rosehearty, Sc,UK
141/H7 Roseira, Braz.
165/P16 Roselle, Il,US
167/D2 Roselle, NJ,US
167/H9 Roselle Park, NJ,US
164/F7 Rosemead, Ca,US
161/N6 Rosemère, Qu,Can
162/E4 Rosenberg, Tx,US
64/G5 Rosenheim, Ger.
75/G1 Roses, Sp.
80/D1 Roseto degli Abruzzi, It.
156/G3 Rosetown, Sk,Can
91/B4 Rosetta (Rashīd), Egypt
165/M9 Roseville, Ca,US
165/G6 Roseville, Mi,US
91/F7 Rosh Ha'Ayin, Isr.
91/D3 Rosh HaNiqra (pt.), Isr.
83/G3 Roşiori de Vede, Rom.
62/E4 Roskilde, Den.
64/F1 Roskilde (co.), Den.
63/T9 Roskilde (fjord), Den.
63/S7 Roslags-Näsby, Swe.
86/E1 Roslavl', Rus.
66/C5 Rosmalen, Neth.
54/B4 Rosneath, Sc,UK
53/T10 Rosny-sous-Bois, Fr.
80/D4 Rosolini, It.
72/B3 Rosporden, Fr.
69/G2 Rösrath, Ger.
113/M Ross (isl.), Ant.
113/P Ross (sea), Ant.
157/J2 Ross (isl.), Mb,Can
161/S8 Ross (pt.), On,Can
54/C1 Ross (dist.), Sc,UK
73/K3 Rossa (peak), It.
57/E4 Rossall (pt.), Eng,UK
80/E3 Rossano, It.
76/D2 Rossberg (mtn.), Fr.
70/B3 Rossdorf, Ger.
120/E6 Rossel (isl.), PNG
113/N Ross Ice Shelf, Ant.
161/H2 Rossignol (lake), NS,Can
55/G9 Rosskeeragh (pt.), Ire.
156/D3 Rossland, BC,Can
60/D5 Rosslare (bay), Ire.
60/D5 Rosslare (pt.), Ire.
56/A3 Rosslea, NI,UK
128/B2 Rosso, Mrta.
58/D3 Ross on Wye, Eng,UK
86/F2 Rossosh', Rus.
151/M3 Ross River, Yk,Can
77/E4 Rossstock (peak), Swi.
70/D4 Rosstal, Ger.
157/G2 Rosthern, Sk,Can
64/G1 Rostock, Ger.
86/F3 Rostov, Rus.
87/G2 Rostov Obl., Rus.
56/B3 Rostrevor, NI,UK
163/G3 Roswell, Ga,US
159/F4 Roswell, NM,US
77/F1 Rot (riv.), Ger.
120/D3 Rota (isl.), NMar.
74/B4 Rota, Sp.
67/G2 Rotenburg, Ger.
67/G7 Rotenburg an der Fulda, Ger.
71/E2 Roter Main (riv.), Ger.
77/F3 Rote Wand (peak), Aus.
69/F2 Rötgen, Ger.
77/G1 Roth (riv.), Ger.
64/E3 Rothaargebirge (mts.), Ger.
70/E4 Roth bei Nürnberg, Ger.
57/G1 Rothbury, Eng,UK
70/E4 Röthenbach an der Pegnitz, Ger.
70/D4 Rothenburg ob der Tauber, Ger.
57/G5 Rother (riv.), Eng,UK
59/F5 Rother (riv.), Eng,UK
57/G5 Rotherham, Eng,UK
54/C1 Rothes, Sc,UK
54/A5 Rothesay, Sc,UK
69/E2 Rotheux-Rimière, Belg.
59/F2 Rothwell, Eng,UK
111/F6 Roti (isl.), Indo.
115/S10 Rotorua, NZ
69/D2 Rotselaar, Belg.
71/F6 Rott (riv.), Ger.
69/F6 Rotte (riv.), Fr.
76/E5 Rotten (riv.), Swi.
70/C2 Rottenberg, Ger.
70/B6 Rottenburg am Neckar, Ger.
71/F5 Rottenburg an der Laaber, Ger.
66/B5 Rotterdam, Neth.
116/B4 Rottnest (isl.), Austl.
77/F1 Rottum (riv.), Ger.
66/D2 Rottumeroog (isl.), Neth.
66/D2 Rottumerplaat (isl.), Neth.
70/B6 Rottweil, Ger.
120/G6 Rotuma (isl.), Fiji
68/C2 Roubaix, Fr.
72/F4 Roubion (riv.), Fr.
71/H2 Roudnice nad Labem, Czh.
72/D2 Rouen, Fr.
161/R8 Rouge (riv.), On,Can
160/F2 Rouge (riv.), Qu,Can
165/F6 Rouge (riv.), Mi,US
163/G2 Rough (riv.), Ky,US
168/G6 Round (hill), Oh,US
166/B2 Round (hill), Pa,US
166/B3 Round (hill), Pa,US
118/C4 Round Hill (pt.), Austl.
56/B1 Round Knowe (mtn.), NI,UK
165/P15 Round Lake, Il,US
165/P15 Round Lake Beach, Il,US
158/C3 Round Mountain, Nv,US

162/D4 Round Rock, Tx,US
156/F4 Roundup, Mt,US
166/D2 Round Valley (res.), NJ,US
58/E4 Roundway (hill), Eng,UK
55/N13 Rousay (isl.), Sc,UK
118/G8 Rouse Hill, Austl.
72/F4 Roussillon, Fr.
69/E5 Rouvres-en-Woëvre, Fr.
160/E1 Rouyn-Noranda, Qu,Can
61/H2 Rovaniemi, Fin.
78/D1 Rovato, It.
79/E1 Rovereto, It.
109/D3 Rovieng Tbong, Camb.
79/E2 Rovigo, It.
79/E2 Rovigo (prov.), It.
79/G2 Rovinj, Cro.
86/C2 Rovno, Ukr.
86/C2 Rovno Obl., Ukr.
130/B5 Rovuma (riv.), Moz.
114/B3 Rowley (shoals), Austl.
153/J2 Rowley (isl.), NW,Can
128/B4 Roxa (isl.), GBis.
112/B3 Roxas, Phil.
112/C1 Roxas, Phil.
111/F1 Roxas City, Indo.
163/J2 Roxboro, NC,US
62/F2 Roxen (lake), Swe.
128/A3 Roxo (cape), Sen.
159/F4 Roy, NM,US
158/D2 Roy, Ut,US
73/G4 Roya (riv.), Fr.
60/D3 Royal (can.), Ire.
161/Q9 Royal Botanical Garden, On,Can
152/H4 Royale (isl.), Mi,US
59/E2 Royal Leamington Spa, Eng,UK
59/G4 Royal Military (can.), Eng,UK
132/E3 Royal Natal Nat'l Park, SAfr.
118/H9 Royal Nat'l Park, Austl.
165/F6 Royal Oak, Mi,US
101/D4 Royal Paekje Tombs, SKor.
109/D2 Royal Tombs, Viet.
59/G4 Royal Tunbridge Wells, Eng,UK
72/C4 Royan, Fr.
68/B4 Roye, Fr.
62/D2 Røyken, Nor.
59/F2 Royston, Eng,UK
57/F4 Royton, Eng,UK
82/E4 Rožaje, Yugo.
71/H4 Rožmberk (lake), Czh.
65/L4 Rožňava, Slvk.
68/D4 Rozoy-sur-Serre, Fr.
65/M3 Roztoczański Nat'l Park, Pol.
71/H2 Roztoky, Czh.
78/C2 Rozzano, It.
162/E3 R.S. Kerr (lake), Ok,US
87/G1 Rtishchevo, Rus.
57/E6 Ruabon, Wal,UK
126/B4 Ruacana (falls), Ang.
126/B4 Ruacana, Namb.
130/B4 Ruaha Nat'l Park, Tanz.
94/E5 Rub' al Khali (des.), SAr.
130/C4 Rubeho (mts.), Tanz.
53/U11 Rubelles, Fr.
100/C2 Rubeshibe, Japan
86/F2 Rubezhnoye, Ukr.
75/G2 Rubí, Sp.
164/C3 Rubidoux, Ca,US
79/D3 Rubiera, It.
140/B5 Rubim, Braz.
130/A3 Rubondo Nat'l Park, Tanz.
71/G4 Rubřina (riv.), Czh.
102/D1 Rubtsovsk, Rus.
130/B4 Rubuga, Tanz.
158/D2 Ruby (lake), Nv,US
158/D2 Ruby (mts.), Nv,US
158/D2 Ruby Valley, Nv,US
66/B5 Rucphen, Neth.
116/D2 Rudall River Nat'l Park, Austl.
65/K2 Ruda Woda (lake), Pol.
57/G6 Ruddington, Eng,UK
65/G2 Rüdersdorf, Ger.
70/A3 Rüdesheim, Ger.
130/B5 Rudewa, Tanz.
130/C4 Rudi, Tanz.
65/M3 Rudnik, Pol.
87/M1 Rudnyy, Kaz.
88/F1 Rudolf (isl.), Rus.
64/F3 Rudolstadt, Ger.
103/E4 Rudong, China
93/G2 Rūdsar, Iran
57/H3 Rudston, Eng,UK
56/B1 Rue (pt.), NI,UK
53/S10 Rueil-Malmaison, Fr.
54/A4 Ruell (riv.), Sc,UK
72/D4 Ruelle-sur-Touvre, Fr.
82/F4 Ruen (Rujen) (peak), Bul., Mac.
131/D3 Ruenya (riv.), Zim.
77/H3 Ruetzbach (riv.), Aus.
125/M5 Rufā'ah, Sudan
81/F3 Ruffano, It.
130/C4 Rufiji (riv.), Tanz.
142/E2 Rufino, Arg.
131/C2 Rufunsa, Zam.
103/E4 Rugao, China
59/E2 Rugby, Eng,UK
157/J3 Rugby, ND,US
58/E1 Rugeley, Eng,UK
65/G1 Rügen (isl.), Ger.
63/K3 Ruhnu saar (isl.), Est.
66/D6 Ruhr (riv.), Ger.
67/D6 Ruhrgebiet (reg.), Ger.
103/B4 Ruicheng, China
159/F4 Ruidoso, NM,US
66/D3 Ruinen, Neth.
130/C5 Ruipa, Tanz.
53/M7 Ruislip, Eng,UK
146/D4 Ruiz, Mex.
138/C3 Ruiz, Nevado del (peak), Col.
82/F4 Rujen (Ruen) (peak), Bul., Macd.
125/J8 Ruki (riv.), Zaire
130/B5 Rukwa (lake), Tanz.
130/A4 Rukwa (prov.), Tanz.
70/B4 Rülzheim, Ger.
77/H3 Rum, Aus.
150/C2 Rum (cay), Bahm.
82/D3 Ruma, Yugo.
130/B2 Ruma Nat'l Park, Kenya
125/L6 Rumbek, Sudan
93/N6 Rumeli Hisar, Turk.
161/G2 Rumford, Me,US
65/K1 Rumia, Pol.
76/B6 Rumilly, Fr.
58/C4 Rumney, Wal,UK
100/B2 Rumoi, Japan
131/D1 Rumphi, Malw.
167/E3 Rumson, NJ,US
68/D1 Rumst, Belg.
130/C2 Rumuruti, Kenya
56/B1 Runabay Head (pt.), NI,UK
103/C4 Runan, China
57/F5 Runcorn, Eng,UK
130/B3 Runere, Tanz.
63/T9 Rungsted, Den.
125/L7 Rungu, Zaire
130/A4 Rungwa, Tanz.
130/B4 Rungwa, Tanz.
130/B4 Rungwa (riv.), Tanz.
130/B4 Rungwa Game Rsv., Tanz.
130/B5 Rungwe (peak), Tanz.
70/B2 Runkel, Ger.
62/F1 Runn (lake), Swe.
166/C4 Runnemede, NJ,US
159/G4 Running Water Draw (cr.), NM, Tx,US
126/C4 Runtu, Namb.
96/D3 Ruo (riv.), China
63/N1 Ruokolahti, Fin.
102/E4 Ruoqiang, China
108/D2 Rūpar, India
110/B3 Rupat (isl.), Indo.
83/G2 Rupea, Rom.
68/D1 Rupel (riv.), Belg.
160/E1 Rupert (riv.), Qu,Can
156/E5 Rupert, Id,US
153/J3 Rupert House (Waskaganish), Qu,Can
69/G2 Ruppichteroth, Ger.
69/F1 Rur (riv.), Ger.
136/E6 Rurrenabaque, Bol.
121/K7 Rurutu (isl.), FrPol.
131/D3 Rusape, Zim.
165/G7 Ruscom (riv.), On,Can
59/E4 Rushall, Eng,UK
103/E3 Rushan, China
157/K4 Rush City, Mn,US
59/F2 Rushden, Eng,UK
160/C4 Rushville, In,US
159/G2 Rushville, Ne,US
162/E4 Rusk, Tx,US
57/H5 Ruskington, Eng,UK
140/C2 Russas, Braz.
118/F7 Russell (isl.), Austl.
157/H3 Russell, Mb,Can
157/H1 Russell (lake), Mb,Can
152/F1 Russell (isl.), NW,Can
163/H3 Russell (lake), Ga, SC,US
159/H3 Russell, Ks,US
163/G3 Russellville, Al,US
162/E3 Russellville, Ar,US
160/C4 Russellville, Ky,US
70/B3 Rüsselsheim, Ger.
87/G2 Russia
158/B3 Russian (riv.), Ca,US
87/H4 Rustavi, Geo.
132/D2 Rustenburg, SAfr.
162/E3 Ruston, La,US
130/A3 Rutana, Buru.
74/C4 Rute, Sp.
111/F5 Ruteng, Indo.
131/C4 Rutenga, Zim.
158/D3 Ruth, Nv,US
67/F6 Rüthen, Ger.
167/D2 Rutherford, NJ,US
54/B5 Rutherglen, Sc,UK
57/E5 Ruthin, Wal,UK
77/E3 Rüti, Swi.
161/F3 Rutland, Vt,US
59/F1 Rutland Water (res.), Eng,UK
77/E4 Rütli, Swi.
102/C5 Rutog, China
130/A3 Rutshuru, Zaire
130/A3 Rutshuru (riv.), Zaire
66/D4 Ruurlo, Neth.
80/E2 Ruvo di Puglia, It.
130/C4 Ruvu, Tanz.
130/C4 Ruvu (riv.), Tanz.
130/A3 Ruvubu (riv.), Buru.
130/C5 Ruvuma (prov.), Tanz.
130/B5 Ruvuma (riv.), Tanz.
131/C3 Ruwa, Zim.
92/D3 Ruwaq, Jabal ar (mts.), Syria
130/A2 Ruwenzori (range), Ugan.
131/C3 Ruya (riv.), Zim.
103/C4 Ruyang, China
140/B4 Ruy Barbosa, Braz.
130/A3 Ruyigi, Buru.
87/H1 Ruzayevka, Rus.
130/A3 Ruzizi (riv.), Buru., Zaire
65/K4 Ružomberok, Slvk.
130/A2 Rwanda
130/A2 Rwenjaza, Ugan.
130/A3 Rwenzori Nat'l Park, Ugan.
56/C2 Ryan, Loch (inlet), Sc,UK
118/A1 Ryan, Mount (peak), Austl.
119/D2 Ryan, Mount (peak), Austl.
86/F1 Ryazan', Rus.
84/J5 Ryazan' Obl., Rus.
86/G1 Ryazhsk, Rus.
84/G1 Rybachiy (pen.), Rus.
102/C3 Rybach'ye, Kyr.
84/H4 Rybinsk, Rus.
84/H4 Rybinsk (res.), Rus.
65/K3 Rybnik, Pol.
83/J2 Rybnitsa, Mol.
156/D2 Rycroft, Ab,Can
118/H8 Ryde, Austl.
59/E5 Ryde, Eng,UK
63/T9 Rydebäck, Swe.
59/G5 Rye, Eng,UK
59/G5 Rye (bay), Eng,UK
57/H3 Rye (riv.), Eng,UK
167/L8 Rye, NY,US
158/C2 Rye Patch (res.), Nv,US
62/D2 Rygge, Nor.
65/L3 Ryki, Pol.
63/J1 Rymättyla (isl.), Fin.
87/J2 Ryn-Peski (des.), Kaz.
99/F1 Ryōtsu, Japan
99/M9 Ryōzen-yama (peak), Japan
65/K2 Rypin, Pol.
86/B2 Rysy (peak), Slvk.
57/G2 Ryton, Eng,UK
59/E2 Ryton on Dunsmore, Eng,UK
62/F4 Rytterknægten (peak), Den.
99/G3 Ryūgasaki, Japan
100/H8 Ryukyu (Nansei-Shotō) (isls.), Japan
99/M9 Ryūō, Japan
65/M3 Rzeszów, Pol.
65/L3 Rzeszów (prov.), Pol.
84/G4 Rzhev, Rus.

S

63/K1 Sääksjärvi (lake), Fin.
70/B4 Saalbach (riv.), Ger.
67/G4 Saale (riv.), Ger.
76/D1 Saales, Col de (pass), Fr.
64/F3 Saalfeld, Ger.
73/K3 Saalfelden am Steinernen Meer, Aus.
76/D4 Saane (riv.), Swi.
156/C3 Saanich, BC,Can
130/C2 Saanta (peak), Kenya
69/F5 Saar (riv.), Ger.
69/F5 Saarbrücken, Ger.
63/K2 Saaremaa (isl.), Est.
69/F5 Saarland (state), Ger.
69/F5 Saarlouis, Ger.
76/D5 Saastal (vall.), Swi.
109/D3 Sab (riv.), Camb.
150/F3 Saba (isl.), NAnt.
82/D3 Šabac, Yugo.
75/G2 Sabadell, Sp.
98/E3 Sabae, Japan
111/E2 Sabah (state), Malay.
149/F1 Sabana (arch.), Cuba
138/C2 Sabanalarga, Col.
150/D3 Sabaneta, DRep.
110/A2 Sabang, Indo.
149/G4 Sabanita, Pan.
125/M6 Sabat (riv.), Eth., Sudan
95/H2 Şāberī, Hāmūn-e (lake), Afg.
124/H2 Sabhā, Libya
127/B3 Sabie, Egypt
133/F2 Sabie (riv.), Moz.
127/B3 Sabie, SAfr.
133/E2 Sabierivier (riv.), SAfr.
149/G1 Sabinal (cay), Cuba
75/E1 Sabiñánigo, Sp.
162/E4 Sabine (lake), La, Tx,US
162/E4 Sabine (riv.), La, Tx,US
159/J5 Sabine Pass (waterway), US
159/J5 Sabine Pass (waterway), La, Tx,US
80/C1 Sabini (mts.), It.
141/D1 Sabinópolis, Braz.
94/F4 Sabkhat Maṭṭī (salt marsh), UAE
112/C2 Sablayan, Phil.
161/J3 Sable (isl.), Can.
161/H3 Sable (cape), NS,Can
163/H5 Sable (cape), Fl,US
72/C3 Sablé-sur-Sarthe, Fr.
75/H1 Sablon, Pointe du (pt.), Fr.
140/C2 Saboeiro, Braz.
74/B2 Sabor (riv.), Port.
111/H4 Sabra (cape), Indo.
113/J Sabrina (coast), Ant.
93/J2 Sabzevār, Iran
156/D4 Sacajawea (peak), Or,US
158/E4 Sacaton, Az,US
74/A3 Sacavém, Port.
78/A4 Saccarello, Monte (Mont Saccarel), Fr.
78/A4 Saccarel, Mont (Monte Saccarello) (mtn.), Fr.
80/C2 Sacco (riv.), It.
83/G3 Săcele, Rom.
157/L2 Sachigo (lake), On,Can
157/L2 Sachigo (riv.), On,Can
168/C3 Sachuest Point Nat'l Wild. Ref., RI,US
79/F1 Sacile, It.
76/D2 Säckingen, Ger.
161/H2 Sackville, NB,Can
53/S10 Saclay, Fr.
161/G3 Saco, Me,US
141/C1 Sacramento, Braz.
144/C2 Sacramento (plain), Peru
165/M9 Sacramento (cap.), Ca,US
165/M10 Sacramento (co.), Ca,US
158/B2 Sacramento (riv.), Ca,US
158/B3 Sacramento (val.), Ca,US
159/F4 Sacramento (mts.), NM,US
165/L10 Sacramento River Deep Water Ship (can.), Ca,US
74/D4 Sacratif (cape), Sp.
154/W12 Sacred (falls), Hi,US
57/G2 Sacriston, Eng,UK
80/E2 Sacro (peak), It.
78/B1 Sacro Monte, It.
147/L7 Sacromonte Nat'l Park, Mex.
74/A1 Sada, Sp.
130/C4 Sadani, Tanz.
156/C2 Saddle (hills), Ab, BC,Can
167/J8 Saddle (riv.), NJ,US
167/J8 Saddle Brook, NJ,US
54/A2 Saddle, The (mtn.), Sc,UK
57/G4 Saddleworth, Eng,UK
109/D4 Sa Dec, Viet.
108/D2 Sādhaura, India
95/K3 Sādiqābād, Pak.
104/B3 Sadiya, India
99/F2 Sado (isl.), Japan
74/A3 Sado (riv.), Port.
98/B4 Sadowara, Japan
106/B2 Sādri, India
112/D3 Sadripante (mtn.), Phil.
127/C3 Safājah, Bi'r (well), Egypt
124/H1 Safāqis, Tun.
123/X18 Safāqis (gov.), Tun.
108/A1 Safed Koh (range), Pak.
94/E3 Saffānīyah, Ra's as (pt.), SAr.
62/E2 Säffle, Swe.
158/E4 Safford, Az,US
59/G2 Saffron Walden, Eng,UK
124/D1 Safi, Mor.
95/H2 Safīd (mts.), Afg.
95/J1 Safīd (riv.), Afg.
95/K1 Safid Khers (mts.), Afg., Taj.
91/E2 Şāfītā, Syria
84/G5 Safonovo, Rus.
92/C1 Safranbolu, Turk.
106/E2 Saga, China
98/B4 Saga, Japan
98/A4 Saga (pref.), Japan
99/G1 Sagae, Japan
104/B4 Sagaing, Burma
104/B3 Sagaing (div.), Burma
99/H7 Sagami (bay), Japan
99/H7 Sagami (riv.), Japan
99/F3 Sagami (sea), Japan
99/F3 Sagamihara, Japan
99/H7 Sagamiko, Japan
167/E2 Sagamore Hill Nat'l Hist. Site, NY,US
130/C3 Sagana, Kenya
106/C3 Sāgar, India
151/J2 Saganavirktok (riv.), Ak,US
112/C3 Sagay, Phil.
112/D3 Sagay, Phil.
160/D3 Saginaw, Mi,US
160/D3 Saginaw (bay), Mi,US
153/K3 Saglek (bay), Nf,Can
80/A1 Sagone (gulf), Fr.
74/A4 Sagres, Port.
102/F2 Sagsay (riv.), Mong.
67/E2 Sagter Ems (riv.), Ger.
149/H1 Sagua de Tánamo, Cuba
149/F1 Sagua la Grande, Cuba
158/E4 Saguaro Nat'l Mon., Az,US
161/G1 Saguenay (riv.), Qu,Can
124/C2 Saguia el Hamra (wadi), Mor., WSah.
75/E3 Sagunto, Sp.
53/R9 Sagy, Fr.
106/E2 Sa'gya, China
87/K2 Sagyz (riv.), Kaz.
91/E4 Saḥāb, Jor.
127/B5 Sahaba, Sudan
138/C2 Sahagún, Col.
93/F2 Sahand (mtn.), Iran
124/G3 Sahara (des.), Afr.
95/L3 Sahāranpur, India
106/E2 Saharsa, India
123/T15 Sahel (riv.), Alg.
106/E2 Sāhibganj, India
108/B2 Sāhīwāl, Pak.
124/H2 Şaḥrā Awbārī (des.), Libya
125/K2 Sahra' Rabyānah (des.), Libya
146/E4 Sahuayo de Díaz, Mex.
106/D2 Sai (riv.), India
99/E2 Sai (riv.), Japan
123/R16 Saïda, Alg.
123/R16 Saïda (wilaya), Alg.
106/D2 Saidpur, India
98/C2 Saigō, Japan
109/D4 Saigon (Ho Chi Minh City), Viet.
98/C4 Saijō, Japan
98/A4 Saikai Nat'l Park, Japan
98/B4 Saiki, Japan
106/C4 Sailu, India
63/M1 Saimaa (lake), Fin.
68/C4 Sains-Richaumont, Fr.
54/D5 Saint Abbs, Sc,UK
54/D5 Saint Abb's Head (pt.), Sc,UK
72/E5 Saint-Affrique, Fr.
58/A6 Saint Agnes, Eng,UK
58/A6 Saint Agnes (pt.), Eng,UK
161/L2 Saint Alban's, Nf,Can
53/N6 Saint Albans, Eng,UK
53/M6 Saint Albans (val.), Eng,UK
161/F2 Saint Albans, Vt,US
160/D4 Saint Albans, WV,US
156/E2 Saint Albert, Ab,Can
58/D5 Saint Aldhelm's Head (pt.), Eng,UK
68/C3 Saint-Amand-les-Eaux, Fr.
72/E3 Saint-Amand-Montrond, Fr.
161/G1 Saint-Ambroise, Qu,Can
68/C2 Saint-André, Fr.
133/R15 Saint-André, Reun.
72/F2 Saint-André-les-Vergers, Fr.
54/D4 Saint Andrews, Sc,UK
54/D4 Saint Andrews (bay), Sc,UK
128/B5 Saint Ann (cape), SLeo.
72/B2 Saint Anne, Chl,UK
161/Q9 Saint Anns, On,Can
58/A3 Saint Ann's (pt.), UK
161/L1 Saint Anthony, Nf,Can
156/F5 Saint Anthony, Id,US
161/N6 Saint-Antoine, Qu,Can
68/D6 Saint-Armand-sur-Fion, Fr.
53/R11 Saint-Arnoult-en-Yvelines, Fr.
56/E5 Saint Asaph, Wal,UK
56/E4 Saint Athan, Wal,UK
72/B2 Saint Aubin, Chl,UK
161/N6 Saint-Augustin, Qu,Can
163/H4 Saint Augustine, Fl,US
163/H4 Saint Augustine Beach, Fl,US
58/B6 Saint Austell, Eng,UK
58/B6 Saint Austell (bay), Eng,UK
72/B3 Saint-Avé, Fr.
69/F5 Saint-Avold, Fr.
150/F3 Saint Barthélemy (isl.), Fr.
72/D5 Saint-Barthélemy, Pic de (peak), Fr.
56/E3 Saint Bees, Eng,UK
56/E2 Saint Bees Head (pt.), Eng,UK
161/M6 Saint-Benoît, Qu,Can
133/R15 Saint-Benoît, Reun.
161/P7 Saint-Blaise, Qu,Can
132/C4 Saint Blaize (cape), SAfr.
54/D5 Saint Boswells, Sc,UK
58/D3 Saint Briavels, Eng,UK
53/T10 Saint-Brice-sous-Forêt, Fr.
58/A3 Saint Brides (bay), Wal,UK
72/B2 Saint-Brieuc, Fr.
72/B2 Saint-Brieuc (bay), Fr.
161/P6 Saint-Bruno (co.), Qu,Can
161/P6 Saint-Bruno-de-Montarville, Qu,Can
161/M6 Saint-Canut, Qu,Can
161/R9 Saint Catharines, On,Can
150/F4 Saint Catherine (mtn.), Gren.
59/E5 Saint Catherine's (hill), Eng,UK
59/E5 Saint Catherine's (pt.), Eng,UK
72/F4 Saint-Chamond, Fr.
165/P16 Saint Charles, Il,US
160/E4 Saint Charles, Md,US
159/K3 Saint Charles, Mo,US
53/S11 Saint-Chéron, Fr.
150/D4 Saint Christoffel (peak), NAnt.
165/G7 Saint Clair (lake), On,Can, Mi,US
165/H6 Saint Clair (riv.), On,Can, Mi,US
165/G6 Saint Clair (co.), Mi,US
165/G7 Saint Clair (lake), On,Can, Mi,US
165/H6 Saint Clair (riv.), On,Can, Mi,US
165/G6 Saint Clair Shores, Mi,US
76/B5 Saint-Claude, Fr.
58/B3 Saint Clears, Wal,UK
53/S10 Saint-Cloud, Fr.
157/K4 Saint Cloud, Mn,US
58/B6 Saint Columb Major, Eng,UK
54/E1 Saint Combs, Sc,UK
161/N7 Saint-Constant, Qu,Can
116/B3 Saint Cricq (cape), Austl.
157/K4 Saint Croix (riv.), Mn, Wi,US
160/A2 Saint Croix (riv.), Mn, Wi,US
150/E3 Saint Croix (isl.), USVI
151/M3 Saint Cyr (mtn.), Yk,Can
53/S10 Saint-Cyr-l'École, Fr.
53/S11 Saint-Cyr-sous-Dourdan, Fr.
54/D3 Saint Cyrus, Sc,UK
58/A3 Saint David's, Wal,UK
58/A3 Saint David's Head (pt.), Wal,UK
53/T10 Saint-Denis, Fr.
133/R15 Saint-Denis, Reun.
76/A5 Saint-Didier-sur-Saône, Fr.
76/C1 Saint-Dié, Fr.
72/F2 Saint-Dizier, Fr.
72/E3 Saint-Doulchard, Fr.
160/F2 Sainte-Agathe-des-Monts, Qu,Can
161/H1 Sainte-Anne-des-Monts, Qu,Can
161/N6 Sainte-Anne-des-Plaines, Qu,Can
161/G2 Sainte-Foy, Qu,Can
159/K3 Sainte Genevieve, Mo,US
53/T11 Sainte-Geneviève-des-Bois, Fr.
161/P6 Sainte-Julie-de-Verchères, Qu,Can
161/J2 Saint Eleanors, PE,Can
151/K3 Saint Elias (mts.), Can., US
151/K4 Saint Elias (cape), Ak,US
151/K3 Saint Elias (mtn.), Ak,US
151/K3 Saint Elias (mts.), Yk,Can, Ak,US
151/K3 Saint Elias-Wrangell Nat'l Park and Prsv., Ak,US
161/H1 Sainte-Marguerite (riv.), Qu,Can
161/G2 Sainte-Marie, Qu,Can
76/D1 Sainte-Marie-aux-Mines, Fr.
133/J7 Sainte Marie, Nosy (isl.), Madg.
73/G5 Sainte-Maxime, Fr.
68/C5 Sainte-Erme-Outre-et-Ramecourt, Fr.
157/J3 Sainte Rose du Lac, Mb,Can
72/C4 Saintes, Fr.
161/M6 Sainte-Scholastique, Qu,Can
72/E5 Saint-Estève, Fr.
161/N6 Sainte-Thérèse, Qu,Can
161/N6 Sainte-Thérèse-Ouest, Qu,Can
72/F4 Saint-Étienne, Fr.
72/D2 Saint-Étienne-du-Rouvray, Fr.
161/N6 Saint-Eustache, Qu,Can
150/F3 Saint Eustatius (isl.), NAnt.
53/T11 Saint-Fargeau-Ponthierry, Fr.
161/F1 Saint-Félicien, Qu,Can
76/B6 Saint-Felix, Fr.
54/E1 Saint Fergus, Sc,UK
56/C3 Saintfield, NI,UK
72/E2 Saint-Florentin, Fr.
72/E3 Saint-Florent-sur-Cher, Fr.
125/K6 Saint-Floris Nat'l Park, CAfr.
72/E4 Saint-Flour, Fr.
132/D4 Saint Francis (cape), SAfr.
159/K4 Saint Francis (riv.), Ar, Mo,US
159/G3 Saint Francis, Ks,US
165/Q14 Saint Francis, Wi,US
163/F4 Saint Francisville, La,US
163/F2 Saint Francois (mts.), Mo,US
72/D5 Saint-Gaudens, Fr.
161/K1 Saint George (cape), Can.
161/H2 Saint George, Nb,Can
161/K1 Saint George (cape), Nf,Can
151/E4 Saint George (isl.), Ak,US
158/A2 Saint George (pt.), Ca,US
167/J9 Saint George, NY,US
163/H3 Saint George, SC,US
158/D3 Saint George, Ut,US
161/K1 Saint George's, Nf,Can
161/K1 Saint George's (bay), Nf,Can
161/J2 Saint Georges (bay), NS,Can
161/G2 Saint-Georges, Qu,Can
150/F4 Saint George's (cap.), Gren.
56/C6 Saint George's (chan.), Ire., UK
53/S10 Saint-Germain-en-Laye, Fr.
53/T11 Saint-Germain-lès-Corbeil, Fr.
53/U10 Saint-Germain-sur-Morin, Fr.
68/A5 Saint-Germer-de-Fly, Fr.
68/C3 Saint-Ghislain, Belg.
72/F5 Saint-Gilles, Fr.
72/C3 Saint-Gilles-Croix-de-Vie, Fr.
72/D5 Saint-Girons, Fr.
77/E4 Saint Gotthard (pass), Swi.
58/B3 Saint Govan's Head (pt.), Wal,UK
53/S10 Saint-Gratien, Fr.
118/F6 Saint Helena (isl.), Austl.
132/B4 Saint Helena (bay), SAfr.
122/B6 Saint Helena (isl.), UK
165/J9 Saint Helena (mtn.), Ca,US
119/D4 Saint Helens (pt.), Austl.
57/F5 Saint Helens, Eng,UK
156/C4 Saint Helens, Or,US
156/C4 Saint Helens, Mount (vol.), Wa,US
72/B2 Saint Helier, Chl,UK
72/C3 Saint-Herblain, Fr.
161/M6 Saint-Hermas, Qu,Can
106/E3 Sainthia, India
161/G1 Saint-Honoré, Qu,Can
161/P7 Saint-Hubert, Qu,Can
161/F2 Saint-Hyacinthe, Qu,Can
160/C1 Saint Ignace (isl.), On,Can
160/C2 Saint Ignace, Mi,US
118/H8 Saint Ives, Austl.
58/A6 Saint Ives, Eng,UK
59/F2 Saint Ives, Eng,UK
58/A6 Saint Ives (bay), Eng,UK
161/P7 Saint-Jacques-le-Mineur, Qu,Can
152/C3 Saint James (cape), BC,Can
157/K5 Saint James, Mn,US
167/E2 Saint James, NY,US
161/P7 Saint-Jean (co.), Qu,Can
161/G1 Saint-Jean (lake), Qu,Can
161/H1 Saint-Jean (riv.), Qu,Can
72/C4 Saint-Jean-d'Angély, Fr.
72/D3 Saint-Jean-de-la-Ruelle, Fr.
72/C5 Saint-Jean-de-Luz, Fr.
155/M2 Saint-Jean, Lac (lake), Qu,Can
161/G2 Saint-Jean-Port-Joli, Qu,Can
161/F2 Saint-Jean-sur-Richelieu, Qu,Can
161/N6 Saint-Jérôme, Qu,Can
156/D4 Saint Joe (riv.), Id,US
154/C2 Saint Joe (riv.), Id, Wa,US
161/H2 Saint John, NB,Can
161/H2 Saint John (riv.), NB,Can
161/G2 Saint John (riv.), Can., US
72/B2 Saint John, Chl,UK
161/G2 Saint John (riv.), NB,Can, Me,US
150/E3 Saint John (isl.), USVI
150/F3 Saint John's (cap.), Anti.
161/L2 Saint John's (cap.), Nf,Can
56/C3 Saint John's (pt.), IM,UK
158/E4 Saint Johns, Az,US
155/K6 Saint Johns (riv.), Fl,US
161/F2 Saint Johnsbury, Vt,US
166/C5 Saint Jones (riv.), De,US
160/B1 Saint Joseph (lake), On,Can
133/R15 Saint-Joseph, Reun.
160/C2 Saint Joseph (isl.), Mi,US
160/C3 Saint Joseph (riv.), Mi,US
159/J3 Saint Joseph, Mo,US
72/E5 Saint-Juéry, Fr.
76/C5 Saint-Julien-en-Genevois, Fr.
72/D4 Saint-Junien, Fr.
58/A6 Saint Just, Eng,UK
58/A6 Saint Just in Roseland, Eng,UK
119/F5 Saint Kilda, Austl.
55/G8 Saint Kilda (isl.), Sc,UK
150/F3 Saint Kitts (isl.), StK.
150/F3 Saint Kitts and Nevis
161/P6 Saint-Lambert, Qu,Can
157/J3 Saint Laurent, Mb,Can
161/N6 Saint-Laurent, Qu,Can
68/B3 Saint-Laurent-Blangy, Fr.
139/H3 Saint-Laurent du Maroni, FrG.
161/J1 Saint Lawrence (gulf), Can.
161/L2 Saint Lawrence, Nf,Can
161/P6 Saint Lawrence (riv.), Can., US
151/D3 Saint Lawrence (isl.), Ak,US
160/E2 Saint Lawrence Islands Nat'l Park, Can.
161/M7 Saint-Lazare, Qu,Can
119/G5 Saint Leonard (mtn.), Austl.
161/N6 Saint-Léonard, Qu,Can
133/R15 Saint-Leu, Reun.
53/S9 Saint-Leu-la-Forêt, Fr.
72/C2 Saint-Lô, Fr.
161/N7 Saint Louis (lake), Qu,Can
157/G2 Saint Louis, Sk,Can
76/D2 Saint-Louis, Fr.
133/R15 Saint-Louis, Reun.
128/A2 Saint-Louis, Sen.
128/B3 Saint-Louis (reg.), Sen.
156/A2 Saint Louis (riv.), Mn,US
159/K3 Saint Louis, Mo,US
161/H2 Saint-Louis-de-Kent, NB,Can
149/H2 Saint-Louis du Nord, Haiti
161/P7 Saint-Luc, Qu,Can
150/F4 Saint Lucia
150/F4 Saint Lucia (passg.), Mart., StL.
133/F3 Saint Lucia (cape), SAfr.
133/F3 Saint Lucia, Lake (lag.), SAfr.
55/P12 Saint Magnus (bay), Sc,UK
72/C3 Saint-Maixent-L'École, Fr.
157/J3 Saint Malo, Mb,Can
72/B2 Saint-Malo, Fr.
72/B2 Saint-Malo (gulf), Fr.
53/T10 Saint-Mandé, Fr.
72/F5 Saint-Mandrier-sur-Mer, Fr.
149/H2 Saint-Marc, Haiti
149/H2 Saint-Marc, Pointe de (pt.), Haiti
53/U9 Saint-Mard, Fr.
59/H4 Saint Margaret's at Cliffe, Eng,UK
55/N13 Saint Margaret's Hope, Sc,UK
156/D4 Saint Maries, Id,US
157/J3 Saint Martin (lake), Mb,Can
150/F3 Saint Martin (isl.), Fr.
76/A5 Saint-Martin-Belle-Roche, Fr.
68/A2 Saint-Martin-Boulogne, Fr.
68/C6 Saint-Martin-d'Ablois, Fr.
72/F4 Saint-Martin-d'Hères, Fr.
53/T9 Saint-Martin-du-Tertre, Fr.
104/A4 Saint Martins (isl.), Bang.
150/F3 Saint Martin (Sint Maarten) (isl.), Fr.
117/H4 Saint Mary (peak), Austl.
128/A3 Saint Mary (cape), Gam.
118/G8 Saint Marys, Austl.
160/D3 Saint Mary's, Nf,Can
161/J2 Saint Marys (riv.), NS,Can
55/N13 Saint Mary's, Sc,UK
151/F3 Saint Marys, Ak,US
163/H4 Saint Marys, Ga,US
160/E3 Saint Marys, Pa,US
131/B2 Saint Mary's, Zam.
161/N7 Saint-Mathieu, Qu,Can
151/D3 Saint Matthew (isl.), Ak,US
163/H3 Saint Matthews, SC,US
120/E5 Saint Matthias (isls.), PNG
53/T10 Saint-Maur-des-Fossés, Fr.
160/F1 Saint-Maurice (riv.), Qu,Can
76/C5 Saint-Maurice, Swi.
76/B6 Saint-Maurice-de-Gourdans, Fr.
58/A6 Saint Mawes, Eng,UK
69/F6 Saint-Max, Fr.
58/C3 Saint Mellons, Wal,UK
68/D6 Saint-Memmie, Fr.
53/S11 Saint-Michel-sur-Orge, Fr.
54/D4 Saint Monance, Sc,UK
72/B3 Saint-Nazaire, Fr.
59/F2 Saint Neots, Eng,UK
69/E2 Saint-Nicolas, Belg.
53/S10 Saint-Nom-la-Bretèche, Fr.
68/B2 Saint-Omer, Fr.
68/A4 Saint-Omer-en-Chaussée, Fr.
53/S9 Saint-Ouen-l'Aumône, Fr.
161/G2 Saint-Pamphile, Qu,Can
161/G2 Saint-Pascal, Qu,Can
53/U9 Saint-Pathus, Fr.
50/H5 Saint Paul (isls.), Braz.
156/F2 Saint Paul, Ab,Can
51/N7 Saint Paul (isl.), FrAnt.
129/F5 Saint Paul (cape), Gha.
128/C5 Saint Paul (riv.), Gui., Libr.
133/R15 Saint-Paul, Reun.

217

Saint – San M

151/E4 Saint Paul (isl.), Ak,US
159/J3 Saint Paul, Ks,US
157/K4 Saint Paul (cap.), Mn,US
72/C5 Saint-Paul-lès-Dax, Fr.
118/B1 Saint Pauls (peak), Austl.
167/E2 Saint Paul's Church Nat'l Hist. Site, NY,US
72/F4 Saint-Paul-Trois-Châteaux, Fr.
117/G5 Saint Peter (isl.), Austl.
157/K4 Saint Peter, Mn,US
137/M3 Saint Peter and Saint Paul (rocks), Braz.
72/B2 Saint Peter Port, Chl,UK
59/H4 Saint Peter's, Eng,UK
163/H5 Saint Petersburg, Fl,US
84/F4 Saint Petersburg (Leningrad), Rus.
85/V7 Saint Petersburg (Leningrad) (inset), Rus.
84/G3 Saint Petersburg Obl., Rus.
161/P7 Saint-Philippe-de-La Prairie, Qu,Can
133/R15 Saint-Pierre, Reun.
161/K2 Saint Pierre (isl.), StP.
161/K2 Saint Pierre (isl.), StP,Fr
161/K2 Saint Pierre & Miquelon (dpcy.), Fr
72/D3 Saint-Pierre-des-Corps, Fr.
72/C5 Saint-Pierre-du-Mont, Fr.
53/T11 Saint-Pierre-du-Perray, Fr.
157/J3 Saint Pierre-Jolys, Mb,Can
76/C4 Saint-Point (lake), Fr.
72/B2 Saint-Pol-de-Léon, Fr.
68/B1 Saint-Pol-sur-Mer, Fr.
72/E5 Saint-Pons (mtn.), Fr.
53/S9 Saint-Prix, Fr.
68/C4 Saint-Quentin, Fr.
68/C4 Saint Quentin, Canal de (can.), Fr.
73/G5 Saint-Raphaël, Fr.
72/F5 Saint-Rémy-de-Provence, Fr.
53/S10 Saint-Rémy-lès-Chevreuse, Fr.
68/A3 Saint-Riquier, Fr.
72/B2 Saint Sampson's, Chl,UK
68/C3 Saint-Saulve, Fr.
163/H4 Saint Simons (isl.), Ga,US
163/H4 Saint Simons Island, Ga,US
53/U9 Saint-Soupplets, Fr.
161/H2 Saint Stephen, NB,Can
58/B6 Saint Stephen in Brannel, Eng,UK
160/D3 Saint Thomas, On,Can
150/E3 Saint Thomas (isl.), USVI
161/N7 Saint-Urbain-Premier, Qu,Can
72/F3 Saint-Vallier, Fr.
68/B2 Saint-Venant, Fr.
117/H5 Saint Vincent (gulf), Austl.
119/C4 Saint Vincent (pt.), Austl.
150/F4 Saint Vincent (passg.), StL., StV.
150/F4 Saint Vincent (isl.), StV.
150/F4 Saint Vincent and the Grenadines
69/F3 Saint Vith, Belg.
53/T11 Saint-Vrain, Fr.
156/F2 Saint Walburg, Sk,Can
53/T9 Saint-Witz, Fr.
106/D2 Sāipal (mtn.), Nepal
120/D3 Saipan (isl.), NMar.
99/F2 Saitama (pref.), Japan
98/B4 Saito, Japan
130/B2 Saiwa Swamp Nat'l Park, Kenya
109/B3 Sai Yok Nat'l Park, Thai.
144/D5 Sajama Nat'l Park, Bol.
82/E1 Sajószentpéter, Hun.
132/C3 Sak (riv.), SAfr.
99/H7 Sakado, Japan
99/J7 Sakae, Japan
99/M9 Sakahogi, Japan
98/E2 Sakai, Japan
99/F2 Sakai, Japan
99/H7 Sakai (riv.), Japan
98/C3 Sakaide, Japan
98/C3 Sakaiminato, Japan
157/H3 Sakakawea (lake), ND,US
153/J3 Sakami (lake), Qu,Can
131/C2 Sakania, Zaire
83/K5 Sakarya (prov.), Turk.
86/D4 Sakarya (riv.), Turk.
92/B2 Sakarya (str.), Turk.
100/A4 Sakata, Japan
98/C4 Sakawa, Japan
133/H7 Sakay (riv.), Madg.
130/A3 Sake, Zaire
133/H7 Sakeny (riv.), Madg.
89/Q4 Sakhalin (gulf), Rus.
89/Q4 Sakhalin (isl.), Rus.
100/C1 Sakhalin Obl., Rus.
94/F1 Sakht Sar (Ramsar), Iran
86/E3 Saki, Ukr.
100/G8 Sakishima (isls.), Japan
87/L1 Sakmara (riv.), Rus.
109/D2 Sakon Nakhon, Thai.
168/C3 Sakonnet (pt.), RI,US
95/J3 Sakrand, Pak.
99/F2 Saku, Japan
99/J7 Sakura, Japan
99/L10 Sakurai, Japan
122/K10 Sal (isl.), CpV.
148/E3 Sal (pt.), Hon.
87/G3 Sal (riv.), Rus.
65/J4 Šal'a, Slvk.
62/G2 Sala, Swe.
80/D2 Sala Consilina, It.
146/A1 Salada (dry lake), Mex.
135/E2 Saladas, Arg.
142/E2 Saladillo, Arg.
143/S12 Saladillo (riv.), Arg.
142/D3 Salado (riv.), Arg.
142/F2 Salado (riv.), Arg.
149/G1 Salado (riv.), Cuba
158/F4 Salado (dry riv.), NM,US
134/C5 Salado del Norte (riv.), Arg.
129/E4 Salaga, Gha.
93/E3 Şalāḩ ad Dīn (gov.), Iraq
111/G4 Salahatu (mtn.), Indo.
82/F2 Sălaj (co.), Rom.
124/J5 Salal, Chad
127/D4 Şalālah, Sudan
148/D3 Salamá, Guat.
142/D5 Salamanca (plain), Arg.
142/C1 Salamanca, Chile
147/E4 Salamanca, Mex.
74/C2 Salamanca, Sp.
160/E3 Salamanca, NY,US
125/J6 Salamat (riv.), Chad
138/C3 Salamina, Col.
81/H3 Salamís, Gre.
81/L7 Salamís (isl.), Gre.
91/E2 Salamīyah, Syria
109/C1 Sala Mok, Laos
74/B1 Salas, Sp.
75/G1 Salat (riv.), Fr.
87/K1 Salavat, Rus.
120/B5 Salayar (isl.), Indo.
50/D7 Sala y Gomez (isls.), Chile
72/E3 Salbris, Fr.
144/C4 Salcantay (peak), Peru
150/D3 Salcedo, DRep.
112/D3 Salcedo, Phil.
58/C6 Salcombe, Eng,UK
132/K10 Saldanhabaai (bay), SAfr.
63/K3 Saldus, Lat.
119/C3 Sale, Austl.
123/L13 Salé, Mor.
57/F5 Sale, Eng,UK
111/G3 Salebabu (isl.), Indo.
88/G3 Salekhard, Rus.
77/F2 Salem, Ger.
108/G3 Salem, India
63/R7 Salem, Swe.
160/C4 Salem, In,US
159/K3 Salem, Mo,US
161/G3 Salem, NH,US
166/C4 Salem, NJ,US
166/C4 Salem (co.), NJ,US
166/C4 Salem (cr.), NJ,US
168/G6 Salem, Oh,US
156/C4 Salem (cap.), Or,US
160/D4 Salem, Va,US
80/C4 Salemi, It.
80/F2 Salentina (pen.), It.
80/D2 Salerno, It.
80/D2 Salerno (gulf), It.
59/G3 Sales (pt.), UK
57/F5 Salford, Eng,UK
82/D1 Salgótarján, Hun.
140/C3 Salgueiro, Braz.
159/F3 Salida, Co,US
92/B2 Salihli, Turk.
131/D2 Salima, Malw.
127/B4 Salīmah (oasis), Sudan
74/B1 Salime (res.), Sp.
130/C5 Salims, Tanz.
150/C2 Salina (pt.), Bahm.
80/D3 Salina (isl.), It.
159/H3 Salina, Ks,US
158/E3 Salina, Ut,US
146/D3 Salina Cruz, Mex.
140/B5 Salinas, Braz.
138/A5 Salinas, Ecu.
147/E4 Salinas, Mex.
158/B3 Salinas, Ca,US
158/B3 Salinas (riv.), Ca,US
75/G3 Salinas, Cabo de (cape), Sp.
159/F4 Salinas Nat'l Mon., NM,US
144/D4 Salinas y Aguada Blanca Nat'l Rsv., Peru
80/D2 Saline (marsh), It.
54/C4 Saline, Sc,UK
159/J4 Saline (riv.), Ar,US
159/G3 Saline (riv.), Ks,US
165/E7 Saline (riv.), Mi,US
137/J4 Salinópolis, Braz.
117/M8 Salisbury, Austl.
153/J2 Salisbury (isl.), NW,Can
59/E4 Salisbury, Eng,UK
58/D4 Salisbury (plain), Eng,UK
160/F4 Salisbury, Md,US
163/H3 Salisbury, NC,US
140/B3 Salitre (riv.), Braz.
138/B5 Salitre, Ecu.
61/J2 Salla, Fin.
76/C6 Sallanches, Fr.
66/D4 Salland (reg.), Neth.
128/B4 Sallatouk (pt.), Gui.
68/B3 Sallaumines, Fr.
75/F2 Sallent, Sp.
159/J4 Sallisaw, Ok,US
127/D5 Sallūm, Sudan
106/D2 Sallyāna, Nepal
60/D3 Sally Gap (pass), Ire.
69/F3 Salm (riv.), Ger.
93/F2 Salmās, Iran
156/D4 Salmon (riv.), Id,US
156/D3 Salmon Arm, BC,Can
158/D2 Salmon Falls (riv.), Id, Nv,US
156/E4 Salmon River (mts.), Id,US
156/E4 Salmon, South Fork (riv.), Id,US
63/K1 Salo, Fin.
78/D1 Salò, It.
76/B2 Salon (riv.), Fr.
72/F5 Salon-de-Provence, Fr.
125/K8 Salonga Nat'l Park, Zaire
81/H3 Salonika (Thermaic) (gulf), Gre.
81/H2 Salonika (Thessaloníki), Gre.
82/E2 Salonta, Rom.
74/B3 Salor (riv.), Sp.
128/B3 Saloum, Vallée du (wadi), Sen.
63/M1 Salpausselkä (mts.), Fin.
75/G1 Salses, Fr.
87/G3 Sal'sk, Rus.
80/C4 Salso (riv.), It.
78/C3 Salsomaggiore Terme, It.
108/B1 Salt (range), Pak.
132/C3 Salt (riv.), SAfr.
149/J1 Salt (cay), Trks.
158/E4 Salt (riv.), Az,US
165/Q16 Salt (cr.), Il,US
146/D2 Salt (cr.), Tx,US
135/C1 Salta, Arg.
58/B6 Saltash, Eng,UK
57/H2 Saltburn, Eng,UK
54/B5 Saltcoats, Sc,UK
60/D5 Saltee (isls.), Ire.
61/E2 Saltfjorden (fjord), Nor.
58/D4 Saltford, Eng,UK
63/T9 Saltholm (isl.), Den.
163/H4 Saltilla (riv.), Ga,US
147/E3 Saltillo, Mex.
158/E2 Salt Lake City (cap.), Ut,US
168/B3 Salt Meadow Nat'l Wild. Ref., Ct,US
159/J2 Salt, North Fork (riv.), Mo,US
142/E2 Salto, Arg.
141/C2 Salto, Braz.
80/C1 Salto (riv.), It.
135/E3 Salto, Uru.
143/F1 Salto (dept.), Uru.
140/C5 Salto da Divisa, Braz.
135/F1 Salto del Guairá, Par.
158/C4 Salton Sea (lake), Ca,US
141/A3 Salto Santiago (res.), Braz.
63/S7 Saltsjöbaden, Swe.
163/H3 Saluda (riv.), SC,US
112/C3 Salug, Phil.
106/D4 Sālūr, India
77/H5 Salurn (Salorno), It.
137/H2 Salut (isls.), FrG.
78/A3 Saluzzo, It.
143/J7 Salvación (bay), Chile
140/C4 Salvador, Braz.
74/A3 Salvaterra de Magos, Port.
74/A1 Salvatierra de Miño, Sp.
90/J8 Salween (riv.), Asia
87/J5 Sal'yany, Azer.
160/D4 Salyersville, Ky,US
65/H5 Salza (riv.), Aus.
71/F6 Salzach (riv.), Aus., Ger.
67/E4 Salzbergen, Ger.
73/K3 Salzburg, Aus.
73/K3 Salzburg (prov.), Aus.
67/H4 Salzgitter, Ger.
67/G4 Salzhemmendorf, Ger.
67/F5 Salzkotten, Ger.
64/F2 Salzwedel, Ger.
74/C1 Sama, Sp.
110/C4 Samak (cape), Indo.
112/C4 Samales (isls.), Phil.
106/D4 Sāmalkot, India
127/B2 Samālūţ, Egypt
150/D3 Samaná, DRep.
150/D3 Samaná (cape), DRep.
108/D2 Samāna, India
149/H1 Samana (Atwood) (cay), Bahm.
91/D1 Samandağı, Turk.
93/N7 Samandira, Turk.
100/C2 Samani, Japan
91/B4 Samannūd, Egypt
112/D2 Samar (isl.), Phil.
112/D2 Samar (sea), Phil.
87/J1 Samara, Rus.
87/K1 Samara (riv.), Rus.
87/J1 Samara Obl., Rus.
78/B1 Samarate, It.
97/M2 Samarga (riv.), Rus.
91/G7 Samaria (reg.), WBnk.
91/G7 Samaria Nat'l Park, WBnk.
81/H5 Samarias Gorge Nat'l Park, Gre.
111/E4 Samarinda, Indo.
88/G6 Samarkand, Uzb.
93/E3 Sāmarrā', Iraq
95/K3 Samasata, Pak.
140/A2 Sambaíba, Braz.
106/D3 Sambalpur, India
126/C2 Samba Lucala, Ang.
133/H7 Sambao (riv.), Madg.
110/D4 Sambar (cape), Indo.
110/C3 Sambas, Indo.
133/J6 Sambava, Madg.
86/B2 Sambor, Ukr.
143/F2 Samborombón (bay), Arg.
143/T12 Samborombón (riv.), Arg.
109/D3 Sambor Prei Kuk (ruins), Camb.
68/C3 Sambre (riv.), Belg.,Fr.
68/C4 Sambre à l'Oise, Canal de (can.), Fr.
130/C3 Samburu, Kenya
130/C2 Samburu Nat'l Rsv., Kenya
101/E4 Samch'ŏk, SKor.
101/E5 Samch'ŏnp'o, SKor.
130/C4 Same, Tanz.
131/C1 Samfya Mission, Zam.
144/C2 Samiria (riv.), Peru
109/C4 Samit (cape), Camb.
109/C3 Samkos (peak), Camb.
165/C2 Sammamish (lake), Wa,US
101/E5 Samnangjin, SKor.
82/B3 Samobor, Cro.
78/D4 Samoggia (riv.), It.
83/F4 Samokov, Bul.
75/Q10 Samora (riv.), Port.
75/Q10 Samora Correia, Port.
81/J2 Samothráki (isl.), Gre.
142/D2 Sampacho, Arg.
110/D4 Sampit, Indo.
110/D4 Sampit (riv.), Indo.
162/E4 Sam Rayburn (res.), Tx,US
109/C1 Sam Sao (mts.), Laos, Viet.
62/D4 Samsø (isl.), Den.
62/D4 Samsø Bælt (chan.), Den.
118/E6 Samson (mtn.), Austl.
109/D2 Sam Son, Viet.
118/E6 Samsonvale (lake), Austl.
92/D1 Samsun, Turk.
92/C1 Samsun (prov.), Turk.
109/B4 Samui (isl.), Thai.
99/H7 Samukawa, Japan
108/B2 Samundri, Pak.
87/J4 Samur (riv.), Azer., Rus.
109/C3 Samut Prakan, Thai.
109/C3 Samut Sakhon, Thai.
109/C3 Samut Songkhram, Thai.
109/D3 San (riv.), Camb.
97/H5 San (riv.), China
128/D3 San, Mali
65/M3 San (riv.), Pol.
82/C3 Sana (riv.), Bosn.
144/B2 Saña, Peru
94/D5 Sanaa (Sana) (cap.), Yem.
74/A1 San Adrián, Cabo de (cape), Sp.
122/D4 Sanaga (riv.), Afr.
112/D4 San Agustin (cape), Phil.
138/B4 San Agustín Archaeological Park, Col.
75/N8 San Agustin de Guadalix, Sp.
151/F5 Sanak (isl.), Ak,US
111/G4 Sanama (isl.), Indo.
134/B5 San Ambrosio (isl.), Chile
93/F3 Sanandaj, Iran
165/K11 San Andreas (lake), Ca,US
149/F3 San Andrés (isl.), Col.
148/B1 San Andrés (lag.), Mex.
112/D2 San Andres, Phil.
158/F4 San Andres (mts.), NM,US
143/S12 San Andrés de Giles, Arg.
74/C1 San Andrés del Rabanedo, Sp.
147/G5 San Andrés Tuxtla, Mex.
141/B3 Sananduva, Braz.
162/E4 San Angelo, Tx,US
165/J11 San Anselmo, Ca,US
149/H4 San Antero, Col.
143/F3 San Antonio (cape), Arg.
142/C2 San Antonio, Chile
138/B4 San Antonio, Ecu.
112/C2 San Antonio, Phil.
164/C2 San Antonio (mtn.), Ca,US
158/F4 San Antonio, NM,US
162/D4 San Antonio, Tx,US
162/D4 San Antonio (riv.), Tx,US
75/F3 San Antonio Abad, Sp.
149/E1 San Antonio, Cabo de (cape), Cuba
147/M8 San Antonio Cañada, Mex.
142/F2 San Antonio de Areco, Arg.
139/F2 San Antonio del Golfo, Ven.
138/C3 San Antonio del Táchira, Ven.
142/D4 San Antonio Oeste, Arg.
146/B2 San Antonio, Punta (pt.), Mex.
162/E4 San Augustine, Tx,US
108/D2 Sanaur, India
106/C3 Sānāwad, India
80/D2 San Bartolomeo in Galdo, It.
79/E5 San Benedetto (mts.), It.
80/C1 San Benedetto del Tronto, It.
146/C5 San Benedicto (isl.), Mex.
147/R10 San Bernardino (riv.), Mex.
112/D2 San Bernardino (str.), Phil.
164/C2 San Bernardino, Ca,US
164/C2 San Bernardino (co.), Ca,US
164/C2 San Bernardino (mts.), Ca,US
147/L7 San Bernardino Contla, Mex.
164/C2 San Bernardino Nat'l For., Ca,US
142/C2 San Bernardo, Chile
138/C2 San Bernardo (pt.), Col.
146/C3 San Blas, Mex.
163/G4 San Blas (cape), Fl,US
162/E3 San Bois (mts.), Ok,US
79/E2 San Bonifacio, It.
136/E6 San Borja, Bol.
161/S9 Sanborn, NY,US
165/K11 San Bruno, Ca,US
164/A2 San Buenaventura (Ventura), Ca,US
142/C3 San Carlos, Chile
112/C2 San Carlos, Phil.
143/G2 San Carlos, Uru.
158/E4 San Carlos (lake), Az,US
165/K11 San Carlos, Ca,US
138/D2 San Carlos, Ven.
142/C4 San Carlos de Bariloche, Arg.
138/D2 San Carlos del Zulia, Ven.
79/E5 San Casciano in Val di Pesa, It.
81/F2 San Cataldo, It.
104/E3 Sancha (riv.), China
146/E4 Sánchez Román, Mex.
142/C2 San Clemente, Chile
74/D3 San Clemente, Sp.
164/C4 San Clemente, Ca,US
158/C4 San Clemente (isl.), Ca,US
78/C2 San Colombano al Lambro, It.
135/D3 San Cristóbal, Arg.
149/F1 San Cristóbal, Cuba
150/D3 San Cristóbal, DRep.
144/K7 San Cristóbal (isl.), Ecu.
148/E3 San Cristobal (vol.), Nic.
120/F6 San Cristobal (isl.), Sol.
146/B1 San Cristobal (cr.), Az,US
138/C3 San Cristóbal, Ven.
148/C2 San Cristóbal de las Casas, Mex.
149/G1 Sancti Spíritus, Cuba
156/F2 Sand (riv.), Ab,Can
132/D3 Sand (riv.), SAfr.
58/D4 Sand (pt.), Eng,UK
159/G2 Sand (hills), Ne,US
98/D3 Sanda, Japan
56/C1 Sanda (isl.), Sc,UK
109/D3 Sandan, Camb.
83/F5 Sandanski, Bul.
55/N13 Sanday (isl.), Sc,UK
57/F5 Sandbach, Eng,UK
67/F2 Sande, Ger.
62/D2 Sandefjord, Nor.
113/Q Sanders (coast), Ant.
162/C4 Sanderson, Tx,US
163/H3 Sandersville, Ga,US
118/F6 Sandgate, Austl.
56/D2 Sandhead, Sc,UK
161/Q8 Sandhill, On,Can
59/F4 Sandhurst, Eng,UK
143/L8 San Diego (cape), Arg.
164/C5 San Diego, Ca,US
164/C4 San Diego (aqueduct), Ca,US
164/C5 San Diego (bay), Ca,US
164/C4 San Diego (co.), Ca,US
164/C5 San Diego (riv.), Ca,US
162/D5 San Diego, Tx,US
164/C4 San Diego Wild Animal Park, Ca,US
164/C5 San Diego Zoo, Ca,US
164/C5 San Diequito (riv.), Ca,US
92/B2 Sandıklı, Turk.
164/C2 San Dimas, Ca,US
80/D4 San Dimitri, Ras (pt.), Malta
111/E3 Sandkan, Malay.
62/A2 Sandnes, Nor.
61/E2 Sandnessjøen, Nor.
126/D2 Sandoa, Zaire
65/L3 Sandomierz, Pol.
138/B4 Sandoná, Col.
79/F1 San Donà di Piave, It.
128/B3 Sandougou (riv.), Gam., Sen.
117/G2 Sandover (riv.), Austl.
59/E5 Sandown, Eng,UK
156/D3 Sandpoint, Id,US
119/F5 Sandringham, Austl.
59/G1 Sandringham, Eng,UK
131/C4 Sandrivier (riv.), SAfr.
167/L8 Sands (pt.), NY,US
105/E3 Sandu Shuizu Zizhixian, China
160/D3 Sandusky, Mi,US
160/D3 Sandusky, Oh,US
62/D2 Sandvika, Nor.
62/G1 Sandviken, Swe.
118/B2 Sandwich (cape), Austl.
59/H4 Sandwich, Eng,UK
118/D4 Sandy (cape), Austl.
157/K2 Sandy (lake), On,Can
59/F2 Sandy, Eng,UK
168/F6 Sandy (cr.), Oh,US
168/H5 Sandy (cr.), Pa,US
168/C3 Sandy (pt.), RI,US
158/E2 Sandy, Ut,US
157/H2 Sandy Bay, Sk,Can
167/D3 Sandy Hook (bay), NJ,US
167/J10 Sandy Hook (pen.), NJ,US
167/D3 Sandy Hook Lighthouse, NJ,US
163/G3 Sandy Springs, Ga,US
69/E4 Sanem, Lux.
80/C2 San Felice Circeo, It.
142/C2 San Felipe, Chile
147/E4 San Felipe, Mex.
138/D2 San Felipe, Ven.
144/A2 San Felipe de Vichayal, Peru
134/A5 San Félix (isl.), Chile
143/S12 San Fernando, Arg.
142/C2 San Fernando, Chile
147/F3 San Fernando, Mex.
112/C1 San Fernando, Phil.
112/C2 San Fernando, Phil.
74/B4 San Fernando, Sp.
150/F5 San Fernando, Trin.
164/B2 San Fernando, Ca,US
164/B2 San Fernando (val.), Ca,US
139/E3 San Fernando de Apure, Ven.
75/N9 San Fernando-de-Henares, Sp.
61/E3 Sånfjällets Nat'l Park, Swe.
151/K3 Sanford (mtn.), Ak,US
163/H4 Sanford, Fl,US
161/G3 Sanford, Me,US
163/J3 Sanford, NC,US
135/D3 San Francisco, Arg.
112/D3 San Francisco, Phil.
158/E4 San Francisco (riv.), Az, NM,US
165/K11 San Francisco, Ca,US
165/K11 San Francisco (bay), Ca,US
165/K11 San Francisco (co.), Ca,US
138/D2 San Francisco, Ven.
165/K11 San Francisco Bay Nat'l Wild. Ref., Ca,US
138/A4 San Francisco, Cabo de (cape), Ecu.
150/D3 San Francisco de Macorís, DRep.
142/C2 San Francisco de Mostazal, Chile
138/B4 San Gabriel, Ecu.
164/B2 San Gabriel, Ca,US
164/B2 San Gabriel (mts.), Ca,US
164/C2 San Gabriel (res.), Ca,US
164/C2 San Gabriel (riv.), Ca,US
147/M8 San Gabriel Chilac, Mex.
146/B2 San Gabriel, Punta (pt.), Mex.
164/C2 San Gabriel, West Fork (riv.), Ca,US
164/C2 San Gabriel Wilderness, Ca,US
106/B4 Sangamner, India
160/B3 Sangamon (riv.), Il,US
95/H2 Sangān (mtn.), Afg.
138/B5 Sangay (vol.), Ecu.
138/B5 Sangay Nat'l Park, Ecu.
130/A3 Sange, Zaire
74/A1 Sangenjo, Sp.
149/G1 San Germán, Cuba
103/C2 Sanggan (riv.), China
110/D3 Sanggau, Indo.
101/B4 Sanggou (bay), China
124/J7 Sangha (riv.), CAfr., Congo
95/J3 Sanghar, Pak.
112/D5 Sangihe (isl.), Indo.
120/B4 Sangihe (isls.), Indo.
138/C3 San Gil, Col.
80/E2 San Giorgio Ionico, It.
80/C4 San Giovanni Gemini, It.
80/E3 San Giovanni in Fiore, It.
79/E3 San Giovanni in Persiceto, It.
79/E2 San Giovanni Lupatoto, It.
79/E5 San Giovanni Valdarno, It.
96/D2 Sangiyn Dalay (lake), Mong.
101/E4 Sangju, SKor.
111/E3 Sangkulirang, Indo.
108/B2 Sāngla, Pak.
112/E6 Sangley Point Nav. Air Sta., Phil.
106/B4 Sāngli, India
124/H7 Sangmélima, Camr.
99/L10 Sangō, Japan
158/C4 San Gorgonio (peak), Ca,US
104/B3 Sangpang (mts.), Burma
159/F3 Sangre de Cristo (mts.), Co, NM,US
150/F5 Sangre Grande, Trin.
107/F2 Sangri, China
80/D2 Sangro (riv.), It.
108/C2 Sangrūr, India
136/G6 Sangue (riv.), Braz.
129/E4 Sanguie (prov.), Burk.
78/C2 San Guiliano Milanese, It.
103/D3 Sanhe, China
146/B3 San Hipólito, Punta (pt.), Mex.
132/E3 Sani (pass), SAfr.
148/D2 San Ignacio, Belz.
136/E6 San Ignacio, Bol.
136/F7 San Ignacio, Bol.
142/B3 San Ignacio, Chile
146/B2 San Ignacio (riv.), Mex.
112/C1 San Ildefonso (cape), Phil.
98/D3 San'in Kaigin Nat'l Park, Japan
149/F4 San Isidro, CR
148/D2 San Isidro, Mex.
148/E3 San Isidro, Nic.
138/C2 San Jacinto, Col.
112/C2 San Jacinto, Phil.
164/C3 San Jacinto (riv.), Ca,US
142/C2 San Javier, Chile
75/E4 San Javier, Sp.
131/B2 Sanje, Zam.
99/F2 Sanjō, Japan
136/F6 San Joaquín, Bol.
144/K7 San Joaquín (peak), Ecu.
148/C2 San Joaquín, Mex.
165/M11 San Joaquin (co.), Ca,US
164/G8 San Joaquin (hills), Ca,US
165/L10 San Joaquin (riv.), Ca,US
158/B3 San Joaquin (val.), Ca,US
142/E1 San Jorge, Arg.
142/D5 San Jorge (cape), Arg.
142/D5 San Jorge (gulf), Arg.
138/C3 San Jorge (riv.), Col.
146/B2 San Jorge (bay), Mex.
148/E4 San Jorge, Nic.
75/F2 San Jorge (gulf), Sp.
142/D4 San José (gulf), Arg.
149/E4 San José (cap.), CR
148/D3 San José, Guat.
146/C3 San José (isl.), Mex.
144/B2 San José, Peru
112/C2 San Jose, Phil.
75/F3 San José, Sp.
143/F2 San José (dept.), Uru.
143/T11 San José (riv.), Uru.
165/L12 San Jose, Ca,US
164/G7 San Jose (hills), Ca,US
112/C3 San Jose de Buenavista, Phil.
136/F7 San José de Chiquitos, Bol.
139/E2 San José de Guanipa, Ven.
139/E2 San José de Guaribe, Ven.
135/C3 San José de Jáchal, Arg.
112/F6 San Jose del Monte, Phil.
144/C4 San José de Los Molinos, Peru
142/Q9 San José de Maipo, Chile
143/F2 San José de Mayo, Uru.
147/E4 San José Iturbide, Mex.
142/C1 San Juan, Arg.
143/M8 San Juan (cape), Arg.
142/C1 San Juan (prov.), Arg.
135/C3 San Juan (riv.), Arg.
138/B3 San Juan (riv.), Col.
149/E4 San Juan (riv.), CR, Nic.
150/D3 San Juan, DRep.
148/D3 San Juan (pt.), ESal.
112/C2 San Juan, Phil.
112/D3 San Juan, Phil.
112/F6 San Juan (riv.), Phil.
150/E3 San Juan (cap.), PR
164/C3 San Juan (cr.), Ca,US
158/F3 San Juan (mts.), Co,US
158/E3 San Juan (riv.), Co, Ut,US
162/A2 San Juan (basin), NM,US
135/E2 San Juan Bautista, Par.
164/C3 San Juan Capistrano, Ca,US
75/E3 San Juan de Alicante, Sp.
74/B4 San Juan de Aznalfarache, Sp.
146/D5 San Juan de Lima, Punta (pt.), Mex.
112/F6 San Juan del Monte, Phil.
139/E2 San Juan de los Morros, Ven.
146/B3 San Juanico, Punta (pt.), Mex.
147/M8 San Juan Ixcaquixtla, Mex.
147/M7 San Juan Ixtenco, Mex.
147/R9 San Juan Teotihuacan, Mex.
143/K7 San Julián, Gran Bajo de (val.), Arg.
135/D3 San Justo, Arg.
128/C4 Sankanbiriwa (peak), SLeo.
108/F4 Sankaranāyinarkovil, India
128/C4 Sankoroni (riv.), Gui., Mali
73/L3 Sankt Andrä, Aus.
69/G2 Sankt Augustin, Ger.
77/F3 Sankt Gallen, Swi.
77/F3 Sankt Gallen (canton), Swi.
70/B6 Sankt Georgen im Schwarzwald, Ger.
77/G5 Sankt Gertraud (Santa Gertrude), It.
69/G5 Sankt Ingbert, Ger.
77/H4 Sankt Jakob (San Giacomo), It.
73/K3 Sankt Johann im Pongau, Aus.
73/K3 Sankt Johann in Tirol, Aus.
77/H4 Sankt Leonhard in Passeier (San Leonardo in Passiria), It.
77/H4 Sankt Martin in Passeier (San Martino in Passiria), It.
77/H5 Sankt Michael (San Michele), It.
76/D5 Sankt Niklaus, Swi.
73/L2 Sankt Pölten, Aus.
73/L3 Sankt Veit an der Glan, Aus.
69/G5 Sankt Wendel, Ger.
146/B3 San Lázaro, Cabo (cape), Mex.
79/E4 San Lazzaro, It.
165/K11 San Leandro, Ca,US
165/K11 San Leandro (res.), Ca,US
136/E6 San Lorenzo, Bol.
143/J6 San Lorenzo (peak), Chile
138/B4 San Lorenzo, Ecu.
136/B4 San Lorenzo (cape), Ecu.
148/E3 San Lorenzo, Hon.
80/A3 San Lorenzo (cape), It.
146/D3 San Lorenzo (riv.), Mex.
148/E3 San Lorenzo, Nic.
165/K11 San Lorenzo, Ca,US
74/C2 San Lorenzo de El Escorial, Sp.
74/B4 Sanlúcar de Barrameda, Sp.
148/E3 San Lucas, Nic.
146/C4 San Lucas, Cabo (cape), Mex.
142/D2 San Luis, Arg.
142/D2 San Luis (mts.), Arg.
142/D2 San Luis (prov.), Arg.
149/H1 San Luis, Cuba
148/D2 San Luis, Guat.
162/B2 San Luis (val.), Co,US
147/E4 San Luis de la Paz, Mex.
158/B4 San Luis Obispo, Ca,US
147/E4 San Luis Potosí, Mex.
147/E4 San Luis Potosí (state), Mex.
164/C4 San Luis Rey (riv.), Ca,US
158/E4 San Manuel, Az,US
138/C2 San Marcos, Col.
148/D3 San Marcos, Guat.
164/C4 San Marcos, Ca,US
162/D4 San Marcos, Tx,US
79/G5 San Maria di Porto Novo, It.
112/C1 San Mariano, Phil.
79/F5 San Marino
79/F5 San Marino (cap.), SMar.
164/F7 San Marino, Ca,US
142/C2 San Martín, Arg.
143/J7 San Martín (lake), Arg.
136/F6 San Martín (riv.), Bol.
138/C4 San Martín, Col.
147/L7 San Martín de las Pirámides, Mex.
142/C4 San Martín de los Andes, Arg.
144/B2 San Martín-La Libertad (dept.), Peru
79/E2 San Martino Buon Albergo, It.
79/E1 San Martino di Lupari, It.
147/L7 San Martín Texmelucan, Mex.
129/E3 Sanmatenga (prov.), Burk.
112/F6 San Mateo, Phil.
165/K11 San Mateo, Ca,US
165/K12 San Mateo (co.), Ca,US
164/C4 San Mateo (cr.), Ca,US
162/B3 San Mateo (mts.), NM,US
147/K7 San Mateo Atenco, Mex.
142/D4 San Matías (gulf), Arg.
136/G7 San Matías, Bol.
147/L7 San Matías Tlalancaleca, Mex.
78/A2 San Mauro Torinese, It.

218

Sanm – Sawm

103/B4 **Sanmenxia,** China
77/H5 **San Michele** (Sankt Michael), It.
136/F6 **San Miguel** (riv.), Bol.
138/B4 **San Miguel** (riv.), Col., Ecu.
148/D3 **San Miguel,** ESal.
149/G4 **San Miguel** (gulf), Pan.
112/C2 **San Miguel** (bay), Phil.
147/E4 **San Miguel de Allende,** Mex.
142/F2 **San Miguel del Monte,** Arg.
138/B4 **San Miguel de los Bancos,** Ecu.
135/C2 **San Miguel de Tucumán,** Arg.
147/L6 **San Miguel Regla,** Mex.
147/K8 **San Miguel Totomaloya,** Mex.
147/K7 **San Miguel Zinacantepec,** Mex.
105/H3 **Sanming,** China
79/D5 **San Miniato,** It.
99/L9 **Sannan,** Japan
125/M5 **Sannār,** Sudan
80/D2 **Sannicandro Garganico,** It.
158/C4 **San Nicolas** (isl.), Ca,US
142/E2 **San Nicolás de los Arroyos,** Arg.
147/M7 **San Nicolás Terrenate,** Mex.
147/E4 **San Nicolás Tolentino,** Mex.
89/P2 **Sannikova** (str.), Rus.
100/B3 **Sannohe,** Japan
53/S10 **Sannois,** Fr.
99/F2 **Sano,** Japan
65/M4 **Sanok,** Pol.
138/C2 **San Onofre,** Col.
164/C4 **San Onofre** (mtn.), Ca,US
142/B4 **San Pablo,** Chile
165/K11 **San Pablo,** Ca,US
165/K10 **San Pablo** (bay), Ca,US
165/K11 **San Pablo** (res.), Ca,US
165/K10 **San Pablo Bay Nat'l Wild. Ref.,** Ca,US
112/C2 **San Pablo City,** Phil.
112/C2 **San Pascual,** Phil.
142/F2 **San Pedro,** Arg.
142/C2 **San Pedro,** Chile
135/C1 **San Pedro** (vol.), Chile
149/G1 **San Pedro** (riv.), Cuba
148/D2 **San Pedro** (riv.), Guat., Mex.
128/D5 **San Pédro,** IvC.
146/D3 **San Pedro** (riv.), Mex.
135/E1 **San Pedro,** Par.
74/B3 **San Pedro** (range), Sp.
158/E4 **San Pedro** (riv.), Az,US
164/F8 **San Pedro,** Ca,US
164/B3 **San Pedro** (bay), Ca,US
164/B3 **San Pedro** (chan.), Ca,US
148/D3 **San Pedro Carchá,** Guat.
144/C3 **San Pedro de Cajas,** Peru
146/E3 **San Pedro de las Colinas,** Mex.
144/B2 **San Pedro de Lloc,** Peru
75/E4 **San Pedro del Pinatar,** Sp.
150/D3 **San Pedro de Macorís,** DRep.
146/B2 **San Pedro Martir** (mts.), Mex.
148/D3 **San Pedro Sula,** Hon.
80/A3 **San Pietro** (isl.), It.
54/C6 **Sanquhar,** Sc,UK
138/B4 **Sanquianga Nat'l Park,** Col.
146/B2 **San Quintín, Cabo** (cape), Mex.
142/C2 **San Rafael,** Arg.
147/H4 **San Rafael,** Mex.
165/J11 **San Rafael,** Ca,US
164/F7 **San Rafael** (hills), Ca,US
158/E3 **San Rafael** (riv.), Ut,US
149/J4 **San Rafael,** Ven.
138/D2 **San Rafael del Moján,** Ven.
149/E4 **San Ramón,** CR
144/C3 **San Ramón,** Peru
143/G2 **San Ramón,** Uru.
165/L11 **San Ramon,** Ca,US
135/D1 **San Ramón de la Nueva Orán,** Arg.
78/A5 **San Remo,** It.
150/D4 **San Román** (cape), Ven.
74/C4 **San Roque,** Sp.
142/B3 **San Rosendo,** Chile
162/D4 **San Saba,** Tx,US
159/H5 **San Saba** (riv.), Tx,US
150/C1 **San Salvador** (isl.), Bahm.
144/J7 **San Salvador** (isl.), Ecu.
148/D3 **San Salvador** (cap.), ESal.
143/S11 **San Salvador** (riv.), Uru.
135/C1 **San Salvador de Jujuy,** Arg.
147/M7 **San Salvador el Seco,** Mex.
147/M8 **San Salvador Huixcolotla,** Mex.
80/D1 **San Salvo,** It.
74/E1 **San Sebastián,** Sp.
74/D2 **San Sebastián de los Reyes,** Sp.
148/E3 **San Sebastían de Yali,** Nic.
78/D1 **San Sebastiano,** It.
79/F5 **Sansepolcro,** It.
80/D2 **San Severo,** It.
105/F3 **Sansui,** China
96/F2 **Sant,** Mong.
144/B3 **Santa,** Peru
144/B3 **Santa** (riv.), Peru
136/E6 **Santa Ana,** Bol.
136/E7 **Santa Ana,** Bol.
138/A5 **Santa Ana,** Ecu.
148/D3 **Santa Ana,** ESal.
148/D3 **Santa Ana** (vol.), ESal.
146/C2 **Santa Ana,** Mex.
164/C3 **Santa Ana,** Ca,US
164/C3 **Santa Ana** (mts.), Ca,US
164/C3 **Santa Ana** (riv.), Ca,US
147/L7 **Santa Ana Chiautempan,** Mex.
138/D2 **Santa Ana, Falcón,** Ven.
138/D2 **Santa Ana, Trujillo,** Ven.
141/D1 **Santa Bárbara,** Braz.
142/B3 **Santa Bárbara,** Chile
138/C3 **Santa Bárbara,** Col.
148/D3 **Santa Bárbara,** Hon.
112/C2 **Santa Barbara,** Phil.
164/A2 **Santa Barbara,** Ca,US
164/A2 **Santa Barbara** (chan.), Ca,US
164/A1 **Santa Barbara** (co.), Ca,US
138/D3 **Santa Bárbara,** Ven.
141/C2 **Santa Bárbara d'Oeste,** Braz.
112/C3 **Santa Catalina,** Phil.
164/C4 **Santa Catalina** (gulf), Ca,US
164/B4 **Santa Catalina** (isl.), Ca,US
141/B3 **Santa Catarina** (isl.), Braz.
141/B3 **Santa Catarina** (state), Braz.
141/B3 **Santa Cecília,** Braz.
147/Q9 **Santa Cecilia Pyramid,** Mex.
149/G1 **Santa Clara,** Cuba
74/A4 **Santa Clara** (res.), Port.
165/L12 **Santa Clara,** Ca,US
165/L12 **Santa Clara** (co.), Ca,US
164/B2 **Santa Clara** (riv.), Ca,US
75/G2 **Santa Coloma de Farners,** Sp.
75/L7 **Santa Coloma de Gramanet,** Sp.
74/A1 **Santa Comba,** Sp.
79/D5 **Santa Croce sull'Arno,** It.
143/K7 **Santa Cruz** (prov.), Arg.
143/K7 **Santa Cruz** (riv.), Arg.
136/F7 **Santa Cruz,** Bol.
140/C2 **Santa Cruz,** Braz.
142/C2 **Santa Cruz,** Chile
148/E4 **Santa Cruz,** CR
144/J7 **Santa Cruz** (isl.), Ecu.
112/B2 **Santa Cruz,** Phil.
112/C1 **Santa Cruz,** Phil.
112/C2 **Santa Cruz,** Phil.
112/D4 **Santa Cruz,** Phil.
120/F6 **Santa Cruz** (isls.), Sol.
158/E5 **Santa Cruz** (dry riv.), Az,US
158/B3 **Santa Cruz,** Ca,US
164/A2 **Santa Cruz** (isl.), Ca,US
75/S12 **Santa Cruz da Graciosa,** Azor.,Port.
75/R12 **Santa Cruz das Flores,** Azor.,Port.
140/C4 **Santa Cruz da Vitória,** Braz.
148/D3 **Santa Cruz del Quiché,** Guat.
75/X16 **Santa Cruz de Tenerife,** Canl
149/G1 **Santa Cruz del Sur,** Cuba
140/C2 **Santa Cruz do Capibaribe,** Braz.
140/B2 **Santa Cruz do Piauí,** Braz.
141/B2 **Santa Cruz do Rio Pardo,** Braz.
135/F2 **Santa Cruz do Sul,** Braz.
148/D3 **Santa Cruz, Sierra de** (range), Guat.
148/B2 **Santa Cruz Zenzontepec,** Mex.
75/L7 **Sant Adrià de Besòs,** Sp.
142/D5 **Santa Elena** (peak), Arg.
148/E4 **Santa Elena** (bay), CR
148/E4 **Santa Elena** (cape), CR
138/A5 **Santa Elena,** Ecu.
146/E3 **Santa Elena,** Mex.
74/A1 **Santa Eugenia de Ribeira,** Sp.
75/F3 **Santa Eulalia del Río,** Sp.
142/E1 **Santa Fé,** Arg.
142/E2 **Santa Fé** (prov.), Arg.
74/D4 **Santa Fé,** Sp.
163/H4 **Santa Fe** (riv.), Fl,US
159/F4 **Santa Fe** (cap.), NM,US
141/B2 **Santa Fe do Sul,** Braz.
164/B2 **Santa Felicia** (dam), Ca,US
164/F8 **Santa Fe Springs,** Ca,US
80/D3 **Sant'Agata di Militello,** It.
77/G5 **Santa Gertrude** (Sankt Gertraud), It.
77/H5 **Santa Giustina** (lake), It.
140/A1 **Santa Helena,** Braz.
141/B1 **Santa Helena de Goiás,** Braz.
140/A1 **Santa Inês,** Braz.
140/C4 **Santa Inês,** Braz.
143/J8 **Santa Inés** (isl.), Chile
147/L7 **Santa Inés Zacatelco,** Mex.
141/G8 **Santa Isabel,** Braz.
144/B1 **Santa Isabel,** Ecu.
148/D2 **Santa Isabel** (riv.), Guat.
120/E5 **Santa Isabel** (isl.), Sol.
124/G7 **Santa Isabel, Pico de** (peak), EqG.
141/C1 **Santa Juliana,** Braz.
138/B5 **Santa Lucía,** Ecu.
143/F2 **Santa Lucía,** Uru.
143/G2 **Santa Lucía** (riv.), Uru.
140/C3 **Santa Luz,** Braz.
140/A1 **Santa Luzia,** Braz.
140/C2 **Santa Luzia,** Braz.
141/D1 **Santa Luzia,** Braz.
122/J10 **Santa Luzia** (isl.), CpV.
142/E2 **Santa Magdalena,** Arg.
146/B3 **Santa Magdalena** (isl.), Mex.
146/B3 **Santa Margarita** (isl.), Mex.
164/C4 **Santa Margarita** (riv.), Ca,US
78/C4 **Santa Margherita Ligure,** It.
135/F2 **Santa Maria,** Braz.
140/A4 **Santa Maria** (hills), Braz.
142/C2 **Santa María,** Chile
142/B3 **Santa María** (isl.), Chile
144/J7 **Santa María** (isl.), Ecu.
147/L7 **Santa Mariá,** Mex.
146/C3 **Santa María** (bay), Mex.
146/D2 **Santa María** (riv.), Mex.
148/A1 **Santa María** (riv.), Mex.
112/C1 **Santa Maria,** Phil.
112/D4 **Santa Maria,** Phil.
75/T13 **Santa Maria** (isl.), Azor.,Port.
158/B4 **Santa Maria,** Ca,US
131/D5 **Santa Maria, Cabo de** (cape), Moz.
74/B4 **Santa María, Cabo de** (cape), Port.
80/D2 **Santa Maria Capua Vetere,** It.
140/C3 **Santa Maria da Boa Vista,** Braz.
140/A4 **Santa Maria da Vitória,** Braz.
81/F3 **Santa Maria di Leuca** (cape), It.
141/D1 **Santa Maria do Suaçi,** Braz.
148/B3 **Santa María Huatulco,** Mex.
138/C2 **Santa Marta,** Col.
141/B4 **Santa Marta Grande, Cabo de** (cape), Braz.
138/C2 **Santa Marta, Nevada de** (mts.), Col.
164/B2 **Santa Monica,** Ca,US
164/B3 **Santa Monica** (bay), Ca,US
164/B2 **Santa Monica** (mts.), Ca,US
164/B2 **Santa Monica Mts. Nat'l Rec. Area,** Ca,US
140/A4 **Santana,** Braz.
140/B1 **Santana** (isl.), Braz.
75/P11 **Santana,** Port.
75/V15 **Santana,** Madr.,Port.
140/B1 **Santana do Acaraú,** Braz.
140/C2 **Santana do Cariri,** Braz.
140/C3 **Santana do Ipanema,** Braz.
135/E3 **Santana do Livramento,** Braz.
138/B4 **Santander,** Col.
138/C3 **Santander** (dept.), Col.
112/C3 **Santander,** Phil.
74/D1 **Santander,** Sp.
78/C2 **Sant'Angelo Lodigiano,** It.
80/A3 **Sant'Antioco,** It.
80/A3 **Sant'Antioco** (isl.), It.
79/D2 **Sant'Antonio,** It.
164/A2 **Santa Paula,** Ca,US
164/A2 **Santa Paula** (peak), Ca,US
75/E3 **Santa Pola,** Sp.
75/E3 **Santa Pola, Cabo de** (cape), Sp.
79/F4 **Sant'Apollinare in Classe,** It.
140/B2 **Santa Quitéria,** Braz.
140/B1 **Santa Quitéria do Maranhão,** Braz.
79/F4 **Santarcángelo,** It.
139/H5 **Santarém,** Braz.
74/A3 **Santarém,** Port.
74/A3 **Santarém** (dist.), Port.
140/A2 **Santa Rita,** Braz.
140/D2 **Santa Rita,** Braz.
138/D2 **Santa Rita,** Ven.
140/A3 **Santa Rita de Cássia,** Braz.
141/H7 **Santa Rita do Sapucaí,** Braz.
142/D3 **Santa Rosa,** Arg.
142/D4 **Santa Rosa** (val.), Arg.
135/F2 **Santa Rosa,** Braz.
144/B1 **Santa Rosa,** Ecu.
147/F4 **Santa Rosa,** Mex.
158/B3 **Santa Rosa,** Ca,US
158/B4 **Santa Rosa** (isl.), Ca,US
159/F4 **Santa Rosa,** NM,US
158/C2 **Santa Rosa** (range), Nv,US
142/D2 **Santa Rosa de Calamuchita,** Arg.
148/D3 **Santa Rosa de Copán,** Hon.
138/C3 **Santa Rosa de Osos,** Col.
141/C2 **Santa Rosa de Viterbo,** Braz.
146/B3 **Santa Rosalía,** Mex.
138/D2 **Santa Rosalía,** Ven.
146/B2 **Santa Rosalia, Punta** (pt.), Mex.
148/E4 **Santa Rosa Nat'l Park,** CR
164/B2 **Santa Susana** (mts.), Ca,US
137/J6 **Santa Teresa** (riv.), Braz.
117/G2 **Santa Teresa Abor. Land,** Austl.
143/G2 **Santa Teresa Nat'l Park,** Uru.
137/H6 **Santa Teresinha,** Braz.
143/F3 **Santa Teresita,** Arg.
141/B1 **Santa Vitória,** Braz.
143/G2 **Santa Vitória do Palmar,** Braz.
164/A2 **Santa Ynez** (mts.), Ca,US
164/A1 **Santa Ynez** (riv.), Ca,US
75/L7 **Sant Boi de Llobregat,** Sp.
75/F2 **Sant Carles de la Ràpita,** Sp.
75/G2 **Sant Celoni,** Sp.
75/G2 **Sant Cugat del Vallès,** Sp.
164/D5 **Santee,** Ca,US
163/H3 **Santee** (dam), SC,US
163/J3 **Santee** (riv.), SC,US
146/E5 **San Telmo, Punta** (pt.), Mex.
78/A3 **Santena,** It.
79/E4 **Santerno** (riv.), It.
80/D3 **Sant'Eufemia** (gulf), It.
75/L7 **Sant Felíu,** Sp.
75/G2 **Sant Feliu de Guíxols,** Sp.
75/G2 **Sant Feliu de Llobregat,** Sp.
75/F1 **Sant Gervàs** (peak), Sp.
78/B2 **Santhia,** It.
135/F2 **Santiago,** Braz.
142/C2 **Santiago** (cap.), Chile
143/J7 **Santiago** (cape), Chile
150/D3 **Santiago,** DRep.
144/B1 **Santiago** (riv.), Ecu., Peru
147/E3 **Santiago,** Mex.
162/B5 **Santiago** (riv.), Mex.
149/F4 **Santiago,** Pan.
149/F4 **Santiago** (mtn.), Pan.
112/C1 **Santiago,** Phil.
164/C3 **Santiago** (peak), Ca,US
164/C3 **Santiago** (res.), Ca,US
162/C4 **Santiago** (mts.), Tx,US
144/B2 **Santiago de Cao,** Peru
74/A1 **Santiago de Compostela,** Sp.
149/H1 **Santiago de Cuba,** Cuba
135/D2 **Santiago del Estero,** Arg.
146/D4 **Santiago Ixcuintla,** Mex.
148/B2 **Santiago Jocotepec,** Mex.
147/M8 **Santiago Miahuatlán,** Mex.
146/D3 **Santiago Papasquiaro,** Mex.
142/Q9 **Santiago, Región Metropolitana de** (reg.), Chile
147/G5 **Santiago Tuxtla,** Mex.
78/D3 **Sant'Ilario d'Enza,** It.
77/F3 **Säntis** (peak), Swi.
75/K6 **Sant Jeroni** (mtn.), Sp.
75/K6 **Sant Llorenc del Munt Nat'l Park,** Sp.
99/K9 **Santō,** Japan
140/C4 **Santo Amaro,** Braz.
141/G8 **Santo Amaro** (isl.), Braz.
140/C3 **Santo Amaro das Brotas,** Braz.
141/B2 **Santo Anastácio,** Braz.
141/G8 **Santo André,** Braz.
135/F2 **Santo Ângelo,** Braz.
122/J9 **Santo Antão** (isl.), CpV.
124/G7 **Santo António,** SaoT.
140/C4 **Santo Antônio de Jesus,** Braz.
141/D2 **Santo Antônio de Pádua,** Braz.
140/B5 **Santo Antônio do Jacinto,** Braz.
140/A2 **Santo Antônio dos Lopes,** Braz.
149/F1 **Santo Domingo,** Cuba
150/D3 **Santo Domingo** (cap.), DRep.
138/B5 **Santo Domingo de los Colorados,** Ecu.
146/B3 **Santo Domingo, Punta** (pt.), Mex.
140/C4 **Santo Estêvão,** Braz.
135/E3 **Santo Grande** (res.), Uru.
75/E3 **Santomera,** Sp.
74/D1 **Santoña,** Sp.
140/B4 **Santo Onofre** (riv.), Braz.
81/J4 **Santorini** (Thíra), Gre.
141/G8 **Santos,** Braz.
141/K6 **Santos Dumont,** Braz.
144/J7 **Santo Tomás** (vol.), Ecu.
112/C1 **Santo Tomas** (mtn.), Phil.
146/A2 **Santo Tomás, Punta** (pt.), Mex.
142/E1 **Santo Tomé,** Arg.
75/K7 **Sant Pere de Ribes,** Sp.
75/K7 **Sant Sadurní d'Anoia,** Sp.
78/B2 **Santuario di Crea,** It.
78/A1 **Santuario di Oropa,** It.
74/D1 **Santurce-Antiguo,** Sp.
75/K6 **Sant Vincenç de Castellet,** Sp.
75/L7 **Sant Vincenç dels Hort,** Sp.
142/B5 **San Valentin** (peak), Chile
142/C2 **San Vicente,** Chile
148/D3 **San Vicente,** ESal.
164/D5 **San Vicente** (res.), Ca,US
74/B3 **San Vicente de Alcántara,** Sp.
144/B4 **San Vicente de Cañete,** Peru
75/E3 **San Vicente del Raspeig,** Sp.
79/G6 **San Vicino, Monte** (peak), It.
80/B1 **San Vincenzo,** It.
80/C3 **San Vito** (cape), It.
79/F1 **San Vito al Tagliamento,** It.
105/F5 **Sanya,** China
131/C3 **Sanyati** (riv.), Zim.
140/B2 **São Benedito,** Braz.
140/B1 **São Benedito do Rio Prêto,** Braz.
140/A1 **São Bento,** Braz.
141/H7 **São Bento do Sapucaí,** Braz.
140/C3 **São Bento do Una,** Braz.
141/G8 **São Bernardo do Campo,** Braz.
135/E2 **São Borja,** Braz.
141/C2 **São Carlos,** Braz.
140/C3 **São Cristóvão,** Braz.
140/A4 **São Desidério,** Braz.
140/A4 **São Desidério** (riv.), Braz.
140/A4 **São Domingos,** Braz.
140/A4 **São Domingos** (riv.), Braz.
141/B1 **São Domingos** (riv.), Braz.
140/A2 **São Domingos do Maranhão,** Braz.
137/H5 **São Félix do Xingu,** Braz.
141/D2 **São Fidélis,** Braz.
140/A4 **São Francisco,** Braz.
135/G2 **São Francisco** (isl.), Braz.
140/B3 **São Francisco** (mts.), Braz.
137/L5 **São Francisco** (riv.), Braz.
141/B3 **São Francisco do Sul,** Braz.
141/B4 **São Fransisco de Paula,** Braz.
135/F3 **São Gabriel,** Braz.
141/D1 **São Gabriel da Palha,** Braz.
141/K7 **São Gonçalo,** Braz.
141/C1 **São Gonçalo do Abaeté,** Braz.
141/H6 **São Gonçalo do Sapuçaí,** Braz.
141/C1 **São Gotardo,** Braz.
130/B5 **Sao Hill,** Tanz.
141/C2 **São Joachim da Barra,** Braz.
137/K4 **São João,** Braz.
136/F5 **São João** (mts.), Braz.
140/A1 **São João Batista,** Braz.
141/B3 **São João Batista,** Braz.
141/D2 **São João da Barra,** Braz.
141/G6 **São João da Boa Vista,** Braz.
74/A2 **São João da Madeira,** Port.
140/A4 **São João da Ponte,** Braz.
75/P10 **São João das Lampas,** Port.
141/C2 **São João del Rei,** Braz.
141/K7 **São João de Meriti,** Braz.
140/B4 **São João do Paraíso,** Braz.
140/B3 **São João do Piauí,** Braz.
140/B2 **São João dos Patos,** Braz.
141/D1 **São João Evangelista,** Braz.
141/K6 **São João Nepomuceno,** Braz.
141/B4 **São Joaquim,** Braz.
141/B4 **São Joaquim Nat'l Park,** Braz.
75/S12 **São Jorge** (isl.), Azor.,Port.
141/B3 **São José,** Braz.
140/D2 **São José de Mipibu,** Braz.
140/C2 **São José de Piranhas,** Braz.
140/A1 **São José de Ribamar,** Braz.
140/C2 **São José do Belmonte,** Braz.
140/D2 **São José do Campestre,** Braz.
140/C2 **São José do Egito,** Braz.
141/A5 **São José do Norte,** Braz.
141/G6 **São José do Rio Pardo,** Braz.
141/B2 **São José do Rio Preto,** Braz.
141/H8 **São José dos Campos,** Braz.
141/B3 **São José dos Pinhais,** Braz.
141/B4 **São Leopoldo,** Braz.
141/H7 **São Lourenço,** Braz.
137/G7 **São Lourenço** (riv.), Braz.
75/Q10 **São Lourenço,** Port.
141/B4 **São Lourenço do Sul,** Braz.
126/C3 **São Lucas,** Ang.
140/A1 **São Luís,** Braz.
140/D3 **São Luís do Quitunde,** Braz.
141/B2 **São Manoel,** Braz.
140/A1 **São Marcos** (bay), Braz.
140/A5 **São Marcos** (riv.), Braz.
141/E1 **São Mateus,** Braz.
141/D1 **São Mateus** (riv.), Braz.
140/A2 **São Mateus do Maranhão,** Braz.
141/B3 **São Mateus do Sul,** Braz.
140/C2 **São Miguel,** Braz.
75/T13 **São Miguel** (isl.), Azor.,Port.
141/C2 **São Miguel Arcanjo,** Braz.
140/C3 **São Miguel dos Campos,** Braz.
140/B2 **São Miguel do Tapuio,** Braz.
150/D3 **Saona** (isl.), DRep.
76/C3 **Saône,** Fr.
76/A4 **Saône** (riv.), Fr.
76/B4 **Saône-et-Loire** (dept.), Fr.
122/J10 **São Nicolau** (isl.), CpV.
141/G8 **São Paulo,** Braz.
141/H8 **São Paulo** (state), Braz.
136/E4 **São Paulo de Olivença,** Braz.
140/D2 **São Paulo do Potengi,** Braz.
141/D2 **São Pedro da Aldeia,** Braz.
140/B2 **São Pedro do Piauí,** Braz.
140/C2 **São Rafael,** Braz.
140/A2 **São Raimundo das Mangabeiras,** Braz.
140/B3 **São Raimundo Nonato,** Braz.
99/M9 **Saori,** Japan
140/A5 **São Romão,** Braz.
134/F3 **São Roque** (cape), Braz.
140/D2 **São Roque, Cabo de** (cape), Braz.
75/S12 **São Roque do Pico,** Azor.,Port.
141/H8 **São Sebastião,** Braz.
141/H8 **São Sebastião** (isl.), Braz.
131/D4 **São Sebastião** (pt.), Moz.
141/C2 **São Sebastião do Paraíso,** Braz.
141/B1 **São Simão** (res.), Braz.
74/A4 **São Teotónio,** Port.
141/C2 **São Tiago,** Braz.
122/K10 **São Tiago** (isl.), CpV.
134/E5 **São Tomé** (cape), Braz.
124/G7 **São Tomé** (cap.), SaoT.
124/G7 **São Tomé** (isl.), SaoT.
124/F7 **São Tomé and Príncipe**
141/D2 **São Tomé, Cabo de** (cape), Braz.
124/E1 **Saouru** (dry riv.), Alg.
141/G8 **São Vicente,** Braz.
122/J10 **São Vicente** (isl.), CpV.
74/A4 **São Vicente, Cabo de** (cape), Port.
83/K5 **Sapanca,** Turk.
81/H1 **Sapareva Banya,** Bul.
140/D2 **Sapé,** Braz.
163/H4 **Sapelo** (isl.), Ga,US
81/G4 **Sapiéndza** (isl.), Gre.
76/D1 **Sapin Sec, Roche du** (mtn.), Fr.
149/G5 **Sapo, Serraniía de** (range), Pan.
66/D2 **Sappemeer,** Neth.
100/B2 **Sapporo,** Japan
80/D2 **Sapri,** It.
141/H7 **Sapucaí** (riv.), Braz.
93/F2 **Saqqez,** Iran
138/B5 **Saquisilí,** Ecu.
82/E4 **Šar** (mts.), Yugo.
112/C3 **Sara,** Phil.
93/F2 **Sarāb,** Iran
109/C3 **Sara Buri,** Thai.
75/E2 **Saragossa** (Zaragoza), Sp.
144/B1 **Saraguro,** Ecu.
108/B1 **Sarāi Alamgir,** Pak.
82/D4 **Sarajevo** (cap.), Bosn.
163/F4 **Saraland,** Al,US
139/H3 **Saramacca** (dist.), Sur.
104/B3 **Saramati** (mtn.), India
110/D4 **Saran** (peak), Indo.
102/B2 **Saran',** Kaz.
160/F2 **Saranac Lake,** NY,US
130/B4 **Saranda,** Tanz.
81/L6 **Sarandapótamos** (riv.), Gre.
81/G3 **Sarandë,** Alb.
143/G2 **Sarandí Del Yi,** Uru.
112/D4 **Sarangani** (isls.), Phil.
106/C3 **Sārangpur,** India
87/H1 **Saransk,** Rus.
85/M4 **Sarapul,** Rus.
138/D3 **Sarare** (riv.), Ven.
163/H5 **Sarasota,** Fl,US
165/K12 **Saratoga,** Ca,US
156/G5 **Saratoga,** Wy,US
160/F3 **Saratoga Springs,** NY,US
87/H2 **Saratov,** Rus.
87/J1 **Saratov** (res.), Rus.
87/H2 **Saratov Obl.,** Rus.
95/H3 **Sarāvān,** Iran
110/D3 **Sarawak** (state), Malay.
92/A1 **Saray,** Turk.
92/B2 **Sarayköy,** Turk.
92/C2 **Sarayönü,** Turk.
82/D2 **Sárbogárd,** Hun.
77/G5 **Sarca** (riv.), It.
53/T10 **Sarcelles,** Fr.
106/B2 **Sardārshahar,** India
80/A2 **Sardegna** (reg.), It.
73/G5 **Sardinaux, Cap de** (cape), Fr.
80/A2 **Sardinia** (isl.), It.
159/K4 **Sardis** (lake), Ms,US
159/J4 **Sardis** (lake), Ok,US
61/F2 **Sareks Nat'l Park,** Swe.
61/F2 **Sarektjåkko** (peak), Swe.
111/E4 **Sarempaka** (peak), Indo.
78/D1 **Sarezzo,** It.
108/B1 **Sargodha,** Pak.
125/J6 **Sarh,** Chad
93/H2 **Sārī,** Iran
111/J4 **Saribi** (cape), Indo.
120/D3 **Sarigan** (isl.), NMar.
92/B2 **Sarıgöl,** Turk.
92/E1 **Sarıkamış,** Turk.
92/C2 **Sarıkaya,** Turk.
92/C2 **Sarikaya** (prov.), Turk.
76/D4 **Sarine** (riv.), Swi.
125/K2 **Sarīr Kalanshiyū** (des.), Libya
125/J3 **Sarīr Tibasti** (des.), Libya
162/D5 **Sarita,** Tx,US
82/E2 **Sarkad,** Hun.
87/L4 **Sarkamyshskoye** (lake), Trkm., Uzb.
88/H5 **Sarkand,** Kaz.
92/B2 **Şarkîkaraağaç,** Turk.
92/D2 **Şarkışla,** Turk.
83/H5 **Şarköy,** Turk.
72/D4 **Sarlat-La-Canéda,** Fr.
143/K8 **Sarmiento** (peak), Chile
76/E4 **Sarnen,** Swi.
165/H6 **Sarnia,** On,Can
86/C2 **Sarny,** Ukr.
100/C1 **Saroma** (lake), Japan
81/H4 **Saronic** (gulf), Gre.
81/L7 **Saronikós** (gulf), Gre.
78/C1 **Saronno,** It.
83/H5 **Saros** (gulf), Turk.
82/E1 **Sárospatak,** Hun.
62/D2 **Sarpsborg,** Nor.
69/F6 **Sarre** (riv.), Fr.
69/G6 **Sarrebourg,** Fr.
69/G5 **Sarreguemines,** Fr.
74/B1 **Sarria,** Sp.
67/G4 **Sarstedt,** Ger.
148/D3 **Sarstsún** (riv.), Belz., Guat.
89/P3 **Sartang** (riv.), Rus.
72/C3 **Sarthe** (riv.), Fr.
53/S10 **Sartrouville,** Fr.
92/A2 **Saruhanlı,** Turk.
82/D2 **Sárvítz** (riv.), Hun.
82/D2 **Sárvíz** (riv.), Hun.
102/C2 **Sary Ishikotrau** (des.), Kaz.
102/B2 **Saryshagan,** Kaz.
102/A2 **Sarysu** (riv.), Kaz.
78/C4 **Sarzana,** It.
157/K3 **Sasaginnigak** (lake), Mb,Can
106/D3 **Sasarām,** India
99/L9 **Sasayama,** Japan
99/L9 **Sasayama** (riv.), Japan
98/A4 **Sasebo,** Japan
152/F3 **Saskatchewan** (prov.), Can.
156/F3 **Saskatchewan** (riv.), Can.
156/G2 **Saskatoon,** Sk*,Can
149/E3 **Saslaya** (mtn.), Nic.
149/E3 **Saslaya Nat'l Park,** Nic.
87/G1 **Sasovo,** Rus.
166/B5 **Sassafras** (riv.), Md,US
128/D5 **Sassandra,** IvC.
128/D5 **Sassandra** (riv.), IvC.
80/A2 **Sassari,** It.
67/F5 **Sassenberg,** Ger.
66/B4 **Sassenheim,** Neth.
65/G1 **Sassnitz,** Ger.
79/D3 **Sassuolo,** It.
66/A6 **Sas Van Gent,** Neth.
102/D2 **Sasykkol** (lake), Kaz.
98/B5 **Sata-misaki** (cape), Japan
106/B4 **Sātāra,** India
120/E4 **Satawan** (atoll), Micr.
62/F1 **Säter,** Swe.
144/C3 **Satipo,** Peru
57/G2 **Satley,** Eng,UK
106/D3 **Satna,** India
82/E1 **Sátoraljaújhely,** Hun.
102/A2 **Satpayev,** Kaz.
106/C3 **Satpura** (range), India
108/F4 **Sāttānkulam,** India
108/F4 **Sāttūr,** India
82/F2 **Satu Mare,** Rom.
82/F2 **Satu Mare** (co.), Rom.
109/C5 **Satun,** Thai.
121/R9 **Satupaitea,** WSam.
108/F3 **Satyamangalam,** India
142/E3 **Sauce Grande** (riv.), Arg.
140/B3 **Saúde,** Braz.
94/D4 **Saudi Arabia**
64/D4 **Sauer** (riv.), Fr.
67/F5 **Sauer** (riv.), Ger.
69/F4 **Sauer** (riv.), Ger., Lux.
69/G1 **Sauerland** (reg.), Ger.
136/G6 **Sauêruiná** (riv.), Braz.
167/E1 **Saugatuck** (riv.), Ct,US
157/K4 **Sauk** (riv.), Mn,US
157/K4 **Sauk Centre,** Mn,US
157/K4 **Sauk Rapids,** Mn,US
137/H3 **Saül,** FrG.
72/D3 **Sauldre** (riv.), Fr.
70/C6 **Saulgau,** Ger.
160/C2 **Sault Sainte Marie,** On,Can
160/C2 **Sault Sainte Marie,** Mi,US
69/E6 **Saulx** (riv.), Fr.
118/D3 **Saumarez** (reefs), Austl.
72/C3 **Saumur,** Fr.
116/E3 **Saunders** (peak), Austl.
58/B3 **Saundersfoot,** Wal,UK
126/D2 **Saurimo,** Ang.
165/K11 **Sausalito,** Ca,US
53/S9 **Sausseron** (riv.), Fr.
82/C3 **Sava** (riv.), Eur.
80/E2 **Sava,** It.
164/D5 **Savage** (dam), Ca,US
121/H6 **Savai'i** (isl.), WSam.
161/G1 **Savane** (riv.), Qu,Can
116/L6 **Savannah** (brook), Austl.
163/H3 **Savannah,** Ga,US
163/H3 **Savannah** (riv.), Ga, SC,US
163/F3 **Savannah,** Tn,US
107/H4 **Savannaket,** Laos
109/D2 **Savannakhet,** Laos
149/G2 **Savanna la Mar,** Jam.
160/B1 **Savant** (lake), On,Can
106/B4 **Sāvantvādi,** India
92/A2 **Savaştepe,** Turk.
126/C4 **Savate,** Ang.
131/D4 **Save** (riv.), Moz., Zim.
93/G3 **Sāveh,** Iran
79/E4 **Savena** (riv.), It.
83/H2 **Săveni,** Rom.
69/G6 **Saverne,** Fr.
78/A3 **Savigliano,** It.
79/F4 **Savignano sul Rubicone,** It.
53/T11 **Savigny-le-Temple,** Fr.
53/T10 **Savigny-sur-Orge,** Fr.
168/B2 **Saville** (dam), Ct,US
79/F5 **Savio** (riv.), It.
156/C3 **Savona,** BC,Can
78/B4 **Savona,** It.
78/B4 **Savona** (prov.), It.
61/J3 **Savonlinna,** Fin.
76/C6 **Savoy Alps** (mts.), Fr.
62/F3 **Sävsjö,** Swe.
111/F5 **Savu** (sea), Indo.
79/G2 **Savudrija,** Cro.
110/B4 **Sawahlunto,** Indo.
127/D5 **Sawākin,** Sudan
109/B2 **Sawankhalok,** Thai.
99/G3 **Sawara,** Japan
99/F2 **Sawasaki-bana** (pt.), Japan
158/F3 **Sawatch** (range), Co,US
59/G3 **Sawbridgeworth,** Eng,UK
124/J2 **Sawdā** (mts.), Libya
94/D5 **Sawdā', Jabal** (mtn.), SAr.
125/L5 **Sawdirī,** Sudan
111/H4 **Saweba** (cape), Indo.
56/A2 **Sawel** (mtn.), NI,UK
127/B3 **Sawhāj,** Egypt
127/B3 **Sawhāj** (gov.), Egypt
107/F6 **Sāwi,** India
131/C3 **Sawmills,** Zim.

94/G5 Sawqirah, Ghubbat (bay), Oman
95/G5 Şawqirah, Ra's (pt.), Oman
59/G2 Sawston, Eng,UK
119/E1 Sawtell, Austl.
156/E4 Sawtooth (range), Id,US
111/F6 Sawu (isls.), Indo.
75/E3 Sax, Sp.
63/T9 Saxån (riv.), Swe.
63/S7 Saxarfjärden (sound), Swe.
57/H5 Saxilby, Eng,UK
59/H2 Saxmundham, Eng,UK
65/G3 Saxony (state), Ger.
64/F3 Saxony-Anhalt (state), Ger.
99/F3 Sayama, Japan
92/C3 Şaydā, Leb.
147/H4 Sayil (ruins), Mex.
69/G2 Saynbach (riv.), Ger.
96/G3 Saynshand, Mong.
102/D3 Sayram (lake), China
167/D3 Sayreville, NJ,US
167/E2 Sayville, NY,US
81/F2 Sazan (isl.), Alb.
71/H3 Sázava (riv.), Czh.
93/M6 Sazli Dere (riv.), Turk.
57/E3 Scafell Pikes (mtn.), Eng,UK
55/H8 Scalasaig, Sc,UK
57/H3 Scalby, Eng,UK
54/C5 Scald Law (mtn.), Sc,UK
80/D3 Scalea, It.
79/D4 Scale, Corno alle (peak), It.
77/F5 Scalino, Pizzo (peak), It.
55/P12 Scalloway, Sc,UK
79/D3 Scandiano, It.
79/E5 Scandicci, It.
55/N13 Scapa Flow (chan.), Sc,UK
116/K6 Scarborough, Austl.
161/R8 Scarborough, On,Can
57/H3 Scarborough, Eng,UK
68/B3 Scarpe (riv.), Fr.
167/E1 Scarsdale, NY,US
56/E1 Scar Water (riv.), Sc,UK
60/A4 Scattery (isl.), Ire.
53/S10 Sceaux, Fr.
68/D2 Schaerbeek, Belg.
77/E2 Schaffhausen, Swi.
77/E2 Schaffhausen (canton), Swi.
66/B3 Schagen, Neth.
66/C5 Schaijk, Neth.
67/E6 Schalksmühle, Ger.
119/C3 Schanck (cape), Austl.
77/H2 Scharfreiter (peak), Aus.
67/F1 Scharhorn (isl.), Ger.
77/H3 Scharnitz (pass), Ger.
165/P15 Schaumburg, Il,US
66/D2 Scheemda, Neth.
67/G2 Scheessel, Ger.
68/C2 Schelde (Scheldt) (riv.), Belg.
68/C2 Scheldt (Schelde) (riv.), Belg.
70/C6 Schelklingen, Ger.
158/D3 Schell Creek (range), Nv,US
67/H4 Schellerten, Ger.
160/F3 Schenectady, NY,US
67/G1 Schenefeld, Ger.
165/R16 Schererville, In,US
66/D5 Schermbeck, Ger.
66/C3 Scherpenzeel, Neth.
77/F3 Schesaplana (peak), Aus.
70/E3 Schesslitz, Ger.
66/B5 Schiedam, Neth.
67/G5 Schieder-Schwalenberg, Ger.
54/B3 Schiehallion (mtn.), Sc,UK
71/F5 Schierling, Ger.
66/D2 Schiermonnikoog (isl.), Neth.
69/G5 Schiffweiler, Ger.
66/C5 Schijndel, Neth.
68/D1 Schilde, Belg.
66/D2 Schildmeer (lake), Neth.
67/F1 Schillighörn (cape), Ger.
69/G6 Schiltigheim, Fr.
69/E2 Schinnen, Neth.
79/E1 Schio, It.
66/D4 Schipbeek (riv.), Neth.
81/G2 Schkumbin (riv.), Alb.
77/G4 Schlanders (Silandro), It.
67/F5 Schlangen, Ger.
69/F2 Schleiden, Ger.
64/E1 Schleswig, Ger.
67/H1 Schleswig-Holstein (state), Ger.
64/E1 Schleswig-Holsteinisches Wattenmeer Nat'l Park, Ger.
70/D2 Schleuse (riv.), Ger.
77/E3 Schlieren, Swi.
71/F7 Schloss Herrenchiemsee, Ger.
67/F5 Schloss Holte-Stukenbrock, Ger.
67/G4 Schloss Wilhelmstein, Ger.
76/D1 Schlucht, Col de la (pass), Fr.
70/C2 Schlüchtern, Ger.
77/G4 Schluderns (Sluderno), It.
64/F3 Schmalkalden, Ger.
67/F6 Schmallenberg, Ger.
70/C6 Schmeich (riv.), Ger.
77/F1 Schmeie (riv.), Ger.
69/F5 Schmelz, Ger.
70/B2 Schmitten, Ger.
70/D6 Schmutter (riv.), Ger.
71/E3 Schnaittach, Ger.
71/F1 Schneeberg, Ger.
71/E2 Schneeberg (peak), Ger.
69/F3 Schneifel (plat.), Ger.
64/D4 Schneifel (upland), Ger.
67/G2 Schneverdingen, Ger.
154/V12 Schofield Barracks, Hi,US
143/L7 Scholl, Cerro (mtn.), Arg.
70/B5 Schömberg, Ger.
70/C5 Schönaich, Ger.
76/D2 Schönau, Ger.
70/C2 Schondra (riv.), Ger.
64/F2 Schönebeck, Ger.
77/G2 Schongau, Ger.
71/F2 Schönheide, Ger.
64/F2 Schöningen, Ger.
71/F2 Schonwald, Ger.
66/D3 Schoonebeek, Neth.
66/B5 Schoonhoven, Neth.
66/B3 Schoorl, Neth.
70/A3 Schopfheim, Ger.
71/G7 Schörfling am Attersee, Aus.
70/C5 Schorndorf, Ger.
67/E1 Schortens, Ger.
68/D1 Schoten, Belg.
70/C2 Schotten, Ger.
119/D4 Schouten (isl.), Austl.
120/C5 Schouten (isls.), Indo.
66/A5 Schouwen (isl.), Neth.
72/D5 Schrader (peak), Fr.
124/H3 ŞChrā Marzūq (des.), Libya
70/B6 Schramberg, Ger.
77/H3 Schrankogel (peak), Aus.
76/E4 Schreckhorn (peak), Swi.
160/C1 Schreiber, On,Can
70/B4 Schriesheim, Ger.
70/E5 Schrobenhausen, Ger.
132/B2 Schroffenstein (peak), Namb.
162/D4 Schulenburg, Tx,US
67/H4 Schunter (riv.), Ger.
77/F2 Schussen (riv.), Ger.
77/F1 Schussenried, Ger.
70/A6 Schutter (riv.), Ger.
70/E5 Schutter (riv.), Ger.
70/A6 Schutterwald, Ger.
67/E4 Schüttorf, Ger.
166/B2 Schuylkill (co.), Pa,US
166/C3 Schuylkill (riv.), Pa,US
70/E4 Schwabach, Ger.
70/D5 Schwäbische Alb (range), Ger.
70/C5 Schwäbisch Gmünd, Ger.
70/C4 Schwäbisch Hall, Ger.
70/D6 Schwabmünchen, Ger.
70/C4 Schwaigern, Ger.
69/F5 Schwalbach, Ger.
70/B2 Schwalbach am Taunus, Ger.
67/G6 Schwalm (riv.), Ger.
66/D6 Schwalmtal, Ger.
71/F4 Schwandorf im Bayern, Ger.
110/D4 Schwaner (mts.), Indo.
67/F2 Schwanewede, Ger.
65/G3 Schwartz Elster (riv.), Ger.
132/B2 Schwartzerberg (peak), Namb.
70/E4 Schwarzach (riv.), Ger.
71/F4 Schwarzach (riv.), Ger.
71/E4 Schwarze Laber (riv.), Ger.
67/H2 Schwarzenbek, Ger.
70/E4 Schwarzenbruck, Ger.
69/F3 Schwarzer Mann (peak), Ger.
71/F4 Schwarzer Regen (riv.), Ger.
77/H3 Schwarzhorn (peak), Aus.
70/B6 Schwarzwald (Black Forest) (for.), Ger.
73/J3 Schwaz, Aus.
65/J4 Schwechat, Aus.
65/H2 Schwedt, Ger.
70/D2 Schweinfurt, Ger.
67/E6 Schwelm, Ger.
64/F2 Schwerin, Ger.
64/F2 Schweriner (lake), Ger.
67/E6 Schwerte, Ger.
70/B4 Schwetzingen, Ger.
67/G1 Schwinge (riv.), Ger.
67/G5 Schwülme (riv.), Ger.
77/E3 Schwyz, Swi.
77/E3 Schwyz (canton), Swi.
80/C4 Sciacca, It.
80/D4 Scicli, It.
55/H11 Scilly (isls.), Eng,UK
160/D4 Scioto (riv.), Oh,US
168/D1 Scituate, Ma,US
168/C2 Scituate (res.), RI,US
157/G3 Scobey, Mt,US
59/G1 Scolt (pt.), UK
80/D4 Scordia, It.
57/G3 Scotch Corner, Eng,UK
166/D2 Scotch Plains, NJ,US
113/W Scotia (sea), Ant.
55/J8 Scotland, UK
113/M Scott, Ant.
113/L Scott (coast), Ant.
117/M9 Scott (cr.), Austl.
114/C2 Scott (reef), Austl.
152/D3 Scott (cape), BC,Can
153/R7 Scott (cape), NW,Can
152/F2 Scott (lake), NW,Can
159/G3 Scott City, Ks,US
116/B5 Scott Nat'l Park, Austl.
117/M9 Scotts (cr.), Austl.
159/G2 Scottsbluff, Ne,US
159/F2 Scotts Bluff Nat'l Mon., Ne,US
163/G3 Scottsboro, Al,US
160/C4 Scottsburg, In,US
158/E4 Scottsdale, Az,US
119/C4 Scotts Peak (dam), Austl.
160/C4 Scottsville, Ky,US
160/C3 Scottville, Mi,US
55/K7 Scrabster, Sc,UK
166/C1 Scranton, Pa,US
164/C5 Scripps Aquarium/Museum, Ca,US
78/B3 Scrivia (riv.), It.
57/H4 Scunthorpe, Eng,UK
165/N14 Scuppernong (riv.), Wi,US
55/K8 Scurdie Ness (pt.), Sc,UK
82/D4 Scutari (lake), Alb., Yugo.
155/K5 Sea (isls.), Ga,US
140/B4 Seabra, Braz.
59/G5 Seaford, UK
167/M9 Seaford, NY,US
56/C3 Seaforde, NI,UK
57/G2 Seaham, Eng,UK
153/H2 Seahorse (pt.), NW,Can
152/G3 Seal (riv.), Mb,Can
142/B5 Seal (pt.), Chile
132/C4 Seal (cape), SAfr.
53/P8 Seal, Eng,UK
164/B3 Seal Beach, Ca,US
164/F8 Seal Beach Nat'l Wild. Ref., Ca,US
57/H3 Seamer, Eng,UK
141/A3 Seara, Braz.
158/D4 Searchlight, Nv,US
162/F3 Searcy, Ar,US
56/E3 Seascale, Eng,UK
156/C4 Seaside, Or,US
165/C3 SeaTac, Wa,US
58/C5 Seaton, Eng,UK
58/B6 Seaton (riv.), Eng,UK
57/G2 Seaton Carew, Eng,UK
57/G1 Seaton Valley, Eng,UK
165/C2 Seattle, Wa,US
165/C2 Seattle Art Museum, Wa,US
165/C2 Seattle Ctr., Wa,US
167/E2 Seatuck Nat'l Wild. Ref., NY,US
168/F5 Sea World, Oh,US
148/E3 Sébaco, Nic.
123/T15 Sebaou (riv.), Alg.
163/H5 Sebastian, Fl,US
146/B2 Sebastián Vizcaíno (bay), Mex.
119/B3 Sebastopol, Austl.
112/B4 Sebatik (isl.), Malay., Indo.
110/D4 Sebayan (peak), Indo.
123/Q16 Sebdou, Alg.
83/F3 Sebeş, Rom.
131/B4 Sebina, Bots.
92/D1 Şebinkarahisar, Turk.
82/F2 Sebiş, Rom.
65/H3 Sebnitz, Ger.
112/C4 Seboto (pt.), Phil.
123/M13 Sebou (riv.), Mor.
163/H5 Sebring, Fl,US
112/B5 Sebuku (bay), Indo.
111/E4 Sebuku (isl.), Indo.
167/J8 Secaucus, NJ,US
79/D3 Secchia (riv.), It.
144/A2 Sechura, Peru
144/A2 Sechura (bay), Peru
144/A2 Sechura (des.), Peru
68/C2 Seclin, Fr.
143/L7 Seco (riv.), Arg.
127/B4 Second Cataract (falls), Sudan
166/B3 Second Mtn. (ridge), Pa,US
164/C4 Second San Diego (aqueduct), Ca,US
167/H8 Second Watchung (mtn.), NJ,US
106/C4 Secunderābād, India
136/E7 Securé (riv.), Bol.
159/J3 Sedalia, Mo,US
69/D4 Sedan, Fr.
109/B3 Sedaung (mtn.), Burma
57/F3 Sedbergh, Eng,UK
127/B4 Seddenga Temple (ruins), Sudan
91/D4 Sederot, Isr.
57/G2 Sedgefield, Eng,UK
151/L2 Sedgwick (mtn.), Yk,Can
128/B3 Sedhiou, Sen.
71/H3 Sedlčany, Czh.
158/E4 Sedona, Az,US
123/V17 Sedrata, Alg.
65/L3 Sędziszów, Pol.
72/C2 Sée (riv.), Fr.
60/A6 Seefin (mtn.), Ire.
60/C5 Seefin (mtn.), Ire.
70/B3 Seeheim-Jugenheim, Ger.
71/G7 Seekirchen am Wallersee, Aus.
168/C2 Seekonk, Ma,US
132/D3 Seekooi (riv.), SAfr.
67/H5 Seesen, Ger.
67/G2 Seeve (riv.), Ger.
71/G7 Seewalchen am Attersee, Aus.
92/C2 Şefaatli, Turk.
131/B4 Sefare, Bots.
93/G2 Sefīd Rūd (riv.), Iran
123/M14 Sefrou, Mor.
112/B5 Segama (riv.), Malay.
110/B3 Segamat, Malay.
83/F3 Segarcea, Rom.
80/C4 Segesta (ruins), It.
84/G3 Segezha, Rus.
75/E3 Segorbe, Sp.
128/D3 Ségou, Mali
128/D3 Ségou (reg.), Mali
138/C3 Segovia, Col.
74/C2 Segovia, Sp.
84/G3 Segozero (lake), Rus.
78/C2 Segrate, It.
72/C3 Segré, Fr.
75/F2 Segre (riv.), Sp.
151/D5 Seguam (isl.), Ak,US
151/D5 Seguam (passg.), Ak,US
124/H3 Séguédine, Niger
128/D5 Séguéla, IvC.
162/D4 Seguin, Tx,US
74/D3 Segura (riv.), Sp.
126/D5 Sehithwa, Bots.
106/C3 Sehore, India
95/J3 Sehwān, Pak.
99/L10 Seika, Japan
100/B3 Seikan (tunnel), Japan
76/B4 Seile (riv.), Fr.
159/H3 Seiling, Ok,US
69/F6 Seille (riv.), Fr.
61/G3 Seinäjoki, Fin.
157/L3 Seine (riv.), On,Can
72/C2 Seine (bay), Fr.
72/D2 Seine (riv.), Fr.
53/U10 Seine-et-Marne (dept.), Fr.
53/T10 Seine-Saint-Denis (dept.), Fr.
61/G3 Seitsemisen Nat'l Park, Fin.
99/M10 Seiwa, Japan
75/P10 Seixal, Port.
62/D4 Sejerø (isl.), Den.
130/B3 Seke, Tanz.
130/B4 Sekenke, Tanz.
99/E3 Seki, Japan
91/A1 Seki (riv.), Turk.
99/M9 Sekigahara, Japan
99/H6 Sekiyado, Japan
131/A5 Sekoma, Bots.
129/E5 Sekondi, Gha.
156/C4 Selah, Wa,US
80/A3 Selargius, It.
111/H5 Selaru (isl.), Indo.
110/D4 Selatan (cape), Indo.
151/F2 Selawik (lake), Ak,US
151/G2 Selawik Nat'l Wild. Ref., Ak,US
111/F5 Selayar (isl.), Indo.
71/F2 Selb, Ger.
71/E2 Selbitz (riv.), Ger.
57/G4 Selby, Eng,UK
157/H4 Selby, SD,US
92/A2 Selçuk, Turk.
167/E2 Selden, NY,US
80/D2 Sele (riv.), It.
131/B4 Selebi-Phikwe, Bots.
130/B5 Seleli (hill), Tanz.
97/L1 Selemdzha (riv.), Rus.
92/B2 Selendi, Turk.
96/F1 Selenga (riv.), Rus.
96/E2 Selenge, Mong.
96/E2 Selenge (riv.), Mong.
76/D1 Sélestat, Fr.
102/B1 Selety (riv.), Kaz.
102/B1 Seletyteniz (lake), Kaz.
84/G4 Seliger (lake), Rus.
158/D4 Seligman, Az,US
131/B4 Selika, Bots.
80/C4 Selinunte (ruins), It.
156/D3 Selkirk (mts.), BC,Can
157/J3 Selkirk, Mb,Can
54/D5 Selkirk, Sc,UK
158/E5 Sells, Az,US
58/E2 Selly Oak, Eng,UK
67/E5 Selm, Ger.
163/G3 Selma, Al,US
163/F3 Selmer, Tn,US
151/M3 Selous (mtn.), Yk,Can
131/C3 Selous, Zim.
130/C5 Selous Game Rsv., Tanz.
59/F5 Selsey, Eng,UK
59/F5 Selsey Bill (pt.), Eng,UK
72/C2 Sélune (riv.), Fr.
136/E5 Selvas (for.), Braz.
117/H2 Selwyn (range), Austl.
70/B3 Selz (riv.), Ger.
124/C2 Semara, WSah.
110/D5 Semarang, Indo.
112/B4 Sembakung (riv.), Indo.
71/H2 Sembera (riv.), Czh.
93/F2 Şemdinli, Turk.
85/K4 Semenov, Rus.
110/D5 Semeru (peak), Indo.
151/G4 Semidi (isls.), Ak,US
86/F2 Semiluki, Rus.
156/G5 Seminoe (res.), Wy,US
163/G4 Seminole (lake), Ga,US
162/C3 Seminole, Tx,US
102/D1 Semipalatinsk, Kaz.
112/C2 Semirara (isl.), Phil.
151/B5 Semisopochnoi (isl.), Ak,US
110/D4 Semitau, Indo.
93/H3 Semnān, Iran
93/H3 Semnān (gov.), Iran
72/C3 Semnon (riv.), Fr.
69/E4 Semois (riv.), Belg.
76/C2 Semouse (riv.), Fr.
76/B1 Semoutiers, Fr.
69/D4 Semoy (riv.), Fr.
76/E3 Sempacher See (lake), Swi.
84/B2 Semskefjellet (peak), Nor.
109/D3 Sen (riv.), Camb.
109/C3 Sena, Thai.
140/C2 Senador Pompeu, Braz.
131/A3 Senanga, Zam.
163/F3 Senatobia, Ms,US
59/E2 Sence (riv.), Eng,UK
98/B5 Sendai, Japan
99/G1 Sendai (bay), Japan
98/B5 Sendai (riv.), Japan
98/D3 Sendai (riv.), Japan
67/E5 Senden, Ger.
70/D6 Senden, Ger.
67/E5 Sendenhorst, Ger.
65/J4 Senec, Slvk.
68/D2 Seneffe, Belg.
128/B3 Senegal
128/B2 Sénégal (riv.), Afr.
132/D3 Senekal, SAfr.
160/C2 Seney Nat'l Wild. Ref., Mi,US
65/H3 Senftenberg, Ger.
130/A5 Senga Hill Mission, Zam.
141/B3 Sengés, Braz.
102/D5 Sênggê (riv.), China
142/C5 Senguerr (riv.), Arg.
131/C3 Sengwe (riv.), Zim.
140/B3 Senhor do Bonfim, Braz.
65/J4 Senica, Slvk.
79/G5 Senigallia, It.
79/E4 Senio (riv.), It.
92/B2 Senirkent, Turk.
80/E2 Senise, It.
82/B3 Senj, Cro.
61/F1 Senja (isl.), Nor.
100/G8 Senkaku-Shotō (isls.), Jap.
68/B5 Senlis, Fr.
99/L10 Sennan, Japan
125/M5 Sennar (dam), Sudan
68/D2 Senne (riv.), Belg.
160/E1 Senneterre, Qu,Can
58/C3 Sennybridge, Wal,UK
129/F3 Séno (prov.), Burk.
72/E2 Sens, Fr.
148/D3 Sensuntepeque, ESal.
82/E3 Senta, Yugo.
126/E2 Sentery, Zaire
156/C2 Sentinel (peak), BC,Can
120/E4 Senyavin (isls.), Micr.
106/C3 Seoni, India
106/C3 Seonī Mālwā, India
89/N6 Seoul (cap.), SKor.
101/G7 Seoul Grand Park, SKor.
101/F6 Seoul (inset) (cap.), SKor.
101/D4 Seoul-Jikhalsi, SKor.
101/D4 Seoul (Sŏul) (cap.), SKor.
141/K8 Sepetiba (bay), Braz.
120/D5 Sepik (riv.), PNG
65/J2 Sępólno Krajeńskie, Pol.
83/G4 Septemvri, Bul.
161/H1 Sept-Îles, Qu,Can
164/F7 Sepulveda (dam), Ca,US
165/A1 Sequim (bay), Wa,US
158/C3 Sequoia Nat'l Park, Ca,US
78/C1 Serada, Monte (peak), It.
69/E2 Seraing, Belg.
76/B6 Séran (riv.), Fr.
110/C5 Serang, Indo.
110/C3 Serasan (str.), Indo., Malay.
82/E4 Serbia (rep.), Yugo.
78/D5 Serchio (riv.), It.
87/H1 Serdobsk, Rus.
151/D2 Serdtse-Kamen, Mys (pt.), Rus.
92/C2 Şereflikoçhisar, Turk.
78/C1 Seregno, It.
72/F3 Serein (riv.), Fr.
110/B3 Seremban, Malay.
130/B3 Serengeti (plain), Tanz.
130/B3 Serengeti Nat'l Park, Tanz.
131/C2 Serenje, Zam.
130/B2 Serere, Ugan.
85/K5 Sergach, Rus.
88/J2 Sergeya Kirova (isls.), Rus.
140/C3 Sergipe (state), Braz.
84/H4 Sergiyev Posad, Rus.
112/A4 Seria, Bru.
78/C1 Seriate, It.
81/J4 Sérifos (isl.), Gre.
91/B1 Serik, Turk.
137/H5 Seringa (mts.), Braz.
79/E2 Serio (riv.), It.
111/G5 Sermata (isl.), Indo.
77/G5 Serottini, Monte (peak), It.
88/G4 Serov, Rus.
131/B4 Serowe, Bots.
74/B4 Serpa, Port.
80/A3 Serpeddi (peak), It.
119/C4 Serpentine (dam), Austl.
117/F4 Serpentine (lakes), Austl.
139/F2 Serpent's Mouth (str.), Trin., Ven.
128/C3 Serpent, Vallée du (wadi), Mali
84/H5 Serpukhov, Rus.
141/D2 Serra, Braz.
141/J8 Serra da Bocaina Nat'l Park, Braz.
141/C2 Serra da Canastra Nat'l Park, Braz.
140/B3 Serra de Capivara Nat'l Park, Braz.
141/D1 Serra do Cipo Nat'l Park, Braz.
141/K7 Serra dos Órgãos Nat'l Park, Braz.
81/H2 Sérrai, Gre.
80/E3 Serralta di San Vito (peak), It.
80/A3 Serramanna, It.
78/D5 Serra, Monte (peak), It.
136/E3 Serranía de la Neblina Nat'l Park, Ven.
149/G3 Serranilla Bank (reef), Col.
141/B1 Serranópolis, Braz.
123/W17 Serrat (cape), Tun.
140/C2 Serra Talhada, Braz.
68/C4 Serre (riv.), Fr.
140/C3 Serrinha, Braz.
74/A3 Sertã, Port.
140/C3 Sertânia, Braz.
141/C2 Sertãozinho, Braz.
91/C1 Sertavul (pass), Turk.
96/C4 Serteng (mts.), China
131/B4 Serule, Bots.
131/B4 Serurumi (dry riv.), Bots.
110/D4 Seruyan (riv.), Indo.
112/B5 Sesayap (riv.), Indo.
130/B3 Sese (isls.), Ugan.
127/B4 Sesebi (ruins), Sudan
131/B3 Sesheke, Zam.
78/B2 Sesia (riv.), It.
74/A3 Sesimbra, Port.
63/N1 Seskar (isl.), Rus.
164/A1 Sespe (cr.), Ca,US
164/B1 Sespe Condor Sanct., Ca,US
74/D1 Sestao, Sp.
78/B1 Sesto Calende, It.
79/E5 Sesto Fiorentino, It.
78/C1 Sesto San Giovanni, It.
78/C4 Sestri Levante, It.
63/N1 Sestroretsk, Rus.
80/A3 Sestu, It.
77/G4 Sesvenna, Piz (peak), It.
82/C3 Sesvete, Cro.
100/A2 Setana, Japan
72/E5 Sète, Fr.
140/B2 Sete Cidades Nat'l Park, Braz.
141/C1 Sete Lagoas, Braz.
95/J3 Sethārja, Pak.
123/U17 Sétif, Alg.
123/U17 Sétif (wilaya), Alg.
99/E3 Seto, Japan
98/C3 Seto-Naikai Nat'l Park, Japan
100/K6 Setouchi, Japan
78/B4 Settepani, Monte (peak), It.
78/A2 Settimo Torinese, It.
157/J2 Setting (lake), Mb,Can
57/F3 Settle, Eng,UK
150/B1 Settlement (pt.), Bahm.
99/L10 Settsu, Japan
74/A3 Setúbal, Port.
75/Q11 Setúbal (bay), Port.
74/A3 Setúbal (dist.), Port.
72/C4 Seudre (riv.), Fr.
72/C4 Seugne (riv.), Fr.
160/A1 Seul (lake), On,Can
87/H4 Sevan (lake), Arm.
93/F1 Sevan Nat'l Park, Arm.
86/E3 Sevastopol', Ukr.
57/H3 Seven (riv.), Eng,UK
60/B6 Seven Heads (pt.), Ire.
168/F5 Seven Hills, Oh,US
55/F10 Seven Hogs, The (isls.), Ire.
53/P8 Sevenoaks, Eng,UK
157/L2 Severn (riv.), On,Can
58/D3 Severn (riv.), Eng,UK
166/B5 Severn, Md,US
166/B5 Severn (riv.), Md,US
166/B5 Severna Park, Md,US
85/P3 Severnaya Sos'va (riv.), Rus.
90/K2 Severnaya Zemlya (arch.), Rus.
58/C4 Severn, Mouth of the (estuary), Eng,UK
85/Q2 Severnyy, Rus.
65/G3 Severočeský (reg.), Czh.
86/F2 Severodonetsk, Ukr.
84/H2 Severodvinsk, Rus.
89/R4 Severo-Kuril'sk, Rus.
65/J4 Severomoravský (reg.), Czh.
84/G1 Severomorsk, Rus.
85/N3 Severoural'sk, Rus.
78/C1 Seveso, It.
158/D3 Sevier (des.), Ut,US
158/D3 Sevier (riv.), Ut,US
163/H3 Sevierville, Tn,US
138/C3 Sevilla, Col.
119/G5 Seville, Austl.
74/C4 Seville, Sp.
83/G4 Sevlievo, Bul.
53/T10 Sevran, Fr.
53/S10 Sèvres, Fr.
128/C5 Sewa (riv.), SLeo.
151/E2 Seward (pen.), Ak,US
159/H2 Seward, Ne,US
151/M5 Sewell Inlet, BC,Can
156/D2 Sexsmith, Ab,Can
123/V17 Seybouse (riv.), Alg.
123/H5 Seychelles
92/B2 Seydişehir, Turk.
91/D1 Seyhan (dam), Turk.
91/D1 Seyhan (riv.), Turk.
119/C3 Seymour, Austl.
162/D3 Seymour, Tx,US
76/C6 Seynod, Fr.
93/N6 Şeytan (riv.), Turk.
68/C6 Sézanne, Fr.
74/A3 Sezimbra, Port.
80/C2 Sezze, It.
83/G3 Sfîntu Gheorghe, Rom.
123/Q16 Sfizef, Alg.
66/C4 's-Graveland, Neth.
66/B5 's-Gravendeel, Neth.
66/B4 's-Gravenhage (The Hague) (cap.), Neth.
54/A2 Sgurr a' Chaorachain (mtn.), Sc,UK
54/B2 Sgurr a' choire Ghlais (mtn.), Sc,UK
54/B1 Sgurr a' Mhuilinn (mtn.), Sc,UK
54/A1 Sgurr Mór (mtn.), Sc,UK
54/A2 Sgurr na Ciche (mtn.), Sc,UK
54/A2 Sgurr na Lapaich (mtn.), Sc,UK
103/C4 Sha (riv.), China
105/H3 Sha (riv.), China
103/B4 Shaanxi (prov.), China
130/A4 Shaba (reg.), Zaire
130/C2 Shaba Nat'l Rsv., Kenya
125/P7 Shabeelle, Webi (riv.), Som.
126/E1 Shabunda, Zaire
102/C4 Shache, China
113/M Shackleton (coast), Ant.
113/G Shackleton Ice Shelf, Ant.
166/A2 Shade Mtn. (ridge), Pa,US
85/P4 Shadrinsk, Rus.
162/B4 Shafter, Tx,US
58/D4 Shaftesbury, Eng,UK
102/C2 Shagan (riv.), Kaz.
108/D2 Shāhābād, India
95/J3 Shāhdādkot, Pak.
95/J3 Shāhdādpur, Pak.
106/D3 Shahdol, India
125/K1 Shaḥḥāt, Libya
106/C2 Shāhjahānpur, India
108/B2 Shāh Kot, Pak.
108/B1 Shāhpur, Pak.
95/K3 Shahpura, India
106/A2 Shāhpur Chākar, Pak.
127/C3 Shā'ib al Banāt, Jabal (mtn.), Egypt
106/C3 Shājāpur, India
108/C1 Shakargarh, Pak.
126/D4 Shakawe, Bots.
168/F5 Shaker Heights, Oh,US
88/H5 Shakhtinsk, Kaz.
86/G3 Shakhty, Rus.
84/K4 Shakhun'ya, Rus.
100/B2 Shakotan (pen.), Japan
87/H4 Shalbuzdag, Gora (peak), Rus.
58/C5 Shaldon, Eng,UK
117/M8 Shallow Reach (inlet), Austl.
104/C2 Shaluli (mts.), China
130/B4 Shama (riv.), Tanz.
91/C4 Shamal Sīnā' (gov.), Egypt
157/M2 Shamattawa (riv.), On,Can
106/C3 Shāmgarh, India
106/C2 Shāmli, India
92/E5 Shammar, Jabal (mts.), SAr.
166/B2 Shamokin, Pa,US
166/B2 Shamokin (cr.), Pa,US
151/L3 Shamrock (mtn.), Yk,Can
162/C3 Shamrock, Tx,US
131/C3 Shamva, Zim.
104/C4 Shan (plat.), Burma
104/C4 Shan (state), Burma
105/H3 Shan (pass), China
123/W18 Sha'nabī, Jabal ash (peak), Tun.
125/M4 Shandī, Sudan
103/D3 Shandong (pen.), China
101/A4 Shandong (prov.), China
131/C3 Shangani, Zim.
131/C3 Shangani (riv.), Zim.
103/C4 Shangcai, China
103/C5 Shangcheng, China
105/G4 Shangchuan (isl.), China
105/G3 Shangdu, China
103/E5 Shanghai, China
103/E5 Shanghai (mun.), China
103/L8 Shanghai (inset), China
103/D3 Shanghe, China
107/J3 Shanglin, China
103/C4 Shangqiu, China
105/H2 Shangrao, China
103/C4 Shangshui, China
109/E1 Shangsi, China
103/C2 Shangyi, China
105/G3 Shangyou (riv.), China
59/E5 Shanklin, Eng,UK
105/F3 Shanmatang (mtn.), China
60/A3 Shannawona (mtn.), Ire.
104/C3 Shan-ngaw (range), Burma
60/B4 Shannon (riv.), Ire.
96/C3 Shanshan, China
89/P4 Shantar (isls.), Rus.
105/H4 Shantou, China
130/B3 Shanwa, Tanz.
103/B3 Shanxi (prov.), China
103/C3 Shanyin, China
105/F3 Shaodong, China
105/G3 Shaoguan, China
105/J2 Shaoxing, China
105/F3 Shaoyang, China
57/F2 Shap, Eng,UK
113/L Shapeless (peak), Ant.
85/M2 Shapkina (riv.), Rus.
93/F2 Shaqlāwah, Iraq
95/G5 Sharbatāt, Ra's ash (pt.), Oman
100/D2 Shari, Japan
116/B3 Shark (bay), Austl.
150/A1 Shark (pt.), Fl,US
167/E3 Shark River (inlet), NJ,US
127/C3 Sharm ash Shaykh, Egypt
59/F2 Sharnbrook, Eng,UK
168/G5 Sharon, Pa,US
157/K2 Sharpe (lake), Mb,Can
157/J4 Sharpe (lake), SD,US
108/C2 Sharqpur, Pak.
85/K4 Shar'ya, Rus.
131/B4 Shashe, Bots.
131/C4 Shashe (riv.), Bots., Zim.
125/N6 Shashemenē, Eth.
103/C5 Shashi, China
158/B2 Shasta (dam), Ca,US
158/B2 Shasta (lake), Ca,US
158/B2 Shasta (peak), Ca,US
86/B2 Shatskiy Nat'l Park, Ukr.
93/F4 Shatt al Arab (riv.), Iran, Iraq
124/G1 Shaṭṭ al Jarīd (dry lake), Tun.
159/H3 Shattuck, Ok,US
156/F3 Shaunavon, Sk,Can
59/E4 Shaw, Eng,UK
163/H3 Shaw A.F.B., SC,US
160/B2 Shawano, Wi,US
161/M6 Shawbridge, Qu,Can
58/D1 Shawbury, Eng,UK
161/F2 Shawinigan, Qu,Can
159/H4 Shawnee, Ok,US
93/E2 Shaykhān, Iraq
92/C3 Shaykh, Jabal ash (mtn.), Leb.
86/C1 Shchara (riv.), Bela.
86/F1 Shchekino, Rus.
85/X9 Shchelkovo, Rus.
86/F2 Shchigry, Rus.
102/B1 Shchuchinsk, Kaz.
167/K8 Shea Stadium, New York City, NY,US
125/P6 Shebelē Wenz (riv.), Eth.
95/J1 Sheberghān, Afg.
160/C3 Sheboygan, Wi,US
161/H2 Shediac, NB,Can
54/C3 Shee (riv.), Sc,UK
60/C2 Sheelin, Lough (lake), Ire.
151/F2 Sheep (mtn.), Ak,US
167/K9 Sheepshead Bay, NY,US
66/D5 's-Heerenberg, Neth.
57/G5 Sheffield, Eng,UK
163/G3 Sheffield, Al,US
167/M7 Sheffield (isl.), Ct,US
168/E5 Sheffield Lake, Oh,US
59/F2 Shefford, Eng,UK
125/P6 Shēh Husēn, Eth.
143/K7 Shehuen (riv.), Arg.
60/A6 Shehy (mts.), Ire.
103/B3 Shejaping, China
160/C1 Shekak (riv.), On,Can
108/B2 Shekhūpura, Pak.
87/H4 Sheki, Azer.
89/T2 Shelagskiy (cape), Rus.
161/H3 Shelburne, NS,Can
163/F3 Shelby, Ms,US
156/F3 Shelby, Mt,US
163/H3 Shelby, NC,US
163/F2 Shelbyville (lake), Il,US
160/C4 Shelbyville, In,US
163/G3 Shelbyville, Tn,US
89/R3 Shelekhov (gulf), Rus.
151/H4 Shelikof (str.), Ak,US
157/G2 Shellbrook, Sk,Can
166/B3 Shelley (isl.), Pa,US
160/B2 Shell Lake, Wi,US
59/G4 Shell Ness (pt.), UK
157/K5 Shell Rock (riv.), Ia,US
167/F1 Shelter (isl.), NY,US
167/F1 Shelter Island (sound), NY,US
168/A3 Shelton, Ct,US
165/A3 Shelton, Wa,US
87/J4 Shemakha, Azer.
151/A5 Shemya (isl.), Ak,US
157/K5 Shenandoah, Ia,US
166/B2 Shenandoah, Pa,US
160/E4 Shenandoah Nat'l Park, Va,US
168/G5 Shenango (riv.), Pa,US
168/G5 Shenango River (res.), Oh, Pa,US
103/C3 Shenchi, China

Shenc – Smela

123/V17 Smendou (riv.), Alg.
66/D3 Smilde, Neth.
113/V Smith (pen.), Ant.
156/B3 Smith (inlet), BC,Can
153/J2 Smith (isl.), NW,Can
156/F4 Smith (riv.), Mt,US
156/B2 Smithers, BC,Can
163/J3 Smithfield, NC,US
158/E2 Smithfield, Ut,US
160/E4 Smith Mtn. (lake), Va,US
160/E2 Smiths Falls, On,Can
167/E2 Smithtown, NY,US
167/E2 Smithtown (bay), NY,US
161/Q9 Smithville, On,Can
159/J4 Smithville, Ok,US
166/D5 Smithville, Hist. Homes of, NJ,US
119/E1 Smoky (cape), Austl.
156/D2 Smoky (riv.), Ab,Can
159/H3 Smoky (hills), Ks,US
159/G3 Smoky Hill (riv.), Ks,US
156/E2 Smoky Lake, Ab,Can
61/C3 Smøla (isl.), Nor.
84/G5 Smolensk, Rus.
84/F5 Smolensk Obl., Rus.
81/G2 Smólikas (peak), Gre.
83/G5 Smolyan, Bul.
160/D1 Smooth Rock Falls, On,Can
71/G5 Smrčina (peak), Czh.
71/H4 Smutná (riv.), Czh.
113/U Smyley (isl.), Ant.
166/C5 Smyrna (riv.), De,US
163/G3 Smyrna, Ga,US
56/D3 Snaefell (mtn.), IM,UK
151/M2 Snake (riv.), Yk,Can
156/D4 Snake (riv.), US
159/G2 Snake (riv.), Ne,US
156/E5 Snake River (plain), Id,US
115/Q12 Snares (isls.), NZ
66/C2 Sneek, Neth.
66/C2 Sneekermeer (lake), Neth.
132/D3 Sneeuberg (mts.), SAfr.
132/B4 Sneeuberg (peak), SAfr.
132/L11 Sneeuwkop (peak), SAfr.
161/Q8 Snelgrove, On,Can
59/G1 Snettisham, Eng,UK
65/H3 Sněžka (peak), Czh.
82/B3 Snežnik (peak), Yugo.
65/L2 Śniardwy (lake), Pol.
59/G4 Snodland, Eng,UK
61/D3 Snøhetta (peak), Nor.
165/C2 Snohomish, Wa,US
165/D2 Snohomish (co.), Wa,US
165/C2 Snohomish (riv.), Wa,US
165/D2 Snoqualmie (falls), Wa,US
165/D2 Snoqualmie (riv.), Wa,US
165/D3 Snoqualmie, Middle Fork (riv.), Wa,US
165/D3 Snoqualmie-Mount Baker Nat'l For., Wa,US
165/D2 Snoqualmie, North Fork (riv.), Wa,US
165/D3 Snoqualmie, South Fork (riv.), Wa,US
61/E2 Snøtind (peak), Nor.
56/D5 Snowdon (mtn.), Wal,UK
56/D5 Snowdonia Nat'l Park, Wal,UK
158/E4 Snowflake, Az,US
157/H2 Snow Lake, Mb,Can
119/D3 Snowy (riv.), Austl.
151/K2 Snowy (peak), Ak,US
119/D3 Snowy River Nat'l Park, Austl.
166/A2 Snyder (co.), Pa,US
162/C3 Snyder, Tx,US
138/C3 Soacha, Col.
133/H7 Soalala, Madg.
78/A2 Soana (riv.), It.
133/J7 Soanierana-Ivongo, Madg.
57/G6 Soar (riv.), Eng,UK
101/D5 Sobaek (mts.), SKor.
149/G4 Soberania Nat'l Park, Pan.
71/H4 Soběslav, Czh.
111/K4 Sobger (riv.), Indo.
95/J3 Sobhādero, Pak.
140/B3 Sobradinho (res.), Braz.
140/B1 Sobral, Braz.
77/G5 Sobretta, Monte (peak), It.
99/M9 Sobue, Japan
79/G1 Soča (riv.), Slov.
144/D5 Socabaya, Peru
65/L2 Sochaczew, Pol.
86/F4 Sochi, Rus.
121/K6 Society (isls.), FrPol.
141/G7 Socorro, Braz.
138/C3 Socorro, Col.
146/C5 Socorro (isl.), Mex.
158/F4 Socorro, NM,US
162/B4 Socorro, Tx,US
90/E8 Socotra (isl.), Yem.
109/D4 Soc Trang, Viet.
74/D3 Socuéllamos, Sp.
61/H2 Sodankylä, Fin.
156/F5 Soda Springs, Id,US
99/H7 Sodegaura, Japan
62/G1 Söderhamn, Swe.
62/G2 Söderköping, Swe.
62/G2 Sodermanland (co.), Swe.
62/G2 Södertälje, Swe.
63/R7 Södertorn (pen.), Swe.
125/N6 Sodo, Eth.
63/R7 Södra Björkfjärden (bay), Swe.
63/S7 Södra Ljusterö (isl.), Swe.
131/C4 Soekmekaar, SAfr.
67/F5 Soest, Ger.
66/C4 Soest, Neth.
67/E3 Soeste (riv.), Ger.
131/D3 Sofala (prov.), Moz.
133/J6 Sofia (riv.), Madg.
83/F4 Sofia (Sofiya) (cap.), Bul.
82/F4 Sofiya (reg.), Bul.
83/F4 Sofiya (Sofia) (cap.), Bul.
130/C4 Soga, Tanz.
138/C3 Sogamoso, Col.
138/C3 Sogamoso (riv.), Col.
62/A1 Sognafjorden (fjord), Nor.
62/B2 Søgne, Nor.
62/A1 Sogn og Fjordane (co.), Nor.
112/D3 Sogod, Phil.
124/J4 Sogollé (well), Chad
92/C1 Soğuksu Nat'l Park, Turk.
92/B2 Söğüt, Turk.
130/B2 Sogwass (peak), Ugan.
97/K5 Sŏgwip'o, SKor.
59/G2 Soham, Eng,UK
68/D2 Soignies, Belg.
53/U11 Soignolles-en-Brie, Fr.
68/C5 Soissons, Fr.
53/T11 Soisy-sur-Seine, Fr.
98/C3 Sōja, Japan
106/B2 Sojat, India
101/C3 Sŏjosŏn (bay), NKor.
87/J1 Sok (riv.), Rus.
109/C3 Sok (pt.), Thai.
99/H7 Sōka, Japan
101/E3 Sokch'o, SKor.
92/A2 Söke, Turk.
96/F1 Sokhor (peak), Rus.
82/E4 Sokobanja, Yugo.
129/F4 Sokodé, Togo
71/G4 Sokol (peak), Czh.
84/J4 Sokol, Rus.
65/M2 Sokółka, Pol.
71/F2 Sokolov, Czh.
65/M2 Sokołów Podlaski, Pol.
129/G4 Sokoto (plains), Nga.
129/G4 Sokoto (riv.), Nga.
129/G3 Sokoto (state), Nga.
62/A2 Sola, Nor.
112/C1 Solana, Phil.
164/C5 Solana Beach, Ca,US
140/D2 Solânea, Braz.
138/B3 Solano (pt.), Col.
112/C1 Solano, Phil.
165/L10 Solano (co.), Ca,US
77/H3 Solbad Hall in Tirol, Aus.
74/C4 Sol, Costa del (coast), Sp.
75/P10 Sol, Costa do (reg.), Port.
159/J2 Soldier (riv.), Ia,US
138/C2 Soledad, Col.
164/B2 Soledad (canyon), Ca,US
139/F2 Soledad, Ven.
147/N7 Soledad de Doblado, Mex.
141/A4 Soledade, Braz.
59/E5 Solent (chan.), Eng,UK
79/E2 Solesino, It.
69/E4 Soleuvre (mtn.), Lux.
92/E2 Solhan, Turk.
86/C1 Soligorsk, Bela.
59/E2 Solihull, Eng,UK
85/N4 Solikamsk, Rus.
87/K2 Sol'-Iletsk, Rus.
139/E5 Solimões (Amazon) (riv.), Braz.
67/E6 Solingen, Ger.
61/F3 Sollefteå, Swe.
62/G2 Sollentuna, Swe.
75/G3 Sóller, Sp.
63/T9 Søllerød, Den.
67/G5 Solling (mts.), Ger.
70/B2 Solmsbach (riv.), Ger.
61/D3 Søln (peak), Nor.
63/S7 Solna, Swe.
76/B5 Solnan (riv.), Fr.
110/D5 Solo (riv.), Indo.
110/B4 Solok, Indo.
148/D3 Sololá, Guat.
120/E5 Solomon (sea), PNG, Sol.
162/D2 Solomon (riv.), Ks,US
120/E6 Solomon Islands
159/G3 Solomon, North Fork (riv.), Ks,US
168/F5 Solon, Oh,US
87/L4 Solonchak Goklenkui (salt marsh), Trkm.
76/D3 Solothurn, Swi.
76/D3 Solothurn (canton), Swi.
84/G2 Solovetskiy (isls.), Rus.
75/F2 Solsona, Sp.
82/D2 Solt, Hun.
82/B4 Šolta (isl.), Cro.
67/G3 Soltau, Ger.
82/D2 Soltvadkert, Hun.
82/E5 Solunska (peak), Macd.
58/A3 Solva (riv.), Wal,UK
158/B4 Solvang, Ca,US
62/F3 Sölvesborg, Swe.
56/E2 Solway Firth (inlet), Sc,UK
131/B2 Solwezi, Zam.
99/G2 Sōma, Japan
92/A2 Soma, Turk.
131/C3 Somabhula, Zim.
68/C3 Somain, Fr.
123/G4 Somalia
161/F1 Somaqua (riv.), Qu,Can
82/D3 Sombor, Cro.
146/E4 Sombrerete, Mex.
141/B4 Sombrio, Braz.
57/G5 Somercotes, Eng,UK
66/C6 Someren, Neth.
63/K1 Somero, Fin.
156/E3 Somers, Mt,US
152/G1 Somerset (isl.), NW,Can
58/D4 Somerset (co.), Eng,UK
160/C4 Somerset, Ky,US
168/C2 Somerset, Ma,US
166/D3 Somerset, NJ,US
166/D2 Somerset (co.), NJ,US
161/S9 Somerset, NY,US
119/C4 Somerset-Burnie, Austl.
132/D4 Somerset East, SAfr.
132/B4 Somerset West, SAfr.
59/F2 Somersham, Eng,UK
166/D5 Somers Point, NJ,US
161/G3 Somersworth, NH,US
58/D4 Somerton, Eng,UK
158/D4 Somerton, Az,US
168/C1 Somerville, Ma,US
166/D2 Somerville, NJ,US
159/H5 Somerville (lake), Tx,US
83/F2 Someş (riv.), Rom.
83/G2 Someşul Mare (riv.), Rom.
101/D5 Sŏmjin (riv.), SKor.
78/B1 Somma Lombardo, It.
123/T15 Sommam (riv.), Alg.
72/D1 Somme (bay), Fr.
68/B4 Somme (dept.), Fr.
68/A3 Somme (riv.), Fr.
68/D6 Somme (riv.), Fr.
68/B4 Somme, Canal de La (can.), Fr.
62/F3 Sommen (lake), Swe.
68/D5 Somme-Soude (riv.), Fr.
82/C2 Somogy (co.), Hun.
59/F5 Somptin, Eng,UK
62/C4 Sønderborg, Den.
132/L11 Sonderend (riv.), SAfr.
62/C4 Sønderjylland (co.), Den.
77/F5 Sondrio, It.
77/F5 Sondrio (prov.), It.
106/C2 Sonepat, India
106/D3 Sonepur, India
109/E3 Song Cau, Viet.
109/D4 Song Dinh, Viet.
130/B5 Songea, Tanz.
103/F1 Songhua (riv.), China
103/E5 Songjiang, China
103/L8 Songjiang, China
102/B3 Song-Kel' (lake), Kyr.
109/C5 Songkhla, Thai.
109/C3 Songkhram (riv.), Thai.
97/J2 Songling, China
109/C1 Song Ma, Viet.
104/D3 Songming, China
101/D4 Sŏngnam, SKor.
131/D2 Songo, Moz.
126/B2 Songololo, Zaire
103/C4 Song Shan (peak), China
101/D4 Songt'an, SKor.
105/F2 Songtao Miaozu Zizhixian, China
105/H3 Songxi, China
103/C4 Song Xian, China
103/B5 Songzi, China
105/G2 Songzi Guan (pass), China
105/G2 Songzi Hudu (riv.), China
109/E3 Son Ha, Viet.
99/M10 Soni, Japan
96/G3 Sonid Youqi, China
96/G3 Sonid Zuoqi, China
95/J3 Sonmiāni (bay), Pak.
70/E2 Sonneberg, Ger.
59/F4 Sonning, Eng,UK
77/H3 Sonnjoch (peak), Aus.
64/G5 Sonntagshorn (peak), Ger.
140/A3 Sono (riv.), Braz.
140/A5 Sono (riv.), Braz.
98/D3 Sonobe, Japan
165/K10 Sonoma, Ca,US
165/J10 Sonoma (co.), Ca,US
165/J10 Sonoma (cr.), Ca,US
165/J10 Sonoma (mts.), Ca,US
146/C2 Sonora (riv.), Mex.
158/B3 Sonora, Ca,US
162/C4 Sonora, Tx,US
93/F3 Sonqor, Iran
66/D5 Sonsbeck, Ger.
74/D3 Sonseca, Sp.
138/C3 Sonsón, Col.
148/D3 Sonsonate, ESal.
120/C4 Sonsorol (isls.), Palau
82/D3 Sonta, Yugo.
109/D1 Son Tay, Viet.
77/G2 Sonthofen, Ger.
67/G6 Sontra, Ger.
111/G3 Sopi (cape), Indo.
109/C1 Sopka, Laos
95/K2 Sopore, India
83/G4 Sopot, Bul.
65/K1 Sopot, Pol.
82/C2 Sopron, Hun.
58/D3 Sôr (riv.), Wal,UK
80/C2 Sora, It.
101/E3 Sŏrak-san (mtn.), SKor.
101/E3 Sŏraksan Nat'l Park, SKor.
161/F2 Sorel, Qu,Can
91/F8 Soreq, Nabel (dry riv.), Isr.
78/C2 Soresina, It.
72/F5 Sorgues, Fr.
92/C2 Sorgun, Turk.
74/D2 Soria, Sp.
143/F2 Soriano (dept.), Uru.
110/A3 Sorikmerapi (peak), Indo.
87/K3 Sor Karatuley (salt pan), Kaz.
87/K3 Sor Kaydak (salt marsh), Kaz.
87/K3 Sor Mertvyy Kultuk (salt marsh), Kaz.
68/D4 Sormonne (riv.), Fr.
62/D4 Sorø, Den.
141/C2 Sorocaba, Braz.
87/K1 Sorochinsk, Rus.
83/J1 Soroki, Mol.
120/D4 Sorol (atoll), Micr.
111/H4 Sorong, Indo.
139/G3 Sororieng (mtn.), Guy.
130/B2 Soroti, Ugan.
61/G1 Sørøya (isl.), Nor.
61/G1 Sørøysundet (chan.), Nor.
67/E6 Sorpestausee (res.), Ger.
74/A3 Sorraia (riv.), Port.
80/D2 Sorrento, It.
126/B5 Sorris-Sorris, Namb.
80/A2 Sorso, It.
112/D2 Sorsogon, Phil.
84/F3 Sortavala, Rus.
63/K3 Sörve (pt.), Est.
101/D4 Sŏsan, SKor.
101/C4 Sŏsan Haean Nat'l Park, SKor.
67/H5 Söse (riv.), Ger.
86/F1 Sosna (riv.), Rus.
142/C2 Sosneado (peak), Arg.
85/M3 Sosnogorsk, Rus.
85/L4 Sosnovka, Rus.
65/K3 Sosnowiec, Pol.
130/B3 Sotik, Kenya
79/F2 Sottomarina, It.
68/D6 Soude (riv.), Fr.
150/F3 Soufrière (peak), Guad.
150/F4 Soufrière (peak), StV.
123/V17 Souk Ahras, Alg.
123/V17 Souk Ahras (gov.), Alg.
161/M7 Soulanges (co.), Qu,Can
101/D4 Sŏul (Seoul) (cap.), SKor.
69/G1 Soultz-sous-Forets, Fr.
129/E3 Soum (prov.), Burk.
69/E2 Soumagne, Belg.
132/E3 Sources, Mont aux (peak), Les.
137/J4 Soure, Braz.
74/A2 Soure, Port.
123/S15 Sour El Ghozlane, Alg.
157/H3 Souris, Mb,Can
161/J2 Souris, PE,Can
157/H3 Souris (riv.), Can., US
128/E3 Sourou (prov.), Burk.
124/D2 Sous (wadi), Mor.
140/C2 Sousa, Braz.
74/B3 Sousel, Port.
132/C3 Sout (dry riv.), SAfr.
132/M11 Sout (riv.), SAfr.
118/G8 South (cr.), Austl.
161/H2 South (mts.), NS,Can
153/H2 South (bay), NW,Can
60/A3 South (sound), Ire.
115/Q12 South (cape), NZ
115/Q11 South (isl.), NZ
126/D6 South Africa
53/M7 Southall, Eng,UK
59/E2 Southam, Eng,UK
167/H10 South Amboy, NJ,US
153/H2 Southampton (cape), NW,Can
145/J3 Southampton (isl.), NW,Can
153/H2 Southampton (isl.), NW,Can
160/D2 Southampton, On,Can
59/E5 Southampton, Eng,UK
59/E5 Southampton Water (inlet), Eng,UK
107/F5 South Andaman (isl.), India
163/J2 South Anna (riv.), Va,US
50/J6 South Atlantic (ocean)
163/H3 South Augusta, Ga,US
153/K3 South Aulatsivik (isl.), Nf,Can
117/F4 South Australia (state), Austl.
163/F3 Southaven, Ms,US
56/D3 South Barrule (mtn.), IM,UK
160/C3 South Bend, In,US
53/P8 Southborough, Eng,UK
168/C1 Southborough, Ma,US
160/E4 South Boston, Va,US
59/F5 Southbourne, Eng,UK
58/C6 South Brent, Eng,UK
168/B1 Southbridge, Ma,US
130/A3 South Buganda (prov.), Ugan.
161/F2 South Burlington, Vt,US
168/A3 Southbury, Ct,US
149/J1 South Caicos (isl.), Trks.
163/H3 South Carolina (state), US
90/L8 South China (sea), Asia
157/H4 South Dakota (state), US
58/D5 South Dorset Downs (uplands), Eng,UK
59/F5 South Downs (hills), Eng,UK
51/S8 South East (cape), Austl.
119/C3 South East (pt.), Austl.
150/C2 Southeast (pt.), Bahm.
131/B5 South-East (dist.), Bots.
149/G2 Southeast (pt.), Jam.
151/E3 Southeast (cape), Ak,US
165/P16 South Elgin, Il,US
57/G4 South Elmsall, Eng,UK
56/C1 Southend, Sc,UK
59/G3 Southend-on-Sea, Eng,UK
116/K7 Southern (riv.), Austl.
131/B5 Southern (dist.), Bots.
91/D4 Southern (dist.), Isr.
131/D2 Southern (reg.), Malw.
128/B5 Southern (prov.), SLeo.
130/A3 Southern (prov.), Ugan.
131/B3 Southern (prov.), Zam.
115/Q11 Southern Alps (range), NZ
121/J6 Southern Cook (isls.), Cookls.
152/G3 Southern Indian (lake), Mb,Can
163/J3 Southern Pines, NC,US
54/C5 Southern Uplands (mts.), Sc,UK
85/N5 Southern Ural (mts.), Rus.
59/G1 Southery, Eng,UK
119/C4 South Esk (riv.), Austl.
54/C5 South Esk (riv.), Sc,UK
54/D3 South Esk (riv.), Sc,UK
116/E2 Southesk Tablelands (plat.), Austl.
168/F4 South Euclid, Oh,US
165/F7 Southfield, Mi,US
59/H4 South Foreland (pt.), Eng,UK
158/F3 South Fork, Co,US
163/F2 South Fulton, Tn,US
53/N7 Southgate, Eng,UK
164/B3 South Gate, Ca,US
165/F7 Southgate, Mi,US
113/X South Georgia (isl.), UK
58/C4 South Glamorgan (co.), Wal,UK
168/B1 South Hadley, Ma,US
58/C6 South Hams (plain), Eng,UK
59/F5 South Hayling, Eng,UK
160/E4 South Hill, Va,US
66/B5 South Holland (prov.), Neth.
165/Q16 South Holland, Il,US
53/N8 South Holmwood, Eng,UK
130/C2 South Horr, Kenya
168/B2 Southington, Ct,US
130/C2 South Island Nat'l Park, Kenya
130/C3 South Kinangop, Kenya
57/G4 South Kirkby, Eng,UK
130/C3 South Kitui Nat'l Rsv., Kenya
101/D4 South Korea
158/C3 South Lake Tahoe, Ca,US
159/H2 South Loup (riv.), Ne,US
131/C2 South Luangwa Nat'l Park, Zam.
113/K South Magnetic Pole, Ant.
165/Q14 South Milwaukee, Wi,US
59/G3 Southminster, Eng,UK
58/C4 South Molton, Eng,UK
157/J2 South Moose (lake), Mb,Can
151/M5 South Moresby Nat'l Park Rsv., BC,Can
166/A3 South Mtn. (ridge), Pa,US
57/G5 South Normanton, Eng,UK
53/P7 South Ockenden, Eng,UK
167/H9 South Orange, NJ,US
113/W South Orkney (isls.), UK
87/G4 South Ossetian Aut. Obl., Geo.
53/M7 South Oxhey, Eng,UK
167/M9 South Oyster (bay), NY,US
120/G7 South Pacific (ocean)
117/M8 South Para (res.), Austl.
117/M8 South Para (riv.), Austl.
164/F7 South Pasadena, Ca,US
116/K6 South Perth, Austl.
58/D5 South Petherton, Eng,UK
118/E6 South Pine (riv.), Austl.
166/D2 South Plainfield, NJ,US
159/G2 South Platte (riv.), Co, Ne,US
113/W South Polar (plat.), Ant.
113/A South Pole, Ant.
57/E4 Southport, Eng,UK
163/J3 Southport, NC,US
165/C3 South Prairie (cr.), Wa,US
54/C5 South Queensferry, Sc,UK
166/D3 South River, NJ,US
55/N13 South Ronaldsay (isl.), Sc,UK
131/D1 South Rukuru (riv.), Malw.
113/Y South Sandwich (isls.), UK
165/K11 South San Francisco, Ca,US
156/F3 South Saskatchewan (riv.), Ab, Sk,Can
113/W South Shetland (isls.), UK
57/G2 South Shields, Eng,UK
159/H2 South Sioux City, Ne,US
159/J2 South Skunk (riv.), Ia,US
106/E3 South Suburban, India
115/R10 South Taranaki (bight), NZ
130/B2 South Turkana Nat'l Rsv., Kenya
57/F2 South Tyne (riv.), Eng,UK
112/C4 South Ubian, Phil.
55/H8 South Uist (isl.), Sc,UK
158/B2 South Umpqua (riv.), Or,US
53/N7 Southwark (bor.), Eng,UK
57/H5 Southwell, Eng,UK
119/C4 South West (cape), Austl.
150/B1 Southwest (pt.), Bahm.
150/C2 Southwest (pt.), Bahm.
119/C4 South West Nat'l Park, Austl.
164/F8 South Whittier, Ca,US
168/B1 Southwick, Ma,US
166/B1 South Williamsport, Pa,US
59/H2 Southwold, Eng,UK
59/G3 South Woodham Ferrers, Eng,UK
118/C4 Southwood Nat'l Park, Austl.
57/G5 South Yorkshire (co.), Eng,UK
131/C4 Soutpansberg (mts.), SAfr.
83/G2 Sovata, Rom.
80/E3 Soverato Marina, It.
63/J4 Sovetsk, Rus.
97/N2 Sovetskaya Gavan', Rus.
131/B4 Sowa Pan (salt pan), Bots.
57/G4 Sowerby Bridge, Eng,UK
132/D2 Soweto, SAfr.
100/B1 Sōya-misaki (cape), Japan
84/J2 Soyana (riv.), Rus.
101/D4 Soyang (lake), SKor.
72/D4 Soyaux, Fr.
113/E Soyuz, Ant.
86/D1 Sozh (riv.), Eur.
69/E3 Spa, Belg.
113/U Spaatz (isl.), Ant.
163/H4 Spaceport USA, Fl,US
165/D2 Spada (lake), Wa,US
74/C2 Spain
57/H6 Spalding, Eng,UK
165/C3 Spanaway, Wa,US
60/A4 Spanish (pt.), Ire.
55/J9 Spanish Head (pt.), IM,UK
149/G2 Spanish Town, Jam.
77/E4 Spannort (peak), Swi.
158/C3 Sparks, Nv,US
163/H2 Sparta, NC,US
166/D1 Sparta, NJ,US
163/G3 Sparta, Tn,US
160/B3 Sparta, Wi,US
163/H3 Spartanburg, SC,US
81/H4 Sparta (Spárti), Gre.
123/M13 Spartel (cape), Mor.
81/H4 Spárti (Sparta), Gre.
80/A3 Spartivento (cape), It.
80/E4 Spartivento (cape), It.
156/E3 Sparwood, BC,Can
97/L3 Spassk-Dal'niy, Rus.
81/H5 Spátha, Ákra (cape), Gre.
54/B3 Spean (riv.), Sc,UK
54/B3 Spean Bridge, Sc,UK
157/H4 Spearfish, SD,US
77/F3 Speer (peak), Swi.
130/B3 Speke (gulf), Tanz.
57/F5 Speke, Eng,UK
117/H5 Spencer (cape), Austl.
117/H5 Spencer (gulf), Austl.
151/E2 Spencer (pt.), Ak,US
157/K5 Spencer, Ia,US
168/C1 Spencer, Ma,US
67/F4 Spenge, Ger.
57/G2 Spennymoor, Eng,UK
81/H3 Sperkhiós (riv.), Gre.
56/A2 Sperrin (mts.), NI,UK
70/C3 Spessart (range), Ger.
54/C1 Spey (bay), Sc,UK
54/C1 Spey (riv.), Sc,UK
70/B4 Speyer, Ger.
70/B4 Speyerbach (riv.), Ger.
161/Q8 Speyside, On,Can
80/E3 Spezzano Albanese, It.
71/F2 Špičák (peak), Czh.
153/H2 Spicer (isl.), NW,Can
67/E1 Spiekeroog (isl.), Ger.
66/B5 Spijkenisse, Neth.
151/K2 Spike (mtn.), Ak,US
82/A2 Spilimbergo, It.
57/J5 Spilsby, Eng,UK
80/A2 Spina, Bruncu (peak), It.
95/J2 Spin Būldak, Afg.
69/E5 Spincourt, Fr.
78/B3 Spinetta Marengo, It.
156/D2 Spirit River, Ab,Can
156/G2 Spiritwood, Sk,Can
65/L4 Spišská Nová Ves, Slvk.
59/E5 Spithead (chan.), Eng,UK
108/D1 Spiti (riv.), India
88/B2 Spitsbergen (isl.), Sval.
73/K3 Spittal an der Drau, Aus.
157/K2 Split (lake), Mb,Can
82/C4 Split, Cro.
167/H8 Splitrock (res.), NJ,US
77/F4 Splügenpass (pass), It.
156/D4 Spokane (riv.), Id, Wa,US
156/D4 Spokane, Wa,US
77/G5 Spöl (riv.), It.
80/C1 Spoleto, It.
160/B3 Spoon (riv.), Il,US
160/B2 Spooner, Wi,US
166/D3 Spotswood, NJ,US
157/K3 Sprague, Mb,Can
66/C5 Sprang-Capelle, Neth.
110/D2 Spratly (isls.)
65/H2 Spree (riv.), Ger.
79/F1 Spresiano, It.
69/E3 Sprimont, Belg.
163/G4 Spring (cr.), Ga,US
162/E4 Spring, Tx,US
131/C5 Springbokvlakte (val.), SAfr.
161/K1 Springdale, Nf,Can
162/E2 Springdale, Ar,US
67/G4 Springe, Ger.
159/F3 Springer, NM,US
158/E4 Springerville, Az,US
159/G3 Springfield, Co,US
160/B4 Springfield (cap.), Il,US
168/B1 Springfield, Ma,US
159/J3 Springfield, Mo,US
167/H9 Springfield, NJ,US
160/D4 Springfield, Oh,US
156/C4 Springfield, Or,US
163/G2 Springfield, Tn,US
166/A6 Springfield, Va,US
161/F3 Springfield, Vt,US
161/H2 Springhill, NS,Can
162/E3 Springhill, La,US
132/E2 Springs, SAfr.
157/H3 Springside, Sk,Can
119/G5 Springvale
164/D5 Spring Valley, Ca,US
157/K5 Spring Valley, Mn,US
167/D1 Spring Valley, NY,US
67/E6 Sprockhövel, Ger.
59/H1 Sprowston, Eng,UK
160/E4 Spruce (peak), WV,US
166/C2 Spruce Run (res.), NJ,US
66/B5 Spui (riv.), Neth.
57/J4 Spurn Head (pt.), Eng,UK
156/C3 Squamish, BC,Can
165/B3 Squaxin I. Ind. Res., Wa,US
168/D3 Squibnocket (pt.), Ma,US
80/E3 Squillace (gulf), It.
81/F2 Squinzano, It.
117/E3 Squires (peak), Austl.
82/D3 Srbobran, Yugo.
109/C4 Sre Ambel, Camb.
82/D3 Srebrenica, Bosn.
83/G4 Sredna (mts.), Bul.
83/G4 Srednogorie, Bul.
109/D3 Sre Khtum, Camb.
65/J2 Śrem, Pol.
82/E3 Sremčica, Yugo.
82/D3 Sremska Mitrovica, Yugo.
109/C3 Sreng (riv.), Camb.
109/D3 Sre Noy, Camb.
109/D3 Srepok (riv.), Camb.
97/H1 Sretensk, Rus.
95/K3 Sri Dungargarh, India
95/K3 Sri Gangānagar, India
106/D4 Srikākulam, India
104/B5 Sri Kshetra (ruins), Burma
106/D6 Sri Lanka
95/K2 Srīnagar, India
108/G3 Srīrangam, India
108/F4 Srīvaikuntam, India
106/B4 Srīvardhan, India
108/F4 Srīvilliputtūr, India
65/J3 Środa Śląska, Pol.
65/J2 Środa Wielkopolska, Pol.
118/A2 Staaten (riv.), Austl.
118/A2 Staaten River Nat'l Park, Austl.
61/H1 Stabbursdalen Nat'l Park, Nor.
62/D4 Staberhuk (pt.), Ger.
66/B6 Stabroek, Belg.
67/G1 Stade, Ger.
68/C2 Staden, Belg.
66/D3 Stadskanaal, Neth.
70/D6 Stadtbergen, Ger.
67/G4 Stadthagen, Ger.
66/D5 Stadtlohn, Ger.
77/E3 Stäfa, Swi.
62/E4 Staffanstorp, Swe.
70/E2 Staffelberg (peak), Ger.
76/E3 Staffelegg (pass), Swi.
77/H2 Staffelsee (lake), Ger.
78/C3 Staffora (riv.), It.
57/F6 Stafford, Eng,UK
168/B2 Stafford, Ct,US
58/D2 Stafford & Worcester (can.), Eng,UK
57/F5 Staffordshire (co.), Eng,UK
80/B4 Stagnone (isls.), It.
57/G2 Staindrop, Eng,UK
53/M7 Staines, Eng,UK
53/T10 Stains, Fr.
54/B5 Stake, Hill of (hill), Sc,UK
165/M12 Stakes (mtn.), Ca,US
86/F2 Stakhanov, Ukr.
58/D5 Stalbridge, Eng,UK
59/H1 Stalham, Eng,UK
153/S6 Stallworthy (cape), NW,Can
65/M3 Stalowa Wola, Pol.
57/F5 Stalybridge, Eng,UK
83/G4 Stamboliyski, Bul.
59/F1 Stamford, Eng,UK
167/E1 Stamford, Ct,US
57/H4 Stamford Bridge, Eng,UK
61/E1 Stamsund, Nor.
60/D2 Stamullin, Ire.
132/E2 Standerton, SAfr.
57/F4 Standish-with-Langtree, Eng,UK
59/G4 Stanford le Hope, Eng,UK
53/P6 Stanford Rivers, Eng,UK
62/D1 Stange, Nor.
133/E3 Stanger, SAfr.
57/F2 Stanhope, Eng,UK
165/M12 Stanislaus (co.), Ca,US
158/B3 Stanislaus (riv.), Ca,US
83/F4 Stanke Dimitrov, Bul.
117/F2 Stanley (peak), Austl.
161/H2 Stanley, NB,Can
108/F3 Stanley (res.), India
57/G2 Stanley, Eng,UK
143/N7 Stanley (cap.), Falk.
54/C4 Stanley, Sc,UK
157/H3 Stanley, ND,US
125/L8 Stanley (falls), Zaire
82/E4 Stanovo, Yugo.
89/N4 Stanovoy (range), Rus.
53/P8 Stansted, Eng,UK
59/G3 Stansted Mountfitchet, Eng,UK
59/G2 Stanton, Eng,UK
164/C3 Stanton, Ca,US
160/D4 Stanton, Ky,US
162/C3 Stanton, Tx,US
53/M7 Stanwell, Eng,UK
66/D3 Staphorst, Neth.
59/E4 Stapleford, Eng,UK
53/P7 Stapleford Abbotts, Eng,UK
59/G4 Staplehurst, Eng,UK
65/L3 Starachowice, Pol.
82/E3 Stara Pazova, Yugo.
82/F3 Stara Planina (mts.), Yugo.
84/F4 Staraya Russa, Rus.
83/G4 Stara Zagora, Bul.
121/K5 Starbuck (isl.), Kiri.
118/B1 Starcke Nat'l Park, Austl.
65/H2 Stargard Szczeciński, Pol.
168/F6 Stark (co.), Oh,US
163/H4 Starke, Fl,US
163/F3 Starkville, Ms,US
77/H2 Starnbergersee (lake), Ger.
86/F3 Staroderevyan-kovskaya, Rus.
86/E1 Starodub, Rus.
65/K2 Starogard Gdański, Pol.
86/F3 Staroshcher-binovskaya, Rus.
58/C6 Start (bay), Eng,UK
58/C6 Start (pt.), Eng,UK
55/N13 Start (pt.), Sc,UK
65/L3 Staszów, Pol.
160/E3 State College, Pa,US
166/C6 State Fairgnds., De,US
167/D2 Staten (isl.), NY,US
163/H3 Statesboro, Ga,US
163/H3 Statesville, NC,US
167/J9 Statue of Liberty Nat'l Mon., NY,US
64/E3 Staufenberg, Ger.
76/D2 Staufen im Breisgau, Ger.
58/D3 Staunton, Eng,UK
160/E4 Staunton, Va,US
58/D2 Staunton on Wye, Eng,UK
77/G4 Stausee Gepatsch (lake), Aus.

222
Staus – Tachi

71/E1 Stausee-Hohenwarte (res.), Ger.
62/A2 Stavanger, Nor.
57/F3 Staveley, Eng,UK
57/G5 Staveley, Eng,UK
87/G3 Stavropol', Rus.
87/G3 Stavropol' Kray, Rus.
119/B3 Stawell, Austl.
156/C4 Stayton, Or,US
165/L10 Steamboat (slough), Ca,US
158/F2 Steamboat Springs, Co,US
67/H3 Stederau (riv.), Ger.
119/F5 Steele (cr.), Austl.
157/J4 Steele, ND,US
54/C4 Steele's Knowe (hill), Sc,UK
168/G5 Steel Museum, Youngstown, Oh,US
133/E2 Steelpoortrivier (riv.), SAfr.
66/B5 Steenbergen, Neth.
158/C2 Steens (mtn.), Or,US
153/J1 Steensby (inlet), NW,Can
66/D3 Steenwijk, Neth.
116/B3 Steep (pt.), Austl.
157/G1 Steephill (lake), Sk,Can
58/C4 Steep Holm (isl.), Eng,UK
57/J5 Steeping (riv.), Eng,UK
151/J2 Steese Nat'l Rec. Area, Ak,US
152/F1 Stefansson (isl.), NW,Can
142/C5 Steffen (peak), Chile
76/D4 Steffisburg, Swi.
82/A2 Steiermark (prov.), Aus.
70/D3 Steigerwald (for.), Ger.
131/C4 Steilloopbrug, SAfr.
64/F4 Stein, Ger.
69/E2 Stein, Neth.
77/E2 Steina (riv.), Ger.
70/E2 Steinach (riv.), Ger.
157/J3 Steinbach, Mb,Can
70/E4 Stein bei Nürnberg, Ger.
76/D2 Steinen, Ger.
67/F3 Steinfeld, Ger.
67/F5 Steinhagen, Ger.
77/E3 Steinhausen, Swi.
67/G5 Steinheim, Ger.
70/D5 Steinheim am Albuch, Ger.
70/C5 Steinheim an der Murr, Ger.
67/G4 Steinhuder Meer (lake), Ger.
61/D2 Steinkjer, Nor.
68/D1 Stekene, Belg.
77/F5 Stella, Pizzo (peak), It.
161/J2 Stellarton, NS,Can
67/H2 Stelle, Ger.
132/B4 Stellenbosch, SAfr.
73/H5 Stello (mtn.), Fr.
77/G5 Stelvio Nat'l Park, It.
77/G4 Stelvio, Passo di (pass), It.
64/F2 Stendal, Ger.
83/G4 Steneto Nat'l Park, Bul.
63/R7 Stenhamra, Swe.
54/C4 Stenhousemuir, Sc,UK
63/T9 Stenløse, Den.
62/D2 Stenungsund, Swe.
87/H5 Stepanakert, Azer.
119/B1 Stephens Creek, Austl.
161/K1 Stephenville, Nf,Can
162/D3 Stephenville, Tx,US
159/G2 Sterling, Co,US
168/C1 Sterling, Ma,US
162/C4 Sterling City, Tx,US
165/F6 Sterling Heights, Mi,US
87/K1 Sterlitamak, Rus.
71/H5 Sternstein (peak), Aus.
77/H4 Sterzing (Vipiteno), It.
71/H2 Štěti, Czh.
156/E2 Stettler, Ab,Can
168/G7 Steubenville, Oh,US
59/F3 Stevenage, Eng,UK
117/G3 Stevenson (cr.), Austl.
157/J2 Stevenson (lake), Mb,Can
151/H4 Stevenson (str.), Ak,US
168/A3 Stevenson (dam), Ct,US
160/B2 Stevens Point, Wi,US
54/B5 Stevenston, Sc,UK
156/E4 Stevensville, Mt,US
66/C3 Stevinsluizen (dam), Neth.
114/E2 Stewart (cape), Austl.
151/L3 Stewart (riv.), Yk,Can
115/Q12 Stewart (isl.), NZ
151/L3 Stewart Crossing, Yk,Can
54/B5 Stewarton, Sc,UK
151/L3 Stewart River, Yk,Can
56/B2 Stewartstown, NI,UK
157/K5 Stewartville, Mn,US
59/F5 Steyning, Eng,UK
71/H6 Steyr, Aus.
71/H6 Steyr (riv.), Aus.
165/D2 Stickney (mtn.), Wa,US
66/C2 Stiens, Neth.
159/J4 Stigler, Ok,US
151/M4 Stikine (riv.), BC,Can
166/C2 Still Creek (res.), Pa,US
157/K4 Stillwater, Mn,US
158/C3 Stillwater (range), Nv,US
159/H3 Stillwater, Ok,US
166/C1 Stillwater (lake), Pa,US
159/J4 Stilwell, Ok,US
56/D1 Stinchar (riv.), Sc,UK
162/C3 Stinnett, Tx,US
82/F5 Štip, Macd.
69/F5 Stiring-Wendel, Fr.
71/G4 Stírka (peak), Czh.
116/K6 Stirling, Austl.
117/G2 Stirling, Austl.
117/M9 Stirling, Austl.
116/C4 Stirling (peak), Austl.
54/C4 Stirling, Sc,UK
116/C5 Stirling Range Nat'l Park, Austl.
78/C3 Stirone (riv.), It.
61/D3 Stjørdal, Nor.
54/B4 Stob a' Choin (mtn.), Sc,UK
54/B3 Stob Choire Claurigh (mtn.), Sc,UK
77/F2 Stockach, Ger.
59/E4 Stockbridge, Eng,UK
65/J4 Stockerau, Aus.
71/E2 Stockheim, Ger.
62/H2 Stockholm (cap.), Swe.
63/S7 Stockholm (inset) (cap.), Swe.
76/D4 Stockhorn (peak), Swi.
146/E2 Stockon (plat.), Tx,US
131/B4 Stockpoort, SAfr.
57/F5 Stockport, Eng,UK
57/F4 Stocks (res.), Eng,UK
57/G5 Stocksbridge, Eng,UK
70/C3 Stockstadt am Main, Ger.
165/M11 Stockton, Ca,US
159/J3 Stockton (lake), Mo,US
162/C4 Stockton (plat.), Tx,US
57/G2 Stockton-on-Tees, Eng,UK
109/D3 Stoeng Treng, Camb.
58/B6 Stoke (pt.), Eng,UK
57/F5 Stoke-on-Trent, Eng,UK
119/B4 Stokes (pt.), Austl.
116/D5 Stokes Nat'l Park, Austl.
82/C4 Stolac, Bosn.
69/F2 Stolberg, Ger.
89/P2 Stolbovoy (isl.), Rus.
132/K10 Stompneuspunt (pt.), SAfr.
57/F6 Stone, Eng,UK
104/D3 Stone Forest, China
54/D3 Stonehaven, Sc,UK
59/E4 Stonehenge (ruins), Eng,UK
58/D3 Stonehouse, Eng,UK
54/C5 Stonehouse, Sc,UK
157/J3 Stonewall, Mb,Can
54/C5 Stoneyburn, Sc,UK
161/Q9 Stoney Creek, On,Can
157/J2 Stony (pt.), Mb,Can
165/F6 Stony (cr.), Mi,US
166/B3 Stony (cr.), Pa,US
167/E2 Stony Brook, NY,US
165/F6 Stony Creek (lake), Mi,US
157/J3 Stony Mountain, Mb,Can
167/E1 Stony Point, NY,US
88/K3 Stony Tunguska (riv.), Rus.
160/D1 Stooping (riv.), On,Can
153/S7 Stor (isl.), NW,Can
67/G1 Stör (riv.), Ger.
62/D2 Stora Le (lake), Swe.
61/F2 Stora Sjöfallets Nat'l Park, Swe.
61/F2 Storavan (lake), Swe.
62/A2 Stord (isl.), Nor.
62/D4 Store Bælt (chan.), Den.
61/D3 Støren, Nor.
79/G1 Storje, Slov.
119/C4 Storm (bay), Austl.
157/K5 Storm Lake, Ia,US
56/C2 Stormont, NI,UK
55/H7 Stornoway, Sc,UK
59/F5 Storrington, Eng,UK
168/B2 Storrs, Ct,US
55/H8 Storr, The, Sc,UK
62/G1 Storsjön (lake), Swe.
61/F1 Storsteinsfjellet (peak), Nor.
62/D4 Storstrøm (co.), Den.
59/G3 Stort (riv.), Eng,UK
61/F2 Storuman, Swe.
156/G4 Story, Wy,US
143/J7 Stosch (isl.), Chile
59/F2 Stotfold, Eng,UK
77/G2 Stötten, Ger.
157/H3 Stoughton, Sk,Can
168/C1 Stoughton, Ma,US
58/D5 Stour (riv.), Eng,UK
59/E2 Stour (riv.), Eng,UK
59/H3 Stour (riv.), Eng,UK
59/H4 Stour (riv.), Eng,UK
58/D2 Stourbridge, Eng,UK
59/G4 Stour, Great (riv.), Eng,UK
58/D2 Stourport on Severn, Eng,UK
54/D5 Stow, Sc,UK
166/C5 Stow (cr.), NJ,US
168/F5 Stow, Oh,US
59/G2 Stowmarket, Eng,UK
59/E3 Stow on the Wold, Eng,UK
55/H9 Strabane, NI,UK
56/A2 Strabane (dist.), NI,UK
54/D2 Strachan, Sc,UK
54/A4 Strachur, Sc,UK
78/C2 Stradella, It.
66/D6 Straelen, Ger.
71/G4 Strakonice, Czh.
83/H4 Straldzha, Bul.
64/G1 Stralsund, Ger.
132/B4 Strand, SAfr.
56/C3 Strangford, NI,UK
56/C3 Strangford Lough (inlet), NI,UK
84/C4 Strängnäs, Swe.
117/G2 Strangways (peak), Austl.
56/B1 Stranocum, NI,UK
56/C2 Stranraer, Sc,UK
157/G3 Strasbourg, Sk,Can
76/D1 Strasbourg, Fr.
160/D3 Stratford, On,Can
115/R10 Stratford, NZ
168/A3 Stratford, Ct,US
167/L7 Stratford (har.), Ct,US
167/E1 Stratford (pt.), Ct,US
166/C4 Stratford, NJ,US
59/E2 Stratford upon Avon, Eng,UK
54/B5 Strathaven, Sc,UK
54/E1 Strathbeg (bay), Sc,UK
54/B5 Strathblane, Sc,UK
54/B5 Strathclyde (reg.), Sc,UK
54/C4 Strathearn (val.), Sc,UK
156/E3 Strathmore, Ab,Can
54/D3 Strathmore (val.), Sc,UK
54/B1 Strathpeffer, Sc,UK
54/C2 Strathspey (val.), Sc,UK
54/B4 Strathyre, Sc,UK
58/B5 Stratton, Eng,UK
71/F5 Straubing, Ger.
61/M6 Straumnes (pt.), Ice.
65/G2 Strausberg, Ger.
164/B2 Strawberry (peak), Ca,US
117/G5 Streaky (bay), Austl.
165/P15 Streamwood, Il,US
53/N7 Streatham, Eng,UK
59/E3 Streatley, Eng,UK
160/B3 Streator, Il,US
71/H3 Středočeská Žulová Vrchovina (mts.), Czh.
71/G2 Středočeský (reg.), Czh.
65/K4 Středoslovenský (reg.), Slvk.
58/D4 Street, Eng,UK
168/F5 Streetsboro, Oh,US
161/Q8 Streetsville, On,Can
83/F3 Strehaia, Rom.
116/D4 Streich (peak), Austl.
71/G3 Střela (riv.), Czh.
116/C2 Strelley Abor. Land, Austl.
84/H2 Strel'na (riv.), Rus.
57/F5 Stretford, Eng,UK
59/G2 Stretham, Eng,UK
70/D2 Streu (riv.), Ger.
71/G3 Stříbro, Czh.
54/D1 Strichen, Sc,UK
66/B5 Strijen, Neth.
81/H2 Strimón (gulf), Gre.
81/H2 Strimónas (riv.), Gre.
54/A5 Striven (inlet), Sc,UK
143/K7 Strobel (lake), Arg.
81/G4 Strofádhes (isls.), Gre.
80/D3 Stromboli (isl.), It.
55/J8 Stromeferry, Sc,UK
62/D2 Strømmen, Nor.
55/N13 Stromness, Sc,UK
62/D2 Strömstad, Swe.
61/E3 Strömsund, Swe.
77/E6 Strona (riv.), It.
168/F5 Strongsville, Oh,US
65/J3 Stronie Śląskie, Pol.
55/N13 Stronsay, Sc,UK
55/N13 Stronsay Firth (inlet), Sc,UK
71/H5 Stropnice (riv.), Czh.
58/D3 Stroud, Eng,UK
55/H8 Struan, Sc,UK
62/C3 Struer, Den.
82/E5 Struga, Macd.
132/C4 Struisbaai (bay), SAfr.
56/A2 Strule (riv.), NI,UK
81/H2 Struma (riv.), Bul., Gre.
58/A2 Strumble Head (pt.), UK
82/F5 Strumica, Macd.
168/G5 Struthers, Oh,US
61/C3 Stryn, Nor.
65/J3 Strzegom, Pol.
65/H2 Strzelce Krajeńskie, Pol.
117/J4 Strzelecki (cr.), Austl.
117/G2 Strzelecki (peak), Austl.
119/D4 Strzelecki (peak), Austl.
65/J3 Strzelin, Pol.
65/L4 Strzyżów, Pol.
156/B2 Stuart (lake), BC,Can
156/B2 Stuart (riv.), BC,Can
163/H5 Stuart, Fl,US
160/E4 Stuarts Draft, Va,US
65/G1 Stubbenkammer (pt.), Ger.
59/E5 Studland, Eng,UK
59/E2 Studley, Eng,UK
65/J4 Stupava, Slvk.
84/H5 Stupino, Rus.
78/A4 Stura di Demonte (riv.), It.
78/A2 Stura di Lanzo (riv.), It.
157/J3 Sturgeon (bay), Mb,Can
160/B1 Sturgeon (lake), On,Can
160/D2 Sturgeon (riv.), On,Can
160/C2 Sturgeon Bay, Wi,US
160/E2 Sturgeon Falls, On,Can
160/C3 Sturgis, Mi,US
157/H4 Sturgis, SD,US
58/D5 Sturminster Newton, Eng,UK
59/H4 Sturry, Eng,UK
117/J4 Sturt (des.), Austl.
119/B1 Sturt (peak), Austl.
117/M8 Sturt (riv.), Austl.
119/B1 Sturt Nat'l Park, Austl.
132/D4 Stutterheim, SAfr.
70/C5 Stuttgart, Ger.
162/F3 Stuttgart, Ar,US
163/F3 Stuttgart, Ar,US
86/C2 Styr (riv.), Ukr.
73/L3 Styria (prov.), Aus.
141/D1 Suaçui Grande (riv.), Braz.
127/D5 Suakin (arch.), Sudan
130/B2 Suam (riv.), Kenya
135/C3 Suárez (riv.), Col.
110/C5 Subang, Indo.
105/F3 Subao (mtn.), China
80/C1 Subasio (peak), It.
123/W18 Subaytilah, Tun.
96/C4 Subei, China
110/C3 Subi (isl.), Indo.
82/D2 Subotica, Yugo.
166/D2 Succasunna-Kenvil, NJ,US
78/D4 Succiso, Alpe di (peak), It.
83/H2 Suceava, Rom.
83/G2 Suceava (co.), Rom.
65/L3 Suchedniów, Pol.
60/B3 Suck (riv.), Ire.
136/E7 Sucre (cap.), Bol.
138/C2 Sucre (dept.), Col.
138/A5 Sucre, Ecu.
139/F2 Sucre (state), Ven.
138/B5 Sucúa, Ecu.
136/G5 Sucunduri (riv.), Braz.
141/B2 Sucuriú (riv.), Braz.
53/T10 Sucy-en-Brie, Fr.
84/H4 Suda (riv.), Rus.
125/L5 Sudan
124/H5 Sudan (phys. reg.), Afr.
160/D2 Sudbury, On,Can
59/G2 Sudbury, Eng,UK
168/C1 Sudbury, Ma,US
67/H2 Sude (riv.), Ger.
65/H3 Sudeten (mts.), Czh., Pol.
130/C5 Sudi, Tanz.
66/D5 Südlohn, Ger.
129/H5 Sud-Ouest (prov.), Camr.
125/L6 Sue (riv.), Sudan
75/E3 Sueca, Sp.
83/G4 Süedinenie, Bul.
91/C4 Suez (can.), Egypt
91/C5 Suez (gulf), Egypt
91/C5 Suez (As Suways), Egypt
91/D3 Şūf, Jor.
167/D1 Suffern, NY,US
59/G2 Suffolk (co.), Eng,UK
168/C1 Suffolk (co.), Ma,US
167/F2 Suffolk (co.), NY,US
167/E4 Suffolk, Va,US
159/K2 Sugar (riv.), Il, Wi,US
168/F6 Sugar (cr.), Oh,US
168/H5 Sugar (cr.), Pa,US
165/P14 Sugar (cr.), Wi,US
162/E4 Sugar Land, Tx,US
115/J6 Sugarloaf (pt.), Austl.
58/C3 Sugar Loaf (mtn.), Wal,UK
163/H2 Sugarloaf (peak), Ky,US
112/C4 Sugbai (passg.), Phil.
92/C2 Suğla (lake), Turk.
112/B4 Sugut (riv.), Malay.
112/B4 Sugut, Tanjong (cape), Malay.
96/F1 Sühbaatar, Mong.
70/D1 Suhl, Ger.
92/B2 Şuhut, Turk.
109/B4 Sui (pt.), Thai.
137/H6 Suiá-Missu (riv.), Braz.
97/L2 Suibin, China
107/K2 Suichuan, China
97/L3 Suifenhe, China
97/K2 Suihua, China
104/D2 Suijiang, China
97/K2 Suileng, China
103/D4 Suining, China
104/E2 Suining, China
103/C4 Suiping, China
68/D5 Suippe (riv.), Fr.
60/C5 Suir (riv.), Ire.
100/D2 Suishō (isl.), Rus.
165/K10 Suisun (bay), Ca,US
165/K10 Suisun (cr.), Ca,US
165/K10 Suisun City, Ca,US
99/L10 Suita, Japan
166/B6 Suitland-Silver Hill, Md,US
103/D4 Suixi, China
105/F4 Suixi, China
103/C4 Sui Xian, China
105/E3 Suiyang, China
76/B2 Suize (riv.), Fr.
103/C3 Suizhong, China
103/E2 Suizhou, China
106/B2 Sūjāngarh, India
110/C5 Sukabumi, Indo.
110/C4 Sukadana, Indo.
110/C4 Sukadana (bay), Indo.
99/G2 Sukagawa, Japan
108/B2 Sukheke, Pak.
86/E1 Sukhinichi, Rus.
63/N1 Sukhodol'skoye (lake), Rus.
84/J4 Sukhona (riv.), Rus.
109/B2 Sukhothai, Thai.
109/B2 Sukhothai (ruins), Thai.
87/G4 Sukhumi, Geo.
95/J3 Sukkur, Pak.
98/C4 Sukumo, Japan
105/G3 Sul (riv.), China
111/G4 Sula (isls.), Indo.
85/L2 Sula (riv.), Rus.
95/J3 Sulaimān (range), Pak.
111/E4 Sulawesi (Celebes) (isl.), Indo.
127/B4 Sulb Temple (ruins), Sudan
56/D3 Sulby (riv.), IM,UK
65/H2 Sulechów, Pol.
65/H2 Sulęcin, Pol.
65/L2 Sulejówek, Pol.
67/F3 Sulingen, Ger.
96/D4 Sulin Gol (riv.), China
61/F2 Sulitjelma (peak), Nor.
144/A2 Sullana, Peru
60/A6 Sullane (riv.), Ire.
156/F3 Sullivan (lake), Ab,Can
160/C4 Sullivan, In,US
160/E1 Sullivan Mines, Qu,Can
58/C4 Sully, Wal,UK
80/C1 Sulmona, It.
159/J4 Sulphur (riv.), Ar, Tx,US
162/E4 Sulphur, La,US
159/H4 Sulphur, Ok,US
159/G4 Sulphur Spring Draw (cr.), NM, Tx,US
162/E3 Sulphur Springs, Tx,US
165/D2 Sultan (cr.), Wa,US
130/C3 Sultan Hamud, Kenya
112/D4 Sultan Kudarat, Phil.
112/C4 Sulu (sea), Malay., Phil.
112/C4 Sulu (arch.), Phil.
92/C1 Suluova, Turk.
125/K1 Sulūq, Libya
69/G2 Sülz (riv.), Ger.
71/E4 Sulz (riv.), Ger.
70/D4 Sulzach (riv.), Ger.
70/B6 Sulz am Neckar, Ger.
69/G5 Sulzbach, Ger.
71/F6 Sulzbach (riv.), Ger.
71/E4 Sulzbach-Rosenberg, Ger.
113/P Sulzberger (bay), Ant.
113/Q Sulzberger Ice Shelf, Ant.
77/F3 Sulzfluh (peak), Aus.
82/E3 Šumadija (reg.), Yugo.
112/B4 Sumangat, Tanjong (cape), Malay.
138/C4 Sumapaz Nat'l Park, Col.
110/B4 Sumatra (isl.), Indo.
71/G4 Šumava (uplands), Czh.
110/E5 Sumba (isl.), Indo.
111/E5 Sumba (str.), Indo.
87/L5 Sumbar (riv.), Trkm.
110/E5 Sumbawa (isl.), Indo.
111/E5 Sumbawa Besar, Indo.
130/A4 Sumbawanga, Tanz.
126/B3 Sumbe, Ang.
96/F2 Sümber, Mong.
55/P13 Sumburgh Head (pt.), Sc,UK
151/M4 Sumdum (mtn.), Ak,US
140/C2 Sumé, Braz.
82/C2 Sümeg, Hun.
110/D5 Sumenep, Indo.
87/J4 Sumgait, Azer.
57/G3 Summer Bridge, Eng,UK
156/D3 Summerland, BC,Can
161/J2 Summerside, PE,Can
160/D4 Summersville, WV,US
163/G3 Summerville, Ga,US
163/H3 Summerville, SC,US
166/D2 Summit, NJ,US
168/F5 Summit (co.), Oh,US
165/C3 Sumner, Wa,US
98/D3 Sumoto, Japan
65/J4 Šumperk, Czh.
163/H3 Sumter, SC,US
86/E2 Sumy, Ukr.
86/E2 Sumy Obl., Ukr.
104/B4 Sun (peak), Burma
156/E4 Sun (riv.), Mt,US
100/B2 Sunagawa, Japan
108/C2 Sunām, India
99/M9 Sunami, Japan
119/C3 Sunbury, Austl.
166/B2 Sunbury, Pa,US
59/F4 Sunbury on Thames, Eng,UK
101/D5 Sunch'ŏn, SKor.
158/D4 Sun City, Az,US
164/C3 Sun City, Ca,US
161/G3 Suncook, NH,US
90/J10 Sunda (isls.), Indo.
110/B5 Sunda (str.), Indo.
157/G4 Sundance, Wy,US
106/E3 Sundarbans (reg.), Bang., India
106/D3 Sundargarh, India
108/D2 Sundarnagar, India
132/D4 Sundays (riv.), SAfr.
57/G2 Sunderland, Eng,UK
67/F6 Sundern, Ger.
119/D1 Sundown Nat'l Park, Austl.
156/E3 Sundre, Ab,Can
61/F3 Sundsvall, Swe.
63/R7 Sundyberg, Swe.
110/B4 Sungaipenuh, Indo.
110/B2 Sungai Petani, Malay.
92/C1 Sungurlu, Turk.
103/C3 Suning, China
164/F7 Sunland, Ca,US
162/B4 Sunland Park, NM,US
61/D3 Sunndalsøra, Nor.
62/E2 Sunne, Swe.
59/F4 Sunninghill, Eng,UK
165/K12 Sunnyvale, Ca,US
99/H8 Su-no-saki (cape), Japan
160/B3 Sun Prairie, Wi,US
166/D1 Sunrise (mtn.), NJ,US
119/B2 Sunset Country (reg.), Austl.
158/E4 Sunset Crater Nat'l Mon., Az,US
119/F5 Sunshine, Austl.
89/P3 Suntar-Khayata (mts.), Rus.
67/G4 Süntel (mts.), Ger.
164/F7 Sun Valley, Ca,US
97/K2 Sunwu, China
129/E5 Sunyani, Gha.
130/A5 Sunzu (peak), Zam.
98/B4 Suo (sea), Japan
109/D1 Suoi Rut, Viet.
63/L1 Suomenlinna, Fin.
61/H3 Suomenselkä (reg.), Fin.
109/D4 Suong, Camb.
144/B3 Supe, Peru
160/C2 Superior (lake), Can., US
158/E4 Superior, Az,US
156/E4 Superior, Mt,US
160/A2 Superior, Wi,US
160/B2 Superior (upland), Wi,US
109/C3 Suphan Buri, Thai.
111/J4 Supiori (isl.), Indo.
101/C2 Sup'ung (res.), China, NKor.
101/C2 Sup'ung (dam), NKor.
93/F4 Sūq ash Shuyūkh, Iraq
91/E2 Şuqaylabīyah, Syria
103/D4 Suqian, China
143/F3 Sur (pt.), Arg.
69/E4 Sûr (riv.), Belg.
71/F7 Sur (riv.), Ger.
158/B3 Sur (pt.), Ca,US
87/H1 Sura (riv.), Rus.
110/D5 Surabaya, Indo.
106/D4 Surada, India
62/G2 Surahammar, Swe.
110/D5 Surakarta, Indo.
101/G6 Suraksan (mtn.), SKor.
112/D4 Surallah, Phil.
108/G3 Sūramangalam, India
76/B5 Suran (riv.), Fr.
65/K4 Šurany, Slvk.
106/B3 Surat, India
106/B2 Sūratgarh, India
109/B4 Surat Thani, Thai.
69/G6 Surbourg, Fr.
143/J7 Sur, Campo de Hielo (glacier), Chile
82/E3 Surčin, Yugo.
82/F4 Surdulica, Yugo.
69/E4 Sûre (riv.), Belg., Lux.
106/B3 Surendranagar, India
72/C3 Surgères, Fr.
88/H3 Surgut, Rus.
106/E3 Sūri, India
75/F2 Súria, Sp.
112/D3 Surigao, Phil.
109/C3 Surin, Thai.
139/G3 Suriname
102/A4 Surkhob (riv.), Taj.
166/B6 Surrattsville (Clinton), Md,US
156/C3 Surrey, BC,Can
53/M8 Surrey (co.), Eng,UK
76/E3 Sursee, Swi.
124/J1 Surt, Libya
61/D3 Sur-Trøndelag (co.), Nor.
91/D3 Şūr (Tyre), Leb.
140/D2 Surubim, Braz.
92/D2 Sürüç, Turk.
99/F3 Suruga (bay), Japan
139/F4 Surumu (riv.), Braz.
117/F3 Surveyor General's Corner, Austl.
53/T9 Survilliers, Fr.
139/F3 Surwakwima (falls), Guy.
123/X18 Sūsah, Tun.
123/X17 Sūsah (gov.), Tun.
98/C4 Susaki, Japan
93/G4 Sūsangerd, Iran
158/B2 Susanville, Ca,US
92/D1 Suşehri, Turk.
103/B4 Sushui (riv.), China
71/G4 Sušice, Czh.
151/J3 Susitna (riv.), Ak,US
103/D5 Susong, China
99/F3 Susono, Japan
160/E3 Susquehanna (riv.), US
166/B5 Susquehanna Nat'l Wild. Ref., Md,US
161/H2 Sussex, NB,Can
166/C6 Sussex (co.), De,US
166/D1 Sussex (co.), NJ,US
59/F4 Sussex, Vale of (val.), Eng,UK
77/E4 Sustenhorn (peak), Swi.
77/E4 Sustenpass (pass), Swi.
66/C6 Susteren, Neth.
89/Q3 Susuman, Rus.
92/B2 Susurluk, Turk.
118/H9 Sutherland, Austl.
82/D4 Sutjeska Nat'l Park, Bosn.
108/B2 Sutlej (riv.), India, Pak.
165/L9 Sutter (co.), Ca,US
57/H6 Sutterton, Eng,UK
53/N7 Sutton, Eng,UK
53/N7 Sutton (bor.), Eng,UK
168/C1 Sutton, Ma,US
57/J6 Sutton Bridge, Eng,UK
59/E1 Sutton Coldfield, Eng,UK
57/G5 Sutton in Ashfield, Eng,UK
57/J5 Sutton on Sea, Eng,UK
57/H5 Sutton on Trent, Eng,UK
63/K2 Suur (str.), Est.
132/D4 Suurberge (mts.), SAfr.
120/G6 Suva (cap.), Fiji
99/F2 Suwa, Japan
65/M1 Suwałki, Pol.
65/M2 Suwałki (prov.), Pol.
163/H4 Suwannee (riv.), Fl,US
100/K6 Suwanose (isl.), Japan
121/J6 Suwarrow (atoll), CookIs.
91/D3 Şuwaylih, Jor.
101/D4 Suwŏn, SKor.
76/D3 Suze (riv.), Swi.
103/D4 Suzhou, China
103/E5 Suzhou, China
101/C2 Suzi (riv.), China
99/E2 Suzu, Japan
98/E3 Suzuka, Japan
99/M10 Suzuka (range), Japan
99/M10 Suzuka (riv.), Japan
99/E2 Suzu-misaki (cape), Japan
79/D3 Suzzara, It.
88/C2 Svalbard (arch.), Nor.
63/U9 Svalöv, Swe.
63/R7 Svartsjölandet (isl.), Swe.
71/F2 Svatava (riv.), Czh.
109/D4 Svay Rieng, Camb.
62/F2 Svealand (reg.), Swe.
62/D4 Svendborg, Den.
153/S7 Svendsen (pen.), NW,Can
62/E3 Svenljunga, Swe.
85/P4 Sverdlovsk (Yekaterinburg), Rus.
153/S7 Sverdrup (chan.), NW,Can
153/R7 Sverdrup (isls.), NW,Can
88/H2 Sverdrup (isl.), Rus.
86/D1 Svetlogorsk, Bela.
87/G3 Svetlograd, Rus.
82/E4 Svetozarevo, Yugo.
61/P7 Svíahnúkar (peak), Ice.
82/E3 Svilajnac, Yugo.
83/H5 Svilengrad, Bul.
83/G4 Svishtov, Bul.
65/J4 Svitavy, Czh.
97/K1 Svobodnyy, Rus.
83/F4 Svoge, Bul.
61/E1 Svolvær, Nor.
89/Q2 Svyatyy Nos (cape), Rus.
59/E1 Swadlincote, Eng,UK
59/G1 Swaffham, Eng,UK
118/D3 Swain (reefs), Austl.
163/H3 Swainsboro, Ga,US
121/H5 Swains Island (atoll), ASam.
126/C2 Swa-Kibula, Zaire
126/B5 Swakopmund, Namb.
57/G3 Swale (riv.), Eng,UK
59/H4 Swalecliffe, Eng,UK
59/G4 Swale, The (chan.), Eng,UK
66/D6 Swalmen, Neth.
117/G2 Swan (peak), Austl.
116/K7 Swan (riv.), Austl.
156/D2 Swan (hills), Ab,Can
157/H2 Swan (riv.), Mb, Sk,Can
149/F2 Swan (isls.), Hon.
165/F7 Swan (cr.), Mi,US
59/E5 Swanage, Eng,UK
119/B2 Swan Hill, Austl.
156/E2 Swan Hills, Ab,Can
53/P7 Swanley, Eng,UK
59/G4 Swanley Hextable, Eng,UK
165/F7 Swan, North Branch (cr.), Mi,US
157/H2 Swan River, Mb,Can
53/P7 Swanscombe, Eng,UK
58/C3 Swansea, Wal,UK
58/C3 Swansea (bay), Wal,UK
168/C2 Swansea, Ma,US
166/C4 Swarthmore, Pa,US
132/D3 Swart Kei (riv.), SAfr.
166/D1 Swartswood (lake), NJ,US
165/E6 Swartz (cr.), Mi,US
65/J2 Swarzędz, Pol.
71/E2 Swarzenbach an der Sächsischen Saale, Ger.
132/B2 Swarzrand (mts.), Namb.
166/B3 Swatara (cr.), Pa,US
56/B2 Swatragh, NI,UK
59/E5 Sway, Eng,UK
133/E2 Swaziland
61/E3 Sweden
156/C4 Sweet Home, Or,US
164/D5 Sweetwater (res.), Ca,US
162/C3 Sweetwater, Tx,US
156/F5 Sweetwater (riv.), Wy,US
132/C4 Swellendam, SAfr.
65/J3 Świdnica, Pol.
65/M3 Świdnik, Pol.
65/H2 Świdwin, Pol.
65/J3 Świebodzice, Pol.
65/H2 Świebodzin, Pol.
65/K2 Świecie, Pol.
156/G3 Swift Current, Sk,Can
55/H9 Swilly, Lough (inlet), Ire.
167/D3 Swimming River (res.), NJ,US
59/E3 Swindon, Eng,UK
57/H6 Swineshead, Eng,UK
60/B2 Swinford, Ire.
65/H2 Świnoujście, Pol.
57/G5 Swinton, Eng,UK
76/D4 Swiss (plat.), Swi.
69/F2 Swist Bach (riv.), Ger.
76/D4 Switzerland
60/D3 Swords, Ire.
84/G3 Syamozero (lake), Rus.
65/J3 Syców, Pol.
119/D2 Sydney, Austl.
161/J2 Sydney, NS,Can
118/H8 Sydney (inset), Austl.
121/H5 Sydney (Manra) (atoll), Kiri.
161/J2 Sydney Mines, NS,Can
67/F3 Syke, Ger.
85/L3 Syktyvkar, Rus.
163/G3 Sylacauga, Al,US
61/E3 Sylarna (peak), Swe.
107/F3 Sylhet, Bang.
64/E1 Sylt (isl.), Ger.
85/N4 Sylva (riv.), Rus.
160/D3 Sylvania, Oh,US
165/F6 Sylvan Lake, Mi,US
77/H2 Sylvenstein-Stausee (lake), Ger.
81/L6 Syntagma Square, Gre.
167/E2 Syosset, NY,US
113/C Syowa, Ant.
159/G3 Syracuse, Ks,US
160/E3 Syracuse, NY,US
80/D4 Syracuse (Siracusa), It.
88/G5 Syrdar'ya (riv.), Asia
92/D3 Syria
107/G4 Syriam, Burma
92/D3 Syrian (des.), Asia
85/L3 Sysola (riv.), Rus.
59/E1 Syston, Eng,UK
87/J1 Syzran', Rus.
82/E1 Szabolcs-Szatmár-Bereg (co.), Hun.
65/J2 Szamotuły, Pol.
82/E2 Szarvas, Hun.
82/D2 Százhalombatta, Hun.
65/H2 Szczecin, Pol.
65/H2 Szczecin (prov.), Pol.
65/J2 Szczecinek, Pol.
65/L2 Szczytno, Pol.
82/E2 Szeged, Hun.
82/E2 Szeghalom, Hun.
82/E2 Szegvár, Hun.
82/D2 Székesfehérvár, Hun.
82/D2 Szekszárd, Hun.
82/D2 Szentendre, Hun.
82/E2 Szentes, Hun.
82/E2 Szerencs, Hun.
65/M1 Szeskie (peak), Pol.
84/D5 Szeskie Wzgorza (peak), Pol.
82/C2 Szigetvár, Hun.
82/E2 Szolnok, Hun.
82/C2 Szombathely, Hun.
65/H3 Szprotawa, Pol.
65/K2 Sztum, Pol.
65/J2 Szubin, Pol.
65/L3 Szydłowiec, Pol.

T

112/C2 Tabaco, Phil.
112/D3 Tabango, Phil.
93/J3 Tabas, Iran
149/F4 Tabasará, Serranía de (range), Pan.
147/G5 Tabasco (state), Mex.
140/A3 Tabatinga (mts.), Braz.
130/D2 Tabda, Som.
124/E2 Tabelbala, Alg.
156/E3 Taber, Ab,Can
75/E3 Tabernes de Valldigna, Sp.
140/C2 Tabira, Braz.
120/G5 Tabiteuea (atoll), Kiri.
112/C2 Tablas (isl.), Phil.
112/C3 Tablas (str.), Phil.
60/D3 Table (mtn.), Ire.
132/B4 Table (bay), SAfr.
132/L10 Table (peak), SAfr.
159/J3 Table Rock (lake), Ar, Mo,US
74/B1 Taboada, Sp.
71/H4 Tábor, Czh.
130/C5 Tabora, Tanz.
130/B4 Tabora (prov.), Tanz.
128/D5 Tabou, IvC.
93/F2 Tabrīz, Iran
121/K4 Tabuaeran (Fanning) (atoll), Kiri.
112/C1 Tabuk, Phil.
92/D4 Tabūk, SAr.
140/C2 Tabuleiro do Norte, Braz.
120/F6 Tabwemasana (mtn.), Van.
63/S6 Täby, Swe.
148/C3 Tacaná (vol.), Mex.
149/G4 Tacarcuna (mtn.), Pan.
102/D2 Tacheng, China
105/J3 Tachia (riv.), Tai.

223

Tachi – Teres

98/A4 Tachibana (bay), Japan
99/F3 Tachikawa, Japan
71/F7 Tachinger See (lake), Ger.
138/C2 Táchira (state), Ven.
71/F3 Tachov, Czh.
112/D3 Tacloban, Phil.
144/D5 Tacna, Peru
165/C3 Tacoma, Wa,US
144/D5 Tacora (vol.), Chile
75/X16 Tacoronte, Canl.,Sp.
143/G1 Tacuarembó, Uru.
143/G2 Tacuarembó (dept.), Uru.
112/D4 Tacurong, Phil.
139/F4 Tacutu (riv.), Braz., Guy.
99/F2 Tadami (riv.), Japan
99/L10 Tadaoka, Japan
57/G4 Tadcaster, Eng,UK
124/F2 Tademaït (plat.), Alg.
106/D4 Tādepallegūdem, India
121/V12 Tadine, NCal.
59/E4 Tadley, Eng,UK
92/D3 Tadmur, Syria
99/M9 Tado, Japan
101/C5 Tadohae Hasang Nat'l Park, SKor.
98/C3 Tadotsu, Japan
106/C5 Tādpatri, India
124/H2 Tadrart (mts.), Alg., Libya
53/N8 Tadworth, Eng,UK
101/D2 T'aebaek (mts.), NKor., SKor.
101/E4 T'aebaek, SKor.
101/F7 Taebudo (isl.), SKor.
101/D4 Taech'ŏn, SKor.
101/C4 Taech'ŏng (isl.), SKor.
101/D3 Taedong (riv.), NKor.
101/D3 Taegang-got (pt.), NKor.
101/E5 Taegu, SKor.
101/E5 Taegu-Jikhalsi (prov.), SKor.
101/C5 Taehŭksan (isl.), SKor.
101/D4 Taejŏn, SKor.
101/C2 Taeryŏng (riv.), NKor.
58/B3 Taf (riv.), Wal,UK
74/E1 Tafalla, Sp.
58/C3 Taff (riv.), Wal,UK
135/C2 Tafí Viejo, Arg.
93/H4 Taft, Iran
112/D3 Taft, Phil.
95/H3 Taftān (mtn.), Iran
99/M9 Taga, Japan
86/F3 Taganrog, Rus.
86/F3 Taganrog (gulf), Rus., Ukr.
128/C2 Tagant (reg.), Mrta.
93/J2 Tagarav (peak), Trkm.
98/B4 Tagawa, Japan
112/C3 Tagbilaran, Phil.
78/A5 Taggia, It.
124/E1 Taghit, Alg.
112/F6 Tagig, Phil.
151/M3 Tagish, Yk,Can
79/G1 Tagliamento (riv.), It.
68/D5 Tagnon, Fr.
112/C3 Tagolo (pt.), Phil.
112/D3 Tagoloan, Phil.
149/G1 Taguasco, Cuba
140/A4 Taguatinga, Braz.
112/C1 Tagudin, Phil.
120/E6 Tagula (isl.), PNG
112/D4 Tagum, Phil.
85/P4 Tagun (riv.), Rus.
74/C3 Tagus (Tajo) (riv.), Sp.
74/B3 Tagus (Tejo) (riv.), Port.
110/B3 Tahan (peak), Malay.
99/N10 Tahara, Japan
124/G3 Tahat (peak), Alg.
123/R16 Tahat, Oued et (riv.), Alg.
97/J1 Tahe, China
121/L6 Tahenea (atoll), FrPol.
92/E2 Tahir (pass), Turk.
121/L6 Tahiti (isl.), FrPol.
63/K2 Tahkuna (pt.), Est.
162/E3 Tahlequah, Ok,US
151/J3 Tahneta (pass), Ak,US
158/C3 Tahoe (lake), Ca, Nv,US
162/C3 Tahoka, Tx,US
129/G3 Tahoua, Niger
129/G3 Tahoua (dept.), Niger
156/B3 Tahsis, BC,Can
127/B3 Taḩtā, Egypt
144/D3 Tahuamanu (riv.), Peru
121/L6 Tahuata (isl.), FrPol.
111/G3 Tahulandang (isl.), Indo.
165/B3 Tahuyo (riv.), Wa,US
103/L8 Tai (lake), China
101/B2 Tai'an, China
121/X15 Taiarapu (pen.), FrPol.
96/F5 Taibai (peak), China
103/C3 Taibai Shan (mtn.), China
96/H3 Taibus Qi, China
103/E5 Taicang, China
105/J3 Taichung, Tai.
103/C3 Taigu, China
103/C3 Taihang (mts.), China
103/C4 Taihe, China
103/D5 Taihu, China
103/C4 Taikang, China
100/C2 Taiki, Japan
97/J2 Tailai, China
99/L10 Taima, Japan
54/B1 Tain, Sc,UK
105/J4 Tainan, Tai.
81/H4 Taínaron, Ákra (cape), Gre.
128/D5 Taï Nat'l Park, IvC.
140/B4 Taiobeiras, Braz.
121/L5 Taiohae, FrPol.
105/J3 Taipei (cap.), Tai.
103/D5 Taiping, China
97/J2 Taiping (peak), China
110/B3 Taiping, Malay.
140/D2 Taipu, Braz.
98/C3 Taisha, Japan
105/G4 Taishan, China
99/L10 Taishi, Japan
105/H3 Taishun, China
142/B5 Taitao (pen.), Chile
130/B2 Taiti (peak), Kenya
105/J3 Taiwan
105/H4 Taiwan (str.), China, Tai.
103/E4 Tai Xian, China
103/E4 Taixing, China
81/H4 Taíyetos (mts.), Gre.
103/C3 Taiyuan, China
103/D4 Taizhou, China
103/E2 Taizi (riv.), China
110/C4 Tajam (peak), Indo.
124/H3 Tajarhī, Libya
88/H6 Tajikistan
99/F2 Tajima, Japan
99/E3 Tajimi, Japan
99/L10 Tajiri, Japan
148/D3 Tajmulco (vol.), Guat.
74/C3 Tajo (Tagus) (riv.), Sp.
93/G3 Tajrīsh, Iran
74/D2 Tajuña (riv.), Sp.
109/B2 Tak, Thai.
99/G2 Takahagi, Japan
98/D3 Takahama, Japan
98/C3 Takahashi, Japan
98/C3 Takahashi (riv.), Japan
99/G2 Takahata, Japan
99/L10 Takaishi, Japan
98/D3 Takamatsu, Japan
99/M10 Takami-yama (peak), Japan
98/B4 Takanabe, Japan
100/B3 Takanosu, Japan
99/E2 Takaoka, Japan
115/R10 Takapuna, NZ
99/L10 Takarazuka, Japan
121/L6 Takaroa (isl.), FrPol.
99/F2 Takasaki, Japan
99/M9 Takashima, Japan
99/L10 Takatori, Japan
98/D3 Takatsuki, Japan
130/C3 Takaungu, Kenya
99/E2 Takayama, Japan
98/E3 Takefu, Japan
98/C3 Takehara, Japan
93/G2 Takestān, Iran
98/B4 Taketa, Japan
99/M10 Taketoyo, Japan
109/D4 Takev, Camb.
107/H4 Ta Khli, Thai.
125/R2 Takht-e Jamshīd (Persepolis) (ruins), Iran
99/M10 Taki, Japan
152/E2 Takijuq (lake), NW,Can
99/E3 Takikawa, Japan
99/K10 Takino, Japan
159/J2 Takio (cr.), Ia,US
156/B2 Takla (lake), BC,Can
102/D4 Takla Makan (des.), China
129/E5 Takoradi, Gha.
123/V17 Takouch (cape), Alg.
91/B4 Talā, Egypt
130/C3 Tala, Kenya
57/E5 Talacre, Wal,UK
108/B1 Talagang, Pak.
142/Q9 Talagante, Chile
106/B3 Talāja, India
129/G2 Talak (reg.), Niger
149/F4 Talamanca, Cordillera de (range), CR
126/C2 Tala Mugongo, Ang.
110/B4 Talang (peak), Indo.
148/E3 Talanga, Hon.
69/F5 Talange, Fr.
76/A3 Talant, Fr.
144/A2 Talara, Peru
102/B3 Talas (riv.), Kaz.
92/C2 Talas, Turk.
111/G3 Talaud (isls.), Indo.
74/C3 Talavera de la Reina, Sp.
106/D6 Talawakele, SrL.
125/M5 Talawdī, Sudan
74/C3 Talayuela, Sp.
114/D2 Talbot (cape), Austl.
116/E3 Talbot (peak), Austl.
166/B6 Talbot (co.), Md,US
142/C2 Talca, Chile
142/B3 Talcahuano, Chile
106/E3 Tālcher, India
102/C3 Taldy-Kurgan, Kaz.
72/C4 Talence, Fr.
76/C4 Talent (riv.), Swi.
77/H4 Talfer (Talvera) (riv.), It.
88/H5 Talgar, Kaz.
58/C3 Talgarth, Wal,UK
111/F4 Taliabu (isl.), Indo.
112/C4 Talipaw, Phil.
125/M6 Tali Post, Sudan
112/D3 Talisayan, Phil.
111/E5 Taliwang, Indo.
91/B4 Ṭalkhā, Egypt
163/G3 Talladega, Al,US
92/E2 Tall 'Afar, Iraq
163/G4 Tallahassee (cap.), Fl,US
163/F3 Tallahatchie (riv.), Ms,US
91/G8 Tall 'Āsūr (Ba'al Hazor) (mtn.), WBnk.
116/B4 Tallering (peak), Austl.
166/C4 Talleyville, De,US
63/L2 Tallinn (cap.), Est.
91/E2 Tall Kalakh, Syria
93/E2 Tall Kayf, Iraq
168/F5 Tallmadge, Oh,US
163/H3 Tallulah (falls), Ga,US
163/F3 Tallulah, La,US
125/N5 Talo (peak), Eth.
106/B3 Taloda, India
95/J1 Tāloqān, Afg.
146/D4 Talpa, Mex.
71/F1 Talsperre Pöhl (res.), Ger.
135/B2 Taltal, Chile
152/E2 Taltson (riv.), NW,Can
109/C4 Talumphuk (pt.), Thai.
77/H4 Talvera (Talfer) (riv.), It.
108/C2 Talwāra, India
99/H7 Tama, Japan
99/H7 Tama (riv.), Japan
112/A5 Tama Abu (range), Malay.
99/H6 Tamagawa, Japan
99/M10 Tamaki, Japan
129/E4 Tamale, Gha.
138/B3 Tamana (peak), Col.
120/G5 Tamana (atoll), Kiri.
122/C2 Tamanghasset, Alg.
129/F1 Tamanghasset (wilaya), Alg.
166/C2 Tamaqua, Pa,US
58/B5 Tamar (riv.), Eng,UK
100/H8 Tamara (isl.), Japan
138/C3 Tamar, Alto de (peak), Col.
148/E4 Tamarindo Nat'l Wild. Ref., CR
77/E5 Tamaro, Monte (peak), Swi.
82/D2 Tamási, Hun.
146/E5 Tamazula, Mex.
147/F4 Tamazunchale, Mex.
99/L9 Tamba, Japan
99/L9 Tamba (hills), Japan
130/B2 Tambach, Kenya
128/B3 Tambacounda, Sen.
128/B3 Tambacounda (reg.), Sen.
128/C3 Tambaoura, Falaise de (escarp.), Mali
131/D3 Tambara, Moz.
110/C3 Tambelan (isls.), Indo.
144/C3 Tambo (riv.), Peru
144/C4 Tambo Colorado (ruins), Peru
144/A2 Tambo Grande, Peru
144/D4 Tambopata (riv.), Bol., Peru
77/F5 Tambo, Pizzo (peak), Swi.
111/E5 Tambora (peak), Indo.
140/B2 Tamboril, Braz.
119/C3 Tamboritha (peak), Austl.
87/G1 Tambov, Rus.
87/G1 Tambov Obl., Rus.
74/A1 Tambre (riv.), Sp.
125/L6 Tambura, Sudan
59/E1 Tame (riv.), Eng,UK
74/B2 Tâmega (riv.), Port.
129/H2 Tamgak (peak), Niger
128/B3 Tamgue, Massif du (reg.), Gui., Sen.
147/F4 Tamiahua, Mex.
148/B1 Tamiahua (lag.), Mex.
108/F3 Tamil Nadu (state), India
91/B5 Ṭāmiyah, Egypt
109/E3 Tam Ky, Viet.
109/D2 Tam Le, Viet.
166/C2 Tammany (mtn.), NJ,US
63/K2 Tammisaari (Ekenäs), Fin.
163/H5 Tampa, Fl,US
108/H4 Tampalakamam, SrL.
63/K1 Tampere, Fin.
147/F4 Tampico, Mex.
139/H4 Tampoc (riv.), FrG.
110/A3 Tampulonanjing (peak), Indo.
147/F4 Tamuín, Mex.
148/B1 Tamuín (riv.), Mex.
119/D1 Tamworth, Austl.
59/E1 Tamworth, Eng,UK
101/D5 Tamyang, SKor.
107/K3 Tan (riv.), China
125/N5 Tana (lake), Eth.
130/D3 Tana (riv.), Kenya
61/H1 Tana (riv.), Nor.
98/D4 Tanabe, Japan
141/B2 Tanabi, Braz.
61/J1 Tanafjorden (fjord), Nor.
151/C6 Tanaga (isl.), Ak,US
151/C6 Tanaga (vol.), Ak,US
80/D2 Tanagro (riv.), It.
99/G2 Tanagura, Japan
109/C5 Tanah Merah, Malay.
114/E3 Tanami (des.), Austl.
117/F2 Tanami Desert Wild. Sanct., Austl.
109/D4 Tan An, Viet.
151/J3 Tanana (riv.), Ak,US
130/B4 Tanangozi, Tanz.
130/D3 Tana River Primate Nat'l Rsv., Kenya
78/B3 Tanaro (riv.), It.
103/D4 Tancheng, China
146/E5 Tancitaro, Pico de (peak), Mex.
106/C2 Tānda, India
106/D2 Tānda, India
128/D3 Tanda (lake), Mali
112/D3 Tandag, Phil.
125/M5 Tandaltī, Sudan
83/H3 Ţăndărei, Rom.
142/F3 Tandil, Arg.
108/B2 Tāndliānwāla, Pak.
95/J3 Tando Ādam, Pak.
95/J3 Tando Allāhyār, Pak.
95/J3 Tando Muhammad Khān, Pak.
119/B2 Tandou (lake), Austl.
56/B3 Tandragee, NI,UK
98/B5 Tanega (isl.), Japan
104/C5 Tanem (range), Burma, Thai.
124/E3 Tanezrouft (des.), Alg., Mali
103/C3 Tang (riv.), China
103/C4 Tang (riv.), China
130/C4 Tanga, Tanz.
130/C4 Tanga (prov.), Tanz.
133/H8 Tangainony, Madg.
130/A4 Tanganyika (lake), Afr.
137/G6 Tangará da Serra, Braz.
151/G1 Tangent (pt.), Ak,US
64/F2 Tangerhütte, Ger.
123/M13 Tanger (Tangier), Mor.
102/E5 Tanggula (mts.), China
102/F5 Tanggula Shankou (pass), China
103/C4 Tanghe, China
123/M13 Tangier (Tanger), Mor.
165/B3 Tanglewilde-Thompson Place, Wa,US
168/A1 Tanglewood, Ma,US
102/E5 Tangra (lake), China
103/D3 Tangshan, China
112/C3 Tangub, Phil.
105/F2 Tangyan (riv.), China
103/C4 Tangyin, China
97/K2 Tangyuan, China
140/B4 Tanhaçu, Braz.
104/C2 Taniantaweng (mts.), China
111/H5 Tanimbar (isls.), Indo.
112/C3 Tanjay, Phil.
110/A3 Tanjungbalai, Indo.
110/C5 Tanjungkarang-Telukbetung, Indo.
110/C4 Tanjungpandan, Indo.
110/A3 Tanjungpura, Indo.
108/A1 Tānk, Pak.
120/F6 Tanna (isl.), Van.
99/L9 Tannan, Japan
102/F1 Tannu-Ola (mts.), Mong., Rus.
129/E5 Tano (riv.), Ghana, IvC.
147/F4 Tanquián, Mex.
140/C3 Tanquinho, Braz.
125/M1 Tanṭā, Egypt
91/B4 Ṭanṭā, Egypt
124/C2 Tan-Tan, Mor.
147/F4 Tantoyuca, Mex.
106/D4 Tanuku, India
112/E7 Tanza, Phil.
130/B3 Tanzania
99/H7 Tanzawa-yama (peak), Japan
105/G3 Tao (riv.), China
109/B4 Tao (isl.), Thai.
97/J2 Tao'er (riv.), China
96/F4 Taole, China
97/J2 Taonan, China
80/D4 Taormina, It.
159/F3 Taos, NM,US
124/E3 Taoudenni, Mali
123/N13 Taourirt, Mor.
107/K2 Taoyuan, China
105/J3 Taoyuan, Tai.
63/L2 Tapa, Est.
148/C3 Tapachula, Mex.
139/H5 Tapajós (riv.), Braz.
139/H4 Tapanahoni (riv.), Sur.
148/C2 Tapantatepec, Mex.
136/F5 Tapauá, Braz.
136/E5 Tapauá (riv.), Braz.
112/C3 Tapaz, Phil.
141/B4 Tapejara, Braz.
141/B4 Tapes, Braz.
144/C2 Tapiche (riv.), Peru
104/C3 Taping (riv.), Burma
110/B3 Tapis (peak), Malay.
129/F3 Tapoa (prov.), Burk.
82/C2 Tapolca, Hun.
54/D2 Tap O'Noth (hill), Sc,UK
160/E4 Tappahannock, Va,US
167/K7 Tappan (lake), NJ, NY,US
167/E1 Tappan, NY,US
168/F7 Tappan (dam), Oh,US
168/F7 Tappan (res.), Oh,US
167/E1 Tappan Zee (reach), NY,US
100/B3 Tappi-zaki (pt.), Japan
165/C3 Tapps (lake), Wa,US
106/B3 Tāpti (riv.), India
112/C4 Tapul (isls.), Phil.
127/B5 Taqab, Sudan
127/D5 Taqātu' Hayyā, Sudan
141/B4 Taquara, Braz.
141/B4 Taquari, Braz.
137/G7 Taquari (riv.), Braz.
141/B2 Taquaritinga, Braz.
141/B2 Taquarituba, Braz.
144/B1 Taquil, Ecu.
79/G2 Tar, Cro.
60/B5 Tar (riv.), Ire.
102/B3 Tar (riv.), Kyr.
82/D4 Tara (riv.), Bosn., Yugo.
88/H4 Tara, Rus.
131/B3 Tara, Zam.
129/H4 Taraba (riv.), Nga.
91/D2 Ţarābulus (Tripoli), Leb.
124/H1 Ţarābulus (Tripoli) (cap.), Libya
60/D2 Tara, Hill of, Ire.
56/B4 Tara, Hill of (hill), Ire.
111/E3 Tarakan, Indo.
100/E2 Taraku (isl.), Rus.
74/D2 Tarancón, Sp.
130/C3 Tarangire Nat'l Park, Tanz.
80/E2 Taranto, It.
80/E3 Taranto (gulf), It.
144/B2 Tarapoto, Peru
72/F4 Tarare, Fr.
72/F5 Tarascon, Fr.
144/D3 Tarauacá, Braz.
144/D2 Tarauacá (riv.), Braz.
121/M7 Taravai (isl.), FrPol.
120/G4 Tarawa (atoll), Kiri.
74/E2 Tarazona, Sp.
74/E3 Tarazona de la Mancha, Sp.
102/D2 Tarbagatay (mts.), Kaz.
130/D2 Tarbaj, Kenya
54/C1 Tarbat Head (pt.), Sc,UK
55/K8 Tarbat Ness (pt.), Sc,UK
95/K2 Tarbela (res.), Pak.
54/A5 Tarbert, Sc,UK
72/D5 Tarbes, Fr.
54/B6 Tarbolton, Sc,UK
163/J3 Tarboro, NC,US
82/A2 Tarcento, It.
72/E3 Tardes (riv.), Fr.
72/D4 Tardoire (riv.), Fr.
97/M2 Tardoki-Jani (peak), Rus.
119/E1 Taree, Austl.
123/V18 Tarf (lake), Alg.
127/C2 Ţarfā', Wādī al (dry riv.), Egypt
127/B4 Tarfāwī, Bi'r (well), Egypt
56/D2 Tarf Water (riv.), Sc,UK
167/E2 Target Rock Nat'l Wild. Ref., NY,US
124/H1 Tarhūnah, Libya
144/B1 Tarifa, Ecu.
74/C4 Tarifa, Sp.
136/F8 Tarija, Bol.
111/J4 Tariku (riv.), Indo.
111/J4 Tariku-taritatu (plain), Indo.
96/B4 Tarim (basin), China
102/D3 Tarim (riv.), China
130/B3 Tarime, Tanz.
95/J2 Tarin (riv.), Afg.
111/J4 Taritatu (riv.), Indo.
86/E3 Tarkhankut, Mys (cape), Ukr.
129/E5 Tarkwa, Gha.
112/C2 Tarlac, Phil.
54/D2 Tarland, Sc,UK
144/C3 Tarma, Peru
72/D5 Tarn (riv.), Fr.
96/E2 Tarna (riv.), Mong.
95/J2 Tarnak (riv.), Afg.
63/T9 Tårnby, Den.
65/L3 Tarnobrzeg, Pol.
65/L3 Tarnobrzeg (prov.), Pol.
65/L3 Tarnów, Pol.
65/L3 Tarnów (prov.), Pol.
108/C2 Tarn Tāran, India
102/D5 Taro (lake), China
78/D3 Taro (riv.), It.
100/B4 Tarō, Japan
105/J3 Taroko Nat'l Park, Tai.
124/D1 Taroudannt, Mor.
163/H4 Tarpon Springs, Fl,US
57/F5 Tarporley, Eng,UK
80/B1 Tarquinia, It.
75/F2 Tarragona, Sp.
75/F2 Tàrrega, Sp.
130/D2 Tarri, Som.
167/E1 Tarrytown, NY,US
91/D1 Tarsus, Turk.
91/D1 Tarsus (riv.), Turk.
135/D1 Tartagal, Arg.
79/E2 Tartaro (riv.), It.
63/M2 Tartu, Est.
91/D2 Ţarţūs, Syria
91/D2 Ţarţūs (dist.), Syria
99/M9 Tarui, Japan
98/B5 Tarumizu, Japan
109/B5 Tarutao Nat'l Park, Thai.
96/D2 Tarvagatay (mts.), Mong.
57/F5 Tarvin, Eng,UK
164/E7 Tarzana, Ca,US
109/D3 Ta Seng, Camb.
102/E2 Tashanta, Rus.
88/F5 Tashauz, Trkm.
87/L4 Tashauz Obl., Trkm.
93/H4 Ţashk (riv.), Iran
102/A3 Tashkent (cap.), Uzb.
102/B3 Tash-Kumyr, Kyr.
110/C5 Tasikmalaya, Indo.
91/C1 Taşkent, Turk.
92/C1 Taşköprü, Turk.
119/C4 Tasman (pen.), Austl.
115/R11 Tasman (bay), NZ
51/S7 Tasman (sea)
119/C4 Tasman Head (cape), Austl.
119/C4 Tasmania (state), Austl.
82/F3 Tăşnad, Rom.
92/D1 Taşova, Turk.
147/K6 Tasquillo, Mex.
63/T9 Tåstrup, Den.
82/D2 Tata, Hun.
124/D2 Tata, Mor.
130/A2 Tata, Zaire
82/D2 Tatabánya, Hun.
160/D2 Tatachikapika (riv.), On,Can
121/M6 Tatakoto (isl.), FrPol.
96/D4 Tatalin (riv.), China
97/N2 Tatar (str.), Rus.
85/L5 Tatar Aut. Rep., Rus.
88/H4 Tatarsk, Rus.
124/H1 Tatāwīn, Tun.
99/F3 Tateyama, Japan
99/E2 Tate-yama (mtn.), Japan
152/E2 Tathlina (lake), NW,Can
128/B2 Tatilt (well), Mrta.
152/G3 Tatnam (cape), Mb,Can
129/H3 Tatokou, Niger
65/K4 Tatranský Nat'l Park, Slvk.
65/K4 Tatrzański Nat'l Park, Pol.
53/P8 Tatsfield, Eng,UK
99/E3 Tatsuno, Japan
57/H5 Tattershall, Eng,UK
92/E2 Tatvan, Turk.
140/B2 Tauá, Braz.
141/H8 Taubaté, Braz.
70/C3 Tauber (riv.), Ger.
70/C3 Tauberbischofsheim, Ger.
73/K3 Tauern, Hohe (mts.), Aus.
71/F6 Taufkirchen, Ger.
70/C1 Taufstein (peak), Ger.
159/K3 Taum Sauk (peak), Mo,US
104/B4 Taungdwingyi, Burma
104/C4 Taunggyi, Burma
104/B3 Taungthonlon (peak), Burma
104/B5 Taungup (pass), Burma
108/A2 Taunsa, Pak.
161/S8 Taunton, On,Can
58/C4 Taunton, Eng,UK
168/C2 Taunton, Ma,US
168/C2 Taunton (riv.), Ma,US
70/B2 Taunus (range), Ger.
70/B2 Taunusstein, Ger.
115/S10 Taupo, NZ
115/S10 Taupo (lake), NZ
63/K4 Tauragė, Lith.
115/S10 Tauranga, NZ
72/D3 Taurion (riv.), Fr.
91/B1 Taurus (mts.), Turk.
74/E2 Tauste, Sp.
72/C2 Taute (riv.), Fr.
121/X15 Tautira, FrPol.
120/E5 Tauu (isls.), PNG
158/E3 Tavaputs (plat.), Ut,US
163/H4 Tavares, Fl,US
92/B2 Tavas, Turk.
85/Q4 Tavda (riv.), Rus.
59/H1 Taverham, Eng,UK
53/S9 Taverny, Fr.
130/C3 Taveta, Kenya
121/Z17 Taveuni (isl.), Fiji
74/B4 Tavira, Port.
58/B5 Tavistock, Eng,UK
109/B3 Tavoy, Burma
109/B3 Tavoy (pt.), Burma
97/L3 Tavrichanka, Rus.
92/B2 Tavşanlı, Turk.
58/B5 Tavy (riv.), Eng,UK
58/B4 Taw (riv.), Eng,UK
99/L10 Tawaramoto, Japan
160/D2 Tawas City, Mi,US
111/E3 Tawau, Malay.
58/C3 Tawe (riv.), Wal,UK
108/C1 Tāwi (riv.), India
130/C5 Tawi, Tanz.
112/B4 Tawi-tawi (isl.), Phil.
127/D5 Ţawkar, Sudan
124/G1 Tawzar, Tun.
147/F5 Taxco, Mex.
147/K8 Taxco de Alarcón, Mex.
108/B1 Taxila, Pak.
108/B1 Taxila (ruins), Pak.
102/C4 Taxkorgan Tajik Zizhixian (Taxkorgan), China
102/C4 Taxkorgan (Taxkorgan Tajik Zizhixian), China
54/C4 Tay (firth), Sc,UK
54/C4 Tay (riv.), Sc,UK
148/D2 Tayasal, Guat.
54/B3 Tay, Loch (lake), Sc,UK
159/H2 Taylor, Ne,US
160/B4 Taylorville, Il,US
89/L2 Taymyr (isl.), Rus.
88/K2 Taymyr (pen.), Rus.
88/K2 Taymyr (riv.), Rus.
88/J2 Taymyr Aut. Okr., Rus.
109/D4 Tay Ninh, Viet.
54/D4 Tayport, Sc,UK
138/C2 Tayrona Nat'l Park, Col.
88/K4 Tayshet, Rus.
54/C3 Tayside (reg.), Sc,UK
112/B3 Taytay, Phil.
112/C3 Taz (riv.), Rus.
123/M13 Taza, Mor.
100/B4 Tazawako, Japan
123/M13 Tazekka (peak), Mor.
163/H2 Tazewell, Tn,US
160/D4 Tazewell, Va,US
125/K2 Tāzirbū (oasis), Libya
148/D3 Tazumal (ruins), ESal.
87/H4 Tbilisi (cap.), Geo.
126/B1 Tchibanga, Gabon
124/H6 Tcholliré, Camr.
65/K1 Tczew, Pol.
139/E5 Tea (riv.), Braz.
57/H5 Tealby, Eng,UK
115/Q12 Te Anau, NZ
115/Q12 Te Anau (lake), NZ
167/D2 Teaneck, NJ,US
57/G5 Teapa, Mex.
115/S10 Te Araroa, NZ
115/S10 Te Aroha, NZ
115/S10 Te Awamutu, NZ
110/B4 Tebak (peak), Indo.
123/W18 Tébessa, Alg.
123/V18 Tébessa (gov.), Alg.
123/W18 Tebessa (mts.), Alg., Tun.
129/F2 Tebesselamane (well), Mali
135/E2 Tebicuary (riv.), Par.
110/A3 Tebingtinggi, Indo.
87/H4 Tebulos-mta (peak), Rus.
146/E5 Tecalitlán, Mex.
147/M8 Tecamachalco, Mex.
75/G1 Tech (riv.), Fr.
83/J3 Techirghiol, Rom.
142/C4 Tecka (riv.), Arg.
63/U9 Teckomatorp, Swe.
147/F4 Tecolutla, Mex.
148/B1 Tecolutla (riv.), Mex.
146/E5 Tecomán, Mex.
147/K6 Tecozautla, Mex.
146/D4 Tecuala, Mex.
83/H3 Tecuci, Rom.
165/G7 Tecumseh, On,Can
160/D3 Tecumseh, Mi,US
159/H2 Tecumseh, Ne,US
95/H1 Tedzhen, Trkm.
88/G6 Tedzhen (riv.), Trkm.
57/G2 Tees (bay), Eng,UK
57/G2 Tees (riv.), Eng,UK
136/F4 Tefé, Braz.
136/E4 Tefé (riv.), Braz.
110/C5 Tegal, Indo.
66/D6 Tegelen, Neth.
124/H2 Tegheri (well), Libya
56/E6 Tegid, Llyn (lake), Wal,UK
129/H3 Tégouma (wadi), Niger
148/E3 Tegucigalpa (cap.), Hon.
152/G2 Tehek (lake), NW,Can
93/G3 Tehrān (cap.), Iran
93/G2 Tehrān (gov.), Iran
102/C5 Tehri, India
147/F5 Tehuacán, Mex.
148/C3 Tehuantepec (gulf), Mex.
147/G5 Tehuantepec (isth.), Mex.
148/C2 Tehuantepec (riv.), Mex.
147/M8 Tehuipango, Mex.
75/X16 Teide (peak), Canl.,Sp.
58/B2 Teifi (riv.), Wal,UK
58/B2 Teifiside (vall.), Wal,UK
125/L4 Teiga (plat.), Sudan
58/C5 Teignmouth, Eng,UK
71/F7 Teisendorf, Ger.
54/B4 Teith (riv.), Sc,UK
74/B3 Tejo (Tagus) (riv.), Port.
159/H2 Tekamah, Ne,US
115/R9 Te Kao, NZ
147/H4 Tekax, Mex.
102/C3 Tekeli, Kaz.
102/D3 Tekes (riv.), China
94/C6 Tekezē Wenz (reg.), Eth.
125/N5 Tekezē Wenz (riv.), Eth., Sudan
102/D4 Tekiliktag (peak), China
83/H5 Tekirdağ, Turk.
92/A1 Tekirdağ (prov.), Turk.
106/D4 Tekkali, India
92/D1 Tekkeköy, Turk.
115/S10 Te Kuiti, NZ
106/D3 Tel (riv.), India
148/E3 Tela, Hon.
123/Q16 Télagh, Alg.
87/H4 Telavi, Geo.
91/D3 Tel Aviv (dist.), Isr.
91/D3 Tel Aviv-Yafo, Isr.
128/E2 Télé (lake), Mali
102/G2 Telem (lake), Mong.
141/B3 Telemaco Borba, Braz.
62/C2 Telemark (co.), Nor.
111/E3 Telen (riv.), Indo.
83/G4 Teleorman (co.), Rom.
124/G3 Telertheba (peak), Alg.
137/G5 Teles Pires (riv.), Braz.
58/D1 Telford, Eng,UK
77/H3 Telfs, Aus.
67/E5 Telgte, Ger.
148/E3 Telica, Nic.
128/B4 Télimélé, Gui.
148/B2 Telixtlahuaca, Mex.
91/G8 Tel Jericho Nat'l Park, WBnk.
156/B2 Telkwa, BC,Can
123/Q16 Tell Atlas (mts.), Alg.
160/C4 Tell City, In,US
108/E3 Tellicherry, India
158/F3 Telluride, Co,US
91/G6 Tel Megiddo Nat'l Park, Isr.
96/D2 Telmen (lake), Mong.
110/B3 Telok Anson, Malay.
147/F5 Teloloapan, Mex.
102/E1 Telotskoye (lake), Rus.
63/K4 Telšiai, Lith.
65/G2 Teltow (reg.), Ger.
129/E5 Tema, Gha.
160/D2 Temagami (lake), On,Can
132/E2 Tembisa, SAfr.
126/C2 Tembo, Zaire
131/D2 Tembue, Moz.
58/D2 Teme (riv.), Eng,UK
164/C4 Temecula, Ca,US
82/D3 Temerin, Yugo.
110/B3 Temerloh, Malay.
102/B1 Temirtau, Kaz.
161/F1 Témiscamie (riv.), Qu,Can
160/E2 Témiscaming, Qu,Can
96/E1 Temnik (riv.), Rus.
121/M7 Temoe (isl.), FrPol.
158/E4 Tempe, Az,US
80/A2 Tempio Pausania, It.
162/D4 Temple, Tx,US
56/B2 Templepatrick, NI,UK
119/G5 Templestowe, Austl.
65/G2 Templin, Ger.
147/F4 Tempoal, Mex.
148/B1 Tempoal (riv.), Mex.
148/B1 Tempoal de Sanchez, Mex.
126/C3 Tempué, Ang.
86/F3 Temryuk, Rus.
68/D1 Temse, Belg.
142/B3 Temuco, Chile
115/R11 Temuka, NZ
138/B5 Tena, Ecu.
167/K8 Tenafly, NJ,US
124/D5 Tena Kourou (peak), Burk.
106/D4 Tenāli, India
147/F3 Tenamaxtle, Mex.
147/F5 Tenancingo, Mex.
147/K7 Tenango, Mex.
148/B2 Tenango, Mex.
147/F5 Tenango de Río Blanco, Mex.
109/B3 Tenasserim (range), Burma
109/B4 Tenasserim (Thanintharyi) (div.), Burma
66/D2 Ten Boer, Neth.
58/D2 Tenbury, Eng,UK
58/B3 Tenby, Wal,UK
78/A4 Tenda, Colle di (pass), It.
125/P5 Tendaho, Eth.
99/G1 Tendō, Japan
76/C4 Tendre (peak), Swi.
124/G3 Ténéré du Tafassasset (des.), Niger
129/H2 Ténéré, 'Erg du (des.), Niger
75/X16 Tenerife (isl.), Canl
123/R15 Ténès, Alg.
75/L6 Tenes (riv.), Sp.
104/C4 Teng (riv.), Burma
104/C3 Tengchong, China
111/E4 Tenggarong, Indo.
96/E4 Tengger (des.), China
102/A1 Tengiz (lake), Kaz.
138/B5 Tenguel, Ecu.
103/D4 Teng Xian, China
73/G4 Tenibres (peak), It.
135/D1 Teniente Enciso Nat'l Park, Par.
76/D1 Teningen, Ger.
82/D3 Tenja, Cro.
108/F4 Tenkāsi, India
129/E4 Tenkodogo, Burk.
158/D4 Tenmile (cr.), Az,US
163/F2 Tennessee (riv.), US
163/G3 Tennessee (state), US
142/C2 Teno, Chile
61/H1 Tenojoki (riv.), Fin.
147/H5 Tenosique, Mex.
99/L10 Tenri, Japan
99/E3 Tenryū, Japan
99/E3 Tenryū (riv.), Japan
59/G4 Tenterden, Eng,UK
109/B2 Ten Thousand Buddhas, Cave of, Burma
111/F3 Tentolomatinan (peak), Indo.
130/B2 Tenus (peak), Kenya
74/A1 Teo, Sp.
146/E4 Teocaltiche, Mex.
147/N7 Teocelo, Mex.
141/A2 Teodoro Sampaio, Braz.
141/D1 Teófilo Otoni, Braz.
130/A2 Te'Okutu, Ugan.
149/H4 Teorama, Col.
147/L7 Teotihuacán (ruins), Mex.
146/E5 Tepalcatepec, Mex.
147/L8 Tepalcingo, Mex.
146/E4 Tepatitlán, Mex.
147/M7 Tepatlaxco de Hidalgo, Mex.
147/F5 Tepeaca, Mex.
147/F5 Tepeapulco, Mex.
147/K7 Tepeji del Río, Mex.
71/F2 Tepelská Plošina (mts.), Czh.
147/M8 Tepexi de Rodríguez, Mex.
146/D4 Tepic, Mex.
71/F2 Teplá (riv.), Czh.
71/G5 Teplá Vltava (riv.), Czh.
65/G3 Teplice, Czh.
146/B2 Tepoca, Cabo (cape), Mex.
121/L6 Tepoto (isl.), FrPol.
147/Q9 Tepotzotlán, Mex.
147/K8 Tepoztlán, Mex.
146/E4 Tequila, Mex.
75/G1 Ter (riv.), Sp.
129/F3 Téra, Niger
74/B1 Tera (riv.), Sp.
66/B4 Ter Aar, Neth.
121/K4 Teraina (Washington) (atoll), Kiri.
80/C1 Teramo, It.
92/E2 Tercan, Turk.
75/S12 Terceira (isl.), Azor.,Port.
142/E2 Tercero (riv.), Arg.
83/K2 Terderovsk (bay), Ukr.
83/K2 Terderovsk (spit), Ukr.
87/H4 Terek (riv.), Rus.
138/D2 Terepaima Nat'l Park, Ven.
140/B2 Teresina, Braz.
141/L7 Teresópolis, Braz.

224

Tergn – Tongc

68/C4 Tergnier, Fr.
96/D4 Tergun Daba (mts.), China
66/B5 Terheijden, Neth.
84/G1 Teriberskiy, Mys (pt.), Rus.
66/C2 Terkaplesterpoelen (lake), Neth.
83/H5 Terkirdağ (prov.), Turk.
77/H4 Terlan (Terlango), It.
95/J1 Termez, Uzb.
80/C4 Termini Imerese, It.
147/H5 Términos (lag.), Mex.
158/B2 Termo, Ca,US
80/D1 Termoli, It.
58/D1 Tern (riv.), Eng,UK
111/G3 Ternate, Indo.
66/A6 Terneuzen, Neth.
80/C1 Terni, It.
72/F3 Ternin (riv.), Fr.
68/B3 Ternoise (riv.), Fr.
86/C2 Ternopol', Ukr.
86/C2 Ternopol' Obl., Ukr.
97/N2 Terpeniya (bay), Rus.
97/N2 Terpeniya (cape), Rus.
156/A2 Terrace, BC,Can
160/C1 Terrace Bay, On,Can
80/C2 Terracina, It.
161/Q8 Terra Cotta, On,Can
80/A3 Terralba, It.
140/B4 Terra Nova, Braz.
140/C3 Terra Nova, Braz.
161/L1 Terra Nova Nat'l Park, Nf,Can
75/G2 Terrassa, Sp.
72/D4 Terrasson-la-Villedieu, Fr.
161/N6 Terrebonne, Qu,Can
161/N6 Terrebonne (co.), Qu,Can
163/G2 Terre Haute, In,US
118/H8 Terrey Hills, Austl.
59/G1 Terrington Saint Clement, Eng,UK
77/F4 Terri, Piz (peak), Swi.
157/G4 Terry, Mt,US
102/A1 Tersakkan (riv.), Kaz.
66/C2 Terschelling (isl.), Neth.
75/E2 Teruel, Sp.
109/B5 Terutao (isl.), Thai.
83/H4 Tervel, Bul.
73/K3 Terza Grande (peak), It.
96/C1 Tes, Mong.
96/D2 Tes, Mong.
72/D5 Tescou (riv.), Fr.
151/G1 Teshekpuk (lake), Ak,US
100/D2 Teshikaga, Japan
100/B1 Teshio, Japan
100/C1 Teshio (riv.), Japan
100/C2 Teshio-dake (mtn.), Japan
96/D2 Tesiyn (riv.), Mong.
96/C1 Tes-Khem (riv.), Rus.
82/C3 Teslić, Bosn.
152/C3 Teslin (lake), BC,Can
151/M3 Teslin, Yk,Can
152/C2 Teslin (riv.), Yk,Can
129/G3 Tessaoua, Niger
69/E1 Tessenderlo, Belg.
59/E4 Test (riv.), Eng,UK
75/G1 Têt (riv.), Fr.
58/D3 Tetbury, Eng,UK
131/D3 Tete, Moz.
131/D2 Tete (prov.), Moz.
76/D1 Tête de Faux (peak), Fr.
73/G4 Tête de l'Estrop (peak), Fr.
76/C6 Tête du Torraz (peak), Fr.
147/L8 Tetela del Volcán, Mex.
147/M7 Tetela de Ocampo, Mex.
76/D5 Tête Ronde (peak), Swi.
62/E5 Teterow, Ger.
83/G4 Teteven, Bul.
57/H5 Tetford, Eng,UK
121/L6 Tetiaroa (isl.), FrPol.
69/F5 Teting-sur-Nied, Fr.
151/K3 Tetlin Nat'l Wild. Ref., Ak,US
156/F4 Teton (riv.), Mt,US
123/M13 Tétouan, Mor.
82/E4 Tetovo, Macd.
77/F2 Tettnang, Ger.
75/N9 Tetuan, Sp.
71/F4 Teublitz, Ger.
135/D1 Teuco (riv.), Arg.
80/A3 Teulada (cape), It.
157/J3 Teulon, Mb,Can
100/B1 Teuri (isl.), Japan
67/F4 Teutoburger Wald (for.), Ger.
79/F5 Tevere (Tiber) (riv.), It.
91/D3 Teverya (Tiberias), Isr.
54/D6 Teviot (riv.), Sc,UK
54/D6 Teviotdale (vall.), Sc,UK
118/D4 Tewantin-Noosa, Austl.
58/D3 Tewkesbury, Eng,UK
162/E3 Texarkana, Ar, Tx,US
162/C4 Texas (state), US
162/E4 Texas City, Tx,US
147/L7 Texcoco de Mora, Mex.
147/R9 Texcoco, Lago del (lake), Mex.
66/B2 Texel (isl.), Neth.
66/B3 Texelstroom (chan.), Neth.
159/G3 Texoma, Ok,US
84/J4 Teykovo, Rus.
147/F5 Teziutlán, Mex.
147/F5 Tezoatlán, Mex.
147/L7 Tezontepec, Mex.
104/B3 Tezpur, India
109/C1 Tha (riv.), Laos
152/G2 Tha-anne (riv.), NW,Can
132/E3 Thabana-Ntlenyana (peak), Les.
133/E2 Thabankulu (peak), SAfr.
132/D2 Thabazimbi, SAfr.
109/B3 Tha Chin (riv.), Thai.
109/B4 Thaen (pt.), Thai.
109/D1 Thai Binh, Viet.
109/C3 Thailand
109/C4 Thailand (gulf), Thai.
109/D1 Thai Nguyen, Viet.
108/A1 Thal, Pak.
108/A2 Thal (des.), Pak.
109/C5 Thaleban Nat'l Park, Thai.
77/E3 Thalwil, Swi.
94/E6 Thamar, Jabal (mtn.), Yem.
59/F3 Thame, Eng,UK
59/F3 Thame (riv.), Eng,UK
160/D3 Thames (riv.), On,Can
115/S10 Thames, NZ
53/P7 Thames (riv.), Eng,UK
53/P7 Thames Barrier, Eng,UK
106/B4 Thāna, India
59/H4 Thanet, Isle of (isl.), Eng,UK
107/J5 Thang Duc, Viet.
109/D2 Thanh Hoa, Viet.
107/J4 Thanh Lang Xa, Viet.
109/D4 Thanh Phu, Viet.
109/D4 Thanh Tri, Viet.
109/B4 Thanintharyi (Tenasserim) (div.), Burma
108/G3 Thanjavur, India
76/D2 Thann, Fr.
76/C1 Thaon-les-Vosges, Fr.
95/J3 Thar (des.), India, Pak.
106/B3 Tharād, India
104/B5 Tharrawaddy, Burma
81/J2 Thásos (isl.), Gre.
59/E4 Thatcham, Eng,UK
109/D1 That Khe, Viet.
104/C5 Thaton, Burma
104/B3 Thaungdut, Burma
107/H4 Tha Uthen, Thai.
59/G3 Thaxted, Eng,UK
65/H4 Thaya (riv.), Aus.
104/B5 Thayetmyo, Burma
104/C4 Thazi, Burma
59/E4 Theale, Eng,UK
127/C3 Thebes (ruins), Egypt
162/C3 The Caprock (cliffs), NM,US
60/D3 The Curragh, Ire.
156/C4 The Dalles, Or,US
119/B3 The Grampians (mts.), Austl.
117/F2 The Granites (peak), Austl.
66/B4 The Hague (s'-Gravenhage) (cap.), Neth.
119/C3 The Lakes Nat'l Park, Austl.
152/F2 Thelon (riv.), NW,Can
56/B2 The Loup, NI,UK
108/F4 Theni-Allinagaram, India
117/F2 Theo (peak), Austl.
157/H3 Theodore, Sk,Can
158/E4 Theodore Roosevelt (lake), Az,US
157/G4 Theodore Roosevelt Nat'l Park, ND,US
157/H2 The Pas, Mb,Can
68/B5 Thérain (riv.), Fr.
131/C3 The Range, Zim.
81/H3 Thermaic (Salonika) (gulf), Gre.
81/H3 Thermopílai (Thermopylae) (pass), Gre.
156/F5 Thermopolis, Wy,US
81/H3 Thermopylae (Thermopílai) (pass), Gre.
53/U9 Thérouanne (riv.), Fr.
160/D2 Thessalon, On,Can
81/H2 Thessaloníki (Salonika), Gre.
81/H3 Thessaly (reg.), Gre.
55/H8 The Storrs, Sc,UK
59/G2 Thet (riv.), Eng,UK
59/G2 Thetford, Eng,UK
161/G2 Thetford Mines, Qu,Can
69/E2 Theux, Belg.
53/T9 Thève (riv.), Fr.
59/G1 The Wash (bay), Eng,UK
59/G4 The Weald (reg.), Eng,UK
162/E4 The Woodlands, Tx,US
58/D1 The Wrekin (hill), Eng,UK
53/P7 Theydon Bois, Eng,UK
53/T10 Thiais, Fr.
81/G3 Thiamis (riv.), Gre.
163/F4 Thibodaux, La,US
157/J3 Thief River Falls, Mn,US
76/C4 Thielle (riv.), Swi.
156/C5 Thielsen (peak), Or,US
79/E1 Thiene, It.
109/D4 Thien Ngon, Viet.
72/E4 Thiers, Fr.
53/T9 Thiers-sur-Thève, Fr.
128/A3 Thiès, Sen.
128/A3 Thiès (reg.), Sen.
104/E4 Thiet Tra, Viet.
130/C3 Thika, Kenya
106/E2 Thimphu (cap.), Bhu.
61/N7 Thingvellir Nat'l Park, Ice.
69/F5 Thionville, Fr.
81/J4 Thíra (isl.), Gre.
127/B5 Third Cataract (falls), Sudan
57/E2 Thirlmere (lake), Eng,UK
57/G3 Thirsk, Eng,UK
116/D5 Thirsty (peak), Austl.
62/C3 Thisted, Den.
61/P6 Thistilfjördhur (bay), Ice.
117/G5 Thistle (isl.), Austl.
151/L3 Thistle (mtn.), Yk,Can
121/Z18 Thithia (isl.), Fiji
81/H3 Thívai, Gre.
61/N7 Thjórsa (riv.), Ice.
152/G2 Thlewiaza (riv.), NW,Can
131/C4 Thohoyandou, SAfr.
109/D4 Thoi Binh, Viet.
76/A5 Thoissey, Fr.
66/B5 Tholen, Neth.
66/B5 Tholen (isl.), Neth.
69/G5 Tholey, Ger.
166/B6 Thomas (pt.), Md,US
168/A2 Thomaston, Ct,US
163/G3 Thomaston, Ga,US
163/G4 Thomasville, Al,US
163/H4 Thomasville, Ga,US
163/H3 Thomasville, NC,US
115/G4 Thompson (riv.), Austl.
156/C3 Thompson (riv.), BC,Can
157/J2 Thompson, Mb,Can
168/C2 Thompson, Ct,US
159/J2 Thompson (riv.), Ia, Mo,US
156/E4 Thompson Falls, Mt,US
156/D3 Thompson, North (riv.), BC,Can
165/B3 Thompson Place-Tanglewilde, Wa,US
152/E1 Thomsen (riv.), NW,Can
118/A4 Thomson (riv.), Austl.
163/H3 Thomson, Ga,US
109/C3 Thon Buri, Thai.
107/J4 Thon Cam Lo, Viet.
109/B2 Thongwa, Burma
109/E4 Thon Lac Nghiep, Viet.
76/C5 Thonon-les-Bains, Fr.
109/E4 Thon Song Pha, Viet.
158/E4 Thoreau, NM,US
162/E2 Thorhild, Ab,Can
53/U10 Thorigny-sur-Marne, Fr.
165/Q16 Thorn (cr.), Il,US
57/G2 Thornaby-on-Tees, Eng,UK
58/D3 Thornbury, Eng,UK
57/H4 Thorne, Eng,UK
161/R8 Thornhill, On,Can
54/B4 Thornhill, Sc,UK
56/E1 Thornhill, Sc,UK
57/G2 Thornley, Eng,UK
57/G3 Thornthwaite, Eng,UK
57/E4 Thornton Cleveleys, Eng,UK
57/H3 Thornton Dale, Eng,UK
161/R9 Thorold, On,Can
161/R9 Thorold South, On,Can
53/M7 Thorpe, Eng,UK
59/H3 Thorpe le Soken, Eng,UK
57/G2 Thorpe Thewles, Eng,UK
72/C3 Thouars, Fr.
72/C3 Thouet (riv.), Fr.
164/B2 Thousand Oaks, Ca,US
130/C3 Thowa (riv.), Kenya
86/C4 Thracian (sea), Gre., Turk.
165/E6 Thread (cr.), Mi,US
156/F4 Three Forks, Mt,US
151/L4 Three Guardsmen (mtn.), BC,Can
156/E3 Three Hills, Ab,Can
119/C4 Three Hummock (isl.), Austl.
115/R9 Three Kings (isls.), NZ
166/B3 Three Mile (isl.), Pa,US
109/B3 Three Pagodas (pass), Burma
129/E5 Three Points (cape), Gha.
160/C3 Three Rivers, Mi,US
162/D3 Throckmorton, Tx,US
116/E3 Throssell (lake), Austl.
58/B5 Thrushel (riv.), Eng,UK
58/D2 Thruxton, Eng,UK
109/D4 Thu Dau Mot, Viet.
109/D4 Thu Duc, Viet.
68/D3 Thuin, Belg.
72/E5 Thuir, Fr.
70/C2 Thulba (riv.), Ger.
153/T7 Thule Air Base, Grld.
112/B3 Thumb (peak), Phil.
76/D4 Thun, Swi.
160/B1 Thunder Bay, On,Can
76/D4 Thunersee (lake), Swi.
109/C2 Thung Salaeng Luang Nat'l Park, Thai.
77/E2 Thur (riv.), Swi.
77/F2 Thurgau (canton), Swi.
71/E1 Thüringer Schiefergebirge (mts.), Ger.
70/D1 Thüringer Wald (for.), Ger.
64/F3 Thuringia (state), Ger.
59/E2 Thurlaston, Eng,UK
60/C4 Thurles, Ire.
55/K7 Thurso, Sc,UK
113/T Thurston (isl.), Ant.
165/A3 Thurston (co.), Wa,US
113/S Thwaites Iceberg Tongue, Ant.
131/D3 Thyolo, Malw.
136/E7 Tiahuanco (ruins), Bol.
151/M5 Tian (pt.), BC,Can
103/D4 Tianchang, China
105/E4 Tiandeng, China
107/J3 Tian'e, China
140/B1 Tianguá, Braz.
103/D3 Tianjin, China
103/D3 Tianjin (prov.), China
107/J3 Tianlin, China
103/C5 Tianmen, China
103/K9 Tianmu (mts.), China
88/H5 Tian Shan (range), Asia
96/F5 Tianshui, China
103/C5 Tiantangzhai (mtn.), China
107/J3 Tianyang, China
103/C2 Tianzhen, China
105/F3 Tianzhu, China
123/R16 Tiaret, Alg.
123/R16 Tiaret (wilaya), Alg.
121/S9 Tiavea, WSam.
141/B3 Tibagi, Braz.
141/B2 Tibaji (riv.), Braz.
124/H6 Tibati, Camr.
57/F6 Tibberton, Eng,UK
63/R7 Tibble, Swe.
128/C4 Tibé, Pic de (peak), Gui.
80/C1 Tiber (riv.), It.
91/D3 Tiberias (Sea of Galilee) (lake), Isr., Syria
91/D3 Tiberias (Teverya), Isr.
79/F5 Tiber (Tevere) (riv.), It.
124/J3 Tibesti (mts.), Chad, Libya
90/H6 Tibet (reg.), China
104/B2 Tibet (Xizang) Aut. Reg., China
75/L7 Tibidabo (peak), Sp.
124/H1 Ṭīb, Ra's aṭ (Cape Bon) (cape), Tun.
62/F2 Tibro, Swe.
57/G5 Tibshelf, Eng,UK
138/B3 Tibugá, Ensenada de (gulf), Col.
149/H2 Tiburon (cape), Haiti
146/B2 Tiburón (isl.), Mex.
149/G4 Tiburón (cape), Pan.
165/K11 Tiburon, Ca,US
59/G4 Ticehurst, Eng,UK
165/P14 Tichigan (lake), Wi,US
128/C2 Tichīt, Dhar (hills), Mrta.
124/C3 Tichla, WSah.
78/C2 Ticino (riv.), It.
77/E5 Ticino (canton), Swi.
77/E5 Ticino (riv.), Swi.
57/G5 Tickhill, Eng,UK
160/F3 Ticonderoga, NY,US
147/H4 Ticul, Mex.
62/E2 Tidaholm, Swe.
57/G5 Tideswell, Eng,UK
124/F2 Tidikelt (plain), Alg.
128/C2 Tidjikdja, Mrta.
78/C3 Tidone (riv.), It.
111/G3 Tidore (isl.), Indo.
128/A2 Tidra (isl.), Mrta.
75/X16 Tiede Nat'l Park
66/C5 Tiel, Neth.
97/K2 Tieli, China
101/B1 Tieling, China
75/N9 Tielmes, Sp.
68/C1 Tielt, Belg.
69/D2 Tielt-Winge, Belg.
128/D4 Tiemba (riv.), IvC.
102/E3 Tiemen Guan (pass), China
69/D2 Tienen, Belg.
105/H3 Tieniu (pass), China
90/H5 Tien Shan (range), China
109/D1 Tien Yen, Viet.
109/D2 Tien Yen, Viet.
124/J3 Tieroko (peak), Chad
62/G1 Tierp, Swe.
158/F3 Tierra Amarilla, NM,US
147/F5 Tierra Blanca, Mex.
143/L8 Tierra del Fuego (isl.), Arg., Chile
143/L8 Tierra del Fuego, Antártida e Islas del Atlántico Sur (prov.), Arg.
143/K8 Tierra del Fuego Nat'l Park, Arg.
138/B4 Tierradentro (ruins), Col.
74/C2 Tiétar (riv.), Sp.
141/B2 Tietê (riv.), Braz.
124/C2 Tifariti, WSah.
160/D3 Tiffin, Oh,US
163/H4 Tifton, Ga,US
121/V12 Tiga (isl.), NCal.
139/G4 Tiger (falls), Guy., Sur.
54/A6 Tighvein (hill), Sc,UK
124/H6 Tignère, Camr.
143/S12 Tigre, Arg.
144/C1 Tigre (riv.), Peru
139/F2 Tigre (riv.), Ven.
93/F4 Tigris (riv.), Asia
124/J4 Tigui (well), Chad
129/G2 Tiguidit, Falaise de (escarp.), Niger
62/C3 Tihøje (peak), Den.
147/F4 Tihuatlán, Mex.
61/J3 Tiilikkajärven Nat'l Park, Fin.
128/B1 Tijirīt (reg.), Mrta.
141/K8 Tijuca Nat'l Park, Braz.
141/B3 Tijucas, Braz.
141/B1 Tijuco (riv.), Braz.
148/D2 Tikal (ruins), Guat.
148/D2 Tikal Nat'l Park, Guat.
106/C3 Tīkamgarh, India
151/G3 Tikchik (lakes), Ak,US
121/L6 Tikehau (atoll), FrPol.
86/G3 Tikhoretsk, Rus.
84/G4 Tikhvin, Rus.
93/E3 Tikrīt, Iraq
81/H2 Tikveš (lake), Macd.
66/C5 Tilburg, Neth.
53/Q7 Tilbury, Eng,UK
162/D4 Tilden, Tx,US
166/B6 Tilghman (isl.), Md,US
54/D5 Till (riv.), Eng,UK
57/H5 Till (riv.), Eng,UK
156/C4 Tillamook, Or,US
76/B3 Tille (riv.), Fr.
54/C4 Tillicoultry, Sc,UK
62/D3 Tilst, Den.
54/C3 Tilt (riv.), Sc,UK
142/Q9 Tiltil, Chile
92/B5 Ṭimā, Egypt
85/L2 Timan (ridge), Rus.
115/R11 Timaru, NZ
86/F3 Timashevsk, Rus.
140/D2 Timbaúba, Braz.
157/H4 Timber Lake, SD,US
140/B2 Timbiras, Braz.
141/B3 Timbó, Braz.
128/E2 Timbuktu (Tombouctou), Mali
111/H4 Timbuni (riv.), Indo.
81/G3 Timfristós (peak), Gre.
123/V18 Timgad (ruins), Alg.
124/F2 Timimoun, Alg.
128/A2 Timiris (cape), Mrta.
82/E3 Timiş (co.), Rom.
82/E3 Timiş (riv.), Rom.
82/E3 Timişoara, Rom.
129/G2 Ti-m-Mershoï (wadi), Niger
160/D1 Timmins, On,Can
160/B2 Timms (hill), Wi,US
140/B2 Timon, Braz.
166/B5 Timonium, Md,US
114/D2 Timor (sea), Austl.
111/F5 Timor (isl.), Indo.
141/D1 Timóteo, Braz.
89/N4 Timpton (riv.), Rus.
61/F3 Timrå, Swe.
163/G3 Tims Ford (lake), Tn,US
132/E3 Tina (riv.), SAfr.
112/D4 Tinaca (pt.), Phil.
138/D2 Tinaco, Ven.
106/C5 Tindivanam, India
124/D2 Tindouf, Alg.
74/B1 Tineo, Sp.
105/H3 Ting (riv.), China
118/F7 Tingalpa (cr.), Austl.
118/F7 Tingalpa (res.), Austl.
119/D3 Tingaringy Nat'l Park, Austl.
124/H2 Tinghert (upland), Libya
128/C4 Tingi (mts.), Gui., SLeo.
151/F2 Tingmerkpuk (mtn.), Ak,US
144/C3 Tingo María, Peru
142/C2 Tinguirrica (vol.), Chile
137/L6 Tinharé, Braz.
140/C4 Tinharé (isl.), Braz.
109/D2 Tinh Gia, Viet.
120/D3 Tinian (isl.), NMar.
166/C4 Tinicum Nat'l Env. Ctr., Pa,US
159/H4 Tinker A.F.B., Ok,US
128/C4 Tinkisso (riv.), Gui.
165/Q16 Tinley Park, Il,US
135/C2 Tinogasta, Arg.
81/J4 Tínos (isl.), Gre.
68/C5 Tinqueux, Fr.
124/G2 Tinrhert (plat.), Alg.
124/D1 Tinrhir, Mor.
104/B3 Tinsukia, India
58/B5 Tintagel, Eng,UK
58/B5 Tintagel Head (pt.), Eng,UK
58/D3 Tintern Abbey, Wal,UK
74/B4 Tinto (riv.), Sp.
54/C5 Tinto (mtn.), Sc,UK
167/D3 Tinton Falls (New Shrewsbury), NJ,US
57/G5 Tintwistle, Eng,UK
144/B3 Tinyahuarco, Peru
124/F4 Ti-n-Zaouâten, Alg.
157/H3 Tioga, ND,US
110/B3 Tioman (isl.), Malay.
123/S15 Tipaza, Alg.
123/R15 Tipaza (wilaya), Alg.
60/C4 Tipperary (co.), Ire.
59/G3 Tiptree, Eng,UK
106/C5 Tiptūr, India
121/L6 Tiputa, FrPol.
140/A1 Tiracambu (mts.), Braz.
127/C2 Tiran (str.), Egypt
92/C5 Tīrān (isl.), SAr.
81/F2 Tiranë (cap.), Alb.
127/C3 Tiran, Jazīrat (isl.), Egypt
77/G5 Tirano, It.
117/H4 Tirari (des.), Austl.
83/J2 Tiraspol', Mol.
92/A2 Tire, Turk.
86/F4 Tirebolu, Turk.
55/H8 Tiree (isl.), Sc,UK
129/F1 Tirest (well), Mali
83/G3 Tîrgovişte, Rom.
83/H3 Tîrgu Bujor, Rom.
83/F3 Tîrgu Cărbuneşti, Rom.
83/H2 Tîrgu Frumos, Rom.
83/F3 Tîrgu Jiu, Rom.
83/F2 Tîrgu Lăpuş, Rom.
83/G2 Tîrgu Mureş, Rom.
83/H2 Tîrgu Neamţ, Rom.
83/H2 Tîrgu Ocna, Rom.
83/H3 Tîrgu Secuiesc, Rom.
95/K1 Tirich Mīr (mtn.), Pak.
83/G2 Tîrnava Mare (riv.), Rom.
83/G2 Tîrnava Mică (riv.), Rom.
83/G2 Tîrnăveni, Rom.
81/H3 Tírnavos, Gre.
77/G3 Tirol (prov.), Aus.
141/C1 Tiros, Braz.
58/C1 Tir Rhiwiog (mtn.), Wa,UK
71/F3 Tirschenreuth, Ger.
80/A2 Tirso (riv.), It.
108/F3 Tiruchchendūr, India
108/G3 Tiruchchirāppalli, India
108/G4 Tiruchendūr, India
108/F4 Tirumangalam, India
108/F4 Tirunelveli, India
106/C5 Tirupati, India
108/G3 Tiruppattūr, India
108/F3 Tiruppūr, India
108/E3 Tirūr, India
108/G3 Tiruttaraippūndi, India
108/F4 Tiruvalla, India
106/C5 Tiruvannāmalai, India
86/B2 Tisa (riv.), Eur.
83/G1 Tisa (riv.), Ukr.
58/D4 Tisbury, Eng,UK
157/G2 Tisdale, Sk,Can
159/H4 Tishomingo, Ok,US
123/R16 Tissemsilt, Alg.
123/R16 Tissemsilt (wilaya), Alg.
63/T8 Tisvilde, Den.
82/E2 Tisza (riv.), Hun.
82/E2 Tiszaföldvár, Hun.
82/E2 Tiszafüred, Hun.
82/E2 Tiszakécske, Hun.
82/E1 Tiszalök, Hun.
82/E2 Tiszavasvári, Hun.
79/F5 Titano, Monte (peak), SMar.
112/C4 Titay, Phil.
82/E3 Titel, Yugo.
144/D4 Titicaca (lake), Bol., Peru
168/A3 Titicus (mtn.), Ct,US
76/E2 Titisee Neustadt, Ger.
106/D3 Titlagarh, India
77/E4 Titlis (peak), Swi.
82/D4 Titograd, Yugo.
82/D4 Titovo Užice, Yugo.
82/E5 Titov Veles, Macd.
82/E5 Titov vrh (peak), Macd.
117/G2 Ti-Tree Abor. Land, Austl.
53/P8 Titsey, Eng,UK
83/G3 Titu, Rom.
163/H4 Titusville, Fl,US
130/C3 Tiva (riv.), Kenya
128/A3 Tivaouane, Sen.
82/D4 Tivat, Yugo.
58/C5 Tiverton, Eng,UK
168/C2 Tiverton, RI,US
63/T9 Tivoli Gardens, Den.
144/B1 Tixán, Ecu.
147/L7 Tizayuca, Mex.
147/H4 Tizimín, Mex.
123/T15 Tizi Ouzou, Alg.
123/T15 Tizi Ouzou (wilaya), Alg.
95/L1 Tiznap (riv.), China
124/D2 Tiznit, Mor.
66/C3 Tjeukemeer (lake), Neth.
62/D3 Tjorn (isl.), Swe.
147/M7 Tlachichuca, Mex.
148/B2 Tlacolula, Mex.
147/P8 Tlacotalpan, Mex.
147/R10 Tláhuac, Mex.
146/E3 Tlahualilo de Zaragoza, Mex.
147/K6 Tlahuelilpa de Ocampo, Mex.
146/E4 Tlajomulco, Mex.
147/N8 Tlalixcoyan, Mex.
147/R10 Tlalmanalcó de Velásquez, Mex.
147/Q9 Tlalnepantla, Mex.
147/L7 Tlalnepantla de Galeana, Mex.
147/Q10 Tlaloc (mtn.), Mex.
147/Q10 Tlalpan, Mex.
147/K8 Tlaltizapan, Mex.
147/F5 Tlapa, Mex.
147/R10 Tlapacoya (ruins), Mex.
147/F5 Tlapacoyan, Mex.
146/E4 Tlaquepaque, Mex.
147/K8 Tlaquiltenango, Mex.
147/M7 Tlatlauquitepec, Mex.
147/E5 Tlatlaya, Mex.
147/F5 Tlaxcala, Mex.
147/F5 Tlaxcala (state), Mex.
147/L7 Tlaxcala de Xicohténcatl, Mex.
147/K6 Tlaxcoapan, Mex.
147/L7 Tlaxco de Morelos, Mex.
147/L8 Tlayacapan, Mex.
123/Q16 Tlemcen, Alg.
123/Q16 Tlemcen (wilaya), Alg.
131/B5 Tlokweng, Bots.
124/J2 Tmassah, Libya
149/F4 Toabré, Pan.
83/G2 Toaca (peak), Rom.
138/B4 Toachi (riv.), Ecu.
123/G6 Toamasina, Madg.
133/J7 Toamasina (prov.), Madg.
165/B2 Toandos (pen.), Wa,US
121/L6 Toau (atoll), FrPol.
156/B3 Toba (inlet), BC,Can
96/D5 Toba, China
110/A3 Toba (lake), Indo.
99/E3 Toba, Japan
150/F5 Tobago (isl.), Trin.
95/J2 Toba Kākar (range), Pak.
74/E3 Tobarra, Sp.
108/B2 Toba Tek Singh, Pak.
78/B3 Tobbio, Monte (peak), It.
56/B2 Tobermore, NI,UK
117/H2 Tobermorey, Austl.
55/H8 Tobermory, Sc,UK
100/B2 Tōbetsu, Japan
140/C3 Tobias Barreto, Braz.
112/C3 Tobias Fornier, Phil.
116/E2 Tobin (lake), Austl.
157/H2 Tobin (lake), Sk,Can
161/H2 Tobique (riv.), NB,Can
99/M9 Tobishima, Japan
85/Q4 Tobol (riv.), Kaz., Rus.
88/G4 Tobol'sk, Rus.
125/K1 Tobruk, Libya
166/C1 Tobyhanna (cr.), Pa,US
166/C1 Tobyhanna (lake), Pa,US
166/C1 Tobyhanna Saint Park, Pa,US
85/L2 Tobysh (riv.), Rus.
137/J5 Tocantinópolis, Braz.
140/A2 Tocantins (riv.), Braz.
140/A3 Tocantins (state), Braz.
163/H3 Toccoa, Ga,US
77/E5 Toce (riv.), It.
99/F2 Tochigi, Japan
99/F2 Tochigi (pref.), Japan
147/L8 Tochimilco, Mex.
99/F2 Tochio, Japan
74/C4 Tocina, Sp.
135/B1 Tocopilla, Chile
149/G4 Tocumen, Pan.
138/D2 Tocuyito, Ven.
138/D2 Tocuyo (riv.), Ven.
99/H7 Toda, Japan
106/C2 Toda Bhīm, India
59/F3 Toddington, Eng,UK
130/B1 Todenyang, Kenya
80/C1 Todi, It.
77/E4 Tödi (peak), Swi.
57/F4 Todmorden, Eng,UK
101/C5 Todohae Hasang Nat'l Park, SKor.
140/C4 Todos os Santos (bay), Braz.
167/J9 Todt Hill, NY,US
60/A7 Toe Head (pt.), Ire.
139/G3 Toekomstig (res.), Sur.
156/E2 Tofield, Ab,Can
61/E3 Töfsingdalens Nat'l Park, Swe.
121/H6 Tofua (isl.), Tonga
128/C2 Togba (well), Mrta.
77/F3 Toggenburg (val.), Swi.
151/G4 Togiak Nat'l Wild. Ref., Ak,US
101/D2 Togno (riv.), NKor.
129/F4 Togo
99/N9 Tōgō, Japan
103/B2 Togtoh, China
101/D5 Tōgyu-san Nat'l Park, SKor.
158/E4 Tohatchi, NM,US
166/C3 Tohickon (cr.), Pa,US
121/X15 Tohivea (peak), FrPol.
100/B3 Tōhoku (dist.), Japan
99/F2 Tōhoku (prov.), Japan
99/F3 Toi, Japan
99/M9 Tōin, Japan
158/C3 Toiyabe (range), Nv,US
98/C3 Tojō, Japan
99/L10 Tōjō, Japan
100/C2 Tokachi (riv.), Japan
99/E3 Tōkai, Japan
99/F2 Tōkamachi, Japan
127/D5 Tokar, Sudan
100/K6 Tokara (isls.), Japan
127/D5 Tokar Game Rsv., Sudan
92/D1 Tokat, Turk.
92/D1 Tokat (prov.), Turk.
101/C4 Tōkchōk (arch.), SKor.
50/A6 Tokelau (isls.), NZ
121/H5 Tokelau (terr.), NZ
99/N9 Toki, Japan
99/N9 Toki (riv.), Japan
99/H6 Tokigawa, Japan
99/M10 Tokoname, Japan
100/D1 Tokoro, Japan
100/C2 Tokoro (riv.), Japan
115/S10 Tokoroa, NZ
99/F3 Tokorozawa, Japan
96/B2 Toksun, China
102/B3 Toktogul (res.), Kyr.
100/K7 Tokuno (isl.), Japan
100/K7 Tokunoshima, Japan
98/D3 Tokushima, Japan
98/C4 Tokushima (pref.), Japan
98/B3 Tokuyama, Japan
131/C3 Tokwe (riv.), Zim.
99/H7 Tokyo (bay), Japan
99/F3 Tōkyō (cap.), Japan
99/F3 Tōkyō (pref.), Japan
99/H7 Tōkyō Disneyland, Japan
99/H7 Tōkyō (inset) (cap.), Japan
148/E4 Tola, Nic.
123/G7 Tōlañaro, Madg.
83/H4 Tolbukhin, Bul.
135/F1 Toledo, Braz.
112/C3 Toledo, Phil.
74/C3 Toledo, Sp.
74/C3 Toledo (mts.), Sp.
160/D3 Toledo, Oh,US
162/E4 Toledo Bend (dam), La,US
162/E4 Toledo Bend (res.), La, Tx,US
80/C1 Tolentino, It.
142/C3 Tolhuaca Nat'l Park, Chile
102/D2 Toli, China
133/G8 Toliara, Madg.
133/H8 Toliara (prov.), Madg.
138/C4 Tolima (dept.), Col.
138/C3 Tolima, Nevado del (peak), Col.
111/F3 Tolitoli, Indo.
60/D3 Tolka (riv.), Ire.
168/B2 Tolland, Ct,US
168/B2 Tolland (co.), Ct,US
168/A1 Tolland Saint For., Ma,US
82/A2 Tolmezzo, It.
82/D2 Tolna, Hun.
82/D2 Tolna (co.), Hun.
111/F4 Tolo (gulf), Indo.
55/P13 Tolob, Sc,UK
74/D1 Tolosa, Sp.
101/D5 Tolsan (isl.), SKor.
165/D2 Tolt (res.), Wa,US
165/D2 Tolt (riv.), Wa,US
142/B3 Toltén, Chile
142/B3 Toltén (riv.), Chile
165/D2 Tolt, North Fork (riv.), Wa,US
165/D2 Tolt, South Fork (riv.), Wa,US
138/C2 Tolú, Col.
147/K7 Toluca, Mex.
148/B2 Toluca, Mex.
147/Q10 Toluca de Laredo, Mex.
148/B2 Toluca, Nevado de (peak), Mex.
87/J1 Tol'yatti, Rus.
88/J4 Tom' (riv.), Rus.
160/B3 Tomah, Wi,US
100/B2 Tomakomai, Japan
100/B1 Tomamae, Japan
120/G6 Tomanivi (peak), Fiji
74/A3 Tomar, Port.
81/G3 Tómaros (peak), Gre.
92/C2 Tomarza, Turk.
65/M3 Tomaszów Lubelski, Pol.
65/L3 Tomaszów Mazowiecki, Pol.
54/C2 Tomatin, Sc,UK
136/G6 Tombador (mts.), Braz.
125/M6 Tombe, Sudan
163/F4 Tombigbee (riv.), Al, Ms,US
126/B2 Tomboco, Ang.
103/B4 Tomb of Qinshihuang, China
124/E4 Tombouctou, Mali
128/E2 Tombouctou (Timbuktu), Mali
158/E5 Tombstone, Az,US
126/B4 Tombua, Ang.
142/B3 Tomé, Chile
72/B2 Tomé (isl.), Fr.
62/E4 Tomelilla, Swe.
74/D3 Tomelloso, Sp.
111/F4 Tomini (gulf), Indo.
74/A2 Tomiño, Sp.
54/C2 Tomintoul, Sc,UK
99/H7 Tomiura, Japan
99/F3 Tomiyama, Japan
89/N4 Tommot, Rus.
138/D3 Tomo (riv.), Col.
160/C4 Tompkinsville, Ky,US
167/D3 Toms (riv.), NJ,US
88/J4 Tomsk, Rus.
167/D4 Toms River, NJ,US
91/D1 Tömük, Turk.
151/K3 Tom White (mtn.), Ak,US
148/C2 Tonalá, Mex.
77/G5 Tonale, Passo del (pass), It.
156/D3 Tonasket, Wa,US
161/S9 Tonawanda, NY,US
161/S9 Tonawanda (cr.), NY,US
161/S9 Tonawanda Ind. Res., NY,US
53/P8 Tonbridge, Eng,UK
139/G3 Tonckens (falls), Sur.
99/L10 Tondabayashi, Japan
111/F3 Tondano, Indo.
62/C4 Tønder, Den.
108/G4 Tondi, India
125/K6 Tondou (mts.), CAfr.
99/J7 Tone, Japan
99/G3 Tone (riv.), Japan
58/C4 Tone (riv.), Eng,UK
93/G2 Tonekābon, Iran
60/D3 Tonelagee (mtn.), Ire.
96/F5 Tong (riv.), China
121/H7 Tonga
105/H3 Tong'an, China
121/K5 Tongareva (Penrhyn) (atoll), CookIs.
121/H7 Tonga-tapu (isl.), Tonga
103/C4 Tongbai, China
101/G6 Tongbu, SKor.
105/G2 Tongcheng, China

225

Tongc – Twen

105/H2 **Tongcheng**, China
96/F4 **Tongchuan**, China
101/G6 **Tongdaemun**, SKor.
105/F3 **Tongdao Dongzu Zizhixian**, China
101/D4 **Tongduch'ŏn**, SKor.
69/E2 **Tongeren**, Belg.
107/K2 **Tonggu**, China
105/H3 **Tonggu Zhang** (peak), China
101/C2 **Tonghua**, China
101/D3 **Tongjosŏn** (East Korea) (bay), NKor.
103/E2 **Tongliao**, China
103/D5 **Tongling**, China
104/E2 **Tongnan**, China
111/E5 **Tongo** (peak), Indo.
105/F3 **Tongren**, China
106/F2 **Tongsa** (riv.), Bhu.
103/C5 **Tongshan**, China
96/D5 **Tongtian** (riv.), China
55/J7 **Tongue**, Sc,UK
156/G4 **Tongue** (riv.), Mt, Wy,US
150/B1 **Tongue of the Ocean** (chan.), Bahm.
103/C4 **Tongxu**, China
103/E1 **Tongyu**, China
100/C1 **Tonino-Anivskiy** (pen.), Rus.
66/D6 **Tönisvorst**, Ger.
125/L6 **Tonj**, Sudan
106/C2 **Tonk**, India
159/H3 **Tonkawa**, Ok,US
109/D1 **Tonkin** (gulf), China, Viet.
128/D5 **Tonkoui** (peak), IvC.
109/C3 **Tonle Sap** (lake), Camb.
72/D4 **Tonneins**, Fr.
100/B4 **Tōno**, Japan
158/D4 **Tonopah**, Az,US
158/C3 **Tonopah**, Nv,US
98/D3 **Tonoshō**, Japan
131/B4 **Tonota**, Bots.
62/D2 **Tønsberg**, Nor.
158/E4 **Tonto Nat'l Mon.**, Az,US
92/D1 **Tonya**, Turk.
158/D2 **Tooele**, Ut,US
119/G6 **Toomuc** (cr.), Austl.
118/C4 **Toowoomba**, Austl.
117/G2 **Top** (peak), Austl.
164/B2 **Topanga Saint Park**, Ca,US
159/J3 **Topeka** (cap.), Ks,US
93/M6 **Topkapi Palace**, Turk.
156/B2 **Topley**, BC,Can
83/G2 **Toplita**, Rom.
65/K4 **Topoľčany**, Slvk.
83/G3 **Topoloveni**, Rom.
83/H4 **Topolovgrad**, Bul.
84/F2 **Topozero** (lake), Rus.
156/C4 **Toppenish**, Wa,US
58/C5 **Topsham**, Eng,UK
125/M6 **Tor**, Eth.
58/C6 **Tor** (bay), Eng,UK
130/A2 **Tora**, Zaire
99/M9 **Torahime**, Japan
144/D5 **Torata**, Peru
111/G3 **Torawitan** (cape), Indo.
92/A2 **Torbalı**, Turk.
93/J3 **Torbat-e Ḩeydarīyeh**, Iran
72/B1 **Torbay**, Eng,UK
151/H3 **Torbert** (mtn.), Ak,US
53/T10 **Torcy**, Fr.
64/E1 **Törder**, Den.
75/L6 **Tordera** (riv.), Sp.
74/C2 **Tordesillas**, Sp.
75/G1 **Torelló**, Sp.
65/G2 **Torgelow**, Ger.
62/F3 **Torhamnsudde** (pt.), Swe.
68/C1 **Torhout**, Belg.
99/J7 **Toride**, Japan
99/E3 **Torii-tōge** (pass), Japan
74/A1 **Toriñana** (cape), Sp.
78/A3 **Torino** (prov.), It.
78/A2 **Torino** (Turin), It.
120/D1 **Tori-Shima** (isl.), Japan
125/M7 **Torit**, Sudan
95/H1 **Torkestān** (mts.), Afg.
74/C2 **Tormes** (riv.), Sp.
116/C5 **Torndirrup Nat'l Park**, Austl.
57/H4 **Torne** (riv.), Eng,UK
61/G2 **Torneälven** (Torniojoki) (riv.), Swe.
67/G1 **Tornesch**, Ger.
82/D4 **Tornik** (peak), Yugo.
61/G2 **Torniojoki** (Torneälven) (riv.), Fin.
74/C2 **Toro**, Sp.
135/C2 **Toro, Cerro del** (peak), Arg.
82/E2 **Törökszentmiklós**, Hun.
81/H2 **Toronaic** (gulf), Gre.
130/A2 **Toro Nat'l Rsv.**, Ugan.
161/R8 **Toronto**, (cap.), On,Can
161/R8 **Toronto** (isl.), On,Can
168/G7 **Toronto**, Oh,US
63/P3 **Toropets**, Rus.
130/B2 **Tororo**, Ugan.
75/N8 **Torote** (riv.), Sp.
62/E3 **Torpa**, Swe.
54/D2 **Torphins**, Sc,UK
58/B6 **Torpoint**, Eng,UK
58/C6 **Torquay**, Eng,UK
164/B3 **Torrance**, Ca,US
74/D4 **Torre del Campo**, Sp.
78/D5 **Torre del Lago Puccini**, It.
74/D4 **Torredonjimeno**, Sp.
74/D2 **Torrejón de Ardoz**, Sp.
74/C1 **Torrelavega**, Sp.
75/N8 **Torrelodones**, Sp.
118/B3 **Torrens** (cr.), Austl.
117/M8 **Torrens** (isl.), Austl.
117/H4 **Torrens** (lake), Austl.
117/M8 **Torrens** (riv.), Austl.
75/E3 **Torrente**, Sp.
146/E3 **Torreón**, Mex.
75/E4 **Torre-Pacheco**, Sp.
74/D3 **Torreperogil**, Sp.
114/G2 **Torres** (str.), Austl.
141/B4 **Tôrres**, Braz.
120/F6 **Torres** (isls.), Van.
143/J7 **Torres del Paine Nat'l Park**, Chile
74/A3 **Torres Novas**, Port.
74/A3 **Torres Vedras**, Port.
75/E4 **Torrevieja**, Sp.
56/B1 **Torr Head** (pt.), NI,UK
58/B5 **Torridge** (riv.), Eng,UK
74/C3 **Torrijos**, Sp.
168/A2 **Torrington**, Ct,US
157/G5 **Torrington**, Wy,US
77/F5 **Torrone Alto** (peak), Swi.
74/D4 **Torrox**, Sp.
62/E1 **Torsby**, Swe.
52/C2 **Tórshavn**, Den.
72/B2 **Torteval**, Chl,UK
150/E3 **Tortola** (isl.), BVI
80/A3 **Tortoli**, It.
78/B3 **Tortona**, It.
75/F2 **Tortosa**, Sp.
75/F2 **Tortosa** (cape), Sp.
149/H1 **Tortue** (Tortuga) (isl.), Haiti
149/H1 **Tortuga** (Tortue) (isl.), Haiti
149/F4 **Tortuguero Nat'l Park**, CR
102/C3 **Torugart, Pereval** (pass), Kyr.
65/K2 **Toruń**, Pol.
65/K2 **Toruń** (prov.), Pol.
55/G9 **Tory** (isl.), Ire.
65/L4 **Torysa** (riv.), Slvk.
84/G4 **Torzhok**, Rus.
98/C4 **Tosa**, Japan
98/C4 **Tosa** (bay), Japan
138/A5 **Tosagua**, Ecu.
98/C4 **Tosashimizu**, Japan
126/B5 **Toscanini**, Namb.
73/J4 **Tosco-Emiliano** (range), It.
78/D1 **Toscolano-Maderno**, It.
100/A2 **Toshibet** (riv.), Japan
100/C2 **Toshibetsu** (riv.), Japan
63/P2 **Tosno**, Rus.
96/D4 **Toson** (lake), China
96/D2 **Tosontsengel**, Mong.
77/E3 **Töss** (riv.), Swi.
54/E6 **Tosson** (hill), Eng,UK
135/D2 **Tostado**, Arg.
67/G2 **Tostedt**, Ger.
98/B4 **Tōsu**, Japan
92/C1 **Tosya**, Turk.
74/E4 **Totana**, Sp.
131/A4 **Toteng**, Bots.
59/E5 **Totland**, Eng,UK
58/C6 **Totnes**, Eng,UK
147/E5 **Totolapan**, Mex.
142/E2 **Totoras**, Arg.
167/J8 **Totowa**, NJ,US
113/H **Totten** (glac.), Ant.
165/B3 **Totten** (inlet), Wa,US
53/N7 **Tottenham**, Eng,UK
167/H9 **Tottenville**, NY,US
57/F4 **Tottington**, Eng,UK
59/E5 **Totton**, Eng,UK
98/D3 **Tottori**, Japan
98/C3 **Tottori** (pref.), Japan
147/N7 **Totutla**, Mex.
124/D1 **Toubkal, Jebel** (peak), Mor.
157/G3 **Touchwood** (hills), Sk,Can
101/D1 **Toudao** (riv.), China
128/E3 **Tougan**, Burk.
124/G1 **Touggourt**, Alg.
123/S16 **Touiel** (riv.), Alg.
69/E6 **Toul**, Fr.
161/H1 **Toulnustouc** (riv.), Qu,Can
72/F5 **Toulon**, Fr.
72/D5 **Toulouse**, Fr.
124/H3 **Toumo** (well), Niger
128/D5 **Toumodi**, IvC.
104/C5 **Toungoo**, Burma
128/D5 **Toura** (mts.), IvC.
68/C2 **Tourcoing**, Fr.
72/C5 **Tourettes, Pic de** (peak), Fr.
74/A1 **Touriñan** (cape), Sp.
72/C2 **Tourlaville**, Fr.
68/C2 **Tournai**, Belg.
53/U10 **Tournan-en-Brie**, Fr.
76/A4 **Tournus**, Fr.
140/D2 **Touros**, Braz.
72/D3 **Tours**, Fr.
75/E3 **Tous** (res.), Sp.
72/B2 **Toussaines, Signal de** (peak), Fr.
124/J3 **Toussidé** (peak), Chad
125/K6 **Toussoro** (peak), CAfr.
132/C4 **Touws** (riv.), SAfr.
138/D2 **Tovar**, Ven.
59/E2 **Tove** (riv.), Eng,UK
96/E2 **Tövshrüüleh**, Mong.
99/G2 **Towada**, Japan
100/B3 **Towada** (lake), Japan
100/B3 **Towada-Hachimantai Nat'l Park**, Japan
59/F2 **Towcester**, Eng,UK
53/N7 **Tower Hamlets** (bor.), Eng,UK
53/N7 **Tower of London**, Eng,UK
57/G2 **Tow Law**, Eng,UK
157/H3 **Towner**, ND,US
156/F4 **Townsend**, Mt,US
165/A2 **Townsend** (mtn.), Wa,US
166/D5 **Townsends** (inlet), NJ,US
118/C3 **Townshend** (cape), Austl.
118/B2 **Townsville**, Austl.
95/H1 **Towraghondi**, Afg.
166/B5 **Towson**, Md,US
111/F4 **Towuti** (lake), Indo.
102/C3 **Toxkan** (riv.), China, Kyr.
100/B2 **Toya** (lake), Japan
162/C4 **Toyah**, Tx,US
162/C4 **Toyahvale**, Tx,US
99/E2 **Toyama**, Japan
99/E2 **Toyama** (bay), Japan
99/E2 **Toyama** (pref.), Japan
101/D5 **Toyang**, SKor.
99/N9 **Toyoake**, Japan
99/E3 **Toyohashi**, Japan
99/E3 **Toyokawa**, Japan
99/L10 **Toyonaka**, Japan
99/L10 **Toyono**, Japan
98/D3 **Toyo'oka**, Japan
99/M9 **Toyosato**, Japan
99/E2 **Toyoshina**, Japan
99/E3 **Toyota**, Japan
99/M9 **Toyoyama**, Japan
151/H2 **Tozi** (mtn.), Ak,US
109/E3 **Tra Bong**, Viet.
164/C3 **Trabuco, Arroyo** (cr.), Ca,US
92/D1 **Trabzon**, Turk.
92/D1 **Trabzon** (prov.), Turk.
161/H2 **Tracadie**, NB,Can
109/D4 **Tra Cu**, Viet.
161/F2 **Tracy**, QU,Can
165/M11 **Tracy**, Ca,US
78/B1 **Tradate**, It.
74/B4 **Trafalgar** (cape), Sp.
75/P10 **Trafaria**, Port.
142/B3 **Traiguén**, Chile
156/D3 **Trail**, BC,Can
73/L3 **Traisen** (riv.), Aus.
65/J4 **Traiskirchen**, Aus.
60/A5 **Tralee**, Ire.
63/S7 **Trälhavet** (bay), Swe.
109/D1 **Tra Linh**, Viet.
141/B4 **Tramandaí**, Braz.
109/E3 **Tra Mi**, Viet.
77/H5 **Tramin** (Termeno), It.
60/C5 **Tramore** (bay), Ire.
159/G3 **Tramperos** (cr.), NM, Tx,US
62/F2 **Tranås**, Swe.
62/D3 **Tranbjerg**, Den.
62/D4 **Tranebjerg**, Den.
54/D5 **Tranent**, Sc,UK
69/D4 **Tranet** (mtn.), Fr.
109/B5 **Trang**, Thai.
111/H5 **Trangan** (isl.), Indo.
62/E1 **Trängsletsjön** (lake), Swe.
80/E2 **Trani**, It.
108/G3 **Tranquebar**, India
113/W **Transantarctic** (mts.), Ant.
83/F1 **Trans-Carpathian Obl.**, Ukr.
132/E3 **Transkei** (ind. homeland), SAfr.
131/C5 **Transvaal** (prov.), SAfr.
82/F2 **Transylvania** (reg.), Rom.
82/F3 **Transylvanian Alps** (range), Rom.
109/D4 **Tra Ôn**, Viet.
80/C3 **Trapani**, It.
109/D3 **Trapeang Veng**, Camb.
156/E4 **Trapper** (peak), Mt,US
53/S10 **Trappes**, Fr.
119/C3 **Traralgon**, Austl.
128/B2 **Trarza** (reg.), Mrta.
80/C1 **Trasimeno** (lake), It.
74/B2 **Trás-os-Montes e Alto Douro** (dist.), Port.
109/C3 **Trat**, Thai.
71/H6 **Traun**, Aus.
71/G6 **Traun** (riv.), Aus.
71/F7 **Traun** (riv.), Ger.
71/F7 **Traunreut**, Ger.
71/G7 **Traunsee** (lake), Aus.
71/F7 **Traunstein**, Ger.
78/D1 **Travagliato**, It.
64/F2 **Trave** (riv.), Ger.
119/B2 **Travellers** (lake), Austl.
151/G2 **Traverse** (peak), Ak,US
157/J4 **Traverse** (lake), SD,US
160/C2 **Traverse City**, Mi,US
109/D4 **Tra Vinh**, Viet.
162/D4 **Travis** (lake), Tx,US
158/B3 **Travis A.F.B.**, Ca,US
82/C3 **Travnik**, Bosn.
58/C2 **Trawsalt** (mtn.), Wal,UK
56/E6 **Trawsfynydd**, Wal,UK
56/E6 **Trawsfynydd, Llyn** (lake), Wal,UK
82/B2 **Trbovlje**, Slov.
117/G2 **Treachery** (peak), Austl.
78/C3 **Trebbia** (riv.), It.
64/G1 **Trebel** (riv.), Ger.
65/H4 **Třebíč**, Czh.
82/D4 **Trebinje**, Bosn.
80/E3 **Trebisacce**, It.
71/H4 **Třeboň**, Czh.
74/B4 **Trebujena**, Sp.
70/B3 **Trebur**, Ger.
78/B2 **Trecate**, It.
58/C3 **Tredegar**, Wal,UK
58/C2 **Trefeglwys**, Wal,UK
56/E5 **Trefnant**, Wal,UK
58/C2 **Tregaron**, Wal,UK
79/G6 **Treia**, It.
54/B3 **Treig, Loch** (lake), Sc,UK
143/G2 **Treinta y Tres**, Uru.
143/G2 **Treinta y Tres** (dept.), Uru.
76/C6 **Tré-la-Tête** (mtn.), Fr.
131/C3 **Trelawney**, Zim.
72/C3 **Trélazé**, Fr.
58/B3 **Trelech**, Wal,UK
142/D4 **Trelew**, Arg.
72/D4 **Trélissac**, Fr.
62/E4 **Trelleborg**, Swe.
56/D6 **Tremadoc** (bay), Wal,UK
53/T10 **Tremblay-lès-Gonesse**, Fr.
60/C2 **Tremblestown** (riv.), Ire.
156/B2 **Trembleur** (lake), BC,Can
69/D2 **Tremelo**, Belg.
80/D1 **Tremiti** (isls.), It.
158/D2 **Tremonton**, Ut,US
71/G3 **Třemošná** (riv.), Czh.
71/G3 **Třemšín** (peak), Czh.
161/F1 **Trenche** (riv.), Qu,Can
65/K4 **Trenčín**, Slvk.
142/E2 **Trenque Lauquen**, Arg.
57/H5 **Trent** (riv.), Eng,UK
57/F6 **Trent and Mersey** (can.), Eng,UK
77/G5 **Trentino-Alto Adige** (reg.), It.
77/H5 **Trento**, It.
77/H5 **Trento** (prov.), It.
112/D3 **Trento**, Phil.
160/E2 **Trenton**, On,Can
163/H4 **Trenton**, Fl,US
163/G3 **Trenton**, Ga,US
165/F7 **Trenton**, Mi,US
159/J2 **Trenton**, Mo,US
166/D3 **Trenton** (cap.), NJ,US
163/F3 **Trenton**, Tn,US
58/C3 **Treorchy**, Wal,UK
81/F2 **Trepuzzi**, It.
77/E6 **Tresa** (riv.), It.
143/T11 **Tres Arboles**, Uru.
142/E3 **Tres Arroyos**, Arg.
141/H6 **Três Corações**, Braz.
78/D3 **Tresinaro** (riv.), It.
141/E6 **Três Irmãos** (res.), Braz.
135/D2 **Tres Isletas**, Arg.
141/B2 **Três Lagoas**, Braz.
141/C1 **Três Marias**, Braz.
141/C1 **Três Marias** (res.), Braz.
146/D4 **Tres Marías** (isls.), Mex.
142/B5 **Tres Montes** (cape), Chile
138/B3 **Tres Morros, Alto de** (peak), Col.
142/C4 **Tres Picos** (peak), Arg.
142/E3 **Tres Picos** (peak), Arg.
141/H6 **Três Pontas**, Braz.
142/D5 **Tres Puntas** (cape), Arg.
141/K7 **Três Rios**, Braz.
75/F1 **Tres Seigneurs, Pic de** (peak), Fr.
70/D5 **Treuchtlingen**, Ger.
71/F1 **Treuen**, Ger.
64/G2 **Treuenbrietzen**, Ger.
78/C1 **Treviglio**, It.
79/F1 **Treviso**, It.
79/F1 **Treviso** (prov.), It.
166/D3 **Trevose-Feasterville**, Pa,US
58/A5 **Trevose Head** (pt.), Eng,UK
78/C1 **Trezzo sull'Adda**, It.
166/A5 **Triadelphia** (res.), Md,US
131/C4 **Triangle**, Zim.
118/B2 **Tribulation** (cape), Austl.
77/H3 **Tribulaun** (peak), Aus.
81/F3 **Tricase**, It.
108/F3 **Trichūr**, India
111/J4 **Tricora** (peak), Indo.
72/E5 **Trie-Château**, Fr.
53/S10 **Triel-sur-Seine**, Fr.
69/F4 **Trier**, Ger.
79/G1 **Trieste**, It.
79/G1 **Trieste** (gulf), It.
79/G1 **Trieste** (prov.), It.
80/E2 **Triggiano**, It.
83/G4 **Triglav** (peak), Bul.
82/A2 **Triglav** (peak), Slov.
82/A2 **Triglav Nat'l Park**, Slov.
80/D2 **Trigno** (riv.), It.
74/B4 **Trigueros**, Sp.
81/G3 **Tríkala**, Gre.
81/G3 **Trikhonís** (lake), Gre.
76/D3 **Trimbach**, Swi.
57/G2 **Trimdon**, Eng,UK
108/H4 **Trincomalee**, SrL.
108/H4 **Trincomalee** (dist.), SrL.
137/J7 **Trindade**, Braz.
65/K4 **Třinec**, Czh.
59/F3 **Tring**, Eng,UK
142/E3 **Trinidad** (isl.), Arg.
136/F6 **Trinidad**, Bol.
143/J7 **Trinidad** (chan.), Chile
143/J7 **Trinidad** (gulf), Chile
150/F5 **Trinidad** (isl.), Trin.
143/F2 **Trinidad**, Uru.
159/F3 **Trinidad**, Co,US
150/F5 **Trinidad and Tobago**
137/N8 **Trinidade**, Braz.
161/L2 **Trinity** (bay), Nf,Can
151/H4 **Trinity** (isls.), Ak,US
158/B2 **Trinity** (riv.), Ca,US
158/C2 **Trinity** (range), Nv,US
162/E4 **Trinity** (riv.), Tx,US
127/D5 **Trinkitat**, Sudan
78/B2 **Trino**, It.
133/S15 **Triolet**, Mrts.
124/H1 **Tripoli** (cap.), Libya
81/H4 **Trípolis**, Gre.
124/H1 **Tripolitania** (reg.), Libya
91/D2 **Tripoli** (Ţarābulus), Leb.
108/F4 **Tripunittura**, India
107/F3 **Tripura** (state), India
77/G3 **Trisanna** (riv.), Aus.
50/J7 **Tristan da Cunha** (isls.), StH.
128/B4 **Tristao** (isls.), Guin.
142/D4 **Triste** (peak), Arg.
71/G5 **Třístoličník** (peak), Czh.
109/D4 **Tri Ton**, Viet.
67/H1 **Trittau**, Ger.
108/F4 **Trivandrum**, India
65/J4 **Trnava**, Slvk.
120/E5 **Trobriand** (isls.), PNG
68/A5 **Troesne** (riv.), Fr.
73/L3 **Trofaiach**, Aus.
80/D2 **Troia**, It.
75/Q11 **Tróia**, Port.
69/G2 **Troisdorf**, Ger.
69/G6 **Troisfontaines**, Fr.
123/N13 **Trois Fourches, Cap des** (cape), Mor.
161/G1 **Trois-Pistoles**, Qu,Can
161/F2 **Trois-Rivières**, Qu,Can
69/E3 **Troisvierges**, Lux.
85/P5 **Troitsk**, Rus.
62/E2 **Trollhättan**, Swe.
139/G5 **Trombetas** (riv.), Braz.
123/H6 **Tromelin** (isl.), Reu.
54/B3 **Tromie** (riv.), Sc,UK
61/F1 **Troms** (co.), Nor.
61/F1 **Tromsø**, Nor.
142/C4 **Tronador** (peak), Arg., Chile
61/D3 **Trondheim**, Nor.
61/D3 **Trondheimsfjorden** (fjord), Nor.
80/C1 **Tronto** (riv.), It.
91/C2 **Troodos** (mts.), Cyp.
56/D1 **Trool, Loch** (lake), Sc,UK
54/B5 **Troon**, Sc,UK
80/D3 **Tropea**, It.
158/D3 **Tropic**, Ut,US
70/B6 **Trossingen**, Ger.
56/B1 **Trostan** (mtn.), NI,UK
71/F6 **Trostberg an der Alz**, Ger.
53/Q8 **Trottiscliffe**, Eng,UK
149/H2 **Trou du Nord**, Haiti
54/D1 **Troup Head** (pt.), Sc,UK
152/D2 **Trout** (lake), NW,Can
157/K3 **Trout** (lake), On,Can
57/F3 **Troutbeck**, Eng,UK
156/E1 **Trout Lake**, BC,Can
58/D4 **Trowbridge**, Eng,UK
163/G4 **Troy**, Al,US
165/F6 **Troy**, Mi,US
160/F3 **Troy**, NY,US
163/G1 **Troy**, Oh,US
83/G4 **Troyan**, Bul.
83/G4 **Troyanski Prokhod** (pass), Bul.
72/F2 **Troyes**, Fr.
81/K3 **Troy** (Ilium) (ruins), Turk.
82/E4 **Trstenik**, Yugo.
151/M3 **Truitt** (peak), Yk,Can
144/B3 **Trujillo**, Peru
74/C3 **Trujillo**, Sp.
138/D2 **Trujillo**, Ven.
138/D2 **Trujillo** (state), Ven.
120/E4 **Truk** (isls.), Micr.
167/E1 **Trumbull**, Ct,US
168/G5 **Trumbull** (co.), Oh,US
76/D4 **Trümmelbachfälle** (falls), Swi.
58/D2 **Trumpet**, Eng,UK
109/D1 **Trung Khanh**, Viet.
161/J2 **Truro**, NS,Can
58/A6 **Truro**, Eng,UK
168/C3 **Trustom Pond Nat'l Wild. Ref.**, RI,US
158/F4 **Truth Or Consequences**, NM,US
65/H3 **Trutnov**, Czh.
72/E4 **Truyère** (riv.), Fr.
56/D6 **Trwyn Cilan** (pt.), Wal,UK
83/G4 **Tryavna**, Bul.
62/E1 **Trysil**, Nor.
62/D1 **Trysilelva** (riv.), Nor.
65/J2 **Trzcianka**, Pol.
65/H1 **Trzebiatów**, Pol.
65/J3 **Trzebnica**, Pol.
65/J2 **Trzemeszno**, Pol.
82/B2 **Tržič**, Slov.
96/D3 **Tsagaan Bogd** (peak), Mong.
96/G2 **Tsagaan-Ovoo**, Mong.
96/E1 **Tsagaan-Üür**, Mong.
133/J6 **Tsaratanana Massif** (plat.), Madg.
132/B2 **Tsarisberge** (mts.), Namb.
96/C2 **Tsast** (peak), Mong.
102/F2 **Tsast Uul** (peak), Mong.
132/E3 **Tsatsana** (peak), Les.
126/D5 **Tsau**, Bots.
130/C3 **Tsavo**, Kenya
130/C2 **Tsavo East Nat'l Park**, Kenya
130/C2 **Tsavo West Nat'l Park**, Kenya
102/B1 **Tselinograd**, Kaz.
96/F2 **Tsenhermandal**, Mong.
131/A4 **Tsetseng**, Bots.
96/D2 **Tsetsen-Uul**, Mong.
96/E2 **Tsetserleg**, Mong.
131/B1 **Tshangalele** (res.), Zaire
126/B1 **Tshela**, Zaire
131/B4 **Tshesebe**, Bots.
126/D2 **Tshibwika**, Zaire
126/D2 **Tshikapa**, Zaire
131/B2 **Tshinsenda**, Zaire
131/C4 **Tshipise**, SAfr.
131/B3 **Tsholotsho**, Zim.
125/K8 **Tshuapa** (riv.), Zaire
123/G6 **Tsiafajavona** (peak), Madg.
85/L2 **Tsil'ma** (riv.), Rus.
87/G2 **Tsimlyansk** (res.), Rus.
133/H9 **Tsiombe**, Madg.
133/H7 **Tsiribihina** (riv.), Madg.
133/H7 **Tsiroanomandidy**, Madg.
132/C4 **Tsitsikamma Forest & Coastal Nat'l Park**, SAfr.
87/G4 **Tskhinvali**, Geo.
84/G4 **Tsna** (riv.), Rus.
96/D2 **Tsogt**, Mong.
96/F3 **Tsogt-Ovoo**, Mong.
96/F3 **Tsogttsetsiy**, Mong.
96/F2 **Tsöh** (riv.), Mong.
132/D3 **Tsomo** (riv.), SAfr.
98/E3 **Tsu**, Japan
101/E5 **Tsu** (isl.), Japan
98/A3 **Tsu** (isls.), Japan
99/F2 **Tsubame**, Japan
98/E2 **Tsubata**, Japan
99/G2 **Tsuchiura**, Japan
99/M10 **Tsuchiyama**, Japan
100/B3 **Tsugaru** (pen.), Japan
100/B3 **Tsugaru** (str.), Japan
99/L10 **Tsuge**, Japan
100/B4 **Tsukidate**, Japan
99/M10 **Tsukigase**, Japan
99/H7 **Tsukui**, Japan
98/B4 **Tsukumi**, Japan
126/C4 **Tsumeb**, Namb.
99/K10 **Tsuna**, Japan
99/F3 **Tsuru**, Japan
98/E3 **Tsuruga**, Japan
99/H7 **Tsurugashima**, Japan
99/E2 **Tsurugi**, Japan
98/D4 **Tsurugi-san** (mtn.), Japan
100/A4 **Tsuruoka**, Japan
99/M9 **Tsushima**, Japan
98/D3 **Tsuyama**, Japan
131/B4 **Tswapong** (hills), Bots.
110/C5 **Tua** (cape), Indo.
74/B2 **Tua** (riv.), Port.
142/B4 **Tuamapu** (chan.), Chile
121/L6 **Tuamotu** (arch.), FrPol.
103/B4 **Tuan** (riv.), China
110/A3 **Tuan** (pt.), Indo.
109/C1 **Tuan Giao**, Viet.
110/A3 **Tuangku** (isl.), Indo.
109/D2 **Tuan Thuong**, Viet.
112/C1 **Tuao**, Phil.
86/F3 **Tuapse**, Rus.
105/J5 **Tuba**, Phil.
158/E3 **Tuba City**, Az,US
110/D5 **Tuban**, Indo.
94/D6 **Tuban** (riv.), Yem.
141/B4 **Tubarão**, Braz.
112/C3 **Tubbataha** (reef), Phil.
66/D4 **Tubbergen**, Neth.
112/C3 **Tubigon**, Phil.
70/C5 **Tübingen**, Ger.
68/D2 **Tubize**, Belg.
128/C5 **Tubmanburg**, Libr.
120/H6 **Tubou**, Fiji
125/K1 **Ţubruq** (Tobruk), Libya
121/K7 **Tubuaï** (isls.), FrPol.
121/K7 **Tubuaï** (isl.), FrPol.
112/C3 **Tuburan**, Phil.
112/C4 **Tuburan**, Phil.
140/C3 **Tucano**, Braz.
65/J2 **Tuchola**, Pol.
166/C5 **Tuckahoe** (cr.), Md,US
166/D5 **Tuckahoe** (riv.), NJ,US
167/K8 **Tuckahoe**, NY,US
158/E4 **Tucson**, Az,US
159/G4 **Tucumcari**, NM,US
139/E2 **Tucupido**, Ven.
139/F2 **Tucupita**, Ven.
137/J4 **Tucuruí**, Braz.
137/H4 **Tucuruí** (res.), Braz.
74/E1 **Tudela**, Sp.
53/P8 **Tudeley**, Eng,UK
72/E5 **Tude, Rochers de la** (mtn.), Fr.
132/E3 **Tugela** (falls), SAfr.
133/E3 **Tugela** (riv.), SAfr.
163/H2 **Tug Fork** (riv.), WV,US
112/D3 **Tugnug** (pt.), Phil.
112/C1 **Tuguegarao**, Phil.
164/F7 **Tujunga**, Ca,US
111/F5 **Tukangbesi** (isls.), Indo.
91/B4 **Ţūkh**, Egypt
63/K3 **Tukums**, Lat.
110/D4 **Tukung** (peak), Indo.
130/B5 **Tukuyu**, Tanz.
165/C3 **Tukwila**, Wa,US
130/C3 **Tula** (riv.), Kenya
147/K6 **Tula** (riv.), Mex.
86/F1 **Tula**, Rus.
147/K6 **Tula de Allende**, Mex.
102/F4 **Tulagt Ar** (riv.), China
165/C1 **Tulalip Ind. Res.**, Wa,US
147/F4 **Tula Nat'l Park**, Mex.
147/F4 **Tulancingo**, Mex.
86/F1 **Tula Obl.**, Rus.
158/C3 **Tulare**, Ca,US
159/F4 **Tularosa**, NM,US
159/F4 **Tularosa** (val.), NM,US
132/L10 **Tulbagh**, SAfr.
138/B4 **Tulcán**, Ecu.
83/J3 **Tulcea**, Rom.
83/J3 **Tulcea** (co.), Rom.
165/L9 **Tule** (can.), Ca,US
131/C4 **Tuli**, Zim.
131/C4 **Tuli** (riv.), Zim.
162/C3 **Tulia**, Tx,US
131/C4 **Tuli Block** (reg.), Bots.
151/E5 **Tulik** (vol.), Ak,US
120/E5 **Tulin** (isls.), PNG
91/D3 **Ţūlkarm**, WBnk.
163/G3 **Tullahoma**, Tn,US
54/B3 **Tulla, Loch** (lake), Sc,UK
60/C3 **Tullamore**, Ire.
72/D4 **Tulle**, Fr.
54/C4 **Tullibody**, Sc,UK
63/R7 **Tullinge**, Swe.
65/J4 **Tulln**, Aus.
84/G1 **Tuloma** (riv.), Rus.
166/B3 **Tulpehocken** (cr.), Pa,US
159/J3 **Tulsa**, Ok,US
63/T9 **Tulstrup**, Den.
147/K7 **Tultepec**, Mex.
138/B3 **Tuluá**, Col.
147/J4 **Tulum Nat'l Park**, Mex.
89/L4 **Tulun**, Rus.
149/E3 **Tuma** (riv.), Nic.
158/E5 **Tumacacori Nat'l Mon.**, Az,US
137/H3 **Tumac-Humac** (mts.), Braz.
138/B4 **Tumaco**, Col.
62/G2 **Tumba**, Swe.
125/J8 **Tumba** (lake), Zaire
144/A1 **Tumbes**, Peru
109/C3 **Tumbot** (peak), Camb.
131/B1 **Tumbwe**, Zaire
103/B2 **Tumd Youqi**, China
103/B2 **Tumd Zuoqi**, China
97/K3 **Tumen**, China
101/E1 **Tumen** (riv.), China, NKor.
106/C5 **Tumkūr**, India
54/C3 **Tummel** (riv.), Sc,UK
97/M1 **Tumnin** (riv.), Rus.
110/B2 **Tumpat**, Malay.
111/F4 **Tumpu** (peak), Indo.
119/D2 **Tumut**, Austl.
165/B3 **Tumwater**, Wa,US
92/D2 **Tunceli**, Turk.
92/D2 **Tunceli** (prov.), Turk.
105/F5 **Tunchang**, China
131/C3 **Tundazi** (hill), Zim.
130/B5 **Tunduma**, Tanz.
130/C5 **Tunduru**, Tanz.
102/C1 **Tundyk** (riv.), Kaz.
82/H4 **Tundzha** (riv.), Bul., Turk.
63/T9 **Tune**, Den.
106/C4 **Tungabhadra** (res.), India
106/C4 **Tungabhadra** (riv.), India
119/C3 **Tungamah**, Austl.
112/C4 **Tungawan**, Phil.
101/C4 **Tŭngsan-got** (pt.), NKor.
138/B5 **Tungurahua** (prov.), Ecu.
88/K3 **Tunguska, Lower** (riv.), Rus.
88/K3 **Tunguska, Stony** (riv.), Rus.
123/X17 **Tūnis** (cap.), Tun.
80/B4 **Tunis** (gov.), Tun.
123/X17 **Tunis** (gulf), Tun.
123/W18 **Tunisia**
138/C3 **Tunjá**, Col.
112/B4 **Tunku Abdul Rahman Nat'l Park**, Malay.
103/C3 **Tunliu**, China
140/A2 **Tuntum**, Braz.
153/K3 **Tunungayualuk** (isl.), Nf,Can
142/C2 **Tunuyán**, Arg.
142/C2 **Tunuyán** (riv.), Chile
168/A2 **Tunxis Saint For.**, Ct,US
104/E2 **Tuo** (riv.), China
158/B3 **Tuolumne** (riv.), Ca,US
109/D2 **Tuong Duong**, Viet.
103/E3 **Tuoniang** (riv.), China
102/F5 **Tuotuo** (riv.), China
141/B2 **Tupã**, Braz.
141/B1 **Tupaciguara**, Braz.
121/K6 **Tupai** (isl.), FrPol.
140/C2 **Tuparetema**, Braz.
138/D3 **Tuparro** (riv.), Col.
163/F3 **Tupelo**, Ms,US
163/F3 **Tupelo Nat'l Bfld.**, Ms,US
147/G5 **Tupilco**, Mex.
141/B2 **Tupi Paulista**, Braz.
136/E8 **Tupiza**, Bol.
160/F2 **Tupper Lake**, NY,US
142/C2 **Tupungato** (peak), Arg., Chile
97/J2 **Tuquan**, China
106/F2 **Tura**, India
85/Q4 **Tura** (riv.), Rus.
108/G3 **Turaiyūr**, India
97/L1 **Turana** (mts.), Rus.
115/S10 **Turangi**, NZ
88/G5 **Turan Lowland** (plain), Uzb.
138/C2 **Turbaco**, Col.
95/H3 **Turbat**, Pak.
138/C2 **Turbo**, Col.
83/F2 **Turda**, Rom.
121/M7 **Tureia** (atoll), FrPol.
65/K2 **Turek**, Pol.
88/G4 **Turgay Obl.**, Kaz.
160/E1 **Turgeon** (riv.), Qu,Can
83/H4 **Türgovishte**, Bul.
92/A2 **Turgutlu**, Turk.
92/D1 **Turhal**, Turk.
75/E3 **Turia** (riv.), Sp.
137/J4 **Turiaçu**, Braz.
140/A1 **Turiaçu** (riv.), Braz.
52/D4 **Turin**, It.
78/A2 **Turin** (Torino), It.
125/N7 **Turkana** (lake), Eth., Kenya
102/A3 **Turkestan**, Kaz.
82/E2 **Túrkeve**, Hun.
92/C2 **Turkey**
88/F6 **Turkmenistan**
92/D2 **Türkoğlu**, Turk.
150/D2 **Turks** (isls.), Trks.
150/C2 **Turks and Caicos** (isls.), UK
150/D2 **Turks Island** (passg.), Trks.
63/G3 **Turku**, Fin.
63/K1 **Turku** (Åbo), Fin.
63/K1 **Turku Ja Pori** (prov.), Fin.
130/B2 **Turkwel** (riv.), Kenya
158/B3 **Turlock**, Ca,US
141/D1 **Turmalina**, Braz.
139/E2 **Turmero**, Ven.
54/B6 **Turnberry**, Sc,UK
148/E2 **Turneffe** (isls.), Belz.
116/C2 **Turner** (peak), Austl.
66/B6 **Turnhout**, Belg.
156/F1 **Turnor Lake**, Sk,Can
65/H3 **Turnov**, Czh.
83/G4 **Turnu Măgurele**, Rom.
96/B3 **Turpan**, China
102/E3 **Turpan** (depr.), China
149/G2 **Turquino** (peak), Cuba
54/D1 **Turriff**, Sc,UK
128/B5 **Turtle** (isls.), SLeo.
168/H7 **Turtle Creek**, Pa,US
156/F2 **Turtleford**, Sk,Can
57/F4 **Turton**, Eng,UK
102/C3 **Turugart Shankou** (pass), China
141/J6 **Turvo** (riv.), Braz.
163/G3 **Tuscaloosa**, Al,US
80/B1 **Tuscano** (arch.), It.
78/D4 **Tuscany** (reg.), It.
168/F7 **Tuscarawas** (co.), Oh,US
168/F6 **Tuscarawas** (riv.), Oh,US
158/C2 **Tuscarora**, Nv,US
161/S9 **Tuscarora Ind. Res.**, NY,US
166/A3 **Tuscarora Mtn.** (ridge), Pa,US
163/G3 **Tuskegee**, Al,US
164/C3 **Tustin**, Ca,US
65/K3 **Tuszyn**, Pol.
84/H4 **Tutayev**, Rus.
57/G6 **Tutbury**, Eng,UK
108/G4 **Tuticorin**, India
82/E4 **Tutin**, Yugo.
140/B1 **Tutóia**, Braz.
112/A4 **Tutong**, Bru.
83/H3 **Tutrakan**, Bul.
159/H3 **Tuttle Creek** (lake), Ks,US
70/B7 **Tuttlingen**, Ger.
130/B4 **Tutubu**, Tanz.
121/H6 **Tutuila** (isl.), ASam.
144/D5 **Tutupaca** (vol.), Peru
151/F2 **Tututalak** (mtn.), Ak,US
77/H2 **Tutzing**, Ger.
96/F2 **Tuul** (riv.), Mong.
63/L1 **Tuusula**, Fin.
88/K4 **Tuva Aut. Rep.**, Rus.
120/G5 **Tuvalu**
94/E4 **Ţuwayq, Jabal** (mts.), SAr.
57/H5 **Tuxford**, Eng,UK
146/D4 **Tuxpan**, Mex.
147/F4 **Tuxpan**, Mex.
147/F4 **Tuxpan** (riv.), Mex.
147/F5 **Tuxtepec**, Mex.
148/C2 **Tuxtla Gutiérrez**, Mex.
74/A1 **Túy**, Sp.
109/D2 **Tuyen Hoa**, Viet.
109/D1 **Tuyen Quang**, Viet.
109/E3 **Tuy Hoa**, Viet.
85/M5 **Tuymazy**, Rus.
93/G3 **Tūysarkān**, Iran
92/C2 **Tuz** (lake), Turk.
158/D4 **Tuzigoot Nat'l Mon.**, Az,US
93/F3 **Ţūz Khurmātū**, Iraq
82/D3 **Tuzla**, Bosn.
93/N7 **Tuzla**, Turk.
93/E1 **Tuzluca**, Turk.
84/G4 **T'ver**, Rus.
84/G4 **T'ver Obl.**, Rus.
84/G4 **Tvertsa** (riv.), Rus.
83/G4 **Tvŭrditsa**, Bul.
131/C2 **Twapia**, Zam.
65/J3 **Twardogóra**, Pol.
54/D5 **Tweed** (riv.), UK
119/E1 **Tweed Heads**, Austl.
54/D5 **Tweedmouth**, Eng,UK
54/C5 **Tweedsmuir**, Sc,UK
66/D4 **Twente** (can.), Neth.
66/D4 **Twente** (reg.), Neth.
161/Q9 **Twenty Mile** (riv.), On,Can

Twin – Vaud

159/G5 Twin Buttes (res.), Tx,US
156/E5 Twin Falls, Id,US
131/C1 Twingi, Zam.
166/D3 Twin Rivers, NJ,US
168/F5 Twinsburg, Oh,US
67/G6 Twiste (riv.), Ger.
67/F3 Twistringen, Ger.
115/R11 Twizel, NZ
159/G3 Two Buttes (riv.), Co,US
119/D3 Twofold (bay), Austl.
157/L4 Two Harbors, Mn,US
156/F2 Two Hills, Ab,Can
160/C2 Two Rivers, Wi,US
59/E1 Twycross, Eng,UK
59/F4 Twyford, Eng,UK
58/C1 Twymyn (riv.), Wal,UK
56/D2 Twynholm, Sc,UK
104/B4 Tyao (riv.), Burma, India
100/E1 Tyatya Gora (mtn.), Rus.
65/K3 Tychy, Pol.
59/G1 Tydd Saint Giles, Eng,UK
160/E2 Tyendinaga, On,Can
163/H3 Tyger (riv.), SC,US
57/F4 Tyldesley, Eng,UK
162/E3 Tyler, Tx,US
97/N1 Tymovskoye, Rus.
73/L2 Týn, Czh.
159/H2 Tyndall, SD,US
54/B4 Tyndrum, Sc,UK
57/F2 Tyne (riv.), Eng,UK
54/D5 Tyne (riv.), Sc,UK
57/G2 Tyne & Wear (co.), Eng,UK
57/G1 Tynemouth, Eng,UK
92/C3 Tyre, Leb.
62/H2 Tyresö, Swe.
63/S7 Tyresta (reg. park), Swe.
91/D3 Tyre (Şūr), Leb.
62/D1 Tyrifjorden (lake), Nor.
97/L2 Tyrma (riv.), Rus.
87/G4 Tyrnyauz, Rus.
119/B2 Tyrrell (cr.), Austl.
119/B2 Tyrrell (lake), Austl.
80/B2 Tyrrhenian (sea), It.
62/A2 Tysnesøy (isl.), Nor.
166/A6 Tysons Corner, Va,US
87/J3 Tyub-Karagan (pt.), Kaz.
87/J3 Tyulen'i (isls.), Kaz.
87/H3 Tyuleniy (isl.), Rus.
85/Q4 Tyumen', Rus.
85/Q4 Tyumen' Obl., Rus.
102/C3 Tyup, Kyr.
58/B3 Tywi (riv.), Wal,UK
58/B1 Tywyn, Wal,UK
131/C4 Tzaneen, SAfr.

U

112/C2 Uac (mtn.), Phil.
121/M5 Ua Huka (isl.), FrPol.
54/B4 Uamh Bheag (mtn.), Sc,UK
121/L5 Ua Pou (isl.), FrPol.
139/G5 Uatumã (riv.), Braz.
140/C3 Uauá, Braz.
139/E5 Uaupés, Braz.
138/D4 Uaupés (riv.), Braz.
147/H5 Uaxactún, Guat.
148/D2 Uaxactún (ruins), Guat.
82/E3 Ub, Yugo.
141/D2 Ubá, Braz.
69/F2 Übach-Palenberg, Ger.
85/Q5 Ubagan (riv.), Kaz.
140/C4 Ubaíra, Braz.
140/C4 Ubaitaba, Braz.
140/B1 Ubajara, Braz.
140/B1 Ubajará Nat'l Park, Braz.
125/J7 Ubangi (riv.), Zaire
140/C4 Ubatã, Braz.
138/C3 Ubaté, Col.
141/H8 Ubatuba, Braz.
112/D3 Ubay, Phil.
73/G4 Ubaye (riv.), Fr.
66/C5 Ubbergen, Neth.
98/B4 Ube, Japan
74/D3 Úbeda, Sp.
136/G7 Uberaba (lake), Bol.
141/C1 Uberaba, Braz.
69/F5 Überherrn, Ger.
141/B1 Uberlândia, Braz.
77/F2 Überlingen, Ger.
77/F2 Überlingersee (lake), Ger.
111/J4 Ubia (peak), Indo.
109/D3 Ubon Ratchathani, Thai.
74/C4 Ubrique, Sp.
126/E1 Ubundu, Zaire
144/C3 Ucayali (dept.), Peru
144/C2 Ucayali (riv.), Peru
64/C3 Uccle, Belg.
85/N5 Uchaly, Rus.
85/X8 Uchinskoye, Rus.
100/B2 Uchiura (bay), Japan
64/F2 Uchte (riv.), Ger.
89/P4 Uchur (riv.), Rus.
69/F5 Uckange, Fr.
65/G2 Uckermark (reg.), Ger.
59/G5 Uckfield, Eng,UK
156/B3 Ucluelet, BC,Can
96/F1 Uda (riv.), Rus.
106/B3 Udaipur, India
108/F3 Udamalpet, India
108/G4 Udankudi, India
62/D2 Uddevalla, Swe.
54/B5 Uddingston, Sc,UK
61/F2 Uddjaure (lake), Swe.
66/C5 Uden, Neth.
66/C5 Udenhout, Neth.
106/C4 Udgīr, India
108/C1 Udhampur, India
79/G1 Udine, It.
79/G1 Udine (prov.), It.
106/B5 Udipi, India
85/L4 Udmurt Aut. Rep., Rus.
109/C2 Udon Thani, Thai.
65/H2 Ueckermünde, Ger.
99/F2 Ueda, Japan
125/K7 Uele (riv.), Zaire
67/H3 Uelzen, Ger.
98/E3 Ueno, Japan
99/F3 Uenohara, Japan
67/G1 Uetersen, Ger.
67/H4 Uetze, Ger.
85/M5 Ufa, Rus.
85/N5 Ufa (riv.), Rus.
59/E3 Uffington, Eng,UK
130/A4 Ugalla, Tanz.
130/A4 Ugalla (riv.), Tanz.
130/A4 Ugalla River Game Rsv., Tanz.
130/B1 Uganda
81/F3 Ugento, It.
54/E1 Ugie (riv.), Sc,UK
73/G4 Ugine, Fr.
97/N2 Uglegorsk, Rus.
84/H4 Uglich, Rus.
73/L4 Ugljan (isl.), Cro.
86/E1 Ugra (riv.), Rus.
96/F2 Ugtaaltsaydam, Mong.
130/C3 Ugweno, Tanz.
65/J4 Uherské Hradiště, Czh.
70/C5 Uhingen, Ger.
71/G4 Uhlava (riv.), Czh.
71/F3 Uhlavka (riv.), Czh.
140/B3 Uibaí, Braz.
55/H7 Uig, Sc,UK
55/H8 Uig, Sc,UK
126/C2 Uíge, Ang.
101/D4 Ŭijŏngbu, SKor.
87/K2 Uil (riv.), Kaz.
132/L11 Uilkraal (riv.), SAfr.
87/G4 Uilpata, Gora (peak), Rus.
158/E2 Uinta (mts.), Ut,US
140/C2 Uiraúna, Braz.
101/E4 Ŭisŏng, SKor.
132/D4 Uitenhage, SAfr.
66/B3 Uitgeest, Neth.
66/B3 Uithoorn, Neth.
120/F4 Ujae (atoll), Mrsh.
120/F4 Ujelang (atoll), Mrsh.
82/E2 Újfehértó, Hun.
99/L10 Uji, Japan
99/L10 Uji (riv.), Japan
130/A4 Ujiji, Tanz.
99/L10 Ujitawara, Japan
106/C3 Ujjain, India
111/E5 Ujung Pandang, Indo.
130/B3 Ukara (isl.), Tanz.
130/B3 Ukerewe (isl.), Tanz.
85/M3 Ukhta, Rus.
158/B3 Ukiah, Ca,US
63/L4 Ukmergė, Lith.
86/D2 Ukraine
91/C2 U.K. Sovereign Base Area (mil. res.), Cyp.
130/B5 Ukwama, Tanz.
96/F2 Ulaanbaatar (cap.), Mong.
96/C2 Ulaangom, Mong.
96/B2 Ulaanhus, Mong.
96/F1 Ulan-Burgasy (mts.), Rus.
97/J2 Ulanhot, China
103/B2 Ulansuhai (salt lake), China
96/F1 Ulan-Ude, Rus.
102/F5 Ulan Ul (lake), China
165/L10 Ulatis (cr.), Ca,US
130/C4 Ulaya, Tanz.
101/E4 Ulchin, SKor.
82/D5 Ulcinj, Yugo.
96/G2 Uldz (riv.), Mong.
62/C2 Ulefoss, Nor.
97/H2 Ulgain (riv.), China
106/B4 Ulhāsnagar, India
96/D2 Uliastay, Mong.
125/L8 Ulindi (riv.), Zaire
120/D3 Ulithi (atoll), Micr.
74/A1 Ulla (riv.), Sp.
119/D2 Ulladulla, Austl.
55/J8 Ullapool, Sc,UK
144/D4 Ulla Ulla Nat'l Rsv., Bol.
61/F1 Ullsfjorden (fjord), Nor.
57/F2 Ullswater (lake), Eng,UK
98/B2 Ullŭng (isl.), SKor.
70/C6 Ulm, Ger.
63/S7 Ulnasjön (lake), Swe.
131/D2 Ulonguè, Moz.
62/E3 Ulricehamn, Swe.
101/E5 Ulsan, SKor.
70/C1 Ulster (riv.), Ger.
56/A3 Ulster (reg.), Ire.
56/A2 Ulster American Folk Park, NI,UK
148/E3 Ulua (riv.), Hon.
92/B2 Uluborlu, Turk.
92/B1 Uludağ, Tepe (peak), Turk.
93/F2 Uludoruk (peak), Turk.
130/C4 Uluguru (mts.), Tanz.
148/D2 Ulumal, Mex.
96/B2 Ulungur (lake), China
96/B2 Ulungur (riv.), China
117/F3 Uluru (Ayers Rock) (peak), Austl.
117/F3 Uluru Nat'l Park, Austl.
102/A2 Ulutau, Gora (peak), Kaz.
57/E3 Ulverston, Eng,UK
119/C4 Ulverstone, Austl.
63/J1 Ulvila, Fin.
63/P2 Ul'yanovka, Rus.
162/C2 Ulysses, Ks,US
147/H4 Umán, Mex.
86/D2 Uman', Ukr.
112/D3 Umanum (pt.), Phil.
140/C2 Umarizal, Braz.
106/D4 Umarkot, India
95/L2 Umāsi La (pass), India
120/D5 Umboi (isl.), PNG
77/G4 Umbrailpass (pass), Swi.
77/G4 Umbrail, Piz (peak), Swi.
80/C1 Umbria (reg.), It.
79/F5 Umbro-Marchigiano, Appennino (mts.), It.
131/C5 Umbuluze (riv.), Moz., Swaz.
88/B3 Ume (riv.), Swe.
131/C3 Ume (riv.), Zim.
61/G3 Umeå, Swe.
61/F2 Umeälv (riv.), Swe.
133/E3 Umfolozi (riv.), SAfr.
131/C3 Umfuli (riv.), Zim.
133/E3 Umgeni (riv.), SAfr.
95/F4 Umm as Samīm (salt dep.), Oman
125/M4 Umm Durmān (Omdurman), Sudan
91/D3 Umm el Fahm, Isr.
127/C4 Umm Hibal, Bi'r (well), Egypt
125/M5 Umm Ruwābah, Sudan
151/E5 Umnak (isl.), Ak,US
151/E5 Umnak (passg.), Ak,US
131/C3 Umniati, Zim.
131/C3 Umniati (riv.), Zim.
156/C5 Umpqua (riv.), Or,US
132/E3 Umtata, SAfr.
135/F1 Umuarama, Braz.
132/E3 Umzimvubu (riv.), SAfr.
131/C4 Umzingwani (riv.), Zim.
82/B3 Una (riv.), Bosn., Cro.
140/C4 Una, Braz.
115/R11 Una (peak), NZ
140/A5 Unaí, Braz.
151/E5 Unalaska (isl.), Ak,US
92/D3 'Unāzah, Jabal (mtn.), SAr.
158/E3 Uncompahgre (plat.), Co,US
131/C2 Undaunda, Zam.
62/F2 Unden (lake), Swe.
157/H4 Underwood, ND,US
121/Z17 Undu (pt.), Fiji
86/E1 Unecha, Rus.
151/F4 Unga (isl.), Ak,US
130/D3 Ungama (bay), Kenya
153/K3 Ungava (bay), Qu, Can
153/J2 Ungava (pen.), Qu,Can
86/C3 Ungeny, Mol.
140/B2 União, Braz.
141/B3 União da Vitória, Braz.
140/C3 União dos Palmares, Braz.
151/E4 Unimak (isl.), Ak,US
151/E5 Unimak (passg.), Ak,US
139/F5 Unini (riv.), Braz.
54/C5 Union (can.), Sc,UK
159/K3 Union, Mo,US
167/D2 Union, NJ,US
167/D2 Union (co.), NJ,US
166/C5 Union (lake), NJ,US
156/D4 Union, Or,US
166/A2 Union (co.), Pa,US
163/H3 Union, SC,US
167/D3 Union Beach, NJ,US
165/K11 Union City, Ca,US
167/D2 Union City, NJ,US
163/F2 Union City, Tn,US
167/L9 Uniondale, NY,US
149/F1 Unión de Reyes, Cuba
146/D5 Unión de Tula, Mex.
148/C2 Unión Hidalgo, Mex.
163/G3 Union Springs, Al,US
160/E4 Uniontown, Pa,US
161/R8 Unionville, On,Can
159/J2 Unionville, Mo,US
94/F4 United Arab Emirates
55/* United Kingdom
167/K8 United Nations, NY,US
101/E5 United Nations Mem. Cemetery, SKor.
152/* United States
153/T6 United States (range), NW,Can
156/F2 Unity, Sk,Can
162/D4 Universal City, Tx,US
147/Q10 University City, Mex.
168/F5 University Heights, Oh,US
164/G8 Univ. of California-Irvine, Ca,US
164/F7 Univ. of California-Los Angles, Ca,US
164/F7 Univ. of Southern California, Ca,US
106/B3 Unjha, India
117/M8 Unley, Austl.
67/E5 Unna, Ger.
106/D2 Unnāo, India
60/B1 Unshin (riv.), Ire.
55/P12 Unst (isl.), Sc,UK
64/F3 Unstrut (riv.), Ger.
77/F2 Unterargen (riv.), Ger.
70/D3 Unterpleichfeld, Ger.
71/E6 Unterschleissheim, Ger.
77/E2 Untersee (lake), Ger., Swi.
76/E4 Unterwalden (canton), Swi.
92/D1 Ünye, Turk.
98/A4 Unzen-Amakusa Nat'l Park, Japan
98/B4 Unzen-dake (mtn.), Japan
85/K4 Unzha (riv.), Rus.
99/E2 Uozu, Japan
140/C2 Upanema, Braz.
139/F2 Upata, Ven.
126/E2 Upemba (lake), Zaire
126/E2 Upemba Nat'l Park, Zaire
54/C5 Uphall, Sc,UK
112/D4 Upi, Phil.
132/C3 Upington, SAfr.
130/B5 Upiriwombe, Zam.
106/B3 Upleta, India
53/P7 Upminster, Eng,UK
154/U10 Upolu (pt.), Hi,US
121/H6 Upolu (isl.), WSam.
158/C2 Upper (lake), Ca,US
167/D2 Upper (bay), NJ, NY,US
163/H1 Upper Arlington, Oh,US
156/D3 Upper Arrow (lake), BC,Can
71/H6 Upper Austria (prov.), Aus.
166/C4 Upper Darby, Pa,US
139/G3 Upper Demerara-Berbice (reg.), Guy.
59/G5 Upper Dicker, Eng,UK
129/E4 Upper East (reg.), Gha.
77/F5 Upper Engadine (val.), Swi.
115/S11 Upper Hutt, NZ
159/J2 Upper Iowa (riv.), Ia,US
156/C5 Upper Klamath (lake), Or,US
56/B2 Upperlands, NI,UK
60/C1 Upper Lough Erne (lake), NI,UK
160/C2 Upper Peninsula (pen.), Mi,US
157/L5 Upper Peoria (lake), Il,US
157/K3 Upper Red (lake), Mn,US
165/F7 Upper Rouge (riv.), Mi,US
167/J7 Upper Saddle River, NJ,US
139/G4 Upper Takutu-Upper Essequibo (reg.), Guy.
59/E3 Upper Thames (val.), Eng,UK
129/E4 Upper West (reg.), Gha.
59/F1 Uppingham, Eng,UK
62/G2 Upplands-Väsby, Swe.
62/G2 Uppsala, Swe.
62/G1 Uppsala (co.), Swe.
151/D3 Upright (cape), Ak,US
118/B2 Upstart (bay), Austl.
118/B2 Upstart (cape), Austl.
157/G4 Upton, Wy,US
58/D2 Upton upon Severn, Eng,UK
93/F4 Ur (ruins), Iraq
138/B2 Urabá (gulf), Col.
103/B2 Urad Qianqi, China
99/H7 Uraga (chan.), Japan
100/C2 Urahoro, Japan
140/A1 Uraim (riv.), Braz.
100/C2 Urakawa, Japan
88/F3 Ural (mts.), Rus.
88/F5 Ural (riv.), Rus., Kaz.
87/J2 Ural'sk, Kaz.
87/J2 Ural'sk Obl., Kaz.
130/B4 Urambo, Tanz.
140/B4 Urandi, Braz.
152/F3 Uranium City, Sk,Can
139/F4 Uraricoera (riv.), Braz.
100/J7 Urasoe, Japan
99/F3 Urawa, Japan
88/G3 Uray, Rus.
99/H7 Urayasu, Japan
70/C5 Urbach, Ger.
160/B3 Urbana, Il,US
160/D3 Urbana, Oh,US
149/G1 Urbano Noris, Cuba
140/B1 Urbano Santos, Braz.
79/F5 Urbino, It.
77/E3 Urdorf, Swi.
57/G3 Ure (riv.), Eng,UK
158/E5 Ures, Mex.
99/M10 Ureshino, Japan
92/D2 Urfa, Turk.
92/D2 Urfa (prov.), Turk.
67/G6 Urft (riv.), Ger.
88/G5 Urgench, Uzb.
78/C1 Urgnano, It.
61/H1 Urho Kekkosen Nat'l Park, Fin.
77/E4 Uri (canton), Swi.
138/D3 Uribante (riv.), Ven.
54/D2 Urie (riv.), Sc,UK
126/F2 Urimáan, Ven.
139/F3 Urimán, Ven.
146/D3 Urique (riv.), Mex.
77/E4 Uri-Rotstock (peak), Swi.
63/K1 Urjala, Fin.
66/C3 Urk, Neth.
92/A2 Urla, Turk.
83/H3 Urlaţi, Rom.
108/C2 Urmar, India
97/L2 Urmi (riv.), Rus.
93/F2 Urmia (lake), Iran
57/F5 Urmston, Eng,UK
77/E4 Urnersee (lake), Swi.
82/E4 Uroševac, Yugo.
56/E1 Urr Water (riv.), Sc,UK
147/N7 Úrsulo Galván, Mex.
137/J6 Uruaçu, Braz.
146/E5 Uruapan, Mex.
144/C3 Urubamba (riv.), Peru
139/G5 Urubu (riv.), Braz.
140/C1 Uruburetama, Braz.
140/C4 Uruçuca, Braz.
140/A2 Uruçuí, Braz.
140/A3 Uruçuí (mts.), Braz.
140/A5 Uruçuí (riv.), Braz.
140/A3 Uruçuí Prêto (riv.), Braz.
135/E2 Uruguaiana, Braz.
135/E3 Uruguay
135/E2 Uruguay (riv.), SAm.
96/B2 Ürümqi, China
140/B1 Uruoca, Braz.
89/R5 Urup (isl.), Rus.
141/B4 Urussanga, Braz.
130/A4 Uruwira, Tanz.
97/H1 Uryumkan (riv.), Rus.
87/G2 Uryupinsk, Rus.
83/H3 Urziceni, Rom.
53/R9 Us, Fr.
96/C1 Us (riv.), Rus.
98/B4 Usa, Japan
53/J2 Usa (riv.), Rus.
130/B3 Usagara, Tanz.
92/B2 Uşak, Turk.
92/B2 Uşak (prov.), Turk.
126/C5 Usakos, Namb.
143/N7 Usborne (peak), Falk.
166/D6 U.S.C.G. Receiving Ctr., NJ,US
166/A5 U.S. Dept. of Energy, Md,US
130/A4 Usevia, Tanz.
130/B3 Ushashi, Tanz.
130/B4 Ushetu, Tanz.
98/B4 Ushibuka, Japan
99/J7 Ushiku, Japan
130/A3 Ushirombo, Tanz.
102/C2 Ushtobe, Kaz.
143/K8 Ushuaia, Arg.
108/F4 Usilampatti, India
130/A4 Usinge, Tanz.
70/B2 Usingen, Ger.
53/H3 Usinsk, Rus.
58/D3 Usk, Wal,UK
58/D3 Usk (riv.), Wal,UK
83/J5 Üsküdar, Turk.
67/G5 Uslar, Ger.
71/G4 Úslava (riv.), Czh.
86/F1 Usman', Rus.
166/B6 U.S. Naval Academy, Md,US
150/E3 U.S. Naval Res., PR
164/F8 U.S. Nav. Weap. Sta., Seal Beach, Ca,US
130/B4 Usoke, Tanz.
96/E1 Usol'ye-Sibirskoye, Rus.
112/C2 Uson, Phil.
142/C2 Uspallata (pass), Arg., Chile
154/W13 U.S.S. Arizona Mem., Hi,US
72/E4 Ussel, Fr.
70/D5 Ussel (riv.), Ger.
76/C5 Usses (riv.), Fr.
130/B4 Ussure, Tanz.
97/L2 Ussuri (Wusuli) (riv.), Rus., China
97/L3 Ussuriysk, Rus.
77/E3 Uster, Swi.
80/C3 Ustica (isl.), It.
89/L4 Ust'-Ilimsk, Rus.
65/H3 Ústí nad Labem, Czh.
65/J1 Ustka, Pol.
89/S4 Ust'-Kamchatsk, Rus.
102/D2 Ust'-Kamenogorsk, Kaz.
89/L4 Ust'-Kut, Rus.
96/E1 Ust'-Ordynskiy, Rus.
65/M4 Ustrzyki Dolne, Pol.
85/K3 Ust'ya (riv.), Rus.
87/K4 Ustyurt (plat.), Kaz., Uzb.
102/D3 Usu, China
98/B4 Usuki, Japan
148/D3 Usulután, ESal.
148/C2 Usumacinta (riv.), Guat., Mex.
158/E3 Utah (state), US
158/D2 Utah (lake), Ut,US
131/D2 Utale, Malw.
99/L10 Utano, Japan
100/C2 Utashinai, Japan
159/G3 Ute (cr.), NM,US
63/L4 Utena, Lith.
130/B5 Utengule, Tanz.
71/G3 Uterský (riv.), Czh.
130/C4 Utete, Tanz.
109/C3 Uthai Thani, Thai.
160/F3 Utica, NY,US
74/E3 Utiel, Sp.
157/K2 Utik (lake), Mb,Can
156/E2 Utikuma (lake), Ab,Can
148/E2 Utila (isl.), Hon.
140/B4 Utinga, Braz.
120/G3 Utirik (atoll), Mrsh.
120/G5 Utiroa, Kiri.
117/G2 Utopia Abor. Land, Austl.
106/D2 Utraulā, India
66/C4 Utrecht, Neth.
66/C4 Utrecht (prov.), Neth.
74/C4 Utrera, Sp.
99/F2 Utsunomiya, Japan
108/F4 Uttamapālaiyam, India
109/C2 Uttaradit, Thai.
102/C5 Uttarkashi, India
106/C2 Uttar Pradesh (state), India
57/G6 Uttoxeter, Eng,UK
63/R7 Uttran (lake), Swe.
150/E3 Utuado, PR
120/F6 Utupua (isl.), Sol.
121/K6 Uturoa, FrPol.
50/B6 Uturoa (isl.), FrPol.
96/G2 Uulbayan, Mong.
96/E1 Üür (riv.), Mong.
96/C1 Üüreg (lake), Mong.
96/C1 Uus (lake), Mong.
63/J1 Uusikaupunki, Fin.
63/L1 Uusimaa (prov.), Fin.
138/D4 Uva (riv.), Col.
162/D4 Uvalde, Tx,US
85/K4 Uval, Northern (hills), Rus.
71/H2 Uvaly, Czh.
87/G2 Uvarovo, Rus.
130/A4 Uvinza, Tanz.
130/A3 Uvira, Zaire
149/F4 Uvita (pt.), CR
102/F1 Uvs Nuur (lake), Mong.
98/C4 Uwajima, Japan
125/L6 Uwayl, Sudan
53/M7 Uxbridge, Eng,UK
168/C1 Uxbridge, Ma,US
103/B3 Uxin Qi, China
147/H4 Uxmal (ruins), Mex.
85/P5 Uy (riv.), Kaz., Rus.
96/E2 Uyanga, Mong.
96/C2 Uyench, Mong.
104/B3 Uyu (riv.), Burma
136/E8 Uyuni, Bol.
88/G5 Uzbekistan
86/B2 Uzhgorod, Ukr.
86/F1 Uzlovaya, Rus.
92/D2 Üzümlü, Turk.
83/H5 Uzunköprü, Turk.
77/F3 Uzwil, Swi.

V

132/C3 Vaal (riv.), SAfr.
132/E2 Vaaldam (res.), SAfr.
69/F2 Vaals, Neth.
69/E2 Vaalserberg (hill), Neth.
131/C5 Vaalwater, SAfr.
61/G3 Vaasa (prov.), Fin.
61/G3 Vaasa (Vasa), Fin.
66/C4 Vaassen, Neth.
82/D2 Vác, Hun.
165/K10 Vaca (mtn.), Ca,US
165/K10 Vaca (mts.), Ca,US
141/B4 Vacaria, Braz.
165/L10 Vacaville, Ca,US
149/H2 Vache (isl.), Haiti
153/J2 Vachon (riv.), Qu,Can
78/B4 Vado Ligure, It.
77/F4 Vadret, Piz (peak), Swi.
62/F2 Vadstena, Swe.
77/F3 Vaduz (cap.), Lcht.
84/J3 Vaga (riv.), Rus.
82/B3 Vaganski vrh (peak), Cro.
85/R4 Vagay (riv.), Rus.
62/F3 Vaggeryd, Swe.
65/J4 Váh (riv.), Slvk.
121/M6 Vahitahi (isl.), FrPol.
54/B1 Vaich, Loch (lake), Sc,UK
70/B5 Vaihingen an der Enz, Ger.
95/K5 Vaijāpur, India
108/F4 Vaikam, India
159/F3 Vail, Co,US
68/C5 Vailly-sur-Aisnes, Fr.
167/J9 Vailsburg, NJ,US
76/B1 Vair (riv.), Fr.
53/T10 Vaires-sur-Marne, Fr.
120/G5 Vaitupu (isl.), Tuv.
86/F4 Vakfıkebir, Turk.
88/J3 Vakh (riv.), Rus.
95/K1 Vākhān (mts.), Afg.
95/J1 Vakhsh (riv.), Trkm.
76/D5 Valais (canton), Swi.
79/G2 Valalta, Cro.
62/G1 Valbo, Swe.
66/C5 Valburg, Neth.
79/E1 Valdagno, It.
84/G4 Valdai (hills), Rus.
79/E5 Valdarno (vall.), It.
69/F6 Val-de-Bide, Fr.
74/C3 Valdecañas (res.), Sp.
79/E6 Val d'Elsa, Colle di, It.
53/T10 Val-de-Marne (dept.), Fr.
62/G2 Valdemarsvik, Swe.
75/M8 Valdemorillo, Sp.
74/D3 Valdepeñas, Sp.
74/C2 Valderaduey (riv.), Sp.
142/E4 Valdés (pen.), Arg.
138/B4 Valdez, Ecu.
142/B3 Valdivia, Chile
79/F1 Valdobbiadene, It.
68/A5 Val-d'Oise (dept.), Fr.
160/E1 Val d'Or, Qu,Can
163/H4 Valdosta, Ga,US
74/A1 Valdoviño, Sp.
156/D5 Vale, Or,US
156/D2 Valemount, BC,Can
141/K7 Valença, Braz.
140/B2 Valença do Piauí, Braz.
72/F4 Valence, Fr.
138/B5 Valencia, Ecu.
55/F11 Valencia (isl.), Ire.
112/D3 Valencia, Phil.
112/D4 Valencia, Phil.
75/E3 Valencia, Sp.
75/E3 Valencia (aut. comm.), Sp.
75/F3 Valencia (gulf), Sp.
138/E2 Valencia, Ven.
74/B3 Valencia de Alcántara, Sp.
68/C3 Valenciennes, Fr.
83/H3 Vălenii de Munte, Rom.
140/C3 Valente, Braz.
76/C3 Valentigney, Fr.
140/B2 Valentim (mts.), Braz.
159/G2 Valentine, Ne,US
162/B4 Valentine, Tx,US
53/T10 Valenton, Fr.
78/B2 Valenza, It.
112/E6 Valenzuela, Phil.
138/D2 Valera, Ven.
63/M3 Valga, Est.
141/G7 Valhinos, Braz.
72/D5 Valier (mtn.), Fr.
80/A2 Valinco (gulf), Fr.
82/D3 Valjevo, Yugo.
63/K1 Valkeakoski, Fin.
63/M1 Valkeala, Fin.
69/E2 Valkenburg, Neth.
66/C6 Valkenswaard, Neth.
147/H4 Valladolid, Mex.
74/C2 Valladolid, Sp.
75/E3 Vall de Uxó, Sp.
138/B5 Valle, Ecu.
165/L11 Valle (arroyo), Ca,US
75/N9 Vallecas, Sp.
78/A5 Vallecrosia, It.
78/A1 Valle d'Aosta (prov.), It.
78/A1 Valle d'Aosta (reg.), It.
147/E5 Valle de Bravo, Mex.
138/B3 Valle de Cauca (dept.), Col.
139/E2 Valle de la Pascua, Ven.
75/M8 Valle de los Caídos, Sp.
147/E4 Valle de Santiago, Mex.
138/C2 Valledupar, Col.
136/F7 Vallegrande, Bol.
147/F3 Valle Hermoso, Mex.
75/X16 Vallehermoso, Canl.,Sp.
66/C4 Valleikanaal (can.), Neth.
165/K10 Vallejo, Ca,US
135/B2 Vallenar, Chile
69/G3 Vallendar, Ger.
63/S6 Vallentuna, Swe.
63/S6 Vallentunasjön (lake), Swe.
80/D5 Valletta (cap.), Malta
157/J4 Valley City, ND,US
167/E1 Valley Cottage, NY,US
160/D2 Valley East, On,Can
168/C2 Valley Falls, RI,US
161/M7 Valleyfield, Qu,Can
166/C3 Valley Forge Nat'l Hist. Park, Pa,US
167/E2 Valley Stream, NY,US
150/F3 Valley, The, Angu.
156/D2 Valleyview, Ab,Can
79/F3 Valli Bertuzzi (lag.), It.
79/F3 Valli di Comacchio (lag.), It.
76/B4 Vallière (riv.), Fr.
142/E3 Vallimanca (riv.), Arg.
63/R7 Vällingen (lake), Swe.
75/F2 Valls, Sp.
77/G3 Valluga (peak), Aus.
156/G3 Val Marie, Sk,Can
75/M8 Valmayor (res.), Sp.
67/F6 Valme (riv.), Ger.
63/L3 Valmiera, Lat.
53/S9 Valmondois, Fr.
81/F2 Valona (bay), Alb.
108/F3 Vālpārai, India
142/C2 Valparaíso, Chile
142/C2 Valparaíso (reg.), Chile
146/E4 Valparaíso, Mex.
163/G4 Valparaiso, Fl,US
160/C3 Valparaiso, In,US
76/D6 Valpelline (riv.), It.
82/D3 Valpovo, Cro.
72/F4 Valréas, Fr.
132/D2 Vals (riv.), SAfr.
106/B3 Valsād, India
147/L8 Valsaquillo (res.), Mex.
132/B4 Valsbaai (bay), SAfr.
76/B5 Valserine (riv.), Fr.
77/F4 Valserrhein (riv.), Swi.
77/G4 Valsura (riv.), It.
77/F5 Valtellina (vall.), It.
86/F2 Valuyki, Rus.
108/H4 Valvedditturai, SrL.
74/B4 Valverde del Camino, Sp.
63/K1 Vammala, Fin.
93/E2 Van, Turk.
93/E2 Van (lake), Turk.
93/E2 Van (prov.), Turk.
63/K1 Vanajavesi (lake), Fin.
121/L7 Vanavaro (isl.), FrPol.
162/E3 Van Buren, Ar,US
161/H2 Van Buren, Me,US
159/K3 Van Buren, Mo,US
159/H3 Vance A.F.B., Ok,US
167/K8 Van Cortlandt Park, New York City, NY,US
116/C5 Vancouver (cape), Austl.
156/C3 Vancouver, BC,Can
156/B3 Vancouver (isl.), BC,Can
156/C4 Vancouver, Wa,US
151/L3 Vancouver (mtn.), Yk,Can, Ak,US
113/L Vanda, Ant.
160/B4 Vandalia, Il,US
159/K3 Vandalia, Mo,US
158/B4 Vandenberg A.F.B., Ca,US
132/D2 Vanderbijl Park, SAfr.
167/E2 Vanderbilt Museum, NY,US
156/B2 Vanderhoof, BC,Can
114/F3 Vanderlin (isl.), Austl.
114/E2 Van Diemen (cape), Austl.
114/E2 Van Diemen (gulf), Austl.
69/F6 Vandoeuvre-lès-Nancy, Fr.
62/E2 Vänern (lake), Swe.
62/E2 Vänersborg, Swe.
130/C4 Vanga, Kenya
133/H8 Vangaindrano, Madg.
66/C2 Van Harinxmakanaal (can.), Neth.
109/D1 Van Hoa, Viet.
162/B4 Van Horn, Tx,US
153/R7 Vanier (isl.), NW,Can
120/F6 Vanikoro (isl.), Sol.
76/D4 Vanil Noir (peak), Swi.
111/K4 Vanimo, PNG
97/N2 Vanino, Rus.
61/F3 Vännäs, Swe.
72/E2 Vanne (riv.), Fr.
72/B3 Vannes, Fr.
109/E3 Van Ninh, Viet.
164/B2 Van Norman (lakes), Ca,US
164/F7 Van Nuys, Ca,US
73/G4 Vanoise Nat'l Park, Fr.
132/E3 Vanreenenpas (pass), SAfr.
111/J4 Van Rees (mts.), Indo.
62/F1 Vansbro, Swe.
153/H2 Vansittart (isl.), NW,Can
63/L1 Vantaa, Fin.
120/G6 Vanua Levu (isl.), Fiji
120/F6 Vanuatu
53/S10 Vanves, Fr.
160/C3 Van Wert, Oh,US
109/D1 Van Yen, Viet.
73/G5 Var (riv.), Fr.
78/C4 Vara (riv.), It.
62/E2 Vara, Swe.
149/F1 Varadero, Cuba
93/G3 Varāmīn, Iran
106/D2 Vārānasi, India
61/J1 Varangerfjorden (fjord), Nor.
61/J1 Varangerhalvøya (pen.), Nor.
80/D2 Varano (lake), It.
82/C2 Varaždin, Cro.
78/B4 Varazze, It.
62/E3 Varberg, Swe.
81/G2 Vardar (riv.), Gre.
82/E5 Vardar (riv.), Macd.
62/C4 Varde, Den.
67/F2 Varel, Ger.
161/P6 Varennes, Qu,Can
68/A4 Varennes (riv.), Fr.
53/T10 Varennes-Jarcy, Fr.
72/E3 Varennes-Vauzelles, Fr.
82/D3 Vareš, Bosn.
78/B1 Varese, It.
78/B1 Varese (prov.), It.
140/C3 Vargem (riv.), Braz.
141/G6 Vargem do Sul, Braz.
140/B1 Vargem Grande, Braz.
141/H6 Varginha, Braz.
62/A2 Varhaug, Nor.
81/L7 Vari, Gre.
61/H3 Varkaus, Fin.
108/F4 Varkkallai, India
63/T9 Værløse, Den.
63/S7 Värmdo, Swe.
63/S7 Värmdolandet (isl.), Swe.
62/E2 Värmeln (lake), Swe.
62/E2 Värmland (co.), Swe.
83/H4 Varna, Bul.
83/H4 Varna (reg.), Bul.
62/F3 Värnamo, Swe.
82/D2 Várpalota, Hun.
92/E2 Varto, Turk.
60/D3 Vartry (res.), Ire.
60/D3 Vartry (riv.), Ire.
140/C2 Várzea Alegre, Braz.
141/C1 Várzea da Palma, Braz.
137/G7 Várzea Grande, Braz.
140/A4 Varzelândia, Braz.
84/H2 Varzuga (riv.), Rus.
82/C2 Vas (co.), Hun.
140/C3 Vasa Barris (riv.), Braz.
65/M4 Vásárosnamény, Hun.
61/G3 Vasa (Vaasa), Fin.
85/K2 Vashka (riv.), Rus.
165/C3 Vashon (isl.), Wa,US
86/D2 Vasil'kov, Ukr.
83/H2 Vaslui, Rom.
83/H2 Vaslui (co.), Rom.
160/D3 Vassar, Mi,US
62/B2 Vassdalsegga (peak), Nor.
81/G4 Vassés (Bassae) (ruins), Gre.
141/K7 Vassouras, Braz.
62/G2 Västerås, Swe.
61/F3 Västerbotten (co.), Swe.
62/E1 Västerdalälven (riv.), Swe.
62/H2 Västerhaninge, Swe.
61/F3 Västernorrland (co.), Swe.
62/G3 Västervik, Swe.
62/G1 Västmanland (co.), Swe.
84/C3 Vastmanland (co.), Swe.
80/D1 Vasto, It.
62/E3 Västra Silen (lake), Swe.
71/E6 Vaterstetten, Ger.
80/C2 Vatican City
61/P7 Vatnajökull (glac.), Ice.
83/G2 Vatra Dornei, Rom.
62/F2 Vättern (lake), Swe.
121/Y18 Vatukoula, Fiji
76/C4 Vaud (canton), Swi.

227
Vaud – Wadd

161/M7 Vaudreuil, Qu,Can
161/M7 Vaudreuil (co.), Qu,Can
161/Q8 Vaughan, On,Can
159/F4 Vaughn, NM,US
76/A6 Vaulx-en-Velin, Fr.
138/D4 Vaupés (comm.), Col.
138/D4 Vaupés (riv.), Col.
72/F5 Vauvert, Fr.
68/D4 Vaux (riv.), Fr.
156/E3 Vauxhall, Ab,Can
53/R9 Vaux-sur-Seine, Fr.
68/B3 Vaux-Vraucourt, Fr.
121/H6 Vava'u Group (isls.), Tonga
108/H4 Vavuniva (dist.), SrL.
108/H4 Vavuniya, SrL.
63/S7 Vaxholm, Swe.
62/F3 Växjö, Swe.
53/J2 Vaygach (isl.), Rus.
141/C1 Vazante, Braz.
141/G8 Vázea Paulista, Braz.
84/G5 Vazuza (res.), Rus.
66/D4 Vecht (riv.), Neth.
67/F3 Vechta, Ger.
67/E4 Vechte (riv.), Ger.
82/D2 Vecsés, Hun.
78/B1 Vedano Olona, It.
108/G3 Vedāranniyam, India
83/G3 Vedea (riv.), Rom.
142/E2 Vedia, Arg.
66/D2 Veendam, Neth.
66/C4 Veenendaal, Neth.
66/A5 Veersedam (dam), Neth.
66/A5 Veerse Meer (res.), Neth.
61/D2 Vega (isl.), Nor.
151/B6 Vega (pt.), Ak,US
61/D2 Vegafjorden (fjord), Nor.
63/U8 Vegeån (riv.), Swe.
66/C5 Veghel, Neth.
81/G2 Vegoritis (lake), Gre.
156/E2 Vègreville, Ab,Can
63/M1 Vehkalahti, Fin.
142/E2 Veinticinco de Mayo, Arg.
70/C3 Veitshöchheim, Ger.
62/C4 Vejen, Den.
74/C4 Vejer de la Frontera, Sp.
62/C4 Vejle, Den.
62/C4 Vejle (co.), Den.
76/D6 Vélan, Monte (peak), Swi., It.
75/S12 Velas, Azor,Port.
138/B5 Velasco Ibarra, Ecu.
66/E6 Velbert, Ger.
73/L3 Velden am Wörthersee, Aus.
66/C6 Veldhoven, Neth.
66/D5 Velen, Ger.
82/B2 Velenje, Slov.
138/C3 Vélez, Col.
74/C4 Vélez-Málaga, Sp.
74/D4 Vélez-Rubio, Sp.
141/C1 Velhas (Araguari) (riv.), Braz.
82/C3 Velika Gorica, Cro.
82/E3 Velika Plana, Yugo.
63/N3 Velikaya (riv.), Rus.
63/P3 Velikiye Luki, Rus.
53/H2 Velikiy Ustyug, Rus.
83/G4 Veliko Tŭrnovo, Bul.
83/G4 Velingrad, Bul.
53/S10 Vélizy-Villacoublay, Fr.
65/J4 Velké Meziříčí, Czh.
65/K4 Veľký Krtíš, Slvk.
71/F3 Velký Zvon (peak), Czh.
108/G3 Vellār (riv.), India
80/C2 Velletri, It.
67/G6 Vellmar, Ger.
75/N8 Vellón (res.), Sp.
106/C5 Vellore, India
84/J3 Vel'sk, Rus.
66/C4 Veluwe (reg.), Neth.
66/C4 Veluwemeer (lake), Neth.
66/C4 Veluwezoom Nat'l Park, Neth.
157/H3 Velva, ND,US
108/F3 Vembādi Shola (peak), India
108/F4 Vembanād (lake), India
63/T9 Ven (isl.), Swe.
54/B4 Venachar, Loch (lake), Sc,UK
147/L6 Venados, Mex.
142/E2 Venado Tuerto, Arg.
80/D2 Venafro, It.
139/F3 Venamo (peak), Ven.
141/A4 Venâncio Aires, Braz.
168/H5 Venango (co.), Pa,US
78/A2 Venaria, It.
73/G5 Vence, Fr.
141/B2 Venceslau Brás, Braz.
131/C4 Venda (ind. homeland), SAfr.
74/A3 Vendas Novas, Port.
72/D3 Vendôme, Fr.
75/F2 Vendrell, Sp.
79/F2 Veneta (lag.), It.
79/E1 Veneto (reg.), It.
79/F2 Venezia (gulf), It.
79/F1 Venezia (prov.), It.
79/F2 Venezia, Po di (riv.), It.
79/F2 Venezia (Venice), It.
139/E3 Venezuela
138/D2 Venezuela (gulf), Ven.
106/B4 Vengurla, India
151/G4 Veniaminof (vol.), Ak,US
163/H5 Venice, Fl,US
79/F2 Venice (Venezia), It.
72/F4 Vénissieux, Fr.
62/E1 Venjansjön (lake), Swe.
106/C5 Venkatagiri, India
66/D6 Venlo, Neth.
62/B2 Vennesla, Nor.
62/C3 Veno (bay), Den.
76/C4 Venoge (riv.), Swi.
80/D2 Venosa, It.
77/G4 Venosta (vall.), It.
66/C5 Venray, Neth.
63/J3 Venta (riv.), Lat., Lith.
74/C2 Venta de Baños, Sp.
121/L6 Vent, Iles du (isls.), FrPol.
121/K6 Vent, Iles sous le (isls.), FrPol.
78/A5 Ventimiglia, It.
59/E5 Ventnor, Eng,UK
166/D5 Ventnor City, NJ,US
63/J3 Ventspils, Lat.
139/E3 Ventuari (riv.), Ven.
164/A2 Ventura (co.), Ca,US
164/A2 Ventura (riv.), Ca,US
164/A2 Ventura (San Buenaventura), Ca,US
80/B1 Venturina, It.
140/C3 Venturosa, Braz.
121/X15 Vénus (pt.), FrPol.
148/C2 Venustiano Carranza, Mex.
135/D2 Vera, Arg.
147/F5 Veracruz, Mex.
147/F5 Veracruz (state), Mex.
141/B4 Veranópolis, Braz.
106/B3 Verāval, India
78/B1 Verbania, It.
78/B2 Vercelli, It.
78/B2 Vercelli (prov.), It.
76/C3 Vercel-Villedieu-le-Camp, Fr.
161/P6 Verchères (co.), Qu,Can
61/D3 Verdal, Nor.
141/B1 Verdão (riv.), Braz.
142/E3 Verde (bay), Arg.
141/H6 Verde (riv.), Braz.
146/D3 Verde (riv.), Mex.
147/E4 Verde (riv.), Mex.
135/E1 Verde (riv.), Par.
124/B5 Verde (cape), Sen.
158/E4 Verde (riv.), Az,US
78/A5 Verde, Capo (cape), It.
74/B1 Verde, Costa (coast), Sp.
140/B4 Verde Grande (riv.), Braz.
112/C2 Verde Island (chan.), Phil.
67/G3 Verden, Ger.
159/J3 Verdigris (riv.), Ks, Ok,US
141/B1 Verdinho (riv.), Braz.
72/F5 Verdon (riv.), Fr.
164/F7 Verdugo (mts.), Ca,US
161/N7 Verdun, Qu,Can
69/E5 Verdun-sur-Meuse, Fr.
132/D2 Vereeniging, SAfr.
79/E1 Verena, Monte (peak), It.
85/M4 Vereshchagino, Rus.
65/M4 Veretskiy Pereval (pass), Ukr.
128/B4 Verga (cape), Gui.
74/D1 Vergara, Sp.
161/F2 Vergennes, Vt,US
81/H2 Vergína (ruins), Gre.
74/B2 Verín, Sp.
70/C6 Veringenstadt, Ger.
141/B1 Veríssimo, Braz.
84/F1 Verkhnetulomskiy (res.), Rus.
89/N3 Verkhoyansk (range), Rus.
67/F5 Verl, Ger.
68/C4 Vermand, Fr.
140/A3 Vermelho (riv.), Braz.
78/A4 Vermenagna (riv.), It.
156/F2 Vermilion, Ab,Can
156/F2 Vermilion (riv.), Ab,Can
159/K2 Vermilion (riv.), Il,US
168/E5 Vermilion, Oh,US
168/E5 Vermilion (riv.), Oh,US
157/K4 Vermillion (range), Mn,US
157/J5 Vermillion, SD,US
159/H2 Vermillion (riv.), SD,US
161/F2 Vermont (state), US
158/E2 Vernal, Ut,US
72/D2 Verneuil-sur-Avre, Fr.
53/R10 Verneuil-sur-Seine, Fr.
132/C3 Verneukpan (salt pan), SAfr.
76/C5 Vernier, Swi.
156/D3 Vernon, BC,Can
68/A5 Vernon, Fr.
168/B2 Vernon, Ct,US
162/D3 Vernon, Tx,US
165/Q15 Vernon Hills, Il,US
166/D1 Vernon Valley/Great Gorge & Action Park, NJ,US
53/R10 Vernouillet, Fr.
69/F5 Verny, Fr.
163/H5 Vero Beach, Fl,US
81/H2 Véroia, Gre.
79/D2 Verona, It.
79/D1 Verona (prov.), It.
167/J8 Verona, NJ,US
76/C6 Verres, Pointe des (peak), Fr.
53/S10 Verrières-le-Buisson, Fr.
78/B3 Versa (riv.), It.
53/S10 Versailles, Fr.
160/C4 Versailles, Ky,US
53/S10 Versailles, Chateau de, Fr.
86/E2 Verskla (riv.), Rus., Ukr.
67/F4 Versmold, Ger.
76/C5 Versoix, Swi.
74/E1 Vert (riv.), Fr.
73/J3 Vertana (peak), It.
77/G4 Vertana, Cima (peak), It.
76/C6 Verte, Aiguille (peak), Fr.
53/T11 Vert-le-Grand, Fr.
53/T11 Vert-le-Petit, Fr.
72/C3 Vertou, Fr.
53/T11 Vert-Saint-Denis, Fr.
69/E2 Verviers, Belg.
59/E5 Verwood, Eng,UK
58/B6 Veryan (bay), Eng,UK
77/E5 Verzasca (riv.), Swi.
77/E5 Verzasca (Gerra), It.
78/A2 Verzel, Punta (peak), It.
69/F2 Vesdre (riv.), Belg.
71/H4 Veselí nad Lužnicí, Czh.
87/G3 Veselyy (res.), Rus.
63/L1 Vesijärvi (lake), Fin.
68/D5 Vesle (riv.), Fr.
76/C2 Vesoul, Fr.
62/B2 Vest-Agder (co.), Nor.
62/D2 Vestby, Nor.
61/E1 Vesterålen (isls.), Nor.
52/E2 Vestfjorden (bay), Nor.
61/E2 Vestfjorden (fjord), Nor.
62/C2 Vestfold (co.), Nor.
62/D4 Vest-Sjælland (co.), Den.
61/E1 Vestvågøya (isl.), Nor.
82/C2 Veszprém, Hun.
82/C2 Veszprém (co.), Hun.
82/E2 Vészto, Hun.
132/D3 Vet (riv.), SAfr.
62/F3 Vetlanda, Swe.
85/K4 Vetluga (riv.), Rus.
80/C1 Vetralla, It.
72/D3 Veude (riv.), Fr.
68/B1 Veurne, Belg.
76/C5 Vevey, Swi.
69/F2 Veybach (riv.), Ger.
76/B5 Veyle (riv.), Fr.
72/D4 Vézère (riv.), Fr.
92/C1 Vezirköprü, Turk.
136/E7 Viacha, Bol.
78/D3 Viadana, It.
140/A1 Viana, Braz.
74/B1 Viana del Bollo, Sp.
74/A2 Viana do Castelo, Port.
74/A2 Viana do Castelo (dist.), Port.
66/C5 Vianen, Neth.
109/C2 Viangchan (Vientiane) (cap.), Laos
74/C4 Viar (riv.), Sp.
78/D5 Viareggio, It.
53/T9 Viarmes, Fr.
72/E4 Viaur (riv.), Fr.
62/C3 Viborg, Den.
62/C3 Viborg (co.), Den.
80/E3 Vibo Valentia, It.
75/G2 Vic, Sp.
74/D4 Vicar, Sp.
144/A2 Vice, Peru
164/F8 Vicente (pt.), Ca,US
146/E4 Vicente Guerrero, Mex.
143/S12 Vicente López, Arg.
79/E1 Vicenza, It.
79/E1 Vicenza (prov.), It.
77/H6 Vicenza (state), It.
138/D3 Vichada (comm.), Col.
138/D3 Vichada (riv.), Col.
84/J4 Vichuga, Rus.
72/E3 Vichy, Fr.
163/F3 Vicksburg, Ms,US
163/F3 Vicksburg Nat'l Mil. Park, Ms,US
80/C1 Vico (lake), It.
140/C3 Viçosa, Braz.
141/D2 Viçosa, Braz.
140/B1 Viçosa do Ceará, Braz.
81/G3 Vicou Gorge Nat'l Park, Gre.
68/C5 Vic-sur-Aisne, Fr.
69/F6 Vic-sur-Seille, Fr.
130/B3 Victoria (lake), Afr.
142/E2 Victoria, Arg.
114/E3 Victoria (riv.), Austl.
119/C3 Victoria (state), Austl.
148/D2 Victoria (peak), Belz.
104/B4 Victoria (peak), Burma
156/C3 Victoria (cap.), BC,Can
152/E1 Victoria (isl.), NW,Can
152/F2 Victoria (str.), NW,Can
161/Q8 Victoria, On,Can
142/B3 Victoria, Chile
105/G4 Victoria (cap.), HK
112/C2 Victoria, Phil.
112/B3 Victoria (peak), Phil.
83/G3 Victoria, Rom.
162/D4 Victoria, Tx,US
131/B3 Victoria (falls), Zam.
131/B3 Victoria Falls, Zim.
113/L Victoria Land (reg.), Ant.
130/B2 Victoria Nile (riv.), Ugan.
112/C3 Victorias, Phil.
161/G2 Victoriaville, Qu,Can
146/E4 Víctor Rosales, Mex.
164/C1 Victorville, Ca,US
133/F3 Vidal (cape), SAfr.
163/H3 Vidalia, Ga,US
163/F4 Vidalia, La,US
141/B3 Videira, Braz.
83/G3 Videle, Rom.
71/G4 Vidhošt (peak), Czh.
82/F4 Vidin, Bul.
106/C3 Vidisha, India
162/E4 Vidor, Tx,US
62/F3 Vidöstern (lake), Swe.
72/E5 Vidourle (riv.), Fr.
72/C3 Vie (riv.), Fr.
71/F4 Viechtach, Ger.
142/E4 Viedma, Arg.
143/J7 Viedma (lake), Arg.
71/H5 Viehberg (peak), Aus.
74/C1 Vieja (mtn.), Sp.
162/B4 Vieja (mts.), Tx,US
144/B2 Viejo (peak), Peru
69/E3 Vielsalm, Belg.
67/H5 Vienenburg, Ger.
166/A6 Vienna, Va,US
160/D4 Vienna, WV,US
65/J4 Vienna (Wien) (cap.), Aus.
72/F4 Vienne, Fr.
72/D3 Vienne (riv.), Fr.
109/C2 Vientiane (Viangchan) (cap.), Laos
150/E3 Vieques (isl.), PR
69/D6 Viere (riv.), Fr.
66/D5 Vierlingsbeek, Neth.
70/B3 Viernheim, Ger.
69/E4 Vierre (riv.), Fr.
66/D6 Viersen, Ger.
77/E3 Vierwaldstättersee (Lucerne) (lake), Swi.
72/E3 Vierzon, Fr.
80/E2 Vieste, It.
109/D2 Vietnam
109/D1 Viet Tri, Viet.
68/C3 Vieux-Condé, Fr.
150/F4 Vieux Fort, StL.
54/B5 Viewpark, Sc,UK
76/C5 Vieze (riv.), Swi.
112/D2 Viga, Phil.
112/C1 Vigan, Phil.
78/B2 Vigevano, It.
137/J4 Vigia, Braz.
78/B1 Vigliano Biellese, It.
80/C2 Viglio (peak), It.
72/C5 Vignemale (mtn.), Fr.
53/T10 Vigneux-sur-Seine, Fr.
79/E4 Vignola, It.
74/A1 Vigo, Sp.
79/E2 Vigonza, It.
69/F5 Vigy, Fr.
95/K2 Vihāri, Pak.
63/L1 Vihti, Fin.
61/H3 Viitasaari, Fin.
106/D4 Vijayawada, India
81/F2 Vijosë (riv.), Alb.
62/C2 Vikersund, Nor.
83/F5 Vikhren (peak), Bul.
156/F2 Viking, Ab,Can
108/F4 Vikramasingapuram, India
120/F6 Vila (cap.), Van.
75/G2 Viladecans, Sp.
75/V14 Vila de Porto Santo, Madr.,Port.
131/D3 Vila de Sena, Moz.
74/A2 Vila do Conde, Port.
75/T13 Vila do Porto, Azor,Port.
75/K7 Vilafranca del Penedès, Sp.
74/A3 Vila Franca de Xira, Port.
75/T13 Vila Franca do Campo, Azor.,Port.
72/B3 Vilaine (riv.), Fr.
133/H7 Vilanandro (cape), Madg.
131/D4 Vilanculos, Moz.
74/A2 Vila Nova de Gaia, Port.
75/F2 Vilanova i la Geltrù, Sp.
75/K7 Vilanova i la Geltru, Sp.
74/B2 Vila Real, Port.
74/B2 Vila Real (dist.), Port.
74/B4 Vila Real de Santo António, Port.
141/D2 Vila Velha Argolas, Braz.
83/F3 Vîlcea (co.), Rom.
61/F2 Vilhelmina, Swe.
136/F6 Vilhena, Braz.
63/M4 Viliya (riv.), Bela.
63/L2 Viljandi, Est.
89/K2 Vil'kitsogo (str.), Rus.
142/G9 Villa Alemana, Chile
150/D3 Villa Altagracia, DRep.
135/D2 Villa Ángela, Arg.
112/D3 Villaba, Phil.
74/E1 Villaba, Sp.
74/B1 Villablino, Sp.
138/D2 Villa Bruzual, Ven.
142/E3 Villa Cañas, Arg.
74/D3 Villacañas, Sp.
78/D1 Villa Carcina, It.
135/D3 Villa Carlos Paz, Arg.
74/D3 Villacarrillo, Sp.
73/K3 Villach, Aus.
142/E2 Villa Constitución, Arg.
146/C3 Villa Constitución, Mex.
74/A1 Villa de Cruces, Sp.
139/E2 Villa de Cura, Ven.
74/C4 Villa del Río, Sp.
135/C3 Villa Dolores, Arg.
77/E5 Villadossola, It.
148/C2 Villa Flores, Mex.
74/B3 Villafranca de los Barros, Sp.
79/D2 Villafranca di Verona, It.
74/A1 Villagarcía, Sp.
162/E4 Village Mills, Tx,US
143/F3 Villa Gesell, Arg.
142/F1 Villaguay, Arg.
147/G5 Villahermosa, Mex.
149/J2 Villa Jaragua, DRep.
75/E3 Villajoyosa, Sp.
74/B1 Villalba, Sp.
74/B2 Villalcampo (res.), Sp.
142/E2 Villa María, Arg.
74/C4 Villamartín, Sp.
136/F8 Villa Montes, Bol.
77/H4 Villandro, Monte (peak), It.
138/C2 Villanueva, Col.
148/D3 Villa Nueva, Guat.
148/E3 Villanueva, Hon.
148/E3 Villanueva, Nic.
74/A1 Villanueva de Arosa, Sp.
74/C3 Villanueva de Córdoba, Sp.
74/D3 Villanueva del Arzobispo, Sp.
74/C3 Villanueva de la Serena, Sp.
74/D3 Villanueva de los Infantes, Sp.
147/Q10 Villa Obregon, Mex.
79/G1 Villa Opicina, It.
164/C3 Villa Park, Ca,US
165/Q16 Villa Park, Il,US
142/D3 Villa Regina, Arg.
138/C3 Villa Rosario, Col.
75/E3 Villarreal de los Infantes, Sp.
142/B3 Villarrica, Chile
142/B3 Villarrica (lake), Chile
142/C3 Villarrica (vol.), Chile
135/E2 Villarrica, Par.
142/C3 Villarrica Nat'l Park, Chile
74/D3 Villarrobledo, Sp.
74/D3 Villarrubia de los Ojos, Sp.
166/D5 Villas, NJ,US
149/E3 Villa Sandino, Nic.
142/F2 Villa San José, Arg.
78/C1 Villasanta, It.
136/F7 Villa Serrano, Bol.
135/C2 Villa Unión, Arg.
138/C3 Villavicencio, Col.
74/C1 Villaviciosa, Sp.
75/N9 Villaviciosa de Odon, Sp.
136/E8 Villazón, Bol.
53/T10 Villecresnes, Fr.
53/S10 Ville-d'Avray, Fr.
72/E4 Villefranche-de-Rouergue, Fr.
72/F4 Villefranche-sur-Saône, Fr.
53/T10 Villejuif, Fr.
53/T10 Villemomble, Fr.
75/E3 Villena, Sp.
68/C2 Villeneuve-d'Ascq, Fr.
53/S10 Villeneuve-la-Garenne, Fr.
53/U10 Villeneuve-le-Comte, Fr.
53/T10 Villeneuve-le-Roi, Fr.
72/F5 Villeneuve-lès-Avignon, Fr.
68/B6 Villeneuve-Saint-Georges, Fr.
72/D4 Villeneuve-sur-Lot, Fr.
72/D5 Villeneuve-Tolosane, Fr.
53/R10 Villennes-sur-Seine, Fr.
53/T10 Villeparisis, Fr.
53/T10 Villepinte, Fr.
162/E4 Ville Platte, La,US
53/S10 Villepreux, Fr.
68/B4 Villers-Bocage, Fr.
68/C5 Villers-Cotterêts, Fr.
69/F6 Villers-lès-Nancy, Fr.
68/C3 Villers-Outreaux, Fr.
69/E5 Villerupt, Fr.
76/A6 Villeurbanne, Fr.
53/T10 Villevaudé, Fr.
53/T10 Villiers-le-Bel, Fr.
53/T10 Villiers-sur-Marne, Fr.
70/B6 Villingen-Schwenningen, Ger.
70/B2 Villmar, Ger.
108/G3 Villupuram, India
63/L4 Vilnius (cap.), Lith.
61/H3 Vilppula, Fin.
71/E4 Vils (riv.), Ger.
71/F6 Vilsbiburg, Ger.
71/G5 Vilshofen, Ger.
68/D2 Vilvoorde, Belg.
89/M3 Vilyuy (range), Rus.
89/N3 Vilyuy (riv.), Rus.
78/C1 Vimercate, It.
74/B1 Vimianzo, Sp.
62/F3 Vimmerby, Swe.
78/C2 Vimodrone, It.
71/G4 Vimperk, Czh.
68/B3 Vimy, Fr.
124/H6 Vina (riv.), Camr.
142/C2 Viña del Mar, Chile
73/G5 Vinaigre (mtn.), Fr.
75/F2 Vinaroz, Sp.
113/H Vincennes (bay), Ant.
53/T10 Vincennes, Fr.
53/U10 Vincennes (res.), Fr.
160/C4 Vincennes, In,US
164/B1 Vincent, Ca,US
138/B5 Vinces, Ecu.
61/F2 Vindeln, Swe.
161/R9 Vineland, On,Can
166/C5 Vineland, NJ,US
161/R9 Vineland Station, On,Can
168/D3 Vineyard (sound), Ma,US
109/D2 Vinh, Viet.
141/G8 Vinhedo, Braz.
109/D4 Vinh Long, Viet.
109/D2 Vinh Moc, Tunnels of, Viet.
109/D4 Vinh Quoi, Viet.
109/E3 Vinh Thanh, Viet.
109/D1 Vinh Yen, Viet.
82/F5 Vinica, Macd.
159/J3 Vinita, Ok,US
82/F3 Vînju Mare, Rom.
82/D3 Vinkovci, Cro.
86/D2 Vinnitsa, Ukr.
86/D2 Vinnitsa Obl., Ukr.
86/B2 Vinogradov, Ukr.
78/A3 Vinovo, It.
50/E9 Vinson (peak), Ant.
112/C1 Vintar, Phil.
53/R9 Viosne (riv.), Fr.
79/G1 Vipava, Slov.
112/D2 Virac, Phil.
92/D2 Viranşehir, Turk.
106/B4 Virār, India
157/H3 Virden, Mb,Can
72/C2 Vire, Fr.
126/B4 Virei, Ang.
62/F2 Viren (lake), Swe.
140/B5 Virgem da Lapa, Braz.
135/C7 Virgenes (cape), Arg.
161/R9 Virgil, On,Can
150/E3 Virgin (isls.), UK, US
158/D3 Virgin (riv.), US
150/E3 Virgin Gorda (isl.), BVI
160/E5 Virginia (state), US
157/K4 Virginia, Mn,US
160/F4 Virginia Beach, Va,US
158/C3 Virginia City, Nv,US
53/M7 Virginia Water, Eng,UK
150/E3 Virgin Islands Nat'l Park, USVI
109/D3 Virochey, Camb.
53/S10 Viroflay, Fr.
68/D3 Viroin (riv.), Belg.
160/B3 Viroqua, Wi,US
82/C3 Virovitica, Cro.
69/E4 Virton, Belg.
144/B3 Virú, Peru
108/F4 Virudunagar, India
130/A3 Virunga, Zaire
130/A3 Virunga Nat'l Park, Zaire
53/T10 Viry-Châtillon, Fr.
80/D1 Vis (isl.), Cro.
106/D4 Visākhapatnam, India
158/C3 Visalia, Ca,US
112/C3 Visayan (sea), Phil.
67/F3 Visbek, Ger.
62/H3 Visby, Swe.
141/D2 Visconde do Rio Branco, Braz.
153/R7 Viscount Melville (sound), NW,Can
69/E2 Visé, Belg.
82/D4 Višegrad, Bosn.
74/B2 Viseu, Port.
74/B2 Viseu (dist.), Port.
83/G2 Vişeu de Sus, Rom.
85/L3 Vishera (riv.), Rus.
85/N3 Vishera (riv.), Rus.
132/B4 Vishoek, SAfr.
106/B3 Visnagar, India
82/D3 Višnjevac, Cro.
82/D4 Visoko, Bosn.
76/D5 Visp, Swi.
67/G3 Visselhövede, Ger.
164/C4 Vista, Ca,US
81/J2 Vistonis (lake), Gre.
86/B2 Vistula (riv.), Pol.
65/K2 Vistula (Wisł'a) (riv.), Pol.
83/G4 Vit (riv.), Bul.
157/J3 Vita, Mb,Can
73/J5 Vitalba (peak), It.
78/D6 Vitalba, Monte (peak), It.
63/P4 Vitebsk, Bela.
63/N4 Vitebsk Obl., Bela.
80/C1 Viterbo, It.
109/D4 Vi Thanh, Viet.
120/G6 Viti Levu (isl.), Fiji
96/G1 Vitim (plat.), Rus.
96/G1 Vitim (riv.), Rus.
71/H5 Vítkuv Kamen (peak), Czh.
141/D2 Vitória, Braz.
74/D1 Vitoria, Sp.
140/B4 Vitória da Conquista, Braz.
140/D3 Vitória de Santo Antão, Braz.
140/A1 Vitória do Mearim, Braz.
140/A2 Vitorino Freire, Braz.
83/F4 Vitosha Nat'l Park, Bul.
72/C2 Vitré, Fr.
72/F5 Vitrolles, Fr.
68/D6 Vitry-le-François, Fr.
53/T10 Vitry-sur-Seine, Fr.
130/A3 Vitshumbi, Zaire
76/B1 Vittel, Fr.
80/D4 Vittoria, It.
73/K4 Vittorio Veneto, It.
72/F4 Vivarais (mts.), Fr.
74/B1 Vivero, Sp.
78/A2 Viverone (lake), It.
146/B3 Vizcaíno, Sierra de (mts.), Mex.
83/H5 Vize, Turk.
85/K2 Vizhas (riv.), Rus.
106/D4 Vizianagaram, India
79/G2 Vižinada, Cro.
66/B5 Vlaardingen, Neth.
82/F2 Vlădeasa (peak), Rom.
53/H4 Vladikavkaz, Rus.
53/H3 Vladimir, Rus.
84/J5 Vladimir Obl., Rus.
86/C2 Vladimir-Volynskiy, Ukr.
97/L3 Vladivostok, Rus.
67/E2 Vlagtwedde, Neth.
83/G2 Vlăhiţa, Rom.
82/E4 Vlajna (peak), Yugo.
82/D3 Vlasenica, Bosn.
65/H4 Vlašim, Czh.
82/F4 Vlasotince, Yugo.
71/G3 Vlastec (hill), Czh.
66/B2 Vlieland (isl.), Neth.
66/C2 Vliestroom (chan.), Neth.
66/C5 Vlijmen, Neth.
66/A6 Vlissingen, Neth.
81/F2 Vlorë, Alb.
67/F4 Vlotho, Ger.
71/H2 Vltava (riv.), Czh.
71/G6 Vöcklabruck, Aus.
84/H3 Vodlozero (lake), Rus.
71/H4 Vodňany, Czh.
79/G3 Vodnjan, Cro.
66/D5 Voerde, Ger.
70/C1 Vogelsberg (mts.), Ger.
78/C3 Voghera, It.
77/E5 Vogorno, Pizzo di (peak), Swi.
82/D4 Vogošća, Bosn.
71/E2 Vogtland (reg.), Ger.
121/U12 Voh, NCal.
71/F3 Vohenstrauss, Ger.
133/H9 Vohimena (cape), Madg.
133/G7 Vohipeno, Madg.
77/G1 Vöhringen, Ger.
130/C3 Voi, Kenya
165/C3 Voight (cr.), Wa,US
54/B4 Voil, Loch (lake), Sc,UK
72/F4 Voiron, Fr.
72/D2 Voise (riv.), Fr.
153/K3 Voisey (bay), Nf,Can
68/B5 Voisne (riv.), Fr.
82/D5 Vojosë (riv.), Alb.
82/D3 Vojvodina (aut. prov.), Yugo.
69/F5 Völklingen, Ger.
79/E3 Volano, Po di (riv.), It.
149/F4 Volcán Barú Nat'l Park, Pan.
120/C2 Volcano (isls.), Japan
149/E4 Volcán Poás Nat'l Park, CR
130/A3 Volcans Nat'l Park, Rwa.
63/Q1 Volchiy Nos (cape), Rus.
61/C3 Volda, Nor.
66/C4 Volendam, Neth.
53/H4 Volga (riv.), Rus.
84/H3 Volga-Baltic Wtwy., Rus.
53/H4 Volgodonsk, Rus.
87/H2 Volgograd, Rus.
87/H2 Volgograd (res.), Rus.
87/G2 Volgograd Obl., Rus.
70/D3 Volkach, Ger.
70/D3 Volkach (riv.), Ger.
66/B5 Volkerakdam (dam), Neth.
73/L3 Völkermarkt, Aus.
77/E3 Volketswil, Swi.
63/Q2 Volkhov, Rus.
84/F4 Volkhov (riv.), Rus.
64/D4 Völklingen, Ger.
67/G6 Volkmarsen, Ger.
65/N2 Volkovysk, Bela.
133/E2 Volksrust, SAfr.
69/G5 Volmunster, Fr.
84/H4 Vologda, Rus.
84/J3 Vologda Obl., Rus.
76/D5 Vologne (riv.), Fr.
81/H3 Vólos, Gre.
81/H3 Vólos (gulf), Gre.
78/A2 Volpiano, It.
53/H3 Vol'sk, Rus.
129/E4 Volta (lake), Gha.
129/F5 Volta (reg.), Gha.
129/F5 Volta (riv.), Gha.
141/J7 Volta Redonda, Braz.
79/D6 Volterra, It.
80/D2 Volturno (riv.), It.
123/M13 Volubilis (ruins), Mor.
81/H2 Vólvi (lake), Gre.
71/G4 Volyňka (riv.), Czh.
85/L5 Volzhsk, Rus.
53/H4 Volzhskiy, Rus.
151/H3 Von Frank (mtn.), Ak,US
72/D3 Vonne (riv.), Fr.
66/B4 Voorburg, Neth.
66/B5 Voorne (isl.), Neth.
66/B4 Voorschoten, Neth.
66/D4 Voorst, Neth.
77/F4 Vorab (peak), Swi.
77/F3 Vorarlberg (prov.), Aus.
70/C4 Vorbach (riv.), Ger.
71/G7 Vorchdorf, Aus.
66/D4 Vorden, Neth.
77/E4 Vorderrhein (riv.), Swi.
72/F4 Voreppe, Fr.
53/K2 Vorkuta, Rus.
63/K2 Vormsi (isl.), Est.
87/G1 Vorona (riv.), Rus.
53/G3 Voronezh, Rus.
86/F1 Voronezh (riv.), Rus.
87/G2 Voronezh Obl., Rus.
63/Q1 Voronov (cape), Rus.
84/G1 Voron'ya (riv.), Rus.
69/E1 Vorst, Belg.
63/L2 Vörts (lake), Est.
63/M3 Võru, Est.
76/C1 Vosges (dept.), Fr.
76/C2 Vosges (mts.), Fr.
84/H5 Voskresensk, Rus.
62/B1 Voss, Nor.
113/V Vostock (cape), Ant.
113/H Vostok, Ant.
121/K6 Vostok (isl.), Kiri.
53/J3 Votkinsk, Rus.
85/M4 Votkinsk (res.), Rus.
141/C2 Votorantim, Braz.
141/B2 Votuporanga, Braz.
74/B2 Vouga (riv.), Port.
76/B5 Vouglans (lake), Fr.
76/B5 Vouglans, Barrage de (dam), Fr.
81/H5 Voúxa, Ákra (cape), Gre.
157/K3 Voyageurs Nat'l Park, Mn,US
113/J Voyeykov Ice Shelf, Ant.
85/M3 Voy-Vozh, Rus.
84/H3 Vozhe (lake), Rus.
86/D3 Voznesensk, Ukr.
76/B1 Vraine (riv.), Fr.
83/H3 Vrancea (co.), Rom.
90/S2 Vrangelya (isl.), Rus.
82/E4 Vranje, Yugo.
65/L4 Vranov nad Teplou, Slvk.
83/F4 Vratsa, Bul.
82/C3 Vrbas (riv.), Bosn.
82/D3 Vrbas, Yugo.
71/H4 Vrchy (peak), Czh.
132/E2 Vrede, SAfr.
66/D4 Vreden, Ger.
132/B4 Vredenburg, SAfr.
73/L4 Vrhnika, Slov.
108/G3 Vriddhāchalam, India
66/D2 Vries, Neth.
66/D4 Vriezenveen, Neth.
64/B5 Vrin (riv.), Fr.
106/C2 Vrindāban, India
82/E4 Vrnjačka Banja, Yugo.
82/E3 Vršac, Yugo.
79/G2 Vrsar, Cro.
132/D2 Vryburg, SAfr.
133/E2 Vryheid, SAfr.
65/K4 Vsetín, Czh.
151/E5 Vsevidof (mtn.), Ak,US
63/P1 Vsevolozhsk, Rus.
65/K4 Vtáčnik (peak), Slvk.
82/E4 Vučitrn, Yugo.
66/C5 Vught, Neth.
82/D3 Vukovar, Cro.
156/E3 Vulcan, Ab,Can
83/F3 Vulcan, Rom.
80/D3 Vulcano (isl.), It.
83/F4 Vŭlchedrŭm, Bul.
80/B1 Vulci (ruins), It.
109/D2 Vu Liet, Viet.
109/D4 Vung Tau, Viet.
120/G7 Vunisea, Fiji
63/M1 Vuohijärvi (lake), Fin.
63/N1 Vuoksa (lake), Rus.
84/E1 Vuotso, Fin.
130/C3 Vuria (peak), Kenya
83/F4 Vŭrshets, Bul.
130/B5 Vwawa, Tanz.
106/B3 Vyāra, India
53/H3 Vyatka, Rus.
85/L4 Vyatka (riv.), Rus.
85/L4 Vyatka Obl., Rus.
85/L4 Vyatskiye Polyany, Rus.
97/L2 Vyazemskiy, Rus.
84/G5 Vyaz'ma, Rus.
63/N1 Vyborg, Rus.
63/N1 Vyborg (bay), Rus.
85/K3 Vychegda (riv.), Rus.
65/H3 Východočeský (reg.), Czh.
65/L4 Východoslovenský (reg.), Slvk.
84/G3 Vygozero (lake), Rus.
65/M4 Vyhorlat (peak), Slvk.
84/J5 Vyksa, Rus.
85/L3 Vym' (riv.), Rus.
58/C1 Vyrnwy (riv.), Wal,UK
84/G4 Vyshniy Volochek, Rus.
65/J4 Vyškov, Czh.

W

129/E4 Wa, Gha.
66/C5 Waal (riv.), Neth.
66/C6 Waalre, Neth.
66/C5 Waalwijk, Neth.
68/C1 Waarschoot, Belg.
156/E2 Wabasca, Ab,Can
152/E3 Wabasca (riv.), Ab,Can
160/C4 Wabash (riv.), Il, In,US
160/C3 Wabash, In,US
67/G6 Wabern, Ger.
157/K3 Wabigoon (lake), On,Can
157/J2 Wabowden, Mb,Can
65/K2 Wąbrzeźno, Pol.
103/D4 Wabu (lake), China
101/G6 Wabu, SKor.
99/L9 Wachi, Japan
68/C1 Wachtebeke, Belg.
66/D6 Wachtendonk, Ger.
70/C2 Wächtersbach, Ger.
168/C1 Wachusett (res.), Ma,US
162/D4 Waco, Tx,US
162/D2 Waconda (lake), Ks,US
157/K4 Waconia, Mn,US
99/J7 Wada, Japan
119/D3 Wadbilliga Nat'l Park, Austl.
124/J2 Waddān, Libya

66/C2 Waddenzee (sound), Neth.
156/B3 Waddington (mtn.), BC,Can
57/F4 Waddington, Eng,UK
57/H5 Waddington, Eng,UK
66/B4 Waddinxveen, Neth.
118/D4 Waddy (pt.), Austl.
58/B5 Wadebridge, Eng,UK
157/H3 Wadena, Sk,Can
157/K4 Wadena, Mn,US
77/E3 Wädenswil, Swi.
69/F4 Wadern, Ger.
67/F5 Wadersloh, Ger.
69/F5 Wadgassen, Ger.
59/G4 Wadhurst, Eng,UK
91/D4 Wādī As Sīr, Jor.
127/B4 Wādī Ḥalfā', Sudan
166/D4 Wading (riv.), NJ,US
125/M5 Wad Medanī, Sudan
65/K4 Wadowice, Pol.
168/F5 Wadsworth, Oh,US
101/E5 Waegwan, SKor.
101/B3 Wafangdian, China
130/B2 Wagagai (peak), Ugan.
67/F3 Wagenfeld-Hasslingen, Ger.
66/C5 Wageningen, Neth.
152/G2 Wager (bay), NW,Can
119/C2 Wagga Wagga, Austl.
70/B4 Waghäusel, Ger.
71/F7 Waginger See (lake), Ger.
77/E3 Wägitalersee (lake), Swi.
140/B4 Wagner, Braz.
65/J2 Wągrowiec, Pol.
95/K2 Wāh, Pak.
111/G4 Wahai, Indo.
127/B4 Wāḥat Salīmah (well), Sudan
154/V12 Wahiawa, Hi,US
159/H2 Wahoo, Ne,US
157/J4 Wahpeton, ND,US
158/D3 Wah Wah (range), Ut,US
106/B4 Wai, India
154/V13 Waianae, Hi,US
103/D2 Waibamiao, China
73/L3 Waidhofen an der Ybbs, Aus.
111/H3 Waigeo (isl.), Indo.
111/E5 Waikabubak, Indo.
115/R11 Waikari, NZ
154/T10 Wailuku, Hi,US
115/R11 Waimate, NZ
154/V12 Waimea (falls), Hi,US
161/R10 Wainfleet, On,Can
57/J5 Wainfleet All Saints, Eng,UK
106/C3 Waingangā (riv.), India
111/F5 Waingapu, Indo.
139/G2 Waini (riv.), Guy.
156/F2 Wainwright, Ab,Can
154/V13 Waipahu, Hi,US
154/U10 Waipio, Hi,US
115/S11 Waipukurau, NZ
115/S10 Wairoa, NZ
115/R10 Waitara, NZ
115/R10 Waitemata, NZ
121/Z17 Waiyevu, Fiji
99/E2 Wajima, Japan
130/D2 Wajir, Kenya
111/G4 Waka (cape), Indo.
98/D3 Wakasa, Japan
98/D3 Wakasa (bay), Japan
157/G2 Wakaw, Sk,Can
98/D3 Wakayama, Japan
98/D4 Wakayama (pref.), Japan
120/F3 Wake (isl.), PacUS
162/D2 Wakeeney, Ks,US
57/G4 Wakefield, Eng,UK
160/B2 Wakefield, Mi,US
168/C3 Wakefield-Peacedale, RI,US
104/B5 Wakema, Burma
98/D3 Waki, Japan
100/B1 Wakkanai, Japan
99/H7 Wakō, Japan
100/B4 Wakuya, Japan
160/D1 Wakwayowkastic (riv.), On,Can
130/B4 Wala (riv.), Tanz.
83/G3 Walachia (range), Rom.
83/G3 Walachia (reg.), Rom.
116/D2 Walagunya Abor. Land, Austl.
131/C2 Walamba, Zam.
65/J3 Wałbrzych, Pol.
65/J3 Wałbrzych (prov.), Pol.
59/E4 Walbury (hill), Eng,UK
77/H2 Walchensee (lake), Ger.
66/A5 Walcheren (isl.), Neth.
68/D3 Walcourt, Belg.
65/J2 Wałcz, Pol.
77/E3 Wald, Swi.
71/H6 Waldaist (riv.), Aus.
69/G2 Waldbröl, Ger.
70/B5 Waldbronn, Ger.
67/G6 Waldeck, Ger.
159/F2 Walden, Co,US
70/C5 Waldenbuch, Ger.
156/G2 Waldheim, Sk,Can
70/A6 Waldkirch, Ger.
71/F4 Waldmünchen, Ger.
71/F3 Waldnaab (riv.), Ger.
71/F3 Waldsassen, Ger.
77/E2 Waldshut-Tiengen, Ger.
70/C5 Waldstetten, Ger.
73/L2 Waldviertel (reg.), Aus.
167/J7 Waldwick, NJ,US
111/F4 Walea (str.), Indo.
111/F4 Waleabahi (isl.), Indo.
77/F3 Walensee (lake), Swi.
153/H2 Wales (isl.), NW,Can
55/J10 Wales, UK
168/G6 Walford (Bessemer), Pa,US
113/T Walgreen (coast), Ant.
71/F4 Walhalla, Ger.
157/J3 Walhalla, ND,US
163/H3 Walhalla, SC,US
168/E7 Walhonding (riv.), Oh,US
126/E1 Walikale, Zaire
132/L11 Walker (bay), SAfr.
158/C3 Walker (lake), Nv,US
158/C3 Walker (riv.), Nv,US
54/C5 Walkerburn, Sc,UK
131/D2 Walkers Ferry, Malw.
160/D2 Walkerton, On,Can
166/D1 Walkill (riv.), NJ, NY,US
156/E4 Wallace, Id,US
165/H6 Wallaceburg, On,Can
116/D1 Wallal Downs, Austl.
57/E5 Wallasey, Eng,UK
156/D4 Walla Walla, Wa,US
70/B4 Walldorf, Ger.
70/C3 Walldürn, Ger.
165/F6 Walled (lake), Mi,US
101/G7 Walled City, SKor.
165/F6 Walled Lake, Mi,US
67/F4 Wallenhorst, Ger.
68/C3 Wallers, Fr.
71/G7 Wallersee (lake), Aus.
59/E3 Wallingford, Eng,UK
168/B3 Wallingford, Ct,US
167/J8 Wallington, NJ,US
121/H6 Wallis (isls.), Wall.
120/G6 Wallis & Futuna (terr.), Fr.
77/E3 Wallisellen, Swi.
156/D4 Wallowa (mts.), Or,US
55/P12 Walls, Sc,UK
57/G2 Wallsend, Eng,UK
57/E3 Walney, Isle of (isl.), Eng,UK
164/C2 Walnut, Ca,US
158/E4 Walnut Canyon Nat'l Mon., Az,US
165/K11 Walnut Creek, Ca,US
164/F8 Walnut Park, Ca,US
163/F2 Walnut Ridge, Ar,US
165/G6 Walpole I. Ind. Res., On,Can
116/C5 Walpole-Nornalup Nat'l Park, Austl.
151/F4 Walrus (isls.), Ak,US
58/E1 Walsall, Eng,UK
153/K2 Walsingham (cape), NW,Can
59/G1 Walsingham, Eng,UK
67/G3 Walsrode, Ger.
77/G2 Waltenhofen, Ger.
163/H3 Walterboro, SC,US
166/C1 Walter, F. E. (res.), Pa,US
163/G4 Walter F. George (res.), Al, Ga,US
168/C1 Waltham, Ma,US
53/P6 Waltham Abbey, Eng,UK
53/N7 Waltham Forest (bor.), Eng,UK
59/G3 Waltham Holy Cross, Eng,UK
57/F4 Walton-le-Dale, Eng,UK
59/F4 Walton on Thames, Eng,UK
59/H3 Walton on the Naze, Eng,UK
67/E5 Waltrop, Ger.
126/B5 Walvis Bay, Namb.
165/P14 Walworth (co.), Wi,US
116/C4 Walyahmoning (peak), Austl.
116/L6 Walyunga Nat'l Park, Austl.
126/C3 Wama, Ang.
130/C2 Wamba, Kenya
125/L7 Wamba, Zaire
66/C5 Wamel, Neth.
130/C4 Wami (riv.), Tanz.
57/E2 Wampool (riv.), Eng,UK
156/G5 Wamsutter, Wy,US
103/D5 Wan (riv.), China
115/Q11 Wanaka, NZ
167/D1 Wanaque, NJ,US
167/D1 Wanaque (res.), NJ,US
97/L2 Wanda (mts.), China
130/A2 Wandi, Ugan.
104/C3 Wanding, China
53/N7 Wandsworth (bor.), Eng,UK
109/B2 Wang (riv.), Thai.
115/S10 Wanganui, NZ
119/C3 Wangaratta, Austl.
103/C3 Wangdu, China
77/F2 Wangen, Ger.
67/E1 Wangerooge (isl.), Ger.
111/F6 Wanggamet (peak), Indo.
101/A2 Wanghai Shan (peak), China
109/B4 Wang Hip (peak), Thai.
103/D5 Wangjiang, China
97/K2 Wangkui, China
104/E3 Wangmo, China
103/E5 Wangpan (bay), China
97/K3 Wangqing, China
111/F4 Wani (peak), Indo.
139/H3 Wanica (dist.), Sur.
77/H2 Wank (peak), Ger.
131/B3 Wankie (Hwange) Nat'l Park, Zim.
107/K4 Wanning, China
99/M9 Wanouchi, Japan
103/C2 Wanquan, China
102/D5 Wanquan (lake), China
105/F5 Wanquan (riv.), China
103/B4 Wanrong, China
57/G1 Wansbeck (riv.), Eng,UK
53/P7 Wanstead, Eng,UK
59/E3 Wantage, Eng,UK
167/L9 Wantagh, NY,US
105/F2 Wanxian, China
69/E2 Wanze, Belg.
112/D4 Wao, Phil.
160/C3 Wapakoneta, Oh,US
157/G2 Wapawekka (lake), Sk,Can
156/D2 Wapiti (riv.), Ab, BC,Can
111/J4 Wapoga (riv.), Indo.
159/K3 Wappapello (lake), Mo,US
157/K5 Wapsipinicon (riv.), Ia,US
166/B1 Wapwallopen (cr.), Pa,US
99/H7 Warabi, Japan
106/C4 Warangal, India
59/F2 Warboys, Eng,UK
67/G6 Warburg, Ger.
117/H3 Warburton (cr.), Austl.
108/B2 Warburton, Pak.
117/E3 Warburton (Central Australia) Abor. Rsv., Austl.
117/E3 Warburton Range Abor. Rsv., Austl.
69/F3 Warche (riv.), Belg.
115/R11 Ward, NZ
59/G4 Warden (pt.), Eng,UK
67/F2 Wardenburg, Ger.
106/C3 Wardha, India
57/F3 Ward's Stone (mtn.), Eng,UK
59/F3 Ware, Eng,UK
168/B1 Ware, Ma,US
168/B1 Ware (riv.), Ma,US
68/C2 Waregem, Belg.
58/D5 Wareham, Eng,UK
168/D2 Wareham, Ma,US
69/E2 Waremme, Belg.
64/G2 Waren, Ger.
67/E5 Warendorf, Ger.
59/F3 Wargrave, Eng,UK
109/D3 Warin Chamrap, Thai.
56/B3 Waringstown, NI,UK
57/F1 Wark, Eng,UK
65/L3 Warka, Pol.
115/R10 Warkworth, NZ
58/D2 Warley, Eng,UK
53/N8 Warlingham, Eng,UK
157/G2 Warman, Sk,Can
132/E2 Warmbad, SAfr.
67/G6 Warmebach (riv.), Ger.
67/H5 Warme Bode (riv.), Ger.
65/K1 Warmia (reg.), Pol.
58/D4 Warminster, Eng,UK
166/C3 Warminster, Pa,US
158/B2 Warner (mts.), Ca,US
163/H3 Warner Robins, Ga,US
64/G2 Warnow (riv.), Ger.
66/D4 Warnsveld, Neth.
117/G2 Warrabri Abor. Land, Austl.
117/G2 Warramunga Abor. Land, Austl.
117/H3 Warrandirinna (lake), Austl.
119/G5 Warrandyte, Austl.
118/B4 Warrego (range), Austl.
115/H5 Warrego (riv.), Austl.
116/C5 Warren (riv.), Austl.
151/M2 Warren (pt.), NW,Can
162/E3 Warren, Ar,US
165/F6 Warren, Mi,US
157/J3 Warren, Mn,US
166/D2 Warren, NJ,US
166/C1 Warren (co.), NJ,US
168/G5 Warren, Oh,US
160/E3 Warren, Pa,US
168/C2 Warren, RI,US
56/B3 Warrenpoint, NI,UK
159/J3 Warrensburg, Mo,US
168/F5 Warrensville Heights, Oh,US
132/D3 Warrenton, SAfr.
160/E4 Warrenton, Va,US
165/P16 Warrenville, Il,US
57/F5 Warrington, Eng,UK
163/G4 Warrington, Fl,US
119/B3 Warrnambool, Austl.
157/K3 Warroad, Mn,US
119/D1 Warrumbungle Nat'l Park, Austl.
160/C3 Warsaw, In,US
159/J3 Warsaw, Mo,US
65/L3 Warsawa (prov.), Pol.
65/L2 Warsaw (Warszawa) (cap.), Pol.
65/H5 Warscheneck (peak), Aus.
57/G5 Warslow, Eng,UK
57/G5 Warsop, Eng,UK
67/F6 Warstein, Ger.
65/L2 Warszawa (Warsaw) (cap.), Pol.
65/H2 Warta (riv.), Pol.
118/D5 Warwick, Austl.
59/E2 Warwick, Eng,UK
168/C2 Warwick, RI,US
59/E2 Warwickshire (co.), Eng,UK
158/E2 Wasatch (range), Ut,US
158/C4 Wasco, Ca,US
157/K4 Waseca, Mn,US
152/F1 Washburn (lake), NW,Can
57/G4 Washburn (riv.), Eng,UK
157/M3 Washi (lake), On,Can
57/H5 Washingborough, Eng,UK
57/G2 Washington, Eng,UK
156/C4 Washington (state), US
166/A6 Washington (cap.), DC,US
160/B3 Washington, Il,US
160/C4 Washington, In,US
163/J3 Washington, NC,US
161/G2 Washington (mtn.), NH,US
166/D2 Washington, NJ,US
160/D3 Washington, Pa,US
168/G7 Washington (co.), Pa,US
168/C2 Washington (co.), RI,US
165/C2 Washington (lake), Wa,US
160/C2 Washington (isl.), Wi,US
160/D4 Washington Court House, Oh,US
121/K4 Washington (Teraina) (atoll), Kiri.
159/H4 Washita (riv.), Ok, Tx,US
165/E7 Washtenaw (co.), Mi,US
59/G1 Wash, The (bay), Eng,UK
65/M2 Wasilków, Pol.
93/F3 Wāsiṭ (gov.), Iraq
160/E1 Waskaganish (Rupert House), Qu,Can
151/G4 Waskey (mtn.), Ak,US
66/B4 Wassenaar, Neth.
66/D6 Wassenberg, Ger.
71/F6 Wasserburg am Inn, Ger.
70/C2 Wasserkuppe (peak), Ger.
154/C4 Wassuk (range), Nv,US
57/E3 Wast Water (lake), Eng,UK
160/E1 Waswanipi (lake), Qu,Can
111/E4 Watampone, Indo.
99/M10 Watarai, Japan
99/F2 Watarase (riv.), Japan
99/G1 Watari, Japan
58/C4 Watchet, Eng,UK
59/E3 Watchfield, Eng,UK
168/C3 Watch Hill (pt.), RI,US
167/H9 Watchung (mts.), NJ,US
59/G2 Waterbeach, Eng,UK
131/B5 Waterberge (mts.), SAfr.
168/A2 Waterbury, Ct,US
161/Q9 Waterdown, On,Can
163/H3 Wateree (dam), SC,US
163/H3 Wateree (lake), SC,US
163/H3 Wateree (riv.), SC,US
60/C5 Waterford, Ire.
60/C5 Waterford (co.), Ire.
60/D5 Waterford (har.), Ire.
165/F6 Waterford, Mi,US
58/A6 Watergate (bay), Eng,UK
157/J2 Waterhen (lake), Mb,Can
156/F2 Waterhen (riv.), Sk,Can
68/D2 Waterloo, Belg.
160/D3 Waterloo, On,Can
159/J2 Waterloo, Ia,US
160/B4 Waterloo, Il,US
68/D2 Waterloo Battlesite, Belg.
166/D2 Waterloo Village, NJ,US
59/E5 Waterlooville, Eng,UK
68/D2 Watermael-Boitsfort, Belg.
156/E3 Waterton Lakes Nat'l Park, Ab,Can
168/A2 Watertown, Ct,US
168/C1 Watertown, Ma,US
160/F3 Watertown, NY,US
157/J4 Watertown, SD,US
160/B3 Watertown, Wi,US
133/E2 Waterval-Bo, SAfr.
161/G2 Waterville, Me,US
156/C4 Waterville, Wa,US
53/M7 Watford, Eng,UK
157/H4 Watford City, ND,US
116/B4 Watheroo Nat'l Park, Austl.
57/G5 Wath-upon-Dearne, Eng,UK
150/C1 Watling (San Salvador) (isl.), Bahm.
59/F3 Watlington, Eng,UK
109/B2 Wat Mahathat, Thai.
159/H4 Watonga, Ok,US
111/G3 Watowato (peak), Indo.
104/D5 Wat Phra Si Ratana Mahathat, Thai.
109/D3 Wat Phu, Laos
157/G3 Watrous, Sk,Can
130/A2 Watsa, Zaire
160/C3 Watseka, Il,US
152/D2 Watson Lake, Yk,Can
158/B3 Watsonville, Ca,US
73/J3 Wattens, Aus.
68/C2 Wattignies, Fr.
59/G1 Watton, Eng,UK
68/C2 Wattrelos, Fr.
164/F8 Watts, Ca,US
77/F3 Wattwil, Swi.
168/C2 Watuppa (pond), Ma,US
109/C2 Wat Xieng Thong, Laos
163/H5 Wauchula, Fl,US
165/P15 Wauconda, Il,US
116/D2 Waukarlycarly (lake), Austl.
165/Q15 Waukegan, Il,US
165/P13 Waukesha, Wi,US
165/P14 Waukesha (co.), Wi,US
58/C3 Waun Fâch (mtn.), Wal,UK
58/C1 Waun Oer (mtn.), UK
160/B3 Waupun, Wi,US
159/H4 Waurika, Ok,US
160/B2 Wausau, Wi,US
160/C3 Wauseon, Oh,US
165/P13 Wauwatosa, Wi,US
59/H2 Waveney (riv.), Eng,UK
57/E2 Waver (riv.), Eng,UK
119/G5 Waverly, Austl.
163/G2 Waverly, Tn,US
68/D2 Wavre, Belg.
68/B2 Wavrin, Fr.
125/L6 Wāw, Sudan
160/C2 Wawa, On,Can
149/E3 Wawa (riv.), Nic.
160/E1 Wawagosic (riv.), Qu,Can
149/E3 Wawasang (mtn.), Nic.
167/H7 Wawayanda Saint Park, NJ,US
162/D3 Waxahachie, Tx,US
69/F3 Waxweiler, Ger.
163/H4 Waycross, Ga,US
168/C1 Wayland, Ma,US
165/F7 Wayne, Mi,US
165/F7 Wayne (co.), Mi,US
159/H2 Wayne, Ne,US
167/D2 Wayne, NJ,US
168/F6 Wayne (co.), Oh,US
166/C1 Wayne (co.), Pa,US
163/H3 Waynesboro, Ga,US
163/F4 Waynesboro, Ms,US
160/E4 Waynesboro, Pa,US
160/E4 Waynesboro, Va,US
159/J3 Waynesville, Mo,US
163/H3 Waynesville, NC,US
68/C3 Waziers, Fr.
108/C1 Wazīrābād, Pak.
99/L10 Wazuka, Japan
64/K2 Wda (riv.), Pol.
129/F3 W du Niger Nat'l Park, Afr.
110/A2 We (isl.), Indo.
59/G4 Weald, The (reg.), Eng,UK
57/G2 Wear (riv.), Eng,UK
57/F2 Wear Head, Eng,UK
159/H4 Weatherford, Ok,US
162/D3 Weatherford, Tx,US
57/F5 Weaver (riv.), Eng,UK
158/B2 Weaverville, Ca,US
162/C3 Webb A.F.B., Tx,US
168/C1 Webster, Ma,US
168/C1 Webster (lake), Ma,US
157/J4 Webster, SD,US
157/K5 Webster City, Ia,US
130/B2 Webuye, Kenya
113/W Weddell (sea), Ant.
143/M7 Weddell (isl.), Falk.
119/C2 Weddin Mountains Nat'l Park, Austl.
67/G1 Wedel, Ger.
67/G3 Wedemark, Ger.
58/D4 Wedmore, Eng,UK
58/D1 Wednesbury, Eng,UK
58/D1 Wednesfield, Eng,UK
131/C3 Wedza, Zim.
158/B2 Weed, Ca,US
59/E2 Weedon Bec, Eng,UK
167/J8 Weehawken, NJ,US
163/H4 Weeki Wachee Springs, Fl,US
58/B5 Week Saint Mary, Eng,UK
66/D4 Weerselo, Neth.
66/C6 Weert, Neth.
66/C4 Weesp, Neth.
66/D6 Wegberg, Ger.
65/L1 Węgorzewo, Pol.
65/M2 Węgrów, Pol.
76/D2 Wehr, Ger.
76/D2 Wehra (riv.), Ger.
67/G6 Wehre (riv.), Ger.
70/B2 Wehrheim, Ger.
97/H4 Wei (riv.), China
97/H3 Weichang, China
64/G3 Weida, Ger.
71/F3 Weiden, Ger.
103/D3 Weifang, China
166/B4 Weigelstown, Pa,US
101/B4 Weihai, China
70/C4 Weikersheim, Ger.
70/B2 Weil (riv.), Ger.
70/B2 Weilburg, Ger.
70/B5 Weil der Stadt, Ger.
69/F2 Weilerswist, Ger.
77/H2 Weilheim, Ger.
70/C5 Weilheim an der Teck, Ger.
70/B2 Weilmünster, Ger.
64/F3 Weimar, Ger.
77/F2 Weinfelden, Swi.
70/B4 Weingarten, Ger.
77/F2 Weingarten, Ger.
70/B3 Weinheim, Ger.
70/C4 Weinsberg, Ger.
70/C5 Weinstadt, Ger.
65/J4 Weinviertel (reg.), Aus.
168/G7 Weirton, WV,US
156/D4 Weiser, Id,US
156/D4 Weiser (riv.), Id,US
103/D4 Weishan, China
103/D4 Weishan (lake), China
103/C4 Weishi, China
69/F4 Weiskirchen, Ger.
163/G3 Weiss (lake), Al,US
70/B5 Weissach, Ger.
71/F2 Weisse Elster (riv.), Ger.
71/E4 Weisse Laber (riv.), Ger.
70/D4 Weissenburg im Bayern, Ger.
64/F3 Weissenfels, Ger.
70/D6 Weissenhorn, Ger.
76/D3 Weissenstein (mtn.), Swi.
69/G3 Weissenthurm, Ger.
71/E2 Weisser Main (riv.), Ger.
71/F4 Weisser Regen (riv.), Ger.
69/F3 Weisser Stein (peak), Ger.
76/D5 Weisshorn (peak), Swi.
77/G4 Weisskugel (Palla Blanca) (peak), Aus., It.
76/D5 Weissmies (peak), Swi.
65/H3 Weisswasser, Ger.
70/B3 Weiterstadt, Ger.
107/G2 Weixi, China
103/C3 Wei Xian, China
107/J2 Weixin, China
96/E4 Weiyuan, China
104/D4 Weiyuan (riv.), China
73/L3 Weiz, Aus.
105/F4 Weizhou (isl.), China
65/K1 Wejherowo, Pol.
166/A3 Welch (hill), Pa,US
160/D4 Welch, WV,US
125/N5 Weldiya, Eth.
59/F2 Weldon, Eng,UK
125/M6 Welel (peak), Eth.
59/E4 Welford, Eng,UK
53/N6 Welham Green, Eng,UK
106/D6 Weligama, SrL.
69/E2 Welkenraedt, Belg.
132/D3 Welkom, SAfr.
161/R10 Welland, On,Can
161/R10 Welland (can.), On,Can
59/F1 Welland (riv.), Eng,UK
161/R10 Wellandport, On,Can
69/E2 Wellen, Belg.
114/F3 Wellesley (isls.), Austl.
168/C1 Wellesley, Ma,US
59/F2 Wellingborough, Eng,UK
119/C3 Wellington (inlet), Austl.
153/S7 Wellington (chan.), NW,Can
143/J7 Wellington (isl.), Chile
115/R11 Wellington (cap.), NZ
132/B4 Wellington, SAfr.
58/C5 Wellington, Eng,UK
58/D2 Wellington, Eng,UK
162/D2 Wellington, Ks,US
162/C3 Wellington, Tx,US
116/D3 Wells (lake), Austl.
156/C2 Wells, BC,Can
58/D4 Wells, Eng,UK
156/E5 Wells, Nv,US
59/G1 Wells-next-the-Sea, Eng,UK
160/D4 Wellston, Oh,US
71/H6 Wels, Aus.
77/H5 Welshnofen (Nova Levante), It.
58/C1 Welshpool, Wal,UK
67/E5 Welver, Ger.
59/F3 Welwyn, Eng,UK
59/F3 Welwyn Garden City, Eng,UK
70/C5 Welzheim, Ger.
57/F6 Wem, Eng,UK
130/B4 Wembere (riv.), Tanz.
156/D2 Wembley, Ab,Can
53/N7 Wembley Stadium, Eng,UK
58/B6 Wembury, Eng,UK
153/J3 Wemindji, Qu,Can
68/D2 Wemmel, Belg.
54/B5 Wemyss Bay, Sc,UK
156/C4 Wenatchee, Wa,US
105/F5 Wenchang, China
105/J3 Wencheng, China
129/E5 Wenchi, Gha.
67/H4 Wendeburg, Ger.
69/G2 Wenden, Ger.
101/B4 Wendeng, China
59/F3 Wendover, Eng,UK
158/D2 Wendover, Nv,US
58/A6 Wendron, Eng,UK
107/K3 Wengyuan, China
58/D2 Wenlock Edge (ridge), Eng,UK
67/F6 Wenne (riv.), Ger.
67/G4 Wennigsen, Ger.
57/F3 Wennington, Eng,UK
107/H3 Wenshan, China
103/D4 Wenshang, China
103/C3 Wenshui, China
57/F3 Wensleydale (val.), Eng,UK
59/H1 Wensum (riv.), Eng,UK
57/G4 Went (riv.), Eng,UK
103/B4 Wenxi, China
103/C4 Wen Xian, China
105/J3 Wenzhou, China
131/A5 Werda, Bots.
64/G3 Werdau, Ger.
125/Q6 Werdēr, Eth.
67/E6 Werdohl, Ger.
66/B5 Werkendam, Neth.
67/E5 Werl, Ger.
67/E3 Werlte, Ger.
67/E6 Wermelskirchen, Ger.
70/C3 Wern (riv.), Ger.
67/E5 Werne an der Lippe, Ger.
70/D3 Werneck, Ger.
67/H5 Wernigerode, Ger.
119/D2 Werong (peak), Austl.
67/G6 Werra (riv.), Ger.
67/F4 Werre (riv.), Ger.
119/E1 Werrikimbe Nat'l Park, Austl.
57/F5 Werrington, Eng,UK
67/E5 Werse (riv.), Ger.
70/D6 Wertach (riv.), Ger.
70/C3 Wertheim, Ger.
167/F2 Wertheim Nat'l Wild. Ref., NY,US
67/F4 Werther, Ger.
70/D5 Wertingen, Ger.
66/C3 Wervershoof, Neth.
68/C2 Wervik, Belg.
70/B3 Weschnitz (riv.), Ger.
66/D5 Wesel, Ger.
67/E5 Wesel-Datteln-Kanal (can.), Ger.
67/F2 Weser (riv.), Ger.
67/G4 Wesergebirge (ridge), Ger.
162/D5 Weslaco, Tx,US
132/D2 Wes-Rand, SAfr.
114/F2 Wessel (cape), Austl.
114/F2 Wessel (isls.), Austl.
58/D4 Wessex (reg.), Eng,UK
157/J4 Wessington Springs, SD,US
119/C4 West (pt.), Austl.
165/C2 West (pt.), Wa,US
117/G5 Westall (pt.), Austl.
165/P13 West Allis, Wi,US
163/H3 West Augusta, Ga,US
167/E2 West Babylon, NY,US
91/D3 West Bank (occ. zone)
54/D5 West Barns, Sc,UK
160/B3 West Bend, Wi,US
106/E3 West Bengal (state), India
59/G3 West Bergholt, Eng,UK
168/C1 West Boylston, Ma,US
160/C2 West Branch, Mi,US
168/F5 West Branch Saint Pk., Oh,US
168/C1 West Bridgewater, Ma,US
57/G6 West Bridgford, Eng,UK
59/E1 West Bromwich, Eng,UK
58/D4 Westbury, Eng,UK
167/E2 Westbury, NY,US
149/H1 West Caicos (isl.), Trks.
54/C5 West Calder, Sc,UK
167/H8 West Caldwell, NJ,US
116/C5 West Cape Howe Nat'l Park, Austl.
167/E1 Westchester (co.), NY,US
166/C4 West Chester, Pa,US
165/P16 West Chicago, Il,US
130/C3 West Chyulu Game Consv. Area, Kenya
53/M8 West Clandon, Eng,UK
58/B3 West Cleddau (riv.), Wal,UK
163/H3 West Columbia, SC,US
57/G2 West Cornforth, Eng,UK
164/C2 West Covina, Ca,US
58/C5 West Dart (riv.), Eng,UK
66/A6 Westdorpe, Neth.
52/F3 West Dvina (riv.), Eur.
162/B2 West Elk (mts.), Co,US
66/D3 Westerbork, Neth.
53/P8 Westerham, Eng,UK
67/E4 Westerkappeln, Ger.
64/E1 Westerland, Ger.
69/D1 Westerlo, Belg.
168/C3 Westerly, RI,US
91/A5 Western (des.), Egypt
129/E5 Western (reg.), Gha.
130/B2 Western (prov.), Kenya
128/B4 Western (area), SLeo.
130/A2 Western (prov.), Ugan.
131/A2 Western (prov.), Zam.
116/D3 Western Australia (state), Austl.
131/A3 Western Caprivi Game Park, Namb.
98/A3 Western Channel (str.), Japan, SKor.
88/C4 Western Dvina (riv.), Lat., Rus.
106/B4 Western Ghats (mts.), India
124/B3 Western Sahara
121/R9 Western Samoa
96/C1 Western Sayan (mts.), Rus.
66/A6 Westerschelde (chan.), Neth.
67/E2 Westerstede, Ger.
160/D3 Westerville, Oh,US
66/C5 Westervoort, Neth.
69/G2 Westerwald (for.), Ger.
67/F4 Westfalica, Porta (pass), Ger.
143/M8 West Falkland (isl.), Falk.
157/J4 West Fargo, ND,US
120/D4 West Fayu (isl.), Micr.
168/B1 Westfield, Ma,US
168/B1 Westfield (riv.), Ma,US
167/D2 Westfield, NJ,US
68/B2 West Flanders (prov.), Belg.
160/B4 West Frankfort, Il,US
66/C2 West Frisian (isls.), Neth.
58/C3 West Glamorgan (co.), Wal,UK
59/F1 West Glen (riv.), Eng,UK
53/P7 West Ham, Eng,UK
168/B2 West Hartford, Ct,US
168/B3 West Haven, Ct,US
167/E1 West Haverstraw, NY,US
167/C2 West Hazleton, Pa,US
163/F3 West Helena, Ar,US
167/L9 West Hempstead, NY,US
54/D2 Westhill, Sc,UK
164/F7 West Hollywood, Ca,US
53/Q7 West Horndon, Eng,UK
53/M8 West Horsley, Eng,UK
57/F4 Westhoughton, Eng,UK
161/Q8 West Humber (riv.), On,Can
113/F West Ice Shelf, Ant.
115/J4 West Islet (isl.), Austl.
167/E2 West Islip, NY,US
158/E2 West Jordan, Ut,US
54/B5 West Kilbride, Sc,UK
53/P8 West Kingsdown, Eng,UK
168/C3 West Kingston, RI,US
57/E5 West Kirby, Eng,UK
54/D3 West Knock (mtn.), Sc,UK
168/F5 Westlake, Oh,US
164/B2 Westlake Village, Ca,US
165/F7 Westland, Mi,US
54/C5 West Linton, Sc,UK
156/E2 Westlock, Ab,Can
131/B2 West Lunga (riv.), Zam.
131/B2 West Lunga Nat'l Park, Zam.
60/C3 Westmeath (co.), Ire.
163/F3 West Memphis, Ar,US
59/G3 West Mersea, Eng,UK
59/E2 West Midlands (co.), Eng,UK
168/H7 West Mifflin, Pa,US
167/D1 West Milford, NJ,US
164/B3 Westminster, Ca,US
166/B4 Westminster, Md,US
53/N7 Westminster Abbey, Eng,UK
53/N7 Westminster, City of (bor.), Eng,UK
165/Q16 Westmont, Il,US
166/C4 Westmont (Haddon), NJ,US
57/F3 Westmoreland (reg.), Eng,UK
161/N7 Westmount, Qu,Can
57/C3 Westmuir, Sc,UK
167/D2 West New York, NJ,US
131/C4 West Nicholson, Zim.
168/A3 Weston, Ct,US
168/C1 Weston, Ma,US
159/J3 Weston, Mo,US
160/D4 Weston, WV,US
132/P13 Westonaria, SAfr.
58/D4 Weston-super-Mare, Eng,UK
58/D4 Weston Zoyland, Eng,UK
167/D2 West Orange, NJ,US
168/B1 Westover A.F.B., Ma,US
163/H5 West Palm Beach, Fl,US
167/J8 West Paterson, NJ,US
53/Q8 West Peckham, Eng,UK
163/G4 West Pensacola, Fl,US
159/K3 West Plains, Mo,US
163/G3 West Point (lake), Al, Ga,US
163/F3 West Point, Ms,US
159/H2 West Point, Ne,US
167/D1 West Point (mil. res.), NY,US
115/R11 Westport, NZ
167/E1 Westport, Ct,US
55/N13 Westray (isl.), Sc,UK
156/B2 West Road (riv.), BC,Can
165/L9 West Sacramento, Ca,US
161/S10 West Seneca, NY,US
88/H3 West Siberian (plain), Rus.
168/B1 West Springfield, Ma,US
59/F4 West Sussex (co.), Eng,UK
53/P7 West Thurrock, Eng,UK
158/E2 West Valley City, Ut,US
156/C3 West Vancouver, BC,Can
168/G6 West View, Pa,US

160/D4 West Virginia (state), US
58/B4 Westward Ho!, Eng,UK
168/C2 West Warwick, RI,US
54/D3 West Water (riv.), Sc,UK
168/C1 Westwood, Ma,US
167/D2 Westwood, NJ,US
131/C2 Westwood, Zam.
57/G4 West Yorkshire (co.), Eng,UK
162/B2 Wet (mts.), Co,US
111/G5 Wetar (isl.), Indo.
111/G5 Wetar (str.), Indo.
156/E2 Wetaskiwin, Ab,Can
130/C4 Wete, Tanz.
160/E1 Wetetnagami (riv.), Qu,Can
57/F2 Wetheral, Eng,UK
57/G4 Wetherby, Eng,UK
119/B2 Wetherell (lake), Austl.
168/B2 Wethersfield, Ct,US
67/E6 Wetter, Ger.
70/B2 Wetter (riv.), Ger.
70/C2 Wetterau (reg.), Ger.
68/C1 Wetteren, Belg.
76/E4 Wetterhorn (peak), Swi.
77/E3 Wettingen, Swi.
67/E4 Wettringen, Ger.
77/E3 Wetzikon, Swi.
71/E2 Wetzstein (peak), Ger.
68/C2 Wevelgem, Belg.
120/D5 Wewak, PNG
159/H4 Wewoka, Ok,US
60/D5 Wexford, Ire.
60/D5 Wexford (co.), Ire.
60/D5 Wexford (har.), Ire.
53/M8 Wey (riv.), Eng,UK
59/H1 Weybourne, Eng,UK
53/M7 Weybridge, Eng,UK
157/H3 Weyburn, Sk,Can
117/G5 Weyland (pt.), Austl.
58/D5 Weymouth, Eng,UK
58/D5 Weymouth (bay), Eng,UK
168/D1 Weymouth, Ma,US
115/S10 Whakatane, NZ
57/G5 Whaley Bridge, Eng,UK
168/D2 Whaling Museum, Ma,US
57/F4 Whalley, Eng,UK
55/P12 Whalsey (isl.), Sc,UK
115/R10 Whangarei, NZ
57/G3 Wharfe (riv.), Eng,UK
162/D4 Wharton, Tx,US
157/G5 Wheatland, Wy,US
59/E3 Wheatley, Eng,UK
165/P16 Wheaton, Il,US
58/D1 Wheaton Aston, Eng,UK
166/A5 Wheaton-Glenmont, Md,US
166/C5 Wheaton Village, NJ,US
163/G3 Wheeler (lake), Al,US
159/F3 Wheeler (peak), NM,US
158/D3 Wheeler (peak), Nv,US
154/V13 Wheeler A.F.B., Hi,US
165/Q15 Wheeling, Il,US
160/D3 Wheeling, WV,US
57/F3 Whernside (mtn.), Eng,UK
57/G2 Whickham, Eng,UK
117/G5 Whidbey (pt.), Austl.
165/B1 Whidbey (isl.), Wa,US
60/A6 Whiddy (isl.), Ire.
117/F3 Whinham (peak), Austl.
158/B2 Whiskeytown-Shasta-Trinity Nat'l Rec. Area, Ca,US
57/G2 Whitburn, Eng,UK
54/C5 Whitburn, Sc,UK
161/S8 Whitby, On,Can
57/H3 Whitby, Eng,UK
57/F6 Whitchurch, Eng,UK
59/E4 Whitchurch, Eng,UK
59/F3 Whitchurch, Eng,UK
58/C4 Whitchurch, Wal,UK
113/D White (isl.), Ant.
117/F2 White (lake), Austl.
161/K1 White (bay), Nf,Can
160/C1 White (lake), On,Can
84/H2 White (sea), Rus.
151/L4 White (pass), Ak,US
163/F3 White (riv.), Ar,US
158/E2 White (riv.), Co, Ut,US
160/C4 White (riv.), In,US
159/J5 White (lake), La,US
159/K4 White (riv.), La, Mo,US
165/E6 White (lake), Mi,US
159/G2 White (riv.), Ne, SD,US
158/D3 White (riv.), Nv,US
162/C3 White (riv.), Tx,US
160/D4 White (peak), Va,US
165/D3 White (riv.), Wa,US
165/P14 White (riv.), Wi,US
54/D5 Whiteadder Water (riv.), Sc,UK
161/K1 White Bear (riv.), Nf,Can
157/G3 White City, Sk,Can
54/C6 White Coomb (mtn.), Sc,UK
156/E2 Whitecourt, Ab,Can
166/A1 White Deer (cr.), Pa,US
54/C6 White Esk (riv.), Sc,UK
157/K4 Whiteface (riv.), Mn,US
57/F4 Whitefield, Eng,UK
160/C2 Whitefish (bay), On,Can, Mi,US
156/E3 Whitefish, Mt,US
151/L2 Whitefish Station, Yk,Can
58/B3 Whiteford (pt.), Wal,UK
157/G2 White Fox, Sk,Can
55/N13 Whitehall, Sc,UK
156/E4 Whitehall, Mt,US
166/C2 Whitehall (Fullerton), Pa,US
56/E2 Whitehaven, Eng,UK
56/C2 Whitehead, NI,UK
54/D1 Whitehills, Sc,UK
151/L3 Whitehorse (cap.), Yk,Can
59/E3 Whitehorse (hill), Eng,UK
166/B5 White Marsh, Md,US
166/D2 White Meadow Lake, NJ,US
151/J2 White Mountains Nat'l Rec. Area, Ak,US
157/K3 Whitemouth (riv.), Mb,Can
125/M5 White Nile (riv.), Sudan
166/B5 White Oak, Md,US
160/A1 White Otter (lake), On,Can
167/E1 White Plains, NY,US
160/C1 White River, On,Can
158/E4 Whiteriver, Az,US
162/B3 White Rock, NM,US
158/F4 White Sands, NM,US
158/F4 White Sands Nat'l Mon., NM,US
143/K8 Whiteside (chan.), Chile
156/F4 White Sulphur Springs, Mt,US
160/D4 White Sulphur Springs, WV,US
163/J3 Whiteville, NC,US
129/E4 White Volta (riv.), Burk., Gha.
157/L3 Whitewater (lake), On,Can
166/C2 Whitewater Kingdom/ Dorney Park, Pa,US
165/D3 White, West Fork (riv.), Wa,US
157/H3 Whitewood, Sk,Can
56/D2 Whithorn, Sc,UK
54/A6 Whiting Bay, Sc,UK
58/B3 Whitland, Wal,UK
57/G1 Whitley Bay, Eng,UK
168/D1 Whitman, Ma,US
158/C3 Whitney (mtn.), Ca,US
159/H4 Whitney (lake), Tx,US
58/B6 Whitsand (bay), Eng,UK
59/H4 Whitstable, Eng,UK
115/H4 Whitsunday (isl.), Austl.
118/C3 Whitsunday I. Nat'l Park, Austl.
164/B3 Whittier, Ca,US
119/G5 Whittlesea, Austl.
59/F1 Whittlesey, Eng,UK
57/G5 Whitwell, Eng,UK
57/F4 Whitworth, Eng,UK
152/F2 Wholdaia (lake), NW,Can
117/H5 Whyalla, Austl.
109/B2 Wiang Ko Sai Nat'l Park, Thai.
160/D2 Wiarton, On,Can
130/B2 Wiawer, Ugan.
68/C2 Wichelen, Belg.
159/H3 Wichita, Ks,US
159/H4 Wichita (mts.), Ok,US
159/H4 Wichita (riv.), Tx,US
162/D3 Wichita Falls, Tx,US
55/K7 Wick, Sc,UK
158/D4 Wickenburg, Az,US
59/G3 Wickford, Eng,UK
119/C3 Wickham (cape), Austl.
59/H2 Wickham Market, Eng,UK
168/F4 Wickliffe, Oh,US
60/D4 Wicklow (co.), Ire.
60/D4 Wicklow (mts.), Ire.
60/D3 Wicklow Gap (pass), Ire.
56/C6 Wicklow Head (pt.), Ire.
67/F4 Wickriede (riv.), Ger.
57/F5 Widnes, Eng,UK
69/G2 Wied (riv.), Ger.
67/G2 Wiedau (riv.), Ger.
67/F2 Wiefelstede, Ger.
67/F4 Wiehengebirge (ridge), Ger.
69/G2 Wiehl, Ger.
65/L4 Wieliczka, Pol.
68/C2 Wielsbeke, Belg.
65/K3 Wieluń, Pol.
65/J4 Wien (prov.), Aus.
65/J5 Wiener Neustadt, Aus.
65/J4 Wien (Vienna) (cap.), Aus.
73/L2 Wienwald (reg.), Aus.
65/M3 Wieprz (riv.), Pol.
66/D4 Wierden, Neth.
66/B3 Wieringermeerpolder (polder), Neth.
66/C3 Wieringerwerf, Neth.
65/K3 Wieruszów, Pol.
70/B2 Wiesbaden, Ger.
76/D2 Wiese (riv.), Ger.
88/H2 Wiese (isl.), Rus.
70/B1 Wieseck (riv.), Ger.
70/E3 Wiesent (riv.), Ger.
70/B4 Wiesloch, Ger.
67/E2 Wiesmoor, Ger.
67/E3 Wietmarschen, Ger.
67/G3 Wietze, Ger.
67/G3 Wietze (riv.), Ger.
65/K1 Wiezyca (peak), Pol.
57/F4 Wigan, Eng,UK
163/F4 Wiggins, Ms,US
59/E5 Wight, Isle of (isl.), Eng,UK
63/K5 Wigry (lake), Pol.
59/E1 Wigston, Eng,UK
57/E2 Wigton, Eng,UK
56/D2 Wigtown, Sc,UK
56/D2 Wigtown (bay), Sc,UK
66/C5 Wijchen, Neth.
66/D4 Wijhe, Neth.
66/C5 Wijk bij Duurstede, Neth.
125/N5 Wik'ro, Eth.
77/F3 Wil, Swi.
159/H2 Wilber, Ne,US
118/G8 Wilberforce, Austl.
57/H4 Wilberfoss, Eng,UK
168/D2 Wilbur (pt.), Ma,US
156/D4 Wilbur, Wa,US
159/J4 Wilburton, Ok,US
88/G1 Wilczek (isl.), Rus.
70/B5 Wildbad im Schwarzwald, Ger.
70/B5 Wildberg, Ger.
132/E4 Wild Coast (reg.), SAfr.
166/C2 Wild Creek (res.), Pa,US
67/F3 Wildeshausen, Ger.
161/Q8 Wildfield, On,Can
77/G3 Wildgrat (peak), Aus.
76/D5 Wildhorn (peak), Swi.
164/C3 Wildomar, Ca,US
157/J4 Wild Rice (riv.), Mn,US
77/G4 Wildspitze (peak), Aus.
76/D5 Wildstrubel (peak), Swi.
166/B6 Wild World, Md,US
132/E2 Wilge (riv.), SAfr.
168/G5 Wilhelm (res.), Pa,US
113/F Wilhelm II (coast), Ant.
139/G4 Wilhelmina (mts.), Sur.
66/C5 Wilhelminakanaal (can.), Neth.
67/G2 Wilhelmsburg, Ger.
67/F1 Wilhelmshaven, Ger.
166/C1 Wilkes-Barre, Pa,US
163/H2 Wilkesboro, NC,US
113/J Wilkes Land (reg.), Ant.
156/F2 Wilkie, Sk,Can
113/V Wilkins (sound), Ant.
168/H7 Wilkinsburg, Pa,US
151/N4 Will (mt.), BC,Can
165/P16 Will (co.), Il,US
156/C4 Willamette (riv.), Or,US
119/C2 Willandra Nat'l Park, Austl.
156/B4 Willapa (bay), Wa,US
57/F5 Willaston, Eng,UK
158/E4 Willcox, Az,US
67/G5 Willebadessen, Ger.
68/D1 Willebroek, Belg.
150/D4 Willemstad (cap.), NAnt.
53/N7 Willesden, Eng,UK
119/B3 William (peak), Austl.
116/C5 William Bay Nat'l Park, Austl.
158/D4 Williams, Az,US
160/C4 Williamsburg, Ky,US
167/K9 Williamsburg, NY,US
160/E4 Williamsburg, Va,US
156/C2 Williams Lake, BC,Can
160/D4 Williamson, WV,US
166/A1 Williamsport, Pa,US
119/F5 Williamstown, Austl.
166/D4 Williamstown, NJ,US
161/S10 Williamsville, NY,US
66/D6 Willich, Ger.
168/B2 Willimantic, Ct,US
166/D3 Willingboro, NJ,US
57/G2 Willington, Eng,UK
57/G6 Willington, Eng,UK
162/E4 Willis, Tx,US
115/J3 Willis Islets (isls.), Austl.
156/C2 Williston (lake), BC,Can
163/H4 Williston, Fl,US
157/H3 Williston, ND,US
167/L8 Williston Park, NY,US
58/C4 Williton, Eng,UK
158/B3 Willits, Ca,US
157/K4 Willmar, Mn,US
168/F4 Willoughby Hills, Oh,US
156/C2 Willow (riv.), BC,Can
156/D4 Willow (cr.), Or,US
164/F8 Willowbrook, Ca,US
165/Q16 Willowbrook, Il,US
157/G3 Willow Bunch, Sk,Can
166/C3 Willow Grove, Pa,US
166/C3 Willow Grove Nav. Air Sta., Pa,US
117/G2 Willowra Abor. Land, Austl.
156/C2 Willow River, BC,Can
158/B3 Willows, Ca,US
114/D4 Wills (lake), Austl.
76/D1 Willstätt, Ger.
165/Q15 Wilmette, Il,US
53/P7 Wilmington, Eng,UK
164/F8 Wilmington, Ca,US
166/C4 Wilmington, De,US
163/J3 Wilmington, NC,US
160/D4 Wilmington, Oh,US
163/H4 Wilmington Island, Ga,US
57/F5 Wilmslow, Eng,UK
69/H2 Wilnsdorf, Ger.
108/G4 Wilpattu Nat'l Park, SrL.
66/B6 Wilrijk, Belg.
67/G2 Wilseder Berg (peak), Ger.
153/H2 Wilson (cape), NW,Can
164/B2 Wilson (mtn.), Ca,US
163/J3 Wilson, NC,US
161/S9 Wilson, NY,US
166/C2 Wilson, Pa,US
115/H7 Wilsons Promontory (pen.), Austl.
119/C3 Wilsons Promontory Nat'l Park, Austl.
59/E4 Wilton, Eng,UK
168/A3 Wilton, Ct,US
59/E4 Wiltshire (co.), Eng,UK
53/N7 Wimbledon, Eng,UK
58/E5 Wimborne Minster, Eng,UK
68/A2 Wimereux, Fr.
130/B3 Winam (gulf), Kenya
132/D3 Winburg, SAfr.
58/D4 Wincanton, Eng,UK
59/E3 Winchcombe, Eng,UK
59/G5 Winchelsea, Eng,UK
59/E4 Winchester, Eng,UK
168/A2 Winchester, Ct,US
160/C4 Winchester, Ky,US
163/G3 Winchester, Tn,US
160/E4 Winchester, Va,US
165/L12 Winchester Mystery House, Ca,US
165/P14 Wind (lake), Wi,US
156/F5 Wind (riv.), Wy,US
77/G2 Windach (riv.), Ger.
157/G5 Wind Cave Nat'l Park, SD,US
163/H3 Winder, Ga,US
57/F3 Windermere, Eng,UK
57/F3 Windermere (lake), Eng,UK
168/D2 Windham, Ct,US
168/B2 Windham (co.), Ct,US
126/C5 Windhoek (cap.), Namb.
157/K5 Windom, Mn,US
158/E4 Window Rock, Az,US
156/F5 Wind River (range), Wy,US
59/E3 Windrush (riv.), Eng,UK
118/G8 Windsor, Austl.
161/L1 Windsor, Nf,Can
161/H2 Windsor, NS,Can
165/F7 Windsor, On,Can
161/G2 Windsor, Qu,Can
59/F4 Windsor, Eng,UK
168/B2 Windsor, Ct,US
168/B1 Windsor (dam), Ma,US
168/B2 Windsor Locks, Ct,US
149/H2 Windward (passg.), Cuba, Haiti
150/F4 Windward (isls.), NAm.
156/D3 Winfield, BC,Can
159/H3 Winfield, Ks,US
59/F3 Wing, Eng,UK
57/G2 Wingate, Eng,UK
68/C1 Wingene, Belg.
161/R10 Winger, On,Can
59/H4 Wingham, Eng,UK
116/D2 Winifred (lake), Austl.
157/M2 Winisk, On,Can
157/M2 Winisk (lake), On,Can
157/M2 Winisk (riv.), On,Can
157/J3 Winkler, Mb,Can
129/E5 Winneba, Gha.
160/B3 Winnebago (lake), Wi,US
158/C2 Winnemucca, Nv,US
70/C5 Winnenden, Ger.
157/J5 Winner, SD,US
165/Q15 Winnetka, Il,US
156/F4 Winnett, Mt,US
162/E4 Winnfield, La,US
116/B2 Winning, Austl.
157/J3 Winnipeg (cap.), Mb,Can
157/J2 Winnipeg (lake), Mb,Can
157/K3 Winnipeg (riv.), Mb, On,Can
157/J3 Winnipeg Beach, Mb,Can
157/J3 Winnipegosis, Mb,Can
157/H2 Winnipegosis (lake), Mb,Can
162/F3 Winnsboro, La,US
163/H3 Winnsboro, SC,US
161/Q9 Winona, On,Can
157/L4 Winona, Mn,US
66/E2 Winschoten, Neth.
58/D4 Winscombe, Eng,UK
57/F5 Winsford, Eng,UK
58/D4 Winsley, Eng,UK
59/F3 Winslow, Eng,UK
158/E4 Winslow, Az,US
168/A2 Winsted, Ct,US
163/H2 Winston-Salem, NC,US
66/D2 Winsum, Neth.
67/F6 Winterberg, Ger.
132/D4 Winterberge (mts.), SAfr.
58/D3 Winterbourne, Eng,UK
163/H4 Winter Haven, Fl,US
70/C6 Winterlingen, Ger.
163/H4 Winter Park, Fl,US
166/B4 Winters Run (riv.), Md,US
77/F3 Winterstaude (peak), Aus.
66/D5 Winterswijk, Neth.
77/E2 Winterthur, Swi.
166/C4 Winterthur Museum and Gardens, De,US
168/D1 Winthrop, Ma,US
161/G2 Winthrop, Me,US
165/Q15 Winthrop Harbor, Il,US
76/D1 Wintzenheim, Fr.
64/F3 Wipper (riv.), Ger.
67/H2 Wipperau (riv.), Ger.
67/E6 Wipperfürth, Ger.
57/G5 Wirksworth, Eng,UK
57/E5 Wirral (pen.), Eng,UK
59/G1 Wisbech, Eng,UK
76/D1 Wisches, Fr.
160/B2 Wisconsin (state), US
160/B2 Wisconsin Rapids, Wi,US
70/E1 Wisenta (riv.), Ger.
54/C5 Wishaw, Sc,UK
157/J4 Wishek, ND,US
65/K4 Wisła, Pol.
63/H4 Wiślany (lag.), Pol.
65/K2 Wisła (Vistula) (riv.), Pol.
65/L4 Wisłok (riv.), Pol.
65/L4 Wisłoka (riv.), Pol.
64/F2 Wismar, Ger.
69/G5 Wissembourg, Fr.
69/G2 Wissen, Ger.
59/G1 Wissey (riv.), Eng,UK
132/E2 Witbank, SAfr.
132/A2 Witberg (peak), Namb.
59/G3 Witham, Eng,UK
57/H5 Witham (riv.), Eng,UK
58/C5 Witheridge, Eng,UK
57/J4 Withernsea, Eng,UK
151/J3 Witherspoon (mtn.), Ak,US
163/H4 Withlacoochee (riv.), Fl, Ga,US
57/F4 Withnell, Eng,UK
117/G3 Witjira Nat'l Park, Austl.
132/D3 Wit Kei (riv.), SAfr.
65/J2 Witkowo, Pol.
59/E3 Witney, Eng,UK
65/H2 Witnica, Pol.
76/D2 Wittelsheim, Fr.
69/E2 Wittem, Neth.
67/E6 Witten, Ger.
77/F3 Wittenbach, Swi.
64/G3 Wittenberg, Ger.
64/F2 Wittenberge, Ger.
76/D2 Wittenheim, Fr.
59/F1 Wittering, Eng,UK
67/H3 Wittingen, Ger.
69/F4 Wittlich, Ger.
67/E1 Wittmund, Ger.
65/G1 Witton (pen.), Ger.
64/G2 Wittstock, Ger.
130/D3 Witu, Kenya
132/P12 Witwatersrand (reg.), SAfr.
67/G6 Witzenhausen, Ger.
58/C4 Wiveliscombe, Eng,UK
115/J5 Wivenhoe (lake), Austl.
59/G3 Wivenhoe, Eng,UK
165/E6 Wixom, Mi,US
139/H3 W. J. van Blommenstein (lake), Sur.
65/L2 Wkra (riv.), Pol.
65/K1 Władysławowo, Pol.
65/K2 Włocławek, Pol.
65/K2 Włocławek (prov.), Pol.
65/K2 Włocławskie (lake), Pol.
65/M3 Włodawa, Pol.
65/K3 Włoszczowa, Pol.
58/C1 Wnion (riv.), Wal,UK
130/B2 Wobulenzi, Ugan.
59/F3 Woburn Abbey, Eng,UK
59/F2 Woburn Sands, Eng,UK
119/C3 Wodonga, Austl.
65/K4 Wodzisław Śląski, Pol.
66/B4 Woerden, Neth.
69/G6 Woerth, Fr.
66/C3 Wognum, Neth.
77/E3 Wohlen, Swi.
76/D4 Wohlen bei Bern, Swi.
164/D4 Wohlford (lake), Ca,US
69/F5 Woippy, Fr.
111/H5 Wokam (isl.), Indo.
97/K2 Woken (riv.), China
53/M8 Woking, Eng,UK
59/F4 Wokingham, Eng,UK
101/D5 Wŏlch'ul-san Nat'l Park, SKor.
168/B2 Wolcott, Ct,US
161/S9 Wolcottsville, NY,US
53/N8 Woldingham, Eng,UK
120/D4 Woleai (atoll), Micr.
144/J6 Wolf (isl.), Ecu.
144/J7 Wolf (vol.), Ecu.
151/H2 Wolf (mtn.), Ak,US
165/R16 Wolf (lake), In,US
168/F5 Wolf (cr.), Oh,US
159/G3 Wolf (cr.), Ok, Tx,US
168/G5 Wolf (cr.), Pa,US
160/B2 Wolf (riv.), Wi,US
70/B6 Wolfach (riv.), Ger.
151/F3 Wolf Creek (mtn.), Ak,US
156/E4 Wolf Creek, Mt,US
64/G3 Wolfen, Ger.
67/H4 Wolfenbüttel, Ger.
70/B2 Wölfersheim, Ger.
67/G6 Wolfhagen, Ger.
157/G3 Wolf Point, Mt,US
77/H2 Wolfratshausen, Ger.
67/H4 Wolfsburg, Ger.
77/F3 Wolfurt, Aus.
65/G1 Wolgast, Ger.
65/H2 Woliński Nat'l Park, Pol.
152/E2 Wollaston (pen.), NW,Can
152/F3 Wollaston (lake), Sk,Can
143/L8 Wollaston (isl.), Chile
59/F2 Wollaston, Eng,UK
119/D2 Wollemi Nat'l Park, Austl.
119/D2 Wollongong, Austl.
132/D2 Wolmaransstad, SAfr.
73/J3 Wolnzach, Ger.
124/C6 Wologizi (range), Libr.
65/L2 Wołomin, Pol.
65/J3 Wołów, Pol.
132/L10 Wolseley, SAfr.
57/G2 Wolsingham, Eng,UK
65/J2 Wolsztyn, Pol.
68/D2 Woluwé-Saint-Lambert, Belg.
66/D3 Wolvega, Neth.
58/D1 Wolverhampton, Eng,UK
59/F2 Wolverton, Eng,UK
160/D2 Woman (riv.), On,Can
60/B6 Womanagh (riv.), Ire.
58/D1 Wombourne, Eng,UK
57/G4 Wombwell, Eng,UK
165/P15 Wonder (lake), Il,US
131/C2 Wonder Gorge, Zam.
71/F3 Wondreb (riv.), Ger.
119/C1 Wongalarroo (lake), Austl.
101/D4 Wŏnju, SKor.
119/C3 Wonnangatta-Moroka Nat'l Park, Austl.
101/D3 Wŏnsan, NKor.
116/C3 Wonyulgunna (peak), Austl.
157/H2 Wood (lake), Sk,Can
156/G3 Wood (mtn.), Sk,Can
151/K3 Wood (mtn.), Yk,Can
161/Q8 Woodbridge, On,Can
59/H2 Woodbridge, Eng,UK
168/A3 Woodbridge, Ct,US
167/D2 Woodbridge, NJ,US
152/E2 Wood Buffalo Nat'l Park, Ab, Yk,Can
161/Q9 Woodburn, On,Can
56/C2 Woodburn, NI,UK
156/C4 Woodburn, Or,US
166/C4 Woodbury, NJ,US
60/B4 Woodcock (hill), Ire.
165/Q16 Wood Dale, Il,US
118/D4 Woodgate Nat'l Park, Austl.
57/H5 Woodhall Spa, Eng,UK
165/F7 Woodhaven, Mi,US
165/L9 Woodland, Ca,US
164/E7 Woodland Hills, Ca,US
159/F3 Woodland Park, Co,US
120/E5 Woodlark (isl.), PNG
166/B5 Woodlawn, Md,US
59/F4 Woodley, Eng,UK
167/E2 Woodmere, NY,US
165/P16 Woodridge, Il,US
167/J8 Wood-Ridge, NJ,US
117/F3 Woodroffe (peak), Austl.
165/D2 Woods (cr.), Wa,US
57/F6 Woodseaves, Eng,UK
117/M8 Woodside, Austl.
161/H2 Woodstock, NB,Can
59/E3 Woodstock, Eng,UK
168/C2 Woodstock, Ct,US
165/P15 Woodstock, Il,US
160/E4 Woodstock, Va,US
163/F4 Woodville, Ms,US
162/E4 Woodville, Tx,US
159/H3 Woodward, Ok,US
58/D5 Wool, Eng,UK
58/D4 Woolavington, Eng,UK
54/E5 Wooler, Eng,UK
57/G1 Woolsington, Eng,UK
53/P7 Woolwich, Eng,UK
117/G4 Woomera Prohibited Area, Austl.
116/L6 Woonoloo (brook), Austl.
168/C1 Woonsocket, RI,US
159/H1 Woonsocket, SD,US
118/C4 Woorabinda Abor. Community, Austl.
116/B3 Wooramel (riv.), Austl.
57/F5 Woore, Eng,UK
168/F6 Wooster, Oh,US
59/E3 Wootton Basset, Eng,UK
76/D4 Worb, Swi.
132/B4 Worcester, SAfr.
58/D2 Worcester, Eng,UK
168/C1 Worcester, Ma,US
168/C1 Worcester (co.), Ma,US
58/D2 Worcester & Birmingham (can.), Eng,UK
168/C3 Worden (pond), RI,US
73/K3 Wörgl, Aus.
56/E2 Workington, Eng,UK
57/G5 Worksop, Eng,UK
156/G4 Worland, Wy,US
50/* World
167/J9 World Trade Ctr., New York City, NY,US
66/B4 Wormer, Neth.
53/N6 Wormley, Eng,UK
70/B3 Worms, Ger.
70/D5 Wörnitz (riv.), Ger.
67/F2 Worpswede, Ger.
70/B3 Wörrstadt, Ger.
70/B2 Worsbach (riv.), Ger.
57/G4 Worsbrough, Eng,UK
165/Q16 Worth, Il,US
70/B4 Wörth am Rhein, Ger.
59/F5 Worthing, Eng,UK
157/K5 Worthington, Mn,US
70/E6 Wörthsee (lake), Ger.
120/F3 Wotho (atoll), Mrsh.
120/G4 Wotje (atoll), Mrsh.
58/D3 Wotton under Edge, Eng,UK
66/C4 Woudenberg, Neth.
66/C5 Woudrichem, Neth.
149/F3 Wounta (lag.), Nic.
66/B5 Wouw, Neth.
111/F4 Wowoni (isl.), Indo.
57/H5 Wragby, Eng,UK
89/T2 Wrangel (isl.), Rus.
151/A5 Wrangell (cape), Ak,US
151/K3 Wrangell (mts.), Ak,US
151/K3 Wrangell-Saint Elias Nat'l Park & Prsv., Ak,US
57/J5 Wrangle, Eng,UK
55/J7 Wrath (cape), Sc,UK
159/G2 Wray, Co,US
53/M7 Wraysbury, Eng,UK
53/M7 Wraysbury (res.), Eng,UK
57/H6 Wreake (riv.), Eng,UK
115/K4 Wreck (reef), Austl.
132/B3 Wreck (pt.), SAfr.
58/D1 Wrekin, The (hill), Eng,UK
57/F5 Wrenbury, Eng,UK
168/C1 Wrentham, Ma,US
57/F5 Wrexham, Wal,UK
157/G5 Wright, Wy,US
59/G3 Writtle, Eng,UK
65/J3 Wrocław, Pol.
65/J3 Wrocław (prov.), Pol.
53/P8 Wrotham, Eng,UK
152/D1 Wrottesley (cape), NW,Can
58/D1 Wroxeter, Eng,UK
59/H1 Wroxham, Eng,UK
65/J2 Września, Pol.
65/J3 Wschowa, Pol.
105/F3 Wu (riv.), China
105/G3 Wu (riv.), China
103/C3 Wu'an, China
116/C4 Wubin, Austl.
103/C5 Wuchang, China
103/C5 Wuchang (lake), China
103/D3 Wucheng, China
105/H3 Wuchiu (isl.), Tai.
103/B2 Wuchuan, China
97/K2 Wudalianchi, China
105/F1 Wudang (mts.), China
105/F1 Wudang Shan (mtn.), China
103/D3 Wudi, China
103/B3 Wuding (riv.), China
103/B5 Wufeng, China
105/G3 Wugong (mtn.), China
96/F4 Wuhai, China
103/C5 Wuhan, China
103/D4 Wuhe, China
103/D5 Wuhu, China
96/F3 Wujia (riv.), China
103/E5 Wujiang, China
66/E6 Wülfrath, Ger.
103/D4 Wulian, China
104/D3 Wulian (mts.), China
104/D4 Wuliang (mts.), China
105/F2 Wuling (mts.), China
107/J2 Wulong, China
129/H5 Wum, Camr.
104/D3 Wumeng (mts.), China
67/F2 Wümme (riv.), Ger.
106/C3 Wūn, India
130/C3 Wundanyi, Kenya
116/L7 Wungong (brook), Austl.
116/L7 Wungong (res.), Austl.
67/F5 Wünnenberg, Ger.
71/F2 Wunsiedel, Ger.
67/G4 Wunstorf, Ger.
158/E4 Wupatki Nat'l Mon., Az,US
67/E6 Wupper (riv.), Ger.
67/E6 Wuppertal, Ger.
103/B3 Wuqi, China
102/C4 Wuqia, China
103/C3 Wuqiang, China
103/D3 Wuqiao, China
77/H1 Würm (can.), Ger.
69/F2 Würm (riv.), Ger.
71/E6 Würm (riv.), Ger.
129/G3 Wurno, Nga.
69/F2 Würselen, Ger.
70/C3 Würzburg, Ger.
97/H5 Wushan (lake), China
105/G2 Wusheng Guan (pass), China
102/C3 Wushi, China
67/G6 Wüstegarten (peak), Ger.
97/L2 Wusuli (Ussuri) (riv.), China, Rus.
77/E2 Wutach (riv.), Ger.
103/C3 Wutai, China
103/C3 Wutai Shan (peak), China
128/C4 Wuteve (peak), Libr.
70/D1 Wutha-Farnroda, Ger.
66/B6 Wuustwezel, Belg.
103/D5 Wuwei, China
103/E5 Wuxi, China
105/H2 Wuxi (riv.), China
103/C3 Wuxiang, China
103/C5 Wuxue, China
103/C4 Wuyang, China
103/C3 Wuyi, China
105/H3 Wuyi (mts.), China
96/F3 Wuyuan, China
97/K2 Wuyur (riv.), China
103/B3 Wuzhai, China
103/C4 Wuzhi, China
105/F5 Wuzhi (mts.), China
105/F5 Wuzhi Shan (peak), China
105/F4 Wuzhou, China
167/M8 Wyandanch, NY,US
165/F7 Wyandotte, Mi,US
165/F7 Wyandotte Nat'l Wild. Ref., Mi,US
119/D2 Wyangale (dam), Austl.
167/D1 Wyckoff, NJ,US
58/D3 Wye (riv.), UK
131/C4 Wyllie's (pass), SAfr.
58/D4 Wylye (riv.), Eng,UK
57/G6 Wymeswold, Eng,UK
59/H1 Wymondham, Eng,UK
163/F3 Wynne, Ar,US
118/F6 Wynnum, Austl.
157/G3 Wynyard, Sk,Can
156/F5 Wyoming (state), US
160/C3 Wyoming, Mi,US
156/F5 Wyoming (peak), Wy,US
158/E2 Wyoming (range), Wy,US
166/C3 Wyomissing, Pa,US
119/B2 Wyperfeld Nat'l Park, Austl.
116/D5 Wyralinu (peak), Austl.
57/F4 Wyre (riv.), Eng,UK
65/L2 Wyszków, Pol.
160/D4 Wytheville, Va,US

X

109/D4 Xa Binh Long, Viet.
148/B3 Xadani, Mex.
102/E5 Xainza, China
106/E2 Xaitongmoin, China
131/D4 Xaiva, Moz.
131/D5 Xai-Xai, Moz.
104/E4 Xam (riv.), Laos
109/D1 Xam Nua, Laos
109/D3 Xan (riv.), Viet.
66/D5 Xanten, Ger.
81/J2 Xánthi, Gre.
141/A3 Xanxerê, Braz.
125/Q7 Xarardheere, Som.
109/E4 Xa Song Luy, Viet.
126/C3 Xassengue, Ang.
109/D3 Xa Tho Thanh, Viet.
137/J6 Xavantes (mts.), Braz.
141/B2 Xavantes (res.), Braz.
109/D4 Xa Vo Dat, Viet.
102/D3 Xayar, China
147/J4 Xel-há (ruins), Mex.
160/D4 Xenia, Oh,US
109/D2 Xeno, Laos
131/B4 Xhumo, Bots.
103/E2 Xi (lake), China
101/A2 Xi (riv.), China
104/D3 Xiaguan, China
103/C3 Xiajin, China
105/H3 Xiamen, China
103/B4 Xi'an, China
103/B5 Xianfeng, China
105/G3 Xiang (riv.), China
96/G5 Xiangcheng, China
103/C4 Xiangfan, China
103/B4 Xiangfen, China
103/D3 Xianghe, China
105/G3 Xianghua (mtn.), China
109/C2 Xiang Khoang (plat.), Laos
103/B4 Xiangning, China
97/H5 Xiangshui, China
105/G2 Xiangtan, China
105/G3 Xiangtan, China
103/C3 Xiangyuan, China
104/D3 Xiangyun, China
105/J2 Xianju, China
103/C5 Xianning, China
104/D2 Xianshui (riv.), China
103/C5 Xiantao, China
105/H2 Xianxia (mtn.), China
96/F5 Xianyang, China
103/C3 Xiao (riv.), China
104/D3 Xiao (riv.), China
105/F3 Xiao (riv.), China
97/J1 Xiaobole (peak), China
103/C5 Xiaogan, China
97/K2 Xiao Hinggang (mts.), China
104/D2 Xiaojin (riv.), China
105/G3 Xiaomei (pass), China
103/D3 Xiaoqing (riv.), China
103/L9 Xiaoshan, China
103/C3 Xiaowutai Shan (peak), China
103/D4 Xiao Xian, China
103/B3 Xiaoyi, China
148/D2 Xiatil, Mex.
103/D4 Xiayi, China
107/F2 Xibaxa (riv.), China
103/C4 Xicheng Shan (mtn.), China
107/H3 Xichou, China
103/B4 Xichuan, China
147/F4 Xicohténcatl, Mex.
147/F4 Xicotepec, Mex.
105/J2 Xidongting (mtn.), China
103/C4 Xifei (riv.), China
96/F4 Xifeng, China
97/J3 Xifeng, China
106/E2 Xigazê, China
96/E5 Xihan (riv.), China
103/B3 Xihekou, China
103/C4 Xihua, China

230

Xijir – Zhang

102/F4 Xijir Ulan (lake), China
103/E2 Xiliao (riv.), China
107/J3 Xilin, China
104/C4 Ximeng Vazu Zizhixian, China
105/H2 Xin (riv.), China
103/C4 Xin'an, China
103/D5 Xin'an (riv.), China
105/H2 Xin'anjiang (res.), China
131/D5 Xinavane, Moz.
97/H2 Xin Barag Zuoqi, China
101/C2 Xinbin, China
103/C4 Xincai, China
105/J2 Xinchang, China
103/C3 Xincheng, China
107/K3 Xinfeng, China
105/G4 Xinfengjiang (res.), China
105/F3 Xing'an, China
103/E2 Xingcheng, China
126/C2 Xinge, Ang.
103/D4 Xinghua, China
102/D3 Xingjiang Uygur Aut. Reg., China
97/L3 Xingkai (lake), China
103/D2 Xinglong, China
103/B5 Xingshan, China
103/C3 Xingtai, China
137/H4 Xingu (riv.), Braz.
103/C4 Xingyang, China
104/E3 Xingyi, China
103/C3 Xinhe, China
105/F3 Xinhuang Dongzu Zizhixian, China
96/E4 Xining, China
90/K6 Xining Shi, China
103/C5 Xinji, China
103/B4 Xinjiang, China
90/J5 Xinjiang (reg.), China
101/A3 Xinjin, China
103/C3 Xinle, China
101/B2 Xinmin, China
104/D3 Xinping Yizu, China
105/F3 Xinshao, China
103/D4 Xintai, China
103/C4 Xinxiang, China
103/C4 Xinyang, China
103/C4 Xinye, China
103/D4 Xinyi, China
105/G3 Xinyu, China
102/D3 Xinyuan, China
103/C4 Xinzheng, China
103/C5 Xinzhou, China
103/D3 Xiong Xian, China
103/C4 Xiping, China
96/E5 Xiqing (mts.), China
140/B3 Xique-Xique, Braz.
107/J2 Xishui, China
103/E5 Xitang, China
105/H2 Xitianmu (peak), China
105/G2 Xiu (riv.), China
105/D5 Xiuning, China
107/J2 Xiuwen, China
103/C4 Xiuwu, China
101/B2 Xiuyan, China
106/E2 Xixabangma (peak), China
104/D2 Xixi (riv.), China
103/B4 Xixia, China
104/E4 Xiyang (riv.), China
104/B2 Xizang (Tibet Aut. Reg.), China
103/E3 Xizhong (isl.), China
147/K8 Xochicalco (ruins), Mex.
147/Q10 Xochimilco, Mex.
147/M8 Xochitlán, Mex.
105/H3 Xu (riv.), China
103/B5 Xuan'en, China
103/C2 Xuanhua, China
104/E3 Xuanwei, China
103/C4 Xuchang, China
125/P7 Xuddur (Oddur), Som.
104/C3 Xue (mts.), China
103/E5 Xuedou (peak), China
96/D4 Xugin Gol (riv.), China
103/B4 Xun (riv.), China
105/F4 Xun (riv.), China
97/K2 Xunke, China
103/C4 Xun Xian, China
103/B4 Xunyang, China
105/F4 Xuwen, China
103/D4 Xuyi, China
104/E2 Xuyong, China
103/D4 Xuzhou, China

Y

104/D2 Ya'an, China
124/G7 Yabassi, Camr.
125/N7 Yabēlo, Eth.
96/F1 Yablonovyy (ridge), Rus.
150/E3 Yabucoa, PR
99/G2 Yabuki, Japan
102/D3 Yacgam (mtn.), Phil.
104/E3 Yachi (riv.), China
99/J7 Yachiyo, Japan
99/K9 Yachiyo, Japan
141/A4 Yacuí (riv.), Braz.
136/F8 Yacuiba, Bol.
138/D2 Yacumbu Nat'l Park, Ven.
106/C4 Yādgīr, India
100/G8 Yaeyama (isl.), Japan
99/L9 Yagi, Japan
124/J5 Yagoua, Camr.
96/D4 Yagradagzê (peak), China
148/E3 Yaguale (riv.), Hon.
143/G2 Yaguarón (riv.), Uru.
144/D1 Yaguas (riv.), Col., Peru
149/J2 Yague del Sur (riv.), DRep.
99/N10 Yahagi (riv.), Japan
146/E4 Yahualica de Gonzalez Gallo, Mex.
92/C2 Yahyalı, Turk.
99/F2 Yaita, Japan
99/F3 Yaizu, Japan
91/E1 Yakacık, Turk.
97/J2 Yakeshi, China
156/C4 Yakima, Wa,US
156/C4 Yakima (riv.), Wa,US
100/B1 Yakishiri (isl.), Japan
129/E3 Yako, Burk.
125/K7 Yakoma, Zaire
83/F4 Yakoruda, Bul.
98/B5 Yaku (isl.), Japan
98/B5 Yaku-Kirishima Nat'l Park, Japan
100/B2 Yakumo, Japan
99/K9 Yakuno, Japan
151/K4 Yakutat (bay), Ak,US
89/N3 Yakut Aut. Rep., Rus.
89/N3 Yakutsk, Rus.
109/C5 Yala, Thai.
148/E1 Yalahua (lag.), Mex.
117/F4 Yalata Abor. Land, Austl.
148/D2 Yalbac (hills), Belz.
116/B5 Yalgorup Nat'l Park, Austl.
159/K4 Yalobusha (riv.), Ms,US
124/J6 Yaloké, CAfr.
104/D2 Yalong (riv.), China
83/J5 Yalova, Turk.
86/E3 Yalta, Ukr.
97/J3 Yalu (riv.), China, NKor.
92/B2 Yalvaç, Turk.
100/B4 Yamada, Japan
98/B4 Yamaga, Japan
99/G1 Yamagata, Japan
99/F1 Yamagata (pref.), Japan
98/B3 Yamaguchi, Japan
98/B3 Yamaguchi (pref.), Japan
88/G2 Yamal (pen.), Rus.
88/G3 Yamal-Nenets Aut. Okr., Rus.
99/F3 Yamanashi (pref.), Japan
118/B2 Yamanie (falls), Austl.
118/B2 Yamanie Falls Nat'l Park, Austl.
88/F4 Yamantau (peak), Rus.
85/N5 Yamantau, Gora (peak), Rus.
99/N9 Yamaoka, Japan
116/D3 Yamarna Abor. Rsv., Austl.
116/D4 Yamarna Abor. Rsv., Austl.
99/L10 Yamashiro, Japan
99/F2 Yamato, Japan
99/L10 Yamato (riv.), Japan
99/L10 Yamato-Kōriyama, Japan
98/D3 Yamatotakada, Japan
99/M10 Yamazoe, Japan
125/L7 Yambio, Sudan
83/H4 Yambol, Bul.
104/C4 Yamethin, Burma
111/K4 Yamin (peak), Indo.
118/A4 Yamma Yamma (lake), Austl.
99/G1 Yamoto, Japan
128/D5 Yamoussoukro (cap.), IvC.
158/F2 Yampa (riv.), Co,US
106/C2 Yamuna (riv.), India
108/D2 Yamunānagar, India
107/E2 Yamzho Yumco (lake), China
103/B3 Yan (riv.), China
108/H4 Yan (riv.), SrL.
89/P3 Yana (riv.), Rus.
98/B4 Yanagawa, Japan
98/C4 Yanai, Japan
85/M4 Yanaul, Rus.
107/H2 Yanbian, China
103/C4 Yancheng, China
103/E4 Yancheng, China
116/B4 Yanchep Nat'l Park, Austl.
121/T12 Yandé (isl.), NCal.
116/C2 Yandeearra Abor. Rsv., Austl.
104/B5 Yandoon, Burma
125/K7 Yangambi, Zaire
104/C3 Yangbi (riv.), China
103/C4 Yangcheng, China
103/L8 Yangcheng (lake), China
105/H3 Yangdang (mts.), Laos
101/D2 Yanggang-do (prov.), NKor.
102/C2 Yanggao, China
103/C3 Yanggu, China
101/D3 Yanggu, SKor.
105/F4 Yangjiang, China
101/A4 Yangma (isl.), China
105/F3 Yangming (peak), China
104/C5 Yangon (Rangoon) (cap.), Burma
103/C3 Yangqu, China
103/C3 Yangquan, China
107/K3 Yangshan, China
107/K3 Yangshuo, China
104/C3 Yangtouyan, China
105/H2 Yangtze (Chang) (riv.), China
104/D3 Yangtze (Jinsha) (riv.), China
125/P5 Yangudi Rassa Nat'l Park, Eth.
103/D3 Yangxin, China
105/G2 Yangxin, China
101/E3 Yangyang, SKor.
103/C2 Yangyuan, China
103/D4 Yangzhong, China
103/D4 Yangzhou, China
97/K3 Yanji, China
103/C4 Yanjin, China
104/E2 Yanjin, China
129/H4 Yankari Game Rsv., Nga.
167/K8 Yankee Stadium, New York City, NY,US
157/J5 Yankton, SD,US
103/C4 Yanling, China
103/C3 Yanmen Guan (pass), China
103/D3 Yanshan, China
103/C4 Yanshi, China
97/K2 Yanshou, China
103/E3 Yantai, China
104/E2 Yanting, China
103/C2 Yantong Shan (mtn.), China
119/G5 Yan Yean (res.), Austl.
104/D3 Yanyuan, China
103/D4 Yanzhou, China
98/D3 Yao, Japan
107/H2 Yao'an, China
103/B3 Yaodian, China
124/H7 Yaoundé (cap.), Camr.
120/C4 Yap (isls.), Micr.
139/E4 Yapacana Nat'l Park, Ven.
111/J4 Yapen (isl.), Indo.
111/J4 Yapen (str.), Indo.
167/F2 Yaphank, NY,US
146/C3 Yaqui, Mex.
146/C2 Yaqui (riv.), Mex.
59/E5 Yar (riv.), Eng,UK
149/G1 Yara, Cuba
138/D2 Yaracuy (state), Ven.
92/C1 Yaralıgöz (peak), Turk.
111/J4 Yaramaniapuka (mtn.), Indo.
85/K4 Yaransk, Rus.
91/B1 Yardımcı (pt.), Turk.
166/D3 Yardville-Groveville, NJ,US
59/H1 Yare (riv.), Eng,UK
138/C4 Yarí (riv.), Col.
99/E2 Yari-ga-take (mtn.), Japan
83/J5 Yarımca, Turk.
138/D2 Yaritagua, Ven.
102/C4 Yarkant (riv.), China
161/H3 Yarmouth, NS,Can
84/H4 Yaroslavl', Rus.
84/H4 Yaroslavl' Obl., Rus.
119/G5 Yarra (riv.), Austl.
119/G5 Yarra Glen, Austl.
138/C3 Yarumal, Col.
120/G6 Yasawa Group (isls.), Fiji
86/C1 Yasel'da (riv.), Bela.
100/B4 Yashima, Japan
99/H7 Yashio, Japan
99/K10 Yashiro, Japan
87/L2 Yasnyy, Rus.
109/D3 Yasothon, Thai.
94/F4 Yas, Sir Bani (isl.), UAE
99/M9 Yasu, Japan
99/M10 Yasu (riv.), Japan
98/C3 Yasugi, Japan
92/D1 Yasun (pt.), Turk.
138/B5 Yasuni Nat'l Park, Ecu.
99/G2 Yatabe, Japan
92/B2 Yatağan, Turk.
58/D3 Yate, Eng,UK
59/F4 Yateley, Eng,UK
129/E3 Yatenga (prov.), Burk.
159/J3 Yates Center, Ks,US
152/G2 Yathkyed (lake), NW,Can
99/M9 Yatomi, Japan
99/E2 Yatsuo, Japan
98/B4 Yatsushiro, Japan
130/C3 Yatta (plat.), Kenya
91/D4 Yaṭṭah, WBnk.
58/D4 Yatton, Eng,UK
144/C4 Yauca (riv.), Peru
150/E3 Yauco, PR
147/K7 Yautepec, Mex.
144/C2 Yavari (riv.), Peru
144/C2 Yavari Mirim (riv.), Peru
106/C3 Yavatmāl, India
88/H2 Yavay (pen.), Rus.
148/C2 Yaveo, Mex.
139/E4 Yávita, Ven.
149/G4 Yaviza, Pan.
91/F8 Yavne, Isr.
92/D2 Yavuzeli, Turk.
99/J7 Yawahara, Japan
99/L10 Yawata, Japan
98/C4 Yawatahama, Japan
148/D2 Yaxchilán (ruins), Mex.
59/F2 Yaxley, Eng,UK
91/E2 Yayladaği, Turk.
93/H4 Yazd, Iran
93/H3 Yazd (gov.), Iran
163/F3 Yazoo (riv.), Ms,US
163/F3 Yazoo City, Ms,US
71/H7 Ybbs (riv.), Aus.
62/C3 Yding Skovhøj (peak), Den.
109/B3 Ye, Burma
57/G4 Yeadon, Eng,UK
58/B6 Yealmpton, Eng,UK
109/C4 Yeay Sen (cape), Camb.
102/C4 Yecheng, China
75/E3 Yecla, Sp.
147/N7 Yecuatla, Mex.
92/B1 Yedigöller Nat'l Park, Turk.
93/M6 Yedikule, Turk.
86/F1 Yefremov, Rus.
87/G3 Yegorlak (riv.), Rus.
147/M8 Yehualtepec, Mex.
91/F7 Yehud, Isr.
125/M7 Yei, Sudan
85/P4 Yekaterinburg Obl., Rus.
85/P4 Yekaterinburg (Sverdlovsk), Rus.
100/E1 Yekateriny (chan.), Rus.
85/M5 Yelabuga, Rus.
87/G2 Yelan', Rus.
86/F1 Yelets, Rus.
89/Q4 Yelizavety (cape), Rus.
89/R4 Yelizovo, Rus.
55/P12 Yell (isl.), Sc,UK
123/R16 Yellel, Alg.
97/J4 Yellow (sea), Asia
163/G4 Yellow (riv.), Al, Fl,US
168/G6 Yellow (cr.), Oh,US
166/A3 Yellow Breeches (cr.), Pa,US
157/G3 Yellow Grass, Sk,Can
97/H4 Yellow (Huang) (riv.), China
152/E2 Yellowknife (cap.), NW,Can
152/E2 Yellowknife (riv.), NW,Can
168/G6 Yellow, North Fork (cr.), Oh,US
157/G4 Yellowstone (riv.), Mt,US
156/F4 Yellowstone (lake), Wy,US
156/F4 Yellowstone Nat'l Park, Wy,US
162/E2 Yellville, Ar,US
58/B6 Yelverton, Eng,UK
96/D4 Yema (riv.), China
94/E5 Yemen
86/F2 Yenakiyevo, Ukr.
104/B4 Yenangyaung, Burma
109/D1 Yen Bai, Viet.
129/E4 Yendi, Gha.
102/C4 Yengisar, China
86/E4 Yenice (riv.), Turk.
83/J5 Yenişehir, Turk.
88/J3 Yenisey (riv.), Rus.
88/K4 Yeniseysk, Rus.
109/D1 Yen Minh, Viet.
116/E3 Yeo (lake), Austl.
58/D5 Yeo (riv.), Eng,UK
95/K4 Yeola, India
116/E3 Yeo Lake Nature Rsv., Austl.
58/D5 Yeovil, Eng,UK
118/C3 Yeppoon, Austl.
81/H3 Yerakovoúni (peak), Gre.
68/A4 Yères (riv.), Fr.
87/H4 Yerevan (cap.), Arm.
158/C3 Yerington, Nv,US
92/C2 Yerköy, Turk.
102/C1 Yermak, Kaz.
88/H4 Yermentau, Kaz.
91/D4 Yeroḥam, Isr.
72/D2 Yerre (riv.), Fr.
53/T10 Yerres, Fr.
53/U11 Yerres (riv.), Fr.
144/B3 Yerupaja (peak), Peru
91/D4 Yerushalayim (Jerusalem) (cap.), Isr.
104/B4 Yesagyo, Burma
101/D4 Yesan, SKor.
102/A1 Yesil', Kaz.
92/C2 Yeşilhisar, Turk.
86/F4 Yeşilırmak (riv.), Turk.
91/E1 Yeşilkent, Turk.
101/D3 Yesŏng (riv.), NKor.
87/G3 Yessentuki, Rus.
54/D5 Yetholm, Sc,UK
58/D5 Yetminster, Eng,UK
72/B3 Yeu (isl.), Fr.
106/B3 Yevla, India
87/H4 Yevlakh, Azer.
86/E3 Yevpatoriya, Ukr.
103/D3 Ye Xian, China
86/G3 Yeya (riv.), Rus.
87/F3 Yeysk, Rus.
103/C4 Yi (riv.), China
143/G2 Yi (riv.), Uru.
81/H2 Yiannitsá, Gre.
81/J4 Yiaros (isl.), Gre.
104/E2 Yibin, China
103/B5 Yichang, China
103/B4 Yicheng, China
103/C5 Yicheng, China
103/C4 Yichuan, China
105/G3 Yichun, China
107/K2 Yifeng, China
105/H3 Yihuang, China
97/K2 Yilan, China
92/D1 Yıldız (peak), Turk.
92/D2 Yıldızeli, Turk.
93/N6 Yildiz Park, Turk.
97/J1 Yilehuli (mts.), China
104/E3 Yiliang, China
103/B4 Yima, China
104/D3 Yimen, China
97/J2 Yimin (riv.), China
96/F3 Yin (mts.), China
103/D4 Yinan, China
96/F4 Yinchuan, China
116/D4 Yindarlgooda (lake), Austl.
103/C4 Ying (riv.), China
105/G2 Yingcheng, China
107/K3 Yingde, China
101/B2 Yingkou, China
103/C5 Yingshan, China
103/D4 Yingshang, China
105/H2 Yingtan, China
102/D3 Yining, China
104/B2 Yi'ong (riv.), China
125/M6 Yirol, Sudan
105/F3 Yishan, China
103/D4 Yishui, China
103/F2 Yitong (riv.), China
96/C3 Yiwu, China
103/D5 Yixing, China
103/C4 Yiyang, China
105/G2 Yiyang, China
103/D3 Yiyuan, China
107/K2 Yizhang, China
103/D4 Yizheng, China
56/E6 Y Llethr (mtn.), Wal,UK
63/K1 Ylöjärvi, Fin.
62/G2 Yngaren (lake), Swe.
162/D4 Yoakum, Tx,US
101/D5 Yŏch'ŏn, SKor.
98/D3 Yodo (riv.), Japan
89/P4 Yoduma (riv.), Rus.
112/D2 Yog (pt.), Phil.
124/J4 Yogoum (well), Chad
110/D5 Yogyakarta, Indo.
156/D3 Yoho Nat'l Park, BC,Can
100/B2 Yoichi, Japan
148/D3 Yojoa (lake), Hon.
124/J7 Yokadouma, Camr.
98/E3 Yōkaichi, Japan
98/D3 Yokawa, Japan
98/E3 Yokkaichi, Japan
99/F3 Yokohama, Japan
99/H7 Yokohama (inset), Japan
99/F3 Yokosuka, Japan
100/B4 Yokote, Japan
124/H6 Yola, Nga.
149/E4 Yolaina, Serranías de (range), Nic.
165/L9 Yolo (co.), Ca,US
109/C2 Yom (riv.), Thai.
126/B1 Yombi, Gabon
105/F4 Yon (riv.), China
72/C3 Yon (riv.), Fr.
98/C3 Yonago, Japan
100/G8 Yonaguni (isl.), Japan
100/K7 Yonaha-dake (peak), Japan
100/B3 Yoneshiro (riv.), Japan
99/G2 Yonezawa, Japan
105/H3 Yong'an, China
105/F3 Yong'an (pass), China
96/E4 Yongchang, China
103/D4 Yongcheng, China
101/E5 Yŏngch'ŏn, SKor.
107/G3 Yongde, China
103/H7 Yongding (riv.), China
101/E4 Yŏngdŏk, SKor.
101/F6 Yongdungpo, SKor.
107/J3 Yongfu, China
103/B3 Yonghe, China
101/D3 Yŏnghŭng (riv.), NKor.
103/B4 Yongji, China
101/F6 Yŏngjong (isl.), SKor.
101/E4 Yŏngju, SKor.
101/D4 Yongmun-san (mtn.), SKor.
103/C3 Yongnian, China
109/E1 Yongning, China
103/D3 Yongqing, China
103/H7 Yongqing, China
107/H2 Yongren, China
101/D5 Yŏngsan (riv.), SKor.
104/D2 Yongshan, China
105/D3 Yongsheng, China
107/J2 Yongshun, China
101/E4 Yŏngwŏl, SKor.
107/K2 Yongxin, China
105/F3 Yongzhou, China
167/E2 Yonkers, NY,US
72/E2 Yonne (riv.), Fr.
99/H7 Yono, Japan
102/C4 Yopurga, China
164/C3 Yorba Linda, Ca,US
114/G2 York (cape), Austl.
114/G2 York (sound), Austl.
161/R8 York, On,Can
161/Q8 York (co.), On,Can
161/H1 York (riv.), Qu,Can
57/G4 York, Eng,UK
163/F3 York, Al,US
159/H2 York, Ne,US
166/B4 York, Pa,US
166/B3 York (co.), Pa,US
163/H3 York, SC,US
160/E4 York (riv.), Va,US
117/H5 Yorke (pen.), Austl.
157/J1 York Landing, Mb,Can
57/G4 York Minster, Eng,UK
57/F3 Yorkshire Dales Nat'l Park, Eng,UK
57/H3 Yorkshire Wolds (hills), Eng,UK
157/H3 Yorkton, Sk,Can
167/E1 Yorktown Heights, NY,US
57/G3 York, Vale of (val.), Eng,UK
148/E3 Yoro, Hon.
99/M9 Yorō, Japan
99/J7 Yōrō (riv.), Japan
99/M10 Yoroi-zaki (pt.), Japan
100/K7 Yoron (isl.), Japan
96/F2 Yöröö, Mong.
57/F6 Yorton, Eng,UK
129/F4 Yorubaland (plat.), Nga.
158/C3 Yosemite Nat'l Park, Ca,US
98/C4 Yoshida, Japan
98/D3 Yoshii (riv.), Japan
99/H7 Yoshikawa, Japan
98/D3 Yoshimo (riv.), Japan
99/L10 Yoshino, Japan
99/L10 Yoshino (riv.), Japan
98/E3 Yoshino-Kumano Nat'l Park, Japan
85/L4 Yoshkar-Ola, Rus.
101/D5 Yŏsu, SKor.
100/B2 Yōtei-san (mtn.), Japan
99/J7 Yotsukaidō, Japan
105/G3 You (peak), China
105/E4 You (riv.), China
105/F2 You (riv.), China
60/C6 Youghal (bay), Ire.
119/D2 Young, Austl.
143/F2 Young, Uru.
165/C3 Youngs (lake), Wa,US
161/R9 Youngstown, NY,US
168/G5 Youngstown, Oh,US
107/J2 Youyang, China
97/L2 Youyi, China
139/E3 Yovi (peak), Ven.
92/C2 Yozgat, Turk.
165/E7 Ypsilanti, Mi,US
56/D6 Yr Eifl (mtn.), Wal,UK
158/B2 Yreka, Ca,US
68/B2 Yser (riv.), Fr.
62/E4 Ystad, Swe.
58/C3 Ystalyfera, Wal,UK
58/C3 Ystradgynlais, Wal,UK
58/C3 Ystrad Mynach, Wal,UK
58/C2 Ystwyth (riv.), Wal,UK
54/D2 Ythan (riv.), Sc,UK
62/A1 Ytre Sula (isl.), Nor.
107/J3 Yu (riv.), China
105/J4 Yü (peak), Tai.
103/C5 Yuan (lake), China
105/F2 Yuan (riv.), China
105/G3 Yuan (riv.), China
103/B5 Yuan'an, China
105/F3 Yuanbao (mtn.), China
103/C3 Yuanping, China
103/B4 Yuanqu, China
104/D4 Yuan (Red) (riv.), China
103/C3 Yuanshi, China
103/C4 Yuanyang, China
158/B3 Yuba City, Ca,US
100/B2 Yūbari, Japan
100/C1 Yūbetsu, Japan
100/C2 Yūbetsu (riv.), Japan
164/C2 Yucaipa, Ca,US
148/E1 Yucatan (chan.), Cuba, Mex.
148/D2 Yucatan (pen.), Mex.
148/D1 Yucatán (state), Mex.
158/D4 Yucca, Az,US
103/C4 Yucheng, China
103/D3 Yucheng, China
103/C3 Yuci, China
105/G3 Yudu, China
104/E2 Yuechi, China
105/G2 Yuelu (mtn.), China
117/F2 Yuendumu Abor. Land, Austl.
105/J2 Yueqing, China
105/H2 Yuexi, China
104/D2 Yuexi (riv.), China
105/G2 Yueyang, China
85/K3 Yug (riv.), Rus.
85/P1 Yugorskiy (pen.), Rus.
82/D3 Yugoslavia
103/L9 Yuhang, China
105/G3 Yuhua (mtn.), China
105/J2 Yuhuan, China
99/F2 Yūki, Japan
152/B2 Yukon (riv.), Can., US
151/K2 Yukon-Charley Rivers Nat'l Prsv., Ak,US
151/L3 Yukon Crossing, Yk,Can
151/F3 Yukon Delta Nat'l Wild. Ref., Ak,US
151/J2 Yukon Flats Nat'l Wild. Ref., Ak,US
152/C2 Yukon Territory (terr.), Can.
93/F2 Yüksekova, Turk.
98/B4 Yukuhashi, Japan
117/F3 Yulara, Austl.
105/F4 Yulin, China
103/B3 Yulin (riv.), China
103/D5 Yuling Guan (pass), China
104/D3 Yulongxue (peak), China
158/D4 Yuma, Az,US
159/G2 Yuma, Co,US
117/G4 Yumbarra Consv. Park, Austl.
130/A2 Yumbe, Ugan.
142/B3 Yumbel, Chile
126/E1 Yumbi, Zaire
138/B4 Yumbo, Col.
96/D4 Yumen, China
102/D2 Yumin, China
103/C5 Yun (riv.), China
92/B2 Yunak, Turk.
103/B4 Yuncheng, China
103/C4 Yuncheng, China
103/C2 Yungang Caves, China
136/E7 Yungas (reg.), Bol.
142/B3 Yungay, Chile
144/D5 Yunguyo, Peru
105/F4 Yunkai (mts.), China
117/F2 Yunkanjini Abor. Land, Austl.
107/G2 Yunlong, China
104/D3 Yunnan (prov.), China
103/D4 Yuntai Shan (peak), China
103/D2 Yunwu Shan (peak), China
103/B4 Yunxi, China
103/B4 Yun Xian, China
104/D3 Yun Xian, China
103/D4 Yunyan (riv.), China
103/B3 Yunyanzhen, China
103/C3 Yunzhong Shan (mtn.), China
107/J2 Yuping, China
103/H7 Yuqiao (res.), China
98/D3 Yura (riv.), Japan
144/B2 Yuracyacu, Peru
88/J4 Yurga, Rus.
100/E2 Yuri (isl.), Rus.
144/B2 Yurimaguas, Peru
139/F3 Yuruari (riv.), Ven.
102/C4 Yurungkax (riv.), China
85/N5 Yuryuzan' (riv.), Rus.
105/J4 Yushan Nat'l Park, Tai.
103/C3 Yushe, China
103/D4 Yutai, China
103/D3 Yutian, China
69/F5 Yutz, Fr.
103/C3 Yu Xian, China
103/C4 Yu Xian, China
105/J2 Yuyao, China
100/B4 Yuzawa, Japan
100/A4 Yuza, Japan
100/D1 Yuzhno-Kuril'sk, Rus.
97/N2 Yuzhno-Sakhalinsk, Rus.
86/D2 Yuzhnyy Bug (riv.), Ukr.
53/R10 Yvelines (dept.), Fr.
76/C4 Yverdon, Swi.
53/S10 Yvette (riv.), Fr.
69/D3 Yvoir, Belg.
72/E3 Yzeure, Fr.

Z

104/C1 Za (riv.), China
123/N13 Za (riv.), Mor.
66/B4 Zaandam, Neth.
70/C4 Zaber (riv.), Ger.
65/L2 Ząbki, Pol.
65/J3 Ząbkowice Śląskie, Pol.
95/H2 Zābol, Iran
65/J4 Zábřeh, Czh.
65/K3 Zabrze, Pol.
148/D3 Zacapa, Guat.
147/M7 Zacapoaxtla, Mex.
147/E5 Zacapú, Mex.
146/E4 Zacatecas, Mex.
146/E3 Zacatecas (state), Mex.
148/D3 Zacatecoluca, ESal.
147/K8 Zacatepec, Mex.
147/M7 Zacatlán, Mex.
163/F4 Zachary, La,US
148/D3 Zaculeu, Guat.
82/B3 Zadar, Cro.
109/B4 Zadetkyi (isl.), Burma
96/D5 Zadoi, China
74/B3 Zafra, Sp.
65/H3 Żagań, Pol.
123/X17 Zaghwān', Tun.
123/W17 Zaghwān' (gov.), Tun.
82/B2 Zagorjeob Savi, Slov.
82/C3 Zagreb (cap.), Cro.
93/F2 Zagros (mts.), Iran
102/E5 Za'gya (riv.), China
95/H3 Zāhedān, Iran
106/C4 Zahirābād, India
91/D3 Zaḥlah, Leb.
94/D5 Ẓahrān, SAr.
122/E5 Zaire (Congo)
122/E4 Zaire (Congo) (riv.), Zaire
82/F4 Zaječar, Yugo.
131/C4 Zaka, Zim.
96/E1 Zakamensk, Rus.
93/E2 Zākhū, Iraq
81/G4 Zákinthos, Gre.
81/G4 Zákinthos (isl.), Gre.
65/K4 Zakopane, Pol.
125/J5 Zakouma Nat'l Park, Chad
81/J5 Zakro (ruins), Gre.
82/C2 Zala (co.), Hun.
82/C2 Zala (riv.), Hun.
82/C2 Zalaegerszeg, Hun.
74/C3 Zalamea de la Serena, Sp.
97/J2 Zalantun, China
82/C2 Zalaszentgrót, Hun.
82/F2 Zalău, Rom.
124/J2 Zalṭan (well), Libya
66/C5 Zaltbommel, Neth.
99/H7 Zama, Japan
126/F4 Zambezi (riv.), Afr.
131/A2 Zambezi, Zam.
131/D3 Zambézia (prov.), Moz.
131/B3 Zambezi Escarpment (cliff), Zam., Zim.
131/B2 Zambia
112/C4 Zamboanga City, Phil.
65/M2 Zambrów, Pol.
75/P11 Zambujal de Cima, Port.
129/G3 Zamfora (riv.), Nga.
109/B3 Zami (riv.), Burma
144/B2 Zamora, Ecu.
144/B1 Zamora (riv.), Ecu.
74/C2 Zamora, Sp.
144/B2 Zamora-Chinchipe (prov.), Ecu.
146/E5 Zamora de Hidalgo, Mex.
65/M3 Zamość, Pol.
65/M3 Zamość (prov.), Pol.
74/D3 Záncara (riv.), Sp.
102/C5 Zanda, China
66/A5 Zandkreekdam (dam), Neth.
66/B4 Zandvoort, Neth.
163/H2 Zanesville, Oh,US
103/C3 Zanhuang, China
93/G2 Zanjān, Iran
93/G2 Zanjān (gov.), Iran
130/C4 Zanzibar, Tanz.
130/C4 Zanzibar (isl.), Tanz.
130/C4 Zanzibar North (prov.), Tanz.
130/C4 Zanzibar South (prov.), Tanz.
130/C4 Zanzibar West (prov.), Tanz.
130/B3 Zanzuzi (hill), Tanz.
103/C3 Zaoqiang, China
99/G1 Zaō-san (mtn.), Japan
103/C4 Zaoyang, China
103/D4 Zaozhuang, China
97/N2 Zapadno-Sakhalin (mts.), Rus.
71/G3 Západočeský (reg.), Czh.
65/J4 Západoslovenský (reg.), Slvk.
142/C3 Zapala, Arg.
135/C1 Zapaleri (peak), Arg.
149/F1 Zapata (pen.), Cuba
162/D5 Zapata, Tx,US
138/C3 Zapatoca, Col.
138/C2 Zapatosa, Ciénaga de (lake), Col.
71/H4 Záplatský Rybnik (lake), Czh.
84/F1 Zapolyarnyy, Rus.
86/E3 Zaporozh'ye, Ukr.
86/E3 Zaporozh'ye Obl., Ukr.
138/B5 Zapotal, Ecu.
82/B3 Zaprešić, Cro.
92/D2 Zara, Turk.
138/C3 Zaragoza, Col.
147/E2 Zaragoza, Mex.
75/E2 Zaragoza (Saragossa), Sp.
129/H4 Zaranda (hill), Nga.
142/F2 Zárate, Arg.
74/D1 Zarauz, Sp.
139/E2 Zaraza, Ven.
93/G3 Zard (mtn.), Iran
93/H4 Zargān, Iran
129/G4 Zaria, Nga.
95/H2 Zarmast (pass), Afg.
83/G3 Zărneşti, Rom.
93/F2 Zarrīneh (riv.), Iran
93/G3 Zarrin Shahr, Iran
65/J4 Záruby (peak), Slvk.
144/B1 Zaruma, Ecu.
144/A1 Zarumilla, Peru
65/H3 Żary, Pol.
138/B3 Zarzal, Col.
74/A1 Zas, Sp.
95/L2 Zāskar (range), India
71/G2 Žatec, Czh.
68/D2 Zaventem, Belg.
82/D3 Zavidovići, Bosn.
97/K1 Zavitinsk, Rus.
131/D5 Závora (pt.), Moz.
65/K3 Zawadzkie, Pol.
131/C3 Zawi, Zim.
65/K3 Zawiercie, Pol.
96/D6 Zaya (riv.), China
102/D2 Zaysan, Kaz.
102/D2 Zaysan (lake), Kaz.
104/C2 Zayü, China
104/C2 Zayü (riv.), China
149/G1 Zaza (riv.), Cuba
65/H2 Zbąszyń, Pol.
65/H4 Žd'ár nad Sázavou, Czh.
65/K3 Zduńska Wola, Pol.
142/C5 Zeballos (peak), Arg.
123/R16 Zeddine (riv.), Alg.
68/C1 Zedelgem, Belg.
66/A5 Zeeland (prov.), Neth.
160/C3 Zeeland, Mi,US
132/D2 Zeerust, SAfr.
66/C4 Zeewolde, Neth.
91/D3 Zefat, Isr.
65/L2 Zegrzyńskie (lake), Pol.
65/G2 Zehdenick, Ger.
117/G2 Zeil (peak), Austl.
66/C4 Zeist, Neth.
64/G3 Zeitz, Ger.
68/D1 Zele, Belg.
85/L5 Zelenodol'sk, Rus.
63/N1 Zelenogorsk, Rus.
87/G3 Zelenokumsk, Rus.
66/D4 Zelhem, Neth.
70/D1 Zella-Mehlis, Ger.
76/E1 Zell am Harmersbach, Ger.
73/K3 Zell am See, Aus.
71/G7 Zellersee (lake), Aus.
77/E2 Zellersee (lake), Ger.
76/D2 Zell in Wiesental, Ger.
65/K3 Zelów, Pol.
82/B2 Zeltweg, Aus.
68/C1 Zelzate, Belg.
80/B4 Zembra (isls.), Tun.
125/L6 Zemio, CAfr.
123/R16 Zemmora, Alg.
147/N7 Zempoala, Mex.
147/Q10 Zempoala (mtn.), Mex.
148/C2 Zempoaltepec, Cerro (mtn.), Mex.
68/D2 Zemst, Belg.
158/B2 Zenia, Ca,US
82/C3 Zenica, Bosn.
165/C3 Zenith, Wa,US
70/D3 Zenn (riv.), Ger.
157/H2 Zenon Park, Sk,Can
98/C3 Zentsūji, Japan
82/D3 Žepče, Bosn.
123/S15 Zeralda, Alg.
123/L13 Zerga (lake), Mor.
86/G3 Zernograd, Rus.
152/F1 Zeta (lake), NW,Can
67/E2 Zetel, Ger.
67/G2 Zeven, Ger.
66/D5 Zevenaar, Neth.
66/B5 Zevenbergen, Neth.
97/K1 Zeya, Rus.
97/K1 Zeya (res.), Rus.
97/K1 Zeya (riv.), Rus.
97/K1 Zeya-Bureya (plain), Rus.
74/A3 Zêzere (riv.), Port.
91/D2 Zghartā, Leb.
65/K3 Zgierz, Pol.
65/H3 Zgorzelec, Pol.
97/K2 Zhan (riv.), China
103/B5 Zhang (riv.), China
105/G3 Zhang (riv.), China
103/C5 Zhangdu (lake), China
97/K3 Zhangguangcai (mts.), China
103/C2 Zhanghei, China
103/C2 Zhangjiakou, China

Acknowledgements

OXFORD UNIVERSITY PRESS
ADVISORS

Dr C. Board
Department of Geography
London School of Economics and Political
Science

Dr A. S. Goudie
Professor of Geography
University of Oxford

COMPUTERIZED CARTOGRAPHIC
ADVISORY BOARD

Mitchell J. Feigenbaum, Ph.D
Chief Technical Consultant
Toyota Professor, The Rockefeller University
Wolf Prize in Physics, 1986
Member, The National Academy of Sciences

Judson G. Rosebush, Ph.D
Computer Graphics Animation
Producer, Director and Author

Gary Martin Andrew, Ph.D
Consultant in Operations Research,
Planning and Management

Warren E. Schmidt, B.A.
Former U.S. Geological Survey,
Chief of the Branch of Geographic
and Cartographic Research

HAMMOND PUBLICATIONS
ADVISORY BOARD

UNITED STATES AND CANADA
Daniel Jacobson
Professor of Geography and Education,
Adjunct Professor of Anthropology,
Michigan State University

LATIN AND MIDDLE AMERICA
John P. Augelli
Professor and Chairman,
Department of Geography-Meteorology,
University of Kansas

WESTERN AND SOUTHERN EUROPE
Norman J. W. Thrower
Professor, Department of Geography,
University of California, Los Angeles

NORTHERN AND CENTRAL EUROPE
Vincent H. Malmstrom
Professor, Department of Geography,
Dartmouth College

SOUTH AND SOUTHEAST ASIA
P. P. Karan
Professor, Department of Geography,
University of Kentucky

EAST ASIA
Christopher L. Salter
Professor and Chairman,
Department of Geography,
University of Missouri

AUSTRALIA, NEW ZEALAND
& THE PACIFIC AREA
Tom L. McKnight
Professor, Department of Geography,
University of California, Los Angeles

POPULATION AND DEMOGRAPHY
Kingsley Davis
Distinguished Professor of Sociology,
University of Southern California
and Senior Research Fellow,
The Hoover Institution,
Stanford University

BIBLICAL ARCHAEOLOGY
Roger S. Boraas
Professor of Religion,
Upsala College

FLAGS
Whitney Smith
Executive Director,
The Flag Research Center,
Winchester, Massachusetts

LIBRARY CONSULTANT
Alice C. Hudson
Chief, Map Division,
The New York Public Library

SPECIAL ADVISORS

DESIGN CONSULTANT
Pentagram

CONTRIBUTING WRITER
Frederick A. Shamlian

HAMMOND INCORPORATED

Charles G. Lees, Jr., V.P.
Editor in Chief, Cartography

William L. Abel, V.P.
Graphic Services

Chingliang Liang
Director, Technical Services

Ernst G. Hofmann
Manager, Topographic Arts

Martin A. Bacheller
Editor-In-Chief, Emeritus

Joseph F. Kalina, Jr.
Managing Editor

Phil Giouvanos
Manager, Computer Cartography

Philip W. Varrallo
Graphics Project Manager

Shou-Wen Chen
Cartographic Systems Manager